SIXTH EDITION

GROUP DYNAMICS

Donelson R. Forsyth

University of Richmond

WADSWORTH
CENGAGE Learning

Australia • Brazil • ... • United States

WADSWORTH
CENGAGE Learning·

Group Dynamics, **Sixth Edition,**
International Edition
Donelson R. Forsyth

Publisher: Jon-David Hague

Acquisitions Editor: Timothy Matray

Assistant Editor: Lauren Moody

Editorial Assistant: Nicole Richards

Media Editor: Mary Noel

Brand Manager: Elisabeth Rhoden

Market Development Manager: Chris Sosa

Manufacturing Planner: Karen Hunt

Rights Acquisitions Specialist:
Dean Dauphinais

Production Service, Art Direction, and
Composition: PreMediaGlobal

Text Researcher: PreMediaGlobal

Cover Image: Daniela Illing/Shutterstock

International Edition:

ISBN-13: 978-1-285-05144-4

ISBN-10: 1-285-05144-0

Cengage Learning International Offices

Asia
www.cengageasia.com
tel: (65) 6410 1200

Australia/New Zealand
www.cengage.com.au
tel: (61) 3 9685 4111

Brazil
www.cengage.com.br
tel: (55) 11 3665 9900

India
www.cengage.co.in
tel: (91) 11 4364 1111

Latin America
www.cengage.com.mx
tel: (52) 55 1500 6000

UK/Europe/Middle East/Africa
www.cengage.co.uk
tel: (44) 0 1264 332 424

Represented in Canada by Nelson Education, Ltd.
www.nelson.com
tel: (416) 752 9100 / (800) 668 0671

Cengage Learning is a leading provider of customized learning solutions
with office locations around the globe, including Singapore, the United
Kingdom, Australia, Mexico, Brazil, and Japan. Locate your local office at:
www.cengage.com/global

For product information and free companion resources:
www.cengage.com/international

Visit your local office: **www.cengage.com/global**

Visit our corporate website: **www.cengage.com**

Printed in the United States of America
1 2 3 4 5 6 7 16 15 14 13 12

Brief Contents

PREFACE   xv

1 Introduction to Group Dynamics   1

2 Studying Groups   33

3 Inclusion and Identity   62

4 Formation   99

5 Cohesion and Development   133

6 Structure   165

7 Influence   202

8 Power   241

9 Leadership   277

10 Performance   318

11 Decision Making   357

12 Teams   399

13 Conflict   433

14 Intergroup Relations   469

15 Groups in Context   506

16 Groups and Change   541

17 Crowds and Collectives   571

REFERENCES   605
AUTHOR INDEX   694
SUBJECT INDEX   721

Contents

PREFACE   xv

1 Introduction to Group Dynamics   1

The Nature of Groups   2

Defining Groups   2

Describing Groups   6

Types of Groups   11

Perceiving Groups   13

The Nature of Group Dynamics   16

The Scientific Study of Groups   18

A Multilevel Approach to the Study of Groups   22

The Significance of Groups   24

Topics in Contemporary Group Dynamics   27

Group Dynamics Is Dynamic   29

Chapter Review   30

Resources   32

2 Studying Groups   33

Measurement in Group Dynamics   34

Observation   34

Self-Report Measures   41

Research Methods in Group Dynamics   44

Case Studies   44

Experimental Studies   46

Correlational Studies   47

Studying Groups: Issues and Implications   49

Theoretical Perspectives   52

Motivational and Emotional Perspectives   52

Behavioral Perspectives   53

Systems Theory Perspectives   55

Cognitive Perspectives   56

Biological Perspectives   57

Selecting a Theoretical Perspective   58

Chapter Review   59

Resources   61

3 Inclusion and Identity   62

From Isolation to Inclusion   63

The Need to Belong   64

Groups and Loneliness   66

Inclusion and Exclusion   68

Inclusion and Human Nature   73

From Individualism to Collectivism   77

The Micro Level: The Social Self   79

The Meso Level: The Group Culture   82

The Macro Level: Collectivism across Cultures   85

From Personal Identity to Social Identity   88

Social Identity Theory: The Basics   88

Motivation and Social Identity   91

Chapter Review   94

Resources   97

4 Formation   99

Joining Groups   100

Personality   101

Men, Women, and Groups   103

Social Motivation   104

Anxiety and Attachment   106

Attitudes, Experiences, and Expectations   110

Affiliation   112

Social Comparison   112

Stress and Affiliation   115

Social Comparison and the Self   118

Attraction   120

Principles of Attraction   121

The Economics of Membership   128

Chapter Review   129

Resources   131

5 Cohesion and Development   133

The Nature of Cohesion   134

Sources of Cohesion   135

Social Cohesion   136

Task Cohesion   137

Collective Cohesion   138

Emotional Cohesion   139

Structural Cohesion   141

Assumptions and Assessments   144

Developing Cohesion   145

Theories of Group Development   146

Five Stages of Development   146

Cycles of Development   150

Consequences of Cohesion   151

Member Satisfaction and Adjustment   153

Group Dynamics and Influence   154

Group Productivity   155

Application: Explaining Initiations   158

Group Cohesion and Initiations   158

Hazing   160

Chapter Review   162

Resources   164

6 Structure   165

Norms   167

The Nature of Social Norms   167

The Development of Norms   169

The Transmission of Norms   169

The Importance of Norms   171

Roles   174

  The Nature of Social Roles   174

  Role Theories   177

  Group Socialization   180

  Role Stress   183

Intermember Relations   186

  Social Network Analysis   186

  Network Dynamics   189

  Application: The SYMLOG Model   195

Chapter Review   198

Resources   200

7 Influence   202

Majority Influence: The Power of the Many   204

  Conformity and Independence   204

  Conformity across Contexts   207

  Who Will Conform?   211

Minority Influence: The Power of the Few   215

  Conversion Theory of Minority Influence   215

  Predicting Minority Influence   217

  Dynamic Social Impact Theory   219

Sources of Group Influence   220

  Implicit Influence   221

  Informational Influence   222

  Normative Influence   224

  Interpersonal Influence   225

  When Influence Inhibits: The Bystander Effect   228

Application: Understanding Juries   231

  Jury Dynamics   231

  How Effective Are Juries?   234

  Improving Juries   235

Chapter Review   237

Resources   240

8 Power   241

Obedience to Authority   242

  The Milgram Experiments   243

Milgram's Findings 244

The Power of the Milgram Situation 247

Social Power in Groups 250

Bases of Power 250

Bases and Obedience 254

Power Tactics 254

Compliance Tactics 257

Social Status in Groups 258

Claiming Status 258

Achieving Status 260

Status Hierarchies and Stability 263

The Metamorphic Effects of Power 265

Changes in the Powerholder 266

Reactions to the Use of Power 270

Who Is Responsible? 273

Chapter Review 273

Resources 276

9 Leadership 277

The Nature of Leadership 278

Leadership Myths 278

What Is Leadership? 281

What Do Leaders Do? 281

Leadership Emergence 286

Who Will Lead? 286

The Leader's Personality 287

The Leader's Competencies 289

Participation 291

What Do Leaders Look Like? 292

Theories of Leadership Emergence 294

Implicit Leadership Theory 295

Social Identity Theory 298

Social Role Theory 299

Terror Management Theory 299

Evolutionary Theory 300

Leader Effectiveness 301

Fiedler's Contingency Model 301

Style Theories   304

Leader-Member Exchange Theory   306

Participation Theories   308

Transformational Leadership   311

The Future of Leadership   313

Chapter Review   314

Resources   317

10 Performance   318

Working in Groups   320

Groups with a Purpose   320

When to Work in Groups   322

The Process Model of Productivity   322

Social Facilitation   323

Performance in the Presence of Others   324

Why Does Social Facilitation Occur?   327

Conclusions and Applications   331

Social Loafing   333

The Ringelmann Effect   333

Causes of and Cures for Social Loafing   336

The Collective Effort Model   339

Groups versus Individuals   339

Additive Tasks   341

Compensatory Tasks   341

Disjunctive Tasks   342

Conjunctive Tasks   345

Discretionary Tasks   346

Process Gains In Groups   347

Group Creativity   348

Brainstorming   348

Improving Brainstorming   350

Alternatives to Brainstorming   351

Chapter Review   353

Resources   356

11 Decision Making   357

The Functional Perspective   359

The Orientation Stage   360

The Discussion Stage   361

The Decision Stage   365

The Implementation Stage   368

Who Decides?   369

Problems and Pitfalls   371

Failing to Plan Is Planning to Fail   371

The Difficulty of Discussion   372

The Shared Information Bias   374

Cognitive Limitations   376

Dysfunctional Postdecision Tendencies   379

Group Polarization   380

Group Decisions Involving Risk   380

What Causes Group Polarization?   382

The Consequences of Polarization   385

Victims of Groupthink   385

Symptoms of Groupthink   386

Defective Decision Making   388

Causes of Groupthink   388

The Emergence of Groupthink   390

Alternative Models   391

Preventing Groupthink   392

Chapter Review   394

Resources   397

12 Teams   399

The Nature of Teams   400

A Brief History of Teams   401

What Is a Team?   402

Types of Teams   403

A Systems Model of Teams   407

Building the Team   408

The Team Player   409

Knowledge, Skill, and Ability (KSA)   411

Diversity   413

Men, Women, and Teams   416

Working In Teams   417

Team Processes   418

Cognitive Processes   421

Team Cohesion   422

Team Performance   425

Evaluating Teams   425

Suggestions for Using Teams   427

Chapter Review   430

Resources   432

13 Conflict 433

The Roots of Conflict   435

Winning: Conflict and Competition   435

Sharing: Conflict over Resources   441

Controlling: Conflict over Power   446

Working: Task and Process Conflict   446

Liking and Disliking: Personal Conflicts   448

Confrontation and Escalation   450

Uncertainty → Commitment   450

Perception → Misperception   451

Soft Tactics → Hard Tactics   451

Reciprocity → Retaliation   454

Irritation → Anger   454

Few → Many   456

Conflict Resolution   456

Commitment → Negotiation   457

Misperception → Understanding   458

Hard Tactics → Cooperative Tactics   459

Retaliation → Forgiveness   462

Anger → Composure   463

Many → Few   463

The Value of Conflict: Redux   464

Chapter Review   465

Resources   468

14 Intergroup Relations 469

Intergroup Conflict: Us versus Them   471

Competition and Conflict   472

The Discontinuity Effect   473

Power and Domination 475

Intergroup Aggression 478

Norms of Engagement 479

Evolutionary Perspectives 480

Intergroup Bias: Perceiving Us and Them 482

Conflict and Categorization 483

The Ingroup–Outgroup Bias 483

Cognitive Biases 485

Stereotype Content Model 487

Exclusion and Dehumanization 489

Categorization and Identity 491

Intergroup Conflict Resolution: Uniting Us and Them 492

Intergroup Contact 492

Cognitive Cures for Conflict 496

Learning to Cooperate 498

Resolving Conflict: Conclusions 501

Chapter Review 501

Resources 504

15 Groups in Context 506

Places: The Physical Context 508

A Sense of Place 508

Stressful Places 511

Dangerous Places 514

Spaces: The Social Context 515

Personal Space 516

Reactions to Spatial Invasion 518

Seating Arrangements 521

Locations: Group Territoriality 523

Types of Territoriality 524

Group Territories 526

Territoriality in Groups 529

Designing Group Environments 532

The Person-Place Fit 533

Fitting Form to Function 535

Chapter Review 537

Resources 539

16 Groups and Change 541

Group Approaches to Change 542

Therapeutic Groups 543

Interpersonal Learning Groups 548

Support Groups 550

Sources of Change in Groups 554

Universality and Hope 554

Social Learning 556

Group Cohesion 558

Disclosure and Catharsis 560

Altruism 560

Insight 561

The Effectiveness of Groups 562

Empirical Support for Group Treatments 562

Using Groups to Cure: Cautions 564

The Value of Groups 567

Chapter Review 567

Resources 569

17 Crowds and Collectives 571

Collectives: Forms and Features 573

What Are Collectives? 573

Gatherings 575

Crowds 577

Mobs 579

Panics 581

Collective Movements 583

Social Movements 586

Collective Dynamics 587

Contagion 589

Convergence 590

Deindividuation 592

Emergent Norms 595

Social Identity 596

Collectives are Groups 598

The Myth of the Madding Crowd 598

Studying Groups and Collectives 600

Chapter Review   600

Resources   602

REFERENCES   605
AUTHOR INDEX   694
SUBJECT INDEX   721

Preface

Welcome to the study of groups and their dynamics. The cases, theories, concepts, definitions, charts, examples, generalizations, ideas, and observations that fill this book's pages have just one purpose: To describe, explore, and illuminate all things related to human groups. What are groups, and what are their essential qualities? Why do people join groups? How do groups change over time? How do groups influence their members? Why are some groups more productive than others? What is the cause of conflict in groups and between groups? These are just a few of the questions asked, explored, and—in some cases—answered in *Group Dynamics*.

But why study groups? Why learn about the processes that unfold in interacting, dynamic groups? Why study theories that explain these processes? Why extend these theories to explain more and more about groups?

Because groups hold the secret to the universe—the interpersonal universe, at any rate. Understanding people—why they think, feel, and act the way they do—requires understanding their groups. Human behavior is so often group behavior that people must be studied in context—embedded in their families, friendship cliques, work groups, and so on—rather than in isolation. The study of larger social systems, including organizations, communities, and societies, also requires scrutinizing the groups that sustain them, for such social forces as traditions, values, and norms do not reach directly to individuals, but instead work through the groups to which each individual belongs.

On a practical level, much of the world's work is done by groups, so efficiency, achievement, progress—success itself—depends on understanding the strengths and weaknesses of groups. Productivity in the workplace, problem solving in a boardroom, learning in the classroom, and even therapeutic change—all depend on group-level processes. Groups, too, hold the key to solving such societal problems as racism, sexism, and international conflict. Any attempt to change society will succeed only if the groups within that society change.

Groups are also important for personal reasons. You will spend your entire life in groups, getting out of groups, leading groups, and changing groups. Through your membership in groups, you define and confirm your values and beliefs and take on or refine your identity. When you face uncertain situations, in groups you gain reassuring information about your problems and security in companionship. In groups, you learn about relations with others, the types of impressions you make on others, and the ways in which you can relate with others more effectively. Groups influence you in consequential ways, so you ignore their influence at your own risk.

FEATURES

This book is about groups, but it is not based on experts' opinions or common-sense principles. It offers, instead, a scientific analysis of groups, for it draws on theory and research from any and all disciplines to offer empirically supported evidence about the nature of groups. The book reviews hundreds of theories about groups and thousands of empirical studies that test those theories, all in an attempt to better understand what makes a group tick.

- **Organization:** The chapters progress from basic issues and processes to the analysis of more specialized topics. The first two chapters consider questions of definition, history, and methods, and they are followed by chapters dealing with group formation, cohesion, structure, and development. The book then turns to issues of influence and productivity in groups and teams, before examining groups in specific contexts. The order of chapters, however, is somewhat arbitrary, and many may prefer a different sequence.

- **Cases:** Each chapter that examines a specific topic, such as teams, social influence, or cohesion, uses a case study of a particular group to illustrate and integrate the chapter's contents. The study of teams, for example, begins with a cardiac surgical team learning a new operating procedure; the analysis of group formation examines the situational and personal factors that caused the impressionists to form a working coalition; and the chapter dealing with conflict uses theory and research to illuminate the source of the dispute between the business executives at a large U.S. computer manufacturing firm. All the cases are or were real groups rather than hypothetical ones, and the incidents described are documented events that occurred within the group (although some literary license was taken for the case used to illustrate the dynamics of juries).

- **Terms, Citations, and Names:** The approximately 500 key concepts, when first introduced, are set in boldface type and defined at the bottom of the page. Citations to the approximately 3,000 referenced works are given in the style of the American Psychological Association and usually include investigators' last names and the date of the publication of the research report or book. A small number of researchers and theorists are mentioned by name in the text rather than in the citations; in such cases, their first and last names are included.

- **Outlines, Summaries, and Readings:** The first page of each chapter asks several questions examined in that chapter and also outlines the chapter's contents. Each chapter uses three levels of headings. The primary headings are centered and printed in all capitals, the secondary headings are also centered but only the first letter of each word is capitalized. The tertiary headings begin individual paragraphs. Each chapter ends with a summary written in the form of an outline and a list of sources to consult for more information.

- **Focuses:** Each chapter organizes the content into three or four subsections, which can be read easily in a single sitting. But each chapter also includes two thematic boxed inserts that focus on groups that exist in virtual and cross-cultural contexts.

CHANGES FROM THE FIFTH EDITION

This book's aims have changed over the years. The first edition, published 30 years ago, followed in the footsteps of Marv Shaw's *Group Dynamics: The Psychology of Groups* (1978), Paul Hare's *Handbook of Small Group Research* (1976), and Doc Cartwright and Al Zander's *Group Dynamics* (1968). Back then, nearly all of the research on groups was conducted by social psychologists in psychology and sociology, and they published their findings—mostly studies of ad hoc groups working in laboratory settings—in their discipline's journals. But things have changed since then. Now, nearly every science has something to say about groups and their dynamics. And not just anthropology, communication, education, management and organizational behavior, and political science, but also legal studies, biology, and even physics offer insights into issues of group formation, process, and function. As the study of groups continues to thrive intellectually and scientifically, new findings are emerging in such areas as cohesion, conformity, development, identity, networks, justice, leadership, online groups, multicultural groups, negotiation, power, social comparison, status and hierarchy, and teams. This edition strives to summarize the current state of scientific research in the field.

Changes to this edition include:

- **Updating and clarification of the content:** The book remains a research-oriented examination of group-level processes, with an emphasis on social psychological perspectives within the psychological and sociological traditions. Each chapter has been thoroughly revised, however, based on continuing changes in the study of groups and feedback from those who have used the book—both to teach with and to learn from. Classic theories and findings are still given considerable attention, but every chapter has been updated to summarize emerging findings and outlooks.

- **The reorganization of the sequence of topics within and between chapters:** The addition of new material and updating of traditional topics required changes in sequencing and organization to increase the coherence and comprehensiveness of the material. For example, the chapter dealing with inclusion and identity reorganizes the analysis of collectivism and individualism within a multilevel framework, and materials dealing with power, status, and prestige are now examined in one chapter rather than spread across several.

- **Increased focus on interdisciplinary work in the study of groups:** Given that nearly every field of human endeavor is influenced by, and therefore interested in, groups, theory and research on groups sprawls across traditional disciplinary boundaries. This edition draws from many sources for insights into groups and has Google Scholar, and the shift to online publishing, to thank for bringing this elusive goal within closer reach.

- **Both theory and application are amplified:** Specific research findings are examined in detail, but a concerted attempt is made to provide a theoretical synthesis of these findings when possible. Also, the study of groups is an immanently practical pursuit, given the use of groups in organizational, political, military, and industrial settings. The text examines such applied topics as group performance, roles, cohesion, decision making, creativity, teams, and conflict.

- **Online groups and groups in cross–cultural contexts**: The material examined in the previous editions in boxed features has been incorporated into the main text to increase both memorability and flow, but each chapter now has two themed, boxed features pertaining to online groups and groups in multicultural contexts.

ACKNOWLEDGMENTS

Most things in this world are accomplished by groups rather than by single individuals working alone. This book is no exception. Although I am personally responsible for the ideas presented in this book, one group after another helped me along the way. The scientists who study groups deserve much of the credit, for this book summarizes the results of their intellectual work. Within that group, too, is a subgroup of experts who provided specific comments, suggestions, and materials, and those reviewers include Alvin Snadowsky, Brooklyn College of CUNY; LaWanna Gunn-Williams, Grambling State University; Marcus Patterson, University of Massachusetts-Boston; Patricia Mitchell, University of San Francisco; Lorianne Lueders-Yanotti, Suffolk County Community College; Yolanda T. Martinez, Chemeketa Community College; Rufus Barfield, University of Central Florida; and Amy Corbett, State University of New York at Cobleskill. The members of the production teams at Wadsworth/Cengage, including Tim Matray, Nicole Richards, Lauren Moody, and at Pre-PressPMG, also deserve special thanks for their capable efforts. Lindsay Bethoney, in particular, somehow remained constantly supportive and positive as she guided the process of turning the manuscript pages into a final published book.

Four distinct groups at the University of Richmond also deserve special mention: colleagues, students, members of my research group, and administrators. The small group known as SPUR (Social Psychologists of the University of Richmond) includes Jeni Burnette, Scott Allison, Al Goethals, and Crystal Hoyt. I have benefited from their wise counsel on many topics. My classes at the University of Richmond provided me with the opportunity to field-test my ideas about groups, and I very much appreciate my students' tolerance of my unbridled enthusiasm for all things related to groups. Those students, too, who joined with me by undertaking a research project examining group dynamics, leadership, and ethics deserve mention (Matt Eley, Eric Loepp, John McAuliff, Laura Musser, Christina Pfaff, Will Stanton, Max Teschke, and Julie Yermack). The able administrative group of the University of Richmond, including Terry Price, Sandra Peart, Steve Allred, and Ed Ayers, also earns a well-deserved note of appreciation for dealing so effectively with the many challenges that confront a modern institution of higher learning.

One final group deserves far more than just acknowledgment. Claire, David, and Rachel provided me with a stream of much-needed respites from the marathon revision sessions, insights into more modern forms of group communication (e.g., Facebook), and expert editorial suggestions. (Carmen, the family dog, also helped some, but not as much as on the last edition.) So, I thank, as always, my most important group: my family.

—Donelson R. Forsyth, Montebello, Virginia

Introduction to Group Dynamics

CHAPTER OVERVIEW

Group dynamics are the influential actions, processes, and changes that occur within and between groups. Groups come in all shapes and sizes and their functions are many and varied, but their influence is universal. The tendency to join with others in groups is perhaps the single most important characteristic of humans, and the processes that unfold within these groups leave an indelible imprint on their members and on society. To understand people, one must understand groups and their dynamics.

- What is a group?
- What are some common characteristics of groups?
- Are there different types of groups, and do people distinguish between these groups?
- What assumptions guide researchers in their studies of groups and their dynamics?
- Why study groups and their dynamics?
- What topics are included in the scientific study of group dynamics?

CHAPTER OUTLINE

The Nature of Groups

Defining Groups

Describing Groups

Types of Groups

Perceiving Groups

The Nature of Group Dynamics

The Scientific Study of Groups

A Multilevel Approach to the Study of Groups

The Significance of Groups

Topics in Contemporary Group Dynamics

Group Dynamics is Dynamic

Chapter Review

Resources

Most people spend their entire lives in groups. Although some may bemoan the growing alienation of individuals from the small social groups that once linked them securely to society at large, the single man or woman who has no connection to other men and women is an extraordinarily rare human being (Silvia & Kwapil, 2011). People are in many respects individuals seeking personal, private objectives, yet they are also members of groups that constrain them, guide them, and sustain them. Members of the species *Homo sapiens* are capable of surviving alone, but few choose to, for virtually all human activities—working, learning, worshiping, relaxing, playing, and even sleeping—occur in groups. No one knows for certain how many groups exist at this moment, but given the number of people on the planet and their groupish proclivities, 30 billion is a conservative estimate.

Sages, scholars, and laypersons have been puzzling over **group dynamics**—the actions, processes, and changes that occur within groups and between groups—for centuries. Why, they asked, do humans so frequently join with others in groups? How do members coordinate their efforts and energies? What factors give rise to a sense of cohesion, esprit de corps, and a marked distrust for those outside the group? And how do groups and their leaders hold sway over members? Their inquiries provide the scientific basis for the field of group dynamics, which is the scientific discipline devoted to studying groups and group process.

This book unravels many of the mysteries of groups, beginning with two sets of essential questions. First, *what is a group?* What distinguishes a group from a mere collection of people? What features can we expect to find in most groups, and what kinds of processes provide the foundation for their dynamics? Second, *what is this field of study we are calling group dynamics?* What assumptions guide researchers as they describe, analyze, and compare the various groups that populate the planet?

---

group dynamics The influential actions, processes, and changes that occur within and between groups; also, the scientific study of those processes.

THE NATURE OF GROUPS

Fish swimming in synchronized unison are called a *school*. A gathering of kangaroos is a *mob*. A threesome of crows cawing from their perch on a telephone wire is a *murder*. A *gam* is a group of whales. A flock of larks in flight is an *exaltation* (Lipton, 1991). But what is a collection of human beings called? A *group*.

Defining Groups

Take a moment and make a mental list of all the groups of which you are a part. Did you include your family? The people you work or study with? How about your neighbors or people who used to be neighbors but moved away? Are all of the people you have friended on Facebook members of a group? How about people of your same sex, race, and citizenship and those who share your political beliefs? Are African American men, Canadians, and Republicans groups? Are you in a romantic relationship? Did you include you and your partner on your list of groups? Which collections of humans are groups and which are not?

As the sampling of definitions in Table 1.1 suggests, people who study groups are not conformists. Some of their definitions of the word *group* stress the importance of communication or mutual dependence. Still others suggest that a shared purpose or goal is what turns a mere aggregate of individuals into a bona fide group. Most, however, would agree that groups come into existence when people become linked together by some type of relationship. Three persons working on math problems in separate rooms can hardly be considered a group; they are not connected to each other in any way. If, however, we create relationships linking them—for example, we let them send notes to each other or we pick one person to distribute the problems to the others—then these three individuals can be considered a rudimentary group. Neither would we call people who share some superficial similarity, such as eye color, a favorite football team, or birthplace, group members for we expect them to be connected to each other in socially meaningful ways. A family is a group because the

TABLE 1.1   A Sampling of Definitions of the Word *Group*

Central Feature	Definition
Categorization	"Two or more individuals … [who] perceive themselves to be members of the same social category" (Turner, 1982, p. 15)
Communication	"Three or more people … who (a) think of themselves as a group, (b) are interdependent (e.g., with regard to shared goals or behaviors that affect one another), and (c) communicate (interact) with one another (via face-to-face or technological means)" (Frey & Konieczka, 2010, p. 317)
Face-to-face	"Any number of persons engaged in interaction with one another in a single face-to-face meeting or series of such meetings" (Bales, 1950, p. 33)
Influence	"Two or more persons who are interacting with one another in such a manner that each person influences and is influenced by each other person" (Shaw, 1981, p. 454)
Interaction	"Two or more interdependent individuals who influence one another through social interaction" (APA Dictionary of Psychology, 2007, p. 419)
Interdependence	"A dynamic whole based on interdependence rather than similarity" (Lewin, 1948, p. 184)
Interrelations	"An aggregation of two or more people who are to some degree in dynamic interrelation with one another" (McGrath, 1984, p. 8)
Need satisfaction	"A collection of organisms in which the existence of all (in their given relationships) is necessary to the satisfaction of certain individual needs in each" (Cattell, 1951, p. 167)
Psychological significance	"A *psychological group* is any number of people who interact with each other, are psychologically aware of each other, and perceive themselves to be in a group" (Pennington, 2002, p. 3)
Relations	"Individuals who stand in certain relations to each other, for example, as sharing a common purpose or having a common intentionality, or acting together, or at least having a common interest" (Gould, 2004, p. 119)
Shared identity	"Two or more people possessing a common social identification and whose existence as a group is recognized by a third party" (R. Brown, 2000, p. 19)
Shared tasks and goals	"Three or more people who work together interdependently on an agreed-upon activity or goal" (Keyton, 2002, p. 5)
Size	"Two or more people" (Williams, 2010, p. 269)
Structure	"A social unit which consists of a number of individuals who stand in (more or less) definite status and role relationships to one another and which possesses a set of values or norms of its own regulating the behavior of individual members, at least in matters of consequence to the group" (Sherif & Sherif, 1956, p. 144)
Systems	"An intact social system, complete with boundaries, interdependence for some shared purpose, and differentiated member roles" (Hackman & Katz, 2010, p. 1210)
Unity	"A unit consisting of a plural number of separate organisms (agents) who have a collective perception of their unity and who have the ability to act and/or are acting in a unitary manner toward their environment" (Smith, 1945, p. 227)

members are connected, not just by genetic similarities but social and emotional relationships. People who work together are linked not only by the collaborative tasks that they must complete collectively but also by friendships, alliances, and inevitable antagonisms. Students in a class all recognize that they are members of a smaller subset within the larger educational community and that those who are not in their class are outsiders. A **group**, then, is *two or more individuals who are connected by and within social relationships.*

Two or More Individuals   A group can range in size from two members to many thousands. Very small collectives, such as dyads (two members) and triads (three members) are groups, but so are large mobs, crowds, and congregations (Simmel, 1902). Most groups, however, tend to be small, including two to seven members.

Sociologist John James was so intrigued by the variation in the size of groups that he took to the streets of Eugene and Portland, Oregon to record the size of the 9,129 groups he encountered there. He defined a group to be two or more people in "face-to-face interaction as evidenced by the criteria of gesticulation, laughter, smiles, talk, play or work" (James, 1951, p. 475). He studied pedestrians walking down the city streets, people shopping, children on playgrounds, public gatherings at sports events and festivals, patrons during the intermissions at plays and entering movie theaters, and various types of work crews and teams. Most of these groups were small, usually with only two or three members, but groups that had been deliberately created for some specific purpose, such as the leadership team of a company, tended to be larger. His findings, and the results of studies conducted in other settings (cafeterias and businesses) are summarized in Figure 1.1. They suggest that groups tend to "gravitate to the smallest size, two" (Hare, 1976, p. 215).

A group's size influences its nature in many ways, for a group with only two or three members possesses many unique characteristics simply because it includes

group Two or more individuals who are connected by and within social relationships.

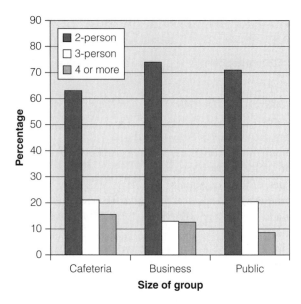

FIGURE 1.1   The percentage of groups of varying sizes (2, 3, and 4+) observed in cafeterias, business settings, and in various public places, such as parks and the lobbies of movie theaters.

SOURCES: Cafeteria data: "Deindividuation as a Function of Density and Group Members," by D. O Jorgenson and F. O. Dukes, *Journal of Personality and Social Psychology*, 1976, *34*, 24–29. Business data: Ruef, M., Aldrich, H. E., & Carter, N. M. (2003). The structure of founding teams: Homophily, strong ties, and isolation among U.S. entrepreneurs. *American Sociological Review, 68*(2), 195–222. Public data: James, J. (1951). A preliminary study of the size determinant in small group interaction. *American Sociological Review, 16*, 474–477.

so few members. The dyad is so small that it ceases to exist when one member leaves, and it can never be broken down into subgroups. The members of dyads are also sometimes linked by a unique and powerful type of relationship—love—that makes their dynamics so intense that they belong in a category all their own (Levine & Moreland, 2012). Larger groups can also have unique qualities, for the members are rarely connected directly to all other members, subgroups are very likely to form, and one or more leaders may be needed to organize and guide the group. By definition, however, all are considered groups. [This issue is not, however, entirely settled. Moreland (2010), for example, offers a strong argument for excluding dyads from the group world, whereas Williams (2010) explains why, in his opinion, a group of two is still a group.]

Who Are Connected   The members of any given group are connected to each other like a series of networked computers. These connections, or social ties, are not of one type. In families, for example, the relationships are based on kinship, but in the workplace the relationships are based on task-related interdependencies. In some groups, members are friends of one another, but in others the members express little mutual attraction. Nor are the relationships linking members of different types of groups equally strong or enduring. Only some relationships, like the links between members of a family or a clique of close friends, are enduring ones that have developed over time and are based on a long history of mutual influence and exchange. Nor need all relationships be mutual ones. In a group of friends, for example, some members may be liked by all the group members but these members may like only a subset of the group members in return. But no matter what the nature of the relations, a group exists when individuals are connected to one another by some type of social tie.

The larger the group, the more ties are needed to join members to each other and to the group. The maximum number of ties within a group in which everyone is linked to everyone else is given by the equation $n(n-1)/2$, where n is the number of people in the group. Only one relationship is needed to create a dyad, but as Figure 1.2 illustrates, the number of ties needed to connect all members grows exponentially as the group gets larger: 10 ties would be needed to join each member of a 5-person group to every other member, 45 for a 10-person group, but over a thousand for a 50-person group. Even more ties are needed if the ties between members are directed rather than reciprocal ones. If knowing A is linked to B does not tell us that B is also linked to A, then twice as many ties are needed to completely link ever member to every other member with directed ties. Hence, in larger groups many group members link to other members only indirectly. Person A might, for example, talk directly to B, but B may talk only to C so that A is linked to C only through B. But even in large groups, members often feel connected to the group as a whole (Katz et al., 2005).

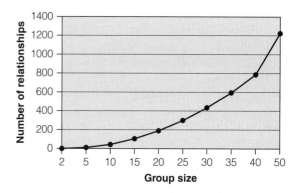

FIGURE 1.2   The number of relationships needed to connect all members to one another in groups ranging in size from 2 members to 50 members.

SOURCE: © Cengage Learning 2014

When the ties linking members are strong, the group is more enduring and its influence on members is more extensive. But weak ties are also essential to the long-term functioning of groups. When information diffuses throughout a group, it flows first along the strong ties, but to permeate the entire group it must also be shared among members who are linked by weaker ties. Individuals who are on the job market, for example, often learn of new openings from acquaintances rather than close friends, because whatever their close friends know, they probably know as well. Weak ties, in contrast, allow the group members to gain access to information that is common knowledge outside of their tight-knit social circles. Sociologist Mark S. Granovetter (1973) called this tendency the "strength of weak ties."

By and Within Social Relationships   Definitions of the word *group* vary, but many stress one key consideration: social relationships among the members. When people are linked by a relationship they become interdependent, for they can influence one another's thoughts, actions, emotions, and outcomes. And a *social* relationship suggests that this interdependence is not caused by some impersonal factor, such as proximity or common origin, but by the "actual, imagined, or implied presence of other human beings" (Allport, 1968, p. 3). This type of relationship even has a name: *membership*. Just as people who are friends are joined in *friendship*, or all the senior members of a law firm form a *partnership*, people in a group are said to be linked by their **membership**.

These social relationships link members to one another but they also enclose members within the group. A group is *boundaried*, in a psychological sense, with those who are included in the group recognized as members and those who are not part of the group excluded as nonmembers. These boundaries, even if unstable and highly permeable, distinguish groups from another psychologically significant aggregate: the **social network**. To become part of a social network, an individual need only establish a relationship of some sort with a person who is already part of the network. If persons A and B already know each other—they are linked by a social relationship—then person C can join their network by establishing a relationship with either A or B. But a group, unlike a network, is more than a chain of individuals joined in dyadic pairings. A group exists when members form a relationship with the group as a whole and when it is the group that sustains, at least in part, the relationships among each of the individual members.

This definition of a group, two or more individuals who are connected by and within social relationships, is consistent with most theoretical perspectives on groups, but it is one definition of many (Greenwood, 2004). The definition is also somewhat hopeful, for it suggests that collections of people can be easily classified into two categories—group and nongroup—when in actuality the line between group and nongroup is fuzzy rather than sharp. Some groups, such as work teams or families, easily meet the definition's "by and within social relationships" requirement, but others do not. For example, five strangers waiting on a city sidewalk for a bus may not seem to fit the definition of a group, but they may become a group when one passenger asks the others if they can change a dollar bill. And what about people playing a Massively Multiplayer Online Role-Playing Game (MMORPG) together on the Web? As Focus 1.1 asks, are people who are connected to one another by computer-based networks a group?

The definition is also limited by its brevity. It defines the barest requirements of a group, and so it leaves unanswered other questions about groups. If we want to understand a group, we need to ask many more questions: What do the people do in the group? Does the group have a leader? How unified is the group? How has the group changed over time? Deciding that a collection of people qualifies as a group is only the beginning of understanding that group.

Describing Groups

Each one of the billions of groups that exist at this moment is a unique configuration of individuals, processes, and relationships. A study group at a university library, for example, will differ in a hundred ways from a team on a soccer field, a rock band performing a well-loved song, or a board of directors selecting a new company CEO. But all groups, despite their distinctive characteristics, possess common properties and dynamics. When researchers study a group, they must go beyond its unique qualities to consider characteristics that appear with consistency in most groups. Some of these qualities, such as what the group members are doing and the tasks they are attempting, are relatively obvious ones. Other qualities, such as the degree of interdependence among members or the group's overall unity, are harder to discern. Here we start with a group's easily detectable qualities before turning to those that are often hidden from view.

Interaction   Groups are the setting for an infinite variety of interpersonal actions. If you were to watch a group for even a few minutes, you would see people doing all sorts of things: talking over issues, getting into arguments, and making decisions. They would upset each other, give each other help and support, and take advantage of each other's weaknesses. They would likely work together to accomplish difficult tasks, find ways to not do their work, and even plot against the best interests of those who are not a part of their group.

---

membership The state of belonging to, or being included in, a social group; also, the collective body of all members of a group.
social network A set of interpersonally interconnected individuals or groups.

F o c u s　1.1　E-groups: The Reality of Online Groups

When people think of a group, they tend to think of a gathering of individuals in some specific location. A family picnicking, a football team practicing, a team of workers assembling a machine, or a clique of friends gossiping about the weekend's events; these are groups. Some groups, however, do not fit people's intuitive conception of the typical group. Consider, for example, 10 people who never see each other face-to-face but only communicate with one another using computers connected to the Internet. Are these people members of a group?

The Internet has transformed people's lives, including their groups. All kinds of groups, from support groups, work teams, clubs, and gameplayers ("gamers") congregate via the Web. These groups go by various names—cybergroups, computer-mediated communication (CMC) groups, e-groups, virtual teams, and **online groups**—but they all rely on computer-based information technologies to build and sustain social relationships among the members (Brandon & Hollingshead, 2007). The unique, technology-mediated environment in which these groups meet undoubtedly influences their dynamics: members of an online group will not interact in the same way as will members of **offline groups**. Yet, in many cases, their dynamics are similar to those of more traditional, face-to-face groups. Such groups develop norms, admit new members, identify goals, and experience conflict. Members of such groups take the lead, offer suggestions, ask questions, and influence one another. New members

must often suffer through a period of initiation; for example, members of many multiplayer game worlds are given the derisive label of *noob* and are ignored until they develop their skills. Members also identify with their online groups and react differently to those who are in their groups and those who are not (McKenna & Seidman, 2005). Members, when they describe their group, endorse such statements as "I really like this group," "I feel at home in this group," and "I get a lot out of being in this group" (Blanchard, 2007). These are the same sentiments that people express when talking about offline, traditional face-to-face groups.

Are online groups true groups? This question is, at core, an empirical one. As researchers explore the dynamics of these groups, they will likely identify aspects of these groups that are consistent with what is known about groups in general: how they form, how members interact with one another, and how they perform over time. But, given their unique setting, researchers will likely also discover these groups are unique in some ways. If their distinctiveness is so substantial that e-group dynamics cannot be explained by the principles that account for the processes studied in offline groups, then a case could be made to place Internet groups in their own category. However, until research suggests otherwise, we will consider e-groups to be groups and will present the latest findings on these groups in Focus sections in each chapter.

As the expression "it takes two to tango" suggests, many of the most interesting, influential, and entertaining forms of human action are possible only when people join with others in a group.

Sociologist Robert Freed Bales (1950, 1999), intrigued by the question "What do people do

when they are in groups?" spent years watching and recording people in relatively small, face-to-face groups. He recognized the diversity of group interaction, but eventually concluded that the countless actions he had observed tend to be of two types: those that focused on the task the group was dealing with and those that sustained, strengthened, or weakened interpersonal relationships within the group. **Task interaction** includes all group behavior that is focused principally on the group's work, projects, plans, and goals. In most

---

online group (or e-group) Two or more individuals who interact with each other solely or primarily through computer-based information technologies (e.g., e-mail, instant messaging, social networking sites) rather than through face-to-face interactions.

offline group Two or more individuals whose interaction with each other occur primarily or solely in conventional, face-to-face situations and not via computer-based technology.

---

task interaction The conjointly adjusted actions of group members that pertain to the group's projects, tasks, and goals.

groups, members must coordinate their various skills, resources, and motivations so that the group can make a decision, generate a product, or achieve a victory. When a jury reviews each bit of testimony, a committee discusses the best course of action to take, or a family plans its summer vacation, the group's interaction is task focused.

But groups are not simply performance engines, for much of what happens in a group is **relationship interaction** (or *socioemotional interaction*). If group members falter and need support, others will buoy them up with kind words, suggestions, and other forms of help. When group members disagree with the others, they are often roundly criticized and made to feel foolish. When a coworker wears a new suit or outfit, others in his or her work unit notice it and offer compliments or criticisms. Such actions sustain or undermine the emotional bonds linking the members to one another and to the group. We will review the method that Bales developed for objectively recording these types of interactions, his *Interaction Process Analysis (IPA)*, in Chapter 2.

Goals   Humans, as a species, seem to be genetically ready to set goals for themselves—"what natural selection has built into us is the *capacity* to strive, the capacity to seek, the capacity to set up short-term goals in the service of longer-term goals" (Dawkins, 1989, p. 142)—and that tendency is only amplified in groups. A team strives to take first place. A study group wants to help members get better grades. A jury makes a decision about guilt or innocence. The members of a congregation seek religious and spiritual experiences. In each case, the members of the group are united by their common goals. The groups Bales (1999) studied spent the majority of their time (63%) dealing with goal-related activities and tasks.

The goals groups pursue are many and varied. One approach to their classification suggests that a

broad distinction can be made between intellectual and judgmental tasks (Laughlin, 1980). Another emphasizes three different categories: production, discussion, and problem-solving goals (Hackman & Morris, 1975). A third model, proposed by social psychologist Joseph E. McGrath (1984) and partially summarized in Table 1.2, distinguishes among four basic group goals: *generating* ideas, plans, or novel solutions, *choosing* between options, *negotiating* solutions to a conflict, and *executing* (performing) performance tasks. Some of these goals require groups to take action, but others require only rational analysis. Others require that group members work together in the pursuit of a group-level goal, but other goals are ones sought by specific group members rather than the group as a whole. As Chapter 10 explains, groups are sources of heightened motivation, for they increase members' commitment to their own personal goals and to the goals that the group has set for itself. In general, the most effective groups are the ones that are most conscientious when examining their purposes and procedures (Katzenbach & Smith, 2001).

Interdependence   The acrobat on the trapeze will drop to the net unless her teammate catches her outstretched arms. The assembly line worker is unable to complete his work until he receives the unfinished product from a worker further up the line. The business executive's success and salary are determined by how well her staff completes its work; if her staff fails, then she fails as well. In such situations, members are obligated or responsible to other group members, for they provide each other with support and assistance. This **interdependence** means that members *depend* on one another; their outcomes, actions, thoughts, feelings, and experiences are partially determined by others in the group.

Some groups create only the potential for interdependence among members. The outcomes of people standing in a queue at a store's checkout

---

relationship interaction (socioemotional interaction) The conjointly adjusted actions of group members that relate to or influence the nature and strength of the emotional and interpersonal bonds within the group, including both sustaining (social support, consideration) and undermining actions (criticism, conflict).

---

interdependence Mutual dependence, as when one's outcomes, actions, thoughts, feelings, and experiences are influenced, to some degree, by other people.

TABLE 1.2 Four Types of Group Goals and Group Tasks

Goals	Tasks	Examples
Generating	Concocting strategies, producing new ideas, developing plans, creating novel solutions	A community group coming up with fund-raising ideas, a task force identifying new markets for a product, military commanders discussing ways to reduce the risk of causalities
Choosing	Selecting between alternatives, settling on a single option among many, making a choice	A legislative body voting, students completing a multiple-choice test as a group, a jury deciding a defendant's guilt, a committee selecting one of three candidates for an award
Negotiating	Managing differences of opinions, resolving conflicts and disputes, improving coordination	A team arguing about who is to blame for losing an account, a leader setting new requirements for attendance, a group taking action to expel one of its members
Executing	Taking action, carrying out a plan, making something, performing a task	A theater group performing a play, a military squad on the attack, a work crew building a house, sports teams in competition, protesters occupying a public park

SOURCE: McGrath, J. E., Groups: Interaction and Performance, 1st Edition, © 1984. Reprinted by permission of Pearson Education, Inc., Upper Saddle River, NJ.

counter, audience members in a darkened theater, or the congregation of a large mega-church are hardly intertwined at all. The individuals within these groups can reach their goals on their own without making certain their actions mesh closely with the actions of those who are nearby. Other groups, such as gangs, families, sports teams, and military squads, create far higher levels of interdependency since members reliably and substantially influence one another's outcomes over a long period of time and in a variety of situations. But even the interdependencies in these tightly meshed groups are rarely invariant or undifferentiated. As Figure 1.3 suggests, in symmetric, "flat" groups, the influence among members is equal and reciprocated (Figure 1.3a). But more typically interdependencies are asymmetric, unequal, and hierarchical (Fiske, 2010). In a business, for example, the boss may determine how employees spend their time, what kind of rewards they experience, and even the duration of their membership in the group (Figure 1.3b). In other cases the employees may be able to influence their boss to a degree, but the boss influences them to a much greater extent (Figure 1.3c). Interdependency can also be ordered sequentially, as when C's outcomes are determined by B's actions, but B's actions are determined by A (Figure 1.3d).

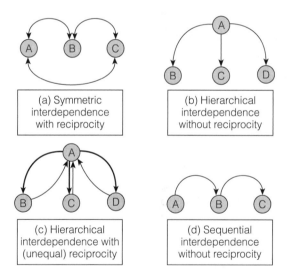

FIGURE 1.3 Examples of interdependence among group members.
SOURCE: © Cengage Learning 2014

Structure Group members are not connected to one another at random, but in organized and predictable patterns. In all but the most ephemeral groups, patterns and regularities emerge that determine the kinds of actions that are permitted or condemned: who talks to whom, who likes whom and who dislikes whom, who can be counted on to perform particular tasks, and whom others look to for guidance and help. These regularities combine to generate **group structure**—the complex of roles, norms, and intermember relations that organizes the group. **Roles**, for example, specify the general behaviors expected of people who occupy different positions within the group. The roles of *leader* and *follower* are fundamental ones in many groups, but other roles—information seeker, information giver, and compromiser—may emerge in any group (Benne & Sheats, 1948). Group members' actions and interactions are also shaped by their group's **norms**—consensual standards that describe what behaviors should and should not be performed in a given context.

Roles, norms, and other structural aspects of groups, although unseen and often unnoticed, lie at the heart of their most dynamic processes. When people join a group, they initially spend much of their time trying to come to terms with the requirements of their role. If they cannot meet the role's demand, they might not remain a member for long. Norms within a group are defined and renegotiated over time, and conflicts often emerge as members violate norms. In group meetings, the opinions of members with higher status carry more weight than those of the rank-and-file members. When several members form a *subgroup* within the larger group, they exert more influence on the rest of the group than they would individually. When people manage to place themselves at the hub of the group's

---

group structure The persistent and interrelated features of a group, such as roles and norms, that influence the functioning of the group as a whole and create regularities in the interactions of its members.

role A socially shared set of behaviors, characteristics, and responsibilities expected of people who occupy a particular position or type of position within a group; by enacting roles, individuals establish regular patterns of exchange with one another that increase predictability and social coordination.

norm A consensual and often implicit standard that describes what behaviors should and should not be performed in a given context.

information-exchange patterns, their influence over others also increases. If you had to choose only one aspect of a group to study, you would probably learn the most by studying its structure.

Cohesiveness Just as a book is not just a set of sequenced pages or a cake just sugar, flour, and other ingredients mixed together and baked, so a group is not just the individual members. A group is an entity that forms when interpersonal forces bind the members together in a unit with boundaries that mark who is in the group and who is outside of it. In consequence, when we speak about groups, we refer to them as single objects: for example, a gang *is* menacing or the club *meets* tomorrow.

In physics, the molecular integrity of matter is known as *cohesiveness*. When matter is cohesive, the particles that constitute it bond together so tightly that they resist any competing attractions. But when matter is not cohesive, it tends to disintegrate over time as the particles drift away or adhere to some other nearby object. Similarly, **group cohesion** is the integrity, solidarity, social integration, unity, and groupiness of a group. All groups require a modicum of cohesiveness or else the group would disintegrate and cease to exist as a group (Dion, 2000).

Groups are so commonplace that their complexities are too often overlooked, but the qualities listed in Table 1.3—interaction, goals, interdependence, structure, and cohesion—provide a place to start when describing a group. The conversations between members that seem so capricious are actually social exchanges that move the task along toward its goals while keeping the group intact. Beneath the surface of the group are a set of structures that regulate actions and outcomes and create a complex web of interdependencies and influence. And even though often unnoticed, you intuitively size up each group you encounter, as you search for

---

group cohesion The solidarity or unity of a group resulting from the development of strong and mutual interpersonal bonds among members and group-level forces that unify the group, such as shared commitment to group goals and *esprit de corps*.

T A B L E 1.3   Five Characteristics of Groups

Feature	Description
Interaction	Groups create, organize, and sustain relationship and task interactions among members
Goals	Groups have instrumental purposes, for they facilitate the achievement of aims or outcomes sought by the members
Interdependence	Group members depend on one another, in that each member influences and is influenced by each other member
Structure	Groups are organized, with each individual connected to others in a pattern of relationships, roles, and norms
Cohesion	Groups unite members in a bonded network of interpersonal relations recognized by both members of the group and those outside of it.

outward signs of unity. Even the most mundane group becomes fascinating when you examine its key qualities more closely.

Types of Groups

Groups come in a variety of shapes and sizes and they perform functions that are vast and varied, so the differences among them are as noteworthy as their similarities. Here we consider four basic types of groups, but admit this simple typology fails to do justice to the wondrous variety of groups.

Primary Groups Sociologist Charles Horton Cooley (1909) labeled the small, intimate clusters of close associates, such as families, good friends, or cliques of peers, **primary groups**. These groups profoundly influence the behavior, feelings, and judgments of their members, for members spend much of their time interacting with one another, usually in face-to-face settings with many of the other members present. Even when the group is dispersed, members nonetheless feel they are still "in" the group, and they consider the group to be a very important part of their lives.

---

primary group A small, long-term group characterized by frequent interaction, solidarity, and high levels of interdependence among members that substantially influences the attitudes, values, and social outcomes of its members.

In many cases, individuals become part of primary groups involuntarily: Most are born into a family that provides for their well-being until they can join other groups. Other primary groups form when people interact in significant, meaningful ways for a prolonged period of time. For example, the Impressionists, a small group of artists who worked together during the second half of the nineteenth century, exhibited many of the key qualities of a primary group. The group originated in 1860 when two struggling artists, Claude Monet and Camille Pissarro, met by happenstance and immediately became friends. They spent hours together sharing their ideas about art and politics, and soon other artists joined with them. The group, challenged by those who criticized their work, became highly unified. They met regularly, each Thursday and Sunday, in a café in Paris to discuss technique, subject matter, and artistic philosophies, and they even painted as a group. When one of them fell ill or faced financial crises, the others were there to provide support. They competed with one another for fame and notoriety, but throughout they worked together to change the public's attitudes about their work. As Chapter 4's more detailed analysis of this group explains, in time the group overcame their critics, and their approach was recognized as a new form of artistic expression (Farrell, 2001).

Cooley (1909) considered such groups to be primary because they so significantly influenced the lives of their members. Primary groups protect members from harm, care for them when they are ill, and provide them with shelter and sustenance, but as Cooley explained, they also create the connection between the individual and society at large:

> They are primary in several senses, but chiefly in that they are fundamental in forming the social nature and ideals of the individual. The result of intimate association, psychologically, is a certain fusion of individualities in a common whole, so that one's very self, for many purposes at least, is the common life and purpose of the group. Perhaps the simplest way of describing this wholeness is by saying that it is a "we." (Cooley, 1909, p. 23)

Social Groups   In earlier eras *Homo sapiens* lived most of their lives in primary groups that were usually clustered together in relatively small tribes or communities. But, as societies became more complex, so did their groups. People began to associate with a wider range of people in less intimate, more public settings, and **social groups** emerged to structure these interactions. Social groups are larger and more formally organized than primary groups, and memberships tend to be shorter in duration and less emotionally involving. Their boundaries are also more permeable, so members can leave old groups behind and join new ones, for they do not demand the level of commitment that primary groups do. People can enjoy membership in a variety of social groups, but it would be unusual to belong to numerous primary groups. Various terms have been used to describe this category of groups, such as *secondary groups* (Cooley, 1909), *associations* (MacIver & Page, 1937), *task groups* (Lickel, Hamilton, & Sherman, 2001), and *Gesellschaften* (Toennies, 1887/1963).

Social groups create networks of interpersonal communication and influence between members,

but often they are task-oriented: their primary purpose is the performance of tasks rather than enjoying relationships. Such groups as military squads, governing boards, construction workers, teams, crews, fraternities, sororities, dance troupes, orchestras, bands, ensembles, classes, clubs, secretarial pools, congregations, study groups, guilds, task forces, committees, and meetings are all social groups whose success at their tasks depends, in part, on the relationships that link members to one another and to the group itself. Consider, for example, the group of advisors newly elected U.S. President John F. Kennedy assembled in 1961. This group's members boasted years of experience in making monumentally important governmental decisions, and various warfare specialists from the CIA and the military attended all the meetings. The group met for many hours devising a plan to help a group of 1,400 Cuban exiles invade Cuba at a place called Bahía de Cochinos, the Bay of Pigs. They believed their plan was nearly perfect, but the attack was a disaster, and the members spent the following months wondering at their shortsightedness and cataloging all the blunders they had made (Janis, 1972, 1982, 1983). As with many social groups, the interpersonal dynamics that members failed to understand set the stage for the group's errors. We will review this particular group in detail in Chapter 11, when we examine how groups make decisions.

Collectives   At exactly 1:30 in the afternoon on a sunny day outside the student union, two students—one dressed in white and another in green—bowed to each other before launching into a barrage of mock karate chops punctuated with shouts of "Wha-cha." At that moment, most of the people near them—30 to 40 fellow college students—also paired off in make-believe mêlées that lasted until one of the original combatants fell to the ground. When he collapsed, all the other fighters collapsed as well, leaving but one person standing. As he walked away, the students all stood up, picked up their knapsacks, and went their separate ways. It was a *flash mob*, organized by the use of cell phone technology and instant messaging (Rheingold, 2002; see Chapter 17).

---

social group A relatively small number of individuals who interact with one another over an extended period of time, such as work groups, clubs, and congregations.

A **collective** is literally any aggregate of two or more individuals, but most theorists reserve the term for larger, more spontaneous, and looser forms of association among people (Blumer, 1951). A list of collectives would include a street crowd watching a building burn, an audience at a movie, a line *(queue)* of people waiting to purchase tickets, a peaceful but nonetheless pepper-sprayed gathering of college students protesting a government policy, and a panicked mob fleeing from danger. But the list would also include mass movements of individuals who, though dispersed over a wide area, display common shifts in opinion or actions. The members of collectives owe little allegiance to such groups, for in many cases such groups are created by happenstance, and the relations joining the group are so transitory that they dissolve as soon as the members separate.

Categories A **social category** is a collection of individuals who are similar to one another in some way. For example, people who live in New York City are *New Yorkers*, Americans whose ancestors were from Africa are *African Americans*, and those who routinely wager sums of money on games of chance are *gamblers*. If a category has no social implications, then it only describes individuals who share a feature in common. If, however, these categories set in motion personal or interpersonal processes—if two students in college become friends when they discover they grew up in the same town, if people respond to a person differently when they see he is an African American, or if a person begins to gamble even more of her earnings because she realizes that she is a *gambler*—then a

category may be transformed into a highly influential group (Galinsky, Ku, & Wang, 2005).

Primary and social groups significantly influence people's conception of themselves, but social categories do as well. As social psychologist Henri Tajfel (1974) explained, members of the same social group or category often share a common identity with one another. They know who is in their category, who is not, and what qualities are typical of insiders and outsiders. This perception of themselves as members of the same group or social category—this **social identity**—is "that part of an individual's self-concept which derives from his knowledge of his membership of a social group (or groups) together with the emotional significance attached to that membership" (Tajfel, 1974, p. 69).

When this sense of *we* and *us* is coupled with a sense of *them* and *they* conflict can erupt between people who belong to different categories (Abrams et al., 2005). Consider, for example, two individuals—Cuneo and his friend Boyle—who worked as bouncers at a local bar. While driving home after work, they stop by another car at a red light and begin shouting insults at the two men seated in it. At the next intersection, a savage fight breaks out between the two groups of men who use baseball bats, a bottle, a knife, a piece of a picket fence, jumper cables, and even a car to injure each other. Why? Were these old enemies who were settling a grudge? Gang members who had sworn a vow to defend their turf? Drug dealers fighting over territory? No. The two sets of men were strangers to one another. But Cuneo and Boyle were white, Wilson and Booker were black, and these categories instigated the conflict (Sedgwick, 1982; see Chapter 14).

Perceiving Groups

Group theorists are not the only ones who divide groups up into coherent clusters like those listed in

---

collective A relatively large aggregation or group of individuals who display similarities in actions and outlook. A street crowd, a line of people (a queue), a panicked group escaping a fire are examples of collectives, as are more widely dispersed groups (e.g., listeners who respond similarly to a public service announcement).
social category A perceptual grouping of people who are assumed to be similar to one another in some ways but different in some ways from individuals who are not members of that grouping.

---

social identity An individual's sense of self derived from relationships and memberships in groups; also, those aspects of the self that are assumed to be common to most or all of the members of the same group or social category.

T A B L E   1.4   Types of Groups

Type of Group	Characteristics	Examples
Primary groups	Small, long-term groups characterized by a high frequency of interaction (usually in face-to-face settings), cohesiveness, and member identification	Close friends, families, gangs, military squads
Social groups	Small groups of moderate duration and permeability characterized by moderate levels of interaction over an extended period of time, often in goal-focused situations	Coworkers, crews, expeditions, fraternities, teams, study groups, task forces
Collectives	Aggregations of individuals that form spontaneously, last only a brief period of time, and have very permeable boundaries	Audiences, bystanders, crowds, mobs, waiting lines (queues)
Categories	Aggregations of individuals who are similar to one another in some way, such as gender, ethnicity, religion, or nationality	Asian Americans, New Yorkers, physicians, U.S. citizens, women

Table 1.4. People not only recognize the difference between groups and nongroups, but they also intuitively draw distinctions between diverse types of groups.

Entitativity: Seeing Groups Social psychologist Donald Campbell (1958a) coined the term **entitativity** to describe the extent to which a group seems to be a single, unified entity—a real group. Campbell grounded his analysis of group entitativity in the principles of perception studied most closely by Gestalt psychologists (e.g., Köhler, 1959). These researchers identified these principles in their studies of the cues people rely on when perceptually organizing objects into unified, well-organized wholes (Gestalts). An automobile, for example, is not perceived to be 4 wheels, doors, a trunk, a hood, a windshield, and so on, but a single thing: a car. Similarly, a collection of individuals—say four young men walking down the street—might be perceived to be four unrelated individuals, but the observer may also conclude the individuals are a group. Entitativity, then, is the "groupiness" of a group, perceived rather than actual group unity or cohesion.

----

entitativity The apparent cohesiveness or unity of an assemblage of individuals; the quality of being a single entity rather than a set of independent, unrelated individuals (coined in Campbell, 1958).

Entitativity, according to Campbell, is substantially influenced by similarity, proximity, and common fate, as well as such perceptual cues as pragnanz (good form) and permeability. Say, for example, you are walking through a library and see a table occupied by four women. Is this a group—four friends or classmates studying together—or just four independent individuals? Campbell predicts that you would, intuitively, notice if the four have certain physical features in common, such as age, skin color, or clothing. You would also take note of the books they were reading, for if they were studying the same subject, you would assume they share a common goal—and hence are more likely to be a true group (Brewer, Hong, & Li, 2004; Ip, Chiu, & Wan, 2006). Their emotional displays would also provide you with information about their entitativity. If the women all seem to be happy or sad, then you would be more likely to think the group is responsible for their emotional state and that the group itself is a unified one (Magee & Tiedens, 2006). Proximity is also a signal of entitativity, for the smaller the distance separating individuals, the more likely perceivers will assume they are seeing a group rather than individuals who happen to be collocated (Knowles & Bassett, 1976). The principle of common fate also predicts perceived entitativity, for if all the members begin to act in similar ways, or move in a relatively coordinated fashion, then your confidence that this

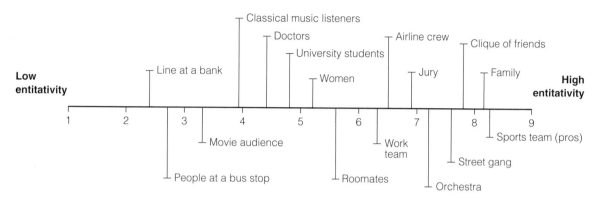

FIGURE 1.4 Entitativity ratings of 16 different groups (Data source: Lickel et al., 2000).
SOURCE: © Cengage Learning 2014

cluster is a unified group would be bolstered (Lakens, 2010).

Types of Groups and Entitativity When do social perceivers conclude the people they encounter are members of a group and when do they instead see them as many individuals? Social psychologist Brian Lickel and his colleagues (2000) examined this question by asking people to rate all sorts of human aggregations in terms of their size, duration, permeability, amount of interaction among members, importance to members, and so on. Lickel and his colleagues then used a statistical procedure called *cluster analysis* to determine if some of these aggregates were rated as more similar than others. These analyses, as they expected, yielded four natural groupings that were very similar to the ones that are listed in Table 1.4 (which they labeled intimacy groups, task groups, loose associations, and social categories). The researchers then asked people to sort the 40 aggregates into stacks. Again, analysis identified the same basic types of groups. They also asked people to list 12 groups that they belong to. When unbiased raters reviewed these lists, once again the four types were in evidence (Lickel et al., 2000).

The research team also asked the perceivers if they considered all these kinds of aggregations of individuals to be true groups. They did not force people to make an either/or decision about each one, however. Recognizing that the boundary between what is and what is not a group is perceptually fuzzy, they instead asked participants to rate the aggregations on a scale from 1 *(not at all a group)* to 9 *(very much a group)*. As Figure 1.4 indicates, primary groups, such as professional sports teams, families, and close friends, received the highest entitativity ratings, followed by social groups (e.g., a jury, an airline crew, a team in the workplace), categories (e.g., women, doctors, classical music listeners), and collectives (e.g., people waiting for a bus, a queue in a bank). These findings suggest that people are more likely to consider aggregations marked by strong bonds and frequent interactions among members to be groups, but that they are less certain that such aggregations as crowds, waiting lines, or categories qualify as groups (Lickel et al., 2000, Study 3). They also suggest that social categories—which include vast numbers of people whose only qualification for membership in the category may be a demographic quality, such as sex or nationality—were viewed as more group-like than such temporary gatherings as waiting lines and audiences and, in some cases, task-focused groups (Spencer-Rogers, Hamilton, & Sherman, 2007).

Lickel and his colleagues also point out that, even though they were studying entitativity, they could not use this word on their questionnaires, because people would have been baffled by this unusual term. Instead, they simply asked "participants to evaluate the degree to which different collections of people 'qualify as a group'" (Lickel et al., 2000, p. 228).

Entitativity's Implications   The sociologist W. I. Thomas stated that "if men define situations as real, they are real in their consequences" (Thomas & Thomas, 1928, p. 572); this statement is now known as the **Thomas Theorem** (Merton, 1976). Applied to groups, this theorem predicts that if people define groups as real, they are real in their consequences. A collection of individuals literally becomes a group when the members, or others outside the group, construe the gathering to be a group.

This shift in thinking—seeing a gathering of people as a true group rather than single individuals—triggers a series of psychological and interpersonal changes for both members and non-members. Entitativity changes people's perceptions of their relationship to their group, for it causes members to identify with the group and its goals, value the importance of membership, and feel bonded to the group (Castano, Yzerbyt, & Bourguignon, 2003; Jans, Postmes, & Van der Zee, 2011). This tendency is particularly strong when people feel uncertain about themselves and the correctness of their beliefs (Hogg et al., 2007). When members feel they are part of a high entitativity group, they are more likely to think that they fit well within the group, they believe that they are similar to other group members in terms of values and beliefs, and they are more willing to accept the consequences of group-level outcomes as their own (Mullen, 1991). For example, when researchers repeatedly told women working in isolation that they were nonetheless members of a group, the women accepted this label and later rated themselves more negatively after the group failed—even though the group existed only in their perceptions (Zander, Stotland, & Wolfe, 1960).

People also think differently about entitative groups and the people in them. When people encounter a person who is a member of a group thought to be high in entitativity, their perceptions of that person are more influenced by any **stereotypes** that they hold about that particular group (Rydell et al., 2007). People tend to think members of such groups are basically interchangeable (Crawford, Sherman, & Hamilton, 2002), and they tend to evaluate the group, in general, more negatively (Dasgupta, Banaji, & Abelson, 1999). Observers are more likely to hold the members of such groups collectively responsible for the actions of one of the group members (Denson et al., 2006), and they assume the group has a relatively strong influence on its members (Waytz & Young, 2012). A sense of **essentialism** tends to permeate perceivers' beliefs about groups that are high in entitativity, for people think that such groups have deep, relatively unchanging essential qualities that give rise to their more surface-level characteristics (Haslam, Rothschild, & Ernst, 2002; Yzerbyt, Judd, & Corneille, 2004). When perceivers think an aggregate of individuals is a group they are more likely to treat it like a group, and this treatment increases the group's actual unity (Alter & Darley, 2009; see Focus 1.2).

THE NATURE OF GROUP DYNAMICS

Group dynamics describes both a subject matter and a scientific field of study. When psychologist Kurt Lewin (1951) described the way groups and

---

Thomas Theorem The theoretical premise, put forward by W. I. Thomas, which maintains that people's understanding of a social situation, even if incorrect, will determine their reactions in the situation; "If men define situations as real, they are real in their consequences" (Thomas & Thomas, 1928, p. 572).

stereotype A socially shared set of qualities, characteristics, and behavioral expectations ascribed to a particular group or category of people.

essentialism The belief that all things, including individuals and groups, have a basic nature that makes them what they are and distinguishes them from other things; a thing's essence is usually inferred rather than directly observed and is generally assumed to be relatively unchanging.

F o c u s 1.2   Cross-Cultural Perspectives: Seeing the Forest (Groups) or the Trees (Individuals)

Groups may be everywhere, doing just about everything, but they stand outside the limelight that shines on most people's explanation of what makes the world go around. Even though people throw concepts like teamwork, networks, gangs, and cliques about in their discussions of contemporary issues, they tend to see only the individuals in these groups and not the groups themselves. Most people are intuitive psychologists searching for the causes of behavior within each person, and they resist explanations that talk about group-level influences (Heider, 1958).

Westerners, that is. This generalization about the perceptual prominence of individuals relative to groups is not a universal, for one's capacity to "see" groups varies depending on one's cultural and community background. People who grew up in non-Western societies, such as China and India, think of themselves as group members first and individuals second and so emphasize the unity of all people in their group rather than each person's individuality. In many cultures, social existence is centered on group relations, for groups create social obligations that form the basis of respect, trust, and community (Triandis & Suh, 2002).

People living in China, for example, resist making judgments of individuals if they do not know anything about the group to which the person belongs. The primary philosophical framework in that culture, Confucianism, takes as given the relatedness of all things, and this perspective is manifested interpersonally by the unrelenting and taken-for-granted emphasis on membership in closely knit collectives (Nisbett et al, 2001). Japanese people similarly begin with the group and only move to consider individual-level factors to account for unexpected, baffling events. This emphasis on the group is reflected in the rich vocabulary of group-level concepts in the Japanese language. Whereas English includes a smattering of words for groups, the Japanese language is rich with words for *group*: kumi, han, gurupu, shudan, kyudan, renchuu, dojo, nakama, kurabu, saakuru, renshukai, kenkyukai, keikokai, and shugyokai. Nor is there an English word that corresponds to the group-level concept of *amae* in Japanese. Amae means "to look to others for affection," but it underscores the strong, unbreakable, and deeply fulfilling bond that joins group members to one another (Niiya, Ellsworth & Yamaguchi, 2006). The Japanese emphasis on groups goes beyond kin relations, as work settings, schools, and social activities are all centered on groups (Yuki, 2003).

This emphasis on groups results in differences in perceptions of the entitativity of groups. People raised in a Western culture, such as England or the United States, do not shift to a group-level perceptual set unless provoked by some aspect of the group. Someone raised in an Asian culture, such as China or Korea, sees unity and connection first and separateness second. Researchers, when asking participants from China and America to judge the degree of entitativity of two fictitious groups discovered that those perceivers from China judged these groups to be higher in entitativity than did American participants. They also felt that changing from one group to another would be a more difficult task than did individuals raised in the West (Spencer-Rodgers et al., 2007). In another study, the participants raised in non-Western cultures differed from Americans in their perceptions of different types of groups—the Japanese perceivers considered task groups to be higher in entitativity than primary, intimate groups (Kurebayashi et al., 2012).

Individuals from Eastern cultures still recognize individuals as entities—they attribute personality characteristics to people, and they view people as possessing an essence that defines who they are—just as Westerners do. However, individuals from three East Asian cultures (Hong Kong, Japan, and Korea) were more likely than those from five Western cultures (Australia, United Kingdom, United States, Belgium, and Germany) to attribute cognitive and emotional states to both groups and individuals (Kashima et al., 2005). This difference in emphasis was apparent in the words used in newspaper articles that covered stories of illegal actions taken by corporate "rogue" traders. Japanese newspapers more frequently focused on the organization and its responsibility, whereas U.S. newspapers concentrated on the perpetrator and his actions (Menon et al., 1999).

These findings urge caution when making sweeping, cross-cultural conclusions about people. Each of the chapters of this book draws on research and theory to offer general conclusions about groups and human behavior in groups, but these generalities are in some cases culturally specific. Conclusions reached by studying the groups in one setting and one time may tell us little about groups in other places and in other eras. As a constant reminder of the dangers of cultural ethnocentrism, each chapter will include a "Focus" section that examines the cultural conditions that influence groups and their dynamics.

individuals act and react to changing circumstances, he named these processes *group dynamics*. But Lewin also used the phrase to describe the scientific discipline devoted to the study of these dynamics. Later, Dorwin Cartwright and Alvin Zander supplied a formal definition, calling it a "field of inquiry dedicated to advancing knowledge about the nature of groups, the laws of their development, and their interrelations with individuals, other groups, and larger institutions" (1968, p. 7).

Group dynamics is about a century old. Although scholars have long pondered the nature of groups, the first scientific studies of groups were not carried out until the 1900s. Cartwright and Zander (1968), in their review of the origins of group dynamics, suggest that its slow development stemmed in part from several unfounded assumptions about groups. Many felt that the dynamics of groups was a private affair, not something that scientists should lay open to public scrutiny. Others felt that human behavior was too complex to be studied scientifically and that this complexity was magnified enormously when groups of interacting individuals became the objects of interest. Still others believed that the causes of group behavior were so obvious that they were unworthy of scientific attention.

The field also developed slowly because theorists and researchers disagreed among themselves on many basic theoretical and methodological issues. The field was not established by a single theorist or researcher who laid down a set of clear-cut assumptions and principles. Rather, group dynamics resulted from group processes. One theorist would suggest an idea, another might disagree, and the debate would continue until consensus would be reached. Initially, researchers were uncertain how to investigate their ideas empirically, but through collaboration and, more often, spirited competition, researchers developed new methods for studying groups. World events also influenced the study of groups, for the use of groups in manufacturing, warfare, and therapeutic settings stimulated the need to understand and improve such groups.

These group processes shaped the field's **paradigm**. The philosopher of science, Thomas S. Kuhn (1970), used that term to describe scientists' shared assumptions about the phenomena they study. Kuhn maintained that when scientists learn their field, they master not only the content of the science—important discoveries, general principles, facts, and so on—but also a way of looking at the world that is passed on from one scientist to another. These shared beliefs and unstated assumptions give them a worldview—a way of looking at that part of the world that they find most interesting. The paradigm determines the questions they consider worth studying, using the methods that are most appropriate.

What are the core elements of the field's paradigm? What do researchers and theorists notice when they observe a group acting in a particular way? What kinds of group processes do they find fascinating, and which ones do they find less interesting? We begin to answer these questions by considering some of the basic assumptions of the field and tracing them back to their source in the work of early sociologists, psychologists, and social psychologists. We then shift from the historical to the contemporary and review current topics and trends in the field. Chapter 2 continues this analysis of the field's paradigm by considering practices and procedures used by researchers when they collect information about groups (Forsyth & Burnette, 2005).

The Scientific Study of Groups

When anthropology, psychology, sociology, and the other social sciences emerged as their own unique disciplines in the late 1800s, the dynamics of groups became a topic of critical concern for all of them. Sociologists studying religious, political, economic, and educational social systems highlighted the role groups played in maintaining social order. Anthropologists, as they studied one culture after another, discovered similarities and differences among the

---

paradigm Scientists' shared assumptions about the phenomena they study; also, a set of research procedures.

world's small tribal groups. Political scientists' studies of voting, public engagement, and political parties led them to the study of small groups of closely networked individuals. In 1895, social theorist Gustave Le Bon, published *Psychologie des Foules* (*Psychology of Crowds*), which claimed that individuals are transformed when they join a group. The psychologist Wilhelm Wundt (1916), recognized as the founder of scientific psychology, also studied groups extensively. His book *Völkerpsychologie* is sometimes translated as "folk psychology," but another translation is "group psychology." It combined elements of anthropology and psychology by examining the conditions and changes displayed by elementary social aggregates and how group memberships influence virtually all cognitive and perceptual processes.

These works laid the basic groundwork for the scientific study of groups. But as the discipline's paradigm took shape, investigators often endorsed disparate sets of assumptions about humans and their groups. Must we study groups as a unit, or can we instead focus on the individuals only? Do groups have minds, just as individuals do? Are groups greater than the sum of their parts?

Which Level: Group or Individual? Almost immediately, theorists disagreed about the **level of analysis** to take when studying groups. Some favored a *group-level analysis*, for they recognized that humans are the constitutive elements of groups and that groups and their processes have a profound impact on their members. Others advocated for an *individual-level analysis* that focused on the person in the group. Researchers who took this approach sought to explain the behavior of each group member, and they ultimately wanted to know if such psychological processes as attitudes, motivations, or personality were the true determinants of social behavior (Steiner, 1974, 1983, 1986).

Sociological researchers tended to undertake group-level analyses, and psychological researchers favored the individual-level analysis. Sociologist Émile Durkheim (1897/1966), for example, traced a highly personal phenomenon—suicide—back to group-level processes. He concluded that individuals who are not members of friendship, family, or religious groups can lose their sense of identity and, as a result, are more likely to commit suicide. Durkheim strongly believed that widely shared beliefs—what he called *collective representations*—are the cornerstone of society. He wrote: "emotions and tendencies are generated not by certain states of individual consciousness, but by the conditions under which the social body as a whole exists" (Durkheim, 1892/2005, p. 76).

Other researchers questioned the need to go beyond the individual to explain group behavior. Psychologist Floyd Allport (1924), for example, chose the individual in the group, and not the group itself, as the unit of analysis when he wrote that "nervous systems are possessed by individuals; but there is no nervous system of the crowd" (p. 5). Because Allport believed that "the actions of all are nothing more than the sum of the actions of each taken separately" (p. 5), he thought that a full understanding of the behavior of individuals in groups could be achieved by studying the psychology of the individual group members. Groups, according to Allport, were not real entities and that people who used such phrasings as "the group felt confident" or "the group thought the proposal was a good idea" were falling prey to the **group fallacy**. "An individual can be said to 'think' or 'feel'; but to say that a group does these things has no ascertainable meaning beyond saying that so many individuals do them" (Allport, 1962, p. 4). He is reputed to have said, "You can't trip over a group."

---

level of analysis The focus of study when examining a multilevel process or phenomenon, such as the micro-level (individuals in a group), the meso-level (the group), or the macro-level (the organization or society where the group is located).

---

group fallacy Explaining social phenomena in terms of the group as a whole instead of basing the explanation on the individual-level processes within the group; ascribing psychological qualities, such as will, intentionality, and mind, to a group rather than to the individuals within the group.

Do Groups Have Minds? The idea of **group mind** (or collective consciousness) brought the group- and individual-level perspectives into clear opposition (Jahoda, 2007). Groups that undertake extreme actions under the exhortation of charismatic leaders fascinate both laypeople and researchers alike. Although groups are so commonplace that they usually go unnoticed and unscrutinized, atypical groups—cults, violent mobs, terrorist cells, communes—invite extensive analysis. Some early commentators on the human condition went so far as to suggest that such groups may develop a collective consciousness that is greater than the sum of the psychological experiences of the members and that it can become so powerful that it can overwhelm the will of the individual. Le Bon (1895/1960, p. 23), for example, wrote "Under certain circumstances, and only under those circumstances, an agglomeration of men presents new characteristics very different from those of the individuals composing [the group]." Durkheim, too, suggested that groups, rather than being mere collections of individuals in a fixed pattern of relationships with one another, were linked by an "esprit de group" (group mind):

> individuals are all that society is made of … the mentality of groups is not that of individuals *(particuliers)*, precisely because it assumes a plurality of individual minds joined together. A collectivity has its own ways of thinking and feeling to which its members bend but which are different from those they would create if they were left to their own devices. (Durkheim, 1900/1973, pp. 16–17)

Durkheim may have been positing the existence of a metaphysical bond that joined members, but more likely he was using the phrase *group mind* metaphorically to suggest that many psychological processes are determined, in part, by interactions with other people, and those interactions are in turn shaped by the mental activities and actions of each individual in the collective. Even so, Durkheim believed that group-level forces were sometimes so strong that they dominated the will of the individual.

The idea of group mind was a controversial one and contributed to a continuing disunity within the developing field of group dynamics. Allport, for example, never backed down from his anti-group position. Even though he conducted extensive studies of such group phenomena as rumors and morale during wartime (Allport & Lepkin, 1943) and conformity to standards (the J-curve hypothesis; Allport, 1934, 1961), he continued to question the scientific value of the term *group*. He did, however, eventually conclude that individuals are often bound together in "one inclusive *collective* structure" but he could not bring himself to use the word *group* to describe such collectives (Allport, 1962, p. 17, italics in original). He also believed that "only through social psychology as a science of the individual can we avoid the superficialities of the crowdmind and collective mind theories" (p. 8).

Allport's reluctance to accept such dubious concepts as group mind into social psychology helped ensure the field's scientific status, but most people recognize that groups are capable of some forms of collective thinking, reasoning, and feeling, so that, in a sense, groups have minds. The researchers in one study, for example, simply asked people if groups have minds. They did this by presenting people with a long list of various types of groups and asking them if each group on the list had a mind: "the capacity to make plans, have intentions, and think for itself" (Waytz & Young, 2012, p. 78). When they examined people's ratings, they discovered that general categories of people, such as all blondes or Facebook users, were not thought to have minds, but that smaller, more cohesive aggregates—such as organizations (e.g., Bank of America), teams (e.g., Boston Red Sox), and decision-making groups (e.g., the Supreme Court)—received higher ratings of mind. Interestingly, they also discovered a trade-off between the group- and individual-level conceptions of mind: as judgments of group mind went up, estimates of individual mind went down. Those who were members of groups that the perceiver thought had mind-like

---

group mind (or collective consciousness) A hypothetical unifying mental force linking group members together; the fusion of individual consciousness or mind into a transcendent consciousness.

qualities were viewed as less mindful individuals, whereas those individuals who were members of groups that did not seem to have group minds were viewed as having minds of their own. Because attributions of mind to groups increased along with perceptions of the group's cohesiveness (entitativity), members of low-cohesive groups were held more accountable for their group's actions, whereas members of highly cohesive groups were given less personal responsibility. Here, the group was held accountable, since it was thought to have a "mind."

Are Group Processes Real? Allport was correct in rejecting the concept of a group mind. Researchers have never found any evidence that group members are linked by a psychic, telepathic connection that creates a single group mind. But just because this group-level concept has little foundation in fact does not mean that other group-level concepts are equally unreasonable. Consider, for example, the concept of a group norm. As noted earlier, a *norm* is a standard that describes what behaviors should and should not be performed in a group. Norms are not just individual members' personal standards, for they are shared among group members. Only when members agree on a particular standard does it function as a norm, so this concept is embedded at the level of the group rather than at the level of the individual.

The idea that a norm is more than just the sum of the individual beliefs of all the members of a group was verified by Muzafer Sherif in 1936. Sherif, a social psychologist, literally created norms by asking groups of men to state aloud their estimates of the distance that a dot of light had moved. He found that the men gradually accepted a standard estimate in place of their own idiosyncratic judgments. He also found, however, that even when the men were later given the opportunity to make judgments alone, they still based their estimates on the group's norm. Moreover, once the group's norm had developed, Sherif removed members one at a time and replaced them with fresh members. Each new member changed his behavior until it matched the group's norm. If the individuals in the group are completely replaceable, then where does the group norm "exist"? It exists at the group level rather than the individual level (MacNeil & Sherif, 1976).

Are Groups More Than the Sum of Their Parts? The debate between individual-level and group-level approaches waned, in time, as theorists developed stronger models for understanding group-level process. Lewin's (1951) theoretical analyses of groups were particularly influential. His *field theory* is premised on the principle of *interactionism*, which assumes that the behavior of people in groups is determined by the interaction of the person and the environment. The formula $\boldsymbol{B} = \boldsymbol{f(P, E)}$ summarizes this assumption. In a group context, this formula implies that the behavior (B) of group members is a function (f) of the interaction of their personal characteristics (P) with environmental factors (E), which include features of the group, the group members, and the situation. Lewin believed that, because of interactionism, a group is a Gestalt—a unified system with emergent properties that cannot be fully understood by piecemeal examination. Adopting the dictum, "The whole is greater than the sum of the parts," he maintained that when individuals merged into a group something new was created and that the new product itself had to be the object of study.

Many group phenomena are consistent with Lewin's belief that a group is more than the sum of the individual members. A group's cohesiveness, for example, goes beyond the mere attraction of each individual member for one another (Hogg, 1992). Individuals may not like each other a great deal and yet, when they join together, they experience powerful feelings of unity and esprit de corps. Groups sometimes perform tasks far better—and far worse—than might be expected, given the talents of their individual members. When individuals combine synergistically in a group, they sometimes accomplish incredible feats and make horrible decisions that no single individual could ever conceive (Larson, 2010). Such a group seems to possess supervening qualities "that cannot be reduced

---

$\boldsymbol{B} = \boldsymbol{f(P, E)}$ The law of interactionism that states each person's behavior (B) is a function of his or her personal qualities (P), the social environment (E), and the interaction of these personal qualities with factors present in the social setting (proposed by Kurt Lewin).

Orientation (forming)
Exchange of background personal information, uncertainty, tentative communication

Conflict (storming)
Dissatisfaction, disagreement, challenges to leader and procedures, cliques form

Structure (norming)
Cohesiveness, agreement on procedures, standards, and roles, improved communication

Performance (performing)
Focus on the work of the group, task completion, decision making, cooperation

Dissolution (adjourning)
Departures, withdrawal, decreased dependence, regret

F I G U R E 1.5   Stages of group development. Tuckman's theory of group development suggests that groups typically pass through five stages during their development: orientation (forming), conflict (storming), structure (norming), performance (performing), and dissolution (adjourning).

SOURCE: © Cengage Learning 2014

to or described as qualities of its participants" (Sandelands & St. Clair, 1993, p. 443).

Groups also become more Gestalt-like as they mature from newly formed, fledgling assemblies of individuals into highly structured, well-developed groups. Educational psychologist Bruce Tuckman's theory of **group development**, for example, assumes that most groups move through the five stages summarized in Figure 1.5 (Tuckman, 1965;

---

group development Patterns of change in a group's structure and interactions that occur over the course of the group's existence.

Tuckman & Jensen, 1977). In the orientation (*forming*) phase, the group members become oriented toward one another. In the conflict (*storming*) phase, conflicts surface in the group as members vie for status and the group sets its goals. These conflicts subside when the group becomes more structured and standards emerge in the structure (*norming*) phase. In the performance (*performing*) phase, the group moves beyond disagreement and organizational matters to concentrate on the work to be done. The group continues to function at this stage until it reaches the dissolution (*adjourning*) stage. As Chapter 5 explains in more detail, groups also tend to cycle repeatedly through some of these stages as group members strive to maintain a balance between task-oriented actions and emotionally expressive behaviors (Bales, 1965).

A Multilevel Approach to the Study of Groups

In time, the rift between individual-level and group-level researchers closed as the unique contributions of each perspective were integrated in a **multilevel perspective** on groups. This perspective does not favor a specific level of analysis when examining human behavior, for it argues for examining processes that range along the micro–meso–macro continuum (see Figure 1.6). *Micro-level* factors include the qualities, characteristics, and actions of the individual members. *Meso-level* factors are group-level qualities of the groups themselves, such as their cohesiveness, their size, their composition, and their structure. *Macro-level* factors are the qualities and processes of the larger collectives that enfold the groups, such as communities, organizations, or societies. Groups, then, are nested at the meso-level, where the bottom-up

---

multilevel perspective The view that recognizes that a complete explanation of group processes and phenomena requires multiple levels of analysis, including individual (micro), group (meso), and organizational or societal (macro) level.

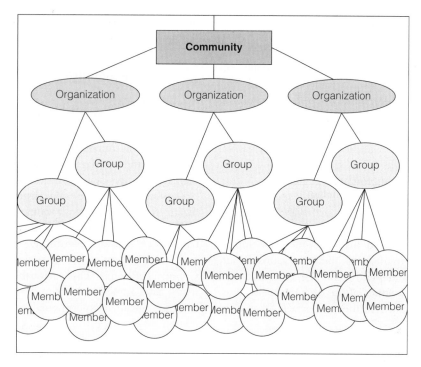

FIGURE 1.6 A multilevel perspective on groups. Researchers who study groups recognize that individuals (micro-level) are nested in groups (meso-level), but that these groups are themselves nested in larger social units, such as organizations, communities, tribes, nations, and societies (the macro-level). Researchers may focus on one level in this multilevel system, such as the group level, but they must be aware that these groups are embedded in a complex of other relationships.

SOURCE: © Cengage Learning 2014

micro-level variables meet the top-down macro-level variables.

Crossing Levels Social psychologist Richard Hackman and his colleagues' studies of performing orchestras illustrate the value of a multilevel approach (Allmendinger, Hackman, & Lehman, 1996; Hackman, 2003). In their quest to understand why some professional orchestras outperformed others, they measured an array of micro-, meso-, and macro-level variables. At the micro-level, they studied the individual musicians: Were they well-trained and highly skilled? Were they satisfied with their work and highly motivated? Did they like each other and feel that they played well together? At the group-level (meso-level), they considered the gender composition of the group (number of men and women players), the quality of the music the orchestra produced, and the financial resources available to the group. They also took note of one key macro-level variable: the location of the orchestras in one of four different countries (United States, England, East Germany, or West Germany).

Their work uncovered complex interrelations among these three sets of variables. As might be expected, one micro-level variable—the skill of the individual players—substantially influenced the quality of the performance of the group. However, one critical determinant of the talent of individual players was the financial health of the orchestra; better-funded orchestras could afford to hire better performers. Affluent orchestras could also afford music directors who worked more closely with the performers, and orchestras who performed better than expected given the caliber of their individual players were led by the most skilled directors. The country where the orchestra was based was also an important determinant of the group members' satisfaction with their orchestra, but only when one also considered the gender composition of the orchestras. Far fewer women were members of orchestras in West Germany, but as the proportion of women in orchestras increased, members became increasingly negative about their group. In contrast, in the United States with its directive employment regulations, more women were included in orchestras, and the proportion of women in the groups was less closely related to attitude toward the group. Given their findings, Hackman and his colleagues concluded that the answer to most of their questions about orchestras was "it depends": on the individuals in the group, on the nature of the orchestra itself, and the social context where the orchestra is located.

Interdisciplinary Orientation The multilevel perspective gives group dynamics an interdisciplinary character. For example, researchers who prefer to study individuals may find themselves wondering what impact group participation will have on individuals' cognitions, attitudes, and behavior. Those who study organizations may find that these larger social entities actually depend on the dynamics of small subgroups within the organization. Social scientists examining such global issues as the development and maintenance of culture may find themselves turning their attention toward small groups as the unit of cultural transmission. Political scientists who study national and international leaders may discover that such leaders are centers of a small network of advisors and that their political actions cannot be understood without taking into account the dynamics of these advisory councils. Although the listing of disciplines that study group dynamics in Table 1.5 is far from comprehensive, it does convey the idea that the study of groups is not limited to any one field. As A. Paul Hare and his colleagues once noted, "This field of research does not 'belong' to any one of the recognized social sciences alone. It is

the common property of all" (Hare, Borgatta, & Bales, 1955, p. vi).

The Significance of Groups

A multilevel perspective makes it clear that many of the most important aspects of human existence—including individuals, organizations, communities, and cultures—cannot be fully understood without an understanding of groups. But, practically speaking, why study groups when one can investigate brain structures, cultures, biological diseases, organizations, ancient civilizations, or even other planets? In the grand scheme of things, how important is it to investigate groups?

Groups Influence Their Members Lewin, who many have argued is the founder of the movement to study groups experimentally, chose the word *dynamic* to describe the activities, processes, operations, and changes that transpire in groups. This word suggests that groups have a profound impact on individuals; they shape actions, thoughts, and feelings (Lewin, 1943, 1948, 1951).

Some of these changes are subtle ones. Moving from isolation to a group context can reduce our sense of uniqueness, but at the same time it can enhance our ability to perform simple tasks rapidly. In one of the earliest experimental studies in the field, Norman Triplett (1898) verified the discontinuity between people's responses when they are isolated rather than integrated, and this shift has been documented time and again in studies of motivation, emotion, and performance. (Many have suggested that Triplett's study marks the start of the scientific investigation of interpersonal processes, but in all likelihood the field's roots reach even further back in time; see Stroebe, 2012.) Groups can also change their members by prompting them to change their attitudes and values as they come to agree with the overall consensus of the group (Newcomb, 1943). As Cooley (1909) explained, people acquire their attitudes, values, identities, skills, and principles in groups and become practiced at modifying their behavior

TABLE 1.5   Interdisciplinary Interest in Groups and Group Processes

Discipline	Topics
Anthropology	Groups in cross-cultural contexts; societal change; social and collective identities; evolutionary approaches to group living
Architecture and Design	Planning spaces to maximize group–environment fit; design of spaces for groups, including offices, classrooms, venues, arenas, and so on
Business and Industry	Work motivation; productivity in organizational settings; team building; goal setting; management and leadership
Communication	Information transmission in groups; discussion; decision making; problems in communication; networks
Computer Science	Virtual groups, computer-based groups support systems, computer programming in groups
Criminal Justice	Organization of law enforcement agencies; gangs and criminal groups; jury deliberations
Education	Classroom groups; team teaching; class composition and educational outcomes
Engineering	Design of human systems, including problem-solving teams; group approaches to software design
Mental Health	Therapeutic change through groups; sensitivity training; training groups; self-help groups; group psychotherapy
Political Science	Leadership; intergroup and international relations; political influence; power
Psychology	Personality and group behavior; problem solving; perceptions of other people; motivation; conflict
Social Work	Team approaches to treatment; community groups; family counseling; groups and adjustment
Sociology	Self and society; influence of norms on behavior; role relations; deviance
Sports and Recreation	Team performance; effects of victory and failure; cohesion and performance

in response to social norms and others' requirements. As children grow older, their peers replace the family as the source of social values (Harris, 1995), and when they become adults, actions and outlooks are then shaped by an even larger network of interconnected groups (Barabási, 2003).

But groups also change people in ways that are not subtle at all. The earliest group psychologists were struck by the apparent madness of people when immersed in crowds, and many concluded that the behavior of a person in a group may have no connection to that person's behavior when alone. Social psychologist Stanley Milgram's (1963) classic studies of obedience offered further confirmation of the dramatic power of groups over their members, for Milgram found that most people placed in a powerful group would obey the orders of a malevolent authority to harm another person. Individuals who join religious or political groups that stress secrecy, obedience to leaders, and dogmatic acceptance of unusual or atypical beliefs (*cults*) often display fundamental and unusual changes in belief and behavior.

Theories about groups have also proven to be particularly resilient, scientifically speaking, when put to an empirical test. In the last 100 years, researchers have conducted more than 25,000 studies involving over 8 million participants. A review of these studies suggests that much can be learned by studying people's attitudes, cognitions, personalities, and relationships, but one area of study surpassed all others in terms of providing an explanation for human social behavior. Leading the way, across all 18 topics examined in the review, was the scientific study of groups and their dynamics (Richard, Bond, & Stokes-Zoota, 2003).

Groups Influence Society   Societies of all types, from the hunter/gatherers through to the postindustrial, are defined by the small groups that create them. Groups are niched at the meso-level, between individuals and society at large, so they are the intermediary through which culture and custom influences the individual. Just as characteristics of the specific individuals who belong to a group shape that group's basic nature, so the groups that belong to society determine that society's culture and institutions. Legal and political systems, religious institutions, and educational and economic systems are based, at core, on small groups and subgroups of connected individuals. For example, individuals often endorse a specific religion, such as Christianity or Islam, but their connection to their religion occurs in smaller groups and congregations. Groups are also the means by which individuals, through their united action, transform society. Single individuals and large, dispersed populations cannot leverage the resources needed to promote social change, but groups can. The ideology of a social movement may initially attract individuals, but it takes a group to sustain their sense of community, identity, and engagement. Groups provide the microstructure "through which individuals mobilize to create social transformation" (Harrington & Fine, 2000, p. 315).

The Usefulness of Groups   Groups are supremely useful forms of social organization. These days much of the work of the world is done by people working in teams, which are, of course, groups that are uniquely task-focused (see Chapter 12). Social

workers have also found themselves dealing with such groups as social clubs, gangs, neighborhoods, and family clusters, and an awareness of group processes helps them crystallize their understanding of group life. Educators also must understand group dynamics, for most learning still takes place in small classes of collocated students. Groups, too, are often used by those in mental health fields to help individuals find the motivation to change their thoughts and behaviors (see Chapter 16).

The application of group dynamics to practical problems is consistent with Lewin's call for **action research**. Lewin argued in favor of the intertwining of basic and applied research, for he firmly believed that there "is no hope of creating a better world without a deeper scientific insight into the function of leadership, of culture, and of the other essentials of group life" (1943, p. 114). To achieve this goal, he assured practitioners that "there is nothing so practical as a good theory" (1951, p. 169) and charged researchers with the task of developing theories that can be applied to important social problems (Bargal, 2008). Understanding groups offers the means to solve many of the most basic problems people face as individuals and as a species: prejudice, personal adjustment and well-being, conflict, intergroup aggression, and abuses of power and influence.

The Dark Side of Groups   Groups offer their members many of the resources they need to prosper, but groups are not all plus with no minus. They are often the arena for profound interpersonal conflicts that end in violence and aggression. Even though group members may cooperate with one another, they may also engage in competition as they strive to outdo one another. When individuals are members of very large groups, such as crowds, they sometimes engage in behaviors that they would never undertake if they were acting individually. Many of the most misguided decisions have

_____

action research Scientific inquiry that both expands basic theoretical knowledge and identifies solutions to significant social problems.

not been made by lone individuals but by groups of people who, despite working together, still managed to make a disastrous decision. Even though people tend to work together in groups, in many cases these groups are far less productive than they should be, given the talents and energies of the individuals in them. Given these problems, psychologist and historian Christian Buys whimsically suggested that all groups be eliminated because "humans would do better without groups" (1978a, p. 123).

Although Buys' suggestion is a satirical one, it does make the point that groups are neither all good nor all bad. Groups are so "beneficial, if not essential, to humans" that "it seems nonsensical to search for alternatives to human groups" (Buys, 1978b, p. 568), but groups can generate negative outcomes for their members. Researchers, however, are more often drawn to studying negative rather than positive processes with the result that theory and research in the field tend to stress conflict, rejection, dysfunction, and obedience to malevolent authorities and to neglect cooperation, acceptance, well-being, and collaboration. This negative bias, Buys suggested, has led to an unfair underestimation of the positive impact of groups on people.

Buys' comments, by the way, have prompted a number of rejoinders by other group researchers. One group-authored response (Kravitz et al., 1978) suggested that Buys wrongly assigned responsibility for the problems; its authors argued that humans would do better without other humans rather than without any groups. Another proposed that groups would do better without humans (Anderson, 1978), whereas a third simply argued that groups would do better without social psychologists (Green & Mack, 1978).

Topics in Contemporary Group Dynamics

Throughout the history of group dynamics, some approaches that initially seemed promising have been abandoned after they contributed relatively little or failed to stimulate consistent lines of research. The idea of group mind, for example, was discarded when researchers identified more likely causes of crowd behavior. Similarly, such concepts as syntality (any effects that the group has as a functioning unit; Cattell, 1948), groupality (the personality of the group; Bogardus, 1954), and life space (all factors that define an individual's psychological reality; Lewin, 1951), initially attracted considerable interest but stimulated little research.

In contrast, researchers have studied other topics continuously since they were first broached (Berdahl & Henry, 2005). Table 1.6 samples the topics that currently interest group experts, and it foreshadows the topics considered in the remainder of this book. Chapters 1 and 2 explore the foundations of the field by reviewing the group dynamics perspective (Chapter 1) and the methods and theories of the field (Chapter 2).

Chapters 3 through 6 focus on group formation and development—how groups come into existence and how they change and evolve over time. Chapters 3 and 4 consider the demands and opportunities of a life in a group rather than alone, including the personal and situational forces that prompt people to join groups or remain apart from them. Chapter 5 focuses more fully on group development by considering the factors that increase the unity of a group and the way those factors wax and wane as the group changes over time. Chapter 6 turns to the topic of group structure—how groups develop systems of roles and relationships—with a particular focus on how structure emerges as groups mature.

A group is a complex social system—a microcosm of powerful interpersonal forces that significantly shape members' actions—and Chapters 7 through 9 examine the flow of information, influence, and interaction in that microcosm. Chapter 7 looks at the way group members sometimes change their opinions, judgments, or actions so that they match the opinions, judgments, or actions of the rest of the group (*conformity*). Chapter 8 extends this topic by considering how group members make use of social power to influence others and how people respond to such influence. Chapter 9 considers issues of leadership in groups.

T A B L E 1.6   **Major Topics in the Field of Group Dynamics**

Chapter and Topic	Issues
Foundations	
1. Introduction to group dynamics	What are groups, and what are their key features? What do we want to know about groups and their dynamics? What assumptions guide researchers in their studies of groups and the processes within groups?
2. Studying groups	How do researchers measure group processes? How do researchers search for and test their hypotheses about groups? What general theoretical perspectives guide researchers' studies of groups and the people in them?
Formation and Development	
3. Inclusion and identity	Do humans, as a species, prefer inclusion to exclusion and group membership to isolation? What demands does a shift from individuality to collectivity make on people? How do group experiences and memberships influence individuals' identities?
4. Formation	Who joins groups, and who remains apart? When and why do people seek out others? Why do people deliberately create groups or join existing groups? What factors influence feelings of liking for others?
5. Cohesion and development	What factors promote the increasing solidarity of a group over time? What is cohesion? As groups become more unified, do they develop a shared climate and culture? How do groups develop over time? What are the positive and negative consequences of cohesion and commitment?
6. Structure	What are norms and roles, and how do they structure interactions in groups? How and why do social networks develop in groups, and what are the interpersonal consequences of relational networks in groups?
Influence and Interaction	
7. Influence	When will people conform to a group's standards, and when will they remain independent? How do norms develop, and why do people obey them? Do nonconformists ever succeed in influencing the rest of the group?
8. Power	Why are some members of groups more powerful than others? What types of power tactics are most effective in influencing others? Does power corrupt? Why do people obey authorities?
9. Leadership	What is leadership? Who do groups prefer for leaders? Should a leader be task-focused or relationship-focused? Is democratic leadership superior to autocratic leadership? Can leaders transform their followers?
Working in Groups	
10. Performance	Do people perform tasks more effectively in groups or when they are alone? Why do people sometimes expend so little effort when they are in groups? When does a group outperform an individual? Are groups creative?
11. Decision making	What steps do groups take when making decisions? Why do some highly cohesive groups make disastrous decisions? Why do groups sometimes make riskier decisions than individuals?
12. Teams	What is the difference between a group and a team? What types of teams are currently in use? Does team building improve team work? How can leaders intervene to improve the performance of their teams?

TABLE 1.6   Major Topics in the Field of Group Dynamics (Continued)

Chapter and Topic	Issues
Conflict	
13. Conflict in groups	What causes disputes between group members? When will a small disagreement escalate into a conflict? Why do groups sometimes splinter into subgroups? How can disputes in groups be resolved?
14. Intergroup relations	What causes disputes between groups? What changes take place as a consequence of intergroup conflict? What factors exacerbate conflict? How can intergroup conflict be resolved?
Contexts and Applications	
15. Groups in context	What impact does the social and physical setting have on an interacting group? Are groups territorial? What happens when groups are overcrowded? How do groups cope with severe environments?
16. Groups and change	How can groups be used to improve personal adjustment and health? What is the difference between a therapy group and a support group? Are group approaches to treatment effective? Why do they work?
17. Crowds and collective behavior	What types of crowds are common? Why do crowds and collectives form? Do people lose their sense of self when they join crowds? When is a crowd likely to become unruly?

Questions of group performance form the focus in Chapters 10 through 12, for people work in groups across a range of contexts and settings. Chapter 10 examines basic questions of group productivity, including brainstorming, Chapter 11 decision-making groups, and Chapter 12 teams.

The next two chapters examine conflict and cooperation in groups. Groups are sources of stability and support for members, but in some cases conflicts erupt within groups (Chapter 13) and between groups (Chapter 14).

The final chapters deal with groups in specific settings. All groups are embedded in a social and environmental context, and Chapter 15 considers how the context in which groups exist affects their dynamics. Chapter 16 reviews groups in therapeutic contexts—helping, supportive, and change-promoting groups. Chapter 17 concludes our analysis by considering groups in public and societal contexts, including such relatively large groups as mobs, crowds, and social movements.

Group Dynamics Is Dynamic

The field of group dynamics emerged in the twentieth century as theorists and researchers concluded that groups are real and that they should be subjected to scientific analysis. In the 1950s and 1960s, in particular, the field grew rapidly as theorists and researchers studied more and more topics, the field became more interdisciplinary, and the accumulated knowledge was applied to practical problems.

This rapid expansion slowed once the study of groups gained acceptance in both sociology and psychology, but even today the field remains vibrant. Groups are studied by a range of investigators in a host of different disciplines. Although these researchers have very different goals, pursuits, and paradigms, they all recognize that groups are essential to human life. Through membership in groups, we define and confirm our values and beliefs and take on or refine our social identity. When we face uncertain situations, we join groups to gain reassuring information about our problems and security in companionship. Even though we must sometimes bend to the will of a group and its leaders, through groups we can reach goals that would elude us if we attempted them as individuals. Our groups are sometimes filled with conflict, but by resolving this conflict, we learn how to relate with others more effectively. Groups are the bedrock of humans' social existence, and we must accept the charge of understanding them (Harrod, Welch, & Kushkowski, 2009; Randsley de Moura et al., 2008).

CHAPTER REVIEW

What is a group?

1. No two groups are identical to each other, but a *group*, by definition, is two or more individuals who are connected by and within social relationships.

    ▪ Groups vary in size from dyads and triads to very large aggregations, such as mobs and audiences. Studies of naturally forming groups, like those conducted by James, indicate that most groups include two or three members.

    ▪ The number of possible relations in a group increases exponentially as groups increase in size, but both strong and weak relations are essential to group functioning (Granovetter's "strength of weak ties" hypothesis).

    ▪ Group-based relations are *memberships*. Unlike *networks*, groups usually have boundaries that define who is in the group.

    ▪ Members of groups that use computer-based technologies—e-groups or *online groups*—possess many unique qualities, but they nonetheless have many of the same characteristics and processes of *offline groups*.

What are some common characteristics of groups?

1. People in groups interact with one another. Bales' Interaction Process Analysis (IPA) system distinguishes between *task interaction* and *relationship interaction*.

2. Groups seek a variety of goals, such as those specified by McGrath: generating, choosing, negotiating, and executing.

3. Groups create *interdependence* among the group members (unilateral, reciprocal, etc.).

4. Interaction is patterned by *group structure*, including *roles, norms*, and interpersonal relations.

5. *Group cohesion*, or cohesiveness, is the unity of a group.

Are there different types of groups, and do people distinguish between these groups?

1. A number of different types of groups have been identified.

    ▪ *Primary groups* are relatively small, personally meaningful groups that are highly unified. Cooley suggested such groups are primary agents of socialization.

    ▪ Members of *social groups*, such as work groups, clubs, and congregations, interact with one another over an extended period of time.

    ▪ *Collectives* are relatively large aggregations or groups of individuals who display similarities in actions and outlook.

    ▪ Members of a *social category* share some common attribute or are related in some way. Such categories, even though based on similarity rather than interaction, often influence members' *social identity*, defined by Tajfel and his colleagues as an aspect of the self based on membership in a group or category.

2. Social perceivers also distinguish between groups and nongroups, and they draw distinctions among different types of groups.

    ▪ The perception of *entitativity* (groupness), according to Campbell, is substantially influenced by common fate, similarity, and proximity cues within an aggregation.

    ▪ Research conducted by Lickel, Hamilton, Sherman, and their colleagues suggests that people spontaneously draw distinctions among primary groups, social groups, collectives, and more general social categories.

    ▪ The *Thomas Theorem*, applied to groups, suggests that if individuals think an aggregate is a true group then the group will have important interpersonal consequences for those in the group and for those who are observing it.

- Groups that are high in entitativity are assumed to have a basic essence that defines the nature of their members (*essentialism*).

- Individuals in Eastern cultures tend to take more notice of groups, whereas those living in Western cultures focus more on individuals.

What assumptions guide researchers in their studies of groups and their dynamics?

1. Lewin first used the phrase *group dynamics* to describe the powerful processes that take place in groups, but group dynamics also refers to the "field of inquiry dedicated to advancing knowledge about the nature of groups" (Cartwright and Zander, 1968, p. 7).

2. The field's basic assumptions and procedures, termed a *paradigm* by Kuhn, were shaped by such early researchers as:

   - Le Bon, a social theorist best known for his book on the psychology of crowds and mobs, *Psychologie des Foules*.

   - Wundt, a psychologist who wrote *Völkerpsychologie*.

   - Durkheim, a sociologist who argued that society is made possible by the collective representations of individuals.

   - Allport, a psychologist who avoided holistic approaches to groups.

3. Early researchers disagreed in both their theorizing about groups and the methods they used to study them.

   - Sociological investigators, such as Durkheim, tended to adopt a group *level of analysis*, whereas psychologists focused on individuals. Allport, for example, objected to such group-level concepts as the *group mind* and collective conscious as examples of the *group fallacy*.

   - Research studies have yet to confirm the existence of a group mind, but Sherif's study of norm formation indicated that such group-level processes as norms can be studied through experimentation.

- Lewin's field theory suggested that in some cases the characteristics of groups cannot be deduced from the individual members' characteristics. Lewin maintained that behavior is a function of both the person and the environment, expressed as the law of interactionism, $B = f(P, E)$.

- Tuckman's theory of *group development* assumes that over time most groups move through the five stages of forming, storming, norming, performing, and adjourning.

4. The study of groups requires a multilevel, interdisciplinary analysis.

   - A *multilevel perspective* to groups recognizes that individuals are nested in groups, and these groups are usually nested in larger social aggregations, such as communities and organizations. Hackman's studies of orchestras illustrate the importance of examining micro-, meso-, and macro-level factors when investigating group dynamics.

   - Groups and their dynamics are the focus of study in a wide variety of fields.

Why study groups and their dynamics?

1. Groups are influential.

   - Groups alter their members' attitudes, values, and perceptions. Triplett's early study of group performance demonstrated the impact of one person on another.

   - Milgram's work demonstrated that a group situation can powerfully influence members to cause harm to others.

   - A review of 25,000 studies indicated that hypotheses about groups yielded clearer findings than studies of other social psychological topics.

2. Groups influence society. Groups mediate the connection between individuals and society-at-large.

3. Applied studies of groups and their dynamics, such as *action research*, yields solutions to a number of practical problems.

4. Despite the many problems caused by groups (competition, conflict, poor decisions), Buys notes that humans could not survive without groups.

What topics are included in the scientific study of group dynamics?

1. Contemporary group research examines both classic topics dealing with group structure and performance, as well as newer topics, such as e-groups and diversity.

2. Topics in the field include group formation, cohesion, group development, structure, influence, power, performance, conflict, and groups in specific settings.

RESOURCES

Introduction to Groups

- *Blackwell Handbook of Social Psychology: Group Processes*, edited by Michael A. Hogg and Scott Tindale in 2001, remains one of the most comprehensive collections of in-depth analyses of critically important topics in the field of group dynamics.

- *Encyclopedia of Group Processes & Intergroup Relations*, edited by John M. Levine and Michael A. Hogg (2010) is a 2-volume, 998-page compendium of current knowledge about groups and their relations, with over 300 entries ranging from *action research* to *xenophobia*.

- *Group Dynamics: Research and Theory*, edited by Dorwin Cartwright and Alvin Zander (1968), is a classic in the scientific field of groups, with chapters dealing with such topics as group membership, conformity, power, leadership, and motivation.

Group Dynamics: History and Issues

- *A History of Social Psychology: From the Eighteenth-Century Enlightenment to the Second World War*, by Gustav Jahoda (2007), is a fascinating history of the early emergence of social psychology in general and group dynamics in particular.

- "A History of Small Group Research," by John M. Levine and Richard L. Moreland (2012), provides a careful, detailed review of the development of the field of group dynamics, divided into the following eras: first 50 years, 1950s, 1960s and 1970s, and 1980s and beyond.

- "The Historical Background of Modern Social Psychology," by Gordon W. Allport (1968), reviews with extraordinary care the first scholarly studies of mobs, groups, and crowds.

Contemporary Group Dynamics

- "Learning More by Crossing Levels: Evidence from Airplanes, Hospitals, and Orchestras," by J. Richard Hackman (2003), provides one lucid example after another of the advantages of a multilevel approach to understanding group behavior.

- "Prospects for Group Processes and Intergroup Relations Research: A Review of 70 Years' Progress," by Georginia Randsley de Moura, Tirza Leader, Joseph Pelletier, and Dominic Abrams (2008), documents the growing interest in group-level analyses of interpersonal behavior across a range of disciplines.

Studying Groups

CHAPTER OVERVIEW

Just as researchers in the natural sciences use exacting procedures to study aspects of the physical environment, so do group researchers use scientific methods to further their understanding of groups. They measure as precisely as possible group processes, develop theories that provide coherent explanations for the group phenomenon they study, and collect evidence to test the adequacy of their predictions and assumptions.

- What are the three critical requirements of a scientific approach to the study of groups?
- How do researchers measure group processes?
- What are the key characteristics of and differences between case, experimental, and correlational studies of group processes?
- What are the strengths and weaknesses of case, experimental, and correlational methods?
- What theoretical perspectives guide researchers' studies of groups?

CHAPTER OUTLINE

Measurement in Group Dynamics
> *Observation*
> *Self-Report Measures*

Research Methods in Group Dynamics
> *Case Studies*
> *Experimental Studies*
> *Correlational Studies*
> *Studying Groups: Issues and Implications*

Theoretical Perspectives
> *Motivational and Emotional Perspectives*
> *Behavioral Perspectives*
> *Systems Theory Perspectives*
> *Cognitive Perspectives*
> *Biological Perspectives*
> *Selecting a Theoretical Perspective*

Chapter Review

Resources

People have always been interested in groups. Aristotle discussed groups in detail, eventually concluding that humans are by nature group-seeking animals. Shakespeare worked groups into his plays, which are all the more interesting for their vivid accounts of unexpected group dynamics and intergroup relations. Centuries ago, Niccolo Machiavelli considered how to best manage groups, particularly if one aims to increase one's power over the people in them. Ralph Waldo Emerson opined, "There need be but one wise man in a company and all are wise, so a blockhead makes a blockhead of his companions." More recently Bob Kraft, owner of the New England Patriots, attributed his team's improvement during the 2012 season to the "strength of spirit in the team," which he believed was created by the support of the team's fans (Kraft, 2012).

These historical and contemporary analyses of groups are insightful but limited in one important way: They are all conjectures based on personal opinion rather than scientific research. Are humans truly social creatures? Is the key to controlling people controlling their groups? What happens when an incompetent person—one "bad apple!"—joins a group? What is esprit de corps, and does this group-level spirit make groups more successful? Why do groups and their members act, feel, and think the way they do? Without scientific analysis, we cannot be certain.

This chapter reviews three basic activities that science requires: measuring, theorizing, and testing hypotheses. As sociologist George Caspar Homans explained, when "the truth of a relationship lies finally in the data themselves" and "nature, however stretched out on the rack, still has a chance to say 'No!'—then the subject is a science" (1967, p. 4). Homans' definition enjoins researchers to "stretch nature out on the rack" by systematically measuring group phenomena and group processes. Scientists must also test "the truth of the relationship" by conducting research that yields the data they need to understand the phenomenon that interests them. Emerson's belief that "one bad apple can ruin the barrel" may apply to groups, but this hypothesis must be tested by gathering evidence about groups that contain one substandard member. But scientists do not just measure things and collect data. They also create conceptual frameworks to organize their findings. Homans recognized that "nothing is more lost than a loose fact" (1950, p. 5) and urged the development of theories that provide a "general form in which the results of observations of many particular groups may be expressed" (p. 21).

MEASUREMENT IN GROUP DYNAMICS

Science often begins with measurement. No one believed that tiny microorganisms were causing illness and infection until the compound microscope made the once invisible visible. Most did not believe that moons circled other planets until the invention of telescopes. Researchers' success in studying groups, too, depended on progress in measuring group members' interpersonal actions and psychological reactions. Here, we trace the growth and impact of two important measurement methods—observing groups and questioning group members—that gave group dynamics a foothold in the scientific tradition.

Observation

Researchers who study groups often begin with **observation**: watching and recording a group's activities and interactions. Groups are complicated, multifaceted, and dynamic, but they are *observable*. Researchers can watch the members communicating with one another, performing their tasks, making decisions, confronting other groups, seeking new members and expelling old ones, accepting direction from their leaders, and so on.

---

observation A measurement method that involves watching and recording the activities of individuals and groups.

Sociologist William Foote Whyte (1943) relied on observation in his classic ethnographic study *Street Corner Society*. He undertook a detailed analysis of the life experiences of a group of young men who joined together regularly, usually at a particular street corner in their neighborhood, in Italian American sections of Boston in the late 1930s. Whyte, to learn about these groups, moved into the neighborhood and joined one of the groups, the Nortons, and also participated in a club known as the Italian Community Club. Whyte studied these groups for three-and-a-half years, gradually becoming an expert on this community and its groups.

Whyte's study documents the relationships that linked the members to their group and to the community, but it also illustrates some key features of observational measures. Whyte described members' actions and avoided making inferences about what they were thinking or feeling if he had no direct evidence of their inner states. He did not count or track the Nortons' actions, but instead described what he observed in his own words and kept track of what the Nortons said and did. He also concentrated on the group's communication, leadership, and status-allocation processes, sampling across time and settings (McGrath & Altermatt, 2001). He also decided to take part in the group's activities, and he revealed his identity and intentions to the group members. These decisions shaped his study and its conclusions.

Covert and Overt Observation Whyte made no attempt to hide what he was doing from the Nortons. Because he used **overt observation**, he let the Nortons know that he was a student of groups and would be studying their behavior for a book he was researching. Other researchers, in contrast, prefer to use **covert observation**, whereby they

---

overt observation Openly watching and recording information with no attempt to conceal one's research purposes.

covert observation Watching and recording information on the activities of individuals and groups without their knowledge.

record the group's activities without the group's knowledge. Researchers interested in how groups organize themselves by race and sex in schools sit quietly in the corner of the lunchroom and watch as students choose their seats. To study gatherings of people in a public park, a researcher may set up a surveillance camera and record where people congregate throughout the day. Overt observation of behavior in public places raises few ethical issues, for such research is less likely to violate people's right to privacy.

Participant Observation Some researchers observe groups from a vantage point outside the group. They may, for example, study video recordings of group meetings or watch the group from behind a special one-way mirror. But some researchers, like Whyte, use **participant observation**: they watch and record the group's activities and interactions while taking part in the group's social process. Whyte went bowling with the Nortons, gambled with the Nortons, and even lent money to some of the members. He worked so closely with the group that Doc, one of the key figures in the Nortons, considered himself to be a collaborator in the research project with Whyte, rather than one of the individuals being studied (Whyte, Greenwood, & Lazes, 1991). A diagram of the Nortons' structure, shown in Figure 2.1, includes a member named "Bill"; that would be Bill Whyte himself.

When researchers immerse themselves in group settings like those sampled in Table 2.1, their accounts are often detailed, nuanced, and compelling, depending on the skill and experience of the observer. Observation yields a particularly rich type of data: the actual words used by members in their discussions and conversations, impressions drawn from nonverbal expressions, information about the member's appearance and location in relationship to each other, and the sequences of behaviors that

---

participant observation Watching and recording group activities as a member of the group or participation in the social process.

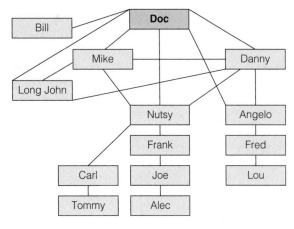

FIGURE 2.1 The core members of the Nortons, the street corner gang described by William Foote Whyte in his book *Street Corner Society*. Lines between each member indicate interdependence, and members who are placed above others in the chart had more influence than those in the lower positions. Doc was the recognized leader of the group, and Mike and Danny were second in terms of status. Whyte ("Bill" in the diagram), the researcher, was connected to the group through Doc (Whyte, 1955).

SOURCE: From *Street Corner Society* by W. F. Whyte, p. 13. Copyright © 1943 by University of Chicago Press. Reprinted by permission.

unfold within the group over time. In many cases, observers can record the actions and events that transpire in the group more accurately than can the members who are too caught up with the group's interaction to document accurately group-level processes. Given the complexity of groups and their dynamics, researchers who use participant observers are enjoined to improve their records by keeping notes during the course of the observation and using these records to develop a more detailed account of the latest group episode as soon as they can following each period of observation (Emerson, Fretz, & Shaw, 2011).

Reactivity and the Hawthorne Effect Whyte, as a participant observer, gained access to information that would have been hidden from an external observer. His techniques also gave him a very detailed understanding of the gang. Unfortunately, his presence in the group may have changed the group itself. As Doc remarked, "You've slowed me down plenty since you've been down here. Now, when I do something, I have to think what Bill Whyte would want to know about it and how I can explain it. Before, I used to do things by instinct" (Whyte, 1943, p. 301).

This tendency for individuals to act differently when they know they are being observed is often called the **Hawthorne effect**, after research conducted by psychologist Elton Mayo and his associates at the Hawthorne Plant of the Western Electric Company. These researchers studied productivity in the workplace by systematically varying a number of features while measuring the workers' output. They moved one group of women to a separate room and monitored their performance carefully. Next, they manipulated features of the work situation, such as the lighting in the room and the duration of rest periods. They were surprised when *all* the changes led to improved worker output. Dim lights, for example, raised efficiency, but so did bright lights. Mayo's team concluded that the shift members were working harder because they were being observed and because they felt that the company was taking a special interest in them (Mayo, 1945: Roethlisberger & Dickson, 1939).

Reviews of the Hawthorne studies suggested that other factors besides the scrutiny of the researchers contributed to the increased productivity of the groups. The Hawthorne groups worked in smaller teams, members could talk easily among themselves, and their managers were usually less autocratic than those who worked the main floor of the factory, and all these variables—and not observation alone—may have contributed to the performance gains. Nonetheless, the term *Hawthorne effect* continues to be used to describe any change in behavior that occurs when people feel they are being observed by others (see Bramel & Friend, 1981; Franke & Kaul, 1978; Olson et al., 2004).

Hawthorne effect A change in behavior that occurs when individuals know they are being observed or studied.

TABLE 2.1   Examples of Participant Observation Research

Type of Group	Summary	Key Concepts
Street corner gangs (Whyte, 1943)	Study of groups in an economically challenged neighborhood in Boston ("Cornerville"), focusing on a group of men in their 20s who congregate on a Norton street corner	leadership, status and performance, mutual obligations, social injustice
Doomsday group (Festinger, Riecken, & Schachter, 1956)	Analysis of a group that formed around a woman who believed the end of the world was approaching and the group's response when the prophecy was disconfirmed	cognitive dissonance, communication following belief disconfirmation
Work teams (Roy, 1959)	Describes the rituals used by a group of workers performing highly repetitive tasks that increase group cohesion and provide entertainment over the course of the workday	rituals, cohesion, conflict, group socialization
Mushroom collectors (Fine, 2003)	Examines the activities and interpersonal dynamics (trust, keeping secrets, storytelling) of voluntary communities (mycological societies) who search for edible mushrooms (morels)	interpersonal trust, social exchange, cohesion, leisure organizations
Search and rescue teams (Lois, 2003)	Reports the dynamics of a search and rescue squad, including status allocations and group-level mechanisms that control individual's attempts to claim heroic status	emotion management, edgework, heroism and altruism, social support
Inner city gangs (Venkatesh, 2008)	Describes the inner workings of the Black Kings, a group of young men living in public housing in Chicago, revealing the economy and stability of a community that nonmembers considered dysfunctional and unstable	negotiation, intergroup conflict, economic factors that sustain alternative community practices
Online groups (Bainbridge, 2010)	Reports the complex dynamics of altruism, competition, and leisure in the online multiplayer game *World of Warcraft*	rituals, trust and deviancy, sources of group satisfaction

Structuring Observations Whyte conducted a **qualitative study** of the Nortons. Like an anthropologist doing fieldwork, he tried to watch the Nortons without any preconceptions so that he would not unwittingly confirm his prior expectations. Nor did he keep track of the frequencies of any of the behaviors he noted or try explicitly to quantify members' reactions to the events that occurred in the group. Instead he watched, took

notes, and reflected on what he saw before drawing general conclusions about the group.

Qualitative methods generate data, but the data describe general qualities and characteristics rather than precise quantities and amounts. Such data are often textual rather than numeric and may include verbal descriptions of group interactions developed by multiple observers, notes from conversations with group members, or in-depth case descriptions of one or more groups. Such qualitative observational methods require an impartial researcher who is a keen observer of groups and one who is careful to remain objective (Dollar & Merrigan, 2002).

---

qualitative study A research procedure that collects and analyzes nonnumeric, unquantified types of data, such as verbal descriptions, text, images, or objects.

F o c u s   2.1   E-groups: Watching Virtual Groups from Within

The group failed, for the third time. What were they doing wrong, they wondered, as they retraced their choices and tried to pinpoint problems. After talking things over they decided, reluctantly, that they would need to add another person to the team to offset the lack of experience of several of its members. When one of the members said she knew someone who was highly proficient and might be willing to join them, one of the most junior members of the group graciously agreed to give this expert her place in the group. As luck would have it, the newly recruited member had solved this problem in another group, and he offered a number of good suggestions about tactics and strategy. The results of this change in personnel and strategy were gratifying. The group succeeded with the help of the newcomer who they invited to join their group. They also shared some of the rewards of their success with the group member who had given up her spot in the group.

This group is an unusual one for two reasons. First, these interactions took place online in Azeroth, a world created in the virtual game *World of Warcraft*, or *WoW*. Azeroth is populated by computer-generated characters, both human-like (gnomes, elves, humans) and nonhuman (undead, orks, dragons), and also characters—avatars—who represent the game players themselves. When players first enter the game, they complete various tasks ("quests") to gain skill and in doing so advance through levels of experience and challenge. Players acquire virtual swords, armor, money, mounts, jewelry, prestige, and experience as they slay various monsters and creatures, nonplayer characters (NPCs), and one another. All characters are members of various races (elf, human, tauren, etc.) and classes (paladin, priests, hunters, etc.) that have shared histories, territories, and skill-sets. They interact with one another in cities, villages, markets, inns, and along the paths, roadways, and trails of the world. The game also encourages collaboration, for even at the lower levels some quests are difficult to complete without help from others. The very difficult quests, called instances, can only be completed when groups of individuals, with complementary skills and talents, join forces to overcome an extremely powerful set of adversaries. Although many of the groups that attempt these instances are pick-up groups (PUGs) of individuals who do not know one another, players also do these runs with their guildmates—players who have joined together in a more formal association with others within the game. The group described earlier

included a mage, a paladin, a druid, a hunter, and a priest, and they were attempting the Hour of Twilight Dungeon, in Tanaris, which is a level 85 heroic for 5-player teams.

This group was also unusual in that it included a social scientist who was studying the group through participant observation. Researchers have used this method to study such groups as gangs, leisure groups, teams, cults, and sororities, but as new forms of group associations have emerged over the years, so have new opportunities for participant observation. Whereas people once traveled long distances to join with other group members, now they frequently join others in virtual, online groups using computer-based technologies. These new forms of human association include Facebook, where people regularly share information with friends and acquaintances; multiplayer game environments where people carry out group-level activities with other users; and larger virtual worlds, such as *Second Life*® and *WoW*, where members interact with one another in a variety of settings using avatars.

Just as groups abound in the offline world, so groups are everywhere, doing just about anything, in these online worlds—and researchers have joined these groups in order to better understand their dynamics (Chen & Duh, 2007; Ducheneaut et al., 2006; Nardi & Harris, 2006). The sociologist William Sims Bainbridge (2007, 2010), for example, studied, via participation, a number of groups, including the Process Church of the Final Judgement, Scientology, the John Birch Society, and Hare Krishna, but for two years he spent 2,300 hours as Maxrohn (a priest), Catullus (a blood elf), and a number of other alts in WoW. As a new member (*noob, newb, nubie*), he learned the world's implicit rules pertaining to privacy, vulgarity, sharing, and collaboration. He discovered, for example, that it is unethical to take loot (resources, rewards) that one has not earned or does not need, and a person who gains a reputation for such misbehavior (a loot ninja) will be shunned by others. He "leveled up" his characters over time by taking on quests, developing skills and crafts, and by learning tricks and techniques by socializing with other players in the taverns, towns, and cities. When he reached the point where he could attempt more difficult instances, he joined a guild and in time became its leader.

Bainbridge's experiences, as reported in his book *The Warcraft Civilization*, attest to the similarity between group-level processes in WoW and in offline environments. The groups in WoW displayed a range of human motivations, from apathy to altruism to greed. Players established various types of social connections with each other, from weak acquaintance ties to more robust alliances that eventually created friendships in the non-WoW world. Players also worked together effectively to achieve their goals but, in some cases, fail miserably despite the best of intentions on the part of all players. As one researcher concluded,

the groups within WoW are "not that different from groups in the physical world like clubs, sports teams, or even workgroups in organizations." This comment, ironically, was made by Kartuni, a character in WoW, played by social network researcher Nicolas Ducheneaut during a research conference convened in WoW itself (Bainbridge, 2010, p. 221).

Social psychologists Albert Hastorf and Hadley Cantril's (1954) classic "They Saw a Game" study demonstrated just how easily one's biases can influence what one "sees" a group doing. They arranged for college students from Dartmouth and Princeton to watch a film of their two teams playing a football game. The game they showed the students was a particularly rough one, with a number of penalties and injuries on both sides. But when Hastorf and Cantril asked Dartmouth and Princeton students to record the number and severity of the infractions that had been committed by the two teams, the Princeton students were not very accurate. Dartmouth students saw Princeton commit about the same number of infractions as Dartmouth. Princeton students, however, saw the Dartmouth team commit more than twice as many infractions as the Princeton team. Apparently, the Princeton observers' preference for their own team distorted their perceptions.

Structured observational methods offer researchers a way to increase the objectivity of their observations. Like biologists who classify living organisms under such categories as phylum and order or psychologists who classify people as to personality type, researchers who use a structured observational method classify each group behavior into an objectively definable category. First, they decide which behaviors to track. Then they develop

unambiguous descriptions of each type of behavior they will code. Next, using these behavioral definitions as a guide, they note the occurrence and frequency of these targeted behaviors as they watch the group. This type of research would be a **quantitative study**, because it yields numeric results (Weingart, 1997).

Sociologist Robert Freed Bales developed two of the best-known structured coding systems for studying groups (Bales, 1950, 1970, 1980). As noted in Chapter 1, Bales spent many years watching group members interact with each other, and he often used the **Interaction Process Analysis,** or **IPA**, to structure his observations. Researchers who use the IPA classify each behavior performed by a group member into one of the 12 categories shown in Figure 2.2. Six of these categories (1 through 3 and 10 through 12) pertain to socioemotional, *relationship interaction*. As noted in Chapter 1, these types of actions sustain or weaken interpersonal ties within the group. Complimenting another person is an example of a positive relationship behavior, whereas insulting a group member is a negative relationship behavior. The other six

---

structured observational method A research procedure that creates a systematic record of group interaction and activities by classifying (coding) each overt expression or action into a defined category.

quantitative study A research procedure that collects and analyzes numeric data, such as frequencies, proportions, or amounts.

Interaction Process Analysis (IPA) A structured coding system used to measure group activity by classifying each observed behavior into one of 12 categories, such as "shows solidarity" or "asks for orientation" (developed by Robert F. Bales).

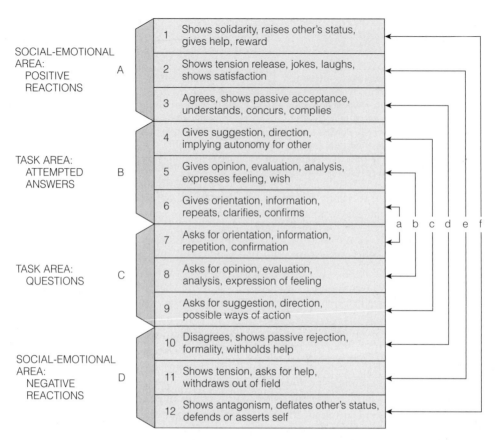

FIGURE 2.2 Robert F. Bales' original Interaction Process Analysis (IPA) coding system for structuring observations of groups. Areas A (1 through 3) and D (10 through 12) are used to code socioemotional, relationship interactions. Areas B (4 through 6) and C (7 through 9) are used to code task interaction. The lines to the right (labeled a through f) indicate problems of orientation (a), evaluation (b), control (c), decision (d), tension management (e), and integration (f).

SOURCE: Bales, R. F., & Strodtbeck, F. L. (1951). Phases in group problem-solving. The *Journal of Abnormal and Social Psychology, 46*(4), 485–495.

categories (4 through 9) pertain to instrumental, *task interaction*, such as giving and asking for information, opinions, and suggestions related to the problem the group faces. When using the IPA, observers must listen to the group discussion, break the content down into behavioral units, and then categorize. If Crystal, for example, begins the group discussion by asking "Should we introduce ourselves?" and Al answers, "Yes," observers write "Crystal–Group" beside Category 8 (Crystal asks for opinion from whole group) and "Al–Crystal"

beside Category 5 (Al gives opinion to Crystal). If Don later angrily tells the entire group, "This group is a boring waste of time," the coders write "Don–Group" beside Category 12 (Don shows antagonism toward the entire group).

Bales (1999, xvi) once wrote, "I have always felt the compulsion to ground my thinking in empirical data." In consequence, he improved his system as he continued to study groups in a variety of contexts. His newer version, which generates more global summaries of group behavior, is called the **Systematic Multiple Level Observation of Groups**, or **SYMLOG**. SYMLOG coders use 26 different categories instead of only 12, with these categories signaling members' dominance–submissiveness, friendliness–unfriendliness, and accepting–opposing the task orientation of established authority (Hare, 2005). When a group begins discussing a problem, for example, most behaviors may be concentrated in the dominant, friendly, and accepting authority categories. But if the group argues, then scores in the unfriendly, opposing authority categories may begin to climb. Chapter 6 uses SYMLOG to describe changes in relationships among group members that occur over time.

Reliability and Validity of Observations Structured observation systems, because they can be used to record the number of times a particular type of behavior has occurred, make possible comparison across categories, group members, and even different groups. Moreover, if observers are carefully trained, a structured coding system, such as IPA and SYMLOG, will yield data that are both reliable and valid. **Reliability** is determined by a measure's consistency across time, components, and raters. If a rater, when she hears the statement, "This group is a boring waste of time," always classifies it as a Category 12 behavior, then the rating is reliable. The measure has *interrater reliability* if different raters, working independently, all think that the statement belongs in Category 12. (Researchers once had to arrange for teams of observers to watch the groups

they studied, but now they usually videorecord the groups for later analysis.) **Validity** describes the extent to which the technique measures what it is supposed to measure. The IPA, for example, is valid only if observers' ratings actually measure the amount of relationship and task interaction in the group. If the observers are incorrect in their coding, or if the categories are not accurate indicators of relationship and task interaction, the scores are not valid (Bakeman, 2000).

Given the greater reliability and validity of structured observations, why did Whyte take a qualitative, unstructured approach? Whyte was more interested in gaining an understanding of the entire community and its citizenry, so a structured coding system's focus on specific behaviors would have yielded an unduly narrow analysis. At the time he conducted his study, Whyte did not know which behaviors he should scrutinize if he wanted to understand the group. Whyte was also unfamiliar with the groups he studied, so he chose to immerse himself in fieldwork. His research was more exploratory, designed to develop theory first and validate hypotheses second, so he used an unstructured observational approach. If he had been testing a hypothesis by measuring specific aspects of a group, then the rigor and objectivity of a structured approach would have been preferable. Qualitative methods, in general, "provide a richer, more varied pool of information" than quantitative ones (King, 2004, p. 175).

Systematic Multiple Level Observation of Groups (SYMLOG) A theoretical and structured coding system for recording the activities of a group and the overall behavioral orientation of members. The system assumes group activities can be classified along three dimensions: dominance versus submissiveness, friendliness versus unfriendliness, and acceptance of versus opposition to authority (developed by Robert F. Bales).

reliability The degree to which a measurement technique consistently yields the same conclusion at different times. For measurement techniques with two or more components, reliability is also the degree to which these components yield similar conclusions.

Self-Report Measures

Whyte often supplemented his observations of Doc, Mike, Danny, and the other Nortons by asking them questions: "Now and then, when I was concerned with a particular problem and felt I needed more information from a certain individual … I would seek an opportunity to get the man alone

---

validity The degree to which a measurement method assesses what it was designed to measure.

and carry on a more formal interview" (Whyte, 1955, pp. 303–304).

Self-report measures, despite their variations, are all based on a simple premise: if you want to know what a group member is thinking, feeling, or planning, then just ask him or her to report that information to you directly. In *interviews* the researcher records the respondent's answer to various questions, but *questionnaires* ask respondents to record their answers themselves. Some variables, such as members' beliefs about their group's cohesiveness or their perceptions of the group's leader, may be so complex that researchers need to ask a series of interrelated questions. When the items are selected and pretested for accuracy, a multi-item measure is usually termed a *test* or a *scale*.

Sociometry   Psychiatrist Jacob Moreno (1934), a pioneer in the field of group dynamics, used self-report methods to study the social organization of groups of young women living in adjacent cottages at an institution. The women were neighbors, but they were not very neighborly, for disputes continually arose among the groups and among members of the same group who were sharing a cottage. Moreno believed that the tensions would abate if he could regroup the women into more compatible clusters and put the greatest physical distance between hostile groups. So he asked the women to identify five women whom they liked the most on a confidential questionnaire. Moreno then used these responses to construct more harmonious groups, and his efforts were rewarded when the overall level of antagonism in the community declined (Hare & Hare, 1996).

Moreno called this technique for measuring the relations between group members **sociometry**. A researcher begins a sociometric study by asking group members one or more questions about the other members. To measure attraction, the

researcher might ask, "Whom do you like most in this group?" but such questions as "Whom in the group would you like to work with the most?" or "Whom do you like the least?" can also be used. Researchers often limit the number of choices that participants can make. These choices are then organized in a **sociogram**, which is a diagram of the relationships among group members.

Figure 2.3 is a sociogram, redrawn from Whyte's original chart of the authority relations in the Nortons (see Figure 2.1). Each member of the Nortons is represented by a symbol, and lines are used to indicate who is most closely connected to whom. In Figure 2.3, the members have been arranged so that individuals with more connections to other members are located near the center of the figure and those with fewer ties occupy the perimeter.

Sociometry was an early form of **social network analysis (SNA)**, a set of procedures for studying the relational structure of groups and networks graphically and mathematically. SNA yields information about individual members, relationships between pairs of members, and the group's overall structure. At the level of the individual group member, Figure 2.3 indicates which Norton had more connections with others and who had relatively few. Doc, for example, would be the "star" of the group (see Table 2.2). Not only is he linked to 5 of the other members, but his connections also have more connections as well. Notice, too, that one

---

self-report measure An assessment method, such as a questionnaire, test, or interview, that asks respondents to describe their feelings, attitudes, or beliefs.

sociometry A method for measuring the relationships among members of a group and summarizing those relationships graphically (developed by Jacob Moreno).

sociogram A graphic representation of the patterns of intermember relations created through sociometry. In most cases, each member of the group is depicted by a symbol, such as a lettered circle or square, and relations among members (e.g., communication links, friendship pairings) are indicated by lines from one member to another.

social network analysis (SNA) A set of procedures for studying the relational structure of groups and networks mathematically and graphically. Using information about the relationships (ties, edges) linking members (nodes, vertexes), the method yields member-level indexes (e.g., centrality, betweenness), group-level indexes (e.g., density, cohesiveness), and a graphic representation of the unit.

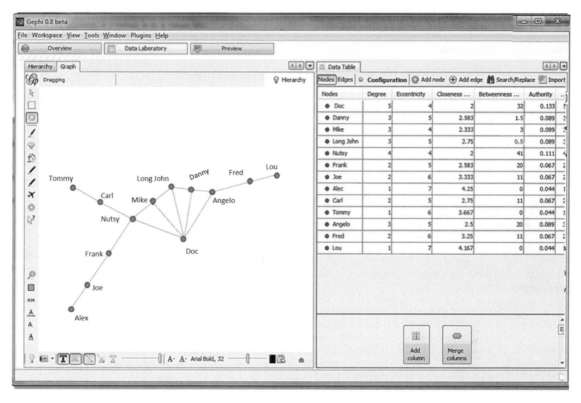

FIGURE 2.3   A network graph of the Nortons, generated by the Gephi.0.8 beta Graph Visualization and Manipulation Software (GNU General Public).

SOURCE: Gephi.0.8 beta Graph Visualization and Manipulation Software (GNU General Public). Reprinted with permission of Gephi.org.

group member—Nutsy—is the bridge between two large subgroups within the group. In such a position, Nutsy could be a gatekeeper who determines what information is passed back and forth from the peripheral members, like a Frank and Carl, to the more central members like Doc and Mike.

Social network analysis also yields information about cliques, schisms, hierarchies, and other relational regularities and oddities in the overall organization of a group (Borgatti, 2002). The Nortons, for example, were a centralized group, for a small number of group members (Doc, Nutsy) were tied to many members, but the majority of the members had only one or two links. The group's network of relationships, however, is not a very dense one. In this group of 13 men, 78 relationships would be required to link every member to every other member (see Chapter 1). But Figure 2.3 shows only 20% of the possible ties (16 relationships) are in place in the Nortons. Chapter 6 will examine, in more detail, the use of social network analysis in the study of groups and their structures.

Reliability and Validity of Self-Report Measures
Self-report methods, such as sociometry, have both weaknesses and strengths. They depend very much on knowing what questions to ask the group members. A maze of technical questions also confronts researchers designing questionnaires. If respondents do not answer the questions consistently—if, for example, Dejun indicates that he likes Gerard the most on Monday but on Tuesday changes his choice to Claire—then his responses are unreliable. Also, if questions are not worded properly, the instrument will lack validity, because the respondents may misinterpret what is being asked. Validity is also a

T A B L E 2.2 **Examples of Group Roles from Sociometry**

Role	Description
Clique members	those who are part of a subcluster within the group
Couples (pairs)	two people who like one another, and so have reciprocal bonds
Gatekeepers	those located between one part of the group and another, and so can control the flow of information
Isolates	loners who are infrequently chosen by any members
Rejecteds (unpopulars)	those who is disliked by many members
Sociables (positives)	those who select many others as their friends
Stars (populars)	the most chosen, well-liked, very popular members (high *choice status*)
Unsociables (negatives)	those who select few others as their friends

problem if group members are unwilling to disclose their personal attitudes, feelings, and perceptions or are unaware of these internal processes.

Despite these limitations, self-report methods provide much information about group phenomena, but from the perspective of the participant rather than the observer. When researchers are primarily interested in personal processes, such as perceptions, feelings, and beliefs, self-report methods may be the only means of assessing these private processes. But if participants are biased, their self-reports may not be as accurate as we would like. Self-reports may also not be accurate indicators of group-level processes, such as cohesiveness or conflict.

RESEARCH METHODS IN GROUP DYNAMICS

Good measurement alone does not guarantee good science. Researchers who watch groups and ask group members questions can develop a detailed description of a group, but they must go beyond description if they are to *explain* groups. Once researchers have collected their data, they must use that information to test hypotheses about group phenomena. They use many techniques to check the adequacy of their suppositions about groups, but the three most common approaches are (1) *case studies*, (2) *experimental studies* that manipulate one or more aspects of the group situation, and (3) *correlational studies* of the naturally occurring relationships between various aspects of groups.

Case Studies

Social psychologist Irving Janis (1972) was puzzled. He had studied a wide variety of groups in many contexts, but when his daughter asked him why U.S. President John F. Kennedy's advisors encouraged him to support an invasion of Cuba, he had no answer. The members of this group were the top political minds in the country, and they had reviewed their recommendation carefully, yet it was a decidedly mistaken one. What caused this group to perform so far below its potential?

Janis decided to study this group in detail. Relying on historical documents, minutes of meetings, diaries, letters, and group members' memoirs and public statements, he analyzed the group's structure, its communication processes, and its leadership. He also expanded his study to include other groups that made disastrous errors, including the military personnel responsible for the defense of Pearl Harbor before it was attacked in World War II and advisors who urged greater U.S. involvement in Vietnam. His analyses led him to conclude that these groups suffered from the same problem. Over time they had become so unified that members felt as though they could not disagree with the group's decisions, and so they failed to examine their assumptions carefully. Janis labeled this loss of rationality caused by strong pressures to conform **groupthink**. Chapter 11 examines Janis's theory in more detail.

---

groupthink A set of negative group-level processes, including illusions of vulnerability, self-censorship, and pressures to conform, that occur when highly cohesive groups seek concurrence rather than objective analysis when making a decision (identified by Irving Janis).

Conducting a Case Study   One of the best ways to understand groups in general is to understand one group in particular. This approach has a long and venerable tradition in all the sciences, with some of the greatest advances in thinking coming from the **case study**—an in-depth examination of one or more groups. If the groups have not yet disbanded, the researcher may decide to observe them directly, but they may also cull facts about the group from interviews with members, descriptions of the group written by journalists, or members' autobiographical writings. Researchers then relate this information back to the variables that interest them and thereby estimate the extent to which the examined case supports their hypotheses (Yin, 2009).

Researchers have conducted case studies of all sorts of groups: adolescent peer groups (Adler & Adler, 1995), artist circles (Farrell, 2001), the casts of Bollywood films (Wilkinson-Weber, 2010), crisis intervention teams in psychiatric hospitals (Murphy & Keating, 1995), cults (Festinger, Riecken, & Schachter, 1956), drug-dealing gangs (Venkatesh, 2008), families coping with an alcoholic member (Carvalho & Brito, 1995), focus groups (Seal, Bogart, & Ehrhardt, 1998), government leaders at international summits (Hare & Naveh, 1986), guilds in online game worlds (Nardi, 2010), industrialists and inventors (Uglow, 2002), Little League baseball teams (Fine, 1987), mountain climbers (Kayes, 2006), naval personnel living in an undersea habitat (Radloff & Helmreich, 1968), presidential advisors (Goodwin, 2005), religious communes (Stones, 1982), rock-and-roll bands (Bennett, 1980), fans of rock-and-roll bands (Adams, 1998), search-and-rescue squads (Lois, 2003), sororities (Robbins, 2004), sports fans (St. John, 2004), support groups (Turner, 2000), the Supreme Court (Toobin, 2007), and, of course, advisory groups making critically important decisions pertaining to national policy and defense (Allison & Zelikow, 1999;

Janis, 1972). Although once considered to be questionable in terms of scientific value, case studies that are carried out with care and objectivity are now widely recognized as indispensable tools for understanding group processes (Yin, 2009).

Advantages and Disadvantages   All research designs offer both advantages and disadvantages, and case studies are no exception. By focusing on a limited number of cases, researchers often provide richly detailed qualitative descriptions of naturally occurring groups. If the groups have disbanded and researchers are relying on archival data, they need not be concerned that their research will substantially disrupt or alter naturally occurring group processes. Case studies also tend to focus on **bona fide groups** that are found in everyday, natural contexts. Unlike groups that are concocted by researchers in the laboratory for a brief period of time and then disbanded, bona fide groups are embedded in a natural context (Frey, 2003). Case methods are also particularly appropriate when the phenomenon of interest has been well documented but when the processes that produced it and are influenced by it remain unknown. A case study, too, may be used when the research has no way of imposing methodological controls in the situation (Griffin & Bengry-Howell, 2008; Yin, 2009).

These advantages are offset by limitations. Researchers who use the case study method must bear in mind that the group studied may be unique, and, unless they embed their work into a general theoretical conceptualization, their findings may say little about other groups' dynamics. Also, if the group being studied is a contemporary one, researchers can use quantitative measures to document some key variables, but if the study is primarily qualitative they must deal with issues of objectivity. In addition, the essential records and artifacts may be inaccurate or unavailable to the researcher. Janis, for example, was forced to "rely

---

case study A research technique that draws on multiple sources of information to examine, in depth, the activities and dynamics of a group or groups.

bona fide group A naturally occurring group, such as an audience, board of directors, club, or team; compare to an ad hoc group created for research purposes.

mainly on the contemporary and retrospective accounts by the group members themselves … many of which are likely to have been written with an eye to the author's own place in history" (1972, p. v). In the case of the Bay of Pigs, when many key documents were eventually declassified, they suggested that the group did not experience group-think but instead was misled deliberately by some of the group members (Kramer, 2008). Finally, case studies only imply but rarely establish causal relationships among important variables in the group under study. Janis believed that groupthink was causing the poor decisions in the groups he studied, but actually some other unnoticed factor could have been the prime causal agent.

Experimental Studies

Psychologists Kurt Lewin, Ronald Lippitt, and Ralph White started with one basic question: Are people more productive and more satisfied when working for a democratic, group-centered leader rather than an autocratic, self-centered leader? To find an answer, they arranged for 10- and 11-year-old boys to meet after school in five-member groups to work on hobbies such as wood-working and painting. An adult led each group by adopting one of three styles of leadership: autocratic, democratic, or laissez-faire. The *autocratic* leader made all the decisions for the group; the *democratic* leader let the boys themselves make their own decisions; and the *laissez-faire* leader gave the group members very little guidance (Lewin, Lippitt, & White, 1939; White, 1990; White & Lippitt, 1968).

The researchers observed the groups as they worked with each type of leader and measured group productivity and aggressiveness. When they reviewed their findings, they discovered that the autocratic groups spent more time working (74%) than the democratic groups (50%), which in turn spent more time working than the laissez-faire groups (33%). Although these results argued in favor of the efficiency of an autocratic leadership style, the observers also noted that when the leader left the room for any length of time, the democratically led groups kept right on working, whereas

the boys in the autocratic groups stopped working. The boys in the autocratically led groups were also more hostile more destructive, and more likely to single out one member to be the target of almost continual verbal abuse. The researchers believed that this **scapegoat** provided members with an outlet for pent-up hostilities that could not be acted out against the powerful group leader.

Conducting Experiments   Lewin, Lippitt, and White's study of leadership styles possesses the three key features of an **experiment**. First, the researchers identified a variable that they believed caused changes in group processes and then systematically manipulated this **independent variable** by giving groups different types of leaders (autocratic, democratic, or laissez-faire). Second, the researchers assessed the effects of the independent variable by measuring such factors as productivity and aggressiveness. The variables that researchers measure are called **dependent variables** because their magnitude depends on the strength and nature of the independent variable. Lewin, Lippitt, and White hypothesized that group leadership style would influence productivity and aggressiveness, so they tested this hypothesis by *manipulating* the independent variable (leadership style) and *measuring* the dependent variables (productivity and aggressiveness).

---

scapegoat An individual or group who is unfairly held responsible for a negative event and outcome; the innocent target of interpersonal hostility.

experiment A research design in which the investigator (a) manipulates at least one variable by randomly assigning participants to two or more different conditions, (b) measures at least one other variable, and (c) controls the influence of other variables on the outcome.

independent variable Something that the researcher changes in an experimental study while holding other variables constant and measuring the dependent variable; the causal mechanism in a cause-effect relationship.

dependent variable The resultant outcomes measured by the researcher; the effect variable in a cause-effect relationship.

Third, the experimenters tried to maintain control over other variables. The researchers never assumed that the only determinant of productivity and aggressiveness was leadership style; they knew that other variables, such as the personality characteristics and abilities of the group members, could influence the dependent variables. In the experiment, however, the researchers were not interested in these other variables. They therefore made certain that these other variables were controlled in the experimental situation. For example, they took pains to ensure that the groups they created were "roughly equated on patterns of interpersonal relationships, intellectual, physical, and socioeconomic status, and personality characteristics" (White & Lippitt, 1968, p. 318). Because no two groups were identical, these variations could have resulted in some groups working harder than others. The researchers used *random assignment* of groups to even out these initial inequalities. Thus, they hoped that any differences found on the dependent measure would be due to the independent variable rather than to uncontrolled differences among the participating groups.

In sum, when researchers conduct experiments, they manipulate one or more independent variables, assess systematically one or more dependent variables, and control other possible contaminating variables. When the experiment is properly designed and conducted, researchers can assume that any differences among the conditions on the dependent variables are produced by the independent variable that is manipulated and not by some other variable outside their control.

Advantages and Disadvantages Why do researchers so frequently rely on experimentation to test their hypotheses about groups? This preference derives, in part, from the inferential power of experimentation. Researchers who design their experiments carefully can make inferences about the causal relationships linking variables. If the investigators keep all variables constant, except for the independent variable, and the dependent variable changes, then they can cautiously conclude that the independent variable caused the dependent

variable to change. Experiments, if properly conducted, can therefore be used to detect causal relationships between variables (Hoyle, 2005).

Experiments offer an excellent means of testing hypotheses about the causes of group behavior, but they are not without their logistical, methodological, and ethical problems. Researchers cannot always control the situation sufficiently to manipulate the independent variable or to keep other variables constant. Lewin and his colleagues, for example, had considerable difficulty manipulating their independent variable in a systematic way (see Chapter 9). Moreover, to maintain control over the conditions of an experiment, researchers may end up studying closely monitored but artificial group situations. Experimenters often work in laboratories with ad hoc groups that are created just for the purpose of research, and these groups may differ in important ways from bona fide groups. Although an experimenter can heighten the impact of the situation by withholding information about the study, such deception can be challenged on ethical grounds. Experiments can be conducted in the field using already existing groups, but they will almost necessarily involve the sacrifice of some degree of control and will reduce the strength of the researchers' conclusions. Hence, the major advantage of experimentation—the ability to draw causal inferences—can be offset by the major disadvantage of experimentation—basing conclusions on contrived situations that say little about the behavior of groups in more naturalistic settings. (These issues are discussed in more detail by Driskell & Salas, 1992 and Reis & Gosling, 2010.)

Correlational Studies

Social psychologist Theodore Newcomb (1943), when teaching at Bennington College in the mid-1930s, noticed his students were changing both politically as well as intellectually. When they first entered school, most of them were conservative, but by the time they graduated, they had shifted to become more liberal. In fact, in 1936 fully 62% of the first-year class preferred the Republican presidential candidate. But only 15% of the juniors and seniors endorsed the Republican candidate, evidence of a profound shift in political beliefs.

Newcomb believed that the first-year students were changing their political beliefs to match the prevailing politics of Bennington. The younger students were, in effect, accepting seniors as their **reference group**, which is a group that provides individuals with guidelines or standards for evaluating themselves, their attitudes, and their beliefs (Hyman, 1942). Any group that plays a significant role in one's life, such as a family, a friendship clique, colleagues at work, or even a group one admires but is not a member of, can function as a reference group (Singer, 1990). When students first enrolled at Bennington, their families served as their reference group, so their attitudes matched their families' attitudes. The longer students remained at Bennington, however, the more their attitudes changed to match the attitudes of their new reference group—the rest of the college population. Their families had conservative attitudes, but the college community supported mainly liberal attitudes, and Newcomb hypothesized that many Bennington students shifted their attitudes in response to this reference-group pressure.

Newcomb tested this hypothesis by administering questionnaires and interviews to an entire class of Bennington students from their entrance in 1935 to their graduation in 1939. He found a consistent trend toward liberalism in many of the students and reasoned that this change resulted from peer-group pressure because it was more pronounced among the popular students. Those who endorsed liberal attitudes were (1) "both capable and desirous of cordial relations with the fellow community members" (Newcomb, 1943, p. 149), (2) more frequently chosen by others as friendly, and (3) a more cohesive subgroup than the conservative students. Individuals who did not become more liberal were less involved in the college's social life, or they were very family-oriented. These reference groups changed the students permanently, for the students who shifted were still liberals when Newcomb measured their political beliefs some 25 years later (Newcomb et al., 1967).

Conducting Correlational Studies Newcomb's Bennington study was a nonexperimental, **correlational study**; he examined the naturally occurring relationships among several variables without manipulating any of them. Newcomb believed, for example, that as students came to identify more closely with other students, their attitudes and values changed to match those of their peers. Therefore, he assessed students' popularity, their dependence on their families, and changes in their political attitudes. Then he examined the relationships among these variables by carrying out several statistical tests. At no point did he try to manipulate the group situation.

Correlational studies are so named because, at least initially, researchers indexed the strength and direction of the relationships among the variables they measured by calculating **correlation coefficients**. A correlation coefficient, abbreviated as r, can range from −1 to +1, with the distance from zero (0), the neutral point, indicating the strength of the relationship. If Newcomb had found that the correlation between students' popularity and liberal attitudes was close to 0, for example, he would have concluded that the two variables were unrelated to each other. If the correlation was significantly different from 0—in either a positive or a negative direction—his study would have shown that these two variables were related to each other. The sign

---

reference group A group or collective that individuals use as a standard or frame of reference when selecting and appraising their abilities, attitudes, or beliefs; includes groups that individuals identify with and admire and categories of noninteracting individuals.

correlational study A research design in which the investigator measures (but does not manipulate) at least two variables and then uses statistical procedures to examine the strength and direction of the relationship between these variables.

correlation coefficient A standardized statistic that measures the strength and direction of a relationship between two variables. Often symbolized by r, correlations can range from −1 to +1.

of the correlation (− or +) indicates the direction of the relationship. If, for example, the correlation between popularity and liberal attitudes was +.68, this positive correlation would indicate that both variables increased or decreased together: The more popular the student, the more liberal her attitude. A negative correlation, such as −.57, would indicate that the variables were inversely related: More popular students would tend to have less liberal attitudes. Thus, a correlation is a handy way of summarizing a great deal of information about the relationship between two variables. Researchers do not always analyze their data by computing correlations, but the term *correlational study* continues to be used to describe studies that rely on measuring variables rather than manipulating them.

Advantages and Disadvantages   Researchers use correlational designs whenever they wish to know more about the relationship between variables. Are group leaders usually older than their followers? Do groups become more centralized as they grow larger? Do people who are more committed to their group tend to express attitudes that match their group's position? These are all questions that researchers might ask concerning the relationship between variables. When coupled with valid measures, correlational studies clearly describe these relationships without disrupting or manipulating any aspect of the group.

Correlational studies, however, yield only limited information about the *causal* relationship between variables because the researcher does not directly manipulate any variables. Newcomb's data, for example, indicated that the attitude changes he measured were related to reference-group pressures, but he could not rule out other possible causes. Perhaps, unknown to Newcomb, the most popular students on campus all read the same books that contained arguments that persuaded them to give up their conservative attitudes. Newcomb also could not be certain about the *direction* of the relationship he documented. He believed that individuals who joined the liberal reference group became more liberal themselves, but the causal

relationship may have been just the opposite: People who expressed more liberal attitudes may have been asked to join more liberal reference groups. Although these alternative explanations seem less plausible, they cannot be eliminated, given the methods used by Newcomb.

Studying Groups: Issues and Implications

Researchers recognize that all conceptual analyses of groups, no matter how intellectually alluring, must be tested with procedures that meet the field's scientific standards, but those who study groups face some unique logistic and statistical problems. Group processes including leadership, communication, and influence, are notoriously difficult to document objectively, for many of the traditional tools of the social scientist fail to provide sufficient detail when the subject of study is a group. Researchers who study groups must also deal with a host of methodological and statistical problems that the researcher who studies only isolated individuals can avoid. "The enduring and often indeterminate time frame of 'real' groups, to say nothing of their inherent complexity, makes their systematic study a daunting exercise" (Kerr, Aronoff, & Messé, 2000, p. 160).

Selecting a Method   Researchers use a variety of empirical procedures to deal with these complexities. Some observe group processes and then perform a qualitative analysis of their observations, whereas others insist on quantitative measurement methods and elaborate controlled experiments. Some conduct their studies in field situations using bona fide groups, whereas others bring groups into the laboratory or even create groups to study. Some undertake exploratory studies with no clear idea of what results to expect, whereas other research studies are designed to test hypotheses carefully derived from a specific theory. Some study group phenomena by asking volunteers to role-play group members, and others simulate group interaction with computers.

Advances in instrumentation, design, and statistical procedures have also eased some of the labor and time costs of conducting group research. Information technologies provide opportunities to study groups using the Internet, and software can now search out and model the structure of groups. Researchers have even begun developing tools that will allow them to create *virtual reality groups*, where computers are used to immerse individuals in groups that seem to be real but are actually created by virtual environment technologies (Blascovich et al., 2002; Sivuneun & Hakonen, 2011).

This diversity of research methods does not reflect researchers' uncertainty about which technique is best. Rather, the diversity stems from the unique advantages and disadvantages offered by each method. Case studies limit the researcher's ability to draw conclusions, to quantify results, and to make objective interpretations. But some topics, such as groupthink, are difficult to study by any other method. As Janis (1982) himself pointed out, it would be difficult to examine groups that make decisions about national policies—including war and civil defense—through traditional quantitative methods such as experimentation. But the real forte of the case study approach is its power to provide grist for the theoretician's mill, enabling the investigator to formulate hypotheses that set the stage for other research methods.

Such stimulation of theory is also frequently a consequence of correlational research. Correlational studies are limited in causal power, but they yield precise estimates of the strength of the relationships between variables. Experimentation provides the firmest test of causal hypotheses by showing that variable *X* will cause such and such a change in variable *Y*. In a well-designed and conducted experiment, the researcher can test several hypotheses about groups, making the method both rigorous and efficient. However, when an artificial setting would yield meaningless results, when the independent variable cannot be manipulated, or when too little is known about the topic even to suggest what variables may be causal, some other approach is preferable. The solution is to study groups using multiple methods, for all "methods have inherent flaws—though each has certain advantages. These flaws cannot be avoided. But what the researcher can do is to bring more than one approach, more than one method, to bear on each" (McGrath, 1984, p. 30).

Dealing with Interdependence Group data are multilevel data, since individuals are nested in groups that are often nested in some larger organization, community, or culture. Researchers must therefore exercise special care when designing their measures and examining their data. Imagine, for example, yourself a member of a research team studying some fascinating group phenomenon, such as the reasons why people become loyal to their group or the way members express displeasure with the group leader by skipping meetings. You locate 20 groups, each with five members, and measure things like loyalty, conscientiousness, and duration of membership. But, when it comes time to analyze the data, you face a basic question. How many subjects are in your study: 100 individuals or 20 groups?

The answer depends on the *level of analysis* you take in your study. If you undertake a micro-level analysis, you may predict that members who have been in a group longer tend to be more loyal to the group or that members with certain personality characteristics will have fewer absences. But if you shift upward to the group, or meso-level, the group will be your unit of analysis. You may decide, for example, to average together each member's responses to the "Are you loyal?" question to get an index of group loyalty, but only if most of the members give similar answers to this question. You may also rephrase the question so that it asks about the group: "Are most members loyal to the group?"

Researchers must also exercise special care when examining their data so that they do not attribute effects caused by group-level processes to individual-level processes and vice versa. You might be thrilled, for example, to find that members' individual loyalty scores predict the regularity of their attendance at meetings, until you realize that people who are in the same groups have unusually similar loyalty scores due to some group-level process. It may be that when the groups formed, the members naturally sorted themselves into groups in which members were relatively similar in their loyalty to the group or a norm of loyalty emerged within a group and most people eventually adopted the group's norm as their own. As a result, most of the variability in loyalty is not between people but between groups, so that when the researchers take into account which group a person belongs to, the effect of individual-level loyalty disappears.

Advances in statistical procedures offer ways to deal with these problems. If you collect data from each group member, you can check for group-level interdependencies by computing intra-class correlations (ICC), average deviation scores (e.g., rWG scores), or within-and-between analysis (WABA) statistics (Sadler & Judd, 2001). These analyses will indicate if you can use each individual member as the unit of analysis or if interdependency among the members' data is so high that you should aggregate their responses at the group level. Some statistical procedures, such as hierarchical linear modeling (HLM), are designed specifically for multilevel data and so are capable of disentangling cause-effect relationships and processes that operate simultaneously at two or more levels (Zyphur, Kaplan, & Christian, 2008).

Ethics of Group Research Group researchers, given their commitment to learning all they can about people in groups, pry into matters that other people might consider private, sensitive, or even controversial. Observers may watch groups—a sports team playing a rival, a class of elementary school children on the playground, a sales team reviewing ways to improve their productivity—without telling the groups that they are being observed. Researchers may deliberately disguise their identities so that they can join a group that might otherwise exclude them. Experimenters often manipulate aspects of the groups they study to determine how these manipulations change the group over time. Do researchers have the moral right to use these types of methods to study groups?

In most cases the methods that group researchers use in their studies—watching groups, interviewing members, changing an aspect of the situation to see how groups respond to these changes—raise few ethical concerns. People are usually only too willing to take part in studies, and investigators prefer to get group members' consent before proceeding. If they do watch a group without the members' knowledge, it is usually a group in a public setting where members have no expectation of privacy or where their identities are completely unknowable (de-identified). Group researchers strive to treat the subjects in their research with respect and fairness.

In some cases, however, researchers have used methods that raise more complex issues of ethics and human rights. One investigator, for example, used participant observation methods in a study of men having sex with one another in a public restroom. He did not reveal that he was a researcher until later, when he tracked them down at their homes (many of them were married) and asked them follow-up questions (Humphreys, 1975). Other researchers, with the permission of a U.S. district judge, made audio recordings of juries' deliberations without the jurors' knowledge. When the tapes were played in public, an angry U.S. Congress passed legislation forbidding researchers from eavesdropping on juries (see Hans & Vidmar, 1991). In other studies researchers have placed participants in stressful situations, as when researchers studied obedience in groups by arranging for an authority to order participants to give an innocent victim painful electric shocks. The shocks were not real, but some participants were very upset by the experience (Milgram, 1963).

These studies are exceptional ones, and they were conducted before review procedures were developed to protect participants. Present-day researchers must now submit their research plans to a group known as an **Institutional Review Board**, or **IRB**. The IRB, using federal guidelines

---

Institutional Review Board (IRB) A group, usually located at a university or other research institution, that reviews research procedures to make certain that they are consistent with ethical guidelines for protecting human participants.

that define what types of procedures should be used to minimize risk to participants, reviews each study's procedures before permitting researchers to proceed. In most cases researchers are expected to give participants a brief but accurate description of their duties in the research before gaining their agreement to take part. Researchers also use methods that minimize any possibility of harm, and they treat participants respectfully and fairly. An investigator might not need to alert people that they are being studied as they go about their ordinary activities in public places, but it is best to let an impartial group—the IRB—make that decision.

THEORETICAL PERSPECTIVES

Researchers do not just develop ingenious methods for measuring and studying group processes. They also develop compelling theoretical explanations for group phenomena. Scientists gather empirical evidence, but they also use this evidence to test the strength of hypotheses derived from theoretical models and general principles. Theories provide the means of organizing known facts about groups and so create orderly knowledge out of discrete bits of information. Theories also yield suggestions for future research. When researchers extend existing theories into new areas, they discover new information about groups, while simultaneously testing the strength of their theories.

Researchers have developed hundreds of theories about groups and their dynamics. Some of these theories are relatively narrow, for they focus on some specific aspect of groups. Others, in contrast, are far broader in scope, for they offer general explanations for groups across a wide variety of times and contexts. These theories, despite their variations, often share certain basic assumptions about what processes are more important than others, the types of outcomes they explain, and the variables that are most influential. This section reviews some of these basic theoretical perspectives

on groups, but with the caveat that these approaches are not necessarily mutually exclusive. Most theories embrace assumptions from more than one of the motivational/emotional, behavioral, systems, cognitive, and biological perspectives.

Motivational and Emotional Perspectives

Why do some people vie for leadership in their groups, whereas others remain content with less prominent roles? Why do some groups struggle against adversity, whereas others give up after the first setback? Why do some people shy away from groups, whereas others join dozens of them? The answers to these "why" questions often lie in people's motivations and emotions. **Motivations** are psychological mechanisms that give purpose and direction to behavior. These inner mechanisms can be called many things—habits, beliefs, feelings, wants, instincts, compulsions, drives—but no matter what their label, they prompt people to take action. **Emotions** often accompany these needs and desires; feelings of happiness, sadness, satisfaction, and sorrow are just a few of the emotions that can influence how people act in group situations. The words *motivation* and *emotion* both come from the Latin word *movere*, meaning "to move."

Motivational approaches offer insight into a wide range of group phenomena, for they focus on the "generative aspect of human behavior, on the forward-moving, internally driven aspect of behavior" (Pittman & Zeigler, 2007). Why, for example, do most people seem to desire to join with others in groups rather than remain alone? Motivational theories suggest that groups are an excellent way for members to satisfy some of their most basic needs. Psychologist Abraham Maslow's (1943)

---

motivation Wants, needs, and other psychological processes that energize behavior and thereby determine its form, intensity, and duration.

emotion A subjective state of positive or negative affect often accompanied by a degree of arousal or activation.

well-known **hierarchy of needs**, for example, describes a ranked series of basic human motives, including physiological and safety needs, belongingness needs, and the need for esteem and respect. Applied to groups, his motivational theory suggests that groups are the most popular of choices for most people because they satisfy these needs. Groups, with their greater resources, offer members food, shelter, and other essentials for survival. Groups offer protection from harm ("safety in numbers"), and they can care for members who are sick or injured. Groups, by their very nature, create a sense of belonging for their members and, by accepting and supporting them, are a source of prestige and esteem. Groups, from a motivational perspective, are a useful means of satisfying psychological needs (Kenrick et al., 2010).

Emotions, too, play a role in prompting individuals to seek membership in groups rather than remain alone. Studies of well-being suggest that one of the ways that people maximize their happiness is by joining with other people in groups—people who are happiest are the ones who report being linked to others in positive social relationships (Helliwell & Putnam, 2004). To be sure, groups, by rejecting and mistreating members, can be sources of such extremely negative emotions as loneliness, despair, sadness, and shame, but groups are also the source of such positive social emotions as contentment, pleasure, bliss, joy, love, gratitude, and admiration (Hareli & Parkinson, 2008). The impact of groups on emotions is, however, to some extent culturally specific. Individuals raised in cultures that stress interdependence and community experience more positive emotions when they are socially engaged than do those raised in cultures that stress independence and individualism (Kitayama, Markus, & Kurokawa, 2000). As Focus 2.2 explains, group behavior, like so many forms of human behavior, varies from one culture and context to another.

---

hierarchy of needs An ordering of needs from the most basic and biologically necessary to the more social and psychological needs, such as aesthetic and actualization needs (developed by Abraham Maslow).

Behavioral Perspectives

Many theories about groups draw on the seminal work of psychologist B. F. Skinner (1953, 1971). Skinner's **behaviorism** was based on two key assumptions. First, Skinner believed that psychological processes, such as motives and drives, may shape people's reactions in groups, but he also believed that such psychological processes are too difficult to index accurately. He therefore recommended measuring and analyzing how people actually behave in a specific context rather than speculating about the psychological or interpersonal processes that may have instigated their actions. Second, Skinner believed that most behavior was consistent with the *law of effect*—that is, behaviors that are followed by positive consequences, such as rewards, will occur more frequently, whereas behaviors that are followed by negative consequences will become more rare.

Social exchange theories use Skinner's behaviorism to explain how relationships are initiated and sustained through the reliable exchange of rewards and the imposition of costs by individuals and groups (Blau, 1964; Homans, 1961; Thibaut & Kelley, 1959). These theories stress the economics of membership by suggesting that members contribute their time and personal resources to their groups in exchange for direct, concrete rewards, such as pay, goods, and services, as well as indirect, socioemotional rewards, such as status and admiration. These exchanges create relationships among members and their group that are strengthened when (a) the rewards are valued ones and any costs created by the group are minimized, (b) the members trust each other to fulfill their obligations over the long term, (c) the exchange is judged to be a fair one with fairness defined primarily by mutual adherence to the norm of reciprocity, and (d) members develop a

---

behaviorism A theoretical explanation of the way organisms acquire new responses to environmental stimuli through conditioning (learning).

social exchange theory An economic model of interpersonal relationships that assumes individuals seek out relationships that offer them many rewards while exacting few costs.

Focus 2.2   Cross-cultural Perspectives: Groups Are Nested in Cultures

When do you feel happiest—contented, jubilant, joyful? Your answer may depend, in part, on where you were born and the culture where you were raised. Most people feel happier when they are members of supportive social groups, but in some cultures happiness is even more dependent on group associations. Researchers studied this cultural difference by asking people from the United States and from Japan how often they felt certain emotions: ones that were usually triggered by feelings of interdependence (respectful, friendly feelings), ones triggered by independence from others (pride, superior, "top of the world"), and more general, context-free emotions, such as happiness. They discovered that in the West happiness went hand-in-hand with emotions that arose from feeling superior to others. In the East, people felt happiness when they could reaffirm the connection between themselves and other people (Kitayama et al., 2000).

Anthropologists have documented extraordinary differences among the world's cultures. The Ghorbat of Central Asia and the Balkans maintain highly egalitarian groups with no permanent leadership roles and no hereditary positions of authority. The Kpelle of Liberia, before westernization, formed secret societies within their villages based on animal magic, and members reaffirm their bonds with one another by regularly performing certain sacred rituals. The Hubeer and the Rahanweyn of Somali cited kinship ties as the basis of their groups, yet many of the groups included "adopted" individuals who were unrelated to anyone in the group (Human Area Relations Files, 2012). Without exception, humans in all societies join with other humans to form groups, but because each society is unique in its traditions, culture, and ecology, the groups within any given culture may display unique interpersonal processes.

Social and organizational psychologist Geert Hofstede's theory of national cultures offers one way of identifying similarities and differences in values and cultural norms. In the late 1960s, Hofstede, working with a large international corporation (IBM), collected data about the beliefs, outlooks, and perspectives of employees in countries located all over the world. He then used these data to describe the culture-specific beliefs, traditions, practices, and philosophies shared by members of a group or region; what Hofstede calls "the collective programming of the mind" (Hofstede, Hofstede, & Minkov, 2010). Over time, he identified four key dimensions that underlie variations in cultural outlooks.

■   The *Power Distance Index* (PDI) is an indicator of inequality within a given culture, across individuals, groups, and classes. When PDI is low, cultures strive to minimize inequalities in the distribution of power within society but, when PDI is high, both those with and without power accept hierarchy as the natural order of things.

■   *Individualism* (IDV) contrasts group-centered and more individualistic cultures. In more individualistic cultures, ties between people are looser, for each person focuses on their own needs (or those of their immediate family). In collective cultures, people are integrated into cohesive groups that support them in exchange for their loyalty.

■   *Masculinity* (MAS) refers to the extent to which masculinity and its associated elements—competition, assertiveness, machismo—is manifested in the culture's practices, including role expectations associated with men and women.

■   *Uncertainty Avoidance Index* (UAI) describes the extent to which the culture's practices minimize uncertainty and ambiguity, generally by developing extensive social and legal guidelines, emphasizing security, and adopting religious or philosophical beliefs that define how one should behave.

These four dimensions form the foundation of his theory, but Hofstede added more as he continued to conduct his research. After studying many Asian cultures, Hofstede added *Long-Term Orientation* (LTO), which pertains to such Confucian dynamics as valuing tradition and meeting social obligations. *Indulgence versus Restraint* (IVR), a possible sixth dimension, describes differences in sources of satisfaction. Cultures that lean in the direction of indulgence are more open to basic pleasures, but those that are restrained emphasize self-regulation and control (Hofstede et al., 2010).

These dimensions of variation leave their mark on the group dynamics that occur within cultures. For example, in cultures with high levels of power distance (e.g., Russia, Panama, Malaysia) rather than low levels (e.g., Austria, New Zealand, Israel), people prefer a group's leader to be directive rather than participative, and they are less interested in seeking feedback about their impact on others in the group. They are more likely to trust others in the group, but do not express

Focus 2.2 (Continued)

that trust openly since they are more guarded in displaying their emotions. The degree of individualism, too, has marked effects on group processes. Most Western, industrialized cultures are individualistic—the United States, Australia, and Great Britain have the highest scores on Hofstede's individualism dimension—whereas Eastern countries and those with more agrarian rather than manufacturing economies tend to be more communal (e.g., Columbia, Pakistan, Thailand). Chapter 3 considers the impact of these cultural differences on a number of group processes, for individualism is associated with self-promotion, confrontation, and independence whereas collectivism increases accommodation,

compromising, the degree of identification with groups and organizations, and a preference to work in teams (Taras, Kirkman, & Steel, 2010).

These differences in group processes across cultures should not be altogether unexpected. Humans in all societies join with other humans to form groups, but the groups within any given culture may display unique interpersonal processes, as may the individuals within those groups and cultures. In consequence, even when a finding is obtained in one particular country, it is best to exercise caution before generalizing those findings to other people, places, and situations.

commitment to the group as indicated by increased affective attachment, a sense of loyalty, and an authentic concern for the other members' and the group's well-being. If, however, groups make too many demands on members—meetings, time commitment, investment of personal resources, and giving up involvement in other groups—then members are less likely to maintain their membership (Cress, McPherson, & Rotolo, 1997). Social exchange theory suggests that people join with others in groups because membership is, in a sense, a good deal (Cook & Rice, 2006).

Systems Theory Perspectives

Researchers in a variety of fields, including engineering, biology, and medicine, have repeatedly found that unique results are obtained when a system is formed by creating dependency among formerly independent components. Systems, whether they are bridges, ecological niches, organisms, or groups, synthesize several parts or subsystems into a unified whole.

A **systems theory** approach assumes groups are complex, adaptive, dynamic systems of interacting individuals. The members are the units of the system who are coupled one to another by relationships. Just as systems can be deliberately designed to function in a particular way, groups are sometimes created for a purpose, with procedures and standards designed with the

overall goal of the system in mind. Groups can, however, be self-creating and self-organizing systems, for they may develop spontaneously as individuals begin to act in coordinated, synchronized ways. Just as a system receives inputs from the environment, processes this information internally, and then outputs its products, groups gather information, review that information, and generate products. Groups are also responsive to information concerning the context in which they operate and their impact on that context and will adapt in response to feedback about their actions. Just as the relaying of information between interdependent units is a key concept in systems theory, so the communication of information between members plays a central role in group systems. Systems theory suggests that parts are, to an extent, interchangeable—specific units can be swapped in and out with no discernable impact on the system—but in some cases, because groups are built up of closely entwined parts, they can change to an extraordinary

---

systems theory A general theoretical approach that assumes that complex phenomena are the result of the constant and dynamic adjustments that occur between and among the interdependent parts of the whole. Applied to groups, systems theory assumes that groups are open systems that maintain dynamic equilibrium among members through a complex series of interrelated adjustments and processes.

degree when one of their constituent components changes (Arrow, McGrath, & Berdahl, 2000).

Systems theory provides a model for understanding a range of group-level processes, including group development, productivity, and interpersonal conflict. **Input–process–output models** of group productivity, or I–P–O models, are systems theories that emphasize *inputs* that feed into the group setting, the *processes* that take place within the group as it works on the task, and the *outputs* generated by the system (see Figure 2.4). Inputs would include any factors that are present in the situation when the group begins its work on the task, such as the characteristics of the individual members (skill, experience, and training) and group-level factors (group structure and cohesiveness). These input factors all influence, through a variety of paths, the processes that take place within the group as members work together to complete the task, including communication, planning, conflict, and leadership. These processes combine to transform inputs into outputs, which include aspects of the group's performance (e.g., products, decisions, errors) and changes in the factors that serve as inputs to the system. If the group performs poorly, for example, it may become less cohesive or it may seek out new members. Members of successful groups, in contrast, may become more satisfied with their group and take steps to make sure that the group uses the same procedures to solve the next problem (Ilgen et al., 2005; Littlepage et al., 1995).

Cognitive Perspectives

A group's dynamics, in many cases, become understandable only by studying the **cognitive processes** that allow members to gather information, make sense of it, and then act on the results of their mental appraisals. When people join a group for the first time, they immediately begin to form an impression of the group. This perceptual work prompts them to search for information about the other group members, rapidly identifying those who are outgoing, shy, and intelligent. Group members also search their memories for stored information about the group and the tasks it must face, and they must retrieve that information before they can use it. A group member must also take note of the actions of others and try to understand what caused the other member to act in this way. Thus, group members are busy perceiving, judging, reasoning, and remembering, and all these mental activities influence their understanding of one another, the group, and themselves (Hinsz, Tindale, & Vollrath, 1997; Hodgkinson & Healey, 2008).

Consider, for example, the impact of groups on the human memory system. Cognitive researchers, in their studies of memory, have discovered that people have better memories for actions and events that they are personally connected to and that thinking about themselves when processing information prompts them to encode the information more deeply. This **self-reference effect** can be demonstrated, for example, by asking people to answer a question about each word in a long list of words. If the question is a superficial one, such as "Does the word start with a vowel?" then people remember very few of the words when their memory is later tested. But, if they were asked "Does the word describe you?" their memories are significantly improved. The self, however, is not the only source of improved memory. When this experiment was repeated, but with a question about groups added, a **group-reference effect** occurred. Instead of asking "Does this word describe you?" respondents were asked "Does this word describe your group?" (family, university, or social category).

---

input–process–output (I–P–O) model Any one of a number of general conceptual analyses of groups that assumes raw materials (inputs) are transformed by internal system processes to generate results (output). For example, an I–P–O model of group performance assumes that group-level processes mediate the relationship between individual, group, and situational input variables and resulting performance outcomes.
cognitive processes Mental processes that acquire, organize, and integrate information. Cognitive processes include memory systems that store data and the psychological mechanisms that process this information.

---

self-reference effect The tendency for people to have better memories for actions and events that they are personally connected to in some way.
group-reference effect The tendency for group members to have better memories for actions and events that are related, in some way, to their group.

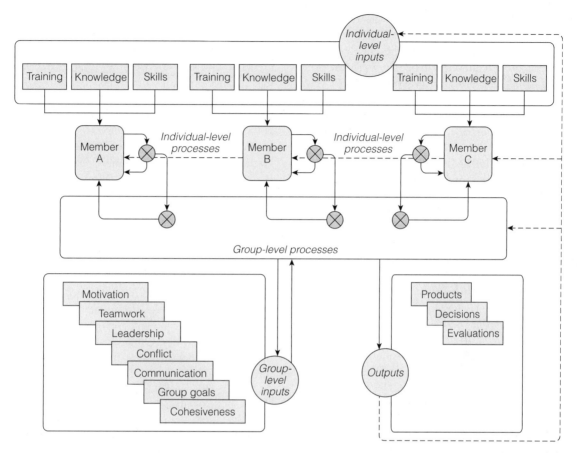

FIGURE 2.4   An example of an input–process–output model of group productivity. A systems theory approach to some complex aspect of a group, such as its productivity, assumes that group processes mediate the relationship between input factors and outputs. Individual-level inputs (shown at the top of the diagram) include training, knowledge, and the skills of each member. Group-level inputs (at the lower left) include motivation, teamwork, leadership, and so on. Individual- and group-level processes are represented by the symbol ⊗. Outputs include products, decisions, and evaluations, and feedback loops are depicted by the dotted lines.

SOURCE: © Cengage Learning

When their memories were later tested, they were able to remember as many of the words as were subjects in the self-reference condition. These findings suggest that "groups have the potential of providing an organizational framework to aid memory" (Johnson et al., 2002, p. 270).

Biological Perspectives

Group members can solve complex problems, communicate with one another using spoken and written language, build and operate massive machines, and plan their group's future. But group members are also living creatures whose responses are often shaped by biological, biochemical, and genetic characteristics. When conflict arises in the group, heart rates escalate, and other body changes occur to help members cope with the stress (Blascovich, Nash, & Ginsburg, 1978). When groups are trapped in confining, cramped spaces, members often become physiologically aroused, and this arousal can interfere with their work (Evans & Cohen, 1987). Men who seek to gain positions of higher status in the group tend to be those who have elevated levels of the testosterone hormone (Dabbs & Dabbs, 2000). The neuropeptide oxytocin, produced in the hypothalamus, increases the likelihood that people will treat other members of their group in positive, prosocial ways, although it also increases rejection of outgroup members (De Dreu et al., 2010).

One biological perspective—**evolutionary psychology**—argues that these processes may be part of the species' anatomical, biological, and neurochemical adaptations produced through natural selection. Evolutionary psychology recognizes that over time the human species has evolved socially as well as physically and that common forms of interpersonal and group behavior are not learned but rather the result of genetic predispositions. Anthropologists have documented the great diversity of human societies, but across all these variations, they have found one constancy: People live in groups rather than alone (Mann, 1988). Careful analysis of the artifacts left behind by prehistoric humans—primarily bones and stone implements—suggest that even ancient humans lived in groups (Caporael, 2007). Other primates, such as chimpanzees and bonobos, also live in small groups with dynamics similar in some respects to those seen in human groups (de Waal, 2006). The young of the human species instinctively form strong emotional bonds with their caregivers, and babies who are deprived of close human contact have higher mortality rates (Bowlby, 1980). Humans are also consistently cooperative in their dealings with other people so long as these other people are members of a group to which they belong and are not outsiders. Cooperative group life is a more stable strategy in evolutionary terms than competition and individualism (Axelrod & Hamilton, 1981).

---

evolutionary psychology A biological approach to understanding behavior which assumes that recurring patterns of behavior in animals ultimately stem from evolutionary pressures that increase the likelihood of adaptive social actions and extinguish nonadaptive practices.

Researchers are only now subjecting the theory to close scrutiny, so its assumptions should be considered skeptically. The theory is difficult to test experimentally, and its basic premise—that characteristics that enhance our fitness have a genetic basis—is arguable. Just because groups are useful does not mean that people are instinctively drawn to them (Francis, 2004). Nonetheless, the evolutionary approach offers insight into a range of group processes, including reactions to exclusion, affiliation, leadership, intergroup conflict, and aggression (Van Vugt, Hogan, & Kaiser, 2008).

Selecting a Theoretical Perspective

Group dynamics is rich with theory. Some of these theories trace group processes back to psychological processes—the motivations of the individual members, the mental processes that sustain their conception of their social environment, and even their instinctive urges and proclivities. Other theories focus more on the group as a social system that is integrated in the surrounding community and society.

These different theoretical perspectives, however, are not mutually exclusive paradigms, struggling for the distinction as *the* explanation of group behavior. Some researchers test hypotheses derived from only one theory; others draw on several perspectives as they strive to describe, predict, control, and explain groups and their members. Just as the questions "How should I measure this aspect of the group?" and "How should I test my hypothesis about groups?" can be answered in more than one way, no one solution can be offered in response to the question "What theory explains group behavior?" Many of the greatest advances in understanding groups have occurred not when one theory has been pitted against another, but when two or more theories have been synthesized to form a new, more encompassing theoretical perspective. As Homans (1950) wrote: "We have a great deal of fact to work with, [and] we also have a great deal of theory. The elements of a synthesis are on hand" (p. 4).

4. Cognitive theories assume that many group processes are understandable only after considering the *cognitive processes* that allow members to gather information, make sense of it, and then act on the results of their mental appraisals. For example, the *self-reference effect* improves memory for information that is relevant to the self-concept, but the group-reference effect improves memories for group-related information.

5. Biological perspectives, such as *evolutionary theory*, argue that some group behaviors, including leadership, may be rooted in people's biological heritage.

RESOURCES

Studying Groups

- "Methods of Small Group Research," by Norbert L. Kerr, Joel Aronoff, and Lawrence A. Messé (2000), examines the techniques and measures used by investigators in a wide variety of group research.

- *The Handbook of Group Research and Practice*, edited by Susan A. Wheelan (2005), includes chapters by experts who offer their insights into problems and approaches to studying groups.

Research Methods

- "Observation and Analysis of Group Interaction Over Time: Some Methodological and Strategic Choices," by Joseph E. McGrath and T. William Altermatt (2001), is a complete analysis of structured approaches to group observation.

- *Applications of Case Study Research*, by Robert K. Yin (2009), explains the logic behind case studies and offers a precise set of procedures to follow to carry out a study that will yield valid results.

- *Street Corner Society*, by William Foote Whyte (1943), remains one of the best examples of applying the case study method to understanding a group's dynamics.

- *The Sage Handbook of Qualitative Research in Psychology*, edited by Carla Willig and Wendy Stainton-Rogers (2008) is a compendium (33 chapters) dealing with all aspects of qualitative research procedures, including ethics, ethnography, observation, interviewing, discussion analysis, and so on.

Advances in Group Research Methods

- "Overcoming Dependent Data: A Guide to the Analysis of Group Data," by Melody S. Sadler and Charles M. Judd (2001), outlines the statistical procedures to use when data are collected from intact groups.

- *Theories of Small Groups: Interdisciplinary Perspectives*, edited by Marshall Scott Poole and Andrea B. Hollingshead (2005), describes, reviews, and synthesizes the full range of theoretical perspectives in groups, including evolutionary approaches, network approaches, and feminist and functionalist perspectives.

- *Small Groups as Complex Systems*, by Holly Arrow, Joseph E. McGrath, and Jennifer L. Berdahl (2000), uses the conceptual framework of systems theory to examine the formation, performance, and dissolution of small, performance-focused groups.

CHAPTER

3

Inclusion and Identity

CHAPTER OVERVIEW

Most people prefer group membership to isolation, but, once they join with others, they find they must sometimes do what is best for the group rather than what benefits them personally. Groups blur the boundary between the self and other, for members retain their personal qualities—their motives, emotions, and outlooks—but add to them a sense of self that is based on their group identity. Groups transform the *me* into the *we*.

- Do humans, by nature, seek solitude or inclusion in groups?

- When do people put the group's needs before their own?

- What processes transform an individual's sense of self into a collective, social identity?

CHAPTER OUTLINE

From Isolation to Inclusion

> *The Need to Belong*
> *Groups and Loneliness*
> *Inclusion and Exclusion*
> *Inclusion and Human Nature*

From Individualism to Collectivism

> *The Micro Level: The Social Self*
> *The Meso Level: The Group Culture*
> *The Macro Level: Collectivism across Cultures*

From Personal Identity to Social Identity

> *Social Identity Theory: The Basics*
> *Motivation and Social Identity*

Chapter Review

Resources

Peak Search and Rescue: From Individualism to Collectivism

Peak Search and Rescue is a pseudonym for a volunteer emergency response team based in a town near a mountainous recreational area in the western region of the United States. Peak first formed when several local outdoor enthusiasts recognized the need for better organized and equipped searches for missing, lost, stranded, trapped, and injured persons in remote wilderness areas. Over the years, the group has grown to include 30 active members as well as many others who support the group's activities as needed.

Patrick attended his first meeting of the group when he moved to the area in his mid-20s. An avid rock climber and hiker, he thought that joining this group would be a good way to sharpen his wilderness skills, meet people, and perhaps gain their admiration and respect. Peak's members risked their own lives to save others, and Patrick relished the idea of joining the ranks of these heroes.

He soon learned, however, that the Peak members eschewed the hero label. Any member who set themselves above others, showed off, or acted in ways that increased the risk of harm to other members or to those they were rescuing—any self-glorification—fell quickly from the group's graces. As one of the group members explained, "If you feel like you have to belong to a group like this to make yourself look better to other people, you know, take it somewhere else" (Lois, 2003, p. 55).

Patrick, like many people who are drawn to challenging wilderness experiences, was by nature self-confident, extraverted, and thrill-seeking, and he struggled to reconcile his natural egoism with Peak's collective focus. When he first joined he pushed to take part in rescue efforts long before the group felt that he had earned the right to full membership. He spoke of personal goals, of wanting to "learn things from these guys" rather than contributing to the group (Lois, 2003, p. 74). But, in time, his individual, personal self grew quieter, and his group-level, collective self flourished. He took part in as many missions as he could, but so as not to take the lead or gain the spotlight, he stepped in and filled any role that needed filling, ranging from the exciting and challenging (leading the search team) to the routine but required (monitoring communications from base camp). He learned to never speak of his individual exploits following a rescue, and he publicly accepted the blame for the risky actions he took during his early years in the group. He learned to act for the good of the group rather than for the good of himself (see Lois, 1999, 2003).

Patrick and Peak illustrate what has been called the "master problem of social life": The connection between the individual and society, including groups, organizations, and communities (Allport, 1962). Many people who were interested in joining Peak attended the required orientation and training sessions, but soon discovered that Peak required too much of them. They remained on the group's fringes, for they resisted Peak's mandate that members act for the good of others rather than for themselves. Others, like Patrick, learned to put the group's interests before his own personal needs. They did not just join Peak; they identified so strongly with the group that their sense of self came to be defined by it.

This chapter examines three essential processes that combine to transform lone individuals into group members: inclusion, collectivism, and identity.

Through *inclusion*, individuals change from outsiders into insiders by joining a group. Through *collectivism*, members begin to think about the good of the group as a whole rather than what the group provides them. Through the transformation of *identity*, individuals change their conception of who they are to include their group's qualities as well as their own individual qualities.

FROM ISOLATION TO INCLUSION

Some species of animals are solitary. The cheetah, giant panda, orangutan, and opossum remain apart from other members of their species and congregate in some cases only to mate or rear offspring. Other animals, such as chimps, hyena, deer, and mice, are social creatures, for they usually forage, feed, sleep, and travel in small groups. What about humans? Do people tend to keep to themselves, guarding their privacy from the incursions of others, or are humans group-oriented animals who prefer the company of other people to a life alone?

The Need to Belong

Healthy adult human beings can survive apart from other members of the species, yet across individuals, societies, and eras, humans consistently seek inclusion over exclusion, membership over isolation, and acceptance over rejection. Social psychologists Roy Baumeister and Mark Leary (1995, p. 497) argued that humans have a **need to belong**: "a pervasive drive to form and maintain at least a minimum quantity of lasting, positive, and impactful interpersonal relationships." They likened the need to belong to other basic needs, such as hunger or thirst. A person who has not eaten will feel hungry, but a person who has little contact with other people will feel unhappy and lonely. In this section we review the evidence that backs up their claim that group membership fulfills a generic need to establish positive, enduring relationships with other people.

Solitude and Social Isolation   Aristotle famously suggested that "Man is by nature a social animal; and an unsocial person who is unsocial naturally and not accidentally is either unsatisfactory or superhuman." Henry David Thoreau disagreed with Aristotle, and, to prove his point, spent two years relatively secluded at Walden Pond. He deliberately kept his social contacts to a minimum, explaining:

> Society is commonly too cheap. We meet at very short intervals, not having had time to acquire any new value for each other.

---

need to belong The generalized desire to seek out and join with other people, which, when unsatisfied, causes a state of tension and want.

We meet at three meals a day and give each other a taste of that old musty cheese that we are. Certainly less frequency would suffice for all important and hearty communication. (Thoreau, 1962, p. 206)

Spending time alone, away from others, can be a rejuvenating, pleasurable experience. Patrick, the Peak member, if asked how he felt about being isolated from others while he hiked, would likely say he found enjoyment in the self-discovery, contemplation, and increased spirituality that occurs when one is physically isolated from others (Long et al., 2003). People say I can "discover who I am," "determine what I want to be," "meditate and reflect," "try out some new behaviors," "recover my self-esteem," "protect myself from what others say," and "take refuge from the outside world" when alone (Pedersen, 1999, p. 399). Some philosophers, writers, and artists reach the apex of their creativity during times of isolation, when they were not distracted by other people (Storr, 1988; Suedfeld, 1997). Many people, if they have the financial resources, prefer to live alone rather than with other people (Klinenberg, 2012).

But most people, both young and old, find protracted periods of social isolation disturbing (Zubek, 1973). The diaries of individuals who have been isolated from others for long periods of time—stranded explorers, secluded scientists, and prisoners in solitary confinement—often speak of the psychological costs of their ordeal. As their isolation wears on, they report fear, insomnia, memory lapses, depression, fatigue, and general confusion. Prolonged periods of isolation are also marked by hallucinations and delusions, as when one solo sailor at sea was startled when he thought he saw a pirate steering his life raft (Burney, 1961).

Better Together   For most people, together is better than alone. Most spend the majority of their waking hours in the company of other people—only unmarried or widowed adults over the age of 45 reported spending more time alone than with others. The sheer number of groups that exist at any moment in time is also clear evidence of

T A B L E 3.1   Percentage of Americans Who Report Membership in Various Types of Groups (as of 2006)

Type of Group	Examples	Percent
Religious services group	Church, synagogue	35.7
Unofficial/informal group	Bridge club, interest group	26.7
Sports team	Softball team, soccer club	20.0
Neighborhood	Neighborhood association	16.6
Religion-based group	Bible studies, prayer group	16.3
Professional society	Association of Architects	14.5
School service	Parent-Teacher Association (PTA)	14.2
Labor union	Association of Autoworkers	13.7
Youth group	Boy Scouts, Civil Air Patrol	10.5
Service group	Little Sisters of the Poor, Lions	9.9
Fraternal organization	Fraternal Order of Police, DAR	9.5
Hobby club	Quilting groups, hunt clubs	9.5
Literary or art group	Book club, film club	8.9
Veterans	Veterans of Foreign Wars (VFW)	7.1
School fraternity	Zeta Phi Beta, Kappa Sigma	4.7
Political club	Young Republicans, Amnesty International	4.0
Farm-related group	Co-operative, 4-H club	3.9
Nationality-based group	Asian Culture Society	3.4

SOURCE: General Social Surveys, 1972–2006 [machine-readable data file]. Chicago: National Opinion Research Center at the University of Chicago. http://www3.norc.org/GSS+Website/.

the strength of the need to belong. Voluntary associations, such as churches, farming cooperatives, fraternal clubs, hobby groups, civic service associations, and community councils, are not rare but extremely common (Bonikowski & McPherson, 2007). With groups ranging from the small and distinctive, such as Peak, the Pecan Grove Garden Club, and the Model T Ford Club of Tulsa, to the large and diverse, such as the American Association of Retired Persons (AARP) and the Assembly of First Nations (AFN), there is a group for anyone who wants to join one, and most people do

(see Table 3.1). Americans are above average in their involvement in voluntary associations, but some countries' citizens—the Dutch, Canadians, Scandinavians—are "groupier" still (Curtis, Baer, & Grabb, 2001).

Even more numerous are the many informal kin-based and social groups, such as family, friends, and acquaintances, that satisfy members' need to belong. When surveyed, 87.3% of Americans reported that they lived with other people, including family members, partners, and roommates (Davis & Smith, 2007). The majority, ranging from 50% to 80%, reported doing things in groups, such as attending a sports event together, visiting one another for the evening, sharing a meal together, or going out as a group to see a movie (Putnam, 2000). People also satisfy their need to belong, at least temporarily, by joining in larger collectives and categories. People could perform a variety of activities alone—they could learn individually by reading books and studying papers, watching DVDs in the privacy of their homes, and dining each night at their kitchen counters—but most do not: They prefer to perform these activities in groups.

Groups and Social Capital   Groups, and the relationships they sustain, are a key source of one's **social capital**. Like financial or economic capital, social capital describes how rich you are, but in interpersonal terms rather than monetary or commercial terms. A person with considerable social capital is well connected to other people across a wide variety of contexts, and these connections provide the means for him or her to accomplish both personal and collective outcomes (Pettit et al., 2011).

The kinds of groups that people are joining are changing, however. Fewer people, for example, are joining traditional social clubs and associations, such as the Kiwanis, bridge clubs, and bowling leagues, prompting political scientist Robert Putnam (2000) to conclude we are now "bowling alone." But as some types of groups lose members, other types, such as book groups, support groups, teams at work, and online associations, are increasing in frequency and in membership (Cigler & Joslyn, 2002). Even though people may not be joining traditional groups, such as bowling leagues, as they once did, they are still bowling with other people—just with friends, coworkers, and family members rather than in organized competitive leagues.

Groups and Loneliness

Just as an inadequate diet can undermine one's health, people often feel pronounced psychological discomfort when they do not belong to groups and social networks. Imagine, for example, how Patrick felt when he first moved to the community served by Peak. He might have only known a few people—neighbors, people who he worked with—but these few relationships were probably insufficient to meet his need to belong. Peak, then, provided an antidote to feelings of loneliness.

Social and Emotional Loneliness   Although group memberships are not often considered as essential an interpersonal relationship as friendships and love relationships, the relationships that groups create and sustain can become so intimate and involving that they serve as a buffer against feelings of isolation and loneliness. **Loneliness** is not the same as being alone, for in some situations people are not troubled by isolation or a relative paucity of relations with others. Loneliness, instead, is an aversive psychological reaction to a perceived lack of personal or social relations. *Emotional loneliness* occurs when the problem is a lack of a long-term, meaningful, intimate relationship with another person; this type of loneliness might be triggered by divorce, a breakup with a lover, or repeated romantic failures. *Social loneliness,* in contrast, occurs when people feel cut off from their network of friends, acquaintances, and group members. People who have moved to a new city, children who are rejected by their peers, and new employees of large companies often experience social loneliness, because they are no longer embedded in a network of friends and acquaintances (Green et al., 2001). Both types of loneliness create feelings of sadness, depression, emptiness, longing, shame, and self-pity.

Some groups alleviate loneliness by fostering both intimate and social relations (Shaver & Buhrmester,

---

social capital The degree to which individuals, groups, or larger aggregates of people are linked in social relationships that yield positive, productive benefits; analogous to economic capital (fiscal prosperity), but determined by extensiveness of social connectedness.

---

loneliness Cognitive and affective malaise, including sadness, dejection, self-deprecation, and boredom, experienced when one's personal relationships are perceived to be too few or too unsatisfying.

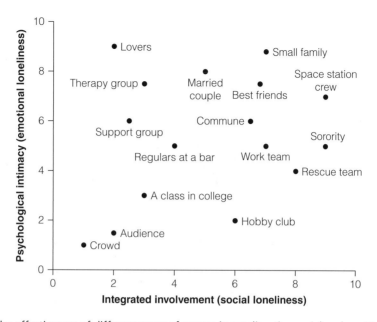

FIGURE 3.1   The effectiveness of different types of groups in ameliorating social and emotional loneliness.

SOURCE: Adapted from "Loneliness, Sex-role Orientation, and Group life: A Social Needs Perspective," by Phillip Shaver and Duane Buhrmester, FIG11-1., p. 263. In Basic Group Processes, Edited by Paul B. Paulus (1983). New York: Springer-Verlag.

1983). College students report less loneliness when they start college if they belong to a cohesive, satisfying group (Buote et al., 2007; Schmidt & Sermat, 1983). Members of groups with extensive interconnections among all the members were less lonely than members of groups with less dense networks (Kraus et al., 1993; Stokes, 1985). Children with friends—even friends who were considered odd or unusual by their peers—were less lonely than friendless children (Asher & Paquette, 2003). People who belonged to groups (e.g., service organizations, religious or church organizations, business or professional organizations, and social clubs) were healthier and happier than individuals who did not (Harlow & Cantor, 1996)—and these effects were stronger still when people contributed their time to several organizations rather than just one (Pilliavin & Siegl, 2007). Those with more connections to others survive environmental disasters, cope more effectively with traumatic events, and live longer lives (Charuvastra & Cloitre, 2008; Klinenberg, 2002; Stroebe, 1994).

The Ties that Bind   All groups are not equally effective in buffering their members from both forms of loneliness. As Figure 3.1 suggests, transitory, impersonal collectives do little to ease either social or emotional loneliness. Sitting with other people in a theater or striking up a conversation with a stranger on a bus creates a connection momentarily, but only groups that sustain stable, reliable alliances among members can ward off social loneliness (Furman & Buhrmester, 2009). Likewise, only groups that connect people together in an intimate, meaningful way reduce feelings of emotional loneliness. Having many superficial relationships with others is far less satisfying than having a few high-quality relationships characterized by high levels of social support, mutual caring, and acceptance (Hawkley & Cacioppo, 2010). In consequence, groups that create connections among their members, such as amateur athletic teams, social clubs, or work groups, will reduce members' feelings of social loneliness, but only more intimate, involving types of groups—families, romantic couples, or very close friendship cliques—will

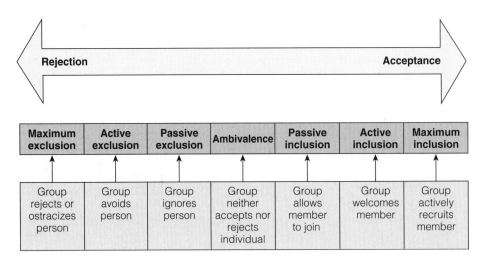

FIGURE 3.2   The inclusion–exclusion continuum. When individuals are actively sought out by groups, they experience maximum inclusion. When groups actively ostracize, people experience maximum exclusion (Leary, 1990).

SOURCE: © Cengage Learning 2014

meet members' social *and* emotional needs (Stroebe et al., 1996).

Loneliness Can Be Contagious   A group usually wards off feelings of loneliness, but not if the group is filled with lonely people. Social network researchers, studying the way such physical ailments as heart disease and obesity are passed along from one person to another, discovered that loneliness also spreads within groups (Cacioppo, Fowler, & Christakis, 2009). By measuring loneliness at different times, researchers found that people who were not initially lonely were more likely to become lonely if they were linked to a lonely person. As a result, loneliness occurred in clusters or at the fringes of the network, possibly because lonely individuals were socially isolated. Loneliness also depended on *degree of separation*: the number of people in the sequence linking one person to another. People were 52% more likely to be lonely if connected to a lonely person (one degree of separation), 25% more likely to be lonely at two degrees of separation (e.g., the friend of a friend was lonely), and 15% more likely to be lonely if linked at three degrees of separation (e.g., a friend

of a friend of a friend was lonely). Loneliness was no longer contagious at four degrees of separation.

Inclusion and Exclusion

The members of Peak did not welcome people to their meetings with open arms. The group guarded its solidarity fiercely, and it required newcomers to prove themselves by withstanding a period of deliberate exclusion. One member recalled feeling like an outsider for months, even though she faithfully attended meeting after meeting: "they didn't really care if I was there or not … no one said hello to me, no one said, 'Welcome, thanks for coming'" (Lois, 2003, p. 80).

Ostracism   People's need to belong is slaked when a group accepts them, but they are most satisfied when a group actively seeks them out. In contrast, people respond negatively when a group ignores or avoids them, and this negative reaction is exacerbated if the group ostracizes, abandons, or banishes them (see Figure 3.2; Leary, 1990). To be isolated from others due to circumstances or accidents is one thing, but to be deliberately ignored and excluded by others—**ostracism**—is particularly distressing (Molden et al., 2009).

The word *ostracism* dates to the Greeks, who voted to punish a member of the community with banishment by inscribing his or her name on potshards called *ostraca* (Williams, 2007). Contemporary forms of ostracism range from formal rejection of a member from a group—as when a church excommunicates a member or a club permanently bans a patron—to more subtle interpersonal tactics such as the "silent treatment" or the "cold shoulder." Cliques of adolescent girls, for example, use the threat of exclusion and ostracism itself to control the activities of members, with excluded girls finding that they are suddenly outcasts instead of trusted friends (Adler & Adler, 1995). Many religious societies shun members who have broken rules or traditions. People who work in offices and business often report feeling left out and alone because others avoid them and exclude them from their conversations and lunches (Ferris et al., 2008). In some cases, too, members are not deliberately excluded, yet they feel as though they are *out of the loop*: that they do not know things that others in the group do, and that the information they are missing is relevant to the group's social or task activities. Individuals who feel out of the loop experience more negative moods, they feel less competent, and they do not feel as close interpersonally to the other group members. These consequences are more pronounced if they feel that the group has deliberately turned against them rather than mistakenly overlooked them (Jones et al., 2009; Jones, Carter-Sowell, & Kelly, 2011).

Even nonhuman groups practice ostracism. A variety of social species, including wolves, bees, and primates, sometimes exclude an individual from the group—usually with fatal consequences (Wilgus, 2003). A shunned male chimpanzee, for example, would be forced to live at the periphery of his group, but remain ever vigilant against straying outside his home group's territory—for lone male chimps are usually killed if they are caught by patrolling chimps from a neighboring troop (Goodall, 1986).

Conclusions drawn from these studies of everyday ostracism are supported by experimental studies that place people in situations where they feel they are being excluded in some way. Social psychologist Kipling Williams (2007) and his colleagues, for example, often use the "ball toss" method. They arrange for people in a waiting room to begin some activity, such as tossing a ball to one another. Unbeknown to the subject of the study, all the others are part of the research team and they deliberately exclude the real subject from the game. Other studies use the "life alone" method, which involves giving people personality tests that indicate their future would be a solitary one. They are told: "You're the type who will end up alone later in life. You may have friends and relationships now, but.... these are likely to be shortlived and not continue.... Relationships don't last, and ... the odds are you'll end up being alone more and more" (Twenge et al., 2007, p. 58). Other studies have people meet briefly in a "get acquainted" session before picking partners or teams. Those targeted for exclusion are rejected by everyone else in the group (Nezlek et al., 1997).

Reactions to Exclusion Most people respond very negatively to ostracism and exclusion. When asked to describe their feelings, excluded people report feeling frustrated, anxious, nervous, and lonely, whereas those who are included in the group feel relaxed, friendly, and comfortable (Williams, 2007). Many feel they have been betrayed by the other group members, and they sometimes report frustration, shock, and surprise. Whereas people who are included value their experiences in the group, the excluded sometimes feel as if they are invisible—as if they do not even exist socially. The desire to belong is so strong that people respond negatively even when rejected by a group whose members they dislike intensely. In one study, researchers arranged for politically liberal college students to be rejected by two members of a socially vilified outgroup—the Ku Klux Klan. Even

---

ostracism Excluding one or more individuals from a group by reducing or eliminating contact with the person, usually by ignoring, shunning, or explicitly banishing them.

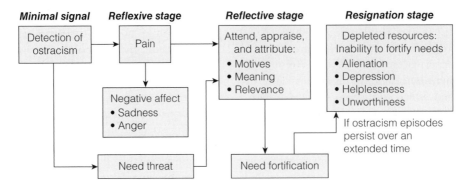

FIGURE 3.3   The temporal need-threat model of ostracism.
SOURCE: (Adapted from Williams, 2009).

though the students reported that they hated this group, they were still upset when the Klan first excluded them (Gonsalkorale & Williams, 2007).

Williams's (2007, 2009) *temporal need-threat model* of ostracism, summarized in Figure 3.3, calls this initial response to ostracism the *reflexive stage*. It is characterized by a flood of negative feelings—pain, disappointment, and distress—that all serve to signal that something is wrong. This period of negative emotions and confusion is followed by the deliberative, *reflective* stage. Patrick, after the meeting, probably reviewed the experience, searching for an explanation for the way he was treated, and, depending on this analysis, he likely would have adopted a specific behavioral strategy to minimize the negative effects of exclusion. If, however, Patrick was never able to gain acceptance in this group or another group, then he would reach the *resignation* stage: alienation, helplessness, loss of self-worth, and depression.

Fight-or-Flight Response   Some people, facing exclusion, fight their way back into the group (a fight response), or they avoid further rejection by seeking membership elsewhere (a flight response). This **fight-or-flight response** is a common

---

fight-or-flight response A physiological and psychological response to stressful events characterized by the activation of the sympathetic nervous system (increased heart rate, pupil dilation) that readies the individual to counter the threat (fight) or to escape the threat (flight).

reaction of people when they face stressful, threatening circumstances, and Williams suggests it is motivated by a desire to gain a sense of control in a deleterious situation. Those who display the *fight response* may confront group members directly, attempt to force their way into the group, insist that the group exclude someone else, or derogate those who have excluded them. They are also more likely to engage in a number of self-defeating behaviors, such as taking unnecessary risks and procrastinating. They also become less helpful toward others and more competitive overall. In more extreme cases, they may lose their temper and try to harm the group in some way (Warburton et al., 2006). This type of reaction is more likely when the exclusion is overt, unwarranted, and unexpected. People who are blindsided by rejection are more likely to fight back (Twenge et al., 2001, 2007).

Those who display a *flight response*, in contrast, attempt to withdraw physically or psychologically from the situation. Rather than tolerate the inattention, those who withdraw inhibit their relational tendencies, keep to themselves, or seek acceptance by some other group (Park & Hinsz, 2006). In one series of studies, researchers created social exclusion in a variety of ways (e.g., reminding people of a time they were excluded, giving them feedback suggesting they would end up living their life alone) and then measured participants' desire to socially reconnect. All these manipulations triggered an upswing in the desire to make friends and a willingness to work with others—but with new people and not with those who excluded them (Maner et al., 2007).

Withdrawal, however, can exacerbate social isolation, for those who too frequently exit rejection-threatening situations may be viewed as unfriendly, unapproachable, and detached by their peers (Doll, Murphy, & Song, 2003). In rare cases, withdrawal also triggers a general shutdown in behavioral and emotional reactivity. Such individuals report little change in mood or emotion other than numbness and lethargy when rejected; they freeze up (DeWall & Baumeister, 2006). Emotional numbing following exclusion is more likely in cases of extreme social injury and insult and, even then, occurs only rarely (Bernstein & Claypool, 2012; Gerber & Wheeler, 2009).

Tend and Befriend Response   Patrick, perhaps because he is a naturally outgoing and very self-confident person, did not respond by fighting or fleeing from the group (Park & Pinkus, 2009). Instead, he coped with his initial rejection in socially positive ways. He volunteered to take on unglamorous but necessary tasks, he kept his opinions to himself, and he tried hard to conform to the group's risk-management and teamwork norms. He displayed what social psychologist Shelley Taylor (2002, 2006) calls the **tend-and-befriend response**. He did not struggle against the group, but instead supported it by backing up others, making sure members' needs were met, reducing risk (tending), and doing what he could to strengthen his connection to others in the group (befriending). Even as the group rejected him, he continued to express an interest in becoming part of the Peak's team and treated his new acquaintances positively.

Those who tend-and-befriend rather than fight-and-flee seek social reconnection: They are more sensitive to social cues, more willing to

work hard for the group, and even tend to sciously mimic the actions of those around them (Lakin, Chartrand, & Arkin, 2008). Those who have recently been excluded or who feel lonely are far more attentive to and more likely to remember accurately the details of a group's interaction: They are searching for social cues that will help them find a way to gain acceptance in the group (Hess & Pickett, 2010). They become more socially perceptive, for they are better able to tell the difference between a false, forced smile and a genuine (Duchenne) smile (Bernstein et al., 2008), but they do tend to focus their attention on people who are responding positively rather than negatively to them (DeWall, Maner, & Rouby, 2009).

Williams and his colleagues demonstrated the earnestness of the excluded in the ball-toss situation. Excluded participants, when later asked how much they liked the other two group members, rated their partners more negatively when they had been ostracized. Women who had been ostracized, however, worked harder on a subsequent collective task, apparently to regain acceptance by the rest of the group. Women were also more likely to blame themselves for their ostracism (e.g., "I have trouble making a good impression with others"). Men, in contrast, did not compensate by working harder nor did they take the blame for their rejection (Williams & Sommer, 1997). These sex differences are consistent with differences between men and women first identified by Taylor when she proposed her tend-and-befriend response to stress: men are more likely to display a fight-or-flight response, whereas women are more likely to tend and befriend (Taylor et al., 2000).

Exclusion and Aggression   The need to belong is a powerful force in human behavior, so much so that individuals can respond violently when that need is thwarted (Ayduk, Gyurak, & Luerssen, 2008). Some individuals experience sadness when excluded; they respond to exclusion passively. But others are angered when excluded, and these individuals are the ones who are more likely to engage in antisocial behavior, including aggression (Chow, Tiedens, & Govan, 2008). Once angry, excluded

---

tend-and-befriend response A physiological, psychological, and interpersonal response to stressful events characterized by increased nurturing, protective and supportive behaviors (tending), and initiating and strengthening relationships with other people (befriending).

people interpret neutral or even accepting actions as negative, with the result that they sometimes feel as if the entire group has ostracized them when they have been rejected by only one or two of the members (Chernyak & Zayas, 2010; DeWall et al., 2009).

Social psychologist Lowell Gaertner and his colleagues demonstrated this tendency to blame the entire group by arranging for four-person groups to take a "Noise Tolerance" test that would require them to listen to painfully loud noise. Three of the four were actually part of the research team, however, and one of them was trained to reject the real subject. Furthermore, in the high entitativity condition of the experiment, all of the researcher's confederates wore the same type of sweatshirt, which indicated they were all members of a sports team. In the other condition, participants were dressed differently from one another (Gaertner, Iuzzini, & O'Mara, 2008).

Just prior to the noise-exposure session, the experimenter explained that the study required only three participants, so one individual would be excluded from the session. In the control condition, the experimenter randomly chose the real subject for exclusion, but, in the exclusion condition, one of the fake group members glared at the subject and said, "He (or she) should be the one who leaves!" The experimenter then escorted the subject from the room before explaining that he needed help in running the experiment and wondered if the subject would assist him by setting the volume level for the noise test. Even though this unexpected turn of events gave the just-rejected subjects the opportunity to exact revenge by turning up the noise dial, very few did, for the noise would harm both the individual who rejected them and innocent bystanders. However, the participants in one particular condition responded more aggressively than all the others by increasing the volume significantly: those in the rejection/high entitativity condition.

Gaertner's findings have implications for understanding cases of extreme violence committed by one or two students against larger groups of students at their schools (Newman et al., 2004). In a case in Kentucky, for example, one student took a handgun to school and shot members of Agape, the Christian group that began each day with a communal prayer. Three students died and five were severely injured. In the spring of 1999, Eric Harris and Dylan Klebold, both students at Columbine High School, used semiautomatic weapons, shotguns, and rifles to kill 13 students and teachers in a carefully planned attack. In 2007, a student at Jokela High School in Finland named Pekka-Eric Auvinen killed six students, the school principal, the school nurse, and then himself after setting fire to the school. In that same year, Seung Hui Cho, a 23-year-old senior at Virginia Tech, killed 32 people and wounded 17 others before committing suicide.

Such horrific actions spring from a complex of interrelated psychological and interpersonal factors, but when Mark Leary and his colleagues (2003) examined 15 cases of post-1995 shootings in schools in the United States, they found that these terrible acts of violence were tied together by a common thread: rejection. In most cases, the aggressors were individuals who did not belong to any groups or take part in social activities. They were often described as loners, as was Seung Hui Cho, the Virginia Tech gunman:

> For all of his 23 years of life the most frequent observation made by anyone about him was that Seung Hui Cho had absolutely no social life. During all of his school years he had no real friends. He had no interest in being with others. In fact, he shied away from other people and seemed to prefer his own company to the company of others. (Dupue, 2007, p. N-3)

Ostracism was not the sole cause of these incidents. In nearly all cases, aggressors had a history of psychological problems, although the severity of their troubles was often unrecognized. They were also often preoccupied with violence and death and were interested in guns and weapons in general. Exclusion, however, was a key social factor in most cases. Some of the perpetrators, such as Cho, were never mistreated by other people, yet they still felt rejected and isolated. In most instances, however, they had been ostracized by others at their schools and were the targets of malicious teasing, ridicule, and bullying. These individuals usually chose their targets deliberately, seeking revenge against those who had excluded them. They did not try to blame their

---

Focus 3.1   E-groups: Ostracism, Even on the Internet, Still Hurts

New technologies, such as cell phones, Internet instant messaging, Web-based meeting spaces, and online multiplayer games, provide new ways for people to slake their need to join—albeit, electronically—with other people, but these interactional spaces also offer new ways for people to exclude each other. People who join into a lively exchange of emails or comments in an online discussion forum may be disappointed when others' comments spark discussion but no one comments on what they offer to the group. Players in online gaming communities often discover that people they have been playing with abandon them or stop inviting them to take part in their group activities. Just as people sometimes exclude others from group activities in face-to-face activities, e-groups sometimes ignore others, effectively excluding them from the interaction. Kipling Williams has labeled this form of exclusion **cyberostracism** (Williams, Cheung, & Choi, 2000).

Given that the members of computer-based groups communicate at a distance and are, in some cases, completely anonymous, one might think that such cyberostracism is relatively inconsequential. However, the work of Williams and his colleagues on cyberostracism suggests otherwise. In one study, people from 62 different countries used the Web to take part in what they thought was a study of creative visualization. They thought they would be linked to two other volunteers and that the three would play a game called Cyberball in which players would pass a virtual disk from one group member to another. The website allowed players to choose whom they would throw the disk to and indicated who possessed the disk, whom it was thrown to, and whether or not the receiver dropped the throw. In actuality, however, the other two players were simulated, and the participants

were randomly assigned to one of four conditions: overinclusion (thrown the disk 50% of the time), inclusion (33%), partial ostracism (20%), and complete ostracism (they never received a throw after the initial round of tosses). When the game was over and the participants completed a brief survey over the Web, those who had suffered ostracism displayed the same sorts of negative reactions as evidenced by people in face-to-face groups. Even though the game was meaningless and their partners were total strangers, their social self-esteem dropped, their moods turned negative, and they admitted that they felt rejected (Williams et al., 2000).

Williams reported similar reactions to exclusion in his studies of chat rooms. In this work, he invited participants to join others in online chat rooms—Internet sites where users can type in messages that are read by others who are logged into the site at the same time. Some of the participants were excluded by the others in the chat room; actually, confederates following a script. Again, the participants reported a variety of negative reactions to the exclusion, but many of them also tried to break into the online conversation by increasing the number of messages they sent. For example, one wrote,

> U 2 can keep talking btw yourselves and ignore me, I don't mind!!! … maybe I should start a conversation with myself … hi how are yah … I'm fine how are you … I'm fine too … come on talk to me…

Williams concluded that these provocative actions provided participants with a way to gain control of the situation and may have partially buffered them from the stressful effects of exclusion (Williams et al., 2002, p. 73; see Wesselmann & Williams, 2011).

---

behavior on psychological problems, their parents, the media, or the influence of their friends. Nearly all claimed that they had been pushed into violence by a specific group of people who excluded them. Exclusion, by itself, is not associated with behavioral problems in adolescents, but those who are isolated and

report "problematic peer encounters" are at risk for a variety of negative outcomes (Kreager, 2004).

Inclusion and Human Nature

Why do people usually choose membership over isolation? Why do people respond so negatively when others exclude them? Why are people so sensitive to signs that others have overlooked them, even when they are connected only by Internet-based technologies (see Focus 3.1)? Evolutionary theory offers a single answer to all of these

---

cyberostracism Excluding one or more individuals from a technologically mediated group interaction, such as a computer-based discussion group, by reducing or eliminating communication with the person.

questions: the need to belong to groups is part of human nature.

The Herd Instinct The idea that humans are instinctively drawn to gather with other humans is not a new one. Over a century ago, psychologist William McDougall (1908) argued that humans are inexorably drawn to "the vast human herd," which "exerts a baneful attraction on those outside it" (p. 303). Advances in evolutionary psychology have revitalized this old idea, however, by specifying both the biological and interpersonal mechanisms that sustain the need to belong.

Evolutionary psychology uses Charles Darwin's theory of natural selection to explain why contemporary humans act, feel, and think the way they do. Darwin dealt primarily with biological and anatomical adaptations, but evolutionary psychologists assume that recurring psychological and social tendencies also stem from evolutionary processes that increase adaptive actions and extinguish nonadaptive practices. Nature not only encouraged the development of webbed feet on ducks and a keen sense of smell in dogs, but also certain psychological and social tendencies in humans. Humans' capacity to introspect, to read the emotion in others' faces, to understand the meaning of others' vocal utterances, and even to consider what future event may become more likely if a specific action is undertaken now, may all reflect adaptations that were shaped by natural selection. Similarly, humans' preference for living in groups rather than alone may also be sustained by psychological and biological mechanisms that evolved over time to help individuals solve basic problems of survival (Kurzban & Leary, 2001).

Living in groups yielded both costs and benefits for early humans. A group of humans foraging probably attracted the attention of more predators than did a single individual. The single individual could keep all the food he or she gathered or successfully hunted, but in groups, the food must be shared. Mingling with many others left one vulnerable to communicable diseases, conflict, and violence. But the benefits of sociality were far more substantial than these costs. Those who joined

with others in an organized band to hunt large animals or forage for patches of food were likely more successful than individuals who remained alone. Individuals in groups could maintain superior surveillance against predators, they could join forces to ward off predators' attacks, and they could rely on other members of their group to protect them from the aggressive actions of other humans. Human infants cannot survive alone. They must be in a group that cares for them until they can reach an age when they can fend for themselves. Groups, too, bring together men and women who can then form the pair-bonds needed for mating and procreation.

Evolutionary theory assumes that these advantages of group life, over multiple generations, eventually sewed sociality into the DNA of the human race. In the modern world, the advantages of group life over solitude are not so clear. People who buy their food in grocery stores and live in houses with deadbolts on the doors do not need to worry much about effective food-gathering strategies or protection from predation. These modern conditions, however, cannot undo 130,000 years of natural selection. Because those individuals who were genetically predisposed to join groups ("joiners") were much more likely to survive and breed than people who avoided social contacts ("loners"), with each passing generation, the genes that promoted solitude-seeking were weeded out of the gene pool, and the genes that encouraged group joining prospered (Marsh & Morris, 1988; see Figure 3.4). In consequence, gregariousness flourished as part of the biological makeup of humans (Kameda & Tindale, 2006).

Sociometer Theory If, as evolutionary theory suggests, humans who joined in groups were most likely to survive and reproduce, then it stands to reason that natural selection would favor those humans who were sensitive to signals of others that they were at risk for exclusion from the group. Evolution would not just favor the joiner, but a special type of joiner: one who is sensitive to signs of social exclusion. It would do you little good to be instinctively drawn to a group, but then to

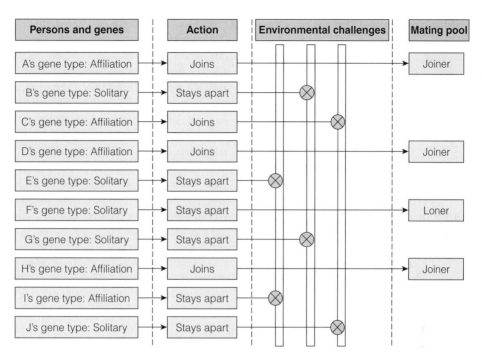

FIGURE 3.4 A schematic representation of the process of natural selection of group-oriented individuals. If human's ancestors lived in an environment that favored those who lived in groups, then over time those who affiliated would gradually outnumber those who were self-reliant loners. Note, too, that one's genetic endowment interacts with the environment, and so not all individuals who are genetically predisposed to affiliate or remain alone will do so (see, for example, person I).

SOURCE: © Cengage Learning

have no way to tell if the group was about to cast you out. What you would need would be a sociometer: a cognitive adaptation that monitors your degree of acceptance by others.

Sociometer theory, proposed by Mark Leary and his colleagues, suggests that feelings of self-worth function as just such a monitor. Many theorists consider the need for self-esteem to be a master motive, but sociometer theory suggests that "self-esteem is part of a sociometer that monitors peoples' relational value in other people's eyes" (Leary, 2007, p. 328). Self-esteem, then, is not an

index of one's sense of personal value, but instead an indicator of acceptance into groups. Like a gauge that indicates how much fuel is left in the tank, self-esteem indicates the extent to which a person is included in groups. If the gauge drops, then exclusion is likely. So when people experience a dip in their self-esteem, they search for and correct characteristics and qualities that have put them at risk of social exclusion. The sociometer model concludes that most people have high self-esteem not because they think well of themselves but because they are careful to maintain inclusion in social groups (Leary & Baumeister, 2000).

Leary and his colleagues (1995) tested the theory experimentally by measuring self-esteem after individuals were excluded from a group. They explained to the students they recruited for the study that they would be comparing decisions

---

sociometer theory A conceptual analysis of self-evaluation processes that theorizes self-esteem functions to psychologically monitor of one's degree of inclusion and exclusion in social groups (proposed by Mark Leary).

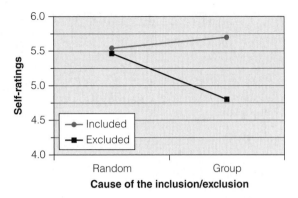

FIGURE 3.5 Group members' reactions to inclusion and exclusion in two different conditions: when the inclusion/exclusion is determined by random assignment or the preferences of the group.

SOURCE: "Self-Esteem as an Interpersonal Monitor: The Sociometer Hypothesis," by M. R. Leary, E. S. Tambor, S. K. Terdal, and D. L. Downs, *Journal of Personality and Social Psychology*, 1995, *68*, 518–530. Copyright 1996 by the American Psychological Association.

made by groups and by people working alone. In half the sessions, the researchers said that the group-versus-individual decision was determined by a random drawing. In such cases, individuals would have to leave the group but it was not because the group rejected them. But in the other half of the groups, students rated each other after a brief get-acquainted session, and those participants who received the fewest votes would be excluded from the group. As predicted, those who were rejected reported feeling less competent, adequate, useful, smart, and valuable than did the included group members—provided the rejection was an interpersonal one. As Figure 3.5 indicates, isolation caused by an impersonal force—the experimenter's random choices—had no effect on self-esteem. Rejection by the group, in contrast, lowered self-esteem, and inclusion raised self-esteem slightly.

The theory is also consistent with correlational studies that find self-esteem rises and falls with increases and decreases in inclusion. One study tracked these two variables with students who met four times in small groups during the course of a month. During that period, the self-esteem of those students who were rated more positively by other group members the week before rose, whereas the self-esteem of the least liked students declined (Srivastava & Beer, 2005). This relationship was also confirmed in a cross-cultural study of friendship and self-esteem. Residents of countries where self-esteem tended to be high, such as Iceland, Ireland, and the United States, also rated their interactions with friends as more enjoyable and inclusive (Denissen et al., 2008).

The Biology of Ostracism and Inclusion   The intensely negative reaction most people experience when they feel excluded has a biological basis. When Patrick first noticed others in the group were ignoring him, his cardiovascular, hormonal, and immune systems likely responded to deal with the stress of exclusion (Stroud et al., 2000). In one study, researchers measured the heart rate, blood pressure, and cardiac output of a person both before and after he or she suffered an interpersonal rejection from a member of their own race or a different race. Same-race rejection prompted deleterious physiological responses that signaled stress and threat, in part because rejection by someone with a different racial background was attributed to prejudice rather than ostracism (Mendes et al., 2008). Inclusion triggers a different set of physiological events: lowered heart rate and blood pressure and an increase in levels of the neuropeptide and hormone oxytocin, which is associated with positive forms of social behavior, including trust and social support (Taylor, 2006). In fact, when individuals who are about to be rejected by others are dosed with oxytocin, some of the negative psychological effects of ostracism are alleviated (Alvares, Hickie, & Guastella, 2010).

Researchers have also explored the close connection between the experience of physical pain and interpersonal pain. People often claim that exclusion is a painful experience—that their feelings are *hurt* or they feel *wounded* when someone slights them—because the pain of exclusion is neurologically similar to pain caused by physical injury (MacDonald & Leary, 2005). As social neuroscientist Naomi Eisenberger (2011, p. 587) explains: "because of the importance of social connection

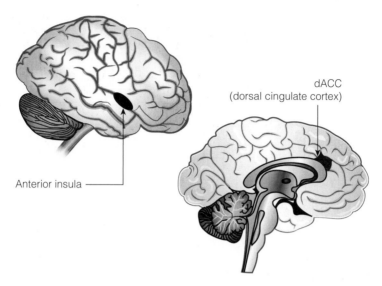

FIGURE 3.6 The brain regions involved in the experience of pain during social exclusion.
SOURCE: © Cengage Learning 2014

for human survival, the social attachment system—which ensures social connection—may have piggybacked directly onto the physical pain system, borrowing the pain signal itself to indicate when social relationships are threatened."

Neuroimaging research confirms the close association between social and physical pain. Eisenberger and her colleagues, for example, used a functional magnetic resonance imaging scanner, or fMRI, to track neural responses to exclusion. Such scanners indicate what portions of the brain are more active than others by measuring cranial temperature and blood flow. When people were left out of a group activity, two specific areas of the brain—the dorsal anterior cingulate cortex (dACC) and the anterior insula—were particularly active (see Figure 3.6). These areas of the brain are associated with the experience of physical pain sensations and other negative social experiences (Eisenberger, Lieberman, & Williams, 2003).

The close association between social and physical pain explains why individuals who are particularly sensitive to pain, in general, are also more likely to respond more negatively to social rejection. The rejection/pain connection also suggests that comforting someone who is in physical pain may do more

than merely provide psychological support—it may activate neuronal mechanisms that alleviate the experience of pain (Eisenberger & Lieberman, 2004). Also, because the pain of exclusion has a neural basis, painkillers that people take for physical pain relieve the pain caused by social exclusion. To test this possibility, volunteers took acetaminophen (Tylenol) or a placebo daily for three weeks. They then played a game of Cyberball while monitored by an fMRI. Those volunteers who took acetaminophen did not respond as negatively as those in the placebo condition when they were excluded from play in the Cyberball game. Another set of volunteers who also took painkillers for three weeks reported feeling less distressed over negative social experiences. They were not necessarily rejected less often—the rejection just did not bother them quite so much (DeWall et al., 2010).

FROM INDIVIDUALISM
TO COLLECTIVISM

Across individuals, societies, and eras, humans consistently prefer to be on the inside of groups rather than the outside. But a social life makes demands

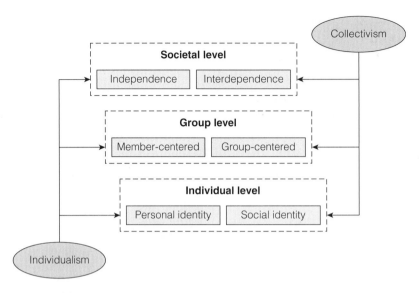

FIGURE 3.7   A multilevel model of individualism and collectivism.
SOURCE: © Cengage Learning 2014

that a life of solitude does not, for once people join with others they must balance their personal needs against the needs of the group. Before Patrick joined Peak, he could do as he pleased without irritating or offending others. He could spend the day working, hiking difficult trails, or skiing unsafe areas. But once Patrick joined with the other members of Peak, his self-centered world became a group-centered one.

Patrick's transition from individual to group member illustrates the fundamental duality of human nature. Patrick, the individual, was independent, opinionated, and self-confident, but Peak expected its members to be interdependent team players, respectful of others' opinions, and unassuming. How did Patrick manage to be both a unique, autonomous individual and a contributing member of Peak Search and Rescue?

Most answers to this question inevitably make their way to the distinction between individualism and collectivism. **Individualism** is a tradition or

worldview based on the independence and uniqueness of each individual. Individualism assumes that people are autonomous and must be free to act and think in ways that they prefer, rather than submit to the demands of the group. Each person is self-governing and should strive to achieve outcomes and goals that will personally benefit them (Kampmeier & Simon, 2001; Simmel, 1902). **Collectivism**, in contrast, puts the group and its goals before those of the individual members. Each person, if even recognized as an independent entity, is inseparably connected to the group or community. Social existence is centered on group relations, which create social obligations based on respect, trust, and a sense of community (Bellah et al., 1985).

The relative emphasis on individualism versus collectivism varies across people, groups, and cultures (see Figure 3.7). Some people, when they describe themselves, are more likely to mention the groups they belong to and their family responsibilities, but others stress their personal attributes and are less likely to refer to other people. Some groups,

individualism A tradition, ideology, or personal outlook that emphasizes the primacy of the individual and his or her rights, independence, and relationships with other individuals.

collectivism A tradition, ideology, or personal orientation that emphasizes the primacy of the group or community rather than each individual person.

T A B L E   3.2   Categories of Information in the Social (Collective) Self

Component	Examples
Roles	athlete, caregiver, churchgoer, community volunteer, daughter, friend, group member, neighbor, parent, relative, secretary, son, spouse, stepparent, student, worker
Groups	book club, class, clique, club, committee, department, executive board, fraternity, gang, neighborhood association, research group, rock band, sorority, sports team, squad, work team
Categories	alcoholic, athlete, Christian, deaf person, Democrat, earthling, feminist, gardener, gay, Hispanic, Republican, retired person, salesperson, scientist, smoker, Southerner, welfare recipient
Relations	friend to others, in love, close to other people, helpful to others in need, involved in social causes

such as Peak, stress cooperation, sharing, and conformity, whereas others condone and even encourage competition, personal achievement, and independence. Some cultures, too, stress connections and interdependence whereas others take independence and autonomy for granted. The following sections explore some of these variations in the nature of interpersonal relationships, norms and roles, motivations, and self-conceptions across the micro (individuals), meso (groups), and macro (cultures) levels. (For more detailed analyses and very differing opinions on the issue of the core dimensions of individualism and collectivism, see Brewer & Chen, 2007; Chen & West, 2008; Forsyth & Hoyt, 2011; Kağitçibaşi, 1997; Oyserman, Coon, & Kemmelmeier, 2002; Triandis & Suh, 2002.)

The Micro Level: The Social Self

William James (1892/1961) offered one of the first psychological analyses of the **self** in his *Principles of Psychology*, where he asserted that the sense of self is an individual's conception of his or her enduring qualities and characteristics. The self (or self-concept) does not necessarily describe one's true characteristics, but it does summarize and organize one's *assumptions* about those characteristics.

Personal and Social Identity   What would you answer if asked the question "Who are you?" Would you include your physical qualities, such as your height, weight, strength, and physical appearance? Would your personality traits, the things you believe in, your politics, or your fears and worries make the list? Might you mention your sex, your age, or where you were born? Would you describe your social roles and memberships, such as daughter, father, citizen of a country, or student at a university (Kuhn & McPartland, 1954)?

When answering the question "Who am I?" people usually mention their individualistic qualities and characteristics: their personality traits (e.g., "I'm kind" or "I am an introvert"), preferences, interests, likes, and dislikes (e.g., "I enjoy group dynamics class"), aspirations, hopes, wishes (e.g., "I hope to find personal fulfillment someday"), habits, and activities ("I play soccer"), abilities, skills, beliefs (e.g., "I am very good at beer pong"), and even their emotional tendencies and current mood state (e.g., "I'm grumpy today"). But they also mention qualities that spring from their relationships with other people and groups (see Table 3.2). Social roles, such as spouse, lover, parent, stepparent, caregiver, and worker, define one's position in groups and social networks. The self may also include memberships in social groups, such as car pools, clubs, or church groups; memberships in larger social categories, based on ethnicity, age, religion, or some other widely shared characteristic; and also information about one's social relations with other people (Brewer & Chen, 2007; Nario-Redmond et al, 2004).

_____

self (or self-concept) A person's perception of his or her enduring qualities and characteristics.

The self, then, is based both on personal qualities and interpersonal qualities. The **personal identity** encompasses all those unique qualities, traits, beliefs, skills, and so on that differentiate one person from another. The **social identity** includes all those qualities that derive from connections with and similarity to other people and groups (Baldwin, 1992). The personal identity is the *me* of the self, and the social identity is the *we* (Rhee et al., 1995).

Individualists and Collectivists   Selves tend to be dualistic with both a personal and social side, but some people stress their personal, individualistic qualities, and others their social, collectivistic qualities. Those who lean toward individualism—variously called **individualists**, independents or idiocentrics—speak of their independence, their personal goals, and their uniqueness (adapted from Oyserman et al., 2002; Triandis et al., 1985):

- Independence: "I tend to do my own thing, and others in my family do the same."

- Goals: "I take great pride in accomplishing what no one else can accomplish."

- Competition: "It is important to me that I perform better than others on a task."

- Uniqueness: "I am unique—different from others in many respects."

- Privacy: "I like my privacy."

- Self-knowledge: "I know my weaknesses and strengths."

- Communication style: "I always state my opinions very clearly."

Collectivists—also called interdependents or allocentrics—stress their connections to others (adapted from Oyserman et al., 2002; Triandis et al., 1985):

- Relating: "To understand who I am, you must see me with members of my group."

- Belonging: "To me, pleasure is spending time with others."

- Duty: "I would help, within my means, if a relative were in financial difficulty."

- Harmony: "I make an effort to avoid disagreements with my group members."

- Advice: "Before making a decision, I always consult with others."

- Context: "How I behave depends on who I am with, where I am, or both."

- Hierarchy: "I have respect for the authority figures with whom I interact."

- Group: "I would rather do a group paper or lab than do one alone."

These differences in individualism and collectivism influence the way individuals think, feel, and act in groups. When explaining why people act as they do, individualists attribute behaviors to the internal, personal characteristics of the person, whereas collectivists recognize that people's actions are often determined by the social circumstance in which they find themselves. Collectivists think of personality differently than individualists do—as a flexible set of tendencies that can change when a person moves from one social situation (e.g., the family) to another (e.g., the workplace). Those who are more individualistic are emotionally detached from their groups; they put their own personal goals above the goals of the group, and they find more enjoyment in personal success and competition. Collectivists are more respectful of other members of their groups, and they are more

---

personal identity An individual's perception of those aspects of his or her self-concept that derive from individualistic, personal qualities such as traits, beliefs, and skills.
social identity (or collective self) An individual's perception of those aspects of his or her self-concept that derive from his or her relationships with other people, groups, and society.
individualists (or independents or idiocentrics) Individuals predisposed to put their own personal interests and motivations above the group's interests and goals.

---

collectivists (or interdependents or allocentrics) Individuals predisposed to put the group's goals and needs above their own.

likely to be good corporate citizens who help co-workers rather than compete with them (Leung, 2008). Individualists and collectivists do not differ in their tendency to join groups, but collectivists value their memberships in their groups more, consider these relationships to be stable and long-lasting, and are less willing to sever their memberships. Collectivists seek jobs that will enhance the quality of their relationships with other people, and their satisfaction with their work depends on the quality of their relationships with their coworkers. Individualists choose jobs that are personally fulfilling and that offer them opportunities for advancement. Collectivists, compared to individualists, have a more favorable attitude toward group-level rewards for collective work (for reviews, see Gelfand et al., 2004; Triandis & Gelfand, 2012). Collectivists are more firmly rooted in their communities: they report having moved less frequently than individualists (Oishi, Lun, & Sherman, 2007).

Sex and Generational Differences Researchers, taking note of the converging content of collectivism and women's reputed tendency to be more relational, have checked for sex differences in their studies—but the results are not conclusive. Some studies suggest that women lean more toward collectivism, at least in Western cultures that place more value on independence and autonomy, but other studies find no consistent differences (Cross & Madson, 1997; Gabriel & Gardner, 1999; Kashima et al., 1995). In general, however, individuals who are members of social groups that are ranked lower in that society in terms of prestige and power—for example, minorities, recent immigrants, and those who are less wealthy—tend to be more collectivistic. Individuals who are low in social status may find that the values of collectivism provide them with the security and support they need to cope with their more difficult social circumstances.

Entire generations of individuals living in a given culture may also display overall differences in individualism and collectivism. Robert Putnam (2000) notes that the generation of Americans born

during the first portion of the twentieth century were so willing to sacrifice for the collective good that they were dubbed the Greatest Generation. Their children—the baby boomers born after the Second World War—displayed a strong work ethic, but their commitment to their employers meant that they had less time to donate to volunteer activities. Gen-Xers, born between 1965 and 1980 or so, and the most recent generation, variously labeled Gen-Y, the Millennials, or the Me Generation, are characterized by stronger needs for autonomy, individualism, confirmation, and support. Social psychologist Jean Twenge and her colleagues maintain that the youngest generation is more individualistic than any previous one. When surveyed, they express less empathy for others, reduced civic orientation, and are not as committed to environmental causes. Many members of this generation have performed community service, but they usually did not volunteer to do so: rather, their schools required them to get involved in some civic activity. Given that members of this generation are more interested in gratifying their personal needs, less likely to be concerned with the recommendations of authority and less likely to follow social rules, Twenge calls them "Generation Me" rather than "Generation We" (Twenge, 2006; Twenge, Campbell, & Freeman, 2012).

Maintaining Optimal Distinctiveness Collectivists are often contrasted with individualists, but these two orientations are continuous dimensions of personality that vary in their influence across time and situations. Most people's selves are a combination of both personal and collective elements, and so their view of themselves can shift along the continuum from individualistic to collectivistic, depending on the situation. People's answers to the question "Who am I?" will change to include more collectivistic elements if they are first asked to imagine themselves in a group or if they have just read texts that contain many plural pronouns such as we or us. Asking them to think about how different they are from others or reading texts with many *I*'s and *me*'s, in contrast, switches on the individualistic self (Oyserman & Lee, 2008).

Optimal distinctiveness theory, proposed by social psychologist Marilynn Brewer (2012), argues that most people have at least three fundamental needs: the need to be assimilated by the group, the need to be connected to friends and loved ones, and the need for autonomy and differentiation. She hypothesized that individuals are most satisfied if they achieve optimal distinctiveness: Their unique personal qualities are noted and appreciated, they are emotionally bonded with intimates, and they feel similar to other group members in many respects.

Groups offer the members a convenient means to meet all these needs. Peak may have restrained Patrick's individuality to some degree, but membership in this group was itself a distinguishing credential. When individuals join a small, distinctive group like Peak, their feeling of uniqueness increases—many of the newcomers mentioned that one of the reasons they initially sought membership was because they wanted to do something that set them apart from the mainstream (Hornsey & Jetten, 2004). Groups, also provide many means for each member to act in ways that are unique, for even within a group as small as Peak members gravitated to specific role assignments, which they enacted in ways that were distinctively their own. Peak also included a variety of overlapping subgroups, so while all were members of the overall group, it was easy for members to feel a common bond with a few other members who remained set apart to a degree from the rest of the group. Groups, then, offer something to both the collectivist and the individualist, for they provide the means to maximize both a sense of uniqueness as well as satisfying the need to belong (Maslach, Stapp, & Santee, 1985; Snyder & Fromkin, 1980).

optimal distinctiveness theory A conceptual analysis that assumes individuals strive to maintain a balance between three basic needs: the need to be assimilated by the group, the need to be connected to friends and loved ones, and the need for autonomy and differentiation (proposed by Marilyn Brewer).

The Meso Level: The Group Culture

As Peak Search and Rescue evolved into an organized group of dedicated rescue experts, its members came to accept a relatively coherent set of beliefs, values, and practices. The group valued most of all members who had few obligations outside of the group and so were ready to take on a mission at a moment's notice. Members were also expected to spend time socializing with other members of the team after a mission as they reviewed the experience and identified ways to improve their service. Because of the complexity and physically challenging nature of the work, Peak respected people who were strong and skilled, but they also stressed that no role within the group was more important than any other. Who people were, in terms of their personalities or their work outside of the group, mattered less than skill and level of experience. And Peak never tolerated anyone who considered themselves to be better than anyone else.

Taken together, these shared values, attitudes, beliefs, practices, and preferences made up Peak's **group culture**. As the psychologist Edgar Schein explains, "any definable group with a shared history can have a culture" and "once a group has learned to hold common assumptions, the resulting automatic patterns of perceiving, thinking, feeling, and behaving provide meaning, stability, and comfort" (1990, p. 111). But, just as a society's cultures vary along a continuum from individualism to collectivism, so do groups and organizations vary in their emphasis on individuals within the group and the group as a whole (Earley & Gibson, 1998; Zhou & Shi, 2011). In some groups, members are together but still separate: Members are encouraged to realize their unique potential, those who stand out from the group are valued, and competition among members is encouraged, as is independence. Other groups, in contrast, are more like communities: Loyalty is prized above all, decisions are often

group culture The distinct ways that members of a group represent their experiences, including shared knowledge, beliefs, rituals, custom, rules, language, norms, and practices.

made collectively, members take each other's views into consideration, and once a person becomes a member, the group takes care of them (Robert & Wasti, 2002). Naturally, the obligations, relations, and dynamics of the individualistic group will differ in predictable ways from those of the more collectivistic group.

Conformity and Uniqueness   Because collectivism elevates the group's rights above those of the individual, in collectivistic groups members are expected to conform to the group's norms and heed the directives of those in positions of authority in the group. A collectivistic group "binds and mutually obligates" each member (Oyserman et al., 2002, p. 5), and so members have no right to create disagreement or to disrupt convened group proceedings. Such groups therefore prefer acquiescence to disagreement and compromise to conflict. Their operating principle is "The tall nail gets pounded down." Members are expected to carry out their duties, and the successful fulfillment of their roles and responsibilities is the primary source of self-satisfaction (Schwartz, 1994).

Individualistic groups, in contrast, often set in place reward structures that favor individual achievement rather than group-level success. Members do not display as high a degree of uniformity in their behavior or even respect for the group's traditions and leadership, for members are expected to act on the basis of their attitudes, beliefs, and preferences. Members believe they have the right to speak their minds and to disagree with others (Triandis, 1996). In consequence, individualistic groups are more reserved in their reactions to nonconformity per se, for they assume that "the squeaky wheel gets the grease." Collectivists hold rule-breakers in contempt, but individualists tend to display anger toward those who disregard the group's emphasis on autonomy by seeking to impose their will on others (Rozin et al., 1999).

Exchange and Communal Relations   Groups create relationships among members, but individualistic groups stress the *exchange* of resources and collectivistic groups focus on sharing *communal* resources.

Individuals in **exchange relationships** monitor their inputs into the group, strive to maximize the rewards they personally receive through membership, and will become dissatisfied if their group becomes too costly for them. They expect to receive rewards in exchange for their investment of time, energy, and other personal resources. If individuals cannot identify any personal benefit from helping others in the group or community, then they will not offer any help (Ratner & Miller, 2001). In contrast, people in **communal relationships** are more concerned with what their group receives than with their own personal outcomes. When individuals work in communal groups, they help fellow members more, prefer to think of their work as a joint effort, and feel disappointed if other members insist on reciprocating any help given. They are also more likely to consider the consequences of their actions for others and are more diligent in making sure that others' needs are met (Clark & Mills, 2012).

The difference between a communal and an exchange relationship is made clear by a simple bargaining simulation called the **Ultimatum Game**. Imagine that you have been allotted $20 that you must share with your partner. You do not know your partner's identity except that he or she is a member of your group. You may offer your partner any portion of the $20—from 1¢ to $19.99—but your partner knows you have been allocated $20. If your partner accepts your offer, the $20 will be divided just as you proposed, but if your partner rejects your offer, no one gets any money at all. You cannot communicate with your partner, and you will not be given a second chance if your partner turns you down.

---

exchange relationship   A reciprocal interdependency that emphasizes the trading of gratifying experiences and rewards among members.

communal relationship   A reciprocal interdependency that emphasizes meeting the needs and interests of others rather than maximizing one's own personal outcomes.

Ultimatum Game   An experimental bargaining situation in which one individual, the allocator, must propose a division of a shared resource to other members; if they reject the allocator's proposal, no one receives any of the resource.

How much will you offer? If you are motivated solely by profit, then you should offer very little to your partner. Economically speaking, even if you only offer $1, your partner should take it because $1, although much less than the $19 you will receive, is better than $0. Yet, when people play the Ultimatum Game, they rarely offer or accept so little. People, on average, generally offer between 35% to 50% of the total sum; in the example, between $7 and $10. People are also quite willing to reject too low an offer, even though it means that they will receive nothing (Henrich et al., 2004). Both the person who offers and their partner recognize that a fair distribution is a nearly equal one—selfishness may prompt a person to want to keep as much as they can, but they realize that their partner is willing to pay to make clear the importance of fairness (Kameda, Takezawa, & Hastie, 2005).

Enterprising researchers have gathered data on responses to the Ultimatum Game in dozens of indigenous societies located around the world. Only one group averaged offers of more than 50% of the endowment: the Lamalara of East Indonesia. The lowest offer was made by the Quichua of South America. This variability, although pronounced, was related to each group's level of collectivism. Some communities stressed the importance of individuality and the family, whereas in others "one's economic well-being depends on cooperation with non-relatives" (Henrich et al., 2004, p. 29). These more cooperative communities tended to be more generous in their allocations in the game, as were those societies that created more elaborate economic and social connections among various households. As for the Lamalara: Their high level of generosity reflects their unique living conditions. The Lamalara are whalers, and traditionally the catch is divided equally among all members of the community—even those who did not participate in the hunt. The Lamalara are quintessential collectivists.

Reciprocity This difference between an exchange and communal orientation is particularly clear when the group must allocate resources to members. Individualism defines relations with others as a "strictly economic exchange" (Fiske, 1992, p. 702). When faced with a common resource pool or a project that requires combined effort, such groups favor an evenly balanced, one-for-one exchange. They "often mark their relationship with very concrete operations of balancing, comparing, or counting-out items in one-for-one correspondence" (Fiske, 1992, p. 691). Such group's exchanges are also guided by the **norm of reciprocity** that requires members to pay back in kind what others give to them. The members cooperate with others, but they do so to pay back past favors and to create obligations for future favors (Gouldner, 1960).

If a group's culture is collectivistic, in contrast, members are not so concerned with matching inputs and outputs. When sharing a resource, members would be more likely to "take what they need and contribute what they can, without anyone attending to how much each person contributes or receives. A person does not need to give something in order to get something in return—simple membership in the group is sufficient to entitle one to the use of whatever resources the group controls, and long-run imbalance is not a violation of the relationship" (Fiske, 1992, p. 693). Individualists tend to be **egocentric**, or self-serving—they strive to extract all the resources they can while minimizing their contribution of personal resources. Collectivists, in contrast, are **sociocentric**, or group serving—they strive to increase the well-being of the community as a whole.

Reciprocity can become problematic when members of the groups do not share equally in the work, but nonetheless seek an equal share of the rewards (Leung, 1997). Whenever groups earn

---

norm of reciprocity A social standard that enjoins individuals to pay back in kind what they receive from others.

egocentric (or self-serving) Emphasizing one's own needs, perspective, and importance, particularly in contrast to those of other individuals or the group.

sociocentric (or group serving) Emphasizing the group's needs, perspectives, and importance, particularly in contrast to those of individual members or oneself.

rewards or cover costs, a fair means must be developed to determine how these rewards and costs are distributed across members. Imagine, for example, that your group has earned a reward by winning a lottery or must pay a fine because one of the group members accidentally broke something. The **equity norm** recommends that group members should receive outcomes in proportion to their inputs. If an individual has invested a good deal of time, energy, money, or other types of inputs in the group, then he or she could expect to receive a good deal of the group payoff. Similarly, individuals who contribute little should not be surprised when they receive little. The **equality norm**, on the other hand, recommends that all group members, irrespective of their inputs, should be given an equal share of the payoff. In collectivistic settings members would likely favor allocating the winnings on an equal-share basis: All should benefit, even if just one of the group members was the one who picked the winning lottery numbers. However, collectivists may also require that the costs be borne more heavily by the individual member who caused a problem, because the group as a whole must be protected against injury (Utz & Sassenberg, 2002). Individualism, in contrast, would favor an equity norm, because the contributions of each member are recognized and rewarded (or punished).

Favoring the Ingroup   One of the ironies of collectivism is apparent when individualists and collectivists encounter a member of another group. Collectivists may be benevolent, trusting, and caring, but this goodwill is reserved for the ingroup. When individualists think about group membership, they consider it to consist of relatively loose associations that are selected by members and not the groups themselves. Collectivists, in contrast, define belonging as "belonging securely," and they tend to view boundaries between one group

---

equity norm A social standard that encourages distributing rewards and resources to members in proportion to their inputs.

equality norm A social standard that encourages distributing rewards and resources equally among all members.

and another to be relatively impermeable. Individualists are less likely to restrict their relationships to the ingroup, and they are more trusting of strangers than are collectivists. Collectivists spend more time in ingroup interactions, and they are not as trusting of people who are not members of their groups. Collectivists divide the world up into "us" and "we"—the ingroup—versus "them" and "they"—the outgroup.

The Macro Level: Collectivism across Cultures

When the French historian Alexis de Tocqueville visited the United States in the 1830s, he was struck by Americans' self-reliance and independence. He noted they frequently joined together to achieve some collective goal, but even when they were working in groups, they still took inordinate pride in their personal autonomy and self-reliance. It seemed to him that all Americans act as if they "owe no man anything and hardly expect anything from anybody. They form the habit of thinking of themselves in isolation and imagine that their whole destiny is in their own hands" (de Tocqueville, 1831/1969, p. 508). He used the word *individualism* to capture this uniquely American spirit of self-reliance (Daniels, 2011).

Cultural Differences   The view of people as independent, autonomous creatures may be peculiar to Western society's individualistic leanings. When researchers measured the relative emphasis on the individual and the group in countries all around the world, they found that the United States, other English-speaking countries (e.g., England, Australia), and Western European countries (e.g., Finland, Germany) tended to be more individualistic than Asian, Eastern European, African, and Middle Eastern countries (Hofstede, 1980; Oyserman et al., 2002). Latin and South American countries were more varied, with such countries as Puerto Rico and Chile exhibiting greater individualism than others (e.g., Mexico, Costa Rica).

The Gahuku-Gama of Highland New Guinea, for example, do not recognize individuals apart from their roles as father, mother, chief, and so on. They do not even grasp the concept of friendship, for such a concept requires liking between two individuals (Read, 1986). The Akaramas of Peru paint their bodies so elaborately that individuals are unrecognizable. Tribes sleep in same-sex groups of 10 or 12, and when individuals die, their passing goes unnoticed (Schneebaum, 1969). Students in the United States, more than students in China, assume that people's behaviors are caused by personality traits rather than by factors in the situation (Chiu, Hong, & Dweck, 1997). People from individualistic and collectivistic cultures even insult one another differently. Personal insults, such as "You are stupid," characterize conflicts in individualistic cultures, whereas remarks about one's family and group typify disputes between two collectivists (Semin & Rubini, 1990).

Culture and the Self   The very idea of self may differ across cultures. In Japan, a relatively collectivistic culture, the word for self, *Jibun,* means "one's portion of the shared space" (Hamaguchi, 1985). To the Japanese, "the concept of a self completely independent from the environment is very foreign," as people are not perceived apart from the existing social context, much less controlling it (Kojima, 1984, p. 973).

Cross-cultural psychologist Harry Triandis and his colleagues illustrated this difference by asking people from various countries to describe themselves. As expected, these self-descriptions contained more references to roles and relationships when people were from collectivistic countries (e.g., Japan, China). Some individuals from the People's Republic of China described themselves exclusively in interpersonal terms. And some U.S. residents used only personal descriptors—they reported no elements of a collective self (Triandis, McCusker, & Hui, 1990; cf. Oyserman et al., 2002). Other research has suggested that people from collectivistic countries resist describing their qualities if the social context is not specified. Japanese, for example, described themselves differently when they were with different people and in different social situations. Americans, in contrast, described themselves similarly across different situations (Cousins, 1989).

These observations are only generalities, however, for people within a culture may not adopt their home country's orientation. Triandis believes that about 60% of the people in collectivistic cultures are interdependent (allocentrics), just as about 60% of the people in individualistic cultures are independent (idiocentric) types. He also reports that interdependent individuals in individualistic countries tend to join more groups, but that independent individuals in collectivistic cultures "feel oppressed by their culture and seek to leave it" (Triandis & Suh, 2002, p. 141). Each culture, too, likely expresses its collectivism and individualism in unique ways. Some collectivistic cultures, for example, are much more hierarchically structured (*vertical*) than others, like the culture of India with its caste system, which stresses tradition, duty, and compliance with authority. Other collectivistic cultures, however, stress commonality, and so their society's status and authority structures are relatively flat (*horizontal*). Many Latin American and Hispanic countries, for example, are collectivistic, but they also place great value on helping strangers—the culture of *simpatia* (Levine, Norenzayan, & Philbrick, 2001). Other collectivistic societies tolerate considerable conflict within their groups. Members of Israeli kibbutzes, for example, often engage in heated debates, whereas Koreans strive for harmony and avoid discord. Both cultures are relatively collectivistic, yet their approaches to resolving disputes differ substantially (Triandis, 1995, 1996). In contrast, Scandinavians are extremely individualistic, but they are also noncompetitive (Fiske, 2002). It may be that the dichotomy between individualism and collectivism reflects, in part, the cognitive biases of the Western theorists who first proposed this distinction.

Regional and Ethnic Differences   Classifying entire cultures along a continuum from individualistic to collectivistic also overlooks significant variations across subgroups within a culture (Miller, 2002). In the United States, for example, certain areas are more individualistic, whereas others are more collectivistic (Vandello & Cohen, 2004). Collectivism is prominent in the south of the United States, which remains more rural, agricultural, and hierarchically structured than the rest of the country. When polled, its residents were more likely to agree to such statements as, "It is better to fit in with people around you," and "It is more important to be a cooperative person who works well with others." Individuals living in the western portions of the United States, where the frontier, pioneer tradition stresses self-reliance, are more

individualistic. Residents of this part of the country felt that "It is better to conduct yourself according to your own standards, even if that makes you stand out" and "It is more important to be a self-reliant person able to take care of oneself" (Vandello & Cohen, 1999, p. 285; see Focus 3.2).

F o c u s   3 . 2   Cross-cultural Perspectives: Culture of Honor, Face, and Dignity

How would you react if someone who you had never met before—a stranger who was outside of your group—insulted you or said disrespectful things about your family, hometown, or close friends. Would you laugh it off, say something insulting in return, or perhaps even use physical force to settle things?

Social psychologists Richard E. Nisbett and Dov Cohen (1996) studied people's responses to this type of situation by recruiting male college students for what was described as an experiment dealing with response time and social judgment. Each student first filled out a questionnaire and was told to put it on a table at the end of the hall. To reach the table, the subject had to pass by a young man filing materials in a cabinet—once to drop off the questionnaire and once to return to the testing area. As the subject passed the second time, the person doing the filing, who was actually part of the research team, feigned irritation at the interruption, slammed the file drawer shut, bumped into him with his shoulder, and called him an insulting name ("asshole").

Some of the men in this study seemed mostly amused by the entire incident, but others showed signs of anger—nonverbal displays of hostility, a readiness to respond to an insult in a hostile way, and elevated levels of stress-related hormones (testosterone and cortisol)—and this difference was based on place of birth. Men whose hometown addresses were located in the northern part of the United States were amused by the incident, whereas men who hailed from the states located in the southern part of the United States were angered (Cohen et al., 1996).

Cohen and Nisbett believe these differences in responses were caused by regional variations in the *culture of honor*. They speculate that when Europeans displaced the indigenous populations of the area now known as the United States, the south and north developed different social and economic structures. The north, with a greater reliance on industry and farming, developed centralized authority structures and urban centers. The south, in contrast, was populated by individuals whose ancestors were herders who were used to guarding their livestock personally rather

than relying on civil authority. They therefore needed to create their own system of order, and this system required developing a reputation of strength and ferocity in the face of challenge; "the individual must project a stance of willingness to commit mayhem and to risk wounds or death for himself" (Nisbett & Cohen, 1996, p. xv). Southerners are not more positive about aggression in general, but they are more likely to recommend aggressive responses for self-defense and in response to insults. White Southern men were more likely to approve of killing to protect their home or family. They were also more likely to advocate fighting when insulted and felt that their sons should be taught to fight (Nisbett & Cohen, 1996).

Cohen and his colleagues have recently compared honor cultures to two other types of cultural syndromes: dignity cultures and face cultures (Kim, Cohen, & Au, 2010; Leung & Cohen, 2011). *Honor cultures* emerge in rural economies where civil authority is too weak to protect individuals from harm. *Dignity cultures* emerge in more economically prosperous, individualistic cultures, for they stress the importance of personal integrity. In such cultures, individuals learn that each individual has inherent value, and the quality of their character is not defined by other people—such individuals may laugh at a person who insults them for, after all, "sticks and stones may break my bones, but names will never hurt me." The third syndrome, *face cultures*, is characterized by hierarchy, humility, and harmony. Face cultures, like honor cultures, value respect and deference, but individuals in face cultures cooperate with one another to maintain one another's respectability. A person who is insulted by another person need not react aggressively, for, in a culture of face, the social group will deal with the offender. Taking matters into one's own hands is a selfish act, for it disrupts harmony and circumvents the system of social hierarchy. Anglo Americans raised in the north and western parts of the United States tend to be guided by a culture of dignity, southern Anglo Americans and Latino Americans a culture of honor, and the responses of Asian Americans are more likely guided by a culture of face.

Ethnic groups in the United States also exhibit remarkable variations in individualism and collectivism. When researchers combined the findings obtained across a number of studies, they found that Asian Americans tended to be more collectivistic than European Americans, but that Japanese and Koreans are more similar to European Americans than were the more collectivistic Chinese Americans. Hispanic Americans did not differ from European Americans in their level of individualism, but they were more collectivistic. Even though Afrocentric cultural traditions, like those emphasized in the African American celebration of Kwanzaa, stress strong family ties and mutual help, the researchers discovered that African Americans tended to score higher than European Americans on measures of individualism and lower than European Americans on measures of collectivism (Oyserman et al., 2002).

FROM PERSONAL IDENTITY TO SOCIAL IDENTITY

Before he joined Peak, Patrick probably answered the question "Who are you?" by listing his accomplishments, his personal qualities, and his goals. But his answer changed after spending two years as an active member of the rescue squad. His need for inclusion prompted him to seek membership in Peak. The group taught him to put the collective's needs before his own. In time he came to identify with Peak and its members. Now, if asked "Who are you?" Patrick likely explained "I'm a member of Peak Search and Rescue."

How does a group become a part of one's social identity? What impact does this acceptance of the group into one's identity have on one's self-concept and self-esteem? In this final section we consider one compelling theoretical answer to these questions: social identity theory. (For detailed analyses of groups and identity, see Ashmore, Deaux, & McLaughlin-Volpe, 2004; Ellemers & Haslam, 2012; Hogg, 2005; Roccas et al., 2008.)

Social Identity Theory: The Basics

Social psychologists Henri Tajfel, John Turner, and their colleagues originally developed **social identity theory** in an attempt to understand the causes of conflict between people who belonged to different groups. Tajfel, who was a Jewish survivor of World War II, wondered why people who shared so much in common sometimes become enemies if the groups they identify with come into conflict. To investigate this process, they started by first creating the **minimal intergroup situation**: just gatherings of people with no history, no future together, and no real connection to one another. They randomly assigned participants to one of two groups, but they told the participants that the division was based on some irrelevant characteristic, such as art preference. Next, the participants were given a series of booklets asking them to decide how a certain amount of money should be allocated to other participants in the experiment. The names of the individuals were not given in the booklets, but the participant could tell which group a person belonged to by looking at his or her code number.

Tajfel and Turner (1979, 1986) assumed that the members of such minimalistic groups would not even notice which group they were in or who belonged to some other group, but that conflict would occur when they added complexities—such as competition, status markers, inequality in resources, and so on. But they were wrong. Even though participants did not know one another, they would not be working together in the future, and their membership in the so-called group had absolutely no personal or interpersonal implications,

---

social identity theory A theoretical analysis of group processes and intergroup relations that assumes groups influence their members' self-concepts and self-esteem, particularly when individuals categorize themselves as group members and identify with the group.

minimal intergroup situation A research procedure used in studies of intergroup conflict that involves creating temporary groups of anonymous, unrelated people (developed by Henri Tajfel and John Turner).

they still favored the ingroup over the outgroup. How could these "purely cognitive" groups—groups that had no interpersonal meaning whatsoever—nonetheless influence people's perceptions and actions? Social identity theory's answer: Two cognitive processes—*categorization* and *identification*—combine to transform a group membership into an identity.

Self-Categorization One's social identity depends, fundamentally, on the process of **social categorization** (Turner, 1991, 1999). Perceivers, to make sense of and understand other people, quickly and automatically classify those they encounter into groups based on age, race, nationality, and other categories. Once classified, individuals' perceptions of people are influenced by any stereotypes they may have about the qualities of people in such groups. If we met Patrick on the street, we would rapidly slot him into such social groupings as man, 20s, American, and white, for example. And once categorized, our perceptions of Patrick would be influenced by our beliefs about the qualities and characteristics of the prototypical American, 20-something white man. These beliefs, which are termed **stereotypes** (or prototypes), describe the typical characteristics of people in various social groups. They also include information about how a group is different from other groups (the *metacontrast principle*).

People do not, however, only categorize other people; they also classify themselves into various groups and categories. Patrick would realize that he is a man, an American, white, and in his 20s—that he belongs in these social categories. He might then apply stereotypes about the people in those categories to himself. He might, for example, believe that the prototypical American man his age tends to act as a leader, is involved in business

outside the home, is logical and objective in his thinking, and does not get his feelings hurt easily (Abele, 2003). Then, through **self-stereotyping** (or autostereotyping), he would also apply those stereotypes to himself and would come to believe that he, like most American men his age, leads rather than follows, is engaged in his work, bases his decisions on logical analysis, and is emotionally tough (Abrams & Hogg, 2001; Mackie, 1980).

Identification Most people belong to many groups and categories, but many of these memberships have no influence on their social identities. Patrick may have been a right-hander, a Democrat, and brown-eyed, but he may not give much thought to these categories. Only some of his memberships, such as his involvement with Peak or his colleagues where he works, are core elements of his sense of self. He *identifies* with these social categories and accepts the group as an extension of himself. He also knows that the other group members similarly identify with Peak, and so they too possess the qualities that this group stresses as essential ones for its most qualified members. As Michael Hogg (2005, p. 136), a leading theorist and researcher in the area of social identity, explains:

> They identify themselves in the same way and have the same definition of who they are, what attributes they have, and how they relate to and differ from specific outgroups or from people who are simply not ingroup members. Group membership is a matter of collective self-construal—*we, us,* and *them.*

As **social identification** increases, individuals come to think that their membership in the group is personally significant. They feel connected and

---

social categorization The perceptual classification of people, including the self, into categories.

stereotypes (or prototypes) A socially shared set of cognitive generalizations (e.g., beliefs, expectations) about the qualities and characteristics of the typical member of a particular group or social category.

self-stereotyping (or autostereotyping) Accepting socially shared generalizations about the prototypical characteristics attributed to members of one's group as accurate descriptions of oneself.

social identification Accepting the group as an extension of the self and therefore basing one's self-definition on the group's qualities and characteristics.

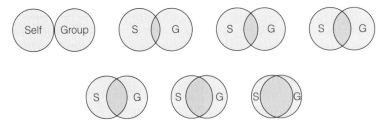

FIGURE 3.8   The inclusion of the group in the self. If asked to select the set of circles that best indicates the extent to which the group (G) overlaps with the self (S), people who do not identify with their group select circles that don't overlap. Increasing identification is indicated by selecting circles where the self and the group overlap to a large degree.

SOURCE: From "Ingroup Identification as the Inclusion of Ingroup in the Self," by Linda R. Tropp & Stephen C. Wright, 2001, *Personality and Social Psychology Bulletin, 27*, pp. 585–600. Copyright 2001 by the Society for Personality and Social Psychology, Inc. Adapted with permission.

interdependent with other members, are glad they belong to the group, feel good about the group, and experience strong attachment to the group. Their connection to the group also becomes more affectively toned—a "hot" cognitive reaction rather than a "cold" recognition of membership—as individuals incorporate the group into their social identity, "together with the value and emotional significance attached to that membership" (Tajfel, 1981, p. 255). Their self-descriptions also become increasingly *depersonalized* as they include fewer idiosyncratic elements and more characteristics that are common to the group. As indicated by Figure 3.8, the sense of self changes as the group is, literally, included in the self (Wright, Aron, & Tropp, 2002).

Self and Identity   Research suggests that in some cases, identification with a group is so great that across situations people think of themselves as group members first and individuals second, and, within their self-concept, their personal idiosyncratic qualities are far outnumbered by their group-level qualities (Phinney & Ong, 2007). More typically, however, the self will shift from *me* to *we* if something in the situation increases the salience of one's membership. Individuals who find that they are the only representative of a particular group—for example, the only man in a group of five women or the only left-hander in a class of otherwise all right-handers—may become very aware of that aspect of themselves (McGuire &

McGuire, 1988). People are also more likely to think of themselves collectively if they are part of a group that others have labeled a group, even if the group members are minimally interdependent (Gaertner et al., 2006). But one of the most important situational triggers of a collective self-representation is the presence of members of the outgroup. As Tajfel and Turner (1986) confirmed in their initial studies of the minimal intergroup situation, categorization and identification become more likely when one group encounters another group. For example, if 10 men are seated in a room, they may not think of themselves as men, but when a group of 10 women enters the room, then their sense of membership in the category *man* is activated.

Researchers have also confirmed that individuals sometimes generalize from their stereotypes about their groups to themselves. Children as young as five years of age, when their identity as boys and girls is made salient, are more likely to describe themselves in stereotypical ways (Bennett & Sani, 2008). When women in sororities rated themselves and other women in their sorority on traits often ascribed to sorority women (e.g., popular, well dressed, conceited, shallow, spoiled), they gave themselves and their group nearly identical ratings—the correlation between self-rating and group rating was .98 (Biernat, Vescio, & Green, 1996). In groups that included both men and women, men's self-descriptions emphasized their masculinity and women's their femininity only when a disagreement had split members along sex lines—men taking one side in the argument and the women the other (Hogg & Turner, 1987).

Another group-level determinant of self-categorization is the relative size of one's group compared to other groups. People in groups with fewer members, such as minority groups based on ethnicity, race, or religion, tend to categorize themselves as members more quickly than do those people who are members of the larger, dominant, majority group. The experience of being in the minority apparently increases the salience of the social identity based on that membership, and so people are more likely to apply the stereotypical features of the minority group to themselves. Researchers informed some participants that a survey they had just completed suggested that they were extraverted and that only 20% of the general population is extraverted. These individuals then gave themselves higher ratings on such traits as *sociable* and *lively* than did people who were told that 80% of the population is extraverted (Simon & Hamilton, 1994).

Motivation and Social Identity

Social identity theory provides key insights into a host of psychological and interpersonal processes, including collectivism, perceptions of the outgroup, presumptions of ingroup permeability, tolerance of deviance within the group, increased satisfaction with the group, and feelings of solidarity (Leach et al., 2008). Later chapters will elaborate on the further implications of this theory, but here we conclude this chapter by considering the role social identity processes play in helping individuals protect and maintain their sense of self-worth.

Evaluating the Self Hogg (2005) suggests that at least two basic motives influence the way social categorization and identification processes combine to shape one's sense of self. In general, individuals are motivated to think well of themselves, and, since their groups comprise a significant portion of their selves, they maintain their self-worth by thinking well of their groups. Second, Hogg suggests that self-understanding is a core motive for most people and that groups offer people a means of understanding themselves.

When individuals join groups, their self-concept becomes connected to that group, and the value of that group influences their feelings of personal worth. People who belong to prestigious groups tend to have higher self-esteem than those who do not (Branscombe, 1998). Sports fans' moods swing up and down as their favorite team wins and loses (Crisp et al., 2007; Hirt et al., 1992). By *basking in reflected glory*, or BIRGing, people stress their association with successful groups, even if they did not contribute to that success (Cialdini et al., 1976). Adolescent boys and girls are known to seek out membership in a particular peer group, and these group memberships influence their identity and their self-esteem. The four most commonly reported groups, in order of prestige: the elites, athletes, academics, and deviants (Sussman et al., 2007). Those who are members of the most prestigious groups generally report feeling very satisfied with themselves and their group. Those students who want to be a part of an "in crowd" but are not accepted by this clique are the most dissatisfied (Brown & Lohr, 1987), and this interpersonal failure can lead to long-term negative effects (Barnett, 2006; Wright & Forsyth, 1997).

Jennifer Crocker and her colleagues examined the relationship between people's self-esteem and their feelings about the groups to which they belonged by developing a measure of **collective self-esteem**. Instead of asking people if they felt good or bad about themselves, they asked individuals to evaluate the groups to which they belonged. Drawing on prior work on social identity and self-esteem, the researchers developed

collective self-esteem A person's overall assessment of that portion of their self-concept that is based on their relationships with others and membership in social groups.

T A B L E 3.3   Items from the Collective Self-Esteem Inventory

Subscale	Issue	Example Item
Membership Esteem	Am I a valuable or an ineffective member of the groups to which I belong?	I am a worthy member of the social groups I belong to.
Private Collective Self-Esteem	Do I evaluate the groups I belong to positively or negatively?	I feel good about the social groups I belong to.
Public Collective Self-Esteem	Do other people evaluate the groups I belong to positively or negatively?	In general, others respect the social groups that I am a member of.
Identity	Are the groups I belong to an important or unimportant part of my identity?	In general, belonging to social groups is an important part of my self-image.

SOURCE: "A Collective Self-Esteem Scale: Self-Evaluation of One's Social Identity" by R. Luhtanen and J. Crocker, *Personality and Social Psychology Bulletin, 18*, 1992.

items that tapped four basic issues: membership esteem, private collective self-esteem, public collective self-esteem, and importance to identity (see Table 3.3). When they compared scores on the collective self-esteem scale to scores on more traditional measures of self-esteem, they found that people with high membership esteem and public and private collective self-esteem scores had higher personal self-esteem, suggesting that group membership contributes to feelings of self-worth (Crocker & Luhtanen, 1990; Crocker et al., 1994; Luhtanen & Crocker, 1992).

Protecting the Collective Self People protect their collective self-esteem just as they protect their personal self-esteem. They deny that their group possesses negative qualities. They consider their group to be superior to alternative groups. They give their group credit for its successes, but blame outside influences when their group fails. Should other, more rewarding groups stand willing and ready to take them in, individuals remain loyal to their original group. Identity is the glue that binds individuals to their groups (Van Vugt & Hart, 2004).

When individuals identify with their group, they also tend to exaggerate the differences between their group and other groups. Once people begin to think in terms of *we* and *us,* they also begin to recognize *them* and *they.* The tendency to look more favorably on the ingroup is called the

ingroup–outgroup bias. Gang members view their group more positively than rival gangs. Teammates praise their own players and derogate the other team. If Group A and Group B work side by side, members of A will rate Group A as better than B, but members of B will rate Group B more favorably than A.

The ingroup–outgroup bias contributes to the self-esteem and emotional well-being of group members. Social identity theory posits that people are motivated to maintain or enhance their feelings of self-worth, and, because members' self-esteem is linked to their groups, their feelings of self-worth can be enhanced by stressing the relative superiority of their groups to other groups. Even membership in a group that others may not admire is generally associated with higher levels of self-esteem (Crocker & Major, 1989). Adolescents with mental retardation do not necessarily have lower self-esteem, even though they know they belong to the negatively stereotyped social category "special education students" (Stager, Chassin, & Young, 1983). African Americans, despite living in a culture where stereotypes about their group tend to be

---

ingroup–outgroup bias The tendency to view the ingroup, its members, and its products more positively than other groups, their members, and their products. Ingroup favoritism is more common than outgroup rejection.

negative, have higher self-esteem than European Americans (Twenge & Crocker, 2002). Members of groups that are criticized often respond by defending their group and reaffirming their commitment to it (Dietz-Uhler & Murrell, 1998). So long as individuals believe that the groups they belong to are valuable, they will experience a heightened sense of personal self-esteem (Crocker et al., 1994).

Even if the group falters, members can nonetheless find ways to protect the group and, in so doing, protect their own selves. A setback, particularly at the hands of another group, calls for **social creativity:** Group members compare the ingroup to the outgroup on some new dimension. Members of a last-placed ice hockey team (1 win and 21 losses), when asked if their team and their opponents were *aggressive, dirty, skilled,* and *motivated,* admitted that their opponents were more skilled, but they also argued that their opponents were more aggressive and that they played dirty (Lalonde, 1992). When emergency medical technicians (EMTs) were told that their group had performed more poorly than another group of EMTs, they later claimed their group members had nicer personalities (Cadinu & Cerchioni, 2001). Hospital employees, when asked to evaluate their hospital and a second hospital that was larger and better equipped, gave the other hospital higher ratings on such variables as community reputation, challenge, and career opportunity, but claimed that their hospital was a better place to work because everyone got along better (Terry & Callan, 1998).

The ingroup–outgroup bias has a significant negative side effect. As individuals champion their group, they sometimes denigrate those who belong to other groups. The tendency to feel good about one's own group is not as strong as the tendency to derogate other groups, and social identification can still occur even in the absence of a contrasting outgroup (Gaertner et al., 2006). But as Chapter 14's

analysis of intergroup conflict explains, the social and psychological processes that generate social identity can also create conflict between groups.

Stereotype Verification and Threat In social identity theory, stereotypes serve to create identity, but they can also constrain identity. When people are proud members of their groups, they readily admit that they are stereotypical and will also take steps to confirm these stereotypes when they interact with people who are not part of their group. They prefer to interact with people who confirm their stereotype about their group, rather than people who hold beliefs that contradict these beliefs (Chen, Chen, & Shaw, 2004; Gómez et al., 2009). They may even accept, and apply to themselves and to other members of their group, stereotypical qualities that are negative rather than positive. A professor who admits that he left behind all the papers he was to return that day to his class mumbles something about being an "absentminded professor." A fair-haired young woman who complains about the amount of statistical information discussed in a class opines, "I'm just a blonde—I don't really like math."

Such negative ingroup stereotyping has been shown to protect individuals' feelings of self-worth. Women who had just discovered they had done poorly on a math test, when reminded of the stereotype of women as weak at math, had higher self-esteem than those in a control condition. A second study indicated that it was women with higher self-esteem who embraced the stereotype after failure rather than women with lower self-esteem (Burkley & Blanton, 2008). These studies suggest that a social identity can protect the self, even if the identity is one that includes qualities that are objectively negative ones (Simon, Glässner-Bayerl, & Stratenwerth, 1991).

In many cases, however, stereotypes distort the accuracy of people's perceptions of the members of other groups and contribute to intergroup conflict. Stereotypes are resistant to revision, so perceivers continue to apply them even when experience tells them these generalizations about people are distorted. Stereotypes often trigger an unfavorable

---

social creativity Restricting comparisons between the ingroup and other groups to tasks and outcomes when the ingroup is more successful than other groups and avoiding areas in which other groups surpass the ingroup.

rejection of others that is both unfair and irrational, causing perceivers to prejudge people solely on the basis of their membership in a group or category. Stereotypes provide the cognitive foundation of prejudice, discrimination, and intergroup hostility.

Stereotype processes can also trigger a process known as **stereotype threat** when individuals know that others they are interacting with may be relying on group stereotypes to judge them. This worry that they might confirm these stereotypes may, in turn, undermine individuals' actual performance. A college professor may not wish to be labeled absentminded and a blonde-haired woman may prefer to be recognized for her scientific acumen rather than her sense of fashion. But when such individuals enter into situations where they are at risk of being judged on the basis of stereotypes that they wish to resist, they may fail to perform as well as they could, and the stereotype becomes a self-fulfilling prophecy (Derks et al., 2011; Steele & Aronson, 1995).

Protecting the Personal Self   In general, people are more disturbed by threats to their personal self-esteem than to their collective self-esteem. They are more likely to deny the accuracy of negative individualized information relative to negative group information, and they more readily claim positive feedback when it focuses on them rather than on their group. For example, an individual, if told "you did very poorly—you must be slow" or "you are excessively moody," will react more negatively than a person who is part of a group told "your group did very poorly—you must be slow" or "people in your group are excessively moody" (Gaertner et al., 2002; Gaertner & Sedikides, 2005; Sedikides, Gaertner, & Toguchi, 2003). Personal failure is more troubling than collective failure, in most cases.

People will also turn away from a group that continues to threaten their personal self-esteem. When people can choose the groups they belong to or identify with, they often shift their allegiances, leaving groups that are lower in status or prone to failure and seeking membership in prestigious or successful groups (Ellemers, Spears, & Doosje, 2002). The technical term for such a change in allegiance is **individual mobility** (Ellemers, Spears, & Doosje, 1997). More common ways to describe this process include resigning, dropping out, quitting, breaking up, resigning, escaping, bailing, and ditching: The member leaves the group for a more promising one. As the analysis of group formation in Chapter 4 shows, when people's groups are too much trouble, they leave them in search of better ones.

CHAPTER REVIEW

Do humans, by nature, seek solitude or inclusion in groups?

1. Three interrelated processes determine the relationship between individuals to groups:

    ▪   Inclusion and exclusion: the degree to which the individual is included or excluded from the group.

    ▪   Individualism and collectivism: the emphasis on the primacy of the individual versus the group.

    ▪   Personal identity and social identity: basing self-conceptions on personal qualities or shared, interpersonal qualities.

2. Baumeister and Leary suggest that much of human behavior is motivated by the *need to*

---

stereotype threat The anxiety-provoking belief that others' perceptions and evaluations will be influenced by their negative stereotypes about one's group that can, in some cases, interfere with one's ability to perform up to one's capabilities.

---

individual mobility Reducing one's connection to a group in order to minimize threats to individual self-esteem.

belong. Solitude is sometimes rewarding, but most adults prefer the company of others.

- Most adults live with others, they spend most of their time with others, and an enormous number of groups exist.

- Putnam suggests that levels of *social capital* are decreasing due to reductions in involvement in groups, but these shifts may indicate changes in the kinds of associations people seek rather than a reduction per se.

- Groups help members avoid basic forms of *loneliness*: social and emotional.

3. *Ostracism,* or deliberate exclusion from groups, is highly stressful, as indicated by self-reports of negative affect in everyday situations and people's reactions in experimental studies of exclusion.

- The temporal need–threat model of ostracism developed by Williams identifies a three-stage response to exclusion: reflexive, reflective, and resignation.

- Individuals who exhibit a *fight-or-flight response* to exclusion confront or withdraw from the group and, in cases of extreme or unexpected exclusion, may display a freezing response.

- Individuals who exhibit a *tend-and-befriend* response to exclusion seek social reconnection.

- Studies conducted by Gaertner, Leary, and their colleagues trace some violent attacks of individuals on groups to ostracism.

- Individuals also react negatively to exclusion from computer-mediated interaction, or *cyberostracism.*

4. Evolutionary psychology suggests that the need to belong resulted from natural selection as individuals who were affiliated with groups were more likely to survive.

- *Sociometer theory* developed by Leary explains the relationship between

exclusion and self-esteem by hypothesizing that self-esteem provides individuals with feedback about their degree of inclusion in groups.

- The intensely negative reactions most people experience when they feel excluded are associated with specific hormonal and neurological processes.

- Studies of the brain using fMRI technology (like those conducted by Eisenberger and her colleagues) and the effects of analgesics on emotional reactions following rejection suggest that the pain of exclusion is maintained by the same biological systems responsible for the experience of physiological pain.

When do people put the group's needs before their own?

1. *Individualism* and *collectivism* are distinguishable in their relative emphasis on individuals and the collective across people (the micro level), groups (the meso level), and cultures (the macro level).

2. The micro level: Individuals differ in their conception of themselves as individuals or members of the collective.

- A person's conception of his or her *self* includes both individualistic elements (the *personal identity*) and collectivistic elements (the *social identity* or collective identity) in the latter.

- *Individualists* (or independents) stress personal qualities, independence, personal goals, competition, uniqueness, need for privacy, self-knowledge, directness in communication whereas *collectivists* (or interdependents) emphasize relationships, belong, duty, harmony, seeking advice, context, hierarchy, and their groups' goals and needs.

- The sexes do not differ reliably or substantially in individualism/collectivism.

- Research conducted by Twenge and her colleagues suggests that younger individuals (Millenials or the "Me" generation) may be shifting in a more individualistic direction.

- Brewer's *optimal distinctiveness theory* suggests that individuals strive to maintain an optimal balance between their personal and collective identities.

3. The meso level: The *group culture* determines the group's emphasis on the individual members or the group as a whole.

- A collectivistic orientation stresses hierarchy and reacts more negatively to nonconformity.

- Collectivism's emphasis on relationships is manifested in the emphasis on *communal relationships* over *exchange relationships* and differences in allocations of resources in the *Ultimatum Game*. Egocentric (self-serving) tendencies are more likely in individualistic settings in contrast to the *sociocentric* (group-serving) tendencies seen in collectivistic settings.

- The *norm of reciprocity* is implemented differently in individualistic and collectivistic groups, with the former following the *equity norm* and the latter the *equality norm*.

- Collectivists are more likely to favor members of the ingroup.

4. The macro level: Cultures and subgroups within countries vary in their relative emphasis on individualism and collectivism. The United States, for example, was recognized by de Tocqueville as highly individualistic.

- Studies conducted by Triandis and others suggest that people who live in collectivistic cultures (e.g., Asian, Eastern European, African, and Middle Eastern countries) think of themselves as group members first and individuals second, whereas people who live in individualistic cultures (Western countries) are self-centered rather than group-centered.

- Certain subgroups and geographic regions within a larger area may display more or less collectivism. The southern portion of the United States, for example, is more collectivistic than other regions. Some ethnic groups in the United States, such as Asian Americans and Hispanic Americans, are more collectivistic than individualistic.

- The work of Cohen and Nisbett on the culture of honor suggests that white southern males in the United States are more likely to respond aggressively when their honor is challenged, but that individuals raised in dignity and face cultures do not.

What processes transform an individual's sense of self into a collective, social identity?

1. Social identity theory, developed by Tajfel, Turner, Hogg, and their colleagues, traces the development of a collective identity back to two key processes (categorization and identification) that occur even in *minimal intergroup situations*.

2. *Social categorization* involves automatically classifying people into categories.

- Through self-categorization, individuals classify themselves into categories.

- *Self-stereotyping* (or autostereotyping) occurs when individuals apply *stereotypes* (prototypes) based on those categories to themselves.

3. Social identification involves bonding with and taking on the characteristics of one's groups.

- When people identify strongly with a group, their self-descriptions become increasingly depersonalized as they include fewer idiosyncratic elements and more characteristics that are common to the group.

- Identification and categorization become more likely when outgroups are salient and when people are members of smaller groups.

4. Hogg's theory of social identity assumes individuals are motivated to maintain self-esteem and to clarify their understanding of themselves and other people.

   ▪ Self-esteem is shaped both by individuals' personal qualities and by the perceived value of the groups to which they belong.

   ▪ Those who join prestigious groups often have higher collective self-esteem than those who belong to less positively valued groups.

   ▪ Studies of *collective self-esteem* (as defined by Crocker and her associates) indicate people with high membership esteem; public and private collective self-esteem scores have higher personal self-esteem.

5. Individuals seek to protect and enhance both private self-esteem and collective self-esteem.

▪ Members of stigmatized groups, failing groups, or groups that are derogated by nonmembers often protect their *collective self-esteem* by rejecting negative information about their group, stressing the relative superiority of their group (the *ingroup–outgroup bias*), and selectively focusing on their group's superior qualities (*social creativity*).

▪ When *stereotype threat* is high, members become concerned that they will be stereotyped if considered a member of a particular group.

▪ In general, personal failure is more troubling than collective failure. Individuals will minimize their association with groups that are performing poorly or will resign from the group (*individual mobility*).

RESOURCES

Chapter Case: Peak Search and Rescue

▪ *Heroic Efforts: The Emotional Culture of Search and Rescue Volunteers* by Jennifer Lois (2003) details the complex nuances of membership in a high demanding group that regularly engages in heroic and dangerous community service.

Inclusion, Exclusion, and Belonging

▪ "Ostracism" by Kipling D. Williams (2007) provides a theoretically driven description of recent empirical investigations into the nature and consequences of exclusion from groups for both those who are excluded and those who do the excluding.

▪ "Evolutionary Approaches to Group Dynamics" is a special issue of the journal *Group Dynamics* edited by Mark Van Vugt and Mark Schaller (2008) exploring the implications of an evolutionary perspective for understanding

groups and their dynamics, with papers by R.I.M. Dunbar (2008), Rick O'Gorman, Kennon M. Sheldon, and David S. Wilson (2008), Gregory D. Webster (2008), Norbert L. Kerr and John M. Levine (2008), David M. Buss and Joshua D. Duntley (2008), Steven L. Neuberg and Catherine A. Cottrell (2008), and Thomas Kessler and Christopher J. Cohrs (2008).

▪ "Sociometer Theory" by Mark R. Leary (2012) summarizes the evidence that supports the idea that self-esteem is not determined by personal appraisals of one's value, but by the extent to which one is accepted by others.

Individualism and Collectivism

▪ "Rethinking Individualism and Collectivism: Evaluation of Theoretical Assumptions and Meta-Analyses" by Daphna Oyserman, Heather M. Coon, and Markus Kemmelmeier (2002) thoroughly explores the psychological implications of individual and cultural differences in individualism and collectivism and is followed by a number of fascinating commentaries by experts in this area (Bond, 2002; Fiske, 2002; Kitayama, 2002; J. G. Miller, 2002).

- "A Theory of Individualism and Collectivism" by Harry C. Triandis and Michele J. Gelfand (2012) traces the development of cultural variations from the time of Hammurabi's Code through to contemporary anthropological, sociological, and psychological studies of individualism and collectivism.

Social Identity

- "The Social Identity Perspective" by Michael A. Hogg (2005) provides a compact but comprehensive review of the basic theoretical assumptions of social identity theory.

- "Social Identity Theory" by Naomi Ellemers and S. Alexander Haslam (2012) examines the history of the development of the theory of social identity, beginning with the earliest work on minimal group situations through to current theoretical issues pertaining to depersonalization, categorization, and self-esteem.

Formation

CHAPTER OVERVIEW

Groups form through a combination of personal, situational, and interpersonal processes. Formation depends on the members themselves; some people are more likely than others to join groups. Groups also come into existence when the press of environmental circumstances pushes people together rather than keeping them apart. They also spring up, sometimes unexpectedly, when people discover that they like one another, and this attraction provides the foundation for the development of interpersonal bonds.

- Who joins groups?
- When do people seek out others?
- What processes generate bonds of interpersonal attraction between members of groups?

CHAPTER OUTLINE

Joining Groups
> *Personality*
> *Men, Women, and Groups*
> *Social Motivation*
> *Anxiety and Attachment*
> *Attitudes, Experiences, and Expectations*

Affiliation
> *Social Comparison*
> *Stress and Affiliation*
> *Social Comparison and the Self*

Attraction
> *Principles of Attraction*
> *The Economics of Membership*

Chapter Review

Resources

The Impressionists: The Group That Redefined Beauty

The group was born in 1862 in Paris in a small school of the arts on the Rue de l'Ouest. Four young men, all students working with Charles Gleyre, formed its core: Frederic Bazille, Claude Monet, Auguste Renoir, and Alfred Sisley. They banded together to ridicule the traditional schools of art and to learn new styles and techniques. Others soon joined them, including the unconventional Edouard Manet, the detail-oriented Gustave Caillebotte, the contentious Edgar Degas, the irritable Paul Cézanne, and the tactful Camille Pissarro. Separately, they were just a few artists struggling to learn their craft, define their style, and earn enough to pay the bills. But when they joined together to form a group, they transformed themselves and their art, and in time they redefined the world's conception of beauty (Farrell, 1982, 2001).

On the surface, they shared little in common. Some were the sons of wealthy families but others had working-class backgrounds. Some were outgoing and confident but others were quiet and uncertain. Some had been working at their craft for many years and others were struggling to learn the basics. But they were united in their belief that the state-supported Academy of Fine Arts was too restrictive and rigid. The academy alone determined which paintings and sculptures could be displayed at the Exhibition of the Works of Living Artists (the "Salon"), and most artists acquiesced to the academy's guidelines. But this small group of renegade painters shared a different vision. They wanted to capture the beauty of everyday life, outdoor scenes and real people instead of posed portraits and technically precise studio paintings of religious, historical, and mythic scenes.

The young artists developed a new approach to painting, often journeying into the countryside to paint landscapes. They sometimes painted side by side and critiqued one another's work. They also met in cafés in Paris to discuss technique, artistic philosophies, and politics. Art critics rejected their approach for years, and the artists scarcely earned enough money to survive. But, in time, they were recognized by the art community as a new school of painting—the *impressionists*—and their paintings are now worth millions.

We can ask many questions about the **artists circle** that founded impressionism. How did they make decisions and strategize? Why did Manet rank so high in status, and why did one of the group's finest painters—Degas—become the malcontent? How did the group counter the constraints imposed by the status quo? But one question—perhaps the most basic of all—asks why did it come into existence in the first place? In 1858, Manet, Monet, Degas, and the others were busy pursuing their careers independently. But by the late-1860s, they had joined to form the most influential artists circle of all time. What were the circumstances that drove these individuals to combine their resources in a group that endured for more than 30 years?

This chapter answers this question in three parts. It begins with the artists themselves, for people's personalities, preferences, and prior experiences influence the extent to which they seek out membership in groups. Some are *joiners*; some are *loners*. Next, it considers the *situation*, for even a collection of highly sociable joiners must affiliate on at least one occasion before a group will form. Some situations push people together; others keep them apart. Affiliation, however, only sets the stage for group formation. If the individuals who find themselves together are not *attracted* to each other, then a long-lasting group like the impressionists likely will not form. Some people like each other; some do not.

---

artists circle A relatively small group of peers who work together for an extended period of time, exchanging ideas for commentary and critique and developing a shared conception of what their profession's methods and goals should be; more generally, a collaborative circle.

JOINING GROUPS

Monet and Vincent van Gogh were both brilliant artists, both dropped out of traditional schools of art, and both experimented continually as they struggled to perfect their craft. But Monet joined with other artists whereas van Gogh kept to himself. Not everyone who joins a group is a "joiner," and people who prefer independence over association are not necessarily "loners." But people differ from each other in many ways—in personality, motivations, and past experiences—and these differences predispose some people to join groups and others to remain apart.

Personality

When Monet learned that Renoir, Bazille, and Sisley were meeting each evening, he was quick to join the group. Why? Part of the answer lies in his basic **personality**. He was energetic, creative, optimistic, and relentless in the pursuit of his goals. Some described him as egotistical, but most thought he was a warm, friendly person who enjoyed being with other people. Once he joined a group, he quickly became its leader. Monet's style of painting changed over time, but his basic personality remained steady throughout his adult life.

Five Factors of Personality The **Five Factor Model** (FFM) of personality provides one explanation for the idiosyncratic consistencies in individuals' thoughts, feelings, and actions over time. Why was Caillebotte so conscientious in organizing the impressionists' exhibitions? Why was Monet so adept at influencing others and making friends, whereas Cézanne was bad-tempered and melancholy? Why was van Gogh unable to relax, even when physically exhausted? FFM's explanation: Variations among people can be conceptualized in

terms of the "big five" fundamental dimensions summarized in Table 4.1: extraversion, agreeableness, conscientiousness, neuroticism, and openness (or, in some models, culture or intellect). The theory assumes that people differ from one another in many ways, but much of this variability is the observable manifestation of these five basic dimensions (Goldberg, 1993; McCrae & Costa, 1997).

Two of these five dimensions—extraversion and agreeableness—are particularly influential determinants of people's engagement in groups (Ozer & Benet-Martínez, 2006). **Extraversion** is the tendency to move toward people rather than away from people. Those on the introversion end of this personality dimension, the *introverts*, tend to be withdrawn, quiet, and reclusive. Their opposites, the *extraverts*, are sociable, outgoing, and active. Extraverts are likely to prefer the company of others, particularly in pleasant and enjoyable situations (Lucas & Diener, 2001). Different cultures imbue introversion and extraversion with unique, culture-specific meaning, but people all over the world spontaneously appraise their own and others' social tendencies (Yang & Bond, 1990). Monet was, in all likelihood, an extravert; van Gogh, an introvert.

Agreeableness, in contrast, is the tendency to be cooperative, kind, and compassionate. Those who are disagreeable tend to be competitive, aloof, and less concerned about others' appraisals of them, whereas the agreeable are helpful, compliant, considerate, and modest (Graziano & Tobin, 2009). These two types are "obnoxious" and "nice" (Davis & Schmidt, 1977, p. 205): the "best analogy for

---

personality The configuration of distinctive but enduring dispositional characteristics, including traits, temperament, and values, that characterize an individual's responses across situations.

Five Factor Model (FFM, or big five theory) A conceptual model of the primary dimensions that structure individual differences in personality. The five dimensions are extraversion, agreeableness, conscientiousness, neuroticism, and openness to experience. Different theorists sometimes use different labels.

---

extraversion In personality trait theories, the degree to which an individual tends to seek out social contacts, including such related qualities as outgoing, enthusiastic, energetic, and assertive. Introverts are oriented primarily toward inner perceptions and judgments of concepts and ideas, whereas extraverts are oriented primarily toward social experiences.

agreeableness In personality trait theories, the degree to which an individual tends to respond positively across situations, including such related qualities as trusting, straightforward, warm, cooperative, modest, and sympathetic.

TABLE 4.1   The Five Factor Model ("Big Five") of Personality

Factor	Content	
Extraversion	Extraverted • talkative • enthusiastic • bold • energetic	Introverted • reserved • quiet • unsociable • withdrawn
Agreeableness	Agreeable • sympathetic • warm • kind • cooperative	Disagreeable • cold • unsympathetic • critical • quarrelsome
Conscientiousness	Conscientious • organized • efficient • systematic • practical	Careless • disorganized • sloppy • inefficient • careless
Neuroticism	Neurotic • moody • anxious • temperamental • easily upset	Stable • content • relaxed • calm • emotionally stable
Openness to experience	Open • creative • imaginative • complex • intelligent	Closed • uncreative • unintellectual • conventional • unimaginative

SOURCES: Gosling, S. D., Rentfrow, P. J., & Swann, W. B., Jr. (2003). A very brief measure of the Big Five personality domains. *Journal of Research in Personality, 37*, 504–528.

Saucier, G. (1994). Mini-Markers: A brief version of Goldberg's unipolar Big-Five markers. *Journal of Personality Assessment, 63*, 506–516.

obnoxious behavior is garlic (which overpowers other foods' flavors), the best analogy for nice behavior is monosodium glutamate [Accent] (which accentuates other foods' flavors but is itself flavorless)." Pizzaro was agreeable and Cézanne—not so much.

Extraverts may seek out groups because such interactions are stimulating, and extraverts appreciate stimulating experiences more than introverts do (Eysenck, 1990). Extraverts' affinity for being part of a group may also be based on assertiveness, for they tend to be influential group members rather than quiet followers. Groups may also seek out extraverts rather than introverts. Some qualities, like intelligence, morality, and friendliness, are difficult to judge during initial encounters, but observers are particularly good at detecting extraversion in others (Albright, Kenny, & Malloy, 1988). If a group is looking for people who will be sociable and will connect easily with others, it might recruit extraverts more actively than introverts (Judge & Cable, 1997). Groups may also prefer to recruit and keep agreeable people rather than disagreeable ones. When researchers tracked the formation of groups and networks among students who were just starting college, they discovered that extraversion predicted overall interaction rate and the development of new peer relationships. Agreeableness predicted a reduced level of conflict, particularly with opposite-sex friends (Asendorpf & Wilpers, 1998).

Happiness and Extraversion Groups may also seek extraverts because they are, in general, happier people than introverts. Do you enjoy talking to strangers? Enjoy working with others? Like making decisions in groups? Do you like to go to parties? If yes, then you are in all likelihood a happier person than someone who avoids groups and enjoys solitary activities (Lucas et al., 2000, p. 468). This difference appears to know no cultural or national boundaries, for when researchers studied students in 39 countries those who were more extraverted were also the ones who were happiest (Lucas et al., 2000).

Why are extraverts so happy? Primarily because extraverts join more frequently with other people, and strong social relationships are a fundamental determinant of well-being (e.g., Lee, Dean, & Jung, 2008). Extraverts may, however, just be in better moods than introverts, for even when they are alone extraverts report that they are happier than do introverts. They may also be adept at regulating their mood states by dealing with negative events in psychologically healthy ways, and so they keep their mood elevated (Augustine & Hemenover, 2008; Lischetzke & Eid, 2006). Extraverts are more sensitive to rewards than introverts, and so their positivity may be due to their more positive reaction to pleasant experiences (Lucas, 2008). Alternatively, introverts may be more negative in their moods because social demands cause them to associate with people so frequently, even though they would prefer to be alone.

Extraverts' happiness may also be due to the fact that the kinds of behaviors that define extraversion are more pleasurable than those that characterize introversion. When introverts and extraverts recorded their behavior five times a day for two weeks, researchers discovered that even introverts talking to other people, interacting in groups, and so on reported experiencing more positive emotions. The researchers then went one step further. Reasoning that acting in an extraverted way may directly influence happiness, they asked volunteers taking part in a group discussion to be talkative, energetic, and active (extraverted) or reserved, quiet, and passive (introverted). Those who acted in extraverted ways ended the study in better moods than did people who were told to act as if they were introverted (Fleeson, Malanos, & Achille, 2002; McNiel & Fleeson, 2006).

Personality-Group Fit Extraversion and agreeableness predict individuals' overall proclivities with regard to joining groups, but all the traits in the five factor model influence the *types* of groups individuals join. Extraverts are particularly attracted to organizations that are team-oriented. Those who are agreeable would just as soon avoid groups that are aggressive and competitive, but, like extraverts, they prefer groups that emphasize cooperation. Conscientious individuals, in contrast, are more attracted to groups and organizations that are detail- and task-oriented. Who joins groups like the one formed by the impressionists—a group that emphasizes creativity, originality, and aesthetics? People whose personalities include the trait openness to experience (Judge & Cable, 1997).

These findings confirm the importance of the fit between the individual's personality and the type of group they would most like to join. Someone who is highly conscientious, for example, is unlikely to join a gang—instead, gangs attract those who are higher in neuroticism and lower in agreeableness (Egan & Beadman, 2011). The U.S. Navy Sea-Air-Land personnel, Navy SEALs, in contrast, are quite conscientious and also extraverted (Braun, Prusaczyk, & Pratt, 1992). An individual who is open to experience is more likely to join an alternative spiritual movement rather than a traditional religious group (Buxant, Saroglou, & Tesser, 2010). The closer the fit between individuals' personality characteristics and the group's purpose and organization, the more likely the individual will seek to join the group.

Men, Women, and Groups

Nearly all the impressionists were men; Berthe Morisot and Mary Cassatt were exceptions. Is the need to seek out and join groups stronger in men than women?

Studies find that men and women differ in their tendency to join groups, but the differences are not great in magnitude. Women tend to be somewhat more extraverted and agreeable than men, and these differences are pronounced in economically developed nations (Schmitt et al., 2008). Women remember more details about their relationships than do men, and they more accurately recount events that occurred in their social networks (Taylor, 2002). Women are, in general, higher in **relationality**;—that is, their values, attitudes, and outlooks emphasize and facilitate establishing and maintaining connections to others (Gore & Cross, 2006). Women expect more reciprocity and loyalty in their one-to-one friendship relationships, as well as intimacy, solidarity, and companionship (Hall, 2011). Men are more agentic than women and so are more likely to join with other men in order to perform a task or reach a goal (Twenge, 1997).

Other studies, however, find few differences between the sexes. Even though women may put more value on their relationships, they may not be any more social than men. One survey of 800 adults in the United States found that men belonged to more professional groups, governing boards, political parties, and military organizations than women, but women spent more time in their groups than did men (Booth, 1972). The sexes do not differ in the time they spend in solitary activities, their involvement in community groups, or their membership in more unusual types of groups, such as cults and covens (Osgood et al., 1996; Parkum & Parkum, 1980; Pittard-Payne, 1980).

The differences that emerge, although subtle, indicate that women seek membership in smaller, informal, intimate groups, whereas men seek membership in larger, more formal, task-focused groups. These tendencies may reflect women's and men's differing interpersonal orientations, with women more likely to define themselves in terms of their memberships in groups and their relationships. The sexes may also differ in their emphasis on achieving

power and establishing connections with others. Both of these goals can best be achieved in groups, but they require membership in different types of groups. Men, seeking power and influence, join competitive, goal-oriented groups where they can vie for status. Women, seeking intimate relationships and, in some cases, safety, would be more likely to join small, supportive groups (Baumeister, 2010; Baumeister & Sommer, 1997; Taylor, 2002).

These sex differences are also entangled with role differences and cultural stereotypes. In cultures where men and women tend to enact different roles, the roles may shape opportunities for involvement in groups. If women are primarily responsible for domestic duties and childbearing, they may have more opportunities to join informal, localized groups but not occupational groups (Taylor, 2002). Hence, as attitudes toward the role of women have changed in contemporary society, differences in social participation have diminished (Lal Goel, 1980; Smith, 1980). Sexism also works to exclude women and men from certain types of groups. Women, for example, were until recently deliberately excluded from juries in the United States. (The U.S. Supreme Court ruled that women could not be excused from jury duty because of their sex in 1975.) In Paris, in the 1860s, women modeled for artists, but few could be artists themselves. Morisot and Cassatt could not even join the other impressionists in the extended discussions at the Café Guerbois. As sexist attitudes continue to decline, differences in membership in various types of groups will also abate.

Social Motivation

Why did Monet reject his father's advice about studying in a traditional school of the arts? Why did Manet refuse to join the group during its first public exhibition? Why did the group try to exclude Cézanne? Such questions can often be answered by considering motivations, which are psychological processes that energize actions and guide group members in one direction rather than another. Social motivations, unlike the more biologically based motivations such as hunger and thirst, influence people's interpersonal behaviors

---

relationality The degree to which one's values, attitudes, and outlooks emphasize and facilitate establishing and maintaining connections to others.

and include the need for affiliation, intimacy, and power (see Forbes, 2011).

Need for Affiliation   Are you the kind of person who is more attracted to sociable people? Do you go out of your way to be friendly toward others? If you were given a choice, would you work alone on a project or be part of a group? Individuals who are high in the **need for affiliation** tend to join groups more frequently, spend more of their time in groups, communicate more with other group members, and accept other group members more readily (see Hill, 2009, for a review). Overall, they consider group activities to be more enjoyable than do those who are low in the need for affiliation, even in situations that are task-focused rather than interpersonally oriented. For example, in one study, college students spent an entire week in e-groups preparing for a 30-item examination that would significantly influence their grade. Their need for affiliation did not predict the students' level of achievement on the test, but it did predict their satisfaction with the online group learning environment. Those high in need for affiliation were more likely to attribute their learning gains to collaboration among the members than were those with lower affiliation motivation (Brewer & Klein, 2006).

Individuals who are high in the need for affiliation are drawn to groups, but some research suggests that they are also more anxious when they confront social situations, perhaps because they fear rejection. Some years ago social psychologist Donn Byrne (1961) demonstrated this tendency by arranging for college students to complete a series of questionnaires while seated in a room equipped with a two-way mirror. Students in the control condition just filled out their forms, but Byrne told those in the experimental group that observers behind the mirror were watching them carefully, rating each one of them on their general popularity, their attractiveness, and how likeable they seemed. Those who were low in their need for affiliation were unfazed by the idea that their social attractiveness was under review, whereas those who were high in need affiliation reported feeling more anxious and uneasy. This substrate of anxiety about rejection can cause the usual positive relationship between the need for affiliation and joining groups to reverse; those who are high in need for affiliation are *less* likely to join a group when they fear the group will reject them (Hill, 1991).

Need for Intimacy   Individuals who have a high **need for intimacy**, like those who have a high need for affiliation, prefer to join with others. Such individuals, however, seek close, warm relations and are more likely to express caring and concern for other people (McAdams, 1982, 1995). They do not fear rejection but, instead, are more focused on friendship, camaraderie, reciprocity, and mutual help. This pro-group orientation was apparent when investigators used an **experience sampling** method to track the thoughts and actions of college students for an entire week. They gave their participants electronic pagers and asked them to complete a short questionnaire every time they were paged over the course of seven days. They then paged them 49 times during the week, between the hours of 9 AM and 11 PM. As expected, when paged, those who were high in need for intimacy were more frequently either thinking about other people or they were actually interacting with other people rather than alone. If with others, their moods were more positive than if they were by themselves (McAdams & Constantian, 1983).

---

need for intimacy A motivating state of tension that can be relieved by seeking out warm, positive relationships with others.

experience sampling A research method that asks participants to record their thoughts, emotions, or behavior at the time they are experiencing them rather than at a later time or date; in some cases, participants make their entries when they are signaled by researchers using electronic pagers, personal data assistants (PDAs), or similar devices.

---

need for affiliation A motivating state of tension that can be relieved by joining with other people, which frequently includes concerns about winning the approval of other people.

Need for Power   Individuals who are high in the **need for power** (or power motive) exhibit an elevated desire to maintain and enhance their capacity to influence other people (Fodor, 2009). They report, for example, an interest in supervising, leading, and managing people, for they would prefer to be in positions of authority where they can make decisions that impact other people. Such individuals therefore seek out membership in groups, not because they wish to bond with others, but because groups provide them with the means to reach their more primary goal of influencing other people. In consequence, those who are high in power seek to lead the groups they join. When such individuals were asked to think about the groups they participated in recently, those with a high power motive reported taking part in relatively fewer dyadic interactions but in more large-group interactions (groups with more than four members). They also reported exercising more control in these groups by organizing and initiating activities, assuming responsibility, and attempting to persuade others (McAdams, Healy, & Krause, 1984).

This relationship between the need for power and participation in groups was stronger for men, in part due to the relationship between the need for power and testosterone. Individuals with high needs for power also tend to have elevated levels of the hormone testosterone, which is associated with agentic, dominance-seeking actions (Stanton & Schultheiss, 2009). The need for power is also associated with power stress: the physiological and psychological response to situations that arouse the need for power but also thwart the satisfaction of that need (McClelland, 1975). For example, those high in need for power show signs of stress when they encounter someone who is assertive rather than compliant and when someone they are attempting to influence remains unpersuaded (Fodor & Wick, 2009; Fodor, Wick, & Hartsen, 2006).

FIRO   Psychologist William Schutz (1958, 1992) integrated the three basic needs for affiliation, intimacy, and power in his **Fundamental Interpersonal Relations Orientation** theory, or FIRO (rhymes with "*I* row"). He labeled them the need for inclusion, affection, and control, and argued they combine to determine how people treat others and how people want others to treat them. Inclusion (need for affiliation) refers to peoples' desire to join with others but also their need to be accepted by those others. Affection (need for intimacy) is a desire to like others as well as a desire to be liked by them. Control (need for power) includes the need to dominate others but also the willingness to let others be dominant. Schutz developed the FIRO-B scale (the B is for *behavior*), which is sampled in Table 4.2, to measure both the need to express and the need to receive inclusion, affection, and control. Inclusion and agreeableness (both wanted and expressed) are associated with gregariousness and warmth, expressed control with extraversion, and wanted control with neuroticism (Furnham, 2008).

FIRO theory assumes that people join groups, and remain in them, because they meet one or more of these basic needs. If, for example, Monet did not need to receive and express inclusion, he probably would have been content to develop his skills alone or in a more traditional teacher-led class setting. But he had a vigorous need to express inclusion, affection, and control, and so he created and maintained the circle of impressionist painters. Sisley, in contrast, wished to receive inclusion and affection but was not as strongly motivated to include others in his activities.

Anxiety and Attachment

Just as one's personality and social motives may push people *toward* groups, other personal qualities

---

need for power A motivating state of tension that can be relieved by gaining control over other people and one's environment.

Fundamental Interpersonal Relations Orientation (FIRO) A theory of group formation and development that emphasizes compatibility among three basic social motives: inclusion, control, and affection (developed by William Schutz).

T A B L E   4.2   Example Items from the Fundamental Interpersonal Relations Orientation-Behavior (FIRO-B) Scale

	Inclusion (I)	Control (C)	Affection (A)
Expressed toward other people	• I try to be with other people. • I join social groups.	• I try to take charge of things when I am with people. • I try to have other people do things I want done.	• I try to be friendly to people. • I try to have close relationships with people.
Wanted from other people	• I like people to invite me to things. • I like people to include me in their activities.	• I let other people decide what to do. • I let other people take charge of things.	• I like people to act friendly toward me. • I like people to act close toward me.

SOURCE: *FIRO: A Three-Dimensional Theory of Interpersonal Behavior* by W. C. Schutz. Copyright 1958 by Holt, Rinehart, & Winston, Inc.

may push them *away from* groups. Cézanne was both shy and temperamental. He was friends with Pissarro but could not bear the company of most of the other impressionists. Historical accounts of the troubled life of van Gogh comment on his anxiety over his failed relationships. He had some friends, and he tried to join his fellow artists, but he could not sustain these relationships. Many of the artists in Paris at the time of the impressionists preferred to work alone, without distraction, rather than painting with others. Some people are shy, socially anxious, or just less interested in being connected to other people and to groups.

Shyness The dispositional tendency to feel uneasy, uncomfortable, and awkward in social situations is called **shyness** (Zimbardo, 1977). Shy people do not join groups as readily as others, and they do not find group activities to be as enjoyable. As early as age 2, some children begin to display fear or inhibition when they encounter a person they do not recognize (Kagan, Snidman, & Arcus, 1992). Some grade school children consistently seek out other people, whereas others show

signs of shyness and withdrawal when they are in groups (Asendorpf & Meier, 1993). Shy people even react differently than nonshy people, neurologically, when they see a stranger's face. Nonshy people's brains show an activation response in the bilateral nucleus accumbens when they see unfamiliar faces, but shy people's brains display heightened bilateral activity in the amygdala, an area of the brain that is responsible for emotional responses, including fear (Beaton et al., 2008).

Most people who are shy manage to cope with the nervousness they feel when in groups. Shy individuals often form associations with other shy individuals, and these groups adopt interaction styles and activities that better suit the social tendencies of their members (Rubin et al., 2006; See Focus 4.1). Shy individuals are also more comfortable in activity-focused groups, such as sports teams and academic groups, and, through positive interactions within such groups, they gain more social confidence (Rose-Krasnor, 2009). Shy people, when they must enter a new group, often take a friend with them. This "social surrogate" helps them transition into the group by doing much of the work needed to establish connections with others. The surrogate takes the place of the shy members during initial interactions until they overcome their initial social anxieties (Bradshaw, 1998).

---

shyness The tendency to be reserved or timid during social interactions, usually coupled with feelings of discomfort and nervousness.

F o c u s   4.1   Cross-cultural Perspectives: The Meaning of Shyness

Going Solo (Klinenberg, 2012), *Quiet* (Cain, 2012), and *Party of One* (Rufus, 2003) are just a few of the recent books that have spoken, encouragingly, about the contributions shy, introverted people make to their groups and organizations. But those who are shy are, in general, underrepresented in groups for two reasons. First, they tend to not seek out membership in as many groups. Second, groups generally prefer those who are outgoing and vociferous to those who are quiet and reserved. Imagine, for example, that you are about to meet John and are given the following background information to consider (from Rapee et al., 2011, p. 491).

> John is a 22-year-old university student. When he is in a group, he tends to not say very much, but he does answer when people talk to him. When he does talk, he usually speaks in a fairly quiet voice and sometimes starts a little hesitantly. However, he always makes sense when he talks. John usually seems friendly, although he is often reserved and he would rarely start a conversation with anyone. John usually goes to parties and social gatherings when he is directly asked, but he sometimes makes excuses not to go and will never organize a social gathering. He spends most of his time with a small number of friends.

What kind of impression do you have of John? Do you think he is a likeable person? And, what do you think about his career prospects? Will his reticence be a help or a hindrance in a future career?

Most people rated John less positively than someone who was described as socially confident and outgoing, but one's country of origin makes a difference. Researchers presented translations of the personality profiles of the shy person and an outgoing person to people in eight different countries: Australia, Canada,

China, Germany, Japan, Korea, The Netherlands, and the United States. As they expected, people from western countries (e.g., United States, Canada) judged outgoing people more positively and the career prospects of the shy more negatively than did individuals from East Asian countries (e.g., China, Korea).

Western countries prize individualism but they do not revere the *shy* individualist. Instead, they favor the sociable, self-promoting individualist. Studies of peer networks in western countries indicate that it is the extraverted children who tend to be the most popular in classes, and both teachers and parents favor the talkative, sociable child over the quiet one (Cain, 2012). The "strong, silent" type is not as attractive as the "socially dynamic, talkative" type. In consequence, individuals who think of themselves as shy tend to also express less overall life satisfaction (Rapee et al., 2011).

Individuals from the more collectivistic cultures of the East, in contrast, seek out close connections with others as extraverts do, but they do not try to dominate others interpersonally. In consequence, shyness has a different meaning in some Asian countries, for it is associated with one's recognition of one's place in the group and a willingness to fit in rather than stand out from the crowd. Parents of shy children in China are not concerned that they are "too withdrawn" or "friendless," and some evidence suggests that the shyness facilitates adjustment and success rather than impedes it (Chen, 2011). Eastern cultures, by tradition, believe enlightenment requires solitude rather than socializing. And some Westerners, agree. Steve Wosniak, the cofounder of Apple Computing, wrote in his memoirs that one must be wary of spending too much time with other people: "I'm going to give you some advice that might be hard to take. That advice is: Work alone" (Wosniak & Smith, 2006, p. 291).

Social Anxiety Shyness can, in some cases, escalate into **social anxiety**. Social anxiety sets in when people want to make a good impression, but they do not think that their attempts to establish relationships

will succeed (Vertue, 2003). Because of these pessimistic expectations, when these individuals interact with other people, they suffer disabling emotional, physiological, and behavioral side effects. They become physiologically aroused to the point that their pulse races, they blush and perspire, their hands may tremble, and their voices quiver when they speak. Socially anxious people, even when they join groups, do not actively participate; they

---

social anxiety A feeling of apprehension and embarrassment experienced when anticipating or actually interacting with other people.

can be identified by their silence, downcast eyes, and low speaking voices. They may also engage in "innocuous sociability" (Leary, 1983): They merge into the group's background by indicating general interest in the group and agreement with the other group members while consistently minimizing their personal involvement in the group interaction.

This anxiety can cause people to reduce their social contact with others—to *disaffiliate* (Leary & Kowalski, 1995, p. 157). In a study that used experience sampling, college students carried with them small handheld computers that signaled them eight times a day, asking them to complete a short set of questions about their emotions, thoughts, and activities. Those who were socially anxious did not spend more time alone, but they were more likely to wish they were alone when they were with other people they did not know very well. They felt more self-conscious and their emotions were more negative when they were with others (Brown et al., 2007).

If these feelings of anxiety are paired with a pronounced fear of embarrassment or humiliation, the individual may be experiencing **social anxiety disorder**, or SAD. This clinical disorder, which affects approximately 5% of adults (4.2% of men, 5.7% of women), is an excessive and unreasonable fear of social situations, qualifying as a phobia rather than distress and discomfort when facing a social challenge. The anxiety is also relatively unrelieved, in that the individual consistently reacts whenever exposed to the situation, although in most cases individuals cope by avoiding the source of the anxiety—all groups. Group situations that are most disturbing to individuals suffering from SAD are speaking in front of other people, including during a group meeting or a class; attending social events, including parties; and eating with other people. Women are more likely to seek pharmacological treatment for SAD, whereas men tend to use alcohol and illicit drugs to reduce their social anxiety (Xu et al., 2012).

Attachment Theory When individuals join a group, they are agreeing, even if implicitly, to be part of a set of intertwined relationships with one or more other individuals. If you are the type of person, like Monet, who by nature is comfortable forming relationships with other people, then joining groups poses no challenge. But if you are a person who avoids forming relationships with others or experiences problems maintaining relationships, like van Gogh, then groups become one more arena where one's relational style will find expression.

The idea that individuals differ in their orientations to their relationships is the basis of *attachment theory* (e.g., Bowlby, 1980). This theory suggests that, from an early age, children differ in the way they relate to others, with some children developing very secure and comfortable relationships with their caregivers but others exhibiting dependence and uncertainty. The theory suggests that these childhood differences emerge in adulthood as variations in **attachment style**—one's basic cognitive, emotional, and behavioral orientation when in a relationship with others (Hazan & Shaver, 1987). Some people enjoy forming close relationships, and they do not worry about being abandoned by their loved ones. Others, however, are uncomfortable relying on other people, they worry that their loved ones will reject them, or they are simply uninterested in relationships altogether. The four basic styles shown in Figure 4.1—secure, preoccupied, fearful, and dismissing—reflect two underlying dimensions: anxiety about relationships and avoidance of closeness and dependency on others.

Social psychologist Eliot Smith and his colleagues theorized that people also have group-level

---

social anxiety disorder A persistent and pervasive pattern of overwhelming anxiety and self-consciousness experienced when anticipating or actually interacting with other people (also known as *social phobia*).

attachment style One's characteristic approach to relationships with other people; the basic styles include secure, preoccupied, fearful, and dismissing, as defined by the dimensions of anxiety and avoidance.

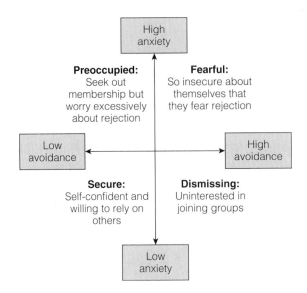

FIGURE 4.1 Group attachment styles. The four basic styles (secure, preoccupied, fearful, and dismissing) are defined by two dimensions: level of anxiety and degree of avoidance. If, for example, individuals who are low in avoidance but high in anxiety would be preoccupied.

SOURCE: © Cengage Learning 2014

attachment styles. They suggested that some individuals are anxious about their group experiences, for they question their acceptance by their group and report feeling as if they were unworthy of membership. They tend to agree with such statements as "I often worry my group will not always want me as a member" and "I sometimes worry that my group doesn't value me as much as I value my group" (Smith, Murphy, & Coats, 1999, p. 110). Others, however, are avoidant; they are not interested in getting close to their group, for they agreed with such statements as "I prefer not to depend on my group or to have my group depend on me" and "I am comfortable not being close to my group" (1999, p. 110). Smith's research team discovered that people with anxious group attachment styles spend less time in their groups, engage in fewer collective activities, and are less satisfied with the level of support they received from the group. Those with avoidant group attachment styles felt that the group was less important to them, and they were more likely to claim that they were planning to leave the group. When researchers followed up these ideas by watching people with varying attachment styles interacting in small groups, they discovered that people with secure attachment styles contributed to both the instrumental and the relationship activities of the group. Those with more anxious attachment styles, in contrast, contributed less to the group's instrumental work, and those with avoidant attachment styles contributed less to both instrumental and relationship activities (Rom & Mikulincer, 2003). Other work suggests that individuals' feelings of anxiety about their personal relationships covary with their anxiety about groups but that avoidance of groups and personal relations are unrelated. Both types of attachment styles, however, predicted how well individuals adjusted when they were transitioning to a new living situation (as new students on a college campus; Marmarosh & Markin, 2007).

Attitudes, Experiences, and Expectations

Not everyone is thrilled at the prospect of joining groups. In many situations, people have the opportunity to join a new group—a club, a group of people who socialize together, an amateur sports team—but decline for personal reasons. Their general attitude about groups and the demands they make on members may be negative. They may have little experience in groups and so are too cautious to take part. They may value individual effort over team engagement. People's attitudes, experiences, and expectations are all factors that influence their decision to join a group.

Beliefs about Groups   Even though humans seem to sort themselves into groups in most contexts, some remain ambivalent about them. Whereas some people look forward with breathless anticipation to their next subcommittee meeting, group-learning experience, or business meeting, others question—quite openly—the worth of these social contrivances. When management researchers Steven J. Karau and Abdel Moneim M. K. Elsaid (2009) investigated these variations, they discovered that people with more negative beliefs about groups and their effectiveness were less likely to take part in them. Karau and Elsaid began their analysis by developing the *Beliefs about Groups* (BAG) scale to measure people's preferences for taking part in groups, expectations about how hard people work in groups, and predictions of the positive and negative effects groups will have on performance (see Table 4.3). Individuals who had more positive

beliefs about a group's capacity to enhance performance and effort expressed a stronger preference to join in groups, whereas those who had more negative expectations about groups were disinclined to take part in them. In addition, preference to work in groups was also related to collectivism (see Chapter 3), trust in others, agreeableness, and experience working in groups in educational settings.

Experiences in Groups   One's previous experience in groups, whether good or bad, influences one's interest in joining groups in the future. College students who receive low scores on assessments based on team-learning activities evaluate group work more negatively than students who get higher grades (Reinig, Horowitz, & Whittenburg, 2011). Participation in organized sports teams in adolescence predicts participation in such groups in adulthood (Walters et al., 2009). Individuals who have had a negative experience in a therapeutic group are less likely to choose that form of treatment in the future (Smokowski, Rose, & Bacallao, 2001). In some cases, too, the experience can be a vicarious one. Children who see their parents joining and enjoying memberships in civic and volunteer associations are more likely to join such groups when they themselves reach adulthood (Bonikowski & McPherson, 2007).

Social psychologists Richard Moreland, John Levine, and their colleagues studied the impact of expectations on students' decisions to join a group

TABLE 4.3   **A Sample of Items from the *Beliefs about Groups* Scale**

Factor	Example items
Group preference	• I'm more comfortable working by myself rather than as part of a group (reversed). • I prefer group work to individual work.
Effort beliefs	• People tend to work especially hard on a group task. • Most people can be trusted to do their fair share of the work.
Negative performance beliefs	• Group projects usually fail to match the quality of those done by individuals. • Assigning work to a group is a recipe for disaster.
Positive performance beliefs	• Generally speaking, groups are highly effective. • Groups often produce much higher quality work than individuals.

SOURCE: Karau, S. J., & Elsaid, A.M.M.K. (2009). Individual differences in beliefs about groups. *Group Dynamics: Theory, Research, and Practice, 13*, 1–13.

when they got to college. In one of their studies, they surveyed more than 1,000 first-year students at the University of Pittsburgh, asking them if they took part in groups in high school and if they expected to join groups in college. They identified those students who had positive experiences in their high school groups—they rated their high school groups as both important and enjoyable. These students, when they enrolled in college, actively investigated the groups available to them. They tried harder to find a group on campus to join, and they were also more optimistic in their evaluations of potential groups; they expected that the positive aspects of joining a group would be particularly rewarding. Experience in groups in high school dampened that enthusiasm somewhat, at least for the specific groups that interested them. For example, those who were in student government in high school and were interested in taking part in student politics in college felt that this group would be rewarding, but they also recognized that it would impose costs as well. These students tended to be more deliberate in their review of potential groups and displayed a commitment to a specific group throughout the search process (Brinthaupt, Moreland, & Levine, 1991; Pavelchak, Moreland, & Levine, 1986).

Taking Collective Action   The impressionists were part artists circle but also part **social movement**, for its members were attempting to undo the academy's tight hold on the Salon and the art world, in general. Many factors influence people's decisions to join a social movement, but two factors—a sense of injustice and strong emotions—are particularly critical. Many artists in Paris in the 1860s were rejected by the Salon judges, but those who joined the impressionists were certain that the existing system was an unfair one. Time and again the artists submitted to the Salon, and only a few of them

were ever permitted to display their work. The Salon's refusal to consider alternative, emerging views of art was considered unjust, for it harmed not only the individual artists, but the group itself. This sense of injustice against the ingroup also fueled the artists' emotions. They were angered by the situation, and anger has been identified as a key factor in distinguishing between who will join a movement and who will not. A person may feel that a situation is unjust, but the person who is also angry about the unfairness is more likely to join with others to redress the wrong. Contempt, too, can be critical in motivating people to take action, particularly more extreme, counter-normative forms of civil disobedience (Tausch et al., 2011). Chapter 17 examines the dynamics of collective movements in more detail.

AFFILIATION

Birds flock, insects swarm, fish shoal, and humans affiliate. **Affiliation**, generally speaking, is the gathering together of conspecifics in one location. This process, as the first portion of this chapter explained, depends in part on the personalities, preferences, and other personal qualities of the group members. Affiliation, however, also becomes more likely in some situations and less likely in others. When individuals face uncertain or bewildering conditions, when they experience stressful circumstances, and when they are fearful (but not embarrassed), by joining a group they can gain the information and social support they need to help them cope with difficult circumstances.

Social Comparison

The impressionists faced uncertainty each time they stood before a blank canvas. They were convinced

---

social movement A deliberate, sustained, and organized group of individuals seeking change or resisting a change in a social system. Movements are sustained by individuals who may share a common outlook on issues or by members of identifiable social groups or categories, but not by businesses, political organizations, or governments.

---

affiliation The gathering together of individuals (typically members of the same species) in one location; also, a formalized relationship, as when an individual is said to be affiliated with a group or organization.

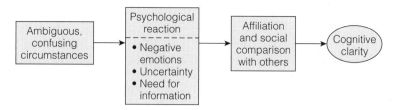

F I G U R E 4.2 Festinger's (1954) theory of social comparison.
SOURCE: © Cengage Learning

that the methods taught by the traditional Parisian art schools were severely limited, but they were not sure how to put their alternative approach into practice. So they often painted together, exchanging ideas about colors and techniques, as they refined their approach to art.

Social psychologist Leon Festinger (1950, 1954) maintained that people often rely on others for information about themselves and the environment. Physical reality is a reliable guide in many cases, but, to validate social reality, people must compare their interpretations to those of other people. Monet, for example, thought that his technique of using bright colors and leaving portions of the work undeveloped was promising, but after a day's painting, he always asked Renoir for his honest appraisal. Festinger called this process **social comparison** and suggested that it begins when people find themselves in ambiguous, confusing situations. Such situations trigger a variety of psychological reactions, most of which are unsettling, and so people affiliate with others to gain the information they need to reduce their confusion. As Figure 4.2 indicates, the final result of social comparison is cognitive clarity, but as the research reviewed in this section suggests, people engage in social comparison for many reasons—to evaluate their own qualities, to set personal goals, to help other people, or to bolster their self-esteem (Suls & Wheeler, 2000, 2012).

social comparison The process of contrasting one's personal qualities and outcomes, including beliefs, attitudes, values, abilities, accomplishments, and experiences, to those of other people.

Misery Loves Company How do people react when they find themselves in an ambiguous, and possibly dangerous, situation? Social psychologist Stanley Schachter (1959) believed that most people, finding themselves in such a predicament, would choose to join with other people to gain the information they need to allay their anxiety. To test his idea, he recruited young women college students to meet at his laboratory. There they were greeted by a researcher who introduced himself as Dr. Gregor Zilstein from the Medical School's Departments of Neurology and Psychiatry. In serious tones, he explained that he was studying the effects of electric shock on human beings. In one condition (*low anxiety*), the room contained no electrical devices; the experimenter explained that the shocks would be so mild that they would "resemble more a tickle or a tingle than anything unpleasant" (p. 14). Participants assigned to the *high-anxiety* condition, however, faced a vast collection of electrical equipment and were informed, "These shocks will hurt, they will be painful … but, of course, they will do no permanent damage" (p. 13). The researcher then asked the participant if she wanted to wait for her turn alone or with others. Approximately two-thirds of the women in the high-anxiety condition (63%) chose to affiliate, whereas only one-third of the women in the low-anxiety condition (33%) chose to wait with others. Schachter's conclusion: "misery loves company" (1959, p. 24).

Misery Loves Miserable Company The majority of the women Schachter studied chose to affiliate, but what was their primary motivation for joining with others? Did they wish to acquire information through social comparison, or were they just so frightened that they did not want to be alone? Schachter examined this question by replicating the high-anxiety condition of his original experiment, complete with the shock equipment and Dr. Zilstein. He held anxiety at a high level, but manipulated the amount of information that could be gained by affiliating with others. He told half of the women that they could wait with other women who were about to receive shocks; these women were therefore *similar* to the participants. He told the others that they could join women who were waiting for advising by their professors; these women could only wait with people who were *dissimilar*. Schachter hypothesized that if the women believed that the others could not provide them with any social comparison information, there would be no reason to join them. The findings confirmed his analysis: 60% of the women asked to wait with others if they all faced a similar situation, but no one in the dissimilar condition wanted to affiliate. Schachter's second conclusion: "Misery doesn't love just any kind of company, it loves only miserable company" (Schachter, 1959, p. 24).

Schachter, by suggesting that people love "miserable company," meant they seek out those who face the same threat and so are knowledgeable. So how would people respond if offered the chance to wait with someone who had participated in the study the previous day? Such individuals would be ideal sources of clarifying information, for they not only faced the same situation—they had survived it. When given such an alternative, participants preferred to join someone who had already gone through the procedure (Kirkpatrick & Shaver, 1988). A similar preference for someone who had "been there, done that" has been documented in patients who are awaiting surgery. When given a choice, 60% of presurgery patients requested a roommate who was recovering from the same type of operation, whereas only 17% wanted "miserable company"—a roommate who was also about to undergo the operation (Kulik & Mahler, 1989). The patients also reported talking with their roommate about the operation more if their roommate had already had the operation and was

recovering (Kulik, Mahler, & Moore, 1996). These studies suggest that people are more interested in gaining clarifying information than in sharing the experience with someone, particularly when the situation is a dangerous one and they can converse openly with other group members (Kulik & Mahler, 2000).

Embarrassed Misery Avoids Company   Even when people need information about a situation, they sometimes refrain from joining others because they do not wish to embarrass themselves. When alone, people might feel foolish if they do something silly, but when they are in a group, foolishness turns into embarrassment. In some cases, this fear of embarrassment can be stronger than the need to understand what is happening, resulting in inhibition instead of affiliation.

Researchers examined this process by changing the Schachter-type situation to include the possibility of embarrassment. The investigators asked four to six strangers to meet in a room labeled with the sign "Sexual Attitudes: Please Wait Inside." In the *fear* condition, the room contained several electrical devices and information sheets that suggested the study involved electric shock and sexual stimulation. In the *ambiguous* condition, the participants found only two cardboard boxes filled with computer forms. In the *embarrassment* (anxiety-provoking) condition, the researchers replaced the equipment and boxes with contraceptive devices, books on sexually transmitted diseases, and pictures of naked men and women. Observers behind a two-way mirror watched the group for 20 minutes, recording the five types of behavior shown in Figure 4.3: *interaction* (talking about the situation), *action* (e.g., examining the equipment), *withdrawal* (e.g., reading a book), *controlled nonreaction* (e.g., talking about something other than the experiment), and *escape* (Morris et al., 1976).

The observers discovered that the group members engaged in social comparison the most when they were fearful. As Figure 4.3 indicates, groups who faced the ambiguous situation spent about 12% of the time talking among themselves, but groups sitting in a room with the fear-inducing

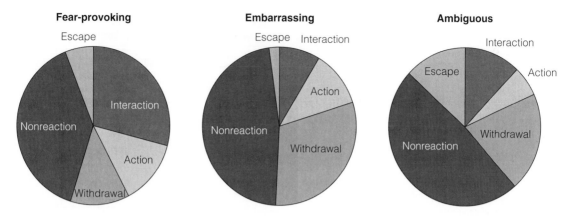

FIGURE 4.3 Five types of behavioral reactions—interaction, action, withdrawal, nonreaction, and escape—to three different kinds of situations: fear-provoking (fear), embarrassing, (embarrassment), and ambiguous. People who faced an ambiguous situation did not talk among themselves as much as people who were fearful. People who were embarrassed, in contrast, interacted the least, and they often withdrew from the group (Morris et al., 1976).

SOURCE: Morris et al., 1976.

electrical equipment spent nearly 30% of the time gathering information through communication. Groups who thought that the study involved sexual behavior did very little talking, and they showed more withdrawal. Embarrassment blocked affiliation in this situation, even though this situation was not a dangerous one. If the need for information or support becomes overwhelming, then embarrassment-related anxiety may not keep people away from their groups (Davison, Pennebaker, & Dickerson, 2000).

Stress and Affiliation

Schachter (1959) did not just confuse people, he frightened people. The women he studied affiliated with others to acquire clarifying information through social comparison, but they were probably also seeking reassurance. Two people, facing the prospect of receiving electric shocks, could analyze the situation, but also they could talk about their misgivings, calm each other down, and help one another should problems arise. Given a choice between people who are equal in their knowledge of the situation but vary in their emotional reaction to the threat—some are very fearful, but others are calm—people usually choose to wait with those who are calm rather than anxious

(Rabbie, 1963) and caring rather than unsupportive (Li et al., 2008).

Safety in Numbers Humans are group-seeking animals, but their gregariousness becomes particularly robust under conditions of stress (Rofé, 1984). In times of trouble, such as illness, divorce, catastrophe, natural disaster, or personal loss, people seek out friends and relatives (Bonanno et al., 2010). College students who are experiencing problems, academically or socially, spend between 28% and 35% of their time interacting with people they feel are supportive (Harlow & Cantor, 1995). Individuals experiencing work-related stress, such as the threat of layoffs, time pressures, or inadequate supervision, cope by joining with coworkers (Bowling et al., 2004; McGuire, 2007). Individuals, when they face a situation that may prove costly to them, join with others, particularly when the likelihood of loss is high rather than low (Suleiman, Aharonov-Majar, & Luzon, 2011). When reminded of their own mortality, they are more likely to sit closer to other people, even if these other individuals do not share their opinions on important social issues (Wisman & Koole, 2003).

People also react to large-scale traumatic events by joining with others. When U.S. President John F. Kennedy was assassinated, 60% of adult

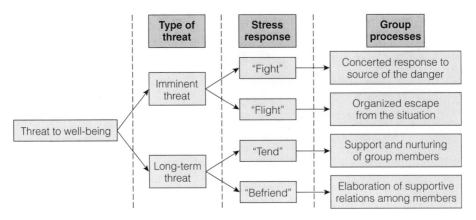

F I G U R E 4.4   Group-level responses to stress.
SOURCE: © Cengage Learning

Americans reported seeking solace by talking to others (Sheatsley & Feldman, 1964). In the days following the terrorist attacks on September 11, 2001, 98% of all adult Americans reported talking to others about the attacks, 60% reported taking part in a group activity, and 77% sought to strengthen their connection to their loved ones (Schuster et al., 2001). Many individuals joined online groups via the Internet. Internet usage declined overall as people watched televised news broadcasts, but discussion areas, forums, and chat room use surged, as did e-mail rates. Individuals who were already heavy users of the Internet tended to be the ones who used this technology to affiliate with others, whereas light users were more likely to rely on more traditional methods (Kim et al., 2004).

As Figure 4.4 suggests, affiliation with others plays a key role in both *fight-or-flight* and *tend-and-befriend* responses to stress (Taylor et al., 2000, see Chapter 3). When members face an imminent threat, they can work together to fight against it; they can rally against attackers, organize a concerted response to a disaster, and so on. Groups also enhance survival as members escape. If escape routes are not restricted, the dispersion of a group can confuse attackers and increase the chances that all members of the group will escape unharmed. A group can also organize its escape from danger, with stronger members of the group helping less able members to reach safety. If, in contrast, the group faces a long-term threat, then the group

may cope by increasing nurturing, protective, and supportive behaviors (*tending*) and by seeking out connections to other people (*befriending*).

Affiliation and Social Support   Monet initially sought to change the art world single-handedly, but he soon found that he needed help from others. When his work was condemned by the critics, he shared his feelings of rejection with the other artists, who offered him encouragement and advice. Frequently penniless, he sold his work to other artists so he could buy food and pay for his lodging. He could not afford his own studio, so Bazille and Renoir invited him to share one with them. When Monet injured his leg, Bazille cared for him. The group did not just provide him with cognitive clarity but with **social support**: comfort, caring, and companionship extended to those who are dealing with turbulence and trouble.

Table 4.4 lists a number of examples of the ways that groups provide support for their members, beginning with *inclusive support*: the group, by letting troubled members know that they are valued members, reassures them that they are not alone in facing their problems (Krause & Wulff,

social support A sense of inclusion, emotional support, advice, guidance, tangible assistance, and spiritual perspective given to others when they experience stress, daily hassles, and more significant life crises.

T A B L E 4.4   Some Forms of Social Support Provided by Groups

Type	Definition	Examples
Inclusive support	Confirming inclusion within the group	• Expressing acceptance • Reassurance of belonging • Reaffirming membership • Encouraging identification • Including in group activities
Emotional support	Expressing caring and concern for one another	• Expressing respect and approval • Providing encouragement • Listening • Sharing feelings • Responding nonverbally in positive ways (e.g., hugging, nodding)
Informational support	Providing advice and guidance	• Sharing helpful information • Giving directions, advice, suggestions • Demonstrating a way to perform a task • Problem solving
Instrumental support	Providing tangible resources	• Doing favors • Lending money or possessions • Assisting with work, duties • Transporting • Providing a place to stay
Spiritual support	Addressing issues of meaning and purpose	• Explaining challenging events • Allaying existential anxiety, fear of death • Sharing faith • Reconfirming one's worldview

2005). Group members provide *emotional support* when they express their caring and concern for one another, often by listening to others' problems without offering criticism or suggestions, encouraging them, and showing general approval (McGuire, 2007). *Informational support* pertains to advice and guidance, *instrumental support* provides members with tangible resources, and *spiritual support* helps members deal with existential dilemmas and threats to their worldview (see Uchino, 2004).

Admittedly, some groups fail to deliver on their promise of support. They may even add stressors by stirring up conflicts, increasing responsibilities, exposing members to criticism, or displaying their own anxieties about the situation (e.g., Newsom et al., 2008). Nor are all members equally adept at providing social support to others, or providing the type of support that the individual experiencing problems most needs. Some work suggests that the men in a group are quicker to provide instrumental support, such as tangible assistance or practical advice, whereas the women in the group provide more emotional support, such as expressions of concern and caring (Verhofstadt, Buysse, & Ickes, 2007). Some people, too, are just naturally better at doing the sorts of things that make other people feel supported. Only some of the individuals in one study reported that they knew how to make sure their friends felt cared for, by treating them with "respect and dignity," considering "her or his message to be valuable and significant," not forgetting "things that this person had told me", and "turning off the TV" so that they could talk without distractions (Hess, Fannin, & Pollom, 2007).

Affiliation and Health   Groups, although they can sometimes irritate their members as much as they support them, are usually a safe haven from the storm of stress. People who enjoy strong social bonds tend to experience less stress in their lives, are less likely to suffer from depression and other psychological problems, and are physically healthier (Stinson et al., 2008). Stressful life circumstances leave people at risk for psychological and physical illness, but groups can serve as protective buffers against these negative consequences. Researchers verified this *buffering effect* in studies of stressors, including health crises, personal tragedies, terrorist attacks, and intergroup conflict. For example, individuals trying to recover from a devastating crisis (e.g., the death of a spouse or child) who were more firmly embedded in a social network of friends, relatives, and neighbors were less depressed than people who were not integrated into groups (Norris & Murrell, 1990). Firefighters who felt they were supported by their peers and their supervisor reported less stress than those who did not feel as closely connected to their group members (Varvel et al., 2007). A survey of New York City residents following the September 11, 2001 terrorist attacks indicated that those who were members of groups or affiliative organizations (e.g., church groups, discussion groups, veterans groups) were more resilient to the stressful effects of the attacks (Bonanno et al., 2007). Participants who played the role of prisoners in a simulation of a prison (in England) provided one another with substantial social support, and, in consequence, they were relatively unaffected by situational stressors (Haslam & Reicher, 2006).

These salutary effects of affiliation occur because of the close connection between the biological systems that maintain and promote health and the quality of one's connection to other people. Just as isolation from others can cause disruptions in immune system functioning, affiliation and social support are associated with healthy changes in a body's immune, hormonal, and neurological systems. Depleted levels of the peptides oxytocin and vasopressin not only trigger an increased desire to affiliate, but these neurochemical control systems also damp down the body's tendency to overreact physiologically to irritating events. In consequence, genetic variants that influence the production of oxytocin and enhance its physiological effects

predict both reactions to stressful circumstances and the likelihood of responding positively to others who need help and support (Poulin, Holman, & Buffone, 2012). Affiliation-related experiences may also recruit areas of the brain that are part of the opioid and dopaminergic systems; these systems have been implicated in reward-based learning and positive emotional reactions, including happiness (Panksepp, Nelson, & Bekkedal, 1996). These social neuroscience studies all suggest that there is health, as well as safety, in numbers.

Social Comparison and the Self

Affiliation, and the social comparison processes it instigates, provide individuals with information about confusing circumstances as well as comfort and companionship in difficult times. But the impact of affiliation does not stop there. Individuals, by joining with others, gain information about their relative standing on skills, competencies, and outcomes; this information has a substantial impact on their self-satisfactions and motivations.

Directed Social Comparison Monet gained information about art and technique when he joined with the other impressionists. This information undoubtedly reduced his confusion, but this cognitive clarity may have come at a psychological cost. Renoir, like Monet, was experimenting with many new methods, but Renoir was prospering in terms of sales. Compared to Renoir, Monet was a failure. And how did Monet feel when he spoke to his friend Sisley? Sisley's work was never considered to be collectible; he lived on the brink of poverty for much of his life. When Monet compared himself to Sisley, he must have felt a sense of relief that his own situation was not so bleak, but at the same time, he must have worried that his own career could take a turn for the worst at any moment.

People compare themselves to others when they lack information about the situation they face, but they are not indiscriminate when selecting targets for comparison. When they want information, they select people who are similar to them or are likely to be particularly well-informed. But when self-esteem is on the line, people engage in **downward social comparison** by selecting targets who are worse off than they are (Wills, 1991). Monet, for example, by contrasting himself to the struggling Sisley, could think to himself, "Things are not going so well for me, but at least I'm better off than poor Sisley." Students reviewing their academic progress with other students, spouses discussing their relationships with other husbands and wives, patients talking with other patients about their success in coping with their illness, medical students taking part in a training class, expectant mothers talking about their pregnancies, and employees reviewing their coworkers' performance all show the tendency to seek out, for comparison purposes, people who are doing more poorly than they are (Buunk & Gibbons, 2007).

What if Monet had, instead, compared himself to the more prosperous Renoir? Such a comparison would be an example of **upward social comparison**, which occurs when people compare themselves to others who are better off than they are. Renoir may have been an inspiration to Monet—when he started to wonder if he would ever be a success, he could find reassurance in Renoir's accomplishments (Collins, 2000). Upward social comparison can also provoke a darker, but highly motivating emotion: envy (van de Ven, Zeelenberg, & Pieters, 2011). But upward social comparison usually leaves people feeling like failures. When students were asked to keep track of the people they compared themselves to over a two-week period, they reported feeling depressed and discouraged when they associated with more competent people (Wheeler & Miyake, 1992). Academically gifted students who attend selective schools are more unsure of their abilities and their intellectual worth than

equally bright students who attend schools with a wide range of student ability—the so-called *big-fish-little-pond effect* (Marsh et al., 2007). Even if people know they have performed better than average, if they compare themselves to someone who has far outperformed them, they feel discouraged (Seta, Seta, & McElroy, 2006). Upward social comparisons generally make people feel worse (Jordan et al., 2011).

Self-Evaluation Maintenance When will people choose upward comparison over downward comparison? Abraham Tesser's **self-evaluation maintenance (SEM) model** suggests that people often graciously celebrate others' accomplishments—but not when they are bested in a domain that they value greatly. In such cases, others' success will more likely trigger resentment, envy, and shame rather than pride and admiration (Smith, 2000). The SEM model, using Monet as an example, predicts he would prefer to join with people who (1) performed worse than he did at tasks that were important to him personally, but (2) performed very well on tasks that were not central to his sense of self-worth (Beach & Tesser, 2000; Tesser, 1988, 1991).

Tesser and his colleagues examined this tension between sharing others' successes and highlighting their failures by asking elementary school students to identify the types of activities (sports, art, music, math) that were personally important to them. The students also identified their most and least preferred classmate. One week later, the students rated their ability, their close classmate's ability, and their distant classmate's ability in one area they felt was important and one area they felt was

---

downward social comparison Selecting people who are less well off as targets for social comparison (rather than individuals who are similar or superior to oneself or one's outcomes).

upward social comparison Selecting people who are superior to oneself or whose outcomes surpass one's own as targets for social comparison.

---

self-evaluation maintenance (SEM) model A theoretical analysis of social comparison processes that assumes that individuals maintain and enhance their self-esteem by associating with high-achieving individuals who excel in areas that are not relevant to the individual's own sense of self-esteem and avoiding association with high-achieving individuals who excel in areas that are important to the individual's sense of self-esteem (developed by Abraham Tesser).

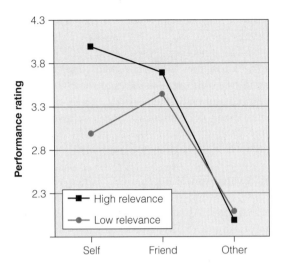

FIGURE 4.5 Ratings of oneself (self), a friend (friend), and some who is less well-liked (other) on tasks that are low and high in self-relevance. Students rated their own performance as superior to their friend's when the task was relevant, but this tendency reversed for the low-relevance task.

SOURCE: Tesser, A., Campbell, J., & Smith, M. (1984). Friendship choice and performance: Self-evaluation maintenance in children. *Journal of Personality and Social Psychology, 46,* 561–574.

unimportant. As Figure 4.5 indicates, if the students thought that the task was important, they judged their performance to be superior to that of their close friend. If the task was not important to them personally, they felt that they had performed relatively worse (Tesser, Campbell, & Smith, 1984). Similarly, in a study of married couples, Tesser and his colleagues discovered that happy couples felt that it was more pleasant to be outdone by one's partner in an area that their partner valued but to outperform the partner in an area that he or she did not value. Unhappy couples did not recognize this secret ingredient for marital bliss (Beach et al., 1998).

In sum, even though social comparison provides an indispensable social and cognitive service, it can also set in motion processes that destabilize rather than sustain the group and its members. Studies of newly formed teams suggest that members feel threatened by teammates who have superior abilities, even if they have had an opportunity to bond with their teammates before they start working together (Cleveland et al., 2011). Group members, to avoid the pain of social comparison, can turn against the highest performing members—the "tall poppies" of their group—ostracizing them or criticizing them unfairly (Feather, 1994). Given the negative consequences of outperforming others, people who perform well often keep their success to themselves—particularly when they do well on tasks that are very important to the other group members (Tal-Or, 2008). Group members may also, unfortunately, maintain their superiority over their friends and teammates by sabotaging, indirectly, others' performances on tasks that are central to their sense of self-worth. The students in one experience sampling study, recorded their interactions over a six-day period and indicated if the interaction involved academic matters or social matters, what their relationship to the person was (e.g., acquaintance, stranger, close friend), and if they shared information with that person that they thought would help the other to improve. These students gave helpful information to their friends when the interactions pertained to social matters, but when it came to academics, they helped their friends less than they helped strangers. This tendency was even more pronounced when the students thought that their friend was already performing better than they were (Pemberton & Sedikides, 2001). A similar finding was obtained when researchers studied recommendations. Individuals were willing to recommend a colleague for promotion who excelled in an area that was unrelated to their expertise, but not one who was proficient in an area where their own accomplishments had earned them high status (Garcia, Song, & Tesser, 2010).

ATTRACTION

Renoir and Bazille met, quite by happenstance, because both were students of Gleyre. Their desire to learn more about their craft and their enrollment in the same school combined to bring them together. But this chance meeting by itself was not sufficient to spark the formation of the group that would, in time, become the impressionists. Bazille and Renoir would not have chosen to spend more and more time together discussing art, politics, and Parisian society if they had disliked each other. Affiliation may set the stage for a group to form, but *attraction* transforms acquaintances into friends.

Principles of Attraction

Social psychologist Theodore Newcomb's classic study of the *acquaintance process* anticipated the methods used in many contemporary reality television programs. Those programs arrange for strangers to live together in a mansion, house, or apartment and then they just record the ebb and flow of likes and dislikes among the members. Similarly, Newcomb offered 17 young men starting their studies at the University of Michigan free rent if they answered a detailed survey of their attitudes, likes, and dislikes each week. Then he watched as the 17 students sorted themselves out into friendship pairs and distinct groups (Newcomb, 1960, 1961, 1979, 1981).

Even though attraction is often thought to be a highly capricious and unpredictable social process, Newcomb identified a small number of principles that explain when liking is more likely. As the sections that follow indicate, people are more likely to associate with certain people—those who are nearby, those who express similar attitudes and values, and those who respond positively to them. Such associations often culminate in the creation of a group (see Clark & LeMay, 2010, for a review).

The Proximity Principle People often assume that their groups result from rational planning or common interests, but the **proximity principle** suggests that people join groups that happen to be close by. Monet, Manet, Renoir, and many other

impressionists lived in the same neighborhood in Paris. Their paths crossed and crossed again, until eventually a group was formed. City dwellers who regularly assemble in the same physical location—commuters at subway stops, patrons at local bars, and frequent picnickers in parks—eventually gel into identifiable groups (see Gieryn, 2000). Newcomb (1960) assigned the participants roommates at random, but by the study's end, most roommates had become close friends. Teachers can create long-lasting cliques and friendships simply by assigning students to adjacent seats in their classrooms (Segal, 1974). In one study, researchers, on the first day of a psychology class in college, assigned the students to their seats at random. Students could sit anywhere in the room after that first day, but one year later the seat assignments still predicted who liked whom (Back, Schmukle, & Egloff, 2008). When people feel that their groups are cohesive or the bonds between members are particularly strong, they describe them as "close"—recognizing, if only implicitly, that propinquity implies intimacy.

Festinger and his colleagues tracked the emergence of networks of attraction in their study of Westgate and Westgate West, two housing developments filled, at random, with students and their families. These housing projects offered him an excellent opportunity to not only study group formation, but also the "relatively subtle influences which are exerted during the normal communication process among members of a group" (Festinger, Schachter, & Back, 1950, p. 7). Festinger discovered that the majority of best friends not only lived in the same building, they lived next door to one another; 41% of the next-door neighbors were identified as people "seen socially." The numbers then dropped with each increase in distance, so that only 22% of the neighbors two doors down were identified as members of the student's social group, 16% of those three doors down, and only 10% of those four doors away. The distances were relatively small ones, but proximity mattered.

People do not form groups with whomever is near them because they are shallow or indiscriminating. First, when people continually encounter other people because their offices, homes, desks,

---

proximity principle The tendency for individuals to form interpersonal relations with those who are close by; also known as the "principle of propinquity."

or rooms are located adjacent to theirs, familiarity increases. And, the *familiarity principle* (or "mere-exposure effect") suggests that people show a preference for the familiar rather than the unknown. Novel, unfamiliar stimuli provoke a wariness that is likely evolutionarily adaptive; the hunter-gatherer who remained cautious when encountering an unrecognized animal, plant, or human was more likely to emerge unscathed than one who risked a closer encounter (Bornstein, 1989).

Second, proximity increases interaction between people, and interaction cultivates attraction. As Festinger's study of Westgate revealed, people encountered some of their neighbors more frequently than others—those who lived close by and those whose apartments they passed by frequently. These were the neighbors who tended to form small groups within the apartment complex. Repeated interactions may foster a sense of groupness as the people come to think of themselves as a group and those outside the group begin to treat them as a group (Arkin & Burger, 1980). One investigator watched, for weeks, the interactions of 12 women who worked at separate desks organized in three rows. The work did not require that the individuals collaborate extensively with one another, but they frequently spoke to each other. Every 15 minutes, the observer would note who was interacting with whom and eventually recorded over 1,500 distinct conversations. The conversations took place primarily between neighbors or at least between the workers who were seated in the same row; these interactions accurately predicted the formation of smaller cliques within the larger group of women (Gullahorn, 1952).

As Focus 4.2 suggests, even when group members are communicating via computers, interaction tends to promote attraction. Exceptions, however, do sometimes occur, particularly when the interactions that proximity promotes yield negative rather than positive outcomes. When people were asked to name their friends, most identified people who lived close by and whom they interacted with very frequently. But when they named someone they disliked, they also tended to pick a near neighbor (Ebbesen, Kjos, & Konečni, 1976). If repeated exposure reveals that those nearby have contemptible qualities, then familiarity will breed contempt rather than contentment (Norton, Frost, & Ariely, 2007).

F o c u s   4.2   E-groups: Translating Proximity into Presence in Online Groups

Susan and Naomi read and reply to each other's status updates on Facebook regularly, even though Susan is in college in California and Naomi is working in New York City. D. K. and Mr. Tiger are arguing about nationalized health care, but their conversation is taking place in the commentary of a blog about politics and D. K. and Mr. Tiger live in different hemispheres. At the push of a button, Lady Gaga can send a message to 25 million people through the miracle of Twitter.

Distance does not apply to people who communicate using the Internet, but the proximity principle's key corollary—frequent interaction tends to promote group formation—does. Online groups, like offline groups, result when individuals find themselves repeatedly interacting with each other. It's just that these interactions do not occur in face-to-face encounters, but through instant messaging, in Facebook, via Twitter and Skype, on e-mail and so on.

Social networking sites are deliberately designed to facilitate social interaction by providing users with tools they can use to communicate with friends and acquaintances. Members of Facebook, for example, can share information about their likes, dislikes, and experiences in their profiles, post updates describing their current activities, communicate with friends publically (by posting on their timeline) and privately (through instant messaging and e-mail), and post pictures of themselves and friends. Studies of Facebook and other social networking sites suggest members use them to both establish new relationships and to maintain existing ones. College students, for example, use Facebook to solidify the emergent social groups and relationships that form when they first arrive on campus. They also use Facebook as a tool

Focus 4.2 (Continued)

for interacting with people they already know (e.g., family, classmates, old friends). Students who report using Facebook more intensively say that they feel more closely connected to other students on their campus and to their friends (Ellison, Steinfield, & Lampe, 2007).

Not all Internet sites are equally effective in promoting social interaction, however. Many areas of the Web that are designed to encourage interaction between people, such as discussion areas and the comment areas of blogs, are nearly empty of commentaries because people visit only once and never return. So when will individuals visit a second time? The best predictor of continuing engagement in the site is how they are treated during their very first visit. In one study, researchers examined the posts of 2,777 newcomers to one of six public discussion areas that dealt with various topics, including dieting, gun rights, and the NY Rangers hockey team. They discovered that 61% of the newcomers received a reply and that the reply increased the likelihood of the person returning to the site in the future by 21%. Getting an answer—interaction itself—was more important than the content of the response. It did not matter if the responder disagreed with the newcomer or if their comment was negative in its emotional tone (Joyce & Kraut, 2006).

These studies suggest that the Internet, by facilitating interaction between remotely located individuals, increases attraction and group formation, but since they make use of correlation designs, it is difficult to determine which came first. Did people who like each other make use of the Internet to interact with one another, or did their interactions on the Internet increase their attraction to one another? To determine the direction of this cause-effect relationship, social psychologist Harry T. Reis and his colleagues (2011) manipulated the frequency of interaction and then measured attraction. In one of their studies, they required same-sex pairs of college

students who were strangers to one another to use instant messaging (IM) to exchange messages in sessions lasting 15 minutes or more. They manipulated the number of IM chat sessions, requiring only one session for some, but two, four, six, or eight sessions for others. As Figure 4.6 indicates, pairs that IM-chatted more frequently liked each other more, and these effects were mediated by increases in knowledge of one another and perceived responsiveness (e.g., "sees the 'real' me," "understands me," "seems interested in what I am thinking and feeling"). These interactions were strictly anonymous ones, but at the end of the study, 62.5% of the dyads who had IM-chatted eight times wanted to know the name and contact information of their partner, but only 17.6% of those dyads who chatted but one time expressed interest in continuing the relationship. These investigators were thus justified in concluding that interaction causes attraction rather than attraction causing interaction—and it matters not if that interaction occurs online or in face-to-face settings.

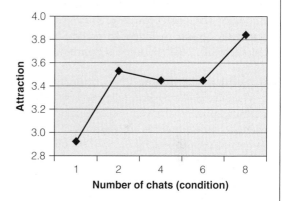

FIGURE 4.6 Attraction to one's partner as a function of the number of instant message chat sessions.

SOURCE: © Cengage Learning 2014

The Elaboration Principle Groups, as self-organizing, dynamic systems, tend to increase in complexity over time. A group that begins with only two members tends to grow in size as these individuals become linked to other nearby individuals. In systems theory, this process is termed elaboration (Parks, 2007) or percolation (Nagler, Levina, & Timme, 2011): "the basic dynamic of elaboration is the proliferation of elements and ties," which "are linked together to form a functional unit called a group" (Arrow et al., 2000, pp. 91–92).

Newcomb's groups, for example, conformed to this **elaboration principle**, for cliques usually evolved from smaller, dyadic pairings. The first friendships were two-person pairs—usually roommates or people living in adjoining rooms who became friends. Over time, these dyads expanded to include other individuals who were attracted to one or both of the original members. This same kind of self-organizing process has been documented in other emerging groups, such as adolescents' peer group associations, leisure groups, and social movements. Gangs, for example, form when three friends refer to themselves with a shared name and recruit other friends to join the group (Tobin, 2008). Friendships are very likely to form between students who were linked to the same individuals (Gibbons & Olk, 2003). Groups form when otherwise unrelated individuals are drawn to a single individual who becomes the hub for gradually developing bonds among the various members (Redl, 1942). The impressionists developed into a group through such a self-organizing process. Each member of the core group drew in others, until in time the group included artists, sculptors, and writers (Farrell, 2001, p. 44; see Figure 4.7).

The Similarity Principle   Newcomb found that the 17 men clustered naturally into two groups containing nine and seven members; one person remained at the fringe of both groups. The seven-man group was particularly unified, for when asked to indicate who they liked out of the total list of 17, they gave relatively high rankings to one another and not to those young men in the other cluster. The members of the other group did not show the same level of mutual attraction as the smaller clique.

When Newcomb (1963) examined these subgroups, he noticed that subgroup members' values, beliefs, and interests were similar. One clique, for example, contained men who endorsed liberal

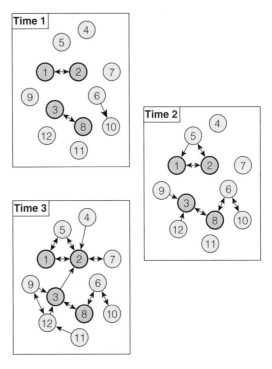

F I G U R E 4.7   The elaboration of groups over time. Groups that begin as simple two-person groups become more complex over time as individuals who are initially linked together only in one-to-one, dyadic relationships (e.g., persons 1 and 2, persons 3 and 8) expand their networks to include additional elements (members).

SOURCE: © Cengage Learning

political and religious attitudes, were all registered in the arts college, came from the same part of the country, and shared similar aesthetic, social, theoretical, economic, political, and religious values. The members of the second subgroup were all veterans, were majors in engineering, and shared similar religious, economic, and political values. Newcomb had found strong evidence for the **similarity principle**: People are attracted to those who are similar to them in some way.

---

elaboration principle   The tendency for groups to expand in size as nonmembers become linked to a group member and thus become part of the group itself; this process is termed *percolation* in network theory.

similarity principle   The tendency for individuals to seek out, affiliate with, or be attracted to an individual who is similar to them in some way; this tendency causes groups and other interpersonal aggregates to be homogenous rather than diverse.

Similarity is a social magnet that creates all kinds of relationships. People tend to marry people who are similar to them; they join groups composed of others who are like them; and they live in communities where people are more alike than different. Although these similarities often reflect agreements in attitudes, values, and beliefs, they are also based on demographic characteristics, such as race, ethnicity, sex, and age (Lazarsfeld & Merton, 1954). As a result, **homophily**—similarity of the members of a group in attitudes, values, demographic characteristics, and so on—is common in groups. The cliques that form in large volunteer organizations tie together people who are similar in some way rather than dissimilar (Feld, 1982). If a group decreases in size, the first individual who is dropped from membership will likely be the one who is the least similar to the other members; ties between similar people are maintained, but ties with dissimilar people dissolve. "Birds of a feather flock together" describes most groups (McPherson, Smith-Lovin, & Cook, 2001).

Homophily appears to be sustained by a number of psychological, sociological, and relational factors that combine to promote contacts between people who share similarities rather than differences. People who adopt the same values and attitudes reassure each other that their beliefs are accurate, and people find association with such people very rewarding (Byrne, 1971). People may also assume, with some justification, that future group interactions will be more cooperative and conflict-free when members are all similar to one another (Insko & Schopler, 1972). Similarity's opposite, dissimilarity, also works to push people away from each other—the dissimilarity-repulsion effect is as influential as the similarity-attraction effect (Drigotas, 1993). Similarity may also increase a sense of connectedness to the other person (Arkin & Burger, 1980). Two

strangers chatting casually on an airplane, for example, feel united if they find that they share even the most trivial similarity, such as the same middle name or favorite television program (Jones et al., 2004). Disliking a person who seems similar may also be psychologically distressing. After all, if a person is similar to us, it follows logically that he or she must be attractive (Festinger, 1957).

Homophily also tends to beget homophily. Because communities, schools, and most workplaces bring people together who are similar in terms of race, attitudes, religion, and ethnicity, people's options for relationships are limited to those who are already similar to them in these ways (McPherson et al., 2001). Also, even when individuals have the opportunity to form relationships with people who are different from them in some way, they nonetheless gravitate toward those who are similar. Researchers demonstrated this tendency by interviewing pairs of students who were attending classes at a large university (25,000 students) or one of several smaller colleges located nearby. Even though the smaller campuses constrained individuals' friendship choices—they offered fewer people to join with—the pairs on the smaller campus were significantly more heterogeneous in their attitudes than the pairs on the larger campus. Ironically, students often choose to attend larger universities because such an environment will offer them more opportunities to make friends with a wider variety of people, but, once on campus, people who are similar in terms of attitudes and values find each other and form stable networks of association. As a result of this natural assortive process, the groups that form in an environment where diversity was greatest tended to be more homogenous (Bahns, Pickett, & Crandall, 2012).

The Complementarity Principle The similarity principle exerts a powerful influence on groups, but in some cases opposites attract. If people's qualities complement each other—they are dissimilar but they fit well together—then this unique form of dissimilarity may encourage people to associate with one another. Claude, for example, may enjoy leading groups, so he is not attracted to other individuals

---

homophily "Love of the same"; the tendency for the members of groups and other collectives to be similar to one another in some way, such as demographic background, attitudes, and values; generally expressed informally as "birds of a feather flock together."

who also strive to take control of the group. Instead, he responds best to those who accept his guidance (Tiedens, Unzueta, & Young, 2007). Similarly, individuals who are forming a group may realize that the members' skills and abilities must complement each other if the group is to be successful (Kristof-Brown, Barrick, & Stevens, 2005). These cases are consistent with the **complementarity principle**, which suggests that people are attracted to those who possess characteristics that complement their own personal characteristics (Miller, 2012).

In all likelihood, group members respond positively to both similarity and complementarity (Dryer & Horowitz, 1997). People who consider themselves to be warm and friendly seek out others who are sociable and positive; those who are cold and critical are more comfortable in the company of those who are cantankerous and negative. However, people generally respond to dominant behaviors by acting submissively and vice versa; so leaders seek out followers, and the strong seek out the weak (e.g., Tracey, Ryan, & Jaschik-Herman, 2001).

Schutz (1958), in his FIRO theory of groups discussed earlier in this chapter, suggested that compatibility can be based on both similarity and on complementarity. **Interchange compatibility** exists when group members have similar expectations about the group's intimacy, control, and inclusiveness. Interchange compatibility will be high, for example, if all the members expect that their group will be formally organized with minimal expressions of intimacy, but it will be low if some think that they can share their innermost feelings whereas others want a more reserved exchange (John et al, 2010). **Originator compatibility** exists when people have dissimilar, but complementary, needs with regard to expressing and receiving control, inclusion, and affection. For example, originator compatibility

would be high if a person with a high need to control the group joined a group whose members wanted a strong leader.

Schutz tested his theory by constructing groups of varying compatibilities. He created originator compatibility by placing in each group one member with a high need for control, one member with a high need for inclusion, and three members with lower needs for control and inclusion. Moreover, interchange compatibility was established by grouping people with similar needs for affection. All the groups in this set were compatible, but levels of affection were high in half of the groups and low in the other half. A set of incompatible groups was also created by including group members who varied significantly in their need for affection, ranging from high to low. As Schutz predicted, (1) cohesiveness was higher in the compatible groups than in the incompatible groups, and (2) the compatible groups worked on problems far more efficiently than the incompatible groups. He found similar results in studies of groups that formed spontaneously, such as street gangs and friendship circles in fraternities (Schutz, 1958).

The Reciprocity Principle When Groucho Marx joked, "I don't want to belong to any club that will accept me as a member," he was denying the power of the **reciprocity principle**—that liking tends to be mutual. When we discover that someone else accepts and approves of us—they give friendly advice, compliment us, or declare their admiration for us—we usually respond by liking them in return. Newcomb (1979) found strong evidence of the reciprocity principle, as did other investigators in a range of different situations (e.g.,

---

complementarity principle A tendency for opposites to attract when the ways in which people are dissimilar are congruent (complementary) in some way.
interchange compatibility Compatibility between group members based on their similar needs for inclusion, control, and affection (defined by William Schutz).

originator compatibility Compatibility between group members that occurs when individuals who wish to express inclusion, control, or affection within the group are matched with individuals who wish to receive inclusion, control, or affection from others (defined by William Schutz).
reciprocity principle The tendency for liking to be met with liking in return; when A likes B, then B will tend to like A.

Kandel, 1978). Some group members, like Groucho Marx, may not like to be liked, but these exceptions to the reciprocity principle are relatively rare. When Person A expresses liking for Person B, it implies that Person A will treat Person B with respect, compassion, and benevolence on future occasions so Person B usually responds favorably by expressing liking for Person A (Montoya & Insko, 2008).

Negative reciprocity also occurs in groups, for disliking someone is a sure way to earn that person's contempt. In one study, college students discussed controversial issues in groups. Unknown to the true participants in the experiment, two of the three group members were confederates of the experimenter, who either accepted or rejected the comments of the participant. During a break between the discussion and the completion of a measure of attraction to the group, the rejecting confederates excluded the participant from their discussion by talking among themselves and giving the participant an occasional dirty look. Naturally, participants were less attracted to their comembers if they had been rejected by them. The rejection also served to lower participants' opinions of themselves (Pepitone & Wilpinski, 1960).

The Minimax Principle Social exchange theory offers one final, and particularly important, principle for predicting group formation. This theory, as noted in Chapter 2, assumes that people are rational creatures who strive to minimize their troubles, their worries, and their losses and instead maximize their positive outcomes, their happiness, and their rewards. Like shoppers searching for a bargain, they are drawn to groups that impose few costs yet offer them the greatest rewards. If a group seems to be a costly one—it will demand much time or will require members to do things that they would rather avoid if possible—then the value of the group will drop and people will be less likely to join. But, if the group offers considerable rewards to its members, such as prestige, desired resources, or pleasant experiences, then they will seek it out. These two basic requirements, taken together, provide the basis for social exchange theory's

minimax principle: People will join groups and remain in groups that provide them with the maximum number of valued rewards while incurring the minimum number of possible costs (Blau, 1964; Homans, 1961; Thibaut & Kelley, 1959).

What kinds of rewards do people seek, and what costs do they hope to avoid? When researchers asked prospective group members to identify the rewards and costs they felt a group might create for them, 40% mentioned such social and personal rewards as meeting people, making new friends, developing new interests, or enhancing their self-esteem. They also mentioned such rewards as learning new skills, increased opportunities for networking, and fun. These prospective members also anticipated costs, however. More than 30% expected to lose time and money by joining a group. Other frequently mentioned costs were social pressures, possible injury or illness, and excessive demands made by the group for their time. Nonetheless, the prospective members in this study optimistically felt that the groups they were considering would offer them far more rewards than costs (Brinthaupt, Moreland, & Levine, 1991; Moreland, Levine, Cini, 1993).

The group members themselves are also an important source of rewards and costs. People are usually attracted to groups whose members possess positively valued qualities and avoid groups of people with objectionable characteristics. People prefer to associate with people who are generous, enthusiastic, punctual, dependable, helpful, strong, truthful, and intelligent (Clark & Lemay, 2010). People tend to dislike and reject as potential group members those individuals who possess socially unattractive personal qualities—people who seem pushy, rude, self-centered, boring, or negative (Kowalski, 1996; Leary et al., 1986). Many of the impressionists, for example, considered having to interact with Degas a major cost of membership. In a letter to

---

minimax principle A general preference for relationships and memberships that provide the maximum number of valued rewards and incur the fewest number of possible costs.

Camille Pissarro, Gustave Caillebotte wrote, "Degas introduced disunity into our midst. It is unfortunate for him that he has such an unsatisfactory character. He spends his time haranguing at the Nouvelle-Athènes or in society. He would do much better to paint a little more" (quoted in Denvir, 1993, p. 181).

The Economics of Membership

Why did such artists as Manet, Pissarro, and Bazille join with Monet to create an artists circle? As we have seen, the group offered its members a number of advantages over remaining alone. By joining Monet, the impressionists gained a sounding board for ideas, social support, help with tasks they could not accomplish alone, and friends. But the group also created costs for members, who had to spend time and personal resources before they could enjoy the benefits the group offered. The minimax principle argues that those who joined the group must have felt that the benefits outweighed the costs (Saavedra & Van Dyne, 1999).

In many cases, people have many options and several may offer a favorable ratio of rewards to costs. How do people choose among the many groups that promise them a favorable reward/cost ratio? According to social exchange theorists John Thibaut and Howard Kelley (1959), the decision to join is based on two factors: the *comparison level* and the *comparison level for alternatives*. **Comparison level (CL)** is the standard by which individuals evaluate the desirability of group membership. The CL derives from the average of all outcomes known to the individual and is usually strongly influenced by previous relationships. If, for example, Degas's prior group memberships yielded very positive rewards with very few costs, his CL should be higher than that of someone who has experienced fewer

rewards and more costs through group membership. According to Thibaut and Kelley (1959, p. 21), groups that "fall above CL would be relatively 'satisfying' and attractive to the member; those entailing outcomes that fall below CL would be relatively 'unsatisfying' and unattractive."

Comparison level, however, only predicts when people will be *satisfied* with membership in a group. If we want to predict whether people will join groups or leave them, we must also take into account the value of other, alternative groups. What if Degas could have joined several artists circles, all of which surpassed his CL? Which one would he then select? According to Thibaut and Kelley (1959), the group with the best reward/cost balance will determine Degas' **comparison level for alternatives (CL$_{alt}$)**. Thibaut and Kelley argued that "CL$_{alt}$ can be defined informally as the lowest level of outcomes a member will accept in the light of available alternative opportunities" (1959, p. 21).

Entering and exiting groups is largely determined by CL$_{alt}$, whereas satisfaction with membership is determined by CL (see Table 4.5). For example, why did Degas initially join the impressionists, but eventually leave the group? According to Thibaut and Kelley, Degas intuitively calculated the positive and negative outcomes that resulted from membership in the group. This index, at least at first, favored the impressionists. If Degas believed that joining the group would surpass his comparison level (CL), then he would likely be satisfied with membership. But over time, the demands of the group became too great and the rewards too small, the group's value dropped below his CL, and he became dissatisfied. If the group's value dropped below Degas's intuitive estimations of the value of other groups (his CL$_{alt}$), then he would likely leave the impressionists and join another, more promising group. He would also be more likely to exit the group if he did not feel committed to it, with

comparison level (CL) In social exchange theory, the standard by which the individual evaluates the quality of any social relationship. In most cases, individuals whose prior relationships yielded positive rewards with few costs will have higher CLs than those who experienced fewer rewards and more costs in prior relationships (described by John Thibaut and Harold Kelly).

comparison level for alternatives (CL$_{alt}$) In social exchange theory, the standard by which individuals evaluate the quality of other groups that they may join (described by John Thibaut and Harold Kelly).

T A B L E   4.5   The Impact of Comparison Level (CL) and Comparison Level for Alternatives (CL$_{alt}$) on Satisfaction with Group Membership and the Decision to Join a Group

		Membership in the group is	
		Above CL	**Below CL**
Membership in the group is	**Above CL$_{alt}$**	Membership is satisfying, will join group	Membership is dissatisfying, but will join group
	Below CL$_{alt}$	Membership is satisfying, but will not join group	Membership is dissatisfying and will not join group

SOURCE: Adapted from Thibaut, J. W., & Kelley, H. H. (1959). *The social psychology of groups*. New York: Wiley.

commitment determined by the resources he had invested in it previously. In Degas' case, the alternative of remaining alone established the lower level of his CL$_{alt}$, and he did not feel sufficiently invested in the group to remain a member (Rusbult, Agnew, & Arriaga, 2012).

The rest of the impressionists, however, remained friends. They often exhibited their works individually and spent months in isolation, but they still provided each other with help as necessary. Indeed, for many years, they met regularly at the Café Riche, where they would discuss art, politics, and literature. In time, they reached their goal of fame and fortune. By the turn of the century, most were invited, at last, to present in traditional shows, and collectors paid handsome prices for their work. As individuals, they came to Paris to learn to paint, but as a group they changed the world's definition of fine art.

CHAPTER REVIEW

Who joins groups?

1. The impressionists were members of an *artists circle* that formed in Paris in the 1860s as a result of three basic sets of influences: personal qualities of the members, the nature of the situation, and their liking for one another.

2. People differ in *personality*, motivations, past experiences, and expectations, and these individual differences influence their degree of interest in joining groups.

   - The Five Factor Model (FFM) of personality identifies five key traits that structure and sustain enduring consistencies in outlook, action, and disposition: extraversion, agreeableness, conscientiousness, neuroticism, and openness.

   - *Extraversion* and *agreeableness* predict general sociability. Extraverts tend to be happier than introverts.

   - Other traits, such as openness, influence the type of group individuals seek to join.

3. Sex differences in group engagement are relatively minor.

   - Women tend to be higher than men in *relationality*.

   - Women seek membership in smaller, informal, intimate groups, whereas men seek membership in larger, more formal, task-focused groups.

   - These differences are likely due, in part, to sex roles and sexism.

4. The strength of social motives, such as the *need for affiliation*, the *need for intimacy*, and the *need for power* also predict one's group-joining proclivities, as demonstrated by:

   - Byrne's studies of the relationship between need for affiliation and rejection sensitivity.

- *Experience sampling* studies of the affiliative tendencies of individuals who are high in the need for intimacy.

- Schutz's work on his *Fundamental Interpersonal Relations Orientation (FIRO)* theory that explains how people use groups to satisfy their need to receive and express inclusion, control, and affection.

5. Individuals who are socially inhibited, shy, and anxious are less likely to join groups.

  - *Shyness* predicts relatively mild nervousness about group situations, but the social meaning of such behaviors are culturally determined. Behaviors that are considered socially problematic in Western countries are viewed more favorably in Asian cultures.

  - Individuals who experience *social anxiety* feel threatened in group settings. When extreme, unreasonable, and debilitating, this reaction can be considered a personality disorder (*social anxiety disorder*).

  - Smith's analysis of group-level *attachment style* (i.e., secure, preoccupied, fearful, and dismissing) indicates that one's anxiety and avoidance pertaining to relationships influence orientation toward groups.

6. People's attitudes, experiences, and expectations are all factors that influence their decision to join a group.

  - Karau and Moneim's *Beliefs about Groups* inventory assesses individuals' general orientation toward working in a group.

  - Moreland and Levine discovered that individuals who had prior positive experiences in groups tended to seek out further group memberships.

  - Two key factors that influence participation in a *social movement* are sense of injustice and angry emotions.

When do people seek out others?

1. Festinger's theory of *social comparison* assumes that *affiliation* is more likely when individuals find themselves in ambiguous, frightening, and difficult circumstances.

2. Schachter, when putting people into a threatening situation, found that they affiliated with others rather than remain alone ("misery loves company").

  - People prefer to affiliate with individuals who likely have useful information about a situation and others who are in a similar situation ("misery loves miserable company").

  - When people worry that they will be embarrassed when they join a group, they usually do not affiliate with others ("embarrassed misery avoids company").

3. Groups provide their members with *social support* during times of stress and tension.

  - Groups facilitate both "fight-or-flight" and "tend-and-befriend" responses to stress.

  - Basic types of support from groups include inclusion and emotional, informational, instrumental, and spiritual support.

  - Group support buffers the negative health consequences of stress, possibly by triggering improved autoimmune and reward system functioning.

4. By choosing comparison targets who are performing poorly compared to themselves (*downward social comparison*), individuals bolster their own sense of competence; by choosing superior targets (*upward social comparison*), individuals refine their expectations of themselves.

  - As the big-fish-little-pond effect suggests, upward social comparison generally lowers self-esteem. Other negative effects include sabotaging other's performances.

- Tesser's *self-evaluation maintenance* (SEM) model argues that people prefer to associate with individuals who do not outperform them in areas that are very relevant to their self-esteem.

What processes generate bonds of interpersonal attraction between members of groups?

1. Newcomb, in his studies of the acquaintance process, found that people who like one another often join together to form groups. Attraction patterns are generally consistent with the following principles:

    - *Proximity principle:* People tend to like those who are situated nearby, in part because it increases familiarity and interaction. Although members of e-groups are not near each other physically, Reis's work and others indicate groups form in online contexts that encourage frequent interaction.

    - *Elaboration principle:* From a systems perspective, groups often emerge when additional elements (people) become linked to the original members.

    - *Similarity principle:* People like others who are similar to them in some way. In consequence, most groups tend toward increasing levels of *homophily*.

    - *Complementarity principle:* People like others whose qualities complement their own qualities. Schutz identified two key forms of compatibility: *interchange compatibility* (based on similarity) and *originator compatibility* (based on complementarity).

    - *Reciprocity principle:* Liking tends to be mutual.

    - *Minimax principle:* Individuals are attracted to groups that offer them maximum rewards and minimal costs.

2. Thibaut and Kelley's social exchange theory maintains that satisfaction with group membership is primarily determined by *comparison level* (CL), whereas the *comparison level for alternatives* (CL_{alt}) determines whether members will join, stay in, or leave a group.

RESOURCES

Chapter Case: The Impressionists

- *Collaborative Circles* by Michael P. Farrell (2001) provides a richly detailed analysis of the impressionists and a number of other influential groups and offers a stage theory that describes how these highly creative groups develop over time.

- *The Chronicle of Impressionism* by B. Denvir (1993) provides the timeline for the development of the impressionists and includes reproductions of both their art and their personal correspondence.

Affiliation

- *Handbook of Social Comparison: Theory and Research*, edited by Jerry Suls and Ladd Wheeler (2000), includes chapters on virtually all aspects of social comparison processes.

- *Is There Anything Good about Men?* by Roy F. Baumeister (2010) is an engaging analysis of sex differences in social behavior that argues that men and women tend to display different, but complementary, approaches to group settings.

- "Social comparison: The end of a theory and the emergence of a field" by Abraham P. Buunk and Frederick X. Gibbons (2007) is a masterful review of the voluminous literature dealing with comparison processes.

- *The Tending Instinct* by Shelley E. Taylor (2002) discusses the scientific support for and implications of her tend-and-befriend theory of sex differences.

Attraction

- "The formation of small groups" by Richard L. Moreland (1987) provides an overall framework for understanding group formation by describing four ways individuals become integrated into a group: environmental integration, behavioral integration, affective integration, and cognitive integration.

- *Intimate Relationships*, by Rowland S. Miller (2012), surveys the copious research and theory examining the causes of attraction and intimacy in relationships.

Cohesion and Development

CHAPTER OVERVIEW

A group is not just a set of individuals, but a cohesive whole that joins the members in interlocking interdependencies. This solidarity or unity is called *group cohesion* and is a necessary, if not sufficient, condition for a group to exist. A group may begin as a collection of strangers, but, as uncertainty gives way to increasing unity, the members become bound to their group and its goals. As cohesion and commitment ebb and flow with time, the group's influence over its members rises and falls.

- What is group cohesion, and what are its sources?

- How does cohesion develop over time?

- What are the positive and negative consequences of cohesion?

- Do initiations increase cohesion?

CHAPTER OUTLINE

The Nature of Cohesion
> *Sources of Cohesion*
> *Social Cohesion*
> *Task Cohesion*
> *Collective Cohesion*
> *Emotional Cohesion*
> *Structural Cohesion*
> *Assumptions and Assessments*

Developing Cohesion
> *Theories of Group Development*
> *Five Stages of Development*
> *Cycles of Development*

Consequences of Cohesion
> *Member Satisfaction and Adjustment*
> *Group Dynamics and Influence*
> *Group Productivity*

Application: Explaining Initiations
> *Group Cohesion and Initiations*
> *Hazing*
> *Chapter Review*
> *Resources*

The U.S. Olympic Hockey Team: Miracle Makers

They were underdogs, and they knew it. Their team's mission: To represent their country, the United States, in the 1980 Winter Olympics hockey competition held in Lake Placid, New York. Their goal: To win a medal, preferably a gold one. Their task: To defeat teams from such hockey-rich countries as Sweden and Germany. Their major obstacle: The powerful U.S.S.R. National Championship Team. At a time when Olympic athletes were amateurs, the Russian players were practically professional players. They were members of the Russian army, and they were paid to practice and play their sport. The Russian team had dominated hockey for many years and was poised to take its fifth consecutive gold medal in the sport. In an exhibition game played on February 9, just a few days before the start of the Olympic Games, Russia soundly defeated the U.S. Olympic team 10 to 3.

But strange things can happen when groups compete against groups. The U.S. team made its way through the preliminary rounds and faced the Russian team in the medal round. The U.S. team fell behind by two goals, and it looked as though the Russians would take the victory with ease. But the Americans struggled on, finally taking the lead with eight minutes left to play. During the game's last minutes, the Russians launched shot after shot, but all the while the U.S. coach, Herb Brooks, calmed his players by telling them "Play your game!" As the game's end neared, the announcer counted down the seconds into his microphone before asking his listeners, "Do you believe in miracles?" What else could explain the game's outcome? The U.S. Olympic team, expected to win a game or two at most in the entire series, had just beaten an unbeatable team.

The U.S. team was inferior to the Russian team in nearly all respects. The Americans were mostly college students or recent graduates. They were smaller, slower, and far less experienced. The team had practiced diligently for months before the tournament, but the Soviet's had been playing as a team for years. But for all their relative weaknesses, they were stronger than the Russian team in one key way: They were more cohesive. They were unified by friendship, a sense of purpose, and esprit de corps. No one player took credit for the victory, but instead spoke only of "we," repeating "we beat those guys" over and over as the bewildered Russian team looked on. As a writer for the magazine *Sports Illustrated* explained (Swift, 1980, p. 32):

> Individually, they were fine, dedicated sportsmen…. But collectively, they were a transcendent lot. For seven months they pushed each other on and pulled each other along, from rung to rung, until for two weeks in February they—a bunch of unheralded amateurs—became the best hockey team in the world. The best team. The whole was greater than the sum of its parts by a mile.

Groups like the U.S. Olympic hockey team are both fascinating and alluring. They are fascinating because their unity is often unexpected and without obvious source. For every group that never quite jells is a group of the unlikeliest of allies that becomes so interlocked that the members fit together like pieces of a jigsaw puzzle. Do they owe their cohesiveness to some unseen "social chemistry" that transforms the members into a team, leaving us to wonder why so many of the groups we belong to lack this mysterious unity? Cohesive groups are also alluring, for they seem to offer their members advantages that no humdrum, uninvolving group can.

But what is group cohesion, after all? Did the U.S. team have this unique quality, and did the Russian team lack it? Why do some groups, as they develop over time, become increasingly cohesive, whereas others' interactions remain forced and uncoordinated? And is cohesiveness such a valuable commodity that it can offset inadequate training and skills and thereby turn a mediocre group into a great group? Is cohesiveness so wondrous that we should strive to make all our groups cohesive ones? This chapter considers the mysteries of cohesiveness by specifying its nature, development over time, and consequences.

THE NATURE OF COHESION

Group cohesion can lay claim to being group dynamics' most theoretically important concept. Uniquely group-level, cohesion comes about if, and only if, a group exists. Cohesiveness signals, if only indirectly, the health of the group. A cohesive group will be more likely to prosper over time, since it retains its members and allows them to reach goals that would elude a more incoherent aggregate. The group that lacks cohesion is at risk, for it may break into subgroups at the first sign of conflict, lose members faster than it can replace them, and fail to reach its agreed upon goals. The concept of group cohesion provides insight into a host of core processes that occur in groups, including productivity, members' satisfaction and turnover, morale, formation, stability, influence, and conflict.

Given the importance of the concept, researchers and theorists have been remarkably diligent in their efforts to better understand why some groups are cohesive and some are not. This section reviews the results of that work, with a focus on three interrelated questions: What is group cohesion? What factors combine to transform an ordinary group into a cohesive one? And how can cohesion be measured?

Sources of Cohesion

The U.S. Olympic team that faced the Russians on that February day in Lake Placid had many noteworthy qualities. The players were handpicked to represent their country, and they had trained diligently for months leading up to the game. They were each one highly skilled, for the majority went on to professional careers in hockey after the Olympics. The team's coach was known for his hard-driving style of leadership, and each player could tell more than one story about the indignities visited upon them by the coach in his dogged pursuit of excellence. But most of all, they were cohesive, and many believed that the team's cohesiveness was the deciding factor in their victory.

The Latin word *haesus* means to cling to; it is the basis of such words as *adhesive*, *inherit*, and, of course, *cohesive*. In physics, when matter is cohesive, the particles that constitute it bond together so tightly that they resist any competing attractions. But when matter is not cohesive, it tends to disintegrate over time as the particles drift away or adhere

to some other nearby object. Something that is cohesive, such as a molecule or compound, forms a single, unified entity that may not appear to have any parts at all, as the various components are unified in a single whole. Similarly, in human groups, cohesion is the integrity, solidarity, and unity of the group. The members of a cohesive group "stick together"; they are fused to form a whole. Members and nonmembers alike consider the group to be high in *entitativity*: those who encounter the group will be convinced that it is a unified, tightly bonded group rather than a loose aggregation of individuals (see Chapter 1).

Cohesive groups are unified groups, but their unity is often the result of different causes and process. Consider, for example, an executive board of a company that is productive and enduring, yet the members never associate with one another after work. In fact, most dislike one another. In contrast, another group may be completely unproductive (most of the groups who star in popular television series—*Friends*, *Big Bang Theory*, *Seinfeld*—fit this category), but the members are so closely interconnected emotionally that they can move from one problematic experience to another without a loss of synchrony. These two groups may be equally cohesive—they are both unified groups—but their cohesiveness is the result of very different group processes. The idea that no one condition or process is a necessary or sufficient condition for a group to become cohesive is consistent with systems theory's principle of **equifinality**: "a system can reach the same final state, from different initial conditions and by a variety of different paths" (Katz & Kahn, 1978, p. 30). What unifies the members of one group may not unify the members of another (Friedkin, 2004).

Increases in cohesiveness, however, are not entirely unpredictable. In many cases, cohesion results from attraction bonds that join members together. For other groups, it is the shared pursuit of group goals—the task the group undertakes—that promotes

---

equifinality In an open system, the potential to reach a given end state through any one of a number of means (identified by Ludwig von Bertalanffy).

cohesion. In others, shared identity, emotions, and the group's structure may be the glue that holds the group together. Recognizing that our review cannot be comprehensive, the following sections examine several different types of cohesive groups. These types correspond to five overlapping, but influential, sources of a group's unity, including attraction relations, task relations, identity, emotions, and structure.

Social Cohesion

The members of the U.S. Olympic team did not gather, as a group, just to play hockey. They lived, traveled, and partied together because their training regimen demanded it, but also because they liked each other. **Social cohesion** is unity based on attraction: "the number and strength of mutual positive attitudes among the members of a group" (Lott & Lott, 1965, p. 259).

Interpersonal Attraction Social psychologists Kurt Lewin, Leon Festinger, and their colleagues conducted some of the earliest studies of group cohesion. As early as 1943, Lewin used the term cohesion to describe the forces that keep groups intact by pushing members together as well as the countering forces that push them apart. Festinger and his colleagues also stressed social forces that bind individuals to groups, for in their studies they defined group cohesion as "the total field of forces which act on members to remain in the group" (Festinger, Schachter, & Back, 1950, p. 164). But when they measured cohesion in their studies of naturally forming groups, they focused on one force more than all others: attraction. They asked the members to identify all their good friends and calculated the ratio of ingroup choices to outgroup choices. The greater the ratio, the greater was the cohesiveness of the group (see, too, McPherson & Smith-Lovin, 2002).

Attraction between individuals is a basic ingredient for most groups (see Chapter 4), but when these relations intensify and proliferate throughout a group, they can transform a conjoined group into a cohesive one. Social psychologists Muzafer and Carolyn Sherif documented this process in a series of unique field studies conducted in 1949, 1953, and 1954. During the summers of those years, the Sherifs ran a camp for 11-and 12-year-old boys that was, for the most part, just a typical summer camp experience—with canoeing, campfires, crafts, hikes, and athletics. But, unbeknownst to the campers, the Sherifs also recorded the behavior of the boys as they reacted to one another and to situations introduced by the investigators. In the 1949 study, conducted in a remote location in northern Connecticut, the 24 campers all bunked in one cabin for three days. During this period, friendships developed quickly based on proximity of bunks, similarities in interests, and maturity. The Sherifs then intervened and broke the large group into two smaller ones that adopted the names Bulldogs and Red Devils. In creating these groups, they deliberately split up any friendship pairs that had formed by assigning one best friend to the Bulldogs and the other to the Red Devils. They equated the members with respect to "size, strength, ability in games, intelligence, and ratings on personality tests" (Sherif & Sherif, 1956, p. 197).

Even under these conditions—with the factors that produced attraction between the boys minimized—new attractions formed quickly and resulted in high levels of cohesion within both groups. The Sherifs made certain that the boys' first few days in their new groups were spent in a variety of positive experiences (hiking, cookouts, games), and before long, the boys, when asked to name their friends, chose members of their new groups rather than the boys they had liked when camp first began. When first split up, 65% of the boys picked as friends those in the other group. But when the groups became cohesive, fewer than 10% named boys as friends who were in the other group. The Sherifs' well-known Robbers Cave Experiment, which is discussed in more detail in Chapter 14's analysis of conflict between groups, yielded similar findings.

Group-level Attraction Social cohesion increases when group members like each other. Cohesion, however, is a *multilevel process*, for group members

---

social cohesion The attraction of members to one another and to the group as a whole.

may be bonded to each other, to their group, and to the organization in which their group is embedded. At the individual level, specific group members are attracted to other group members, but social cohesion also includes group-level attraction: liking for the group rather than specific individuals within the group. The players on the hockey team, for example, described their team as a "great group of guys" and were proud to be members. Since interpersonal attraction usually leads to increased group attraction, friendship among the members of a group tends to generate liking for the group as a whole (Carless & De Paola, 2000). But these forms of attraction need not go hand in hand, particularly if groups focus on work or performance rather than leisure or socializing. When cohesion is based on individual-level attraction and those who are liked leave the group, the remaining members are more likely to quit. When cohesion is based on group-level attraction, people remain members even when specific members leave the group (Ehrhart & Naumann, 2004; Mobley et al., 1979).

Social Attraction Some researchers prefer to reserve the term *cohesion* for group-level attraction only. Social psychologist Michael Hogg and his colleagues, for example, draw on social identity theory in their analysis of cohesion in large aggregates. Hogg noted that although members of cohesive groups usually like one another, this personal attraction is not group cohesion. Rather, group cohesion corresponds to a form of group-level attraction that Hogg labeled *social attraction*—a liking for other group members that is based on their status as typical group members. Unlike personal attraction, which is based on relationships between specific members, social attraction is depersonalized, since it is based on admiration for individuals who possess the kinds of qualities that typify the group. Hogg found that any factor that increases members' tendency to categorize themselves as group members (e.g., conflict with other groups, the presence of outgroups, activities that focus members' attention on their group identity) will reduce personal attraction but increase depersonalized, social attraction. Hogg's analysis means that cohesiveness is not limited to small

groups in which members know one another well but is also a feature of larger collectives and categories (see Hogg, 1992, 2001, for a review).

Task Cohesion

Studies of task-oriented groups, such as teams, military squads, and expeditions, find that members, when asked to describe their team's cohesiveness, stress the quality of their group as a performing unit (MacCoun, Kier, & Belkin, 2005). The U.S. Olympic team players, for example, were not just individuals seeking personal goals, but teammates who combined their strengths and talents to create a single, performance-focused hockey team. They achieved **task cohesion**: a shared commitment among members to achieve a goal that requires the collective effort of the group.

Group Motivation Task cohesion is based on group-level goal motivation. Many of the players on the hockey team were the stars of their college teams, and when they played they wanted to do their personal best by scoring the most goals or defending their own net. But success in hockey is not based on personal performance. A good player may do much to help the team win, but success in hockey requires collaboration, so it requires all members to contribute to the group and its objectives. Group members typically have the choice of working for the group, for themselves, for both the group and themselves, or for neither and thus do not always choose to strive for group success. If, however, group cohesiveness is so strong that all members feel united in a common effort, then group-oriented motives should replace individualistic motives, and the desire among members for group success should be strong (Zander, 1971).

The coach of the hockey team, Herb Brooks, was careful to emphasize the importance of team goals rather than individual performance as he

---

task cohesion A shared commitment among members to achieve a goal and the resulting capacity to perform successfully as a coordinated unit.

prepared his team for the Olympics. Rather than appealing to player-centered motivations by emphasizing personal performance and rewarding individual expertise, Brooks instilled a strong desire for group rather than individual success. He deliberately avoided developing personal relationships with the players and reminded each one frequently that, as a hockey player, he was expendable. As one of the players remarked in describing his coach: "He treated us all the same: rotten" (Swift, 1980, p. 32).

Collective Efficacy and Potency   Groups that are cohesive, in terms of task commitment, tend to exhibit high levels of collective efficacy and group potency. **Collective efficacy** is determined by members' shared beliefs that they can accomplish all the components of their group's tasks competently and efficiently. Unlike self-efficacy, which is confidence in one's own abilities, collective efficacy is a group-level process: Most or all of members must believe the members will competently coordinate their individual actions in a skilled, collective performance (Pescosolido, 2003). Hence, collective efficacy is "a group's shared belief in its conjoint capabilities to organize and execute the courses of action required to produce given levels of attainment" (Bandura, 1997, p. 476). A similar construct, **group potency**, is a generalized positive expectation about the group's chances for success (Guzzo et al., 1993). High-potency groups tend to select more difficult goals to pursue and they tend to outperform their less potent counterparts (Stajkovic, Lee, & Nyberg, 2009).

Collective Cohesion

Brooks, the coach, did not just stress shared goals, but also **collective cohesion**: He wanted each

---

collective efficacy The belief, shared among a substantial portion of the group members, that the group is capable of organizing and executing the actions required to attain the group's goals and successfully complete its tasks.
group potency The level of the group's shared optimism regarding its collective capabilities.
collective cohesion Members' identification with the group; unity based on shared identity and belonging.

player to identify so completely with the team that division between self and other became moot. His goal, he explained, was to "build a 'we' and 'us' in ourselves as opposed to an 'I,' 'me,' and 'myself'" (Warner HBO, 2001). This unity reached its peak in the medal ceremonies after the U.S. team had won its gold medal. Team captain Mike Eruzione waved to the team to join him on the small stage, and somehow the entire team crowded onto the platform. Instead of the team captain representing the group, the entire group, as a whole, received the medal.

Self and Identity   Psychoanalyst Sigmund Freud was one of the first theorists to discuss the tendency for members of groups to identify so strongly with their groups that their sense of individuality is replaced by a shared sense of unity. Although he tended to stress psychological processes in his explanations of adjustment and dysfunction, he also studied groups and was particularly intrigued by members' willingness to sacrifice their personal interests for the good of the group. Perhaps, he speculated, groups come to replace individuals' first, and most fulfilling, group: the family. His replacement hypothesis suggests that in highly cohesive groups, the other group members come to take the place of siblings, and the emotional ties that bind members to their groups are like the ties that bind children to their family (Kohut, 1984). More recently, and with more solid data to support it, social identity theory suggests that when individuals identify with their groups their membership becomes central to their self-definition.

When a substantial number of group members identify with the group, the group is likely to display telltale signs of high collective cohesiveness. Group members often reveal their perceptions of their group's unity in the words that they use to describe their connection to it. When members talk about themselves and their group, they use more plural pronouns than personal pronouns: "We won that game" or "We got the job done" rather than "I got the job done" (Cialdini et al., 1976). They use words like *family*, *community*, or just *we* to describe their group. They may also refuse to differentiate among the members of the group, as when one member refuses to take responsibility for the victory or win and insists that the team as a whole deserves the credit. Members, when asked to comment directly on their sense of belonging to the group, are more likely to say "I feel a sense of belonging to my group" (Bollen & Hoyle, 1990), "I think of this group as a part of who I am" (Henry, Arrow, & Carini, 1999), and "I see myself as a member of the group" (Smith, Seger, & Mackie, 2007).

Identity Fusion When individuals identify with their group, their sense of self combines elements drawn from both their individualized, personal self and their collective, group-level self. But what happens if this distinction between the individual self and collective self dissolves—if the individual's personal self becomes fused with the collective? **Identity fusion theory** suggests that in such cases—which are admittedly rare—both the personal self and the collective selves become amplified, with the result that individuals are willing to engage in extreme forms of behavior on behalf of their group. Individuals who sacrifice themselves for their group—heroes in combat but also suicide bombers—perform actions that seem objectively inexplicable; they sacrifice their own lives to either save group members or to harm others who they believe are their enemies. Identity fusion theory suggests that individuals engage in these actions because their identification with their group is so great that they can no longer distinguish between themselves and their group (Swann et al., 2009, 2010; 2012).

In one study of this process researchers surveyed a large number of students to identify those with fused identities by asking them if they agreed with such items as "I am one with my group" and "I feel immersed in my group" (paraphrased from Gómez et al., 2011, p. 992). Individuals who agreed with these items, when recontacted six months later, were asked if they were willing to fight and die for their group. Many said they would. Fusion also predicted how they responded to a modified version of the trolley-car dilemma used in studies of ethics. Participants were asked to imagine that they were on a footbridge and could see that a runaway trolley was about to run over five members of their group. The only thing they could do to stop the trolley would be to jump from the bridge into its path. More of the individuals with fused identifies said they would do so (Gómez et al., 2011).

Emotional Cohesion

Napoleon is said to have proclaimed that the great strength of an army lies not in the skill of its leaders, but in the élan—the emotional intensity—of its members. The sociologist Émile Durkheim, in discussing the nature of ritualized interactions in cohesive groups, stressed how they develop intense emotional experiences, for when all "come together, a sort of electricity is formed by their collecting which quickly transports them to an extraordinary degree of exaltation" (1912/1965, p. 262). Durkheim was describing the large gatherings of local communities in New Guinea, but he believed that *collective effervescence* resulted from the sharing of emotional reactions within a group. As the positive and elevated mood of one person is picked up by the next, the group members eventually display a shared emotional intensity.

A variety of terms is used to describe group-level emotional states, including élan, morale, esprit de corps, and positive affective tone, but no matter what its label, this shared **emotional cohesion** is one of the most obvious features of many unified groups. The Russian and U.S. teams were equal in confidence and collective efficacy, for both groups had the talent needed to win at hockey. But they differed dramatically in their level of emotionality.

---

identity fusion theory A conceptual analysis that explains the extreme self-sacrifice (such as heroism in the face of danger and terrorism) that sometimes occurs when individual identity is fused with group identity.

emotional cohesion The emotional intensity of the group and individuals when in the group.

The Russian team was confident but unenthusiastic. The U.S. team was not so confident, but the team was brimming with energy, enthusiasm, and team spirit. A group with high levels of collective efficacy may expect to succeed, but a group with emotional cohesion has vitality, passion, vim, and vigor. Emotional cohesion predicts a number of positive group behaviors, including helping teammates, protecting the organization, making constructive suggestions, improving one's personal performance, spreading goodwill, and even enhancing survival (Barsade & Gibson, 2012; Spoor & Kelly, 2004). It was this emotionality that Coach Brooks whipped up to its peak intensity before the U.S. team's game with the Russians. He told them that the Russians were taking their victory for granted, but "we can beat them." He told his team: "you were born to be a player," you were "destined to be here today," and this is "our time." When he told them to "spit in the eye of the tiger," they did.

Affect and Relational Cohesion A number of theorists believe that the positive emotions that generate cohesion arise spontaneously during the course of routine interactions in groups—so long as these interactions are relatively pleasant. For example, sociologists Edward Lawler, Shane Thye, and Jeongkoo Yoon (2008), in their **relational cohesion theory**, argue that group members, because they are linked to one another in recurring (and mostly positive) exchange relationships, eventually experience positive emotions when interacting with one another. Particularly when "jointness" is high—members must align their behaviors with each other in order to reach their goals—then members will attribute their positive feelings to the group and become more strongly committed to it.

Lawler, Thye, and Yoon (2000) tested the theory by arranging for groups of three students seated in separate cubicles to work together on an economic decision-making task. Participants were told on each round they would have the opportunity to draw out points from a common pool and that at the end of 20 rounds the points they earned would be converted into monetary payment. The group members needed to negotiate the amounts each withdrew among them; if too much was taken, no one would receive any points at all. After numerous rounds of these negotiations the members were asked to describe their emotions using such adjectives as *pleased, happy, satisfied*, and *contented*. They also indicated if they felt their group was cohesive (e.g., close, solid, and coming together) or divisive (e.g., distant, fragile, or coming apart). As relational cohesion theory predicts, the more frequently the groups successfully completed their negotiations, the more positive their emotions, and the more positive their emotions, the higher their group's level of cohesion.

Synchronous Movement and Emotion Cohesive groups, particularly those with continuity of membership, often engage in practices, rituals, and collective activities—such as collective singing, chanting, praying, and marching—that require behavioral coordination. Some of these practices involve simple **mimicry**: members must perform identical actions, although not necessarily at the same time. **Behavioral synchrony**, in contrast, requires the properly paced coordination of members' actions. When members act synchronously, they must align their behaviors with the behaviors of other members both in place and in time. Mimicry is a simple form of coordination—when one member yawns, other members follow suit—but synchrony—two hockey players skating together down the ice, passing the puck back and forth to one another—is a complex, demanding task (Semin, 2007).

Cohesive groups, in many cases, are more skilled than less cohesive groups when they undertake complex tasks that require synchrony (Gevers,

---

relational cohesion theory A conceptual analysis of cohesion that assumes members of groups develop stronger ties to groups that are perceived to be sources of positive feelings or emotions and weaker ties to those perceived to be sources of negative feelings or emotions.

mimicry When two or more group members perform the same action, including imitation of emotional and nonverbal displays.

behavioral synchrony The coordination of movement between group members.

van Eerde, & Rutte, 2009). However, just as cohesiveness likely increases synchrony, acting in a behaviorally synchronized way increases group cohesion. In one study, researchers simply asked three-person groups to take a short walk together. In the synchrony condition, the group members were asked to walk in step with each other, but, in the control condition, the group members stayed together but they did not coordinate their steps. Those group members who walked in step reported feeling "more connected" with the other group members than those who walked normally (Wiltermuth & Heath, 2009).

Although synchronicity did not influence participants' feelings in this study, other investigators have found that behavioral coordination causes people to feel positive rather than negative emotions (Valdesolo & DeSteno, 2011). Historian William McNeill (1995), for example, suggests that this positive impact of behavioral synchrony explains why military groups often use marching and drill during training. He writes:

> Marching aimlessly about on the drill field, swaggering in conformity with prescribed military postures, conscious only of keeping in step so as to make the next move correctly and in time somehow felt good. Words are inadequate to describe the emotion aroused by the prolonged movement in unison that drilling involved. A sense of pervasive well-being is what I recalled; more specifically, a strange sense of personal enlargement; a sort of swelling out, becoming bigger than life, thanks to participation in collective ritual. (p. 2)

McNeill suggests that much of the history of modern forms of warfare can be traced to the cohesion-building effects of close-group training. His collective-movement hypothesis offers, for example, a solution to one of military history's great mysteries: How did the Greek forces of Athens and Sparta, in the period from 600 B.C. to 300 B.C., manage to overwhelm vastly superior forces? McNeill's proposal: The Greeks relied on highly cohesive groups of ground forces that moved forward as a synchronized unit. This formation is known as a phalanx, from the Greek word for fingers. These units varied in size, but were typically at least eight rows deep and stretched wide enough across a field of battle to prevent flanking. In some cases, each man's shield was designed so that it covered the soldier beside him as well, thereby further increasing the unity of the group. The men of these phalanxes trained together over long periods of time, and they became synchronized to the point that they acted as a single unit that could inflict great damage against even the best-trained individual soldiers. These phalanxes eventually gave way to other means of organizing men in battle, given their vulnerability to cavalry and more maneuverable adversaries.

Structural Cohesion

Structural cohesion is unity of a group that results from the integrity of its structural features, including norms, roles, and intermember relations. The U.S. Olympic team, for example, was a well-structured group, in the social rather than bureaucratic sense. Each player had a position on the ice that he played, and his responsibilities in that role were well-defined. The players, through practice, knew what they were supposed to do when on offense and defense, and their success in enacting these duties was reviewed regularly by the coaching staff that had authority over all the players. The group also had clear rules about how it operated, what kinds of behaviors were acceptable, and the goals that it sought. The group was also closed, rather than open: only certain individuals could join, and membership was regarded by most as a noteworthy accomplishment (see Focus 5.1). These social structures regulated members' behavior, minimized conflict within the group, routinized communication and interdependencies, and, in doing so, increased the group's cohesiveness (Eys & Carron, 2001; Moody & White, 2003).

---

structural cohesion The unity of a group that derives from the group's structural integrity, including normative coherence, clarity of roles, and strength and density of relationships linking members.

Focus 5.1   E-groups: Closed and Open Groups on the Internet

Many online groups are as collaborative, cohesive, and continuous as their corresponding offline cousins. For example, online project-focused groups and teams—such as groups created in college courses that complete group-level learning activities and groups in organizational contexts that have explicit work-related purposes—are initially less unified than offline groups, but most eventually catch up to groups that interact in face-to-face settings. Granted, some groups become cohesive and others do not, but these fluctuations in cohesion are not substantially influenced by the use of computer-mediated communication technologies (e.g., Bateman, Butler, & Gray, 2010; Faraj & Johnson, 2011; Pazos & Beruvides, 2011).

Some types of online groups, however, are less successful when it comes to reaching high levels of cohesiveness. Groups that form in social networking sites, discussion/forum areas, and multiplayer gaming sites, for example, often exhibit one telling sign of low cohesion: membership instability. In a social network site, such as Facebook, people can leave or join a group or sever a connection ("unfriend" someone) at the push of a button. Facebook users are more likely to take this step when the person is an online-only friend who posts too frequently about unimportant or controversial topics (Sibona & Walczak, 2011). A Yahoo! Group can be created by any Yahoo! user, but of the 6 million groups, less than 1% are thriving (regular postings, a core, stable membership of at least 10 members; Backstrom et al., 2008). Studies of the guilds that form in the multiplayer game World of Warcraft indicates that members join and leave these groups at a relatively high rate (Ducheneaut et al., 2006). This rate is so high that one study that tracked the membership patterns of 2,744 guilds for one month discovered that nearly 21% of these guilds disbanded during this period (Williams et al., 2006). Some of the surviving guilds were highly cohesive, but for many their membership was quite fluid: one guild gained 87 new members during this period and another lost 103 (Ducheneaut et al., 2006).

Robert Ziller's (1965) theory of open and closed groups offers an explanation. Ziller notes that groups differ in the extent to which their boundaries and membership rosters are open and fluctuating versus closed and fixed. In open groups, members can be voted out of the group, they can quit the group for personal reasons, and they are free to join other groups. Regardless of the reasons for these changes in membership, **open groups** are especially unlikely to reach a state of equilibrium, since members recognize that they may lose or relinquish their place within the group at any time. In contrast, **closed groups** are often more cohesive, because members remain in the groups for longer periods of time and so anticipate future collaborations. Thus, in closed groups, individuals tend to focus on the collective nature of the group and are more likely to identify with their group as they work together to accomplish a collective goal.

Ziller's theory suggests that open groups, by their very nature, are less cohesive, and this hypothesis has held up when tested empirically. In one illustrative experiment, four-person study groups were recruited from a college class. Half of these groups were closed: members anticipated working together preparing for classroom examinations in the future. The other half were open: The groups were told that one member of the group would be dropped from the group and that the group members would choose who would stay and who would go. As predicted, the open groups were significantly less cohesive than the closed groups. In addition, the members of open groups were less likely to take leadership roles or personal responsibility for the group's work (Burnette & Forsyth, 2008).

Many e-groups, recognizing the benefits of a stabilized membership and the cohesiveness that stability brings, use various technological and interpersonal strategies to transform their open groups into closed ones. Those who create e-groups often set up the membership procedures so that the group has clear boundaries between those who belong and those who do not. In some cases, those seeking to join must be approved by the group before they are admitted, and only then will they be able to access the contents of the group's communications (Backstrom et al., 2008). Many of the most successful, long-term guilds in World of Warcraft, for example, are highly selective, accepting

---

open group A group whose boundaries are so permeable that membership varies considerably as members enter and leave the group.

closed group A group whose boundaries are closed and fixed; as a result, membership is relatively unvarying.

only applicants with certain credentials or those who have been referred to the guild by a current member. Guilds also increase the commitment of members to the group by requiring each member to contribute some of their resources to a common pool—a "guild bank"—and those resources are forfeited if one leaves the guild (Malone, 2009). Although research is needed

to evaluate the impact of these methods of increasing the unity of online groups, anecdotal evidence suggests they are effective means of increasing the cohesiveness of e-groups. A Google search of the phrase "I love my guild" yielded about 1,340,000 results, whereas a search for "I hate my guild" had only 214,000 hits.

Just as a well-designed building can withstand the vicissitudes of time and weather, so can a structurally cohesive group withstand stresses and strains that would cause a less coherent group to crumble. For example, the two groups studied by the Sherifs (1953, 1956) discussed earlier in the chapter—the Bulldogs and Red Devils—developed very different organizational structures. As Figure 5.1 indicates, the Bulldogs had a dense network of relationships linking members, whereas the Red Devils team was more stratified. When the boys were asked to name

as many as five friends at the camp, 9 of the 12 Bulldogs named each other in a tightly knit pattern of reciprocal and overlapping choices. The remaining three individuals received no friendship nominations, but they picked others who were part of the main cluster as friends and were not rejected. In the Red Devils, liking was more concentrated: the two most-liked individuals in the group garnered 50% of all friendship choices. The Red Devils group structure also included a large subgroup—50% of the members were nested in a

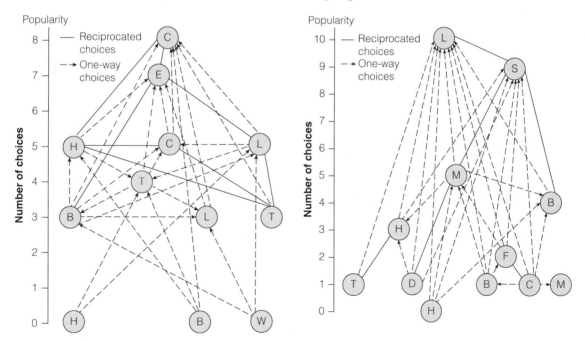

FIGURE 5.1 The attraction relations among the members of the Bulldogs (on the left) and the Red Devils (on the right), as documented by Sherif and Sherif (1956) in their field studies of group processes.

SOURCE: © Cengage Learning

clique linked to one of the mid-level leaders. Such subgroups create *fault lines* in groups, and, when the group experiences turmoil, it can break apart along these lines (Bezrukova et al., 2009). These differences in structure corresponded to differences between the two groups both in cohesiveness and in performance. The Bulldogs were a more tight-knit, cohesive group, and they were the victors when the two teams played each other in a series of competitions. "The results of the intergroup competition for the Bulldogs were elation and heightened ingroup pride and identification" (Sherif & Sherif, 1956, p. 294).

Assumptions and Assessments

The concept of cohesion, given its theoretical importance, has been defined and redefined by dozens of different theorists. Some consider cohesion to be strong feelings of attraction that link members together. Others, in contrast, focus on morale and trust, and still others stress the cohesive group's capacity to combine members in a highly productive unit. Cohesiveness's many definitions have caused some to complain that the concept, ironically, lacks cohesion (e.g., Casey-Campbell & Martens, 2009; Marmarosh & Van Horn, 2010; Mudrack, 1989).

The Multicomponent Assumption A multicomponent approach embraces this definitional diversity by suggesting that many different factors contribute to the unity of a group. The U.S. Olympic team, for example, combined all five of the cohesion-related factors listed in Table 5.1—the members became good friends as well as teammates, they worked well together, they identified with their team, they played with great emotional intensity, and the group was highly structured. But, as is consistent with the concept of equifinality, other cohesive groups may not exhibit all of these qualities.

Some of the factors in Table 5.1 may, however, be more regularly associated with cohesion than others. For example, studies of performance-focused groups, such as military squads and sports teams, identify two components—social cohesion and task cohesion—as the two *primary forms* of cohesion and distinguish between these two forms and *secondary forms* of cohesion (e.g., Carron & Brawley, 2000; Siebold, 2007). Sociological and network studies, in contrast, tend to emphasize the importance of structural features as critical determinants of cohesion (e.g., McPherson & Smith-Lovin, 2002).

The Multilevel Assumption Cohesion is also a *multilevel process* as well as a multicomponent one.

TABLE 5.1   A Multicomponent Conception of Group Cohesion

Component	Description	Examples
Social	Attraction of members to one another and to the group as a whole	• I have many friends in this group. • People get along well in this group. • I love this group.
Task	Commitment to working together as a coordinated unit in the pursuit of group goals	• We work well together. • We pull together to get the job done. • I do my best for this group.
Collective	Consensual identification with the group; unity based on shared identify and belonging	• United we stand. • We are like family. • I identify with this group and its members.
Emotional	Emotional intensity of the group and individuals when in the group	• This group has tremendous energy. • This group has team spirit. • I get excited just being in this group.
Structural	Integrity based on structural features (e.g., norms, roles, and intermember relations)	• The group fits together to make a whole. • All group members feel accepted by the group. • We are tight-knit.

Social cohesion includes both liking for specific members but also liking for the group itself. Task cohesion is commitment to one's personal goals, but also the goals that the group is pursuing. But each of the other sources of cohesion considered in this section—identity, emotions, and structure—also operate at multiple levels. Members of cohesive groups not only identify with other members, mimic their emotions, and meet their role obligations: They embrace the group's identity, share its emotions, and fit into its structure. A multilevel analysis must also take into account vertical and organizational bonding (Seibold, 2007). Cohesion is substantially influenced by the strength of the relations between members and their leaders (vertical bonding) and the relationship between the group and the organization or institution in which it is embedded (organizational bonding).

Alternative Measures   Because of the many types of cohesiveness, researchers use a wide variety of methods to measure it. Some researchers use social network methods, indexing the unity of a group by considering who likes who and group structure. Others rely on observational strategies, monitoring interpersonal relations among members, noting instances of conflict or tension, and judging how smoothly the group works together as a unit (e.g., Fine & Holyfield, 1996). In many cases, too, investigators hope that group members are accurate observers of their group's cohesiveness and, if asked, will share these perceptions. Investigators have used a variety of questions to tap into cohesion, including, "Do you want to remain a member of this group?" and "How strong a sense of belonging do you feel you have to the people you work with?" (Schachter, 1951; Indik, 1965, respectively). Researchers also use multi-item scales that include many questions that can be combined to yield a single index of cohesiveness, such as the *Group Environment Scale* (Moos, Insel, & Humphrey, 1974), *Group Attitude Scale* (Evans & Jarvis, 1986), *Group Environment Questionnaire* (Widmeyer, Brawley, & Carron, 1992), *Perceived Cohesion Scale* (Bollen & Hoyle, 1990), *Group Identification Scale* (Henry et al., 1999), *Sports Cohesiveness Questionnaire* (Martens, Landers, & Loy, 1972), *Gross Cohesion Questionnaire* (Stokes, 1983),

Group Cohesion Scale-Revised (Treadwell et al., 2001), *Questionnaire sur l'Ambiance du Groupe* (Buton et al., 2007), and the *Child Sport Cohesion Questionnaire* (Martin et al., 2012).

Cohesion, as a multilevel concept, can also be measured at multiple levels. Those who consider cohesion to be a psychological quality that is rooted in members' feelings of attraction for others, for the group, and a sense of unity measure cohesion at the individual level. They might ask members of a group to only describe their own attraction to and commitment to the group through such questions as, "Are you attracted to the group?" or "Do you feel a strong sense of belonging to the group?" Other researchers, in contrast, may feel that only a group can be cohesive, and so cohesion should be located at the group level (Mason & Griffin, 2002). These investigators may ask group members to estimate the group's cohesion directly through such questions as, "Are members attracted to this group?" and "Is this group a cohesive one?" They might also decide to have the group answer these types of questions as a group (see Paskevich et al., 1999).

This plethora of operational definitions can create challenges for researchers. When they measure cohesiveness in different ways, they often report different conclusions. A study using a self-report measure of cohesion might find that cohesive groups produce more than cohesive ones, but other investigators may not replicate this finding when they use observational measures (Mullen et al., 1994). Moreover, some operational definitions of cohesion may correspond more closely to the theoretical definition than others. A measure that focuses only on group members' perceptions of their group's cohesiveness, for example, may be assessing something very different than a measure that focuses on the actual strength of the relationships linking individuals to their group.

DEVELOPING COHESION

The U.S. Olympic team that faced the Russian team in February of 1980 was extraordinarily unified, but the group did not become cohesive all at once.

When Coach Brooks invited the best amateur hockey players to a training camp in Colorado Springs in July 1979, the players showed few signs of camaraderie, fellowship, or cohesion. Many had played against one another in college and still held grudges, and some were so temperamental that no one would befriend them. But the hockey team changed over time, transforming from a collection of talented individuals into a cohesive team.

Theories of Group Development

New groups are different from established groups. The committee meeting for the first time will not act the way it will during its tenth meeting. The team playing its first game of the season will not perform in the same way it will on its last game. The partygoers at 2 AM don't do the sorts of things they did at the party's start at 9 PM. Some of the changes that a group and its members undergo are specific to that particular group, for they are the result of the unique characteristics of the members, the distinctive way these individuals interact with each other, and the group's reaction to external pressures that it may encounter. But along with these idiographic changes are more predictable patterns of change that are common to most groups the longer their duration.

Theories of group development seek to describe these recurring patterns of change in a group's structure and interactions that occur over the course of the group's existence. Some theories—*successive-stage models*—suggest that groups move through a series of separable stages as they develop. The U.S. Olympic team, for example, became unified, but only after progressing through earlier stages marked by confusion, conflict, and growing group structure. *Cyclical models*, in contrast, argue that groups repeatedly cycle through periods or phases during their lifetimes, rather than just moving through each stage once. The U.S. Olympic team, for example, experienced substantial shifts in its levels of conflict between the coach and the players throughout its existence, but these shifts triggered processes that worked to control tension and increase harmony. Still other theories mix elements of both stage and cycle models and extend these two basic perspectives in various ways. We consider examples of these approaches to the analysis of group development in this section (Arrow et al., 2005; Brabender & Fallon, 2009).

Five Stages of Development

The clinical psychologist William Fawcett Hill was at one time so intrigued by developmental processes in groups that he diligently filed away each theory that he found on that subject. Over the years, his collection grew and grew, until finally the number of theories reached 100. At that moment, Hill noted, the "collecting bug was exterminated, as the object of the quest had lost its rarity" (Hill & Gruner, 1973, p. 355; see also Hare, 1982; Lacoursiere, 1980).

The morass of theoretical models dealing with group development, though daunting, is not altogether irremediable. Theoreticians are at variance on many points, but many agree that groups pass through several phases, or *stages*, as they develop. Just as humans mature from infancy to childhood, adolescence, adulthood, and old age, stage models of group development theorize that groups move from one stage to the next in a predictable, sequential fashion. The number and names of the stages vary among theorists, but many models highlight certain interpersonal outcomes that must be achieved in any group that exists for a prolonged period. Members of most groups must, for example, discover who the other members are, achieve a degree of interdependence, and deal with conflict (Hare, 1982; Lacoursiere, 1980; Wheelan, 2005). Therefore, most models include the five stages shown in Table 5.2 and illustrated earlier in Chapter 1's Figure 1.5. First, the group members must become oriented toward one another. Second, they often find themselves in conflict, and some solution is sought to improve the group environment. In the third phase, norms and roles develop that regulate behavior, and the group achieves greater unity. In the fourth phase, the group can perform as a unit to achieve desired goals. The final stage ends the sequence of development with the group's adjournment. The educational psychologist Bruce Tuckman (Tuckman, 1965; Tuckman & Jensen, 1977) gave each stage in the

T A B L E   5.2   Stages of Group Development

Stage	Major processes	Characteristics
Orientation: *Forming*	Members become familiar with each other and the group; dependency and inclusion issues; acceptance of leader and group consensus	Communications are tentative, polite; concern for ambiguity, group's goals; leader is active; members are compliant
Conflict: *Storming*	Disagreement over procedures; expression of dissatisfaction; tension among members; antagonism toward leader	Criticism of ideas; poor attendance; hostility; polarization and coalition formation
Structure: *Norming*	Growth of cohesiveness and unity; establishment of roles, standards, and relationships; increased trust, communication	Agreement on procedures; reduction in role ambiguity; increased "we-feeling"
Performance: *Performing*	Goal achievement; high task-orientation; emphasis on performance and production	Decision making; problem solving; mutual cooperation
Dissolution: *Adjourning*	Termination of roles; completion of tasks; reduction of dependency	Disintegration and withdrawal; increased independence and emotionality; regret

five-stage model of group development a poetically pleasant name: *forming* (orientation), *storming* (conflict), *norming* (structure development), *performing* (work), and *adjourning* (dissolution).

Forming: The Orientation Stage   The first few minutes, hours, days, or even weeks of a newly formed group's life are often marked by tension, guarded interchanges, and relatively low levels of interaction. During this initial *forming stage*, members monitor their behavior to avoid any embarrassing lapses of social poise and are tentative when expressing their personal opinions. Because the group's structure has not had time to develop, the members are often uncertain about their role in the group, what they should be doing to help the group reach its goals, or even who is leading the group.

With time, tension is dispelled as the ice is broken and group members become better acquainted.

---

five-stage model of group development A theoretical analysis of the regularities groups exhibit as they change over time that identifies five stages of development: orientation (forming), conflict (storming), structure (norming), performance (performing), and dissolution (adjourning) (identified and labeled by Bruce Tuckman).

After the initial inhibitions subside, group members typically begin exchanging information about themselves and their goals. To better understand and relate to the group, individual members gather information about their leaders' and members' personality characteristics, interests, and attitudes. In most cases, too, members recognize that the others in the group are forming an impression of each other, and so they facilitate this process by revealing some private, personal information during conversations and Internet-based exchanges. This gradual, and in some cases tactical, communication of personal information is termed *self-disclosure*, and it serves the important function of helping members get to know one another (Jourard, 1971). Eventually, the group members feel familiar enough with one another that their interactions become more open and spontaneous.

Storming: The Conflict Stage   As the relatively mild tension caused by the newness of a group wanes, tension over goals, procedures, and authority often waxes. On the U.S. Olympic team, for example, the players from the schools in the eastern part of the United States often excluded the players from the Midwest. Several players were considered hotshots more interested in their personal performance than in team success. And nearly all the players rebelled against the hard-driving coaching style of Herb Brooks. He would yell, insult, swear, and curse the players whenever they failed to perform up to his standards, and he often threatened to cut players from the team.

The *storming stage* is marked by a "lack of unity" (Tuckman, 1965, p. 386), including personal conflicts between individual members who discover that they just do not get along, procedural conflict over the group's goals and procedures, and competition between individual members for authority, leadership, and more prestigious roles. In groups that have an official leader, like the U.S. Olympic team, the conflict often centers on relationships between the leader and the rest of the group. In the orientation stage, members accept the leader's guidance with few questions, but as the group matures, leader–member conflicts disrupt the group's functioning. Members may oscillate between fight (counter dependency) and flight (withdrawal) as some openly challenge the leader's authority and others exude submissiveness. In groups that have no formally appointed leader, conflicts erupt as members vie for status and roles within the group. Once stable patterns of authority, attraction, and communication have developed, conflicts subside, but until then, group members jockey for authority and power (Bennis & Shepard, 1956; Wheelan & McKeage, 1993).

Many group members are discouraged by this outbreak of conflict in their young groups, but conflict is the yang to the yin of group harmony. As Chapter 13's analysis of the roots of conflict suggests, the dynamic nature of the group ensures continual change, but along with this change come stresses and strains that surface in the form of conflict. In rare instances, group members may avoid all conflict because their actions are perfectly coordinated; but in most groups, the push and pull of interpersonal forces inevitably exerts its influence. Low levels of conflict in a group can be an indication of remarkably positive interpersonal relations, but it is more likely that the group members are simply uninvolved, unmotivated, and bored (Fisher, 1980).

Conflict is not just unavoidable, however; it may be a key ingredient for creating group cohesion. If conflict escalates out of control, it can destroy a group. But in some cases, conflict settles matters of structure, direction, and performance expectations. Members of cohesive groups must learn to manage their conflict: when hostility surfaces it must be confronted and resolved (Tekleab, Quigley, & Tesluk, 2009). Conflicts may "serve to 'sew the social system together' by canceling each other out, thus preventing disintegration along one primary line of cleavage" (Coser, 1956, p. 801). Most groups that survive resolve conflicts quickly before the disagreement causes permanent damage to members' relationships (De Dreu, 2010).

Norming: The Structure Stage With each crisis overcome, the U.S. Olympic team became more stable, more organized, and more unified. The players revised their initial impressions of each other and reached more benevolent conclusions about their teammates. The players still complained about the team rules, the practice schedules, and the coach's constant criticisms, but they became fiercely loyal to the team, their teammates, and their coach. Whereas groups in the orientation and conflict stages are characterized by low levels of intimacy, friendship, and continuity, in the norming stage members become more trusting, supportive, and cooperative. The group becomes cohesive.

As the group becomes more organized, it resolves the problems that caused earlier conflicts—uncertainty about goals, roles, and authority—and prepares to get down to the work at hand. Norms emerge more clearly and guide the group members as they interact with one another. The group begins to display interaction rituals that provide structure and meaning for the group and its members, such as regularities in small talk or repetitive mundane practices (Collins, 2004). Differences of opinion still arise, but now they are dealt with through constructive discussion and negotiation. Members communicate openly with one another about personal and group concerns, in part because members know one another better. On the U.S. Olympic team, the players did not always agree with the coach, but they changed the way they dealt with disagreement. Instead of grumbling about their treatment, several players started compiling a book of *Brooksisms*—the odd expressions Coach Brooks used during practice to motivate his players. Nearly every player, interviewed 20 years after they played for Brooks, remembered such Brooksisms as "You are playing worse every day and now you are playing like the middle of next week" and "Gentlemen, you don't have enough talent to win on talent alone."

Performing: The Work Stage The U.S. Olympic team played 41 games against other teams in preparation for the Olympics and won 30 of those matches. They reached their peak of performance when they beat the Russian team to qualify for the final, gold-medal game against Finland. Before that game, Coach Brooks did not give them a pep talk, as he had before the Russian game. Instead, he only said, "You lose this game and you will take it to your [expletive deleted] graves" (Warner HBO, 2001). They won.

Few groups are productive immediately; instead, productivity must usually wait until the group matures. Various types of groups, such as conferences, factory workers assembling relay units, workshop participants, and the members of expeditions, become more efficient and productive later in their group's life cycle (Hare, 1967, 1982; Hare & Naveh, 1984). The more "mature" a group, the more likely the group will spend the bulk of its time working toward its chosen goals rather than socializing, seeking direction, or arguing (Dierdorff, Bell, & Belohlav, 2011). When researchers coded the content of group members' verbal interactions, they discovered task-focused remarks occur later rather than sooner in the group's life (Bales & Strodtbeck, 1951; Borgatta & Bales, 1953; Heinicke & Bales, 1953). Conflict and uncertainty also decrease over time as work-focused comments increase. Groups that have been together longer talk more about work-related matters, whereas younger groups are more likely to express conflict or uncertainty and make requests for guidance (Wheelan, Davidson, & Tilin, 2003). Once the group reaches the *performing stage* "members

shift their attention from what the group is to what the group needs to do" (Bushe & Coetzer, 2007, p. 193).

Not all groups, however, reach this productive work stage. If you have never been a member of a group that failed to produce, you are a rare individual indeed. In a study of neighborhood action committees, only 1 of 12 groups reached the productivity stage; all the others were bogged down at the forming or storming stages (Zurcher, 1969). An early investigation of combat units found that out of 63 squads, only 13 could be clearly classified as effective performance units (Goodacre, 1953). An analysis of 18 personal growth groups concluded that only 5 managed to reach the task performance stage (Kuypers, Davies, & Glaser, 1986). These studies and others suggest that time is needed to develop a working relationship, but time alone is no guarantee that the group will be productive (Gabarro, 1987). Chapters 10, 11, and 12 examine issues pertaining to team performance in detail.

Adjourning: The Dissolution Stage Susan Wheelan's (2005) *Group Development Questionnaire*, summarized in Table 5.3, measures the group's stage of development by asking members to describe their group's success in dealing with issues of orientation, conflict, structure, and productivity. Some groups, however, move through these four basic stages to a fifth one: the *adjourning stage*. The U.S. Olympic team, for example, was invited to the White House to meet the president of the United States after their victory. That ceremony marked the end of the group's existence, for the team never reconvened or played again. After meeting the president, the teammates clapped one another on the back one last time, and then the group disbanded.

A group's entry into the dissolution stage can be either planned or spontaneous. *Planned dissolution* takes place when the group accomplishes its goals or exhausts its time and resources. The U.S. Olympic team meeting the president, a wilderness expedition at the end of its journey, a jury delivering its verdict, and an ad hoc committee filing its final report are all ending as scheduled. *Spontaneous dissolution*, in contrast, occurs when the group's end is not scheduled. In some cases, an unanticipated

TABLE 5.3   A Sampling of Items from the Group Development Questionnaire (GDQ)

Stage	Sample Items
Orientation (forming)	• Members tend to go along with whatever the leader suggests. • There is very little conflict expressed in the group.
Conflict (storming)	• People seem to have very different views about how things should be done in this group. • Members challenge the leader's ideas.
Structure (norming)	• The group is spending its time planning how it will get its work done. • Members can rely on each other. They work as a team.
Work (performing)	• The group gets, gives, and uses feedback about its effectiveness and productivity. • The group encourages high performance and quality work.

SOURCE: Susan A. Wheelan, Judith M. Hochberger, *Small Group Research (Behavior)*, 27, 1, copyright © 1996 by SAGE Publications. Reprinted by Permission of SAGE Publications

problem may arise that makes continued group interaction impossible. When groups fail repeatedly to achieve their goals, their members or some outside power may decide that maintaining the group is a waste of time and resources. In other cases, the group members may no longer find the group and its goals sufficiently satisfying to warrant their continued membership. As social exchange theory maintains, when the number of rewards provided by group membership decreases and the costly aspects of membership escalate, group members become dissatisfied. If the members feel that they have no alternatives or that they have put too much into the group to abandon it, they may remain in the group even though they are dissatisfied. If, however, group members feel that other groups are available or that nonparticipation is preferable to participation in such a costly group, they will be more likely to let their current group die (Vandenberghe & Bentein, 2009).

The dissolution stage can be stressful for members (Birnbaum & Cicchetti, 2005). When dissolution is unplanned, the final group sessions may be filled with conflict-laden exchanges among members, growing apathy and animosity, or repeated failures at the group's task. Even when dissolution is planned, the members may feel distressed. Their work in the group may be over, but they still mourn for the group and suffer from a lack of personal support. Members of disbanding partnerships sometimes blame one another for the end of the group (Kushnir, 1984).

Cycles of Development

Tuckman's model, which can be operationalized using measures like the ones in Table 5.3, is a *successive-stage theory*: It specifies the usual order of the phases of group development. Sometimes, however, group development takes a different course. Although interpersonal exploration is often a prerequisite for group solidarity, and cohesion and conflict often precede effective performance, this pattern is not universal. Some groups manage to avoid particular stages; others move through the stages in a unique order; still others seem to develop in ways that cannot be described by Tuckman's five stages (Bonebright, 2010). Also, the demarcation between stages is not clear-cut. When group conflict is waning, for example, feelings of cohesion may be increasing, but these time-dependent changes do not occur in a discontinuous, stepwise sequence (Arrow, 1997).

Many theorists believe that groups repeatedly cycle through stages during their lifetime, rather than just moving through each stage once (e.g., Arrow, 1997). These *cyclical models* agree that certain issues tend to dominate group interaction during the various phases of a group's development, but they add that these issues can recur later in the life of the group. Very long-term groups, such as teams of software engineers who work on products for many years, show signs of shifting from task-focused stages back to conflict (*re-storming*) and norming (*re-norming*) stages (McGrew, Bilotta, & Deeney, 1999). Production crews in progress meetings spend much of their time discussing the work itself—the tasks they have completed and those still undone—but their conversations also include relational, group-focused topics that increase cohesiveness. Notably, groups that balance the task side with the relational side are more likely to complete their projects on time than are groups whose meetings are all business and no relationships (Gorse & Emmitt, 2009).

The sociologist Robert Freed Bales' **equilibrium model** of group development assumes that group members strive to maintain a balance between accomplishing the task and enhancing the quality of the interpersonal relationships within the group. In consequence, groups cycle back and forth between what Tuckman called the norming and performing stages: A period of prolonged group effort must be followed by a period of cohesion-creating, interpersonal activity (Bales & Cohen, 1979). The discussion groups that Bales studied followed this general pattern of oscillation between the two types of group activity.

Punctuated equilibrium models agree with Bales' view, but they add that groups often go through periods of relatively rapid change. These changes may be precipitated by some internal crisis, such as the loss of a leader, or by changes in the type of task the group is attempting (Eldredge & Gould, 1972). The halfway point in the group's life, too, can trigger dramatic changes in the group, as members realize that the time they have available to them is dwindling (Arrow, 1997; Gersick, 1989). Groups must deal with deadlines and time pressures,

---

equilibrium model A conceptual analysis of group development that assumes the focus of a group shifts back and forth between the group's tasks and the interpersonal relationships among group members (proposed by Robert Bales).

punctuated equilibrium model A group development theory that assumes groups change gradually over time but that the periods of slow growth are punctuated by brief periods of relatively rapid change.

and as time runs out conflict and tension can rise, whereas the group's cohesiveness can drop (Mohammed, Hamilton, & Lim, 2009). The impact of time pressures on groups depends, however, on where the group is located: Some cultures, as Focus 5.2 notes, emphasize deadlines and agendas more than others.

The U.S. Olympic team's development, although stage-like in many respects, changed more rapidly following critical events. Perhaps the most dramatic turning point in the group's life occurred when the team lost an exhibition game to a weak team. Coach Brooks believed the team played without any heart or energy, and after the game he kept them on the ice rather than letting them shower and change. He made the players skate back and forth between the goals (the players called these drills "Herbies") for what seemed like hours. Even when the arena manager turned off the lights and went home, Brooks kept the team skating back and forth in the dark. The experience created a feeling of unity in the group, and this cohesiveness carried them through the remainder of their games and on to victory. Such turning points may, however, be relatively rare in groups. More typically, the shift from an initial orientation focus to a task focus occurs gradually as groups and their members pace their progress toward the completion of their final goal (Seers & Woodruff, 1997).

CONSEQUENCES OF COHESION

Cohesion is something of a purr word. Most people, if asked to choose between two groups—one that is cohesive and another that is not—would likely pick the cohesive group. But cohesiveness has its drawbacks. A cohesive group is an *intense* group, and this intensity affects the members, the group's dynamics, and the group's performance in both positive and negative ways. Cohesion leads to a range of consequences—not all of them desirable.

Focus 5.2   Cross-Cultural Perspectives: The Place and the Pace of Group Processes

Group development is not the inevitable result of the passage of time, but instead depends on dynamic processes that occur within the group that begin when the group first forms and end when the group eventually disbands. Groups must, for example, adapt to their environment, develop and enact methods for attaining their goals, structure and regularize relations, and satisfy members' need to feel connected to and not rejected by the group. These processes combine to produce group development. For example, as the group identifies and deals with sources of strain and tension, it moves into the conflict stage, and when it examines its goals and develops the means to achieve them, it has reached the performance stage. However, because these group-level processes are determined, in part, by cultural expectations and practices, group development will follow a different pace and sequence depending on the cultural background of the group members (Mohammed et al., 2009).

When a group first forms, for example, members reduce uncertainty and start to build trust. But in some cultures, relationship rules differ for public, formal settings and private, personal ones. When interacting in a formal setting, individuals from Japan would be less likely to disclose personal information or expect others to do so. Japanese businessmen and women traditionally exchange business cards during their initial encounters, but little else (Saunders, Van Slyke, & Vogel, 2004). Individuals in the United States and England, in contrast, are quicker to move from the awkward, first stages of group interaction by minimizing formality and revealing personal information (Argyle et al., 1986). Japanese cultural conventions with regard to the expression of emotions also stress reserve rather than exhibition, in contrast to such countries as Italy and Spain (Argyle et al., 1986). But if conflict is a precursor to true cohesiveness, until the group recognizes sources of conflict and resolves those issues, members will not become completely unified. Hence, groups in cultures that deal openly with conflict may move through this stage more rapidly, whereas groups in cultures that

avoid outward discussions of disagreement may skip this stage altogether.

Cultures also differ substantially in their perception of time itself, and these differences likely influence how quickly the group moves through the initial stages of group development to reach the performance stage. Cross-cultural researchers draw a distinction between **polychronic cultures** (P-time cultures), such as Portugal, parts of France, Middle-Eastern countries, Latin America, and some parts of Asia, and **monochronic cultures** (M-time cultures) such as the United States, Switzerland, and Germany (Hall, 1976). P-time cultures view time as flowing and reoccurring and deal with many activities at the same time, without as much concern for deadlines and the passage of time. M-time cultures, in contrast, emphasize a strict adherence to deadlines, agendas, and appointments and are in many cases more task-oriented and superficial in their interpersonal relations. In P-cultures, groups may spend considerable time at the start of a meeting discussing personal issues and not move on to the group's formal task in time to complete it in the allotted time. M-cultures, in contrast, are more task-oriented, and this focus sometimes results in them skipping the conflict stage altogether: They "rarely exhibit dysfunctional group dynamics, such as dealing with jealousy and hurt feelings, because they do not have enough time to do so" (Saunders et al., 2004, p. 23).

These differences in time orientation are particularly apparent in multicultural groups that mix together people from P-time and M-time cultures. One study of such groups conducted in Europe explained that individuals from more southern countries of Europe, such as Spain or Italy, were likely to be late for meetings, as compared to people from more northern countries, such as Germany and Sweden. As one respondent explained (Shachaf, 2008, p. 135):

> People in the north tend to be more precise with respect to time, with respect to quality. People in

---

polychronic cultures (P-time cultures) Collectives whose members view time as a continuous progression from the past into the future and therefore prefer to work on multiple tasks at the same time, without concern for deadline or production pressures.

monochronic cultures (M-time cultures) Collectives whose members view time as a discrete resource that is segmented into units (such as minutes and hours) and prefer to work on tasks in a logical, timely fashion completing one task before beginning another.

the south tend to be loose with time.... They are not actually right on time. It's a matter of appraising time. Time is less important as you go south.... In a European project, everybody knows that we have to be relaxed on that.

In the past, when groups were localized within a single culture and rarely included outsiders, members likely shared similar perspectives on self-disclosure, how to handle conflict, and time. These processes all influenced group dynamics and development, but in ways that were so similar across groups that their influence went unnoticed. Globalization, however, has resulted in groups that interact with groups from other cultures and groups that include members of varying cultural backgrounds, so now these processes have become more salient to members. A skilled group member must now not only understand group dynamics, but also cultural dynamics. Development, and the increases in cohesion and efficiency that are characteristics of mature groups, are important for all groups, but groups with members from many different cultures may benefit, even more substantially, from the process of development. Until such groups deal with issues of conflict, attraction, and performance, the diversity of these groups may be more of a hindrance than an advantage.

Member Satisfaction and Adjustment

Many of the men of the U.S. Olympic team, years later, said that their six months together in 1980 was a special time in their lives. People are usually much more satisfied with their groups when they are cohesive rather than non-cohesive. Across a range of groups in industrial, athletic, and educational settings, people who are members of highly compatible, cohesive groups report more satisfaction and enjoyment than members of non-cohesive groups. One investigator studied teams of masons and carpenters working on a housing development. For the first five months, the men worked at various assignments in groups formed by the supervisor. This period gave the men a chance to get to know virtually everyone working on the project and natural likes and dislikes soon surfaced. The researcher then established cohesive groups by making certain that the teams only contained people who liked each other. As anticipated, the masons and carpenters were much more satisfied when they worked in cohesive groups. As one of them explained, "Seems as though everything flows a lot smoother.... The work is more interesting when you've got a buddy working with you. You certainly like it a lot better anyway" (Van Zelst, 1952, p. 183).

A cohesive group creates a healthier workplace, at least at the psychological level. Because people in cohesive groups respond to one another in a more positive fashion than the members of non-cohesive groups, people experience less anxiety and tension in such groups (Myers, 1962; Shaw & Shaw, 1962). Individuals who are members of cohesive groups—with cohesion defined as a strong sense of belonging to an integrated community—are more actively involved in their groups, are more enthusiastic about their groups, and even suffer from fewer social and interpersonal problems (Hoyle & Crawford, 1994). Members are also more committed to their groups, where commitment is indicated by the degree of attachment to the group, a long-term orientation to the group, and intentions to remain within the group (Arriaga & Agnew, 2001; Wech et al., 1998). They will even sacrifice their own individual desires for the good of the group (Prapavessis & Carron, 1997).

In studies conducted in industrial work groups, for example, employees reported less anxiety and nervousness when they worked in cohesive groups (Seashore, 1954). Cohesion can even make a bad job not so bad, as Donald Roy's (1959) "banana time" case study revealed. Roy worked for two months in 12-hour shifts lasting from 8 AM to 8:30 PM with three other men in an isolated room in a garment factory operating a press machine. The work was not just tedious, but menial, repetitive, and tiring, since he stood the entire day feeding material to the press. He felt he could not last more than a week, but that was before he was drawn into the interaction of the small group. The group filled its workday with jokes, teasing, kidding around, and horseplay that gave structure and meaning to their work. To break up the day into smaller segments, the men stopped from time to time for various refreshments and breaks. There was, of course, lunchtime, but the men added many others, such as coffee time, peach time, fish time, and banana time. These rituals and social activities, collectively called "banana time" by Roy, turned a bad job into a good one.

Cohesive groups can, however, be emotionally demanding (Forsyth & Elliott, 1999). The **old sergeant syndrome**, for example, is more common in cohesive military squads. Although the cohesiveness of the unit initially provides psychological support for the individual, the loss of comrades during battle causes severe distress. When the unit is reinforced with replacements, the original group members are reluctant to establish emotional ties with the newcomers, partly in fear of the pain produced by separation. Hence, they begin restricting their interactions, and these "old sergeants" can eventually become completely isolated within the group (Sobel, 1947). Some highly cohesive groups may also purposefully sequester members from other groups in an attempt to seal members off from competing interests. Individuals who leave high-demand religious groups due to changes in beliefs or social mobility may experience loneliness, chronic guilt, and isolation; a lingering distrust of other people and groups; and anxiety about intimate relationships. As groups become highly cohesive, they can become so self-contained that members' links to nonmembers ("weak ties") are severed, virtually isolating the group (Gulati, Sytch, & Tatarynowicz, 2012).

---

old sergeant syndrome Symptoms of psychological disturbance, including depression, anxiety, and guilt, exhibited by noncommissioned officers in cohesive units that suffer heavy casualties. Strongly loyal to their unit and its members, these leaders feel so responsible for their unit's losses that they withdraw psychologically from the group.

Cohesive groups can also make those few members who are not closely bonded with the group feel like outsiders. Individuals who dropped out of cohesive groups often recognized that the group was cohesive, but they did not feel that they were part of that close-knit unit (Robinson & Carron, 1982). Being part of a cohesive group is not that enjoyable for those on the fringe.

Group Dynamics and Influence

As cohesion increases, the internal dynamics of the group intensify. In consequence, the pressure to conform is greater in cohesive groups, and individuals' resistance to these pressures is weaker. When members of cohesive groups discovered that some others in their group disagreed with their interpretations of three ambiguous stimuli, they tried to exert greater influence over their partners than did members of non-cohesive groups. Partners also conformed more in cohesive dyads, perhaps because they wanted to avoid confrontation (Back, 1951). When the group norms emphasize the value of cooperation and agreement, members of highly cohesive groups avoid disagreement more than members of non-cohesive groups. Irving Janis' (1982) theory of *groupthink* suggests that these pressures undermine a group's willingness to critically analyze its decisions. As Chapter 11 explains, in some cases, this breakdown in decision-making effectiveness can be disastrous.

Anecdotal accounts of highly cohesive groups—military squads, adolescent peer groups, sports teams, fraternities and sororities, and cults—often describe the strong pressures that these groups put on their members (Goldhammer, 1996). Cohesive groups—as the final section of this chapter concludes—are more likely to initiate their members. Drug use and illegal activities are often traced back to conformity pressures of adolescents' peer groups (Giordano, 2003). Cohesive gangs exert strong pressure on members (Coughlin & Venkatesh, 2003). Cults may demand extreme sacrifices from members, including suicide. Even sports teams, if highly cohesive, may extract both compliance and sacrifice from members (Prapavessis & Carron, 1997). Cohesion can also increase negative group processes, including hostility and scapegoating (French, 1941; Pepitone & Reichling, 1955). In one study, cohesive and non-cohesive groups worked on a series of unsolvable problems. Although all the groups seemed frustrated, coalitions tended to form in non-cohesive groups, whereas cohesive groups vented their frustrations through interpersonal aggression: overt hostility, joking hostility, scapegoating, and domination of subordinate members. The level of hostility became so intense in one group that observers lost track of how many offensive remarks were made; they estimated that the number surpassed 600 comments during the 45-minute work period (French, 1941).

Group Productivity

Most people consider cohesion to be a key ingredient for group success. The cohesive, unified group has, throughout history, been lauded as the most productive, the most likely to win in battle, and the most creative. The Spartans who held the pass at Thermopylae were a model of unity, courage, and strength. The explorers on the ship *Endurance*, which was crushed by ice floes during a voyage to the Antarctic, survived by working together under the able leadership of Ernest Shackleton. The engineers at the Palo Alto Research Center (PARC) invented the personal computer and other assorted technologies, including the mouse, a graphical interface (clickable icons), e-mail, and laser printers. When the U.S. Olympic team won, most sports commentators explained the victory by pointing to the U.S. team's cohesiveness, even suggesting that a unified team could work "miracles." But is this folk wisdom consistent with the scientific evidence? Are cohesive groups really more productive?

Do Cohesive Groups Outperform Less Unified Groups? Studies of all kinds of groups—sports teams, work groups in business settings, expeditions, military squads, and laboratory groups—generally confirm the cohesion–performance relationship: Cohesive groups tend to outperform less unified groups. But a series of meta-analytic studies in which researchers combined the results of all available

research, statistically, suggests that the relationship does not emerge in all studies and in all groups (Beal et al., 2003; Gully, Devine, & Whitney, 1995; Mullen & Copper, 1994; Oliver et al., 1999). One analysis of 49 studies of 8,702 members of a variety of groups reported that 92% of these studies supported cohesive groups over non-cohesive ones. However, this cohesion–performance relationship was stronger (1) in bona fide groups than in ad hoc laboratory groups, (2) in correlational studies than in experimental studies, and (3) in smaller groups than in larger groups (Mullen & Copper, 1994). The relationship between cohesion and performance was also strongest in studies of (a) sports teams, somewhat weaker in military squads, weaker still in nonmilitary bona fide groups, and weakest overall in ad hoc, artificial groups (Carron et al., 2002) and (b) project-focused teams rather than production or service teams (Chiocchio & Essiembre, 2009).

Are Cohesion and Performance Causally Connected? Prior studies of groups that work on tasks have found that "nothing succeeds like success" when it comes to cohesion. When a group performs well at its identified task, the level of cohesion in the group increases, but should it fail, disharmony, disappointment, and a loss of esprit de corps are typically observed. These effects of performance on cohesion occur even when groups are identical in all respects except one—when some are arbitrarily told they performed well, but others are told they did not do well. Even under these highly controlled circumstances, groups given positive feedback became more cohesive than groups that are told they performed poorly. These studies suggest that cohesion is related to performance, not because cohesion causes groups to perform better, but because groups that perform better become more cohesive (e.g., Forsyth, Zyzniewski, & Giammanco, 2002).

Social psychologists Brian Mullen and Carolyn Copper (1994) examined the flow of causality in the cohesion–performance relationship by comparing experimental studies that manipulated cohesion with studies that used correlational designs. Because the cohesion–performance relationship emerged in

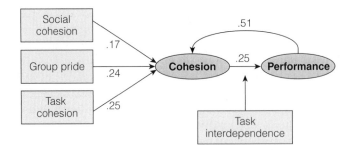

F I G U R E 5.2   The relationship between three forms of cohesion (social and task cohesion and group pride), cohesion, and performance. Meta-analyses suggest that cohesion influences performance, but that the impact of performance on cohesion is stronger than the impact of cohesion on performance.

SOURCE: © Cengage Learning

both types of studies, they concluded that cohesion causes improved performance. However, the relationship between cohesion and performance is stronger in correlational studies. This disparity suggests that cohesion aids performance, but that performance also causes changes in cohesiveness. Mullen and Copper closely examined seven correlational studies that measured cohesion and performance twice rather than once. These studies suggested that a group's cohesiveness at Time 1 predicted its performance at Time 1 and at Time 2. But in these studies, group performance at Time 1 was a particularly powerful predictor of *cohesiveness* at Time 2! These findings prompted Mullen and Copper to conclude that the cohesion–performance relationship is bidirectional: Cohesion makes groups more successful, but groups that succeed also become more cohesive (see Figure 5.2).

What Is It About Cohesive Groups That Makes Them More Effective?   Cohesive groups do outperform less cohesive groups. But what is it about a cohesive group that makes it more successful? Does the high level of attraction among members reduce conflict, making it easier for the group to concentrate on its work? Or perhaps group members are more dedicated to their group if it is cohesive, and this sense of dedication and group pride prompts them to expend more effort on behalf of their group.

The success of cohesive groups lies, in part, in the enhanced coordination of their members. In non-cohesive groups, members' activities are uncoordinated and disjointed, but in cohesive groups,

each member's contributions mesh with those of the other group members. Cohesion thus acts as a "lubricant" that "minimizes the friction due to the human 'grit' in the system" (Mullen & Copper, 1994, p. 213). Members of cohesive groups all share the same "mental model" of the group's task and its demands, and this shared prescription for how the task is to be accomplished facilitates their performance. Hence, cohesive groups are particularly likely to outperform non-cohesive groups when the group's task requires high levels of interaction and interdependence. The degree of interdependency required by the type of tasks the group is working on also determines the size of the cohesion–performance relationship; the more group members must coordinate their activities with one another, the more likely a cohesive group will outperform a less cohesive one (Beal et al., 2003; Gully et al., 1995).

These meta-analytic studies also show support for the value of a multicomponent conceptualization of cohesion, for they suggest that even when cohesion is operationalized in different ways, the cohesion–performance relationship still holds true. In their analysis, Mullen and Copper (1994) gave the edge to task cohesion, particularly in studies involving bona fide groups rather than artificial ones. Subsequent analyses, however, found evidence that all three components—social, task, and perceptual ("group pride") cohesion—were related to performance when one looked only at group-level studies (Beal et al., 2003). Figure 5.2 synthesizes the findings from these meta-analytic reviews.

These analyses confirm the relative performance gains achieved by cohesive groups, but they suggest that attraction and pride are not always enough: Without task cohesion and commitment to the group's goals, a cohesive group may be surprisingly *unproductive*. In a field study of this process, researchers surveyed 5,871 factory workers who worked in 228 groups. They discovered that the more cohesive groups were not necessarily more productive, but their productivity level from one member to the next was less variable. The individuals working in cohesive groups produced nearly equivalent amounts, but individuals in non-cohesive groups varied considerably from one member to the next in their productivity. Furthermore, fairly low standards of performance had developed in some of the highly cohesive groups; thus, productivity was uniformly low in these groups. In contrast, in cohesive groups with relatively high-performance goals, members were extremely productive (Langfred, 1998; Seashore, 1954). As Figure 5.3 indicates, so long as group norms encourage high productivity, cohesiveness and productivity are positively related: a highly cohesive group produces more than a less

cohesive one. If group norms encourage low productivity, however, the relationship is negative.

This tendency for the group's norms about productivity to moderate the strength of the cohesion–performance relationship was also confirmed experimentally by manipulating both cohesion and production norms (Berkowitz, 1954; Gammage, Carron, & Estabrooks, 2001). In one illustrative study, cohesive and non-cohesive groups worked on a simple assembly-line type task. Then, during the task, messages were ostensibly sent from one worker to another to establish performance norms. In some instances, the messages called for increased production (*positive messages*), but in other instances, the messages requested a slowdown (*negative messages*). As expected, the impact of the messages was significantly greater in the cohesive groups than in the non-cohesive groups. Furthermore, the decreases in productivity brought about by the negative messages were greater than the increases brought about by the positive messages (Schachter et al., 1951).

The take-home lesson from these studies—that creating social cohesiveness may make members

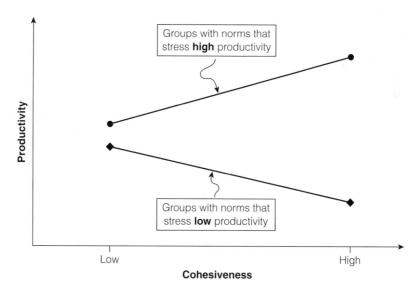

FIGURE 5.3   The relationship between cohesion and productivity when norms stress high and low productivity. If the group's norms encourage productivity, cohesiveness and productivity will be positively correlated. If the group standards for performance are low, however, cohesiveness will actually undermine productivity.

SOURCE: © Cengage Learning

happy but not productive—does not apply to the U.S. team. Every one of the team members was committed to the goal of winning the Olympics, so there was no worry that the performance norm would be set too low. In addition, because of the intervention of a thoughtful coach who skillfully built the group's unity, their cohesion developed over time until its peak during the Olympics. The team's triumph was called a miracle by some, but in retrospect, it was due to effective group dynamics.

APPLICATION: EXPLAINING INITIATIONS

Cohesiveness is no cure-all for what ails the ineffective group, but many groups in a variety of contexts—sports teams, military units, educational fraternities, sororities, clubs, work squads, and so on—nonetheless often take steps to deliberately increase their cohesion in the hopes their performance will improve. As Chapter 12's analysis of teambuilding explains, some of these interventions are effective—when groups identify shared goals, improve coordination, and identify sources of conflict, performance often improves. This section, however, concludes the analysis of cohesion by examining a common, but more controversial, means of unifying a group: initiations.

Group Cohesion and Initiations

Many groups require individuals to demonstrate their commitment to the group before they are allowed to become full-fledged group members. Elite military squads, for example, require a new member to pass extremely demanding tests of physical ability. Religious organizations typically require members to study the group's beliefs and practices and then pass tests on the material before they gain entrance. Other groups require the members to invest considerable time, energy, and personal resources in the group before they can join.

These investments may strengthen the bond between the individual and the group. Groups with admission standards and policies may be more attractive to members, since their exclusiveness may make them seem more prestigious. Since membership must be earned, people who join do so more intentionally and therefore will more likely be active, contributing members. Groups with less stringent requirements are hampered by the unevenness of the contributions of their members: Some may contribute a great deal to the group, but others may actually draw out more resources than they contribute. Groups with strict membership policies, including initiations, avoid this problem by screening and monitoring members closely and dismissing those individuals who do not demonstrate their worth (Iannaccone, 1994).

Initiations and Commitment Leon Festinger's (1957) theory of **cognitive dissonance** offers an intriguing explanation for the relationship between how much new members invest in the group and their commitment to the group. This theory assumes that people prefer to maintain consistency in their thoughts, attitudes, and beliefs. Their belief, for example, that they invested considerable time in a group would be consonant with the belief that this group was of high caliber. But what if, once they joined a group, they discovered it was worthless? Such a situation would generate dissonance and would cause the member psychological discomfort. Although people can reduce cognitive dissonance in many ways, one frequent method is to emphasize the rewarding features of the group while minimizing its costly characteristics.

Festinger developed this theory after his experiences studying a small "doomsday" group (Festinger et al., 1956). This group formed around a psychic named Marion Keech, who believed she was receiving messages from the Guardians, who lived on a planet named Clarion. Through these messages, the Guardians warned Ms. Keech of the impending destruction of the world by flood, but they assured

---

cognitive dissonance An adverse psychological state that occurs when an individual simultaneously holds two conflicting cognitions.

her that the small group of men and women who met regularly to discuss their messages would be rescued by a flying saucer before the December 21 deadline.

Festinger and his colleagues joined this group and recorded members' growing commitment to the group and to Ms. Keech as the deadline loomed. On that date, the faithful gathered in readiness in Ms. Keech's living room, with their bags packed, all metal zippers, buttons, snaps removed from their clothing (metal does strange things in flying saucers), and passwords all memorized. Unfortunately, midnight came and went with no sign of a flying saucer. The prophecy was disconfirmed, but the members did not denounce Ms. Keech as a fraud. Instead, they accepted her rationalization that the tremendous faith and devotion of the group was so impressive that God had decided to call off the flood, and they spread this important message to the news media. Although the central beliefs of the group had been disconfirmed, they refused to abandon them. If they admitted that Ms. Keech was mistaken, they would have no justification for their actions over the previous months; many had quit their jobs, dropped out of school, moved hundreds of miles to be closer to Ms. Keech, and alienated their friends and relatives. If, however, they became more firmly committed to Ms. Keech, then their cognitions and behaviors would all be consistent with one another, and they could avoid the dissonance that arises from inconsistency (cf. Batson, 1975; Hardyck & Braden, 1962).

Severe Initiations and Group Attraction Social psychologists Elliot Aronson and Judson Mills (1959) tested dissonance theory in their classic experimental study of young women's reactions to initiations. Their male experimenter greeted each subject individually and told her that she had been chosen to take part in a group discussion on the psychology of sex. He noted, however, that only women who could discuss sex without embarrassment would be welcome in the group, so all prospective members had to pass an "embarrassment test." Some of the women were then subjected to a severe initiation: They were required to read descriptions of sexual interludes and a series of

obscene words aloud to the male experimenter. (In 1959, women were presumably embarrassed by such vulgarities.) Women who experienced a mild initiation read some mildly provocative passages and words, and women in the control group only agreed to be screened. They randomly assigned female college students to one of three experimental conditions: a severe initiation condition, a mild initiation condition, and a control condition.

After the initiation, the researchers told the women that the group they would be joining was already meeting but that they could listen in using an intercom system. But instead of listening to an actual group, the researchers played a recording of a discussion that was contrived deliberately to be exceedingly boring and dull. After listening for a time, the participants rated the group they had listened to on a number of dimensions. As Figure 5.4 indicates, women who experienced the severe initiation rated the group more positively than those who had experienced a mild initiation or no initiation at all.

Several replications of this unusual study have confirmed the basic finding that initiations influence attraction to and dependency on the group. In one study, researchers used electric shocks rather than obscene readings to manipulate the severity of the initiation into the group and found very similar

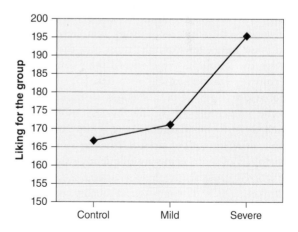

F I G U R E 5.4 The effects of initiation on liking for a group.

SOURCE: © Cengage Learning

results: People who received stronger shocks liked the group the best (Gerard & Mathewson, 1966). In another set of studies, participants completed a series of embarrassing, socially awkward activities (such as acting out demeaning situations or performing silly behaviors) or neutral activities before joining a group. In these studies, individuals who suffered through the more severe initiation were more likely to conform to the group's decisions, rated the group more positively, and felt more comfortable when part of the group (Keating et al., 2005).

Aronson and Mills concluded that the initiation increased cohesion by creating cognitive dissonance, but other factors may also account for the initiation–cohesion relationship. Rather than attempt to reduce cognitive dissonance, their public expressions of liking for such groups may also stem more from a desire to save face after making a faulty decision than from the psychic discomfort of cognitive dissonance (Schlenker, 1975). Initiations also fail to heighten attraction if they frustrate new members or make them angry (Lodewijkx & Syroit, 1997).

Hazing

Some groups do not just require members to meet certain criteria and pass tests of stamina or intellectual fitness before allowing entrance. They instead subject new members to cost-creating experiences that have nothing to do with the actual qualities needed to be a successful group member. Initiates in biker gangs, for example, must earn the right to wear the letters and emblems of their gang—their "colors"—by performing a variety of distasteful behaviors (Davis, 1982). Pledges to fraternities at some universities are ritually beaten, subjected to ridicule and embarrassment, and required to drink unhealthy amounts of alcohol (Nuwer, 1999). New members of sports teams are frequently subjected to ritualized physical, psychological, and sexual abuse (Finkel, 2002). These practices qualify as **hazing**

Hazing An initiation into a group that subjects the new member to mental or physical discomfort, harassment, embarrassment, ridicule, or humiliation.

because they expose the new member to significant risk of psychological and physical harm.

Hazing is an entrenched group practice and has been documented in ancient and modern societies and in all parts of the world. Newcomers to groups are routinely subjected to various abuses for reasons both rational and completely irrational (Cimino, 2011).

- *Bonding and Dependence*: As Festinger's dissonance theory suggests, individuals who suffer to join a group value the group more and become more dependent on the group as a source of support and acceptance. Initiation of groups of newcomers, which is typical of certain groups (e.g., sororities, fraternities, sports teams), increases feelings of unity, for they tend to affiliate more extensively as they deal with the threat and stress. The initiation process thus creates greater cohesion in the overall group, as the individuality of each newcomer is diminished and they learn to rely socially on others (Lodewijkx, van Zomeren, & Syroit, 2005).

- *Dominance*: Initiations serve to introduce new members to the hierarchical order of the group and the requirements to recognize and respect veteran members. The initiation process humbles the newcomers and signals to them their low status, which they can raise only by contributing in substantial ways to the group. The hazing rituals also provide the current members with the means to exercise their power over the newcomers.

- *Commitment*: Hazing requires a substantial commitment from newcomers and serves to weed out individuals who are not willing to meet the group's demands. Hazing provides newcomers with the means to prove their worth.

- *Tradition*: Many groups haze new members because they feel that they must honor the group's traditions, established by founding members of the society (Nuwer, 1999).

Newcomers continue to accept membership in groups that use hazing for many reasons, as well, including a desire to be accepted and to make a good impression with others. In many cases, newcomers are not made aware of the hazing demands and dangers until they are sequestered by the group, and they may fear that refusing to comply with the group's demands will cause more problems and pose greater risks than compliance. Although victims of hazing appear to have voluntarily taken part in the initiation rites, group influence processes create extremely strong pressures that limit hazing victims' capacities to act of their own free will. One emergency room physician, who has experience dealing with hazing-related injuries, recommends treating "hazing patients as victims of violent crime, rather than willing participants in their traumatic injuries" (Finkel, 2002, p. 231).

Is Hazing Effective?   Many members of groups defend their right to haze, citing the benefits of initiation for increasing the cohesion of the group. However, research does not offer very much support for this position. One team of investigators asked the members of a number of groups and teams to differentiate between appropriate and inappropriate activities on a list of 24 practices commonly used in initiations and hazing. Appropriate activities included requirements to take part in group activities, swearing an oath, taking part in skits and team functions, doing community service, and maintaining a specific grade point average. Inappropriate activities, in contrast, included kidnapping and abandonment, verbal abuse, physical punishment (spankings, whippings, and beatings), degradation and humiliation (such as eating disgusting things or drinking alcohol in excessive amounts), sleep deprivation, running errands, and exclusion. Somewhat unexpectedly, a number of the behaviors that the researchers felt belonged on the list of inappropriate hazing behaviors, such as wearing inappropriate clothing, head shaving, and sexual activities, were viewed as relatively innocuous by participants (van Raalte et al., 2007).

Did these experiences work to build a cohesive group? Some of these practices were rarely used by groups, but groups that did use inappropriate hazing methods were judged to be less cohesive rather than more cohesive. Hazing, and illicit hazing in particular, backfired, for it did not contribute to increased cohesion, whereas more positive forms of team-building did (van Raalte et al., 2007).

Should Groups Haze?   Hazing is illegal in a number of states, is aggressive in character, yields unhealthy consequences, and does not even work to increase cohesion, yet this practice continues unofficially. Some mild rites and rituals—as when new members must take a public oath of loyalty, memorize the group's mission, or carry a distinctive object—cause little harm, but in other cases, new members must endure physical and psychological abuse before they are accepted into the group. Emergency room physicians report that they have treated victims of hazing for alcoholic coma, chest trauma, aspiration, 1st, 2nd, and 3rd degree burns, syncope, vomiting, organ damage, heart irregularities, gastrointestinal distress, brain damage, multi-organ system failure, spinal cord injury, exposure, depression, posttraumatic stress, anxiety, and anal, oral, and vaginal trauma (Finkel, 2002). Each year many students are killed or seriously injured in hazing incidents (Goldstein, 2002).

Herb Brooks, the coach of the U.S. Olympic hockey team, did not use hazing, but instead timeworn traditions in sports fitness and training to build the group into a cohesive unit. He was tough on his players, they played dozens of exhibition games leading up to the Olympics, and Brooks kept all of them on edge, threatening to send any one of them home who did not perform up to his standards. Through these experiences, the group reached a very high level of cohesiveness, without recourse to hazing. Given that groups can turn to a variety of equally effective but safe methods to build their groups cohesiveness, the use of hazing is completely unjustified.

CHAPTER REVIEW

What is group cohesion, and what are its sources?

1. Group cohesion is the integrity, solidarity, and unity of the group. Cohesiveness is an indication of the health of the group and is related to a variety of other group processes. Entitativity is, in contrast, perceived cohesiveness.

2. A number of group-level processes contribute to a group's cohesion, so what unifies the members of one group may not unify the members of another. Cohesion, as the principle of *equifinality* suggests, can result from one or more sources, including attraction relations, task relations, identity, emotions, and structure.

3. *Social cohesion* is unity based on bonds of attraction among members and attraction to the group itself.

   ▪ Lewin and Festinger, taking a social psychological approach to cohesion, considered cohesion to be a field of social forces that keeps members in their groups.

   ▪ Sherif and Sherif, using a unique field-study method in a boys' summer camp, found that the same sorts of variables that influence liking and group formation also influence the cohesiveness of the group that is formed.

   ▪ Hogg's concept of social attraction stresses a specific form of group-level attraction based on social identity processes.

4. *Task cohesion* is unity based on members' sharing a common goal that motivates them to work together to achieve that goal.

5. *Collective cohesion* is unity based on members' level of identification with the group.

   ▪ Freud's replacement hypothesis and social identity theory both examine the psychology of identification and cohesion.

   ▪ *Identity fusion theory* suggests that, in extreme cases, self and group identities can be fused into one.

6. *Emotional cohesion* is the affective intensity of the group, often described as élan, morale, esprit de corps, or positive affective tone.

   ▪ Lawler, Thye, and Yoon's *relational cohesion theory* suggests that cohesion results from the positive emotions members' attribute to social exchange in groups.

   ▪ Behavioral coordination, including *mimicry* and *behavioral synchrony*, are not only likely to occur in cohesive groups, but acting in a behaviorally synchronized way (such as marching, as described by McNeill) increases group cohesion.

7. *Structural cohesion* is group unity based on the structural integrity of the group, including roles, norms, and interpersonal networks of member-to-member relationships.

   ▪ According to Ziller, *open groups* display less cohesion than *closed groups*. Online groups (e-groups), because they tend to be open, are lower in cohesiveness and membership stability than offline groups.

   ▪ The Sherifs' study of groups suggested that some structural features (such as the absence of subgroups, less hierarchy, etc.) promote increases in cohesiveness.

8. Cohesion can be defined and measured in many ways, since it is a multicomponent and multilevel process.

How does cohesion develop over time?

1. Cohesion is, in most cases, the consequence of a period of group development—a pattern of growth and change beginning with initial formation and ending, in most cases, with dissolution.

2. As Hill notes, many theories have been developed to explain how groups change over time as they mature. Most, however,

are consistent with Tuckman's *five-stage model of group development*:

- Orientation (forming) stage: Members experience tentative interactions, tension, concern over ambiguity, growing interdependence, and attempts to identify the nature of the situation.

- Conflict (storming) stage: Members express dissatisfaction with the group, respond emotionally, criticize one another, and form coalitions.

- Structure (norming) stage: Unity increases, membership stabilizes, members report increased satisfaction, and the group's internal dynamics intensify.

- Performance (performing) stage: The group's focus shifts to the performance of tasks and goal attainment. Not all groups reach this stage, for even highly cohesive groups are not necessarily productive.

- Dissolution (adjourning) stage: The group disbands. A group's entry into the dissolution stage can be either planned or spontaneous, but even planned dissolution can create problems for members as they work to reduce their dependence on the group.

3. Wheelan's Group Development Questionnaire measures orientation, conflict, structure, and productivity over time.

4. Many groups follow a different developmental course over time.

- Tuckman's model is a successive-stage theory; it specifies the usual order of the phases of group development. Cyclical models, such as Bales' *equilibrium model*, maintain that groups cycle through various stages repeatedly.

- *Punctuated equilibrium models* suggest that groups sometimes move through periods of accelerated change.

- Cultural processes also influence group development. Groups in *polychronic cultures* (P-time cultures), for example, likely develop more slowly and follow a less stage-like progression than groups in *monochronic cultures* (M-time cultures).

What are the positive and negative consequences of cohesion?

1. In most instances, cohesion is associated with increases in member satisfaction and decreases in turnover and stress.

- Roy's analysis of "banana time" in work groups illustrates how groups maintain cohesiveness through ritual and social interaction.

- Cohesive groups can be so psychologically demanding that they cause emotional problems for members (e.g., the old sergeant's syndrome).

2. Cohesion intensifies group processes. Dependence, pressure to conform, and acceptance of influence are greater in cohesive groups and can result in the mistaken decisions identified by Janis in his theory of groupthink.

3. Cohesion and performance are linked, both because success increases a group's cohesion and because cohesive groups tend to perform better than less cohesive groups.

- Meta-analytic studies by Mullen, Copper, and other researchers suggest that each component of cohesion contributes to task proficiency.

- Even though cohesive groups tend to outperform less cohesive groups, this relationship is strongest when members are committed to the group's tasks. If group norms do not encourage high productivity, then cohesiveness and productivity are negatively related.

Do initiations increase cohesion?

1. Many groups require members to pass an initiation before they can join.

2. Festinger's theory of *cognitive dissonance* suggests that initiations create dissonance that new

members resolve by increasing their commitment to the group.

- The increased dedication of the members of the doomsday group formed by psychic Marion Keech supported dissonance theory.

- Aronson and Mills confirmed that people who go through some kind of initiation to join a group tend to like that group more.

3. Hazing is a severe initiation that exposes new members to significant psychological and physical risk.

- Hazing is sustained by a number of group-level processes, including bonding, dominance, commitment, and tradition.

- The use of hazing is unjustified. It is ineffective as a means of increasing cohesion and is illegal.

RESOURCES

Chapter Case: U.S. Olympic Hockey Team

- "A Reminder of What We Can Be," by E. M. Swift (1980) provides many of the basic details about the 1980 U.S. Olympic hockey team and its coach.

Defining and Measuring Cohesion

- "Group Cohesion: From 'Field of Forces' to Multidimensional Construct" by Kenneth L. Dion (2000) reviews key issues in the study of cohesion, with a focus on definitional debates and problems in measurement.

- *The Social Psychology of Group Cohesiveness: From Attraction to Social Identity* by Michael A. Hogg (1992) thoroughly reviews conceptual analyses of the concept of cohesion and bases its integrative theoretical reinterpretation on social identity theory.

Group Development

- *Group Processes: A Developmental Perspective* by Susan A. Wheelan (2005) provides an extensive analysis of each stage that marks the maturation of most groups.

- "Team Development" by Claire B. Halverson (2008) provides a practical guide to dealing with the changes groups experience over time.

Consequences of Cohesion

- "Cohesion and Performance in Groups: A Meta-Analytic Clarification of Construct Relations" by Daniel Beal, Robin Cohen, Michael Burke, and Christy McLendon (2003) carefully considers the methodological issues involved in examining the cohesion–performance relationship and then provides clear documentation of that relationship.

- "The Essence of Military Group Cohesion" by Guy L. Siebold (2007) provides a clear introduction to the standard model of cohesion that guides experts' analyses of cohesion in combat groups.

Hazing

- *Wrongs of Passage: Fraternities, Sororities, Hazing, and Binge Drinking* by Hank Nuwer (1999) remains one of the best researched analyses of hazing on college campuses.

6

Structure

CHAPTER OVERVIEW

The structure of anything, be it a house, a solar system, or a group, is defined by the fixed arrangement of the individual elements. In all but the most ephemeral groups, members are distributed into different roles, and their behavior when in these roles is regulated by norms that dictate what is and what is not proper conduct. The group structure also includes the relationships that join members to one another in an integrated network that regulates interdependencies and increases the group's unity and durability.

- What is group structure?

- What are norms, how do they develop, and how do they work to regulate behavior?

- What kinds of roles are common in groups, and how do they influence members?

- How do social networks shape status, attraction, and communication processes in groups?

CHAPTER OUTLINE

Norms

    The Nature of Social Norms

    The Development of Norms

    The Transmission of Norms

    The Importance of Norms

Roles

    The Nature of Social Roles

    Role Theories

    Group Socialization

    Role Stress

Intermember Relations

    Social Network Analysis

    Network Dynamics

    Application: The SYMLOG Model

Chapter Review

Resources

Andes Survivors: One Group's Triumph over Extraordinary Adversity

The group chartered the Fairchild F-227 to travel from Uruguay to Chile. Most of the passengers on the flight were members of the Old Christians amateur rugby team or their family and friends. But they never reached their destination. The pilots misjudged their course and began their descent far too soon. The plane clipped the peak of Mt. Tinguiririca and crashed in the snow-covered Andes of South America.

Those who survived the crash struggled to stay alive in the harsh, subzero temperatures of the barren Andes. During the first days of the ordeal, they argued intensely over the likelihood of a rescue. Some insisted that searchers would soon find them. Others wanted to climb down from the mountain. Some became so apathetic that they didn't care. But the search planes never spotted them, and their hopes began to fade when a second tragedy struck the group: Early one morning, an avalanche filled the wrecked fuselage where they slept with snow, and many died before they could dig their way out.

A lone individual would have certainly perished in the harsh climate. But the group, by pooling their resources and skills, survived. They organized their work, with some cleaning their sleeping quarters, some tending the injured, and others melting snow into drinking water. When their food ran out, they made the difficult decision to eat the frozen bodies of those who had died in the crash. And when starvation seemed imminent, they sent two men, Fernando Parrado and Roberto Canessa, down the mountain to seek help. After hiking for 14 days, the two explorers, running low on food and supplies, stumbled into a farmer tending his cattle. Parrado himself guided the rescue helicopters back to the crash site. All of them, when asked how they survived, credited the unity of the group. When they read author Pier Paul Read's book about their ordeal, they complained of only one inaccuracy: They felt that he failed to capture the "faith and friendship which inspired them" for 70 days (Read, 1974, p. 310).

The group that came down from the Andes was not the same group that began the flight. Many members were lost to the group forever, and the trauma changed each one of the survivors permanently. But its *group structure* also changed. The structure of a thing is the relatively fixed arrangement of and relations among its constituent elements that links those elements together to form a single integrated whole (which is called, somewhat redundantly, a "structure"). In groups, structure is largely determined by regulatory standards that define how members are supposed to behave (norms) given their position in the group (roles) and the connections among members (intermember relations). When the group was a rugby team, members paid heed to a very different set of *norms* than they did when they were transformed into a group fighting for its very survival. The group began the flight with one set of *roles* and positions—a captain, a coach, parents, supporters, and friends—but ended with an entirely different set of roles, including leaders, helpers, and explorers. The *network* of relationships linking members one to another, in terms of status, liking, and communication, also changed. Men who were at first afforded little respect or courtesy eventually earned considerable status within the group. Some who were well-liked before the crash became outcasts. Some who had hardly spoken to the others before became active communicators within the group.

Any group, whether stranded in the Andes, sitting at a conference table, or working to manufacture some product, can be better understood by examining its structural features. Explaining group behavior in structural terms is analogous to tracing individuals' actions back to their personalities. Personality traits and dispositions cannot be observed directly, yet they influence people's actions across time and settings. Similarly, a structural analysis assumes that group interactions follow a predictable, organized pattern because they are regulated by influential interpersonal structures. This chapter examines three of these core determinants of a group's "personality": norms, roles, and networks (see Biddle, 2001; Hechter & Op, 2001 for reviews).

NORMS

The survivors of the crash needed to coordinate their actions if they were to stay alive. With food, water, and shelter severely limited, they were forced to interact with and rely on each other continually, and any errant action on the part of one person would disturb and even endanger several other people. So members began to abide by a set of unstated rules that defined how the group would sleep at night, what types of duties each healthy individual was expected to perform, and how food and water were to be apportioned. These consensual, regulatory standards are *norms*.

The Nature of Social Norms

Norms are a fundamental element of social structure; the "cement of society" (Elster, 1989, p. 251). Because they are group standards rather than just personal standards, they provide direction and motivation, organize social interactions, and make other people's responses predictable and meaningful. Simple behaviors, such as choice of clothing ("Wear shoes in public"), manners ("Do not interrupt others"), and conventions of address ("Call the professor 'Dr.'"), are based on norms, but so are general societal principles of fairness ("Help others when they are in need"), morality ("Do not lie to members of the group"), and value ("Work hard for the group"). Each group member is restrained to a degree by norms, but each member also benefits from the order that norms provide.

Some norms are specific to a given group. When one group meets, it may be appropriate to interrupt others when they are talking, to arrive late and leave early, and to dress informally. In another group, however, such behaviors would be considered inappropriate violations of group norms of dress and decorum. Some social norms, in contrast, are so widely adopted within a given context and culture that they structure behavior across groups. **Folkways**, for example, are

the influential but ubiquitous standards that define conventional behavior within a culture; they regulate such everyday behaviors as grammar and vocabulary, styles of dress, and conduct in public spaces. **Mores**, in contrast, are more strictly enforced society-wide standards for conduct that apply across situations and individuals. The right to life and self-determination are mores, as are taboos against incest, murder, and cannibalism (Sumner, 1906).

Types of Group Norms Norms prescribe the socially appropriate way to respond in the situation—the normal course of action. Just as a physician's prescription recommends a medicine, so **prescriptive norms** define the socially appropriate way to respond in a situation. **Proscriptive norms**, in contrast, are prohibitions; they define the types of actions that should be avoided if at all possible (Sorrels & Kelley, 1984). For example, some of the prescriptive norms of the Andes group were "Food should be shared equally" and "Those who are not injured should work to help those who are injured," whereas some proscriptive norms were "Do not urinate inside the airplane" and "Do not give up hope."

Norms also differ in their evaluative implications. **Descriptive norms** describe what most people *usually* do, feel, or think in a particular situation. None of the survivors in the Andes groups had ever been in such a desperate situation before, and so they intuitively did what most of the others did: They listened to the radio for information about the rescue and did what the leader told them to do. Everyone did not perfectly match their behavior up to these norms, but most did. This high degree of similarity in everyone's actions

---

folkways The emergent, taken-for-granted ways of acting within a culture or society.

mores The inviolate, morally sanctioned standards of proper action in a culture or society.

prescriptive norm A consensual standard that identifies preferable, positively sanctioned behaviors.

proscriptive norm A consensual standard that identifies prohibited, negatively sanctioned behaviors.

descriptive norm A consensual standard that describes how people typically act, feel, and think in a given situation.

provided members with information about how they should think, feel, and act. As social psychologist Robert Cialdini's (2009) principle of social proof suggests, people assume that a behavior is the correct one when they see others performing it.

Injunctive norms are more evaluative—they describe the sorts of behaviors that people *ought* to perform—or *else* (Morris, 1956). People who do not conform to descriptive norms may be viewed as unusual, but people who violate injunctive norms are negatively evaluated and are open to sanction by the other group members (Rimal & Real, 2005). In the Andes group, for example, those who failed to do their fair share were criticized by the others, given distasteful chores, and sometimes even denied food and water. People who violate injunctive norms are disliked, assigned lower status jobs, pressured to conform, and, in some cases, excluded from membership (Schachter, 1951; see Chapter 7).

Internalization of Norms Norms are not simply external rules but internalized standards; most group members feel duty bound to adhere to norms since they accept the legitimacy of the established norms and recognize the importance of supporting them. They do not conform to norms just because they wish to avoid the social condemnation that might result if they violate the norm, but also because they wish to avoid self-condemnation.

In a study that tested this assumption, pairs of students attending Texas A&M University (the "Aggies") were recruited to work in the same room, each one trying to solve a puzzle (a Rubik's cube). Unbeknown to one of the students, the other student was part of the research team, and she feigned difficulty getting a solution to her cube. When the experimenter returned to check on the group and "discovered" that one of them had failed to solve the puzzle, he told the actual

subject he or she had either conformed to or violated a descriptive norm or an injunctive norm by not doing anything to help. Subjects in the descriptive norm conditions were told they acted "like most Aggies" or "unlike most Aggies" by working independently on their own puzzle. But subjects in the injunctive norm conditions were told their behavior conformed to or violated the "Aggie motto." In these conditions, subjects led to believe they had conformed to an injunctive norm were told "you upheld the Aggie motto of not cheating," but those led to believe they had violated an injunctive norm were told "you did not uphold the Aggie motto of helping others." Also, in half the conditions, the experimenter mentioned the subject's group membership (the Aggies), but in the other conditions, no mention was made of the reference group (Christensen et al., 2004).

The results affirmed the influence of injunctive norms on group members' emotions. When students conformed to the norm—either descriptive or injunctive—their emotions were very positive ones. But when they realized they had violated a norm, their emotions were more negative, but only when the norm was injunctive rather than descriptive. These differences did not hold for students who did not identify with their group and those who were not reminded of their group membership.

Social psychologist Stanley Milgram also documented the personal consequences of violating norms—albeit more informally. In one investigation, he had men and women board a New York City subway and perform a simple counter-normative behavior: asking someone for their seat. In this situation, all interactants recognize and accept the rule "All seats are filled on a first-come, first-served basis," so asking for people to give up their seat is a norm violation. Still, many people gave up their seats, apparently because the request took them by surprise and they wanted to avoid interaction, or because they normalized the situation by concluding that the requestor was ill. Milgram was particularly intrigued, however, by the reactions displayed by the norm-violators. Even though they were volunteers who were deliberately

---

injunctive norm An evaluative consensual standard that describes how people should act, feel, and think in a given situation rather than how people do act, feel, and think in that situation.

breaking the situational norms in the name of research, all experienced severe emotional turmoil as they approached the situation. They "reported that when standing in front of a subject, they felt anxious, tense, and embarrassed. Frequently, they were unable to vocalize the request for a seat and had to withdraw" (Milgram, 1992, p. 42). Milgram, who also performed the norm-violation task, described the experience as wrenching, and concluded that there is an "enormous inhibitory anxiety that ordinarily prevents us from breaching social norms" (p. xxiv).

The Development of Norms

Groups sometimes discuss and formally adopt norms as their group's rules, but more frequently norms are implicit standards rather than explicit ones. Because members gradually align their behaviors until they match certain standards, they are often not even aware that their behavior is dictated by the norms of the situation. People do not, for example, spend a great deal of time wondering "Should I be quiet in the library?" "Should I nap during the group meeting?" or "Should I stop when the light turns red?" Most take these norms for granted so fully that they comply with them automatically (Aarts, Dijksterhuis, & Custers, 2003). Like the members of a concert orchestra tuning their instruments before a performance, this **social tuning** results in the alignment of each individual's action with the actions of others around him or her (Lun et al., 2007).

The Andes survivors, for example, grew up in a culture that condemned cannibalism, but this taboo was largely unstated. But when the group grew weak from starvation, one member casually remarked that the only source of nourishment was the frozen bodies of the crash victims. The others took the remark to be a joke until the tenth day when "the discussion spread as these boys cautiously mentioned it to their friends or those they thought would be sympathetic" (Read, 1974, p. 76). When the topic was discussed by the entire group, two cliques emerged; one favored eating the corpses, but a second group claimed that they could not bring themselves to think of their dead friends as food. The next day, however, they learned by radio that the air force had given up the search. Most of the members then ate a few pieces of meat and, in the end, cannibalism became the norm (Parrado, 2006).

Social psychologist Muzafer Sherif (1936), as noted in Chapter 1, studied this social tuning process by taking advantage of the *autokinetic* (self-motion) *effect*. This visual illusion occurs when a person stares at a pinpoint of light in an otherwise dark room. Ordinarily the visual system compensates for naturally occurring motions of the eye, but when only a single light is visible with no frame of reference, the light appears to wander in unpredictable directions and at variable speeds. Sherif found that when individuals judged the dot's movement repeatedly, they usually established their own idiosyncratic average estimates that varied from 1 to 10 inches. But when people made their judgments in groups, their personal estimates blended with those of other group members. One group, for example, included three people who had already been tested individually. During these initial tests, Person A thought the light moved very little—about 1 inch. Person B estimated the movement at 2 inches, but C's estimates were higher, averaging about 7 inches. When these three people made their estimates of the movement aloud when seated together, their judgments converged. It took three meetings, but by the third session, a norm had emerged: All the members felt the light was moving about 3 inches. Figure 6.1 graphs this convergence process: Over time, individuals with the highest and lowest estimates revise their judgments to match the group average.

The Transmission of Norms

Sherif confirmed that norms emerge, gradually, as group members' behaviors, judgments, and beliefs align over time (Echterhoff, Higgins, & Levine,

---

social tuning The tendency for individuals' actions and evaluations to become more similar to the actions and assumed evaluations of those around them.

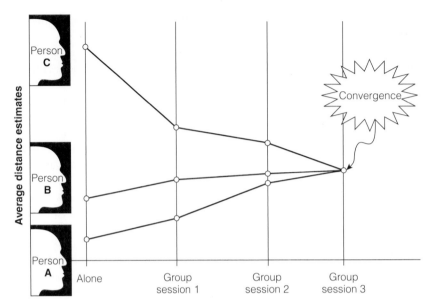

FIGURE 6.1 Sherif's experimental creation of group norms. Individuals' private, pregroup judgments differed markedly, but when they joined with others their judgments converged.

SOURCE: Data from M. Sherif, *The Psychology of Social Norms*, 1936, Harper & Row.

2009). But Sherif also arranged for people to make their judgments alone after taking part in the group sessions when a norm emerged. Did these individuals revert back to their original estimates of movement, or did they continue to base their estimates on the norm that emerged within their group? Sherif discovered that, even though the other group members were no longer present, the individuals' judgments were still consistent with the group's norms (Sherif, 1966). They had *internalized* the norm.

Norms, because they are both consensual (accepted by many group members) and internalized (personally accepted by each individual member), are social facts—taken-for-granted elements of the group's stable structure. Even if the individuals who originally fostered the norms are no longer present, their normative innovations remain a part of the organization's traditions, and newcomers must change to adopt that tradition. Researchers have studied this norm transmission experimentally using a *generational* paradigm: They create a group and then add newcomers to it and retire old-timers

until the entire membership of the group has turned over. Do these succeeding generations of members remain true to the group's original norms, even if these norms are arbitrary or cause the group to make errors and mistakes? In one autokinetic effect study, researchers established an extreme norm by planting a confederate in each three-member group. The confederate steadfastly maintained that the dot of light was moving about 15 inches—an excessive estimate given that most estimates averaged about 3 to 4 inches. Once the confederate deflected the group's distance norm upward, he was removed from the group and replaced by a naive participant. The remaining group members, however, still retained the large distance norm, and the newest addition to the group gradually adapted to the higher standard. The researchers continued to replace group members with new participants, but new members continued to shift their estimates in the direction of the group norm. This arbitrary group norm gradually disappeared as judgments of distance came back down to an average of 3.5 inches, but in most cases, the more reasonable norm did not develop until group membership had changed five or six times (Jacobs & Campbell, 1961; MacNeil & Sherif, 1976). In another generational study, researchers gave groups feedback that suggested that their norm about how decisions should be made was causing them to make errors, but this negative feedback did not reduce the norm's longevity across generations (Nielsen & Miller, 1997).

Studies of the emergence and transmission of norms in a variety of settings—in workgroups, families, sports teams, and children's groups—all demonstrate just how rapidly norms can emerge to structure group behavior (e.g., Bicchieri, 2006; Rossano, 2012). Even children as young as three years old learn norms quickly and respond negatively when newcomers violate these rules. In one study, for example, two- and three-year-olds played for a time with a familiar object—a sponge—in two areas of the day care center. When in the rest area, they were taught to use the sponge to clean. But when in the games area, they were taught to roll the sponge as part of a game. Later, someone else (a puppet, actually) tried to use the sponge for cleaning in the game area or for playing in the rest area, and the researchers watched to see how the children reacted. As they expected, three-year-olds complained when the sponge was misused, saying things like "No! It does not go like this" or "No, you are not allowed to clean up here." These studies suggest that people, when in groups, are by nature ready to follow norms, and, in consequence, group-level consistencies take root easily and can establish a life of their own (Rakoczy et al., 2009; see Focus 6.1).

The Importance of Norms

Because norms tend to resist revision, some group's norms may seem pointless and arbitrary rather than reasonable and functional (see Table 6.1). But norms are essential to group functioning, for even odd or unusual norms organize interactions, increase predictability, and enhance solidarity (Collins, 2004). Why do people feel obligated to help others who help them (Chapter 3)? Why do members of cohesive groups tend to work only as hard as everyone else in the group (see Chapter 5)? Why do people sometimes abandon their own beliefs and adopt the group's position as their own (see Chapter 7)? Why do group members feel justified in retaliating against other members who treat them harshly (Chapter 13)? Why do people who are part of social movements or large crowds sometimes engage in aberrant behavior (Chapter 17)? Because of the influence of norms on members' thoughts, feelings, and actions.

Norms about Drinking Alcohol   Norms regulate interactions in groups, facilitate productivity, and limit conflict, but such negative, unhealthy behaviors as alcohol abuse, overeating, and drug use can also be traced to normative processes. Consider, for example, the impact of social norms on the consumption of alcohol by young adults. Heavy use of alcohol is common on college campuses, even among students who are too young to possess alcohol legally. This excessive use of alcohol is associated with a number of negative outcomes, including lower performance, physical injury, and violence (Hingson et al., 2009; Wechsler & Nelson, 2008). Yet, drinking excessively is considered "normal" on many campuses. Polls of students suggest that most consider drinking five drinks in succession to be appropriate if one is partying, and more than 40% of students conform to that norm (Neighbors et al., 2008). Many students, when asked about the drinking norms endorsed by the groups to which they belong, such as their primary friendship groups, campus clubs, and sororities and fraternities, reported that these groups often approve of "drinking alcohol every weekend" and "drinking enough to pass out" (LaBrie et al., 2010, p. 345)—and the stronger the group's endorsement of drinking, the more heavily students who belong to such groups drank. Many students, when asked about clearly abnormal consequences of drinking—such as substantial loss of memory (e.g., blackouts), loss of consciousness ("passing out"), physical impairment (e.g., dizziness, staggering gait), and illness (vomiting)—considered them to be normal rather than abnormal, but viewing these consequences as acceptable is also associated with excessive drinking (e.g., Mallett et al., 2011).

Focus 6.1   E-groups: Beware the Norms of Social Networking

These days many groups convene virtually in social networking sites, rather than at such physical locations as clubs, conference rooms, and luncheons. Individuals who use the very popular Facebook social networking site, for example, connect with others by "friending" each other. One person sends another person a "friend request," and the person who receives the request must accept this offer to create the friend link. But, just as the interactions that occur in face-to-face groups are guided by a set of rules of comportment, so norms have emerged on social networks that define what is appropriate and what is not. To open an account on Facebook you must agree to follow such rules as:

- You will not upload viruses or other malicious codes.
- You will not bully, intimidate, or harass any user.
- You will not post content that is hateful, threatening, or pornographic; incites violence; or contains nudity or graphic or gratuitous violence.
- You will not use Facebook to do anything unlawful, misleading, malicious, or discriminatory.

Facebook users' actions, however, are also guided by a second set of more informal rules that define what most people do (descriptive norms) and what most people should do (injunctive norms). Communication researchers Erin M. Bryant and Jennifer Marmo (2012) investigated these social norms by asking groups of users to "brainstorm a list of rules that might govern Facebook interaction" (p. 8). These individuals all were relatively well-versed in the use (and abuse) of Facebook, for they possessed an average of 200 Facebook friends and reported spending an average of 38.4 minutes per day on the site. In a second study Bryant and Marmo arranged for another group of users to review the norms that were mentioned frequently during the group sessions and identify those that were the most important ones to follow when using Facebook.

Bryant and Marmo discovered that Facebook norms govern expected actions across five different areas. *Communication norms* set expectations about how frequently one should communicate with friends and the types of messages that should be exchanged. Friends, for example, should write on each other's timeline or wall from time to time, comment on their posts and pictures, and even communicate with them outside of Facebook. *Relationship maintenance norms* encourage using Facebook to strengthen one's relationship with others, primarily by keeping up-to-date on what is happening in others' lives and also by wishing them happy birthday via Facebook. Other norms, however, stressed actions to avoid—to both protect oneself and to protect one's friends. *Negative self-consequences norms* included taking steps to avoid causing oneself harm when using Facebook (e.g., "I should not let Facebook use with this person interfere with getting my work done") and *negative friend-consequences norms* warned against doing things that might harm one's friends (e.g., "I should consider how a post might negatively impact this person's relationships"). Last, *Deception and control norms* defined what steps to take if one violates Facebook norms. For example, "I should delete or block this person if he/she compromises my Facebook image" and "I should intentionally control the level of access this person has to my profile."

Some of these norms were considered more sacred than others: Communicating in positive ways with others and not letting Facebook interfere with one's work were considered more important norms to heed than failing to comment on someone's posted photographs or sending the friend private messages. Different norms, however, applied to different types of Facebook relationships. Bryant and Marmo found that many users distinguished among three types of friends on Facebook: close friends, casual friends, and acquaintances. People were more scrupulous in their compliance with norms of communication and negative friend consequences rules for close friends and deception and control norms for acquaintances. They were also more likely to use Facebook for strengthening the relationship with casual friends and acquaintances, possibly because they used other means of increasing intimacy with their closest friends.

Not heeding these norms will not yield the same consequences that violating a Facebook official users rule will. As Facebook explains, "If you violate the letter or spirit of this Statement, or otherwise create risk or possible legal exposure for us, we can stop providing all or part of Facebook to you." But violating these social norms may be injurious socially. No one is directly taught the norms of Facebook, but those who do not follow them will likely pay the ultimate Facebook price: They will get themselves unfriended.

TABLE 6.1   Characteristics and Varieties of Norms

Common Features	Description
Descriptive	Describe how most members act, feel, and think
Consensual	Shared among group members, rather than personal, individual-level beliefs
Injunctive	Define which behaviors are considered "bad" or wrong and which are "good" or acceptable
Prescriptive	Set the standards for expected behavior; what should be done
Proscriptive	Identify behaviors that should not be performed
Informal	Describe the unwritten rules of conduct in the group
Implicit	Often so taken for granted that members follow them automatically
Self-generating	Emerge as members reach a consensus through reciprocal influence
Stable	Once they develop, resistant to change and passed from current members to new members

Alcohol consumption is also a group-level activity in most cases. On a typical evening, students do not drink alone, but in one group after another. Early in the evening, they "pregame" in dyads or other small groups (Burger et al., 2011). They then continue drinking in larger groups—in bars or at parties in private homes, dorms, or fraternity and sorority houses. The groups in the buildings where students live, such as their dorms and apartment complexes, establish norms about drinking, and those students who live where the norms encourage drinking tend to consume more alcohol and miss more of their classes (Carson, Barling, & Turner, 2007). Parties, too, can set standards for levels of intoxication. One particularly diligent team of investigators sent observers into 224 college parties to record such variables as number of guests, rowdiness, and type of alcohol available (Clapp et al., 2007, 2008). They concluded that people drank less if the party's purpose was to socialize, but they drank more if the party-goers' shared goal was to become intoxicated. The students also drank more alcohol and became more intoxicated as a result if they thought that others were drinking excessively. Parties where the students played drinking games also yielded more intoxicated guests, as did parties where people were costumed (e.g., theme parties and Halloween parties).

Misperceiving Norms: Pluralistic Ignorance
Why do group members continue to conform to norms that are harmful rather than healthy? The answer lies, in part, in the tenacity of norms. Even norms that run counter to society's general traditions can establish a life of their own in small groups within that society. In some cases, too, norms remain in place because of **pluralistic ignorance**: Members privately disagree with the group's norm, but feel that their outlook is shared by few others in the group (Prentice, 2007). So, the norm continues to regulate behavior due to misperception rather than shared consensus. College students, for example, often misperceive the extent to which other students drink excessive amounts of alcohol. Even though most of the students who participated in one study were personally opposed to overindulgence, they believed that their campus's norms encouraged heavy alcohol consumption. The men responded to this norm by gradually internalizing the misperceived norm. They began to drink more the longer they stayed at the school. The women,

---

pluralistic ignorance When members of a group privately vary in outlook and expectations, but publicly they all act similarly because they believe that they are the only ones whose personal views are different from the rest of the group.

in contrast, responded by distancing themselves from their university and its norms about drinking (Prentice & Miller, 1993; see Neighbors et al., 2007, 2008 for a review).

Norms and Health Normative processes also contribute to many other unhealthy behaviors besides excessive use of alcohol. Obesity, for example, tends to spread among individuals who are linked together in a social network, in part because norms encourage lifestyle choices that promote weight gain rather than fitness (Christakis & Fowler, 2007). Interventions designed to help at-risk adolescents by placing them in special programs may actually contribute to increased violence, drug use, and other antisocial behaviors when these groups develop negative rather than positive norms (Dishion & Dodge, 2005). Individuals who are frequent users of "club drugs" (methamphetamine, cocaine, ketamine, ecstasy, GHB, and LSD) are more likely to report that they do so because of social pressure (e.g., "When I was out with friends and they kept suggesting we go somewhere to do drugs," "When I felt pressured to use drugs and felt I couldn't refuse"; Starks et al., 2010, p.1067).

Eating disorders, too, have been linked to normative processes. Social psychologist Chris Crandall (1988), for example, documented the detrimental effects of norms on group members in a study of one particular unhealthy behavior: bulimia—a pernicious cycle of binge eating followed by self-induced vomiting or other forms of purging. Certain social groups, such as cheerleading squads, dance troupes, sports teams, and sororities, tend to have strikingly high rates of eating disorders (Petrie & Greenleaf, 2007). In explanation, Crandall noted that such groups adopt norms that encourage binging and purging. Rather than viewing these actions as abnormal and a threat to health, the sororities that Crandall studied accepted purging as a normal means of controlling one's weight. The women who were popular in such groups were the ones who binged at the rate established by the group's norms. Even worse, women who did not binge when they first joined the group were more likely to take up the practice the longer they remained in

the group. Other studies suggest that unhealthy eating patterns increase with the perceived strength of peer pressure within the sorority and the longer the woman lives in the sorority house itself (e.g., Basow, Foran, & Bookwala, 2007).

Norms may, however, promote healthy actions as well as unhealthy ones. Individuals who wish to reduce their negative indulgences often find success by joining a group and accepting that group's norms as their own. Many fitness, weight-loss, and anti-addiction programs, as noted in more detail in Chapter 16, take a group approach to change. Alcoholics Anonymous, for example, has clear norms about the types of behaviors members must enact in order to stay sober, and those individuals who become highly involved members are less likely to continue to drink heavily (Bond, Kaskutas, & Weisner, 2003). Groups have also been found to be effective in preventing the onset of eating disorders, such as bulimia, in young women. (Stice et al., 2008). Groups, then, can either promote or threaten members' health, depending on their norms. Some groups may put members at risk by encouraging unhealthy actions, whereas others keep members on the path to good health and wellness.

ROLES

On the day after the Andes crash, Marcelo, the captain of the rugby team, organized the efforts of those who could work. Two young men and one of the women administered first aid to the injured. One subgroup of boys melted snow for drinking water, and another team cleaned the cabin of the airplane. These various positions in the group—leader, doctor, snow melter, cabin cleaner—are all examples of *roles*: coherent sets of behaviors expected of people in specific positions (or statuses) within a group or social setting.

The Nature of Social Roles

The concept of roles explains the changes that some people exhibit when they become members of a group. The quiet recluse, taciturn by nature, may become convivial when given responsibility for organizing the group's annual fund-raising event. The otherwise mild-mannered colleague may become habitually critical of process when taking part in group discussions. The staffer with the messiest office may become methodical and precise when elected the group's secretary. Groups may pressure members to conform to the group's norms, but they do not require that members all act the same as one another. Groups instead require members to enact a specific set of behaviors consistently, depending on one's role within the group. Roles define responsibilities and expectations and facilitate coordination by specifying who can be counted on to do what within the group. Over the course of repeated interactions, members not only learn what others in the group usually do, but also what everyone in the group expects of them. By enacting roles, individuals establish an exchange relationship with their fellow members, building the interdependence that is essential for the coordination of behavior, group cohesion, and productivity.

The concept of a social role is similar, in many respects, to a theatrical role. In a play or film, a role is the part the actors portray before the audience. To become Juliet in Shakespeare's *Romeo and Juliet*, for example, an actor must perform certain actions and recite her dialogue accordingly. Similarly, roles in groups structure behavior by dictating the part that members take as they interact. Once cast in a role, such as leader, outcast, or questioner, members perform certain actions and interact with others in a particular way—but this consistency reflects the requirements of their role rather than their personal predilections or inclinations (Stets & Thai, 2010). But just as some variability is permitted in theatrical roles, group roles do not structure group members' actions completely. An actor playing the role of Juliet must perform certain behaviors as part of her role—she would not be Shakespeare's Juliet if she did not fall in love with Romeo. She can, however, recite her lines in an original way, change her stage behaviors, and even ad-lib. In social groups, too, people can fulfill the same role in somewhat different ways, and, so long as they do not stray too

far from the role's basic requirements, the group tolerates this variation. However, like the stage director who replaces an actor who presents an unsatisfactory Juliet, the group can replace members who repeatedly fail to play their part within the group. The role often supersedes any particular group member. When the role occupant departs, the role itself remains and is filled by a new member (Stryker & Burke, 2000).

Role Differentiation As with norms, groups sometimes deliberately create roles to organize the group and thereby facilitate the attainment of the group's goals. A group may decide that its efficiency would be augmented if someone takes charge of the meetings and different tasks are assigned to subcommittees. In some cases, too, someone outside the group, such as the group's supervisor, may mandate roles within the group (Stempfle, Hübner, & Badke-Schaub, 2001). But even without a deliberate attempt at creating a formal group structure, the group will probably develop an informal role structure. Members may initially consider themselves to be just members, basically similar to each other. But in time, some group members will begin to perform specific types of actions and interact with other group members in a particular way. As this **role differentiation** process unfolds, the number of roles in the group increases, whereas the roles themselves gradually become more narrowly defined and specialized. In the Andes survivors, for example, the roles of *leader*, *doctor*, and *cleaner* emerged first, soon followed by the *inventor* who created makeshift snowshoes, hammocks, and water-melting devices; *explorer* who was determined to hike down from the mountain; and *complainer*, *pessimist*, *optimist*, and *encourager*. This rapid proliferation of roles is typical of groups facing difficult problems or emergencies (Bales, 1958).

---

role differentiation An increase in the number of roles in a group, accompanied by a gradual decrease in the scope of these roles as each one becomes more narrowly defined and specialized.

Task and Relationship Roles   What roles emerge more frequently in groups? Certainly, the role of *leader* is a fundamental one in many groups, but other roles should not be overlooked. Many of these roles, such as *expert*, *secretary*, and *organizer*, are similar in that they revolve around the task the group is tackling. People who fulfill a **task role** focus on the group's goals and on the members' attempts to support one another as they work. Marcelo, in the Andes group, was a task-oriented leader, for he organized work squads and controlled the rationing of the group's food supplies; the rest of the members obeyed his orders. He did not, however, satisfy the group members' interpersonal and emotional needs. As if to offset Marcelo's inability to cheer up the survivors, several group members became more positive and friendly, actively trying to reduce conflicts and to keep morale high. Liliana Methol, in particular, provided a "unique source of solace" (Read, 1974, p. 74) to the young men. She came to fill a **relationship role** (also frequently termed *socioemotional role*) in the Andes group. Whereas the *coordinator* and *energizer* structure the group's work, such roles as *supporter*, *clown*, and even *critic* help satisfy the emotional needs of the group members (Mudrack & Farrell, 1995).

Why Differentiation?   Why do task roles and relationship roles emerge in so many different groups? One answer, proposed by Robert Bales (1955, 1958), suggests that very few individuals can simultaneously fulfill both the task and the relationship needs of the group. When group members are task-oriented, they must direct others to act in certain ways, restrict others' options, criticize other members, and prompt them into action. These actions may be necessary to reach the goal, but others may react negatively to these task-oriented activities, so they then look to others in the group for socioemotional, relational support. The peacekeeper who intercedes and tries to maintain harmony is the relationship specialist. Task and relationship roles, then, are a natural consequence of these two partly conflicting demands.

Bales identified these tendencies by tracking role differentiation in decision-making groups across four sessions. Bales used his *Interaction Process Analysis* (IPA) system to identify certain specific types of behavior within the groups. As noted in Chapter 2 (see Figure 2.2), half of the categories in IPA focus on task-oriented behaviors and half focus on relationship behaviors. Bales found that individuals rarely performed both task and relationship behaviors: Most people gravitated toward either a task role or a relationship role. Those who took on a task role (labeled the "idea man") offered mostly suggestions and expressed opinions. Those who gravitated to the relationship roles (labeled the "best-liked man") showed solidarity, more tension release, and greater agreement with other group members. Moreover, this differentiation became more pronounced over time. During the first session, the same leader occupied both the task and the relationship roles in 56.5% of the groups. By the fourth session, only 8.5% of the leaders occupied both roles. In most cases, individuals dropped their role as task leader in favor of the relationship role (Bales, 1958; Bales & Slater, 1955).

Subsequent work suggests that this division of task and relationship roles is not an inevitable occurrence in groups (Turner & Colomy, 1988). Some individuals are the small-group equivalent of master leaders, for they are both well-liked and they focus on the work to be done (Borgatta, Couch, & Bales, 1954). When players on football teams were asked to identify the best players on the team and those who contributed most to the group's harmony, many named the same person— usually a senior or first-string player—to both roles (Rees & Segal, 1984). When students in groups rated each other's role activity, many slotted the

---

task role Any position in a group occupied by a member who performs behaviors that center on tasks and activities, such as initiating structure, providing task-related feedback, and setting goals.

relationship role Any position in a group occupied by a member who performs behaviors that improve the nature and quality of interpersonal relations among members, such as showing concern for the feelings of others, reducing conflict, and enhancing feelings of satisfaction and trust in the group.

same person into both task and relationship roles. Cohesive groups tend to have leaders who can fill both roles, whereas the roles tend to be separated in groups with high levels of conflict (Burke, 1967; Mudrack & Farrell, 1995). Differentiation of these two types of roles is more common than their combination, however, perhaps because few people have the interpersonal and cognitive skills needed to enact both roles successfully.

Role Theories

The concept of role is a redoubtable one and has given rise to a number of alternative theories that describe roles and role-related processes. These conceptualizations agree on many points. Roles, they note, organize group interactions by creating a set of shared expectations that script the behavior of the individuals who occupy them. These theories, however, disagree on other points, including what roles are common to most groups and what functions roles serve. This section reviews a sample of theories that seek to explain roles and role-related processes, focusing on three models that are most relevant to understanding groups: functional role theory, interactionism, and dynamic role theory (Biddle, 1986; R. H. Turner, 2001b).

Functional Role Theories A number of theorists, in seeking to explain why roles develop in groups, stress their functional utility. All groups must, for example, respond in adaptive ways to their environment by recognizing challenges and responding successfully. Most groups, too, usually exist for some purpose, so they must develop methods that facilitate goal attainment—all the while making certain that members are so satisfied with membership that they remain in the group and continue to meet their obligations (Parsons, Bales, & Shils, 1953). Roles exist in groups to fulfill, at least in part, these personal and interpersonal needs (Blumberg et al., 2012).

Education theorists and practitioners Kenneth Benne and Paul Sheats (1948) developed their well-known functional theory of roles by observing the interactions of groups at the National Training Laboratories (NTL), an organization devoted to the improvement of groups. They noted that while much work had been done to train people to lead groups, little had been done to train people to work in groups—even though the "setting of goals and the marshaling of resources to move toward these goals is a group responsibility in which all members of a mature group come variously to share" (pp. 41–42). Leaders, they suggested, are responsible for making sure roles are filled, but members are responsible for fulfilling the demands of the roles.

Like Bales (1950), Benne and Sheats suggested that a group, to survive, must meet two basic demands: The group must accomplish its tasks, and the relationships among members must be maintained. But they identified 19 specific roles within these two broad categories, such as initiator/contributor, opinion seeker, and energizer on the task side, and encourager, harmonizer, and compromiser on the relationship side. They also identified a third set of eight individual roles enacted by group members who are more concerned with their own personal needs rather than the needs of the group. This category includes such roles as aggressor, blocker, and dominator (see Table 6.2).

Benne and Sheats theorize that individuals, given previous experiences in groups and differences in personality, naturally gravitate to a particular type of role across all the groups they join. However, because a group's need for a particular role will vary depending on the type of task it is attempting and the group's stage of development, the most skilled group member is one with role flexibility: the capacity to recognize the current requirements of the group and then enact the role-specific behaviors most appropriate in the given context. A group striving to be creative, for example, has less need of an evaluator/critic than a group examining a range of solutions after extensive deliberation. Individual roles will prove more problematic in the early stage of a group's life.

Interactionist Theories Some theoretical analyses of roles put more emphasis on the generative process of role-related actions, arguing that "the patterning of behavior that constitutes roles arises initially and

T A B L E 6.2   Benne and Sheats' Typology of Roles in Groups

Task Roles
Initiator/contributor: Recommends novel ideas about the problem at hand, new ways to approach the problem, or possible solutions not yet considered
Information seeker: Emphasizes getting the facts by calling for background information from others
Opinion seeker: Asks for more qualitative types of data, such as attitudes, values, and feelings
Information giver: Provides data for forming decisions, including facts that derive from expertise
Opinion giver: Provides opinions, values, and feelings
Elaborator: Gives additional information, examples, rephrasings, implications about points made by others
Coordinator: Shows the relevance of each idea and its relationship to the overall problem
Orienter: Refocuses discussion on the topic whenever necessary
Evaluator/critic: Appraises the quality of the group's methods, logic, and results
Energizer: Stimulates the group to continue working when discussion flags
Procedural technician: Cares for operational details, such as materials, machinery, and so on
Recorder: Takes notes and maintains records

Relationship Roles
Encourager: Rewards others through agreement, warmth, and praise
Harmonizer: Mediates conflicts among group members
Compromiser: Shifts his or her own position on an issue in order to reduce conflict in the group
Gatekeeper/expediter: Smooths communication by setting up procedures and ensuring equal participation from members
Standard setter: Expresses or calls for discussion of standards for evaluating the quality of the group process
Group observer/commentator: Points out the positive and negative aspects of the group's dynamics and calls for change if necessary
Follower: Accepts the ideas offered by others and serves as an audience for the group

Individual Roles
Aggressor: Expresses disapproval of acts, ideas, and feelings of others; attacks the group
Blocker: Negativistic; resists the group's influence; opposes the group unnecessarily
Dominator: Asserts authority or superiority; manipulative
Evader/self-confessor: Expresses personal interests, feelings, and opinions unrelated to group goals
Help seeker: Expresses insecurity, confusion, and self-deprecation
Recognition seeker: Calls attention to him- or herself; self-aggrandizing
Playboy/girl: Uninvolved in the group; cynical, nonchalant
Special-interest pleader: Remains apart from the group by acting as representative of another social group or category

SOURCE: Adapted from "Functional Roles of Group Members" by K. D. Benne and P. Sheats, *Journal of Social Issues*, 1948, *4*(2), 41–49. Copyright 1948 by the Society for the Psychology of Social Issues. Reprinted by permission.

recurrently out of the dynamics of interaction" (R. H. Turner, 2001b, p. 234). Group members share a basic sense of the requirements of the roles that are common in most group settings, but they work out the details of their roles and their demands as they interact with one another. Interactionist approaches recognize that group roles are analogous to theatrical roles, but the group setting is more like improv than a well-rehearsed stage play. Roles are negotiated by all group members through a reciprocal process of *role enactment*—displaying certain behaviors as part of one's role in the group—and *role sending*—the transmission of one's expectations about what kinds of behaviors are expected of people who occupy particular roles (Stryker & Vryan, 2006).

This view is consistent with the dramaturgical approach to social interaction explicated by sociologist Erving Goffman (1959). He maintained that individuals engage in **self-presentation** (also termed impression management) in order to steer others' impressions and expectations. Marcelo, for example, as the rugby team captain, considered himself well-suited for the role of group leader following the crash, so he exhibited the kinds of behaviors appropriate for that role: He assigned tasks to the others, set goals for the group, and sanctioned members who did not do their part. He did so because these actions were required by the role of leader, but also because he wished to define himself as the leader in the other group members' eyes. Roles, then, are negotiated among members through a process that requires motivation, experience, and the ability to step out of one's own role and mentally imagining how others in the groups are seeing you. This process is termed **role-taking**.

---

self-presentation Influencing other people's social perceptions by selectively revealing personal information to them; includes both deliberate and unintentional attempts to establish, maintain, or refine the impression that others have; also known as impression management.
role-taking Perceiving the role requirements of other group members' roles, by taking their perspective; also, the enactment of a role within a group.

It includes not only taking on a role but also a willingness to put oneself into others' roles to see the group as they do (Mead, 1934).

Beth A. Bechky (2006), an ethnographer of work and occupation, applied an interactionist approach to roles in her participant observation study of the interpersonal dynamics of temporary film-production teams. These production groups are common in the construction and film industries. The groups are assembled by production managers or contractors, and they set to work immediately on their task. Bechky, for example, observed crews ranging in size from 35 to 175 set up and film commercials, music videos, and movies. These group members may have worked together previously, but usually as individuals—they were not members of any larger production teams that moved as a unit from project to project. These groups can assemble quickly, however, because each group member's role is relatively well-defined. Filming a commercial, video, or movie requires completion of a number of highly specialized tasks, and these tasks are assigned to specific roles. The production team includes, for example, camera assistants and operators, costume designers, crane and dolly operators, directors, film loaders, gaffers (electrician), grips (lighting and rigging technicians), hair stylists, lighting technicians, location scouts, makeup artists, photographers, producers, and prop managers. Those who occupy these roles work in a highly coordinated manner during the actual production process.

Bechky also discovered, however, that the coordination of these groups is further enhanced on a continual basis through the interactions among the group members on each set. Many of those who work in a particular role have also performed other roles in other projects. An electrician on one shoot, for example, may have worked as a camera loader on another, and so the level of consensual agreement regarding roles is substantial. The complexity of the work, however, required even the most experienced members to modify their actions to suit the needs of others. Throughout every production day, group members were regularly providing each other with corrective feedback about one another's role-based performances, but they did so through "effusive thanking, polite admonishing, and role-oriented joking" (p. 11). Group members openly and routinely thanked each other for completing actions required by their roles, but they were also quick to intervene with suggestions for improvement, if needed, usually phrased as "don't worry about it for now, but next time be sure to…". Humor was often used to give a lighter touch to these suggestions, but also to ridicule someone who had displayed a more jarring role-related misstep. Her observations convinced Bechky (2006, p. 11) that:

> within each project, the generalized role structure is instantiated by a set of crew members who negotiate and modify their particular roles. The generalized role structure and the role enactments mutually support one another, while at the same time establishing a means for almost immediate coordination on each new project.

Dynamic Role Theories Sigmund Freud (1922) is best known for his insightful analyses of personality and adjustment, but he also undertook an analysis of group behavior. He suggested people's actions when in a group are based, in part, on their rational plans, motives, and goals, but also on unconscious interpersonal and psychological processes that are largely unrecognized. He believed, for example, that group members unconsciously respond to the leader of the group as a parental figure, so she or he becomes the "mother" or "father" of the group. Those leaders who identify with the mother role adopt more relational behaviors, whereas those who identified with the father role engaged in more task-oriented, instrumental actions. Freud recognized, however, that members of the group were often not wholly accepting of their leader; they often considered the leader a persecutory, critical "bad mother" rather than a benevolent, supportive, one (Klein, 1948).

Organizational psychologist and group therapist Paul Moxnes (1999) extended Freud's psychodynamic perspective in his theory of "deep roles." Moxnes theorized that group members' early experiences in families, with their apportionment of roles based on biological sex and cultural practices, creates similar structures in groups that are not kin-based. Like functional theorists, Moxnes notes that some roles pertain to the relationships among members and others to the group's tasks. Moxnes, however, suggests that this division is rooted in the structure of the first, and most primary, group—the family—with relational responsibilities associated with the mother and task responsibility to the father. He also suggests that these roles are viewed with some ambivalence by group members, for members distinguish between roles that promote the group's outcomes but others that promote the individual's outcomes. This ambivalence is due, in part, to the differences in power associated with each role. The occupants of some role positions are powerful, whereas the occupants of other roles are less influential. On the basis of these assumptions, Moxnes identified a number of deep roles that are common in many groups: primary roles (good and bad mother and father and good and bad son and daughter) and secondary roles (good and bad followers).

Moxnes' theory is a controversial one (e.g., see Hare, 1999; Robison, 1999) and awaits further empirical testing. Moxnes, however, reports that when group members are asked to categorize each of their fellow group members into one of the roles identified by his theory, members were relatively consistent in placing specific individuals into certain roles. For example, in a class of 30 members, 35% of the members placed the same person in to the "good father" (king) role (Moxnes, 2011).

Group Socialization

An actor answering a casting call may hope to land the lead role of Juliet, but the director may instead offer her only a smaller part, such as the role of the nurse or Lady Capulet. She may decide that the role is too insubstantial for her talents and not accept it, or she may decide that any role in the production is better than no role at all. Similarly, individuals often seek particular roles in groups, but the group may not permit them to occupy these roles. In the Andes group, for example, many sought to be one of the "expeditionaries"—explorers who were selected to hike away from the crash site and seek help. But only three were chosen.

Group Socialization Theory   Richard Moreland and John Levine (1982) developed their theory of **group socialization** to explain how individuals negotiate their role assignments in groups. Their theory, which is summarized in Figure 6.2, recognizes that individuals are often asked to take on roles that they would prefer to avoid. Newcomers must "learn their place" in the group and acquire the behaviors required by the roles to which they have been assigned. Veteran group members must, in some cases, be ready to take on new roles within the group that force them to learn new skills and seek new challenges. But group members also feel that their groups should be flexible enough to change to meet their particular needs. So individuals attempt to influence the group. Hence, group socialization is a mutual process: Through assimilation, the individual accepts the group's norms, values, and perspectives, and through accommodation, the group adapts to fit the newcomer's needs.

Moreland and Levine's theory distinguishes between five classes of roles—*prospective member, new member, full member, marginal member,* and *ex-member.* Prior to actually joining a group, individuals may study the group and the resources it offers, and part of this reconnaissance involves identifying the type of role they will be given should they join. The group, in contrast, seeks to recruit new members, often by promising them roles and responsibilities that once they are in the group they will not actually be given (Kramer, 1998). Should the individuals choose to enter the group (*entry*), their commitment to the group increases, and

their socialization by the full members begins in earnest. To the full members, the newcomers are inexperienced and cannot be completely trusted until they accept the group's norms and role allocations.

The Newcomer Role   The role of newcomer can be a stressful one (Moreland & Levine, 2002). New to the group and its procedures, newcomers lack basic information about their place in the group and their responsibilities. Although the passage of time will eventually transform them into rank-and-file members, newcomers often prolong their assimilation into the group by remaining cautiously aloof or by misinterpreting other members' reactions. Moreland (1985), to study this process, led some members of a newly formed group to think that they were newcomers surrounded by more senior members. He arranged for groups of five unacquainted individuals to meet for several weeks to discuss various topics. He told two of the five that the group had been meeting for some time and that they were the only newcomers. Although the role of newcomer existed only in the minds of these two participants, the people who thought themselves newcomers behaved differently from the others. They interacted more frequently and more positively with each other, they were less satisfied with the group discussion, and their descriptions of the group made reference to members' seniority. Thus, the belief that one is a newcomer who will be treated differently by the old-timers can act as a self-fulfilling prophecy: Just thinking of oneself as a newcomer caused people to act in ways that isolated them from the rest of the group (Major et al., 1995). This "mistreatment," which they themselves partially caused, may undermine their loyalty to the group (Levine, Moreland, & Choi, 2001).

Role Transitions   The socialization process does not end when individuals become full-fledged group members. Even seasoned group members must adjust as the group adds new members, adopts new goals in place of its old objectives, or modifies status and role relationships. Much of this

---

group socialization A pattern of change in the relationship between an individual and a group that begins when an individual first considers joining the group and ends when he or she leaves it.

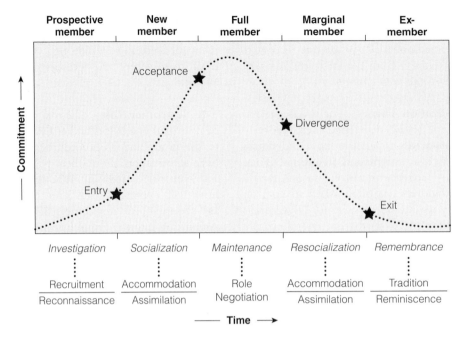

FIGURE 6.2   The Moreland and Levine theory of group socialization. The model identifies five types of roles (top of the figure), five stages and processes of socialization (bottom of the figure), and four transition points (identified as stars on the curve). The curved line represents the gradual increase (and eventual decrease) of a hypothetical member's commitment to the group. Commitment increases as the member moves from prospective member to new member to full member, but then declines as the member moves to the role of marginal member and finally to ex-member.

SOURCE: © Cengage Learning

maintenance phase is devoted to role negotiation. The group may, for example, require the services of a leader who can organize the group's activities and motivate members. The individual, in contrast, may wish instead to remain a follower who is responsible for relatively routine matters. During this phase, the group and the individual negotiate the nature and quantity of the member's expected contribution to the group.

Many group members remain in the maintenance period until their membership in the group reaches a scheduled conclusion. An employee who retires, a student who graduates from college, or an elected official whose term in office expires all leave the group after months or years of successful maintenance. In some cases, however, the maintenance process builds to a transition point that Moreland and Levine labeled *divergence*. The group may, for example, force individuals to take on roles that

they do not find personally rewarding. Individuals, too, may fail to meet the group's expectations concerning appropriate behavior, and role negotiation may reach an impasse.

Resocialization   When the divergence point is reached, the socialization process enters a new phase—*resocialization*. During resocialization, the former full member takes on the role of a marginal member, whose future in the group is uncertain. The individual sometimes precipitates this crisis point, often in response to increased costs and dwindling rewards, waning commitment to the group, and dissatisfaction with responsibilities and duties. The group, too, can be the instigator, reacting to a group member who is not contributing or is working against the group's explicit and implicit purposes. Moreland and Levine identified two possible outcomes of resocialization. The group and the individual, through accommodation and assimilation, can resolve their differences. In this instance, *convergence* occurs, and the individual once more becomes a full member of the group. Alternatively, resocialization efforts can fail (see Figure 6.2). The group may conclude that the individual is no longer acceptable as a member and move to expel him or her. Similarly, the individual may reevaluate his or her commitment to the group and decide to leave. As a result, the divergence between the group and the individual becomes so great that a final role transition is reached: *exit*.

Role Stress

Roles influence group members' happiness and well-being in significant ways. Some roles are more satisfying than others; people prefer to occupy roles that are prestigious and significant rather than roles that are menial and unimportant. They also like roles that require specialized skills and talents more than unchallenging, uninvolving roles (Rentsch & Steel, 1998). The demands of a role can also be stressful for the occupants of that role. A player on a sports team, for example, may be called the *spark plug*, the *comedian*, or the *mentor*, but what are the duties associated with such an amorphous role (Cope et al., 2011)? And what if the leader of a group believes her role involves keeping members on track, but others in the group think that the leader role is synonymous with the "party host" or even the "clown" (Farrell, Schmitt, & Heinemann, 2001). When a role is ambiguously defined, internally inconsistent, or fits the occupant poorly, roles can be great challenges for group members (Kahn et al., 1964).

Role Ambiguity   The responsibilities and activities that are required of a person who occupies a role are not always clear either to the occupant of the role (the *role enactor* or *role taker*) or to the rest of the group (the *role senders*). Even when a role has a long history in the group or the group deliberately creates the role for some specific purpose, the responsibilities of the role may be ill-defined. In such cases, role takers will likely experience

role ambiguity—they wonder if they are acting appropriately, they perform behaviors that others in the group should be carrying out, and they question their ability to fulfill their responsibilities.

Role Conflict   In some instances, group members may find themselves occupying several roles at the same time with the requirements of each role making demands on their time and abilities. If the multiple activities required by one role mesh with those required by the other, role takers experience few problems. If, however, the expectations that define the appropriate activities associated with these roles are incompatible, **role conflict** may occur (Brief, Schuler, & Van Sell, 1981).

Interrole conflict develops when role takers discover that the behaviors associated with one of their roles are incompatible with those associated with another of their roles. When assembly line workers are promoted to managerial positions, for example, they often feel torn between the demands of their new supervisory role and their former roles as friend and workmate. Similarly, college students often find that their student role conflicts with other roles they occupy, such as spouse, parent, or employee. If the student role requires spending every free moment in the library studying for exams, other roles will be neglected.

---

role ambiguity Unclear expectations about the behaviors to be performed by an individual occupying a particular position within the group caused by a lack of clarity in the role itself, a lack of consensus within the group regarding the behaviors associated with the role, or the individual role taker's uncertainty with regard to the types of behaviors expected by others.

role conflict A state of tension, distress, or uncertainty caused by inconsistent or discordant expectations associated with one's role in the group.

interrole conflict A form of role conflict that occurs when individuals occupy multiple roles within a group and the expectations and behaviors associated with one of their roles are not consistent with the expectations and behaviors associated with another of their roles.

Intrarole conflict results from contradictory demands within a single role. A supervisor in a factory, for example, may be held responsible for overseeing the quality of production, training new personnel, and providing feedback or goal-orienting information. At another level, however, supervisors become the supervised because they take directions from a higher level of management. Thus, the members of the team expect the manager to keep their secrets and support them in any disputes with the management, but the upper echelon expects obedience and loyalty (Katz & Kahn, 1978).

Role conflict also arises when role takers and role senders have different expectations. The newly appointed supervisor may assume that leadership means giving orders, maintaining strict supervision, and criticizing incompetence. The work group, however, may feel that leadership entails eliciting cooperation in the group, providing support and guidance, and delivering rewards. As Focus 6.2 explains, because the demands of roles vary from one country to another, in multicultural groups, individuals often misunderstand what their roles require of them.

Person–Role Conflict Sometimes, the behaviors associated with a particular role are completely congruent with the basic values, attitudes, personality, needs, or preferences of the person who must enact the role: A stickler for organization is asked to be in charge of organizing the group's records; a relationship expert must take on a role that requires sensitivity and warmth. In other cases, though, **role fit** is poor. An easygoing, warm person must give performance appraisals to the unit's employees.

An individual with high ethical standards is asked to look the other way when the company uses illegal accounting practices.

When role fit is low, people do not feel that they can "be themselves" in their roles; they also question their capacity to enact the role's demands competently (Talley et al., 2012). In one study, college students who held roles in campus groups were asked if they felt that their role "reflected their authentic self and how much they felt free and choiceful as they fulfilled their role" (Bettencourt & Sheldon, 2001, p. 1136). Those who felt more authentic when enacting their role reported more positive mood, less negative mood, and a higher level of satisfaction with life overall. Feeling competent when enacting one's role was also a powerful predictor of well-being. In another study, students first rated themselves on 20 different traits (e.g., cooperative, outgoing, imaginative). Later in the semester, they were given a list of five discussion roles (idea person, devil's advocate, moderator, secretary, and announcer) and then asked to indicate how valuable these 20 traits were for enacting each role. For example, how important is it for the idea person to be cooperative? Outgoing? Imaginative? Then they were assigned to one of these roles in a class discussion. As the concept of role fit suggests, individuals assigned to roles that required the kinds of characteristics that they believed they possessed felt more authentic, and their moods were more positive (Bettencourt & Sheldon, 2001).

Roles and Well-Being Uncertainty about one's role, including role ambiguity, role conflict, and poor role fit, results in stress and tension, and the results are rarely positive for the group member or for the group itself. In study after study, increases in role ambiguity, role conflict, and person–role conflict are associated with a host of negative psychological and interpersonal outcomes, including heightened levels of tension, employee turnover, absenteeism, interpersonal conflict within the group, and declines in job satisfaction and performance quality (Chiaburu & Harrison, 2008; Örtqvist & Wincent, 2006). Individuals who

---

intrarole conflict A form of role conflict that occurs when the behaviors that make up a single role are incongruous, often resulting from inconsistent expectations on the part of the person who occupies the role and other members of the group.

role fit The degree of congruence between the demands of a specific role and the attitudes, values, skills, and other characteristics of the individual who occupies the role.

F O C U S   6.2   Cross-cultural Perspectives: Role Conflict in 21 Nations

---

Those individuals in the role of the *middle manager* are considered by many organizational experts to be easy targets for role-related stress. In many companies, this role position is located below top management but above first-level supervision and can include general line managers, functional supervisors, and team- or project-based leaders. These individuals serve a boundary spanning role, for they communicate frequently with top management but they are also responsible for organizational strategy and day-to-day activities. In consequence, they often experience the highest level of role conflict of any position in the company since their role is a complex one that links top managers to corporate staff (Wooldridge, Schmid, & Floyd, 2008).

This role's responsibilities and associated stressors may vary, however, with cultural context. In the United States, this role may be a challenging one, rife with ambiguity and conflicting demands, but in companies in other countries, both the responsibilities and the loyalties of those who hold these positions may be more clearly defined and more widely shared. In Mexico, for example, the importance of family may obviate work–family conflict. In Brazil, commercial activities are often carried out within a maze of regulations that are inconsistently enforced, so role ambiguity is an ordinary experience. In some Asian countries, role conflict may be rare because interpersonal relations in workplaces are more formally structured (Kuchinke et al., 2010).

To explore role stress across cultures, organizational psychologist Mark Peterson, cross-cultural psychologist Peter Smith, and their colleagues (1995) had 2,723 managers working in 21 different nations rate themselves on such items as "I do not have clearly planned goals and objectives for my job" (role ambiguity) and "I often get involved in situations in which there are conflicting requirements" (role conflict, p. 440). As expected, role stress varied more by country than by individual, group, or organization.

Managers in some countries, such as France and Germany, reported low levels of role conflict, particularly compared to managers in such countries as Japan and India. Role ambiguity, in contrast, was common across much of the world with only Mexico and Indonesia reporting little ambiguity.

These variations in role ambiguity tracked, to a degree, differences in power distance (PDI) and individualism (IDV), two of the cultural dimensions identified by Hofstede (Hofstede et al., 2010). As Chapter 2 explains, PDI is an indicator of hierarchy; inequalities in power and influence are considered "normal" in high-PDI cultures. In consequence, where power distance is high (e.g., Mexico and Indonesia) role ambiguity is relatively low. Role ambiguity was also related to IDV, which is Hofstede's indicator of collectivism-individualism, for role ambiguity was more pronounced in individualistic cultures. These relations were specific to role ambiguity; they did not hold for role conflict. They did predict, however, how people responded when they ran into difficulties at work. When Smith and his colleagues asked people in many countries who they turned to when they needed guidance or help in solving a problem, they discovered that power distance and individualism predicted a reliance on authorities high in the organization rather than on colleagues or local group norms (Smith et al, 2002).

These tradeoffs may account for the great diversity of the world's cultures, for no one set of values offers only benefits with no cost. Differences in power between people run counter to expectations of equal rights and privileges for all, but such cultural systems lessen the negative impact of role ambiguity. Similarly, even though individualism encourages people to act in ways that they personally prefer, this freedom may keep them from turning to groups when they need help. Whenever something is gained by a culture's accepted practice, something else may be sacrificed.

---

experience conflicts between the work roles and their family roles experience declines in family satisfaction and, to a lesser extent, their work satisfaction (Ford, Heinen, & Langkamer, 2007). Role stress is also associated with physical well-being. One meta-analytic review of 79 studies of the relationship between role stress and physical maladies concluded that role conflict predicts backaches, sleep disturbances, dizziness, and gastrointestinal problems, where as role ambiguity predicted fatigue. Interpersonal conflict—not getting along with people at work—predicted increases in all of these negative physical symptoms (Nixon et al., 2011).

What can groups and organizations do to help their employees cope with role stress? One solution involves making role requirements explicit: Managers should write job descriptions for each role within the organization and provide employees with feedback about the behaviors expected of them (Pritchard et al., 2008). The workplace can also be designed so that potentially incompatible roles are performed in different locations and at different times. In such cases, however, the individual must be careful to engage in behaviors appropriate to the specific role, because slipping into the wrong role at the wrong time can lead to both embarrassment and a loss of coordination within the group (Goffman, 1959). Some companies, too, develop explicit guidelines regarding when one role should be sacrificed so that another can be enacted, or they may prevent employees from occupying positions that can create role conflict (Sarbin & Allen, 1968). Managers and the leaders of groups should also be mindful of the characteristics of the members of their groups and be careful to maximize role fit when selecting members for particular tasks. Work settings should also do what they can to maximize the salutary effects of positive, supportive member relationships. Having antagonistic coworkers increases role stress, but people who work with others who are supportive and helpful experience fewer of the negative consequences of role stress, particularly when they work in settings that are more socially focused (Chiaburu & Harrison, 2008).

INTERMEMBER RELATIONS

On the 17th day of their ordeal, an avalanche swept down on the Andes survivors as they slept, filling their makeshift shelter with snow. Many were killed, and soon a new order emerged in the group. Three young men stepped forward to take over control of the group. They were cousins, and their kinship bonds securely connected them to one another, but they also were friends with many of the remaining group members.

Connections among the members of a group provide the basis for the third component of group structure—the network of intermember relations. The Andes survivors were a group, but they were also many individuals who were connected to one another in different ways. Which one of the three cousins had the most authority? Who in a group is most liked by others, and who is an isolate? How does information flow through a group from one person to the next? The answers depend on social networks.

Social Network Analysis

Social network researchers are the geographers of the human terrain. They seek to map the connections that link individuals to one another and use that information to determine precisely where people are located relative to each other in interpersonal space. This approach dates back to some of the earliest work in sociology and psychology, for these fields' founders all sought to make social relations tangible (Borgatti et al., 2009). These efforts, which included Moreno's (1934) sociometric studies of attraction in groups, experimental studies carried out at the Group Networks Laboratory at the Massachusetts Institute of Technology (e.g., Bavelas, 1948; Leavitt, 1951), and Granovetter's (1973) work on the strength of weak ties laid the foundation for *social network analysis* (SNA): A set of procedures defined by (a) a focus on the structures of social groups and on linkages among group members in particular; (b) the systematic measurement of these structures; (c) the use of graphics to represent these structures; and (d) the application of statistical and mathematic procedures to quantify these structures (Freeman, 2004).

Figure 6.3 illustrates an application of SNA. Each member, or *node*, is represented as a circle, and the lines, or *edges*, connecting nodes indicate who is linked to whom. The arrows indicate the direction of the relationship. An edge with a single arrow indicates the relationship is a *directed* one, linking the sender to the receiver. For example, the links between Zerbino and F. Strauch, Paez, and Delgado go out from Zerbino and are received by Strauch, Paez, and

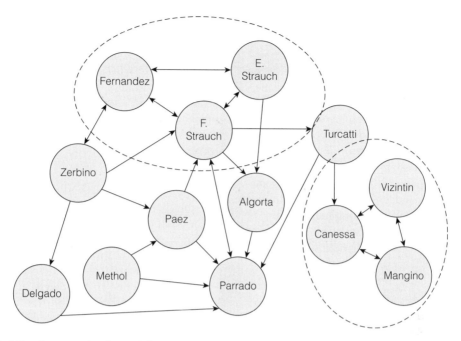

FIGURE 6.3   An example of a social network. Each member, or node, is represented as a circle, and the lines, or edges, connecting nodes indicate who is linked to whom. (The relationships are for illustration only; social network data were not collected for this group.)

SOURCE: © Cengage Learning 2014

Delgado. An edge with arrows at both ends indicates a symmetric, reciprocal relationship (for example, Zerbino and Fernandez). Distance, in social networks, is defined by relationships rather than physical distance. Two people who are directly linked to one another, such as Zerbino and F. Strauch, are separated by a distance of 1. But Zerbino and Vizintin are separated by a distance of 4 because they are linked by three intermediaries (F. Strauch, Turcatti, Canessa). (The relationships in Figure 6.3 are for illustration only; social network data were not collected for this group.)

Individuals in Networks SNA is a multilevel method. It yields information about each member of the network—the egocentric network—as well as insights into the group as a whole—the sociocentric network. Starting with the individual-level indexes, SNA describes each member's location in the network relative to the others. Where, for example, were the cousins, Fito and Eduardo Strauch, located

in the network? Were any members located on the fringes or isolated from the group altogether? Who was in a position to communicate most easily with the most members of the group? SNA answers these questions by calculating and organizing relational information about all the members, including how central they are in the group, how many people link to them, and their location relative to other people in the network. Some key indexes are centrality, betweenness, and closeness.

■ **Degree centrality** is the number of connections or ties to a node. Fito Strauch, for example, was connected by 10 ties to others and to him, whereas Delgado was linked to only 2 others.

---

degree centrality The number of ties between group members; the group's degree centrality is the average of the direct connections among group members.

- **Outdegree and indegree centrality** are more precise indexes of centrality, but they can only be calculated when ties are directed rather than undirected. In such cases, *outdegree* is the number of links directed out from the node, whereas *indegree* is the number of links directed in. Zerbino's outdegree centrality, for example, is 4, since he is linked to Delgado, Paez, F. Strauch, and Fernandez by out-directed relationships, but his indegree centrality is only 1 because only Fernandez directs a relationship to Zerbino. Outdegree and indegree centrality are equivalent when the relationships linking members are undirected, such as the flow of communication in a back-and-forth conversation or friends on Facebook (Wasserman & Faust, 1994; see Borgatti, 2005, for more information about centrality indexes).

- **Betweenness** is also an index of centrality, but it takes into account ties to more distant actors in the network (Freeman, 1979). A position with a high degree of betweenness is one that is located between many of the other individuals in the network. Turcatti, for example, has a much lower degree centrality than F. Strauch, but higher betweenness since he joins the subgroup of Canessa, Vizintin, and Mangino to the rest of the group. An individual in such a position often acts as the go-between or gatekeeper, linking people in the network who could otherwise not contact one another.

- **Closeness** is determined by the distance to all other members of the group. F. Strauch, for example, can reach all other members through short paths, whereas other group members

(such as Delgado or Mangino) are separated from others by greater distances.

Groups as Networks   Unlike egocentric indexes that yield a value for every individual in the network, sociocentric, or group-level, network indexes describe the entire network—or, at least a portion of it. Some common group-level features of networks include size, density, cliques, and holes.

- The *size* of the network is determined by the number of individuals (n) who are connected by some type of tie, which determines the number of relationships possible in the network. The formula for calculating the number of possible relations given group size was mentioned in Chapter 1: $n(n-1)$ if relationships are directed and $n(n-1)/2$ if the relationships are not directed. For the group in Figure 6.3, $n = 13$, so the maximum number of possible relations is 156 (since they are directed).

- **Density** is determined by how many people are linked to one another out of the total possible number of links. Consider, for example, the subgroup formed by Canessa, Vizintin, and Mangino. Since the relationships are directed ones in this example, six relationships are needed to fully link the three individuals, and all six are present. The density of this subgroup is therefore 1.0—the maximum. However, looking at the group as a whole, density is much lower than 1.0 because many group members are only linked to one or two others and not to all the 12 other members. This group would require 156 directed ties to link all the members to one another, but only 29 ties are present in this group. The density of the group is therefore .19 (29/156).

---

outdegree The number of ties initiated by the individual in a directed network.

indegree The number of ties received by the individual in a directed network.

betweenness The degree to which a group member's position in a network is located along a path between other pairs of individuals in the network.

closeness The inverse of the distance, in terms of ties, of an individual from all others in the network.

---

density The degree of connectedness of the group's members, as indexed by the number of actual ties linking members divided by the number of possibilities.

- **Cliques**, or clusters, of subgroups often form in larger networks. Members of the same racial category, for example, may join to form a coalition, or the group may separate naturally into all-male and all-female cliques (Hallinan, 1981; Schofield & Whitley, 1983; Thorne, 1993). Also, group members often deliberately form and manipulate cliques within larger groups by systematically including some individuals and excluding others (Adler & Adler, 1995). In the Andes group, Vizintin, Canessa, and Mangino formed a unified coalition within the larger group based on friendship. Others rarely hesitated to show their disdain for the members of this subgroup, but these three were joined by strong bonds of attraction. Also, F. Strauch, E. Strauch, and Fernandez formed a second clique, in this case based on authority—these three formed a leadership triumvirate within the group.

- **Holes** are "disconnections between nonredundant contacts in a network" (Burt, 1997, p. 339) or the gaps in a network that separate clusters or cliques. Holes may have a positive effect on group members if they buffer them from unwanted or too frequent contact with others, but they can also isolate members from the rest of the network. Turcatti spanned the hole in the Andes group.

Network Dynamics

Psychiatrist Jacob Moreno, in the fall of 1932, faced a serious puzzle. The staff of the Hudson School for Girls needed his help in turning back a sudden surge of runaways—14 girls in a two-week period. They called in Moreno to help. Moreno, as mentioned in Chapter 2, discovered something hidden beneath the surface of the groups at the Hudson School that the staff had overlooked. Using the sociometric methods that he pioneered, he discovered that the girls who ran away were joined together in an unnoticed web of social connections and that these connections facilitated the transmission of influence and ideas—some of which included the notion of leaving Hudson School behind (Moreno, 1934).

SNA is particularly useful in making what is often unseen and unnoticed evident. Dyadic relations—status differences, likes and dislikes, and patterns of communication—may be clearly known by some in the group, but often only a SNA will reveal the actual patterns and processes that sustain these relationships.

Status Differentiation Rare is the group where all members enjoy equal amounts of authority. Group members may start off on an equal footing, but over time **status differentiation** takes place: Certain individuals are granted, or they acquire, authority within the group, and the other members of the group come to accept their influence as legitimate. These stable variations in members' relative status have many names—*authority*, *power*, *status network*, *pecking orders*, *chain of command*, or *prestige ranking*—but whatever their label they result in elevated authority for some and less for others. In the Andes group, Fito Strauch, Eduardo Strauch, and Fernandez formed a coalition that controlled most of the group's activities (see Figure 6.4). Below this top level was a second stratum of members who had less power than the leaders but more prestige than the occupants of lower echelons. The explorers ("expeditionaries") occupied a special niche. These individuals had been chosen to hike down the mountain in search of help. In preparing for their journey, they were given special privileges, including better sleeping arrangements and more clothing, food, and water. The rank-and-file

---

cliques In social network analysis, subgroups of interrelated members within the larger group context.
holes In social network analysis, gaps or schisms within the network.

---

status differentiation The gradual rise of some group members to positions of greater authority, accompanied by decreases in the authority exercised by other members.

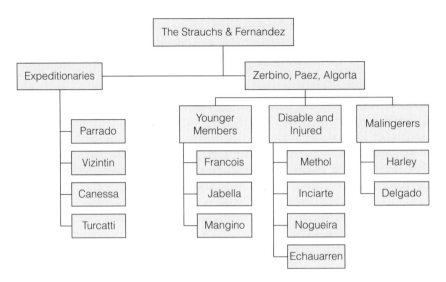

FIGURE 6.4   The status hierarchy in the Andes group.
SOURCE: © Cengage Learning 2014

members included the youngest men in the group, the injured, and those thought to be malingering. The factors that influence who ends up where in the status hierarchy—why, for example, was Fito Strauch influential but Methol was not—are consider in more detail in Chapter 8.

The lines of group authority in the survivors group became hierarchical and centralized, rather like the pyramid-shaped organizational charts of businesses and military organizations (Dale, 1952). Groups tend to adopt such organizational patterns for reasons of efficiency and, perhaps, instinctively. Status hierarchies are ubiquitous across groups, organizations, and cultures, and they arise quickly in both informal, socioemotional groups and in those that are more task-focused (Tiedens & Fragale, 2003). Furthermore, even though individuals often express a preference for more egalitarian structures where each person is equal to every other person in terms of influence and control of resources, people are generally more comfortable when they are members of hierarchical groups (Zitek & Tiedens, 2012). But the lines of authority shown by the organizational chart—the group's *formal structure*—may not correspond to the group's actual structure—often called its *informal structure*

(Krackhardt, 1996; Krackhardt & Hanson, 1993). When the group's informal structure is not congruent with its formal structure, communication flow within the group is disrupted, decisions are sometimes made by the wrong people, and individuals may act in ways that are not consistent with their roles in the group. These problems are illustrated in the network analysis of a group of twelve individuals diagrammed in Figure 6.5. Michael is the designated leader of this hypothetical group. He is responsible for three smaller teams within the group, and these teams are managed by Brandon, Ryan, and Jessica, respectively. At least, that is the way the group is intended to function. The group's actual structure, however, is very different from its formal, mandated structure. Michael is the ostensible group leader, but Jessica (who is the group's executive secretary and staff coordinator) holds the more centralized position within the group (see Figure 6.5b). Given this structure, if Michael does not garner Jessica's support for his leadership initiatives they will likely fail.

Sociometric Differentiation   Just as status differentiation results in variations in status, so, too, **sociometric differentiation** results in a stable

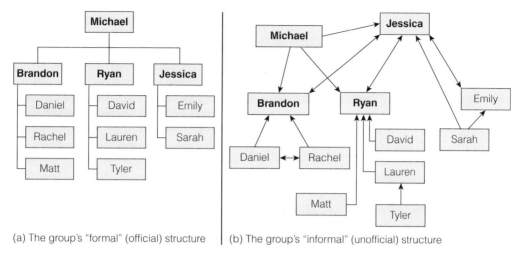

(a) The group's "formal" (official) structure | (b) The group's "informal" (unofficial) structure

F I G U R E   6.5   The informal (actual) structure of a group does not always match the group's mandated (formal) structure.

SOURCE: Krackhardt, 1996. "Social Networks and Liability of Newness for Managers." In C. L. Cooper and D. M. Rousseau (eds.). John Wiley & Sons, Ltd. New York. NY. *Trends in Organizational Behavior*. Volume 3, pp. 159–173. (may be reprinted here from another original source).

ordering of members from least liked to most liked (Maassen, Akkermans, & van der Linden, 1996). Consider, for example, the relationships among the rank-and-file group members and the four designated explorers in the Andes group, Turcatti, Parrado, Vizintin, and Canessa. Nearly everyone admired Turcatti and Parrado; their warmth, optimism, and physical strength buoyed the sagging spirits of the others. Vizintin and Canessa, in contrast, "did not inspire the same affection" (Read, 1974, p. 141). They liked each other but had few other friends within the group. Mangino, one of the younger men, was an exception; he liked them both. Most of the others, however, quarreled with them constantly.

As with status structures, SNA can reveal aspects of a group's sociometric structure that often go unnoticed even by members of the group themselves. Sociologists Pamela Paxton and

James Moody (2003), for example, used SNA to examine the structure of a specific type of group—a sorority in a university located in the southern United States that they gave the fictitious name of Alpha Beta Chi, or ABX. ABX appeared to be a highly cohesive group with strong relations among all members, but SNA revealed the existence of four cliques within the overall group, which Paxton and Moody labeled the Separatists, the Middles, the Random Chapter Members, and the Small Clique. The Separatists were noteworthy in that they were relatively isolated from the other members of the sorority, and their density was much higher than the other groups. The Middles, in contrast, were more likely to have ties to people outside of their clique. The group also included several women who had high levels of betweenness, labeled as "liaisons" by the researchers, and women who were linked to the group by only a single tie ("hangers-on").

Paxton and Moody discovered a member's commitment to her sorority could be predicted by studying her place in the group's social network. Women in the Middles, for example, had a stronger sense of belonging to the group, particularly in comparison to the Separatists. Paxton and Moody

sociometric differentiation   The development of stronger and more positive interpersonal ties between some members of the group, accompanied by decreases in the quality of relations between other members of the group.

also used a specialized method of calculating overall degree centrality. To index an individual's connection to other well-connected members, they weighted each person's centrality by the centrality of those to whom she was tied (Bonacich, 1987). This index was a strong predictor of satisfaction with the group, as well as a sense of belonging. Overall popularity—as indexed by how many times a woman was picked as a friend by others (indegree)—was not, however. Also, within any particular clique, those women with more central locations within the clique tended to be less committed to their sorority as a whole. Devoting one's relational energies to a small subset of the group may leave little time for the interpersonal work required to maintain good relations with the entire group.

A Balance Theory of Network Stability   Moreno (1934) maintained that the tendency to react to one another on a spontaneous, affective level imparts a unique quality to human groups. But these relationships can destabilize, rather than stabilize, the group. According to Fritz Heider's **balance theory**, some patterns of relationships in groups are more structurally sound, or balanced, than others, so groups naturally tend to gravitate toward these rather than toward unbalanced states (Cartwright & Harary, 1956, 1970; Heider, 1958; Newcomb, 1963). Consider, for example, the triad of Vizintin, Canessa, and Mangino. This triad was *balanced* because everyone in it liked one another; all bonds were positive. What would happen, however, if Mangino came to dislike Canessa? According to Heider, this group would be *unbalanced*. Such a group pattern is considered so unstable that it has been given the ominous name "the forbidden triad" (Granovetter, 1973). In general, a group is balanced if (1) all the relationships are positive, or (2) an

even number of negative relationships occurs in the group. Conversely, groups are unbalanced if they contain an odd number of negative relations.

Because unbalanced sociometric structures generate tension among group members, people are motivated to correct the imbalance and restore the group's equilibrium. Heider noted that this restoration of balance can be achieved either through psychological changes in the individual members or through interpersonal changes in the group (Gawronski, Walther, & Blank, 2005). If Mangino initially likes only Vizintin and not Canessa, he may change his attitude toward Canessa when he recognizes the strong bond between Vizintin and Canessa. Alternatively, group members who are disliked by the other group members may be ostracized, as in the case of Delgado (Taylor, 1970). Finally, because the occurrence of a single negative relationship within a group can cause the entire group to become unbalanced, large groups tend to include a number of smaller, better balanced cliques (Newcomb, 1981). The Andes group, for example, was somewhat unbalanced overall, but its subgroups tended to be very harmonious. As a result, the group was high in cohesiveness.

Communication Networks   Patterns of communication among group members, like other structural features of groups, are sometimes deliberately set in place when the group is organized. Many companies, for example, adopt a centralized, hierarchical **communication network** that prescribes how information is passed up to superiors, down to subordinates, and horizontally to one's equals. Even when no formal attempt is made to organize communication, an informal communication network will usually take shape over time. Moreover, this network tends to parallel status and attraction patterns. Take the Andes group as a case in point: Individuals who occupied high-status roles—the explorers, the food preparers, and the lieutenants—communicated

---

balance theory An analysis of social relations that assumes relationships can be either balanced (integrated units with elements that fit together without stress) or unbalanced (inconsistent units with elements that conflict with one another). Unbalanced relationships create an unpleasant tension that must be relieved by changing some element of the system (developed by Fritz Heider).

---

communication network Patterns of information transmission and exchange that describe who communicates most frequently and to what extent with whom.

at much higher rates and with more individuals than individuals who occupied the malingerer and injured roles (Shelly et al., 1999).

Communication networks become more complex and varied as groups increase in size, but some of their basic forms are graphed in Figure 6.6. In a *wheel* network, for example, most group members communicate with just one person. In a *comcon*, all members can and do communicate with all other members. In a *chain*, communication flows from one person to the next in a line. A *circle* is a closed chain, and a *pinwheel* is a circle where information flows in only one direction (Shaw, 1964).

Centrality is a particularly important feature of communication networks. With centralized networks, one of the positions in the group has a

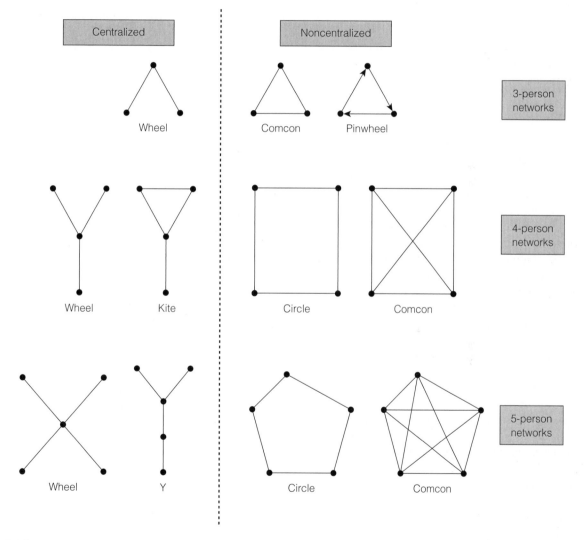

FIGURE 6.6 Examples of common communication networks in small groups. These networks are a sample of the various kinds of communication networks that can be created by opening and closing lines of communication among members. In most of these examples the lines are undirected ones, with information flowing back and forth between members. Only the pinwheel has directed, one-way communication links.

SOURCE: Adapted from "Communication Networks," by M. E. Shaw. In L. Berkowitz (ed.), *Advances in Experimental Social Psychology* (Vol. 1). Copyright © 1964 by Academic Press.

very high degree of centrality—it is located at the crossroads (the *hub*) of communications—relative to the other positions in the group (e.g., the wheel, the kite, or the Y in Figure 6.6). Groups with this type of structure tend to use the hub position as the data-processing center, and its occupant typically collects information, synthesizes it, and then sends it back to others. In decentralized structures, like the circle or comcon, the number of channels at each position is roughly equal, so no one position is more "central" than another. These groups tend to use a variety of organizational structures when solving their problems, including the so-called *each to all* pattern, in which everyone sends messages in all directions until someone gets the correct answer (Shaw, 1964, 1978).

Network Centralization and Performance Early studies of communication networks suggested that groups with centralized networks outperformed decentralized networks (Bavelas, 1948, 1950; Bavelas & Barrett, 1951; Leavitt, 1951). A group with a wheel structure, for example, took less time to solve problems, sent fewer messages, detected and corrected more errors, and improved more with practice than a group with a decentralized structure, such as a circle or comcon (Shaw, 1964, 1978). The only exceptions occurred when the groups were working on complicated tasks such as arithmetic, sentence construction, problem solving, and discussions. When the task was more complex, the decentralized networks outperformed the centralized ones.

These results led social psychologist Marvin E. Shaw to propose that network efficiency is related to *information saturation*. When a group is working on a problem, exchanging information, and making a decision, the central position in the network can best manage the inputs and interactions of the group. As work progresses and the number of communications being routed through the central member increases; however, a saturation point can be reached at which the individual can no longer efficiently monitor, collate, or route incoming and outgoing messages. Shaw noted that saturation can occur in a decentralized network, but it becomes

more likely when a group with a centralized structure is working on complex problems. Because the "greater the saturation the less efficient the group's performance" (Shaw, 1964, p. 126), when the task is simple, centralized networks are more efficient than decentralized networks; when the task is complex, decentralized networks are superior. In consequence, groups tend to gravitate naturally to more decentralized network structures when the tasks they must accomplish become more complex and multifaceted (Brown & Miller, 2000).

These different types of centrality also influence role allocations, overall commitment, and satisfaction with membership in the group (Krackhardt & Porter, 1986; Lovaglia & Houser, 1996). Individuals who occupy positions of high betweenness in centralized communication networks, such as a wheel or a Y (see Figure 6.6), are nearly always thought to be the leader of their group, even when they are randomly assigned to this position (Leavitt, 1951). In studies of employees in work groups, those who are more central in their network are less likely to quit than are employees at the periphery of the company's communication network (Feeley, 2000). Peripheral members are also more likely to quit in clumps. Because individuals in decentralized positions are connected to very few of the other members, when one peripheral member leaves the group, the individuals located near that person in the network also tend to leave the group (Krackhardt & Porter, 1986). Finally, centralized networks, by definition, have fewer centralized positions than decentralized positions. In consequence, the overall level of satisfaction in a centralized group is almost always lower than the level of satisfaction in a decentralized group (Shaw, 1964).

Directional (Up–Down) Effects Only small groups with decentralized communication networks outperform groups with centralized networks. Once the group becomes too large, members can no longer keep up with the high rate and quantity of information they are receiving. Therefore, most larger groups and organizations manage information flow by adopting hierarchical communication networks (Goetsch & McFarland, 1980). In such networks, information can pass either horizontally between members on the same rung of the communication ladder or vertically up and down from followers to leaders and back (Jablin, 1979).

Upward communications tend to be very different from downward communications (Sias, Krone, & Jablin, 2002). Downward-flowing information moves from the leaders to the followers of the group, and generally includes explanations of actions to be taken, the reasons for actions, suggestions to act in a certain manner, and feedback concerning performance. In some cases, too, up-down messages are urgent, sent using more immediate channels of communication, such as e-mail, rather than face-to-face meetings (Byrne & LeMay, 2006). Upward communications from subordinates to superiors, in contrast, include information on performance, insinuations about a peer's performance, requests for information, expressions of distrust, factual information, or grievances concerning the group's policies. These upward communications, moreover, tend to be fewer in number, briefer, and more guarded than downward communications. In larger organizations, the upward flow of information may be much impeded by the mechanics of the transfer process and by the low-status members' reluctance to send information that might reflect unfavorably on their performance, abilities, and skills (Sias, 2009). This reticence of low-status members means that good news travels quickly up the hierarchy, whereas the top of the ladder will be the last to learn bad news.

Application: The SYMLOG Model

Robert Bales' **Systematic Multiple Level Observation of Groups,** or **SYMLOG**, provides

---

Systematic Multiple Level Observation of Groups (SYMLOG) A theoretical analysis of group structure and group observation system that assumes that group activities can be classified along three dimensions (dominance versus submissiveness, friendliness versus unfriendliness, and acceptance versus nonacceptance of authority) and that groups are more effective when these three aspects of the group align (developed by Robert Freed Bales).

a fitting conclusion to the structural analysis of groups. Although it is tempting to treat each of the many and varied groups we commonly encounter as unique, groups possess a basic underlying structure, and SYMLOG provides a way to describe, explain, and control those structures.

Bales and his associates spent years searching for regularities in group interaction (Bales, 1950, 1970, 1980, 1999; Bales, Cohen, & Williamson, 1979). Initially, they assumed that most of the variation in group behavior revolved around role structures. Hence, their initial system, Interaction Process Analysis (IPA), underscored the differences between task-oriented and relational behavior. In time, however, Bales expanded the model to take into account both status and attraction differentiation, and the result was his three-dimensional theory of group structure: SYMLOG (see Table 6.3). Those three dimensions are:

- *Dominance or submissiveness*: Is this member active, outgoing, and talkative or passive, quiet, and introverted? (dominance is **U**p, submissive is **D**own.)

- *Friendliness or unfriendliness*: Is this member warm, open, and positive or negative and irritable? (friendliness is **P**ositive, unfriendliness is **N**egative.)

- *Acceptance or nonacceptance of task-oriented authority*: Is this member analytic and task-oriented or emotional, nontraditional, and (in some cases) resentful? (acceptance of the task-orientation of established authority is **F**orward, nonacceptance is **B**ackward.)

Observers, or the group members themselves, can rate each individual in the group using the 26 categories shown in the table. The group leader's behaviors, for example, might be concentrated in the "active, dominant, talks a lot" category rather than the "passive, introverted, says little" category. A disillusioned group member, in contrast, might get high scores for "irritable, cynical, won't cooperate." These ratings can be used to chart the flow of a group's interaction over time. When a group first begins to discuss a problem, most of the

TABLE 6.3   The SYMLOG Model of Group Structure

Trait (Direction)	General Behaviors	Individual and Organizational Values
Dominant (U)	Dominant, active, talkative	Individual financial success, personal prominence and power
Sociable (UP)	Outgoing, sociable, extroverted	Popularity and social success, being liked and admired
Persuasive (UPF)	Persuasive, convincing, shows task leadership	Active teamwork toward common goals, organizational unity
Managerial (UF)	Business-like, decisive, impersonal	Efficiency, strong impartial management
Moralistic (UNF)	Strict, demanding, controlling	Active reinforcement of authority, rules, and regulations
Tough (UN)	Tough, competitive, aggressive	Tough-minded, self-oriented assertiveness
Rebellious (UNB)	Rebellious, unruly, self-centered	Rugged, self-oriented individualism, resistance to authority
Funny (UB)	Joking, witty, clever	Having a good time, releasing tension, relaxing control
Warm (UPB)	Protects others, sympathetic, nurturant	Protecting less able members, providing help when needed
Equalitarian (P)	Friendly, democratic, group-oriented	Equality, democratic participation in decision making
Cooperative (PF)	Cooperative, reasonable, constructive	Responsible idealism, collaborative work
Task-oriented (F)	Serious, logical, objective	Conservative, established, "correct" ways of doing things ways of doing things
Persistent (NF)	Rule-oriented, insistent, inflexible	Restraining individual desires for organizational goals
Selfish (N)	Self-protective, unfriendly, negativistic	Self-protection, self-interest first, self-sufficiency
Cynical (NB)	Uncooperative, pessimistic, cynical	Rejection of established procedures, rejection of conformity
Unpredictable (B)	Expresses emotions, shows feelings	Change to new procedures, different values, creativity
Likable (PB)	Likeable, affectionate, enjoyable	Friendship, mutual pleasure, recreation
Trustful (DP)	Trustful, accepting, sensitive	Trust in the goodness of others
Responsible (DPF)	Modest, respectful, dedicated	Dedication, faithfulness, loyalty to the organization
Obedient (DF)	Cautious, dutiful, obedient	Obedience to the chain of command, complying with authority
Self-sacrificing (DNF)	Constrained, conforming, self-sacrificing	Self-sacrifice if necessary to reach organizational goals
Resentful (DN)	Depressed, unsociable, resentful	Passive rejection of popularity, going it alone
Withdrawn (DNB)	Alienated, rejects task, withdraws	Admission of failure, withdrawal of effort
Indecisive (DB)	Indecisive, anxious, holds back	Passive non-cooperation with authority
Contented (DPB)	Quietly contented, satisfied, unconcerned	Quiet contentment, taking it easy
Silent (D)	Silent, passive, uninvolved	Giving up personal needs and desires, passivity

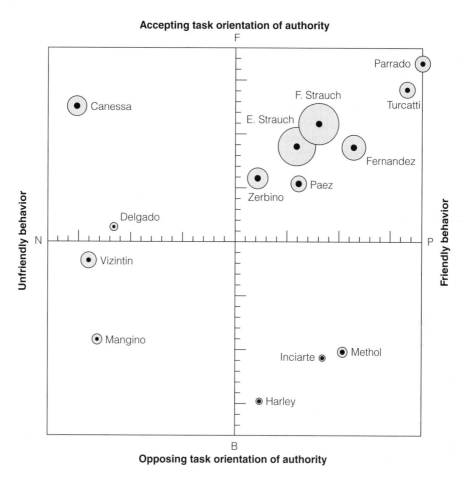

Accepting task orientation of authority

F

Parrado

F. Strauch

Turcatti

E. Strauch

Fernandez

Canessa

Zerbino

Paez

Delgado

N   P

Vizintin

Mangino

Inciarte   Methol

Harley

B

Opposing task orientation of authority

Unfriendly behavior

Friendly behavior

F I G U R E 6.7   Possible locations of a subset of the Andes group members in the three-dimensional space described by the SYMLOG rating system.

SOURCE: © Cengage Learning

behaviors may be concentrated in the dominant, friendly, and accepting authority categories. But if the group is wracked by disagreement, then scores in the unfriendly, nonaccepting authority categories may begin to climb. SYMLOG can also be used to create a graph of the group profile based on dominance, friendliness, and authority dimensions (Hare & Hare, 2005; Isenberg & Ennis, 1981; Polley, 1989).

Although SYMLOG ratings were never completed for the Andes group, Figure 6.7 is a speculative mapping of the group's structure into the three dimensions in Bales' model. The vertical axis corresponds to the role-related behavior in

the group. People like Fito Strauch and Fernandez rank near the task-oriented, accepting of authority end of this dimension, whereas Harley and Mangino are located near the opposing authority end of this dimension because they tended to resist group pressures and to express their feelings and emotions within the group. The horizontal axis pertains to attraction relations among the members. Parrado and Turcatti, for example, occupy positions at the friendly end of this dimension because they were both very popular within the group, whereas Delgado's and Canessa's low social standing places them at the unfriendly end. Bales uses circles of varying size to illustrate the third structural dimension: dominance/submission. The larger the circle, the greater the group member's status in the group; hence, Fito Strauch is represented by a very large circle, whereas Harley (one of the malingerers) is represented by a very small circle.

SYMLOG, by taking into account role, status, and attraction, yields an integrative and in-depth picture of the organization of groups (Hare et al., 2005). The task-oriented acceptance of authority/nonacceptance of authority dimension focuses on role structure, the dominant/submissive dimension

parallels status structure, and the friendly/unfriendly dimension pertains to attraction structure. Also, although communication structure is not considered explicitly, studies of task-performance groups indicate that individuals who are task-oriented and friendly communicate more frequently with others, whereas those who are dominant tend to receive more communications from others. Thus, SYMLOG is a powerful conceptual and methodological tool that provides a clearer understanding of the unseen group structures that underlie recurring patterns of interpersonal behaviors in groups.

CHAPTER REVIEW

What is group structure?

1. Groups are not unorganized, haphazard collections of individuals, but organized systems of interactions and relationships regulated by group structure.

2. Three important elements of group structure are norms, roles, and networks of connections among the members.

What are norms, how do they develop, and how do they work to regulate behavior?

1. Norms are implicit, self-generating, and stable standards for group behavior.

   - *Folkways* are cultural standards that define social conventions in public settings.

   - *Mores* are societal standards of right and wrong.

   - *Prescriptive norms* set the standards for expected group behavior.

   - *Proscriptive norms* identify behaviors that should not be performed.

   - *Descriptive norms* define what most people do, feel, or think in the group.

   - *Injunctive norms* differentiate between desirable and undesirable actions.

2. Norms are internalized standards, so individuals react negatively when they violate them. Milgram confirmed the surprisingly high level of discomfort experienced when one violates a social norm.

3. Sherif's study, involving the autokinetic effect, indicated that norms develop gradually over time as members align their actions with those displayed by others (*social tuning*).

4. Because norms are transmitted to other group members, they tend to be consensual, implicit, self-generating, and stable. Norms influence the actions of children as young as three years, as well as individuals using social networking sites, such as Facebook, as Bryant and Marmo's work suggests.

5. Norms influence a wide range of group processes, including some unhealthy behaviors, such as alcohol consumption, overeating, and eating disorders.

   - Individuals consume more alcohol when their group's norms support overindulgence.

   - In some cases, individuals misperceive their group's norms, and this *pluralistic ignorance* can further contribute to alcohol consumption.

- Crandall documented the influence of norms in his study of eating disorders in groups.

What kinds of roles are common in groups, and how do they influence the members?

1. Roles specify the types of behaviors expected of individuals who occupy particular positions within the group.

2. As members interact with one another, their role-related activities become patterned (*role differentiation*) with

    - *Task roles* pertaining to the work of the group, and

    - *Relationship roles* pertaining to maintaining relations among members.

3. Studies conducted by Bales and his colleagues suggest that the same person rarely holds both the task role and the relationship role in the group.

4. A number of theories examine roles and role-related processes.

    - Beene and Sheats's functional theory identified 27 distinct roles in discussion groups, including task roles, relationship roles, and individualistic roles.

    - Interactionist role theories draw on Goffman's analyses of *impression management* in their descriptions of the dynamic processes involved in role negotiation. Bechky applied this model to her analysis of production crews.

    - Moxnes draws on Freud's psychodynamic model of groups to identify the deep roles in groups, such as "mother" and "father" roles.

5. Moreland and Levine's theory of *group socialization* describes the ways roles are allocated to individuals and the ways in which members transition through the roles of prospective member, new member, full member, marginal member, and former member.

6. The role differentiation and socialization processes often create stress and tension for groups and group members.

    - *Role ambiguity* occurs when the behaviors associated with a role are poorly defined.

    - *Role conflict* occurs when group members occupy two or more roles that call for incompatible behaviors (*interrole conflict*) or when the demands of a single role are contradictory (*intrarole conflict*).

    - When *role fit* is low, members do not feel that they match the demands of their roles.

    - Role ambiguity depends, in part, on the cultural context where the group or organization is located. Research by Peterson, Smith, and their colleagues suggests that role ambiguity is less in high power distance, collectivistic countries.

How do social networks shape status, attraction, and communication processes in groups?

1. Social network analysis, or SNA, offers researchers the means to describe a group's structure both visually and quantitatively.

    - Individual-level (egocentric) indexes used in SNA include degree centrality, indegree, outdegree, betweenness, and closeness.

    - Group-level (sociocentric) indexes include *size, density, cliques, and holes*.

2. As Moreno's sociometric studies demonstrated, SNA is useful in identifying unnoticed, latent aspects of the group's structure.

3. Groups develop a stable pattern of variations in authority and power (e.g., status networks, chains of command) through a *status differentiation* process.

    - Groups naturally gravitate toward hierarchical, centralized status networks.

    - Network analyses, such as the one conducted by Krackhardt in his analysis of the inefficient workgroup, often reveal discrepancies between the group's formal status network and its informal (actual) status network.

4. Groups develop a stable pattern of variations in attraction through *sociometric differentiations.*

- Paxton and Moody's study indicated members with high centrality indexes for a clique within the overall group were less committed to the sorority as a whole.

- Heider's *balance theory* assumes sociometric structures tend to reach a state of equilibrium in which likes and dislikes are balanced within the group.

5. A group's *communication network* may parallel formally established paths, but most groups also have an informal network that defines who speaks to whom most frequently.

- Centralized networks are most efficient, but as Shaw's concept of information saturation suggests, not if tasks are too complex and require high levels of information exchange.

- A group's network, in addition to structuring communication, influences a variety of group and individual outcomes, including performance, effectiveness, and members' level of satisfaction. Individuals who occupy more central positions in communication networks are often more influential than those located at the periphery. Because centralized networks have lower levels of closeness, the overall level of member satisfaction in such groups tends to be lower.

- More information generally flows downward in hierarchical networks than flows upward, and the information that is sent upward is often unrealistically positive.

6. Bales' *Systematic Multiple Level Observation of Groups,* or *SYMLOG,* model of interaction and structure assumes that structure is based on three dimensions: dominance/submissiveness (Up/Down), friendliness/unfriendliness (Positive/Negative) and acceptance of task-orientation of authority/nonacceptance of task-orientation of authority (Forward/Backward).

RESOURCES

Chapter Case: The Andes Survivors

- *Alive* by Piers Paul Read (1974) is the best-selling account of the young men who crashed in the Andes and survived by creating a potent group.

- *Miracle in the Andes* by Nando Parrado (2006), with Vince Rause, is a first-person account of the collective spirit of the rugby team. Parrado, the author, was one of the men who hiked down from the mountain to bring back help.

Norms

- "Managing Normative Influences in Organizations" by Noah J. Goldstein and Robert B. Cialdini (2011) reviews the basic

tenets of the focus theory of normative conduct and the intriguing empirical studies that support it.

- *Social Norms*, edited by Michael Hechter and Karl-Dieter Op (2001), is a collection of solid theoretical and empirical reviews of the nature of norms and their influence in groups.

Roles

- "Role Theory" by Bruce J. Biddle (2001) provides a concise summary of the history of role theory in the social sciences, as well as a review of current applications and trends.

- "A Meta-analysis of Work Demand Stressors and Job Performance: Examining Main and

Moderating Effects" by Simona Gilboa, Arie Shirom, Yitzhak Fried, and Cary Cooper (2008) synthesizes the results of 169 studies of 35,265 employees and their experiences with role-related stress.

Intermember Relations

- "Network Analysis in the Social Sciences" by Stephen P. Borgatti, Ajay Mehra, Daniel J. Brass, and Giuseppe Labianca (2009) provides a concise, but comprehensive, overview of the uses of social network analysis in the social sciences, in general, and in the study of groups, in particular.

- *Analysis of Social Interaction Systems*, edited by A. Paul Hare, Endre Sjøvold, Herbert G. Baker, and Joseph Powers (2005), includes 26 chapters dealing with a variety of aspects of the SYM-LOG method of group analysis with sections pertaining to leadership, organizational development, cross-cultural implications, and methodology.

Influence

CHAPTER OVERVIEW

An interpersonal undercurrent flows beneath the surface of most groups that pushes group members together: toward greater consensus, uniformity, homogeneity, and conformity. But other forces push members in divergent directions: promoting dissension, uniqueness, heterogeneity, and independence. Groups require both conformity and rebellion if they are to endure.

- When do people conform in groups?
- When do people resist the group's influence and, instead, change the group?
- What are the sources of social influence?
- Does social influence shape juries' verdicts?

CHAPTER OUTLINE

Majority Influence: The Power of the Many
   Conformity and Independence
   Conformity across Contexts
   Who Will Conform?

Minority Influence: The Power of the Few
   Conversion Theory of Minority Influence
   Predicting Minority Influence
   Dynamic Social Impact Theory

Sources of Group Influence
   Implicit Influence
   Informational Influence
   Normative Influence
   Interpersonal Influence
   When Influence Inhibits: The Bystander Effect

Application: Understanding Juries
   Jury Dynamics
   How Effective Are Juries?
   Improving Juries
Chapter Review
Resources

Twelve Angry Men: Social Influence in Juries

When the prosecutor and the defendant's attorney finish their closing comments, the judge tells the jury: "If there is a reasonable doubt in your minds as to the guilt of the accused—then you must declare him not guilty. If, however, there is no reasonable doubt, then he must be found guilty. Whichever way you decide, the verdict must be unanimous" (Rose & Sergel, 1958, p. 9).

The jurors file out and make their way to the jury room. There, the foreman reviews their task and its seriousness; a son is accused of attacking, stabbing, and killing his own father. The foreman takes a straw vote, asking who favors a guilty verdict; four jurors immediately raise their hands and then another five join in. When Jurors #9 and #11 slowly raise their hands as well, all eyes turn to look at Juror #8 who looks down at the table in front of him. "Eleven to one," announces the foreman.

The jurors, from that moment onward, begin the task of bending Juror #8 to the will of the group. Juror #3 leans across the table and mutters to #8, "You are in left field." Juror #4 urges Juror #8 to be reasonable—it is far more likely that the eleven who agree on guilt are correct and that the lone individual is wrong. Juror #3 tries to bully the holdout, exclaiming, "You sat right in the court and heard the same things I did. The man's a dangerous killer. You could see it!" (Rose & Sergel, 1958, p. 14). Juror #7, who wants to end the discussion quickly since he has plans for the evening, tells #8 that it is hopeless to resist: "I think the guy's guilty. You couldn't change my mind if you talked for a hundred years" (Rose & Sergel, 1958, p. 15). Juror #8 answers back, "I want to talk for a while."

And, talk they do. As Juror #8 explains the source of his doubts, suggests alternative interpretations of the evidence, and questions the accuracy of some of the witnesses, the jurors become uncertain. They vote time and time again, and with each vote the numbers favoring guilt and innocence shift: from 11 against 1 to 10 against 2 to 9 against 3 until, in time, the tables are turned. Juror #3, who was so sure that the son was guilty, finds that he is now the lone holdout. The group then pressures him to change, and grudgingly, angrily, he admits he was wrong, and the shift of opinion is complete. The jury's verdict: not guilty.

This jury's deliberations were described by Reginald Rose in his play *Twelve Angry Men* (Rose & Sergel, 1955). The play is based on Rose's experiences when he was summoned to jury duty. Like the jurors in the play, Rose found himself in the midst of an angry group of argumentative jurors who struggled to find common ground. Rose explained: "I was overwhelmed. I was on a jury for a manslaughter case, and we got into this terrific, furious, eight-hour argument in the jury room" (Kelly, 2002).

How did the jury reach its verdict? The answer lies in **social influence**—interpersonal activities and processes that change other people. A jury member changing his vote, clique members mimicking the mannerisms of the group's leader, children endorsing the political views of their parents, and the uncertain restaurant patron using her small fork for her salad because everyone else at the table used that fork—all are influenced by other people rather than by their own individual ideation.

Much of this influence flows from the group to the individual, as Figure 7.1 suggests. When the majority of the group's members champion a particular view, they may pressure the few dissenting group members to change for the sake of the group's unity. However, social influence also flows from the individual to the group. If the group is to meet new challenges and improve over time, it must recognize and accept ideas that conflict with the status quo. In the jury described in *Twelve Angry Men,* for example, the lone minority held his ground, offered reasons for his views, and he prevailed. Whereas **majority influence** increases

---

social influence Interpersonal processes that change the thoughts, feelings, or behaviors of another person.

majority influence Social pressure exerted by the larger portion of a group (the majority), directed toward individual members and smaller factions within the group (the minority).

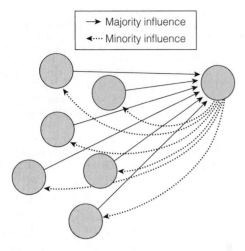

→ Majority influence
◄···· Minority influence

FIGURE 7.1 Majority and minority influence in groups. In many cases, group members change as a result of direct group pressure by the majority (majority influence), but in other cases, one or more group members succeed in changing the entire group. This minority influence is indicated by the curved lines of influence from the lone minority back to the majority group members.

SOURCE: © Cengage Learning

the consensus within the group, **minority influence** sustains individuality and innovation. In this chapter, we consider the nature of this give-and-take between majorities and minorities and the implications of this influence process for understanding how juries make their decisions (Prislin & Crano, 2012).

MAJORITY INFLUENCE: THE POWER OF THE MANY

Lone individuals are free to think and act as they choose, but group members must abandon some of their independence. Once they walked into the jury room, the 12 jurors had to coordinate their actions with the activities of the other group

members. Each one strove to change the group to suit their personal inclinations, but at the same time, the group influenced its members: It swayed their judgments, favored one interpretation of reality over another, and encouraged certain behaviors while discouraging others. When the group first polled the members, several members were uncertain but they voted guilty to go along with others. They displayed **conformity**.

Conformity and Independence

When do people conform? Muzafer Sherif (1936; see Chapter 6) verified that group members modify their judgments so that they match those of others in their groups. Theodore Newcomb's (1943; see Chapter 2) study of Bennington students showed that members of a group will gradually take as their own the group's position on political and social issues. But it was social psychologist Solomon Asch who most clearly demonstrated the power of the many to influence the few (Asch, 1952, 1955, 1956).

The Asch Situation Asch assembled groups of seven to nine male college students and seated them in two rows (see Figure 7.2). He told them he wanted them to look at a series of lines and decide which ones were the same lengths. Asch then showed the subjects two cards like those in Figure 7.3; the card on the left contained the "standard" line and the other card displayed three lines of varying length. The students then picked the one line from the second card that was the same length as the standard line on the first card. This comparison process was repeated 18 times, or 18 trials, and on each occasion the students announced their answers aloud.

The groups seemed ordinary enough, but in this case looks were deceiving. All but one of the

---

minority influence Social pressure exerted by a lone individual or smaller faction of a group (the minority), directed toward members of the majority.

conformity A change in a member's opinions, judgments, or actions that increases their consistency with those expressed by other people.

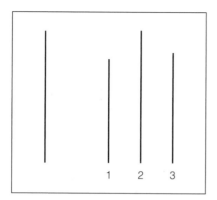

FIGURE 7.2   An example of the problems given to participants in the Asch study. Subjects were told to look at the standard line (on the left) and then match it to one of the three lines on the right. The task was an easy one, but all of the group members, save the one true subject, were Asch's confederates who deliberately made many mistakes.

SOURCE: Asch, 1956.

students were Asch's confederates, who were told to give the wrong answer on 12 of the 18 trials. The one real subject was always seated in the seventh chair, so he could listen to six of the other group members' judgments before he made his own. On one of the rigged trials, the first confederate would glance at the cards and confidently say, "The answer is line 1." The next confederate would nod his head in agreement and say, "Yes, it's line 1." After six wrong answers, it was the subject's turn. He faced a choice: agree with

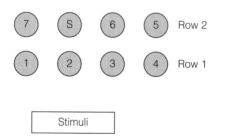

FIGURE 7.3   Seating arrangements for the group members (1 to 7) and the actual subject (S).

SOURCE: Data from Asch, solomon E. (1956). Studies of independence and conformity: I. A minority of one against a unanimous majority. *Psychological Monographs: General and Applied, 70,* No. 9. Whole No. 416.

everyone else's judgments or give the answer that he personally thought was correct.

When the students worked alone, they rarely made an error. But in the **Asch situation**, when confederates all gave the same wrong answer, about one-third of the subjects conformed by also giving that answer. As Figure 7.4 indicates, the average conformity rate across the sessions was 36.8%. Only 5% of the subjects conformed on every trial, but 76.4% of the subjects made at least one blatant error during the experiment. Had Asch's groups been making important decisions—deliberating over a verdict in a murder trial, forging a plan to deal with an emergency, or crafting a solution to a difficult problem—then the participants would have let the group make a mistake at least one out of every three times.

Forms of Social Response   Juror #9 in the *Twelve Angry Men* jury voted guilty on the first straw vote in the jury group but he harbored strong misgivings about the rush to judgment. Juror #3, in contrast, voted guilty on the first straw vote but he was not conforming: He had decided the defendant was guilty independently. Juror #12, in contrast, was convinced that guilty was the right verdict because so many other jurors selected it.

These jurors all agreed with the majority, but each one illustrates a specific type of conformity (Nail & MacDonald, 2007; see Figure 7.5).

- **Compliance** (acquiescence): Members privately disagree with the group but they publicly express an opinion that matches the opinion expressed by the majority of the group.

Asch situation An experimental procedure developed by Solomon Asch in his studies of conformity to group opinion. Participants believed they were making perceptual judgments as part of a group, but the other members were trained to make deliberate errors on certain trials.

compliance (acquiescence) Change that occurs when the targets of social influence publicly accept the influencer's position but privately maintain their original beliefs.

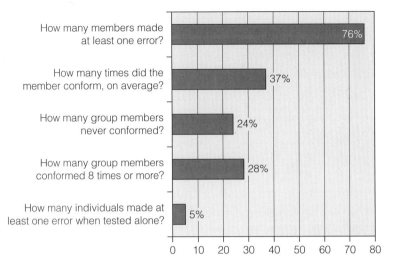

FIGURE 7.4   Results of Asch's study of conformity.

SOURCE: Data from Asch, solomon E. (1956). Studies of independence and conformity: I. A minority of one against a unanimous majority. *Psychological Monographs: General and Applied, 70*, No. 9. Whole No. 416.

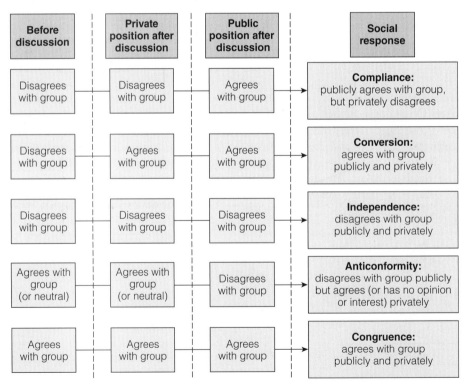

FIGURE 7.5   Forms of social response. When people react to group pressures, conformity can be labeled compliance,and nonconformity can be thought of as anti-conformity. In the opposite situation, when the response is prompted by one's personal standards, conformity becomes conversion, and nonconformity becomes independence. People who agree with the group from the outset are not technically conformists, because they do not shift their opinion in the direction advocated by the group; they already hold that position. They display congruence with their groups.

SOURCE: © Cengage Learning

- **Conversion** (private acceptance): Members change their position on the issue because they think the group is correct; they personally accept the group's position as their own.

- **Congruence** (uniformity): Members agree with the group from the outset, so they are not responding to the group's influence when they express their position publicly. They do not need to shift their opinion in the direction advocated by the group because it was already their position.

Juror #8, in contrast, was no conformist; he refused to vote guilty because he wished to challenge the group's decision to skip the deliberation process. He was unsure of the defendant's innocence, but he disagreed in order to challenge the group's norms (Packer, 2008b). Juror #8's social response in the situation was one of independence rather than anti-conformity.

- **Independence** (dissent): Members disagree by publicly expressing ideas, beliefs, and judgments that are consistent with their personal standards.

- **Anticonformity** (counterconformity): Members express ideas or take actions that are the opposite of whatever the group recommends.

---

conversion (private acceptance) Change that occurs when group members personally accept the influencer's position; also, the movement of all members of a group to a single, mutually shared position, as when individuals who initially offer diverse opinions on a subject eventually come to share the same position.

congruence (uniformity) Unprompted, natural agreement between the individual and the group.

independence (dissent) Expressing opinions, making judgments, or acting in ways that are consistent with one's personal beliefs but inconsistent with the opinions, judgments, or actions of other group members or the group's norms.

anticonformity (or counterconformity) Deliberately expressing opinions, making judgments, or acting in ways that are different from those of the other group members or the group's norms in order to challenge the group and its standards rather than simply for the purpose of expressing one's personal preferences.

Asch's subjects displayed two predominant forms of social response to the group pressure: compliance and independence. Of those who conformed, some questioned their own accuracy and ended up believing that the others were right. Most, however, thought the majority was wrong, but they went along with the group's choice. As Asch explained, they "suspected that the majority were 'sheep' following the first responder, or that the majority were victims of an optical illusion; nevertheless, these suspicions failed to free them at the moment of decision" (1955, p. 33).

Nearly all of the subjects, however, disagreed with the majority more frequently than they agreed. People conformed, on average, 3 of 12 times, but that means they disagreed 9 out of 12 times. Asch's study is often used to suggest that people are, by nature, conformists who tend to go along unthinkingly with whatever the majority favors. The data, however, suggest otherwise. Participants did not comply on all the trials; instead, their more frequent social response was to remain independent. They spoke their minds even when confronted with a unanimous majority and agreed with the others only occasionally—when their error was a slight one or by choosing an answer that was intermediate between the correct answer and the majority's mistaken one (Hodges & Geyer, 2006).

Conformity across Contexts

Asch studied conformity in newly formed groups working on a very easy task that was not particularly consequential. The members did not know each other well; they sat together in a well-lit room, and they made their decisions by announcing their choice aloud. Did these details matter? Did people conform because they had not a single ally who agreed with them? Did people conform so much because the group was so large that it overwhelmed them or because their response was made in such a public way? Once Asch confirmed the ubiquity of conformity, he and other researchers began systematically searching for factors that influence conformity and independence.

Unanimity Juror #8 in *Twelve Angry Men* faced 11 other men who disagreed with him. Asch's participants faced a similar situation, for they were the only ones in the group who favored the correct line; all of the other group members chose a different line as the correct one. Did some of the force of the Asch situation derive from the unanimity of the majority?

Asch examined this possibility by running his study again, but this time he provided each subject with a partner; either another subject or a confederate who publically announced his answer before the subject responded. As predicted, when participants had an ally, their conformity rates were cut to one-fourth their previous levels. In yet another variation, Asch arranged for some confederates to disagree with the majority but still give an incorrect answer. Participants did not agree with the erroneous nonconformist, but his dissent made it easier for them to express their own viewpoint (Asch, 1955, 1956).

Why is a unanimous majority so influential? First, individuals who face the majority alone, without a single ally, bear 100 percent of the group's pressure. Psychologically, being completely alone is very different from having another person join with you against the others (Allen, 1975). Gaining a partner, however, helps one withstand the pressure to conform only as long as the partner remains supportive. Asch discovered that if the partner reverts back to the majority position, then subjects do as well. Second, the larger the size of the minority, the smaller the majority; each time a member of the majority shifts to the minority, the minority grows stronger and the majority weaker (Clark, 1990). Third, a partner makes a very embarrassing situation less so. The kinds of judgments that Asch studied were simple ones, so most participants probably realized that if they dissented, they would make an odd impression on others. After all, "the correct judgment appeared so obvious that only perceptual incompetents, fools, or madmen could err" (Ross, Bierbrauer, & Hoffman, 1976, p. 149). A partner—and particularly one who is the first to dissent—takes much of the risk for going against the group (Sabini, Garvey, & Hall, 2001).

Strength in Numbers (Up to a Point) How many people does it take to create maximum conformity? Is two against one enough? Are smaller groups less influential? Is 11 to 1 too many, since individuals feel so anonymous in large groups they can resist group forces? Asch explored these questions by studying groups with 2 to 16 members. His findings, summarized in Figure 7.6, confirm that larger majorities are more influential—but only up to a point. People in two-person groups conformed very little; most were unsettled by the erroneous choices of their partner, but they did not go along with him or her (3.6% error rate). But the error rate climbed to 13.6% when participants faced two opponents, and when a single individual was pitted against three others, conformity jumped to 31.8%. Asch studied even larger groups, but he found that with more than three opponents, conformity increased only slightly (reaching its peak of 37.1% in the seven-person groups); even 16 against 1 did not raise conformity appreciably above the level achieved with three against one (Asch, 1952, 1955).

Social psychologist Rod Bond (2005), in a meta-analytic review of subsequent studies that used Asch's line-length judgment task, concluded that most studies confirm the pattern shown in Figure 7.6, but that the precise shape of the relationship between size and influence depends on a number of factors. When, for example, individuals in larger groups state their opinions publicly, the findings tend to match the Asch pattern. But when they keep their opinions to themselves, people are more likely to dissent. A large group can also lose some of its influence when its members do not reach their decisions independently of one another. If individuals learn that a six-person group disagrees with them but they believe that the group members worked together as a group to make their decision, then the size of the group matters less. But when individuals believe that the other group members reached their conclusions independently of one another, then their influence increases as the number of sources increases. For example, two two-person groups are more influential than one four-person group whose members worked together (Wilder, 1977, Experiment 2; see also Jackson, 1987; Latané, 1981; Wolf, 1987).

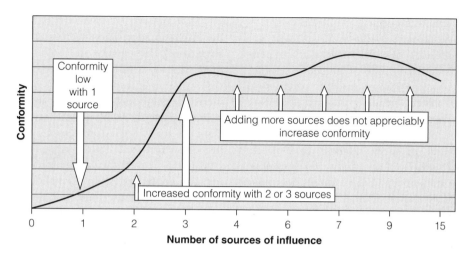

FIGURE 7.6   The relationship between conformity and group size. Studies conducted in a number of settings suggest that few people conform when they face just one other person who disagrees with them, but that conformity rises rapidly when a lone individual faces a group of two or three. Adding more people to the majority beyond three does not appreciably increase conformity.

SOURCE: © Cengage Learning

Social Impact   Social psychologist Bibb Latané, drawing on Asch's findings and his own studies of people responding in a wide range of social situations, concluded that social impact is a function of the strength (S), the immediacy (I), and the number (N) of sources present, or:

Social Impact = f SIN

Latané called his **social impact theory** the "lightbulb theory" of social relations. When a single lightbulb is lit in an otherwise dark room, the room is illuminated, but how brightly? It depends on the strength of the lightbulb in the lamp—a 25-watt bulb gives just enough light to see by, while a floodlight might reach every corner. And where is the lamp located? A lamp in the corner may leave the opposite corner of the room in shadows, but if you want more light, you can always turn on more

lamps. However, if you continue to add light from whatever source, eventually the room will become so bright that turning on more lights will not make much difference.

In an analogous fashion, social impact is contingent on the relative strength of the other group members. Like a 25-watt bulb surrounded by 100-watt bulbs, a person with relatively little status in the group will likely choose to conform (Jetten, Hornsey, & Adarves-Yorno, 2006). Immediacy also matters, for people who are physically nearby will have more of an impact than people who are seated far away or are absent. In the *Twelve Angry Men* jury, for example, the first juror to change to agree with juror #8 was juror #9. Sheer numbers are also critical. As with lightbulbs, the more people, the more impact they will have on you—up to a point. Just as the first light turned on in a dark room has more of an impact than the hundredth, the first person who expresses a different opinion has more impact than the hundredth person. In consequence, "there is a marginally decreasing effect of increased supplies of people" (Latané, 1981, p. 344; see, too, Latané,

---

social impact theory   An analysis of social influence, which proposes that the impact of any source of influence depends upon the strength, the immediacy, and the number of people (sources) present (developed by Bibb Latané).

1996, 1997; Latané & Bourgeois, 2001; Latané & Wolf, 1981; MacCoun, 2012).

Latané's principle of social impact explains people's reactions across a range of influence settings, including Asch's conformity studies, reactions to emergencies, attitude change among dormitory residents, the formation of spontaneous crowds on street corners, donations to charities, and even a society's cultural practices (Harton & Bullock, 2007; Latané, 1997). One study, for example, asked college students to imagine themselves singing the "Star Spangled Banner" alone or with others in front of audiences of one, three, or nine listeners who were either music experts or students who were partially tone deaf. As the theory suggests, performers were more nervous when the audience was high rather than low in strength (experts versus students) and nervousness increased at a decreasing rate as the audience grew larger. Performers also felt less anxiety when they imagined themselves performing, or actually performed, in front of audiences when they themselves were part of a group. Size, however, still mattered. People's anxiety declined when their groups increased from two, to three, to four, but once they reached four members, adding members did not appreciably reduce anxiety (Jackson & Latané, 1981).

Strong and Weak Situations   Asch studied conformity in a social situation that was simple, but also strong. Strong situations are ones that are structured in such a way that they leave very little opportunity for people to act in unusual or idiosyncratic ways. In contrast, weak situations do not pressure people to act as everyone else does, and so their actions in such settings tend to be shaped more by their personal proclivities rather than by social constraints (Mischel, 1977). Pressure to conform, then, varies across social settings. Some of the situational factors listed in Table 7.1 undercut group members' capacity to resist the group—for example, accountability, commitment to the group, and the difficulty of the task—whereas others encourage individuality and dissent (Cialdini & Goldstein, 2004; Cialdini & Trost, 1998).

Consider, for example, the difference between the Asch situation and the so-called **Crutchfield situation**. Participants in Asch's studies stated their choices aloud under the watchful eyes of all the other members, and this procedure likely increased their feelings of embarrassment and of being evaluated. Asch's procedure was also inefficient, for many confederates were required to study just one participant. Psychologist Richard Crutchfield (1955) solved this latter problem by eliminating the confederates. In Crutchfield's laboratory, the participants made their judgments while seated in individual cubicles. They flipped a switch on a response panel to report their judgments to the researcher, and their answers would supposedly light up on the other group members' panels as well. Crutchfield told each person in the group that he or she was to answer last, and he himself simulated the majority's judgments from a master control box. Thus, during the critical trials, Crutchfield could lead participants to think that all the other participants were giving erroneous answers.

The Crutchfield situation sacrificed face-to-face interaction between the participant and the confederates, but was efficient: Crutchfield could study five or more people in a single session, and he did not need to recruit confederates. Because group members' responses were private, however, fewer people conformed in the Crutchfield situation relative to the Asch situation (Bond & Smith, 1996). Indeed, the change that takes place in such groups may reflect conversion rather than a temporary compliance that disappears when the individual is separated from the group and its influence. The procedure, although unusual when he first used it, is now not novel at all: Online groups are, in a sense, the modern form of the Crutchfield situation (see Focus 7.1).

Crutchfield situation An experimental procedure developed by Richard Crutchfield to study conformity. Participants who signaled their responses using an electronic response console believed they were making judgments as part of a group, but the responses of the other members that appeared on their console's display were simulated.

T A B L E   7.1   A Sampling of Group and Situational Characteristics That Reliably Increase and Decrease Conformity

Factor	Conformity is More Likely If	Conformity is Less Likely If
Accountability (Quinn & Schlenker, 2002)	Individuals are striving for acceptance by others whose preferences are known	Individuals are accountable for their actions and are striving for accuracy
Accuracy (Mausner, 1954)	Majority's position is reasonable or accurate	Majority's position is unreasonable or mistaken
Ambiguity (Spencer & Huston, 1993)	Issues are simple and unambiguous	Issues are complex and difficult to evaluate
Anonymity (Deutsch & Gerard, 1955)	Responses are made publicly in face-to-face groups	Responses are anonymous and members cannot see each other
Attraction (Kiesler & Corbin, 1965)	Members are attracted to the group or its members	Members dislike each other
Awareness (Krueger & Clement, 1997)	Individuals are aware they disagree with the majority	Individuals do not realize their position is unusual
Cohesion (Lott & Lott, 1961)	Group is close-knit and cohesive	Group lacks cohesion
Commitment to membership (Kiesler, Zanna, & Desalvo, 1966)	Individuals are committed to remaining in the group	Groups or membership are temporary
Forewarning and depletion (Janssen, Fennis, & Pruyn, 2010)	Individuals are ego-depleted	Individuals are forewarned about a future social influence attempt
Priming (Epley & Gilovich, 1999)	Unnoticed cues in the setting prime conformity	Situational cues prime independence
Public commitment to position (Gerard, 1964)	Individuals did not initially conform but their responses are private	Individuals did not initially conform and their responses are public
Situational motivators (Griskevicius et al., 2006)	Nonconformists could be revealed as incorrect	Individuals are motivated to stand out from the crowd
Size (Asch, 1955)	Majority is large	Majority is small
Task (Baron, Vandello, & Brunsman, 1996)	Task is important but very difficult	Task is important and easy, or task is trivial
Unanimity (Asch, 1955)	Majority is unanimous	Several members disagree with the majority

Who Will Conform?

Asch studied young men (mostly) making public judgments about relatively inconsequential matters. All lived in the United States at a time when their culture was politically conservative. Would his findings hold with other kinds of people, from other cultures, and in other groups facing different issues?

Conformity across People   Asch discovered that people differed, to an extraordinary degree, in their

---

Focus 7.1   E-groups: Conformity across the Internet

When people began to use the Internet to interact with each other, many wondered how users would act once they were free to express themselves without fear of social embarrassment, reprisal, or recrimination. Would not online interactions trigger disinhibition—the reduction in self-regulation—with the result that emotions, thoughts, and opinions that would normally be kept private would be expressed publicly (Joinson, 2007). Interactions on the Internet, it was feared, might be rife with hostility, conflict, inappropriate self-disclosures, and wanton disregard of social conventions.

The Internet, like most social settings, includes its share of nonconformists: angry users who TYPE IN ALL CAPS, "trolls" who post hostile comments in discussion areas, vandals who deface Wikipedia pages, and websites that vilify individuals and social groups. But research suggests that people conform as much when online as when offline (Bargh & McKenna, 2004). Through discussion, consensus emerges within the group, and members move in the direction of agree- ment rather than continually debating issues. Online groups develop norms that structure interactions and status, and new members are socialized to follow these rules. Members sometimes act in ways that violate the group's norms of etiquette ("netiquette") by express- ing hostility and exchanging insults, but such deviations are usually sanctioned, and offenders who do not conform are eventually ostracized from the group (Straus, 1997).

Conformity may actually be more prevalent in online groups rather than offline groups, and the *Social Identity Model of Deindividuation Effects*—or SIDE for short—explains why (Spears et al., 2011). SIDE suggests that in the relatively anonymous online world, individuals tend to define themselves in terms of their collective, social identities rather than their individualistic, personal identities. Online interactions are depersonalized ones, but only in the sense that individual motivations, qualities, and beliefs become less salient. One's collective, shared attributes, in contrast, become more salient, and so the social com- ponent of the self comes to the fore. Some people, faced with increased depersonalization, may strive to reassert their individuality by acting in unusual, dis- tinctive ways, but if their group identity is salient they will more likely conform to the group's norms (Spears et al., 2002).

Because of these "SIDE effects," when individuals receive electronic messages from other individuals—even people they do not know and will not communicate with in the future—they frequently change their decisions to match the recommendations of these anonymous strangers (Lee & Nass, 2002). When small groups of students use e-mail in classes, each group develops idiosyncratic norms that regulate the group's interactions, and conformity to these norms increases through the semester (Postmes, Spears, & Lea, 2000). People comply with norms of reciprocity and cooperation in online groups even when completely anonymous, provided they identify with the group (Cress, 2005). Members of groups will also trust each other to fairly share financial resources, provided these others are members of the same online group (Tanis & Postmes, 2005).

This tendency for individuals on the Internet to match their behaviors to those displayed by other people explains how videos, images, and ideas become *viral*—widely shared in a very short space of time by many users. Millions of videos, for example, have been uploaded by users to the video-sharing site, YouTube, since it was founded in 2005. Most videos that are posted are viewed by only a small number of people, but others attract a much wider audience in a very short period of time. Such videos as *Charlie Bit My Finger*, *Numa Numa*, *Double Rainbow*, *JK's Wedding Dance*, and *Kony 2012* were viewed millions of times over the course of only a few days. Both social networking and conformity processes combine to generate this rapid upswing in attention (Susarla, Oh, & Tan, 2012). First, YouTube makes it easy to recommend a video to others, by posting a link to the video on social networking sites such as Facebook and communication media such as Twitter. As these recommendations prompt other individuals within the network to watch the video, its popularity index increases, attracting even more viewers who equate popularity with quality. Second, when indi- viduals who have many connections to others in the social network of the Internet, such as celebrities, sports figures, Internet information and news sites, and media blogs, endorse a video, a popular video can go viral. The *Kony 2012* video, for example, was viewed 40 million times in only 4 days when it was endorsed by a long list of celebrities and well- respected news sites. Apparently, the urge to con- form, which Asch found so powerful in face-to-face settings, is no less powerful when people who are separated by space and time are united by an Internet connection.

reaction to the conformity situation. Those who conformed often became increasingly disoriented as the study progressed, hesitating before they disagreed and apologizing to the others for their temerity. Others, in contrast, remained confident and self-assured throughout the experiment, never wavering from their convictions as they disagreed time and time again with the others. As one participant remarked, "The answers of the others didn't change my mind—an honest answer was expected. I did not change my answer once." When asked about the others in the group, he simply said "They were wrong" (Asch, 1952, p. 467).

Table 7.2 summarizes some of the differences between those who yield and those who remain resolute in the face of social pressure. Conformists tend to be more rigid in their thinking; their conventionality, conservative values, and unwillingness to confront authority increase their willingness to accept the majority's opinion. They let the situation and other people influence their perceptions, opinions, and outlooks. People who rely on situational cues when making perceptual judgments, self-conscious individuals, and those who are continually checking to see how well they are fitting into the group or situation (high self-monitors) are more likely to make certain that their actions match the group's standards. People who conform show a greater interest, overall, in other people. They have a higher need for social approval, are more interpersonally oriented, and are more fearful of social rejection. Factors that undermine self-confidence—low self-esteem, incompetence, low intelligence—also increase conformity.

Conformity across the Sexes   Did Asch underestimate the urge to conform by studying mostly men? Is it not true that women are more likely to be swayed by others' opinions, whereas men are independent and steadfast? When this possibility was first tested by researchers, they often discovered that the sexes did differ—that women were more likely to conform than men. However, these studies often used tasks that focused on topics that men were more familiar with, and they were also conducted by men rather than women researchers. Once gender-neutral topics were introduced and more women began studying the issue, differences between men and women faded (Bond & Smith, 1996; Cooper, 1979; Eagly & Carli, 1981; Leaper & Ayres, 2007).

If the sexes do differ, it tends to be in groups that meet face-to-face and when responses are made publicly rather than in private, with women conforming more in such settings and men conforming even less. Women tend to use agreement to create consensus and cohesion in their groups. Men, in contrast, use disagreement to dominate others or even to separate themselves from the group. When men and women were primed by a story about a romantic encounter while vacationing, only the men later demonstrated their uniqueness by not conforming to others' choices about personal tastes and preferences (Griskevicius et al., 2006).

These differences may also reflect continuing biases in the allocation of status to women. Despite changes in stereotypes about women and men, groups traditionally reward men for acting in dominant, nonconforming ways and women for acting in cooperative, communal ways. If women feel that they should behave in a traditional way, they may conform more than men (Eagly, Wood, & Fishbaugh, 1981). Women who do not conform to traditional sex roles, however, do not conform more than men (Bem, 1985). Sexism in groups and in society at large may also prevent women from expressing their dissent in groups. The studies of status allocation reviewed in Chapter 8, for example, have indicated that groups only grudgingly allocate status to qualified women. This sexist bias against women undermines their resistance to influence and weakens their power to influence others (Eagly, 1987). As women have become more successful in work and educational settings, their social status has risen, along with their independence and assertiveness (Twenge, 2001).

Conformity across Cultures and Eras   In the years since Asch first published his findings, other researchers have replicated his basic procedure in dozens of countries, including the United States, Britain,

T A B L E 7.2 A Sampling of Personality Characteristics That Are Reliably Associated with Conformity and Nonconformity

Characteristic	Reaction to Influence
Age	Conformity increases until adolescence and then decreases into adulthood (Costanzo & Shaw, 1966).
Authenticity	Individuals who are higher in dispositional authenticity tend to resist external influences (Wood et al., 2008).
Authoritarianism	Authoritarians respect and obey authorities and social conventions (Altemeyer, 1988; Feldman, 2003).
Birth order	Firstborn children tend to conform more than children born later, who tend to be more rebellious and creative (Sulloway, 1996).
Dependency	People who are high in dependency (a strong motivation to please other people) display heightened compliance, conformity, and suggestibility (Bornstein, 1992).
Five-factor model personality traits	Introverts experience more discomfort when disagreeing with a group and so conform more (Matz, Hofstedt, & Wood, 2008). Agreeableness, conscientiousness, and stability are associated with greater conformity (DeYoung, Peterson, & Higgins, 2002), but openness with less conformity (McCrae, 1996).
Gender identity	Masculine individuals and androgynous individuals conform less on gender-neutral tasks than feminine individuals (Bem, 1982).
Individualism–collectivism	People from collectivistic cultures (e.g., Asians) value conformity as a means of achieving harmony with others, whereas those from individualistic cultures (e.g., European Americans) value uniqueness (Kim & Markus, 1999).
Individuation	People with a high desire to publicly differentiate themselves from others (high individuators) are more willing to express dissenting opinions and contribute more to group discussions (Whitney, Sagrestano, & Maslach, 1994).
Intelligence	Less intelligent people and individuals who are uncertain of their abilities conform more (Crutchfield, 1955).
Need for closure	Conformity pressures are stronger in groups with a preponderance of members with a high need for closure (De Grada et al., 1999).
Need for uniqueness	Individuals with a high need for uniqueness are more likely to make unusual choices and resist majority influence (Imhoff & Erb, 2009).
Self-blame	Adolescents who tend to blame themselves for negative outcomes conform more than individuals low in self-blame (Costanzo, 1970).
Self-esteem	Individuals with low self-esteem conform more than individuals with moderate and high self-esteem (Berkowitz & Lundy, 1957); however, adolescents with high self-esteem conform more than those with low self-esteem (Francis, 1998).
Self-monitoring	High self-monitors, because of their higher self-presentational tendencies, conform more when striving to make a positive impression (Chen, Shechter, & Chaiken, 1996).
Yea-saying	Yea-sayers, particularly when working under a cognitive load, say "yes" faster and more frequently than individuals who thoughtfully consider their position (Knowles & Condon, 1999).

Belgium, Fiji, Holland, Kuwait, Portugal, and Zimbabwe. When Rod Bond and Peter Smith (1996) surveyed these studies, they concluded that Asch may actually have underestimated conformity by studying people living in a relatively individualistic culture. As noted in Chapter 3, Western societies tend to place the individual above the collective. Collectivistic societies, which are more prevalent in Asia, Africa, and South America, stress shared goals and interdependence. As a result, people tend to conform more in collectivistic cultures, especially when the source of influence is family members or friends (Frager, 1970).

Bond and Smith also checked for changes in conformity during the period from 1952 to 1994 to determine if conformity rates fluctuated as society's tolerance of dissent waxed and waned. When Asch carried out his work in the 1950s, social norms stressed respect for authority and traditional values, whereas the late 1960s were marked by student activism and social disobedience. This period of rebelliousness was followed by a prolonged period of social stability. Do entire generations of people become more or less conforming, depending on the sociopolitical climate of the times in which they live? Bond and Smith discovered that conformity rates have dropped since the 1950s, but they found no support for the idea that conformity is a "child of its time." Conformity is decreasing, but this decline was not sharper in the 1960s or more gradual in the relatively placid 1970s and 1980s (Larsen, 1982; Perrin & Spencer, 1980, 1981).

MINORITY INFLUENCE: THE POWER OF THE FEW

Sometimes the few influence the many. Juror #8 refused to change his verdict and eventually the other 11 members of the *Twelve Angry Men* yielded to him. Despite pressure from religious authorities, Galileo insisted that the planets revolve around the sun rather than the earth. Many in the U.S. civil rights movement of the 1960s favored using violence, if necessary, to overcome discrimination and racism, but Dr. Martin Luther King Jr. insisted on nonviolent methods. Sigmund Freud actively rebuked critics of his theory of the unconscious mind until it was grudgingly accepted by many psychologists. The composer Igor Stravinsky was denounced as a musical heretic when *The Rite of Spring* was first performed, but he refused to change a note. The majority can bring powerful and potentially overwhelming pressure to bear upon the minority, but minorities can fight back with pressure of their own.

Conversion Theory of Minority Influence

Just as Asch's studies highlighted the power of the majority, so the work of Serge Moscovici and his colleagues underscored the power of the minority. Moscovici, in an insightful analysis of conformity in science itself, suggested that for too long theorists and researchers assumed that change comes from within existing social systems rather than from external revolutionary sources; that the victory of the majority is more democratic than the victory of the minority; and that innovation occurs as a result of direct rather than indirect interaction between the majority and minority. In contrast to this majority-rules model of social influence, Moscovici's **conversion theory** maintains that disagreement within the group results in conflict and that the group members are motivated to reduce that conflict, by getting others to change but also by changing their own opinions (Moscovici, 1976, 1980, 1985, 1994).

Comparison or Validation?   Conversion theory proposes that minorities influence in a different way than majorities do. Minorities, Moscovici

---

conversion theory A conceptual analysis of the cognitive and interpersonal processes that mediate the direct and indirect impact of a consistent minority on the majority (developed by Serge Moscovici).

theorized, influence through the *validation process* shown in Figure 7.7. When someone in the group breaks the group's unanimity—such as Juror #8 arguing "not guilty"—members take notice of this surprising turn of events. The minority captures their attention, and though most do not believe that the minority is correct, they nonetheless consider the arguments closely. The majority's message, in contrast, is less intriguing to members. When people discover where most of the group stands on a position, through a *comparison process*, they check to see if they can join the majority. Because being in the majority is, in most cases, more rewarding than membership in the minority—those in the majority usually find that they control the group's resources whereas those in the minority may have little say in the group's decisions—people usually change to comply with the group's consensus. This compliance reflects a desire to be included within the group, however, rather than any kind of in-depth review of the majority's reasons for their position. In consequence, the change is relatively superficial and may evaporate once the individual leaves the group.

Moscovici maintained that the validation processes instigated by a minority are longer-lasting than those triggered by the comparison processes of majority influence. Comparison results in direct influence as members publicly comply. Validation, in contrast, leads to private acceptance, making minorities a source of innovation in groups. They shake the confidence of the majority and force the group to seek out new information about the situation. This conversion process takes longer, however, than the compliance process, and so the effects of a minority on the majority sometimes do not emerge until some time has passed. In some cases, the influence of minorities becomes evident only when the group has completed its initial deliberations and moved on to another task (see also Nemeth & Goncalo (2011).

Delayed Social Influence   Moscovici and his colleagues, in one of the first tests of the theory,

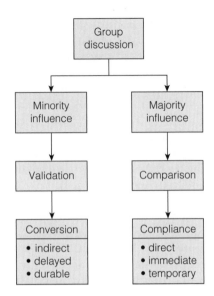

FIGURE 7.7   Moscovici's conversion theory of minority and majority influence.
SOURCE: © Cengage Learning 2014

reversed the usual Asch situation by inserting two confederates in six-person groups and then arranging for the confederates to systematically disagree with the majority's decision. Instead of judging lines, Moscovici's subjects judged, aloud, the color and brightness of a series of color slides. All of the 36 slides were shades of blue, varying only in luminosity. But when it was their turn to name the color of the slides, the confederates consistently said "green" rather than "blue." In some cases, the confederates answered first and second, but in other groups one answered first and the other answered fourth (Moscovici, Lage, & Naffrechoux, 1969).

Moscovici and his colleagues confirmed the power of the minority. When tested alone, only one person of the 22 tested said two of the slides were green. But when in the presence of the green-saying confederates, this error rate jumped to 8.4%—not as much influence as that found by Asch in his studies of majority influence, but a significant amount considering the obviousness of the correct answer. Moscovici also found evidence of the delayed effects of the minority on the majority. After the public judgment task, a second experimenter entered the room and explained that he was also doing a study of vision. Participants were then shown another set of colors that included 3 blue slides, 3 green slides, and 10 slides in the blue-green range, and they privately labeled each one either blue or green. Those who had been previously exposed to a minority-group opinion were more likely to label the ambiguous slides as green rather than blue, and this bias was more marked among those members who *did not* change their public choices when they first encountered the minority. This delayed, indirect impact of minorities on the majority has been documented in a wide variety of laboratory and field studies, which indicate that "minorities tend to produce profound and lasting changes in attitudes and perceptions that generalize to new settings and over time … whereas majorities are more likely to elicit compliance that is confined to the original influence setting" (Maass, West, & Cialdini, 1987, pp. 56–57).

Predicting Minority Influence

Moscovici's conversion theory began as a minority opinion that many researchers rejected, but it eventually won over even the most stubborn members of the opposition—confirming the theory's own predictions. The question changed, over time, from "Are minorities influential?" to "When are minorities influential?" Answers to that question, which are reviewed briefly in the next sections, suggest that given enough time, minorities who argue consistently for their positions but all the while manage to remain members in good-standing in the group will shift the group's consensus away from the majority's position toward the one they favor (see Crano & Seyranian, 2007; Gardikiotis, 2011; Martin & Hewstone, 2010, for reviews).

Consistency and Influence In *Twelve Angry Men*, Juror #8 always voted in favor of "not guilty." He did not waver as the majority pressured him to change his vote. He did not always have compelling arguments to back up his position, but he was always consistent in the defense of his view. He was one inspiring juror (Ellsworth, 2003).

A consistent minority is an influential one. Moscovici verified the importance of maintaining consistency in his original blue-green study by also including a condition in which the confederates labeled the blue slides green on two-thirds of the trials instead of all of the trials. The error rate dropped down to 1.25%—hardly any influence at all (Moscovici et al., 1969; Moscovici & Personnaz, 1980).

Subsequent studies have confirmed the importance of behavioral consistency on the part of the minority, but they also suggest that minorities must walk the line between appearing self-assured and unreasonable. In general, minorities are more influential when they are perceived to be team players who are committed, competent, and group-centered (Levine & Russo, 1987). An influential minority also avoids threatening the integrity of the group itself. Many groups will tolerate debate and disagreement, but if the dissent creates deep divisions in the group, the majority may take steps to quash the minority or exclude its members from the group. If a group is just a loose conglomeration of individuals with no clear sense of identity, then the members of this "group" do not feel threatened by disagreement. But if the group members identify strongly with their group and they feel that the dissenter is undermining its collective identity, they are more likely to feel a sense of loss when members begin to take a minority's arguments seriously (Prislin, Brewer, & Wilson, 2002). In such cases, an individual who is not even a member of the group may be more influential than an ingroup member (Phillips, 2003).

Idiosyncrasy Credits In *Twelve Angry Men*, Juror #8 was influential, but so was Juror #11. That juror voted guilty on the first ballot, as did the other 10 jurors. But, when Juror #8 noted several conflicting aspects of the evidence, Juror #11 changed his mind and shifted his vote. Did prefacing his dissent with conformity increase or decrease his influence?

Edwin Hollander (1971) developed the concept of **idiosyncrasy credits** to explain the group's positive reaction to a minority who prefaces dissent with conformity. According to Hollander, idiosyncrasy credits accumulate as the member contributes to the progress of the group toward desired goals. Because high-status members have usually contributed more in the past and possess more valued personal characteristics, they have more idiosyncrasy credits. Therefore, if they do not conform, their actions are more tolerable to the other members. The low-status members' balance of credits is, in comparison, low, so they are permitted a smaller latitude for nonconformity. The idiosyncrasy model suggests that influence levels in a group are increased by careful conformity to group norms during the early phases of group formation, followed by dissent when a sufficient balance of idiosyncrasy credit has been established (Hollander, 2006).

Hollander's advice about early conformity contrasts to some extent with Moscovici's recommendations concerning consistent nonconformity. Hollander warned that dissenters who challenge the majority without first earning high status in the group will probably be overruled by the majority, but Moscovici argued that consistent nonconformity will lead to innovation and change. Both tactics, however, may prove effective. Researchers compared the two in group discussions of three issues. One minority built up idiosyncrasy credits by agreeing on the first two issues that the group discussed but then disagreeing on the third. The second minority built up consistency by disagreeing with the group on all three issues. Both minorities were influential, but the minority who built up

idiosyncrasy credits was more influential in all-male groups (Bray, Johnson, & Chilstrom, 1982).

Individuals who occupy positions of leadership in their groups typically have accumulated the "innovation credits" they need to remain in the group's good graces should that role require the need to take a counter normative stance on important issues (Morrison & Miller, 2011). However, a consistent dissenter who is also the group's leader is a rarity—in most cases leaders express opinions that are prototypical ones for the group. When, in one study, leaders expressed opinions that ran counter to the group's norms, they were viewed as negatively as a rank-and-file member who favored an unpopular position. The only dissenters who were viewed positively were individuals in the group who had been chosen to take the leadership role in the future. Apparently the period between being selected to lead and then actually leading is recognized as a time for innovation and creativity (Abrams et al., 2008).

The Diligence of Dissenters Part of the secret of the unique influence of minorities lies in the quality of their argumentation. Those who know that they are members of the majority position on an issue feel less pressure to articulate their points clearly, for they expect that, with numbers on their side, they are likely to carry the day. But the individual who holds the minority position feels more intently the need to craft persuasive messages. Disagreeing with others is not a situation most people find enjoyable, and so few enter into this predicament without considering the strength of their own arguments and their reasonableness. Minorities are likely to have put more thought into the issue, and, as a result, they are able to ready a stronger defense of their position (Guinote, Brown, & Fiske, 2006). In a related study, researchers found that individuals who knew they would be arguing against the views of the majority prepared more diligently for their meetings (Van Hiel & Franssen, 2003).

Researchers tested the augmented argumentative skill of minorities by asking individuals to read about a controversial medical case and then decide

---

idiosyncrasy credit An explanation for the leniency groups sometimes display toward high-status members who violate group norms; the hypothetical interpersonal credit or bonus that is earned each time an individual makes a contribution to the group but the credit decreases each time the individual influences others, makes errors, or deviates from the group's norms (proposed by Edwin Hollander).

if they supported the physicians' decision in the matter. Before being given the opportunity to meet with others to discuss the case, the participants were told that 78% of the others agreed with them or that only 22% shared their view. Participants then were asked to provide their arguments and reasons in support of their position in writing. The researchers then gave these written arguments to raters who evaluated the messages for creativity and strength. As expected, the "minorities" crafted better arguments than those in the "majority" (Kenworthy et al., 2008).

Decision Rules and Dissent Juror #8 faced a difficult situation—he alone disagreed with all the others in the group—but one aspect of the group situation helped him cope: the group's decision rule. The law required the group to operate under the rule of unanimity, meaning that all group members had to agree on the decision before the case was closed. If a group operates under a unanimity rule, then the lone minority has far more power over the others. But if the group adopts a majority-rules procedure, then the majority can reach its decision without having to even consider the validity of the minority's position (Thompson, Mannix, & Bazerman, 1988). A unanimity rule helps the minority, and the majority-rules procedure benefits the majority.

Investigators examined the impact of the group's decision rule on the relative influence of majorities and minorities by asking three-person groups to role play owners of three small businesses negotiating to rent a shared marketplace. Two of the members agreed with one another on several of the key issues, but the third member was the lone minority. Some of the groups worked under a unanimity rule, which stipulated that all three parties must agree to the terms of the final decision, but others were bound by the majority-rules stipulation. As expected, the group working under the unanimity rule reached a decision that was fairer to all three of the parties than did the groups that operated under the majority-rules order, but when the group based its decision on majority-rules, the majority formed a coalition that blocked the minority. Group members' personal motivations, however, moderated this tendency in a significant way, for the pernicious effects of the groups' decision rule only occurred when members were motivated to maximize their own personal rewards rather than the rewards for the entire group (Ten Velden, Beersma & De Dreu, 2007).

Dynamic Social Impact Theory

The majority assumes change takes place when members recognize the wisdom of the collective and conform to its choices. The minority, in contrast, thinks change occurs when the majority reexamines and possibly revises its position. But change in groups is actually a mutual process, with the majority influencing the minority and the minority influencing the majority over time (Mason, Conrey, & Smith, 2007).

Dynamic social impact theory, as proposed by Latané and his colleagues, describes the processes underlying this give-and-take between the majority and the minority. As noted earlier in the chapter, social impact theory suggests that influence is determined by the strength, immediacy, and number of sources present. *Dynamic* social impact theory extends this basic principle by describing how groups, as complex systems, change over time. Groups are not static, but constantly organizing and reorganizing in four basic patterns: consolidation, clustering, correlation, and continuing diversity (Harton & Bullock, 2007; Latané, 1996, 1997; Latané & Bourgeois, 1996, 2001; Vallacher & Nowak, 2007).

- *Consolidation.* As individuals interact with one another regularly, their actions, attitudes, and

---

dynamic social impact theory An extension of Latané's social impact theory, which assumes that influence is a function of the strength, the immediacy, and the number of sources present and that this influence results in consolidation, clustering, correlation, and continuing diversity in groups that are spatially distributed and interacting repeatedly over time (developed by Bibb Latané).

opinions become more uniform. For example, even when individuals are assigned at random to rooms in college dormitories, over the course of the academic year their attitudes on a variety of topics become more and more similar (Cullum & Harton, 2007). The opinions held by a majority of the group tend to spread throughout the group, and the minority dwindles in size.

- *Clustering.* As the law of social impact suggests, people are more influenced by their closest neighbors, so clusters of group members with similar opinions emerge in groups. Clustering is more likely when (a) group members communicate more frequently with members who are close by and less frequently with more distant group members, and (b) if members can change locations to join similar others.

- *Correlation.* Over time, the group members' opinions on a variety of issues—even ones that are not discussed openly in the group—converge, so that their opinions become correlated. Students living on the same floor of a dorm, for example, find that they agree on topics that they have discussed during the year—such as the value of certain majors or the best times to work out in the fitness center—but that they also agree on topics they have never discussed or even considered discussing: the value of labor unions, the benefits of the Greek system, and human cloning (Cullum & Harton, 2007).

- *Continuing diversity.* Because of clustering, members of minorities are often shielded from the influence attempts of the majority, and their beliefs continue within the group. Diversity drops if the majority is very large and if the members of the minority are physically isolated from one another, but diversity continues when the minority members who communicate with the majority resist the majority's influence attempts.

Social psychologist Helen Harton and her colleagues identified all four patterns in a study of classroom groups (Harton et al., 1998). They asked students to answer several multiple-choice questions twice—once on their own and once after talking about the questions with the two people sitting on either side of them. *Consolidation* occurred on several of the questions. On one question, 17 of the 30 students favored an incorrect alternative before discussion. After discussion, 5 more students changed their answers and sided with the incorrect majority—including 3 students who had initially answered the question correctly. The majority increased from 57% to 73%. *Clustering* was also apparent; 11 students disagreed with both of their neighbors initially, but after discussion, only 5 students disagreed with both neighbors. Students within clusters also tended to give the same answers on other items (*correlation*), and some individuals refused to change their answers, even though no one else agreed with them (*continuing diversity*).

These four patterns vary depending on the number of times the group holds its discussion, the dispersion of the group members, the group's communication network, the status of particular individuals, the group members' desire to reach agreement, and other aspects of the situation (Miller & Brunner, 2008). The four tendencies are robust, however, and answer some key questions about influence in groups. Do most groups eventually converge on a single opinion that represents the average across all members? Dynamic social impact theory says no—groups tend to become polarized on issues as clusters form within the group. Does social pressure eventually force all those who disagree with the majority to conform? Again, dynamic social impact theory suggests that minorities, particularly in spatially distributed groups, are protected from influence. So long as minorities can cluster together, diversity in groups is ensured (Nowak, Vallacher, & Miller, 2003).

SOURCES OF GROUP INFLUENCE

Many people think of conformity in a negative way. They assume that people who change to agree with others are so weak-willed that they lack the inner fortitude to stand up for their personal beliefs. This pejorative view, unfortunately, underestimates the complexity of social influence, for individuals in any group change their behavior for a variety of reasons. First, conformity is in many cases an automatic, spontaneous reaction rather than a mindful one. Second, conformity is often the most reasonable response in a situation: When others are well-informed but we ourselves are ignorant, it's wise to use them as an informational resource. Third, people often conform because they accept the legitimacy of the group and its norms. Last, conformity is often interpersonally rewarding: Groups tend to be aggregations of like-minded individuals and so those who do not go along with the majority find that they are pressured to change. These causes of conformity—the implicit, informational, normative, and the interpersonal—are examined in the next section (Deutsch & Gerard, 1955; Kelley, 1952).

Implicit Influence

As you watch a tour group moving across a college campus, a queue moving gradually forward toward a ticket window, or a jury deliberating, the individual group members likely believe that they are carefully processing information before making one deliberate choice after another. Their actions, however, are likely produced by implicit cognitive, emotional, and behavioral processes of which they are not aware. The tour group forms a semicircle to listen to the guide, the queue members maintain a set distance between each member, and the jurors' speak in the same tones and cadence as each other—all without any conscious awareness (Pronin, 2008).

Mimicry People often deliberately imitate each other, but mimicry involves an unconscious copying of the behavior others are exhibiting. When, for example, one person adopts a particular nonverbal stance, such as crossing his or her arms, others nearby often mimic that display, but without realizing they are doing so (Chartrand & van Baaren, 2009). If one group member smiles or yawns, others in the group will join in the levity or begin

yawning as well. (Semin, 2007). Frowns, too, are contagious and will spread from one group member to another (Bourgeois & Hess, 2008). In one study, for example, individuals interacted with another person who deliberately shook her foot repeatedly or touched her face during the conversation. Their partners did not notice either type of behavior, but they nonetheless mimicked them as the interaction progressed (Chartrand & Bargh, 1999). Even jurors, dealing with as serious an issue as a murder case, laugh frequently and collectively. When investigators were given access to a jury that deliberated for several days, they identified 51 sequences of group laughter. Most of this laughter involved many of the group members, and it served to relieve tension, increase cohesion, identify errors in judgment, and mark points where the group had moved too far off track (Keyton & Beck, 2010).

Mindlessness Many group situations are so routine that members don't need to concentrate on what they are doing. When standing in a line for fast food, finding a seat in a classroom, or exiting a movie theater, people switch on their automatic pilot and act on the basis of habit and previously formed discriminations. When in a state of **mindlessness**, people aren't asking themselves, "Should I agree?" They aren't even thinking about what they are doing and so conform almost automatically (Langer, 1989).

Ellen Langer and her associates demonstrated mindless conformity by asking adults using a photocopier at a university library: "Excuse me. May I use the Xerox machine?" In the control condition, no justification for the request was offered. In the second condition, a reasonable excuse was provided: "I'm in a rush." In the third condition, the experimenter offered a senseless explanation: "I have to make some copies." (Of course the requester had to make copies; why else

---

mindlessness A state of reduced cognitive processing characterized by actions based on habit, routine, or previously formed discriminations rather than conscious deliberation.

use the machine?). The magnitude of the request was also varied; the experimenter explained that either 5 or 20 copies were needed (Langer, Blank, & Chanowitz, 1978).

Langer felt that subjects would be shocked out of their mindlessness if the experimenters (1) failed to provide any excuse whatsoever, or (2) asked to make a large rather than a small number of copies. But if an explanation were offered—even a senseless one and the favor wasn't too big—Langer felt that subjects would mindlessly agree to the request. These predictions were supported; over 90% of the subjects agreed to the request if some explanation was offered—even a nonsensical one (Langer, 1989).

Informational Influence

In the *Twelve Angry Men* jury, Juror #11 changed his verdict from guilty to not guilty, but he did not mindlessly go along. Rather, when #11 learned that #8 had a "reasonable doubt," he wondered, "Why did #8 draw different conclusions about the case than I did?" and "Am I correct in my interpretation of the evidence?" His reaction illustrates **informational influence**: change that results when group members use the responses of others in the group—the descriptive norms of the situation—as reference points and informational resources. If a group member learns that 99 other people favor Plan A over Plan B, that individual will likely adopt Plan A simply because "everyone else does." Other people provide social proof of the validity of a position or choice (Cialdini, 2009).

Social Comparison   Social comparison theory assumes that group members, as active information processors, evaluate the accuracy of their beliefs and gauge the quality of their personal attributes by comparing themselves to other individuals. If individuals facing questions with no clear solution—"Is the defendant guilty?" "Is Plan A

better than Plan B?" "Is majority influence stronger than minority influence?"—cannot reduce this uncertainty by consulting objective sources of information, they turn to the views endorsed by others in the group (see Chapter 4). In some cases, groups deliberately gather information about their members' opinions. Many deliberating groups, including juries, stop their discussions periodically to take a so-called *straw poll* to see which way the group, as a whole, is leaning (picture the wind blowing across a field of straw). In most cases, however, information about others' views is gathered during routine interactions (Gerard & Orive, 1987). Like pollsters who gauge public sentiment by sampling opinions in surveys of communities, people informally take note of their fellow group members' actions and beliefs and revise their own positions accordingly.

Members' sampling of others' opinions is not, however, systematic or objective. They oversample, for example, the opinions of those in their own group compared to those of people outside of their group (Denrell & Le Mens, 2007). If people happen to interact more frequently with some group members than with others, in time the opinions of those more frequent contacts will come to define their inferences about the group's overall position on issues—even if the frequent contacts are only a small sample of the group. Those on the group's periphery may endorse positions that are not fully consistent with the group, but not because the group ostracized them. Their isolation prevents them from accessing the social information they need to hone their opinions and also prevents the other group members from gaining their unique insights. As a result, both members of the majority and the minority display a **false consensus effect**: They assume that there is more support for their position than there actually is (Krueger & Clement, 1997; Ross, Greene, & House, 1977).

---

informational influence Change-promoting interpersonal processes that are based on the informational value of the responses of others in the situation.

false consensus effect Perceivers' tendency to assume that their beliefs, attributes, and actions are relatively common and appropriate in any given situation.

Dual Process Approaches Why is social information—the data revealed by discovering how most people are thinking, acting, and feeling—so influential? **Dual process theories of influence** suggest that the information contained in other's responses influences people in both direct and indirect ways. *Direct processes* (or central, systematic processes) entail a thoughtful analysis, or elaboration, of the issues at hand. Group members, confronted with an opinion that is different from their own, review the arguments, look for weaknesses, reexamine their own ideas on the topic, and revise their position if revision is warranted. In one study of this route to influence, group members learned that they were part of a minority that disagreed with a majority on such matters as foreign policy and juvenile justice. After they listened to members of both the minority and the majority argue their positions, subjects recorded their thoughts. Those listeners who processed the arguments offered by the majority more extensively changed their opinions to conform to the majority position (Mackie, 1987). Exposure to others' positions—in addition to providing further information and prompting a more thorough analysis of that information—can also cause group members to reinterpret or cognitively restructure key aspects of the issue (see Martin & Hewstone, 2008, for a review).

These direct informational influence processes are complemented by less rational, more *indirect processes* (Moskowitz & Chaiken, 2001). Particularly when members' cognitive resources are limited or when group members are not motivated to do the cognitive work necessary to weigh the information available to them, they will use simplifying inferential principles, termed **heuristics,** to reach decisions quickly. They might, for example, base their decision on their general mood rather than the

---

dual process theories of influence In general, any conceptual analysis that identifies two sources or forms of influence: direct (such as persuasion and discussion) and indirect (such as imitation and herding).

heuristic An inferential principle or rule of thumb that people use to reach conclusions when the amount of available information is limited, ambiguous, or contradictory.

quality of others' arguments—people in good moods tend to conform more than those in bad ones (Tong et al., 2008). If someone in the group speaks eloquently using very general, abstract terms rather than specifics, the group may assume that person knows what they are talking about and will gravitate toward their position (Sigall, Mucchi-Faina, & Mosso, 2006). Is a restaurant a good place to eat? Is this a good book? People tend to assume that a restaurant is a good one if many people dine there and that best-selling books are better than unranked ones. Behavioral economists call this preference for popular choices *herding* and underscore its rational basis: There is information revealed in the choices other people make (Raafat, Chater & Frith, 2009).

Informational Influence of Minorities Minority influence also depends on both direct and indirect processes. As Moscovici argued, minorities create cognitive conflicts that challenge the status quo of the group and call for a reevaluation of issues at hand. Minority dissent can undermine the majority's certainty and force the group to seek out new information about the situation. This increase in elaborative processing causes the group to take longer to reach its conclusions and consider multiple perspectives (Peterson & Nemeth, 1996). In some cases, too, group members can remember the minority's arguments better than the majority's (Nemeth & Goncalo, 2011; cf. Walther et al., 2002).

A minority's influence also depends, in part, on cognitive shortcuts. Because group members are also sensitive to shifts in the group's general opinion, if members notice that the minority position is gaining ground on the majority, then they may shift sides as well, creating a cascade of opinion shift (Chamley, 2004). Social psychologist Russell Clark (1999, 2001) examined this process by measuring observers' verdicts after each round of balloting in a jury trial. He first provided observers with a detailed description of a hypothetical trial and jury deliberation patterned after the one described in *Twelve Angry Men.* He then asked the observers to rate the guilt of the defendant after learning that, on the first ballot, the vote was 11 against 1 with the majority favoring a guilty verdict. Nearly all the observers agreed with the majority, but as the deliberations progressed, the observers learned that the minority position was growing from 9 to 3, to 6 to 6, to 3 to 9, and eventually 0 to 12. With each progressive vote, the observers shifted their own ratings from guilty to not guilty. Other research has suggested that individuals are particularly likely to join an expanding minority when the minority offers cogent arguments supporting its position and when other defectors are thought to have been swayed by the logic of the minority's arguments rather than by self-interest (Gordijn, De Vries, & De Dreu, 2002).

Normative Influence

Informational influence occurs because others' responses convey information concerning the nature of the social setting and how most people are responding to that setting. **Normative influence**, in contrast, occurs when members tailor their actions and attitudes to match the injunctive norms of the group situation. The members of the majority in the *Twelve Angry Men* jury, for example, did more than just think "Most everyone in the group agrees with me." They also recognized that their position was the normative one: "This group has decided the defendant is guilty and anyone who believes differently is going against the norms of this group."

Dissonance and Dissent   As noted in Chapter 6, normative influence causes members to feel, think, and act in ways that are consistent with the group's norms. When people identify with their groups, they feel duty-bound to adhere to the group's norms; they accept the legitimacy of the established norms; and they recognize the importance of supporting

---

normative influence Change-promoting interpersonal processes based on social norms, standards, and convention. Because individuals internalize their group's norms, they strive to act in ways that are consistent with those norms.

these norms. Thus, people obey norms not only because they fear the negative interpersonal consequences—ostracism, ridicule, punishment—that their nonconformity may produce, but also because they feel personally compelled to live up to their own expectations.

This negative psychological reaction to discovering one has managed to wander outside of the group's norms generates a negative reaction that is akin to *cognitive dissonance*. As noted in Chapter 5, Festinger (1957) suggested that cognitive dissonance is such an unpleasant state that people are motivated to take steps to reduce dissonance whenever it occurs. Dissonance theory originally focused on how people respond when they hold two inconsistent cognitions, but researchers have confirmed that people also experience dissonance when they discover that they do not agree with other group members. In one study, individuals with extreme opinions on issues were led to believe they were going to discuss these issues with four or five other people who had directly opposing opinions. Before the discussion, the participants described their emotions, and, as expected, they were not positive: Participants reported feeling more uneasy, uncomfortable, tense, bothered, and concerned— all indications of cognitive dissonance (Matz & Wood, 2005).

The discomfort of disagreeing with others can be so great that it even triggers activity in portions of the brain associated with pain, fear, and stress. To examine brain activity during conformity and independence, investigators used a functional magnetic resonance imaging (fMRI) scanner to monitor participants' neuronal activity. Volunteers were told that the study would examine their spatial-relations abilities by asking them to decide if two rotated three-dimensional objects were identical. To create social influence during the mental rotation task, as participants made their judgments, they were presented with the responses of four peers who, on half of the trials, chose the wrong answer. The researchers discovered that when participants agreed with the group (even when the group was incorrect) portions of their brain associated with processing visual information were most active—they assumed the others' responses were valid and adopted their solution as their own. But when they disagreed with the group, portions of the brain that are responsible for strong emotional responses (the amygdala) showed evidence of high neuronal activity (Berns et al., 2005).

Focus Theory of Normative Influence   Informational influence is based on descriptive norms—what most people do in a situation—whereas normative influence is based on injunctive norms—what most people *should do* in a situation. Of these two forms of influence, which one is more powerful? Do people tend to do what most other people do, or do they tend to do the right thing—even if others do not?

Robert Cialdini's **focus theory of normative conduct** assumes that both types of norms influence behavior but that they work in different ways. Descriptive norms make fewer processing demands on group members—they need only notice what most others do in a situation and then act that way as well. Injunctive norms, in contrast, require more cognitive resources before they will guide behavior. Only when members can focus on the norm and its implications will individuals act accordingly (e.g., Cialdini, Kallgren, & Reno, 1991; Cialdini, Reno, & Kallgren, 1990; Goldstein & Cialdini, 2011).

Cialdini's research team tested focus theory's predictions by putting handbills under the windshield wipers of cars in a parking lot and watching to see if people threw these scraps of paper on the ground when they returned to their cars. They also manipulated the salience of norms about littering across three conditions. To create informational influence, some participants, while walking toward their car, passed by a confederate who carefully dropped a bag of trash into a garbage can. This condition suggested "Most people do not litter." In a second condition, participants saw a confederate

actually pick up a piece of litter (the same bag of trash) and dispose of it in the garbage can. Cialdini and his colleagues believed that this confederate made salient the injunctive norm, "It is wrong to litter!" In the control condition, the confederate merely walked by the participant. Participants encountered the confederate either in the lot where the participant's car was parked or on the path leading to the parking lot.

These researchers discovered that descriptive norms are nearly as influential as injunctive norms but that their impact wears off rapidly. If the encounter between the subject and the confederate occurred in the parking lot, only 17% of the subjects in the descriptive norm condition littered. This percentage jumped to 36%, however, if the confederate's litter-conscious actions had occurred on the path leading to the lot. In contrast, the injunctive norm became more powerful over time. No one who saw the confederate pick up litter on the path leading to the lot littered (Reno, Cialdini, & Kallgren, 1993, Study 3).

Interpersonal Influence

Western societies claim to value nonconformity and independence, but in most situations dissent is not rewarded. In fact, it is met with **interpersonal influence**: social responses that encourage, or even force, group members to conform. In the *Twelve Angry Men* jury, the men did not dispassionately discuss their perceptions of the evidence calmly and carefully. Instead, they complained, demanded, threatened, pleaded, negotiated, pressured, manipulated, insulted, and shouted—even threatening one another with physical harm—in an attempt to change one another's opinions so the group could reach a unanimous decision. When groups discover a nonconformist—a deviant—in their midst, they sometimes use interpersonal pressure to force the member to conform.

---

focus theory of normative conduct An explanation of influence that assumes descriptive and injunctive norms influence behavior when they are made salient and therefore attended to (developed by Robert Cialdini).

interpersonal influence Change-promoting interpersonal processes based on group members selectively encouraging conformity and discouraging or even punishing nonconformity.

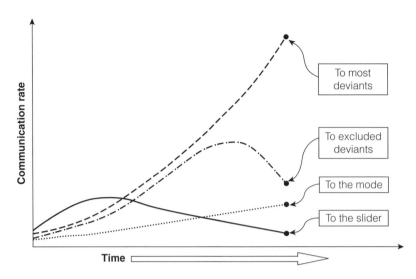

FIGURE 7.8   Communication rates with a mode, a slider, a deviant who is excluded, and a deviant who is included. Schachter's (1951) study of communication found that the person who disagreed with the others (the deviant) usually received the most communication throughout the discussion period. The only exception occurred in cohesive groups working on a relevant task whose members disliked the deviant. In this case, communications tapered off. The average number of communications addressed to the mode increased slightly over the session, while communication with the slider decreased.

SOURCE: © Cengage Learning

Stanley Schachter (1951) documented interpersonal influence by planting three kinds of confederates in a number of all-male discussion clubs. The *deviant* always disagreed with the majority. The *slider* disagreed initially but conformed over the course of the discussion. The *mode* served as a control; he consistently agreed with the majority. Schachter also manipulated the groups' cohesiveness by putting some of the participants in clubs that interested them and others in clubs that did not interest them. He assumed that people with common interests would be more cohesive than those with disparate interests. He also had the groups discuss a topic that was either relevant or irrelevant to the group's stated purpose.

Schachter was interested in how group members would pressure the deviant during the course of the discussion, so he kept track of each comment directed to the deviant, slider, and mode by the other group members. He predicted that the group would initially communicate with the mode, deviant, and slider at equal rates. But once the group became aware of the deviant's and slider's

disagreement, group members would concentrate on these two participants. Schachter believed that communication would continue at a high rate until the dissenter capitulated to the majority opinion (as in the case of the slider) or until the majority concluded that the deviant would not budge from his position (as in the case of the persistent deviant), but that this reaction would be exacerbated by the group's cohesiveness and the relevance of the task.

Influence and Ostracism   Figure 7.8 summarizes Schachter's findings. In most cases, the group communicated with the slider and the mode at a relatively low rate throughout the session, whereas communications with the deviant increased during the first 35 minutes of discussion. At the 35-minute mark, however, some groups seemed to have rejected the deviant. These groups were cohesive, working on a task that was relevant to the group's goals and whose members developed a negative attitude toward the deviant. Schachter discovered that not all groups disliked the deviant and that this level of liking played a key role in how the deviant was treated. If the group developed more positive feelings for the deviant, communication increased all the way up to the final minute. If the group disliked the deviant, communication dropped precipitously.

Schachter's findings highlight the difference between inclusive and exclusive reactions to minorities (see Levine & Kerr, 2007, for a review). Most of the groups displayed an *inclusive* reaction to the deviant: Communication between the majority and the minority was intensive and hostile, but the minority was still perceived to be a member of the ingroup. If an *exclusive* reaction occurred, however, communication with the deviant dwindled along with overt hostility, and the deviant was perceptually removed from the group by the majority members. An exclusive reaction becomes more likely when group members think that their group is very heterogeneous (Festinger, Pepitone, & Newcomb, 1952; Festinger & Thibaut, 1951). Highly cohesive groups, too, will sometimes "redefine the group's boundary" if the dissenter is inflexible and the issue is important (Gerard, 1953). So-called *double minorities*—individuals who disagree with the group and also possess one or more other unique qualities that distinguish them from the rest of the group—are also more likely to face exclusion (Sampson & Brandon, 1964).

Interpersonal Rejection   The group members did not just argue with the deviant—they also rejected the deviant. When Schachter's participants rated each other on likeability, the deviant was the sociometric outcast, whereas the mode was liked the most. The deviant was also saddled with the secretarial chores of the group; the mode and slider were assigned more desirable positions. This rejection was more pronounced in the more cohesive groups.

The group's dislike of dissenters even extended to the slider. Sliders, it could be argued, do little to provoke rejection. They begin the discussion by taking a position that few favor, but after a time they listen to reason and shift. What's not to like about such a reasonable person? Yet, Schachter's findings show that the slider was not as well-liked as someone who sided with the majority all along

(the mode). Indeed, any disagreement with a group is enough to lower one's interpersonal acceptance. Social psychologist John Levine and his associates, across a series of studies, have examined reactions to all types of deviants: those who start off neutral and then conform, others who begin as extreme deviants and then shift over to the majority, and even those who start off with the majority and then slide toward dissent (see Levine, 1980; Levine & Kerr, 2007). Levine, like Schachter, found that nonconformists and those who were initially neutral but eventually disagreed were liked the least. Moreover, even the individual who abandons his or her initial position to agree with the group is liked less than a conformist. These reactions to the dissenter likely reflect group members' sensitivity to the size of shifting majorities and minorities. Majority members are gratified when a member of the minority converts, but they are particularly troubled when a member of the majority "goes over to the other side" (Prislin, Limbert, & Bauer, 2000).

Subsequent studies have replicated this relationship between rejection and nonconformity, although these studies also identify certain situational factors that increase the magnitude of this relationship. Task relevance, cohesiveness, group consensus, interdependence, behavior extremity, newcomer status, and the degree of threat posed by the dissenter all work to increase rejection. The deviant's contribution to the task, apologies for deviation, and history of previous conformity reduce the likelihood of rejection, as do norms that encourage deviation and innovation (Levine & Kerr, 2007; Rink & Ellemers, 2011; Tata et al., 1996).

The Black-Sheep Effect   Social identity processes play a particularly critical role in determining members' reactions to deviants and conformists. Social identity theory, as discussed in Chapter 3, suggests that members share a common identity that defines the prototypical qualities of a member and encourages a distinction between members and nonmembers. Group members find deviants within their midst to be distressing because they call into question the group's positive identity and make hazy the distinctiveness of the ingroup relative to outgroups. These psychological processes, which are referred to as **subjective group dynamics**, will cause individuals to react negatively to dissenters with whom they share only category memberships. A fan of the Arsenal soccer team, for example, will react negatively to another Arsenal fan who expresses admiration for the play of the Manchester United forward—even though the two fans might never actually meet. One intriguing consequence of subjective group dynamics: Ingroup members are sometimes judged more harshly than outgroup members when they perform identical behaviors. A statement that Manchester United played brilliantly will be tolerated when spoken by a Man U fan, but if an Arsenal fan expresses such a belief, he or she would be roundly criticized by other Arsenal fans. This tendency is termed the **black-sheep effect** (Marques, 2010).

Identity and Dissent   Social identity processes not only influence the group's reaction to dissent, but also members' decisions about conforming or dissenting. Although individuals who strongly identify with their group may tend to support its decisions out of misguided loyalty, social psychologist Dominic Packer's normative conflict model of dissent argues that members who are strongly committed to the group are more, rather than less, likely to dissent. Those who do not identify with their group tend to display uneasy conformity— they keep quiet and go along with the group— or they withdraw from the group altogether. In contrast, members who identify strongly with the group are willing to accept the interpersonal costs that come with dissent, in the hope that the group will take steps to correct its mistake. Their dissent

is "motivated by a desire to change group norms and initiate improvement within a group" (Packer, 2008b, p. 54). In support of the model, Packer and his colleague have found that members who identify with their groups are more likely to dissent than less committed members, but only when they believe the group's position is collectively harmful. Significantly, people who identify with their group are not more likely to dissent when doing so would improve their own personal circumstances, but would not necessarily benefit the group (Packer, 2008b, Packer, 2009; Packer & Chasteen, 2009).

When Influence Inhibits: The Bystander Effect

Human groups could not form, remain intact, and achieve their goals if their members did not continually, and successfully, influence one another. Groups require coordinated action, and social influence is the means to achieve that coordination. This readiness to cooperate and conform, however, can cause individuals to follow when they should lead and comply when they would be better off resisting. A number of negative, dysfunctional group phenomena—peer pressure, groupthink, hazing, bullying, conflict, and intergroup conflict—are sustained, at least in part, by social influence processes. This section considers one such process in detail: the bystander effect.

Inhibition of Helping in Groups   In the early morning of March 13, 1964, a young woman named Catherine Genovese ("Kitty" to her friends) was attacked and killed in Queens, New York. Many residents of the area were roused from their sleep by the noise of the attack and wondered what was happening, but none of them helped directly. Only one person even called the police (Manning, Levine, & Collins, 2007).

Many blamed this failure on the bystanders, suggesting that the urbanites were cruel, apathetic, or lacking the moral compunction needed to compel them to act. But when social psychologists Bibb Latané and John Darley (1970) read about the

---

subjective group dynamics Psychological and interpersonal processes that result from social categorization and identification processes, including members' desire to sustain the positive distinctiveness of the ingroup and the validity of its shared beliefs.

black-sheep effect The tendency for group members to evaluate a group member who performs an offensive behavior more harshly than an outgroup member who performs the same offense.

murder of Kitty Genovese, they were struck by the large number of witnesses. Could social pressures, they wondered, have interfered with people's capacity to respond in a helpful way to the emergency?

Latané and Darley investigated this possibility by creating a false emergency in their laboratory. While male college students completed some bogus questionnaires, Latané and Darley pumped white smoke through an air vent into the test room. Some participants were alone in the room, but others worked in three-person groups consisting of one participant and two confederates. The confederates pretended to be participants, but they ignored the emergency. As the room filled with smoke, they nonchalantly glanced at the vent, shrugged, and went back to their questionnaires. If the participant mentioned the smoke to them, they said merely "I dunno." In a third condition, all three members of the group were actual participants.

When tested alone, participants usually left the room to report the smoke within two minutes; 75% reported the emergency within the six-minute time limit. Participants tested in groups behaved very differently. Only 10% of the participants tested with the passive confederates ever reported the smoke, and the reporting percentage reached no higher than 15% even when all three group members were actual participants. By the time the six-minute period was up, the room was so smoky that participants could not see the far wall. They coughed and rubbed their eyes, but they stayed at their tables, fanning the fumes away from their papers so they could finish their questionnaires.

Latané and Darley's work demonstrated the **bystander effect**—people are less likely to help

---

bystander effect The tendency for people to help less when they know others are present and capable of helping. The effect was initially thought to be the result of apathy and a selfish unwillingness to get involved, but research suggests a number of cognitive and social processes, including diffusion of responsibility and misinterpretation that help is not needed, contribute to the effect.

when in groups rather than alone—and soon other investigators confirmed these results. A statistical review of approximately 50 studies of nearly 6,000 people who faced various apparent emergencies alone or in a group indicated that groups impede helping. Across these various studies, about 75% of the participants tested alone intervened, but only 53% of the participants in groups helped (Latané & Nida, 1981).

Social Influence and the Bystander Effect   But why do people in groups not help as much as single individuals? First, emergency situations are usually unfamiliar ones, so people who witness them do not fully understand what is happening and how they should respond. This ambiguity causes them to rely on the reactions of others in the situation to guide their interpretation of the event. If, however, each group member is responding similarly—looking to the other group members for information about how to interpret the situation—then each nonresponding bystander sends the same inaccurate message to every other nonresponding bystander: "It's OK; no help is needed." In situations that are obviously emergencies, the bystander effect disappears (Clark & Word, 1972, 1974).

Second, normative influence does not enjoin bystanders to help strangers. Most everyday situations do not require one act as a Good Samaritan (Feigenson, 2000), but they do caution against involvement in others' affairs. In most cultures (but not all), it is not "normal" to interact with others who you do not know, let alone offer them some sort of assistance (see Focus 7.2). Most people prefer to appear poised and normal in social settings and actively avoid doing anything that may lead to embarrassment. In an ambiguous emergency, people fear that they will look foolish if they offer assistance to someone who does not need it, so they look the other way rather than get involved (Schwartz & Gottlieb, 1976). These normative pressures, however, are reduced when the people in an emergency situation (the witnesses and the person needing help) are members of the same group or social

---

F o c u s 7.2 Cross-Cultural Perspectives: Who Will Help?

Brazilians are known for *jeitinho*, a willingness to bend a social norm in order to solve a problem (Ferreira et al., 2012). Whose citizens are happiest? Denmark's (Helman, 2011). If you are doing business in Russia, be prepared to offer a bribe: Russia is ranked first among larger countries where bribery is used to make a sale or close a deal (Riaño & Hodess, 2009). But where are people most likely to offer others help? Imagine your zipper on your backpack breaks as you exit from the taxi at your destination, and now the wind is scattering its contents about on the sidewalk. People are passing by you as you struggle to pick up your things, but will they stop and help? Does it matter if you are in New York City, Tokyo, or Rio de Janeiro? Are people more helpful in some cultures than in others?

Researchers have used a variety of field methods to examine this question. Showing considerable creativity, investigators typically stage a minor accident or make a small request of passersby in different countries and then compare the amount of helping. One researcher, for example, arranged for teams in Paris, Athens, and Boston to slightly overpay for purchases and ask passersby for directions. He discovered that people were sometimes given bad directions and clerks often kept the overpayment, but that it depended on the researcher's apparent nationality. Athenians treated outgroup members (Americans) better than their own compatriots, but Parisians and Bostonians treated ingroup members better than foreigners (Feldman, 1968).

These findings suggest that the degree of collectivism in a culture may influence helping. Collectivists may diffuse responsibility more readily, and they may be less helpful to those who are not part of their group (Levine, Cassidy, & Jentzsch, 2010; Mazar & Aggarwal, 2011). Cultures also differ in trust, for in some parts of the world people assume that others can be trusted to reciprocate help and support, whereas in others trust is slower to develop and requires social structures that detect and sanction those who do not reciprocate (Buchan, Croson, & Dawes, 2002).

To explore these possible differences, social psychologist Robert Levine and his colleagues (2001) tested the responses of passersby in the largest cities of 23 different countries. In each city, a young man staged three types of minor emergencies: (a) he dropped a pen while walking down the street; (b) already limping from a known injury, he struggled to collect a dropped pile of magazines; and (c) while wearing sunglasses and carrying a white cane used by the blind, he paused and waited for help in crossing an intersection.

Helping rates varied substantially across the countries Levine studied. In Rio de Janeiro and San Jose, for example, the young man was helped over 90% of the time, whereas he received help less than 50% of the time in Singapore, New York City, and Kuala Lampur (in Malasia). A culture's degree of collectivism did not predict helping, but the economic prosperity of the residents of the city and cultural *simpatico* did. In more affluent countries, people were less likely to help a blind person or someone who inadvertently dropped his pen. These were also places where the pace of life was quick—as evidenced by the more rapid pace of the passersby as they walked by without helping.

Several of the countries that Levine studied, however, were ones that are unique in their endorsement of a cultural norm that encourages prosocial behavior. This norm, called *simpatia* in Spain and *simpatico* in Portugal, is typical of certain Spanish heritage countries; it encourages people to treat other people in a positive, polite way, including strangers. The five *simpatico* countries in the study, Brazil, Costa Rica, El Salvador, Mexico, and Spain, exhibited higher levels of helping (83%) compared to the other, non-*simpatico* countries (66%).

These findings attest to the impact of cultural norms, and the social influence processes they sustain, on helping. Although humans, as a species, are uniquely helpful relative to other species, this biological tendency is modified to a degree by local cultural constraints. People may be naturally helpful, but this tendency depends on the norms of the places where they live.

---

category. If individuals in the situation know each other, then the bystander effect is minimized— and often reversed—with larger groups providing more help than individuals or smaller groups

(Levine et al., 2005). If "bystanders share group-level psychological relationships, group size can encourage as well as inhibit helping" (Levine & Crowther, 2008, p. 1429).

Third, people feel less responsible when in groups compared to being alone, and this **diffusion of responsibility** leaves bystanders feeling that it is not their responsibility to help. "The pressures to intervene do not focus on any one of the observers; instead, the responsibility for intervention is shared among all the onlookers and is not unique to any one" (Darley & Latané, 1968, p. 378). Simply imagining that one will be with others in a group is sufficient to reduce feelings of accountability and helpfulness (Garcia et al., 2002).

These factors, although relatively mundane social processes in most contexts, combine to cause bystanders to overlook the suffering of others. The bystander effect is not caused by apathy or a loss of humanity that overtakes people when they become part of a collective. The effect is, instead, the predictable result of group-level social influence processes that leave members confused, uncertain of the proper course of action, and unable to take action.

APPLICATION:
UNDERSTANDING JURIES

Groups have served as the final arbiter of guilt and innocence for centuries. As far back as the eleventh century, the neighbors of those accused of wrongdoing were asked both to provide information about the actions of the accused and to weigh the evidence. Witnesses and experts now provide the evidence, but the jury remains responsible for weighing the testimony of each person before rendering a verdict. More than 300,000 juries convene each year in American courtrooms alone (Hyman & Tarrant, 1975).

Jury Dynamics

The jury situation is designed to foster careful decision making and tolerance for all viewpoints, but at its core, a jury is a group. The jury's final decision depends not only on the evidence presented at the trial, the attorneys' arguments, and the judge's instructions, but also on social influence.

Stories, Evidence, and Verdicts   The Chicago Jury Project, conducted in the 1950s, was one of the first attempts to study, systematically, the ways juries carry out their responsibilities and render their verdicts. Using a variety of methods, including jury simulations, recording actual deliberations, and posttrial interviews, the investigators discovered that most juries follow the same basic procedures during deliberation. Juries usually begin by electing a leader and deciding if balloting will be secret or public. Some juries take a straw poll of their initial preferences, and as many as 30% of those groups reach complete consensus on that first ballot (Diamond et al., 2003; Kalven & Zeisel, 1966). But when members disagree, they initiate a consensus-seeking process. During this phase of the deliberation, the group may ask the judge for instructions and request additional information concerning the evidence. The group spends about 75% of its time examining evidence and the remainder discussing points of law or unrelated matters (Ellsworth, 1989; Hans & Vidmar, 1991). Once it reaches a final verdict, the group then spends some time making sure that all members are willing to endorse it (the reconciliation stage; Levett et al., 2005).

The jury's approach to the deliberations depends, in part, on how it structures the task. Jury researchers Reid Hastie, Steven Penrod, and Nancy Pennington (1983), in their **story model** of jury deliberation, noted that jurors generally approach the decision in one of two ways. Some jurors appear to be *verdict driven*. They reach a decision about the verdict before deliberation and

---

diffusion of responsibility A reduction of personal responsibility experienced by individuals in groups and social collectives (identified by John Darley and Bibb Latané in their studies of bystanders' failures to help someone in need).

story model A theory of cognitive processing of trial information that suggests jurors mentally organize evidence in coherent, credible narratives.

cognitively organize the evidence into two categories: evidence that favors a verdict of guilty and evidence that favors a verdict of not guilty. *Evidence-driven* jurors, in contrast, resist making a final decision on the verdict until they have reviewed all the available evidence; then they generate a story that weaves together the evidence of the trial and their own expectations and assumptions about people and similar situations in a coherent narrative (Pennington & Hastie, 1986, 1992). Should the jurors find, during deliberations, that their stories are relatively similar, then the group will be able to reach a verdict quickly. If, however, their stories are different, they spend time discussing alternative stories until a consensus can be reached.

When juries contain both verdict-driven and evidence-driven jurors, the approach preferred by the majority of the jurors is generally used to structure the deliberations. When researchers created mock three-person juries containing two members who shared the same type of cognitive orientation, this cognitive majority dominated the deliberations, and, in most cases, the individual with the alternative viewpoint restructured their approach so that it matched the majority's approach (Kameda, 1994).

Minority Influence in Juries Most of the *Twelve Angry Men* jury, as they listened to the evidence presented during the trial, made sense of it all with a simple story: The ungrateful, disrespectful son fought with his father and, in a fit of anger, killed him. Juror #8, in contrast, developed a different story: The father, who had many enemies in the neighborhood, was attacked by one of them, who stabbed him with a knife identical to one owned by the man's son. These two stories lead in very different directions in terms of the verdict, but over the course of the deliberations, Juror #8 managed to convince all the others that his story was more credible than theirs.

The success of Juror #8 was a rarity. As Figure 7.9 indicates, the verdict favored by the majority of the jurors—7 to 11 jurors in a regular 12-person jury—on the first ballot becomes the jury's final decision in 90% of all jury trials (Devine et al., 2001). Most jurors implicitly adopt a majority-rules decision norm: If a significant majority of the members (say, two-thirds) favor a verdict, then everyone in the group should agree with that verdict. In fact, a computer model that simulates jury deliberations (DICE) assumes that a three-person coalition in a standard 12-person jury will be relatively weak, but a four- or five-person coalition will be fairly influential (Hastie et al., 1983).

Minorities are not powerless, however. Even though the majority tends to prevail in juries, as Figure 7.9 suggests, the minority convinces the majority to change in about 1 trial out of every 10. For example, in the trial of the second defendant in the Oklahoma City Bombing, Terry Nichols, the first vote was 10 to 2 for acquittal (Bartels, 2001). But the two lone jurors who favored a guilty verdict dug in to their position and carefully reviewed the evidence for six long days. One of the jurors, a geophysicist, used his skill, logic, and persuasive talents to craft a compromise verdict of guilty of conspiracy but not guilty of first-degree murder. He was successful, in part, because of his recognized expertise and the rapid change in votes by four of the other jurors. These findings confirm the importance of encouraging juries to take the time they need to deliberate before rendering a final decision (Hans et al. 2003).

Minorities can also deadlock the jury by refusing to conform to the majority's verdict, resulting in a *hung jury* if a unanimous verdict is required. The origin of the term "hung jury" is not certain, but it was apparently first used to describe American juries that could not reach a verdict. It matches "most closely to the meaning of the word hung as caught, stuck, or delayed" (Hans et al., 2003, p. 33). Hung juries generally occur when the evidence does not clearly favor one verdict, and, even then, occur only in approximately 10% of such cases. When a hung jury does occur, it is often just one or two jurors holding out against the majority (Hans et al., 2003).

Status and Influence Some members of the *Twelve Angry Men* jury had higher status within the group than the other rank-and-file members: Juror #4, for example, was a stockbroker, whereas

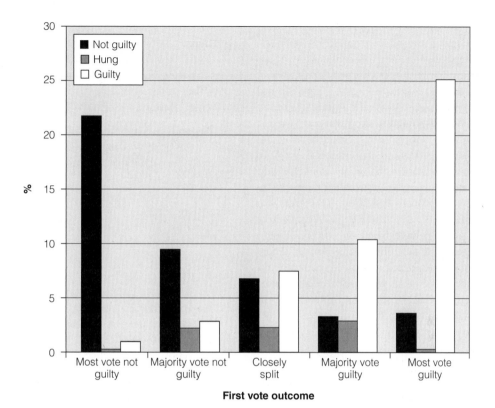

FIGURE 7.9 The percentage of different types of outcomes in jury trials by initial distribution of votes. In most cases, the decision favored by the majority of the jurors when deliberations first begin is the verdict returned by that jury. Minority influence, although rare, occurred in about 10% of the cases when the majority favored acquittal and 15% of the cases when the majority favored conviction.

SOURCE: © Cengage Learning 2014

Juror #6 worked in construction. Is it a coincidence that the jury paid far more attention to the ideas and suggestions of Juror #4 rather than #6?

Fairly or unfairly, people who have high prestige or status are more influential than low-status members. Researchers in the Chicago Jury Project carefully replicated all aspects of an actual trial. They selected sets of 12 individuals from a pool of eligible jurors, simulated the pretrial interview process designed to eliminate biased jurors (voir dire), and assembled the group in the courtroom. A bailiff then played a recording of a trial and asked the group to retire to a jury room to decide on a verdict. Except for the use of a recording, the groups were treated just like actual juries (Strodtbeck &

Hook, 1961; Strodtbeck James, & Hawkin, 1957; Strodtbeck & Mann, 1956).

These juries tended to favor people of higher socioeconomic status (proprietors and office workers) over those of lower socioeconomic status (blue-collar workers) when choosing a foreman, even though no mention of occupation was made (Strodtbeck & Lipinski, 1985). High-status members also participated more frequently in the jury's discussions, often by offering more suggestions and providing more orientation to the task. High-status members were also more successful in convincing the others that their judgments on the case were the most accurate. Proprietors' opinion about the verdict formed before deliberation predicted the jury's decision; the correlation between their private predeliberation opinion and the jury's decision was .50. For laborers, there was no significant relationship ($r = .02$) between their predeliberation opinion and the jury's decision (Strodtbeck et al., 1957).

In these studies, conducted in the 1950s, sex and race differences were also apparent in juries. Women and racial minorities joined in the discussion less frequently than men (James, 1959; Strodtbeck et al., 1957). Furthermore, women's comments were more often relational in nature, showing solidarity and agreement, whereas men's comments were more task-focused (Strodtbeck & Mann, 1956; see also Nemeth, Endicott, & Wachtler, 1976). These inequities, however, have faded over time. Recent analyses suggest that race and sex no longer determine influence in juries, but that social status remains a potent factor; those jurors who are more affluent or well-educated continue to be more influential than others (York & Cornwell, 2006).

How Effective Are Juries?

Given what we know about conformity and nonconformity in groups, should the jury system be modified? Asch's studies tell us that people often conform and that even a correct minority often loses to an incorrect majority. As we have seen, normative, informational, and interpersonal influence are powerful forces in groups, and they can quash individuals' freedom to speak their minds. Juries are a time-honored tradition, but are they effective?

Determining the effectiveness of juries as deciders of guilt or innocence is a complicated task, for we can never know when the jury has been correct or incorrect in condemning or freeing a defendant. If a clear criterion for determining guilt existed, juries would not be necessary in the first place. Several bits of evidence, however, provide partial support for the effectiveness of juries as decision makers. First, jurors seem to take their role very seriously (Gastil, Burkhalter, & Black, 2007). One jury expert, after studying the responses of more than 2,000 jurors participating in the Chicago Jury Project, concluded:

> The most consistent theme that emerged from listening to the deliberations was the seriousness with which the jurors approached their job and the extent to which they were concerned that the verdict they reached was consistent with the spirit of the law and with the facts of the case. (Simon, 1980, p. 521)

Second, jury members themselves, when asked to rate the quality of their group's deliberations, are generally very favorable. Individuals tend to be quite negative when they evaluate the quality of many decision-making groups (e.g., teams at work, organizational meetings, committees), but they give high marks to the juries they have served on. Jurors who were asked to rate their jury experience either agreed or strongly agreed with such statements as: "Jurors thoroughly discussed the relevant facts of the case," "All of the jurors listened respectfully to each other during deliberation," and "The other jurors gave me enough of a chance to express my opinions about the case" (Gastil et al., 2007, p. 350). These jurors did not report an experience like that depicted in the *Twelve Angry Men* jury.

Third, juries do well when compared with judges' decisions. In a survey of nearly 8,000 actual criminal and civil trials, judges and juries disagreed on only 20% of the cases; for criminal trials, the jury was somewhat more lenient than the judge, but for civil trials, the disagreements were evenly split for and against the defendant. Furthermore, 80% of these disagreements occurred when the weight of the evidence was so close that the judge admitted that the verdict could have gone either way. This match between verdicts may explain why 77% of the judges surveyed felt that the jury system was satisfactory, 20% felt that it had disadvantages that should be corrected, but only 3% felt the system to be so unsatisfactory that its use should be curtailed (Kalven & Zeisel, 1966).

Last, jurors are hardly unbiased, rational weighers of evidence; the defendant's physical appearance, the lawyers' style of questioning, and the sequencing of evidence are just a few of the factors that bias jurors' decisions (Dane & Wrightsman, 1982; Hastie et al., 1983; Wrightsman, Nietzel, & Fortune, 1998). These biases are largely controlled, however, by relying on group decisions rather than individual decisions. Simulations of juries suggest that the lone juror's initial biases and preferences have very little impact on the group's final decision, no matter what the size of the jury (Kerr & Huang, 1986). Discourse analyses of the actual content of jury deliberations indicate that members openly address biases, manage their conflict, and reduce decisional regret collectively (Poole & Dobosh, 2010; Sunwolf, 2010).

Each of these pro-jury arguments, however, can also be countered by other, more disquieting data about juries and their capabilities. In recent years, a number of very high-profile juries have made decisions that in retrospect appear to have been based on emotion and prejudice rather than on the thoughtful analysis of the evidence. Studies of their deliberation processes indicate that a handful of group members dominated the group discussion, and these individuals succeeded, in most cases, in determining the final verdict. When investigators have asked jurors about their understanding of the legalities of the case, they discovered that many understood less than half of the judge's instructions to the jury (Ellsworth & Reifman, 2000). Jury members also have a particularly difficult time following the arguments and evidence introduced in complex, time-consuming trials (Cecil, Hans, & Wiggins, 1991; Levett et al., 2005). These findings have prompted some to suggest that the jury system should be abolished, but others favor a more moderate solution—improving juries by modifying their structure and dynamics.

Improving Juries

The judicial system is long on tradition, but in recent years, several innovations have been suggested and even implemented (Vidmar & Hans, 2007). Some of these reforms, such as reducing the size and the decision rules of juries, are designed to improve the general efficiency of juries and the fairness of their procedures. Others, such as note taking, help jurors to process the evidence and testimony that they must consider when reaching their decision.

Jury Size In 1970, the U.S. Supreme Court returned a landmark ruling in the case of *Williams v. Florida*, 1970. Williams sought to have his conviction overturned on the grounds that the deciding jury had included only six persons. The Supreme Court, however, found in favor of Florida, ruling that a six-person jury is large enough to promote group deliberation, protect members from intimidation, fairly represent the community, and weigh the facts in the case. Psychology and law expert Michael J. Saks, however, has suggested that the Supreme Court should have taken group dynamics research into consideration before making its decision. As he noted, modifying jury size could influence:

- *Group structure.* Members of smaller juries participate at more equal rates; smaller juries are more cohesive; and members of larger juries exchange more information.

- *Representativeness.* Smaller groups are not as representative of the community as larger ones. For example, if a community was 10% Latino and 90% Anglo, in all probability, about 80% of the 12-person juries selected from that community would include at least one Latino, but only 40% of the six-person juries would contain Latinos.

- *Majority influence.* The majority's influence may be greater in smaller juries, because the likelihood of finding a partner for one's minority coalition becomes smaller.

- *Voting.* Saks contended that the Supreme Court erred in assuming that a 5 to 1 vote in a six-person jury was the same as a 10 to 2 split in a 12-person group. With the 10 to 2 vote, one is joined by a dissenting partner, whereas in the 5 to 1 vote, one faces the majority alone. As a result, the likelihood of a hung jury is greater in larger juries (Kerr & MacCoun, 1985).

Saks also noted, however, that despite size-related changes in group dynamics, small juries and large juries do not appear to differ significantly in the types of verdicts reached—except in certain civil cases, when smaller juries tend to return larger damages (Saks, 1977; Saks & Hastie, 1978; Saks & Marti, 1997).

Unanimity In 1972, three men were convicted, in separate trials, of assault, grand larceny, and burglary by the court system of Oregon. They appealed to the U.S. Supreme Court on the grounds that their right to a fair trial had been violated because the votes of the juries had not been unanimous. To the defendants' dismay, the Supreme Court ruled in favor of Oregon (*Apodaca v. Oregon,* 1972), concluding that the Sixth Amendment to the U.S. Constitution guarantees only that a "substantial majority of the jury" must be convinced of the defendant's guilt. Later in the ruling, the Supreme Court suggested that a 75% agreement constitutes an acceptable minimum for most juries.

The Court's conclusion is, for the most part, justified by empirical evidence. The verdict preferred by the majority of the jurors on their first vote usually becomes the final verdict in a large percentage of the cases, with or without a unanimity rule. The minority's opinion sometimes prevails, but, in such cases, the minority is usually so substantial that a 9 out of 12 majority would not have been reached anyway. Most juries implicitly operate according to either a basic two-thirds or a 10-out-of-12 rule (Davis, Bray, & Holt, 1977; Davis et al., 1975; Stasser, Kerr, & Bray, 1982). Once most of the members of the group favor a particular verdict, the members of the minority who are uncertain tend to go along with the others to support the "team" and its verdict (Meyers, Seibold, & Kang, 2010).

Relaxing the requirement for unanimity, however, changes the decision-making process in juries. Juries that do not have to reach a unanimous decision render their judgments twice as quickly and are far less likely to come to a stalemate (Foss, 1981; Kerr et al., 1976). Saks and Hastie (1978) feared that juries that do not deliberate to unanimity do not deliberate sufficiently and make more mistakes—"convictions when the correct decision is acquittal; acquittals when the correct decision is conviction" (pp. 84–85).

Procedural Innovations Whereas jurors were once forbidden from taking notes or discussing the case prior to deliberations, in a series of modifications, courts have experimented with various types of procedural changes to determine if notes help jurors to remember and process the volumes of information they receive during the trial. For example, the courts have worked to try to clarify information about the legal terms used in the case under consideration. The revised wording of such concepts as "reasonable doubt" and "preponderance of evidence," for example, has triggered changes in how long juries deliberate and in their eventual verdicts (Horowitz & Kirkpatrick, 1996). Courts have studied ways to make the instructions given to the jurors prior to deliberation clearer and more understandable (Ellsworth & Reifman, 2000). Some courts also permit jurors to (1) take notes during the presentation of evidence and use these notes during deliberation; (2) submit questions to the court that, after review by judge and legal counsel, can be considered in summary statements during the trial or in the presentation of additional evidence; and (3) discuss the trial among themselves while the trial is ongoing (Vidmar & Hans, 2007). These innovations are generally associated with increased involvement of jurors in the deliberation process, but their impact on decision outcomes appears to be modest (Devine et al., 2001).

Voir Dire The selection of jury members from a pool of potential participants occurs through a process known as **voir dire**. Voir dire—an alteration of the French phrase *vrai dire*, which means "to speak truly"—calls for verbal or written questioning of prospective jurors to uncover any biases or prejudices that may stand in the way of fairness and impartiality (Hans & Vidmar, 1982).

Until the 1970s, voir dire was left primarily to the judge's discretion; defense lawyers could submit questions, but judges were free to disregard them if they desired. However, when convictions were overturned on appeal because trial judges had disallowed defense participation in voir dire (e.g., *Ham v. S. Carolina*, 1973), trial courts began opening up the jury selection procedure to attorneys. Systematic jury selection, when lawyers carefully

----

voir dire The oral or written questioning of prospective jurors by counsel or the judge.

study the prospective jurors in the pool and use voir dire to identify sympathetic and antagonistic jurors, is now a common practice in major trials. Voir dire is regularly used, for example, in cases in which the defendant, if convicted, faces the death penalty. By rejecting from the jury anyone who objects to the death penalty, the prosecution can assemble what is termed a *death-qualified jury*.

Systematic jury selection is controversial. Proponents argue that in many political and criminal trials, biases produced by unfair publicity, regional prejudices, and unrepresentative jury rosters must be controlled if the defendant is to receive just treatment. Critics feel that systematic jury selection is tantamount to jury rigging, as it produces biased rather than fair juries and works to exclude certain types of people from juries. Death-qualified juries,

for example, are not just willing to impose a death sentence, but they are also more conviction prone than non-death-qualified juries (Filkins, Smith, & Tindale, 1998).

Social psychologist Lawrence Wrightsman, an expert on psychology and the law, has argued that judges should limit the number of jurors that lawyers can challenge during voir dire. He also recommended stricter guidelines for lawyers, who sometimes use the voir dire process to influence the jurors in their favor. Wrightsman suggested that voir dire questioning be carried out carefully, so that jurors will respond honestly and that judges supervise the process more closely. Voir dire is a useful way of identifying highly biased individuals, but it should not be a means of manipulating the composition of the jury (Wrightsman, Nietzel, & Fortune, 1998).

CHAPTER REVIEW

When do people conform in groups?

1. *Social influence* in groups occurs when the majority of the members influence smaller subgroups within the group to change (*majority influence*) and when the minority members succeed in converting the majority of group members to their position (*minority influence*).

2. Asch studied *conformity* by measuring people's decisions when the majority of their group's members made errors judging line lengths.

   ▪ People in the *Asch situation* conformed, on average, on one-third of the test trials, but nearly all of the subjects disagreed with the majority more frequently than they agreed.

   ▪ When group members change their position, their conformity may result from temporary *compliance* to the group's pressure rather than true *conversion* (private acceptance). Those who do not comply may be displaying *independence* or deliberate defiance of the group (*anticonformity*). When *congruence* occurs, members were in agreement from the outset.

3. Conformity increased when the majority was large and unanimous, but increasing the majority beyond four did not significantly increase conformity.

   ▪ This decreasing impact of increased numbers of sources of influence is consistent with Bond's meta-analytic review and Latané's *social impact theory*.

   ▪ The principle of social impact suggests that impact depends on the strength (S), the immediacy (I), and the number (N) of sources present, or Impact = *f* SIN.

4. Majority influence varies in strength depending on the size, structure, cohesiveness, and goals of the group and the nature of its tasks.

   ▪ Fewer group members conformed in the test situation developed by Crutchfield (the *Crutchfield situation*), where their responses were not identifiable.

   ▪ Individuals in groups engaged in computer-mediated interactions conform at rates equal to and sometimes greater than face-to-face groups (Social Identity

Model of Deindividuation Effects, or SIDE effects).

5.   Conformity rates vary across time, cultures, sexes, and group settings.

- Certain personality traits are related to conformity. People who conform consistently in groups tend to be more authoritarian but seek social approval. Nonconformists are more self-confident.

- Women conform slightly more than men, primarily in face-to-face groups. Women may use conformity to increase group harmony, whereas men use nonconformity to create the impression of independence.

- Bond and Smith's review suggests that group members in collectivistic societies yield to majority influence more often than those in individualistic societies.

- Conformity rates dropped slightly in the last half of the twentieth century.

When do people resist the group's influence and instead change the group?

1.   Moscovici's *conversion theory* suggests that consistent minorities will be influential, although that influence may in some cases be indirect and delayed. Minorities, therefore, create more conversion and innovation, whereas majorities tend to create compliance.

- Moscovici found that a minority, particularly if behaviorally consistent, can influence the majority.

- Hollander suggests that minorities that are accorded high status in the group can also influence the majority, for their *idiosyncrasy credits* protect them from sanctions when they display nonconformity.

- Minorities exert more effort in their attempts to influence than do majorities, and the decision rule the group adopts will differentially influence the success of majorities (majority-rules) and minorities (unanimity).

2.   Latané's *dynamic social impact theory* uses the processes of consolidation, clustering, correlation, and continuing diversity to explain majority and minority influence in spatially distributed groups that interact repeatedly over time.

What are the sources of social influence?

1.   Implicit influence is produced by cognitive, emotional, and behavioral processes that are neither consciously controlled nor frequently noticed.

- Group members tend to mimic each other, without realizing they are doing so.

- Langer suggests that *mindlessness* can cause individuals to conform automatically.

2.   *Informational influence* takes place whenever group members use others' responses as reference points and informational resources.

- As social comparison theory notes, people are a valuable source of information, although individuals often misjudge the extent to which others agree with their viewpoint (the *false consensus effect*).

- *Dual process theories* recognize that social influence occurs when group members systematically process available information (*direct process*) or base their choices on nonrational processes, such as *heuristics* and emotional responses (*indirect process*).

3.   *Normative influence* prompts group members to feel, think, and act in ways that are consistent with their group's social standards.

- Disagreeing with others can trigger cognitive dissonance, an unpleasant and neurologically detectable psychological state that individuals are motivated to reduce.

- Cialdini's *focus theory of normative influence* suggests that, in some cases, normative influence is a more potent and longer-lasting form of influence than informational influence.

4. *Interpersonal influence* includes verbal and nonverbal tactics—complaining, demanding, threatening, pleading, negotiating, pressuring, manipulating, rejecting, and so on—designed to induce change.

   - Schachter's analysis of group rejection indicates that a nonconformist is generally less liked by others in the group.

   - Communication with a disliked deviant eventually diminishes, at least when cohesive groups are working on relevant tasks. Schachter's findings, as well as those by Levine and his colleagues, indicate that any dissent from the group mode will reduce likeability.

   - Reaction to deviants results, in part, from *subjective group dynamics* triggered by social identity processes. Group members who violate norms can lead to the *black-sheep effect*—they will be evaluated more negatively than an individual who is not a group member who performs the same type of action.

   - Packer's normative conflict model suggests that strongly identified members are more willing to bear social costs associated with dissent in order to improve group outcomes.

5. Social influence can cause individuals to fail to respond in emergency situations.

   - The *bystander effect* occurs when individuals help less in groups rather than when alone. Interest in the effect was generated by the Kitty Genovese incident.

   - Latané and Darley confirmed the effect of groups on helping by studying people's reactions to staged emergencies.

   - Informational and normative influences contribute to the bystander effect, as does *diffusion of responsibility*.

   - Cross-cultural studies of helping, such as Levine's work, suggest that the norms of some cultures (such as *simpatico* cultures)

prompt residents to respond more positively to those who are in need.

Does social influence shape juries' verdicts?

1. The magnitude of social influence suggests that the decisions reached by groups, including juries, are shaped by social processes rather than by an unbiased weighing of evidence.

   - The Chicago Jury Project and work by Hastie, Penrod, and Pennington suggest that jurors, through deliberation, develop narratives to account for evidence (*story model*).

   - Juries tend to use either *verdict-driven* or *evidence-driven* deliberation strategies. In most cases, they choose the method of deliberation favored by the majority of the members.

   - The verdict favored by the majority of the members prior to deliberation (or on the first straw poll) is usually the jury's final verdict.

   - Jurors who have higher status occupations tend to dominate the group's discussion.

2. Available evidence suggests that juries are satisfactory vehicles for making legal decisions.

   - Despite size-related changes in group dynamics, small and large juries do not appear to differ significantly in the types of verdicts reached.

   - Juries that do not have to reach a unanimous decision render their judgments twice as quickly and are far less likely to be hung juries.

   - Several alterations of procedure have been developed to help jurors remember and process trial information, but their impact is not yet known.

   - Voir dire procedures are often used to select jury members, but Wrightman maintains this process can undermine the representativeness of the jury.

RESOURCES

Chapter Case: Twelve Angry Men

- *Twelve Angry Men: A Play in Three Acts* by Reginald Rose and Sherman L. Sergel (1958) is a play based on Rose's experience while serving on a jury. Although a fictional dramatization, the play demonstrates the pressures to conform present in groups. Both movie versions of the play, one made in 1957 starring Henry Fonda as Juror #8 and a 1997 version with Jack Lemon taking the role, are excellent depictions of group processes.

Majority and Minority Influence

- "Dynamic Social Impact: A Theory of the Origins and Evolution of Culture" by Helen C. Harton and Melinda Bullock (2007) reviews recent studies of dynamic social impact theory and applies the theory to explain the origins of consistencies in human culture.

- "Majority and Minority Influence" by William D. Crano and Viviane Seyranian (2007) is a concise summary of the last 30 years of research investigating minority and majority influence in groups.

- "Minority Iinfluence" by Antonis Gardikiotis (2011) summarizes the history of the empirical study of minority influence and identifies key theoretical and empirical issues.

Sources of Social Influence

- *Influence: Science and Practice* by Robert B. Cialdini (2009) examines the basic methods people use to persuade and extract compliance.

- *Rebels in Groups: Dissent, Deviance, Difference and Defiance*, edited by Jolanda Jetten and Matthew J. Hornsey (2011), draws together in one place the leading experts on minority/majority influence in groups and offers insight after insight into the dynamics of opinion change in small groups.

- *The Science of Social Influence: Advances and Future Progress*, edited by Anthony R. Pratkanis (2007), is a collection of 13 chapters written by experts on various aspects of social influence, dealing with both normative influence and compliance.

Juries

- *Investigating Jury Deliberations*, a special issue of the journal *Small Group Research* (2010), includes six articles based on the analysis of the deliberations of a jury in a death-sentence trial.

- *Inside the Jury* by Reid Hastie, Steven D. Penrod, and Nancy Pennington (1983) presents a masterful analysis of communication, influence, and decision-making in juries.

- *American Juries: The Verdict* by Neil Vidmar and Valerie P. Hans (2007) is a carefully researched analysis of the strengths and possible weaknesses of the jury system.

Power

CHAPTER OVERVIEW

Power is a group-level process, for it involves some members of a group doing what others require in situations that range from the purely cooperative and collaborative to those rife with conflict, tension, and animosity. Power can be used for the group and against it, for authorities sometimes demand actions that members would otherwise never consider. We would not be social beings if we were immune to the impact of power, but power can corrupt.

- What are the limits of an authority's power over group members?

- What are the sources of power in groups?

- What are the sources of status in groups?

- How do people react when they use their power to influence others?

- How do those without power react when power is used to influence them?

CHAPTER OUTLINE

Obedience to Authority

The Milgram Experiments

Milgram's Findings

The Power of the Milgram Situation

Social Power in Groups

Bases of Power

Bases and Obedience

Power Tactics

Compliance Tactics

Social Status in Groups

Claiming Status

Achieving Status

Status Hierarchies and Stability

The Metamorphic Effects of Power

Changes in the Powerholder

Reactions to the Use of Power

Who Is Responsible?

Chapter Review

Resources

> ### The People's Temple: The Metamorphic Effects of Power
>
> Jim Jones was the founder and minister of the People's Temple Full Gospel Church of San Francisco. Jones was an inspiring leader who decried the racism, inequality, and spiritual emptiness of American society. Jones was respected by his community, and, under his charismatic leadership, the congregation grew to 8,000 members. But the church, and Jones, had a dark side. Former members reported that at some services, people were beaten before the whole congregation, with microphones used to amplify their screams. Jones, some said, insisted on being called Father, and he demanded absolute dedication and obedience from his followers. He asked members to donate their property to the church, and he even forced one family to give him their six-year-old son.
>
> Jones, to transform his church into a collective society free from the interference of outsiders, moved his entire congregation to Guyana, in South America. He called the isolated settlement Jonestown and claimed that it would be the model for a new way of living where all would find love, happiness, and well-being. But the men, women, and children of Jonestown did not find contentment. They found, instead, a group that exercised incredible power over their destiny. Jones asked members to make great personal sacrifices for the group, and time and again they obeyed. They worked long hours in the fields. They were given little to eat. They were forbidden to communicate with their loved ones back in the United States. Then disaster struck: An armed group of church members attacked and killed visitors who were part of a congressional delegation from the United States.
>
> Jones, fearing the dismantling of his empire, ordered his followers to take their own lives. When authorities reached the settlement, they could not believe the scope of the tragedy. On Jones's orders, 908 men, women, and children had either killed themselves or been killed by other followers. One resident, Dick Tropp, wrote in his journal that day: "We are begging only for some understanding. It will take more than small minds … to fathom these events. Something must come of this" (quoted in Scheeres, 2011, p. 237).

Why did the group members obey Jones's order? What force is great enough to make parents give poison to their children? Many blamed Jim Jones—his persuasiveness, his charisma, his depravity. Others emphasized the kind of people who join such groups—their psychological instability, their willingness to identify with causes, and their religious fervor. Still others suggested more fantastic explanations—mass hypnosis, government plots, and even divine intervention.

Such explanations underestimate the power of groups and their leaders to influence members, even when members try to resist this influence (Cartwright, 1959). As Chapter 7 noted, groups influence the way their members feel, think, and act. But in some cases this influence can be extraordinarily strong. Rather than subtly shaping opinions and choices, powerful people and groups can compel obedience among members who would otherwise resist the group's wishes. Here we consider the sources of that power and the consequences of

power for those who wield it as well as those who are subjected to it.

OBEDIENCE TO AUTHORITY

Few interactions advance very far before elements of power and influence come into play. The police officer asking the driver for the car's registration, the teacher scowling at the errant student, and the boss telling an employee to get back to work—all are exerting their **social power** over others. Powerful people can influence other people in significant ways: "A has power over B to the extent that he can get B to do something that B would not otherwise do" (Dahl, 1957, p. 202). But can power generate such a heartrending outcome as the

---

social power The capacity to influence others, even when these others try to resist influence.

Jonestown mass suicide? Can group members be so bent to the will of an authority that they would follow any order, no matter how noxious? Social psychologist Stanley Milgram's (1963, 1974) laboratory studies of obedience to authority suggest that the answer to these questions is *yes*.

The Milgram Experiments

Stanley Milgram carried out his now-famous studies in the early 1960s. Intrigued by people's tendency to yield to the demands of authorities, Milgram tested American subjects' reactions to an experimenter who ordered them to do something they would normally not do—to inflict significant harm on another person who was innocent of any wrongdoing.

The Obedience Situation Milgram studied obedience—a change in response to an order from another person—by creating small groups in his laboratory at Yale University. In most cases, he studied three-man groups: One member was a volunteer who had answered an advertisement; one member was the experimenter who was in charge of the session; and one member appeared to be another participant but was in actuality part of the research team. This confederate looked to be in his late 40s, and he seemed friendly and a little nervous. The experimenter, in contrast, acted self-assured as he set the group's agenda, explained their task, and issued orders. He assigned the participants to one of two roles—teacher or learner. The one given the teacher role read a series of paired words (*blue box*, *nice day*, *wild day*, etc.) to the learner who was supposed to memorize the pairings. The teacher would later check the learner's ability to recall the pairs by reading the first word in the pair and several possible answers (e.g., *blue*: *sky*, *ink*, *box*, *lamp*). Failures would be punished by an electric shock. What the volunteer did not know, however, was that the confederate was always assigned to the learner role and that the learner did not actually receive shocks.

After assigning the participants to their roles, the experimenter took both group members into the next room where he strapped the learner into a chair that was designed "to prevent excessive movement during the shock." As the experimenter attached an electrode to his wrist, the confederate asked if shocks were dangerous. "Oh, no," answered the experimenter, "although the shocks can be extremely painful, they cause no permanent tissue damage" (Milgram, 1974, p. 19).

The experimenter then led the participant back to the other room and seated him at the shock generator. This bogus machine, which Milgram himself fabricated, featured a row of 30 electrical switches. Each switch, when depressed, would supposedly send a shock to the learner. The shock level of the first switch on the left was 15 volts (*v*), the next switch was 30, the next was 45, and so on, all the way up to 450 *v*. Milgram also labeled the voltage levels, from *Slight Shock* to *Danger: Severe Shock* as shown in Figure 8.1. The final two switches were marked *XXX*. The rest of the face of the shock generator was taken up by dials, lights, and meters that flickered whenever a switch was pressed.

The experimenter administered a sample shock of 45 *v* to "strengthen the subject's belief in the authenticity of the generator" (Milgram, 1974, p. 20). The session then began in earnest. Using a microphone to communicate with the learner, the teacher read the list of word pairs and then began "testing" the learner's memory. Each time the teacher read a word and the response alternatives, the learner indicated his response by pushing one of four numbered switches that were just within reach of his bound hand. His response lit up on the participant's control panel. Participants were to deliver one shock for each mistake and increase the voltage one step after delivering a punishment.

The Demands (Prods) Milgram set the stage for the order-giving phase by having the learner make mistakes deliberately. Although participants punished that first mistake with just a 15-*v* jolt, each subsequent failure was followed by a stronger shock. At the 300-*v* level, the learner also began to protest the shocks by pounding on the wall, and, after the next shock of 315 *v*, he stopped responding altogether. Most participants assumed that the session was over at this point, but the

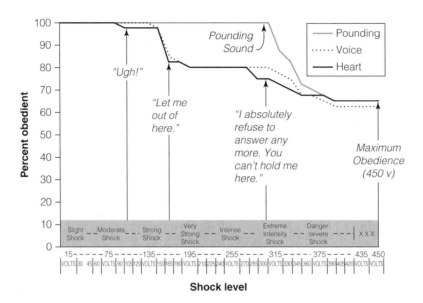

FIGURE 8.1   Level of obedience in three conditions of the Milgram experiment: original (pounding on the wall), voice-feedback (voice), and heart-condition (heart).

SOURCE: Adapted from *Obedience to Authority: An Experimental View*, by Stanley Milgram. Copyright © 1974 by Stanley Milgram.

experimenter told them to treat a failure to respond as a wrong answer and to continue delivering the shocks. When the participants balked, the experimenter, who was seated at a separate desk near the teacher's, would use a sequence of prods to goad them into action (Milgram, 1974, p. 21):

- *Prod 1:* "Please continue," or "Please go on."

- *Prod 2:* "The experiment requires that you continue."

- *Prod 3:* "It is absolutely essential that you continue."

- *Prod 4:* "You have no other choice; you must go on."

The situation was extremely realistic and served as a laboratory analog to real-world groups when authorities give orders to subordinates. The experimenter acted with self-assurance and poise. He gave orders crisply, as if he never questioned the correctness of his own actions, and he seemed surprised that the teacher would try to terminate the shock sequence. Yet from the participant's point of view, this authority was requiring them to act in a way that was harmful to another person. When they accepted the $4.50 payment, they implicitly agreed to carry out the experimenter's instructions, but they were torn between this duty and their desire to protect the learner from possible harm. Milgram designed his experiment to determine which side would win in this conflict.

Milgram's Findings

Milgram was certain that very few of his participants would carry out the experimenter's orders. He went so far as to purchase special equipment that would let him record the duration of each shock administered, expecting that few participants would give more than four or five shocks (Elms, 1995). So he was surprised when 26 of the 40 (65%) individuals who served as teachers in the initial experiment administered the full 450 *v* to the presumably helpless learner (see Figure 8.1). Most of the participants resisted, challenging the experimenter again and again each time he told them to continue. But no one broke off before the 300-v level or checked on the learner when he failed to answer. The comments made by the participants during the shock procedure and their obvious psychological distress revealed that they were reluctant to go on but felt unable to resist the experimenter's demands for obedience. Perplexed, Milgram studied over 800 people in a series of replications and extensions of his original study. Although he continued to search for the limits of obedience, again and again his participants buckled under the pressure of the experimenter's power.

Harm versus Rights In the original version of the study, the participants heard only a pounding on the wall when they pressed down the switch for 300 v. So Milgram added additional cues that signaled the learner's suffering and an emotional entreaty for release. In the *voice-feedback condition*, the learner's shouts and pleas (carefully rehearsed and tape-recorded) could be heard through the wall. The learner grunted when shocked at levels below 120 v and complained about the pain. At 150 v, he cried out, "Experimenter, get me out of here! I won't be in the experiment anymore! I refuse to go on!" (Milgram, 1974, p. 23). He continued screaming and demanding release until the 330-v level, when he refused to answer any more questions.

These changes did not substantially reduce the level of obedience, for 62.5% of the participants still obeyed to the 450-v level. Moreover, those who did disobey seemed to be responding more to the learner's demand to be released than to his suffering. If participants were going to disobey, they usually did it when the learner retracted his consent to continue—after receiving the 150-v shock. Those who passed that milestone usually continued to 450 v, even though the learner screamed in pain until he eventually lapsed into silence (Packer, 2008a). Faced with the orders of the authority to continue and the learner's demand to be released, the majority sided with the authority.

To test whether participants would respond explicitly to the learner's signs of suffering, Milgram increased the possibility of significant harm in the *heart problem condition*. When the experimenter connected the wires to his arm, the learner mentioned that he had a heart condition and asked about complications. The experimenter said that the shocks would cause no permanent damage. When shocked, the learner's groans and shouts of protest could be heard through the wall, and he also repeatedly complained that his heart was bothering him. Even when the learner stopped responding after 330 v, 65% of the participants continued to administer shocks to the 450-v level.

Proximity and Surveillance Effects In earlier versions of the study, the teacher and learner were separated by a glass observation window. Milgram noticed that, even though teachers could see the learner react to the shocks, most averted their eyes and expressed discomfort at having to watch. So, to make the consequences of their actions even clearer to subjects, Milgram moved the learner into the same room as the teacher. In the *proximity condition*, the learner sat in the same room as the teacher, voicing the same complaints used in the voice-feedback condition and writhing with pain at each shock. Obedience dropped to 40%. In the most extreme of all the variations, the *touch-proximity condition*, the learner sat next to the teacher and received his shock when he put his hand on a shock plate. At the 150-v level, he refused to put his hand down on the plate, so the experimenter gave the participant an insulated glove and told him to press the learner's hand down onto the plate as he depressed the shock switch. Still, 30% obeyed.

Milgram also examined the impact of increased distance between the experimenter and the teacher on rates of obedience by having the experimenter leave the room after he reviewed the procedures with the participant. He continued giving orders to the participant by telephone, but he lost his ability to monitor the subject's actions. In this *low surveillance condition*, 25% of the participants stopped as soon as the learner insisted on release (the 150-v level). Only 20% of the participants were obedient to the 450-v level, and many participants disobeyed by deceiving the authority—they assured the experimenter that they were administering increasingly large shocks with each mistake when they were actually only delivering 15 *v*.

Prestige and Legitimacy   Milgram conducted his initial studies on the campus of Yale University, which most people recognize as a prestigious center of learning and science. Milgram was concerned that people obeyed the experimenter because he was perceived to be a "Yale scientist" and could therefore be trusted to act appropriately. So, in the *office-building condition*, Milgram moved the study to a building located in a shopping area. "When subjects inquired about professional affiliations, they were informed only that we were a private firm conducting research for industry" (Milgram, 1974, pp. 68–69). Obedience dropped to 48%—still a surprisingly large figure given the unknown credentials of the staff. However, two individuals refused to give any shocks at all.

Milgram next lowered the legitimacy of the experimenter by arranging for the orders to come from someone other than the expert experimenter. In the *ordinary-man variation*, he added a fourth member to the group who was given the task of recording the shock levels used. The experimenter explained the study, as in the other conditions, but gave no instructions about shock levels before he was called away. The new participant, who was actually a confederate, filled the role of the authority; he suggested that shocks be given in increasingly strong doses and ordered the participant to continue giving shocks when the learner started to complain. Obedience dropped to 20%. But when the participants refused to continue, the confederate left the experimenter's desk and began administering the shocks. In this case, most of the participants (68.75%) stood by and watched without stopping the confederate—although one "large man, lifted the zealous shocker from his chair, threw him to a corner of the laboratory, and did not allow him to move until he had promised not to administer further shocks" (1974, p. 97).

Milgram further explored the legitimacy of the authority in the *authority-as-victim condition*. Here the experimenter agreed to take the role of the learner, supposedly to convince a reluctant learner

that the shocks were not harmful. The experimenter tolerated the shocks up to 150 *v*, but then he shouted, "That's enough, gentlemen!" The confederate, who had been watching the procedure, then insisted, "Oh, no, let's go on. Oh, no, come on, I'm going to have to go through the whole thing. Let's go. Come on, let's keep going" (Milgram, 1974, p. 102). In all cases, the participant released the experimenter; obedience to the ordinary person's command to harm the authority was nil.

Group Effects   Milgram (1974) studied obedience rather than conformity, since the authority did not himself engage in the action he demanded of the teacher and the teacher faced the power of the authority alone. But Milgram recognized that in many cases authorities give orders to groups rather than lone individuals, and the group may be a second source of power in the situation—either in standing against the authority or taking sides with him. So Milgram arranged for groups to administer the shocks. In the *two peers rebel condition*, Milgram added two more confederates to the situation. They posed as fellow participants and the three worked together to deliver the shocks to the learner. One read the list of words, one gave the verbal feedback to the learner, and the participant pushed the shock button. As shown in Figure 8.2, the subject sat before the shock machine, and the other group members sat on either side.

The confederates played out their roles until the learner cried out in pain at 150 *v*. Then, one of the confederates refused to continue and left the table. The experimenter could not convince him to return and ordered the remaining two to continue. However, at the 210-*v* mark, the second confederate quit as well, explaining, "I'm not going to shock that man against his will" (1974, p. 118). Only the real subject was left to give the shocks, and, in most cases, he sided with the group and refused to obey. Only 10% of the participants were fully obedient. Membership in a group helped participants defy the authority.

But what if an individual is part of a group that was obedient? In the *peer administers shock condition*, the subject was given subsidiary tasks, such as reading the questions and giving feedback, but he did not push the shock button; a second subject

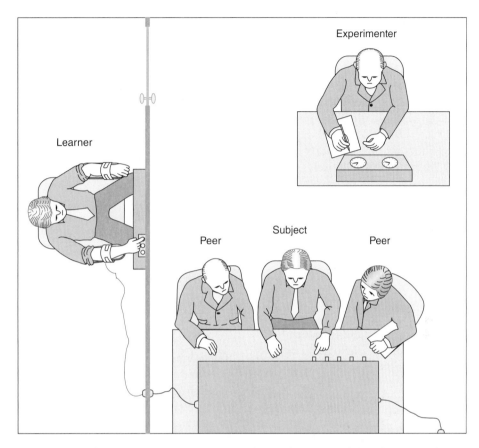

FIGURE 8.2 Layout of the experimental situation in which Milgram tested the obedience of groups. When the subject worked with others who obeyed the experimenter's orders, very few disobeyed. But if the others refused to continue to shock the learner, most of the subjects also refused to obey the experimenter.

SOURCE: Adapted from *Obedience to Authority: An Experimental View*, by Stanley Milgram. Copyright © 1974 by Stanley Milgram.

(actually, a confederate), who was fully compliant, did so. In this variation, 37 of the 40 people tested (92.5%) obediently fulfilled their tasks without intervening. As Milgram explained, "They are accessories to the act of shocking the victim, but they are not psychologically implicated in it to the point where strain arises" (1974, p. 122).

The Power of the Milgram Situation

The people of Jonestown obeyed the orders of their leader, Jim Jones, and took their own lives, as well as the lives of their loved ones. Their actions seem

inexplicable, yet Milgram discovered that the majority of people he studied—ordinary people who were not even dedicated members of an isolated and relationally intensive group—obeyed a malevolent authority. But Milgram's results sparked controversies and raised questions that are unresolved even today (Blass, 2009; Miller, 2004; Russell & Gregory, 2011).

Are the Findings Valid? Most people, including both experts and laypersons alike, were surprised by the level of obedience Milgram discovered in his research. When Milgram asked panels of psychiatrists, college students, and middle-class adults to make predictions about how people would act in his experiment, only a few predicted anyone would give more than 180 v. The high levels of obedience Milgram recorded prompted some to suggest that the participants were not taken in by Milgram's subterfuge. They suggested that the participants knew that no shocks were being administered, but they played along so as not to ruin the study (Orne & Holland, 1968). Milgram's research team, however, interviewed all the participants, and fewer than 20% challenged the reality of the situation (Elms, 1995). Moreover, if participants saw through the elaborate duplicity, then why did they become so upset? According to Milgram,

> Many subjects showed signs of nervousness in the experimental situation, and especially upon administering the more powerful shocks. In a large number of cases the degree of tension reached extremes that are rarely seen in sociopsychological laboratory studies. Subjects were observed to sweat, tremble, stutter, bite their lips, groan, and dig their fingernails into their flesh. (1963, p. 375)

The distress of the participants was so great that the publication of the study sparked a controversy over the ethics of social–psychological research (Blass, 2004).

Other experts, when trying to explain why so many people obeyed, pointed to the participants themselves, suggesting they were unusual individuals and unrepresentative in some way. Just as many people, when first hearing of the Guyana tragedy, wondered, "What strange people they must have been to be willing to kill themselves," when people are told about Milgram's findings, they react with the question, "What kind of evil, sadistic men did he recruit for his study?" Yet, by all accounts, Milgram's participants were normal and well-adjusted (see Blass, 1991, for an analysis). Many believe that the level of obedience that Milgram documented in his laboratory matches levels found in military, organizational, and educational settings (Fiske, Harris, & Cuddy, 2004; Hinrichs, 2007; Pace & Hemmings, 2007).

Are People Still Obedient?   Many things have changed since Milgram conducted his study, and one of those things might be obedience to authority. Would people born in the second half of the twentieth century be so willing to obey an authority (Twenge, 2009)?

Milgram's study can never be exactly replicated given the level of distress his participants experienced and procedures that are now required to protect subjects from harm. However, social psychologist Jerry Burger (2009), by modifying aspects of the Milgram situation that caused the greatest stress for participants, was able to test 70 men and women in 2006. Burger used a facsimile of the original shock machine (complete with the "Shock Generator, Type ZLB, Dyson Instrument Company, Waltham, Mass. Output 15 volts–450 volts" label on the side), an innocent male victim who cried out in pain and demanded to be released, and an experimenter who delivered well-rehearsed prods if participants balked. But Burger ended the study when participants administered 150 v and appeared to be continuing on to the next set of word pairs. He also hired a clinical psychologist who interviewed each potential participant so as to eliminate anyone who might have "a negative reaction to participating in the study" (Burger, 2009, p. 6).

Back in the 1960s, 82.5% of the men continued past the 150-v level. But in 2006, 70% of the men and women Burger tested were similarly obedient—a decline, but not a statistically significant one. Women were just as obedient as men, and those subjects tested in a group with a confederate who refused to continue were only slightly less obedient (63.3%). People are still obedient after all these years.

Who Obeys?   The people who took part in Milgram's study differed from one another in age, personality, and life experiences, and they also differed in their response to the experimenter's orders. Some broke off at the first sign of trouble from the learner, others obeyed until the learner stopped answering, and others continued until the shocks reached levels they felt were too dangerous. Age

---

Focus 8.1 Cross-cultural Perspectives: Obedience around the World

Milgram initially planned to measure levels of obedience in both America and Germany, but he soon changed his plans. "I found so much obedience in America," Milgram explained, "I hardly saw the need for taking the experiment to Germany" (quoted in Meyer, 1970, p. 73; for more information, see Milgram, 1963, 1965, 1974).

Other investigators, however, have examined the extent to which culture and context determine willingness to obey an authority's orders. A study carried out in Germany, for example, carefully replicated Milgram's procedures (Mantell, 1971). The participants were all recruited from government agencies and private industry (except for seven who were described as "hippies"). The sessions were run in a relatively respectable office building in Munich, which was identified as a center sponsored by the prestigious Max-Planck Institute. As in the "voice-feedback" condition of Milgram's experiment, the teacher could hear the learner's "surprised and painful cries" at the 165–v level and "desperate screams, moaning, sobbing, and searching pleas" at higher levels. Once the teacher moved beyond the 390-v level, the teacher stopped responding altogether. Under these conditions, 85% of the participants administered the full range of shocks.

Australians, too, were obedient when tested. In one study of "self-immolation," researchers created a situation where subjects not only delivered the harm, but were themselves the target of the injurious action. Participants were led to believe that the study investigated auditory acuity and that they would be given the choice of setting the intensity of the sounds they would be exposed to via headphones. At the lowest level, the sound would cause no damage, but, as they moved up from level 0 to level 10, the possibility of permanent hearing loss increased with the highest levels rated as extremely harmful (participants were not actually exposed to any sounds). Some participants (8%) refused outright to take part, but once they had their headphones in place, a full 95% chose the most

damaging level, without any prodding (Martin et al., 1976). Australia was also the site of a study that explored group-level obedience by creating two separate roles for participants in a Milgram-like experimental situation. The subject assigned to the "transmitter role" relayed orders from the experimenter, whereas the subject assigned to the "executant" role delivered the shocks. As expected, 54% of the transmitters obeyed, compared to 28% of the executants. Nearly twice as many men (54%) than women (23%) were obedient (Kilham & Mann, 1974).

And what about Canadians? In one particularly ingenious variation, participants were recruited to serve as the experimenter rather than the teacher in a Milgram-like situation. Although they were led to believe that the teacher was the subject, in reality the teacher was part of the research procedure and became increasingly upset as the experiment progressed—complaining of illness and displaying signs of stress as the learner made mistake after mistake and the voltage level increased toward 450 v. Most of the subjects (over 90%) pressured the teacher to continue even when the teacher pleaded to be permitted to stop (Shelton, 1982).

Social psychologist Thomas Blass (2012), after surveying previous studies of obedience, concluded that obedience levels are relatively uniform in all the cultures where the Milgram's study has been replicated. In Austria, South Africa, Germany, and Italy, a larger percentage of people obeyed than in the United States, Jordan, India, and Spain, but obedience was generally substantial everywhere—with 50% or more of those tested obeying no matter what their country or cultural background. Although surveys of cultural values suggest that countries differ in their degree of endorsement of power and power differences between people, the experimental evidence—limited as it is—suggests that these values do not substantially influence obedience to authority. As Blass (2012, p. 203) concludes, "authority may be one of the universals of social behavior."

---

and occupation did not predict these variations, but personality did. Individuals who evidenced a rigid adherence to conventional values paired with a submissive, uncritical acceptance of authority—an authoritarian personality—were somewhat more

likely to give more intense shocks than were nonauthoritarians (Elms, 1972, 2009). Burger (2009), in his replication of Milgram's study, found that individuals who were higher in dispositional empathy were quicker to show reluctance to continue with the study. Obedience in the Milgram study may have also been linked to the respondents' level of moral maturity—they tended to report thinking about moral dilemmas in more sophisticated ways that emphasized basing decisions on principles of social justice than those who obeyed (Sprinthall, 2009). Milgram, however, only studied U.S. citizens. As Focus 8.1 suggests, people raised in other cultures may respond differently when they confront a malevolent authority.

SOCIAL POWER IN GROUPS

Milgram created a complex social situation in his Yale laboratories. Those who entered into it were pressured to act in ways that were inconsistent with their personal beliefs and social values, and some yielded to this pressure. He succeeded in controlling others' actions to promote his own goals "without their consent, against their will, or without their knowledge or understanding" (Buckley, 1967, p. 186). But just as Jim Jones did not use physical force to coerce his followers into leaving their homes in the United States and joining him in Jonestown, Milgram's experiment did not resort to threats of violence or punishment to extract high levels of obedience from participants. But both the Jonestown residents and many of the Milgram subjects followed orders. Why?

Bases of Power

Nobel laureate Bertrand Russell concluded many years ago that "the fundamental concept in social science is Power, in the same sense in which Energy is the fundamental concept in physics" (1938/2004, p. 4). The conquest of one civilization by another, the development of architecture and engineering, political intrigues and social policy, and the obedience of the members of the People's Temple and Milgram's subjects—all are inexplicable if one does not understand power. Russell added, however, that

power takes many forms, so to understand the "laws of social dynamics … it is necessary first to classify the forms of power" (1938/2004, p. 6).

Social psychologists John R. P. French and Bertram Raven's (1959) theory of **power bases** answers Russell's challenge. French and Raven recognized that power is relational and rooted in inequalities in control over resources and punishments. When a person's experience of positive and negative outcomes depends on another person who is not similarly dependent in return, differences in power result. French and Raven identified and differentiated the five forms of power shown in Table 8.1: reward, coercive, legitimate, referent, and expert power. Raven (1965), drawing on his subsequent studies of influence, added a sixth base: informational power.

Reward Power Jones's **reward power** was considerable given his control over both impersonal and personal rewards. Impersonal rewards are material resources, such as food, shelter, protection, promotions, wages, and awards. Personal rewards are positive interpersonal reinforcements, such as verbal approbation, compliments, smiles, and promises of liking or acceptance. Both types of rewards are potent sources of power, particularly during times of scarcity (Emerson, 1962). Money and food, for example, are valued resources, but they become a source of power when the rest of the group is penniless and starving. Rewards that one controls exclusively are also more likely to augment one's power, for group members who depend on someone for a reward will likely comply with that

---

power bases Sources of social power in a group, including one's degree of control over rewards and punishment, authority in the group, attractiveness, expertise, and access to and control over information needed by group members (Originally described by John French and Bertram Raven).

reward power Power based on one's control over the distribution of rewards (both personal and impersonal) given or offered to group members.

TABLE 8.1   French and Raven's Six Bases of Power

Power Base	Sample Indicators
Reward: The capability of controlling the distribution of rewards given or offered to the target.	• determines pay level • gives desirable job assignments • can promote • compliments and praises
Coercive: The capacity to threaten and punish those who do not comply with requests or demands.	• can terminate employment (fire) • controls who is given undesirable assignments • can suspend without pay • verbal reprimands and warnings
Legitimate: Authority that derives from the legitimate right to require and demand obedience.	• duly appointed supervisor, manager, etc. • representative of the group or organization • role is sanctioned by the group or organization • has the right to make demands of others
Referent: Influence based on the identification with, attraction to, and respect of others.	• is a person meriting respect • is someone who is admired by others • is someone with whom others identify • is a nice person
Expert: Influence based on others' belief that the powerholder possesses superior skills and abilities.	• can devise clever solutions to problems • can provide sound task-related advice • source of needed technical knowledge • shares considerable experience/training
Informational: Influence based on the potential use of informational resources, including rational argument, persuasion, or factual data.	• explains the basis for requests • gives good reasons for requests • uses reason to handle problems • promotes an understanding of procedures and changes

SOURCE: Adapted from French & Raven, 1959; Raven, Schwarzwald, & Koslowsky, 1998; Schriesheim, Hinkin, & Podsakoff, 1991.

individual's requests. Once Jones moved the church to Jonestown, his power increased since he became the sole source of rewards that members once acquired from non-church sources (Cook, Cheshire, & Gerbasi, 2006). Unfortunately, research suggests that when followers' dependence on a leader increases, this dependence triggers increases in respect, trust, and deference (van der Toorn, Tyler, & Jost, 2011).

Ironically, rewards that powerful people dispense are viewed as more valuable than the identical rewards one receives from those with less power. A smile from Jim Jones, for example, was far more rewarding than a smile from Shirley Baisy,

a rank-and-file member. Researchers investigated this phenomenon by giving group members the opportunity to trade goods of equal monetary value with other group members. Oddly, most were willing to pay more for goods they received from a high-status group member, and they considered those resources to be more valuable, important, and worth having. As a result, because powerful individuals' rewards were overvalued by others, they did not need to expend as many of their resources to achieve the same level of success in the exchange as did those members with low power, so their resources tended to grow rather than diminish (Thye, 2000).

Coercive Power   Jones used threats and punishment as a means of exacting obedience from his followers. When members broke the rules or disobeyed his orders, he was quick to punish them with beatings, solitary confinement, denials of food and water, and long hours of labor in the fields.

Coercive power derives from one's capacity to dispense punishments, both impersonal and personal, to others. Terrorists attacking other countries, employers threatening employees with the loss of pay or dismissal, and teachers punishing mischievous students with extra assignments are all relying on impersonal coercive bases of power. Disagreeing friends insulting and humiliating one another, the boss shouting angrily at his secretary, and religious leaders threatening members with loss of grace or ostracism derive their power from personal sources (Pierro, Kruglanski, & Raven, 2012; Raven, 1992).

Certain people consistently rely on coercion to influence others, but most only turn to coercive power when they feel it is the only means they have to influence others (Kramer, 2006). In consequence, and paradoxically, individuals in positions of authority who feel relatively powerless are more likely to use coercion than more powerful individuals. Adults dealing with children, for example, are the recognized authorities in such relationships, yet the adults often feel relatively powerless. In consequence, in contentious situations, they tend to use coercive threats, punishments, and abuse more than do empowered authorities (Bugental, 2010). In contrast, when individuals who are equal in coercive power interact, they often learn over time to avoid the use of their power (Lawler & Yoon, 1996). Group members also prefer to use reward power rather than coercive power if both are available and they fear reprisals from others in the group should they act in a coercive way (Molm, 1997).

Legitimate Power   Individuals who have **legitimate power** have the socially sanctioned right to ask others to obey their orders. The security personnel at the airport telling a passenger to remove her shoes, the drill sergeant ordering the squad to attention, the professor waiting for the class to become quiet before a lecture, and the minister interpreting the Gospel for the congregation are powerful because they have the right to command others, and others are obligated to obey. Jones, for example, was the legitimate head of the People's Temple. He was an ordained minister; his work had been commended by many political and religious leaders, and he had received such honors as the Martin Luther King Jr. Humanitarian Award. When individuals joined the People's Temple, they tacitly agreed to follow Jones's orders.

Those who rely on reward or coercive power often find that their authority dwindles when their control over resources diminishes. In contrast, those who achieve a position of authority through methods that the group considers fair or proper generally find that their decisions are accepted, without resistance, by others in the group (Tyler, 2005). Members obey these legitimate authorities because they personally accept the norms of the group. Their obedience is not coerced but voluntary, for it springs from an internalized sense of loyalty to the group rather than the desire to gain resources or avoid harm. Even duly appointed or selected authorities will lose their legitimate power, however, if they consistently act in ways that are viewed as unfair or they repeatedly cause harm to the group and its members (Lammers et al., 2008). Those who engage in unethical behavior, for example, or do not show proper respect for their subordinates run the risk of losing the members' loyalty—and once loyalty is gone so is the willingness to obey (Tyler & Blader, 2003).

---

coercive power Power based on one's ability to punish or threaten others who do not comply with requests or demands.

legitimate power Power based on an individual's socially sanctioned claim to a position or role that gives the occupant the right to require and demand compliance with his or her directives.

Referent Power Who is the best-liked member of the group? Who is the most respected? Is there someone in the group whom everyone wants to please? The individual with **referent power** occupies the interpersonal center of the group. Just as group members seek out membership in selective, desirable groups, so they identify with and seek close association with respected, attractive group members. The members of the People's Temple were devoted to Jones—to the point where they loved, admired, and identified with him. Many made financial and emotional sacrifices in the hope of pleasing him. As one of his followers explained, Jones "was the God I could touch" (quoted in Reston, 2000, p. 25).

The concept of referent power explains how charismatic leaders manage to exert so much control over their groups (Flynn, 2010). Sociologist Max Weber first used the term **charisma** to account for the almost irrational devotion that some followers exhibit for their leaders. People often refer to a charming leader as charismatic, but Weber reserved the term to describe the tremendous referent and legitimate power of the "savior–leader." Charisma originally described a special power given by God to certain individuals. These individuals were capable of performing extraordinary, miraculous feats, and they were regarded as God's representatives on earth (Weber, 1956/1978). Weber argued that charismatic leaders do not have unique, wondrous powers, but they succeed because their followers *think* they have unique, wondrous powers. Weber himself was struck by the charismatic leader's power to demand actions that contradict established social norms: "Every charismatic authority … preaches, creates, or demands *new* obligations—most typically, by virtue of revelation, oracle, inspiration, or of his own will" (1956/1978, p. 243). Charismatic leaders, such as Jones, usually appear on the scene when a large group of people is dissatisfied or faces a stressful situation. The leader offers these people a way to escape their problems, and the masses react with intense loyalty.

Expert Power Group members often defer to and take the advice of those who seem to possess superior skills and abilities. A physician interpreting a patient's symptoms, a local resident giving directions to an out-of-towner, a teacher spelling a word for a student, and a computer technician advising a user—all transform their special knowledge into **expert power**.

As with most of the power bases identified by French and Raven, a person does not actually need to be an expert to acquire expert power; the person must only be *perceived* by others to be an expert (Kaplowitz, 1978; Littlepage & Mueller, 1997). Researchers demonstrated the impact of perceived expertise on influence by arranging for dyads to work on a series of problems. Half of the participants were led to believe that their partner's ability on the task was superior to their own, and the rest were told that their partner possessed inferior ability. As the concept of expert power suggests, individuals who thought that their partners were experts accepted their recommendations an average of 68% of the time, whereas participants paired with partners perceived as inferior accepted their recommendations only 42% of the time (Foschi, Warriner, & Hart, 1985).

Informational Power In 1965, Raven separated out **informational power** from expert power: Group members can turn information into power

---

referent power Power based on group members' identification with, attraction to, or respect for the powerholder.
charisma From the Greek *xarisma* (a divine gift of grace), the ascription of extraordinary or supernatural acumen, ability, and value to a leader by his or her followers (coined by Max Weber).

---

expert power Power that derives from subordinates' assumption that the powerholder possesses superior skills and abilities.
informational power Power based on the potential use of informational resources, including rational argument, persuasion, or factual data.

by providing it to others who need it, by keeping it from others, by organizing it, increasing it, or even falsifying it. Some individuals achieve informational power by deliberately manipulating or obscuring information or at least making certain that the information remains a secret shared by only a few group members (Messick, 1999). Other individuals are recognized as the keepers of the group's truths or secrets, and these individuals must be consulted before the group makes a decision (Fine & Holyfield, 1996). People who share information with others can achieve informational power, even by passing unverified and, in some cases, private information through the group's "grapevine" (Kurland & Pelled, 2000). Individuals who pass along the latest gossip (personal and, in many cases, scurrilous information about others) or rumors (information that is potentially useful and relevant, but is unsubstantiated) are using informational power to influence others (DiFonzo, 2008).

Bases and Obedience

Was the experimenter in the Milgram study powerful, as French and Raven define power? Even though the experimenter was not an authority in a traditional sense—he was not formally identified as the group's leader and given an impressive title, such as captain, president, director, or doctor—he did draw power from all six of the bases identified by French and Raven (1959). His power to reward was high, because he gave out the payment and also because he was an important source of positive evaluations; participants wanted to win a favorable appraisal from this figure of authority. He also used coercive prods (e.g., "You have no other choice, you must go on") to warn of possible negative consequences of disobedience. Many participants also assumed that the experimenter had a legitimate right to control their actions and that the learner had no right to quit the study. The participants also respected Yale University and recognized the importance of scientific research, so the experimenter had referent power.

Very few participants knew much about electricity, either, so they considered the experimenter an expert. He also persuaded them to continue by telling them that the study was important and that its findings would answer questions about how people learn.

Blass (2000a) confirmed the power of the experimenter in the Milgram study by asking a group of unbiased observers to review a 12-minute videotape of Milgram's procedures. The observers then ranked six possible reasons, derived from French and Raven's power base theory, as explanations for why the participants obeyed. For example, did Milgram's experimenter have coercive power? Did he "warn of negative consequences" should people not obey (Blass, 2000a, p. 42)? Did he have expert power? Did participants assume that the experimenter was a professional and knew what he was doing? Using these items, the observers ranked the experimenter as higher on expert, legitimate, coercive, and informational power, but lower on reward power, and lower still on referent power. The experimenter adopted a very brusque manner during the study, so he did not seem particularly likable; hence his low referent power. His stern, no-nonsense manner, however, apparently made him seem like a duly appointed expert whose orders could not be disobeyed.

Power Tactics

The French and Raven (1959) theory of power bases identifies and differentiates the six most common sources of influence in groups, but they did not claim their list was exhaustive. When people need to poke, prod, or prompt others into action, their choice of **power tactic** is limited only by their ingenuity, self-regulation, and willingness to ignore social controls.

---

power tactics Specific strategies used to influence others, usually to gain a particular objective or advantage.

Types of Tactics Table 8.2 gives examples of some of these tactics that differ in terms of their hardness, rationality, laterality, and social acceptability (Falbo & Peplau, 1980; Raven, Schwarzwald, & Koslowsky, 1998).

- *Hard and soft tactics.* Hard tactics are more coercive than soft tactics; they limit the "freedom an influence recipient is allowed in choosing whether or not to comply with a request or a demand" (Pierro et al., 2012, p. 41). Bullying, enforcing or invoking standards, punishing, and delivering contingency-based rewards are examples of hard tactics. Soft tactics, in contrast, exploit the relationship between the influencer and the target to extract compliance. When individuals use such methods as collaboration, socializing, friendships, personal rewards, and ingratiation, they influence more indirectly and interpersonally. Hard tactics are often described as harsh, forcing, or direct, but they are not necessarily more powerful than soft tactics; threatening people with exclusion from a group or public embarrassment may lead to substantially greater change than the threat of some deprivation or corporal punishment (Fiske & Berdahl, 2007).

- *Rational and nonrational tactics.* Tactics that emphasize reasoning, logic, and good judgment are rational tactics; bargaining and persuasion are examples. Tactics such as ingratiation and evasion are nonrational tactics of influence, because they rely on emotionality and misinformation.

- *Unilateral and bilateral tactics.* Some tactics are interactive, involving give-and-take on the part of both the influencer and the target of the influence. Such bilateral tactics include persuasion, discussion, and negotiation. Unilateral tactics, in contrast, can be enacted without the cooperation of the target of influence. Such tactics include demands, faits accomplis, evasion, and disengagement.

TABLE 8.2   A Sampling of the Many Power Tactics People Use to Influence Other People in Everyday Situations

Tactic	Examples
Apprise	• I point out what she will gain. • I note the personal benefits he'll receive.
Bully	• I yell at him. • I push him around.
Claim expertise	• I let her know I'm an expert. • I rely on my experience.
Collaborate	• I offer to help. • I provide assistance as needed.
Complain	• I gripe about all the work I have to do. • I grumble about having to study.
Consult	• I ask him to help me with the project. • I get her involved in the work.
Criticize	• I point out her limitations. • I find fault with their work.
Demand	• I demand that the problem be solved. • I order her to continue.
Discuss	• I give him supporting reasons. • We talk about it.
Disengage	• I give him the cold shoulder. • I stop talking to her.
Enforce	• I remind him about the rules. • I make it clear what the standards are.
Evade	• I change the subject when it comes up. • I skip the meeting.
Fait accompli	• I just do it. • I don't get anyone's permission.
Ingratiate	• I flatter her. • I compliment him on the way he looks.
Inspire	• I appeal to her sense of fair play. • I cheer him on.

(Continued)

TABLE 8.2   (Continued)

Tactic	Examples
Instruct	• I teach him how to do it. • I set an example.
Join forces	• I get the boss to agree with me. • I turn the group against her.
Manipulate	• I lie. • I leave out important details.
Negotiate	• I offer her a bargain. • I wheel and deal.
Persist	• I don't take no for an answer. • I reiterate my point.
Persuade	• I coax her into it. • I convert him to my side.
Promise	• I promise to never do it again. • I offer to do some of his work for him.
Punish	• I fire her. • I slap him.
Put down	• I insult him. • I say something like, "You are an idiot."
Request	• I ask him to do me a favor. • I tell her what I expect.
Reward	• I increase his pay. • I give her a present.
Socialize	• I make small talk for a while. • I ask about the family.
Supplicate	• I plead. • I beg humbly for permission.
Threaten	• I threaten legal action. • I tell him that he might get fired.
Use humor	• I try to make a joke out of it. • I tell a funny story.

SOURCES: Drawn from various studies of influence, including Caldwell & Burger, 1997; Dillard & Fitzpatrick, 1985; Emans, Munduate, Klaver, & Van de Vliert, 2003; Falbo, 1977; Falbo & Peplau, 1980; Fu, Peng, Kennedy, & Yukl, 1997; Howard, Blumstein, & Schwartz, 1986; Instone, Major, & Bunker, 1983; Kipnis, 1984; Littlepage, Nixon, & Gibson, 1992; Stets, 1997; Wiseman & Schenck-Hamlin, 1981; Yukl & Michel, 2006.

How People "Get Their Way"   People vary in their habitual use of one type of power tactic over another. When asked the question "How do you get your way?" more interpersonally oriented people—those more concerned with being liked and accepted—showed a preference for soft, indirect, and rational power tactics (Falbo, 1997). Those who espoused a Machiavellian, manipulative philosophy when dealing with others tended to use indirect/nonrational tactics, as did those who scored lower in terms of agreeableness and emotional stability (Butkovic & Bratko, 2007). Extraverts use a greater variety of tactics than introverts (Caldwell & Burger, 1997). Men and women also differ somewhat in their choice of power tactics (Keshet et al., 2006). Men and women who supervised an ineffective employee used both rewards and criticism, but women intervened less frequently with a more limited range of tactics. Women promised fewer pay raises and threatened more pay deductions than men, and they were more likely to criticize subordinates (Instone, Major, & Bunker, 1983). The sexes also differ in their use of power in more intimate relationships, for men tend to use bilateral and direct tactics, whereas women report using unilateral and indirect methods (Falbo & Peplau, 1980).

People also choose different power tactics depending on the nature of the group situation (Yukl & Michel, 2006). A person who has high status in a group that is already rife with conflict will use different tactics than an individual who is low in status and wants to minimize conflict. In a corporate setting, authorities rely on referent and expert power, but in an educational setting, teachers may turn to reward and punishment power (Krause & Kearney, 2006). Who one is attempting to influence can also dictate the choice of power tactic; for example, people report using a variety of soft and hard methods to influence subordinates but, when dealing with superiors, they rely heavily on rational methods such as persuasion and discussion (Kipnis et al., 1984). People also shift from soft to hard tactics when they encounter resistance (Carson, Carson, & Roe, 1993; Teppner, 2006).

The interpersonal consequences of the use of these various types of influence methods will be considered later in this chapter.

Compliance Tactics

Social psychologist Robert Cialdini's (2009) studies of salespersons, recruiters, fundraisers, and telemarketers—people who make their living by influencing other people—identified another category of influence methods: **compliance tactics**. These tactics, like all influence methods, are designed to increase acquiescence in response to a request that may be inconsistent with the target person's privately held beliefs or best interests, but they are uniquely subtle and difficult to detect (Cialdini & Griskevicius, 2010). These tactics work by creating a favorable cognitive and emotional response in the targets of the influence attempt and disrupting their capacity to think critically about what they are being asked to do.

The Foot-in-the-Door Technique Many compliance tactics work by exploiting people's desire to act consistently across situations. The **foot-in-the-door technique**, for example, works by prefacing a major request with a minor one that is so inconsequential that few people would refuse to comply. Investigators demonstrated the strength of this technique by asking home owners to post a large, unattractive sign in their yards. Nearly all refused—unless this major request had been preceded by a smaller one (Freedman & Fraser, 1966). Similar studies have also found that the two requests called for by the foot-in-the-door technique are superior to a single request for many types of behaviors, although such factors as the sex of the influencer and the amount of time

---

compliance tactics Subtle, indirect, and difficult to detect techniques used to influence another person, usually without his or her awareness.

foot-in-the-door technique A method of influence in which the influencer first makes a very small request that the target will probably agree to; once the target agrees to the minor request, he or she is more likely to agree to the influencer's more important request.

that elapses between the two requests moderate the power of the foot-in-the-door method (Beaman et al., 1983; Dillard, 1991).

Commitment and Compliance Milgram, when he designed his procedures for studying obedience, may have unwittingly made use of the foot-in-the-door technique to increase compliance. He did not ask participants to push a lever that would deliver 450 v to the learner at the outset of the study. Instead, he asked them only to give the learner a mild shock if he answered incorrectly. No one refused. Over time, however, the demands escalated, and participants were unable to extricate themselves from the situation. Once they began, they could not stop (Gilbert, 1981; Modigliani & Rochat, 1995).

Jim Jones may have also capitalized on behavioral commitment to counter his followers' natural rejection of his order to take their own lives. Jones did not suddenly order his followers to commit suicide. Instead, he prefaced his request with months of demands that increased in their intensity. Jones had talked about mass suicide even before the People's Temple moved to Guyana. On more than one occasion, Jones had told the congregation that he had poisoned the sacramental wine and that all would be dead within the hour. He went so far as to plant confederates in the audience who feigned convulsions and death. He repeated this ceremony in Jonestown, calling it the White Night. After enough repetitions, the thought of suicide, so alien to most people, became commonplace in the group.

Brainwashing Interrogators often exploit behavioral commitment to extract compliance from detainees. Chinese military personnel, for example, used the foot-in-the-door tactic in their so-called brainwashing methods during the Korean War. They began by subjecting U.S. prisoners of war to physical hardships and stressful psychological pressures. The men were often fatigued from forced marches, and their sleep was disrupted. Their captors broke down the chain of command in these units by promoting non-ranking soldiers to positions of authority, and friendships among the men were systematically discouraged.

Although the Chinese relied heavily on traditional methods of influence, such as persuasion, compliance tactics proved more effective. The prisoners were initially asked to perform inconsequential actions, such as copying an essay out of a notebook or answering some questions about life in the United States. Once the men agreed to a minor request, a more significant request followed. They might be asked to write their own essays about communism or discuss the problems of capitalism. Each small concession led to a slightly larger one, until the men found themselves collaborating with the Chinese. The Chinese rarely succeeded in permanently changing the men's attitudes and values, but they did extract obedience to their authority: Morale within the prison was poor, and the men rarely tried to escape (Schein, 1961; Segal, 1954).

SOCIAL STATUS IN GROUPS

Jonestown was founded on principles of equality and social justice, but like most groups its members' rights, responsibilities, and privileges were determined by their position in the group's status hierarchy. As Chapter 6's analysis of group structure noted, the members of a newly formed group may begin as equals, but before long, some members gain greater power, influence, and control over others. In this section we examine this status-organizing process, focusing on the factors that determine status, personal qualities that influence who seeks status, and biases in the status-allocation process.

Claiming Status

The human brain is adept at detecting and processing information about status. Perceivers notice the difference between people displaying signals of dominance and deference (based on directness of eye gaze and head tilt) in as little as 33 milliseconds (Chiao, 2006). People are also remarkably accurate in their estimations of their own and others' status within a group. Although individuals often overestimate their own standing on valued

social characteristics, their estimates of their status in the group tend to match up well with other people's appraisals (Anderson et al., 2001; Anderson et al., 2006)

Status Signals   All social animals know how to communicate the message "I am in charge." Dominant chimpanzees chatter loudly at potential rivals, the leader of the wolf pack growls and bares his teeth at low-ranking wolves, and the ranking lioness in the pride swats another with her paw. Members of these social groups compete for status, for the individual at the top of the hierarchy—the so-called alpha male or female—enjoys greater access to the group's resources. These high-ranking members maintain their position by threatening or attacking low-ranking members, who in turn manage to avoid these attacks by performing behaviors that signal deference and submissiveness. This system of dominance and submission is often called a **pecking order** because (at least in chickens) it determines who will do the pecking and who will be pecked.

Humans, too, compete for status in their groups. Humans rarely snarl at one another to signal their status, but they do use such nonverbal cues as a firm handshake, intense facial expressions, a relaxed, open posture, or an unsmiling countenance to let others know that they should be respected (Chaplin et al., 2000; Hall, Coats, & LeBeau, 2005). People also seek status by speaking clearly, loudly, confidently, and directly, whereas those who speak softly and pepper their comments with nervous giggles are afforded less authority (Fiske, 2010b). Displays of emotion also signal differences in status. Group members who seem angry are thought to be more influential and are accorded higher status, whereas those who seem sad are thought to be lower in status (Tiedens, 2001; Tiedens, Ellsworth, & Mesquita, 2000).

---

pecking order A stable, ordered pattern of individual variations in prestige, status, and authority among group members.

People also signal their authority through their verbal communications. Those seeking status often initiate conversations and shift the discussion to their own areas of competence (Godfrey, Jones, & Lord, 1986). A person seeking high status would be more likely to (1) tell other people what they should do, (2) interpret other people's statements, (3) confirm or dispute other people's viewpoints, and (4) summarize or reflect on the discussion (Stiles et al., 1997). In a study group, for example, a high-status member may say, "I've studied this theory before," "I know this stuff backward and forward," or "I think it's more important to study the lecture notes than the text." A low-status individual, in contrast, may lament that "I always have trouble with this subject" or "I'm not sure I understand the material." Status seekers tend to dominate conversations and are quicker to voice their opinions (Bonito & Hollingshead, 1997; Islam & Zyphur, 2005). Group members also assert their authority over the group by interrupting other speakers frequently (Schmid Mast, 2002).

Who Seeks Status?   Not everyone seeks power over others. Some members are content to be rank-and-file members, equal in responsibilities and influence to most of the others in the group, and do not desire to rise upward in the group's hierarchy. Other individuals seek only personal power. They wish to control their own individual outcomes and experiences, but they are not concerned about controlling other's outcomes (van Dijke & Poppe, 2006). Some, however, strive for power, and they pursue it across time, groups, and situations (Winter, 2010).

People who are high in their need for power, for example, tend to pursue status and prestige more vigorously than others. They describe themselves as hoping to have power in the future: "I want to have power in every aspect of my life" (Harms, Roberts, & Wood, 2007). The need for power, measured when people are first hired for a large company, predicts their rise to positions of authority in the corporation's management hierarchy some 8 to 16 years later (McClelland & Boyatzis, 1982). They are more likely to hold offices in groups and organizations. As noted in Chapter 4, individuals who are strong in their need for power are more likely to experience power stress when that need is thwarted (Fodor & Wick, 2009). Also, the quest for power is linked to testosterone, which is the primary androgen that determines masculine sexual features, both physical and psychological. (Women's bodies produce testosterone, but at a substantially reduced level.) Testosterone predicts aggression, assertiveness, and toughness, all of which improve one's chances of besting others in contests of dominance (Rivers & Josephs, 2010). However, testosterone's effects are muted when men are members of stable rather than contested dominance hierarchies (e.g., McIntyre et al., 2011).

Some individuals are more motivated to engage fully in the politics of status-seeking in groups. One measure of such willingness, the *Political Skill Inventory*, includes such items as "I spend a lot of time and effort at work networking with others," "I am able to make most people feel comfortable and at ease around me," and "I am good at building relationships with influential people at work" (Ferris et al., 2005, p. 149). Those with political skills are more likely to be affable, likeable, outgoing, proactive, and task-oriented; when they seek to influence others, they are more likely to succeed (Ferris et al., 2007).

Social Dominance Orientation   Individuals who seek and use power tend to view the world—and the individuals and groups within it—as ordered in terms of relative dominance. As described by Jim Sidanius and Felicia Pratto, **social dominance orientation** (SDO) is a general predisposition toward anti-egalitarianism within and between groups; a preference for "group-based hierarchy and the domination of 'inferior' groups by 'superior' groups" (Sidanius & Pratto, 1999, p. 48). Those who are high in SDO strive to protect and even increase the differences between group members, and they

---

social dominance orientation A dispositional tendency to accept and even prefer circumstances that sustain social inequalities, combined with a general preference for hierarchical social structures (identified by Jim Sidanius and Felicia Pratto).

prefer membership in hierarchical groups. They are dominant and assertive rather than submissive and passive, and they match the prototype of the driven, tough, and relatively uncaring seeker of power who views the world as a "dog-eat-dog" jungle where only the strong survive. Individuals who are high in SDO are more likely to be identified as group leaders, and they also report using social influence tactics, including "forceful pressure," to win the position (Son Hing et al., 2007). Men tend to be higher in SDO than women (Lee, Pratto, & Johnson, 2011).

SDO also predicts reactions to outgroups. Just as individuals who are high in SDO believe that a pecking order structures groups, they feel that a group-level pecking order ranks all societies. They would tend to agree with such statements as, "Some groups of people are simply inferior to other groups" and "It's probably a good thing that certain groups are at the top and other groups are at the bottom" (Sidanius & Pratto, 1999, p. 67). In consequence, and as Chapter 14 explains, SDO predicts prejudice and reactions to intergroup conflict (Whitley, 1999).

Bullying   Unchecked, pathological levels of dominance over others can lead to bullying. **Bullying** involves deliberately inflicting injury or discomfort on another person repeatedly through physical contact, verbal abuse, exclusion, or other negative actions. Although bullying was originally considered to be a characteristic of childrens' and adolescents' groups, bullying also occurs in military, business, and professional organizations (Geffner et al., 2004). Both males and females bully, but they tend to do so in different ways: Females are relationally aggressive, for they use gossip, criticism, and exclusion against their victims. Males tend to use noncontingent punishment: they treat people negatively for no reason (Hoel et al., 2010). Jim Jones was a bully.

---

bullying Repetitively teasing, ridiculing, provoking, or tormenting others through various types of irritating, harassing, or aggressive actions, such as name-calling, threats, insults, and physical injury.

Bullying signals a marked imbalance in the power relationship between the bully and his or her victim. The victim of abuse "has difficulty in defending himself or herself and is somewhat helpless against" the bully (Olweus, 1997, p. 216). Bullying, then, is not retaliation between parties in a dispute or conflict, but the mistreatment of a less powerful person by someone with power. Bullying is also a group behavior. Victims are sometimes isolated and friendless individuals abandoned to their fate by the rest of the group, but in many cases, groups of individuals are abused by groups of bullies. Similarly, although bullies are often thought to be poorly adjusted individuals who are expressing anger by picking on those who cannot defend themselves, bullies are often relatively popular group members. Bullies in school settings, for example, are often involved in sports if boys and considered attractive and more mature if girls. They tend to be recognized as school leaders and trend setters, but they are also disliked for the way they treat other people of lower status in the group (Vaillancourt, Hymel, & McDougall, 2003). Bullying also involves more than just the bully and the victim, as other group members are drawn into the harmful bully–victim exchange. Some group members take the role of henchmen or facilitators; they do not initiate the abuse, but they take an active part once the bullying event has begun. Others encourage bullies or signal support by smiling and laughing. Others impassively watch the interaction without speaking, and a few members of the bystander group may intercede on behalf of the victim, either directly or by seeking help from authorities (Giacalone & Promislo, 2010). Because bullying is rooted in both power dynamics and group dynamics, experts recommend organization- and group-level interventions for preventing peer abuse (Giannetti & Sagarese, 2001; Horne, Stoddard, & Bell, 2007; Olweus, 1997).

Achieving Status

People's status-seeking efforts will be for naught if the group rejects them. This process, unfortunately, is often unfair—individuals whose influence should be accepted are not always recognized by the group, just as the group sometimes takes direction from people who are not qualified to lead.

Expectation-States Theory Sociologist Joseph Berger and his colleagues developed **expectation-states theory** to explain how groups determine who will be granted status and who will not be. This theory assumes that status differences are most likely to develop when members are working collectively in the pursuit of shared goals that they feel are important ones. Because the group seeks to use its resources to its best advantage, members intuitively take note of one another's *status characteristics*— personal qualities that they think are indicative of ability or prestige. Those who possess numerous status characteristics are implicitly identified and permitted to perform more numerous and varied group actions, to provide greater input and guidance for the group, to influence others by evaluating their ideas, and to reject the influence attempts of others (Berger, Ridgeway, & Zelditch, 2002; Ridgeway, 2001).

Expectation-states theorists believe that group members base their expectations on two types of status cues. **Specific status characteristics** are indicators of ability at the task to be performed in the given situation. On a basketball team, for example, height may be a specific status characteristic, whereas prior jury duty may determine status in a jury (Strodtbeck & Lipinski, 1985). In Jonestown, given the physically challenging tasks the group faced in building a community in a South American rain forest, strong, energetic individuals who were

experienced in building and farming moved upward in the status hierarchy relative to those who are not so skilled.

Diffuse status characteristics are more general qualities that the members assume are relevant to ability and evaluation. Sex, age, wealth, ethnicity, status in other groups, or cultural background can serve as diffuse status characteristics if people associate these qualities with certain skills, as did the members of the People's Temple. Age and spiritual wisdom were both considered important diffuse status characteristics, with older, more devout members gaining status. In other groups—those that value youth, for example—the opposite might hold true (Oldmeadow, 2007).

Researchers have largely confirmed expectation-states theory's prediction that individuals with positively evaluated specific status and diffuse status characteristics usually command more authority than those who lack status-linked qualities (Wilke, 1996). In police teams, officers with more work experience exercised more authority than their less experienced partners (Gerber, 1996). Members of dyads working on a perceptual task deferred to their partner if he or she seemed more skilled at the task (Foddy & Smithson, 1996). People who are paid more are permitted to exert more influence over people who are paid less (Stewart & Moore, 1992). When air force bomber crews work on nonmilitary tasks, rank predicts influence (Torrance, 1954). Juries allocate more status to jurors who have previously served on juries or who have more prestigious occupations (Strodtbeck et al., 1957). The bulk of the research also confirms the following causal sequence in status allocation: First, group member X displays specific and diffuse status characteristics. Second, other members form positive expectations about X. Last, members permit X to influence them (Driskell & Mullen, 1990).

---

expectation-states theory An explanation of status differentiation in groups, which assumes that group members allocate status to group members judged to be competent at the task at hand and to group members who have qualities that the members think are indicators of competence and potential.

specific status characteristics In status characteristics theory, task-specific behavioral and personal characteristics that people consider when estimating the relative competency, ability, and social value of themselves and others.

---

diffuse status characteristic In status characteristics theory, general personal qualities, such as age, race, and ethnicity, that people consider when estimating the relative competency, ability, and social value of themselves and others.

Status Generalization   Because status in a group is determined by both specific and diffuse status characteristics, groups do not always allocate status fairly (Schneider & Cook, 1995). Imagine, for example, a jury that includes these three individuals:

- Dr. Prof, a 40-year-old European American woman who teaches in the School of Business and who has written several books on management.

- Mr. Black, a 35-year-old African American high school principal.

- Dr. White, a 58-year-old European American male physician who has an active practice.

Considerable evidence suggests that, when selecting a foreman, a jury of middle-class European Americans would be biased against Dr. Prof and Mr. Black and in favor of Dr. White. Dr. Prof and Mr. Black, despite their specific status credentials, may be disqualified from positions of status in the group by their (completely irrelevant) diffuse status characteristics. In contrast, Dr. White poses little incongruence for the group if the group members unfairly consider advanced age, pale skin, an MD degree, and upper-class social status to be positive features (York & Cornwell, 2006). This phenomenon is known as **status generalization**: Group members let general status (i.e., diffuse status) characteristics influence their expectations, even though these characteristics may be irrelevant in the given situation (Molm, 1986; Ridgeway & Balkwell, 1997).

Status generalization explains why women and African Americans are given less status and authority in groups than men and European Americans, respectively (Ridgeway et al., 2009). Women and racial minorities report more dissatisfaction about how status is allocated in groups (Hembroff 1982).

---

status generalization The tendency for individuals known to have achieved or been ascribed authority, respect, and prestige in one context to enjoy relatively higher status in other, unrelated, contexts (e.g., a celebrity who exercises influence in a group even though this diffuse status characteristic is not relevant in the current group context).

Women are less likely to be selected as leaders of their groups, and they are more likely to be assigned to lower status roles (Eagly & Carli, 2007). Women and minorities must put extra effort into their groups and reach higher performance standards just to reach the same level of respect and authority granted to less productive European American men (Biernat & Kobrynowicz, 1997; Foschi, 1996). Groups, failing to recognize women's expertise, tend to under-perform when women, rather than men, have the expertise a task demands (Thomas-Hunt & Phillips, 2004).

Solo Status   These unfair status-allocation processes are magnified when individuals who are members of stereotyped minority societal groups are also underrepresented in the group itself. **Solo status** causes minority members to feel that the other members are categorizing them in terms of their social group and are not fully accepted as members. In consequence, they are less likely to identify with the group, will not be as loyal to the group, and feel their performance will be unfairly evaluated. They also expect that their contributions will be devalued, and these concerns are generally justified. Despite their many contributions, solo members are rarely allocated high status in groups (e.g., Biernat et al., 1998; Sekaquaptewa & Thompson, 2003).

These negative status effects often fade over time as groups revise their hierarchies as they recognize the skills and abilities of previously slighted members and as solos learn how to cope with the challenges of status generalization (Johnson & Richeson, 2009). Women and minorities who communicate their involvement in the group to the other members tend to gain status more rapidly, as do those who act in a group-oriented rather than a self-oriented way (Anderson & Kilduff, 2009). If a solo woman in an otherwise all-male group remains actively involved in the group by asking questions, the

---

solo status The state of being the only group member who is a representative of a specific social category in an otherwise homogenous group (e.g., a man in an otherwise all-female group).

negative effects of her solo status are eliminated (Fuegen & Biernat, 2002). External authorities can also undo unfair status generalizations by explicitly stressing the qualifications of women and minorities or by training group members to recognize their biases (Ridgeway, 1989). Moreover, groups may reduce biases in the allocation of status to their members by making use of computer-based technology to make decisions and exchange information (see Focus 8.2).

Status Hierarchies and Stability

Humans, like many social species, live in groups with organized systems of power relations. Field studies of chimpanzees, baboons, and bonobos reveal complex patterns of power relations that determine various privileges and responsibilities. As Milgram (1974, p. 124) concluded, "Each member's acknowledgement of his place in the hierarchy stabilizes the pack."

Dominance and Cooperation   Evolutionary theory suggests that the system of dominance and deference in human groups is an adaptive one, designed to enhance survival by increasing group coordination and decision making, improving defense, and providing a means to resolve conflict. A group that must move regularly in search of food and water requires some means to determine whose advice to take and whose advice to ignore. When conflicts occur between members, someone in the group must mediate the dispute, either by negotiating a peace or by requiring it through a show of force. When a group encounters a threat, the group that is organized will likely fare better than one that is not. Because the environment in which human groups lived favored those with a stable dominance hierarchy, modern humans are instinctively prepared to accept, understand, and even prefer status differences. So long as the authority is motivated to advance the interests of the group, those lower in the status hierarchy prosper by cooperating with those of higher status. Not everyone can lead nor should everyone follow (see, for example, de Kwaadsteniet & van Dijk, 2010; Tiedens, Unzueta, & Young, 2007; Van Vugt, Hogan, & Kaiser, 2008).

Interpersonal Complementarity   The naturalness of dominance hierarchies is in evidence when people join with several others in a "leaderless" group. Even when no explicit instructions are provided, within minutes such groups form status hierarchies that all members can accurately describe without having ever explicitly discussed who will lead and who will follow (Keltner et al., 2010). Leaderless groups do not stay leaderless for long. This tendency translates into a small-group version of sociologist and political theorist Robert Michels' (1915/1959) **iron law of oligarchy**—the rule of the many by the few.

This shift from status homogeneity to hierarchy results, in part, from the behavioral complementarity of dominance and deference. According to the **interpersonal complementarity hypothesis**, each member's action tends to evoke, or "pull," a predictable set of actions from the other group members (Carson, 1969). If, for example, an individual seems agreeable, pleasant, and cooperative, the other group members would tend to react in kind: They would behave in positive, friendly ways. Friendly behaviors are reciprocated by friendly behaviors. But what if group members act in dominant, firm, directive ways—issuing orders, taking charge, giving advice? Such behaviors would tend to evoke submissive responses from the others. People also report feeling more comfortable when interacting with someone who displays complementary rather than similar reactions. Group members who display signs of submissiveness when talking to someone who seems

---

iron law of oligarchy The principle of political and social control that predicts that, in any group, power is concentrated in the hands of a few individuals (an oligarchy) who will act in ways that protect and enhance their power (described by Robert Michels).

interpersonal complementarity hypothesis The predicted tendency for certain behaviors to evoke behaviors from others that are congruous with the initial behavior, with positive behaviors evoking positive behaviors, negative behaviors evoking negative behaviors, dominant behaviors evoking submissive behaviors, and submissive behaviors evoking dominant behaviors.

F o c u s   8.2   E-groups: Status Generalization in Online Groups

When people meet offline in face-to-face groups to make decisions or solve problems, their impact on the final outcome is often a function of their status in the group. Those who have risen to the top of the group's hierarchy speak as much as 40% to 50% of the time (Stephan & Mischler, 1952), even when the meeting is supposed to be a discussion. The remainder of the speaking will be done by two or three other group members, but these people will have higher status than the rank-and-file members (Gibson, 2003). Those at the bottom of the "speaking order" may say nothing at all during the course of a meeting. Contributions to the discussion also tend to be clustered. Once individuals enter the discussion stream, they tend to concentrate their comments during periods of high vocality, or megaturns (Dabbs & Ruback, 1987; Parker, 1988). This pattern occurs, in part, because some individuals are too slow to speak when the previous speaker concludes, so they never manage to capture the floor. Moreover, as expectation-states theory suggests, individuals who are more influential are given more latitude in speaking than are those who are low in status (Bonito & Hollingshead, 1997).

What happens when groups meet online rather than face to face? In many online groups, the effects of status on participation are muted, resulting in a *participation equalization effect* (Hollingshead, 2001b). One early investigation of participants who varied in status tracked their involvement in discussions conducted via e-mail or in face-to-face meetings. E-mail reduced the participation differences between group members with the result that low-status members participated more and high-status members participated less (Dubrovsky, Kiesler, & Sethna, 1991). Studies of online discussions in college classes also indicated that students participate more equally than they do in face-to-face discussions and that differences in participation due to the cultural background or the student's sex are reduced (Davidson-Shivers, Morris, & Sriwongkol, 2003; Kim & Bonk, 2002). Students who eventually earn better grades are more active in such online discussions, but these differences in contribution likely reflect motivational differences rather than status differences (Wang, Newlin, & Tucker, 2001).

But recent studies suggest that people in online groups behave, in most respects, like those in offline groups. Many of the cues that people implicitly use to allocate status to others are minimized when people interact via computers—a group member's height, age, sex, and race can be kept private in online groups, and the computer-mediated format prevents the

exchange of nonverbal signs of dominance and authority. There can be no raised voice, no long stare, and no rolling of the eyes when members are connected only by a computer. Online groups, however, still exhibit signs of status differentiation. Participants, through the content of their messages, level of involvement, and style of communication (e.g., punctuation; capitalization such as I AGREE TOTALLY!!!!; slang; humor; and emoticons—text-based faces created with periods, commas, parentheses, semicolons, and so on) lay claim to characteristics that define their place within the group. In some cases, group members may even be more influenced by irrelevant diffuse status characteristics in online groups because they have no other information to use to guide their perceptions of the other members. If all Ed knows about his partner in a discussion is that his or her name is Jolina, then he may inevitably draw conclusions about her personality and interests from her name alone (Spears, Lea, & Postmes, 2007).

Some online communities, however, have succeeded in minimizing the impact of irrelevant social category cues on status by stressing competence, merit, and level of contribution as the key sources of status within the group. Open source software programmers, for example, work collectively in online development communities. These communities are based on a philosophy of openness, and so the projects are shared with all computer users. Rewards are primarily social ones—contributing to a collaborative effort and being respected by others in the group. In one such community, participants are "certified" at one of four levels—observer, apprentice, journeyer, and master—based on ratings by peers. When researchers studied these certifications, they found that rankings were based on the number of projects completed and the years spent programming and not on less relevant qualities such as age or level of education. Status was also unrelated to sex, but only because there were so few women in the group (Bianchi, Kang, & Stewart, 2012).

Why did this online community resist status inequities whereas others do not? The explanation may lie in the norms of the group. The programmers, "as part of the hacker culture, demonstrate a strong commitment to objectivity and meritocracy in rewarding contributions to the community" (Bianchi et al., 2012, p. 351). These findings suggest that other groups, through concerted effort, can learn to resist sexism, racism, nepotism, cronyism, and other social biases when allocating status (Son Hing et al., 2011).

powerful are better liked, as are those who take charge when interacting with docile, submissive individuals (Tiedens & Fragale, 2003). The interpersonal complementary hypothesis thus predicts that (1) positive behaviors evoke positive behaviors and negative behaviors evoke negative behaviors, and (2) dominant behaviors evoke submissive behaviors and submissive behaviors evoke dominant behaviors (Sadler & Woody, 2003).

Researchers put this hypothesis to the test by arranging for young women to work, for a short period of time, with a partner who was trained to enact a particular behavioral style. When the partner enacted a dominant, leading style, she exuded confidence and authority. In some cases, she added a degree of friendliness to her dominance, frequently intervening to keep the group working. In others, she was dominant, but less friendly; she stressed her superiority and autonomy, and her self-confidence bordered on self-absorption and conceit. In other conditions, she acted in more submissive, self-effacing ways. Rather than take charge, she would seem timid, uncertain, passive, and inhibited (Strong et al., 1988).

The videorecordings of the sessions revealed clear evidence of complementarity. Participants who were paired with a dominant confederate acted submissively; they acquiesced, behaved passively, and showed respect for their partner. Only rarely did a participant respond in a dominant manner when faced with a dominant interaction partner. Conversely, if the confederate behaved in a docile manner, the participants tended to take charge by acting in a dominant fashion—strong evidence of the power of complementarity.

Hierarchy and Harmony Hierarchy is not all gain without cost. Individual's whose status is low in groups sometimes fail to perform to their full capabilities, because their low level status undercuts their motivation and cognitive functioning (Kishida et al., 2012). High status group members often exceed their authority, and cause far more harm than good for their groups (Smith, Larimer, et al., 2007). As the final section of this chapter warns, excessive and unfair differences in the distribution of power within a group can lead to a wide-range of negative consequences.

A group whose hierarchy of authority is stable, however, will be more productive than one with unsettled status ranks. To test this hypothesis experimentally, researchers manipulated groups' status structures by carefully distributing people who differed in their levels of testosterone into groups. Testosterone, as noted earlier in the chapter, is associated with one's tendency to seek influence over others. So the researchers created three kinds of groups, expecting groups with all high-testosterone members to be more unstable ones in comparison to (a) groups with just one high-testosterone, low-testosterone, and average-testosterone participants and (b) groups with all low-testosterone participants. As they anticipated, levels of conflict were much higher in the high-testosterone groups, with members reporting problems communicating and connecting to each other. Productivity was also lower in these groups, for groups with a mix of high, average, and low testosterone members outperformed both the all-high and all-low testosterone groups. These researchers verified these results in a second study where they manipulated power psychologically rather than biologically. They created groups with different hierarchies by prompting some members to feel more or less powerful. Given the consistency of these results, the researchers concluded hierarchy "enhances rather than undermines group effectiveness" (Ronay et al., 2012, p. 669).

THE METAMORPHIC EFFECTS OF POWER

The system for organizing status in human groups is not a perfect one. Individuals sometimes engage in dominance competitions that are so disruptive they create disunity in the group and undermine its productivity. Groups too often fail to extend respect and deference to those who deserve it. Sometimes exploitive, self-serving individuals manage to secure substantial influence within the group, and, when they do, the entire group suffers or, as in the case of the People's Temple, perishes. Sometimes, the power process can disrupt, rather than facilitate, group functioning.

Changes in the Powerholder

Probably for as long as humans have joined together in groups, they have puzzled over the nature of power and its influence on those who have it, those who lack it, and those who seek it (Kipnis, 1974). In their tragedies, the Greeks dramatized the fall of heroes, who, swollen by past accomplishments, conceitedly compared themselves to the gods. Myth and folklore are replete with tales of the consequences of too much power, as in the case of Icarus, whose elation at the power of flight caused his own death. Although some celebrated the liberating effects of power, others spoke of its corruptive side effects. As Lord Acton warned, "Power tends to corrupt, and absolute power corrupts absolutely."

Priming Power   Power is, in part, a state of mind —a feeling of authority rather than authority per se. Some individuals who occupy positions of authority and influence report that they feel powerless and without any control over events that transpire in their lives. Yet, other individuals, who face situations that seem to be those they cannot in any way influence and control, report feeling very powerful and in charge (Anderson & Galinsky, 2006). A sense of power also depends on the situation; if you win an election, are appointed to a position of influence in an organization, or are granted membership in a high-status group, in all likelihood you will experience a feeling of heightened power that comes from the circumstances (Keltner et al., 2008). A sense of power can also be triggered in more subtle ways. Environmental or cognitive cues can prime a sense of power by activating preexisting beliefs, concepts, or memories of experiences relevant to power. College students meeting in a professor's office act in more powerful ways if they are seated in the professor's chair behind the desk facing out into the room than those seated in the chair reserved for visitors (Chen, Lee-Chai, & Bargh, 2001).

The Paradoxical Effects of Power   Social psychologist Dacher Keltner and his colleagues (2003, 2008), synthesizing previous analyses of both power and motivation, theorize that power—having power, using power, even thinking about power— leads to psychological and interpersonal changes for both those who have power and those who do not. Their **approach/inhibition theory** recognizes that most organisms display one of two basic types of reactions to environmental events. One reaction, approach, is associated with action, self-promotion, seeking rewards and opportunities, increased energy, and movement. The second reaction, inhibition, is associated with reaction, self-protection, avoiding threats and danger, vigilance, loss of motivation, and an overall reduction in activity. Significantly, the approach/inhibition model suggests that power increases approach tendencies, whereas reductions in power trigger inhibition. Power activates people—it causes them to experience increases in drive, energy, motivation, and emotion—and often leads to positive consequences. The powerful can bring their heightened energy, clearer insights, and positive emotions to bear on the issues facing the group and help the group overcome difficulties and reach its goals. But power, and the activation it brings, also has a dark side, for it can create a Jim Jones or an Adolph Hitler as often as a Mahatma Gandhi or an Abraham Lincoln.

Power's Positive Effects   Power influences those who wield it. Individuals who are powerful (powerholders), or at least, feel powerful, act, feel, and think differently than individuals who feel they are powerless.

- *Power and action.* Power increases activity levels, prompting people to take action rather than remain passive. Powerholders are usually the busiest people in the group or organization.

---

approach/inhibition theory An integrative conceptual analysis of the transformative effects of power that finds power to be psychologically and behaviorally activating but the lack of power inhibiting (posited by Dacher Keltner and his colleagues).

They are proactive; they would rather speak first during a debate, make the first move in a competition, or make the first offer during a negotiation (Magee, Galinsky, & Gruenfeld, 2007). In one study, researchers first asked some people to think back to a time when they had power over other individuals. Others thought of a time when they had little power. They were then left to wait for the next phase of the study at a table positioned too close to an annoying fan blowing directly on them. Some of the participants just put up with this irritation, but others took steps to solve the problem: They moved the fan or turned it off. As predicted, 69% of the individuals who recalled a time they were powerful removed the bothersome fan, compared to only 42% of less powerful participants (Galinsky, Gruenfeld, & Magee, 2003).

- *Power and emotion.* Powerful people also tend to experience, and express, more positive emotions than those who are lower in power. Powerholders usually feel good about things— their moods are elevated, they report higher levels of such positive emotions as happiness and satisfaction, and they even smile more than low-power group members (Berdahl & Martorana, 2006; Watson & Clark, 1997). Power is also associated with optimism about the future, apparently because more powerful individuals tend to focus their attention on more positive aspects of the environment (Anderson & Galinsky, 2006). Powerful people seek rewards more actively than people without power who are motivated to avoid negative outcomes (Keltner, Gruenfeld, & Anderson, 2003). Some evidence even suggests that powerful people cope more effectively with stress because they are positively challenged, rather than threatened, by difficult circumstances (Scheepers et al., 2012).

- *Power and goal-striving.* Powerful individuals also exhibit more intense and resilient goal-striving. When working toward a goal that is illusive, they are able to maintain high levels of motivation, for power is associated with increased levels of self-regulation—provided they are working at tasks that they feel are appropriate ones for the purposes and procedures of the given situation (DeWall et al., 2011). In a work setting, for example, they plan more task-related activities, unless their role requires them to be sensitive to other individuals' needs and experiences. In such circumstances, the goal-striving orientation of the powerful prompts them to be more empathic and prosocial (Côté et al., 2011; Guinote, 2008; Schmidt Mast, Jonas, & Hall, 2009).

- *Power and cognitive functioning.* Power facilitates executive cognitive functions by enhancing attentional focus, decision-making, planning, and goal-selection (Smith et al., 2008). Power seems to sharpen mental acuity to a degree, helping the powerful to selectively focus on important information and reducing their distractibility (Guinote, 2007). When researchers tracked the brain functioning of people working in a group solving intellectual problems the high-status members displayed (a) increased blood oxygenation in the prefrontal cortex over time, indicating increased mental activity and (b) decreased oxygenation in the amygdala, suggesting decreases in fear and nervousness. This pattern of neuronal change was reversed for lower status members (Kishida et al., 2012).

- *Power and influence.* Power insulates individuals, to a degree, from the influence of others. Powerful people are more likely to act on the basis of their own personal preferences. When people are primed by thoughts of power, their public statements and actions are more authentic in the sense that they correspond to their private beliefs and dispositions. Powerful people feel freer to express their ideas and resist conformity pressures that influence less powerful people (Kraus, Chen, & Keltner, 2011).

Power's Negative Effects   These consequences of power, in terms of action orientation, emotions, and judgmental tendencies, can also be liabilities.

- *Power and risk-taking.* Powerful people are proactive, but in some cases their actions are risky, inappropriate, or unethical (Emler & Cook, 2001). Some individuals, driven by their need for power, overstep the boundaries of their authority or engage in inappropriate actions. If they feel that they have a mandate from their group or organization, they may do things they are not empowered to do (Clark & Sechrest, 1976). They are, in some cases, not just optimistic, but overly optimistic, for they assume the group can accomplish more in a given amount of time than is rationally possible (Weick & Guinote, 2010).

- *Power and emotion.* Powerful people may be happier, but they often generate negative emotional reactions in their subordinates, particularly when there is disagreement and conflict in the group (Fodor & Riordan, 1995). In a study of dyads, those with more power than their partner reported feeling such positive emotions as happiness, pride, and amusement. Their partners, unfortunately, reported more anger, fear, tension, and sadness (Langner & Keltner, 2008). When people in work settings are asked to identify the sources of their stress and dissatisfaction, the number one cause reported is powerful people: bosses, managers, and supervisors.

- *Power and empathy.* Powerful people often misjudge, misunderstand, and even derogate their subordinates. Powerholders can be discerning judges of those who work for them, but often only when their personal success depends on recognizing the strengths and weaknesses of subordinates (Overbeck and Park, 2001). Power tends to weaken one's social attentiveness with the result that powerful people have a more difficult time understanding other people's point of view (Galinsky et al., 2006). Researchers documented the pernicious effects of power by arranging for two people to discuss an experience that caused them emotional pain and suffering. During and after the conversation, the researchers tracked participants' feelings of compassion, using both physiological measures and self-reports, as they listened to their partner's outpouring of emotional angst. As expected, people who did not describe themselves as powerful and influential became more and more distressed themselves when their partners became more upset as they related their experience—their emotions were relatively synchronized. Powerful people, in contrast, did not respond emotionally to their partner's distress, and their levels of compassion declined as their partner's became more troubled (see Figure 8.3). These findings suggest that power may insulate the powerful from feeling troubled by the harm they inflict on others (van Kleef et al., 2008).

- *Power and self-satisfaction.* The successful use of power as a means of controlling others can lead to self-satisfaction, unrealistically positive self-evaluations, and over-estimations of interpersonal power (Galinsky, Jordan, & Sivanathan, 2008). When Kipnis (1974) asked participants if their subordinates were performing well because of (1) the workers' high self-motivation levels, (2) their manager's comments and suggestions, or (3) their desire for money, the high-power managers believed that their workers were only in it for the money (which the manager could control). The low-power managers believed that the workers were "highly motivated." Other studies have also revealed this tendency for powerful individuals to assume that they themselves are the prime cause of other people's behavior (Kipnis et al., 1976). Powerholders tend to (1) increase the social distance between themselves and non-powerful individuals, (2) believe that non-powerful individuals are untrustworthy and in need of close supervision, and (3) devalue the work and ability of less powerful individuals (Kipnis, 1974; Strickland, Barefoot, & Hockenstein, 1976). This tendency is all the more pronounced when powerholders use harsh rather than soft tactics. This reevaluation of self and others also occurs

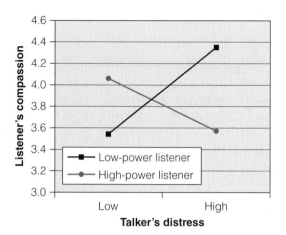

FIGURE 8.3 The relationship between the listener's compassion and the talker's distress for people who are low and high in power. Low-power people respond with more compassion as the talker becomes more distressed. For high-power people, their initially somewhat higher levels of compassion decline as the talker becomes more distressed.

SOURCE: van Kleef, G. A., Oveis, C., van der Löwe, I., LuoKogan, A., Goetz, J., & Keltner, D. (2008). Power, distress, and compassion: Turning a blind eye to the suffering of others. *Psychological Science*, 19, 1315–1322. doi: 10.1111/ 1467-9280 2008 02241.x

when powerholders use methods that are not congruent with the base of power. Individuals with expert power who use soft power tactics, or people with legitimate power who use harsh power tactics, reevaluate themselves and their targets less than those who use power tactics that do not match their power base (Klocke, 2009).

- *Power and coercion.* Powerful people also tend to use their power to influence others even when a display of power is unnecessary. Social psychologist David Kipnis (1974) examined this tendency by arranging for advanced business students to participate as managers in a simulated manufacturing company. Some had considerable power, in that they could award bonuses, cut pay, threaten and actually carry out transfers to other jobs, give additional instructions, and even fire a worker, but others could not. Kipnis controlled the level of

productivity of the fictitious workers (all performed adequately), but powerful managers nonetheless initiated roughly twice as many attempts at influence as the less powerful managers. Moreover, power determined the power tactics managers used—the powerless ones relied on persuasion, whereas the powerful ones coerced or rewarded their workers. Other studies have yielded similar support for the idea that people with power tend to make use of it, but the magnitude of this effect depends on many other factors (Fiske & Berdahl, 2007).

- *Power and ethics.* When individuals feel powerful, they sometimes treat others unfairly, particularly if they are more self-centered rather than focused on the overall good of the group (Chen, Lee-Chai, & Bargh, 2001). Some individuals (primarily men) associate power with sexuality, so when they are empowered, they engage in inappropriate sexual behaviors, including sexual harassment (MacKinnon, 2003). This tendency, termed the **Bathsheba syndrome**, takes its name from the biblical story of David and Bathsheba. King David is smitten by Bathsheba, the wife of one of his generals, and he seduces her. David compounds his moral failure with one misdeed after another, until he eventually orders Bathsheba's husband killed. A powerholder acting immorally is not, apparently, a new phenomenon in human societies (Ludwig & Longenecker, 1993).

Power and Power Seeking In small, stable groups, individuals in positions of authority wish to maintain their status relative to those lower in the hierarchy, but once they maintain this relative difference, they do not continue to seek more and more status. Power is not addictive or so alluring that people are never satisfied with the level of

---

Bathsheba syndrome The tendency for high-status members to claim unfair and inappropriate privileges and honors, including predacious sexual activities.

power they currently enjoy (van Dijke & Poppe, 2007). In some cases, however, the experience of power is so positive—energizing, emotionally satisfying, psychologically stimulating—that powerholders may become preoccupied with seeking power, driven by a strong motivation to acquire greater and greater levels of interpersonal influence (McClelland, 1975, 1985; Winter, 1973). They seek power, not because they can use it to achieve their goals, but because they value power per se. Hence, once such people attain power, they take steps to protect their sources of influence.

Reactions to the Use of Power

Humans, like many social species, are willing to accept guidance from other members of their group. However, in some cases, power does not just include power with people and over people, but also power against people. Powerholders can influence, sometimes dramatically, the outcomes of those who have little power, prompting them to do things they would rather not. How do people respond—behaviorally, cognitively, and emotionally—when the directives of authorities conflict with the goals they have set for themselves?

Reactions to Hard Influence Tactics Approach/inhibition theory suggests that individuals who find themselves without power, relative to others, avoid rather than approach. They not only lack resources, but they are dependent on others for the resources that they need. They therefore tend to display more negative affect, they are sensitive to threats and punishments, and they follow closely the dictates of the norms of the group (Keltner et al., 2003). In general, however, these effects of power are more pronounced when the powerholder uses hard (e.g., punishment, sanctions, nonpersonal rewards) rather than soft (personal rewards, referent power) influence methods. Harsh tactics generate a range of negative emotions, including hostility, depression, fear, and anger, whereas those influenced by softer methods tend to reciprocate with cooperation (Fiske & Berdahl, 2007; Pierro, Cicero, & Raven, 2008). Group members are also more likely to resist

an authority who uses coercive influence methods and asks the group members to carry out unpleasant assignments (Yukl, Kim, & Falbe, 1996); this resistance may cause the powerholder to turn to even more negative forms of influence (Youngs, 1986). Hence, although coercive powerholders may be successful in initial encounters, influence becomes more difficult in successive meetings as the group's anger and resistance to pressure grow. Groups will, however, tolerate the use of coercive methods when the group is successful (Michener & Lawler, 1975), the leader is trusted (Friedland, 1976), and the use of such tactics is justified by the group's norms (Michener & Burt, 1975).

Coercion and Conflict The conflict created by coercive influence can disrupt the entire group's functioning. Studies of classrooms, for example, indicate that many teachers rely heavily on coercion, but that these methods cause rather than solve disciplinary problems (Kounin, 1970). Coercive tactics, such as physical punishment, displays of anger, and shouting, not only fail to change the target student's behavior but also lead to negative changes in the classroom's atmosphere (Kounin & Gump, 1958). When misbehaving students are severely reprimanded, other students often become more disruptive and uninterested in their schoolwork, and negative, inappropriate social activity spreads from the trouble spot throughout the classroom. This disruptive contagion, or *ripple effect*, is especially strong when the reprimanded students are powerful members of the classroom status structure or when commands by teachers are vague and ambiguous.

Resistance and Rebellion In some cases, group members may rebel against an authority who they consider to be unfair, incompetent, or both (Ciulla & Forsyth, 2011). They may escape the powerholder's region of control or apply influence in return. Members contend against those in power as individuals, particularly when they feel that others in the group have more power than they do. But when members feel a sense of shared identity with the other low-power members of the group, they are

T A B L E 8.3   **Kelman's Compliance-Identification-Internalization Theory of Conversion**

Stage	Description
Compliance	Group members comply with the powerholder's demands, but they do not personally agree with them. If the powerholder does not monitor the members, they will likely not obey.
Identification	Group members' compliance with the actual or anticipated demands of the powerholder is motivated by a desire to imitate and please the authority. The members mimic the powerholder's actions, values, characteristics, and so on.
Internalization	Group members follow the orders and advice of the powerholder because those demands are congruent with their own personal beliefs, goals, and values. They will perform the required actions even if not monitored by the powerholder.

SOURCE: Kelman, 1958.

more likely to join with them in a **revolutionary coalition** that opposes the powerholder (van Dijke & Poppe, 2004; Haslam & Reicher, 2012). In one study of group rebellion, two group members worked under the direction of a leader who was appointed to that post because he or she had outscored them on a bogus test of ability. The leader then proceeded to keep more than half of the money earned by the group, giving each participant less than one-fourth. If the leader had personally decided how to apportion payment, 58% of the participants rebelled by forming a coalition with the other low-status participant. If the leader was not responsible for the payment scheme, only 25% revolted (Lawler & Thompson, 1978, 1979).

Identification and Conversion Both Milgram's participants and the People's Temple members did as they were told, but the two groups differed in one crucial respect: Most of Milgram's participants struggled to withstand the authority's pressure, for they believed that the learner should not be held against his will. Many of Jones's followers, in contrast, zealously followed his orders. They did not strain against his authority; they had converted to his way of thinking (Darley, 1995; Lutsky, 1995; Staub, 1989, 2004).

_____

revolutionary coalition A subgroup formed within the larger group that seeks to disrupt or change the group's authority structure.

Social psychologist Herbert Kelman (1958, 1961, 2006) identified three basic reactions that people display in response to coercive influence (see Table 8.3). In some cases, the powerholder only produces compliance—the group members do what they are told to do, but only because the powerholder demands it. Privately, they do not agree with the powerholder, but publicly they yield to the pressure. Like Milgram's participants, they obey only when the powerholder maintains surveillance. Identification occurs when the target of the influence admires and therefore imitates the powerholder. When group members identify with the powerholder, their self-image changes as they take on the behaviors and characteristics of the person with power. Many members of the People's Temple admired Jones and wanted to achieve his level of spirituality. They obeyed his orders because they identified with him.

Identification, if prolonged and unrelenting, can lead to the final stage—internalization. When internalization occurs, the individual "adopts the induced behavior because it is congruent with his value system" (Kelman, 1958, p. 53). The group members are no longer merely carrying out the powerholder's orders; instead, their actions reflect their own personal beliefs, opinions, and goals. Even if the powerholder is not present, the group members will still undertake the required actions. Extreme obedience—such as occurred with Jonestown, the murder of millions of Jews by the Nazis during World War II, the My Lai massacre, and suicidal cults—often requires internalization. The group members' actions reflect their private acceptance of the authority's value system (Hamilton & Sanders, 1995, 1999; Kelman & Hamilton, 1989).

Kelman's three-step model of conversion explains how groups convert recruits into fervent members over time. Cults, for example, insist that the members adopt the group's ideology, but in the early stages of membership, they only require compliance. New recruits are invited to pleasant group functions where they are treated in a warm, positive way. Once they agree to join the group for a longer visit, the veteran members disorient them by depriving them of sleep, altering their diet, and persuading them to join in physically exhilarating activities. The recruits are usually isolated from friends and family to prevent any lapses in influence, subjected to lectures, and asked to take part in group discussions. Compliance with these small requests is followed by greater demands, as with the U.S. prisoners of war in Korea. Eventually, the recruits freely agree to make personal sacrifices for the group, and these sacrifices prompt a further consolidation of their attitudes (Baron, 2000; Baron, Kerr, & Miller, 1992). Once recruits reach the consolidation stage, they have fully internalized the group's ideology and goals.

Destructive Obedience In both the Milgram experiment and at Jonestown, power led to destructive obedience, as group members failed to question the authority's motivation, interpretations, and orders. For example, Jack Washington, a participant in Milgram's experiment, administered all the shocks up to 450 *v* with barely a hesitation. When later asked why he followed orders, he said, "I merely went on. Because I was following orders. I was told to go on. And I did not get a cue to stop" (Milgram, 1974, p. 50).

Milgram believed that destructive obedience becomes more likely when individuals no longer take responsibility for their own actions. They enter what Milgram called the **agentic state**; they

---

agentic state A psychological state that occurs when subordinates in an organized status hierarchy experience such a marked reduction in autonomy that they are unable to resist authorities' orders (proposed by Stanley Milgram).

become agents of a higher authority (Milgram, 1974). They feel "responsibility to the authority" but "no responsibility for the content of the actions that the authority prescribes" (Milgram 1974, pp. 145–146). Like Jack Washington, who was just "following orders" when he shocked the screaming learner, many individuals who have little power in the group assume that they are supposed to carry out the orders of the authority without questioning those orders. They no longer feel that they are in control of their own actions and become willing cogs in the group machine, carrying out the orders of an authority without considering their implications or questioning their effects (Hinrichs et al., 2012; Kelman & Hamilton, 1989).

Social psychologist Philip Zimbardo and his colleagues documented this kind of "blind obedience" to authority in their well-known Stanford Prison Study. Zimbardo, seeking to simulate a prison environment, randomly assigned male student volunteers to the role of prison guard or prisoner. The study was scheduled to run for two weeks, but was ended early due to the extreme reaction of the subjects. The prisoners seemed literally to become prisoners; although some rebelled, the majority became withdrawn and depressed. The guards also became increasingly tyrannical and arbitrary in their control of the prisoners. Some of their actions crossed the line between intimidation and abuse. They threatened the prisoners with physical injury, ran hooded prisoners into walls as they walked them to the bathrooms at night, and forced them to engage in feigned sexual activities. Zimbardo himself sank deeply into the role of superintendent, worrying over possible "prison breaks" and autocratically controlling visiting procedures (Haney, Banks, & Zimbardo, 1973; Zimbardo, Maslach, & Haney, 2000; Zimbardo, 2004, 2007).

Zimbardo concluded that the participants were overwhelmed by the "power of the situation." All of the participants had a general idea of the power differences between the role of a prisoner and the role of a guard. As the study progressed, to be a guard meant controlling all aspects of the prison and protecting this control with force if necessary. Prisoners, on the other hand, were supposed to accept this control and try to get through the experience as easily as possible by obeying all the prison's rules. Participants who refused to obey these norms were pressured by the other participants to bring their behavior back in line; nonconformity was not tolerated. Zimbardo concluded that his study "made it evident that initially our guards were 'good apples,' some of whom became soured over time by powerful situational forces" (2007, p. 329). Zimbardo calls the tendency for people to be corrupted by negative group environments the **Lucifer effect**.

Who Is Responsible?

A church member obediently swallowing poison. A soldier executing innocent civilians. A worker installing substandard building materials. A participant in an experiment giving an innocent victim painful shocks. On first hearing about such events, people sometimes fall prey to the **fundamental attribution error** (FAE): They blame the personalities of the individuals rather than the powerful group processes at work that forced them to obey—even though a closer, more informed

analysis of the situation would reveal the power pressures the members faced (Reeder, Monroe, & Pryor, 2008). In extreme instances, when a powerholder inflicts tremendous suffering and misfortune on people, the group members blame themselves for their misery. The members of the People's Temple may have felt so deserving of their fate that they chose to suffer rather than escape suffering. These feelings of self-condemnation may account for their willingness to take their own lives (Clark, 1971; Fanon, 1963).

Yet obedience is not a reflection of the nature of the individuals in the group, but an indication of the power of the group itself. By controlling key bases of power, using power tactics, and exploiting the nature of the subordinate–authority relationship, authorities exert great influence on group members. As John Darley explained, "Many evil actions are not the volitional products of individual evil-doers. Instead, they are in some sense societal products, in which a complex series of social forces interact to cause individuals to commit multiple acts of stunning evil" (Darley, 1992, p. 204).

CHAPTER REVIEW

What are the limits of an authority's power over group members?

1. *Social power* is the capacity to influence others, even when these others try to resist this influence.

2. Milgram tested people's ability to resist a powerful authority who ordered them to give painful and potentially harmful electric shocks to a confederate.

   - A majority (65%) of Milgram's participants obeyed, apparently because they felt powerless to refuse the orders of the authority.

   - Obedience rose and fell systematically as Milgram manipulated various aspects of the setting, including the risk of the procedure to the victim, the proximity of the victim to the group member, the prestige of the research location, surveillance by the experimenter, the legitimacy of the authority, and the presence of groups.

Lucifer effect The transformation of benign individuals into morally corrupt individuals by powerful, but malevolent, social situations; named for the biblical character Lucifer, an angel who fell from grace and was transformed into Satan (proposed by Philip Zimbardo).

fundamental attribution error The tendency to overestimate the causal influence of dispositional factors and underemphasize the causal influence of situational factors.

3. Milgram's studies suggest that obedience is common in hierarchically organized groups, such as those found in military, educational, and organizational settings.

   - Critics noted methodological flaws of the procedures and suggested that the personal characteristics of Milgram's participants prompted them to obey, but the findings have been replicated in other laboratories. Blass's review concludes that obedience is common in cultures throughout the world.

   - Burger recently replicated the Milgram study and found a level of obedience comparable to that reported by Milgram.

   - Obedience is related to differences in personality, including authoritarianism and moral maturity.

What are the sources of power in groups?

1. French and Raven's theory of *power bases* emphasizes six sources of power—*reward power, coercive power, legitimate power, referent power, expert power,* and *informational power.* Blass confirmed empirically that Milgram's experimenter derived power from all six bases.

2. Group members' influence over others depends on their control of these six power bases. Weber's concept of *charisma* suggests that certain leaders, for example, exert their influence by relying on legitimate power and referent power.

3. *Power tactics* are specific methods, such as persuasion, bargaining, and evasion, that people use to attain the goal of influencing others. These methods vary in a number of ways (hard–soft, rational–irrational, lateral–bilateral), with individuals selecting particular tactics depending on their personal characteristics and the nature of the group setting.

4. Cialdini's studies of compliance professionals identified a number of subtle techniques—*compliance tactics*—that people use to indirectly influence others' actions and choices.

   - One tactic, which may explain the levels of obedience in the Milgram experiment and Jonestown, is the *foot-in-the-door technique:* prefacing major demands with minor, inconsequential ones.

   - The so-called "brainwashing" methods used by Chinese military personnel during the Korean War relied on various methods of influencing, including behavioral commitment.

What are the sources of status in groups?

1. The status structure in a group defines differences in power and influence.

   - In some instances, members compete with one another for status in groups; the resulting pecking order defines who is dominant and who is submissive.

   - Personal characteristics, such as the need for power and *social dominance orientation,* predict those individuals who are more likely to strive for power over others.

   - *Bullying* is the use of coercive influence against another, less powerful person. It can involve physical contact, verbal abuse, exclusion, or other negative actions.

2. Group members' perceptions of one another also determine status. Berger's *expectation-states theory* argues that group members allocate status by considering *specific status characteristics* and *diffuse status characteristics.*

3. When *status generalization* occurs, group members unfairly allow irrelevant characteristics, such as race, age, or ethnicity, to influence the allocation of prestige.

   - Status allocations are particularly unfair when individuals who are members of stereotyped minority societal groups are also underrepresented in the group itself, with the most extreme case being *solo status* (being the only individual of that category in the group).

- In some online groups, the effects of status on participation are muted, resulting in a participation equalization effect.

4. Status differences in groups may be an evolved adaptation.

- In leaderless groups, status organizing processes rapidly create status differences.

- Michel's *iron law of oligarchy* predicts the emergence of status differences.

- Individuals tend to respond submissively when they confront authority, and they tend to behave assertively when they encounter someone who is submissive (the *interpersonal complementarity hypothesis*).

How do people react when they use their power to influence others?

1. People differ in the disposition level of personal power, but situational factors can also prime a sense of power.

2. The idea that "power corrupts, and absolute power corrupts absolutely" is consistent with Keltner's *approach/inhibition theory*, which suggests that power activates the approach response system whereas the loss of power inhibits actions.

3. The positive effects of power include increased activity levels, more positive emotions, consistent goal-striving, enhanced executive functioning, increased authenticity, and lower levels of conformity.

4. The negative effects of power include an increased tendency to act in a risky or inappropriate way, a negative impact on others' emotional states, loss of perspective-taking, the tendency to misjudge others, and increased self-satisfaction.

- Kipnis's studies of the metamorphic effects of power found that people who are given coercive power will use this power, and that once it is used, the powerholders tend to overestimate their control over others and devalue their targets.

- The *Bathsheba syndrome* occurs when authorities use their power to exploit others, particularly in a sexual way.

- Powerholders may become so enamored of power that they are preoccupied with gaining it and using it.

How do those without power react when power is used to influence them?

1. Approach/inhibition theory predicts that individuals who do not feel powerful will display more negative emotion and reduced motivation. These negative effects are more likely when powerholders use coercive influence methods.

2. Coercive methods have been linked to a number of dysfunctional group processes, including increases in conflict as more group members rebel against authority (the ripple effect), disrupted interpersonal relations, and revolutionary coalitions.

3. Kelman's compliance–identification–internalization model predicts that targets of influence may begin by merely complying with the authority's request, but over time, they may experience identification and internalization. When group members identify with the authority or internalize the authority's demands, their obedience reflects their personal beliefs rather than the constraints of the situation.

4. Individuals who are dominated by authorities sometimes engage in destructive obedience.

- Milgram's theory of the agentic state traces obedience back to the nature of the authority–subordinate relationship. When individuals become part of an organized hierarchy, they tacitly agree to follow the leader's orders. They also experience a reduction of responsibility.

- Zimbardo's simulated prison study was terminated prematurely when participants became too dominant and too submissive.

5. People who blame obedience on the individuals in the situation may be displaying the *fundamental attribution error* (FAE), which underestimates the power of group-level processes.

RESOURCES

Chapter Case: The People's Temple

- *Our Father Who Art in Hell: The Life and Death of Jim Jones* by James Reston, Jr. (2000) relies on the analysis of over 800 hours of recordings, as well as personal interviews with Jonestown survivors, to develop a full analysis of the People's Temple.

- *A Thousand Lives: The Untold Story of Hope, Deception, and Survival at Jonestown* by Julia Scheeres (2011) draws on FBI documents and audiotapes to describe the experiences of individuals who lived and died in Jonestown.

Obedience to Authority

- *Obedience to Authority: Current Perspectives on the Milgram Paradigm*, edited by Thomas Blass (2000b), provides both a personal and an objective analysis of the study that some feel is "one of the best carried out in this generation" (Etzioni, 1968, pp. 278–280).

- *Obedience to Authority* by Stanley Milgram (1974) describes his classic obedience studies in graphic detail.

Source of Power in Groups

- "Interpersonal Stratification: Status, Power, and Subordination" by Susan T. Fiske (2010) is an extensive analysis of the social psychology of status structures and influence in groups.

- *Naturally Selected: The Evolutionary Science of Leadership* by Mark Van Vugt and Anjana Ahuja (2010) provides an up-to-date review of the basic principles of evolutionary psychology and applies those principles to the analysis of status differences in groups.

Metamorphic Effects of Power

- "A Reciprocal Influence Model of Social Power: Emerging Principles and Lines of Inquiry" by Dacher Keltner, Gerben A. Van Kleef, Serena Chen, and Michael W. Kraus (2008) discusses power as an interactional outcome, possibly rooted in evolutionary mechanisms.

- *The Social Psychology of Power*, edited by Ana Guinote and Theresa K. Vescio (2010), includes chapters dealing with theoretical perspectives, negotiating power, and power in intergroup contexts, all by leading experts in the field.

- *The Lucifer Effect: Understanding How Good People Turn Evil* by Philip Zimbardo (2007) describes in detail the methods and results of the Stanford Prison Study and applies the insights gained to suggest ways to resist situational influences.

Leadership

CHAPTER OVERVIEW

Groups generally require guidance as they strive to reach their goals, and the individual who coordinates and motivates the group can fundamentally shape the group's future. If asked, "What one thing would you change to turn an inept group into a productive one?" most people would answer, "The leader."

- What is leadership?
- Who will emerge as a leader?
- Why do some lead and others follow?
- Why do some leaders succeed and others fail?

CHAPTER OUTLINE

The Nature of Leadership
   Leadership Myths
   What Is Leadership?
   What Do Leaders Do?

Leadership Emergence
   Who Will Lead?
   The Leader's Personality
   The Leader's Competencies
   Participation
   What Do Leaders Look Like?

Theories of Leadership Emergence
   Implicit Leadership Theory
   Social Identity Theory
   Social Role Theory
   Terror Management Theory
   Evolutionary Theory

Leader Effectiveness
   Fiedler's Contingency Model
   Style Theories
   Leader–Member Exchange Theory
   Participation Theories
   Transformational Leadership
   The Future of Leadership

Chapter Review

Resources

Wendy Kopp: Transforming Groups through Leadership

Wendy Kopp kept putting off writing her senior thesis until she finally found a topic that she truly cared about: the uneven quality of public education in America. How, she wondered, could injustices and discrimination in American society be eliminated if the quality of schooling depends so much on the wealth of the community where one was raised? For her thesis, she proposed the creation of a national teacher corps, similar to the Peace Corps, whose members would be recent college graduates who were willing to spend two years teaching before starting their corporate careers or graduate studies.

After graduation, she decided to follow through on her idea. That first summer she worked alone in donated office space in New York City, sending out an endless stream of letters seeking donations of the funds she needed to get the program started. She called her corps Teach For America (TFA) and worked tirelessly talking to potential corporate sponsors. Many of those who met her told her to start small to see if the approach would work before shifting to a larger scale. But she held fast to her original vision, explaining that "this was not going to be a little non-profit organization or model teacher-training program. This was going to be a *movement*" (Kopp, 2003, p. 23).

By late fall, she had appointed boards of directors and advisors and hired a staff. They worked tirelessly in a hive-like office space deep in Manhattan, but they also traveled out across the nation to recruit potential students on college campuses. By spring, they had attracted thousands of applicants from across the country, and Kopp had succeeded in gaining commitments from funders for the 2.5 million dollars needed to run TFA for a single year. So, in the spring of 1990, five hundred new corps members attended a summer institute in Los Angeles in preparation for two years of teaching in schools located in low-income areas of the United States. Asked how she managed to succeed at such a monumental task so quickly, Kopp explained, "There was nothing magical about it. I simply developed a plan and moved forward step by step" (2003, p. 47).

Over the years since Kopp first founded Teach for America, her company has placed thousands of teachers in schools, many of whom decided to become permanent teachers once their two-year term ended. The board, the staff, and the teachers of TFA deserve much of the credit for the success of the organization, but it was Wendy Kopp's **leadership** that made the difference. She developed a long-range vision and then a plan to reach her goals. She assembled a staff and organized their work to maximize efficiency. Her organization nearly collapsed under the pressure of criticism, funding limitations, and internal restructuring. Yet Kopp managed to guide her organization successfully through each quagmire, and each year TFA attracted applicants from the best colleges and universities. Why did she succeed where others might have failed?

---

leadership Guidance of others in their pursuits, often by unifying, directing, coordinating, supporting, and motivating their efforts; also, the ability to lead others.

THE NATURE OF LEADERSHIP

People have probably been puzzling over leadership since the first hominid cave dweller told the rest of the group, "We're doing this all wrong. Let's get organized." Egyptian hieroglyphics written five thousand years ago include the terms *leader* and *leadership* (Bass, 2008). The great epics, such as *Beowulf*, the *Song of Roland*, and the *Odyssey*, are filled with the exploits of leaders of small bands of adventurers. Leadership, like sex, language, and groups, make the anthropologist's list of universals that have been identified as common to all cultures and all civilizations, without exception (Brown, 1991). But what is leadership?

Leadership Myths

The political scientist James McGregor Burns (1978) has asserted that leadership is "one of the most observed and least understood phenomena on earth" (p. 2). Other experts have expressed dismay at the prevalence of misunderstanding about leadership, complaining that most people "don't have the faintest concept of what leadership is all about" (Bennis, 1975, p. 1) and that "the nature of leadership in our society is very imperfectly understood" (Gardner, 1965, p. 3). Many prescriptive suggestions are offered to leaders, but they are too often based on some questionable assumptions about leadership.

Is Leadership Power?   Many people, including some prominent political leaders, assume that good leaders are those capable of manipulating, controlling, and forcing their followers into obedience. Adolf Hitler, for example, defined leadership as the ability to move the masses, whether through persuasion or violence, and Ho Chi Minh once said that a good leader must learn to mold, shape, and change people just as a woodworker must learn to use wood. But people who use domination and coercion to influence others—whether they are kings, presidents, bosses, or managers—are not necessarily leaders. Leadership is a form of power, but power *with* people rather than *over* people—a cooperative relationship rather than a coercive one.

Are Leaders Born or Made?   Aristotle believed that nature, rather than nurture, determined one's leadership potential: "Men are marked out from the moment of birth to rule or be ruled." Some people do possess certain stable personal qualities—such as particular temperaments, intelligence, or skill in dealing with people—that increase the likelihood that they will be selected as leaders and be successful in that role. But researchers, by studying the similarity of twins, have discovered leadership is not entirely a matter of genetic destiny (Arvey & Chaturvedi, 2011). If one member of a set of identical twins holds a leadership position in a group or organizational setting, there is a 30% chance the other twin will, as well (Arvey et al., 2006, 2007). Genetics thus creates a biological readiness to lead, but a person's leadership potential is determined more by environmental forces—exposure to mentors and role models, opportunities to take on leadership challenges, the diligent development of leadership competencies, and so on—than biological ones.

Do All Groups Have Leaders?   Groups can function without a leader, but this role is usually the first to emerge in a newly formed group (see Chapter 6). In groups that exist only briefly, all members may share leadership responsibilities, but groups working for an extended duration on more complex tasks require coordinated action, as do those experiencing conflict. The size of the group is also critical: Members of larger groups are more likely to rely on one of their members to make rules clear, keep members informed, and make group decisions. In general, leaders appear in groups when (1) members feel that success on the group task is within their reach, (2) the rewards of success are valued, (3) the task requires group effort rather than individual effort, and (4) an individual with previous experience in the leadership role is present in the group. A group that is facing a stressful situation—such as a potential failure or danger—is also likely to embrace a leader's guidance (Guastello, 2007; Hemphill, 1950).

Some evidence suggests that a group of men will be more likely to include a leader than will a group of women (Schmid Mast, 2002). Investigators tested for this sex difference by arranging for three- to five-person groups to meet over three weeks. Some of the groups were all male, some were all female, and some included two men and two women. At the end of each day's session, the group members rated one another on leadership, and the researchers used these ratings to determine if control over the group's activities was concentrated, by consensus, on one group member. Centralization decreased, over time, in all the groups, but it remained higher across the three weeks in the all-male groups. The investigators concluded that men, in general, are more tolerant of inequality than women, so they favor social hierarchy and centralization (Berdahl & Anderson, 2005).

Do Followers Resist Leaders?   Some laypersons and experts have suggested that groups function best without leaders—that reliance on a central authority figure weakens the group and robs members of their self-reliance. Some, too, have noted that groups chafe under the control of a leader, for they begrudge the authority and power of the leader (Gemmill, 1986). Yet most people prefer to be led rather than to be leaderless. When in groups, people must often coordinate their actions with those of others in the group, and leaders are often the ones in the group who are responsible for ensuring that harmonization (see Chapter 8). Group members are usually more satisfied and productive when their groups have leaders (Berkowitz, 1953). Group members often complain about the quality of their leaders—surveys that ask employees to identify the worst thing about their job find these complaints tend to converge on the leader—but they seek out better leaders rather than avoiding them altogether (Hogan & Kaiser, 2005). Most people do not just accept the need for a leader but appreciate the contribution that the leader makes to the group and its outcomes (Friedman & Saul, 1991; Stewart & Manz, 1995).

This "need for a leader" becomes particularly strong in groups that are experiencing interpersonal turmoil or stressful, life-threatening circumstances (Goethals & Hoyt, 2011). Individuals who take pride in their independence may find, when difficult circumstances overtake them, that they are relieved to find a leader who is ready to take charge of the group and coordinate its reaction to the threat. Such circumstances can even cause members to see leadership potential in people where none exists. Members of troubled groups, compared to more tranquil groups, exaggerate the potential of possible leaders. They even misremember crucial details, tending to recall their prospective leader as having performed any number of leader-consistent behaviors and forgetting any past behaviors that conflict with their image of the person as a suitable leader. Thus, members do not resist having a leader; instead, they actively create leaders both interpersonally and psychologically (Emrich, 1999).

Do Leaders Make a Difference?   In 1991, Kopp got a job offer. An entrepreneur was starting up a new company devoted to educational reform, and he wanted Kopp to join his staff. What would have happened if Kopp had taken that job? Would TFA be as successful today? Would it even exist at all?

Leaders influence their groups in significant ways. Studies of leaders in all kinds of group situations—flight crews, politics, schools, military units, and religious groups—all suggest that groups prosper when guided by good leaders. Groups, when discussing solutions to problems, tend to spend too much time discussing information shared by many members—unless a leader is present in the group who controls the group's tendency to focus on shared information (Larson et al., 1996). When a company gets a new chief executive officer (CEO), its performance tends to climb (Jung, Wu, & Chow, 2008). Newly appointed leaders who inspire and excite members with fresh ideas and strategies can spur the group on to great achievements and successes (Kaiser, Hogan, & Craig, 2008). Groups, as noted in Chapter 7, often fail to help in emergency situations. But what happens if a leader is present in the group? In one study of the bystander effect, only 35% of the groups helped a person in need, but when the group had a leader, 80% of the groups delivered assistance (Baumeister et al., 1988).

Unfortunately, the difference leaders make is not always a positive one. Leaders sometimes take their group in directions it should not go. They act to promote their own personal outcomes and overlook the good of the group. Leaders manipulate followers, persuading them to make sacrifices, while the leaders enjoy the rewards of their power and influence. They push their agendas too hard, their groups obey their demands, and only later do all realize their mistakes (Schyns & Hansbrough, 2010). Such leaders are influential—but in a negative way.

Do Leaders Make *All* the Difference?   Leaders significantly influence their group's dynamics, but sometimes people think that leaders do *everything*. In Western cultures, in particular, people assume that leaders are so influential that they, and they alone, determine their group's outcomes. This romanticized view of leaders as rescuers and heroes has been aptly termed the **romance of leadership** (Meindl, Ehrlich, & Dukerich, 1985).

---

romance of leadership The tendency to overestimate the amount of influence and control leaders exert on their groups and their groups' outcomes.

This romance of leadership ignores both the limited influence wielded by most leaders and the many other factors that influence a group and its dynamics. When a team fails, those in charge often replace the group's leaders, for they assume that a different leader could have rescued the failing team. When people give all the credit for a group's success to the leader or blame him or her for a failure, they overlook the contributions of the other group members. Leaders like Wendy Kopp are influential, but few leaders deserve all the blame for their group's failures and fewer still are heroes who can fairly claim the lion's share of credit for their group's achievements (Bligh, Kohles, & Pillai, 2011).

What Is Leadership?

Leadership is a complex social process, and, over the years, different people have defined it in very different ways (see Table 9.1). Most of these definitions, however, stress the same themes: influence, relationships, and shared goals. Leadership is not the power to coerce others, an inborn trait, a necessity of group life, or a mysterious capacity to turn foundering groups into effective ones. Instead, leadership is the process by which individuals guide others in their pursuits, often by unifying, directing, coordinating, supporting, and motivating their efforts. These processes are reciprocal, transactional, transformational, cooperative, and adaptive.

- Leadership is a *reciprocal* process, involving the leader, the followers, and the group situation. The leader does not just influence the group members; rather, the leader–follower relationship is mutual. An interactional view assumes that leadership cannot be understood independently of **followership**—the skills and qualities displayed by non-leaders (Hollander, 2006; Messick, 2005).

- Leadership is a *transactional* process in which leaders and followers work together,

followership Working effectively with a leader and other group members.

exchanging their time, energies, and skills to increase their joint rewards (Avolio, 2004).

- Leadership is a *transformational* process, for leaders heighten group members' motivation, confidence, and satisfaction by uniting members and changing their beliefs, values, and needs (Burns, 2003).

- Leadership is a *cooperative* process of legitimate influence rather than sheer power. The right to lead is, in most instances, voluntarily conferred on the leader by some or all members of the group, with the expectation that the leader is motivated by the group's collective needs rather than his or her own interests (Avolio & Locke, 2002).

- Leadership is an *adaptive*, *goal-seeking* process, for it organizes and motivates group members' attempts to attain personal and group goals (Parks, 2005).

A distinction is often drawn between leadership and other forms of influence in groups and organizations, such as management and supervision. Leaders may hold supervisory positions in groups, but holding a position does not always translate into leadership; there are many bosses, supervisors, and managers who are not leaders. Conversely, many individuals in groups and organizations who do not hold formal positions of authority are leaders, for they influence others as they pool their efforts in the pursuit of shared goals (Bedeian & Hunt, 2006; Kotter, 1990; see Mintzberg, 2009 and Rost, 2008 for discussions of issues involved in defining leadership and management).

What Do Leaders Do?

Wendy Kopp, as the leader of TFA, hired personnel and supervised them closely, providing them with feedback about their strengths and weaknesses. She spent much of her time planning and organizing the organization, focusing on both day-to-day operations as well as long-range goals years in the future. She made minor and major decisions every day, from picking furnishings for the offices to the difficult choice of who to let go when the organization

T A B L E   9.1   A Sampling of One Hundred Years of Definitions of Leadership

Decade	Definition
1900s	Leadership is the preeminence of one or a few individuals in a group in the process of control of societary phenomena (Mumford, 1902, p. 221).
1910s	Integrity in personal relations and that broad spirit of fair-mindedness which is back of all enduring cooperation, back of managerial team-work (Merton, 1917, p. 194).
1920s	Leadership is the setting up by one person of unusual or original behavior patterns which are responded to, accepted, adopted by other persons (Bogardus, 1928, p. 573).
1930s	Leadership-followership is a type of interaction which consists of inter-stimulation and inter-response of a leader and one or more followers (Smith, 1935, pp. 350–351).
1940s	That relationship which is characterized by love of the members for the central person, leading to incorporation of the personality of the central person in the ego ideal of the followers (Redl, 1942, p. 576).
1950s	Leadership is viewed as the performance of those acts which help the group achieve its objectives (Cartwright & Zander, 1953, p. 538).
1960s	By leadership behavior we generally mean the particular acts in which a leader engages in the course of directing and coordinating the work of group members (Fiedler, 1967, p. 36).
1970s	Leadership is the reciprocal process of mobilizing persons with certain motives and values, various economic, political, and other resources, in a context of competition and conflict, in order to realize goals independently or mutually held by both leaders and followers (Burns, 1978, p. 425).
1980s	Leadership involves the process of influence between a leader and followers to attain group, organizational, or societal goals (Hollander, 1985, p. 486).
1990s	Leadership is an influence relationship among leaders and followers who intend real changes that reflect their mutual purposes (Rost, 1993, p. 102)
2000s	The ability to motivate, influence, and enable individuals to contribute to the objectives of organizations of which they are members (House, 2004, p. xxii).
2010s	Leadership is the process of influencing others to understand and agree about what needs to be done and how to do it, and the process of facilitating individual and collective efforts to accomplish shared objectives (Yukl, 2013, p. 7).

could no longer afford to pay the salaries of all the staff members. Kopp also represented TFA in dealings with funding agencies and school systems, coordinated the meetings held regularly among the staff, and delivered motivational speeches to the corps members before they began their workshops on teaching skills. Leading, for Kopp, involved a number of interrelated activities, including analyzing, communicating, consulting, controlling, coordinating, deciding, developing, monitoring, negotiating, organizing, planning, representing, supporting, and supervising (Lord, 1977; Mintzberg, 1973).

Leadership's Two Sides: Tasks and Relationships
Wendy Kopp carried out a staggering array of diverse activities as the CEO of TFA, but the **task–relationship model** of leadership assumes that these many and varied behaviors cluster into one of two basic categories described in Table 9.2.

---

task–relationship model A descriptive model of leadership, which maintains that most leadership behaviors can be classified as either performance maintenance or relationship maintenance.

TABLE 9.2   **Task and Relationship Leadership: Definitions, Related Terms, and Sample Behaviors**

Factor	Terms	Sample Behaviors
Task leadership Promoting task completion; regulating behavior, monitoring communication, and reducing goal ambiguity	Task-oriented, agentic, goal-oriented, work facilitative, production-centered, administratively skilled, goal achievement	• Assigns tasks to members • Makes attitudes clear to the group • Critical of poor work • Sees to it that the group is working to capacity • Coordinates activity
Relationship leadership Maintaining and enhancing positive interpersonal relations in the group; friendliness, mutual trust, openness, recognizing performance	Relationship-oriented, communal, socioemotional supportive, employee-centered, relations skilled, group maintenance	• Listens to group members • Easy to understand • Friendly and approachable • Treats group members as equals • Willing to make changes

- *Task leadership* focuses on the group's work and its goals. To facilitate the achievement of group goals, the leader initiates structure, sets standards and objectives, identifies roles and positions members in those roles, develops standard operating procedures, defines responsibilities, establishes communication networks, gives evaluative feedback, plans activities, coordinates activities, proposes solutions, monitors compliance with procedures, and stresses the need for efficiency and productivity (Lord, 1977; Yukl, 2013).

- *Relationship leadership* focuses on the interpersonal relations within the group. To increase socioemotional satisfaction and teamwork in the group, the leader boosts morale, gives support and encouragement, reduces interpersonal conflict, helps members to release negative tensions, establishes rapport, and shows concern and consideration for the group and its members (Lord, 1977; Yukl, 2013).

Different situations require different skills of leaders, but researchers in many countries have repeatedly confirmed this two-dimensional model of leadership behaviors. Although the labels vary—*task-oriented* versus *relational-oriented* (DeRue et al., 2011), *work-facilitative* versus *supportive* (Bowers & Seashore, 1966), *production-centered* versus *employee-centered* (Likert, 1967), *administratively skilled* versus *relations-skilled* (Mann, 1965), and *performance* versus

maintenance (Misumi, 1995)—the two basic clusters emerge with great regularity (Shipper & Davy, 2002). For example, in the Ohio State University Leadership Studies conducted in the 1950s, investigators first developed a list of hundreds of types of behaviors observed in military and organizational leaders—behaviors that included initiating new practices, providing praise, interacting informally with subordinates, delegating responsibilities, representing the group, and coordinating group action. They then refined the list by asking members of various groups to indicate how many of these behaviors their leaders displayed. Using factor analysis, a statistical technique that identifies clusters of interrelated variables, they discovered that 80% of the variability in followers' ratings could be explained by the two basic factors: *task leadership* (initiation of structure) and *relationship leadership* (consideration for group members; Fleishman, 1953; Halpin & Winer, 1952).

Leadership Behavior Description Questionnaire The Ohio State researchers built these two dimensions into their *Leader Behavior Description Questionnaire* (LBDQ). Group members completed the LBDQ by rating their leader on items such as those presented in the right-hand column of Table 9.2; the totals from the two separate sets of behaviors index the two dimensions of leadership specified in the task–relationship model (Kerr et al., 1974; Schriesheim & Eisenbach, 1995).

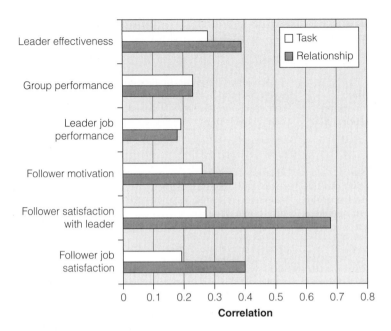

FIGURE 9.1   The relationship between the task-oriented leadership (structuring), relational leadership (support), and leadership outcomes. When researchers used meta-analysis to combine the results of over 320 correlational findings generated in 130 studies of leadership behavior, they found that both facets of leadership predicted critically important leadership outcomes, but that relationship leadership was more closely associated with follower satisfaction (Judge, Piccolo, & Ilies, 2004).

SOURCE: From tabled data in "The forgotten ones? The validity of consideration and initiating structure in leadership research," by T. A. Judge, R. F. Piccolo, & R. Ilies, *Journal of Applied Psychology,* 87, 2004.

People tend to favor one of the two facets when leading groups—some people are naturally task-focused and others are more relational. But as Figure 9.1 illustrates, both facets predict positive leadership outcomes. A meta-analytic review of the responses of over 20,000 people who took part in over 100 studies—many of which made use of the LBDQ to measure leadership—indicates the overall correlation between task leadership and leadership outcomes is .29, and the correlation for relationship leadership is .48. The correlation between relationship leadership and follower satisfaction was particularly strong (r = .68; Judge, Piccolo, & Ilies, 2004; see, too, DeRue et al., 2011).

Leadership Substitutes The task-relationship model assumes that leaders, despite their widely varying methods and styles, tend to do two basic things when they lead others—they coordinate

the work that the group must accomplish and they attend to the group's interpersonal needs. But these two forms of leadership, though commonplace, are not needed in every leadership situation. Kopp, for example, spent much of her time initiating structure: planning, strategizing, organizing, and soliciting funding. She did not need to spend very much time attending to the interpersonal needs of the group members because of the high level of enthusiasm, personal commitment, and cohesion in the group.

The TFA case is consistent with **leadership substitutes theory,** which maintains that *substitutes*

---

leadership substitutes theory A conceptual analysis of the factors that reduce or eliminate the need for a leader (substitutes) or prevent the leader from dispatching his or her responsibilities (neutralizers).

for leadership obviate the need to provide task or relational support to the group members (Kerr & Jermier, 1978). In some cases, something about the group members may reduce their need for task, relational, or both task and relational leadership. For example, experienced, professional, and well-trained members may need little in the way of task leadership. In other cases, aspects of the task and the group or organizational setting may substitute for leadership. If the group is highly cohesive and the members are providing all the support to each other they need, relational leadership becomes less important, just as a task that is highly structured or routine will negate the need for task structuring. In TFA, for example, the staff members were chosen for their commitment to equality in education, and this shared vision served as a substitute for relationship leadership. TFA was not, however, a formally organized group with specified staff functions. Thus, the group responded well to, and very much needed, Kopp's task-oriented approach to leadership (Dionne et al., 2005).

Other features of the members, the task, or the group and organizational setting may work to neutralize leadership. Whereas substitutes take the place of leadership interventions, *neutralizers* interfere with or completely prevent the leader from effectively dealing with the task or relational needs of the group. When members work at extremely simple, boring tasks, even the most energetic and well-meaning leader may be unable to transform the work into an intellectually satisfying experience (Howell et al., 1990).

Do Women Lead Differently Than Men? Leadership has two sides—the task side and the relational side—and humans come in two varieties—man and woman. Do these variations in leadership correspond to sex differences in leadership?

Despite changes in the roles of men and women in contemporary society, when men and women gather in groups, the men tend to be *agentic*—task-oriented, active, decision-focused, independent, goal-oriented—whereas women are more *communal*—helpful to others, warm in relation to others, understanding, aware of others' feelings (Abele, 2003). Women, to speak in generalities, when asked to describe themselves to others in just-formed groups, stress their communal qualities with such adjectives as open, fair, responsible, and pleasant. Men describe themselves as influential, powerful, and skilled at the task to be done (Forsyth et al., 1985). Women, more so than men, engage in relationship maintenance, including giving advice, offering assurances, and managing conflict (Leaper & Ayres, 2007). Women connect more positively to other group members by smiling more, maintaining eye contact, and responding more tactfully to others' comments (Hall, 2006). These differences can be seen in groups of children, with boys undertaking physical activities, competing with one another, and playing in rough ways, and girls carrying out coordinated activities with a minimum of conflict (Maccoby, 2002). These differences may even reflect evolutionary pressures that encouraged the development of communal tendencies in women and task-focused activity in men.

This sex difference is only a tendency; it does not manifest itself across all groups and situations. Kopp, for example, remains a task-focused leader: She is not the type of leader who likes to "walk around, rally the troops, and make sure that everyone was feeling good" (2003, p. 66). Nor does it determine how men and women respond when they become a group's leader. When social psychologists Alice Eagly and Blair Johnson (1990) reviewed more than 150 studies that compared the leadership styles adopted by men and women, they discovered that as the agentic–communal tendency suggests, women performed more relationship-oriented actions in laboratory groups and also described themselves as more relationship-oriented on questionnaires. The sexes did not differ, however, in studies conducted in organizational settings (Dobbins & Platz, 1986). Indeed, as leaders, women tended to be both task-and relationship-oriented, whereas men were primarily task-oriented (Stratham, 1987). Women and men often adopted different styles of leadership, but they did not differ in their agentic and communal tendencies.

LEADERSHIP EMERGENCE

Manet was the leader of the impressionist painters. Fito Strauch took control of the day-to-day activities of the Andes survivors. Jim Jones was the charismatic leader of the People's Temple. John F. Kennedy was elected president of the United States. Wendy Kopp is the CEO of TFA. But why Manet and not Degas? Why Strauch and not Canessa? Why Kennedy and not Nixon? Why did Kopp, armed with just her senior thesis written in her last semester in college, emerge as the CEO of an internationally successful nonprofit organization and remain the leader of that group for all these years? What determines who will lead their groups, organizations, and countries? What determines **leadership emergence**?

Who Will Lead?

You are assigned to a five-person group to complete a project. The group has three weeks to complete its work and each member's performance review will be based on the project's quality. Edna is very familiar with the topic of the project and seems like a hardworker. Frank is very friendly and makes certain everyone is satisfied with the group's decisions. Lamar is the intellectual giant of the group; he rarely speaks, but the things he says are insightful. Rachel typically sits at the head of the table and checks her cellphone frequently. Who would you predict would emerge (excluding yourself) as your group's leader?

Great Leader or Zeitgeist? Scholars down through the centuries have searched for the source of leadership inside of people and in the situations where they lead. In the nineteenth century, for example, the historian Thomas Carlyle (1841) offered up his **great leader theory** of history (Carlyle called it the "great man" theory). He asserted that leaders do not achieve their positions by accident or twist of fate. Rather, these individuals possess certain characteristics that mark them for greatness. Carlyle believed that leaders are unique individuals, and so history could be best studied by considering the contributions of the few great men and women.

The Russian novelist Leo Tolstoy disagreed with Carlyle's great leader theory. To Tolstoy, such leaders as Alexander the Great and Napoleon came to prominence because the spirit of the times—the *Zeitgeist*—was propitious for the dominance of a single individual, and the qualities of the person were largely irrelevant to this rise to power. Tolstoy's **Zeitgeist theory** posited that the conquests and losses of military leaders such as Napoleon were caused not by their decisions and skills but by uncontrollable aspects of the historical situation (Tolstoy, 1887/1952).

These two perspectives—Carlyle's great leader theory and Tolstoy's Zeitgeist approach—continue to shape theoretical analyses of leadership emergence. The great leader theory is consistent with a *trait approach* to leadership, which assumes that leaders possess certain personality traits and characteristics and that these characteristics are responsible for their rise in the leadership ranks. Tolstoy's Zeitgeist view, in contrast, is consistent with *situationism*, which suggests that leadership is determined by a host of variables operating in the leadership situation, including the size of the group, its cohesion, the quality of leader–member relations, and the type of task to be performed.

---

leadership emergence The process by which an individual becomes formally or informally, perceptually or behaviorally, and implicitly or explicitly recognized as the leader of a leaderless group.

great leader theory A view of leadership, attributed to historian Thomas Carlyle, which states that successful leaders possess certain characteristics that mark them for greatness and that such great leaders shape the course of history.

Zeitgeist theory A view of leadership, attributed to Leo Tolstoy, which states that history is determined primarily by the "spirit of the times" rather than by the actions and choices of great leaders.

Traits and Situations Combined: An Interactional Perspective Contemporary theories about leadership, true to Kurt Lewin's (1951) *Behavior = f(P,E)* formula discussed in Chapter 1, integrate the trait approach (*P*) and the situational approach (*E*) by taking an interactional approach to leadership. The approach assumes that traits are not necessarily rigid, inborn qualities of the person, but are in most cases fluid enough to flex to fit the demands of a given situation. Extraversion, for example, is a tendency to act in a gregarious manner, but well-adjusted extraverted people do not strive to connect with others in situations that require minimal interaction among participants (Kiesler, 1991). Different types of leadership situations will also favor individuals with different types of personality traits. If a group is about to disintegrate because of heated conflicts among the members, for example, the effective leader will be someone who can improve the group's interpersonal relations (Katz, 1977). Similarly, if individuals possess skills that facilitate performance on intellectual tasks but undermine performance on artistic tasks, then they are likely to emerge as effective leaders only if the group is working on intellectual tasks (Stogdill, 1974).

The Leader's Personality

Early leadership researchers believed that leaders possessed certain personality traits that set them apart from others. This trait approach, which in its strongest form assumed that some people were natural-born leaders, faded in popularity as researchers reported a series of failures to find any consistent impact of personality on leadership behavior across a wide variety of situations. After conducting hundreds of studies, researchers began to wonder if personality made much of a difference when trying to predict who would emerge as a leader and who would not (Mann, 1959; Stogdill, 1948).

Searching for Leadership Traits In retrospect, this rejection of the trait approach was premature. When researchers used more precise measures of personality, stronger relationships were identified. Table 9.3, for example, samples the results of just a few of the hundreds of studies of the relationship between such personality qualities as assertiveness, authenticity, strength of character, dominance, narcissism, self-efficacy, self-monitoring, and social motivation, and leadership emergence and effectiveness. These studies suggest that the relationship between traits and leadership is strongest for those characteristics that predict stable individual differences in the two core behavioral components of leadership—task-orientation and relationality. Individuals who are dispositionally conscientious, organized, achievement-oriented, and high in self-control are more likely to emerge in situations that favor a task-oriented leader, whereas situations that require a relationally skilled leader favor those individuals with more extraverted, gregarious, interpersonally skilled personalities (DeRue et al., 2011). Researchers also discovered that single traits sometimes said little about emergence, but when they looked at personality profiles that took into account several traits, then clearer patterns emerged (e.g., Zaccaro, Kemp, & Bader, 2004).

More sophisticated research procedures also yielded stronger evidence of the power of personality as a predictor of leadership emergence. Longitudinal and rotational designs proved to be particularly useful, for these types of studies could detect consistencies in leadership tendencies over time and situations. For example, longitudinal studies that measured young adults' personality at age 19 used that information to successfully predict who would occupy a leadership position in their workplace 12 years later (Reichard et al., 2011). Rotational designs separate the causal influence of the person versus the situation by studying individuals as they rotate from one group to another, working on different tasks. Such studies suggest the same individual often emerges as the leader again and again across groups, despite the changes in group composition and the tasks the groups are attempting (Borgatta, Couch, & Bales, 1954; Foti & Hauenstein, 2007).

T A B L E 9.3   A Sampling of Personality Characteristics That Are Reliably Associated with Leadership Emergence

Characteristic	Relationship to Leadership Emergence
Assertiveness	The relationship between assertiveness and leadership emergence is curvilinear; individuals who are either low in assertiveness or very high in assertiveness are less likely to be identified as leaders (Ames & Flynn, 2007).
Authenticity	Individuals who are more aware of their personality qualities, including their values and beliefs and exhibiting less bias when processing self-relevant information, are more likely to be accepted as leaders (Ilies, Morgeson, & Nahrgang, 2005).
Birth order	Those born first in their families and only children are hypothesized to be more driven to seek leadership and control in social settings. Middle-born children tend to accept follower roles in groups, and children born later are thought to be rebellious and creative (Grose, 2003).
Character strengths	Those seeking leadership positions in a military organization had elevated scores on a number of indicators of strength of character, including honesty, hope, bravery, industry, and teamwork (Matthews et al., 2006).
Dominance	Individuals with dominant personalities—they describe themselves as high in their desire to control their environment, to influence other people, and to express their opinions in a forceful way—are more likely to act as leaders in small-group situations (Smith & Foti, 1998).
Five factors of personality	Those who emerge as leaders tend to be more extraverted, conscientious, emotionally stable, and open to experience, although these tendencies are stronger in laboratory studies of leaderless groups (Judge et al., 2002).
Gender identity	Masculine individuals are more likely to emerge as leaders than are feminine individuals (Lord, De Vader, & Alliger, 1986).
Narcissism	Individuals who take on leadership roles in turbulent situations, such as groups facing a threat or those in which status is determined by intense competition among rivals within the group, tend to be narcissistic, arrogant, self-absorbed, hostile, and very self-confident (Rosenthal & Pittinsky, 2006).
Self-efficacy for leadership	Confidence in one's ability to lead is associated with increases in willingness to accept a leadership role and success in that role (Hoyt & Blascovich, 2007).
Self-monitoring	High self-monitors are more likely to emerge as the leader of a group than are low self-monitors, since they are more concerned with status-enhancement and are more likely to adapt their actions to fit the demands of the situation (Bedeian & Day, 2004).
Social motivation	Individuals who are both success-oriented and affiliation-oriented, as assessed by projective measures, are more active in group problem-solving settings and are more likely to be elected to positions of leadership in such groups (Sorrentino & Field, 1986).

Five-Factor Model of Personality and Leadership Statistical advances also provided better tools for testing the strength of relationships, allowing researchers to distinguish between group-level determinants of leadership emergence and personality factors. Meta-analysis also helped researchers sift through all the findings, for this type of review catalogs the results from multiple studies more precisely by using statistics rather than subjective interpretation (Zaccaro, 2007; Zaccaro, Gulick, & Khare, 2008). Figure 9.2, for example, presents the results of one such meta-analytic study of the relationship between the personality traits identified by the five-factor model and leadership. As Chapter 4 explained, the five-factor model identifies five sets of interrelated personality traits: extraversion, agreeableness, conscientiousness, stability (or, its inverse, neuroticism), and openness (see Table 4.1). The two personality traits that correspond to task-orientation and relationality—conscientiousness and extraversion—are the two traits that are correlated at the higher levels with leadership emergence. Openness and emotional stability also predict leadership, although to a lesser degree, leaving only agreeableness as a relatively poor predictor of leadership emergence; leaders, apparently, need not be warm and kind (Hogan, 2005). Note, though, these two caveats. First, studies involving students generally found stronger relationships between personality and leadership emergence than studies of leaders in military, government, and business settings. Second, what predicts leadership emergence may not also predict effectiveness once one has

become a leader. Narcissists, for example, are often selected for positions of leadership, given their outgoing, confident interpersonal styles. However, once they take on the leadership role, their abrasive personal tendencies often cause them to perform poorly as leaders (O'Boyle et al., 2012). Similarly, and as Figure 9.2 indicates, agreeableness did not predict leadership emergence, but it did predict effectiveness—even more so than conscientiousness (Judge et al., 2002).

The Leader's Competencies

Wendy Kopp was fresh out of college when she started TFA and had no experience as an educational professional. However, she knew how to organize people to work together on tasks. In college she was the manager of a staff of 60 working for a nonprofit called Foundation for Student Communications. She was also a quick study. When people describe her, they often start with one word: smart.

Intelligence Leaders tend to be above average in intelligence: The correlation between leadership (both emergence and effectiveness) and intelligence ranges from .25 to .30 across studies, populations, and settings (Stogdill, 1948, 1974). Leaders tend to score higher than average on standard intelligence tests, and they make superior judgments with greater decisiveness. They tend to be knowledgeable both generally and about their particular field, and their verbal skills—both written and oral—are superior relative to non-leaders.

Leaders, however, typically do not exceed their followers' intellectual prowess by a wide margin (Simonton, 1985). Groups generally prefer leaders who are more intelligent than the average group member, but too great a discrepancy introduces problems in communication, trust, and social sensitivity. Although highly intelligent individuals may be extremely capable and efficient leaders, their groups may feel that large differences in intellectual abilities translate into large differences in interests, attitudes, and values. Hence, although high intelligence may mean skilled leadership, a group prefers

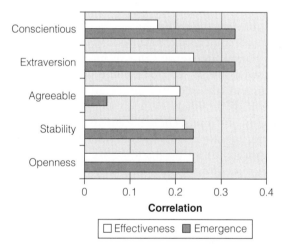

FIGURE 9.2 The relationship between the personality factors identified in the five-factor model of personality and leadership emergence and effectiveness. When researchers used meta-analysis to combine the results of 222 correlational findings generated in 73 samples of the personality–leadership relationship, they found that extraversion and conscientiousness were the strongest predictors of emergence and agreeableness the weakest (Judge, Bono, Ilies, & Gerhardt, 2002).

SOURCE: From tabled data in "Personality and leadership: A qualitative and quantitative review" by T. A. Judge, J. E. Bono, R. Ilies, & M. W. Gerhardt, *Journal of Applied Psychology, 87,* 2002.

to be "ill-governed by people it can understand" (Gibb, 1969, p. 218).

Emotional Intelligence When people think of intelligence, they often stress cognitive abilities such as mathematics, verbal skills, and intellectual problem solving. But some people are also interpersonally intelligent: They have the ability to understand and relate to people, for they deal with others wisely and effectively. They have elevated **emotional intelligence**: "the ability to perceive emotions in self and others; to understand how emotions blend, unfold, and influence cognition and behavior; to use emotions to facilitate thinking; and to manage emotions in self and others" (Joseph & Newman, 2010; Lopes & Salovey, 2008, p. 81).

Skill in communicating and decoding emotions is essential for an effective leader. The emotionally intelligent leader can see problems coming, for such problems are often conveyed indirectly by others' moods and emotions. Better able to read the politics of the situation, such leaders can detect shifting alliances and recognize where to put their energies and when to bide their time. They can also communicate their ideas to others in more robust ways, for they can use their own emotional energy to influence others. They are also less likely to lose control of their emotions—they are not inappropriately angry, critical, or histrionic. In consequence, emotional intelligence is associated with various aspects of leadership, including emergence as a leader, willingness to cooperate with others, empathy for others, the tendency to take others' perspectives, and the emotional intensity of one's interpersonal relations (Goleman, Boyatzis, & McKee, 2002).

Practical and Creative Intelligence During World War II, Germany, America, and England all experimented with various methods for identifying leaders to serve in the military. In many cases they used the so-called leaderless-group tests, in which a group of individuals, strangers to one another, were given a task to complete. For example, a group might be assembled on one side of a ravine and told to use the available boards, ropes, and beams to build a temporary bridge to the other side (Eaton, 1947). Some individuals within these groups could master these tasks by identifying the solution and persuading others in their group to follow their directions. Individuals who succeeded in the leaderless-group tests had *practical intelligence*.

Psychologist Robert Sternberg (2007, 2011) includes practical intelligence as one of the cornerstones of his systems model of leadership. Sternberg recognizes that good leaders are often intellectually strong individuals, capable of acquiring and processing information in a logical, sensible, and rapid way. But leaders are also skilled problem-solvers. They have the "know how" needed for success in the given situation, and they are sufficiently skilled to convince others to follow their recommendations. Sternberg also includes *creative intelligence* in his theory, recognizing that in many cases leaders must be able to recognize future goals and directions and take steps to help the group accept their vision of the future. Wendy Kopp, for example, was not just intelligent in the analytical and practical sense, but also in the creative sense: she recognized the need for an organization like TFA, and she was successful in convincing others to share this vision.

Expertise Practical intelligence comes with experience, and groups are more likely to recognize the leadership potential of one who is experienced rather than inexperienced. One review of 52 studies of characteristics typically ascribed to a leader discovered that technical, task-relevant skills were mentioned in 35% of the studies (Stogdill, 1974). Groups are more accepting of leaders who have previously demonstrated task ability and are more willing to follow the directions of a task-competent person than those of an incompetent person (Goldman & Fraas, 1965; Hollander, 1965). Furthermore, although high task ability facilitates

---

emotional intelligence The component of social intelligence that relates to one's capacity to accurately perceive emotions, to use information about emotions when making decisions, and to monitor and control one's own and others' emotional reactions.

leadership, low task ability seems to be an even more powerful factor in disqualifying individuals from consideration as leaders (Palmer, 1962). Initially, if group members do not know one another well, then they may rely on diffuse status characteristics, such as rank, age, and tenure with the group, to infer expertise, but over time they will shift to specific, behavioral cues to determine who is competent and who is not (Bunderson, 2003). Given enough experience in working together, most group members can distinguish between the skilled and the unskilled (Littlepage, Robison, & Reddington, 1997; Littlepage & Silbiger, 1992).

Field studies of leadership in organizational and military settings suggest that individuals who possess valued skills are more often recognized as leaders. The successful head of the accounting department, for example, is usually recognized as a better accountant than his or her subordinates or other, less highly regarded managers (Tsui, 1984). Studies of ratings of military leadership ability have also found that physical ability and task-performance skills are highly correlated with leadership emergence (Rice, Instone, & Adams, 1984). Particular, task-specific skills are more important in determining leadership emergence in performance-oriented, service–delivery-oriented groups, whereas interpersonal and conceptual skills are more important in upper-echelon leadership positions (Yukl, 2013).

Participation

Individuals with much to offer the group—those who are intelligent, emotionally adept, and highly skilled at the tasks the group must complete—may nonetheless not emerge as a leader if they are disengaged from the group and its activities. Leaders are active within their groups rather than aloof; they show up for meetings, they ask questions, they offer comments and suggestions, they talk to other members on the phone, and they send out e-mails. The correlation between leadership emergence and most personal characteristics usually averages in the low .20s, but the correlation between participation rate and leadership ranges from .61 to .72 (Littlepage & Mueller, 1997; Malloy & Janowski, 1992; Stein & Heller, 1979).

Group members take note of participation rate in part because it tells them who is interested in the group and is willing to take responsibility for its performance. One of the surest ways to escape serving as the leader of a group is to not say much during meetings. But which matters more: quality or quantity of participation? Do people who talk a lot at meetings but add little of substance rise to positions of leadership, or does quality count more: the value of the ideas expressed rather than the volume of one's words?

Some studies support the so-called **babble effect**: The quantity of participation is more important than the quality of the contribution. One study, for example, examined this effect by manipulating both the quantity and quality of the statements of a trained confederate in a problem-solving group. The researchers created four-person groups and set them to work, but one of the group members was a confederate who systematically offered either many comments or few comments that were either high in quality (they promoted success on the tasks) or low in quality (they promoted failure on the tasks). When the participants later rated the confederate's confidence, influence, and contributions, both quantity and quality counted, but the effects due to quantity were still stronger (Sorrentino & Boutillier, 1975).

Other work, however, calls into question the generality of the babble effect. Social psychologists Eric Jones and Janice Kelly (2007) noted that comparing quality to quantity is like comparing apples to oranges. Since they are two different variables that can range in intensity from high to low, comparing their relative impact on leadership requires that they be matched in terms of strength. They therefore conducted a series of studies where they

---

babble effect The tendency for group members who talk at a high rate in the group to emerge as leaders, even if the information they share with the group is of low quality.

pitted quantity against quality, but they first calibrated the strength of these two variables so that each one had a fair chance of overpowering the other one. As in prior research, they created low- and high-quality arguments and low- and high-quantity messages, but they also made sure the high conditions were twice the level of the low conditions for both variables. What they discovered was that quantity did matter, but only if the comments offered were of high quality. People who made low-quality comments during the group discussion received relatively low ratings on leadership potential, even when they offered a substantial number of these comments. Quantity did boost one's leadership ratings, but only if the comments were of high quality. Rationality (quality) trumped babble (quantity), at least in this case.

What Do Leaders Look Like?

When Kopp first met with funders and other experts in education, they often expressed their incredulity, for they did not think that a young woman in her twenties could lead the organization successfully. One executive asked her, point blank, "Who is going to run this?" When Kopp answered that she was, the executive said, "That's just not going to work" (quoted in Kopp, 2003, p. 19). Kopp's qualities were not those that these people expected in a leader, for leadership emergence depends not only on personal qualifications and achievements but also on general demographic characteristics, such as age, race, and sex.

Physical Appearances Leaders tend to differ physically from their subordinates. They are often older, taller, and heavier than the average group member. Ralph Stogdill (1948, 1974), a clinical psychologist who studied leadership for many years, after thoroughly reviewing the relationship between height and leadership, noted that correlations varied from −0.13 to +0.71, but the average was about +0.30. Group members seem to associate height with power, but the relationship is not so strong that height is a prerequisite for leadership.

Leaders also tend to be more physically fit. The smaller a man's waist-to-hip ratio (an indicator of fitness, because those with larger ratios tend to be out of shape), the more others rated him as leader-like when working in leaderless groups that were observed by others (Campbell et al., 2002).

Stogdill found that the link between age and leadership emergence is more complicated. Leaders in informal discussion groups vary in age, whereas political and business leaders are often older than their subordinates. Stogdill suggested that in organizations and political settings, the climb up the ladder of leadership takes time. Fewer than 1% of the corporate executives for the top Fortune 700 companies are under 40 years of age, and 81% are 50 or older (Spencer Stuart, 2004). As Stogdill noted, "Organizations tend to rely upon administrative knowledge and demonstration of success that comes with experience and age" (1974, p. 76). Furthermore, if group members assume that age is an indicator of wisdom, experience, and sagacity, they are likely to prefer a leader who is older rather than younger.

Even hair color predicts who will lead and who will follow. A study of the 500 top CEOs in England discovered fewer blondes and more redheads than might be expected given the distribution of these hair colors in the overall population of the country. The authors suggest that stereotypes about blondes—that they are less cognitively swift—and redheads—that they are mean but competent—may be sufficient to cause their under- and overrepresentation in leadership positions. However, of these 500 CEOs, only two were women, and they both had brown hair (Takeda, Helms, & Romanova, 2006).

Diversity The CEO of TFA (Wendy Kopp) is white, and the majority (65%) of the corps members are white as well. The president of the student government association of Spelman College, which is a traditionally African American school, is a black woman. The executive director of the Organization of Chinese Americans is a Chinese American. The director of the Mexican American Community

Services Agency is a Latino woman. In 2012, how many African Americans were leaders (CEOs) of a Fortune 500 company in the United States? Only six. Only 13 African-Americans have served in that position, total (Isidore, 2012).

Leadership is not limited to any particular cultural, ethnic, or racial group, for the role of leader is firmly embedded in the traditions of African, European, Latino, Asian, and Native American groups (Smith & Bond, 1993). But how do the members of a subculture fare in groups where they are outnumbered by members of another ethnic group?

First, minorities tend to be less influential in heterogeneous small groups and, as a result, are less likely to emerge as leaders (Bass, 2008). For example, when Mexican American and European American women interacted in groups, the Mexican American women exerted less influence than the European American women (Roll, McClelland, & Abel, 1996). In a study conducted in Australia that paired Chinese students with Australian students, the Chinese students were less influential than the Australian students (Jones et al., 1995).

Second, minorities tend to be underrepresented in leadership roles in business and organizational settings (Bass, 2008). Only two African Americans have been elected as state governors (Douglas Wilder of Virginia and Deval Patrick of Massachusett), and Barak Obama was the first African American U.S. president. African Americans in U.S. organizations and military groups are less likely to lead in racially diverse groups, even if their experience qualifies them for these roles (Molm, 1986; Webster & Driskell, 1983). When senior managers review the leadership potential of lower-level managers, they give higher marks to European Americans than to African Americans and Asian Americans (Carton & Rosette, 2011; Landau, 1995). Asian Americans, despite their success in scientific and technical fields, are less likely than European Americans and African Americans to achieve positions of leadership in their fields (Tang, 1997). Ethnic and racial minorities are underrepresented in the leadership world (Hooijberg & DiTomaso, 1996; Scandura & Lankau, 1996).

Sex Kopp, as both a woman and a leader, is something of an exception. Although the gender gap in leadership has narrowed in recent years, it has not closed. Both men and women, when surveyed, express a preference for a male rather than a female boss (Eagly & Carli, 2007). Women receive lower evaluations and fewer promotions than men, even when actual performance data or behaviors are held constant (Heilman, Block, & Martell, 1995). A recent survey of over 40 countries, including Austria, Israel, and Singapore, indicated that women hold 20% to 30% of the governmental, legislative, and managerial positions in those countries (Schein, 2007). The percentage has risen steadily over the years, but men still hold a near monopoly on high-level leadership positions (Carli & Eagly, 2011). In 2012, only 18 women (3.6%) were the CEOs of Fortune 500 companies. Female managers are more likely to feel excluded from career-related and informal interactions with senior managers than are male managers (Cianni & Romberger, 1995), and some have also expressed less confidence in their leadership abilities (Watson & Hoffman, 1996). The term *glass ceiling* describes the hidden situational and interpersonal factors that prevent women from gaining leadership positions.

This gender difference also shapes men's and women's actions in small-group settings. Men are five times more likely to enact leadership behaviors than women in small, mixed-sex, leaderless groups and so are more likely to emerge as leaders (Walker et al., 1996). Both leaders and subordinates perceive female leaders to be less dominant than male leaders (Carli, 2001). The lone man in an otherwise all-female group often becomes the leader, whereas the lone woman in an otherwise all-male group has little influence (Crocker & McGraw, 1984). When a woman exerts influence in a group, members tend to frown and tighten their facial muscles; but when a man takes charge, members are more likely to nod in agreement (Butler & Geis, 1990). The tendency for men to dominate women in informal discussion groups was observed even when the men and women were all deemed to be androgynous (Porter et al., 1985), when group members were personally committed to equality for men and women (Sapp, Harrod, & Zhao, 1996), when the women in the group were dispositionally more dominant than the men (Megargee, 1969; Nyquist & Spence, 1986), and when the men and women were equally extraverted (Campbell et al., 2002). When researchers paired together a person who tended to be interpersonally powerful with one who was more submissive, the dispositionally dominant person emerged as the leader in 73% of same-sex dyads. But in mixed-sex dyads, the dominant man became the leader 90% of the time, and the dominant woman became the leader only 35% of the time (Nyquist & Spence, 1986).

This tendency for men to emerge as leaders more frequently than women is particularly ironic because studies of sex differences in the qualities that have been shown to predict leadership effectiveness—extraversion, conscientiousness, skill in working with others, acknowledging the good work of subordinates, communicating clearly, and facilitating others' development—all suggest that women are superior in these qualities to men.

Hence, although women's personality traits and competences qualify them to be leaders, they are less likely to gain such positions (Eagly, Johannesen-Schmidt, & van Engen, 2003).

THEORIES OF LEADERSHIP EMERGENCE

Leadership emergence in small groups isn't an erratic phenomenon, for leaders differ, physically and psychologically, from their subordinates. They tend to be older, taller, and heavier than the average group member. They are generally more accomplished at the tasks facing the group, and they tend to talk more than the average member. Leaders are outgoing rather than shy, and dominant rather than submissive. Leaders, too, are more often men rather than women and more likely masculine than feminine in their sex-role orientation. But why do these factors influence people's choices of leaders?

FIGURE 9.3 A representation of the associations that make up an implicit leadership theory.
SOURCE: © Cengage Learning 2014

Implicit Leadership Theory

When people meet for the first time, they quickly appraise one another's potential as leaders, and, within the first few minutes, those with more potential are permitted to exert more influence over the group than others. **Implicit Leadership Theory** (ILT), developed by social psychologist Robert Lord and his colleagues, traces these preferences to individuals' expectations, beliefs, and assumptions about leaders and leadership. These cognitive structures are termed **implicit leadership theories** or *leader prototypes*. These structures are described as *implicit* because they are not overtly stated; followers may not even be aware they have intuitive beliefs about leadership or that these beliefs influence their reactions to leaders. They are called *theories* because, like formal theories, they include generalities about leadership and hypotheses about the qualities that characterize most leaders (Lord, Foti, & De Vader, 1984; Lord & Maher, 1991).

Consider the hypothetical ILT shown in Figure 9.3. A follower whose thoughts about leadership were organized by this ILT would believe that outstanding leaders should be intelligent, inspirational, visionary, relational, dedicated, team-oriented, diplomatic, and have integrity. This ILT also indicates how these general traits are linked to more specific qualities. How do you know if a leader is dedicated? See if he or she is hard-working and knows how to get things done. And what about inspiration? An inspiring leader should be motivating, dynamic, positive, and encouraging. Although each group member may have a unique

conception of leadership, most people's ILTs include task skills—the leader should be active, determined, influential, and in command—and relationship skills—the leader should be caring, interested, truthful, and open to others' ideas, (Epitropaki & Martin, 2004; House et al., 2004). ILTs are also sensitive to the specifics of a given situation. Some leadership traits, such as persistence, likeability, and charisma, are considered to be essential qualities only in particular contexts, such as politics, business, or sports (Lord et al., 1984). As Focus 9.1 explains, ILTs are also sometimes unique to a specific culture. A person who would be recognized as a leader in one culture may not match the expectations of followers in another.

The Prototype-Matching Hypothesis Lord suggests that ILTs provide followers with a psychological standard or *prototype* they can use to distinguish between effective and ineffective leaders and leaders and followers (Lord, 2005; Lord & Maher, 1991). If, for example, a follower thinks that a leader should be bold, energetic, and daring, then she will likely rate a gung-ho leader more positively than a low-key consensus builder. In contrast, if the follower believes that a leader should be considerate and reflective, then he will respond more positively to one who shows concern for others and deliberates extensively before making a decision. To test this *prototype-matching hypothesis*, Lord and his colleagues (1984) asked people to evaluate one of three hypothetical leaders. One, the prototypical leader, displayed qualities that were congruent with most people's ILTs: He set goals, provided directive information, talked with subordinates a great deal, and identified problems needing solutions. The second leader displayed qualities that were inconsistent with most ILTs; he admitted mistakes, he paid little attention to details, was critical without reason, and withheld rewards. A third leader displayed positive qualities that were neither consistent nor inconsistent with most ILTs. This leader sought out information, clarified his attitudes, and prevented conflicts. As the prototype-matching hypothesis predicts,

---

implicit leadership theory A cognitive explanation for leadership emergence that assumes members' implicit expectations and assumptions about leaders influence their appraisals of the leadership potential of other group members (developed by Robert Lord and his colleagues).

implicit leadership theories Group members' taken-for-granted assumptions about the traits, characteristics, and qualities that distinguish leaders from the people they lead; also known as leader prototypes.

the prototypical leader was judged to be more effective than the atypical leader, with a match to ITL explaining the majority of the variance in leadership evaluations.

Biases and Errors ILTs help followers to sift through and organize a welter of information about current or future leaders, but they provide this service at a cost. If individuals' ILTs are based on factors

---

Focus 9.1   Cross-cultural Perspectives: The GLOBE Studies of Leadership

Most countries have a word for someone who guides the group—in England, *leader*; in Spain, *el líder*; in the Netherlands, *leider*; in Germany, *leiter* (and not *führer*). But all concepts—motherhood, compassion, friendship, law, and freedom—have different shades of meaning depending on place, people, and era, so a person who grew up in the United States and one from Mozambique who both declare "I am an outstanding leader" may be making very different claims.

To study how people think about leaders in countries across the world, management scholar Robert J. House and his colleagues (2004) launched the highly ambitious Global Leadership and Organizational Behavior Effectiveness (GLOBE) Program in 1992. The project itself was an example of strong teamwork and leadership. House assembled a core group of experts, who worked with research teams located in 62 countries. The GLOBE researchers, drawing on previous studies of leadership, developed a set of items to give respondents who were to indicate if these qualities were those that inhibit, or contribute to, a person being an outstanding leader. The list included mostly behavioral and trait items, such as autocratic, intuitive, trustworthy, and collaborative, and was translated to the language of each country, usually by a professional translator. The items were then translated back into English by a second party to verify that the translated term matched the meaning of the original English word.

To be certain that the findings they obtained were not caused by differences in the background and experiences of the individuals within each country—its findings would be difficult to interpret if, for example, the survey was completed by mostly college students in one country but military officers in another—the researchers asked over 17,000 managers in 951 businesses in financial services, food processing, and telecommunication industries to complete the survey. The participants were also asked to describe the values of the organization where they worked and the country where they lived. These data were then examined to identify those leadership qualities and cultural values that were shared within an organization or country. Items only made it to the list of a culture's beliefs

about leadership if a significant majority of the individuals in the survey from that country agreed with each other on the relative importance of the item. In terms of level of analysis, this step shifted the data from the individual level to the group level.

The GLOBE project yielded a wealth of information about leadership and its cultural specificity. Table 9.4, for example, summarizes just a small portion of the study's findings. It indicates that leadership is not just a process common to all cultures, but that people worldwide also share some basic beliefs about leadership. People expect leaders to be diplomatic, moral, charismatic (inspirational and visionary), and team-oriented, as well as dependable, intelligent, decisive, and administratively skilled. Those qualities that were considered to be most undesirable in a leader were those associated with a lack of integrity, self-centeredness, and asocial tendencies (Dorfman, Hanges, & Brodbeck, 2004).

In addition to these universal qualities, the GLOBE researchers also identified leadership qualities that were unique to a specific country or world region. Whereas most people surveyed expected effective leaders to be visionary and team-focused, some cultures stressed these qualities more than others. Highly collectivistic societies, for example, favored charismatic leaders more so than more individualistic cultures. Cultures that displayed higher levels of gender egalitarianism stressed participative, team-focused leadership. Those individuals who lived in cultures marked by hierarchical power structures and greater levels of elitism were more tolerant of self-centered leaders who were status-conscious and formalistic. The GLOBE researchers also discovered that certain specific traits were highly valued in some cultures but seen as harmful to leadership in others. Even such questionable qualities as risk-taking, cunning, elitism, micromanagement, and willfulness were viewed as positive qualities in some cultures. Given these findings, the GLOBE researchers recommend those who lead multicultural teams should remember that not everyone in the group will value all forms of leadership similarly (Dorfman et al., 2004).

Focus 9.1   (Continued)

TABLE 9.4   Shared Conceptions of Leaders Identified by the GLOBE Study of Sixty-Two Different Countries

Leadership Dimension	Leader Attribute Questionnaire Items
Diplomatic: skilled at interpersonal relations, tactful	• *effective bargainer*: able to negotiate effectively • *win/win problem solver*: able to identify solutions that satisfy individuals with diverse and conflicting interests
Integrity: moral respectability	• *trustworthy*: deserves trust, can be believed and relied upon to keep his or her word • *just*: acts according to what is right or fair • *honest*: speaks and acts truthfully
Inspirational: inspires others to be motivated to work hard	• *encouraging*: gives courage, confidence, or hope through reassuring and advising • *positive*: generally optimistic and confident • *dynamic*: highly involved, energetic, enthused, motivated • *motive arouser*: mobilizes and activates followers • *confidence builder*: instills others with confidence by showing confidence in them • *motivational*: stimulates others to put forth efforts above and beyond the call of duty and make personal sacrifices
Team-oriented: interpersonal and organizational skills	• *communicative*: communicates with others frequently • *informed*: knowledgeable; aware of information • *coordinator*: integrates and manages work of subordinates • *team builder*: able to induce group members to work together
Visionary: vision and imagination of the future	• *foresight*: anticipates possible future events • *plans ahead*: anticipates and prepares in advance
Other qualities	• *dependable*: reliable • *intelligent*: smart, learns and understands quickly • *decisive*: makes decisions firmly and quickly • *administratively skilled*: able to plan, organize, coordinate, and control work of large numbers of individuals • *excellence-oriented*: strives for excellence in performance of self and subordinates

SOURCE: Adapted from TBL21.2 (p. 677) in Dorfman, P. W., Hanges, P. J., & Brodbeck, F. C. (2004). Leadership and cultural variation (669–719). In R. J. House, P. J. Hanges, M. Javidan, P. W. Dorfman, & V. Gupta (Eds.), *Culture, leadership, and organizations: The GLOBE study of 62 societies.* Thousand Oaks, CA: Sage.

that are irrelevant to successful leadership—such as skin color or sex—then people will sometimes see leadership when none actually exists and overlook leadership when they do not expect it. When voters must select a leader, they sometimes fall prey to the *Warren Harding Effect*; they think a handsome candidate has great leadership potential, even when he is thoroughly incompetent (Gladwell, 2005). If members are satisfied with a leader, they may attribute characteristics to him or her that are consistent with their ILT, but inconsistent with the leader's actual qualities. ILTs can even bias memories, for people remember their favored leaders acting in ways that confirm their ILTs, even when the leader performed no such action (Foti & Lord, 1987). If their group or organization performs poorly, members are quicker to blame the leader for the failure if he or she has ITL-inconsistent qualities (Ryan et al., 2011).

The biasing influence of ILTs on followers' perceptions and evaluations of leaders may also explain continuing sex differences in leadership. If ILTs were like actual scientific theories, then group members would discard them when they fail to explain who is and who is not an effective leader. But ILTs, because they are *implicit* theories, are rarely recognized or revised. In consequence, if individuals' ILTs are biased in favor of individuals who are white, masculine, tall, or just highly vocal, then members with these qualities will rise to positions of authority in the group, even if they are not qualified for these positions (Forsyth & Nye, 2008).

Social Identity Theory

Social psychologist Michael Hogg and his colleagues believe that social identity processes influence a wide range of leadership processes, including who the group selects to be their leader. They theorize that individuals who identify with their group include in their self-definition—their social identity—qualities that they share in common with other group members. They also develop an idealized image of the prototypical member of the group, similar to an ILT, and over time consensus will emerge on these characteristics. Applied to leadership, social identity theory predicts that when group members share a social identity, they will favor individuals in the group who best represent that identity. For example, groups that prize cooperation and sensitive communication among members should favor relationship-oriented leaders, whereas groups of individuals who pride themselves on their action and productivity will support task-oriented leaders (Hogg, 2010; Haslam, Reicher, & Platow, 2011).

Prototypicality and Identity The leader's prototypicality is particularly important for group members who strongly identify with their group. If, for example, the group is newly formed or members are not committed to continuing in the group, they are less likely to base their leadership preferences on prototypicality. But "as group membership becomes more important to self-definition and members identify more strongly with the group, leaders who are perceived to be more group prototypical" are more likely to emerge and be effective as leaders (Hogg, 2010, p. 1195). In a test of this hypothesis, Hogg and his colleagues formed ad hoc groups in the laboratory and appointed one member as leader of each group. They manipulated the psychological salience of the groups by telling some members that everyone in the group shared certain qualities, whereas others were told the groups were just loose aggregations with no commonalities. They also circulated within the group some background information about the leader to indicate that he or she matched the fictitious group prototype or did not match it. As predicted, group members who identified with the group were more positive about the prototypical leader (Hains, Hogg, and Duck, 1997).

Leadership in Intergroup Situations Social identity theory also suggests that people will favor individuals who not only exemplify the group, but also those with qualities that demonstrate what makes the group different from, and superior to, other groups. In general, members expect their leader to champion the ingroup and its unique strengths. In consequence, leaders who, during intergroup conflict, make conciliatory gestures toward the outgroup may lose the support of their own group. A skilled leader, recognizing this appeal, may use self-presentational strategies to lay claim to qualities that are prototypical ones for the group and to bolster their popularity by creating conflicts with, and denigrating, other groups (Haslam et al., 2011). Those who convince the other group members that they are "one of us," while at the same time offering a unique and socially desirable vision of the group's future, are particularly likely to be endorsed by group members (Halevy, Berson, Galinsky, 2011).

Social Role Theory

Alice Eagly's **social role theory**, like ILT and social identity theory, suggests that group members have definite expectations about what kind of qualities are needed in a person who will fill the role of leader. These expectations tend to emphasize the agentic, task-oriented side of leadership rather than the communal and interpersonal. When group members are asked to describe the qualities needed in a leader, they stress the importance of competition with peers, high energy, dominance, forcefulness, and skill at taking command and controlling a situation (Eagly & Karau, 2002).

These expectations, however, favor men relative to women as leaders. Although gender stereotypes vary across time and place, people in virtually all cultures, when asked to describe women, speak of their expressive qualities, including nurturance, emotionality, and warmth. They expect a "she" to be sentimental, affectionate, sympathetic, soft-hearted, talkative, gentle, and feminine. When describing men, they stress their instrumental qualities, including productivity, energy, and strength (Williams & Best, 1990). In consequence, the expectations associated with leadership mesh with the male gender role stereotype, but the leadership role is inconsistent with stereotypes about women (Forsyth, Heiney, & Wright, 1997). When people think "leader," they think "male" (Koenig et al., 2011; Schein, 2007).

This *role incongruity* not only disqualifies women from taking the lead in groups, but it also creates a double standard for women once they achieve a position of leadership. Women, to be evaluated as positively as men, must outperform men. When Eagly and her colleagues reviewed 61 different studies that asked people to evaluate the performance of male and female leaders, they found that the behaviors and outcomes achieved by men were viewed more positively than the exact same outcomes achieved by women (Eagly, Makhijani, & Klonsky,

1992). Ironically, this bias reaches its peak when a female leader adopts a more task-oriented approach to leadership. In a classic example of a "Catch-22," women are urged to act more like male leaders, but when they do, they are denigrated for not being "ladylike" (Hoyt, 2010; Rudman & Glick, 2001). Caught in this double-bind, women respond by avoiding the role of leader, by underperforming as leaders due to the pressure of the negative stereotypes, or by actively resisting the stereotypes and doing what they can to invalidate members' negative expectations (Hoyt & Chemers, 2008).

Terror Management Theory

The idea that people are drawn to powerful leaders for less than rational reasons is consistent with **terror management theory (TMT).** This theory assumes that humans, perhaps uniquely, are aware that someday their earthly existence will come to an end. This awareness of one's inevitable demise, if cognitively inescapable, would be the source of continuous existential anguish, so the human mind has developed defenses against thoughts of death. TMT suggests, for example, that culture diminishes this psychological terror by providing meaning, organization, and a coherent worldview. Self-esteem and pride, too, function to elevate one's sense of worth and serve as a defense against the intrusive thoughts of death (Greenberg, Solomon, & Pyszczynski, 1997).

TMT explains why the popularity of a leader often grows, exponentially, during times of tumult and crisis. The theory, as an explanation of leadership emergence and endorsement, suggests that followers will show a marked preference for strong, iconic leaders when their mortality is made salient to them. After the terrorist attacks on the United States in 2001, for example, U.S. citizen's approval ratings of then-president George W. Bush jumped from 40% to 50% to 90%. TMT suggests that the attack made citizens aware of their mortality and also threatened their worldview. Bush, by

---

social role theory A conceptual analysis of sex differences that recognizes men and women take on different types of roles in many societies and that these role expectations generate gender stereotypes and differences in the behavior of women and men (proposed by Alice Eagly).

---

terror management theory (TMT) A conceptual analysis of the implicit psychological processes thought to defend individuals from the emotionally terrifying knowledge that they are mortal and will someday die.

promising to find the terrorists responsible for this horrible action and bring them to justice swiftly, provided an antidote to their existential concerns.

Researchers have put TMT to the test by reminding some people of their mortality and then assessing their preferences for different types of leaders (Cohen et al., 2004, 2005; Landau et al., 2004). One study, for example, compared preferences for three candidates for political office.

- The *task-oriented leader* stressed setting difficult but achievable goals, strategic planning, and initiating structure.

- The *relationship-oriented leader* communicated compassion, respect, trust, and confidence in others.

- The *charismatic leader* spoke of long-term goals, the unique value of the nation, and working together.

Before evaluating these candidates, participants in the mortality-salience condition were reminded of their eventual demise in a not-so-subtle way: They were asked to describe the emotions that the thought of their own death aroused in them and to write down what will happen to them, physically, when they die. Those in the control condition were asked parallel questions, but about their next exam rather than their death. The results indicated that, in the control condition, people were more positive toward the task- and relationship-oriented leaders relative to the charismatic one. Conversely, in the mortality-salience condition, ratings of the charismatic leader climbed and ratings of the relationship-oriented leader dropped. The task-oriented leader was the most favorably rated in both conditions (Cohen et al., 2004). Other research finds that, as social role theory might suggest, individuals reminded of their mortality prefer as their leaders (a) members of their own group, or (b) men rather than women (Hoyt, Simon, & Reid, 2009).

Evolutionary Theory

Charles Darwin's theory of evolution explains why humans, who are autonomous, self-reliant animals, are so often willing to turn over some of the control

of their lives to someone else. Could both following and leading be evolutionary adaptations that are characteristics of the fittest?

Leadership as an Adaptation Evolutionary psychology suggests that leadership is an *adaptation*: a heritable characteristic that developed in a population over a long period of time. Adaptations enhance individuals' fitness, for they increase the chances of their genetic material being represented in future generations of the species. Leadership and followership, as adaptations, evolved because they contributed so substantially to the survival of human beings in the *environment of evolutionary adaptation* (EEA). For much of their evolutionary past, humans likely lived in relatively small groups, or tribes, of genetically related individuals. These groups moved in search of water and food and in response to seasonal and climate changes. Like most ground-dwelling primates (gorilla, baboons, chimpanzees), such groups required coordinated movement (King & Cowlishaw, 2009). The leader was, quite literally, the individual who guided the group from one place to the next. But in time the role of leader expanded as the leader's facilitative impact on coordinated movement extended to coordination in general. A leader made plans and recruited other members to put them into effect, made decisions about alternative courses of action that were available to the group, quelled conflict that could undermine the group's unity, and stepped forward when the group confronted danger (Johnstone & Manica, 2011).

Leadership and Dominance Evolutionary theory does not consider leadership to be the same as a dominance contest, where the strongest member of the group—most likely a male—bests all others in the group through force. Leadership benefited both those who led and those who followed, for in scarce resource environments competition among members, struggles for dominance, and uncoordinated defensive and domestic activities were deadly to all. The anthropologist Napoleon Chagnon's (1997) description of the leadership processes in the Yanomamö illustrates the coopted, rather than contested, nature of leadership in early groups. The leadership among the Yanomamö was not based on heredity or physical strength, but rather on record of service to the village. Leaders gained some special rewards for themselves and their kin, but they frequently proved their worth to the entire group by settling arguments, planning the group's hunting activities, seeking out connections with other villages, and providing for the defense of the village. This final responsibility put the leader at risk in many cases, for the Yanomamö are known as the "fierce people"—neighboring villages are in a constant state of war with each other.

Mismatch Hypothesis Evolutionary theory maintains that the adaptive advantages of leadership are achieved only if the group selects the most qualified individual to lead. In consequence, over time humans developed the mental apparatus needed to evaluate those who sought the position of leadership, so, even in modern times, people instinctively favor certain leaders over others. Followers, for example, recognize that leaders may be tempted to use their position of authority to maximize their self-interests, so they monitor their leaders closely and are quick to detect evidence of bias or unfairness (Smith, Larimer, et al., 2007). Their preference for older, more experienced, and those who are both task and relationally skilled may also be genetically prescribed.

These tendencies, however, evolved in human groups that existed in an EEA that differed in dramatic ways from the groups and communities where humans currently live. As a result, the psychological and interpersonal reactions of both followers and leaders are influenced by genetic tendencies that are not as behaviorally adaptive as they were in earlier evolutionary contexts. Social and evolutionary psychologist Mark Van Vugt and his colleagues term this possibility the *evolutionary mismatch hypothesis* (Vugt & Ahuja, 2010; Van Vugt, Hogan, & Kaiser, 2008). This mismatch may, for example, cause people to prefer men as leaders in political contexts. Van Vugt and his colleagues reasoned that humans do not consistently favor males over females, but moderate their

choices depending on the situation. They suggest that groups, for millennia, relied on male leaders to lead their groups when they confronted other rival tribes. These same groups, however, relied on women leaders to make certain that the relations within the group were strong and that any intragroup conflicts were minimized so that the group's cohesion was not damaged. In their research, they supported this hypothesis by finding that individuals playing an investment-type game preferred a woman as leader during intragroup competition, but a man as leader during intergroup competition. In further work, people tended to prefer more masculine-looking leaders in situations involving intergroup conflict (Spisak et al., 2012; Van Vugt & Spisak, 2008).

LEADER EFFECTIVENESS

Alexander the Great controlled a huge empire without any modern means of transportation or communication. General George S. Patton inspired those under his command by displaying high levels of personal confidence, sureness, and an immense strength of character. Wendy Kopp built TFA from the ground up and steered the company through a period of organizational and funding nightmares. Alexander, Patton, and Kopp are not simply leaders. They are *effective* leaders. But what is the key to their effectiveness?

Fiedler's Contingency Model

Industrial/organizational psychologist Fred Fiedler spent years studying groups that worked to achieve collective goals under the direction of an appointed, elected, or emergent leader. He focused his attention on groups that generated products and performances that could be evaluated, and he measured aspects of the groups' settings and their leaders to see what combinations consistently led to good results. His basic conclusion was that a leader's effectiveness cannot be predicted just by considering the leader's qualities. Nor can it be predicted on the basis of the situation. Rather, Fiedler's **contingency theory** assumes that leadership effectiveness is contingent on both the leader's motivational style and the leader's capacity to control the group situation (Fiedler, 1964, 1978, 1996).

Motivational Style Consistent with the task-relationship model of leadership, Fiedler suggests that leaders naturally tend to adopt one of two leadership styles, which he measured using the **Least Preferred Coworker Scale (LPC).** Respondents first think of the one individual with whom they have had the most difficulty working at some time. They then rate this person, dubbed the *least preferred coworker*, on bipolar adjective scales such as "pleasant–unpleasant," "friendly–unfriendly," and "tense–relaxed." People with high scores on the LPC are assumed to be relationship-oriented; after all, they even rate the person they do not like to work with positively. Low LPC scorers are assumed to be task-oriented.

Situational Control Just as leadership style is the key *personal* variable in contingency theory, control is the key *situational* factor in the model. If leaders can control the situation, they can be certain that decisions, actions, and suggestions will be carried out by the group members. Leaders who have trouble gaining control, in contrast, cannot be certain that the group members will carry out their assigned duties. As Figure 9.4 indicates, leader control is determined by the quality of leader–member relations, the degree of task structure, and the

---

contingency theory Any theory that suggests a leader's effectiveness is contingent on situational factors; usually used in reference to Fred Fiedler's conceptual analysis of leadership, which posits that a leader's success is determined by his or her leadership style and the favorability of the group situation; more generally, any analysis of leadership that suggests that the effectiveness of leaders depends on the interaction of their personal characteristics and the group situation.

Least Preferred Coworker Scale (LPC) An indirect measure of the tendency to lead by stressing the task (low LPC) or relationships (high LPC) (developed by Fred Fiedler).

leader's position power. Octant I in the chart is the most favorable setting—leader–member relations are good, the task is structured, and the leader's power is strong. Octant VIII is the least favorable situation, for all three variables combine in a group that is difficult for the leader to control.

Predicting Leadership Effectiveness Fiedler did not believe that either type of leader—task-motivated or relationship-motivated—is better overall. Instead, he predicted that task-oriented leaders (low LPC score) would be most effective in situations that are either highly favorable or highly unfavorable, whereas relationship-oriented leaders (high LPC score) would be most effective in middle-range situations. If, for example, Kopp is a low-LPC leader (task-motivated), she will get the most out of groups in Octants I, II, and III where situational favorability is high, as well as in Octant VIII, the least favorable situation. Were she a high-LPC leader, her groups would perform best in the middle-range situations—Octants IV to VII. Why? Fiedler suggested that in difficult groups (Octant VIII), task-motivated leaders drive the group toward its goals, but relationship-motivated leaders spend too much time repairing relations. In highly favorable (Octants I through III) situations, in contrast, task-oriented leaders become more considerate, yielding a more satisfied workgroup.

Studies of a variety of working groups support the complex predictions charted in Figure 9.4 (Ayman, Chemers, & Fiedler, 2007). For example, when Fiedler (1964) studied antiaircraft artillery crews, he measured both the commander's leadership style (high or low LPC) and the favorability of the situation. In most crews, the leaders enjoyed a strong position of power because their authority was determined by rank. Moreover, task structure was high because the same sequence of decisions had to be made for each target. In some crews, however, the commander was well liked—placing the crew in the most favorable situation (Octant I), whereas, in other crews, the commander was disliked (Octant V). Thus, a low-LPC leader should be more effective for Octant I crews, but groups in Octant V should perform better with a high-LPC

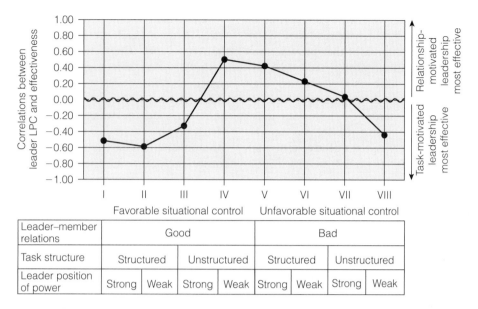

Leader–member relations	Good				Bad			
Task structure	Structured		Unstructured		Structured		Unstructured	
Leader position of power	Strong	Weak	Strong	Weak	Strong	Weak	Strong	Weak

FIGURE 9.4 Fiedler's contingency model of leadership. The theory assumes that effectiveness depends on three aspects of the group situation: leader–member relations, task structure, and the leader's position of power. Octant I corresponds to the most controllable and favorable situation, and Octant VIII corresponds to the least controllable and least favorable setting. The vertical axis indicates the predicted relationship between LPC scores and task performance. If the correlation is greater than 0 (positive), effectiveness is positively related to LPC; that is, relationship-motivated leaders are more effective. If the correlation is smaller than 0 (negative), effectiveness is negatively related to LPC; task-motivated leaders are more effective. The graph suggests that a task-oriented leader is more effective when the situation is favorable (Octants I, II, and III) or unfavorable (Octant VIII) for the leader.

SOURCE: Adapted from "The Contingency Model and the Dynamics of the Leadership Process." *Advances in Experimental Social Psychology*, Volume 11, 1978, Pages 59–112, by Fred E. Fiedler. Adapted by permission of Elsevier.

leader. Supporting this prediction, Fiedler (1955) found that LPC scores were negatively correlated with effectiveness for artillery squads in Octant I ($r = -0.34$) but positively correlated with effectiveness in Octant V ($r = 0.49$).

The effectiveness of a unique leadership training program, called *Leader Match,* also supports the validity of contingency theory. Although many different programs and techniques have been developed to train leaders, the results of these procedures are typically disappointing (Stogdill, 1974). Fiedler, however, suggested that these programs fail because they place too much emphasis on changing the leaders—making them more supportive, more decisive, more democratic, and so on. He suggested instead that the situation should be engineered to

fit the leader's particular motivational style. He called his training program *Leader Match* because he taught trainees to modify their group situation until it matched their personal motivational style (Fiedler, Chemers, & Mahar, 1976). Studies of the effectiveness of this innovative training program suggest that trained leaders outperform untrained leaders, although degree of improvement depends on who is doing the evaluations (Burke & Day, 1986; Taylor, Russ-Eft, & Taylor, 2009).

Questions and Conclusions Contingency theory, like all theories, has both weaknesses and strengths. Despite years of research, experts are divided on the model's validity, with some arguing that evidence supports the model and others arguing against it (see Chemers, 1997, for a review). Investigators have challenged not only the strength of the relationships that provide the basis of the predictions in the eight octants in Figure 9.4, but they have also questioned the methods that Fiedler used to measure leaders' motivational style. In defense of contingency theory, however, the contingency model was one of the first theories of leadership effectiveness that fully considered both personal factors (LPC score) and situational factors (situational control). Few would dispute its key take-home message—that the effectiveness of a leader cannot be predicted without taking into account both the leader's perceptions of his or her followers and the leader's degree of control in the situation (Chemers, 2000; Rice, 1979). The work also led Fiedler to examine how leaders respond to stressful leadership settings (Fiedler, 1986).

Style Theories

Fiedler's contingency model assumes that leaders have a preferred "style" of leading: Some tend to be relationship-oriented leaders and others are task-oriented leaders. Many other leadership theories accept this basic premise, but add that some leaders integrate both task and relationship elements in their approach to leadership. These style theories argue that effective leaders balance these two basic ingredients in the groups they lead (see Bass, 2008, for a review).

The Leadership Grid Psychologist Robert Blake and management expert Jane Mouton hypothesized that leadership style depends on how one answers two basic questions: (1) How important is the production of results by the group? (2) How important are the feelings of group members? To some leaders, the key goal is achieving results. For others, positive feelings in the group are so important that they emphasize teamwork and personal satisfaction. Others may feel that both of these goals are important (Blake & McCanse, 1991; Blake & Mouton, 1964, 1982).

Blake and Mouton summarized these differences in their **Leadership Grid** (formerly called the *Managerial Grid*), which is presented in Figure 9.5. Both dimensions—concern for people and concern for results—are represented as 9-point scales ranging from *low concern* to *high concern*. Although a person's orientation could fall at any of 81 possible positions on the grid, Blake and Mouton emphasized the five located at the four corner positions and the center. An apathetic, impoverished 1, 1 leader is hardly a leader, for he or she is not interested in subordinates' feelings or the production of results. The 9, 1 individual (high on concern for production, but low on concern for people, located in the lower right corner of the grid) is a taskmaster who seeks productivity at any cost. The 1, 9 leader, in contrast, adopts a "country club" approach that makes subordinates feel comfortable and relaxed in the group. The "middle-of-the-roader," located at 5, 5, tries to balance both performance and morale but sometimes sacrifices both when results and individuals' feelings come into conflict. Finally, the 9, 9 leader highly values both people and products and therefore tackles organizational goals through teamwork—"a high degree of shared responsibility, coupled with high participation, involvement, and commitment" (Blake & Mouton, 1982, p. 41).

Blake and Mouton (1982) were not contingency theorists; they felt that the 9, 9 leadership style was the most effective style overall. In their initial studies, they found that managers who adopted the 9, 9 styles were far more successful in their careers than managers who adopted other methods. They also noted that studies conducted in educational, industrial, and medical organizations supported the utility of the 9, 9 leadership style, as did the favorable results of their management training system. These results are impressive, but many

---

Leadership Grid A theory of management and leadership assuming that people vary in their concern for results and their concern for people and that individuals who are high on both dimensions (9,9) are the best leaders (developed by Robert Blake and Jane Mouton).

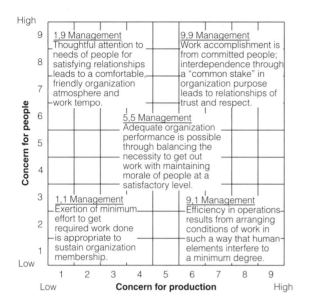

High

experts still question their strong claim that the 9, 9 style works in *all* situations.

Situational Leadership Theory Management experts Paul Hersey and Kenneth Blanchard also described leadership in terms of the relationship and task dimensions. Unlike Blake and Mouton's grid, however, their **situational leadership theory** suggests that effective leaders combine supportive behaviors with directive behaviors depending on the developmental level, or *maturity*, of the group or subordinate. Mature individuals or groups are those that are committed to the group and its task, and they are usually confident, self-assured, and highly motivated. Maturity is also related to

competence, for mature members possess the skills and knowledge needed to perform their assigned tasks, perhaps because they have been trained or because they have experience (Hersey & Blanchard, 1976, 1982; Hersey, Blanchard, & Johnson, 2001).

The theory recommends that leaders start with a task-focused, directive style. When group members are low in both commitment and competence, they work most effectively with a *directing* leader who is not supportive (S1). As the group develops and gains experience on the task and commitment to the group's goals, the leader can increase relationship behavior and adopt a *coaching* style (S2; high direction and support). Still later in the group's development, the leader can ease off on both types of leadership, starting first with direction. In moderately mature groups, the *supporting* leader is most effective (S3), and in fully mature groups, a *delegating* leadership style is best (S4). Thus, an effective leader must display four different leadership styles as the group moves through its life cycle—directing, coaching, supporting, and delegating (Hersey et al., 2001).

Some critics have argued that situational leadership theory puts too much emphasis on matching the maturity of the members; these experts call for a careful balancing of task and relationship orientation at all developmental levels (Vecchio, Bullis, & Brazil, 2006). But the basic premise on which the model rests—that different groups need varying amounts of task and relationship leadership—is consistent with research findings. One of the key sources of leadership success is flexibility in providing to the group more or less relational support and task-orientation, depending on the group's needs (Zaccaro, Foti, & Kenny, 1991). Newly hired employees, for example, need and appreciate greater task structuring from their manager than do veteran employees (Vecchio, 1987). Conversely, members with higher levels of education and greater levels of job tenure may prefer a leader who provides less task structure (Vecchio & Boatwright, 2002). The theory's training methods and measures are also very popular among business professionals. Situational leadership theory forms the basis for the "one-minute management" approach to leadership in organizational settings (Blanchard & Johnson, 1981).

situational leadership theory A theory of leadership suggesting that groups benefit from leadership that meshes with a group's stage of development (developed by Paul Hersey and Kenneth Blanchard).

Leader–Member Exchange Theory

Most theories of leadership, such as Fiedler's (1978) contingency theory and Blake and Mouton's (1982) Leadership Grid, focus on the leader's style or strategy and how the group responds as a whole to various interventions. But such a "one size fits all" approach does not always match the needs of specific group members. Whereas one group member may work well with a task-oriented leader, others may prefer a leader who provides them with support.

Leader–member exchange theory (LMX theory) uniquely stresses the quality of the one-to-one relationship between a leader and a subordinate. LMX theory (and its predecessor, *vertical dyad linkage theory*) notes that leaders have *dyadic* relationships with each group member and that these *dyadic* relationships may be substantially different within the total group. Some leaders may work well with only a subset of the group members who are more engaged in the group and its tasks. Other group members, however, may not respond as positively to the leader, so their responses are defined by their role and their fixed responsibilities (Dansereau, Graen, & Haga, 1975; Graen & Uhl-Bien, 1995).

LMX theory suggests that group members tend to cleave into subgroups within the overall group. One group, the *ingroup*, or *inner group*, includes those individuals with positive linkages to the leader. Leaders spend more time working with these members, value their inputs more, and also provide them with more resources. These group members respond by working harder for the group, taking on additional role responsibilities, and declaring their loyalty to the leader and the group. They are less likely to leave the group and more likely to earn higher performance evaluations,

get promoted more rapidly, express more commitment to the organization, voice more positive attitudes about their work and the group, and garner more attention and support from their leader. They often view their relationship with their boss as a *partnership*. The second group, the *outgroup*, or *outer group*, includes individuals with less satisfying linkages to the leader. These individuals do their work, but do not contribute as much to the group. They also express less loyalty and support for the leader (Dienesch & Liden, 1986).

LMX theory's basic assumptions have been verified empirically (Dulebohn et al., 2012; Gerstner & Day, 1997; cf. Schriesheim, Castro, & Cogliser, 1999). Researchers have documented the natural tendency for subgroups to develop within groups and for disparities in performance to exist between these two cliques (Bass, 2008). Those who enjoy a positive LMX are more likely to do things that benefit their group and organization. These *organizational citizenship behaviors* include helping other group members, common courtesy, job dedication, civic virtue, supporting organizational changes, and so on (Ilies, Nahrgang, & Morgeson, 2007). Individuals who are not satisfied with their LMX tend to perform more poorly, but the strength of this relationship depends, in part, on the degree of differentiation within the group. In undifferentiated groups, there is little variation in LMX—no ingroup and outgroup at all. In highly differentiated groups, in contrast, the LMX relation varies substantially from one member to the next; there are those who work well with the leader and those who do not. Such variation can lead to dissatisfaction, overall, since it is inconsistent with principles of fairness and equal treatment (Hooper & Martin, 2008). Therefore, leaders who recognize this tendency can improve their overall relations with their group by minimizing the number of people in the outer group (Graen & Uhl-Bien, 1991). However, some research suggests that differentiation can be motivating. In such groups, low LMX members recognize that they may, through hard work, meet the leader's standards, for they view the leader as a discriminating judge of group members

---

leader–member exchange theory A dyadic, relational approach to leadership assuming that leaders develop exchange relationships with each of their subordinates and that the quality of these leader–member exchange (LMX) relationships influences subordinates' responsibility, decision influence, access to resources, and performance.

(Liden et al., 2006). LMX also provides a way of understanding the unique demands a leader faces when working with online groups, since the leader-member relation may be more prominent in this environment than member–member relations. In consequence, "for those who work in a virtual mode extensively, a high quality LMX relationship becomes especially instrumental to enhancing their organizational commitment, job satisfaction, and work performance" (Golden & Veiga, 2007, p. 79; see Focus 9.2).

LMX theory's dyadic approach—stressing the relationship between each member and the leader—also provides an additional way of looking at leadership in general. Researchers have returned to other leadership theories, such as Fiedler's contingency model, and have begun to explore the type of leadership style that leaders use with each group member. These dyadic-level approaches add a second layer of information about leadership to the more common group-level analysis (Yammarino & Dansereau, 2008; Yammarino et al., 2005).

Focus 9.2   E-groups: E-leadership in Online Groups

A well-received manual for leadership from the 1950s (Heyel, 1949) offered hundreds of excellent suggestions for working with people in groups, including modeling the skills needed for the work to be done, delivering lectures on "fatigue, personal hygiene, safety, production theory, and other topics" (p. 200), maintaining "at all times the dignity of ... authority" (p. 210), and working "out a simple, short, clear code of social behavior" (p. 214). But, as groups have moved from shared physical locations to multiple locations linked by various telecommunication technologies, the work of the group leader has changed as well. Leadership in online groups—**e-leadership**—requires unifying, directing, coordinating, supporting, and motivating group members as they pursue individual and collective goals, but these functions must be fulfilled at a distance rather than through face-to-face interaction (Avolio, Walumbwa, & Weber, 2009; Hoyt, in press).

Surveys of e-groups and their goals suggest that some of these groups succeed, but others are often significant failures. One team of eight volunteers in the United States and England worked for months planning an international conference for their professional association. They completed dozens of complicated, interrelated tasks that required careful sequencing and execution (May, Carter, & Dewey, 2002). But another virtual team, working in Australia developing a software program for data archiving and analysis, had less luck pulling their product together. This group relied on technology to bridge two subgroups that were collocated, but the two halves of the

group were unable to coordinate their activities, and the result was a product that was delivered late and did not meet performance standards (Jarman, 2005). Another team of engineers who worked with no face-to-face meetings whatsoever developed the full design specifications for a new thrust chamber for a rocket engine that far exceeded the development goals set by their company's executives (Majchrzak et al, 2000).

When these cases were examined to identify what went right and wrong, the definitive determinants of a satisfactory outcome were the decisions, interventions, and choices of the groups' leaders. Leaders must monitor the work of the group, intervene to help if progress is too slow, and provide accurate feedback about performance, but e-leaders must learn how to "observe" the group's work virtually. They must, for example, require more frequent progress reports from members, but they also should make use of the electronic footprints the members leave behind as they interact with one another. If individuals rarely post messages to the group's discussion board, e-mail only occasionally, and never post to a threaded discussion relevant to their area of expertise, a corrective intervention may help to increase the members' level of engagement (Malhotra, Majchrzak, & Rosen, 2007).

Task structuring is also particularly important in e-groups, since individual members are less able to examine the relationship between their individual activities and the group's overall purposes. In the conference-planning group, for example, the e-leader (who was also a volunteer) organized the various tasks that had to be completed into "blocks" of work, and

---

e-leadership Leading individuals in multiple locations through the use of such telecommunication technologies as teleconferencing, Internet communication, and file-sharing systems.

asked members to take responsibility for working on a particular block. This method increased the members' motivation to complete their assigned tasks successfully and also improved the leader's ability to monitor progress. This method increased camaraderie, as well, for members took to calling each other "blockheads" (May et al., 2002). When people who worked in virtual teams were asked to identify behaviors that were particularly important for leaders to perform, they stressed "setting clear tasks for team members," "ensuring a common understanding of the tasks," "stimulating information sharing," and setting forth "clear role definitions" (Zimmermann, Wit, & Gill, 2008, p. 328).

Virtual work groups also require the investment of more time in developing connections to individual group members (Golden & Veiga, 2008). Although some technologies can be used to hold meetings with multiple parties synchronously—ranging from multi-party videoconferencing and online live-narrated presentations to avatar-based meetings in virtual worlds—e-leaders often spend much of their time in one-to-one correspondence with group members.

When 20 e-leaders who had worked with e-groups for an average of eight years or more were surveyed, they stressed building strong dyadic relationships with their followers as critical for reducing the negative interpersonal side effects of working with others across distances. As one leader explained, "I build trust among team members by getting to know each one as an individual. I like to find out their strengths and build on those and find out their weak points and work on those" (Van Pelt, 2009, p. 70).

More sophisticated technologies, however, may not necessarily ease the demands of leading an e-group. Most virtual teams rely heavily on e-mail for communication, and, while some augment this relatively ancient form of communication with more sophisticated technologies, these technologies are useful only because they serve the basic purposes of helping group members exchange information, form relationships with each other, make decisions, and coordinate activities. Technology should serve the group, rather than the group serving the technology (Lee-Kelley & Sankey, 2008).

Participation Theories

Some leaders do all the leading—they, and they alone, make decisions, dole out assignments, supervise work quality, communicate with other groups, set goals, and so on. Such leaders adopt a *command-and-control* leadership style; they give the orders and subordinates carry them out. Other leaders, however, share their leadership duties with the group members. Kopp, for example, set the general goals for TFA, but she expected the other staff members and recruiters to make choices, create structures, and recommend changes in procedures. She adopted a *participatory leadership style*.

Autocratic versus Democratic Leadership Kurt Lewin and his colleagues Ronald Lippitt and Ralph White conducted one of the earliest laboratory studies of interacting groups to determine the relative effectiveness of a democratic, group-centered approach to leadership versus an autocratic,

leader-centered approach. As mentioned briefly in Chapter 2, they arranged for groups of 10- and 11-year-old boys to meet after school to work on various hobbies. In addition to the boys, each group included a man who adopted one of three leadership styles (Lewin, Lippitt, & White, 1939; White & Lippitt, 1960, 1968):

- The *authoritarian*, or *autocratic*, leader took no input from the members in making decisions about group activities, did not discuss the long-range goals of the group, emphasized his authority, dictated who would work on specific projects, and arbitrarily paired the boys with their work partners.

- The *democratic* leader made certain that all activities were first discussed by the entire group. He allowed the group members to make their own decisions about work projects or partners and encouraged the development of an egalitarian atmosphere.

The *laissez-faire* leader rarely intervened in the group activities. Groups with this type of atmosphere made all decisions on their own without any supervision, and their so-called leader functioned primarily as a source of technical information.

In some cases, the boys were rotated to a different experimental condition so they could experience all three types of participation.

The three types of leadership resulted in differences in efficiency, satisfaction, and aggressiveness. As Figure 9.6 indicates, the groups in the study reacted to the autocratic leader in one of two distinctive ways. Some groups accepted the leader's control and became very submissive. Although these groups became aggressive if the autocratic leader was replaced with a more permissive one, when he was present, the group members worked hard, demanded little attention, only rarely engaged in horseplay, and closely followed his recommendations. Several other groups with an autocratic leader, in contrast, rebelled aggressively against the leader's control. These groups were as productive as the democratically led groups if the leader was present (see "work" in Figure 9.6), but once the leader left the room, productivity dropped significantly. Members of groups with an autocratic leader displayed greater reliance on the leader, expressed more critical discontent, and made more aggressive demands for attention. Democratic groups tended to be friendlier and more group-oriented. Overall, the boys preferred democratic leaders to the other two varieties.

These findings suggest that, at least in terms of productivity, a directive, autocratic style can be as effective as a participatory, democratic style. In terms of interpersonal relations and member satisfaction, however, the democratically led groups were superior to all others. These findings also indicate that the laissez-faire leadership climate—group anarchy—was the least effect in both task and relational terms. These groups were unproductive, disorganized in their activities, and prone to loafing. As a methodological aside, the

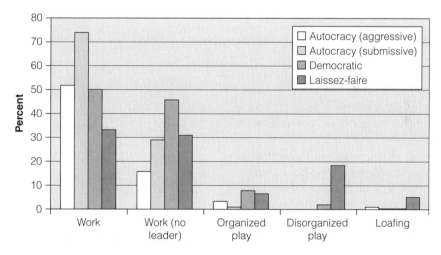

FIGURE 9.6 The results of Lewin, Lippitt, and White's 1939 study of authoritarian, democratic, and laissez-faire leaders. The investigators identified four different "leadership climates" in the groups they studied: autocracy with aggression, autocracy with submissiveness, democratic, and laissez-faire. The autocratic and democratic leaders were more productive than the laissez-faire groups, but the autocratic groups were less productive when the leader left the room. Other findings suggest that the democratic groups were more cohesive.

SOURCE: From tabled percentages reported in "The 'social climate' of children's groups," by Ronald Lippitt and Ralph K. White. In Roger G. Barker, Jacob S. Kounin, and Merbert F. Wright (Eds.), *Child behavior and development: A course of representative studies.* (pp. 485–508). New York: McGraw-Hill.

findings should also be interpreted with caution because the laissez-faire condition was not originally included when Lewin and his team designed the study. But when one of the experimenters was unable to enact the democratic style correctly and instead just distanced himself from the groups, the investigators relabeled the leadership style he used as laissez-faire leadership (White & Lippitt, 1960, p. 21).

Shared Leadership Lewin, Lippitt, and White's (1939) findings suggested shared leadership is as effective as centralized leadership. Such decentered leadership models go by many names—co-leadership, collective leadership, democratic leadership, delegated leadership, empowerment, peer leadership, self-leadership, shared leadership, team leadership, and participatory leadership—but underlying these various models is a common emphasis on breaking the leader's monopoly on power, influence, and authority in the group and distributing responsibility for core leadership functions to all the group members (Pearce & Conger, 2003).

When people think about leadership, they tend to assume that it is concentrated in a single position rather than distributed across a group (Seers, Keller, & Wilkerson, 2003). In consequence, groups sometimes move away from shared leadership to more vertical forms of leadership—with an up-down form of organization rather than side-to-side and up-and-down (Pearce, Conger, & Locke, 2008). However, if the members' reactions to their work are a key factor in maintaining and evaluating success, a participatory approach will be superior to a more leader-centered method (Levin, 2006; Miller & Monge, 1986). As Stogdill (1974) noted after reviewing more than 40 studies of various leadership methods that ranged along the participation continuum, satisfaction with the group seems to be highest in democratic groups, as opposed to autocratic and laissez-faire groups. Shared methods of leadership are also more effective in smaller rather than in larger groups and are well-suited to organizations that rely on small, self-directed teams or networks of distributed, relatively independent employees (Vroom & Mann, 1960). Groups often

share leadership when making decisions and when organized to function as a team; we will reexamine issues related to participatory leadership in Chapters 11 (Decision Making) and 12 (Teams).

Followership Theory If leadership is not concentrated in a single person but shared across the group, then knowing who is in the group becomes as important as knowing who leads it. Even though group members are often described with words that lack the potency of the word *leader*—they are *followers*, *subordinates*, *assistants*, or merely *reports*—the group depends as much on the actions of those who accept others' influence as it does on those who provide guidance and direction.

But just as bad leaders are mixed with the good ones, so followers vary in their effectiveness. Robert Kelley (1988, 2004), an organizational researcher and consultant who has closely examined the nature of followership, asks two basic questions about followers: Are they active or passive, and are they independent or dependent? First, the best followers are committed to the group and their role within it; they are actively engaged in their work rather than passive and withdrawn. Second, effective followers can be self-reliant, when necessary. By definition, they follow the leader, but they must also be able to exercise their independence and monitor themselves and their progress. Ineffective followers are overly dependent on the leader, and they are unable to think for themselves. Kelley, by considering these two aspects of followers—the degree of active engagement and independence—identifies five types of followers:

- *Conformist followers* (yes people) are active and energized, but they are devoted to the leader; they do not think to question the leader's directions and will defend him or her vigorously.

- *Passive followers* (sheep) follow the lead of others, but without great enthusiasm or commitment. They put time into the group and will eventually finish their assignments, but they must be continually monitored or they will simply stop contributing.

- *Pragmatic followers* are the rank-and-file members of the group; they are not clearly active, passive, conforming, or independent, but make up the group's basic, and essential, workforce.

- *Alienated followers* are not committed to the group or its goals, in part because they steadfastly maintain their independence from others' influence. They are often sullenly silent, but when they speak they are critical of their fellow members for remaining true to the group, and they question the leader's choices. They often think of themselves as the rightful leader of the group and refuse to invest in the group or its activities until they are accorded their rightful position.

- *Exemplary followers* (stars) are actively engaged in the group, but they do not simply do what they are told. If they have issues with the leader's position, they express their dissent openly, but constructively. The leader can delegate responsibilities to them, and they can be trusted to complete the task with an enthusiasm that springs from their concern for the group's interests.

The leader's task, suggests Kelley (1988, 2004), is to transform the followers into exemplary followers, using any means possible. Groups with "many leaders," he concludes, "can be chaos. Groups with none can be quite productive" (1988, p. 148)—so long as these followers are exemplary ones who are actively engaged in their work, treat one another as colleagues, and engage in constructive debate with their leaders.

Transformational Leadership

Wendy Kopp is no ordinary CEO. She does not just set goals and plan future initiatives, but she inspires, excites, and captures the imaginations of those who work for her. When she spoke to the first group of future teachers at the start of their summer training, she inspired them with her vision of their work and their future. TFA's mission: "One day, all children in this nation will have the opportunity to attain an excellent education" (Kopp, 2003, p. 185).

Leaders, as we have seen in this chapter, contribute substantially to their groups by structuring and facilitating the completion of tasks and also by providing members with relational support. But leaders also face a third set of responsibilities: planning and making possible changes. The leader who maintains the group's status quo is a good leader, but an excellent leader will elevate the group. Kopp, for example, is not content with merely making certain TFA functions smoothly; she seeks to change the people who work in TFA, the teachers who join her corps, the school systems where the teachers are placed, and America itself. She focuses on change or, more precisely, transformation: She seeks to elevate herself, her followers, her organization, and even society. Kopp is a transformational leader.

Charismatic Leadership and Change Early theory pertaining to transformational leaders focused on their charismatic qualities. Such leaders, like Kopp, through the force of their personality, their spoken words, and their dynamic presentational style, profoundly affect others. Max Weber (1921/1946), as noted in Chapter 8, used the word *charisma* to describe such leaders, for they seem to possess a "divinely inspired gift" that sets them apart from other, more commonplace leaders. Charismatic leaders inspire others, often by expressing ideas that are both appealing and easily understood. They tend to act in ways that provide their group members with a model that they can emulate (Conger, 2011).

But it was political scientist James McGregor Burns (1978) who set forth the basic assumptions of the transformational approach to leadership in his book *Leadership*. Burns argued that most leaders engage primarily in what he called **transactional leadership.** The follower and the leader cooperate with one another in the pursuit of a shared goal, but their relationship is based on the exchange of

---

transactional leadership A traditional form of leadership that involves contributing time, effort, and other resources in the pursuit of collaborative goals in exchange for desired outcomes.

resources that can include time, money, help, and instruction. Transactional leadership "occurs when one person takes the initiative in making contact with others for the purpose of an exchange of valued things" (Burns, 1978, p. 19). It is "pursuit of change in measured and often reluctant doses" (Burns, 2003, p. 24). The only thing that unites the leader and follower are the resources that are exchanged. In contrast, **transformational leadership** "occurs when one or more persons *engage* with others in such a way that leaders and followers raise one another to high levels of motivation and morality" (1978, p. 20, italics in original). Burns believed that transformational leaders not only change their groups, organizations, and societies, but they also transform themselves and their followers.

Measuring Transformational Leadership   Industrial and organizational psychologist Bernard Bass (1997), drawing on Burns's work, identified the components of both transactional and transformational leadership and contrasted these two methods with laissez-faire leadership. Most leaders, Bass suggests, are transactional: They define expectations, offer rewards, "formulate mutually satisfactory agreements, negotiate for resources, exchange assistance for effort, and provide commendations for successful follower performance" (Bass, 1997, p. 134). Transformational leaders, however, go beyond rewards and punishments. These leaders tend to be self-confident and determined, and their communications with their followers are usually eloquent and enthusiastic (Yammarino & Bass, 1990). In contrast to both transactional and transformational leadership, some leaders adopt a passive/avoidant, or laissez-faire, style. They point out members' failings or ignore problems until they become dire.

Bass and his colleagues developed the *Multifactor Leadership Questionnaire* (MLQ) to measure these key components of transformational leadership

(Avolio and Bass, 1995; Bass, 1997). As summarized in Table 9.5, transformational leadership includes four basic components: the so-called 4Is of idealized, inspirational, intellectual, and individualized consideration. Transformational leaders stand for something and make their position clear to others in the group. They challenge others to join them in their pursuit of exciting endeavors, but at the same time, they provide each member with individualized support and consideration. They are, in a word, charismatic.

The MLQ also includes, however, measures of two other approaches to leadership: transactional leadership and passive (or avoidant) leadership (see Table 9.5). Transactional leadership is more routine, traditional leadership, for it involves monitoring members' behaviors, providing them with rewards and corrections as needed, and stepping in only when errors have occurred (management by exception). Passive leadership does not, in many cases, even qualify as leadership, for the so-called leader is so uninvolved with the group and its members that he or she does not meet the role requirements of a "leader."

Both transactional and transformational leaders are more effective than passive leaders, but groups working with transformational leaders often achieve the best results of all. A meta-analytic review of 87 studies concluded that transformational leadership was more strongly associated with followers' job satisfaction, satisfaction with the leader, motivational levels, performance quality, and ratings of the leader's effectiveness than transactional leadership—although transactional leadership predicted these positive outcomes as well. Passive forms of leadership were unrelated to these outcomes or were negatively related (Judge & Piccolo, 2004). Meta-analysis also suggests that women tend to be more likely to use transformational styles of leadership, whereas men are more likely to enact laissez-faire and transactional styles (Eagly et al., 2003; Eagly & Johnson, 1990). Cross-cultural research supports Bass's (1997) belief that the transactional–transformational distinction applies across all world cultures. Last, confirming the

---

transformational leadership An inspirational method of leading others that involves elevating one's followers' motivation, confidence, and satisfaction, by uniting them in the pursuit of shared, challenging goals, and changing their beliefs, values, and needs.

TABLE 9.5   The Multifactor Leadership Questionnaire

Transformational Leadership	
Idealized influence	Expressing one's conviction clearly and emphasizing the importance of trust; taking stands on difficult issues and urging members to adopt their values; emphasizing the importance of purpose, commitment, and the ethical consequences of decisions.
Inspirational motivation	Articulating an appealing vision of the future; challenging followers with high standards, talking optimistically with enthusiasm, and providing encouragement and meaning for what needs to be done.
Intellectual stimulation	Questioning old assumptions, traditions, and beliefs; stimulating in others new perspectives and ways of doing things, and encouraging the expression of ideas and reasons.
Individualized consideration	Dealing with others as individuals; considering individual needs, abilities, and aspirations; listening attentively and furthering individual members' development; advising, teaching, coaching.

Transactional Leadership	
Contingent rewards	Providing rewards to followers contingent on performance, recognizing achievements, and providing direction and positive feedback; defining expectations, arranging mutually satisfactory agreements, and negotiating for resources.
Management by exception (active)	Supervising followers' performances and intervening if they detect failures to reach goals or maintain standards.

Avoidant/Passive Leadership	
Passive management by exception	Being uninvolved in the group activity until a serious problem occurs; not taking action until mistakes are brought to their attention.
Laissez-faire	Do not accept responsibility for the leadership role; often absent when needed; ignoring their followers' requests for help; not making their views and values known to others. According to Bass, these individuals are not leaders.

SOURCE: Paraphrased from B. M. Bass (1997). Does the transactional-transformational leadership paradigm transcend organizational and national boundaries? *American Psychologist, 52,* pp. 133–134.

idea that "there is nothing so practical as a good theory" (Lewin, 1951, p. 169), leadership training programs based on the model have also proven to be a relatively effective means of improving performance in businesses and other organizations (e.g., Dvir et al., 2002).

The Future of Leadership

The future promises many changes in the nature and application of leadership principles. As organizations continue to become more decentralized—flatter rather than hierarchical—leadership methods will likely shift from leader-centered approaches to group-centered ones. Also, the increase in the use of information technologies likely will also change the way leaders interact with their followers, as traditional forms of leadership give way to new forms of e-leadership (Avolio et al., 2009; Coovert & Burke, 2005). Increases in diversity across groups will also create challenges for leaders, particularly if they must adapt their methods and style to match the varied needs of heterogeneous work groups (Klein et al., 2011). Leaders of the future will not only be leading individuals, but also the many subgroups that exist within their groups and organizations (Pittinsky, 2010).

The future may see increased numbers of women rising to positions of leadership in groups and organizations. As noted earlier, male and female leaders differ to a degree in their basic approaches to leadership, but the sexes are equivalent when it comes to providing members with task-orientation and relational support (Eagly, Karau, & Makhijani, 1995). However, given that women tend to be participative and transformational leaders rather than autocratic, laissez-faire, and transactional leaders and given that these styles are more effective methods of leadership, as prejudicial biases give way to fairer promotional practices, the Wendy Kopps of the world will become the standard rather than the exception.

CHAPTER REVIEW

What is leadership?

1. Contrary to common myths, leadership is not power over group members and members do not resist the influence of effective leaders.

   - Certain personality variables are associated with effective leadership, but leadership is not a fixed, inborn trait. Only 30% of a person's leadership tendencies are heritable.

   - Not all groups have leaders, but as groups increase in size and complexity, most select someone to lead.

   - Most people prefer to be led rather than to be leaderless.

   - Leaders make a difference, for groups prosper when guided by good leaders.

   - People sometimes assume that leaders are so influential that they, and they alone, determine their group's outcomes. This tendency is termed the *romance of leadership*.

2. *Leadership* is the process by which an individual guides others in their pursuits, often by organizing, directing, coordinating, supporting, and motivating their efforts. This process can be characterized as reciprocal, transactional, transformational, cooperative, and adaptive. *Followership*, in contrast, is the process of interacting—usually in a positive, cooperative way—with a leader.

3. The *task-relationship model* identifies two basic sets, or clusters, of leadership behavior:

   - Task leadership focuses on the group's work and its goals.

   - Relationship leadership focuses on the interpersonal relations within the group.

   - The Ohio State University Leadership Studies identified these clusters, and the *Leader Behavior Description Questionnaire* (LBDQ) assesses both task and relationship leadership.

4. *Leadership substitutes theory* suggests that certain features of the members and the situation can fulfill critical interpersonal and task functions and so reduce the need for a leader (substitutes). Other factors (neutralizers) interfere with leadership.

5. Men tend to be more agentic and task-oriented in groups, whereas women are more communal and relationship-oriented. The sexes differ only negligibly, however, in their emphasis on task versus relationship leadership when they occupy positions of leadership.

Who will emerge as a leader?

1. Paralleling Carlyle's *great leader theory* and Tolstoy's *Zeitgeist theory,* early analyses of *leadership emergence* adopted either a trait model or a situational model. Most modern theories are interactional models that base predictions on the reciprocal relationships among the leader, the followers, and the nature of the group situation.

2. Early researchers questioned the strength of the relationship between personality and leadership, but more recent, and more sophisticated, analyses indicate personality does predict leadership tendencies.

- Improved research procedures, such as longitudinal and rotational designs, have provided clearer evidence of personality's influence on leadership.

- All the trait clusters in the five-factor model of personality are related to leadership emergence and effectiveness.

3. Certain competencies are associated with leadership emergence.

   - Groups prefer leaders who are somewhat more intelligent than the average group member.

   - *Emotional intelligence* is related to leadership emergence and effectiveness.

   - Sternberg's systems model of leadership stresses the importance of practical and creative intelligence.

   - Emergent leaders are generally more experienced.

   - People who speak more in groups are likely to emerge as leaders (*the babble effect*), although work by Jones and Kelly suggests that quality of comments is more influential than sheer quantity.

4. Leadership is also associated with demographic variables.

   - Leaders tend to be older, taller, and heavier than the average group member.

   - Ethnic minorities and women are less likely to be selected as leaders in groups. The term *glass ceiling* suggests hidden situational and interpersonal factors prevent women from gaining leadership positions.

   - The bias against women is ironic because, in general, women possess more of the skills needed to be a successful leader.

Why do some lead and others follow?

1. Lord's *implicit leadership theory* is based on the idea that individuals' beliefs about what qualities they expect in a leader—their *implicit leadership theories*—influence their perceptual and cognitive reactions to leaders and potential leaders.

   - Most ILTs include task and relationship qualities.

   - The GLOBE studies, conducted by House and his colleagues, identified a number of common elements in ILTs worldwide, including diplomatic, moral integrity, charismatic (inspirational and visionary), and team-oriented.

   - The prototype matching hypothesis suggests that individuals prefer leaders who match their ILTs, but ILTs can distort members' perceptions of and reactions to their leaders.

2. Hogg's *social identity theory* predicts that leader endorsement depends on leader prototypicality and the members' social identity.

3. Eagly and her colleagues' *social role theory* maintains that stereotypes of sex roles and leadership roles can create negative expectations for women leaders.

4. *Terror management theory* suggests that individuals may have a deep-seated need for leaders, particularly in times of crisis, when mortality is salient.

5. Evolutionary theory suggests that leadership is an evolutionary adaptation that improves the fitness of both leaders and followers.

   - Leadership is a cooperative process, as illustrated by Chagnon's studies of the Yanomamö.

   - Van Vugt and his colleagues' evolutionary mismatch hypothesis suggests that because of the difference between the demands of the modern world and the environment of evolutionary adaptiveness (EEA), members sometimes instinctively respond to leaders in less than optimal ways—as when favoring males when facing intergroup conflict and females when dealing with intragroup conflict.

Why do some leaders succeed and others fail?

1. Fiedler's *contingency theory* suggests that leadership effectiveness is determined by the leader's motivational style and the favorability of the situation.

   - The leader's motivational style can be either task motivated or relationship motivated, as measured by the *Least Preferred Coworker (LPC) Scale.*

   - Situational favorability is determined by leader–member relations, the task structure, and the leader's power.

   - Fiedler's theory predicts that task-motivated (low-LPC) leaders will be most effective in situations that are either extremely unfavorable or extremely favorable, whereas relationship-motivated leaders are most effective in intermediate situations.

2. Leadership style theorists assume that effectiveness depends on the leader's task and relationship behaviors.

   - The *Leadership Grid*, proposed by Blake and Mouton, assumes that people vary in their concern for results and in their concern for people and that individuals who are high on both dimensions (9,9) are the best leaders.

   - The *situational leadership theory*, proposed by Hersey and Blanchard, suggests that groups benefit from leadership that meshes with the developmental stage of the group.

3. *Leader–member exchange theory* (LMX) focuses on the *dyadic* relationship linking the leader to each member of the group and notes that, in many cases, two subgroups of linkages exist (the inner group and the outer group). Groups with more inner-group members are more productive.

   - Members with a positive LMX are more likely to engage in organizational citizenship behavior.

   - *E-leaders*, who guide virtual groups, must learn to improve leader–member relations, task structure, and goal striving through the use of various telecommunication technologies.

4. Participation theories suggest that leadership should be distributed throughout the group rather than concentrated on a single individual.

   - Lewin, Lippitt, and White compared three types of "group climates": autocratic, democratic, and laissez-faire. Laissez-faire leadership was ineffective compared to democratic and autocratic, with members preferring democratic.

   - Shared leadership models, such as co-leadership, collective leadership, and peer leadership, encourage member-centered leadership methods.

   - Kelly's theory of followership suggests that followers vary along two dimensions: active/passive and independent/dependent. He identifies five types of followers: conformist, passive, pragmatic, alienated, and exemplary.

5. Transformational theories of leadership examine how charismatic leaders promote change.

   - Burns distinguished between *transactional leaders* and *transformational leaders* and suggested that the latter are able to elevate both themselves and their followers.

   - Bass identified four components of transformational (rather than transactional) leadership: idealized influence (or charisma), inspirational motivation, intellectual stimulation, and individualized consideration; they can be measured by the *Multifactor Leadership Questionnaire.*

6. Women tend to adopt participative and transformational styles of leadership, whereas men are more likely to enact autocratic, laissez-faire, and transactional styles. Women's skills are particularly well suited for organizations of the future, which will be less hierarchical and require a collaborative, shared approach to leadership.

RESOURCES

Chapter Case: Wendy Kopp

- *One Day, All Children …* by Wendy Kopp (2003) provides a first-person account of the founder of Teach For America, a highly successful educationally focused nonprofit corporation.

The Nature of Leadership

- *The Bass Handbook of Leadership: Theory, Research, & Managerial Applications* (2008) by Bernard M. Bass (with Ruth Bass) is a comprehensive and finely detailed analysis of the scientific findings and theories dealing with leadership.

- *Encyclopedia of Leadership*, edited by George R. Goethals, Georgia J. Sorenson, and James McGregor Burns (2004), is a massive compilation of scholarship dealing with all aspects of leaders and leadership: 1,927 pages filled with 1.2 million words written by 311 scholars.

- *Leadership in Organizations* by Gary Yukl (2013) is a masterful integration of theory, research, and application of leadership studies in businesses and organizations.

Theoretical Perspectives

- *Leadership and Psychology,* edited by Crystal L. Hoyt, George R. Goethals, and Donelson R. Forsyth (2008), collects in a single volume a variety of papers that examine the relationship between a range of social psychological processes—such as motivation, personality, and social cognition—and leadership.

- *Culture, Leadership, and Organizations: The GLOBE Study of 62 Societies*, edited by Robert J. House, Paul J. Hanges, Mansour Javidan, Peter W. Dormfan, and Vipin Gupta (2004), describes in detail this monumental study of cultural values and people's perceptions of leadership.

Women and Leadership

- "Women and Leadership" by Crystal L. Hoyt (2010) is a concise review of research examining sex differences in leadership style and effectiveness, with a focus on the impact of sex stereotypes on biases against women as leaders.

- *Through the Labyrinth* by Alice Eagly and Linda L. Carli (2007) examines closely the findings from hundreds of studies of women and leadership, including trends in biases against women as leaders and differences between men and women in their leadership styles.

Performance

CHAPTER OVERVIEW

People join with others in groups to get things done. Groups are the world's workers, protectors, builders, decision makers, and problem solvers. When individuals combine their talents and energies in groups, they accomplish goals that would overwhelm individuals. People working collectively inevitably encounter problems coordinating and maximizing their efforts, but groups are the crucible for creativity.

- What processes promote group performance, and what processes inhibit it?

- Do people work as hard when in groups as they do when working by themselves?

- When do people give their all when working in a group?

- When do groups outperform individuals?

- What steps can be taken to encourage creativity in groups?

CHAPTER OUTLINE

Working in Groups

Groups with a Purpose

When to Work in Groups

The Process Model of Productivity

Social Facilitation

Performance in the Presence of Others

Why Does Social Facilitation Occur?

Conclusions and Applications

Social Loafing

The Ringelmann Effect

Causes of and Cures for Social Loafing

The Collective Effort Model

Groups versus Individuals

Additive Tasks

Compensatory Tasks

Disjunctive Tasks

Conjunctive Tasks

Discretionary Tasks

Process Gains In Groups

Group Creativity

Brainstorming

Improving Brainstorming

Alternatives to Brainstorming

Chapter Review

Resources

The Miracle on the Hudson: Working with Others in Groups

US Airways Flight 1549 from New York's LaGuardia Airport to Charlotte, North Carolina, began uneventfully. The flight attendants helped the 150 passengers settle into their seats. The baggage handlers packed the cargo hold of the Airbus A320 with luggage and sealed the doors. Nothing was amiss as the two-man crew piloting the aircraft—Captain Chesley B. "Sully" Sullenberger and first officer Jeffrey B. Skiles—completed the preflight checklist. Flight 1549, with Skiles at the controls, lifted off from Runway 4, and the local controller passed the flight to Patrick Harten, the air traffic controller for LaGuardia departures. The time was 3:26 PM.

Less than five minutes later, the Airbus A320 was sinking in the freezing waters of Hudson River. As Sully and Skiles readied the plane for its ascent to cruising altitude, it collided with a flock of large geese, resulting in the destruction of the craft's engines. The A320 was designed to be flyable with a single engine functioning, but the loss of two engines was catastrophic. Sully, who was more experienced flying the A320, immediately started the auxiliary power unit before telling Skiles, "My aircraft." Skiles responded, "Your aircraft," before turning his attention to restarting the damaged engines (Brazy, 2009, p. 38).

Sully radioed Harten:"Mayday. Mayday. Mayday. This is, uh, Cactus fifteen thirty-nine. Hit birds. We've lost thrust in both engines. We're turning back towards LaGuardia" (Sullenberger, 2009, p. 217). Harten initiated emergency procedures, including communicating the problem to airport and municipal emergency response personnel. The engines would not restart, however, and the plane—now gliding without any engine power—did not have enough altitude or speed to reach LaGuardia. Sully considered taking the plane to an airport he could see nearly seven miles away in New Jersey (Teterboro Airport), but decided he could not reach that airport, either. He radioed Harten, "We're gonna be in the Hudson." Harten's response: "I'm sorry, say again, Cactus?" (Brazy, 2009, p. 39).

New Yorkers watched as the A320, traveling at about 150 MPH, splashed down in the middle of the Hudson River, just south of the George Washington Bridge. The ditching damaged the underside of the aircraft, which began sinking as water flooded the rear of the passenger cabin. Sully gave the order to evacuate, and the passengers exited as quickly as they could onto the wings and an emergency slide at the front exit. Within minutes, a flotilla of rescue vessels assembled around the aircraft, and the passengers and crew were pulled from the icy water to safety. Some required hospitalization, but not a single life was lost. The event was dubbed the "Miracle on the Hudson," and the crew members were awarded the Master's Medal of the Guild of Air Pilots and Air Navigators for their skillful handling of this emergency.

Flight 1549 is a study of groups that get things done. The three flight attendants worked together to seat all the passengers and review with them the steps they should follow in case of an emergency. The pilots worked on a series of complex, interdependent tasks that changed from the routine to the exceptional after the bird strike. As the emergency unfolded, air traffic controllers and airport personnel working the incident communicated with each other, identifying and readying alternative landing locations. When the plane ditched in the river, other groups swung into action: Firefighters, the Coast Guard, ferry boat crews, and search and rescue teams converged on the scene. The passengers, too, worked together as they escaped the doomed aircraft and waited in the freezing January weather for help to arrive.

This chapter examines task-oriented groups—those with goal-related purposes. It begins by surveying the many different types of tasks groups attempt, with a focus on proficiency. Even though groups do much of the world's work, not all of them are as successful as the groups that combined their efforts to see that Flight 1549 ended safely. What processes promote good group performance, and what processes inhibit it? Chapters 11 and 12 examine groups making decisions and working as teams, respectively, but this chapter explores productivity and performance in all types of groups—from the simplest situation (two people working side-by-side on separate tasks) to more complex forms of interlocking interdependency.

WORKING IN GROUPS

Most of the billions of groups in the world exist to get a particular job done. People use groups to discuss problems, concoct plans, forge products, and make decisions. When a task would overwhelm a single person's time, energy, and resources, individuals turn to groups. Even when tasks can be accomplished by people working alone (such as studying group dynamics), people often prefer to work in the company of others.

Groups with a Purpose

Some groups concentrate on only one type of task in their work, whereas others perform dozens of very different tasks (Arrow & McGrath, 1995). For example, following the terrorist attacks on New York City in 2001, the Office of Emergency Management for the city revised its procedures to follow in the event of large-scale disasters, including air crashes. This group focused on one basic task: planning the city's response to emergencies. The pilots of Flight 1549, in contrast, performed a variety of tasks: They sought a solution to their problem, chose from alternatives, and they "landed" the plane in the Hudson.

The Task Circumplex Model Social psychologist Joseph McGrath's (1984) task circumplex model brings order to the many goal-related activities that groups undertake. As noted briefly in Chapter 1 (Table 1.2), McGrath's model distinguishes among four basic group goals: generating ideas or plans, choosing a solution, negotiating a solution to a conflict, or executing (performing) a task. As Figure 10.1 indicates, each of these basic categories can be further subdivided, yielding a total of eight goal-related activities.

- *Generating*: Groups concoct the strategies they will use to accomplish their goals (Type 1: planning tasks) or create altogether new ideas

and approaches to their problems (Type 2: creativity tasks).

- *Choosing*: Groups make decisions about issues that have correct solutions (Type 3: intellective tasks) or questions that can be answered in many ways (Type 4: decision-making tasks).

- *Negotiating*: Groups resolve differences of opinion among members regarding their goals or decisions (Type 5: cognitive conflict tasks) or settle competitive disputes among members (Type 6: mixed-motive tasks).

- *Executing*: Groups do things, including taking part in competitions (Type 7: contests/battles/competitive tasks) or creating some product or carrying out collective actions (Type 8: performances/psychomotor tasks).

McGrath's task circumplex model also distinguishes between conceptual-behavioral tasks and cooperation-conflict tasks. Groups dealing with conceptual tasks (Type 2, 3, 4, and 5) generally exhibit high levels of information exchange, social influence, and process-oriented activity (Morris, 1966). Groups dealing with behavioral tasks (Type 1, 6, 7, 8) are those that produce things or perform services. Members of these groups perform a series of motor tasks that range from the simple and relatively individualistic through to the complex and highly interdependent (Wildman et al., 2012). Conflict tasks (Types 4, 5, 6, and 7) pit individuals and groups against each other, whereas cooperative tasks require collaboration (Types 1, 2, 3, and 8). The group in the cockpit of Flight 1549, for example, was a highly cooperative one. Sully and Skiles, both before and after the "bird ingestion," worked together in the pursuit of shared goals, without a hint of rivalry, disagreement, or tension. The passengers, too, were a highly collaborative group—at least until the time came to evacuate the aircraft. In the rush to escape, some members of the group acted selfishly, pushing people aside, grabbing flotation cushions, and refusing to heed the orders of the flight attendants. These passengers changed their Type 8 task into a Type 6 or even a Type 7 task.

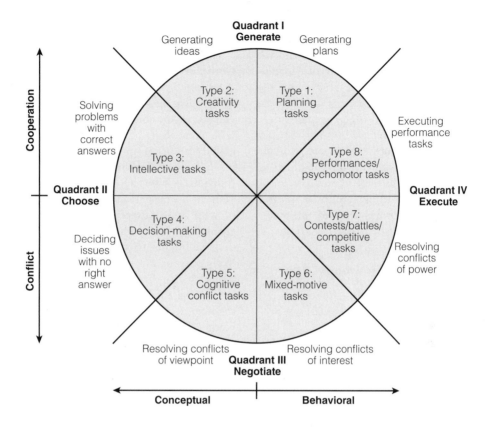

FIGURE 10.1 McGrath's task circumplex model of group tasks.

SOURCE: McGrath, *Groups: Interaction and Performance*, 1st Edition, © 1984. Reprinted by permission of Pearson Education, Inc., Upper Saddle River, New Jersey.

Collective Intelligence Just as some individuals are specialists—uniquely trained or talented at a particular task—some groups are more effective when working at one type of task rather than another. Sully and Skiles, for example, were skilled as pilots, but their proficiency at this task does not guarantee success when they attempt some other type of task. Similarly, groups in military contexts may be skilled when dealing with hostile forces and protecting the group members from harm, but this same group may prove inadequate when asked to act as a peacekeeping police force. The group may be quite capable when dealing with situations rife with conflict—contests, battles, and competition—but not when the situation requires cooperation and creative problem solving (Weiss, 2011).

But some groups may be jacks-of-all-trades—skilled at many of the types of tasks in the McGrath task circumplex. One team of researchers examined groups' generalized proficiency—which they called *collective intelligence*, or *c-factor*—by assembling groups of two to five members and having them work for up to five hours on tasks from all the quadrants of the McGrath task circumplex. The groups spent time brainstorming possible uses for a brick, solving problems taken from intelligence tests, discussing an issue that required moral sensitivity, planning a shopping trip, typing a shared Google document, playing a game of checkers against a computerized opponent, generating as many words as possible that started with "s" and ended in "n" and so on. The researchers then added together the scores on all these different tests to generate each group's "collective intelligence" (only the morality test was unrelated to all the other tasks). Like individuals, some groups had higher levels of "intelligence" than others, for they were able to master most of the diverse set of problems they faced. Group intelligence was related to the average intelligence of the group members, but also to the group's composition. Groups with more women performed better than those with few or none, as did groups with higher average scores on social sensitivity. The best performing groups were also those where members contributed to the tasks more equally (Woolley et al., 2010).

When to Work in Groups

Not all tasks require the skills, attentions, and resources of a group of people. Individuals can perform any and all of the tasks in the McGrath task circumplex—one pilot can fly a small single-engine aircraft, an author can write every word of his or her book, and individual investors can choose which stocks to buy and sell. Groups, with their greater intellectual and motivational resources, may be the best choice in a given situation, but that choice should be shaped by an analysis of the task at hand. As tasks become more challenging, complex, and consequential, the more likely a well-organized group will succeed where an individual may fail (Zander, 1985).

Level of Difficulty   In some circumstances, people are faced with tasks that are well beyond the skills and resources of a single individual. No one person, no matter how talented, can compile a dictionary of all the words in the English language, construct a nuclear power plant, or overthrow a political dictator. Other tasks are difficult ones because they require enormous amounts of time, effort, or strength. One talented individual could build a car or dig a 100-yard-long trench, but a crew of workers will accomplish these tasks far more quickly and with better results. Projects that take months or years to complete are best attempted by multiple individuals, so that the work continues even when specific individuals leave and join the

group. Unfamiliar tasks are also more difficult ones, as are those with many possible solutions (Shaw, 1981).

Complexity and Interdependence   A single person cannot perform Beethoven's Fifth Symphony or compete against the New York Yankees. Individuals may be able to carry out specific assignments with great skill, but tasks that require the "integrated action of group members" (Shaw, 1981, p. 364) create dependencies among the members. Individuals who agree with such statements as "I have a one-person job; I rarely have to check or work with others" have little need to work in groups on tasks, whereas those who depend on their colleagues to complete their work are more likely to tout the benefits of working collectively rather than individually (Haines & Taggar, 2006). In general, as interdependency increases, group members feel more responsible for successfully completing their work (Shaw, Duffy, & Stark, 2000).

Importance   Changing a flat tire or reformatting a document pale in importance when compared to rescuing the wildlife harmed by an oil spill or landing a jet airliner whose engines have failed. Important tasks are those that have significant effects on many, rather than a few people, and these effects are long-lasting rather than temporary. Important tasks are also those that concern health, safety, and survival, as well as those that have significant financial consequences. When circumstances are dire and the consequences of a mistake would be catastrophic, the wisdom of a group is preferred to intervention of the lone expert. Groups may also help individuals deal with the stress of decision making and the consequences of their actions should they fail. Even individuals who question the wisdom of a group's judgment may turn to groups in an effort to shield themselves from liability should the outcome be a negative one.

The Process Model of Productivity

The world relies on groups to achieve its goals, but people sometimes challenge the wisdom of this custom. Although groups usually turn out excellent products, they sometimes fall short of expectations. One task force may formulate an effective plan for dealing with a problem, whereas another may create a plan that ends in disaster. A team may practice diligently, yet still play miserably during the big game. Sully and Skiles piloted their disabled Airbus A320 successfully, but other flights have ended in tragedy when the crew's response to an emergency was inadequate. Why do some groups perform impressively whereas others fail?

Actual Productivity ≠ Potential Productivity Ivan Steiner (1972), in his classic work *Group Process and Productivity*, drew on the concept of **process loss** to predict when groups will perform well or poorly. Steiner recognized that groups have great potential, for their resources outstrip those of any single individual. But Steiner also realized that groups rarely reach their full potential because no group can perfectly coordinate its resources, members, and processes. When individuals work by themselves, their performance depends strictly on their personal resources, including their talents, skills, and effort. But when individuals join together to work in groups, their performance depends on each individual's resources plus the interpersonal processes that determine how these resources are combined. Even Sully and Skiles—experienced, well-trained, highly motivated—did not coordinate their actions perfectly during the emergency. In consequence, their potential productivity did not match their actual productivity.

In Steiner's (1972, p. 8) model, task-related processes are the steps group members take as they complete a task, including "all those intrapersonal and interpersonal actions by which people transform their resources into a product, and all those nonproductive actions that are prompted by frustration, competing motivations, or inadequate

---

process loss A reduction in performance effectiveness or efficiency caused by actions, operations, or dynamics that prevent the group from reaching its full potential, including reduced effort, faulty group processes, coordination problems, and ineffective leadership.

understanding." Although a group's *potential productivity* (PP) can be predicted by determining if its resources match the requirements of the task it is attempting, *process loss* (PL)—the grit in the interpersonal machinery of a working group—determines how effectively the group makes use of its resources. Steiner's "law" of group productivity

$$AP = PP - PL$$

predicts that *actual productivity* (AP) is determined by a group's potential productivity (PP) less all the process losses (PL) the group experiences.

Predicting Performance Steiner's theory of group productivity pinpoints two basic causes of poor group performance. First, the group may lack the resources it needs to complete the particular task it is attempting—the group may be too small, the members too weak, and the rock too heavy. Second, even if the group has the potential to be successful, for it has the resources the task requires, the group may not use its resources effectively. The remainder of this chapter applies these basic ideas to the analysis of potential and actual productivity in groups. We begin with tasks with minimal interpersonal demands, for they require little in the way of coordinated effort. We then turn to other questions about working groups: When do people give their all when working in a group? When do groups outperform individuals? And how can groups be coaxed into finding creative, unusual solutions rather than remaining entrenched in their traditional ways of thinking?

SOCIAL FACILITATION

When the last passenger on Flight 1549 was seated and the flight attendants closed the door, first officer Skiles completed the preflight checklist and taxied to the departure runway. The procedures Skiles followed were complex ones, but they were very familiar ones for him, for during his long career as a pilot he had flown thousands of take-offs at airports all over the United States. Skiles, however, was not alone in the cockpit. Captain Sullenberger was seated beside him, completing a second set of procedures required at take-off, but also monitoring Skiles' actions. Did Sully's presence facilitate Skiles' performance as he worked to fly the plane, or was Sully a source of process loss?

Performance in the Presence of Others

When individuals work alone, social forces are minimized. But add another person to the situation, and social processes immediately begin to shape group members' actions and outcomes. In some situations, individuals perform more effectively when working in the presence of others; **social facilitation** results. In others—particularly more complex, challenging ones—another person's presence hurts performance rather than helping it.

Triplett's Experiment   One of the first studies in the field of group dynamics examined performance in the presence of other people. Psychologist Norman Triplett's (1898) inspiration for the study came when he was watching a series of bicycle races. In some events, cyclists raced alone and their performance was timed. Other events were competitions with cyclists racing each other. In a third type of race, a rider was paced by a motor-driven cycle. Invariably, riders achieved their best times when they competed or they were paced, and they were slowest when racing alone.

Many observers at the time thought the differences were caused by drafting: the lead cyclist creates a partial vacuum that pulls followers along while also breaking down wind resistance. Triplett, however, was more interested in "dynamogenic factors":

> The bodily presence of another rider is a stimulus to the racer in arousing the competitive instinct; that another can thus be the means of releasing or freeing nervous energy for him that he cannot of himself

release; and, further, that the sight of movement in that other by perhaps suggesting a higher rate of speed, is also an inspiration to greater effort. (p. 516)

To eliminate the possibility of drafting, he arranged for 40 children to perform a simple reel-turning task in pairs and when alone. His study was a success, for he was able to experimentally document social facilitation: The children in pairs outperformed those who worked alone.

Triplett is still recognized for his noteworthy contribution to the scientific study of groups, even though a reanalysis of his findings using modern statistics indicated the differences between the conditions he studied were not very substantial. In all likelihood, had he performed his study today instead of in 1898, his fellow researchers would have sent him back to his laboratory to find more convincing evidence of those mysterious dynamogenic factors (Strube, 2005).

Coaction, Audiences, and Inconsistencies   Triplett studied **coaction**: people working in the presence of other people, but not necessarily interacting with one another. People digging separate holes in a field, taking a test in a classroom, or riding bicycles with friends are common coaction situations that could trigger social facilitation. But researchers soon discovered that social facilitation also occurs when individuals perform for an *audience*. One investigator discovered that audiences can trigger social facilitation when he watched people exercising in a weight room. He noted that people who were watched when working out suddenly could lift heavier weights (Meumann, 1904).

Other studies, however, did not confirm the "presence of people improves performance" effect. Floyd Allport (1920), for example, arranged for participants to complete tasks twice—once while alone

---

social facilitation An improvement in task performance that occurs when people work in the presence of other people.

coaction Performing a task or another type of goal-oriented activity in the presence of one or more other individuals who are performing a similar type of activity.

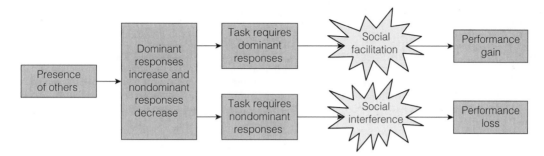

FIGURE 10.2 Zajonc's theory of social facilitation.
SOURCE: © Cengage Learning

in a small testing cubicle, and once with others at a table. To reduce competition, Allport cautioned participants not to compare their scores with one another, and he also told them that he himself would not be making comparisons. He found that people in groups produced more than isolated individuals, but their products were often lower in quality. Likewise, other researchers sometimes reported gains in performance through coaction or when an audience was watching, but they also documented performance decrements (Aiello & Douthitt, 2001).

Zajonc's Resolution Confusion reigned until Robert Zajonc (1965) explained why different studies yielded such divergent results. Some behaviors, he noted, are easier to learn and perform than others. These *dominant responses* are located at the top of the organism's response hierarchy, so they dominate all other potential responses. Behaviors that are part of the organism's behavioral repertoire but are less likely to be performed are *nondominant responses*. Zajonc observed that studies documenting social facilitation focused on well-learned or instinctual responses, such as lifting weights, bicycling, or eating rapidly. Studies involving novel, complicated, or unpracticed actions, such as solving difficult math problems or writing poetry, usually found little evidence of social facilitation.

Zajonc's insight was that the presence of others increases the tendency to perform dominant responses and decreases the tendency to perform nondominant responses. If the dominant response is the correct or most appropriate response in a particular situation, then social facilitation occurs; people will perform better when others are present than when they are alone. If the task calls for nondominant responses, however, then the presence of other people interferes with performance (see Figure 10.2). Imagine that you must memorize some pairs of words. If the pairs are common associations, such as *blue–sky* or *clean–dirty*, then the task is an easy one, for which the dominant response is correct. Hence, your performance will be better if other people are present. If, however, you are trying to learn some uncommon associations—such as *blue–dynamogenic* or *clean–nondominant*—then you are required to make a nondominant response and an audience will hurt more than help.

Speed, Quantity, and Quality Zajonc's analysis has been supported by a number of studies, including those sampled in Table 10.1. Novice drivers perform more poorly when an audience is present in the car. Individuals dress more quickly when another person is present, provided they are putting on familiar articles of clothing. Right-handed people can write faster with that hand when another person is present, but even more slowly if they are trying to write with their left hand. Social facilitation has even been documented in other species. Cockroaches, horses, puppies, chickens, mice, rats, monkeys, armadillos, ants, beetles, and opossums are on the list of animals that show signs of increased performance in the presence of other members of their species (Clayton, 1978).

In general, the effect that Zajonc identified—the improved performance on simple tasks that require dominant responses—is strongest when

T A B L E 10.1   **A Sampling of Empirical Demonstrations of Social Facilitation**

Situation	Findings
Dressing	People were asked to perform a familiar task (taking off their own shoes and socks) and a less familiar task (putting on a robe that tied in the back) when alone and when with another person. People removed their shoes and socks three seconds faster if another person was in the room. They were even faster—by two seconds on average—when the observer watched as they removed their footwear. In contrast, they donned the unfamiliar clothes more slowly when the observer was present and watchful (Markus, 1978).
Driving	Individuals seeking their license to drive an automobile took their driving test, with only the tester in the car or with another test-taker in the car, seated in the rear seat. Forty-nine percent of the applicants passed the test when alone, but only 34% passed when an audience was present (Rosenbloom et al., 2007).
Handwriting	College students were told to copy a list of words as quickly as they could. They wrote one list with their dominant hand (easy task) and one using their nondominant hand (hard task). They worked in the presence of an image of their favorite television personality (displayed on a computer screen) or an image of another character from the same program. If the task was easy, they wrote more words in the presence of their favorite character; if the task was difficult, the favorite character inhibited their performance (Gardner & Knowles, 2008).
Jogging	Solitary women jogging along a footpath encountered, when they rounded a bend, a woman who either watched them as they ran or sat facing away from them. Joggers accelerated when they encountered the watchful observer (Worringham & Messick, 1983).
Playing	People playing pool were surreptitiously watched to identify skilled and unskilled players. Skilled players made at least two-thirds of their shots, and unskilled players missed at least two-thirds. The observer then moved near the pool table and watched their play. Skilled players' performance improved 14% when they were observed, but unskilled players' performance dropped by more than 30% (Michaels et al., 1982).
Running	Roaches (Blatta orientalis) were timed as they scurried away from a light source in a simple maze or a complex one. In the simple maze, single roaches reached the goal in an average of 40.6 seconds, but coacting roaches averaged only 33 seconds. This tendency reversed when the maze was complex: Single roaches crawled to the finish line 19.6 seconds faster than did coacting roaches. Roaches watched by an audience—several roaches sealed in small plastic boxes adjacent to the maze—were particularly slow when the maze was complex, taking nearly two minutes longer than single roaches (Zajonc, Heingartner, & Herman, 1969).
Speaking	When asked to write out as many words as they could in response to a word, most people (93%) produced more words when another person was present than when they were alone (Allport, 1920). When this study was replicated with individuals who stuttered when they spoke, 80% of the subjects produced more words when alone rather than with another person (Travis, 1928).

speed and quantity count more than correctness and quality. When researchers reviewed hundreds of studies of over 24,000 humans meta-analytically, they concluded that social facilitation is most likely to occur on tasks where speed and quantity matter more than accuracy. So long as the task is a simple one, people tend to work more quickly when others are present, and the result is a small, but consistent, uptick in productivity. The presence of other people interferes with speed, however, when the task is complex, so other people significantly inhibited both the quantity and quality of their performance. Overall, the gains that occurred when people worked together on simple tasks were not as great as the losses that occurred when people worked on complex tasks (Bond & Titus, 1983).

Why Does Social Facilitation Occur?

The situations studied by Triplett and Zajonc barely qualify as groups, for they involved strangers working on individualized tasks without any interaction, influence, shared identity, or common goals. Yet, even these circumstances were sufficient to trigger psychological and interpersonal processes that sometimes facilitated, and sometimes interfered with, performance (see Aiello & Douthitt, 2001; Strauss, 2002).

Drive Processes Zajonc coined the word *compresence* to describe the state of responding in the presence of others. Compresence, he hypothesized, touches off a basic arousal response in most social species "simply because one never knows, so to speak, what sorts of responses—perhaps even novel and unique—may be required in the next few seconds" when others are nearby (Zajonc, 1980, p. 50). Zajonc believed that compresence in and of itself elevated drive levels that triggered social facilitation when tasks were so easy that only dominant responses would be needed to perform them.

Zajonc's **drive theory** uniquely predicts that social facilitation will occur even when all forms of social interaction, communication, and evaluation between the individual and the observer are blocked. Investigators tested this hypothesis by asking people to work on simple or complex tasks in the presence of an "observer" who was blindfolded and wore earplugs. Even though the observer could not interact with participants in any way, his mere presence still enhanced their performance when they worked on simple tasks and slowed their performance on complex ones (Schmitt et al., 1986).

---

drive theory In general, an analysis of human motivation that stresses the impact of psychological or physiological needs or desires on individuals' thoughts, feelings, and actions; also an explanation of social facilitation that maintains that the presence of others evokes a generalized drive state characterized by increased readiness and arousal (proposed by Robert Zajonc).

Physiological Processes Zajonc's drive theory suggests that people react, physiologically, to the presence of people—but the magnitude of this change depends on the type of situation and on who is watching. Social psychologist James Blascovich and his colleagues (1999), for example, verified that an audience triggers increases in cardiac and vascular reactivity. Blascovich's team also discovered, however, that this arousal was physiologically very different when people worked on an easy task rather than on a hard one. When the task was easy, people displayed a *challenge response*. At the physiological level, they appeared to be ready to respond to the challenge that they faced (elevated heart rate and sympathetic nervous system activation). But when the task was difficult, people displayed a *threat response*; they appeared to be stressed rather than ready for effective action. Other studies found that the presence of certain people—such as close friends—can have a calming rather than an arousing influence. When women performed a difficult math test with a friend who was merely present—the friend could touch the participant's wrist but was preoccupied with another task and was wearing a headset that blocked all sound—the participant's cardiovascular responses were lowered (Kamarck, Manuck, & Jennings, 1990).

Neurological Processes Social neuroscientists have also offered suggestive evidence as to the basic neurological reactivity of the human brain to the presence of other humans. In one fMRI study (see Chapter 3), researchers imaged the brains of volunteers when they were watching video clips of a single individual or two people interacting. While watching these clips, areas of the volunteers' brains that are thought to be dedicated to monitoring social information (the medial parietal and dorsomedial prefrontal cortex) showed signs of increased activity, suggesting that simply seeing other human beings triggers a cortical reaction (Iacoboni et al., 2004, p. 1171). These findings were partly confirmed in a second study that used a different imaging method, near-infrared spectroscopy (NIRS), to monitor brain activity when individuals performed a task alone or in the presence of another person. In this study, activity in the dorso-lateral prefrontal cortex increased in the presence of others, and this increase was associated with inhibited performance on complex, but not simple, tasks. This study, however, found that changes in heart rate and blood pressure were not associated with increased error rates, prompting investigators to conclude that it is the brain, and not the heart, that overreacts to the presence of others (Ito et al., 2011).

Motivational Processes   The forty-nine-year-old Skiles earned his pilot license when he was sixteen. With over 20,000 hours logged as a commercial pilot, he was nearly as experienced as the plane's captain, Sully. But Skiles had only recently completed his training for this particular aircraft, and this was his first flight without an instructor. Skiles and Sully did know each other particularly well, for they had only begun working together as a flight crew four days earlier on the first leg of their seven-leg flight rotation. As Skiles maneuvered the plane along the tarmac, he knew that Sully was watching his every move.

Psychologist Nickolas Cottrell (1972) suggested that this evaluative pressure is one of the reasons why people tend to be more productive in the presence of others. His **evaluation apprehension theory** assumes that individuals have learned through experience that other people are the source of most of the rewards and punishments they receive. Thus, individuals learn to associate social situations with evaluation, so they feel apprehensive whenever other people are nearby. This evaluation apprehension enhances performance on simple tasks, but it becomes debilitating when people attempt more difficult projects. Cottrell thus believed that apprehension, and not the arousal

response identified by Zajonc, is the source of social facilitation effects.

Sociologist Erving Goffman's (1959) analysis of self-presentational processes, noted in Chapter 6, also underscores the motivational impact of impression management pressures. **Self-presentation theory** assumes that group members actively control others' impressions of themselves by displaying social behaviors that establish and maintain a particular social image, or *face*. Group members do not want the others to think that they possess negative, shameful qualities and characteristics, so they strive to make a good impression. Performance situations create self-presentational challenges for members, particularly when they feel they might fail. To avoid that embarrassment, group members redouble their efforts when self-presentational pressures are strong—as they were in the cockpit when Skiles was piloting and Sully was watching (Bond, Atoum, & VanLeeuwen, 1996).

Researchers have tested, and in many cases confirmed, the primary hypothesis that derives uniquely from such motivational models—that any stimulus increasing the organism's apprehension over future rewards or punishments should increase drive levels. When people find themselves in evaluative situations, they tend to perform dominant rather than nondominant responses (Seta et al., 1989). When, for example, individuals who were watched by an observer were told that the observer was evaluating them, their performance improved, but only when they were working on a simple task (Bartis, Szymanski, & Harkins, 1988). When people who had already failed once tried the task a second time, they performed worse when others were present (Seta & Seta, 1995). Also, situational factors that decrease evaluation apprehension, such as allowing for private responses, nonevaluative audiences, and the absence of a definable task that can be evaluated, often eliminate social facilitation

----

evaluation apprehension theory An analysis of performance gains in groups arguing that individuals working in the presence of others experience a general concern for how these others are evaluating them and that this apprehension facilitates their performance on simple, well-learned tasks.

----

self-presentation theory An analysis of performance gains in groups assuming that social facilitation is caused by individuals striving to make a good impression when they work in the presence of others.

effects (Henchy & Glass, 1968). Finally, individuals who are highly confident perform better when evaluated by others, whereas those who doubt their ability perform better when alone (Sanna, 1992).

The presence of other people—even friends— also increases physiological reactivity if these friends are evaluative. As noted earlier, people were more relaxed when working on a task with a friend nearby. Their friend, however, was wearing earphones and could not evaluate the participant's performance (Kamarck et al., 1990). What would happen if the friend was a potential source of evaluation? When people are watched closely by a friend, they tend to show signs of physiological arousal rather than relaxation. In fact, people are more relaxed when they are with their pets rather than with other people. Pets are an ideal source of social support, for they provide reassurance through their presence but they do not (we assume) evaluate their owner's performance (Allen et al., 1991; Allen, Blascovich, & Mendes, 2002).

Other findings, though, do not support this emphasis on evaluation. Even when the companion refrains from attending to the individual in any way, social facilitation still occurs (Berger, 1981; Platania & Moran, 2001). Also, social facilitation occurs in animals that likely lack the capacity to feel nervous or embarrassed—rats, armadillos, and roaches, for example. Moreover, activities that involve little threat of evaluation, such as eating, drinking, or getting dressed, still show social facilitation effects.

Attentional Processes Zajonc stressed drive levels, Cottrell underscored the importance of evaluation, but several cognitive theories have suggested that the presence of others changes people's capacity to process information adequately. When people work in the presence of other people, they must split their attention between the task they are completing and the other person (Guerin & Innes, 1982). The presence of an audience may also increase individuals' self-awareness, and, as a result, they may focus their attention on themselves and fail to pay sufficient attention to the task (Mullen & Baumeister, 1987).

Distractions, however, do not inevitably undermine performance. **Distraction-conflict theory** suggests that distraction interferes with the attention given to the task, but that these distractions can be overcome with effort. Therefore, on simple tasks that require dominant responses, the interference effects are inconsequential compared with the improvement that results from concentrating on the task so performance is facilitated. On more complex tasks, the increase in drive is insufficient to offset the effects of distraction, and performance is therefore impaired (Baron, 1986; Sanders, Baron, & Moore, 1978).

People are, in most cases, distracting. But, oddly enough, if people are working in the presence of other people and those people are not at all distracting, then social facilitation does not occur even when tasks are simple ones (Bond et al., 1996; Sanders et al., 1978). Distractions have also been shown to improve performance on certain tasks, such as the *Stroop Task*. In the Stroop task, participants are shown a color name (e.g., *Red, Blue*) printed in a primary color (such as red or blue) and are asked to name the color of the *ink*. For example, if the word *Red* is printed in blue ink, the participant should answer *blue*. When the ink and the color word match, people have no problems. But when the ink and the color word are incongruent, reaction time and errors increase. These errors, however, decrease when individuals complete the task with others. The presence of others may work by helping people narrow their focus of attention and by filtering out the distracting color name cue (Huguet et al., 1999). The effect may also be due to the (a) extra cognitive demands imposed on participants by the presence of the observer and the need to evaluate the task itself (Klauer, Herfordt, & Voss, 2008) or (b) increased attentional focusing on the task that is triggered

---

distraction-conflict theory An analysis of performance gains in groups assuming that when others are present, attention is divided between the other people and the task; this attentional conflict increases motivation, and it facilitates performance on simple, well-learned tasks.

by a threat of self-evaluation (Muller & Butera, 2007).

Cognitive Processes   When Sully announced "my aircraft" and took over the control of the mortally wounded Airbus A320, his mind was busy calculating any number of possible courses of action, factoring in the craft's altitude and speed, distance to available airports, the hazards of a water-landing, the number of civilians on the ground who could be injured, and so on. But the stress of the situation undoubtedly influenced the way he processed that information, helping him to narrow his focus to concentrate on his best options while ignoring more untenable alternatives.

Social psychologist Stephen Harkins' *mere-effort model* suggests that the gains and losses in performance individuals exhibit when they work on simple and complex tasks are due, in part, to changes in the way they process information (Harkins, 2006; McFall, Jamieson, & Harkins, 2009). His model proposes that when people think they are being evaluated, they exert more effort—but this effort causes them to concentrate more on ideas and information that is readily accessible to them. If this information is relevant to the task at hand, then facilitation will occur. However, if this information is not relevant, then thinking about this information will inhibit performance.

To test this hypothesis Harkins (2006) measured the performance of individuals who worked on simple and complex versions of the Remote Associates Test—the RAT. Each item on the RAT consists of three words, and the test-taker's task is to provide a single word that the three stimulus words have in common. A simple RAT item would be birthday-playing-shark, since the correct answer (card) is a close associate of all three words in the list. A complex RAT item, such as elephant-lapse-vivid, is more difficult because the correct answer (memory) is a remote rather than close associate, and so the test-taker must discard the close associates and search for more distant ones to solve the problem.

Harkins discovered that evaluative pressures improve performance on simple RATs but slowed performance on complex RATs, as evaluation apprehension theory would suggest. But he also discovered that this effect occurs because the evaluative pressure increased the availability of close associates (the "pre-potent responses"), which were only correct when people were working on the simple RAT. People could solve the more complex RAT items, but they needed time to move beyond the close associates that came to mind so easily.

Personality Processes   Sully, in the months following the crash, became a public figure: He appeared on talk shows, testified before Congress, accepted awards and accolades from various groups, and even threw out the first pitch at a couple of baseball games. He took it all in stride, rising to each occasion as he did when he landed Flight 1549 on the Hudson.

Social orientation theory suggests that people differ in their overall orientation toward social situations, and these individual differences in social orientation predict who will show facilitation in the presence of others and who will show impairment. According to this theory, individuals who display a *positive orientation* are so self-confident that they react positively to the challenge the group may throw their way. Others, in contrast, display a *negative orientation*. They approach social situations apprehensively, for they feel inhibited and threatened by other people. People may be capable of adopting either orientation in a given situation, but people tend to be either positive or negative in their orientations. Some people, like Sully, are naturally positive in their orientation toward tasks. Others, in contrast, possess personality traits that prompt them to be more negative, such as low self-esteem, self-consciousness, and anxiety. A meta-analysis of previous studies of social

---

social orientation theory   An analysis of performance gains in groups suggesting individual differences in social orientation (the tendency to approach social situations apprehensively or with enthusiasm) predict when social facilitation will occur.

T A B L E   10.2   Four General Explanations of Social Facilitation

Theory	Mediating Process	Evidence
Drive theory	*Drive process:* The mere presence of others elevates drive levels; this drive triggers social facilitation when tasks are so easy that only dominant responses are needed to perform them. (Zajonc, 1965)	• People show signs of physiological arousal when others are present. • Many species perform basic tasks more efficiently in the presence of other species' members. • Arousal facilitates performance on simple tasks.
Evaluation apprehension theory; self-presentation theory	*Motivational process:* Through experience, people learn to associate the presence of others with evaluation; this concern for evaluation facilitates performance on well-learned tasks. (Cottrell, 1972)	• The presence of others is facilitative only when the observers can evaluate the quality of the performance. • Facilitative effects are strongest when individuals are striving to make a good impression.
Distraction-conflict theory; mere-effort model	*Cognitive process:* When others are present, attention is divided between the other people and the task; attentional conflict increases motivation, which facilitates performance so long as the task is a simple one. (Baron, 1986; Harkins, 2006)	• Recall is poorer when a stimulus is presented in the presence of others, suggesting others are distracting. • Facilitation is reduced if the others in the situation are not noticed. • The presence of others improves performance on interference tasks (e.g., the *Stroop Task*, the *RAT*).
Social orientation theory	*Personality process:* Individuals who display a positive interpersonal orientation are more likely to show social facilitation effects. (Uziel, 2007)	• The presence of others improves performance among individuals with high self-esteem and low anxiety. • Those with an attention-seeking tendency (exhibitionism) perform better than self-conscious individuals in coaction settings.

facilitation, focusing only on those studies that included measures that might be indicators of participants' degree of positive or negative orientation, supported the theory. Individuals with qualities that suggested their social orientation was positive usually showed social facilitation effects, whereas those with a negative orientation showed a social interference effect (Uziel, 2007, 2010).

Conclusions and Applications

Social facilitation occurs because humans, as social beings, respond in predictable ways when joined by other members of their species (see Table 10.2). Some of these reactions, as Zajonc suggested, are very basic ones, for the mere presence of other people elevates drive levels. But arousal becomes more substantial when group members realize that the people around them are evaluating them and might form a negative impression of them if they perform badly. Cognitive and personality mechanisms that govern how individuals process information and monitor the environment also come into play when people work in the presence of others. As the following examples illustrate, these physiological, motivational, cognitive, and personality processes influence group members' reactions across a wide range of performance settings.

Prejudice and Social Facilitation   *Prejudices* are deeply ingrained negative attitudes about the members of other groups. Such prejudices as racism and sexism are increasingly recognized as unfair and socially inappropriate, so individuals who are prejudiced often try to keep their prejudices to themselves to avoid being labeled a racist or sexist (Kleinpenning & Hagendoorn, 1993). But prejudice is often a well-learned, *dominant* response; ironically, the presence of other people may lead individuals to express even more biased opinions when they are in public rather than in private. The presence of others may work to facilitate prejudice, rather than keep it in check (Lambert et al., 1996; Lambert et al., 2003).

Eating in Groups   The presence of other people facilitates one of the most dominant of basic responses in humans: eating. Most people report that they prefer to eat with others rather than dine alone (Clendenen, Herman, & Polivy, 1994). When researchers ask people to keep track of how much and with whom they eat, they usually find that people eat more—sometimes 40% to 50% more—when they dine in groups (e.g., de Castro et al., 1997; Patel & Schlundt, 2001). As meals eaten by groups are longer in duration than those eaten by solo individuals, people have more opportunity to keep eating when in groups than alone. Watching someone else eat also increases social imitation of the eating response. When the participants in one study witnessed another person eating 20 soda crackers, they ate far more crackers themselves than did participants who saw someone eat only one (Nisbett & Storms, 1974). People even seem to prepare relatively larger portions for meals to be eaten in groups than individually, as if they anticipate that the group members will be able to consume more than they would if alone. So long as the group does not include a substantial portion of dieters, the group may continue to eat until all the available food is consumed. Solitary eaters are more likely to eat only until they are sated (Herman, Roth, & Polivy, 2003). Larger groups trigger greater increases in eating, although at a decreasing rate, similar to response patterns suggested by social impact theory (Latané, 1981).

Groups do not always facilitate eating, however. The social facilitation of eating is weak when co-eaters are strangers or disliked, and strongest when people dine with families and friends. The social facilitation of eating is also limited to coaction rather than audience situations. People eat more when others with them are eating, but they tend to eat less when the other people who are present are observing them (Herman et al., 2003).

Electronic Performance Monitoring (EPM)   Social facilitation is not limited to face-to-face, or collocated, group settings. The *presence* of others in a virtual sense—made possible when people join with others via computers, telephones, or other communication systems—can also enhance performance on simple tasks but undermine performance on complicated ones. Social psychologist John Aiello, for example, drew on studies of social facilitation in his analyses of **electronic performance monitoring**, or **EPM**. Many businesses can now track the performance of their employees throughout the workday with computer information networks. When workers use their computer to enter data, communicate with one another, or search databases for stored information, their activity can be monitored automatically. Does EPM enhance performance, or does it create so much evaluation anxiety that performance suffers? Aiello found that EPM may enhance employees' productivity, but in ways that are consistent with social facilitation effects. He studied people working on a data entry task. Some were alone, some were working with others, and some were members of a cohesive group. Aiello discovered that EPM enhanced the performance of highly skilled workers, but interfered with the performance of less skilled participants. Monitoring also increased workers' feeling of stress, except among those who were part of a cohesive work group (Aiello & Kolb, 1995). Individuals responded more positively to monitoring when they believed that they could turn off the monitoring and that only their job-related activities were being monitored, as well as when they had the opportunity to participate in decisions about the use

---

electronic performance monitoring (EPM) The use of information technologies, such as computer networks, to track, analyze, and report information about workers' performance.

of the monitoring system (Alge, 2001; Douthitt & Aiello, 2001; Samaranayake & Gamage, 2012).

Social Facilitation in Educational Settings
Much can be learned when one is alone, but until recently most formalized learning activities occurred in the presence of other people. In some cases, the student may work with one other person, the teacher or mentor, but more frequently a class of learners is assembled in one place with the hope that learning will occur en masse (see Focus 10.1).

But even though learning in a social context is a common practice, the presence of other people may actually inhibit the acquisition of new concepts and skills. Others can be distracting, and, during the early phases of learning, this distraction can interfere with overt and covert practicing. When the participants in one project needed to learn a list of words, they were too embarrassed to rehearse the material by saying it aloud, and their performance suffered (Berger et al., 1981, 1982). Studies of athletes acquiring new skills, students learning a second language, and clinicians developing their therapeutic skills have indicated that learning proceeds more rapidly, at least initially, when learners work alone (Ferris & Rowland, 1983; MacCracken & Stadulis, 1985; Schauer, Seymour, & Geen, 1985).

Zajonc (1965, p. 274), however, suggests that once students have learned their skills well, then they should perform with others present if possible (Utman, 1997). He recommends the student:

> study all alone, preferably in an isolated cubicle, and arrange to take his examinations in the company of many other students, on stage, and in the presence of a large audience. The results of his examination would be beyond his wildest expectations, provided, of course, he had learned his material quite thoroughly.

SOCIAL LOAFING

Modern air travel requires not only the services of the group of pilots who fly the planes, but dozens of other groups who handle service, ticketing, security,

maintenance, transportation, and so on. The work of these groups is often outstanding, but anyone who has traveled has likely encountered a group that was neither efficient nor effective. Captain Sullenberger, describing his own experience in the industry, writes: "The gate agent hasn't pulled the jetway up to the plane in time. The skycap is supposed to bring the wheelchair and hasn't…. The caterer hasn't brought all the first-class meals…. You get tired of constantly trying to correct what you corrected yesterday" (Sullenberger, 2009, pp. 158–159). Some groups, it seems, are not so intent on minimizing the gap between their potential performance and their actual performance.

The Ringelmann Effect

Max Ringelmann (1913), a nineteenth-century French agricultural engineer, was one of the first researchers to study the relationship between process loss and group productivity. Ringelmann's questions were practical ones: How many oxen should be yoked in one team? Should you plow a field with two horses or three? Can five men turn a mill crank faster than four? But Ringelmann, instead of speculating about the answers to these questions, set up teams of varying sizes and measured their collective power.

Productivity Losses in Groups Ringelmann's most startling discovery was that workers—and that includes horses, oxen, and men—all become less productive in groups. A team pulling a rope is stronger than a single opponent or an audience applauding makes more noise than an individual. But even though a group outperforms an individual, the group does not usually work at maximum efficiency. When Ringelmann had individuals and groups pull on a rope attached to a pressure gauge, groups performed below their predicted potential productivity (Steiner, 1972). If person A and person B could each pull 100 units when they worked alone, could they pull 200 units when they pooled their efforts? No, their output reached only 186. A three-person group did not produce 300 units, but only 255. An eight-person group managed only

---

F o c u s   10.1   Cross-cultural Perspectives: Learning Experiences in Groups

Learning is considered to be a process best achieved collectively. Groups are used in a variety of ways in many educational settings, including small seminars, group discussions, problem-based learning teams, study groups, and so on, with student-centered approaches gaining in popularity relative to traditional, teacher-centered methods. Group projects, for example, teach students how to work effectively in groups and teams, and they can help students stay focused on their academic goals (Gillies, 2007). Moreover, students who are members of effectively functioning **study groups** outperform students who do not work in groups (Webb, Troper, & Fall, 1995).

Group approaches to learning, however, are not enthusiastically embraced by everyone. As noted in Chapter 4, some people's beliefs about groups are decidedly negative, and they avoid taking classes that make use of group learning methods. One survey of college students found that many had taken classes that used group-based experiences, but only 32% of the students rated their small-group experiences positively in terms of learning outcomes. The best predictors of negative attitudes toward learning groups were the instructor's failure to explain the goals of the group activity, the lack of preparedness of other students, and the tendency for one or two people in the group to do most of the work (Hillyard, Gillespie, & Lettig, 2010).

These reactions may also be related to people's beliefs about how people best learn. As educator and social psychologist David A. Kolb (1984) explains in his theory of learning styles, not everyone likes to learn new things in the same way. People differ, for example, in their preference for concrete experiences versus abstract conceptualizations. Some prefer learning in situations that provide them with immediate, direct experiences, but others feel they learn best by studying abstract, theoretical concepts. People also differ in their preference for active versus reflective learning. Some prefer to observe situations and then reflect on the meaning and implications of the events they have witnessed. Others are more action-focused; they wish to test things out, initiate action, and seek solutions through active experimentation.

These differences in learning styles influence people's reactions to group-learning experiences. Those who prefer to learn through active, concrete experiences are more positive when evaluating group learning, particularly in comparison to those who like to learn through abstract, reflective experiences. Active, concrete learners were more likely to agree with such items as "Group work helps me learn better," "Group work is a productive use of class time," and "Group work engages my interest," whereas students' whose learning style emphasized reflection and observation were more likely to say "I learn best when I am working alone." They also rated listening to lectures as more educationally beneficial than most other students (Gardner & Korth, 1998, p. 31).

Kolb's concept of learning styles may also explain how people from different cultures approach learning in small-group settings. One review of studies of the residents of many different countries, including Australia, Germany, Japan, the United States, Russia, France, and China, identified country-level differences in preference for active, experiential (direct), reflective, and more abstractive learning experiences. Learners in Australia, the United States, and, to a lesser degree, France and Quebec, favored experiential learning more than students in Japan, China, and Germany. These differences may have been due, in part, to perceptions of power and hierarchy. In countries such as Japan, China, and Greece, which are higher in power distance, students preferred teacher-centered approaches to learning, such as lecturing. In low power-distance countries, like Australia and the United States, group approaches were preferred (Yamazaki, 2005; see, too, Ioakimidis & Myloni, 2010). Other researchers have found that practical, skill-based learning is more valued in some cultures than others, and if students associate group activities with skill-based learning, then these cultural values may also influence their reaction to group methods. One study of students from several European countries found that French learners had no preference for either practical or conceptual learning, but that Spanish and East European learners preferred a more practical approach (Jackson, 1996).

Researchers have only begun to explore these cultural differences, but the available research suggests that they are more expectations than deeply held cultural standards. As one researcher discovered after surveying students taking classes in 11 different countries, students may prefer one method of learning to another, but they all recognized the value of learning in groups rather than in traditional, authority-based classes (Littlewood, 2001). Moreover, as Kolb (1984) makes clear, even though individuals may prefer one mode of learning, all the methods in his model—concrete experiences, active exploration, reflective observation, and abstract conceptualization— are necessary steps to take to achieve a full understanding of a topic. Thus, the best course in groups will involve not only group activities, but also reflection, observation, exploration, and theorizing.

---

study group A self-organized, self-directed group formed by students for the purpose of studying course material.

392, not 800. Groups certainly outperformed individuals—but as more and more people were added, the group became increasingly inefficient (see Figure 10.3). To honor its discoverer, this tendency for groups to become less productive as group size increases is now known as the **Ringelmann effect** (Ingham et al., 1974; Kravitz & Martin, 1986, present an excellent summary and interpretation of Ringelmann's work.)

Ringelmann believed that this reduction in productivity had two sources. First, *coordination losses*, or "the lack of simultaneity of their efforts," introduced inefficiencies into each group (Ringelmann, 1913, p. 9). Even on a simple task, such as rope pulling, people tend to pull and pause at different times, resulting in some process loss and a failure to reach their full productive potential. Ringelmann's groups often sang a song together in an attempt to synchronize their efforts and minimize coordination losses. Second, *motivation losses* were also sapping group productivity: People did not work as hard when they were in groups rather than alone. After watching a group of prisoners turning the crank of a flour mill, for example, he noted that their performance was "mediocre because after only a little while, each man, trusting in his neighbor to furnish the desired effort, contented himself by merely following the movement of the crank, and sometimes even let himself be carried along by it" (p. 10; translation from Kravitz & Martin, 1986, p. 938). This reduction of effort by individuals working in groups is now known as **social loafing** (Williams, Harkins, & Latané, 1981).

Many Hands Make Light the Work   Bibb Latané, Kipling Williams, and Stephen Harkins disentangled the effects of both coordination loss and

---

Ringelmann effect The tendency, first documented by Max Ringelmann, for people to become less productive when they work with others; this loss of efficiency increases as group size increases, but at a gradually decreasing rate.

social loafing The reduction of individual effort exerted when people work in groups compared to when they work alone.

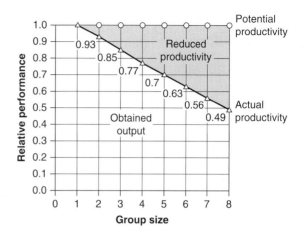

FIGURE 10.3   The Ringelmann effect. Ringelmann (1913) found that the level of productivity of each group member decreased as groups increased in size. For example, members of three-person groups reached only 85% of productive potential, whereas those in eight-person groups reached only 49% of their productive potential.

SOURCE: From tabled data in Ringelmann, M. (1913). Recherches sur les moteurs animes: Travail de homme [Research on animate sources of power: The work of man]. *Annales de l'Institut National Agronomique, 2e serie—tome XII*, 1–40.

social loafing in a series of cleverly designed studies. They told the men they recruited for their groups that they were researching "the effects of sensory feedback on the production of sound in social groups" and that all they needed to do was to cheer as loudly as they could. They asked the participants to wear blindfolds and headsets, so their performance would not be influenced by "the effects of sensory feedback" (1979, p. 824). They then asked participants to shout as loudly as they could while the headsets played a stream of loud noise. Consistent with the Ringelmann effect, groups of participants made more noise than individuals, but groups failed to reach their potential. When the participants were tested alone, they averaged a rousing 9.22 dynes/cm^2 (about as loud as a pneumatic drill). In dyads, each participant shouted at only 66% of capacity and in six-person groups at 36% of capacity. This drop in productivity is charted in Figure 10.4 (Latané, Williams, & Harkins, 1979, Experiment 2, p. 826; see also Harkins, Latané, & Williams, 1980; Williams et al., 1981).

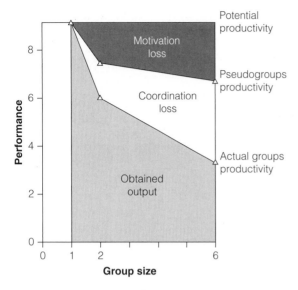

FIGURE 10.4 Social loafing and coordination losses in groups. Latané and his colleagues disentangled the two major causes of productivity losses in groups by leading people to think they were working in groups when they actually were not. The people in these "groups" (labeled "Pseudogroups productivity") suffered from motivation loss, but not from coordination loss since they were actually working alone. The shaded portion represents motivation loss (social loafing) and the unshaded portion represents coordination loss. They combine to create the Ringelmann effect.

DATA SOURCE: Adapted from "Many hands make light the Work: The Causes and Consequences of Social Loafing," by B. Latané, K. Williams, & S. Harkins, *Journal of Personality and Social Psychology, 37*, 1979.

But how much was this drop in productivity due to social loafing and how much due to coordination problems? Latané and his colleagues separated out these sources of process loss by testing noise production in "pseudogroups." In these conditions, participants were led to believe that either one other participant or five other participants were shouting with them, but in actuality, they were working alone. (The blindfolds and headsets made this deception possible.) Thus, any loss of production obtained in these pseudogroup conditions could not be due to coordination problems, because there were no other group members shouting. Instead, any decline in production could only be blamed on the reduced effort brought about by social loafing. As

Figure 10.4 indicates, when participants thought that one other person was working with them, they shouted only 82% as intensely. If they thought that five other persons were shouting, they reached only 74% of their capacity. These findings suggest that even if work groups are so well organized that virtually all losses due to faulty coordination are eliminated, actual productivity will not equal the potential productivity due to social loafing.

Causes of and Cures for Social Loafing

People carrying out all sorts of physical and mental tasks—including brainstorming, evaluating employees, monitoring equipment, interpreting instructions, and formulating causal judgments—have been shown to exert less effort when they combine their efforts in a group situation. Even worse, loafing seems to go unrecognized by group members. When people in groups are asked if they are working as hard as they can, they generally claim that they are doing their best, even though the objective evidence indicates that they are loafing. Evidently, people are not aware that they are loafing, or they are simply unwilling to admit it (Karau & Williams, 1993). Fortunately, researchers have identified a number of steps that can be taken to reduce the level of social loafing in a group.

Increase Identifiability   Studies of social loafing suggest that people are *less* productive when they work with others. But studies of social facilitation, discussed earlier in this chapter, find that people are *more* productive when others are present (at least when the task is easy). Which is it?

Both. When people feel as though their level of effort cannot be ascertained because the task is a collective one, then social loafing becomes likely. But when people feel that they are being evaluated, they tend to exert more effort and their productivity increases. If the task is an individualistic one, and is easy, social facilitation occurs. But when group members are anonymous and their contributions are unidentifiable, the presence of others reduces evaluation apprehension, and social loafing becomes more likely (Arterberry, Cain, & Chopko, 2007; Harkins & Szymanski, 1987, 1988; Jackson & Latané, 1981).

Researchers illustrated the importance of evaluation by asking the members of a four-person group to generate as many ideas as possible for a common object. The participants did not discuss their ideas out loud but simply wrote them on slips of paper. Some of the participants thought that their ideas were individually identifiable, whereas others thought that their ideas were being collected in a common pool. Moreover, some participants believed that everyone was devising uses for the same object, but others thought that each group member was working with a different object. In this study, loafing occurred not only when ideas were pooled, but also when the participants believed that their individual outputs were not comparable or could not be evaluated (Harkins & Jackson, 1985). When each individual member's output was identifiable, on the other hand, loafing was virtually eliminated (Hardy &Latané, 1986; Kerr & Bruun, 1981; Sanna, 1992; Williams et al., 1981).

Minimize Free Riding   Thousands of people listen to public radio without making a contribution when the radio asks for donations. Some audience members do not clap during the call for an encore because they know their applause will not be missed. Many students avoid group projects where the entire group receives the same grade, because inevitably one or more members of the group will not do their share of the work (Hoffman & Rogelberg, 2001).

All these situations invite **free riding**—members doing less than their share of the work because others will make up for their slack. Although norms of fairness warn members to do their part, if they feel that the group does not need them or their contribution, they will be tempted to free-ride. When group members think that they are an indispensable part of the group—perhaps because their contribution is unique or essential for the group's success—they work harder (Kerr & Bruun, 1983). They also free-ride less in smaller groups because each person plays a larger role in determining the group's outcomes (Kameda et al., 1992). But free riding sometimes increases when members become suspicious of the level of effort being invested by the other group members. Rather than looking like a "sucker" by working harder than the others, group members reduce their efforts to match the level they think other group members are expending. This **sucker effect** is strongest when they feel that their fellow group members are competent but lazy (Hart, Bridgett, & Karau, 2001).

Set Goals   Groups that set clear, challenging goals outperform groups whose members have lost sight of their objectives (Kleingeld, van Mierlo, & Arends, 2011). When truck drivers who hauled logs from the woods to the mill were initially told to do their best when loading the logs, the men only carried about 60% of what they could legally haul (Latham & Baldes, 1975). When the drivers were later encouraged to reach a goal of 94% of the legal limit, they increased their efficiency and met this specific goal. In a study of groups generating ideas, members were more productive when they had a clear standard by which to evaluate the quality of their own work and the group's work (Harkins & Szymanski, 1989). Other research has suggested that clear goals stimulate a number of production-enhancing processes, including increases in effort, better planning, more accurate monitoring of the quality of the group's work, and increased commitment to the group (Weldon, Jehn, & Pradhan, 1991). The group's goals should also be challenging rather than too easily attained.

---

free riding Contributing less to a collective task when one believes that other group members will compensate for this lack of effort.

sucker effect The tendency for members to contribute less to a group endeavor when they expect that others will think negatively of those who work too hard or contribute too much (considering them to be a "sucker").

The advantages of working in a group are lost if the task is so easy that it can be accomplished even if the group loafs, so care should be taken to set the standards high—but not so high that they are unattainable (Hinsz, 1995; Latham & Locke, 2007; Weldon & Weingart, 1993).

Increase Involvement Sullenberger (2009) was very involved in his work as a pilot. Hardworking, attentive to detail, and serious about providing quality service, his wife described him as a "pilot's pilot" (p. 276). People like Sully do not loaf in groups. When researchers first screened people on a set of questions that measured their approach to work—the Protestant Ethic Scale—they discovered people with high scores loafed very little. Such sentiments as "People who fail at a job have usually not tried hard enough" and "There are few satisfactions equal to the realization that one has done his best at a job" are antithetical to not doing one's share of the work (Smrt & Karau, 2011). Individuals who enjoy competition and working with others in groups are also less likely to loaf (Stark, Shaw, & Duffy, 2007).

In general, the more engaged people are in the group or the group's work, the less likely they will loaf. So long as the competition remains "friendly," group members may persevere with much greater intensity when they are vying with others in the group for the best score (Hinsz, 2005). Challenging, difficult tasks reduce loafing, but so do those that will determine group members' personal outcomes—either by reward or by punishment (Brickner, Harkins, & Ostrom, 1986; Shepperd, 1993, 1995; Shepperd & Wright, 1989). Social loafing is also reduced when rewards for successful performance are group-based rather than individually based—so long as the group is not too large in size (DeMatteo, Eby, & Sundstrom, 1998) and the reward is divided nearly equally among all the group members (Honeywell-Johnson & Dickinson, 1999; Liden et al., 2004).

Involvement may even prompt group members to compensate for the expected failures or incompetencies of their fellow group members by expending extra effort. Kipling Williams and Steven Karau (1991) documented **social compensation** by convincing individuals that their group's task was a meaningful one, but that the motivation of other group members was in doubt (apparently because one of the other experimenters considered the research topic to be boring). Participants were also led to expect that their partners were either skilled or unskilled at the task. Williams and Karau discovered that group members worked hardest when the task was meaningful and the members believed that their coworkers' ability was minimal. A field study of loafing in a classroom setting even suggests that a high level of involvement may trump the sucker effect. If students' grades were on the line, when they discovered that one of their group members was a loafer, they tended to work harder themselves, rather than reducing their own effort to look less like a sucker (Liden et al., 2004).

Increase Identification with the Group Social identity theory also suggests a way to reduce loafing: increase the extent to which group members identify with their group or organization (Haslam, 2004). Social identity theory suggests that the difference between a hardworking group and a loafing group is the match between the group's tasks and its members' self-definitions. If people are working together but the group and its tasks have no meaning to them, they care very little if their group succeeds or fails. But when individuals derive their sense of self and identity from their membership in the group, then *social loafing* is replaced by *social laboring* as members expend extra effort for their group. Individuals sometimes work hard when they think "This task is important to me," but they are likely to work even harder when they think "This task is

---

social compensation The tendency for group members to expend greater effort on important collective tasks to offset the anticipated insufficiencies in the efforts and abilities of their co-members.

important to *us*" (Haslam, 2004; cf. Gockel et al., 2008).

The Collective Effort Model

Karau and Williams's (1993, 2001) **collective effort model (CEM)** provides a comprehensive theoretical framework for understanding the causes and cures of social loafing. Drawing on classic expectancy-value theories of motivation, they suggested that two factors determine group members' level of motivation: their expectations about reaching a goal and the value of that goal. Motivation is greatest when people think that the goal is within their reach (expectations are high) and they consider the goal to be valuable. Motivation diminishes if expectations are low or individuals do not value the goal. Working in a group, unfortunately, can diminish both expectations about reaching a goal and the value that is placed on that goal. In groups, the link between our effort and the chance of success is ambiguous. Even if we work hard, others may not, and the group may fail. Moreover, even if the group does succeed, we personally may not benefit much from the group's good performance. Earning a good grade on a project completed by a group may not be as satisfying as earning a good grade on a project that we complete working on our own.

Karau and Williams tested the CEM's basic predictions in a meta-analysis. Their review of 78 studies supported their basic theoretical contention that loafing is reduced if individuals' expectations for success are high and they feel that the goal they are seeking is a valuable one. They also identified a number of other consistencies that emerged across studies. For example, loafing was greater among men than women, in Western countries compared to Eastern countries, and for simple tasks rather than complex tasks.

---

collective effort model (CEM) A theoretical explanation of group productivity that traces losses of productivity in groups to diminished expectations about successful goal attainment and the diminished value of group goals (developed by Steven Karau and Kipling Williams).

GROUPS VERSUS INDIVIDUALS

Groups tend to lose some of their productivity due to social loafing, but they usually outperform individuals. A lone individual in a tug-of-war with a group will lose. Individuals racing each other will run faster than they would if racing against the clock. A group taking a multiple-choice test will probably get a higher score than an individual taking the same test. Three flight attendants will be able to seat and service 150 passengers far more effectively than only one could.

But how well do groups perform on more complex tasks that require coordination and collaboration? Companies and businesses must monitor, regulate, and organize the activities of hundreds of employees—should they organize their workers into teams? When quality matters, will a single, dedicated craftsperson build a more beautiful product than a work crew that must plan each action as raw construction materials are transformed into a finished product? Mountaineers can climb alone, but can they reach the highest peaks only by working with others? When do groups outperform individuals?

Steiner's theory of group productivity, introduced earlier in the chapter, suggests the answer to this question depends on the type of task being attempted. Some tasks, Steiner explained, require high levels of coordinated activity but others do not; even if group members make little or no attempt to adapt their actions to match those of others, the group will still succeed. A group working on an assembly line, for example, must combine members' products in ways that differ from the combination process used by a team playing baseball or pilots flying a commercial jetliner.

Steiner called the combination processes dictated by the problem or group activity the **task demands** and suggested that they vary depending on the divisibility of the task, the type of output

---

task demands The effect that a problem or task's features, including its divisibility and difficulty, have on the procedures the group can use to complete the task.

T A B L E 10.3   **A Summary of Steiner's Taxonomy of Tasks: Types, Qualities, and Examples**

Divisibility: Can the task be broken down into sub-tasks?		
Divisible	The task has subcomponents that can be identified and assigned to specific members.	• Playing a football game • Preparing a six-course meal
Unitary	The task does not have subcomponents.	• Pulling on a rope • Reading a book
Quantity versus quality: Is quantity produced more important than the quality of the performance?		
Maximizing	*Quantity*: The more produced the better the performance.	• Generating many ideas • Lifting a great weight • Scoring the most goals
Optimizing	*Quality*: A correct or optimal solution is needed.	• Developing the best answer • Solving a math problem
Interdependence: How are individual inputs combined to yield a group product?		
Additive	Individual inputs are added together.	• Pulling a rope • Shoveling snow
Compensatory	A decision is made by averaging together individual decisions.	• Estimating an ox's weight by asking three people to guess and averaging their averaging the guesses • Averaging ratings of job applicants
Disjunctive	The group selects one solution or product from a pool of members' solutions or products.	• Picking one answer to a math problem to be the group's answer • Letting one art project represent the entire school
Conjunctive	All group members must contribute to the product for it to be completed.	• Climbing a mountain • Eating a meal as a group
Discretionary	The group decides how individual inputs relate to the group product.	• Deciding to shovel snow together • Choosing to vote on the best answer to a problem

SOURCE: Adapted from *Group Processes and Productivity* by I. D. Steiner. © 1972 by Academic Press.

desired, and the combination rules required to complete the task (see Table 10.3).

First, some tasks are *divisible*—they can be broken down into subtasks that can be assigned to different members—whereas other tasks are *unitary*. Building a house, planting a large garden, or working a series of math problems by assigning one to each group member are all **divisible tasks**, because the entire task can be split into parts. **Unitary tasks**, however, cannot be divided: Only one painter is needed for a small closet in a house, only one gardener can plant a single seed, and only one person is needed to solve a simple math problem.

Second, some tasks call for a high rate of production (*maximization*), whereas others require a high-quality, correct outcome (*optimization*). With

divisible task A task that can be broken down into subcomponents that can then be assigned to individuals or to subgroups within the group.

unitary task A task that cannot be performed piecemeal because it does not break down into any subcomponents.

maximizing tasks, quantity is what counts. In a relay race, tug-of-war, or block-stacking problem, performance depends on sheer quantity; the emphasis is on maximal production. For **optimizing tasks**, a good performance is the one that most closely matches a predetermined criterion. Examples of optimizing tasks include estimating the number of beans in a jar or coming up with the best solution to a problem.

Third, members' contributions to the group task can be *combined* in different ways. On an assembly line, for example, the members perform a specific task repeatedly, and the product is finished when each member has made his or her contribution. The members of a rock band, in contrast, all play and sing together, so each member's contribution must mesh with the other members' contributions. Steiner (1972) describes five basic combinatorial strategies: *additive, compensatory, disjunctive, conjunctive,* and *discretionary*. By taking into account the type of task the group is attempting, the performance of groups relative to individuals can be predicted with more accuracy.

Additive Tasks

On the surface, **additive tasks** are the easiest types of tasks for a group to complete. Since they are both divisible and maximizing, group members need only add their contribution to the group's output, so coordination demands are minimal. So long as each group member can perform his or her assigned task—such as pulling on a rope, editing an online encyclopedia, cheering at a football game, processing documents, clapping after a concert, responding to customer complaints in a call center,

or raking leaves in a yard—the productivity of the group will probably exceed the productivity of the single individual.

Studies of both social facilitation and social loafing, however, warn that working on additive tasks is more complicated than it seems. If working in the presence of others, people may perform their piece of the additive task particularly well—but only if their subtask is a relatively simple one. People shucking green beans together on the front porch may work more effectively than individuals working separately, but once the task gets more challenging, the benefits of social facilitation will likely be negligible. Social loafing is also likely given the structure of an additive task. Adding more and more members will increase a group's productivity when it works on an additive task, but at an ever decreasing rate of gain. One solution to this very basic problem is to create "groups within groups." When large groups are split into smaller ones, members loaf less (Waber et al., 2010).

Compensatory Tasks

When groups attempt **compensatory tasks**, the members average their individual judgments or solutions together to generate an answer. For example, each one of the passengers of Flight 1549 could be contacted and asked to estimate how long it took to rescue them from the cold waters of the Hudson after the crash. The estimates could then be averaged to generate a group judgment, which could be compared to the actual time taken: only 24 minutes (Miracle on the Hudson Survivors, 2009).

The Wisdom of Crowds Effect Legendary nineteenth-century polymath Francis Galton was surprised by the accuracy of groups when making compensatory decisions. Known for his studies of

---

maximizing task A task or project that calls for a high rate of production.

optimizing task A task or project that has a best solution and outcome, thus the quality of the group's performance can be judged by comparing the product to a quality-defining standard.

additive task A task or project that a group can complete by cumulatively combining individual members' inputs.

---

compensatory task A task or project that a group can complete by literally averaging together (mathematically combining) individual members' solutions or recommendations.

intelligence, Galton questioned whether a group could possibly make more accurate judgments than an expert. He had the opportunity to test his hypothesis when he came across a "Guess the weight of an Ox" contest at a local fair. Each contestant estimated the ox's weight, and the person who came closest to the ox's actual weight won a prize. Galton took the estimates home and examined them, expecting that the crowd would be far off the mark. Yet, the weight of the ox was 1,198 pounds, and the average of the judgments of the 800 contestants was 1,197, confirming the *wisdom of the crowd effect* (Surowiecki, 2004). Some people overestimated the ox's weight, but others underestimated, so the "group" judgment, which was an average of all the estimates offered, was more accurate than the judgments made by experts and by most of the individuals.

Crowds are wiser than individuals for at least two reasons. First, the compensatory method is relative immune to group process loss caused by poor coordination, loafing, or undue influence of the persuasive but unwise. In face-to-face groups, those who are well-respected by the group—but not necessarily any better informed—often sway the group's decision. They do not when groups work on compensatory tasks—provided the group members make their judgments independently of others. Second, a statistically derived group score is more accurate because it is based on multiple measures. When single individuals make multiple estimates, and their estimates are averaged, their judgments are also more accurate (Stoop, 1932). Because of the importance of basing the final estimate on a sufficient number of responses, the compensatory method requires a large enough number of judgments to compensate for any extreme judgments.

Swarm Size and Problem Difficulty Crowds may be wise, but what happens when they encounter a very difficult problem (Krause et al., 2011)? Researchers in Germany tested the limits of "swarm intelligence" by asking visitors to a science exhibit to step up to a computer console and enter in their best guesses for two questions. One problem was easy: All

they had to do was estimate the number of marbles in a jar next to the computer console. The second problem was more difficult: "Estimate how many times a coin needs to be tossed for the probability that the coin will show heads each time to be roughly as small as that of winning the German lotto" (p. 942). Statisticians who were also active lotto players may have known that it would take about 24 consecutive heads to equal the very remote chances of winning the lottery (1 in 35 million), but most visitors found the second question to be very challenging.

The crowd was quite wise when answering the easy question. The mean for the group was 553.6, coming within 1.5% of the actual number of marbles (562). But the crowd's average estimate for the second question, 498 flips of the coin, was not accurate at all, suggesting a crowd will not be wise when its members lack the knowledge needed to solve the problem. These findings also affirmed the importance of recruiting enough people to form the crowd (see Figure 10.5). Even for the easy question (shown in the top chart), groups with ten members or fewer were not as accurate as the majority of the individual members. Groups that ranged in size from 10 to 40 members outperformed most of the individuals in the group, but not the top 25% of individuals. Once the group included more than 40 members, the group's accuracy surged past most of the group's members, but this effect occurred only for the relatively easy estimation problem. Estimates for the difficult problem, shown in the lower chart in Figure 10.5, were always inferior to individual member's scores—because so many of the group members' estimates were massively incorrect. Errors did not have a chance to cancel each other out.

Disjunctive Tasks

Sully, Skiles, and Harten had a decision to make. Without power, Flight 1549 needed a place to land. Harten, the air traffic controller, favored a return to LaGuardia. Skiles did not express any preference. Sully initially considered the nearby Teterboro airport, but then changed his choice to the Hudson. There could be only one

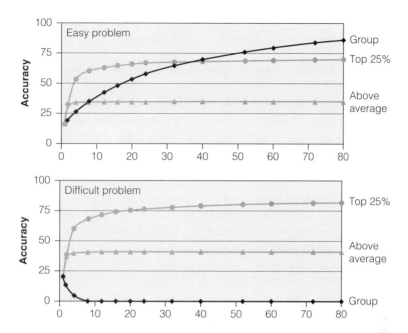

FIGURE 10.5 The "wisdom of the crowd" when attempting an easy problem (top chart) and a difficult problem (bottom chart). Scores could range from 0, indicating low accuracy, to 100, indicating high accuracy. The three plotted lines correspond to the "group" estimate (black diamond lines), the average score of randomly picked individuals from the top half of the distribution (grey triangles), and the average score of randomly picked individuals from the top 25% of the estimators (grey circles).

SOURCE: From "Swarm Intelligence in Humans: Diversity Can Trump Ability," by S. Krause, R. James, J. J. Faria, G. D. Ruxton, & J. Krause, *Animal Behavior, 81,* 941–948, 2011.

solution—they could not switch to Plan B if Plan A failed.

When groups work at **disjunctive tasks**, they must generate a single solution that will stand as the group's outcome. Juries making decisions about guilt or innocence, computer technicians deciding which program bug to fix first, or the coaching staff setting the lineup for the day's game, are all performing disjunctive tasks. These types of tasks tend to be both unitary and optimizing, for they cannot be broken down into subtasks, and they require a high-quality or correct solution rather than a large quantity of product.

---

disjunctive task A task or project that is completed when a single solution, decision, or recommendation is adopted by the group.

Disjunctive tasks often require discussion and decisions; Chapter 11 provides a more detailed analysis of how groups tackle such tasks. In general, however, groups perform disjunctive tasks better than most of the individual members. For example, if four students complete a quiz as a group, the group will likely outscore most of the individual students because more heads means more information and better detection of errors. In an actual class where students were permitted to take tests in pairs or alone, pairs scored nearly 4% points higher than individuals (Pandey & Kapitanoff, 2011).

When Does "Truth" Win? When aviation experts reviewed all the facts related to Flight 1549 they concluded Sully's solution was the best one given the circumstances. The flight crew's choice of that alternative illustrates the *truth-wins rule*.

The best solution (truth), when suggested during the group's deliberations, was the one the group adopted (wins).

Truth, however, does not always win, for in some cases even though the correct answer is known by at least one group member, the group fails to select it as the group's solution. Rosa may be certain that the answer to the question "Who first documented the reduction of individual productivity when in groups?" is "Ringelmann," but her group may not accept her solution because they doubt her skills or because someone of higher status may propose a different solution. Ringelmann is the correct answer, but this truth will not win out over error unless someone in the group supports Rosa and her answer—a *truth-supported-wins rule*.

When we are told the answer to a *Eureka problem*, we are very certain that the answer offered is correct. It fits so well, we react with an "Aha!" or "Eureka!" The answers to *non-Eureka problems*, in contrast, are not so satisfying. The truth–wins rule usually holds for groups working on *Eureka problems*, whereas the truth-supported-wins rule holds for groups working on *non-Eureka problems*. Even after arguing about them, we often wonder if the recommended answer is the correct one. Consider, for example, the famous horse-trading problem:

> A man bought a horse for $60 and sold it for $70. Then he bought it back for $80 and again sold it for $90. How much money did he make in the horse-trading business? (Maier & Solem, 1952, p. 281)

When 67 groups discussed this problem, many included a member who knew the correct answer, but even these groups often adopted the wrong solution. In this case, truth lost because knowledgeable members had a difficult time persuading the other members to adopt their solutions. In fact, some people later changed their answers to match the incorrect solution advocated by their groups (Maier & Solem, 1952; the answer, by the way, is $20). Thus, groups perform at the level of the best member of the group only if (1) the member who knows the answer shares his or her answer with the others, and (2) the group decides to adopt this answer as the solution (Davis, 1973; Littlepage, 1991; Steiner, 1972).

Intellective and Judgmental Tasks   Groups are also more likely to recognize, and accept, the correct solution when the person who proposes it can demonstrate that the solution is the correct one. If a group member backs up a solution with a proof, a citation, or a quote from an authority, the rest of the group may accept it. But if he or she says, "It's hard to explain, I just have a feeling that is the answer," then even the correct answer may not find acceptance within the group.

Social psychologist Patrick Laughlin (1980) bases his distinction between intellective and judgmental tasks on confirmability. **Intellective tasks**, like some Eureka tasks, yield solutions that can be objectively reviewed and judged as right or wrong. They have a demonstrably correct solution. **Judgmental tasks**, in contrast, require evaluative judgments for which no correct answer can be authoritatively determined. Logic and math problems are intellective tasks, whereas a jury's decision in a trial or the question "Was Captain Sullenberger a hero?" would be judgmental tasks. As tasks move along the continuum from clearly intellective to clearly judgmental, the superiority of groups relative to individuals also changes: Groups are more clearly superior when performing intellective tasks (Bonner & Baumann, 2008; Laughlin, Bonner, & Miner, 2002; Laughlin et al., 2003).

When the Leader Makes a Mistake   Groups can also fail at disjunctive tasks when a too-confident leader rejects a superior solution offered by a subordinate. Although Skiles and Sully worked well together, the formal lines of authority in the airline industry sometimes cause groups to make

---

intellective task A project, problem, or other type of task with results that can be evaluated objectively using some normative criterion, such as a mathematics problem with a known solution or the spelling of a word.
judgmental task A project, problem, or other type of task with results that cannot be evaluated objectively because there are no clear criteria to judge them against.

room is a **discretionary task**, because the members themselves can choose the method for combining individual inputs.

Process Gains In Groups

Steiner's (1972) analysis of task demands and their impact on group performance is summarized in Table 10.4. Groups perform additive tasks fairly well, although their productivity is often limited by social loafing. Groups also perform better than the average group member on many other kinds of tasks (compensatory, disjunctive, divisible conjunctive tasks when weaker members are assigned easier subtasks, and discretionary), but only when process losses are minimized. As Steiner's (1972) formula, $AP = PP - PL$, predicts, process losses turn potential productivity into actual productivity.

But don't groups sometimes achieve results that surpass what Steiner's theory predicts? Can't group members, by collaborating on a shared task, sometimes gain new solutions, energy, and insights into old problems that they would never have achieved as individuals? Aren't some groups greater than the sum of their parts? Does $1 + 1 + 1$ sometimes equal 4 instead of 3?

Searching for Synergy Group researchers have long sought definitive evidence of **synergy** in groups. Synergy occurs whenever the combined effect of two or more discrete systems is greater than the effect of these systems when they operate independently. Two drugs, for example, combine synergistically if their effects are greater when they are taken together rather than separately. In groups,

---

discretionary task A relatively unstructured task that can be completed by using a variety of social combination procedures, thus leaving the methods used in its completion to the discretion of the group or group leader.
synergy Producing an outcome as a group that is superior to the results that could have been achieved by a simple aggregation or accumulation of group members' individual efforts; a gain in performance caused by performance-enhancing group processes.

if synergy occurs, the group as a whole performs better than what would be expected given the skills and abilities of its members. Synergy, as defined by group researchers, is not group-level energy or a heightened sense of connectedness among members, but a process gain generated by performance-enhancing group processes. Synergy is sometimes called an *assembly bonus effect* because "the group is able to achieve collectively something which could not have been achieved by any member working alone or by a combination of individual efforts" (Collins & Guetzkow, 1964, p. 58).

Strong and Weak Synergy Social psychologist James Larson (2010) draws a distinction between weak and strong synergy. Imagine, for example, four students who, working separately, earn 70%, 80%, 80%, and 90% on a test. If, when they take the test as a group, they earn an 85%—which is a score above the average of the four individual scores and a better score than three of the four would have achieved working individually—then the group would demonstrate weak synergy. The group would be showing strong synergy, however, if it scored a 91% or higher—better than even the best member of the group.

Synergy eludes most groups. Steiner did not write his formula as $AP = PP - PL + PG$, where PG indicates process gains due to synergy. When individuals work on a collective task, the whole is often much less than the sum of the parts, as members exert less effort (social loafing) or let others do their share of the work (free-riding). Groups often outperform the most incompetent group member (the "better than the worst" effect), and, in most cases, they perform as well as the most typical group member. Rarely, however, do they perform above and beyond the level of the typical group member (weak synergy) or the better-than-the-best member (strong synergy; see Carey & Laughlin, 2012).

But synergy, although rare, does happen, particularly when the group members are highly motivated—when grades, jobs, or lives are on the line. For example, in one study, 222 classroom groups took tests that counted toward their course grades. These groups often outperformed their best

T A B L E   10.4   **A Summary of the Potential Productivity of Groups Working on Various Tasks**

Type of Task	Productivity Effect
Additive	*Better than the best*: The group exceeds the performance of even the best individual member.
Compensatory	*Better than most*: The group exceeds the performance of a substantial number of the individual members.
Disjunctive	*Better than average and sometimes equal to the best*: The group performs best if it accepts the most capable member's input as the group solution; groups rarely perform *better than the best* member. (Process gains resulting in synergy are rare.)
Conjunctive: Unitary	*Equal to the worst*: The group equals the performance of its least capable member.
Conjunctive: Divisible	*Better than the worst*: Performance will be superior if subtasks are matched to members' capabilities.
Discretionary	*Variable*: Performance depends on the combination rules adopted by the group.

members, suggesting that the groups could identify new and better solutions when they worked together (Michaelsen, Watson, & Black, 1989). Other investigators replicated these findings, although they concluded that the synergistic effects occurred primarily because someone in the group other than the best member knew the right answer and could correct the best member (Stasson & Bradshaw, 1995). Such groups apparently make this critically important judgment by considering the level of confidence each member expresses in his or her answer. The group is more likely to perform well when the member who is correct is also the most confident (Bahrami et al., 2010; see too Koriat, 2012).

Other researchers have examined the use of specialized performance methods designed to minimize all process loss, while maximizing the possibility of achieving process gain. The final section of this chapter examines several of these methods, particularly those that can be used by groups searching for creative solutions to difficult problems.

GROUP CREATIVITY

Sully and Skiles did not have much time to troubleshoot the problem and discuss alternatives. Their air traffic controller had proposed a few alternatives.

They tried to restart the engines, but as the plane lost altitude, Sully turned to Skiles and asked, "Got any ideas?" Their final solution, however, if not creative was certainly unusual. Commercial jets rarely land in the Hudson River.

Brainstorming

Had the crew of Flight 1549 more time they may have used a group method known as **brainstorming** to identify solutions to their problem. This method was developed by Alex Osborn (1957), an advertising executive, to help his colleagues identify novel, unusual, and imaginative solutions. The technique requires an open discussion of ideas and is guided by four basic rules:

- *Be expressive.* Express any idea that comes to mind, no matter how strange, wild, or fanciful. Do not be constrained or timid; freewheel whenever possible.

brainstorming A method for enhancing creativity in groups that calls for heightened expressiveness, postponed evaluation, quantity rather than quality, and deliberate attempts to build on earlier ideas.

- *Postpone evaluation.* Do not evaluate any of the ideas in any way during the idea-generation phase. All ideas are valuable.

- *Seek quantity.* The more ideas, the better. Quantity is desired, for it increases the possibility of finding an excellent solution.

- *Piggyback ideas.* Because all ideas belong to the group, members should try to modify and extend others' ideas whenever possible. Brainstorming is conducted in a group, so that participants can draw from one another.

Does Brainstorming Work? When groups need to think of new ideas, the call to "brainstorm" is often raised, but their faith in this method may be misplaced. Researchers began testing this method by comparing brainstorming groups to individuals and to so-called **nominal groups**: groups created by having individuals work alone and then pooling their ideas (a group "in name" only). Their studies offered support to brainstorming. A four-person brainstorming group, for example, would not only outperform any single individual but also a nominal group of four individuals. However, these investigations stacked the deck against the nominal groups; brainstorming groups were told to follow the four basic brainstorming rules, whereas the individuals composing the nominal group were not given any special rules concerning creativity. When individuals working alone were better informed about the purposes of the study and the need for highly creative responses, they often offered more solutions than individuals working in groups. In one study, for example, four-person groups came up with an average of 28 ideas in their session, whereas four individuals working alone suggested an average of 74.5 ideas when their ideas were pooled. The quality of ideas was also lower in groups—when the researchers rated each idea on creativity, they found that individuals had 79.2% of the good ideas. Groups also performed more poorly even when given more time to complete the task (Diehl & Stroebe, 1987; Mullen, Johnson, & Salas, 1991; see Paulus & Brown, 2007, for a review).

Production Blocking Brainstorming groups, like many performing groups, must struggle to overcome process losses as they strive to generate ideas. Even though members strive to expend maximum effort, social loafing detracts from their performance unless such safeguards as high identifiability, clear goals, and involvement prevent the undercutting of individual effort (Wegge & Haslam, 2005). But brainstorming groups also suffer coordination and cognitive losses. The originators of brainstorming thought that hearing others' ideas would stimulate the flow of ideas, but the clamor of creative voices instead resulted in **production blocking**. In brainstorming groups, members must wait their turn to get the floor and express their ideas, and, during that wait, they forget their ideas or decide not to express them. Hearing others is also distracting and can interfere with one's ability to do the cognitive work needed to generate ideas. Even when researchers tried to undo this blocking effect by giving brainstormers notepads and organizing their speaking turns, the groups still did not perform as well as individuals who were generating ideas alone (Diehl & Stroebe, 1987, 1991; Nijstad & Stroebe, 2006).

Evaluation Apprehension Evaluation apprehension can also limit the effectiveness of brainstorming groups, even though the "no evaluation" rule was

---

nominal group A collection of individuals that meets only the most minimal of requirements to be considered a group and so is a group in name only; in studies of performance, a control or baseline group created by having individuals work alone and then pooling their products.

---

production blocking A loss of productivity that occurs when group and procedural factors obstruct the group's progress toward its goals, particularly when individuals in a brainstorming session are delayed in stating their ideas until they can gain the floor and when group members are distracted by others' ideas and so generate fewer of their own.

designed to free members from such concerns (Diehl & Stroebe, 1987). Groups become even less effective when an authority watches them work. Apparently, members worry that the authority may view their ideas negatively (Mullen et al., 1991). Individuals with high social anxiety are particularly unproductive brainstormers and report feeling more nervous, anxious, and worried than group members who are less anxiety prone (Camacho & Paulus, 1995).

Social Matching   Social comparison processes also conspire to create a **social matching effect**. Although under-contributors are challenged to reach the pace established by others, over-contributors tend to reduce their contributions to match the group's mediocre standards. Since over-contribution is more effortful than under-contribution, over time the high performers tend to adjust their rate downward to match the group's lower norm (Brown & Paulus, 1996; Seta, Seta, & Donaldson, 1991).

Illusion of Group Productivity   Brainstorming groups are also unproductive because they often overestimate their productivity. In many cases, a group has no standard to determine how well it is performing, so individual members can only guess at the quantity and quality of their group's product and their personal contributions to the endeavor. These estimates, however, are often unrealistically positive, resulting in a robust **illusion of group productivity** (Stroebe, Diehl, & Abakoumkin, 1992). Members of groups working on collective tasks generally think that their group is more productive than most (Polzer, Kramer, & Neale, 1997). Nor do group members feel that they are doing less than their fair share. When members of a group trying to generate solutions to a problem were

---

social matching effect The tendency for individuals in brainstorming groups to match the level of productivity displayed by others in the group.
illusion of group productivity The tendency for members to believe that their group is performing effectively.

asked to estimate how many ideas they provided, each group member claimed an average of 36% of the ideas, when in reality they generated about 25% of the ideas (Paulus et al., 1993).

Several processes appear to combine to sustain this error in performance appraisal. Group members may intuitively mistake others' ideas for their own, and so, when they think about their own performance, they cognitively claim a few ideas that others actually suggested (Stroebe et al., 1992). When they brainstorm in groups, they can also compare themselves to others who generate relatively few ideas, reassuring them that they are one of the high performers (Paulus et al., 1993). Group brainstorming may also "feel" more successful since the communal process means that participants rarely experience failure. When alone and trying to think creatively, people repeatedly find that they are unable to come up with a new idea. In groups, because others' ideas are being discussed, people are less likely to experience this failure in their search for new ideas (Nijstad, Stroebe, & Lodewijkx, 2006).

Improving Brainstorming

Studies of brainstorming offer a clear recommendation: Do not use face-to-face deliberative groups to generate ideas unless special precautions are taken to minimize production blocking, evaluation apprehension, social matching, and social loafing. Groups can be creative, but Osborn's original suggestions should be augmented with additional requirements (see Paulus & Brown, 2007; Paulus et al., 2006), such as:

- *Stick to the rules*: Members should be trained to follow brainstorming rules and be given feedback if they violate any of the basic principles. Groups that have not practiced brainstorming methods usually generate only mediocre ideas.

- *Pay attention to everyone's ideas*: The key to brainstorming is exposure to other's ideas, but people tend to focus on their own suggestions and pay little attention to other people's suggestions. Many techniques can be used to force members' attention onto others' ideas, including listing the ideas on a board or asking members to repeat others' ideas.

- *Mix individual and group approaches*: Members should be given the opportunity to record their ideas individually during and after the session. One technique, called **brainwriting**, involves asking members to write down ideas on paper and then pass the paper along to others who add their ideas to the list. A post-group session during which members generate ideas by themselves enhances idea generation (Dugosh et al., 2000).

- *Take breaks*: Members should deliberately stop talking periodically to think in silence (Ruback, Dabbs, & Hopper, 1984).

- *Do not rush*: Members should have plenty of time to complete the task. Groups that work under time pressure often produce more solutions initially, but the quality of those solutions is lower than if they had spent more time on the task (Kelly, Futoran, & McGrath, 1990; Kelly & Karau, 1993).

- *Persist*: Members should stay focused on the task and avoid telling stories, talking in pairs, or monopolizing the session; they must continue to persist at the task even through periods of low productivity.

- *Facilitate the session*: Members' efforts should be coordinated by a skilled discussion leader. A skilled leader can motivate members by urging them on ("We can do this!"), correcting mistakes in the process ("Remember, the rules of brainstorming forbid criticism."), setting a clear standard ("Let's reach 100 solutions!"). and stressing the importance of individuality, uniqueness, and novelty (Goncalo & Staw, 2006). A facilitator can also record all of the ideas in full view of the participants, as

exposure to others' ideas is critical for successful brainstorming,

- *Use technology*: Various computer-mediated communication tools, including sophisticated idea-generating software packages, minimize various types of process loss, including production blocking and social matching (see Focus 10.2).

Alternatives to Brainstorming

Most groups, when faced with the challenge of generating creative solutions, uncreatively suggest brainstorming. But given the difficulties in implementing brainstorming techniques correctly, groups should consider turning to other methods in their quest for fresh ideas and new insights into old problems (Sunwolf, 2002).

The Nominal Group Technique Several creativity-building methods take advantage of the "wisdom" of groups by integrating individual idea-generating sessions with group-level methods. The **nominal group technique (NGT)**, for example, minimizes blocking and loafing by reducing interdependence among members; it achieves this improvement by starting with a nominal group phase before turning to a group session (Delbecq & Van de Ven, 1971).

- *Step 1*. The group discussion leader introduces the problem or issue in a short statement that is written on a blackboard or flip chart. Once members understand the statement, they silently write ideas concerning the issue, usually working for 10 to 15 minutes.

- *Step 2*. The members share their ideas with one another in a round-robin; each person states an idea, which is given an identification letter and written beneath the issue statement, and the

---

brainwriting Brainstorming sessions that involve generating new ideas in writing rather than orally, usually by asking members to add their own ideas to a circulating list.

nominal group technique (NGT) A group performance method wherein a face-to-face group session is prefaced by a nominal-group phase during which individuals work alone to generate ideas.

Focus 10.2 E-groups: Electronic Brainstorming (EBS)

Computer technology offers yet another alternative to face-to-face brainstorming. **Electronic brainstorming (EBS)** allows members to communicate via the Internet rather than meeting face-to-face. Using software designed specifically for groups (called *group decision support systems* or *groupware*), group members seated at individual computers can share information rapidly and more completely. One program, *GroupSystems*, opens up several windows on each group member's computer—one window is for entering ideas, another displays all the ideas, and still another shows a counter that tracks how many ideas the group has generated (see http://www.groupsystems.com/).

EBS offers practical advantages over more traditional face-to-face sessions, such as reduced travel, time, and cost. But EBS may also be more effective than face-to-face brainstorming since the format may reduce factors that lead to creative mediocrity. Members do not need to wait their turn, so EBS reduces production blocking. Working from a distance, participants may also feel less evaluation apprehension and nervousness about contributing, and they may be able to persist longer at the task. EBS also enhances one of the key features of brainstorming—idea building—for online exposure to others' ideas tends to stimulate the production of additional novel ideas (Michinov, 2012).

Groups using EBS, although they are freed from some of the constraints created by face-to-face meetings, still display problems of social coordination and motivation. Computer-mediated discussions can overwhelm group members with a flood of information to process (Nagasundaram & Dennis, 1993). Social matching can also occur in groups if members know how

many ideas each group member has contributed (Roy, Gauvin, & Limayem, 1996). EBS sessions are also not particularly productive if the group members become so focused on generating ideas that they ignore the ideas generated by other members. When researchers arranged for groups and individuals to use *GroupSystems* to generate solutions to a problem, they discovered that EBS groups reached high levels of creativity only when members were told that their memory of the ideas expressed by others would be tested later (Dugosh et al., 2000). Individuals can also show marked declines in motivation when they could not take personal credit for their contributions to the pool of creative ideas (McLeod, 2011).

More research is needed to explore fully the gains and losses associated with EBS methods, but preliminary results are positive. In a meta-analysis, investigators compared EBS to (a) traditional face-to-face groups, (b) nominal groups, and (c) *e-nominal groups*, individuals who generated ideas in isolation using a computer. They discovered that EBS was clearly superior to traditional brainstorming groups, both in terms of productivity and also members' satisfaction: They liked the EBS approach better. EBS was generally equal to nominal and e-nominal groups, unless the size of the group was large (greater than eight); in this case, EBS was superior even to nominal groups (DeRosa, Smith, & Hantula, 2007). Osborn, the inventor of brainstorming, surely never could have imagined the possibility that people in locations widely dispersed around the world could work together creatively using an adaptation of his brainstorming methods.

---

next individual then adds his or her contribution.

- *Step 3*. The group discusses each item, focusing primarily on clarification.

- *Step 4*. The members rank the five solutions they most prefer, writing their choices on an index card.

---

electronic brainstorming (EBS) Generating ideas and solving problems using computer-based communication methods such as online discussions and synchronous e-mail rather than face-to-face sessions.

The leader then collects the cards, averages the rankings to yield a group decision, and informs the group of the outcome. The group may wish to add two steps to further improve the procedure: a short discussion of the vote (optional Step 5) and a re-voting (optional Step 6). These methods are particularly useful when groups discuss issues that tend to elicit highly emotional arguments. NGT groups produce more ideas and also report feeling more satisfied with the process than unstructured groups. The ranking and voting procedures also provide for an explicit mathematical solution that fairly weights all members' inputs and provides a balance between task concerns and interpersonal forces (Delbecq & Van de Ven, 1971; Gustafson et al., 1973).

The Delphi Technique   The **Delphi technique** eliminates the group-level discussion altogether. This method, named for the legendary Delphic oracle, involves surveying members repeatedly with the results of each round of surveys informing the framing of the questions for subsequent rounds. The Delphi coordinator begins the process by developing a short list of questions on the topic and gathering the answers of a carefully selected group of respondents. Their answers are then pooled and communicated back to the entire group; members are asked to restate their responses to the original items, comment on others' responses, or respond to new questions that emerged in the first round of surveying. This process is repeated until a solution is reached. The method is particularly well-suited for problems that cannot be solved by a systematic review of the available data (Forsyth, 2010).

Buzz Groups, Bug Lists, and Beyond   When stumped for new ideas, members can break up into buzz groups, which are small subgroups that generate ideas that can later be discussed by the entire group. Members can jot down a bug list of small irritations pertaining to the problem under discussion, and the group can then discuss solutions for each bug. Groups can use the *stepladder technique*, which requires asking each new member of the group to state his or her ideas before listening to the group's position (Rogelberg & O'Connor, 1998). Groups can even use elaborate systems of idea-generation with such exotic-sounding names as synectics and TRIZ. In synectics, a trained leader guides the group through a discussion of members' goals, wishes, and frustrations using analogies, metaphors, and fantasy (Bouchard, 1972). TRIZ is used primarily in science and engineering and involves following a specific sequence of problem analysis, resource review, goal setting, and review of prior approaches to the problem (Moehrle, 2005).

CHAPTER REVIEW

What processes promote group performance and what processes inhibit it?

1. Groups carry out a wide range of tasks. McGrath's task circumplex model distinguishes between generating, choosing, negotiating, and executing tasks. These tasks differ along two dimensions: conceptual-behavioral and cooperation-conflict.

2. The proficiency of groups with high levels of collective intelligence (c-factor) is due, in part, to member intelligence and social sensitivity.

3. Groups are best used for dealing with tasks that are difficult, complex, and important.

4. Steiner, in his analysis of group productivity, suggests that few groups reach their potential, because negative group processes (*process loss*) place limits on their performance. He believed that Actual Productivity = Potential Productivity − Losses owing to faulty Processes, AP = PP − PL.

Do people work as hard when in groups as they do when working by themselves?

1. Triplett's 1898 study of *social facilitation* confirmed that people work more efficiently when other people are present. Social facilitation occurs for both *coaction* tasks and audience tasks.

2. As Zajonc noted, social facilitation usually occurs only for simple tasks that require dominant responses, whereas social interference or impairment occurs for complex tasks that require nondominant responses. Studies conducted in a variety of settings, such as

---

Delphi technique A group performance method that involves repeated assessment of members' opinions via surveys and questionnaires as opposed to face-to-face meetings.

classrooms and jogging trails, have confirmed the effect, which also holds for a variety of species—including cockroaches.

3. Researchers have linked social facilitation to several personal and interpersonal processes, including arousal, evaluation apprehension, distraction, and personality differences (see Table 10.2).

    ■   Zajonc's *drive theory* argues that the mere presence of a member of the same species (compresence) raises the performer's arousal level by touching off a basic alertness response; Blascovich's studies of the challenge-threat response and brain imaging work have confirmed that people respond physiologically and neurologically to the presence of others.

    ■   Cottrell's *evaluation apprehension theory* proposes that the presence of others increases arousal only when individuals feel that they are being evaluated. *Self-presentation theory* suggests that this apprehension is greatest when performance may threaten the group member's public image. This theory, however, cannot account for social facilitation effects in nonhuman species.

    ■   *Distraction-conflict theory* emphasizes the mediational role played by distraction, attentional conflict, and increased motivation. Distractions due to the presence of other people have been shown to improve performance on certain tasks, such as the *Stroop Task*. Harkins' mere-effort model traces facilitation effects back to changes in how information is processed.

    ■   *Social orientation theory* suggests that individuals who display a positive interpersonal orientation (extraverted and low anxiety) are more likely to display social facilitation effects.

4. Social facilitation effects are related to a number of interpersonal processes, including prejudice, eating, *electronic performance monitoring, study groups, and learning styles* (Kolb).

When do people give their all when working in a group?

1. Groups become less productive as they increase in size. This *Ringelmann effect* is caused by coordination losses and by *social loafing*—the reduction of individual effort when people work in a group.

2. Latané, Williams, and Harkins identified the relative contributions of coordination losses and social loafing to the Ringelmann effect by studying groups and pseudogroups producing noise.

3. Social loafing depends on a number of group-level factors, including,

    ■   Identifiability: When people feel as though their level of effort cannot be ascertained because the task is a collective one, then social loafing becomes likely. But when people feel that they are being evaluated, they tend to exert more effort, and their productivity increases (leading to social facilitation if the task is easy).

    ■   *Free riding*: Individuals in collective work sometimes work less, knowing that others will compensate for their lack of productivity. They also work less to avoid being the "sucker" who works too hard (the *sucker effect*).

    ■   Goals: Groups that set clear, challenging goals outperform groups whose members have no clear standard to evaluate their performance.

    ■   Involvement: Loafing is less likely when people work at exciting, challenging, and involving tasks. Williams and Karau confirmed that such tasks reduce loafing and even trigger *social compensation* (highly involved group members work harder to compensate for the poor performance of others in the group).

    ■   Identity: According to social identity theory, when individuals derive their identity from their membership in a group, social loafing is replaced by social laboring as members expend extra effort for their groups.

4. Karau and Williams's *collective effort model* (CEM) draws on expectancy-value theories of motivation to provide a comprehensive theoretical framework for understanding social loafing.

When do groups outperform individuals?

1. Steiner's typology of group tasks argued that group effectiveness depends on the task the group is attempting. *Task demands* are defined by the task's divisibility (*divisible tasks* versus *unitary tasks*), the type of output desired (*maximizing tasks* versus *optimizing tasks*), and the social combination rule used to combine individual members' inputs.

   ■ Groups outperform individuals on *additive tasks* and *compensatory tasks*. Galton confirmed the "wisdom of the crowd" effect by finding that independent individuals' judgments, when averaged together, tend to be highly accurate. Other work indicates the a crowd must be sufficiently large, and the problem not too difficult, for a crowd to be wise.

   ■ Groups perform well on *disjunctive tasks* if the group includes at least one individual who knows the correct solution. The truth-wins rule usually holds for groups working on Eureka problems, whereas the *truth-supported-wins* rule holds for groups working on non-Eureka problems.

   ■ Groups are more effective decision makers than individuals, particularly when dealing with problems that have a known solution (*intellective tasks*) rather than problems that have no clear right or wrong answer (*judgmental tasks*).

   ■ Reviews of plane crashes suggest that crews, in some cases, fail to communicate critical information clearly, resulting in pilot error.

   ■ Groups perform poorly on *conjunctive tasks*, unless the task can be subdivided with subtasks matched to members' abilities. The *Köhler effect* occurs when the poorest-performing members increase their productivity due to competitive strivings and the recognition that their poor performance is holding the group back from success.

   ■ The effectiveness of groups working on *discretionary tasks* covaries with the method chosen to combine individuals' inputs.

2. Groups perform better than the average group member on many kinds of tasks (see Table 10.4), but only when process losses are minimized.

   ■ *Synergy* results in the group achieving collectively results that could not be achieved by any member working alone.

   ■ As Larson notes, weak synergy occurs when the group's performance is superior to that of the typical member. Strong synergy occurs when the group outperforms its best member. Strong synergy, or the assembly bonus effect, rarely occurs in groups.

What steps can be taken to encourage creativity in groups?

1. *Brainstorming* groups strive to find creative solutions to problems by following four basic rules that encourage the flow of ideas among members: "Be expressive," "Postpone evaluation," "Seek quantity," and "Piggyback ideas."

2. Brainstorming groups rarely generate as many ideas as individuals in *nominal groups*. Their less-than-expected performance has been linked to social loafing, *production blocking*, social matching, and the *illusion of productivity*.

3. Other methods, including *brainwriting*, *synectics*, the *nominal group technique* (*NGT*), the *Delphi technique*, and *electronic brainstorming* (*EBS*), offer advantages over traditional brainstorming.

RESOURCES

Chapter Case: Miracle on the Hudson

- *Highest Duty* by Chesley "Sully" Sullenberger (with Jeffrey Zaslow, 2009), the autobiographical account of the crash of Flight 1549, provides critical details about the processes that occurred on the flight deck before and after the bird collision.

- *Miracle on the Hudson* by the Survivors (with William Prochnau and Laura Parker, 2010) provides details about what occurred in the passenger area of Flight 1549, drawn from the passengers' personal statements about the experience.

Group Productivity

- *Group Process and Productivity* by Ivan D. Steiner (1972) is a timeless analysis of groups that includes entire chapters examining the relationship between group composition, motivation, size, and performance.

- "Group Behavior and Performance" by J. Richard Hackman and N. Katz (2010) provides an excellent overview of key issues pertaining to group performance.

Social Facilitation and Loafing

- "Social Facilitation: From Triplett to Electronic Performance Monitoring" by John R. Aiello and Elizabeth A. Douthitt (2001) reviews the literature on social facilitation before offering an integrative model of performance processes in groups.

- "Understanding Individual Motivation in Groups: The Collective Effort Model" by Steven J. Karau and Kipling D. Williams (2001) is an updated review of work examining the factors that contribute to motivation loss in groups. This chapter is one of many excellent papers in *Groups at Work*, edited by Marlene E. Turner (2001).

Group Synergy and Creativity

- "Group Idea Generation: A Cognitive-Social-Motivational Perspective of Brainstorming" by Paul B. Paulus and Vincent R. Brown (2007) organizes much of the research on brainstorming within a cognitive-social-motivational model.

- *In Search of Synergy in Small Group Performance* by James R. Larson, Jr. (2010) is a high-level introduction to the scientific study of group performance.

Decision Making

CHAPTER OVERVIEW

People turn to groups when they must solve problems and make decisions, for the wisdom of the many is greater than even the genius of the one. But groups, constituted as they are of individuals, sometimes make mistakes. When a group sacrifices rationality in its pursuit of unity, the decisions it makes can yield calamitous consequences.

- How do groups make decisions?
- What problems undermine the effectiveness of decision making in groups?
- Why do groups make riskier decisions than individuals?
- What is groupthink, and how can it be prevented?

CHAPTER OUTLINE

The Functional Perspective
The Orientation Stage
The Discussion Stage
The Decision Stage
The Implementation Stage
Who Decides?

Problems and Pitfalls
Failing to Plan Is Planning to Fail
The Difficulty of Discussion
The Shared Information Bias
Cognitive Limitations
Dysfunctional Postdecision Tendencies

Group Polarization
Group Decisions Involving Risk
What Causes Group Polarization?
The Consequences of Polarization

Victims of Groupthink
Symptoms of Groupthink
Defective Decision Making
Causes of Groupthink
The Emergence of Groupthink
Alternative Models
Preventing Groupthink
Chapter Review
Resources

The Bay of Pigs Planners: Disastrous Decisions and Groupthink

The group is meeting in the Cabinet Room of the White House, just down the hall from the Oval Office of the president of the United States. The date is February 17, 1961; the group has gathered at the request of then-President John F. Kennedy to discuss "CIA Para-Military Plan, Cuba." The Central Intelligence Agency (CIA) had developed this plan after Fidel Castro gained control of the government of Cuba. The CIA used various methods during this period to curtail the spread of communism in Latin and South American countries, and it hoped to apply these covert operational strategies to overthrow Castro and his communist government.

The plan assumed that a squad of well-trained troops could capture and defend a strip of land in the Bahía de Cochinos (Bay of Pigs) on the southern coast of Cuba. The men would then launch raids and encourage civilian revolt in Havana. All they needed was Kennedy's approval, but Kennedy did not want to make this decision by himself. So he assembled his advisors, and together they discussed the strengths and weaknesses of the proposal. The Bay of Pigs advisory group, as diagrammed in Figure 11.1, included White House senior advisors and staff members, cabinet members, the CIA and their subject matter experts (SMEs), and military advisors from the Department of Defense—all highly skilled individuals well-trained in making critically important policy and military decisions. This group, after a thorough review, advised the president to give the CIA the go-ahead.

The Bay of Pigs invasion took place on April 17, 1961. The assault that was so carefully planned was a disaster. For the plan to succeed, the attacking force needed to secure and hold the beachhead at Playa Girón, but Castro's forces' counterattack overwhelmed them. Several key elements of the plan, including air support and supplying the ground forces with munitions, were either aborted or poorly executed. The entire attacking force was killed or captured within days, and the U.S. government had to send food and supplies to Cuba to ransom them back. Group expert Irving Janis described the decision as one of the "worst fiascoes ever perpetrated by a responsible government" (1972, p. 14), and President Kennedy lamented, "How could I have been so stupid?" (quoted in Wyden, 1979, p. 8).

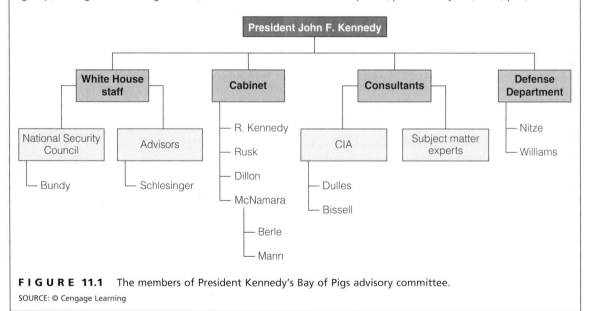

F I G U R E 11.1   The members of President Kennedy's Bay of Pigs advisory committee.

SOURCE: © Cengage Learning

The Bay of Pigs advisory committee was not unique. Like many other groups, the committee faced a problem needing a solution. Through discussion, the members pooled their expertise and knowledge. They sought out information from available sources, and they thoroughly weighed alternatives and considered the ramifications of their actions. When their alternatives were narrowed down to two—to invade or not to invade—they made the decision as a group. But the committee was typical in another way. Like so many other groups, it made the wrong decision.

We owe much to groups. Groups put humans on the moon, built the Empire State Building, performed the first symphony, and invented the personal computer. But groups also killed innocent civilians at My Lai, marketed thalidomide, doomed the space shuttles *Challenger* and *Columbia*, and decided that the best way to deal with the communist regime in Cuba was to invade it. This chapter examines both the pros and the cons of making decisions in groups before examining one potentially catastrophic group process—groupthink—in detail.

THE FUNCTIONAL PERSPECTIVE

In office buildings, executives hold conferences to solve problems of management and production; at the dinner table, families talk over moving to a new neighborhood; in courthouses, juries weigh evidence to determine guilt and innocence; on the battlefield, a combat squad identifies a target and plans an attack. In these and thousands of other similar settings, interdependent individuals make decisions in groups.

Why turn to a group when an important decision must be made? As noted in Chapter 10, even though groups are far from perfect, their choices, judgments, estimates, and solutions are generally superior to those tendered by lone individuals (Stasser & Dietz-Uhler, 2001). Teams of scientists outpace the progress made by lone scientists (Stokols et al., 2008). Groups' perceptions of other people are more accurate than individuals' impressions (Ruscher & Hammer, 2006). Small groups working together on Google searching for information will find more relevant information more quickly than a single searcher can (Lazonder, 2005). Teams of physicians making a diagnosis are more accurate than single physicians (Glick & Staley, 2007). Students permitted to take a test in groups get better grades than individual students (Zimbardo, Butler, & Wolfe, 2003). Burglars who work in groups are less likely to be caught than are thieves who work alone (Warr, 2002). Even very powerful leaders—presidents of the

United States, for example—rarely make decisions without consulting others. Instead, they rely on groups, for the weighty problems that they must handle on a daily basis would overwhelm a lone individual. In most situations, the wisdom of the many is greater than even the genius of the one.

What is the secret to groups' superiority in making decisions? A **functional theory of group decision making** suggests that groups engage in a sequence of activities and operations as they move from uncertainty to decisional conviction and that each step in the series serves some purpose. Decision makers, for example, often need to learn more about the situation before they can make an informed choice, so the "gather information" stage is one that occurs with great regularity when people make decisions. Not all functions are essential ones for making a decision, and some are not necessarily adaptive ones. Some enhance members' sense of satisfaction and increase the unity of the group, but in supporting the group's structure, these functions may undermine its capacity to generate high-quality decisions (Gouran & Hirokawa, 1996).

Although no two groups reach their decisions in precisely the same way (and no two theorists agree on *the* definitive list of decision functions), the stages in the *Orientation-Discussion-Decision-Implementation* (ODDI) model shown in Figure 11.2 and examined in this section are often in evidence when groups make decisions. The group defines the problem, sets goals, and develops a strategy in the orientation phase. Next, during the discussion phase, the group gathers information about the situation and, if a decision must be made, identifies and considers options. In the decision phase, the group chooses its solution by reaching consensus, voting, or using some other social decision process. In the implementation phase, groups put the decision into action and assess the

---

functional theory of group decision making A conceptual analysis of the steps or processes that groups generally follow when making a decision, with a focus on the intended purpose of each step or process in the overall decision-making sequence.

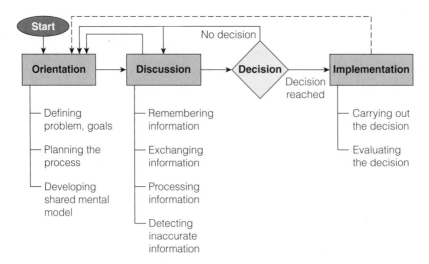

FIGURE 11.2 The Orientation-Discussion-Decision-Implementation (ODDI) model of group decision making.
SOURCE: © Cengage Learning

consequences of their choice. Groups that follow these four stages are more likely to make better decisions than those who sidestep or mishandle information along the way (Hollingshead et al., 2005; Wittenbaum et al., 2004).

The Orientation Stage

Decisions begin with a problem that needs a solution. A group of students in a class are required to complete a project that includes a written paper and a presentation. The president of the United States is briefed by the CIA on the invasion of Cuba. The combat unit is under attack and running low on ammunition. Such situations trigger a decision-making process that often begins with the recognition of the unsatisfactory state of the current situation and the need for a solution. Groups also meet, more routinely, to check progress, review feedback, identify any possible issues, and to identify new goals.

In the first stage of problem solving, orientation, the group reviews its objectives and organizes the procedures it will use in its work. Members clarify the group's goals, identify the resources needed to make the decision, enumerate obstacles that must be overcome or avoided, specify the procedures to be followed in gathering information

and making the decision, and agree on procedures to follow during the meeting (paraphrased from Gouran & Hirokawa, 1996, p. 76–77). All this planning provides the blueprint for "the order in which a sequence of operations is to be performed" (Miller, Galanter, & Pribram, 1960, p. 16), so that actions are structured effectively. The group should, by the end of the orientation phase, understand its purpose, its procedures, and the tasks that it will undertake. Armed with a shared plan, groups no longer simply react to situations; rather, they pro-actively influence events so that their expectations are affirmed.

Setting Goals and Objectives Members of even the best run groups sometimes lose sight of their original purpose. As multiple meetings are held, ambiguous issues are raised, and divergent opinions are voiced, members can become sidetracked, pursuing questions that are only tangentially related to their real goals. By clarifying goals and objectives, the group can review its organizational and communication structures to make sure they will support the work, identify any subtasks that must be accomplished, and assign different individuals to specific roles and tasks. When possible, the group itself should be involved in identifying its goals and procedures, and the project launch should make it clear how each subtask relates to the broad goals of the group and organization (Ericksen & Dyer, 2004).

Timing should also be considered during the planning stage. Groups are notorious for the injudicious use of time, but groups that recognize that their time is limited plan out their work better than groups that do not (Sanna et al., 2005). In one survey of 48 self-managing teams, those who spent time during their initial stages with temporal planning developed strong norms about time, and these norms helped these groups perform better than groups that did not put enough time into time planning (Janicik & Bartel, 2003).

Shared Mental Models   One particularly valuable outcome of this period of orientation is the development of a **shared mental model**—knowledge structures that organize declarative and procedural information pertaining to the problem and the group that are held in common by the group members (Cannon-Bowers & Salas, 2001). Because of differences in prior experiences, knowledge, expectations, and so on, each individual may have a differing view of the history of the issue, the current situation, and even the methods that will be used to reach a decision. Some of these differences may lead to misunderstandings and inefficiencies as the group does its work, so the emergence of agreement—the shared mental model—will facilitate the group's functioning. When group members adopt the same general conceptualization of their tasks, goals, and procedures, their final choices reflect the group's preferences rather than the group members' personal biases (DeChurch & Mesmer-Magnus, 2010).

The Benefits of Planning   Some groups take goal planning very seriously, particularly when dealing with difficult problems with many criteria that will determine success. For example, planners in

investment banking, manufacturing, human resource development, and other fields have adapted mathematically sophisticated goal-planning programs for use in groups, and the results are, in most cases, improvements in forecasting accuracy (see Munro & Aouni, 2012, for a review). But in a time-urgent world, groups sometimes rush through the orientation stage; they want to get on with the work and not waste time with preliminaries (Varela, 1971). However, research clearly favors delaying the discussion of the issue at hand until the group reviews its goals, procedures, and time constraints (Weingart, 1992; Weldon, Jehn, & Pradhan, 1991). The importance of planning is so great that in some cases it is the only thing that differentiates successful groups from unsuccessful ones (Hirokawa, 1980). In a study of six conferences in which panels of experts evaluated new medical technologies, participants were more satisfied when the decisional procedures had been discussed in advance (Vinokur et al., 1985). Similarly, in a project that experimentally manipulated the use of process planning, groups were more productive when they were encouraged to discuss their performance strategies before working on a task requiring intermember coordination (Hackman, Brousseau, & Weiss, 1976).

The Discussion Stage

If information is the lifeblood of decision making, then the discussion phase must be the heart of that process (Kowert, 2002). Group members, asked to provide an answer to a question, problem, or puzzle without recourse to external informational sources, use **discussion** to expand their information base, make explicit the values that should shape their preferences, and appraise all possible solutions before making the best decision they can (Gastil et al., 2008). The Bay of Pigs planners examined

---

shared mental model Knowledge, expectations, conceptualizations, and other cognitive representations that members of a group have in common pertaining to the group and its members, tasks, procedures, and resources.

discussion The communication of information between two or more people undertaken for some shared purpose, such as solving a problem, making a decision, or increasing participants' mutual understanding of the situation.

all kinds of issues—the strength of Cuba's forces, the tactical advantages of surprise, the morale of the invading force, the possibility of intervention by other communist countries—through the exchange of information among the members.

What is the value of all this discussion and debate? An *information processing model* of decision making assumes that people strive, in most cases, to make good decisions by acquiring the information that is relevant to the issue and processing that information thoroughly, so that its implications are clearly understood. A **collective information processing model** also assumes that people seek out and process relevant information but that they do this cognitive work during the group discussion (Hinsz, Tindale, & Vollrath, 1997). When people discuss the problem as a group, they improve their memory for information, exchange information with each other, process the information more thoroughly, and identify errors and mistakes (see Figure 11.2).

Collective Memory Processes   Two heads are better than one because groups have superior memories for information relative to individuals. Arthur Schlesinger, for example, knew a great deal about international relations, but he could not compete with the combined informational resources of all the Bay of Pigs planners. Their memories, when combined, contained a vast assortment of information about Cuba, Castro, weaponry, and even the terrain of the beach where the troops would land (Clark, Stephenson, & Kniveton, 1990; Harris, Paterson, & Kemp, 2008; Hirst & Manier, 2008).

A group's **collective memory** is the shared reservoir of information held in the memories of two or more members of a group. Groups remember more than individuals, because groups draw on more memories that contain different types of information. The CIA operatives who met with the Bay of Pigs planners knew all about the weapons, tactics, and the morale of Castro's troops, but Rusk was an expert on the relationship between Cuba and the Soviet Union. When they joined together, they could pool their individual expertise to form the group's decisions. (Unfortunately, no one in the group knew that the Bay of Pigs was Castro's favorite fishing spot, so he was thoroughly familiar with every path, road, and hill in the area.) Similarly, when students are permitted to take examinations as a group, they usually outperform individuals, for the student who is stumped by the question "Name four common phases of group decision making" may be saved by a group member who remembers the mnemonic acronym ODDI: Orientation, Discussion, Decision, and Implementation (Bonner & Baumann, 2012). Groups can also get more information than individuals can. In many cases, decision-making groups are staffed by individuals who have widely differing experiences, backgrounds, and associations, so each one can contribute unique information to the discussion (Henningsen & Henningsen, 2007).

Transactive memory processes also enhance the group's capacity to store and quickly access information by dividing data among the members. Members working in the same group often specialize, to a degree, in different areas. These individuals not only have more information on a given topic, but they are also the ones who should be more responsible for storing any new information that is relevant to their area of expertise. In the committee, for example, the CIA was recognized as the source of all information about the invasion force, so other group members spent little effort deliberately storing information on that topic. When anyone needed to check a fact pertaining to the commandos, they turned to the CIA and their

---

collective information processing model A general theoretical explanation of group decision making assuming that groups use communication and discussion among the members to gather and process the information needed to formulate decisions, choices, and judgments.

collective memory A group's combined memories, including each member's memories, the group's shared mental models, and transactive memory systems.

---

transactive memory processes Information to be remembered is distributed to various members of the group who can then be relied upon to provide that information when it is needed.

memory stores (Hollingshead, 2001a; Wegner, Giuliano, & Hertel, 1985). But the Bay of Pigs planners had not spent enough time together to develop a strong transactive memory system. As discussed in more detail in Chapter 12, transactive memory is enriched by the experience of working as a team and by trust among members. The Bay of Pigs planners had neither.

Groups can also improve their access to information stored in members' memories through **cross-cuing**. This process occurs when one member says something that jogs other members' memories. For example, President Kennedy may not remember where the force will land, but perhaps he will say, "I think it's a bay." This cue may trigger someone else's memories, so that the name "Bay of Pigs" is retrieved by the group, even though none of the members could generate this name initially (Meudell, Hitch, & Kirby, 1992). Unfortunately, if a group member offers up a misleading cue—instead of saying, "I think it's a bay," a committee member said, "I think it's near a lagoon"—then such cueing can inhibit memory retrieval rather than facilitate it (Andersson, Hitch, Meudell, 2006).

Information Exchange If the human mind is an information processing network, then a group is a "network of networks" (Van Overwalle & Heylighen, 2006, p. 606). Groups do not merely draw on a larger pool of information than individuals. They can also exchange information among the members of the group, thereby further strengthening their access to information as well as their recall of that information. One study group, asked to make a simple estimate such as "What is the population of the state of Utah?" exchanged, on average, 27 pieces of information before drawing a conclusion (Bonner & Baumann, 2012). The general discussion groups that Bales and his colleagues (1955) studied exchanged, on average, 960 pieces of information in *each* of their sessions. More than 50%

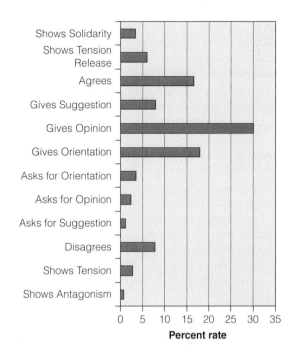

F I G U R E 11.3 Average interaction profile for discussion groups (Bales, 1999).

SOURCE: *Social Interaction Systems: Theory and Measurement*, by Robert Freed Bales, Transaction Publishers, 1999, p. 240.

of all comments made by members were suggestions, expressions of opinion, and attempts at orientation (see Figure 11.3). Group members also shared information about the problem, expressed agreement or disagreement, and asked for more information and clarification. The proportion of comments in each category will vary depending on the nature of the group discussion and its level of intensity, but in most groups communication peaks during the discussion phase.

Processing Information Groups not only recall and exchange information more effectively than individuals, they also process that information more thoroughly through discussion. Members ask questions, and others offer answers. Alternative options are discussed, and the strengths and weaknesses of each option are considered. Group members analyze each other's ideas and offer corrections when they note errors. Members dialogue with one

---

cross-cueing The enhancement of recall that occurs during group discussion when the statements made by group members serve as cues for the retrieval of information from the memories of other group members.

another, sharing viewpoints and seeking a shared meaning. Ideas are debated, with some group members seeking to convince others that their position is better. The group members also monitor their work and intervene as necessary to bring the group back on task. Most group discussions also include an interpersonal element that complements the focus on the work to be done. Decision-making groups not only share and evaluate information; they also encourage each other, express commitment to the group, and help each other (Jehn & Shah, 1997; Weingart & Weldon, 1991).

Just as the orientation period is essential to effective decision making, so the time spent in active discussion increases the quality of the group's decision (Katz & Tushman, 1979). When researchers monitored group members' communications while working on a problem that could be solved only by properly sequencing individuals' responses, they found that the group's use of essential information through discussion proved to be the best predictor of success (Lanzetta & Roby, 1960). Groups working on *collective induction problems*—tasks that require a cycle of hypothesis generation and testing—performed best when members discussed the problems actively and focused their analysis on evidence rather than on hypotheses (Laughlin & Hollingshead, 1995). Flight crews that confront sudden emergencies often overcome the problem if they share information with one another; but those crews that do not take advantage of group discussion often make errors in judgment that are not corrected by the group (Paris, Salas, & Cannon-Bowers, 1999). Physicians trying to diagnose an illness were more successful when they spent more time "talking to the room"—expressing ideas about the problem openly, so the entire group can hear them (Tschan et al., 2009). Studies of online groups have found that the online format substantially hampers the group's ability to make an informed decision if the rate of information exchange is too low and too slow (Baltes et al., 2002). When researchers watched groups make decisions, they found that information sharing (talking a great deal, free expression of ideas, thoughts, and feelings) and critical evaluation of ideas (critically evaluating each other's ideas or works, differences of opinion, disagreement among group members, disagreements on who should do what or how something should be done) were correlated with judgmental accuracy (Jehn & Shah, 1997).

Error Detection and Correction As groups discuss information, they appraise the validity of ideas being shared, seeking increased accuracy and identifying any errors of fact or implications. This error-checking process was identified as a crucial determinant of successful decision making by psychologist Marjorie Shaw (1932) in one of the earliest experimental studies of group performance. She examined the sagacity of groups by putting 21 individuals and 5 four-person groups to work on several intellective tasks, including the famous (at least to people who study groups) missionary–cannibal dilemma:

> Three missionaries and three cannibals are on one side of the river and want to cross to the other side by means of a boat that can only hold two persons at a time. All the missionaries can row, but two cannibals cannot. For obvious reasons, the missionaries must never be outnumbered by the cannibals, under any circumstances or at any time, except where no missionaries are present at all. How many crossings will be necessary to transport the six people across the river?

When the groups and individuals finished the first set of problems, Shaw reorganized them, so that those who worked alone initially solved several new problems in groups and those who initially worked in groups solved several new problems individually.

Shaw's groups performed well for two reasons. First, compared to individuals, her groups generated more correct solutions. Second, however, the groups were better at checking for errors in calculations and faulty inferences about the problems. If a group member recommended a solution that was inaccurate, groups were more likely to reject that solution. Groups, when they did make mistakes, also erred later in the decision process than did individuals, in part because groups were more proficient at noticing and correcting errors than were individuals. Groups, however, took longer to complete the task than did individuals. (The answer to the missionary–cannibal problem, by the way, is 13 crossings! Note, too, that this study was conducted by Marjorie E. Shaw—no relation to Marvin E. Shaw who also studied groups and whose classic 1981 text, *Group Dynamics*, is this book's intellectual progenitor.)

The Decision Stage

By early April, the Bay of Pigs committee was ready to make its decision. The members had spent days examining the CIA's plan, and even though many questions remained unanswered, the group could delay no longer. Word of the plan had leaked to the press, and the group was worried that Castro might begin to shore up his defenses. They needed to make up their minds.

A **social decision scheme** is a group's method for combining individual member's inputs in a single group decision. Some groups have clearly defined ways of making a decision—their bylaws may state, for example, that they will follow a particular rule of order (such as *Robert's Rules*). In many cases, though, the social decision scheme is an implicit one that is taken for granted by groups. Not until someone says, "Let's take a vote" does the group realize that a decision must be made about how to make decisions. Some common social decision schemes are *delegating*, *averaging*, *voting*, and *reaching consensus* (Hastie & Kameda, 2005; Kameda et al., 2011). Each decision scheme has strengths as well as weaknesses.

---

social decision scheme A strategy or rule used in a group to select a single alternative from among various alternatives proposed and discussed during the group's deliberations, including explicitly acknowledged decision rules (e.g., the group accepts the alternative favored by the majority) and implicit decisional procedures (e.g., the group accepts the alternative favored by the most powerful members).

Delegating: Shared Decisions The group as a whole does not make the decision when the decision is delegated to one of the members, a subgroup within the group, or someone outside of the group. Under an *authority scheme*, the leader, president, or other individual makes the final decision with or without input from the group members. When an *oligarchy* operates in a group, a coalition speaks for the entire group. Other forms of delegation include asking an expert to answer (the best-informed member) or forming a subcommittee made up of a few members to study the issue and reach a conclusion. Delegation saves the group time and is appropriate for less important issues. As noted later in the chapter, mandates from authorities can leave members feeling disenfranchised and ignored.

Averaging: Statisticized Decisions In some cases, groups make decisions by combining each individual's preferences using some type of computational procedure. If the group must select the best option among five alternatives, for example, each member could make his or her decision individually (either before or after a group discussion), and these private recommendations could then be averaged to yield a group decision. As with compensatory tasks discussed in Chapter 10, such decisions do not necessarily require any interaction among members, and they are often surprisingly accurate (see Focus 11.1). They weight equally all the group members' opinions, and errors tend to cancel each other out. Unfortunately, there are equally important disadvantages associated with the timing of the ranking process. If the group just averages without discussion, then the benefits of discussion will be lost. If, however, the group averages after a discussion, biases and inaccuracies introduced during the discussion may skew the group's conclusions. Members may also feel that process is too arbitrary and so feel little responsibility for implementing the decision.

Voting: Plurality Decisions Most groups, at least in Western cultures, use some type of voting procedure to make decisions (Mann, 1986). Members express their individual preferences publicly or, to reduce social pressure, by secret ballot. In most

---

Focus 11.1 **E-groups: Solving Problems through Crowdsourcing**

At this moment, groups are busy making decisions—but these groups will never meet together in a corporate boardroom, the conference room of a business, or even in a threaded discussion forum on a webpage. The members of these groups are scattered around the world, but are linked together in an online network of distributed production called **crowdsourcing**. This term combines both the idea of a crowd—a large and often dispersed group of people—with the idea of outsourcing—assigning a task to individuals outside of the group or organization. Crowdsourcing takes many forms, and that diversity has created considerable debate over definitions and distinctions, but the method nearly always involves recruiting a group of volunteer workers from the general public and asking them to perform some type of task. Rewards are sometimes offered, but engagement in the process itself is voluntary.

Crowdsourcing, as used by businesses, often involves harnessing the creative energies of Internet users to review, evaluate, create, develop, and even market new products, procedures, and applications. One of the best-known examples of corporate crowdsourcing, Threadless.com, sells clothing featuring clever sayings, unusual designs, and artful images. But the employees of Threadless.com do not create these designs. Instead, members of the Threadless community—and that is anyone who has registered at Threadless.com for a free account—submit their ideas, and they are posted on the Threadless webpage. The community votes on each submitted design for a one-week period, and votes are then averaged to gauge the potential popularity of a suggestion. Threadless then manufactures only the designs that are ranked highly and so is assured that its products will find buyers. Similar methods have been used to identify new slogans, products, and software design features (Howe, 2008).

InnoCentive.com uses another form of crowdsourcing—staged competitions—to identify solutions to challenging scientific and technical problems. InnoCentive's clients, called "seekers," post "challenges" to the InnoCentive community, offering monetary awards to the "solver" who offers the best solution. Many of its members are scientists—chemists, physicists, biologists, engineers, and so on—but anyone can join the InnoCentive community and submit a solution

to any challenge. For example, a challenge asking for solutions to a specific problem often encountered when processing wastewater generated 266 proposed solutions. The seeker selected the best solution from this pool and awarded the solver a prize of $10,000. Another seeker sought schemes for "large scale removal of chlorinated hydrocarbon impurities from metal salt solutions." The reward for winning this competition: $25,000.

Other crowdsourcing projects call for more collaboration among group members. Some consider Wikipedia to be a crowdsourced resource, for this online encyclopedia is edited by volunteers who continually upgrade and monitor the entries. The open source software program Linux also makes use of crowdsourcing, as programmers work on its code and applications voluntarily and without direct compensation. Uniting all these varied forms of crowdsourcing is the reliance on a "group of individuals of varying knowledge, heterogeneity, and number" to perform a task or make a decision for little or no recompense (Estellés-Arolas & González-Ladrón-de-Guevara, 2012, p. 197).

Just as group decisions made by averaging together the decisions made by the individual members are often superior to those that groups generate through face-to-face consensus building and politicking, so crowdsourced products, even though they are generated by large numbers of relatively anonymous and independent individuals, often rival the work of dedicated (and often highly paid) experts and professionals. One team of researchers, seeking to classify a large set of documents for a research project, turned to the workers of the Mechanical Turk for assistance. This service links requesters—those who are seeking people to perform Human Intelligence Tasks (HITs)—with people who are interested in performing these tasks (turkers) in an online network. Turkers are paid for their time, if the work is adequate, although the amount paid is usually quite small—in this study, for example, two cents per HIT. The investigators provided the turkers with a statement of the criteria for rating the documents and a document to review and rate on a scale from 0 (not relevant) to 3 (excellent). When the ratings were returned from the hundreds of turkers who did the work, the researchers just averaged the ratings and compared these ratings to those provided

---

crowdsourcing Obtaining information, estimates, ideas, and services from a large number of individuals, often using Internet-based technologies.

by experts. In all but four cases, the experts and turkers agreed, but when the researchers reviewed those four, they concluded that the turkers were right on three of them (Alonso & Mizzaro, 2009).

The Greek philosopher Plato distrusted the wisdom of the masses. He believed that nations (and, perhaps groups as well) should be ruled by a wise individual—preferably a philosopher—who would

make decisions for the group, for the masses are too influenced by their emotions and too little by their rationality (Plato, 380 BC/1992). Plato, however, was just one person. He might have been mistaken. Perhaps a random assortment of independent and widely distributed individuals—a crowd—would provide a more accurate answer to the challenge "Who is wiser, the crowd or the single expert?"

cases, the group selects the alternative favored by the majority of the members (the very common *majority-rules scheme*), but in some cases, a more substantial plurality (such as a *two-thirds majority scheme*) is needed before a decision becomes final. Some groups also use ranking methods with more points awarded to alternatives that are ranked higher than others (the *Borda count method*). In even rarer cases, the group's decision rules may give single individuals the authority to rule against any impending decision (*veto scheme*).

When researchers compared these decision rules, plurality was the most consistent in yielding a superior decision, and it involved the least amount of effort from individual group members (Hastie & Kameda, 2005). Even groups that do not officially "take a vote" implicitly adopt a plurality decision scheme. When people are asked to estimate what the final decision a group will make given the distribution of various opinions within the group, their predictions coincide with the majority-rules decisional scheme. People assume that if more group members think option A is better than option B, the group will be picking option A—even if it is the wrong one (Ladbury & Hinsz, 2009). But plurality, despite its overall effectiveness, has limitations. When the vote is close, some members of the group may feel alienated and defeated. In consequence, they become dissatisfied with their membership and are less likely to lend support to the decision (Castore & Murnighan, 1978). Voting can also lead to internal politics, as members get together before meetings to apply pressure, form coalitions, and trade favors to ensure the passage

of proposals that they favor. Also, if the vote is taken publicly, individuals may (a) conform to others' opinions rather than expressing their personal views or (b) refuse to change their public opinion so as to maintain the image of independence and consistency (Davis et al., 1988).

Reaching Consensus: Unanimous Decisions

The Bay of Pigs advisory committee took several polls of the members, but, in the final review, the group's position was unanimous—all agreed that the covert invasion of Cuba should proceed as planned. Some groups, such as juries, officially adopt a consensus rule, but, in many cases, groups that adopt a plurality decision scheme reach consensus at the final vote. This outcome can occur when all in the group actually agree, but it also happens when the minority who disagree vote for the favored solution for various reasons, including not wanting to be on the side that loses.

Consensus decision schemes are often galvanizing and can lead to high levels of commitment to the decision and to the group; people usually express more satisfaction with this procedure than any other decision-making method (Schweiger, Sandberg, & Ragan, 1986). However, consensus building takes a good deal of time, and if rushed, the strategy can misfire. When most of the members of a decision-making group favor an invasion, for example, the three individuals who think that it is a terrible idea may hold back information that they believe would cause dissent within the group (Kameda et al., 2002). Groups often prefer to reach consensus on questions that require sensitive judgments, such as issues of morality, but they favor a majority-rules voting scheme on problem-solving tasks (Kaplan & Miller, 1987).

Consensus, no matter if achieved by voting or through prolonged discussion ending in unanimity, has long-term positive effects on performance. When researchers combined the results of dozens of previous studies that examined the level of consensus among decision makers and the performance of their groups and organizations, they discovered that higher levels of agreement went hand-in-hand with superior performance. This relationship was strongest, however, when the group was discussing strategic priorities, rather than more specific issues, such as the means to implement those strategies (Kellermanns et al., 2011).

The Implementation Stage

When the die is cast and the decision made, two significant pieces of work remain to be done. First, the decision must be *implemented*. If a union decides to strike, it must put its strike plan into effect. If a city planning commission decides that a new highway bypass is needed, it must take the steps necessary to begin construction. If an advisory committee approves an invasion, its members must mobilize the necessary military forces. Second, the quality of the decision must be *evaluated*. Was the strike necessary? Did we put the highway where it was needed the most? Was invading Cuba really such a good idea?

Evaluating the Plan   The Bay of Pigs invasion plan was implemented by the United States and its operatives on April 17, 1961. It was a high-risk plan to begin with, but its implementation was fraught with its own ambiguities and inadequacies. The invasion failed not only because it was based on incorrect information about the region and the forces that were involved in the conflict, but also because the planners did not agree on the basic purpose of the mission. As the attack unfolded, changes were made to deal with circumstances, and these choices did not have the desired effects. The mission failed.

Kennedy and his staff did not execute the planning, discussion, and decision stages well, but they did respond relatively well during the implementation stage. When it became clear that the decision was a faulty one, the group took steps to evaluate the cause of the fiasco. Kennedy created a task force headed by an outside expert rather than a member of the advisory group and provided considerable support to the fact-finding group. Kennedy then used that report to change the way his advisors made decisions.

Social Justice   Implementation is, in some cases, more or less successful depending on perceptions of the fairness of the decision. Fairness judgments are determined by two forms of social justice: distributive and procedural. **Distributive justice** concerns how rights, resources, and costs are granted to, shared with, and imposed on (distributed across) a group's members. When the group decides that your project will only be given a grade of C, that the Cubans who live near the Bay of Pigs will be subjected to aerial bombardments, or all of the group members will be getting raises, one wonders about distributive justice. **Procedural justice**, in contrast, is concerned with the methods used to make decisions about the allocation of resources. Procedural justice asks, "Did we make the decision in a fair way?" (Tyler, 2011).

Successful implementation depends on both forms of justice. People generally consider decisions that benefit them personally to be superior to those that run counter to their interests; they define them as fair and worthy of their support. How the decision was made also matters. When fair procedures are followed, group members feel more satisfied with the decision and will be more likely to perform the tasks that are required to implement the decision. For example, many of the members of the

---

distributive justice Perceived fairness of the distribution of rights, resources, and costs.

procedural justice Perceived fairness and legitimacy of the methods used to make decisions, resolve disputes, and allocate resources; also, in judicial contexts, the use of fair and impartial procedures.

president's advisory group were against the Bay of Pigs plan, but they believed that the group had examined the issue in a fair, impartial way, and so, when the decision was made, they went to work implementing it. People are more likely to regard a decision as a fair one if the decisional procedures are implemented "(a) consistently, (b) without self-interest, (c) on the basis of accurate information, (d) with opportunities to correct the decision, (e) with the interests of all concerned parties represented, and (f) following moral and ethical standards" (Brockner & Wiesenfeld, 1996, p. 189). The group that uses procedurally just methods for making decisions will be more successful during the implementation stage (Colquitt & Greenberg, 2003; Skitka, Winquist, & Hutchinson, 2003).

Participation and Voice   Many factors influence perceptions of procedural fairness, but when people believe that they had a voice in the matter—that they could have expressed any concerns they had and others would have listened and responded—then they tend to be far more engaged in the implementation of the final decision. This *voice effect* was examined in an early study by psychologists Lester Coch and John R. P. French (1948). The management of a clothing mill asked Coch and French to identify a way to improve employees' commitment to new production methods. Coch and French suspected that employees would respond more positively if they were involved in planning changes, so they devised three different training programs. Employees in the *no-participation* program were just given an explanation for the innovations. Those in the *participation-through-representation* program attended group meetings where the need for change was discussed openly and an informal decision was reached. A subgroup was then chosen to become the "special" operators who would serve as the first training group. Employees in the third program—*total participation*—followed much the same procedures as those in the second program, but here *all* the employees, not a select group, took part in the training system.

Confirming the voice effect, hostility, turnover, and inefficiency was highest in the no-

participation group; 17% quit rather than learn the new procedures, and those who remained never reached the goals set by management. Those in the two participation conditions, in contrast, learned their new tasks quickly, and their productivity soon surpassed prechange levels and management goals. Morale was high, only one hostile action was recorded, and none of the employees quit in the 40 days following the change. Furthermore, when the members of the no-participation control condition were run through a program of increased voice and involvement several months later, they, too, reached appropriate production levels (cf. Bartlem & Locke, 1981).

Autonomous work groups and *self-directed teams* are the modern-day counterparts to Coch and French's total-participation groups (Cascio, 1995). These groups vary considerably in composition and goals, but in most cases, they are charged with identifying problems that are undermining productivity, efficiency, quality, or job satisfaction. These groups spend considerable time discussing the causes of the problems and suggesting possible solutions, either with or without a formal leader or supervisor. Once decisions are made about changes (usually by consensus), these changes are implemented and evaluated. If the changes do not have the desired effect, the process is repeated. These groups are considered in more detail in Chapter 12.

Who Decides?

President Kennedy was given the secret document describing the invasion plan in early February (Wyden, 1979, p. 90). It suggested that the United States should arm and train a group of Cuban exiles, who would then return to their homeland and lead a revolt against that country's leader. Kennedy could have studied the report and made a decision at that moment. Instead, he turned to a group to help him make a decision.

Making a decision in a group offers a number of advantages over making a decision alone. Groups, with their greater informational resources and capacity to process that information, may be able to identify better solutions and to detect errors in reasoning. Members may also find a group's decision more satisfying than that of a single individual, particularly if the group uses a consensus-building decision process. Group decisions, however, can take more time than people wish to give to them, and so groups too often sacrifice quality for timeliness. Some issues, too, are so trivial, so convoluted, or so contentious that a group approach may end in failure.

Normative Model of Decision Making Industrial/organizational psychologist Victor Vroom, recognizing the pros and cons of using groups to make decisions, developed the **normative model of decision making** to determine when to use groups and when to avoid them (Vroom, 2003; Vroom & Jago, 2007). Although decisional methods can fall anywhere along the continuum from authoritarian leader-centered to democratic group-centered decision making, Vroom's (2003) most recent model identifies these five basic types of decision-making methods:

- *Decide:* The leader solves the problem or makes the decision and announces it to the group. The leader may rely on information available to him or her at that time, but may also obtain information from group members. The members only provide information to the leader, and the leader may not tell the group members why the information is needed.

- *Consult (Individual):* The leader shares the problem with the group members individually, getting their ideas and suggestions one-on-one without meeting as a full group. The leader then makes the decision, which may not reflect the group members' influence.

- *Consult (Group):* The leader discusses the problem with the members as a group,

collectively obtaining their input. Then the leader makes the decision, which may not reflect the group members' influence.

- *Facilitate:* The leader coordinates a collaborative analysis of the problem, helping the group reach consensus on the issue. The leader is active in the process, but does not try to influence the group to adopt a particular solution. The leader accepts the will of the group and implements any decision that is supported by the entire group.

- *Delegate:* If the group already functions independently of the leader, then he or she can turn the problem over to the group. The group reaches a decision without the leader's direct involvement, but the leader provides support, direction, clarification, and resources as the group deliberates.

Selecting a Decision-Making Method Vroom's normative model does not advocate one decision-making method as superior to another. Rather, the situation must be considered and an approach selected that is most suited to the given context. One of the most important of all factors to consider is the significance of the decision itself; if the problem is not very important, then it can be solved using a method that involves the least amount of time and the fewest individuals. But when the problem becomes increasingly important, other situational factors must also be considered: Does the leader have substantial knowledge about the issue? Does the group know even more about the problem? Will the group be committed to the solution and its implementation if it does not get involved in the decision-making process, and does that even matter? How well do the group members work together? Is conflict so high in the group that members may not be able to work together on the problem? In general, when problems are simple ones, the leader is well informed and the consequences for a poor decision are relatively minor, then in the interest of time the leader should decide. A group-focused approach, in contrast, is best whenever a high-quality solution is needed, along with support

---

normative model of decision making A theory of decision making and leadership that predicts the effectiveness of group-centered, consultative, and autocratic decisional procedures across a number of group settings (developed by Victor Vroom and his associates).

from the group to implement it. However, choosing between an individual and a group approach is so complex that Vroom and his colleagues have developed a computer program that guides the choice between deciding, consulting, facilitating, and delegating (Vroom, 2003).

The normative model synthesizes studies of leadership, group decision making, and procedural fairness to predict when a choice should be made by an authority and when it should be handled by the group. Although the model may oversimplify this complex process, it translates theoretical ideas into concrete suggestions and thus is a practical approach to group decision making. Existing research also supports the basic assumptions underlying the model (Vroom, 2003).

PROBLEMS AND PITFALLS

People often have harsh words to say about the decisions made by groups. Members complain about time wasted in groups and swap jokes such as "An elephant is a mouse designed by a committee," "Trying to solve a problem through group discussion is like trying to clear up a traffic jam by honking your horn," and "Committees consist of the unfit appointed by the unwilling to do the unnecessary." Although groups, with their vastly greater informational and motivational resources, have the *potential* to outperform individuals, they do not always reach that potential. At each point in the functional model—from orientation, discussion, decision, and implementation—groups can go wrong, and they often do.

Failing to Plan Is Planning to Fail

Given the clear benefits of spending time setting goals and making plans, it is unfortunate that few groups show much interest in planning their procedures (Tindale et al., 2001). When a group member raises the issue of planning, very rarely do any of the other group members respond positively (Hackman & Morris, 1975). When groups are given a problem to solve or a decision to make,

their first tendency is to get started on the task itself rather than consider process-related issues. Even when enjoined to plan, groups believe that planning activities are less important than actual task activities (Shure et al., 1962). This antiplanning bias stems, in part, from the tendency of groups to apply whatever method they used in the past to current and future projects (Hackman & Morris, 1975). Even Kennedy's group moved through the orientation stage too hastily. Kennedy had just become the president of the United States, and his advisors had not worked together before, so the members should have spent several meetings talking about the problem and the strategy they would take in solving it. Instead, they immediately began to discuss logistics and operations (Stern, 1997).

The Planning Fallacy   Even if groups make plans, they will likely underestimate the time it will take them to reach their objectives (Kahneman and Tversky, 1973). This **planning fallacy** occurs because most people assume that the future will be pleasant rather than bleak, that issues that come up along the way will be handled quickly and without great expenditure and effort, and that one's choices will be right rather than wrong. People are basically optimists, so when they envision the future, they tend to construct mental scenarios that err on the positive side and underestimate the possibility of negative, time-draining problems and missteps (Dunning, 2007).

Both individuals and groups are prone to this bias, but groups are even less accurate than individuals. When college students were asked to make predictions about the time needed to complete a written case analysis that would count as 25% of their final grade, their estimates were less accurate after they talked the project over as a group. Even though the projects had been divided into subtasks, each with its own distinct deadline, the group members grossly underestimated the time they would need to complete

---

planning fallacy The tendency for individuals and groups to underestimate the time, energy, and means needed to complete a planned project successfully.

each one. During their discussion of deadlines, the groups focused primarily on factors promoting successful task completion and overlooked possible problems (Buehler, Messervey, & Griffin, 2005).

Contingency Planning   Even if the group spends considerable time initially planning its procedures, this attention to objectives does not mean the group will be able to maintain its focus over time. Even groups that are careful to begin with a deliberate planning session may fail to develop contingency plans or be skilled in revisiting and revising their plans along the way (DeChurch & Haas, 2008). The group planning the Bay of Pigs invasion, for example, did not have a clear set of backup plans to follow should the initial invasion force fail to hold the beachhead. Some members of the group believed the group could escape to the hills and join existing rebel forces, but others in the group assumed that Kennedy, recognizing the importance of the mission, would commit to sending in a full complement of United States forces.

The Difficulty of Discussion

People meet in groups to exchange and process information, but most people's capacity to express themselves clearly and to listen to and understand what others are saying is limited. People assume their skills are sufficient for dealing with problems through discussion, but their confidence is often misplaced.

Misunderstandings and Mistakes   Most experts on group communication agree that misunderstanding seems to be the rule in groups, with accurate understanding being the exception. On the sender side, many group members lack the skills needed to express themselves clearly. They fail to make certain that their verbal and nonverbal messages are easily decipherable and so unintentionally mislead, confuse, or even insult other members. One study of college students reported that 33% could not give accurate directions, 49% could not summarize the points made by a person who disagreed with them, and 35% could neither state their point of view

clearly nor defend it (Rubin, 1985). On the receiver side, inaccuracies also arise from the information-processing limitations and faulty listening habits of human beings. Listeners tend to *level* (simplify and shorten), *sharpen* (embellish distinctions made by the speaker), and *assimilate* (interpret messages so that they match personal expectations and beliefs) information offered by others during a discussion (Campbell, 1958b; Collins & Guetzkow, 1964).

These limitations are apparent to anyone who attends meetings with any frequency. When researchers asked 569 full-time employees who worked at jobs ranging from clerical positions to upper-level management to describe "in their own words what happens during a meeting that limits its effectiveness," they received nearly 2500 answers. About a quarter of the complaints had to do with meeting planning. In many cases the groups included the wrong people, the time needed for the work was inadequate, and the agenda used to structure the meeting was unhelpful or inaccurate. Another category of problems pertained to the implementation phase: nothing ever happened as a follow-up to the meeting. The majority of the complaints, however, suggested too many members either (a) did not have the skills needed to work well with others in a group setting or (b) they did not bother to make use of their skills once in the group. *Lack of skill in communication* was a commonly reported complaint (10%): Not only did members frequently fail to listen to what others had to say, but they rarely communicated their ideas and opinions in engaging and informative ways. Speakers did little to make their message heard by others, they were often repetitive and boring, and they did not express their ideas clearly. *Egocentric behavior* was also a frequently reported problem (8%), for many members used the meetings to flaunt their idiosyncrasies, intimidate others, and to show- and goof-off. Such behaviors served the individual members' needs, but at the expense of the group's productivity. Perhaps for these reasons many members did not take part in an active way in the sessions (*nonparticipation*, 7%): they attended, but they did not speak, volunteer to join with others working on projects, and sometimes just stared silently at others. Members also complained of *sidetracking* (6.5%) as the discussions too frequently went off topic; frequent *interruptions* (6%), such as engaging in side conversations or taking a phone call during the meeting; *inadequate leadership* (6%) by the group facilitator; and excessive displays of *negative attitudes and emotions* (5%). The participants in this research suggested that the groups failed more frequently than they succeeded. As one respondent explained, "No one, not even the leader, ever listens to what anybody else has to say" (Di Salvo, Nikkel, & Monroe, 1989, p. 557).

Death by Meeting   When Kennedy needed to make a decision about the CIA's plan, he called a meeting, and in doing so he was not doing anything particularly extraordinary. Meetings are the default choice used by many organizations to make decisions: One source estimates the number of meetings held in the United States in a year's time to be about three billion (Nunamaker et al., 1997).

Meetings may be essential tools for making decisions and organizing productivity, but those who attend often consider them to be boring, uninteresting, and inefficient. They can, in some cases, be filled with conflict, so that they are not just boring but also threatening. They can also be viewed as interruptions of the work that must be done, particularly by those who do not need to coordinate their activities with others.

Industrial/organizational psychologist Steve Rogelberg and his colleagues explored the downside of meetings by asking workers in England, Australia, and the United States about their involvement in meetings and to rate them on a scale from 1 (extremely ineffective) to 5 (extremely effective). The researchers also measured such variables as job satisfaction, stress (e.g., tension, anxiety, worry, gloom, depression, and misery), and the degree of interdependence required by their job. People who thought their meetings were effective felt more enthusiastic about their work, more satisfied, and more productive. But if they rated their meetings as ineffective, they were more depressed, more anxious, and more likely to be thinking about quitting—particularly if they did not feel that they needed to work closely with other people to

accomplish their work-related tasks. Many saw meetings as interruptions—not as ways to get more work done, but as obstacles to productivity (Luong & Rogelberg, 2005; Rogelberg et al., 2006). These findings suggest that most people would appreciate two things: a reduction in the number of meetings and an improvement in the quality of those that take place.

Wasting Time   The humorist C. Northcote Parkinson's (1957) time management laws are particularly apt when applied to groups. Parkinson's first law, which he modestly named **Parkinson's Law**, states that a task will expand to fill the time available for its completion. Hence, if a group gathers at 1 PM for a one-hour meeting, the group will likely adjourn at 2 PM, no matter how simple or routine the issues they examine.

Parkinson's second law, the **law of triviality**, states that the time a group spends on discussing any issue will be in inverse proportion to the consequentiality of the issue (Parkinson, 1957, paraphrased from p. 24). Parkinson described a hypothetical finance committee dealing with Item 9 on a long agenda: a $10-million allocation to build a nuclear reactor. Discussion is terse, lasting about 2½ minutes, and the committee unanimously approves the item. However, when the group turns to Item 10, the allocation of $2350 to build a bicycle shed to be used by the office staff, everyone on the committee has something to say. As Parkinson (1957, p. 301) explained:

> A sum of $2350 is well within everybody's comprehension. Everybody can visualize a bicycle shed. Discussion goes on, therefore, for forty-five minutes, with the possible result of saving some $300. Members at length sit back with a feeling of achievement.

Parkinson's Law A task will expand to fill the time available for its completion.

law of triviality The amount of time a group spends on discussing any issue will be in inverse proportion to the consequentiality of the issue.

Muddling Through Sometimes groups use discussion to *avoid* rather than make a decision. People tend to be "reluctant decision makers" who will do anything to avoid making a hard choice (Anderson, 2003; Janis & Mann, 1977). Avoidance tactics include the following:

- *Procrastination.* The group postpones the decision rather than studying alternatives and arguing their relative merits.

- *Bolstering.* The group quickly but arbitrarily formulates a decision without thinking things through completely and then bolsters the preferred solution by exaggerating the favorable consequences and minimizing the importance and likelihood of unfavorable consequences.

- *Denying responsibility.* The group avoids taking responsibility by delegating the decision to a subcommittee or by diffusing accountability throughout the entire assembly.

- *Muddling through.* The group muddles through the issue (Lindblom, 1965) by considering "only a very narrow range of policy alternatives that differ to only a small degree from the existing policy" (Janis & Mann, 1977, p. 33).

- *"Satisficing"* ("what satisfies will suffice"). Members accept a low-risk, easy solution instead of searching for the best solution.

- *Trivializing the discussion.* Groups obey Parkinson's laws by spending most of their time on trivial issues and too little time on important, consequential ones.

The Shared Information Bias

The Bay of Pigs planners spent much time talking about the incompetence of Castro's forces and how U.S. citizens would react to the invasion. They did not spend as much time talking about the weapons that the troops would carry, the political climate in Cuba, or the type of communication system used by Cuban military forces. Only the CIA representatives knew that the morale of the invasion force was low, but they never mentioned that information during the discussion. Kennedy, as a result of other briefings, was privy to many facts relevant to the initiative, but he kept this information to himself (Kramer, 2008).

The Common Knowledge Effect The good news is that groups can pool their individual resources to make a decision that takes into account far more information than any one individual can consider. The bad news is that groups often fall prey to **shared information bias**: they spend too much of their discussion time examining *shared information*—details that two or more group members know in common—rather than unshared information (Stasser, 1992; Wittenbaum, Hollingshead, & Botero, 2004). If all the members of a group discussing an invasion plan know that the majority of U.S. citizens oppose communism, then this topic will be discussed at length. But if only the CIA representative knows that the invading troops are poorly trained or only Kennedy knows that Cuban citizens support Castro, these important—but unshared—pieces of information might never be discussed. This tendency is also known as the *common knowledge effect* (Gigone, 2010; Gigone & Hastie, 1997).

The Hidden Profile Problem The harmful consequences of this shared information bias are substantial when the group must consider carefully the unshared information to make a good decision. If a group is working on a problem when the shared information suggests that Alternative A is correct, but the unshared information favors Alternative B, then the group will only discover this so-called *hidden profile* if it discusses the unshared information. Social psychologists Garold Stasser and William Titus (1985) studied this problem by giving the members of four-person groups 16 pieces of information about three candidates for student body president. Candidate A was the best choice for the post, for he possessed eight positive qualities, four

---

shared information bias (or *common knowledge effect*) The tendency for groups to spend more time discussing information that all members know (shared information) and less time examining information that only a few members know (unshared).

neutral qualities, and four negative qualities. The other two candidates had four positive qualities, eight neutral qualities, and four negative qualities. When the group members were given all the available information about the candidates, 83% of the groups favored Candidate A—an improvement over the 67% rate reported by the participants before they joined their group. But groups did not fare so well when Stasser and Titus manipulated the distribution of the positive and negative information among the members to create a hidden profile. Candidate A still had eight positive qualities, but Stasser and Titus made certain that each group member received information about only two of these qualities. Person 1, for example, knew that Candidate A had positive qualities P1 and P2; Person 2 knew that he had positive qualities P3 and P4; Person 3 knew that he had positive qualities P5 and P6; and Person 4 knew that he had positive qualities P7 and P8. But they all knew that Candidate A had negative qualities N1, N2, N3, and N4.

Had the group members pooled their information carefully, they would have discovered that Candidate A had positive qualities P1 to P8 and only four negative qualities. But they oversampled the shared negative qualities and chose the less qualified candidate 76% of the time (Stasser & Titus, 1985, 1987). Subsequent studies have repeatedly confirmed groups' inability to dig deeper than the information known to all: Groups working with hidden profiles are eight times less likely to find the solution than are groups having full information (Lu, Yuan, & McLeod, 2012).

What Causes the Shared Information Bias?   The shared information bias reflects the dual purposes of discussion. As a form of *informational influence*, discussions help individuals marshal the evidence and information they need to make good decisions. But as a form of *normative influence*, discussions give members the chance to influence each other's opinions on the issue. Discussing unshared information may be enlightening, but discussing shared information helps the group reach consensus. Hence, when group members are motivated more by a desire to get closure or to convince the group to back their initial preferences, biases are stronger; but if members are striving to make the best decision, the shared information bias becomes less pronounced (Postmes, Spears, & Cihangir, 2001; Scholten et al., 2007). The bias is strongest when groups work on judgmental tasks that do not have a demonstrably correct solution (Stewart & Stasser, 1998) but is attenuated if groups are working under time pressure and have relatively few alternatives to consider (Reimer, Reimer, & Czienskowski, 2010).

The shared information bias also reflects the psychological and interpersonal needs of the group members. If group members enter into the group discussion with a clear preference, they will argue in favor of their preference and resist changing their minds. If the shared information all points in one direction—as it did in Stasser and Titus's (1985) study of hidden profiles—then all the group members begin the discussion with a negative opinion of Candidate A. The group's final choice reflects these initial preferences. Discussion should have caused them to change their opinions, as additional (unshared) information came to light, but it did not (Nijstad, 2009 for a review).

At the interpersonal level, discussions aren't only about making good decisions. Members are striving to reach the best decision possible, but they have other motivations as well: They are trying to establish reputations for themselves, secure tighter bonds of attraction with others, and possibly compete with and succeed against other group members (Wittenbaum et al., 2004). Therefore, they are selective regarding when they disclose information and to whom they disclose it, often emphasizing shared information to express their agreement with others in the group. Ironically, people consider shared information to be highly diagnostic, so they mistakenly believe that people who discuss shared information are more knowledgeable, competent, and credible than are group members who contribute unshared information to the discussion (Wittenbaum, Hubbell, & Zuckerman, 1999). Members, to make a good impression with the group, dwell on what everyone knows rather than on the points that only they understand. Group members who anticipate a group discussion implicitly focus on information that they know others also possess, instead of concentrating on their unique informational resources (Wittenbaum, Stasser, & Merry, 1996).

Can the Shared Information Bias Be Avoided?
Even though groups prefer to spend their time discussing shared information, experienced members avoid this tendency, and they often intervene to focus the group's attention on unshared data (Wittenbaum, 1998). When researchers studied medical teams making decisions, they noted that the more senior group members repeated more shared information, but they also repeated more unshared information than the other group members. Moreover, as the discussion progressed, they were more likely to repeat unshared information that was mentioned during the session—evidence of their attempt to bring unshared information out through the discussion (Larson et al., 1996). Groups can also avoid the shared information bias if they spend more time actively discussing their decisions. Because group members tend to discuss shared information first, groups are more likely to review unshared information in longer meetings (Bowman & Wittenbaum, 2012; Winquist & Larson, 1998). Other methods of avoiding the bias include increasing the diversity of opinions within the group (Smith, 2008), using an advocacy approach rather than a general discussion (Greitemeyer et al., 2006), emphasizing the importance of dissent (Klocke, 2007), and introducing the discussion as a new topic (new business) rather than a return to a previously discussed item (Reimer, Reimer, & Hinsz, 2010).

Technology also offers a solution to the bias. **Group decision support systems** (GDSS) offer members a way to catalog, more comprehensively, the group's total stock of information and then share that information collectively. Depending on

the GDSS, the group would have access to an array of decision-making tools, such as databases, search engines for locating information, communication tools for sending messages to specific individuals and to the entire group, shared writing and drawing areas where members can collaborate on projects, and computational tools that will poll members automatically and help them to estimate costs, risks, probabilities, and so on (Hollingshead, 2001b). The value of a GDSS has not, however, been confirmed consistently by researchers. Some investigators have found that even a simple GDSS, that only promotes communication, reduces the biasing effects by a half (Lam & Schaubroeck, 2000). Other studies, however, suggest that the common knowledge effect is as common in e-groups as it is in face-to-face groups (Lu, Yuan, & McLeod, 2012).

Cognitive Limitations

Groups generate decisions through processes that are both active and complex. Members formulate initial preferences, gather and share information about those preferences, and then combine their views in a single group choice. Although these tasks are relatively ordinary ones, they sometimes demand too much cognitive work from members. The president's committee, for example, wanted to weigh all the relevant factors carefully before making its choice, but the complexity of the problem outstripped the members' relatively meager cognitive capacity.

Decisional Sins The discussion stage of decision making provides members with the opportunity to gather and exchange information about the problem at hand, but, when the flow of information is too great, it can overwhelm the information-processing capabilities of the members. People use the information they have available to them inappropriately, putting too much emphasis on interesting information and ignoring statistical information. People sometimes form conclusions very quickly and then do not sufficiently revise those conclusions once they acquire additional information. When people cannot easily imagine an outcome, they

---

group decision support systems A set of integrated tools groups use to structure and facilitate their decision making, including computer programs that expedite data acquisition, communication among group members, document sharing, and the systematic review of alternative actions and outcomes.

TABLE 11.1   **Types of Information Processing Errors Made by Individuals and by Groups When Making Decisions**

Type of Error	Examples
Sins of commission	*Belief perseverance:* reliance on information that has already been reviewed and found to be inaccurate
	Sunk cost bias: reluctance to abandon a course of action once an investment has been made in that action
	Extra-evidentiary bias: the use of information that one has been told explicitly to ignore
	Hindsight bias: the tendency to overestimate the accuracy of one's prior knowledge of an outcome
Sins of omission	*Base rate bias:* failure to pay attention to information about general tendencies
	Fundamental attribution error: stressing dispositional causes when making attributions about the cause of people's behaviors
Sins of imprecision	*Availability heuristic:* basing decisions on information that is readily available
	Conjunctive bias: failing to recognize that the probability of two events occurring together will always be less than the probability of just one of the events occurring
	Representativeness heuristic: excessive reliance on salient but misleading aspects of a problem

SOURCE: Adapted from Di Salvo, Nikkei, & Monroe, 1989.

assume that such an outcome is less likely to occur than one that springs easily to mind. People overestimate their judgmental accuracy because they remember all the times their decisions were confirmed and forget the times when their predictions were disconfirmed. People make mistakes.

Groups, unfortunately, do not mitigate these judgmental biases. When social psychologist Norbert Kerr and his colleagues reviewed the research literature looking for studies of these mental glitches in decision making, they identified the three general categories of potential bias summarized in Table 11.1:

- *sins of commission:* the misuse of information
- *sins of omission:* overlooking useful information
- *sins of imprecision:* relying inappropriately on mental rules of thumb, or heuristics, that oversimplify the decision

After reviewing studies that compared individuals' and groups' resistance to these types of biases, Kerr and his colleagues cautiously ruled against groups: Groups amplify rather than suppress these biases. For example, they use information that has already been discredited or they have been told to ignore; they overlook statistical information about general tendencies; they overemphasize personality as a cause of behaviors that are due, in part, to the pressures of the situation; and they base decisions on information that is readily available rather than actually diagnostic. More so even than individuals, groups know decisional sin (Kerr, MacCoun, & Kramer, 1996a, 1996b).

Minimizing Bias   Groups can err in the ways noted in Table 11.1, but they can take steps to minimize their susceptibility. Consider, for example, the **confirmation bias**. The members of a group usually hold certain preferences, even before they begin their discussions. A discussion gives them the opportunity to test their initial inclinations, but this review tends to be a biased one: People usually seek out information that confirms their preferences, and

---

confirmation bias The tendency to seek out information that confirms one's inferences rather than disconfirms them.

they avoid disconfirming evidence. Groups, however, can minimize this bias if they deliberately ban any public statements of initial preferences (Dawes, 1988) or include individuals with a wide range of initial preferences in the group itself.

Researchers studied this method of reducing bias by giving individuals some background information about a company that was considering relocating its production facilities. Participants indicated their initial preference on the matter, and the experimenters then used those choices to create three kinds of groups: (1) unanimous groups, composed of individuals who shared the same initial preference; (2) groups with one member who took a minority position on the issue; and (3) groups with two minority members. Participants in these three conditions were given the opportunity to select and review ten additional background readings, which were summarized by short thesis statements indicating they either supported or opposed relocation. A fourth set of participants made these choices as individuals. As Figure 11.4 indicates, the confirmation bias was robust—particularly in the homogeneous group. The inclusion of one dissenter lowered the tendency somewhat, such that the bias was equal to that shown by lone individuals. Including two dissenters, however, tended to subdue the bias, and it also prompted the group to seek out more information that conflicted with its initial preferences. These results confirm the value of including people with a range of experiences and opinions as members of groups that must make critical decisions (Schulz-Hardt et al., 2000; see also Schulz-Hardt, Jochims, & Frey, 2002).

Failures of Memory   As noted earlier in the chapter, groups can make use of cognitive mechanisms such as cross-cueing and transactive memory to improve their recall of information, but groups are not mnemonic marvels (Van Swol, 2008). When researchers compared the memories of collaborative groups, nominal groups (groups of noninteracting individuals), and individuals, collaborative groups outperformed both the average single individual and the best single individual. Collaborative groups did not, however, perform as well as nominal groups, and the groups displayed many of the characteristics

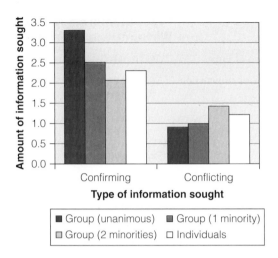

FIGURE 11.4   The seeking of confirming and conflicting information by individuals, unanimous groups, and groups with dissenters. Unanimous groups preferred confirming information and avoided conflicting information, but groups that included two dissenting members resisted this bias.

SOURCE: © Cengage Learning 2014

typically seen in individual memory. Individuals, for example, generally have better memory for information that they process more deeply and better memory for pictures than for words. Groups displayed these same tendencies when their memories were tested (Weldon & Bellinger, 1997). Groups also reported words that were not on the original list, and their memories were also less well structured (Finlay, Hitch, & Meudell, 2000).

The loss of motivation that occurs in group settings—social loafing (see Chapter 10)—also results in an overall decline in the processing efficiency of the members (Weldon, Blair, & Huebsch, 2000). People do not put maximum effort into group discussions, so, as a result, a group's potential productivity is never realized. The complexity of the group setting, combined with lowered motivation, even disrupts members' ability to organize information in memory so that it can be retrieved later. In consequence, collaborating groups perform particularly poorly when trying to remember badly organized information, but they perform the same as noninteracting (nominal) groups when trying to remember organized information (Basden et al., 1997). These inadequacies in collective memory may be so substantial that groups cannot remember their decisions unless they keep a written record of them (minutes). Although few group members relish the role of recorder, without minutes, details of the group's actions may be forgotten.

Dysfunctional Postdecision Tendencies

In theory, after groups implement their decision, they should then expend considerable time and energy reviewing their efforts and outcomes. They should gather and weigh information about their performance and review the strategies they used to make their decision and implement their solution. But, in reality, group members tend to respond defensively after making a decision, so the postdecision review process is either attenuated, biased, or skipped altogether (Umble, Haft, & Umble, 2003).

Denying Responsibility for Group Decisions
When a group's postdecision review indicates the group has erred, members quickly begin their search for the cause. The officers at the Enron Corporation, when explaining their company's abuses, blamed their accountants for using the wrong auditing methods. When the Challenger space shuttle exploded, NASA scientists blamed the engineers who designed the O-rings, but the engineers blamed NASA for launching the shuttle in cold weather. In the aftermath of the failed invasion of Cuba, President Kennedy publicly took the blame for the failure, but he also ended the careers of several group members who he believed were at actually fault.

As these examples suggest, groups prefer to deny responsibility for their failures (Leary & Forsyth, 1987). In some cases, members settle on *group-serving* attributions of responsibility—they blame failures and mistakes on factors outside of the group, but they credit the group for its successful accomplishments. In other cases—particularly when the group lacks cohesion or the mistake is a disastrous one—the group-serving pattern is replaced by

more egocentric, *self-serving* attributions of responsibility; members deny personal responsibility for failure but claim all the credit for successes. Members of failing groups may, for example, blame another group member ("Ed really ruined it for us"), remind the group that they personally performed well ("I warned them not to proceed"), or even disavow membership in the group ("I'm not really part of that group"). Group-serving attributions tend to unite the group, whereas blaming other members for failure tends to reduce cohesion (Forsyth, Berger, & Mitchell, 1981).

Entrapment and the Abilene Paradox   The tendency to deny failure can cause groups to continue too long with projects that are irretrievably flawed. Organizational expert Jerry Harvey named this tendency the **Abilene paradox** after experiencing it, firsthand, during a family visit. For reasons that were never clear to anyone in the group, in the afternoon of a relaxing day, they decided to travel from the comfort of their home to Abilene, Texas, even though none of them as individuals wanted to take such a pointless, uncomfortable trip. As Harvey (1988, p. 14) explains:

> After blaming each other for the bad decision, we all sat back in silence. Here we were, four reasonably sensible people who—of our own volition—had just taken a 106-mile trip across a godforsaken desert in furnace-like heat and dust storm to eat unpalatable food in a hole-in-the-wall cafeteria in Abilene, when none of us had really wanted to go. To be concise, we'd just done the opposite of what we wanted to do.

Two factors contributed to the **Abilene paradox**. First, the Abilene group suffered from a severe case of pluralistic ignorance (see Chapter 6). The

---

Abilene paradox The counterintuitive tendency for a group to decide on a course of action that none of the members of the group individually endorses, resulting from the group's failure to recognize and manage its agreement on key issues (identified by Jerry Harvey).

group members mistakenly believed that their private opinion about the Abilene outing was discrepant from the other group members' opinions. Therefore, each group member, wishing to be seen as a cooperative member of the family, publicly conformed to what they thought was the group's norm, each one erroneously assuming that he or she was the only one with misgivings. Jerry went to Abilene because that is what everyone else wanted to do—or so he thought. Unfortunately, everyone else was thinking the same thing, so the group mismanaged its consensus.

Second, the group committed to its decision quickly and did not reconsider its choice when negative consequences—the heat, the cost, the discomfort—mounted. This process is sometimes termed **entrapment**—a special form of escalation that occurs when the group expends "more of its time, energy, money, or other resources than seems justifiable by external standards" (Pruitt & Kim, 2004, p. 165). Entrapment occurs when groups become so invested in a course of action that they refuse to reverse their decisions (Brockner, 1995; Brockner & Rubin, 1985). Such situations often lure in groups by raising concerns over investments the group has already made in the choice (Arkes & Blumer, 1985). If a group discovers that the costs for a project are escalating, the members will rarely consider canceling the project altogether. Instead, they will continue to fund the project, because the initial investment, or **sunk cost**, must be honored. Unfortunately, the money and time invested in a plan of action is already spent and should no longer be considered in weighing the ultimate value of the project. Sunk costs, however, can cause groups to continue to expend resources on projects that will ultimately fail. Analyses of truly massive, much-criticized projects that cost millions of dollars—such as the Millennium Dome in London, EuroDisney, and the Denver International Airport—can be traced to entrapment (Nutt, 2002).

---

entrapment A form of escalating investment in which individuals expend more of their resources in pursuing a chosen course of action than seems appropriate or justifiable by external standards.

sunk cost An investment or loss of resources that cannot be recouped by current or future actions.

GROUP POLARIZATION

President Kennedy decided to create a committee to help him review the invasion plan. Was he acting on the intuitively appealing notion that groups have a moderating impact on individuals? Did he assume that a group, if faced with a choice between a risky alternative, such as "Invade Cuba," and a more moderate alternative, such as "Use diplomatic means to influence Cuba," would prefer the moderate route? Unfortunately for Kennedy, for his advisers, and for the members of the attack force, groups' decisions are often more extreme than individuals' decisions. Groups do not urge restraint; instead, they *polarize*.

Group Decisions Involving Risk

At about the time that Kennedy's committee was grappling with the problems inherent in the invasion plan, group researchers were initiating the first experimental studies of groups making risky decisions. They created groups in their laboratories and asked these groups to consider a range of options that varied in their level of risk. They fully expected that groups would be more cautious than individuals, but they instead discovered the **risky-shift effect**: group's decisions were riskier than decisions made by individuals (Lamm & Myers, 1978).

Risky Shifts in Groups Many of the early studies of the risky shift used the **Choice-Dilemmas Questionnaire** to measure the level of risk people were willing to accept (Stoner, 1961, 1968). This self-report measure asks respondents to read a series of scenarios—like the one shown in Figure 11.5—that may or may not yield financial, interpersonal, or educational benefits. They then indicate what the odds of success would have to be before they would recommend the course of action. When individuals

---

risky-shift effect: The tendency for groups to make riskier decisions than individuals.

Choice-Dilemmas Questionnaire A self-report measure of willingness to make risky decisions; respondents indicate what the odds of success would have to be before they would recommend the course of action.

What Would You Recommend?

Mr. A, an electrical engineer, who is married and has one child, has been working for a large electronics corporation since graduating from college five years ago. He is assured of a lifetime job with a modest, though adequate, salary and liberal pension benefits upon retirement. On the other hand, it is very unlikely that his salary will increase much before he retires. While attending a convention, Mr. A is offered a job with a small, newly founded company which has a highly uncertain future. The new job would pay more to start and would offer the possibility of a share in the ownership if the company survived the competition of the larger firms.

★★★

Imagine that you are advising Mr. A. Listed below are several probabilities or odds of the new company proving financially sound. Please check the lowest probability that you would consider acceptable to make it worthwhile for Mr. A to take the new job.

❏ **The chances are *1 in 10* that the company will prove financially sound.**
❏ **The chances are *3 in 10* that the company will prove financially sound.**
❏ **The chances are *5 in 10* that the company will prove financially sound.**
❏ **The chances are *7 in 10* that the company will prove financially sound.**
❏ **The chances are *9 in 10* that the company will prove financially sound.**
❏ **Place a check here if you think Mr. A should not take the new job no matter what the probabilities.**

F I G U R E   11.5   A sample question from the Choice-Dilemmas Questionnaire (from Pruitt, 1971, p. 359).

SOURCE: From Pruitt, D. G. (1971). Choice shifts in group discussion: An introductory review. *Journal of Personality and Social Psychology, 20,* 359.

completed the questionnaire individually and in groups, the groups' choices tended to be slightly riskier. For example, in one study that used the *Choice-Dilemmas Questionnaire*, the mean of prediscussion individual decisions was 5.5 on the scale from 1 (most risky) to 9 (least risky). The mean of the groups' consensual decision, however, was 4.8—a shift of 0.7 in the direction of greater risk. This shift also occurred when individual judgments were collected after the group discussion and when the individual postdiscussion measures were delayed two to six weeks. (The delayed posttests were collected from male participants only.) Participants in a control condition shifted very little (Wallach, Kogan, & Bem, 1962).

Cautious Shifts in Groups   The risky-shift was replicated in countries around the world, including

Canada, the United States, England, France, Germany, and New Zealand, and with many kinds of group participants (Pruitt, 1971). Although commentators sometimes wondered about the generality and significance of the phenomenon (Smith, 1972), laboratory findings were eventually corroborated by field studies (Lamm & Myers, 1978).

During this research period, however, some studies hinted at the possibility of the opposite process—a *cautious shift*. For example, when the early risky-shift researchers examined the amount of postdiscussion change revealed on each item of the *Choice-Dilemmas Questionnaire*, they frequently found that group members consistently advocated a less risky course of action than did individuals on one particular item (Wallach et al., 1962). Intrigued by this anomalous finding, subsequent researchers wrote additional choice dilemmas, and they, too, occasionally found evidence of a cautious shift. Then, in 1969, researchers reported some groups moving toward risk after a discussion, but others becoming more cautious, suggesting both types of shifts were possible (Doise, 1969).

Researchers also discovered that group discussions can cause shifts in members' attitudes, beliefs, values, judgments, and perceptions (Myers, 1982). In France, for example, where people generally like their government but dislike Americans, group discussions improved their attitude toward their government but exacerbated their negative opinions of Americans (Moscovici & Zavalloni, 1969). Similarly, strongly prejudiced people who discussed racial issues with other prejudiced individuals became even more prejudiced. However, when mildly prejudiced persons discussed racial issues with other mildly prejudiced individuals, they became less prejudiced (Myers & Bishop, 1970).

Polarization in Groups Researchers eventually realized that risky shifts after group discussions were a part of a more general process. When people discuss issues in groups, they sometimes draw a more extreme conclusion than would be suggested by the average of their individual judgments. The direction of this shift depends on their average initial preferences. When supporters gather to discuss a candidate's strengths and weaknesses, by the meeting's end their opinions will likely become even more favorable toward the candidate. A gathering of students who are moderately negative about a professor's teaching methods will become openly hostile after a discussion. Social psychologists David Myers and Helmut Lamm called this process **group polarization** because the "average postgroup response will tend to be more extreme in the same direction as the average of the pregroup responses" (Myers & Lamm, 1976, p. 603; see also Lamm & Myers, 1978). Group discussion

---

group polarization The tendency for members of a deliberating group to move to a more extreme position with the direction of the shift determined by the majority or average of the members' predeliberation preferences.

polarizes, in the sense that it tends to push people away from the center toward the extremes.

Imagine two groups of four individuals whose opinions vary in terms of preference for risk. As Figure 11.6 indicates, when the average choice of the group members before discussion is closer to the risky pole of the continuum than to the cautious pole (as would be the case in a group composed of Persons A, B, C, and D), a risky shift will occur. If, in contrast, the group is composed of Persons C, D, E, and F, a cautious shift will take place, because the pregroup mean of 6.5 falls closer to the cautious pole. This example is, of course, something of an oversimplification, because the shift depends on the distance from the psychological rather than the mathematical midpoint of the scale. As Myers and Lamm (1976) noted, on choice dilemmas, an initial pregroup mean of 6 or smaller is usually sufficient to produce a risky shift, whereas a mean of 7 or greater is necessary to produce a cautious shift. If the pregroup mean falls between 6 and 7, a shift is unlikely.

What Causes Group Polarization?

How do groups intensify individuals' reactions? Early explanations suggested that groups feel less responsible for their decisions and are overly influenced by risk-prone leaders, but in time, investigators recognized that polarization results from social influence processes that operate routinely in groups, including *social comparison*, *persuasion*, and *social identity* (Friedkin, 1999; Liu & Latané, 1998).

Social Comparison and Cultural Values When individuals discuss their opinions in a group, they shift in the direction that they think is consistent with the values of their group or culture (Clark, 1971). If they are part of a group that, on average, favors risk, the members will shift in that direction after discussion. Similarly, individuals who are raised in cultures that are relatively risk-averse are more likely to endorse more cautious choices when in groups (see Focus 11.2).

Several processes likely sustain this value-determined shift. As social comparison theory

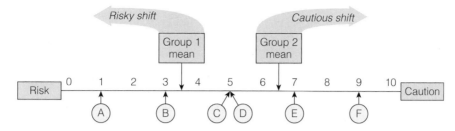

FIGURE 11.6 A schematic representation of polarization in groups. Imagine that Group 1 includes Person A (who chose 1), Person B (who chose 3), and Persons C and D (who both chose 5); the average of pregroup choices would be (1 + 3 + 5 + 5)/4, or 3.5. Because this mean is less than 5, a risky shift would probably occur in Group 1. If, in contrast, Group 2 contained Persons C, D, E, and F, their pregroup average would be (5 + 5 + 7 + 9)/4, or 6.5. Because this mean is closer to the caution pole, a cautious shift would probably occur in the group.

SOURCE: © Cengage Learning 2014

suggests, when people make decisions individually, they have no way to determine whether they are risk-averse or risk-takers; whether they are responding as most people do or are overreacting; whether the position they are defending is reasonable or whether they are arguing for an idea that most people think is bizarre. But when group members make choices together, they use others as reference points to evaluate their own preferences and positions (Goethals & Zanna, 1979; Myers, 1978). Moreover, if the group discussion indicates that the majority of the group likes risk, then a desire to create a positive impression in the group may prompt members to claim that they *really* like risk (Weigold & Schlenker, 1991): "To be virtuous … is to be different from the mean—in the right direction and to the right degree" (Brown, 1974, p. 469).

Persuasive Arguments Group members also change their opinions in response to others' arguments and ideas. If, for example, the discussion reveals several strong arguments that favor risk rather than caution, members will shift in that direction. But as **persuasive-arguments theory**

---

persuasive-arguments theory An explanation of polarization in groups assuming that group members change their opinions during group discussion, generally adopting the position favored by the majority of the members, because the group can generate more arguments favoring that position.

notes, groups usually generate more arguments that support the position endorsed by the majority of the group or the position that is most consistent with dominant social values—in part because members may be more willing to express arguments that are consistent with social norms. As a result, the group persuades itself, as more arguments favoring the dominant viewpoint are brought up during the discussion (Burnstein & Vinokur, 1973, 1977; Vinokur & Burnstein, 1974, 1978). As discussants restate their own and other members' arguments during the discussion, they will tend to gravitate toward which ever position is best supported by the pool of available arguments (Brauer, Judd, & Gliner, 1995). The group's social decision scheme may also favor a more extreme position rather than a moderate one. If, for example, a group adopts a "risk-supported-wins" rule and two members of the group express a willingness to tolerate extreme risk, then the group may shift in that direction (Davis, Kameda, & Stasson, 1992; Zuber, Crott, & Werner, 1992).

Social Identity Curiously, at least for persuasive-arguments theory, group members sometimes shift their opinions when they discover others' positions but not their arguments (Blascovich, Ginsburg, & Howe, 1975, 1976). Why? Social identity theory suggests that people are not persuaded by the content of other's arguments, but by consensus of opinion. If, through discussion, members come to believe that the prototypical group member holds a relatively extreme

---

Focus 11.2 Cross-cultural Perspectives: Risk as a Cultural Value

Deliberation is considered by many to be an elevating and unifying force. As the philosopher John Rawls (1971, p. 358) opined, "the exchange of opinion with others checks our partiality and widens our perspective; we are made to see things from the standpoint of others and the limits of our vision are brought home to us." Unfortunately, deliberation is more often polarizing rather than subduing. When people discuss issues in groups, they move away from neutrality and temperance toward the extremes.

A number of social and psychological processes combine to generate this shift, including the tendency to adopt and express opinions that are consistent with, rather than counter to, cultural norms. When people gather in groups and discuss issues, they may find that in time they can reach agreement, but the group's consensus will more than likely crystalize closer to the position that is valued within the cultural context. A group that exists in a culture that values risk, for example, is more likely to shift toward risk following a group discussion, whereas the post-deliberation position of members of a group in a conservative culture will become more cautious.

And cultures do differ in their tolerance of risk (Rohrmann, 2000). The !Kung San, for example, exhibit a high level of caution that is well-matched to the challenging environment where they live. In contrast, the Baganda of Uganda seek risk and adventure, due in part to the tribe-level conflicts prevalent in their region. Many Asian countries, particularly those that follow the teachings of Confucius, stress moderation and a willingness to allow events to unfold over time, without manipulation. These cultures are more cautious ones, particularly in contrast to many Western, industrialized nations. In these countries, risk is not just tolerated but admired, for in more economically advantaged societies, such as the United States and Germany, wealth and abundance buffer the hardships that a too-risky choice may bring.

Sociologist Lawrence Hong (1978), intrigued by the possibility that culture would determine the direction groups would shift to after a discussion, arranged for 150 American and Chinese college students to complete the Choice-Dilemmas Questionnaire twice: once individually and again in small groups with others who shared their cultural background. As Hong expected, before the discussion, the Americans' choices were closer to the risky side of the cautious-risk continuum (4.7 using the scale shown in Figure 11.6), but the Chinese students' choices, when averaged, were more cautious (6.3). Also, as Hong predicted, when the students discussed the items in their culture-based groups, the Americans displayed a risky shift (to 4.0) and the Chinese students a cautious shift (to 7.3). He concluded that "risky and cautious shifts have a cultural base, and group decisions could be either more risky or more cautious, depending on the value-orientation of the culture" (Hong, 1978, p. 345).

The students in Hong's study met in groups with other students from their cultural group, but what would have happened if he had mixed the cautious Chinese with the more risky Americans? Will diversity magnify, or minimize, group polarization? To answer these questions, researchers compared culturally homogenous groups of students to culturally diverse student groups. All the members of the homogenous groups were Anglos, but the diverse groups included an African-American student and a Latino student or a student from a foreign country. These groups had been working together for a month prior to sitting down to complete the Choice-Dilemmas Questionnaire as a group. As expected, the culturally diverse groups were more cautious than the less diverse groups (Watson & Kumar, 1992). Similarity was associated with risk and diversity with conservatism.

These studies suggest that even though the specific type of behavior displayed by a group—in this case, a shift toward risk or toward caution—depends on the culture in which the group members live and work; this shift is produced by a set of social processes common to groups in all cultures. Groups everywhere discuss and debate important issues, but these discussions will tend to drift toward, rather than away from, traditional values for that culture. In consequence, groups more often serve to reify, rather than challenge, members' cultural worldview.

---

attitude on the issue, those who identify with the group will shift in that direction (Haslam, 2004). This shift causes the diversity of opinions in the group to decrease, as members converge on what they hold to be the opinion of the prototypical group member. This conception of the prototype may also shift toward more extreme positions to differentiate the ingroup from other groups. When, for example, group members learned another group had taken a risky position on an issue, the group members differentiated themselves from that group by becoming more cautious. When the group learned the other group was cautious, then the group shifted in the direction of risk (Hogg, Turner, & David, 1990). Polarization may also result because people are far more likely to respond positively to the arguments offered by ingroup members than outgroup members, and so those who hold a shared social identity may end up persuading each other to take increasingly more extreme positions (Mackie & Queller, 2000).

The Consequences of Polarization

Would people who believe that environmental pollution is a serious problem be more likely, after their discussion, to insist on severe measures to prevent pollution? Would bringing together two sides in a community conflict and allowing them to meet separately for an hour before a joint meeting create even more tensions between the two groups? Would a group of government experts who slightly favored an invasion plan enthusiastically endorse the plan after they discussed it? Do groups amplify group members' shared tendencies? Studies of polarization say *yes* (Sunstein, 2002).

Polarization may, in some cases, yield positive effects. Groups, when viewed from an evolutionary perspective, were designed to monitor risk, hence, they are sensitive to threats and urge caution when alarmed (Kameda & Tamura, 2007). A group's collective efficacy may rise as individually optimistic members join together and discuss their chances for success. The members of a support group may become far more hopeful of their chances for recovery when they gather together with others who are moderately optimistic. Innovations and new ideas may be adopted by large numbers of people as polarization amplifies enthusiasm for the new products, methods, or outlooks. Polarization may also encourage the strengthening of positions within the group that might go unexpressed or even be suppressed. Thus, polarization, though sometimes a source of error and bias, can in some cases have a beneficial impact on the group and its members.

VICTIMS OF GROUPTHINK

Social psychologist Irving Janis was intrigued by President Kennedy's advisory group. The committee, like so many others, failed to make the best decision it could. Its failure, though, was so spectacular that Janis wondered if something more than such common group difficulties as faulty communication and judgmental biases were to blame.

Janis pursued this insight by searching for other groups that made similar errors in judgment. And he found many that qualified: Senior naval officers who ignored repeated warnings of Japan's aggressive intentions regarding Pearl Harbor and took few steps to defend it; President Truman's policy-making staff who recommended that U.S. troops cross the 38th parallel during the Korean War, prompting China to ally with North Korea against the United States; President Nixon's staff who decided to cover up involvement in the break-in at Watergate. After studying these groups and their gross errors of judgment, he concluded that they suffered from *groupthink*—"a mode of thinking that people engage in when they are deeply involved in a cohesive ingroup, when the members' strivings for unanimity override their motivation to realistically appraise alternative courses of actions" (Janis, 1982, p. 9). During groupthink, members try so hard to agree with one another that they make mistakes and commit errors that could easily be avoided.

Janis sought to identify both the causes of groupthink, as well as the symptoms that signal that a group may be experiencing this malady. As Figure 11.7 indicates, Janis identified three key sets of antecedent conditions that set the stage for groupthink, including cohesion, structural faults of the group or organization, and provocative situational contexts. These conditions cause members to seek out agreement with others (concurrence-seeking tendency), which in turn leads to two classes of observable consequences: symptoms of groupthink and symptoms of defective decision making. In this section, we will work backward through the model shown in Figure 11.7: We will start with the warning signs of groupthink and then consider the antecedent conditions.

Antecedent conditions   *Observable consequences*

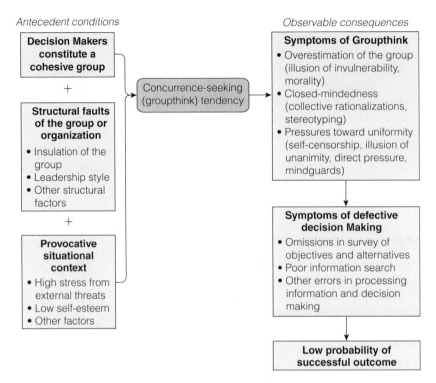

FIGURE 11.7   Irving Janis's (1982) theory of groupthink.

SOURCE: Janis, I. L. (1982). *Groupthink: Psychological studies of policy decisions and fiascos* (2nd ed.). Boston: Houghton Mifflin.

Symptoms of Groupthink

Like a physician who searches for symptoms that signal the onset of the illness, Janis identified a number of recurring patterns that occur in groupthink situations. He organized these symptoms into three categories: *overestimation of the group*, *closed-mindedness*, and *pressures toward uniformity* (Janis, 1972, 1982, 1989; Longley & Pruitt, 1980; Wheeler & Janis, 1980).

Overestimation of the Group   Groups that have fallen into the trap of groupthink are actually planning fiascoes and making all the wrong choices. Yet the members usually assume that everything is working perfectly. They even express enthusiasm in their public statements about their wrong-headed decisions (Tetlock, 1979). Janis traced this unwarranted optimism to illusions of invulnerability and illusions of morality.

The Bay of Pigs planners, like many groups, overestimated their group's decisional savvy. Members felt that they were performing well, even though they were not. This illusory thinking, though commonplace, becomes so extreme during groupthink that Janis called it an *illusion of invulnerability*. Feelings of assurance and confidence engulfed the group. The members felt that their plan was virtually infallible and that their committee could not make major errors in judgment. Such feelings of confidence and power may help athletic teams or combat units reach their objectives, but the feeling that all obstacles can be easily overcome through power and good luck can cut short clear, analytic thinking in decision-making groups (Silver & Bufanio, 1996).

The planners also believed in the inherent morality of their group and its decisions. The plan to invade Cuba could unsympathetically be described as an unprovoked sneak attack by a major world power on a virtually defenseless country. But the decision makers, suffering from *illusions of morality*, seemed to lose their principles in the group's desire to bravely end Castro's regime. Although groups are capable of reaching admirable levels of moral thought, this capability is unrealized during groupthink (McGraw & Bloomfield, 1987).

Closed-Mindedness   Groups that are overtaken by groupthink are not open-minded groups searching for new ideas and perspectives. Rather, they are *closed-minded*—rigidly shut off from alternatives, merely seeking to bolster their initial decision through *rationalization*. One key element of this closure is the tendency to view other groups in biased, simplistic ways. For example, the members of the planning group shared an inaccurate and negative opinion of Castro and his political ideology; They often expressed these *stereotypes about the outgroup* during group discussions. Castro was depicted as a weak leader, an evil communist, and a man too stupid to realize that his country was about to be attacked. His ability to maintain an air force was discredited, as was his control over his troops and the citizenry. The group participants' underestimation of their enemy was so pronounced that they sent a force of 1,400 men to fight a force of 200,000 and expected an easy success. The group wanted to believe that Castro was an ineffectual leader and military commander, but this oversimplified picture of the dictator turned out to be merely wishful thinking.

Pressures toward Uniformity   The struggle for consensus is an essential and unavoidable aspect of life in groups, but in groupthink situations, interpersonal pressures make agreeing too easy and disagreeing too difficult. Tolerance for any sort of dissent seems virtually nil, and groups may use harsh measures to bring those who disagree into line. In the president's committee, criticism was taboo, and members who broke this norm were pressured to conform. Janis highlighted four indicators of this pressure: self-censorship, the illusion of unanimity, direct pressure on dissenters, and self-appointed mindguards.

Self-censorship is Janis's term for a personal ban on expressing disagreements about the group's decisions. In the planning group, many of the members of the group privately felt uncertain about the plan, but they kept their doubts to themselves. Some even sent private memorandums to the president before or after a meeting; but when the group convened, the doubting Thomases sat in silence. As Schlesinger (1965) later wrote,

> In the months after the Bay of Pigs I bitterly reproached myself for having kept so silent during those crucial discussions in the Cabinet Room, though my feelings of guilt were tempered by the knowledge that a course of objection would have accomplished little save to gain me a name as a nuisance. I can only explain my failure to do more than raise a few timid questions by reporting that one's impulse to blow the whistle on this nonsense was simply undone by the circumstances of the discussion. (p. 225)

This self-imposed gag order created an *illusion of unanimity* in the group. The members seemed to agree that the basic plan presented by the CIA was the only solution to the problem. In later discussions, they appeared to just be "going through the motions" of debate. Retrospective accounts reveal that many of the group's members objected to the plan, but these objections never surfaced during the meetings. Instead, a "curious atmosphere of assumed consensus" (Schlesinger, 1965, p. 250) characterized the discussion, as each person wrongly concluded that everyone else liked the plan. As Janis (1972) explained, the group members played up "areas of convergence in their thinking, at the expense of fully exploring divergences that might disrupt the apparent unity of the group" (p. 39). The Bay of Pigs planners apparently felt that it would be "better to share a pleasant, balmy group atmosphere than be battered in a storm" (p. 39).

This easygoing, supportive atmosphere did not extend to those who disagreed with the group, however. *Direct pressure* was applied to dissenters, often by self-appointed vigilantes, or **mindguards**, who shielded the group from information that would shake the members' confidence in themselves or their leader. The mindguard diverts controversial information away from the group by losing it, forgetting to mention it, or deeming it irrelevant and thus unworthy of the group's attention. Alternatively, the mindguard may take dissenting members aside and pressure them to keep silent. The mindguard may use a variety of strategies to achieve this pressure: requesting the change as a personal favor, pointing out the damage that might be done to the group, or informing the dissenter that in the long run, disagreement would damage his or her position in the group (Uris, 1978). But whatever the method, the overall goal is the same—to contain dissent before it reaches the level of group awareness.

President Kennedy, Rusk, and the president's brother, Robert Kennedy, all acted as mindguards. Kennedy, for example, withheld memorandums condemning the plan from both Schlesinger and Fulbright. Rusk suppressed information that his own staff had given him. One extreme example of this mindguarding occurred when Rusk, unable to attend a meeting, sent Undersecretary of State Chester Bowles. Although Bowles was said to be horrified by the plan under discussion, President Kennedy never gave him the opportunity to speak during the meeting. Bowles followed bureaucratic channels to voice his critical misgivings, but his superior, Rusk, did not transmit those concerns to the committee, and he told Bowles that the plan had been revised. Bowles was fired several weeks after the Bay of Pigs defeat—partly because a scapegoat was needed, but also because President Kennedy disliked him intensely (Kramer, 2008).

Defective Decision Making

If luck had been on the side of the Bay of Pigs planners—if, for example, one of Castro's generals

---

Mindguard A group member who shields the group from negative or controversial information by gatekeeping and suppressing dissent.

had decided to stage a coup d'état on the same day as the invasion—then the attack might have succeeded. But the Bay of Pigs planners would still have been a groupthink group. Janis did not consider the group to be one overtaken by groupthink only because it made a bad decision, but because it displayed symptoms of groupthink *and* symptoms of defective decision making. The committee, for example, discussed two extreme alternatives—either endorse the Bay of Pigs invasion or abandon Cuba to communism—while ignoring all other potential alternatives. Moreover, the group lost sight of its overall objectives as it became caught up in the minor details of the invasion plan, and it failed to develop contingency plans. The group actively avoided any information that pointed to limitations in its plans, while seeking out facts and opinions that buttressed its initial preferences. The group members did not just make a few small errors. They committed dozens of blunders. The invasion was a fiasco, but it was the faulty decisional strategies of the group that indicated that the group suffered from groupthink.

Causes of Groupthink

To Janis, groupthink is like a disease that infects healthy groups, rendering them inefficient and unproductive. The symptoms of this disease, such as conformity pressures, illusions, misperceptions, and faulty decision-making strategies, all signal the group's decline, but they are not the root causes of groupthink. These processes undoubtedly contribute to poor judgments, but Janis (1989) distinguished between symptoms of groupthink and its causes: *cohesiveness*, *structural faults* of the group or organization, and *provocative situational factors* (see Figure 11.7).

Cohesiveness The members of the president's committee felt fortunate to belong to a group that boasted such high morale and esprit de corps. Problems could be handled without too much internal bickering, personality clashes were rare, the atmosphere of each meeting was congenial, and replacements were never needed, because no one ever left the group. However, these benefits of cohesiveness did not offset one fatal consequence of a close-knit group—group pressures so strong that critical thinking degenerates into groupthink.

Of the many factors that contribute to the rise of groupthink, Janis emphasized cohesiveness above all others. He agreed that groups that lack cohesion can also make terrible decisions—"especially if the members are engaging in internal warfare"—but they cannot experience groupthink (Janis, 1982, p. 176). In a cohesive group, members refrain from speaking out against decisions, avoid arguing with others, and strive to maintain friendly, cordial relations at all costs. If cohesiveness reaches such a level that internal disagreements disappear, then the group is ripe for groupthink.

Measures of cohesiveness were, of course, never collected for the president's committee. But many signs point to the group's unity. The committee members were all men, and they were in many cases close personal friends. These men, when describing the group in their memoirs, lauded the group, suggesting that their attitudes toward the group were exceptionally positive. The members also identified with the group and its goals; all proudly proclaimed their membership in such an elite body. Robert Kennedy's remarks, peppered with frequent use of the words *we* and *us*, betrayed the magnitude of this identification:

> It seemed that with John Kennedy leading *us* and with all the talent he had assembled, nothing could stop *us*. *We* believed that if *we* faced up to the nation's problems and applied bold, new ideas with common sense and hard work, *we* would overcome whatever challenged *us*. (quoted in Guthman, 1971, p. 88; italics added)

Other evidence, however, suggests that the advisory group was not as unified as Janis believed. The membership of the group was not stable, so different people were present at different meetings, and therefore it is likely that no strong sense of identity actually developed. Also, like many groups composed of influential, successful individuals, personalities and differences in style and strategy caused

tension within the group. To a large extent, group members were not motivated by group-centered motives, but by their own political ambitions (Kramer, 2008).

Structural Faults of the Group or Organization
Cohesion is a necessary condition for groupthink, but the syndrome is more likely to emerge when the group is organized in ways that inhibit the flow of information and promote carelessness in the application of decision-making procedures. *Insulation* of the group from other groups, for example, can promote the development of unique, potentially inaccurate perspectives on issues and their solution. The Bay of Pigs planners worked in secret, so very few outsiders ever came into the group to participate in the discussion. The committee was insulated from criticism. Many experts on military questions and Cuban affairs were available and, if contacted, could have warned the group about the limitations of the plan, but the committee closed itself off from these valuable resources.

President Kennedy's *leadership style* also shaped the way the Bay of Pigs planners worked and may have contributed to groupthink. By tradition, the committee meetings, like cabinet meetings, were very formal affairs that followed a rigid protocol. The president could completely control the group discussion by setting the agenda, permitting only certain questions to be asked, and asking for input only from particular conferees (Stasson, Kameda, & Davis, 1997). He often stated his opinion at the outset of each meeting; his procedures for requiring a voice vote by individuals without prior group discussion paralleled quite closely the methods used by Asch (1952) to heighten conformity pressures in discussion groups. Ironically, Kennedy did not give his advisors opportunities to advise him (Kowert, 2002).

Provocative Situational Context   A number of provocative situational factors may push the group in the direction of error rather than accuracy. As humans tend to be reluctant decision makers in the best of circumstances, they can unravel when they must make important, high-stakes decisions. Such decisions trigger greater tension and anxiety, so group members cope with this provocative *decisional stress* in less than logical ways. Through collective discussion, the group members may rationalize their choice by exaggerating the positive consequences, minimizing the possibility of negative outcomes, concentrating on minor details, and overlooking larger issues. Because the insecurity of each individual can be minimized if the group quickly chooses a plan of action with little argument or dissension, the group may rush to reach closure by making a decision as quickly as possible (Callaway, Marriott, & Esser, 1985). Janis also suggested that any factors that work to lower members' self-esteem, such as a history of mistakes or prior lapses of morality, may further increase the possibility of groupthink.

The Emergence of Groupthink

Because of the complexity of the groupthink model, few tests of the entire model have been conducted. Researchers have, however, attempted to replicate Janis's findings through archival case studies of other historical and political groups. They have also examined specific aspects of the theory—such as the impact of cohesion and stress on decision-making groups—to determine if its key assumptions hold up under empirical scrutiny. These studies, which are reviewed briefly here, sometimes support, sometimes challenge, and sometimes clarify Janis's theory.

Archival Case Studies   Janis, using an archival method, compared groups that made very poor decisions to groups that made excellent choices to determine if error-prone groups exhibited more of the symptoms of groupthink. In later work, he enlarged his pool of cases to a total of 19 decision-making groups and had external raters who worked from the same historical texts rate the groups' symptoms. As predicted, the higher the number of groupthink symptoms, the more unfavorable the outcome of the group's deliberations ($r = .62$; Herek, Janis, & Huth, 1987, 1989; Welch, 1989).

Other archival studies have, for the most part, supported the key elements of the Janis's groupthink model (Esser, 1998; Turner & Pratkanis, 1998b). One study of the content of leaders' public speeches when in groupthink and vigilant decision-making situations, for example, revealed signs of reduced complexity and ingroup favoritism in leaders of groupthink groups (Tetlock, 1979). Another indicated that the structural faults identified by Janis were related to groupthink, but cohesiveness and provocative situational context factors were not (Peterson et al., 1998; Tetlock et al., 1992). When political scientists coded governmental groups that made both good decisions (e.g., Clinton's handling of the proliferation of nuclear capabilities in South Asia) and bad decisions (e.g., Reagan's funding of the Contras) on the variables specified by Janis in his theory, they found considerable correspondence between variables Janis identified and symptoms displayed by poor-performing groups—although, their analysis suggested leadership was even more influential than what Janis suggested (Schafer & Crichlow, 2010).

Cohesion and Groupthink   Janis maintained that groupthink was a characteristic of cohesive groups only. If a group lacked cohesion, it might make poor decisions, but those decisions would be due to processes other than groupthink. His basic prediction was that cohesion, combined with one or more of the other potential causes of groupthink (e.g., structural faults, provocative situational context), would trigger groupthink. He admitted that cohesive groups are not necessarily doomed to be victims of groupthink, but "a high degree of group cohesiveness is conducive to a high frequency of symptoms of groupthink, which, in turn, are conducive to a high frequency of defects in decision-making" (Janis, 1972, p. 199).

A meta-analytic review of the results of seven different studies involving more than 1,300 participants provided some support for this prediction (Mullen et al, 1994). High cohesiveness impaired decision making, provided that one or more of the other triggering conditions for groupthink were present in the situation. If the other causes of groupthink were absent, then cohesiveness increased the quality of a group's decision-making processes. The cohesion–groupthink relationship may also depend on the source of the group's cohesion. In a laboratory study of women college students, groups that derived their cohesiveness from their members' commitment to the task displayed significantly fewer symptoms of groupthink, whereas groups that were interpersonally cohesive displayed more symptoms of groupthink (Bernthal & Insko, 1993). However, a case study of two groups that made catastrophic errors and displayed many of the symptoms of groupthink described by Janis displayed little social cohesion, but instead were united by task cohesion (Burnette, Pollack, & Forsyth, 2011).

Structural Faults and Groupthink Janis identified several structural features of groups that can contribute to groupthink, but researchers have concentrated most of their attention on the group leader (Chen et al., 1996; Flowers, 1977). In one project, group members discussed evidence pertaining to a civil trial. Researchers told some of the groups' assigned leaders to adopt a *closed style* of leadership: They were to announce their opinions on the case prior to the discussion. *Open-style* leaders were told to withhold their own opinions until later in the discussion. Groups with a leader who adopted a closed style were more biased in their judgments, particularly when many of the group members had a high need for certainty (Hodson & Sorrentino, 1997). Groups with leaders with a strong need for power also performed less effectively, irrespective of the group's level of cohesion (Fodor & Smith, 1982). Other evidence, however, suggests that leaders who are highly directive improve their group's decisions, provided that they limit their control to the group's decisional processes rather than the group's decisional outcomes (Peterson, 1997).

Provocative Situational Context Studies of groups under stress suggest that they are more likely to make errors, lose their focus on the primary goals, and make use of procedures that members know have not been effective in the past. Social psychologist Janis Kelly and her colleagues, for example, have documented the negative impact of time pressures on both group performance and process (Kelly & Karau, 1999; Kelly & Loving, 2004). They find that when groups work under time pressure, members focus much of their attention on the task, but doing so leaves them at risk of overlooking important contextual information. They also tend to concentrate on getting the task completed quickly and so become more concerned with efficiency and quick results rather than accuracy and quality. In consequence, time pressures cause groups to "produce a less creative, less adequate, and less carefully reasoned decision. However, when a decision is routine or straightforward, these strategies can lead to adequate or even good decision making" (Kelly & Loving, 2004, p. 186).

Alternative Models

Groupthink is not an obscure idea known only to those who study groups. A mere three years after the publication of Janis's 1972 analysis, the term *groupthink* appeared in *Webster's New Collegiate Dictionary* (Turner & Pratkanis, 1998b). The theory offers insight into very puzzling groups—those that make wrong-headed decisions—and has been applied to political decision makers, cults, businesses, and communities. In 2004, for example, the U.S. Senate Select Committee on Intelligence concluded that the intelligence community of the U.S. government had displayed a number of the symptoms of groupthink when it erroneously concluded that the country of Iraq was assembling weapons of mass destruction (U.S. Senate Select Committee on Intelligence, 2004). The theory serves as a reminder that if we are to understand political events that change the lives of people the world over, we must understand groups.

Researchers, however, continue to debate the validity of the model itself (Baron, 2005). Some, noting the theory's limited support, suggest that it should be drastically revised. Others feel that the jury is still out and encourage more research. Others have proposed alternative models.

Group-Centrism   Theory   Social   psychologist Arie   Kruglanski   and   his   colleagues   (2006),   like Janis, have identified a syndrome that characterizes groups and often causes them to make faulty decisions. They term this syndrome **group-centrism**, because it springs primarily from the group members' striving to maintain and support their group's unity. Group-centric groups tend to rush to make judgments on the basis of insufficient information, particularly if they face situations that interfere with their capacity to process information—time pressures, severe ambiguity, noise, or fatigue. They are more likely to reject a member who disagrees with the group, and they express a strong desire for agreement   with   other   members.   Stereotyped thought and tendencies to favor the ingroup over the outgroup increase and willingness to compromise in order to reach integrative solutions during bargaining   decreases.   The   group   also   strives   for **cognitive closure**—"a desire for a definite answer to a question, any firm answer, rather than uncertainty, confusion, or ambiguity" (Kruglanski et al., 2002, p. 649)—and so adopts a more centralized structure with autocratic leaders. These groups' discussions are dominated by high-status group members   who   have   a   much   greater   impact   on   the group's communications and decisions than the rank-and-file members. These consequences of group-centrism are consistent with the symptoms of groupthink identified by Janis (De Dreu, 2003).

Social Identity and the Ubiquity Model   Social psychologist Robert Baron (2005), after reviewing much of the existing research on Janis's theory, agrees with Janis that members of groups often strive for consensus and that, in doing so, they tend to limit dissent, denigrate the outgroup, and

---

group-centrism A group-level syndrome caused by members' excessive strivings to maintain and support their group's unity that results in perturbations in a group's decision-making capability and intergroup relations.
cognitive closure The psychological desire to reach a final decision swiftly and completely; also, the relative strength of this tendency, as indicated by a preference for order, predictability, decisiveness, and closed-mindedness.

misjudge their own group's competence. Baron's *ubiquity model* of groupthink, however, suggests that these qualities are ubiquitous features of groups, rather than rare ones. They only lead to problems, Baron suggests, when three conditions are met. First, it is not group unity per se that increases groupthink symptoms, but rather a threat to a shared social identity that may result should the group fail (Haslam et al., 2006; Turner & Pratkanis, 1998a). Second, the group must be one that has developed a set of norms that constrains members' opinions with regard to the topic under discussion. Third, groupthink is more likely if group members lack self-confidence. In such cases, they are likely to rely on others' judgments, with the result that the group does not adequately consider its alternatives (Sniezek, 1992).

Preventing Groupthink

Kennedy did not take his Bay of Pigs failure lightly. In the months following the defeat, he explored the causes of his group's poor decision making. He fired those he felt had misled him, put in place improved procedures for handling information, and learned how to decipher messages from his military staff. These changes prepared him for the next great issue to face his administration—the Cuban missile crisis of 1962. When Kennedy learned that the Soviet Union was constructing a missile base in Cuba, he called in his advisors again. But this time, the group made the right decision. Many of the same people meeting in the same room and guided by the same leader worked equally hard under similar pressures. Both crises occurred in the same area of the world, involved the same foreign powers, and could have led to equally serious consequences. Why did the missile crisis advisors succeed when the Bay of Pigs committee had failed?

Limiting Premature Seeking of Concurrence   If conformity was the norm in the Bay of Pigs group, dissent was championed by the group during the missile crisis. Kennedy deliberately suspended the rules of discussion that guided such meetings; agendas were avoided, and new ideas were welcomed.

Although pressures to conform surfaced from time to time during the discussion, the members felt so comfortable in their role as skeptical, critical thinkers that they were able to resist the temptation to go along with the consensus. In fact, the group never did reach 100% agreement on the decision to turn back the Soviet ships.

The atmosphere of open inquiry can be credited to changes designed and implemented by Kennedy. He dropped his closed style of leadership to become an open leader as he (1) carefully refused to state his personal beliefs at the beginning of the session, waiting instead until others had let their views be known; (2) required a full, unbiased discussion of the pros and cons of each possible course of action; (3) convinced his subordinates that he would welcome healthy criticism and condemn "yea-saying"; (4) arranged for the group to meet without him on several occasions; and (5) encouraged specific members of the group to take the role of dissenter, or *devil's advocate*, during the group discussions. Kennedy also reduced pressures to conform by sometimes breaking the advisors into separate groups to reduce their size and spur increased debate (Wheeler & Janis, 1980). Kennedy also gave the group an official name and identity. In a memorandum dated October 22, 1962, Kennedy established, named, and populated the "Executive Committee of the National Security Council" and mandated that this group would meet regularly for the purpose of conducting governmental operations.

Correcting Misperceptions and Biases The new and improved advisory committee did not take success for granted. The group recognized the challenge they faced and did not try to ease their discomfort by overestimating American superiority, belittling the Russians, and denying the magnitude of the dangers. According to the official version of this incident, no trace of the illusion of superiority that had permeated the planning sessions of the Bay of Pigs invasion was in evidence during the executive committee meetings. Each solution was assumed to be flawed and, even when the blockade had been painstakingly arranged, the members developed contingency plans in case it failed.

As members admitted their personal inadequacies and ignorance, they willingly consulted experts who were not members of the group. No group member's statements were taken as fact until independently verified, and the ideas of younger, low-level staff members were solicited at each discussion. Participants also discussed the group's activities with their own staffs and entered each meeting armed with the misgivings and criticisms of these unbiased outsiders.

The committee discussed the ethics of the situation and the proposed solutions. For example, although some members felt that the Russians had left themselves open to any violent response the Americans deemed appropriate, the majority argued that a final course of action had to be consistent with "America's humanitarian heritage and ideals" (Janis, 1972, p. 157). Illusions of morality and invulnerability were supposedly minimized along with biased perceptions of the outgroup (see, for an alternative interpretation of this incident, Alterman, 2004).

Using Effective Decision-Making Techniques The executive committee is not an example of an effective decision-making body simply because its solution to the missile crisis worked. Rather, just as the decision-making methods used by the Bay of Pigs committee ensured its failure, the executive committee's use of effective decision-making techniques increased its chances of success ('t Hart, 1998). Members analyzed a wide range of alternative courses of action, deliberately considered and then reconsidered the potential effects of their actions, consulted experts, and made detailed contingency plans in case the blockade failed to stop the Russians. Many initially favored military intervention, but the majority of the group's members insisted that other alternatives be explored. This demand led to an expanded search for alternatives, and soon the following list emerged:

1. Do nothing.
2. Exert pressure on the Soviet Union through the United Nations.
3. Arrange a summit meeting between the two nations' leaders.
4. Secretly negotiate with Castro.

5. Initiate a low-level naval action involving a blockade of Cuban ports.

6. Bombard the sites with small pellets, rendering the missiles inoperable.

7. Launch an air strike against the sites with advance warning to reduce loss of life.

8. Launch an air strike without advance warning.

9. Carry out a series of air attacks against all Cuban military installations.

10. Invade Cuba.

Once this list was complete, the men focused on each course of action before moving on to the next option. They considered the pros and cons, fleshed out unanticipated drawbacks, and estimated the likelihood of success. During this process, outside experts were consulted to give the members a better handle on the problem, and contingency plans were briefly explored. Even those alternatives that had initially been rejected were resurrected and discussed, and the group invested considerable effort in trying to find any overlooked detail. When a consensus on the blockade plan finally developed, the group went back over this alternative, reconsidered its problematic aspects, and meticulously reviewed the steps required to implement it. Messages were sent to the Russians, military strategies were worked out to prevent any slipups that would escalate the conflict, and a graded series of actions was developed to be undertaken should the blockade fail. Allies were contacted and told of the U.S. intentions, the legal basis of the intervention was established by arranging for a hemisphere blockade sanctioned by the Organization of American States; African countries with airports that could have been used by Russia to circumvent the naval blockade were warned not to cooperate. To quote Robert Kennedy, "Nothing, whether a weighty matter or a small detail, was overlooked" (1969, p. 60).

CHAPTER REVIEW

How do groups make decisions?

1. Groups frequently make decisional errors, but, in general, their decisions tend to be superior to those offered by single individuals.

2. No two groups make decisions in precisely the same way, but a *functional theory of group decision making* identifies four sets of operations that groups tend to perform as they deal with decisions: orientation, discussion, decision, and implementation (see Figure 11.2). The functional approach assumes that groups that enact each stage in the decision-making process effectively will make superior decisions.

3. During the orientation stage, the group identifies the problem to be solved and plans the process to be used in reaching the decision.

   ■ Many groups bypass this stage, but time spent in orientation predicts effectiveness.

   ■ Groups develop a *shared mental model* at this stage, and they may also take steps to better manage their time.

4. During the *discussion* stage, members communicate with one another as they develop a mutual understanding of the situation.

   ■ A *collective, information processing model* assumes that groups gather information and process that information to identify and weigh options, test assumptions, and formulate decisions.

   ■ Four information processing gains that result from a discussion are improved memory, exchange of information, processing of information, and error detection.

   ■ A group's *collective memory* includes the combined memories of all individual members; *cross-cueing* and *transactive memory* systems work to enhance group memory.

- The more information the group members exchange, the more accurate the group's decision. Bales's observations indicate that groups spend the majority of the time during the discussion dealing with suggestions, expressing opinions, and developing a shared orientation to the task.

- Shaw's study of groups working on intellective tasks suggested that the superiority of group decisions was due to improved error-checking in groups.

5. During the decision stage, the group relies on an implicit or explicit *social decision scheme* to combine individual preferences into a collective decision.

- Common schemes include delegating (shared decisions), averaging (statisticized decisions), voting (plurality decisions), and reaching consensus (unanimous decisions). Each decision scheme has both strengths and weaknesses.

- Crowdsourcing, including crowd voting, can be used to gather information needed to make decisions.

- Groups generally use consensus when dealing with sensitive issues, but they tend to use a plurality voting scheme when making simple choices.

6. During the implementation stage, the group carries out the decisions and assesses its impact.

- Groups are more likely to accept a decision that is perceived to be a just one, as determined by *distributive justice* and *procedural justice* beliefs.

- Coch and French's classic study of motivation in the workplace suggests that members are more satisfied and more likely to implement decisions when they were actively involved in the decision-making process (the *voice effect*).

- Contemporary group-management methods are based on increasing participation in the decision-making process.

7. Vroom's *normative model of decision making* suggests that different types of situations call for either autocratic (decide), consultative (individual and group), facilitating, or delegating group decision-making methods.

What problems undermine the effectiveness of decision-making groups?

1. A functional approach assumes that groups that fail to plan, discuss, decide, or implement fully or effectively will not reach their potential as decision-makers.

- Most groups spend too little time planning, but when they do plan, they (a) underestimate how much time they will need to complete their tasks (the *planning fallacy*) and (b) fail to develop contingency plans.

- Group discussion is limited, in part, by members' inability to express themselves clearly and by their limited listening skills.

- Research conducted by Rogelberg suggests that meetings are often viewed by group members as interruptions of their work-flow rather than as a means to increase productivity.

- Groups often act in ways that confirm both *Parkinson's law* and Parkinson's *law of triviality*.

- Groups sometimes use discussions to avoid making decisions, and they often spend more time muddling through issues rather than dealing with them.

2. Groups are prone to the common knowledge effect, or *shared information bias*; they spend more of their discussion time examining details that two or more of the group members know in common than discussing unshared information.

- Work by Stasser and Titus confirms that this oversampling of shared information leads to poorer decisions when a hidden profile would be revealed by considering the unshared information more closely.

- The shared information bias increases when tasks have no demonstrably correct solution and when group leaders do not actively draw out unshared information.

- Multiple factors combine to generate the bias, including normative influence and informational influence processes.

- Groups can avoid the shared information bias if they spend more time actively discussing their decisions or if they make use of *group decision support systems* (GDSS).

3. Judgment errors that cause people to overlook important information and overuse unimportant information are often exacerbated in groups.

- Kerr and his colleagues describe three types of errors—sins of commission, sins of omission, and sins of imprecision—and research suggests that groups exacerbate these errors.

- Groups, more so than individuals, fall prey to the *confirmation bias*—they start off with an initial preference and then seek out additional information to confirm the accuracy of their inclinations. More diverse groups are less likely to display this bias.

4. Group memory is weakened by social loafing and by the complexity of the group setting that disrupts group members' ability to organize information in memory and subsequently to retrieve that information.

5. Groups sometimes mishandle the implementation stage of decision making.

- Groups fail to accurately appraise the quality of their decisions, and they frequently avoid blame for failure through self-serving and group-serving claims of responsibility.

- The *Abilene paradox*, as described by Harvey, occurs when groups mismanage agreement. Studies of *pluralistic ignorance*

have verified the tendency for group members to erroneously assume that their private opinion is discrepant from the other group members' opinions.

- Groups also experience *entrapment* when they become committed too quickly to a decision and continue to invest in it despite high *sunk costs*.

Why do groups make riskier decisions than individuals?

1. Common sense suggests that groups would be more cautious than individuals, but early studies carried out using the *Choice-Dilemmas Questionnaire* found that group discussions generate a shift in the direction of a more risky alternative (the *risky shift effect*).

2. When researchers, such as Myers and Lamm, later found evidence of cautious shifts as well as risky shifts and a tendency for various types of attitudes to become more extreme in groups, they realized that the risky shift was a specific case of *group polarization*: a shift in the direction of greater extremity in individuals' responses (e.g., choices, judgments, expressions of opinions) when in groups.

3. Group polarization is sustained by the desire to evaluate one's own opinions by comparing them to those of others (social comparison theory), by exposure to other members' pro-risk or pro-caution arguments (*persuasive-arguments theory*), and by social identity processes.

4. Individuals from cultures that do not value risk are less likely to exhibit the risky shift effect, as are groups that include people from many different cultures.

What is groupthink, and how can it be prevented?

1. Janis argued that fiascoes and blunders, such as the decision to invade Cuba at the Bay of Pigs, occur when group members strive for solidarity and cohesiveness to such an extent that any questions or topics that could lead to disputes are avoided. Janis called this process *groupthink*.

2. Groupthink has multiple symptoms that Janis organized into three categories:

- Overestimation of the group: illusion of invulnerability and illusion of morality.

- Closed-mindedness: rationalizations, stereotypes about the outgroup.

- Pressures toward uniformity: self-censorship, the illusion of unanimity, direct pressure on dissenters, and self-appointed *mindguards*.

3. Groupthink groups also display defective decision-making processes.

4. Janis identified three sets of causes of groupthink: cohesiveness, structural faults of the group or organization (such as isolation and a closed leadership style), and provocative situational factors (including decisional stress).

5. Research has yielded mixed support for many of Janis's hypotheses regarding decision making in groups:

- Archival studies, taken as a whole, support the theory's most basic prediction—groups that display more of the symptoms of groupthink tend to make poorer decisions.

- Studies have suggested that cohesive groups sometimes display groupthink tendencies, provided that one or more of the other triggering conditions for groupthink are present.

6. Given these limitations, researchers have proposed alternative models, including:

- Kruglanski's *group-centrism* theory suggests that groups whose members have a high *need for cognitive closure* are more likely to make poorer decisions.

- Baron's ubiquity model suggests that many groups display the negative decisional features identified by Janis, but that these factors combined with a shared social identity, restrictive norms, and lack of confidence will trigger groupthink-like decisions.

7. Janis noted that groups need not sacrifice cohesiveness to avoid the pitfall of groupthink. Rather, he recommended limiting premature seeking of concurrence, correcting misperceptions and errors, and improving the group's decisional methods.

RESOURCES

Chapter Case: The Bay of Pigs Planners

- *Bay of Pigs: The Untold Story* by Peter Wyden (1979) offers a wealth of detail about the group that planned the invasion and draws on personal interviews with many of the original group members.

- "Ships in the Night: The CIA, the White House and the Bay of Pigs" by Piero Gleijeses (1995) relies on interviews with group members to develop an explanation for the advisory committee's error in judgment that emphasizes mistakes in communication and misunderstanding.

Making Decisions in Groups

- "A Look at Groups from a Functional Perspective" by Andrea A. Hollingshead,

Gwen M. Wittenbaum, Paul B. Paulus, Randy Y. Hirokawa, Deborah G. Ancona, Randall S. Peterson, Karen A. Jehn, and Kay Yoon (2005) uses a functional perspective to examine group composition, structure, and task performance.

- *Group Performance* by Bernard A. Nijstad (2009), examines a wide range of topics related to group performance, including groups charged with making decisions.

- "Group Performance and Decision Making" by Norbert L. Kerr and R. Scott Tindale (2004) reviews recent studies of group decision making.

- *Why Decisions Fail: Avoiding the Blunders and Traps that Lead to Debacles* by Paul C. Nutt (2002) uses a functional approach to explain terrible mistakes made by corporate leaders in the United States, including the construction of EuroDisney and the failure to recall dangerous automobiles with known risks.

Groupthink

- "Presidential Leadership and Group Folly: Reappraising the Role of Groupthink in the Bay of Pigs Decisions" by Roderick M. Kramer (2008) uses declassified documents and historical records not available to Janis

before concluding that many aspects of the Bay of Pigs decision are inconsistent with the groupthink theory.

- "So Right It's Wrong: Groupthink and the Ubiquitous Nature of Polarized Group Decision Making" by Robert S. Baron (2005) reviews the basic evidence supporting Janis's theory of groupthink before offering a novel interpretation that identifies a new set of critical causes of groupthink.

Teams

CHAPTER OVERVIEW

When the work to be done is difficult, complicated, and important—such as building a bridge, flying a spacecraft to the moon, or performing cardiac surgery—people turn to teams. When a group becomes a true team, it is transformed into a complex, adaptive, dynamic task-performing system. Teams are groups, but not all groups are teams.

- Are teams groups?
- How does the team's composition influence its effectiveness?
- What group processes mediate the input–output relationship?
- How effective are teams, and how can they be improved?

CHAPTER OUTLINE

The Nature of Teams
A Brief History of Teams
What is a Team?
Types of Teams
A Systems Model of Teams

Building the Team
The Team Player
Knowledge, Skill, and Ability (KSA)
Diversity
Men, Women, and Teams

Working in Teams
Team Processes
Cognitive Processes
Team Cohesion

Team Performance
Evaluating Teams
Suggestions for Using Teams
Chapter Review
Resources

Mountain Medical Cardiac Surgery Team

The cardiac surgery team was ready to undertake the most technically challenging of all surgeries: repair of the heart. Only last week they had been using the traditional, open-heart procedure that requires splitting the patient's chest at the breastbone, stopping the heart and transferring its duties to a heart–lung bypass machine, clamping off arteries and valves, isolating and repairing the damaged portions of the heart, and then closing the eight-inch long wound in the chest. But they would not be using those methods today. Instead, the team would be carrying out a minimally invasive surgical procedure. The surgeon would make a small incision between the patient's ribs and snake high-tech instruments to the heart, guided by feedback from a network of technicians, computers, cameras, and ultrasound scanners.

These new procedures would make entirely new demands of the surgical team. Traditional surgical teammates work closely with one another, but they are not continually interdependent. The anesthesiologist sedates the patient and monitors his or her breathing. The perfusionist is the technician who operates the heart–lung machine. The surgeon makes the incision, splits the chest, repairs the heart, and then closes the incision. The scrub nurse or technician prepares the sterile field, suctions blood from the site, and passes instruments to the surgeon as needed. The new procedure is not so modularized. The surgeon can no longer see the heart, but must rely on the computer-enhanced images provided by the perfusionist and anesthesiologist. Because the surgeon cannot apply clamps directly to the heart to stop the flow of blood, that work is done by the anesthesiologist who threads a catheter into the aorta through the femoral vein. The scrub nurse monitors and maintains pressures and vital signs and attaches, when needed, forceps, scissors, scalpels, and other surgical tools to the surgeon's operating mechanicals.

The new procedures require an unprecedented degree of teamwork, but the Mountain Medical team was ready for the challenge. They had practiced for months to learn the new method, and their diligence showed in their level of coordination and communication in the operating room. The operation took somewhat longer than they had expected it would, but there were no surprises: Their first patient recovered fully but also more quickly because of their use of the minimally invasive, and team-intensive, technique (Healey, Undre, & Vincent, 2006; Pisano, Bohmer, & Edmondson, 2001).

The Mountain Medical surgical team is not the first team we have encountered in our analysis of groups and their dynamics. Peak Search and Rescue, the U.S. Olympic hockey team, the Old Christian rugby team stranded in the Andes, and the crew of Flight 1549 were all teams. **Teams**, as groups, include multiple members who are interdependent and share a collective goal. Members' actions are guided by norms and roles, information flows from one to another via channels of communication, and some members are more influential than others. Teams, like all groups, include leaders and followers, interpersonal stars and isolates, and hard workers and loafers. Those who understand groups are well on their way to understanding teams, since teams are groups.

But teams, unlike many groups, require more from the members in the way of collaboration and coordination. Teams are often spawned when one or more individuals confront an obstacle, a problem, or a task they wish to overcome, solve, or complete, but they recognize that the solution is beyond the reach of a single person. Such situations require that members combine their personal energies and resources in such a way that the group, and not just the individuals in the group, reaches its goals. This chapter examines these unique aspects of teams—their nature, design, processes, and effectiveness.

THE NATURE OF TEAMS

In the past, most teams were either pulling plows or playing games. Groups assembled for work that required many hands and much muscle, but less

---

team A unified, structured group that pursues collective goals through coordinated, interdependent interaction.

physically demanding labor was given over to skilled craftsmen and artisans. Over time, however, the complexity of the tasks that humans undertook grew, and so did their need to work in teams in order to achieve their ends. A very talented person could potentially perform coronary surgery, design a new telecommunication device, create an online database of all knowledge, or pilot a spacecraft to the moon, but such tasks are now done by people working in teams.

A Brief History of Teams

Teams may be de rigueur in most organizations today, but for centuries humans did not work in teams—the word was reserved for harnessed animals. The first documented use of the word team to describe groups of humans working collectively did not occur until the 1600s, when Ben Jonson wrote in Bartholomew Fayre, "Twere like falling into a whole Shire of butter: they had need be a teeme of Dutchmen, should draw him out" (OED Online, 1989). The word team apparently derives from the old English and Norse word "for a bridle and thence to a set of draught animals harnessed together" (Annett & Stanton, 2001, p. 1045).

Scientific Management Teams were rarely used outside of sports and military settings even into the 1950s. Their use was, after all, inconsistent with commonly accepted assumptions about the nature of work and the nature of human beings. In the early years of the twentieth century, theories based on **scientific management** maintained that very few people like to work and so most must be prodded into action by the promise of financial incentives, close supervision, and clear goals that they can attain with little effort. The experts considered workers to be mere "adjuncts to machines," and they designed workplaces in which employees

---

scientific management One of the first attempts to apply scientific methods to the analysis of workplace efficiency and productivity; it stressed time management, routinized tasks, and close supervision of the workforce.

did not waste time talking to one another (Taylor, 1923). There were notable exceptions to this tendency— including the famous Hawthorne studies of productivity that suggested that gains in performance could be achieved if individuals worked in collaborative, cohesive groups under favorable conditions—but it was not until the second half of the twentieth century that teams began their ascension to prominence (Sundstrom et al., 2000).

The Rise of Teams In the early 1960s, concerns about the inflexible, autocratic nature of most large organizations prompted a search for alternatives (Likert, 1967; McGregor, 1960). Heeding the call for worker autonomy and participation in decision making, a number of companies began experimenting with employees working in small groups. General Motors, for example, used teams rather than an assembly line in one of its truck factories; General Foods set up autonomous work teams at its Topeka, Kansas plant; the Banner Company, a large manufacturer, set up work groups with varying levels of authority and organizational overlap; and Volvo and Saab both began using teams in their production plants.

From these initial beginnings, organizations began relying on teams for production, management, distribution, and general decision making. Half of the workers in the United States now belong to at least one team at work. Teams are used by a majority of all larger organizations in the United States, and in countries like Sweden and Japan, the use of teams approaches 100% (Devine et al., 1999). Nonprofit organizations, such as health care organizations and public service corporations, are particularly heavy adopters of team approaches to work (81%), followed by blue-collar industries such as construction, manufacturing, and retail sales (50%) and white-collar industries like banking, real estate, and insurance (34%). In many organizations, employees serve not on one team, but on many; recent estimates suggest between 65% to 95% of knowledge workers are members of more than one team (Maynard et al., 2012). The modern organization is no longer a network of individuals, but rather a network of interconnected teams (DeChurch & Mathieu, 2009).

What Is a Team?

Nowadays the word *team* is used to describe a wide assortment of groups. In business settings, work units are sometimes referred to as production teams or management teams. At a university, professors and students form research teams to conduct research cooperatively. In the military, small squads of soldiers train as special operations teams. In schools, teaching teams may be responsible for the education of hundreds of students. In online multiplayer games, people join carefully composed teams to attempt challenges that require the skills of many types of characters. Can all these groups be considered teams?

Despite this diversity in terms of focus, composition, and design, teams are fundamentally groups—two or more individuals who are connected by and within social relationships—with the same basic qualities one can expect in any group: interaction, goals, interdependence, structure, and cohesiveness (see Chapter 1). But it is the nature and intensity of these qualities when manifested in teams that sets them apart from other types of groups. Teams are groups, but hyper-groups: They possess the basic qualities of any group, but to a more extreme degree.

Coordinated Interaction Teams do things as single, coordinated units. The members of all groups engage in a mixture of task and relational *interactions*, but in teams the interaction rate is higher and the flow more continuous. In addition, teams are work-focused groups, so a greater proportion of their interactions pertains to group tasks: monitoring of progress, improving coordination, structuring the work process, assisting one another, strategizing, and so on (Rousseau, Aubé, & Savoie, 2006). Members of teams are attentive to each other's interpersonal needs—they continuously maintain, build, and even question the quality of their social connections—but they spend the bulk of their time on their work. When researchers used the Bales (1999) Interaction Process Analysis to record the communication among team members, they discovered relational statements were used only rarely. In the groups Bales studied, nearly 40% of the commentary was classified as relational, whereas teams made relational comments (e.g., shows solidarity, shows tension) only 11% of the time (Gorse & Emmitt, 2009).

Compelling Purpose The sine qua non of teams is their pursuit of *goals*—and collective ones at that. Teams have been defined in many different ways, but nearly all definitions suggest teams "work toward shared and valued goals" (Salas et al., 2009, p. 39); they seek a "common purpose" (Hackman, 2011, p. 51); and team members are "committed to a common purpose, performance goals, and approach for which they hold themselves accountable" (Katzenbach & Smith, 2001, p. 7). All these definitions stress the consensual nature of a team's goals: members share an understanding of the group's recognized purpose and—in effective teams, at any rate—willingly contribute their time and energy in the group's pursuit of its goals. Shared goals increase coordination within the group and reduce the tendency for members to work at cross-purposes to one another.

Social psychologist and team expert Richard Hackman (2002, 2011) stresses the importance of goals in his **real teams model**. Real teams, he suggests, embrace shared goals that guide the work of the group and heighten members' motivation. According to Hackman, a team's purposes should be clear, challenging, and consequential, but not overly specified, impossibly difficult, or so daunting that team members are motivated by a fear of failure. Teams stress outcomes to such an extent that their very existence is threatened should they fail to achieve their agreed-upon goals.

Interlocking Interdependence All group members are *interdependent* to a degree, but members of teams are so tightly coupled that no member can

----

real teams model A theoretical analysis of teams that identifies key factors that distinguish effective ("real") teams from other collective enterprises, including a compelling direction, an enabling structure, a supportive context, and effective leadership (developed by J. Richard Hackman).

determine his or her own outcome. As Figure 1.3 in Chapter 1 suggested, teams create many types of interdependencies among members. For example, a team on an assembly line may pass work from one person to the next in a fixed order, so the level of interdependence is unequal and sequential. In other teams, however, all members interact jointly to complete their tasks, so they are fully rather than partially interdependent, with members reliably and substantially influencing one another's outcomes over a long period of time and in predictable ways (Saavedra, Earley, & van Dyne, 1993). In a traditional operating room, for example, surgeons have been known to control the entire operation, so the outcome was largely determined by the surgeon's skills rather than the effectiveness of the "support staff." In the Mountain Medical team, in contrast, the contributions of each member of the team were vital to the successful outcome. The interdependencies in a team tend to be equal and reciprocal rather than asymmetric and unequal (see Figure 1.3).

This high level of interdependence, combined with the team's pursuit of consensual goals, means that the members of a team cannot succeed unless their group succeeds. The members of a team may strive to outperform each other or achieve personally important goals, but each member's outcomes are tied to the team's outcomes, such that if the team is successful, so are the individual members. But, should the team fail, the members do as well.

Adaptive Structure Teams are *well-structured*, for their roles, norms, and intermember relations are defined rather than nebulous. The members of an athletic team, for example, are assigned to roles, usually on the basis of their effectiveness in meeting the requirements of that particular position. Similarly, in the Mountain Medical surgical team, each member played a specific role in the operation, and the outcome of the surgery depended on each team member meeting the demands of his or her role. Other aspects of a team's structure, including performance norms, status structures, communication networks, and so on, also tend to be clearer and consensual than in more informal types of groups.

Teams, although they tend to develop formalized procedures and a fixed division of labor, are not miniature bureaucracies. Bureaucracies are highly organized systems, but they tend to become inefficient as structures that are no longer needed are retained, and changes that would improve the system are not implemented. Teams, in contrast, continuously review and revise their structures to improve their functioning (Bunderson & Boumgarden, 2010).

Cohesive Alliance Teams are unified, *cohesive* groups, for the relations linking members to the group are strong, rather than weak, so the group tends to remain intact over time and in difficult circumstances. Teams are united in their pursuit of a common goal, so a team's unity usually springs from its task cohesion, but teams may exhibit one or more of the other forms of cohesion considered in Chapter 5. Teammates are often socially and emotionally close to each other (social cohesion), they strongly identify with their team (collective cohesion), and they are affectively bonded (emotional cohesion). The team's dense network of interdependencies, combined with its stability in membership and clear boundaries, may also heighten its structural cohesion. External pressures may magnify this unity, for teams usually work under some kind of pressure, such as a heavy workload, limited time, or competition with other groups.

Types of Teams

Teams, like groups in general, vary considerably in form and function. Some exist for long periods of time, whereas others disband as soon as they reach some specific goal. Some teams require members to be experts and specialists, but others require less differentiation in terms of members' skills and experience levels (Hollenbeck, Beersma, & Schouten, 2012). Some teams meet in face-to-face contexts, whereas others rely on communication technologies to conduct their work. Some, too, meet more of the criteria expected in a team (e.g., coordinated interaction, compelling purpose, interlocking interdependences, etc.), but others are more pseudo-teams than actual teams (West & Lyubovnikova,

2012). Teams also differ substantially in size, although few teams have more than ten members. Larger teams experience problems in performance and coordination—including communication breakdowns, social loafing, absenteeism, and misuse of team resources—that smaller teams do not (Aubé, Rousseau, & Tremblay, 2011).

Team Goals and Functions   Teams can be differentiated by considering where they are located and the kinds of goals that they pursue. Psychologist Dennis Devine (2002), for example, draws a general distinction between teams that carry out cognitive functions, such as planning and making choices among alternatives, and teams that carry out a production function, such as providing a service or making something. But he breaks these categories down into the more fine-grained subcategories described in Table 12.1 and as follows.

- *Executive teams* and *command teams* carry out both management and leadership functions within an organization. These teams identify and solve problems, make decisions about day-to-day operations and production, and set the goals for the organization's future. They coordinate the actions of others and deal with unexpected issues and difficulties.

- *Negotiation teams*, *commissions*, and *design teams* are all project teams, created to complete a task that requires judgment, discernment, creativity, or persuasiveness. Negotiation teams represent their constituencies and, in most cases, are paired with a team representing another group or faction. Commissions make judgments on specific issues, often in situations that require both objectivity and sensitivity to the needs of many parties. Design teams grapple with ill-defined problems—tasks that require creativity

T A B L E   12.1   Devine's Taxonomy of Teams

Type	Function	Examples
Executive	Plan, direct	Board of directors, top management team
Command	Integrate, coordinate	Control tower, emergency response center
Negotiation	Deal, persuade	Labor management, international summit
Commission	Choose, investigate	Search committee, jury
Design	Create, develop	Research and development team, marketing group
Advisory	Diagnose, suggest	Quality circle, steering committee
Service	Provide, repair	Fast food, auto service team
Production	Build, assemble	Home construction, automotive assembly
Performance	Enact, display	Theatrical company, orchestra
Medical	Treat, heal	Surgery, emergency room
Response	Protect, rescue	Fire station, paramedics
Military	Neutralize, protect	Infantry squad, tank crew
Transportation	Convey, haul	Airline crew, train crew
Sports	Compete, win	Baseball, soccer

SOURCE: Adapted from "A Review and Integration of Classification Systems Relevant to Teams in Organizations," by Dennis J. Devine (2002). *Group Dynamics: Theory, Research, and Practice, 6*, 291–310. Reprinted by permission.

and innovation rather than those that are routine and have a demonstrably correct solution (Wildman et al., 2012). Negotiation teams and commissions often disband once their focal issue has been resolved.

- *Advisory teams*, such as review panels and steering committees, are investigatory teams, tasked to examine both routine and unanticipated problems related to the organization's structure and functioning. These teams often produce a set of conclusions or an official report that makes recommendations regarding how things should be done differently.

- *Service teams* and *production teams* are the work groups that are responsible for the organization's tangible output. They provide services (*service teams*), create products (*production teams*), and include repair teams, wait staff, nurses, sales forces, and so on.

- *Performance*, *medical*, *response*, *military*, *transportation*, and *sports teams* are all action teams that provide a specialized, and often highly desired, good or service through coordinated actions. Performance teams are the many entertainment ensembles that enact elaborate behavior sequences for the purpose of entertaining an audience. Medical teams, like the Mountain Medical surgical team, provide both routine health care but also perform more advanced medical interventions. Response teams, like the Peak Search and Rescue team, travel to the location of an accident or disaster to provide help. Military teams are relatively small, specialized squads within larger military units that acquire specific responsibilities and training, such as a sniper squad or tank crew. Transportation crews operate machinery that moves people and cargo, including large teams that staff oceangoing vessels to the two-person teams that haul freight cross-country by truck. Sports teams play games and contests, usually paired against other sports teams (Devine, 2002; Sundstrom et al., 2000).

A team from any one of these categories may be very different from a team in another category, so generalizations about all teams that cut across type are often inaccurate. Many teams also perform many tasks, and so these types are not necessarily mutually exclusive categories (see Wildman et al., 2012, for a detailed review of team classification systems).

Crews and Ad Hoc Teams Distinctions can also be drawn between teams depending on their duration and the scope of their tasks. Members of **crews**, for example, have very specific responsibilities, and they tend to use specialized tools or equipment to accomplish their appointed tasks. The staff of an emergency room and the men and women piloting an airliner would be crews (Arrow & McGrath, 1995). Crews tend to work together for a specified period of time on highly structured tasks with clear interdependency requirements. They are similar in some ways to **ad hoc teams**, whose ranks are filled by slotting individuals from a pool of available candidates into specific roles, with members sometimes swapped in and out as the team works (Leach et al., 2009). Many surgical teams, for example, are ad hoc teams, with the roles of nurse, anesthesiologist, surgeon, and so on filled with whomever is trained for the role and is available at the time of the operation. Such teams are sometimes known as *knots*, since their members are tied together by relational knots, but only briefly—for the knot will soon be untied (Engeström, 2008).

Founded and Mandated Teams Teams also differ in terms of their source or origin. Some teams, such as the young engineers building a prototype of a computer in a garage, a highly organized study team, or an expedition would all be *member-founded teams*. Other teams, in contrast, are begun by individuals or authorities outside the team. The

---

crews Trained teams that perform standardized, technical tasks that require coordinated actions, often using tools, equipment, or technology.

ad hoc teams Teams, usually of limited duration, formed by selecting members from a pool of eligible and available prospective members; also known as knots.

T A B L E 12.2   **The Authority Matrix: Four Levels of Team Self-Management**

Responsibilities	Type of Team			
	Manager-led	Self-managing	Self-designing	Self-governing
Executes tasks	✓	✓	✓	✓
Monitors and manages work processes		✓	✓	✓
Designs the team and its context			✓	✓
Sets overall direction				✓

SOURCE: Adapted from "The Psychology of Self-Management in Organizations" by J. Richard Hackman (1986). In M. S. Pallak and R. O. Perloff (Eds.), *Psychology and Work: Productivity, Change, and Employment*, pp. 89–136. Washington, DC: American Psychological Association.

team that pulls the tarp over the baseball field when the rain starts and the teams that play on that field during the game would be *mandated teams* (or *concocted* teams), because those who created them are not actually members of the team (Arrow, McGrath, & Berdahl, 2000). Complex organizations, such as large corporations, usually include both types of teams.

Cross-Functional Teams   A number of organizations use **cross-functional teams** to create connections between subgroups or divisions. These teams bring together representatives with different backgrounds and responsibilities, with the goal of reducing the insularity of each segment of the organization and increasing the pool of available information needed to make an informed decision. Although this interdivisional coupling has proven to be an effective means of developing innovative products and solutions to problems, cross-functional teams tend to be unstable. Levels

of conflict are often too great for these groups to become cohesive, and their goals are not always consensual—particularly when resources are limited (DeDreu, 2007).

Self-Managing Teams   Most groups require the services of a leader, and teams are no different. But whereas some work best by recognizing one person within the group as the leader, others adopt a distributed leadership structure whereby members share the responsibilities among themselves on a rotating basis. Some teams, too, work under the guidance of an external leader, who may or may not monitor the team's procedures closely, regulate its activities, and determine its overall purposes (Keyton & Beck, 2008; Stewart, 2006).

Hackman (2002) developed his *authority matrix model* to account for these variations in a team's autonomy. This model, summarized in Table 12.2, describes (in the left column) four critically important team and executive responsibilities: execution of the task itself, managing the work process, designing the team within the organization context, and determining the team's overall mission and objectives. The model also identifies, along the top row of the chart, four types of teams that differ in their degree of responsibility and autonomy. In a *manager-led team*,

---

cross-functional teams Project groups composed of people with differing types of functional expertise, often drawn from various levels, divisions, or segments of an organization.

members provide a service or generate a product, but that is their sole responsibility: An external leader or manager monitors the work, designs the team, and sets the team's direction. Members of *self-managing teams* have more autonomy, for they are charged with both executing the task and managing the team's work. These teams can gauge the quality of their work product, but only an authority external to the team can adjust its procedures and structures. *Self-designing teams* enjoy more discretion in terms of control over their team's structure, for they have the authority to change the team itself. The team's leader sets the direction, but the members have full responsibility for doing what needs to be done to get the work accomplished. Finally, members of *self-governing teams* have responsibility for all four of the major functions listed in Table 12.2. They decide what is to be done, structure the team and its context, manage their own performance, and actually carry out the work. The Mountain Medical cardiac surgery team was a self-governing team. The surgeon who founded the team was the one who lobbied the hospital to try the new procedure, and he worked closely with the staff to design the team.

A Systems Model of Teams

When Ludwig von Bertalanffy, the originator of open systems theory, defined a system to be a "complex of mutually interacting components," he could have just as well have been describing a team. Teams emerge from and then sustain patterns of coordinated interdependencies among individual members. Teams, because of their emphasis on the achievement of desired goals, are more likely than most groups to plan a strategy to enact over a given time period, seek feedback about the effectiveness of the plan and implementation, and make adjustments to procedures and operations on the basis of that analysis. Teams strive for regularity and order, but they also adapt spontaneously to deal with new circumstances or internal changes. Their internal relations are always drifting toward entropy—disorganization—but they counter this tendency through monitoring outcomes and efficiencies (Arrow et al., 2000; Kozlowski et al., 1999).

The Input–Process–Output (I-P-O) Model

Rather than assuming that variables in the system are linked to one another in simple, one-to-one relationships, systems theory recognizes factors that set the stage for teamwork (inputs), that facilitate or inhibit the nature of the teamwork (processes), and a variety of consequences that result from the team's activities (outputs). This assumption is the basis of the well-known *input–process–output (I-P-O) model* first introduced in Chapter 2 and shown (in a simplified form) in Figure 12.1.

- *Inputs* include any antecedent factors that may influence, directly or indirectly, the team members and the team itself. These antecedents include individual-level factors (e.g., who is on the team, and what are their strengths and weaknesses), team-level factors (e.g., how large is the team, and what resources does it control), and environmental-level factors (e.g., how does this team work with other units within the organization).

- *Processes* are operations and activities that mediate the relationship between the input factors and the team's outcomes. These processes include the steps taken to plan the team's activities; initiating actions and monitoring processes; and processes that focus on interpersonal aspects of the team's system, such as dealing with conflict and increasing members' sense of commitment to the team (Marks, Mathieu, & Zaccaro, 2001).

- *Outputs* are the consequences of the team's activities. The team's emphasis on outcome means that the tangible results of the team effort draw the most attention—did the team win or lose, is the team's product high in quality or inadequate, did the team successfully complete the operation or did it kill the patient—but other outcomes are also important, including changes in the team's cohesiveness or the degree to which it changed so that it will be able to deal with similar tasks more efficiently in the future.

Beyond the I-P-O Model The I-P-O model, despite years of steady service to researchers studying

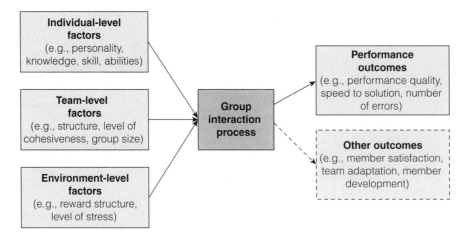

FIGURE 12.1   The traditional Input–Process–Output (I-P-O) model of team performance.

SOURCE: Adapted from J. R. Hackman and C. G. Morris, "Group Tasks, Group Interaction Process, and Group Performance Effectiveness: A Review and Proposed Integration" by Jr. R. Hackmand and C. G. Morris. *Advances in Experimental Social Psychology*, 1975, *8*.

teams, is a relatively simplistic model of a highly complex interpersonal system, and three specific limitations are worth noting. First, the model, with its categorization of factors as inputs, processes, or outputs, understates the complex interdependencies among the variables that influence team performance. Second, some of the so-called "processes" within the process category are not actually processes at all, but rather characteristics of the team that emerge over time as members interact with one another. These emergent states certainly influence the team's outcomes, but it would be more accurate to call them mediators of the relationship between inputs and outputs rather than processes. Third, given that the I-P-O model is a systems theory, it is essential to always consider feedback processes that occur over time. The model is often interpreted as a sequential one, with inputs leading to processes/mediators and these leading to outcomes; but the reverse causal sequences are also a part of the complete model. In consequence, some suggest that the I-P-O model should be reconfigured into an Input–Mediator–Output–Input model (the I-M-O-I) to indicate the diversity of elements in the process stage and the fact that the outputs feed back to become inputs (Ilgen et al., 2005; Marks et al., 2001).

These limitations notwithstanding, the I-P-O model provides a heuristic framework for this chapter's examination of teams. The next section considers team composition, with a focus on who is recruited to the team and how their personal qualities shape the team's interactions. The chapter then turns to issues of process, including teamwork and cognitive work, before considering ways to evaluate the effectiveness of teams.

BUILDING THE TEAM

In 1996, hospitals around the United States began considering adopting noninvasive surgical methods for cardiac surgeries. Technological developments ensured that the procedure was a safe one, but each hospital needed to determine how to change from the traditional method to the newer procedure (Pisano et al., 2001).

Nearly all hospitals settled on a team approach: They would create teams of physicians, nurses, and technicians who would study the method and implement it locally once they had mastered its demands. One hospital, given here the fictitious name of Chelsea Hospital, put the chief of cardiac surgery in charge of building the team. He was an extremely skilled surgeon, but he did not view the new surgery as much of a challenge. He was also very busy and did not get involved in selecting the members of his team. The composition of the Chelsea team was determined by seniority and who was available to attend the three-day offsite training session.

Mountain Medical did things a little differently from Chelsea. A young surgeon, who was new to the hospital, volunteered to get the team started. He talked with the staff in all the departments, and he picked people for the team "based on their experience working together" rather than their seniority (Edmondson, Bohmer, & Pisano, 2001, p. 128). He was part of the team during the training sessions and held meetings with physicians in other departments to share information about the procedure and to identify the best patients for referrals. The members of the team met regularly, prior to the procedure, to walk through the basic steps and to share information about what each of them would be doing and how their actions fit with what the other members of the team were doing.

Gary Pisano, Richard Bohmer, and Amy Edmondson (2001), who studied 16 hospitals that used the new method, discovered that things worked out differently for Chelsea Hospital and Mountain Medical. The Chelsea team did not lose patients, but the operations took longer than they should have, even after they gained experience with the procedure. Mountain Medical, in contrast, performed the first few operations slowly, but then became one of the fastest and most effective surgical teams in the group of 16 studied—despite being led by one of the least experienced surgeons.

Mountain Medical, like most teams, owes much of its success to its composition: the individuals who were selected to make up the team. All teams are composites formed by the joining together of multiple, relatively independent individuals. Each member of the group brings to the team a set of unique personal experiences, interests, skills, abilities, and motivations, that merge together with the personal qualities of all the other individual members to form the team as a whole (Moreland, Levine, & Wingert, 1996).

The Team Player

Mountain Medical deliberately sought out "team players" for their surgical team. Such people are often identified on the basis of their personalities, for some people, by temperament, make better teammates than others. Is a cold, emotionally unstable, narrow-minded person someone to recruit for a team that is attempting a challenging task when lives are at stake? Or, would the team be more likely to prosper if composed of people who are outgoing, stable, and conscientious?

The Five-Factor Model The personality traits identified in the five-factor model of personality—extraversion, agreeableness, conscientiousness, emotional stability (or low neuroticism), and openness—all reliably predict how people respond in group settings (see Table 4.1). Depending on their personality, some people are more likely to enjoy affiliating with others (see Chapter 4), and personality also predicts emergence as a group leader (see Chapter 9). These traits are also related, in predictable ways, to people's responses when part of a team. Teams, as task-focused groups, seek and reward the efforts of those who are conscientious. Individuals with the qualities associated with conscientiousness, for example (dependability, dutifulness, achievement orientation, and efficacy), are very much appreciated when work demands are unpredictable and success depends on each person completing his or her portion of the group's task. Extraversion, too, is consistent with a number of desirable qualities in a teammate (dominance, affiliation, social perceptiveness, expressivity), as is agreeableness. Even emotional stability and openness are likely associated with success working with others, since they are indicators of adjustment, confidence (self-esteem), and flexibility (Bell, 2007; Morgeson, Reider, & Campion, 2005).

The magnitude of the relationship between personality and team performance depends, in part, on the type of team and the work it does. In a work or project team, for example, conscientiousness may be critically important, particularly if the group is self-managing. In action teams that require higher levels of cohesion, in contrast, agreeableness and emotional

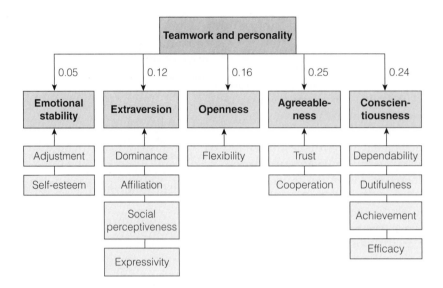

FIGURE 12.2 Hierarchical model of personality characteristics and facets related to teamwork.

SOURCE: Adapted from "What Makes A Good Team Player? Personality and Team Effectiveness" by J. E. Driskell, G. F. Goodwin, E. Salas, & P. G. O'Shea. In *Group Dynamics: Theory, Research, and Practice,* 2006, *10,* 249–271.

stability may be more critical (Bell, 2007). Overall, however, comprehensive meta–analytic reviews find that "team players" tend to be conscientious and agreeable and also extraverted and open (see Figure 12.2; Driskell et al., 2006; Peeters et al., 2006). Only emotional stability was unrelated to how well the team member performed once on the team. Other studies offer a partial explanation: Individuals who do not possess these qualities tend to exhibit behaviors that limit their interpersonal successes, including absence from work, low motivation, burnout, and various forms of counterproductive work behavior (Berry, Ones, & Sackett, 2007).

Team Composition Researchers have also examined other personality variables besides those emphasized by the five-factor model, including assertiveness (Pearsall & Ellis, 2006), psychological collectivism (Dierdorff, Bell, & Belohlav, 2011), emotional intelligence (McCallin & Bamford, 2007), locus of control (Boone et al., 2005), and achievement motivation (LePine, 2003). These differences in personality influence people's behaviors when they are part of a team, but in many cases their effects are configural: They depend on the personality traits of the others who are in the team. Certain combinations of people, given their personal motivations, are more effective than others (Schutz, 1958). Teams composed of all highly dominant individuals are less stable and less productive than groups that include a mix of people who are dominant and less dominant (Ronay et al., 2012). An individual who is conscientious may fit in well with a team when other members are highly motivated to perform well, but that individual may not fit the requirements of other, less task-focused teams.

Researchers tested the importance of a team's total configuration of personality types by comparing teams that included many individuals who were Type A personalities to teams with more Type Bs. Type A individuals tend to be aggressive, competitive, and excessively time-oriented, but they are also high in their achievement orientation. Type B individuals, in contrast, are more relaxed and slow-going. To determine what would happen when these two types mixed in teams, researchers experimentally manipulated team memberships to create all Type A teams, all Type B teams, and some teams with a mixture of both types. After they worked together for a time, the members of these teams were asked to indicate their level of satisfaction with their team and its members. In general, people were more satisfied when their teammates were similar in terms of personality. Teams composed of all Type As or all Type Bs were rated as more satisfying by their members than were teams when Type As and Bs were mixed together. Teams of only Type As did, however, get a lot more done (Keinan & Koren, 2002).

Team Orientation   Even though some people value working in an organized, task-focused group, others are quick to announce "I don't like working in teams" at any opportunity. Individuals who have negative beliefs about groups, for example, generally perform more poorly when they are forced to work in them (Karau & Elsaid, 2009). Individualists, in contrast to collectivists, tend to respond less positively when part of a team (see Chapter 3). Teams with many such individuals in their ranks perform more poorly, as a group, than teams composed of fewer anti-team types (Bell, 2007).

This negativity toward teams is sustained, in part, by two interrelated components: a preference for working alone rather than with others and an unwillingness to accept input from other people. Those who expressed the most negative attitudes toward working in groups agreed strongly with such statements as "I would rather take action on my own than to wait around for others' input" and "I prefer to complete a task from beginning to end with no assistance from others." But they also tended to exhibit a low opinion of other people as a source of useful information. They agreed with such statements as "When I have a different opinion than another group member, I usually try to stick with my own opinion" and "When others disagree, it is important to hold one's own ground and not give in." Individuals with these beliefs tended to perform poorly on a series of team-based tasks, particularly those that called for high levels of interdependence among the team members (Driskell, Salas, & Hughes, 2010).

Knowledge, Skill, and Ability (KSA)

Some teams fail because they simply do not include people with the qualities and characteristics needed for success at the task. A team struggling to generate solutions to math puzzles may not have any mathematicians at the table. A soccer team made up of slow-moving defensive fullbacks but no offensive goal scorers will likely lose. A team's performance depends, in part, on its members' *knowledge, skills, and abilities*, or **KSAs**. Those KSAs are generally of two types: task-relevant proficiencies and interpersonal skills.

Task-specific Proficiencies   A team of mediocre individuals can, with enough practice, good leadership, and determination, reach lofty goals, but teams cannot work miracles; mediocre members make for mediocre teams (Devine & Philips, 2001; Ellis et al., 2003). As influential as teams are in terms of organizing and motivating members, even they can rarely work the transformational magic needed to turn adequate into excellent. Careful design and leadership cannot take a group beyond the limits set by the skills and capabilities of the individual members.

Studies of sport teams indicate that "the best individuals make the best team" (Gill, 1984, p. 325). In many sports, the players' offensive and defensive performances can be tracked so that their skill levels can be identified accurately. These qualities can then be used to calculate the statistical aggregation of the talent level of the team, which can be compared to the team's outcomes. Such analyses indicate that the correlation between the aggregation of individual members' ability and team performance is very strong: .91 in football, .94 in baseball, and .60 in basketball (Jones, 1974; Widmeyer, 1990). The relationship is somewhat reduced in basketball because this sport requires more coordination among members and the teams are smaller in size. Hence, the team members' ability

---

KSAs Acronym for knowledge, skills, abilities, and other characteristics that are needed to complete a job or task successfully.

to play together may have a larger impact on the outcome of a basketball game, whereas the sheer level of ability of players has a greater impact on a football or baseball game's outcome.

Teams that succeed in creating new products and solutions to long-standing problems are generally staffed by individuals of high intelligence, motivation, and energy. For example, Warren Bennis and Patricia Ward Biederman (1997), in a series of case studies of high-performance teams in such organizations as Disney Studios, Lockheed, and the Palo Alto Research Center (PARC), traced much of their success of these teams back to their composition. Many of the members of these groups were individually highly motivated: "fueled by an invigorating, completely unrealistic view of what they can accomplish" (Bennis & Biederman, 1997, p. 15). But their most essential characteristics were their talent and expertise.

A team of experts, however, does not necessarily make an expert team. In one study, researchers had four people work on a task that simulated the work of teams in the intelligence services, detecting possible terrorists from email messages, images taken from surveillance cameras, archives and databases, and so on. Each member of the group reviewed substantial quantities of information individually before meeting collectively to make a team decision. The researchers screened members of the groups, identifying individuals with the particular qualities that would enhance their performance in this kind of situation (good verbal memories and facial recognition). A group with experts in these two areas should have helped their teams perform more effectively—and they did, but only if the teams had spent time organizing their team's procedures. Groups with two experts in them performed particularly poorly—even worse than groups with no experts—if the teams immediately began their work without discussing how they would collaborate to make a decision (Wooley et al., 2008).

Interpersonal Skills   On the social side, teams function best when the members have sufficient social skills to get along well with other people. Social skills are those basic cognitive and behavioral competencies that allow people to interact with other people in an effective, respectful, and supportive way. They include skill in understanding other people, communicating with them effectively, and responding appropriately during social exchanges. Basic social skills include conversational skill, emotional sensitivity, maintaining self-control, making appropriate self-disclosures, giving praise and encouragement as needed, and expressing agreement (Fontana, 1990; Riggio & Kwong, 2009).

In addition to these basic skills—ones that help people work with others in a range of situations—team members must also understand the unique interpersonal dynamics of teams themselves—they require *team knowledge* (Stevens & Campion, 1994). Although different teams require different skills of their members, many performance settings reward individuals who are skilled in conflict resolution, can collaborate with others to solve problems, and are good communicators. Conflict resolution knowledge, skills, and abilities (KSAs), for example, include the ability to distinguish between harmful and constructive conflicts and an emphasis on integrative dispute resolution skills rather than a confrontational orientation. Collaborative problem-solving KSAs involve skill in using group approaches to decision making. Communication KSAs require a range of finely tuned listening and messaging skills, including the capacity to engage in small talk: "to engage in ritual greetings and small talk, and a recognition of their importance" (Stevens & Campion, 1994, p. 505).

How, for example, would you respond if you found yourself in the following situation: You and your coworkers do not agree about "who should do a very disagreeable, but routine task" (Stevens & Campion, 1999, p. 225)? Should you:

A. have your supervisor decide, because this would avoid any personal bias?
B. arrange a rotating schedule so everyone shares the chore?
C. let the workers who show up earliest choose on a first-come, first-served basis?
D. randomly assign a person to do the task and not change it?

Or what if you wanted to improve the quality and flow of conversations among the members of the teams. Should you:

A. use comments that build upon and connect to what others have already said?
B. set up a specific order for everyone to speak and then follow it?
C. let team members with more to say determine the direction and topic of conversation?
D. do all of the above?

According to the *Teamwork-KSA Test* (Stevens & Campion, 1999), the best choice, in the situation in which you were arguing with others about who must do the unpleasant chore, is option B. In contrast, the best choice in terms of KSAs for interpersonal skill for the second question is option A. An individual who scores well on the *Teamwork-KSA Test* is more likely to cooperate "with others in the team," "help other team members accomplish their work," and talk "to other team members before taking actions that might affect them" (Morgeson, Reider, & Campion, 2005, p. 611).

Diversity

The Mountain Medical team was, in some ways, a relatively homogeneous team. Members were similar in terms of ethnicity, skill level, age, motivation, background, and experience with the new procedure. They were, however, heterogeneous with regard to sex, status in the hospital, and training. Would these differences make a difference when they pulled together to form a team?

The diversity of a team is determined by the extent to which members are different from one another. A sample of the many ways that people do, in fact, differ from each other is shown in Table 12.3 that identifies six general clusters of differences: social categories, knowledge and skills, values and beliefs, personality, status, and social connections (Mannix & Neale, 2005). Some of these differences pertain to demographic qualities of people, such as race and sex. Others refer to acquired, functional differences between the members, such as variations in experience, knowledge and skills.

TABLE 12.3   Categories and Types of Diversity

Categories	Types of Diversity
Social-category differences	Race, ethnicity, gender, age, religion, sexual orientation, physical abilities
Differences in knowledge or skills	Education, functional knowledge, information, expertise, training, experience, abilities
Differences in values or beliefs	Cultural background, ideological beliefs, political orientation
Personality differences	Cognitive style, affective disposition, motivational factors
Organizational or community-status differences	Tenure or length of service, title
Differences in social and network ties	Work-related ties, friendship ties, community ties, ingroup membership

SOURCE: E. Mannix and M. A. Neale, *Psychological Science in the Public Interest*, 6, 31–55, copyright © 2005 Association for Psychological Science. Reprinted by Permission of SAGE Publications.

Diversity and Team Performance From a strictly informational perspective, diverse teams should win out against less diverse ones. Diversity brings variety to the team and with that variety should come a broader range of expertise, knowledge, insight, and ideas. If a team is composed of highly similar individuals, they bring the same information and insights to the team so they are less able to identify new strategies and solutions. A diverse team, in contrast, should maximize performance, particularly in situations where success is not determined by the capacity to apply traditional solutions. For example, the team of researchers who conducted the studies of Mountain Medical were a diverse group, at least in terms of sex and disciplinary training. One had a background in organizational behavior and engineering. Another was an economist and the third a physician. When the researchers first started their investigation, each one expected his or her discipline's theories and models would explain why some of the cardiac units were more successful in learning the new procedures than others. But their final conclusions were based on the combined insights drawn from the intertwining of all three disciplinary outlooks (Edmondson, 2011).

But diversity has a possible downside. Diversity can also separate members of the team from one another (Harrison & Klein, 2007). As social categorization theory suggests (Chapter 3), individuals are quick to categorize other people based on their membership in social groups. Although the members of a team should think of each other as "we" or "us," when members belong to a variety of social categories, some members of the team may be viewed as "they" and "them" (van Knippenberg, De Dreu, & Homan, 2004). Diversity may therefore create **faultlines** within the team, and when the team experiences tension, it may break apart along these divisions (Lau & Murnighan, 1998). As Chapter 5 noted, because people are attracted to those who are similar to them, homogeneous teams tend to be cohesive teams and so members may be more willing to perform the supportive, cooperative actions that are so essential for team success.

Studies of Team Diversity   Diversity is a mixed blessing for teams, contributing to gains in performance but at the same time adding the potential for process loss (Horwitz & Horwitz, 2007; Stewart, 2006). Diversity, when based on information and expertise, tends to improve team outcomes, particularly on difficult tasks (Bowers, Pharmer, & Salas, 2000). When members vary in ability, then by definition the team will include at least one individual with high ability. Some homogeneous teams will be uniformly unskilled, so these teams will perform particularly badly at their task. As studies of social compensation discussed in Chapter 10 suggest, heterogeneous teams may also become more productive because the low-performing members are motivated by the high standards set by the others in the team, and the others in the team may also be a source of

help and assistance as the low performers work to increase their performance.

But other types of diversity, such as variations in ethnicity, race, age, and sex, influence performance less reliably. Teams of researchers were more productive when they joined with researchers from other disciplines (Pelz, 1956, 1967), but top management teams and work groups were less productive and experienced more turnover when their members varied noticeably in age and tenure (Pelled, Eisenhardt, & Xin, 1999). Management teams in banks that were diverse in terms of their educational histories and backgrounds were more innovative than teams that were homogeneous (Jackson, 1992), but diversity in affective levels—substantial and continuing variations in positive and negative mood—within top management teams was associated with declines in the firm's financial performance (Barsade et al., 2000). Teams that included Asian, African, Hispanic, and European Americans outperformed teams that only included European Americans (McLeod, Lobel, & Cox, 1996), but a study of 151 teams in three large organizations indicated that those individuals who were more unlike the other members of their teams felt the least psychologically connected to them and had higher rates of absenteeism (Tsui, Egan, & O'Reilley, 1992).

Designing for Diversity   These conflicting findings attest to the mixed benefits and limitations offered by diversity in teams. Diverse teams may be better at coping with changing work conditions because their wider range of talents and traits enhances their flexibility. Diverse teams, however, may lack cohesion because members may perceive one another as dissimilar. Heterogeneity may increase conflict within the team (see Focus 12.1; Mannix & Neale, 2005; van Knippenberg & Schippers, 2007; Williams & O'Reilly, 1998).

Steps can, however, be taken to minimize the negative side effects of diversity and maximize diversity's gains. First, diverse teams will need time to work through the initial period in which differences between people based on their *surface-level qualities*—race, sex, age—lower the team's overall level of cohesiveness. Intervention may also be

---

faultlines Hypothetical divisions that separate the members of a heterogeneous group into smaller, more homogeneous subgroups.

| F o c u s   **12.1** | **Cross-cultural Perspectives: On the Wisdom of Putting Diverse Teams into Space** |

Author Thomas Friedman (2005), in his book *The World is Flat*, speaks of how global changes in communication, commerce, technology, and international relations have broken down the boundaries between the world's nations and their citizens. People from different cultural groups who would have rarely, if ever, ended up together in a work group now find themselves working side-by-side (or computer-to-computer) with people from other regions, nations, and countries. The diversity of these groups is perhaps the deepest of all, for these teammates differ from one another in nearly every way possible: racially, ethnically, experientially, cognitively, culturally, ideologically, and geographically (see Table 12.3).

Cultural diversity, like other forms of diversity, is a valuable resource for teams, for it augments informational resources needed for creative, innovative solutions. A diverse group will likely be able to examine, more critically, an idea and therefore expose its weaknesses. A diverse group, for example, probably would not have supported U.S. President John Kennedy's planned invasion of Cuba at the Bay of Pigs: groupthink is an unlikely event in diverse groups. But diversity adds a layer of interpersonal complications to most team interactions. Communication is more challenging in diverse groups, not only because of differences in spoken language, but also in the interpretation of nonverbal gestures and paralinguistic cues. Diverse groups tend to be less unified than more homogeneous ones, with the result that the social integration needed for effective functioning when tasks require high levels of coordination is diminished. Diverse groups are also more likely to experience both interpersonal and task-related conflict, which in some cases can cause the team to disintegrate.

These advantages and pitfalls are possibilities for all types of diverse teams, including those that work in one of the most remote locations: space. Although both the United States and the Soviet Union have successfully staffed space stations in orbit around earth, in 1991 these countries joined Canada, Japan, and ten other European countries as partners in the International Space Station (ISS) program. Once operational, these countries each sent astronauts and cosmonauts to the station, creating multicultural teams responsible for building, servicing, and operating this incredibly complex piece of equipment.

Differences between Russians and Americans were in evidence from the start of the collaboration (Boyd et al., 2009). Whereas Americans tend to be individualistic in their cultural orientation, Russians are collectivistic. In consequence, when working together in small teams in

the confines of the ISS, Americans were focused more on their own projects, and they were more likely to respond slowly to requests for action from mission control. Russians, in contrast, were more emotionally expressive, more attentive to the demands of the group, and more respectful of hierarchy. Russia is also a high-contact culture (Hall, 1966). In conversation, Russians stand closer to each other, and they are likely to touch each other in some way—backslapping, hugs, and exchanges of kisses on the cheeks. Their conversation style is termed sociocentric. Americans, and particularly those who made the trip to ISS, were more likely to express themselves directly and vocally, rather than nonverbally and indirectly. As idiocentric communicators, they were more likely to discuss task-related concerns rather than background and personal information (David et al., 2010).

In a number of cases, Americans made requests of Russians in such a direct, open way that the Russians felt like the Americans were issuing orders. When, for example, an American photographing a Russian preparing to leave the ISS for a spacewalk said "Smile," the Russian interpreted this request to be an order to smile. In contrast, when a Russian was about to photograph an American, he made a more respectful request, explaining "We are going to capture this historic moment. If *you* have no objections, of course" (David et al., 2010, p. 18). The cosmonaut also used a more formal Russian word for "you," although it is doubtful that the American detected this subtlety.

The Russian and American teammates also differed to a degree in their standards of politeness, and these differences caused an occasional loss of affective synchrony. In one case, for example, as an American was exercising using the fitness equipment, one of the Russian crewmen received a message from mission control assigning a task to the American. The Russian dutifully asked the American if he would perform the task, to which the American replied "no." The American considered his response to be justified—he did not want to perform this relatively routine task—but the Russian considered this answer to be a rude one.

Despite the diversity of the teams that live and work in the ISS, these groups perform their tasks with great proficiency, and it may well be that their success is due, in no small measure, to their diversity. Such a conclusion is consistent with results obtained in studies of less rarefied, ground-based teams. When researchers weighed the relative costs and gains of team diversity in a meta-analytic review of 108 studies of over 10,000 teams, they discovered that process losses

---

F o c u s 12.1   (Continued)

associated with culturally diverse groups were tempered, significantly, by process gains (Stahl et al., 2010). Conflict was greater in diverse groups, and social integration was reduced. However, diverse groups were more creative than less diverse ones, and—somewhat unexpectedly—people enjoyed

membership more in diverse groups compared to less diverse ones. Given these counteracting forces, the impact of diversity on team performance depends on the team's success in managing the interpersonal problems that diversity may cause while taking full advantage of the resources their diversity provides.

---

required when, after time, members have discovered that these surface-level differences are unimportant, but that their *deep-level differences* in values and principles are causing unexpected turbulence in the team (Harrison et al., 2002). Second, because teams exist in an organizational context, the nature of that organization's culture will influence how teammates respond to diversity. If the organization's culture encourages collectivistic values and minimizes distinctions based on tenure and status, then diverse teammates tend to behave more cooperatively than they would in more traditional organizations (Chatman & Spataro, 2005). Third, to minimize conflict between team members from different social categories, steps should be taken to minimize any tendency to draw distinctions between people based on their category memberships (Cunningham, 2005; Homan et al., 2010). Team leaders should remind members of the importance of involving all members of the team in the process and make certain that individuals in the minority do not become isolated from the rest of the team (see Chapter 7's analysis of minority influence).

Men, Women, and Teams

Same-sex teams are becoming increasingly anachronistic. Whereas women were once barred from many types of teams in business and organizational settings, changes in the social climate—and in employment law—have increased sex-based diversity in the workforce.

The Myth of Male Bonding   These changes are not welcomed as progress in all quarters of society or recognized as adaptive by all theories of collective action. Some evolutionary anthropologists, for

example, argue that the presence of women in previously all-male teams may disrupt the functioning of such teams in substantial ways. This perspective suggests that it was males, and not females, who affiliated in same-sex groups for adaptive reasons, so that over time male bonding became a stronger psychological force than female bonding. In consequence, heterogeneously gendered teams may be less productive than same-sex teams, since all-male teams would be more cohesive than mixed-sex teams. Bonding theorists also suggest "the difficulty females experience in male work groups is not that males dislike females but rather that the force of their enthusiasm for females can disrupt the work and endanger the integrity of groups of men" (Tiger & Fox, 1998, p. 145).

The data do not support either the idea that males bond more cohesively in all-male groups than females bond in all-female groups or that, in consequence, male teams outperform female teams. Social psychologist Wendy Wood (1987), after reviewing 52 studies of sex differences in group performance, identified two factors that influence the effectiveness of all-male and all-female teams— task content and interaction style. First, in the studies that favored men, the content of the task was more consistent with the typical skills, interests, and abilities of men than of women. Groups of men were better at tasks that required math or physical strength, whereas women excelled on verbal tasks. Second, Wood suggested that sex differences in performance are influenced by the different interaction styles that men and women often adopt in groups. Men more frequently enact a task-oriented interaction style, whereas women tend to enact an interpersonal-oriented interaction style. Thus, men outperform women (to a small extent) when success is predicated on a high rate of task activity, and women outperform men when success depends on a high level of social activity (Wood, Polek, & Aiken, 1985).

Heterogeneously Gendered Teams But what of mixed-gender teams—teams that include both men and women? Studies of men and women working together in teams suggest that such teams, because of their diversity, have greater information resources than same-sex teams and so excel at tasks that require a broad range of expertise, experience, and information. However, sexism, sexual harassment, and stereotyping continue to dog such teams (Raghubir & Valenzuela, 2010). As with other forms of diversity, sex-based diversity can create subgroups within the team and increase levels of conflict. Diverse teams must also deal with problems of proportion, particularly when very few men are entering into groups that were traditionally staffed by women and vice versa. Teams that achieve diversity by adding only one or two members of a social category, such as a team with one woman and many men, tend to encounter more problems than homogeneous teams. When work groups include a single token or "solo" woman, for example, coworkers are more likely to categorize each other in terms of their sex. Solo members are also scrutinized more than other group members, and this unwanted attention may be emotionally depleting and may contribute to stereotype threat (Johnson & Richeson, 2009). Token members are more often targets of sexism and prejudice and must, in many cases, work harder and express higher levels of commitment to the group to overcome other members' biases (see Chapter 8).

In some cases, teams with token members will outperform homogeneous teams, even when the teams attempt tasks that are traditionally reserved for homogeneous teams. For example, one team of researchers watched groups working on a wilderness survival exercise—an activity that favors people who have knowledge of the outdoors. Groups of men generally outperformed women, but groups of men that included one woman performed best of all. The researchers speculated that the addition of a woman to the otherwise all-male groups may have tempered the men's tendency to compete

with one another and, thus, helped them to function as a team (Rogelberg & Rumery, 1996). Other research, however, confirms one of the speculations offered by the proponents of male-bonding theory: Some men do exhibit impaired cognitive functioning when working in the presence of women, particularly when they consider the women to be attractive (Karremans et al., 2009).

Hackman and his colleagues have explored the complex relationships of gender diversity, the proportion of men and women, and the organizational context in their studies of a particular type of team: the concert orchestra (Allmendinger, Hackman, & Lehman, 1996; Hackman, 2003). Many of the orchestras they studied were in the midst of a transition from all-male groups to groups that included both men and women. Some orchestras were only beginning this transition, for they included very few women (2% was the lowest) whereas others were more heterogeneous (up to 59% women). When they measured members' work motivation and overall satisfaction with their orchestras, they discovered that orchestras with a larger proportion of female members were viewed more negatively. This tendency was more pronounced among the men in the group and also in countries with traditional conceptions of the role of men and women in society. Hackman wrote:

> Life in a homogeneously male orchestra surely is not much affected by the presence of one or two women, especially if they play a gendered instrument such as a harp. Larger numbers of women, however, can become a worrisome presence on high-status turf that previously had been an exclusively male province, engendering intergroup conflicts that stress all players and disrupt the social dynamics of the orchestra. (2003, p. 908)

WORKING IN TEAMS

Chelsea Hospital and Mountain Medical both faced the same problem, and they both decided to solve the problem by forming a team. But they designed their teams differently. Both teams included a scrub nurse, a perfusionist, an anesthesiologist, and a cardiac surgeon, and each trained so carefully that they were skilled at the tasks they needed to perform. But the leaders of the two teams had different views about how they should work together. The young surgeon who headed the team at Mountain Medical insisted that everyone's ideas would be considered, and, during the operation itself, he asked that everyone communicate with everyone else and not focus on only their own duties. Chelsea's head surgeon, in contrast, believed that most members of the staff were so well-trained that they were interchangeable. He did not stress the importance of teamwork and explained, "Once I get the team set up, I never look up [from the operating field]. It's they who have to make sure that everything is flowing" (Edmondson, et al., 2001, p. 128).

Team Processes

Before Mountain Medical carried out its first surgery the members of the team had already worked, for weeks, as a team. They met regularly to discuss the procedure, and all had trained together for three days offsite in a simulated operation procedure. They had discussed the sequence of steps that would begin with an anesthetized patient and end with a repaired heart, so that when it was time to work together, they functioned as a team.

Teamwork is the psychological, behavioral, and mental work that members of the team carry out as they collaborate with one another on the various tasks and subtasks that they must complete to reach their desired goal. A team may include many talented individuals, but they must learn how to pool their individual abilities and energies to maximize the team's performance. Team goals must be set, work patterns structured, and a sense of group identity developed. Individual members must learn how to coordinate their actions, and any strains

---

Teamwork The process by which members of the team combine their knowledge, skills, abilities, and other resources, through a coordinated series of actions, to produce an outcome.

and stresses in interpersonal relations need to be identified and resolved (Cannon-Bowers et al., 1995; Cohen & Bailey, 1997).

A functional approach to teamwork begins with a simple question: What does an effective team look like as it carries out its work? Such an analysis recognizes that teams are complex systems, but examines closely the tendencies and patterns of teams' interactions, searching for the core processes that sustain that complexity. What, for example, did the Mountain Medical team do as it prepared for, conducted, and completed each of its operations? And how did Mountain Medical differ from less effective teams—those that were more dysfunctional rather than effective?

Table 12.4 presents one such functional analysis, developed by organizational experts Michelle Marks, John Mathieu, and Stephen Zaccaro (2001). Their teamwork process model stresses three key processes: transitioning, acting, and managing interpersonal relations among members. Marks and her associates point out that teams, unlike some performance groups, act episodically. During the initial phase of their work, teams plan what they will do in later stages, set their goals, and plan strategy. The group then transitions to the actual action stage when it carries out its assigned tasks through coordinated activity. Once this action phase is completed, the team reenters the transition phase and begins preparing for subsequent tasks. Across all phases, the members are also managing the interpersonal aspects of the team in order to minimize conflict and maximize motivation. Thus, as Table 12.3 indicates, Marks and her associates break teamwork down into three fundamental components: transition processes, action processes, and interpersonal processes.

Transition Processes   Often, teams attempt tasks that are so complex that they cannot be completed, at least with any degree of success, without advance planning. The first type of transition process, *mission analysis*, focuses on the current situation: the tasks and subtasks that must be completed, the resources available to the team, and any environmental conditions that may influence the team's work. Teams also engage in *goal specification* and *strategy formulation*

T A B L E 12.4   Taxonomy of Team Processes

Process Dimension	Definition
Transition processes	
Mission analysis	Interpretation and evaluation of the team's mission, including identification of its main tasks as well as the operative environmental conditions and team resources available for mission execution
Goal specification	Identification and prioritization of goals and subgoals for mission accomplishment
Strategy formulation	Development of alternative courses of action for mission accomplishment and identification of the sequence in which subtasks will be completed
Action processes	
Monitoring progress toward goals	Tracking task and progress toward mission accomplishment, interpreting system information in terms of what needs to be accomplished for goal attainment, and transmitting progress to team members
Systems monitoring	Tracking team resources and environmental conditions as they relate to mission accomplishment, which involves (1) internal systems monitoring (tracking team resources such as personnel, equipment, and other information that is generated or contained within the team), and (2) environmental monitoring (tracking the environmental conditions relevant to the team)
Team monitoring and backup behavior	Assisting team members to perform their tasks. Assistance may occur by (1) providing a teammate with verbal feedback behavior or coaching, (2) helping a teammate behaviorally in carrying out actions, or (3) assuming and completing a task for a teammate
Coordination	Orchestrating the sequence and timing of interdependent action
Interpersonal processes	
Conflict management	Preemptive conflict management involves establishing conditions to prevent, control, or guide team conflict before it occurs. Reactive conflict management involves working through task and interpersonal disagreements among team members
Motivation and confidence building	Generating and preserving a sense of collective confidence, motivation, and task-based cohesion with regard to mission accomplishment
Affect management	Regulating member emotions during mission accomplishment, including (but not limited to) social cohesion, frustration, and excitement

SOURCE: "A Temporally Based Framework and Taxonomy of Team Processes," by Michelle A. Marks, John E. Mathieu, and Stephen J. Zaccaro (2001). *Academy Of Management Review, 26*, 356–376. Reprinted by permission of Academy of Management via Copyright Clearance Center.

between action episodes, since experience working together will provide the members with a clearer idea of the team's potential and limitations. Strategy formulation is particularly essential if the team is unable to reach the goals it has set for itself, for, by reviewing the causes of failure, team members may find ways to improve their efficiency and outcomes (Cannon & Edmondson, 2005).

Action Processes When teams are at work, their task-related actions are so perceptually vivid that the action processes that make up the teamwork portion of their activities often go undetected. When, for example, the Mountain Medical team began to repair the patient's heart, an observer watching the team would see a physician incising and suturing, a nurse monitoring the patient's vital signs, and an anesthesiologist sedating the patient. But Marks, Mathieu, and Zaccaro's teamwork process model suggests that four other, teamwork-related actions are also taking place during the action period. First, the group is *monitoring progress* toward its goals as members implicitly check their own actions as well as those performed by others. Second, *systems monitoring* involves keeping track of the resources the team needs, whether they be physical resources, time, or even energy. Third, *team monitoring and backup behavior*, considered by some to be a key difference between teams and task groups, occurs when one member of the team delivers assistance to another member, simply because that team member needs help. Finally, *coordination* of action involves a change in the behaviors of the team members so that each one's actions mesh with other's actions, resulting in synchrony.

Interpersonal Processes Consistent with studies of work groups in general, during both the transition and action periods, teammates must spend some of their time tending to the relational side of their team. To reach a high level of effectiveness, teams require a degree of unity; yet the pressures often encountered by groups as they strive to reach their goals can produce tension within the group. Members of effective teams tend to reduce the threat of such conflict to the group's cohesion through *conflict management*. Other types of interpersonal work required of the group members include *motivation and confidence building* and *affect management*.

Testing the Teamwork Process Model The teamwork process model developed by Marks and her colleagues (2001) is complex, but a complex model is needed to take into account the many processes that contribute to team functioning (see Figure 12.3). The model has also fared well when subjected to empirical tests. For example, a meta-analytic review of over 150 studies that examined team effectiveness and had measured, in some way, one or more of the processes in Table 12.4, supported the theory (LePine et al., 2008). This review

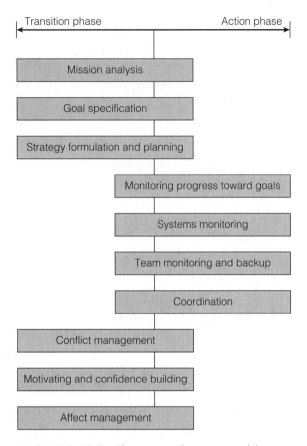

FIGURE 12.3 The teamwork process model.

SOURCE: "A Temporally Based Framework and Taxonomy of Team Processes," by Michelle A. Marks, John E. Mathieu, and Stephen J. Zaccaro (2001). *Academy Of Management Review, 26*, 356–376. Reprinted by permission of Academy of Management via Copyright Clearanc Center.

concluded that the 10 second-order indicators of teamwork specified in the teamwork process model were organized, as predicted, into three superordinate clusters. The analysis also indicated that each of the 10 factors was significantly correlated with performance, ranging from a low of .12 for systems monitoring to a high of .30 for both strategy formulation and motivation. The average correlation was .24. These findings are encouraging; but even so, the list in Table 12.4 may not be complete. Such factors as communication (Kozlowski & Ilgen, 2006), pacing (Nieva, Fleishman, & Rieck, 1978), role clarification (Ross, Jones, & Adams, 2008), and creativity (Gibson et al., 2005) may also belong on the list of key processes that help groups function as teams (Salas et al., 2009).

Cognitive Processes

Teams need to spend time working together before they jell into an effective working unit. However, time alone is not what enhances the team's expertise but also what happens during the passage of that time. As noted in the last chapter, teams improve their performance over time as they develop a shared understanding of the team and the tasks they are attempting. Some semblance of this *shared mental model* is present nearly from its inception, but as the team practices, differences among the members in terms of their understanding of their situation and their team diminish as a consensus becomes implicitly accepted (Tindale, Stawiski, & Jacobs, 2008).

The shared mental model includes the team's joint representations of the task—how it is to be performed, the type of results sought, the kinds of behaviors that are recognized as useful by the team, and so on—as well as shared representations of the team. Although team members, initially, are often poor judges of members' abilities, given time they become more proficient at recognizing, and taking advantage of, the strengths of each team member. In one study of this process, members of groups completed two geography quizzes about U.S. cities, with such questions as "What city is known as the Crescent City?" and "Through what city does the Trinity River run?" Unbeknown to the group, one of their members was a confederate who had been prepped with the answers, and he answered seven of the eight questions correctly on the first test. The group used some of his answers (60.3%) on the first test, but when they were given feedback and a chance to do a second quiz, they used his answers almost exclusively (84.7%). They had learned to rely on his expertise (Littlepage, Robison, & Reddington, 1997; see, too, Littlepage et al., 2008; Littlepage & Silbiger, 1992).

Transactive Memory   Teams also need time to develop *transactive memory systems* (Wegner, 1987).

In the complex world of the operating room during heart surgery, there is too much information about the equipment, the proper settings, the instruments, the heart–lung machine, and so on, for a single individual to retain it all with any degree of accuracy. The surgical team therefore distributes the information to specific members of the team, depending on their role and responsibilities. Then, when the information is required, the team consults with the member known to be the "expert" on that particular matter who then supplies the necessary information to the best of his or her ability (see Chapter 11).

Social psychologist Richard Moreland and his colleagues (Moreland, Argote, & Krishnan, 1996) examined the development of transactive memory systems by training volunteers to build radios from hobby kits. Each kit included a circuit board and dozens of components that had to be put in the correct locations and connected before the radio would function. All the participants received the same training in the first session, but some of them worked alone practicing building the radio whereas others practiced in three-person teams. One week later, the participants returned and assembled a radio, this time with an offer of a cash prize if they performed well. All the subjects worked in teams, but only some of them were assigned to the same team they had worked with originally. These individuals outperformed the subjects who were trained individually, apparently because they were able to form a collaborative, transactive memory for the procedures in the first session. Moreland and his colleagues discovered that teams that performed the best showed signs of (a) memory differentiation—some of the team members were better at remembering certain parts of the assembly procedures than others; (b) task coordination—the team-trained teams worked with less confusion; and (c) task credibility—the teams with stronger transactive memories trusted one another's claims about the assembly process.

Team Learning   Because these cognitive foundations of teamwork develop as the teammates experience working together, teams require group rather than individual practice. Although in years past, organizations often sent their personnel offsite to individually receive training in team skills at institutes and workshops, team members need to be trained together—as a unit—rather than separately. Only by confronting the learning situation as a group can the team engage in team learning, a "process in which a group takes action, obtains and reflects upon feedback, and makes changes to adapt or improve" (Sessa & London, 2008, p. 5).

The success of the Mountain Medical Center's cardiac surgery team illustrates the importance of learning as a team. The 16 hospitals that Pisano, Bohmer, and Edmondson (2001) studied all used the same equipment, and the operating room staff were all trained by the equipment's manufacturer. These highly trained surgical teams performed their work well, and nearly all of the patients fully recovered after their surgery. Some, however, recovered more rapidly and with fewer complications than others, and this gain was indicated by the speed of the operation. None of the teams operated too quickly, but some were relatively slow. With each patient, the teams improved—minimizing the amount of time that the patient was on the heart–lung machine is an indicator of recovery time—but some teams learned more quickly than others. Surprisingly, the educational backgrounds and surgical experience of the teams did not predict learning rates nor did the overall support for the new procedure by the hospital's administrative staff. The status of the head surgeon on the team was also unrelated to learning rate, as was the amount of time the teams spent in formal debriefing sessions after each case.

What did predict learning rates? The way the teams were designed and trained. In the slow-to-learn teams, the surgeons assigned to the team happened to be the ones who were available to attend the training session. They showed little interest in who was on their surgical team—in fact, the members of the team varied from case to case, violating a basic rule of good team design (Hackman, 2002). These teams did not fully realize how intense the new surgical methods would be in terms of coordination demands, and the surgeons did not explicitly discuss the need for greater attention to teamwork.

At places like Mountain Medical, in contrast, the team surgeon was usually an advocate for the procedure, and he or she was actively involved in selecting all the other members of the team. These individuals worked together during the training sessions as a team, and they remained together longer during the first cases using the new methods. The surgeons in these teams also stressed the importance of working together as a team rather than stressing the acquisition of new individual skills: "They made it clear that this reinvention of working relationships would require the contribution of every team member" (Edmondson et al., 2001, p. 130). These fast learners also continued to increase their efficiency, as they developed an open pattern of communication where all felt free to make suggestions for improving the work.

Figure 12.4 provides a partial summary of the findings for one of the fast-learning teams. This team began slowly, taking much longer to finish the procedure than most other teams. By the fifth case, however, this team was performing at the same speed as most other teams, and they continued to improve their rate with each new case until they were able to conduct the operation faster than all the other teams.

Team Cohesion

Teams owe part of their success to their united approach to their work. They need not be interpersonally cohesive, but given the importance of interdependency, strong commitment to the shared task, and willingness to put team interests before individual interests, cohesiveness is in most cases associated with performance gains in teams (Kozlowski & Ilgen, 2006; see Focus 12.2).

Sources of Cohesion As noted earlier in the chapter, cohesion is one of the defining characteristics of teams, for teams are unified groups. That unity, however, can derive from one or more sources examined in Chapter 5 and as follows.

- *Social cohesion*: Any factor that promotes attraction of the members to one another or to the group as a whole, such as proximity, similarity

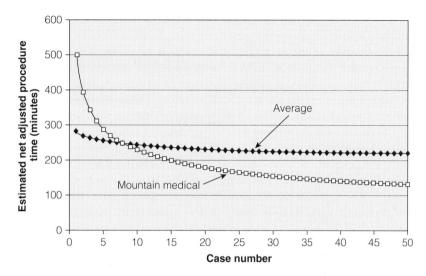

FIGURE 12.4   Estimated net-adjusted procedure times for the Mountain Medical team and the average of teams at all other hospitals.

SOURCE: Reprinted by permission, Gary P. Pisano, Richard M. J. Bohmer, and Amy C. Edmondson, "Organizational Differences in Rates of Learning: Evidence from the Adoption of Minimally Invasive Cardiac Surgery," *Management Science*, Volume 47, 752–768. © 2001 The Institute for Operations Research and the Management Sciences (INFORMS), 7240 Parkway Drive, Suite 300, Hanover, MD 21076 USA.

in attitudes, and the absence of members with negative personal qualities, will augment a group's cohesion. Even though team members need not be close friends, teams with strong social bonds among members outperform less socially cohesive teams (Chiocchio & Essiembre, 2009).

- *Task cohesion*: Teams are unified by members' shared drive to accomplish their goals. Groups that are cohesive, in the sense that they work as a team to achieve chosen goals, are characterized by positive expectations about the group's capabilities and enthusiasm for the group and its work (Guzzo et al., 1993).

- *Collective cohesion*: When members identify with their team—when their sense of self is based on both their personal identity but also on their team-level social identity—the team will likely show heightened unity, increased levels of motivation, and stronger support of the team during periods of stress or crisis (Haslam, 2004). Organizations can communicate a communal perspective through rhetoric that stresses unity by not singling out individual members and

by providing financial incentives for good team work rather than for individual work (Hinds & Mortensen, 2005).

- *Emotional cohesion*: Some teams are cohesive at an affective, emotional level. Jennifer George's (1995) theory of **group affective tone**, applied to teams, suggests cohesive teams are more likely to display collective mood states. This general affective tone is not tied to any specific aspect of the group's activities or to any one individual, but rather pervades all the group's day-to-day activities. The group's mood may be so taken-for-granted that members do not realize its influence, but George believes that a positive group affect will lead to increases in a number of pro-group actions, including helping out other members, protecting the team, making constructive suggestions, and "spreading goodwill" during interpersonal encounters (George & Brief, 1992, p. 310).

————

group affective tone The collective emotional mood of a group.

- *Structural cohesion*: Smaller teams tend to be more cohesive than larger ones, in part because there are too many member-to-member ties to maintain in larger groups. Teams with high density social networks—multiple ties linking members to each other—outperform teams with less integrated social networks (Balkundi & Harrison, 2006), as do teams with performance-focused norms (Hackman, 2002).

Cohesion and Performance   When teams are first formed or when they show signs of performance decrements, the first intervention applied to improve the team's function usually involves building the team's cohesion (Hackman, 2002). However, and as discussed in detail in Chapter 5, the cohesion–performance relationship is a complex one. Meta-analytic studies suggest that cohesion improves teamwork among members, but that performance quality influences cohesion more than cohesion influences performance (Mullen & Copper, 1994). The work group may not be successful because it is cohesive, but instead it may be cohesive because it has succeeded in the past. Cohesive teams can also be spectacularly unproductive if the group's norms stress low productivity rather than high productivity.

F o c u s   12.2   E-groups: Building and Maintaining Trust in Virtual Teams

Teams require a group-level commitment to shared goals, but that does not mean members must sacrifice their own personal objectives for the good of the group. It does, however, require **interpersonal trust**: the mutual assurance that other members of the group will do what they are supposed to do and do so without too much supervision, pestering, or application of pressure (Kramer, 1999). As sociologist Gary Alan Fine concludes, "trust, which originates in confidence in information provided by groups and individuals and builds on personal commitment to the group, is translated into a 'pure' relationship that, when generalized to the collectivity, produces organizational loyalty. Trust anchors cohesion" (2003, p. 189).

Trust develops gradually as members interact with one another, for members require time to gather the information they need to estimate the strength of the relationships before they risk testing those relationships. Many factors influence trust in groups, but one particularly influential theory of trust—the **organizational trust model**—ties trust in others to perceptions of ability, benevolence, and integrity (Mayer, Davis, & Schoorman, 1995; Schoorman, Mayer, & Davis, 2007). At first, trust is largely determined by appraisals of the skills and abilities of other group members; individuals who are thought to be incompetent or untrained cannot be trusted to complete their tasks. Integrity, too, is also salient to group members early in the life of the group, as members determine if others accept the group's norms and standards as their own. Members will also, in time, add to ability and integrity a third quality—benevolence—as they learn about members' degrees of concern for their personal outcomes and for other members' outcomes (Aubert & Kelsey, 2003; Yakovleva, Reilly, & Werko, 2010).

All of these calculations are more difficult to make when team members collaborate using information technologies. Variously termed *e-teams*, *virtual teams* (VTs), and *distributed teams*, e-teams interact via computer-based communication technologies, and so the nature of these teams has changed as technology has changed. Whereas these teams once used e-mail and telephone-based conference calls as their primary means of communicating, most now augment these tools with videoconferencing, decision support software, file store systems, and even virtual-world conferencing. When teams first turned to these technologies, they often encountered difficulties in planning and strategizing relative to offline groups, and, in some cases, performance outcomes were disappointing. Over time, however, improvements in technological tools have increased the richness of e-team interactions, and members have become more skilled in using them. This improvement is due, in part, to a generational shift

---

interpersonal trust The confidence or certainty that other individuals will do what they are supposed to do even in the absence of social surveillance or pressure.

organizational trust model A theory of trust in groups and organizational settings that assumes people's trust in others is based on perceptions of ability, benevolence, and integrity.

in team composition: The newest members of teams grew up using technology in all aspects of their lives (Maynard et al., 2012).

How do members of e-teams learn to trust each other as they collaborate on projects from a distance? Sirkka Jarvenpaa, a researcher in business and management, examined this question by arranging for students in college classes at dozens of universities located around the world to work together virtually (Jarvenpaa et al., 1998, 2004). The groups were given eight weeks to complete a series of tasks, including a written paper and a working website that would count toward their course grade. These groups varied considerably in their overall levels of productivity, but also in their levels of trust. The high-trust groups expressed a high degree of confidence in each other and in their group, in part because members believed that their partners in the work had the skills they needed to be successful. Then, as the group worked on the project, members of high-trust groups also attributed integrity (e.g., "I am never doubtful about whether the other team members will do what they promised") and benevolence (e.g., "the other team members will do everything within their capacity to help the team perform") to the group and its members. The groups where trust was high tended to communicate with one another at much higher rates, with the content focused both on clarifying ambiguities about the group's task, but also exchanging personal information. Team B, for example, was a high-trusting group:

> Team B was above all characterized by frequent communication with a positive tone, by a very explicit division of labor, by acute attention to time management, and by proactive action. From the start, the team members sought to establish clear

goals for the project and also to minimize redundant efforts…. [T]his group exchanged more messages on "how," not just "what." That is, the members did not just divide work and work independently, but rather divided the work and gave each other detailed comments on how to accomplish the work….[T]eam B communicated their excitement and optimism in their first messages ("I am very excited about working on the project with all of you … "; "I am really looking forward to work with you … the assignments do look very interesting") ….Team B engaged in a continuous stream of communication. (Jarvenpaa et al., 1998, p. 46)

Team F, in contrast, was low in trust:

> Team F was characterized by both lack of individual initiative and an unwillingness to give substantial feedback to others' work….[T]eam F suffered from infrequent participation. Two individuals were primarily responsible for the total output of the project and both of them refused to put forth full individual effort given the lack of commitment from the other members. Although the team members expressed their interest and commitment in early messages, no member was willing to take charge. Each time something was needed, a member would ask who was going to do the activity rather than volunteering. This began with the first exercise in which a member said that someone needed to coordinate the activity and asked for a volunteer. No one volunteered. (Jarvenpaa et al., 1998, p. 51)

Team F never completed the assignment, whereas members of Team B stayed in touch with each other even after the project ended.

TEAM PERFORMANCE

Organizational experts recommend using teams to achieve excellence. No matter what system the experts propose—job enrichment, balanced score-card management, business process reengineering, activity-based management, or an updated version of management by objectives—most will tout the benefits of using teams to get work done. But do teams offer the best means to maximize human potential? This section examines the final segment

of the input–process–output model of teams: What do teams generate by way of direct and indirect outcomes? The analysis raises the question of evaluation—how effective are teams?—and also considers ways to improve teams.

Evaluating Teams

Viewed from an evolutionary perspective, teams are highly successful social organisms. From relatively humble beginnings in athletics, farming, and agriculture, teams have spread out to populate much of the world. Teams are gaining popularity as preferred approaches to management, and "how to" books on team methods continue to make the bestseller lists. Teams have also taken the place of some traditional groups as people's source of social connection, for more people report belonging to teams than they do to hobby, community, and social groups. Teams now have only one group to overtake in terms of popularity: religious groups. But do teams live up to their promise as systems for increasing productivity and members' well-being?

The Success of Teams Anecdotal evidence and research findings converge on a verdict that favors teams, but with reservations. Case study approaches are generally, but not uniformly, positive (Applebaum & Blatt, 1994). Texas Instruments, for example, increased productivity when it organized its employees into small groups whenever possible, took steps to build up team cohesiveness, and went to great lengths to establish clear goals based on realistic levels of aspiration (Bass & Ryterband, 1979). When a manufacturer in the United States shifted to teams, supportive supervision, participant leadership, organizational overlap among groups, and intensified group interaction, employee satisfaction increased and turnover decreased (Seashore & Bowers, 1970). Case studies have, however, uncovered examples of spectacularly ineffective teams. For example, Hackman (1990), after examining the effectiveness of 33 teams, had to revise the proposed title of the book he had planned: *Groups That Work* was given the subtitle (*and Those That Don't*) because he found considerable variation in performance quality across the teams he studied.

Field studies of the use of groups and team development generally support the wisdom of relying on teams (Sundstrom et al., 2000). The Harley-Davidson Motor Company, for example, dramatically transformed their production methods by shifting from a traditional command-and-control culture to one based on self-managing work teams, and the positive results of this conversion appear to depend in large part on the high level of cohesiveness maintained by these groups (Chansler, Swamidass, & Cammann, 2003). When researchers, through meta-analysis, examined the link between organizational change and performance, they found that companies that made multiple changes usually improved their performance and that group-level interventions were more closely linked to productivity than individual-level interventions (Macy & Izumi, 1993). A recent survey of people's satisfaction with their team memberships, however, suggests that members themselves are not so happy with their teams. Only 13% of the 23,000 managers, workers, and executives in one survey agreed that their "teams work smoothly across functions" (Covey, 2004, p. 371).

Beyond Productivity Teams are task-focused groups, and so the major criterion for determining their success is their performance: Do they reach the goals they, and others, set for them? By this standard, Mountain Medical was a success. The team learned to perform the new surgery quickly and safely, and this efficiency meant a better recovery for the patients *and* substantial savings for the hospital. The team needed less time in the operating room, and its efficiency was so high that it could do more operations than other teams. At a price of approximately $36,000 per case, the team proved to be both medically sound and economically profitable.

A team's productivity, however, is only one of the outputs that should be considered when determining its effectiveness. Mountain Medical may have become a crack surgical team, but what if the demands of the task were so great that members, feeling great pressure, decided to leave the group? What if the team was productive, but over time members grew to dislike working with each other? What if the Mountain Medical group became stagnant—repeating the motions required for the operation with each case, but losing the capacity to adapt and change that had made them a high-performance team in the first place?

Hackman (2002) suggests three key factors that should be considered when evaluating the success of a team. Task performance is the first and foremost criterion. Teams are created for the purpose of generating results, and a successful group is one that meets or exceeds agreed-upon "standards of quantity, quality, and timeliness" (Hackman, 2002, p. 23). But Hackman adds to this criterion two other, more indirect, outcomes: adaptive growth of the team as a whole and individual development of the members. Many teams can perform their basic work effectively, but over time they fail to profit from their experiences of working together. A truly successful team is one that grows stronger over time so that it can undertake even more challenging tasks in the future. Hackman (2002, p. 28) also feels that a high-performing team should contribute, in positive ways, "to the learning and personal well-being of individual team members":

> If the group prevents members from doing what they want and need to do, if it compromises their personal learning, or if members' main reactions to having been in the group are frustration and disillusionment, then the costs of generating the group product were too high. (Hackman, 2002, p. 29).

Suggestions for Using Teams

Teams are perhaps the most popular of all groups. No longer does a lone mechanic change your car's engine oil; most automotive shops claim a team of technicians will take care of your car's needs. Powerful moguls once ran all the large companies, but now executive leadership teams are in charge. Even scientists, long portrayed as loners working in solitude to unlock the secrets to the universe, are doing their work in groups: Science is now "team science" (Fiore, 2008).

But even the most optimistic appraisal of the available data on team effectiveness would suggest that there is room for improvement in the use of teams in performance settings. Teams are a group with extraordinary promise, but to fulfill that promise they must be implemented correctly, and members must be given assistance to use them to

their full advantage (Cordery, 2004; Kozlowski & Ilgen, 2006).

The Romance of Teams Teams, with their greater resources, goal-focus, and promise of increased productivity, are becoming the default choice in a variety of performance settings, but some caution is needed before rushing to form a team to deal with the task. Teams are also sometimes used because they are popular, rather than effective or appropriate. Just as the "romance of leadership" describes people's tendency to put too much faith in their leaders as saviors who will rescue them when they face difficult circumstances, the **romance of teams** is a "faith in the effectiveness of team-based work that is not supported by, or is even inconsistent with, relevant empirical evidence" (Allen & Hecht, 2004, p. 440). As the industrial/ organizational psychologist Edwin Locke and his colleagues (2001, p. 501) put it: "the emphasis on groups and teams has gone far beyond any rational assessment of their practical usefulness. We are in the age of groupomania."

A team approach may be the best choice in a given situation, but teams perform remarkably badly when given a task to do that is so simple, routine, or individualistic that collaboration is not only unnecessary; it is irritating. Teams should also be avoided when constraints in the situation are such that the basic requirements for a highly effective team (e.g., high rates of interaction, interdependence, consensual goals) cannot be met.

Fidelity of Team Innovations The popularity of team approaches has brought with it a significant drawback—in the rush to claim that they are using team methods, individuals sometimes call work

---

romance of teams The intuitive appeal of teams as effective means of improving performance in business and organizational settings, despite the relative lack of definitive evidence supporting their utility.

groups "teams" even though they lack the defining features of real teams. More than 80% of the executives, managers, and team members surveyed in one study reported that their teams lacked clear goals; that their members did not engage in creative discussion; that team members did not hold each other accountable for their assigned tasks; and that members of their team rarely initiated actions to solve problems (Covey, 2004). These are basic, essential qualities of teams, and, if they are lacking, these work groups likely are not actually teams.

These responses may indicate that the very concept of a team—individuals joining together in unified groups to pursue shared goals—is unworkable, but it may also be that team-based methods have not been properly implemented. Members of true teams cannot complete their work without interacting with each other. That interaction may involve exchanging information, sharing resources, or even lifting, carrying, or moving something together rather than individually, but the work requires each team member to contribute in some way (Aubé & Rousseau, 2005; Kauffeld & Lehmann-Willenbrock, 2012). Members of successful teams are also committed to group-level goals, and the rewards they receive should be based on attaining those goals rather than individual ones. Teams are also relatively well-structured and cohesive. If a team fails because it lacked these key ingredients, then the blame most likely rests with those who built the team rather than the team itself.

Training in Teamwork   Too many organizations create teams but then do little to help team members develop the skills they need to work in those teams. Only 29% of the organizations in one survey gave their teams any kind of training in teamwork or interpersonal relations, and only 26% based compensation (salary, bonuses) on team performance (Devine et al., 1999). Given the complexity of interpersonal and cognitive demands that teams require, members will likely need assistance in learning how to work effectively in them.

Fortunately, **team training** has robust effects on team effectiveness (Kozlowski & Ilgen, 2006). When team expert Eduardo Salas and his colleagues examined the effectiveness of several types of training interventions using meta-analysis, they concluded that (a) most methods work, but (b) the best ones focus on improving member coordination rather than communication strategies (Salas, Nichols, & Driskell, 2007). Cross-training, which involves rotating members throughout the various positions within the group, was particularly helpful, in that it provided members with a clear understanding of the demands associated with each role and the interconnections among members' responsibilities. Crew Resource Management (CRM), developed for training flight crews in teamwork procedures, has also been successfully applied to teams working in many other settings with considerable success. Salas, summarizing the available data, concludes that training team members yields demonstrably positive results, and he encourages organizations to make use of scientific principles and findings to improve their training of team members (Salas et al., 2012; Shuffler, DiazGrandados, & Salas, 2011).

Team Building   When well-meaning leaders and managers wish to help their teams work more effectively, they often turn to **team building** exercises, social events, and offsite training experiences. In the name of team building, organizations often place their teams in challenging environments so that the members will learn teamwork skills but also develop a sense of unity as a result of surviving the ordeal. Team building adventures, such as backpacking together in the wilderness, spending

---

team training Empirically supported instructional methods used to teach individuals and teams the cognitive, behavioral, and affective skills required for effective team performance.

team building Instructional methods used to promote the development of interpersonal and teamwork skills in individuals and teams.

the day in a ropes course, or playing a paintball game against a rival team, continue to be popular methods for increasing team unity.

These activities often function as group-level rewards for participating in teams, but they are no substitute for research-based team building interventions. Unlike team training—which is skill-focused and usually involves practice and feedback—team building is less structured and targets general relational skills. Team building, however, when properly implemented, does tend to improve team functioning (Klein et al., 2009). Salas and his colleagues identified four basic approaches to team building that target more specific problems that teams often face: goal setting, interpersonal relations (e.g., trust, communication, teamwork), role clarification, and problem solving procedures (Salas et al., 1999; Salas, Priest, & DeRouin, 2005). A meta-analytic review of studies of these types of team building methods suggests that all are relatively effective, but that goal-setting and role-clarification interventions led to more significant improvements (Klein et al., 2009).

Situational Support   A final condition for implementing teams is the degree of organizational support available to the teams (Kennedy et al., 2009). Organizations may, in the rush to implement teams, create them but then fail to provide them with the support they need to flourish. Features of the organizational context, such as support for technologically based group support systems, development of group-level reward systems to supplement or complement individual rewards, degree of collectivism in the organizational culture, and the availability of external coaches who can assist the team to navigate trouble spots, will increase the probability that team-based approaches will be successful (Mathieu et al., 2008). Other organizational features, such as traditional leadership styles, hierarchical patterns of organization, and individually based compensation systems, will increase the likelihood that team approaches will not prosper.

The case of **quality circles (QCs)** provides a lesson in the importance of providing support for group-level innovations. QCs were popular in the 1980s. These small, self-regulated decision-making groups usually included 5 to 10 employees who performed similar jobs within the organization. The groups were often led by a supervisor who had been trained for the role, but participation in the circle was often voluntary, and no monetary incentives were offered to those involved. These groups were thought to be excellent ways to increase workers' participation in the management of the organization and to increase productivity, efficiency, quality, and job satisfaction. Yet, by the 1990s, most of these groups were gone—the failure rate was between 60 and 70% (Tang & Butler, 1997). What happened?

QCs were not teams, and they had their own unique limitations—participants volunteered and were not compensated, and, in many cases, conflicts developed between participants and non-participants. Worse, however, was the lack of support provided the QCs. They were originally viewed as an easy means of increasing involvement and satisfaction, but the suggestions of QCs were rarely heeded by management. They were essentially powerless, and members soon realized that they were an ineffective means of achieving valued outcomes. A few transformed from QCs into true self-managing teams, but most were just abandoned (Lawler & Mohrman, 1985).

The lesson of QCs should not be ignored. As many as 90% of Fortune 500 companies implemented such methods in their plants, factories, and meeting rooms at the peak of their popularity, but the method did not take. Without institutional support or proper design, QCs rapidly disappeared. It would be unfortunate if teams went the way of quality circles, due to failures to implement them correctly, failures to train individuals to work effectively in them, and failures to support them.

---

quality circles (QCs) Small self-regulated groups of employees charged with identifying ways to improve product quality.

CHAPTER REVIEW

Are teams groups?

1. *Teams* are unified, structured groups that pursue consensual goals through coordinated, interdependent interaction.

   - Teams have become increasingly popular as a means of organizing work in a variety of settings, replacing alternative approaches, including *scientific management*.

   - Teams possess the basic qualities of a group—coordinated interaction, compelling purpose, interlocking interdependence, adaptive structures, and cohesive alliance—but teams exhibit these qualities with greater intensity than do groups in general.

   - Hackman's *real team model* stresses the unifying functions of a clear, challenging, and consequential task.

2. Devine's taxonomy of teams distinguishes between teams that focus on intellective, informational tasks and those that perform action tasks.

   - Teams that process information include management (executive, command), project (negotiation, commission, design), and advisory teams.

   - Teams that generate products include service, production, and action (performance, medical, response, military, transportation, sports) teams.

   - More specific types of teams include *crews and ad hoc*, member-founded, mandated (or concocted), and *cross-functional teams*.

3. Hackman's model of team autonomy distinguishes between four types of teams on the basis of their control over their processes and goals: manager-led, self-managing, self-designing, and self-governing.

4. The input–process–output (I-P-O) systems model guides much of the theoretical and empirical study of teams.

How does the team's composition influence its effectiveness?

1. Pisano, Bohmer, and Edmondson examined the performance of medical teams and related their effectiveness to composition and design.

2. Personality, as conceptualized within the five-factor model, is related to performance in teams. Conscientiousness and agreeableness are the two personality traits most closely linked to team effectiveness, followed by extraversion and openness.

3. A configural approach to team composition assumes that each member's fit within the team depends on the personal qualities of the other individuals who are on the team.

4. Members' team orientation and their knowledge, skills, and abilities, or KSAs, predict team effectiveness.

   - KSAs include both task competence and interpersonal skills.

   - The teams studied by Bennis and Biederman were staffed with highly motivated, skilled experts, and they were highly effective. Not all groups staffed with all experts are, however.

   - Individuals who function effectively in groups possess a working knowledge of how teams work (team knowledge KSAs).

5. There are advantages and disadvantages associated with team diversity.

   - Diversity increases the team's resources, providing more perspectives and sources of information.

   - Diverse groups may lack cohesion, because their members may perceive each other as dissimilar. If cohesion is essential for the group to succeed, a diverse group will be disadvantaged.

- Teams can minimize the negative side effects of diversity and maximize diversity's gains.

- Culturally diverse groups, such as the crews of the International Space Station, are generally less cohesive than less diverse groups, but this disadvantage is offset by increases in overall satisfaction and creativity.

6. Wood's meta-analysis of sex differences found that men and women do not differ in their effectiveness as team members.

- Research does not support the idea that all-male groups are more cohesive than all-female groups (the male bonding hypothesis).

- Groups that include a lone representative of a particular social category (tokens, or solos) may encounter problems of fairness, influence, and so on.

- Hackman's studies of performing orchestras indicate that the group's history and the larger social context in which the group is embedded influence the impact of a group's gender heterogeneity on performance.

What group processes mediate the input–output relationship?

1. The three key components of working in teams are teamwork, team cognition, and interpersonal engagement.

2. *Teamwork* is the psychological, behavioral, and mental work that members of the team carry out as they collaborate with one another on the various tasks and subtasks that they must complete to reach their desired goal.

3. Marks, Mathieu, and Zaccaro's teamwork process model stresses three key processes: transitioning, acting, and managing interpersonal relations among members.

4. Cognitive processes sustain team processes, including mental models, transactive memory, and learning.

- Members develop a collective understanding of the group and its task over time (mental model).

- Moreland and his associates examined the development of transactive memory by training individuals either in groups or individually, and then examining how much of that training transferred to a subsequent group situation.

- The Pisano, Bohmer, and Edmondson study of surgical teams identified the factors that promoted learning in some groups and reduced the learning capacity of others.

5. The five sources of a team's cohesion are social, task, collective, emotional, and structural.

- George's (1995) theory of *group affective tone*, applied to teams, suggests cohesive teams are more likely to display collective mood states.

- Cohesiveness promotes the exchange of information and trust, but cohesive teams do not necessarily outperform less cohesive ones.

- According to Fine, team members develop *interpersonal trust* over time as they learn which members of their team can be trusted to perform their requisite tasks adequately.

- Research conducted by Jarvenpaa and her colleagues indicates that teams that meet online rather than offline (e-teams or virtual teams) develop trust in a manner consistent with the *organizational trust model*.

How effective are teams, and how can they be improved?

1. Team approaches do not ensure success, but they are reliably associated with increases in effectiveness and member satisfaction.

2. Hackman identified three factors that define the success of a team: task performance, adaptive growth of the team, and individual development of the members.

3. In many cases, teams that perform poorly do not even qualify as teams, but are instead work groups. Also, teams are sometimes used because they are popular management tools

(the *romance of teams*) rather than effective ones. Locke describes the excessive use of teams in performance settings as "groupomania."

4. Salas and his colleagues have identified a number of ways to improve team function and have developed *team training* and *team building* techniques that can be used to teach team members the skills they need to perform more effectively in groups.

5. Experience with past group-level methods, such as *quality circles*, suggests that fidelity, training, and support are required to maximize effectiveness.

RESOURCES

Chapter Case: Mountain Medical's Cardiac Surgery Team

- "Organizational Differences in Rates of Learning: Evidence from the Adoption of Minimally Invasive Cardiac Surgery" by Gary P. Pisano, Richard M. J. Bohmer, and Amy C. Edmondson (2001) examined how the surgery teams at 16 different medical centers adjusted to a new surgical procedure that required a higher degree of teamwork (see, too, Edmondson, Bohmer, & Pisano, 2001).

The Nature of Teams

- "Group Behavior and Performance" by J. Richard Hackman and Nancy Katz (2010) is an integrative review of theories, models, and empirical studies of teams and organizations.

- "Team Effectiveness 1997–2007: A Review of Recent Advancements and a Glimpse into the Future" by John Mathieu, M. Travis Maynard, Tammy Rapp, and Lucy Gilson (2008) carefully examines the ever-expanding research literature dealing with teams in organizations by offering, for each primary topic, a set of exemplars that illustrate core concerns and conclusions.

- "Unraveling the Effects of Cultural Diversity in Teams: A Meta-Analysis of Research on Multicultural Work Groups" by Gunter K Stahl, Martha L Maznevski, Andreas Voigt, and Karsten Jonsen (2010) synthesizes the findings from 108 studies of over 10,000 teams to draw conclusions about the relationship between team diversity and performance.

Working in Teams

- "Enhancing the Effectiveness of Work Groups and Teams" by Steve W. J. Kozlowski and Daniel R. Ilgen (2006) reviews the current state of knowledge with regard to teams, with particularly detailed sections pertaining to cognitive processes, cohesion, emotions, and team design.

- *Team Effectiveness in Complex Organizations: Cross-disciplinary Perspectives and Approaches*, edited by Eduardo Salas, Gerald F. Goodwin, and C. Shawn Burke (2009), is a core resource of state-of-the-art chapters on teams in organizational settings.

Improving Teams

- *Collaborative Intelligence* by J. Richard Hackman (2011) combines years of experience working with teams with extensive research to offer a useful model of ways to help groups working on problems of security and intelligence reach their maximum effectiveness.

- "The 'Romance of Teams': Toward an Understanding of Its Psychological Underpinnings and Implications" by Natalie J. Allen and Tracy D. Hecht (2004) explores some of the practical and psychological factors that may be sustaining business and industry's current fascination for group-level approaches to productivity before reviewing research that suggests the use of teams may not be appropriate in many contexts.

CHAPTER

Conflict

CHAPTER OVERVIEW

Group members do not always get along well with one another. Even in the most serene circumstances, the group's atmosphere may shift rapidly so that once close collaborators become hostile adversaries. Because conflict is a ubiquitous aspect of group life, it must be managed to minimize its negative effects.

- What is conflict?
- What are the sources of conflict in groups?
- Why does conflict escalate?
- How can group members manage their conflict?
- Is conflict an unavoidable evil or a necessary good?

CHAPTER OUTLINE

The Roots of Conflict

Winning: Conflict and Competition

Sharing: Conflict over Resources

Controlling: Conflict over Power

Working: Task and Process Conflict

Liking and Disliking: Personal Conflicts

Confrontation and Escalation

Uncertainty → Commitment

Perception → Misperception

Soft Tactics → Hard Tactics

Reciprocity → Retaliation

Irritation → Anger

Few → Many

Conflict Resolution

Commitment → Negotiation

Misperception → Understanding

Hard Tactics → Cooperative Tactics

Retaliation → Forgiveness

Anger → Composure

Many → Few

The Value of Conflict: Redux

Chapter Review

Resources

Jobs versus Sculley: When Group Members Turn against Each Other

It was a time before the iPod, iPhone, and iMac. Apple Computers had started strong under the leadership of cofounder Steve Jobs, but now it was struggling to hold its own during a downturn in sales of technology and software. Jobs and the executive board decided they needed a chief executive officer (CEO) with a more traditional background in business. They picked John Sculley, president of PepsiCo, hoping that he would stabilize Apple, improve efficiency, and increase sales.

All worked well, for a time. Jobs and Sculley admired each other's strengths as leaders and visionaries, and they conferred constantly on all matters of production and policy. But they did not see eye-to-eye on key issues of corporate goals. Their working relationship dissolved into a series of disagreements, each one more problematic than the last. Both men played central roles as leaders in the company, but their differences in direction, vision, and style were disruptive. As the conflict over Jobs' pet project, the Macintosh (predecessor of the iMac), reached a peak, Sculley asked the executive board to strip Jobs of much of his authority. The group did so, reluctantly (Linzmayer, 2004).

Jobs did not go quietly into the night. He met individually with the board members, seeking to reverse the decision and win approval for his plan to fire Sculley in a corporate coup. He waited to spring his plan when Sculley was traveling in China, but Sculley was tipped off by one of the board members. Sculley cancelled his trip, called a board meeting, and confronted Jobs:

"It's come to my attention that you'd like to throw me out of the company, and I'd like to ask if that's true."

Jobs' answer: "I think you're bad for Apple, and I think you're the wrong person to run this company.... You really should leave this company.... You don't know how manufacturing works. You're not close to the company. The middle managers don't respect you."

Sculley, his voice rising in anger, replied, "I made a mistake in treating you with high esteem.... I don't trust you, and I won't tolerate a lack of trust."

Sculley then polled the board members. Did they support Sculley or Jobs? All of them declared great admiration for Jobs, but they felt that the company needed Sculley's experience and leadership. Jobs then rose from the table and said, "I guess I know where things stand," before bolting from the room (Sculley, 1987, pp. 251–252). Jobs later resigned from the company he had founded. He would return, eventually, but not until Sculley had resigned.

Jobs versus Sculley was one of corporate America's most spectacular conflicts, but it was no anomaly. Groups of all kinds experience periods of disagreement, discord, and friction. Good friends disagree about their weekend plans and end up exchanging harsh words. Families argue over finances, rules, and responsibilities. Struggling work teams search for a person who can be blamed for their inefficiency. College classes, angered by their professors' methods of teaching, lodge formal complaints with the dean. Rock bands split up due to artistic differences. When **conflict** occurs in a group, the actions or beliefs of one or more members of the group are unacceptable to and resisted by one or more of the other group members. Members stand against each other rather than in support of each other (De Dreu, 2010; Pruitt & Kim, 2004).

Why do allies in a group sometimes turn into adversaries? This chapter answers that question by tracing the course of conflict in groups. As Figure 13.1 suggests, the process begins when the group's routine interactions are disrupted by some sort of initial *disagreement*—differences of opinion, confusion about the group's goals, complaints about some group members not working hard enough, and the like. The group resolves some conflicts easily (*false* or *autistic conflicts*; Holmes & Miller, 1976). But others create a lack of alignment in the group and trigger the conflict cycle. The conflict intensifies as discussion gives way to arguing, emotions take the place of logic, and the once unified group splits into factions (*conflict escalation*). Eventually the conflict peaks and

---

conflict Disagreement, discord, and friction that occur when the actions or beliefs of one or more members of the group are unacceptable to and resisted by one or more of the other group members.

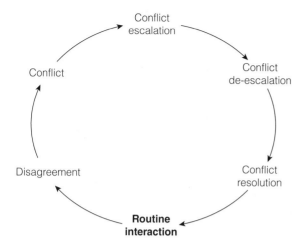

FIGURE 13.1 The course of conflict in groups.
SOURCE: © Cengage Learning 2014

begins to dissipate (*conflict de-escalation*) and the members seek and implement a way to resolve their differences (*conflict resolution*). The board of directors at Apple, for example, decided to support Sculley and so they demoted Jobs—a rather severe means of dealing with the dispute. This chapter focuses on conflict inside a group—between two or more members—or **intragroup conflict**. A second form of conflict—conflict between groups or **intergroup conflict**—is examined in the next chapter.

THE ROOTS OF CONFLICT

Conflict is everywhere. When the members of 71 groups were asked, "Did your group experience any conflict?" they identified 424 instances of interpersonal irritation (Wall & Nolan, 1987). When Robert Freed Bales and his colleagues used the *Interaction Process Analysis* (IPA) to record group

___

intragroup conflict Disagreement or confrontation between members of the same group.
intergroup conflict A disagreement or confrontation between two or more groups and their members that can include physical violence, interpersonal discord, and psychological tension.

interactions, some of the groups they observed spent as much as 20% of their time making hostile or negative comments (Bales & Hare, 1965). Researchers who asked group members to work together on a frustrating, impossible-to-solve task were startled by the intensity of the conflict that overtook the groups. In one particularly hostile group, members averaged 13.5 antagonistic comments *per minute* (French, 1941).

Most people, if given the choice, avoid situations that are rife with conflict (Witteman, 1991). Yet conflict seems to be an unavoidable consequence of life in groups. When individuals are sequestered away from other people, their ambitions, goals, and perspectives are their own concern. But a group, by its very nature, brings individuals into contact with other people—people who have their own idiosyncratic interests, motivations, outlooks, and preferences. As these individuals interact with one another, their diverse interests and preferences can pull them in different directions. Instead of working together, they compete against one another. Instead of sharing resources and power, members selfishly claim more than their fair share. Instead of accepting each other for who they are, members treat those they like better than those they dislike.

Winning: Conflict and Competition

Before Sculley joined Apple, Sculley was *independent* of Jobs. Sculley's success or failure in manufacturing and marketing did nothing to influence Jobs and vice versa. But when they both worked at Apple, they became *interdependent*, for they could influence each other's outcomes through individual and coordinated action (Schelling, 1960). At first, the two worked together cooperatively, for each one's success helped the other succeed. That relationship changed when they ran headlong into a dispute over the Mac. The two men refused to change their minds, and so their once *cooperative* relationship turned into a *competitive* one. For Sculley to succeed, Jobs would have to fail. For Jobs to succeed, Sculley would have to fail.

Cooperation and Competition   The solitary artist and rock climber struggle alone in the pursuit of their goals. Their **independence** from others means that, should they succeed or fail, only they are influenced. But people in groups are interdependent, so their outcomes are linked together. In some groups that link is based on **cooperation**, for the success of any one member of the group will improve the chances of success for the other members. Social psychologist Morton Deutsch (1949b) called this form of interaction *promotive interdependence*. But some groups pit individuals against one another. When playing backgammon, one person must win and the other must lose. When two coworkers both want to be promoted to office manager, if one succeeds the other will fail. In a footrace, only one runner will end up in first place. As Deutsch explained, such situations involve **competition**: The success of any one person means that someone else must fail. Deutsch (1949b) called this form of interaction *contrient interdependence*.

Cooperation and competition trigger different motivational systems. Because people cooperate *with* others, rather than *against* others, cooperative interdependence encourages sharing, trust, and collaboration rather than selfishness, suspicion, and sequestration. People describe group situations that call for cooperation as *friendly*, *involving*, and *pleasant*, and they feel *at ease* and *unconstrained* when they are in them (King & Sorrentino, 1983). Work units with high levels of cooperation have fewer latent tensions, personality conflicts, and verbal confrontations (Tjosvold, 1995). Members of cooperative groups, when negotiating their way through a problem, make fewer negative remarks but more positive statements, and they are more likely to discuss shared priorities (Scheia, Rognes, & Shapiro, 2011).

---

independence A performance situation that is structured in such a way that the success of any one member is unrelated to the chance of other members' succeeding.
cooperation A performance situation that is structured in such a way that the success of any one member of the group improves the chances of other members' succeeding.
competition A performance situation that is structured in such a way that success depends on performing better than others.

Competition, in contrast, causes people to expend greater effort in the pursuit of personal goals, and they often express more interest and satisfaction in their work (Tjosvold et al., 2006). However, because people compete *against* others instead of *with* others, competition also promotes conflict. When people compete, they cannot take pride in other group members' accomplishments, for each time someone else in the group excels, their own outcomes shrink. Competition also tends to elevate levels of greed and fear. Greed is an appetitive motive—a desire to seek and retain resources. Fear, in contrast, is an aversive motive—a worry that others will act in ways that maximize their outcomes but harm your own (Kelley et al., 2003). When members of a group have competing interests, during negotiations they make fewer positive remarks but more negative statements, and they are less likely to discuss shared priorities (Scheia et al., 2011).

The difference between these two orientations was evident when social neuroscientists used fMRI methods to examine the brain functioning of individuals who were cooperating and competing (Decety et al., 2004). They discovered that both forms of interaction recruited areas of the brain that have been implicated in the production of behavioral choices, particularly in uncertain circumstances. The cooperating brain, however, evidenced more activity in regions associated with the processing of social rewards and overall psychological satisfaction (the orbitofrontal cortex). In contrast, the competing brain evidence increased activation in two distinct areas: those responsible for intuiting the motivations of other people (medial prefrontal cortex) and those associated with distinguishing between the self and others (right inferior parietal cortex). In another study, researchers found that individuals who were suspicious of others' motives when interacting in a competitive situation showed elevated activity in the amygdala, an area of the brain thought to be responsible for feelings of fear (Bhatt et al., 2012).

Mixed-Motive Conflict Few situations involve pure cooperation or pure competition; the motive to compete is often mixed with the motive to cooperate. Sculley wanted to gain control over the Mac division but he needed Jobs' help with product development. Jobs valued Sculley's organizational expertise but he felt that Sculley misunderstood the company's goals. The men found themselves in a **mixed-motive situation**—they were tempted to compete and cooperate at the same time.

Researchers use a specialized technique known as the **prisoner's dilemma game (PDG)** to study mixed-motive situations. This procedure takes its name from an anecdote about two prisoners. The criminals, when interrogated by police detectives in separate rooms, are both offered a deal. They are told they can retain their right to remain silent, or they can confess and implicate their accomplice. If both remain silent, then they will be set free. If both confess, both will receive a moderate sentence. But if one confesses and the other does not, then the one who confesses will receive a minimal sentence and his partner will receive the maximum sentence. The prisoners, as partners in crime, want to cooperate with each other and resist the demands of the police. However, by defecting—competing with each other by confessing—then they may end up with a lighter sentence (Luce & Raiffa, 1957; Poundstone, 1992).

The PDG simulates this type of conflict by asking two people to choose cooperation or competition before knowing if their partner is going to cooperate or compete. The logic of the game is summarized in Figure 13.2. The two participants must individually pick one of two options, here labeled C and D. Option C is the *cooperative choice*. If both players pick C, then both will earn money. Option D is the defecting, *competitive choice*. If only one of the two players defects by picking D, that player will make money and the other will lose

---

mixed-motive situation A performance setting in which the interdependence among interactants involves both competitive and cooperative goal structures.
prisoner's dilemma game (PDG) A simulation of social interaction in which players must make either cooperative or competitive choices in order to win; used in the study of cooperation, competition, and the development of mutual trust.

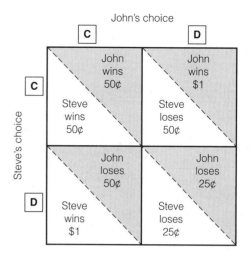

FIGURE 13.2 The prisoner's dilemma game. Two players, John and Steve, must select either option C (cooperation) or option D (defection). These choices are shown along the sides of the matrix. The payoffs for these joint choices are shown within each cell of the matrix. In each cell, John's outcomes are shown above the diagonal line and Steve's outcomes are shown below. For example, if Steve picks C and John picks C, they each earn 50¢. But if Steve picks C and John picks D, then Steve loses 50¢ and John wins $1.

money. But if both pick D, both will lose money. Figure 13.2 shows the payoff matrix that summarizes how much money the two will win or lose in each of the four possible situations:

1. If John chooses C and Steve chooses C, both earn 50¢.

2. If John chooses C and Steve chooses D, John loses 50¢ and Steve earns $1.

3. If John chooses D and Steve chooses C, John earns $1 and Steve loses 50¢.

4. If John chooses D and Steve chooses D, both lose 25¢.

The PDG captures the essence of a mixed-motive situation. Players want to maximize their own earnings, so they are tempted to defect (Option D). But most people realize that their partner also wants to maximize his or her profit—and if both defect, then they will both lose money. So they are drawn to cooperate (Option C), but they fear that their partner may defect. Players usually cannot communicate with each other, and they cannot wait to pick until after they learn their partner's choice. In the *single-trial* version, players only make their choices one time. In the *iterated* version, players play multiple rounds. Each pair of choices is termed a *trial* or *round*.

Which option do most people pick in the PDG? Some cooperate and some compete, with the proportion of cooperators to competitors varying depending on the relationships between members, their expectations, personalities, and a variety of other factors (Weber & Messick, 2004). If, for example, the gains for competing relative to cooperating are increased (e.g., people would earn $2 instead of only $1 by competing in the game shown in Figure 13.2), people compete more. When people are told they are playing the "Wall Street Game," they compete more than if the simulation is called the "Community Game" (Ross & Ward 1995). If the instructions refer to the other person as the "opponent," then competition increases, but the label "partner" shrinks competitiveness (Burnham, McCabe, & Smith, 2000). And, if people know they will be playing multiple trials against the same person, then cooperation increases (Van Lange, Klapwijk, & Van Munster, 2011). In one study, for example, people played the PDG in large groups of 30 to 50 other people. The game randomly paired people together on each trial, but the odds of being paired with the same person repeatedly were varied experimentally from low to high. The greater the chances of playing with a person in the future, the more cooperative players became (Bó, 2005).

Behavioral Assimilation When people play the iterated PDG, their choices are usually influenced by their partner's prior choices. When playing with someone who consistently makes cooperative choices, people tend to cooperate themselves. Those who encounter competitors, however, soon adopt this strategy, and they, too, begin to

compete. Gradually, then, **behavioral assimilation** occurs as group members' choices become synchronized over time.

The *norm of reciprocity* is to blame (or credit) for this assimilative process. As noted in Chapter 3, the norm of reciprocity sustains mutuality in exchange: When people who help you later need help, the norm of reciprocity urges you to help them in return. However, the norm of reciprocity also implies that people who harm you are deserving of harm themselves. The converse of "You scratch my back and I'll scratch yours" is "An eye for an eye, a tooth for a tooth." If one group member criticizes the ideas, opinions, or characteristics of another, the victim of the attack will feel justified in counterattacking unless some situational factor legitimizes the aggression of the former (Falk & Fischbacher, 2006).

Unfortunately, negative reciprocity tends to be stronger than positive reciprocity. Although people consistently return kindness with kindness and thereby maintain equity in their relationship and reward positive behavior, they are even more likely to punish an unkindness with hostility. A cooperative person who runs into a competitive partner is more likely to begin to compete before the competitive person begins to cooperate, so as a result a partner turns into an opponent faster than an opponent turns into an ally (Kelley & Stahelski, 1970a, 1970b, 1970c). This asymmetry in reciprocity is even greater when members believe others' acted deliberately. A person who intentionally treats another person in a positive way may receive a positive response back, but when a person deliberately mistreats another person, a negative payback is assured (Offerman, 2002).

Social Value Orientation (SVO) Jobs was born in 1955 in San Francisco, California. He never finished college, and he was a practicing Zen Buddhist. John Sculley was born in 1939, but as a

---

behavioral assimilation The eventual matching of the behaviors displayed by cooperating or competing group members.

child lived in Bermuda, Brazil, and Europe. He attended Brown University and received an MBA from the Wharton School of Business at the University of Pennsylvania. But the two were alike in one respect: They were both highly competitive.

What makes one person more competitive than another? According to **social value orientation (SVO)** theory, people's willingness to cooperate or compete is determined by two sets of values: their concern for their own outcomes and their concern for other people's outcomes. Proself individuals seek to maximize their personal gains; when they play the PDG, they want to earn as many points as they can. Prosocials, in contrast, are also concerned with others' gains and losses; they want to maximize others' outcomes (Van Lange et al., 2007). When both orientations are taken into account, SVO theory identifies four distinct orientations:

- *Individualists* are proself and concerned only with their own outcomes. They make decisions based on what they think they personally will achieve, without concern for others' outcomes. They neither interfere with nor assist other group members, for they focus only on their own outcomes. Their actions may indirectly impact other group members, but such influence is not their goal.

- *Competitors* are proself and strive to maximize their own outcomes, but they also seek to minimize others' outcomes (their prosocial value is low). They view disagreements as *win–lose situations* and find satisfaction in forcing their ideas on others. Concessions and compromise, they believe, are only for losers. A competitor believes that "each person should get the most he can" and plays to win even when playing a game with a child (Brenner & Vinacke, 1979, p. 291).

_____

social values orientation (SVO) The dispositional tendency to respond to conflict settings in a proself or prosocial way; cooperators, for example, tend to make choices that benefit both parties in a conflict, whereas competitors act to maximize their own outcomes.

- *Cooperators* are both prosocial and proself, so they strive to maximize their own outcomes and others' outcomes as well. They value accommodative interpersonal strategies that generate *win–win situations*. A cooperator would argue that "when people deal with each other, it's better when everyone comes out even." If they play a game with a child, they would be more likely to make sure "no one really wins or loses" (Brenner & Vinacke, 1979, p. 291).

- *Altruists* are prosocial but not proself, so they are motivated to help others who are in need. They willingly sacrifice their own outcomes in the hopes of helping others achieve some gain.

Competitors are more likely to find themselves in conflicts. Their style is abrasive, spurring cooperative members to react with criticism and requests for fairer treatment. Competitors, however, rarely modify their behavior in response to these complaints, because they are relatively unconcerned with maintaining smooth interpersonal relations (De Dreu, Weingart, & Kwon, 2000). Hence, competitors try to overwhelm cooperators who sometimes respond by becoming competitive themselves. For cooperators, the perception of others' cooperativeness is *positively* correlated with their own cooperativeness. If they think that others will cooperate, they cooperate. For competitors, perceptions of others' cooperativeness is *negatively* correlated with their own cooperativeness. If they think that others will cooperate, they compete (Smeesters et al., 2003). When two competitors meet, the result is an intense conflict like that seen at Apple. When competitors lose, they often withdraw from the group altogether (Shure & Meeker, 1967).

Competitors (and altruists, for that matter) are relatively rare; most people are either cooperators or individualists. However, individualists seek their own outcomes without regard for others, so more individualists usually means more conflict (Balliet, Parks, & Joireman, 2009). In one study, researchers first measured peoples' SVOs and then created four-person groups with varying mixtures of individualists and cooperators. The groups were then set to work on a task that required considerable negotiation and compromise. As expected, the groups composed entirely of cooperators were more likely to use more diplomatic negotiation tactics than were groups of individualists. This effect, however, was the result of cooperators adapting their styles to match the composition of the group. Finding themselves in a group with all cooperators, they cooperated. But if they were members of groups with individualists, they became less cooperative. Individualists, however, did not make adjustments—they maintained their confrontational style of interaction when interacting with other cooperators and with other individualists (Weingart et al., 2007).

Men, Women, and Competition   What if John Sculley were Joanna Sculley—a woman rather than a man? Would she and Jobs have battled as fiercely? Or would Joanna have used less competitive methods for settling the dispute?

Common sex role stereotypes generally assume that men are more competitive than women. Stories of executives conjure up images of individuals who are driven, ruthless, self-seeking, and male. But some versions of evolutionary theory suggest that men are more cooperative than women. The male bonding hypotheses—the idea that men's survival was dependent on their ability to form cohesive groups with other men—suggests that men may be more cooperative than women, at least when interacting with other men (Thayer & Hudson, 2010).

The data on the matter are also mixed. Some studies find men to be more competitive, but others suggest women are. For example, men are somewhat more competitive than women when competition is a riskier alternative or will yield a greater payoff (Simpson, 2003). Women are more likely to endorse prosocial SVOs relative to men (Knight & Dubro, 1984). Women's reactions during conflicts are also more nuanced than men's. If, for example, their partner is attractive, women make more cooperative choices. If they do not like their partner, they are more likely to compete (Kahn, Hottes, & Davis, 1971). Men do tend to cooperate more in

all-male groups than do women in all-female groups, but women are also more likely to cooperate in situations that involve sharing rather than competing (Balliet et al., 2011). Given these various findings, when researchers used meta-analytic methods to combine the results of 272 studies of the responses of over 30,000 participants, they discovered that the relationship between sex and cooperativeness was negligible (Balliet et al., 2011).

Competition in High Stakes Situations   Laboratory studies of conflict often involve relatively small amounts of remuneration, leading some to wonder how individuals respond when the benefits of winning are much greater. Fortunately, a number of televised game shows, such as *Weakest Link* and *Survivor*, create situations in which the individuals who out-compete others have much to gain. On *Survivor*, for example, only one contestant can win the grand prize, and members must vote a person out of the group each time their team loses. On *Weakest Link*, members cooperate by answering strings of questions, but after each round they vote to identify and eliminate the weakest player from their teams. The competition among players invariably introduces tension, conflict, and hostility, dividing the players one against the other.

Researchers, to determine if people become more competitive when the stakes are high, systematically analyzed the results on one particular televised game show, *Friend or Foe*. The six players pair up into three teams who compete to build up winnings. After each round, the team with the lowest score drops out until only one team is left. But all the teams, as they leave, must decide how they will split their earnings. Each player has a button that no one else can see, and they can press the button if they wish to compete instead of cooperate. The possible outcomes are: (a) Friend–Friend: Neither player presses the button and they split their earnings; (b) Friend–Foe: The player who presses the button keeps all the earnings; and (c) Foe–Foe: Both players press the button and they lose all their earnings. Unlike choices made in experimental studies, their choice to cooperate or compete will be a very public one, and they are also negotiating for real money. The average amount that the group plays for is $3,705, although some teams try for much more—as much as $16,400 in one case.

When researchers examined the choices of over 100 teams making their choice in the game, they discovered that players defected, trying to take all the money, 50% of the time. Men tended to compete more than women (55% vs. 46%), and younger players were much more competitive than older ones (59% vs. 37%). Hence, competitive men who were paired with older women tended to take home much more money than all other players. The size of the stake, however, was unrelated to competitiveness. Even when people were playing for substantial amounts, they were as likely to cooperate as they were to compete. This competitive urge ended up saving the game show producers a considerable amount of money. Contestants left nearly $100,000 behind as a result of two players making the fatal Foe–Foe choice (List, 2006; Oberholzer-Gee, Waldfogel, & White, 2010).

Application: Cooperative and Competitive Classrooms Despite the strong causal relationship between competition and conflict, most educational settings are competitive places—students compete for grades, honors, and class rank. Competition prompts many students to expend greater effort, but it also focuses attention on performance rather than mastery, and some students eventually conclude that "learning something new" is not nearly as important as "performing better than others" (Ames, 1987, p.134). In cooperative classes, students enhance their outcomes by helping others achieve success, but in competitive classes, students profit from others' errors. Students in competitive settings have two options open to them. First, they can improve their own work in the hopes that they rise above the others. Second, they can undermine, sabotage, disrupt, or interfere with others' work so that their own becomes better by comparison (Amegashie & Runkel, 2007).

Deutsch studied the dark side of competition by creating two different grading systems in his college classes. In competitive classes, students' grades were relative: The individual who did the best in the group would get the highest grade, whereas the individual who did the worst would get the lowest grade. Deutsch created cooperative groups as well. These students worked together in groups to learn the material, and everyone in the group received the same grade. As Deutsch predicted, conflict was much more pronounced in the competitive groups. Members reported less dependency on others, less desire to win the respect of others, and greater interpersonal animosity. Members of cooperative groups, in contrast, acted friendlier during the meetings, were more encouraging and supportive, and communicated more frequently (Deutsch, 1949a, 1949b, 1979, 1980).

Deutsch is not the only educator and researcher who has tested the relative benefits of cooperative and competitive classroom goals (Meece, Anderman, & Anderman, 2006). When educational psychologists David Johnson and Roger Johnson (2009) undertook a meta-analytic review of research in this area, they identified 1,200 studies that examined cooperation, competition, and learning. Their analysis indicated that students in classrooms that stress cooperation rather than individualism or competition work harder, display better psychological adjustment, and have higher self-esteem. Just as importantly, students in cooperative classes outperformed those in competitive ones: They displayed better reasoning skills, perspective-taking ability, and higher levels of achievement overall. Given these robust results, Johnson and Johnson strongly encourage educators to reevaluate their reliance on competitive goal structures and shift to more group-centered, cooperative methods of instruction.

Sharing: Conflict over Resources

Steve Jobs faced a dilemma. The board of directors of Apple had hired John Sculley to be the CEO, and they expected all the company's employees to support Sculley's initiatives. But Sculley called for sacrifices, for he wanted to shift personnel and financial resources away from Jobs' division. Jobs could have accepted this decision and gone along with the group's decision, but instead he chose his own path.

Group life, by its very nature, can be a **social dilemma** for group members. As individuals, members try to extract resources from the group and minimize the amount of time and energy the group takes from them. Yet, as group members, they also wish to contribute to the group, for they realize that their selfishness can destroy the group. Conflicts arise when individualistic motives trump group-oriented motives, and the collective intervenes to redress the imbalance.

Commons Dilemmas Consider the "tragedy of the commons." Shepherds with adjoining farms all share a common grazing field. The large pastures can support many sheep, so the shepherds grow prosperous. Then, one or two shepherds decide to add a few sheep to their flock so that they can make more profit. Others notice the extra sheep, so they, too, add to their flocks. Soon, the commons is overgrazed, and all the sheep die of starvation (Hardin, 1968).

This **social trap**, or **commons dilemma**, occurs when members share a common resource that they want to maintain for their group, but individual members are tempted to take more than their fair share (Pruitt, 1998). But if everyone acts selfishly, the common resource will be destroyed. Members are tempted by the short-term gains that will bring about long-term losses to the collective (Kramer, 2011).

Researchers have studied when people choose self-interest over group interest using a harvesting game. Participants are told that they are being given the opportunity to make a withdrawal from a pool that contains some type of valued resource, such as tokens that can be exchanged for money. They can draw as many tokens as they want from a pool, but the pool is a renewable resource: After each round of harvesting, it regenerates in proportion to the number of tokens remaining in the pool. So, if members draw out too many tokens, the pool is permanently exhausted; cautious removal of only a small number of tokens ensures replenishment of the resource. Nonetheless, the harvesters usually deplete the pool quickly, even when they know the pool is quite small and will grow if they leave some behind (Brewer & Kramer, 1986; Yamagishi, 1994).

How can groups escape this dilemma? Experience in dealing with the situation, communication, and social pressures that encourage conservation are all critical factors. People who are given two chances to harvest a pool are much more cooperative the second time, for they have learned what can happen if they act selfishly (Allison & Messick, 1985a). Communication, so long as it focuses on strategy, also increases prosocial resource conservation (Brechner, 1977). The commons dilemma can also be partially remedied by developing, within the group, normative standards that stress efficient consumption of the resource rather than greedy exploitation. When members are aware of others' choices, they tend to conform to those choices so long as the group is harvesting very little from a small pool but is taking more from a larger one (Brucks, Reips, Ryf, 2007).

Public Goods Dilemmas The commons is a "take some" dilemma: Members can draw on the resource, but they must not take too much. A **public goods dilemma**, in contrast, is a "give some" dilemma: Members are asked to contribute to the group, but members often don't fulfill this obligation. For example, some residents who use their community's resources, such as public parks, highways, and libraries, may not contribute back to the community by paying taxes. Similarly, not all

---

social dilemma An interpersonal situation where individuals must choose between maximizing their personal outcomes or maximizing their group's outcomes.

social trap (or **commons dilemma**) A social dilemma when individuals can maximize their outcome by seeking personal goals rather than the collective goals, but if too many individuals act selfishly, then all members of the collective will experience substantial long-term losses.

---

public goods dilemma A social dilemma when one may or may not not contribute any resources in support of a public good (such as a park or a highway system) but also cannot be excluded for failing to contribute.

group members who enjoy the benefits of membership contribute their share to the group's resources. When students work on class projects as teams, one member may miss meetings and leave assignments undone, but still get a good grade because the group scores well on the final project. When everyone is asked to bring a covered dish to a reception, a few attendees will show up empty-handed. We met these people in Chapter 10's analysis of social loafing: These individuals are *free riders*.

Free riding can spark group conflict. When group members in a college class described the sources of conflicts in their project groups, more than 35% of their comments targeted disputes over workload. People had much to say about the dedication of their comembers to the group's goals, for some members of the group did not put in as much time, effort, and resources as the others expected (Wall & Nolan, 1987). Free riding can also be contagious, for some group members, seeing that others are free riding, may reduce their own contributions or withdraw from the group altogether (the "sucker effect"; see Komorita & Parks, 1994, for a review). Fortunately, the opposite of free riding—consistent contributing—is also contagious: Free riding decreases in groups where one or more of the members consistently contributes at a high level even though others in the group do not (Weber & Murnighan, 2008). A note of warning, however, for those who pride themselves on doing more than their fair share: Paradoxically, members who are too self-sacrificing—they give much to the common good but take nothing for themselves—are sometimes excluded from the group. They set a standard that others in the group cannot reach (Parks & Stone, 2010).

Free riding poses a significant threat to effective group functioning. As an evolutionary perspective suggests, humans' ancestral groups could not survive if too many of their members failed to do their share of their group's work. In consequence, humans are equipped with the mental apparatus needed to detect free riders. Groups can tell the difference, for example, between a person whose lack of contribution is unintentional—someone, for example, who is incompetent, ill, or just confused about the group's requirements—and a person who is intentionally avoiding work (Delton et al., 2012). But once the group identifies a shirker in their midst, they intervene in various ways. Some groups remind those who contribute too little of their obligations and extract promises of improved performance. Others publically reward those who do their share. Groups also impose costs on the free riders—criticism, public humiliation, physical punishment, and fines are all ways to punish free riders. People are even willing to impose costs on themselves if it means that free riders can be punished in some way (Balliet, Mulder, & Van Lange, 2011).

Fairness Dilemmas Jobs and Sculley, even many years after their conflagration, disagreed not only about the causes, but also the essential facts. Sculley (2011) denied ever firing Jobs. He admits that he reassigned Jobs, but it was Jobs' decision to resign. Jobs, in contrast, remembers being fired. In a commencement address given at Stanford University in 2005, he asked, "How can you get fired from a company you started?" (quoted in Ong, 2012). Jobs did not consider the board's decision to be a fair one, but Sculley did.

Fairness judgments are determined by two forms of social justice: procedural and distributive. As discussed in Chapter 11, *procedural justice* is based on the methods used to make decisions about the allocation of resources, whereas *distributive justice* concerns how rewards and costs are shared by (distributed across) the group members. In the case of Jobs versus Sculley, the fairness of firing Jobs depends in part on how the board of directors made their decision. If they weighed the decision carefully, sought all the data they needed, and discussed the problem with all concerned parties, then the decision would be a fair one—at least in terms of procedural justice (van Prooijen et al., 2008). Distributive justice, however, asks, "Did Jobs get what he deserved?" When one's piece of cake seems smaller than it should be, when others get the best seats right up near the front of the bus, when workers who do the same job are paid different salaries, when the person who started the company is fired by the person he hired to help him run the company, some may feel that distributive justice has not been done.

Distributive justice depends, in part, on the norms the group uses to allocate rewards. In some groups, such as Apple, rewards are given for productivity and performance—and individuals who contribute little can expect little in return. Other groups, in contrast, base the distribution of rewards on other factors, such as status, duration of membership, or need. Some common distributive norms follow:

- *Equity:* The group gives more to members who have done more for the group. Someone who has invested a good deal of time, energy, money, or other type of input in the group receives more than individuals who have contributed little.

- *Equality:* The group treats all members equally, no matter what their contribution to the group. For example, a person who contributes 20% of the group's resources receives as much as the person who contributes 40%.

- *Power:* The group allocates more of its resources to those with more authority, status, or control over the group and less to those in lower-level positions ("to the victor go the spoils").

- *Need:* The group takes into consideration the level of need of each of its members and allocates more of its resources to those with the greatest needs and less to those who need less, irrespective of how much these individuals contributed to the group. This norm is sometimes termed the *social responsibility norm* since those who have more are expected to share with those who have less.

Equity versus Equality   Money (and other resources) may not be the root of all evil, but its distribution often causes conflicts within groups (Allison & Messick, 1990; Samuelson & Allison, 1994). Members who contribute less to the group often argue in favor of the equality norm, whereas those who contribute more tend to favor the equity norm. Women prefer equality over equity even when they outperform their coworkers (Wagner, 1995). Members of larger groups prefer to base allocations on equity, whereas members of smaller groups stress equality (Allison, McQueen, & Schaerfl, 1992). Some countries stress equality and need more than equity, as do different organizations and groups within each country (Fischer et al., 2007). Members of groups working on tasks when one individual's contributions are critically important for success prefer equitable distributions over egalitarian ones.

Group members who feel that they are receiving too little for what they are giving—*negative inequity*—sometimes withdraw from the group, reduce their effort, or turn in work of lower quality. Receiving too much for what one has given—*positive inequity*—sometimes causes people to increase their efforts so they deserve what they get, but it is negative inequity that causes conflict (Fortin & Fellenz 2008; Rivera & Tedeschi, 1976). These reactions are driven, in part, by self-interest. Most people strive to maximize their personal rewards, so they react negatively when they are denied what they feel they deserve. But people also react to negative inequity because they recognize that the rewards the group gives them are an indication of their status and prestige within the group—if the group gives more to Sculley than to Jobs, then the group must think Sculley is better than Jobs. In general, however, members' reactions are shaped more by procedural justice than distributive justice. Members who believe that their group has acted with integrity while allocating rewards feel a sense of pride in their group (Blader & Tyler, 2003, 2009).

Inequity in Nonhuman Groups   Humans are not the only species with a highly evolved sense of distributive justice, at least according to research conducted by primatologists Sarah Brosnan, Frans de Waal, and their colleagues. They trained capuchin monkeys to work for food rewards. The monkeys, when given a token, would be rewarded with a small portion of food when they handed the token back. These monkeys would work for a bit of cucumber (low-value reward), but they preferred a grape above all else (high-value reward).

Once trained, Brosnan and de Waal set up different payment conditions to see how the monkeys would respond. In the equity condition, two monkeys worked side-by-side for the same low-value reward; and work they did, diligently exchanging a coin for food. In the inequity condition, the monkeys did the same amount of work, but one of them received the high-value reward and the other was only given the low-value reward. The latter monkeys were none too pleased. In addition to vocalized complaints and gestures of defiance, they refused to continue exchanging the tokens for food, and, when given their food reward, they would indicate their displeasure by returning it—aiming for the researchers. These reactions were worse still in a third, "free food" condition. Conflict reached its peak when the one monkey was given grapes without even having to trade coins back and forth (Brosnan & de Waal, 2003; de Waal, 2006).

De Waal and Brosnan conclude that these monkeys' reactions were guided by their instinctive sense of fairness, for they appeared to recognize the inequity of the situation. But not all primate species react so negatively to such inequities. Rhesus monkeys, for example, do not seem to be sensitive to distributive justice, perhaps because they live in small groups with very differentiated chains of authority that create great inequalities in the distribution of rewards. They also note that the monkeys that prospered under the inequitable arrangement showed no sign of concern over getting more than their fair share. They were not so altruistic that they shared their ill-gotten gains with their unrewarded partner.

Responsibility Dilemmas When a group completes its work, members often dispute who deserves credit and who deserves blame. The board of directors at Apple blamed Jobs' emphasis on design over functionality for the company's economic misfortunes. Sculley credited his skilled marketing interventions for Apple's prosperity in the years following Jobs' dismissal. Jobs blamed Sculley for ruining the company.

Just as individuals carry out extensive appraisals of their own successes and failures, so do group members devote significant cognitive resources to the analysis and comprehension of their collective endeavors. This appraisal, however, is complicated by the collaborative nature of group activities. Group members must identify the factors that contributed to each member's performance, assign credit and blame, and make decisions regarding rewards, power, and status. Each group member, however, generally sees himself or herself as somewhat more worthy of credit than others in the group. This tendency, termed **egocentrism**, can be easily documented just by asking people to indicate how responsible they feel they are for any group activity, where 0% means they are not responsible at all and 100% that they alone are responsible for what the group has achieved. These scores, when summed across group members, invariably exceed 100% (Ross & Sicoly, 1979; Savitsky, 2007).

This bias occurs, in part, because people are far more aware of their own contributions than those of others—they literally see themselves busily contributing to the group effort and overlook the work of others. Thus, egocentrism can be reduced by asking group members to think about their collaborators' contributions, a process termed *unpacking*. When, for example, the authors of multiauthored research articles were asked to estimate their responsibility for the joint project, they were less egocentric if they were also asked to estimate how much the other coauthors had contributed (Caruso, Epley, & Bazerman, 2006; Savitsky et al., 2005).

Group members' claims of responsibility can be either group-serving (*sociocentric*) or self-serving (*egocentric*). After success, members may praise the entire group for its good work with such comments as "We all did well" or "Our hard work really paid off." Likewise, after failure, members may join together in blaming outside forces and absolving one another

---

egocentrism Giving oneself more responsibility for an outcome or event than is warranted; often indexed by comparing one's own judgments of personal responsibility to judgments of responsibility allocated by others.

of blame. Because these types of responsibility claims protect and enhance the group, they lower the levels of relationship conflict within the group (Peterson & Behfar, 2003). Frequently, however, self-serving members blame one another for the group's misfortunes or take the lion's share of the credit after a success (Forsyth et al., 2002; Rantilla, 2000).

These self-serving attributions result in conflict and a loss of cohesion (Leary & Forsyth, 1987). In one study, members of successful and unsuccessful groups were asked to complete a confidential report of their responsibility and others' responsibilities for the outcome. Then, to their surprise, this report was shared with other group members. Unbeknown to the group members, the actual reports were switched with standard ones indicating that another group member either took high, moderate, or low responsibility for the outcome. Group members who blamed others for failure or tried to claim the lion's share of responsibility after success were not well-liked (Forsyth et al., 1981). Other studies confirmed that those who engage in self-serving attributions in groups are often viewed as braggarts, narcissists, or even untrustworthy liars, but that those who share responsibility appropriately are considered trustworthy teammates (Greenberg, 1996; Schlenker, Pontari, & Christopher, 2001).

Controlling: Conflict over Power

The Sculley versus Jobs conflict was rooted in each one's desire to control the company. Jobs thought that he would be content to allow another person to make key decisions about Apple's future, but when those decisions did not mesh with his own vision, he sought to regain control. Sculley believed that Jobs was undermining his authority. Both Jobs and Sculley sought the power they needed to control the company, and their power struggle caused turmoil within the group.

As noted in earlier chapters, the differentiation of members in terms of status, prestige, and power is a ubiquitous feature of groups. As the group strives to coordinate its members' task-directed activities, some individuals will begin to assert more authority over the others. Those who occupy

positions of authority have the right to issue orders to others who are expected to follow those directives. Once individuals gain power over others, they tend to defend their sources of power through manipulation, the formation of coalitions, information control, and favoritism. These power processes occur with great regularity in groups, but they nonetheless cause waves of tension, conflict, and anger to ripple through the group (Coleman, 2000; Sell et al., 2004).

Infighting, power struggles, and disputes are particularly common in business and corporate settings. Sociologist Calvin Morrill (1995) spent several years collecting ethnographic data on the sources and consequences of conflict between executives in corporations. His analysis confirmed the image of companies as arenas for power struggles, when group members compete with each other for power, promotions, and prominence, often by using manipulative, illicit tactics. Contests of authority and power were so commonplace in one company that the executives developed an elaborate set of terms and expressions pertaining to company politics, which Morrill recorded much like an anthropologist would record the rituals and incantations of the members of an isolated tribe. An *ambush* was a "covert action to inconvenience an adversary" (synonyms: *bushwhack* and *cheap shot*); *blindsiding* was "an intentional and surprising public embarrassment by one executive at another's expense"; an *outlaw* was "an executive who handles conflict in unpredictable ways but who is regarded as especially task competent." In some cases, this maneuvering would result in a *meltdown*—a "physical fight between executives" (1995, pp. 263–265).

Working: Task and Process Conflict

When Sculley first went to work at Apple, he and Jobs disagreed about such things as marketing, research and development, and long-term strategy, but they worked through these disagreements. They also disagreed about the way the company should operate and how decisions should be made. These disagreements, in the end, were their undoing.

Task Conflict   As the group goes about its work on shared tasks and activities, members sometimes disagree with one another. This type of conflict is termed **task conflict** (or *content conflict* or *substantive conflict*), because it stems from disagreements about issues that are relevant to the group's goals and objectives. No group of people is so well-coordinated that its members' actions mesh perfectly, so conflicts over group tasks are inevitable. Groups and organizations use such conflicts to make plans, increase creativity, solve problems, decide issues, and resolve misunderstandings. Periods of tension and disunity are so typical in groups that a "storming stage" or "fight-and-flight" stage is included in most theories of group development (see Chapter 5). Sculley and Jobs, as the leaders of Apple, were supposed to argue and debate over substantive issues having to do with making and selling computers.

Process Conflict   Task conflict occurs when ideas, opinions, and interpretations clash. **Process conflict**, or procedural conflict, occurs when strategies, policies, and methods clash. Group members may find themselves uncertain about how to resolve a problem, with some championing continued discussion and others favoring a vote. The leader of the group may make decisions and initiate actions without consulting the group; but the group may become irritated if denied an opportunity to participate in decision making (Smoke & Zajonc, 1962). Members dislike the way roles have been allocated within the group, and they try to change their positions and responsibilities (Spell et al., 2011). Members who are assigned particular tasks do not do them or they do them very poorly (Behfar et al., 2011). Members disagree about how they are supposed to be working together.

Short-term task-focused groups end up arguing over process and not completing their work. Long-term groups, in contrast, minimize procedural ambiguities by formulating and adopting bylaws, constitutions, statements of policies, rules of procedure, and mission and procedure statements that specify goals, decisional processes, and responsibilities (Houle, 1989). Many groups, for example, adopt **rules of order** to regulate their discussions. The best-known set of rules was developed by Henry M. Robert, an engineer who was irritated by the conflict that characterized many of the meetings he attended. *Robert's Rules of Order*, first published in 1876, explicated not only "methods of organizing and conducting the business of societies, conventions, and other deliberative assemblies," but also such technicalities as how motions should be stated, amended, debated, postponed, voted on, and passed (Robert, 1915/1971, p. i). No less than seven pages were used to describe how the group member "obtains the floor," including suggestions for proper phrasings of the request, appropriate posture, and timing. More complex issues, such as the intricacies of voting, required as many as 20 pages of discussion. Robert purposely designed his rules to "restrain the individual somewhat," for he assumed that "the right of any individual, in any community, to do what he pleases, is incompatible with the interests of the whole" (1915/1971, p. 13). As a result, his rules promote a formal, technically precise form of interaction, sometimes at the expense of openness, vivacity, and directness. Additionally, the rules emphasize the use of voting procedures, rather than discussion to consensus, to resolve differences.

The Benefits of Task and Process Conflict   When groups disagree about issues of substance and about process, as they often do, resolving these disagreements eliminates problems that may undermine their performance in the future. Group

---

task conflict (content conflict or substantive conflict) Disagreements over issues that are relevant to the group's recognized goals and procedures.

process conflict (or procedural conflict) Disagreement over the methods the group should use to complete its basic tasks.

---

rules of order Prescriptive rules and principles that describe the processes groups and organizations should use when working collaboratively.

members must understand one another's perspectives, and such understanding sometimes deepens when conflict has surfaced, been confronted, and been resolved (Greer, Jehn, & Mannix, 2008).

But both content and process conflict, if not skillfully managed by the group's members, will destabilize the group and undermine its performance (De Dreu & Weingart, 2003). People who disagree with the group, even when their position is a reasonable one, often provoke considerable animosity. The dissenter who refuses to accept others' views is liked less, assigned low-status tasks, and sometimes ostracized. As the group struggles to reach consensus on the substantive issues at hand, it responds negatively to those group members who slow down this process (Kruglanski & Webster, 1991). Researchers studied this process by planting a confederate in discussion groups. The confederate deliberately slowed down the group with such interruptions as "What do you mean?" "Do you think that's important?" or "I don't understand." In some groups, the confederate had an excuse: He told the group that his hearing aid was not working that day. Other groups, in contrast, received no exculpating explanation. At the end of the session, members were asked to identify one person to exclude from the group. Everyone (100%) picked the disruptive confederate if there was no excuse for his actions (Burnstein & Worchel, 1962). Both task and process conflict can instigate personal conflict.

Liking and Disliking: Personal Conflicts

When school psychologists studied children playing together during recess, they discovered this period of relatively unsupervised interaction was rife with conflict: arguments about a game's rules, disputes about what is fair and what is not, and who gets to make decisions. But the most intense conflicts were personal. Children who disliked each other got into fights. Children who had irritating personal habits were routinely excluded by others. Children in one clique were mean to children in other cliques and to those who were excluded from all cliques.

When children who said they had a rotten time at recess were asked why, in most cases they explained, "I had to play alone" and "Other kids would not let me join in" (Doll, Murphy, & Song, 2003).

Adults do not always play well together either. **Personal conflicts**, also called *affective conflicts* (Guetzkow & Gyr, 1954), *personality conflicts* (Wall & Nolan, 1987), *emotional conflicts* (Jehn, 1995), or *relationship conflicts* (De Dreu & Weingart, 2003), are rooted in individuals' antipathies for other group members. Personal likes and dislikes do not always translate into group conflict, but people often mention their disaffection for another group member when they air their complaints about their groups (Alicke et al., 1992). Morrill's (1995) study of high-level corporate executives, for example, revealed both task and power conflicts, but more than 40% of their disputes were rooted in "individual enmity between the principals without specific reference to other issues." Disputants questioned each other's moral values, the way they treated their spouses, and their politics. They complained about the way their adversaries acted at meetings, the way they dressed at work and at social gatherings, their hobbies and recreational pursuits, and their personality traits. They just did not like each other very much (Morrill, 1995, p. 69).

Sources of Personal Conflicts   Just as any factor that creates a positive bond between people can increase a group's cohesion, so any factor that creates disaffection can increase conflict. In many cases, people explain their conflicts by blaming the other person's negative personal qualities, such as moodiness, compulsivity, incompetence, communication difficulties, and sloppiness (Kelley, 1979). People usually dislike others who evaluate them negatively, so criticism—even when deserved—can generate conflict (Ilgen, Mitchell, & Fredrickson, 1981). Group members who treat others unfairly or impolitely engender more conflict than those who behave politely (Ohbuchi, Chiba, & Fukushima, 1996).

---

personal conflict Interpersonal discord that occurs when group members dislike one another.

People who have agreeable personalities are usually better liked by others, and they also exert a calming influence on their groups. In a study of dyads that included people who were either high or low in agreeableness, dyads with two highly agreeable individuals displayed the least conflict, whereas dyads that contained two individuals with low agreeableness displayed the most (Graziano, Jensen-Campbell, & Hair, 1996). Agreeable people also responded more negatively to conflict overall. When people described their day-to-day activities and their daily moods, they reported feeling unhappy, tense, irritated, and anxious on days when they experienced conflicts—especially if they were by nature agreeable people (Suls, Martin, & David, 1998). Because, as Chapter 4 explained, similarity usually triggers attraction and dissimilarity disliking, diverse groups must deal with conflict more frequently than more homogenous ones.

Conflict and Balance in Groups   Mature adults who do not like each other can usually manage to overlook their personal differences and work well with one another. Until, that is, they find themselves on different sides of a substantive issue. Once Sculley and Jobs' personal liking for each other deteriorated, each time they discussed matters of substance their personal hostility spilled over into task and process conflict.

Sociologist Howard Taylor examined the connection between personal and task conflict by arranging for male college students to discuss an issue with another student whom they liked or disliked. This student was Taylor's confederate who, unbeknown to the group members, was trained to deliberately agree or disagree on key issues. Taylor then watched the groups for evidence of conflict, including tension (nervousness, stammering, blushing, expressions of frustration, and withdrawal), tension release (giggling, joking, cheerfulness, and silliness), and antagonism (anger, hostility, taunting, and defensiveness).

Taylor, drawing on balance theory, predicted that conflicts between friends would elevate levels of tension, but that conflicts with enemies would generate more open hostility. As noted in Chapter 6's

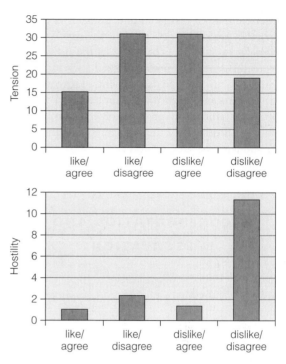

FIGURE 13.3   Levels of tension and hostility when people who disagreed or agreed on an issue and either liked or disliked each other talked for 30 minutes.

DATA SOURCE: From *Balance in small groups* by H. F. Taylor, H. F. 1970. New York: Van Nostrand Reinhold.

analysis of the stability of group structures, balance theory suggests that arguing and fighting with a friend is unpleasant. Disagreeing with someone who is liked is an imbalanced state that will create psychological discomfort. Disagreeing with someone you dislike, in contrast, is cognitively "harmonious"— the elements of the situation all "fit together without stress" (Heider, 1958, p. 180). Such a situation may not cause psychological tension, but it will likely cause conflict, for it combines both task conflict with personal conflict.

Figure 13.3 partly summarizes the findings. As balance theory suggests, tension was highest in the unbalanced pairs—when disagreeing people liked each other or when people who disliked each other agreed. People did not like disagreeing with friends or agreeing with their foes. The greatest amount of antagonism, however, occurred when discussants both disagreed and disliked each other. So, the predictions of balance theory were only partially confirmed. The most harmonious groups were those whose members liked each other and found themselves in agreement. However, the least harmonious groups were balanced, but by negative rather than positive forces: Members disliked each other and they disagreed. Taylor (1970) concluded that such groups would likely not long endure outside the confines of the laboratory.

CONFRONTATION AND ESCALATION

Early in 1985, Sculley and Jobs began moving toward a showdown, pushed into conflict by their incompatibilities, their marked differences of opinion about the company, the competitive nature of their interdependence, and their refusal to take less than they felt was their due. They tried to quell the tension, but by spring, the men were trapped in an upward spiral of hostility.

Conflicts *escalate*. Although the parties to the conflict may hope to reach a solution to their dispute quickly, a host of psychological and interpersonal factors can frustrate their attempts to control the conflict. As Sculley continued to argue with Jobs, he became more committed to his own position, and his view of Jobs and his position became biased. Sculley used stronger influence tactics, and soon other members of Apple were drawn into the fray. All these factors fed the conflict, changing it from a disagreement to a full-fledged corporate war.

Uncertainty → Commitment

As conflicts escalate, group members' doubts and uncertainties are replaced by a firm commitment to their position. Sculley, for example, became more certain that his insights were correct, and his disagreement with Jobs only increased his commitment to them (Staw & Ross, 1987). When people try to persuade others, they search out supporting arguments. If this elaboration process yields further consistent information, they become even more committed to their initial position. People rationalize their choices once they have made them: They seek out information that supports their views, they reject information that conflicts with their stance, and they become entrenched in their original position (Ross & Ward, 1995). Moreover, people feel that once they commit to a position publicly, they must stick with it. They may realize that they are wrong, but to save face, they continue to argue against their opponents (Wilson, 1992).

The *dollar auction* illustrates the impact of conflict on commitment. Members bid for $1, but one special rule is added. The highest bidder gets to keep the dollar bill, but the second highest bidder gets no money *and* must pay the amount he or she bid. Bids flow slowly at first, but soon the offers climb over 50 cents toward the $1 mark. As the stakes increase, however, quitting becomes costly. If a bidder who offers 50 cents for the $1 is bested by someone offering 60 cents, the 50-cent bidder will lose 50 cents. So he or she is tempted to beat the 60-cent bid. This cycle continues upward—well beyond the value of the dollar bill in some cases. On occasion, players have spent as much as $20 for the $1 (Teger, 1980).

Reactance can also cause a person to become overly committed to their position and resistant to compromise. When reactance occurs, individuals strive to reassert their sense of freedom by affirming their autonomy. In one study in which teammates had to make a choice between two alternatives marked 1-A and 1-B, 73% chose 1-A if their partner said, "I prefer 1-A," but only 40% chose 1-A if the partner demanded, "I think we should both do 1-A" (Brehm & Sensenig, 1966). In another study, 83% of the group members refused to go along with a group participant who said, "I think it's pretty obvious all of us are going to work on Task A" (Worchel & Brehm, 1971, p. 299; see also Brehm & Brehm, 1981; Curhan, Neale, & Ross, 2004).

---

reactance A complex emotional and cognitive reaction that occurs when individuals feel that their freedom to make choices has been threatened or eliminated.

Perception → Misperception

Individuals' reactions during conflict are shaped in fundamental ways by their perception of the situation and the people in that situation. Group members' inferences about each other's strengths, attitudes, values, and other personal qualities provide the basis for mutual understanding, but during conflict these perceptions tend to be so distorted that they inflame rather than smooth conflict (Thompson & Nadler, 2000).

Misattribution Sometimes group members settle on explanations that sustain and enhance members' interpersonal relations. Jobs, in trying to explain Sculley's actions, may have assumed Sculley was under pressure from the board, was unaccustomed to the demands of running a high-tech firm, or was dealing with the stress of his relocation. But frequently, people explain their conflicts in ways that make the problem worse. For example, Jobs would think that Sculley's actions were caused by his personal qualities, such as incompetence, belligerence, argumentativeness, greed, or selfishness. Jobs might also believe that Sculley was deliberately trying to harm him and that Sculley therefore deserved to be blamed and punished (Fincham & Bradbury, 1992, 1993). In short, Jobs would fall prey to the *fundamental attribution error* (FAE) and assume that Sculley's behavior was caused by personal (dispositional) rather than situational (environmental) factors (Ross, 1977). If the conflict continued, he may have eventually decided it was an intractable one. People expect intractable conflicts to be prolonged, intense, and very hard to resolve (Bar–Tal, 2007).

Misperceiving Motivations When conflict occurs in a group, members begin to wonder about one another's motivations. "Why," Steve Jobs may have wondered, "is Sculley not supporting my work with the Mac? He must know how important this project is to the company, so why is he not giving it the attention it deserves?"

During conflict, members often become distrustful of one another, wondering if their once cooperative motivations have been replaced by competitive ones. This loss of trust is one of the primary reasons why people, when they begin to compete with one another, have difficulty returning to a cooperative relationship. Researchers examined just this process by pairing people playing a PDG-like game with partners who used one of four possible strategies described earlier: competition, cooperation, individualism, and altruism. When later asked to describe their partners' motives, the players recognized when they were playing with an individualist or a competitor, but they had more trouble accurately perceiving cooperation and altruism (Maki, Thorngate, & McClintock, 1979).

People with competitive SVOs are the most inaccurate in their perceptions of cooperation. When cooperators play the PDG with other cooperators, their perceptions of their partner's strategy are inaccurate only 6% of the time. When competitors play the PDG with cooperators, however, they misinterpret their partner's strategy 47% of the time, mistakenly believing that the cooperators are competing (Kelley & Stahelski, 1970a, 1970b, 1970c; Sattler & Kerr, 1991). Competitors are also biased in their search for information, for they are more likely to seek out information that confirms their suspicions—"I am dealing with a competitive person"—rather than information that might indicate the others are attempting to cooperate (Van Kleef & De Dreu, 2002). Competitors also tend to deliberately misrepresent their intentions, sometimes claiming to be more cooperative than they actually are (Steinel & De Dreu, 2004).

Soft Tactics → Hard Tactics

People can influence other people in dozens of different ways; they can promise, reward, threaten, punish, bully, discuss, instruct, negotiate, manipulate, supplicate, ingratiate, and so on. Some of these tactics are harsher than others. Threats, punishment, and bullying are all hard, contentious tactics because they are direct, nonrational, and unilateral. People use softer tactics at the outset of a conflict, but as the conflict escalates, they shift to stronger and stronger tactics. Sculley gradually shifted from relatively mild methods of influence (discussion, negotiation) to stronger tactics (threats). Eventually, he demoted Jobs (Carnevale & Pruitt, 1992).

T A B L E 13.1   **Influence Methods Used in Groups Sharing Scarce Resources**

Behavior	Example	Percentage
Requests	May I use the glue?	100.0
Statements	We need the glue.	100.0
Demands	Give me the glue, now!	88.9
Complaints	What's wrong with you? Why don't you share?	79.2
Problem solving	You can use our stapler if you will share the glue.	73.6
Third party	Make them share!	45.8
Anger	I'm mad now.	41.7
Threat	Give me the glue or else.	22.2
Harassment	I'm not giving you any more ribbon until you return the glue.	16.7
Abuse	You are a selfish swine.	0.7

SOURCE: Escalation in Response to Persistent Annoyance: Groups versus Individuals and Gender Effects by J. M. Mikolic, J. C. Parker, & D. G. Pruitt, D. G. *Journal of Personality and Social Psychology, 72*, 151–163, 1997.

Social psychologist Dean Pruitt and his colleagues (1997) studied this escalation process by creating a simulated birthday card factory where people were paid a small amount for each card they manufactured using paper, colored markers, and ribbons. The work went well until one of the group members, a confederate of the researchers, began acting selfishly by hoarding materials that the other members needed. As the hour wore on, it became clear that this person was going to make far more money than everyone else, and the group became more and more frustrated. It responded by using stronger and more contentious influence tactics. As Table 13.1 indicates, the group tried to solve the problem initially with statements and requests. When those methods failed, they shifted to demands and complaints. When those methods failed, they tried problem solving and appeals to a third party (the experimenter). In the most extreme cases, they used threats, abuse, and anger to try to influence the irritating confederate (Mikolic, Parker, & Pruitt, 1997).

The Trucking Game Experiment People who use harder tactics often overwhelm their antagonists,

and such methods intensify conflicts. Social psychologists Morton Deutsch and Robert Krauss (1960) examined this intensification process in their classic **trucking game experiment**. They asked pairs of women to role-play the owners of a trucking company. The two companies, Acme and Bolt, carried merchandise over the roads mapped in Figure 13.4. Acme and Bolt each earned 60 cents after each completed run, minus 1 cent for each second taken up by the trip.

The truck route set the stage for competition and conflict between Acme and Bolt. The shortest path from start to finish for Acme was Route 216 and for Bolt was Route 106, but these routes merged into a one-lane highway. When trucks encountered each other along this route, one player had to back up to her starting position to let the other through. Acme and Bolt could avoid this confrontation by taking the winding alternate route, but this path took longer.

---

trucking game experiment A research procedure developed by Morton Deutsch and Robert Krauss in their studies of conflict between individuals who differ in their capacity to threaten and punish others.

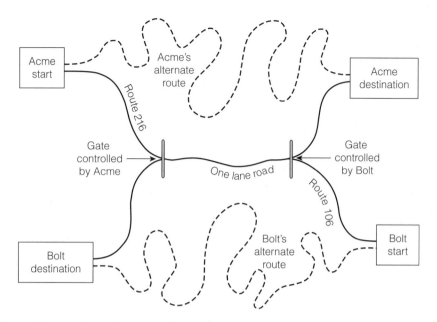

F I G U R E   13.4   The Deutsch and Krauss trucking game simulation. Players took the role of either Acme or Bolt and maneuvered their trucks along Route 216, Route 106, or the longer, alternate routes. In some cases one or both of the players were given gates that they could close to bar access by the other player.

SOURCE: *The Resolution of Conflict: Constructive and Destructive Processes*, by M. Deutsch. Copyright 1973 by Yale University Press. Reprinted by permission.

All the pairs played the same basic game, but some were provided with the power to threaten their opponents and others were not. In the *unilateral threat* condition, Acme was told that a gate, which only she could open and close, was located at the fork in Route 216. When the gate was closed, neither truck could pass this point in the road, making control of the gate a considerable benefit to Acme. If Bolt attempted to use the main route, all Acme had to do was close the gate, forcing Bolt to back up and enabling Acme to reopen the gate and proceed quickly to her destination. Thus, when only Acme possessed the gate, Bolt's profits were greatly threatened. In the *bilateral threat* condition, both sides had the use of gates located at the ends of the one-lane section of Route 216, and, in the *control* condition, no gates were given to the players.

Deutsch and Krauss's control participants soon learned to resolve the conflict over the one-lane road. Most of these pairs took turns using the main route, and, on average, each participant made a $1 profit. Winnings dwindled, however, when one of the players was given a gate. Participants in the unilateral threat condition lost an average of $2.03. Bolt's losses were twice as great as Acme's, but even Acme lost more than $1 at the game. Conflict was even worse when both Acme and Bolt had gates. In the bilateral threat condition, both players usually took the longer route because the gates on the main route were kept closed, and their losses in this condition averaged $4.38.

Power and Conflict These findings convinced Deutsch and Krauss that the capacity to threaten others intensifies conflict. They also noted that establishing a communication link between adversaries does not necessarily help them to solve their dispute (Krauss & Morsella, 2000). If one party can or does threaten the other party, the threatened party will fare best if he or she cannot respond with a counterthreat (Borah, 1963; Deutsch & Lewicki, 1970; Froman & Cohen, 1969; Gallo, 1966). Equally powerful opponents, however, learn to avoid the use of their power if the fear of retaliation is high (Lawler, Ford, & Blegen, 1988).

Reciprocity → Retaliation

Conflict-ridden groups may seem normless with hostility and dissatisfaction spinning out of control. Yet upward conflict spirals are in many cases sustained by the norm of reciprocity. If one group member criticizes the ideas, opinions, or characteristics of another, the victim of the attack will feel justified in counterattacking unless some situational factor legitimizes the hostility of the former (Schumann & Ross, 2010).

If members comply exactly with the norm of reciprocity, a mild threat would elicit a mild threat in return, and an attack would lead to a counterattack. But most people apply the rule of *rough* reciprocity—they give too much (*overmatching*) or too little (*undermatching*) in return. Those who retaliate tend to overmatch: They feel that their response is a fair one, whereas the punished transgressor thinks the level of retaliation is excessive (Stillwell, Baumeister, & Del Priore, 2008).

This tendency tends to cause conflicts to escalate. One researcher studied this process by arranging for women to play a PDG-like game, but modified it so they could send messages back and forth and penalize each other. When a woman received a note from her partner threatening her with a penalty, she sent back a threat in return. When one woman sent multiple threats, her partner did as well. This reciprocity, however, was rough rather than exact. At low levels of conflict, the participants' threats were somewhat stronger, and the penalties they warned of were somewhat greater. At higher levels of conflict, most of the participants undermatched their partner's threats. The overmatching that occurs initially may serve as a strong warning, whereas the undermatching at high levels of conflict may be used to send a conciliatory message (Youngs, 1986).

Irritation → Anger

When disputes arise, tempers flare, and this increase in negative emotions exacerbates the initial conflict. Most people, when asked to talk about a time when they became angry, said that they usually lost their temper when arguing with people they knew rather than with strangers. They admitted that their anger increased the negativity of the conflict; 49% became verbally abusive when they were angry and 10% said they became physically aggressive (Averill, 1983). Participants in another study reported physically attacking someone or something, losing emotional control, or imagining violence against someone else when they were angry (Shaver et al., 1987). Even when group members began by discussing their points calmly and dispassionately, as they became locked into their positions, emotional expression begins to replace logical discussion (De Dreu et al., 2007). Individuals who endorse the principle of negative reciprocity—they agree with such statements as "If someone treats me badly, I feel I should treat them even worse"—tend to become angry when they feel they have been treated badly (Eisenberger et al., 2004, p. 791).

Emotions serve important functions in groups, and anger is no exception. Anger is a way to communicate one's displeasure to others in the group and, in some contexts, is considered appropriate and justified. Anger can be an effective means of influencing others, for individuals who express anger during one meeting tend to be treated more circumspectly in the next, and their demands are more likely to be met (Van Kleef, 2010; Van Kleef & Côté, 2007).

Anger, however, can trigger all manner of negative interpersonal behaviors, including the rejection of concessions, the tendering of unworkable initial offers, and the use of contentious influence strategies (Pillutla & Murnighan, 1996; Van Kleef, De Dreu, & Manstead, 2004). When people express their anger, it redefines the situation, changing it from a cooperative one into one of conflict (Van Doorn, Heerdink, & Van Kleef, 2012). Others often interpret a display of anger as an expression of contempt, and expressing contempt for fellow group members is rarely a good thing (Fischer & Roseman, 2007). Anger is also a contagious emotion in groups (Kelly, 2001). Group members, when negotiating with someone who has become angry, tend to become angry themselves (Van Kleef et al., 2004). As Focus 13.1 explains, even when people are physically separated from each other and interacting via the Internet, they still manage

---

Focus 13.1   E-groups: Taming Flaming in Internet Communications

People use the Internet for all kinds of constructive purposes, such as accessing and exchanging information, discussing important issues, and strengthening interpersonal connections, but online interaction can also instigate conflict: angry emails; name-calling and insults on discussion forms; messages laced with profanities. These types of behaviors are termed **flaming**. According to *The Hackers Dictionary* (Steele, 1983, p. 63), flaming originally meant "to speak rapidly or incessantly on an uninteresting topic or with a patently ridiculous attitude." But as more and more people began using the Internet to communicate with each other in the 1990s, the word came to be used for offensive messages and postings (Turnage, 2008).

Just as people differ in their interpretation of conversational speech—one person's clever repartee can be viewed as a hostile retort by someone else—people also differ in their response to emotion-laden emails and Internet postings (O'Sullivan & Flanagin, 2003). Communications researcher Anna Turnage (2007), to determine when people will call a message a flame, asked people to rate an assortment of Internet messages that varied in their use of profanity, emoticons, acronyms, and emotional expressiveness. Her analysis indicated that messages that included profanities and rudeness were rated as flames (e.g., "I don't care. I just don't have time for this @&#$%! right now!" and "Now how in the hell would I know that if nobody tells me???"; Turnage, 2007, p. 51). Messages that conveyed anger, disappointment, and other forms of displeasure were usually not considered to be flames, so long as they did not use profanity or capitalization (e.g., "What happened to the news release for the department name change?" or "I need an update from you on each of your funded projects ASAP"; Turnage, 2007, p. 51). The ratings provided an empirically based definition for flaming: a computer-mediated communication that the recipient construes as hostile, aggressive, intimidating, insulting, offensive, or unfriendly.

Flaming is triggered by the same factors that cause conflict in offline groups: competitiveness, personality differences, concerns about fairness and distribution of workload and resources, struggles for power, disagreement over the group's tasks and processes, and personal likes and dislikes. E-groups, too, develop over

time, and part of that development includes a period of tension that often generates hostilities and conflicts (Ayoko, Konrad & Boyle, 2012). But the online context adds a few unique and influential elements to the conflict mix. Working online can lead to disinhibition so people express sentiments and opinions that they would never say aloud in face-to-face conversations where they are inhibited by norms of civility or by self-control mechanisms. E-groups, too, allow members to express themselves immediately, so there is no opportunity for members to regain their composure after something or someone irritates them. In consequence, "members are prone to immediate articulation of negative emotions in response to a conflict" (Ayoko et al., 2012, p. 169). The technology itself can also be a source of irritation—a group sitting in a room conversing does not encounter the irksome technical problems that online groups often do.

The discourse of e-groups, however, is regulated by social norms; individuals are not free to express themselves in ways that are openly contemptuous of others' preferences or the group's standards. In some Internet groups, such as Usenet groups, a post that is hostile, rude, or contains profanity will generate a strong reproach from the community, warning the individual to refrain from such behaviors. In most cases, the individual who flamed accepts the reproach and either leaves the group or complies with the group's communication standards (Smith, McLaughlin, & Osborne, 2007). In some Internet-based discussion groups flaming never occurs—in over 1,000 postings on one site not a single one could be considered hostile or insulting. In other groups (e.g., alt.fan.warlords and alt.flame), however, flaming is a common, taken-for-granted mode of self-expression.

Some groups, too, have established rules about how disputants should communicate. The contents of the online encyclopedia *Wikipedia*, for example, are created, reviewed, and revised by a community of volunteers, and the community's norms, termed the *Five Pillars*, include "interact with each other in a respectful and civil manner" (http://en.wikipedia.org/wiki/Wikipedia:Five_pillars). However, Wikipedians (as the editors of pages are called) do not always agree about either the content of a given entry

---

flaming An online communication, such as an e-mail or posting, that is perceived to be hostile, aggressive, intimidating, insulting, offensive, or unfriendly.

(task conflict) or the way in which another editor went about making a change (process conflict). Wikipedia therefore offers an area for every entry where editors can discuss their issues and resolve their disputes in a "respectful and civil manner." In many cases, however, the Wikipedians cannot meet this high standard, and an edit war breaks out. "An edit war occurs when editors who disagree about the content of a page repeatedly override each other's contributions, rather than trying to resolve the disagreement by discussion" (http://en.wikipedia.org/wiki/Wikipedia:Edit_warring). Even though the community spends considerable time editing its policies, when researchers examined the communication of editors working behind the scenes at Wikipedia, they found little evidence of the

application of basic principles of civil discourse (Black et al., 2011).

These studies of flaming underscore again the similarity of the dynamics of online groups to offline groups. Disputes and disagreements occur online just as they do offline, as people try to impress each other with their wisdom, convince them of the error of their opinions, or redress what is perceived to be a wrong of some type. People sometimes become angry, and, when they do, the conflict escalates. Fortunately, however, the parallel between online and offline groups stops there. In some cases when people lose their tempers in offline groups, the dispute can become physically violent. In e-groups, such extreme forms of violence are practically impossible.

---

to communicate their displeasure to one another, and the result is often increased rather than decreased conflict.

Few → Many

During the Jobs versus Sculley conflict, Jobs tried to persuade each member of the board to side with him in the dispute. His goal was to form a powerful coalition that would block Sculley's plans and swing the vote of the board in his favor.

Coalitions exist in most groups, but when conflict erupts, group members use coalitions to shift the balance of power in their favor. The initial disagreement may involve only two group members, but as conflicts intensify, previously neutral members often join with one faction. Similarly, even when members initially express many different views, with time, these multiparty conflicts are reduced to two-party blocs through coalition formation. Coalitions can even link rivals who decide to join forces temporarily to achieve a specific outcome (a mixed-motive situation). Although allies may wish to compete with one another, no single individual has enough power to succeed alone. Hence, while the coalition exists, the competitive motive must be stifled (Komorita & Parks, 1994).

Coalitions draw more members of the group into the fray. Coalitions are often viewed as contentious, heavy-handed influence tactics because individuals in the coalition work not only to ensure their own outcomes but also to worsen the outcomes of noncoalition members. Coalitions form with people and against other people. In business settings, for example, the dominant coalition can control the organization, yet it works outside the bounds of the formal group structure. Those who are excluded from a coalition react with hostility to the coalition members and seek to regain power by forming their own coalitions. Thus, coalitions must be constantly maintained through strategic bargaining and negotiation (Mannix, 1993; Murnighan, 1986; Stevenson, Pearce, & Porter, 1985).

CONFLICT RESOLUTION

In one way or another, conflicts subside. Even when members are committed to their own viewpoints, high levels of tension cannot be maintained indefinitely. Disputants may regain control of their tempers and break the upward conflict spiral. The group may fissure, splitting into two or more subgroups whose members are more compatible.

One member may leave the group, as was the result in the Jobs versus Sculley dispute. In time, group hostility abates.

Commitment → Negotiation

Just as conflicts escalate when group members become firmly committed to a position and will not budge, conflicts de-escalate when group members are willing to negotiate with others to reach a solution that benefits all parties. **Negotiation** is a reciprocal communication process whereby two or more parties to a dispute examine specific issues, explain their positions, and exchange offers and counteroffers.

Distributive and Integrative Negotiations Negotiation sometimes amounts to little more than simple bargaining or mutual compromise. In such **distributive negotiations**, both parties retain their competitive orientation and take turns making small concessions until some equally dissatisfying middle ground is reached. Haggling and bartering ("I'll give you $20 for it, and not a penny more!") illustrate this form of negotiation. **Integrative negotiation**, in contrast, is a collaborative conflict resolution method. Rather than trying to only maximize one's own outcomes, integrative negotiators search for solutions that will benefit both sides. Bargainers need not be motivated by a concern for the other's well-being, but they recognize that a solution that benefits everyone will be one that will likely be more readily adopted and implemented (Lewicki, Saunders, & Barry, 2010; Pruitt, 2012).

---

negotiation A reciprocal communication process whereby two or more parties to a dispute examine specific issues, explain their positions, and exchange offers and counteroffers to reach agreement or achieve mutually beneficial outcomes.

distributive negotiation Resolving differences of opinion and transactions by claiming or dividing resources, making offers and responding with counteroffers, and the guarded disclosure of interests.

integrative negotiation Resolving differences of opinion and transactions by identifying common and complementary interests and proposing solutions that satisfy all concerned parties.

Negotiation Styles Individuals differ in their approach to negotiations. The Harvard Negotiation Project, for example, identified three basic types of negotiators—soft, hard, and principled (see Table 13.2). *Soft bargainers* see negotiation as too close to competition, so they choose a gentle style of negotiation. They make offers that are not in their best interests, they yield to others' demands, they avoid any confrontation, and they maintain good relations with fellow negotiators. *Hard bargainers*, in contrast, use tough, competitive tactics during negotiations. They begin by taking an extreme position on the issue, and then they make small concessions only grudgingly. The hard bargainer uses contentious strategies of influence and says such things as "Take it or leave it," "This is my final offer," "This point is not open to negotiation," "My hands are tied," and "I'll see you in court" (Fisher, 1983).

Principled negotiators, meanwhile, seek integrative solutions by sidestepping a commitment to specific positions. Instead of risking entrapment, principled negotiators focus on the problem rather than the intentions, motives, and needs of the people involved. Positional bargaining, they conclude, is too dangerous:

> When negotiators bargain over positions, they tend to lock themselves into those positions. The more you clarify your position and defend it against attack, the more committed you become to it. The more you try to convince the other side of the impossibility of changing your opening position, the more difficult it becomes to do so. Your ego becomes identified with your position. (Fisher & Ury, 1981, p. 5)

The Harvard Negotiation Project recommends that negotiators explore a number of alternatives to the problems they face. During this phase, the negotiation is transformed into a group problem-solving session with the different parties working together in search of creative solutions and new information that the group can use to evaluate these alternatives. Principled negotiators base their choice on objective criteria rather than on power,

TABLE 13.2 **Comparisons between the Three Approaches to Negotiation**

Element	Soft Negotiation	Hard Negotiation	Principled Negotiation
Perception of others	Friends	Adversaries	Problem solvers
Goals	Agreement	Victory	A wise outcome reached efficiently and amicably
Concessions	Make concessions to cultivate the relationship	Demand concessions as a condition of the relationship	Separate the people from the problem
People vs. problems	Be soft on the people and the problem	Be hard on the problem and the people	Be soft on the people, hard on the problem
Trust	Trust others	Distrust others	Proceed independently of trust
Positions	Change your position easily	Dig into your position	Focus on interests, not positions
Negotiation	Make offers	Make threats	Explore interests
Bottom line	Disclose your bottom line	Mislead as to your bottom line	Avoid having a bottom line
Losses and gains	Accept one-sided losses to reach agreement	Demand one-sided gains as a price of agreement	Invent options for mutual gains
Search	Search for a single answer— the one they will accept	Search for a single answer— the one you will accept	Develop multiple options to choose from; decide later
Criteria	Insist on agreement	Insist on your position	Insist on using objective criteria
Contest of wills	Avoid a contest of wills	Win the contest of wills	Reach a result based on standards, independent of wills
Pressure	Yield to pressure	Apply pressure	Reason and be open to reason; yield to principle, not pressure

SOURCE: Adapted from Getting to YES: *Negotiating Agreement without Giving In* by R. Fisher, W. Ury With B. Patton (ed.). Boston: Houghton Mifflin. 1981.

pressure, self-interest, or an arbitrary decisional procedure. Such criteria can be drawn from moral standards, principles of fairness, objective indexes of market value, professional standards, tradition, and so on, but they should be recognized as fair by all parties (Kolb & Williams, 2003).

Misperception → Understanding

Many conflicts are based on misperceptions. Group members often assume that others are competing with them, when in fact those other people only wish to cooperate. Members think that people who criticize their ideas are criticizing them personally. Members do not trust other people because they are convinced that others' motives are selfish ones. Group members assume that they have incompatible goals when they do not (Simpson, 2007).

Group members must undo these perceptual misunderstandings by actively communicating information about their motives and goals through discussion. In one study, group members were given the opportunity to exchange information about their interests and goals, yet only about

20% did. Those who did, however, were more likely to discover shared goals and were able to reach solutions that benefited both parties to the conflict (Thompson, 1991). Other studies have suggested that conflict declines when group members communicate their intentions in specific terms, make explicit references to trust, cooperation, and fairness, and build a shared ingroup identity (Cohen, Wildschut, & Insko, 2010; Harinck, 2004; Weingart & Olekalns, 2004).

Communication is no cure-all for conflict, however. Group members can exchange information by communicating, but they can also create gross misunderstandings and deceptions. Communication offers group members the means to establish trust and commitment, but it can also exacerbate conflict if members verbalize feelings of hatred, disgust, or annoyance. For example, when Deutsch and Krauss (1960) let participants in their trucking game experiment communicate with each other, messages typically emphasized threats and did little to reduce conflict (Deutsch, 1973). Communication is detrimental if these initial messages are inconsistent, hostile, and contentious (McClintock, Stech, & Keil, 1983). Communication can be beneficial, however, if interactants use it to create cooperative norms, if it increases trust among participants, and if it generates increased cohesion and unity in the group (Messick & Brewer, 1983).

Hard Tactics → Cooperative Tactics

Group members cope with conflict in different ways. Some ignore the problem. Others discuss the problem, sometimes dispassionately and rationally, sometimes angrily and loudly. Still others push their solution onto others, no matter what the others may want. Some actually resort to physical violence (Sternberg & Dobson, 1987). Some of these tactics escalate conflicts, but others are reliably associated with reduced hostility.

Dual Concerns   As with social values orientations, variations in methods of dealing with conflict can be organized in terms of two essential themes: concern for self and concern for the other person.

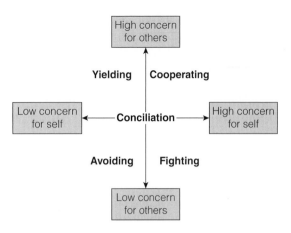

F I G U R E 13.5   The dual concern model of conflict resolution. Avoiding, yielding, cooperating, and fighting, as means of dealing with conflict, differ in the degree to which they are based on concern for oneself and concern for the other person.
SOURCE: © Cengage Learning 2014

According to the **dual concern model** of conflict resolution, some strategies aim to maximize one's own outcomes; others—such as overlooking a problem until it subsides—de-emphasize proself goals. Some conflict resolution strategies are also more other-focused. Yielding, for example, is prosocial, whereas contending and forcing are less prosocial (Pruitt, 1983; Sheppard, 1983; Thomas, 1992; van de Vliert & Janssen, 2001).

When both concern for self and concern for other are taken into account, the dual concern model identifies the four core conflict resolution modes shown in Figure 13.5.

- *Avoidance:* Inaction is a passive means of dealing with disputes. Those who avoid conflicts adopt a "wait and see" attitude, hoping that problems will solve themselves. Avoiders often tolerate conflicts, allowing them to simmer without doing anything to minimize them. Rather than openly discussing disagreements, people who

dual concern model A conceptual perspective on methods of dealing with conflict that assumes avoiding, yielding, fighting, and cooperating differ along two basic dimensions: concern for self and concern for other.

rely on avoidance change the subject, skip meetings, or even leave the group altogether (Bayazit & Mannix, 2003). Sometimes they simply agree to disagree (a modus vivendi). Avoidance tactics are considered to be more skillful methods of dealing with conflict in Eastern cultures (see Focus 13.2).

- *Yielding:* Accommodation is a passive but prosocial approach to conflict. People solve both large and small conflicts by giving in to the demands of others. Sometimes, they yield because they realize that their position is in error, so they agree with the viewpoint adopted by others. In other cases, however, they may withdraw their demands without really being convinced that the other side is correct, but—for the sake of group unity or in the interest of time—they withdraw all complaints. Thus, yielding can reflect either genuine conversion or superficial compliance.

- *Fighting:* Contending is an active, proself means of dealing with conflict that involves forcing others to accept one's view. Those who use this strategy tend to see conflict as a win–lose situation and so use competitive, powerful tactics to intimidate others. Fighting (*forcing, dominating,* or *contending*) *can* take many forms, including authoritative mandate, challenges, arguing, insults, accusations, complaining, vengeance, and even physical violence (Morrill, 1995). These conflict resolution methods are all contentious ones because they involve imposing one's solution on the other party.

- *Cooperation:* Cooperation is an active, prosocial, and proself approach to conflict resolution. Cooperating people identify the issues underlying the dispute and then work together to identify a solution that is satisfying to both sides. This orientation, which is also described as collaboration, problem solving, or a win–win orientation, entreats both sides in the dispute to consider their opponent's outcomes as well as their own.

- *Conciliation.* Some theorists consider conciliation to be a fifth distinct way to resolve conflicts—a middle ground between yielding

and fighting (Euwema & Van Emmerik, 2007). Conciliation, however, is often difficult to distinguish from the other modes of conflict resolution (van de Vliert & Euwema, 1994).

Cooperation and Conflict When conflict erupts, group members can use any or all of the basic modes of conflict resolution shown in Figure 13.5, but most conflict-management experts recommend cooperation above all others: "work things out," "put your cards on the table," and "air out differences," they suggest. This advice assumes that avoidance, fighting, and yielding are only temporary solutions, for they quell conflicts at the surface without considering the source. Avoiding and fighting are generally considered to be negative methods, for they tend to intensify conflicts (Sternberg & Dobson, 1987), and they are viewed as more disagreeable (Jarboe & Witteman, 1996; van de Vliert & Euwema, 1994). The more positive, prosocial methods, yielding and cooperation, mitigate conflict and are viewed as more agreeable. They are more likely to involve more of the members in the solution, and hence they tend to increase unity (Euwema & Van Emmerik, 2007).

Groups may respond well to cooperation when it is used to deal with task conflicts, but what if the problems stem from personal conflicts—differences in personalities, values, lifestyles, likes, and dislikes? Research conducted by Carsten De Dreu and his colleagues suggests that, in such cases, collaborative approaches may aggravate the group conflict more than they mollify it (e.g., De Dreu, 1997; De Dreu & Van Vianen, 2001; De Dreu & Weingart, 2003). In one field study, members of semiautonomous teams working on complex, nonroutine tasks were asked about the ways they handled conflicts in their teams. All these teams included both men and women, and they ranged in size from four to thirteen members. Members of these teams typically interacted with each other in face-to-face settings at least once a week in planning sessions, and they reported interacting with each other informally nearly every day. As expected, negative methods of dealing with conflicts, such as arguing and forcing one's views onto others, were associated with negative team functioning. In these

---

F o c u s 13.2 Cross-cultural Perspectives: Dealing with Conflict in Multicultural Groups

---

Yao was an attorney working in an American law firm located in Shanghai. The firm had been hired by an electronics manufacturer, Yang Shen, to represent them in a dispute with a plastics manufacturer. Unfortunately, Yao had represented the plastics company in a matter several years previously, and so she did not think that she could take the case. She felt it would be an ethics violation (a conflict of interest), since she had too much insider information about the company. The managing partner of the firm, however, disagreed and assigned her the case anyway. She asked him to reconsider and met with him to explain why it would be better for her, the firm, and for both the companies involved in the lawsuit if she did not take the case. He refused to change his position. Yao felt she had no choice but to resign (Chen, Tjosvold, & Su Fang, 2005).

This example illustrates the difficulties multicultural groups face when dealing with conflict. In some cultures, disagreements between people present opportunities to find solutions that all will find satisfying. Rather than letting disagreements threaten the quality of the bonds that link people together, people maneuver around their disagreements to stop them from escalating into full-fledged disputes. In other cultures, in contrast, conflict is considered more of a test between competitors and is framed as a win–lose situation. Many Western societies, for example, openly value competition. Their economic systems are based on competition, their schools teach children the importance of surpassing others' achievements, and popular games and sports have winners and losers. Cooperative societies, in contrast, stress accord rather than individual achievement and competition (Gibson & McDaniel, 2010).

The differences across societies are linked to variations in cultural values pertaining to individuals—collectivism and power hierarchy. Yao, who was raised in China, a collectivistic culture, likely viewed the situation as one requiring compromise. In collectivistic societies, members are more likely to adopt harmony-enhancing strategies that minimize conflict, including following the rules that will yield a fair resolution to the disagreement. Her boss, in contrast, was an American, and he tried to win the argument, as is typical of those raised in more individualistic cultures (Gelfand, Leslie, & Keller, 2008; Gire, 1997).

Most people, across the world, recognize the value of one particular conflict resolution method: cooperation. This approach satisfies both individuals who are seeking their own best outcomes, but also those who

are concerned with the overall well-being of the group (Cai & Fink, 2002). However, in individualistic cultures, conflict is generally viewed as something that should be confronted directly: A person should "directly express what you believe," "verbally defend your views," and "get straight to the point" (Hammer, 2005, p. 685). In more collectivistic cultures, in contrast, people prefer to handle conflict indirectly, with more subtlety: A person should "offer indirect suggestions," "express complaints indirectly," and "talk around disagreements" when possible (Hammer, 2005, p. 685). Individuals in these cultures prefer avoidance, but avoidance does not indicate a low concern for others' outcomes as the dual-process model suggests. In collectivistic countries, avoidance is a more active strategy; a positively valued means of dealing with conflict that sustains, rather than threatens, the group.

Collectivists' preferences for smoothing and compromise, it should be noted, does not necessarily extend to individuals who are not part of their group (Probst, Carnevale, & Triandis, 1999). Collectivists express less anger, hostility, and aggression, but only when dealing with members of their own group (Leung, 1988). When students from countries with collectivistic and individualistic cultures were asked how they would respond to a conflict with another individual (intragroup conflict), to a conflict between their group and another group (intergroup conflict), and to a conflict between their country and another country (international conflict), those from collectivistic countries responded more negatively to intergroup and international conflicts than to interpersonal conflicts. Students from individualistic countries responded similarly to all three types of conflict (Derlega et al., 2002).

These findings offer a warning to people who work in multicultural groups. Even though well-meaning group members may hope to quell a conflict with a deft intervention, they may only make matters worse by using a method that is considered contentious in other cultures (Brew et al., 2011). The collectivist who seeks to deflect the group's attention away from the conflict may be certain that this tactic will be best for the group in the long term. The individualists in the group may consider this tactic irritating and irresponsible—they want to solve the problem, not dodge it. Conversely, the individualist, believing that the conflict can be cleared up if people just speak their minds, pushes everyone to deal with the issues in open discussion. The collectivists in the group will wonder why

Focus 13.2 (Continued)

anyone who seems so intelligent in other ways would use such a clumsy method of dealing with conflict, given that such a discussion may jeopardize the quality of the group's relations. The culturally competent group will, instead, use a variety of methods to deal with conflict,

shifting from one approach to the other depending on the strength of the relations among members, the level of harm the conflict can cause, and the extent to which others in the group have expressed a public commitment to their position.

---

groups, however, collaborative methods of conflict resolution (e.g., "discussing the issues," "cooperating to better understand others' views," "settling problems through give and take") were also negatively correlated with team functioning. Only avoiding responses, such as "avoiding the issues," "acting as if nothing has happened," and "hushing up the quarrel" were associated with increases in group adjustment to the conflict. Apparently, the consistent use of collaboration to deal with intractable differences or petty disagreements distracted the groups from the achievement of their task-related goals (De Dreu & Van Vianen, 2001).

These findings suggest that groups may wish to heed the advice of one member of a successful musical quartet who, when asked how his group managed conflicts, explained, "We have a little saying in quartets—either we play or we fight" (Murnighan & Conlon, 1991, pp. 177–178). Cooperative, prosocial solutions work in many cases, but sometimes groups must ignore the conflict and focus, instead, on the work to be done.

Retaliation → Forgiveness

Consistent cooperation among people over a long period generally increases mutual trust. But when group members continually compete with each other, mutual trust becomes much more elusive (Haas & Deseran, 1981). When people cannot trust one another, they compete simply to defend their own best interests (Lindskold, 1978).

Reversing the Conflict Spiral How can the upward spiral of competition and distrust, once initiated, be reversed? Political scientist Robert

Axelrod (1984) explored this question by comparing a number of strategies in simulated competitions. After studying dozens of different strategies, ranging from always competing with a competitor to always cooperating with one, the most effective competition reverser to emerge was a strategy called **tit for tat** (TFT, or "this for that"). TFT begins with cooperation. If the other party cooperates, too, then cooperation continues. But if the other party competes, then TFT competes as well. Each action by the other person is countered with the matching response—cooperation for cooperation, competition for competition.

The TFT strategem is said to be nice, provocable, clear, and forgiving. It is *nice* because it begins with cooperation and only defects following competition. It is *provocable* in the sense that it immediately retaliates against individuals who compete. It is *clear* because people playing against someone using this strategy quickly recognize its contingencies. It is *forgiving* because it immediately reciprocates cooperation should the competitor respond cooperatively.

TFT is also a *reciprocal* strategy, for it fights fire with fire and rewards kindness in kind. Individuals who follow a tit-for-tat strategy are viewed as "tough but fair"; those who cooperate with a competitor are viewed as weak, and those who consistently compete are considered unfair (McGillicuddy, Pruitt, & Syna, 1984). Because the effectiveness of TFT as a conflict reduction method is based on its

---

tit for tat (TFT) A bargaining strategy that begins with cooperation, but then imitates the other person's choice so that cooperation is met with cooperation and competition with competition.

provocability, any delay in responding to competition reduces the effectiveness of TFT. If a group member competes and this defection is not countered quickly with competition, TFT is less effective (Komorita, Hilty, & Parks, 1991). TFT also loses some of its strength in "noisy" interactions, when behaviors cannot be clearly classified as either competitive or cooperative (Van Lange, Ouwerkerk, & Tazelaar, 2002; Wu & Axelrod, 1995). It is less effective in larger groups, although this decline is minimized if individual members believe that a substantial subgroup within the total group is basing its choices on the TFT strategy (Komorita, Parks, & Hulbert, 1992; Parks & Komorita, 1997).

Forgiveness Greek scholars used the word *aphiemi*, or forgiveness, to describe letting go or voluntarily setting aside an obligation to punish. Viewed from an evolutionary perspective, forgiveness undoes the damaging effects of conflict by reversing the upward spiraling cycle of repeated retaliation following real or perceived injury. Retaliation requires one party to impose sanctions on another, but revenge is risky: It can destroy the social relationship between the wrongdoer and the retaliator and can also provoke counter-retaliatory actions. Forgiveness, in contrast, reduces the likelihood of vengeful behavior and also strengthens the positive relational bonds in the group (McCullough, Kurzban, & Tabak, 2011). Forgiveness may increase both the forgiver's and the forgiven's sense of connectedness to the group (Burnette et al., 2012).

Anger → Composure

Just as negative emotions encourage conflicts, positive affective responses increase concession making, creative problem solving, cooperation, and the use of noncontentious bargaining strategies (Forgas, 1998). Hence, when tempers flare, the group should encourage members to regain control over their emotions. "Count to ten," calling a "time-out," or expressing concerns in a written, carefully edited, letter or e-mail are simple but effective recommendations for controlling conflict, as is the introduction of humor into the group discussion

(Mischel & DeSmet, 2000). Apologies, too, are effective means of reducing anger. When people are informed about mitigating causes—background factors that indicate that the insult is unintentional or unimportant—conflict is reduced (Betancourt & Blair, 1992). Groups can also control anger by developing norms that explicitly or implicitly prohibit shows of strong, negative emotion or by holding meetings on controversial topics online (Yang & Mossholder, 2004).

Many → Few

Conflicts intensify when others take sides, but they shrink when third-party **mediators** help group members reach a mutually agreeable solution to their dispute (Kressel, 2000). Although uninvolved group members may wish to stand back and let the disputants "battle it out," impasses, unflagging conflict escalation, or the combatants' entreaties may cause other group members or outside parties to help by:

- creating opportunities for both sides to express themselves while controlling contentiousness.

- improving communication between the disputants by summarizing points, asking for clarification, and so on.

- helping disputants save face by framing the acceptance of concessions in positive ways and by taking the blame for these concessions.

- formulating and offering proposals for alternative solutions that both parties find acceptable.

- manipulating aspects of the meeting, including its location, seating, formality of communication, time constraints, attendees, and agenda.

- guiding the disputants through a process of integrative problem solving.

However, if the disputants want to resolve the conflict on their own terms, third-party interventions

---

mediator One who intervenes between two persons who are experiencing conflict, with a view to reconciling them.

are considered an unwanted intrusion (Carnevale, 2008).

Go-betweens, facilitators, diplomats, advisers, judges, and other kinds of mediators vary considerably in terms of their power to control others' outcomes (LaTour, 1978; LaTour et al., 1976). In an *inquisitorial procedure*, the mediator questions the two parties and then hands down a verdict that the two parties must accept. In *arbitration*, the disputants present their arguments to the mediator, who then bases his or her decision on the information they provide. In a *moot*, the disputants and the mediator openly and informally discuss problems and solutions, but the mediator can make no binding decisions. Satisfaction with a mediator depends on how well the intermediary fulfills these functions and also on the intensity of the conflict. Mediational techniques, such as arbitration, are effective when the conflict is subdued, but they may not work when conflict intensity is high. Overall, most people prefer arbitration, followed by moot, mediation, and inquisitorial procedures (LaTour et al., 1976; Ross, Brantmeier, & Ciriacks, 2002; Ross & Conlon, 2000).

The Value of Conflict: Redux

Conflict is a natural consequence of joining a group. Groups bind their members and their members' outcomes together, and this interdependence can lead to conflict when members' qualities, ideas, goals, motivations, and outlooks clash. As the group cycles through the phases of disagreement, conflict, conflict escalation and de-escalation, and resolution, relationships are strained or broken, tempers are lost, feelings are hurt, and work is left undone. When Carsten De Dreu and Laurie Weingart (2003) conducted a meta-analysis of dozens of studies of conflict in groups, they discovered that, in study after study, conflict undermined satisfaction and lowered performance. De Dreu and Weingart (2003, p. 748) conclude that:

> Conflict may have positive consequences under very specific circumstances, and we need to detect those circumstances in new research. While waiting for these studies,

however, it seems safe to stop assuming that, whereas relationship conflict is detrimental to team performance, task conflict improves team performance. Clearly, it does not.

Conflict Management But is conflict always harmful—a pernicious process that should be avoided? This question remains open to debate, but it may be that the problem is not conflict, but *mismanaged conflict*. As noted in Chapter 5, many groups pass through a period of conflict as they mature. This conflict phase, so long as it is managed well, expands the range of options, generates new alternatives, and enhances the group's unity by making explicit any latent hostilities and tensions. Conflict can make a group's goals more explicit and help members understand their role in the group. It may force the members to examine, more carefully, their assumptions and expectations and may help the group focus on its strengths and diagnose its weaknesses. A group without conflict may be working so perfectly that no one can identify any improvements, but more likely it is a group that is boring and uninvolving for its members. Conflict, then, is not the culprit. It is poor management of the conflicts that inevitably arise in groups that leads to problems (DeChurch Hamilton, & Haas, 2007; Jehn, 1997; Jehn & Bendersky, 2003).

Organizational and business administration researcher Kristin Behfar and her colleagues (2008) examined the consequences of poorly managed conflict in their detailed quantitative analysis of 57 autonomous work teams. These groups all worked with the same resources, on the same types of projects, and with the same time constraints. Over time, some of the groups became more capable in the task realm, but others did not. Some, too, enjoyed increasingly positive relations among members, whereas others exhibited declines in the quality of their cohesion.

Behfar's group discovered that these changes in task success and interpersonal bonds were related to the group's methods of dealing with conflict. All of the groups experienced conflicts as their work progressed, but they dealt with these problems in different ways. The 21 best teams proactively forecasted possible problems before they happened. They developed schedules and assigned responsibilities carefully, in unemotional, fact-driven discussions, to reach consensus. They did not report dealing with relationship conflict, because they did not have any. A second set of 11 high-performance groups had little cohesiveness, but these groups all expressly discussed their lukewarm interpersonal relations and dismissed the importance of social connections. These groups resolved task and process conflicts by voting. The 14 worst teams, who exhibited both declining performance and interpersonal dysfunction, also used discussion, but the discussion never resolved their problems. These groups reported trying to deal with their problems openly, but members would just give in to more dominant members because they grew tired of arguing. They dealt with their performance problems by rotating duties from one member to another, but they never analyzed the effectiveness of this technique.

These findings suggest that the impact of conflict on a group cannot be predicted until the group's capacity for managing its conflict is known. Groups that take proactive steps to prevent conflict from arising in the first place tend to be more satisfying to members than those that only

respond—and respond poorly at that—to conflicts when they arise. Successful groups also tended to adopt pluralistic strategies for dealing with conflict, rather than particularistic ones. They resolved conflicts using methods that applied to the group as a whole, such as developing rules, standardizing procedures, and assigning tasks to members based on skill and expertise rather than status. Less successful groups, in contrast, used strategies that focused on specific individual complaints or the group's concerns about one or two members. In these groups, the "squeaky wheel would get the grease," but the repair was not sufficient to restore the group to health.

Jobs versus Sculley Did Apple gain from the conflict, or did it suffer a setback as its top executives fought for power and control? In the case of Apple, the dispute between Jobs and Sculley was resolved, but not without a considerable investment of time, resources, and energy. Two men who were once friends parted as enemies. A company that once profited from the leadership of two visionary thinkers lost one of them to a competitor. Before the conflict, Apple was an unconventional, risk-taking trendsetter. After the conflict, the company focused on costs, increasing sales, and turning a profit. Conflict stimulates change—both positive and negative.

CHAPTER REVIEW

What is conflict?

1. When *conflict* occurs in a group, the actions or beliefs of one or more members of the group are unacceptable to and resisted by one or more of the other members.

2. *Intergroup conflict* involves two or more groups, and *intragroup conflict* occurs within a group.

3. Conflict follows a cycle from disagreement to conflict to escalation to de-escalation to resolution.

What are the sources of conflict in groups?

1. Many group and individual factors conspire to create conflict in a group, but the most

common sources are competition, conflicts over the distribution of resources, power struggles, task and process conflicts, and personal conflicts.

2. Competing: Deutsch's early theorizing suggests that *independence* and *cooperation* lower the likelihood of conflict, whereas *competition* tends to increase conflict by pitting members against one another.

- Cooperation is associated with areas of the brain that deal with social rewards, whereas competition stimulates areas pertaining to social perception, self–other distinctions, and fear.

- *Mixed-motive situations*, like the *prisoner's dilemma game* (PDG), stimulate conflict because they tempt individuals to compete rather than cooperate. Individuals tend to compete more in the single-trial PDG and less in the iterated game.

- *Behavioral assimilation* is caused by the norm of reciprocity; competition sparks competition (negative reciprocity) and cooperation (to a lesser extent) provokes cooperation (positive reciprocity).

- Individuals' proself and prosocial values combine to generate a person's *social value orientation* (SVO): individualistic, competitive, cooperative, and altruistic. Cooperators tend to modify their actions depending on the characteristics of others in their groups.

- Men compete more than women in some situations, but women are more competitive in others. Overall, the sexes do not differ in competitive orientation.

- Younger men do tend to compete more on game shows when playing for high stakes against older contestants.

- Although many educational settings stress competition, reviews conducted by Johnson and Johnson suggest cooperation-based classrooms promote both well-being and learning.

3. Sharing: *Social dilemmas* stimulate conflict by tempting members to act in their own self-interest to the detriment of the group and its goals. Disputes arise when members:

   - exploit a shared resource (a *commons dilemma* or *social trap*).

   - do not contribute their share (a *public goods dilemma*, free riding).

   - disagree on the procedures to follow in dividing the resources (procedural justice) and respond negatively to resource distributions (distributive justice).

- do not agree on the norms to follow when apportioning resources (e.g., equality, equity, power, responsibility, and need).

- feel they are receiving less than they should, given their contribution to the group (negative inequity). This reaction is driven, in part, by self-interest, but group members respond negatively to perceived mistreatment because it calls into question their status and inclusion. Work by Brosnan and de Waal suggests that other species are sensitive to unfair distributions of resources.

- take more than their fair share of responsibility for an outcome (*egocentrism*), avoid blame for group failure, or take too much personal responsibility for group successes (self-serving attributions of responsibility).

4. Controlling: Power struggles are common in groups as members vie for control over leadership, status, and position.

   - Morrill, through ethnographic research, traced many of the conflicts he observed in corporate settings back to the struggle for power.

5. Working: As group members collaborate on tasks, differences and disagreements can generate task and process conflict.

   - *Task conflict* stems from disagreements about issues that are relevant to the group's goals and outcomes. Even though such substantive conflicts help groups reach their goals, these disagreements can turn into personal, unpleasant conflicts.

   - *Process conflicts* occur when members do not agree on group strategies, policies, and methods. Groups avoid such conflicts by clarifying procedures and developing or adopting *rules of order*, such as Robert's Rules.

   - Groups, by dealing with work conflict, can improve their functioning, but in most cases such conflict undermines productivity.

6. Liking and Disliking: *Personal conflict* occurs when individual members do not like one another.

   - Researchers studying groups of children at play discovered the most serious, continuing conflicts are personal ones.

   - Any factor that causes disaffection between group members (e.g., differences in attitudes, objectionable personal qualities) can increase personal conflict.

   - Balance theory predicts that group members will respond negatively when they disagree with those they like or agree with those they dislike, but as Taylor's work confirmed, conflict is greatest when group members both disagree with and dislike each other.

Why does conflict escalate?

1. Once conflict begins, it often intensifies before it begins to abate.

2. When individuals defend their viewpoints in groups, they become more committed to their positions.

   - People sometimes refuse to change their mind to save face.

   - *Reactance*, which is the need to reassert one's freedom, can cause people to rigidly adhere to a position.

3. Conflict is exacerbated by members' tendency to misperceive others and to assume that the other party's behavior is caused by personal (dispositional) rather than situational (environmental) factors (fundamental attribution error).

4. As conflicts worsen, members shift from soft to hard tactics. Two studies illustrate this shift:

   - Pruitt and his colleagues found that individuals shift from soft tactics to hard influence tactics when their initial requests are denied.

   - Deutsch and Krauss's *trucking game experiment* indicated conflict escalates when each side could threaten the other.

5. Other factors that contribute to the escalation of conflict in groups include:

   - negative reciprocity, as when negative actions provoke negative reactions in others.

   - angry emotions that trigger expressions of anger among members.

   - the formation of coalitions that embroil formerly neutral members in the conflict.

6. Turnage's research indicates *flaming* is online behavior that is perceived by others to be hostile, aggressive, and intimidating. The level of incivility on the Internet is influenced by norms and community sanctions against norm violators.

How can group members manage their conflicts?

1. In many cases, members use *negotiation* to resolve disagreements and disputes. Distributive negotiation involves dividing up resources whereas integrative negotiation involves identifying the issues underlying the dispute and then working together to find a solution that is satisfying to all parties.

2. The Harvard Negotiation Project maintains that principled, integrative negotiation is more effective than either soft or hard bargaining.

3. Because many conflicts are rooted in misunderstandings and misperceptions, group members can reduce conflict by actively communicating information about their motives and goals through discussion.

4. The *dual concern model* identifies four (or five) means of dealing with conflicts—avoiding, yielding, fighting, and cooperating (and conciliation)—that differ along two dimensions: concern for self and concern for others.

   - In some cases, cooperation is more likely to promote group unity.

   - Personal conflicts—those that are rooted in basic differences in attitude, outlook, and so on—may not yield to cooperative negotiations. De Dreu and his colleagues suggest that the avoiding method may be the best way to cope with such conflicts.

- Most cultures recognize the value of cooperation, but Eastern cultures favor avoidance more than Western ones, whereas Western cultures favor competition more than Eastern ones.

5. Other factors that contribute to the de-escalation of conflict in groups include:

   - responding to competition with a tit-for-tat (TFT) strategy, as described by Axelrod.

   - allowing time for individuals to regain composure.

   - expressing positive rather than negative emotions, including forgiveness.

- using third-party interventions—mediators—who impose solutions (inquisitorial procedures and arbitration) or guide disputants to a compromise (moot and mediation procedures).

Is conflict an unavoidable evil or a necessary good?

1. Conflict is a natural consequence of joining a group and cannot be avoided completely.

2. Research by Behfar and others suggests that conflicts, when managed successfully, promote positive group functioning. However, because of the difficulties groups face when trying to deal with conflict, De Dreu and Weingart conclude that in most cases conflict causes more harm than good.

RESOURCES

Chapter Case: Jobs versus Sculley

- *Apple Confidential 2.0: The Definitive History of the World's Most Colorful Company* by Owen W. Linzmayer (2004) provides a well-researched history of the many conflict-laden episodes in the life of Apple, Inc.

Causes of Conflict

- "A History of Social Conflict and Negotiation Research" by Dean G. Pruitt (2012) reviews the history of conflict studies from the perspective of a leading theorist and researcher in the field.

- *The Psychology of Conflict and Conflict Management in Organizations*, edited by Carsten K. W. De Dreu and Michele J.Gelfand (2008), includes chapters examining how conflict influences communication, diversity, motivation, aggression, leadership, and health in organizational settings, written by leading researchers in the field of conflict management.

- "Social Conflict: The Emergence and Consequences of Struggle and Negotiation" by Carsten K. W. De Dreu (2010) reviews the basic theory and latest research examining

the causes of conflict, factors that cause it to escalate, and ways it can be managed.

- *Social Conflict: Escalation, Stalemate, and Settlement* (3rd ed.) by Dean G. Pruitt and Sung Hee Kim (2004) provides a thorough analysis of the causes and consequences of interpersonal conflict.

Conflict Resolution

- *Getting to YES: Negotiating Agreement without Giving In* (2nd ed.) by Roger Fisher, William Ury, and Bruce Patton (1991) describes a step-by-step strategy for resolving conflicts to the mutual benefit of both parties.

- *The Handbook of Conflict Resolution: Theory and Practice*, edited by Morton Deutsch and Peter T. Coleman (2000), is the definitive source-book for general analyses of conflict resolution but also provides practical recommendations for resolving conflicts.

- *Negotiation* by Roy J. Lewicki, David M. Saunders, and Bruce Barry (2010) is a comprehensive text dealing with all aspects of negotiation, including power, bargaining, and interpersonal and intergroup conflict resolution.

14

CHAPTER

Intergroup Relations

CHAPTER OVERVIEW

As a social species, humans strive to establish close ties with one another. Yet the same species that seeks out connections with others also metes out enmity when it confronts members of another group. Intergroup relations are more often contentious than harmonious.

- What interpersonal factors disrupt relations between groups?
- What are the psychological foundations of conflict between groups?
- How can intergroup relations be improved?

CHAPTER OUTLINE

Intergroup Conflict: Us versus Them
    Competition and Conflict
    The Discontinuity Effect
    Power and Domination
    Intergroup Aggression
    Norms of Engagement
    Evolutionary Perspectives

Intergroup Bias: Perceiving Us and Them
    Conflict and Categorization
    The Ingroup—Outgroup Bias
    Cognitive Biases
    Stereotype Content Model
    Exclusion and Dehumanization
    Categorization and Identity

Intergroup Conflict Resolution: Uniting Us and Them
    Intergroup Contact
    Cognitive Cures for Conflict
    Learning to Cooperate
    Resolving Conflict: Conclusions
Chapter Review
Resources

The Robbers Cave Experiment: Group against Group

On two midsummer days in 1954, twenty-two 11-year-old boys from Oklahoma City boarded buses for their trip to summer camp. They were "normal, well-adjusted boys of the same age, educational level, from similar sociocultural backgrounds and with no unusual features in their personal backgrounds" (Sherif et al., 1961, p. 59). Their parents had paid a $25 fee, signed some consent forms, and packed them off to Robbers Cave State Park, located in the San Bois Mountains of southeast Oklahoma.

Robbers Cave was not a typical summer camp. All the boys had been handpicked by a team of social psychologists that included Muzafer Sherif, O. J. Harvey, Jack White, William Hood, and Carolyn Sherif. The Sherifs and their colleagues had spent more than 300 hours interviewing the boys' teachers, studying their academic records, reviewing their family backgrounds, and unobtrusively recording their behavior in school and on the playground. The parents knew that the camp was actually part of a group dynamics research project, but the boys had no idea that the camp was an experiment. The staff randomly assigned each boy to one of two groups. Each group spent a week hiking, swimming, and playing sports in their area of the camp, and both groups developed norms, roles, and structure. Some boys emerged as leaders, others became followers, and both groups established territories within the park (see Figure 14.1). The boys named their groups the Rattlers and the Eagles and stenciled these names on their shirts and painted them onto flags. The staff members, who were also collecting data, noted clear increases in group-oriented behaviors, cohesiveness, and positive group attitudes.

When the groups discovered another group was nearby, they expressed wariness about these outsiders. After some guarded encounters between members, they asked the staff to set up a competition to determine which group was better than the other. Since a series of competitions between the two groups was exactly what the staff had in mind, they held a series of baseball games, tugs-of-war, tent-pitching competitions, cabin inspections, and a (rigged) treasure hunt.

As the competition wore on, tempers flared. When the Eagles lost a game, they retaliated by stealing the Rattlers' flag and burning it. The Rattlers raided the Eagles' cabin during the night, tearing out mosquito netting, overturning beds, and carrying off personal belongings. The conflict reached its crescendo on the final day of competition when the Eagles won the last event and were declared the overall winners. As they celebrated with a swim in the stream, the Rattlers broke into the Eagles' cabin and absconded with the prizes. The Eagles then confronted the Rattlers, who told the Eagles if they would "get down on their bellies and crawl," then they would give back their prizes (Sherif et al., 1961, p. 115). The Eagles refused, and fistfights broke out between the groups. The staff had to intervene to prevent the boys from seriously injuring one another. They moved the two groups to different parts of the camp, amid shouts of "poor losers," "bums," "sissies," "cowards," and "little babies." It was official: the Rattlers hated the Eagles, and the Eagles hated the Rattlers.

Groups are everywhere and so are conflicts between them. Groups provide the means to achieve humanity's most lofty goals, but when groups oppose each other, they are sources of hostility, abuse, and aggression. Chapter 13 examined the causes of and possible cures for conflict between two or more people—intragroup (or interindividual) conflict—but this chapter examines conflict between groups—*intergroup conflict*. It begins by considering the situational factors that combined during the **Robbers Cave experiment** to push the Rattlers and the Eagles into conflict. As with conflict between group members, intergroup conflict becomes more likely when groups compete against each other, but other factors—power, emotions, and norms—are also influential. Relations between groups are further complicated by psychological processes that sustain divisions between groups rather than alliances, including biased intergroup

Robbers Cave experiment A field study that examined the causes and consequences of conflict between two groups of boys at Robbers Cave State Park in Oklahoma (designed and conducted by Muzafer and Carolyn Sherif and their colleagues).

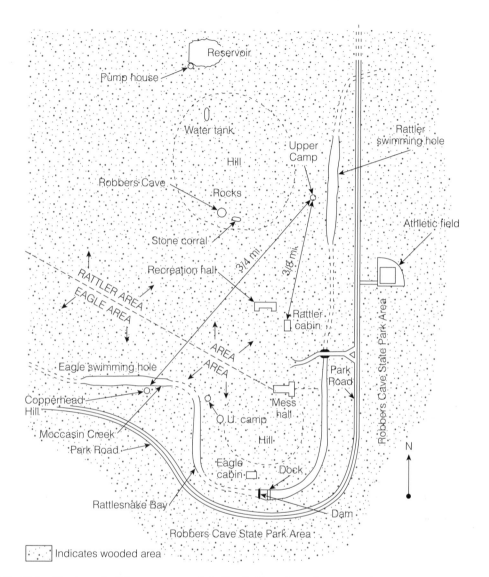

FIGURE 14.1   The layout of the campgrounds in the Robbers Cave Campground.

SOURCE: *Intergroup Conflict and Cooperation. The Robbers Cave Experiment*, by M. Sherif, O. J. Harvey, B. J. White, W. R. Hood, and C. W. Sherif, 1961. Norman, OK: Institute of Group Relations.

perceptions, stereotypes, and group-level emotionality. This analysis will underscore the complexity of intergroup conflict, but not its inevitability: The chapter closes with an analysis of the ways intergroup conflicts can be resolved (for reviews, see Brewer, 2007; Crisp, 2010; Yzerbyt & Demoulin, 2010).

INTERGROUP CONFLICT:
US VERSUS THEM

The researchers' plans for the Robbers Cave experiment worked all too well. In just two weeks, they created a full-fledged war-in-miniature between the Rattlers and the Eagles, complete with violent schemes, hostility, and mistreatment of each side by the other. The Sherifs, by starting with two newly formed groups with no history of rivalry, succeeded in documenting the social and psychological factors that combined to push these two groups into an escalating conflict. Each group at Robbers Cave viewed the other as a rival to be bested, and these perceptions were soon joined by other antecedents of conflict: norms, struggles for status, and ever-strengthening negative emotional reactions. This section examines these causes of conflict, focusing on the Robbers Cave experiment but suggesting implications for other intergroup situations as well.

Competition and Conflict

On the ninth day of the Robbers Cave experiment, the Rattlers and the Eagles saw the tournament prizes for the first time: the shining trophy, medals for each boy, and—best of all—four-blade camping knives. The boys wanted these prizes, and nothing was going to stand in their way. From then on, all group activities revolved around the ultimate goal of winning the tournament. Unfortunately, although both groups aspired to win the prizes, success for one group meant failure for the other. When groups are pitted against each other in a contest for resources, intergroup relations that were once amicable often become antagonistic.

Realistic Group Conflict Theory Many of the things that groups want and need are available in limited supply. Should one group acquire and control a scarce commodity—whether it be food, territory, wealth, power, natural resources, energy, or the prizes so desperately desired by the Rattlers and the Eagles—other groups must do without that resource. According to **realistic group conflict theory**, this struggle between groups over scarce resources inevitably leads to conflict (Campbell,

---

realistic group conflict theory A conceptual framework arguing that conflict between groups stems from competition for scarce resources, including food, territory, wealth, power, natural resources, and energy.

1965; Esses et al., 2005). All groups would prefer to be "haves" rather than "have-nots," so they take steps to achieve two interrelated outcomes—attaining the desired resources and preventing the other group from reaching its goals. Groups often compete economically as they seek to secure resources through manufacturing and trade, but intergroup competition can also trigger intergroup conflict, as groups attempt to dominate one another through the use of force and counterforce. Theorists have traced many negative intergroup dynamics—including struggles between the classes of a society (Marx & Engels, 1947), rebellions (Gurr, 1970), international warfare (Streufert & Streufert, 1986), racism (Gaines & Reed, 1995), religious persecutions (Clark, 1998), tribal rivalries in East Africa (Brewer & Campbell, 1976), police use of lethal force against citizens (Jacobs & O'Brien, 1998), interorganizational conflicts (Jehn & Mannix, 2001), and even the development of culture and social structure (Carneiro, 1970)—to competition over scarce resources.

Competition = Conflict Psychologist Robert Blake and management expert Jane Mouton discovered competition's capacity to create conflict in their work with business executives. They assigned participants in a two-week management training program to small groups charged with solving a series of problems. Blake and Mouton never explicitly mentioned competition, but the participants knew that a group of experts would decide which group had produced the best solution. Many viewed the project as a contest to see who was best, and they wholeheartedly accepted the importance of winning. Leaders who helped the group beat the opponent became influential, whereas leaders of losing groups were replaced. The groups bonded tightly during work and coffee breaks, and only rarely did any participant show liking for a member of another group. In some cases, hostility between the two groups became so intense that the "experiment had to be discontinued" and special steps taken to restore order, tempers, and "some basis of mutual respect" (Blake & Mouton, 1984, 1986, p. 72). These findings and others suggest that *competition*—even competition that is only anticipated—can spark intergroup hostility (Bornstein, 2003; Polzer, 1996; van Oostrum & Rabbie, 1995).

The Discontinuity Effect

During the first week of the Robbers Cave experiment, Mills and Simpson, both Rattlers, competed with each other for status, resources, and respect. But their competition did not result in conflict, for it stabilized when Simpson accepted Mills as the Rattler leader. The competition between the Rattler and the Eagles, in contrast, was more intensive than that between Mills and Simpson, as is consistent with the **discontinuity effect**: the tendency for groups to display a level of competitiveness that is greater than the competitiveness displayed by the individual members. Even though individuals in the group may prefer to cooperate, when they join groups, this cooperative orientation tends to be replaced by a competitive one (see Wildschut et al., 2003, for a review).

Groups Are Uniquely Competitive Social psychologists Chet Insko, John Schopler, and their colleagues documented this discontinuity between interindividual conflict and intergroup conflict by asking individuals and groups to play the *prisoner's dilemma game* (PDG). As noted in Chapter 13, this mixed-motive game offers the two participating parties a choice between cooperation and competition with rewards depending on both parties' choices. This interdependence is illustrated in the sample PDG matrix in Figure 14.2. Option C is the cooperative choice and D is the competitive, defecting-from-cooperation, choice. Cooperation (option C) will yield the best outcomes for both groups if they both select C, but if one picks C and the other picks D, then the cooperative group's

___

discontinuity effect The markedly greater competitiveness of groups when interacting with other groups, relative to the competitiveness of individuals interacting with other individuals.

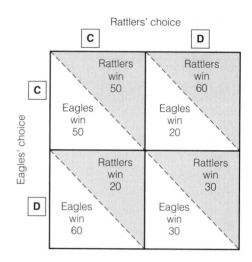

F I G U R E 14.2 The prisoner's dilemma game payoff matrix used to study competition and intergroup conflict. Groups tend to select option D much more frequently than option C.

SOURCE: © Cengage Learning

payoff will be small (20 points) compared to the competitive group's payoff (60 points). If both groups select Option D, then their rewards will be cut in half.

When one person played another person, very few of these singles competed: only 6.6% over the course of the game. Competition was also rare when three individuals—who would share profits at the end of the game but, until then, could not talk to one another—played another set of three independent individuals (7.5%). But when an interacting triad played another interacting triad, 36.2% of their choices were competitive, and when triads played triads but communicated their choices through representatives selected from within the group, competition rose to 53.5% (Insko et al., 1987). These findings are remarkably consistent—a meta-analysis of 48 separate studies conducted in 11 different group dynamics laboratories confirmed that groups are disproportionately more competitive than individuals (Wildschut et al., 2003).

Discontinuity across Social Interactions This discontinuity between individuals and groups is not confined to groups playing a structured conflict game. When researchers examined everyday social interactions, they found that group activities were marked by more competition than one-on-one activities. Participants diligently recorded their interpersonal activities for an entire week, classifying them into one of five categories:

- *One-on-one interactions:* dyadic interactions, such as playing chess, walking to class with another person.

- *Within-group interactions:* interacting with other members of one's group, such as a club meeting or a classroom discussion.

- *One-on-group interactions:* interacting as a single individual with a group, such as a student meeting with the honor council.

- *Group-on-one interactions:* interacting as a part of a group with a single individual, such as a class confronting a teacher over a grading policy.

- *Group-on-group interactions:* interacting as part of a group with another group, such as a soccer game or a joint session of two classes.

As Figure 14.3 indicates, the proportion of competitive interactions within each type of interaction climbed steadily as people moved from one-on-one interactions to group interactions. These effects also emerged when sports activities, which could have exacerbated the competitiveness of groups, were eliminated from the analysis (Pemberton, Insko, & Schopler, 1996). Other research suggests that the discontinuity effect may be intensified in situations that provoke thoughts of physical injury and death (McPherson & Joireman, 2009).

Causes of Discontinuity The consistency of the discontinuity effect suggests that it springs from a number of causes that combine to exacerbate conflicts between groups, including greed, anonymity, fear, ingroup favoritism, and diffusion of responsibility (Pinter et al., 2007). First, individuals are greedy, but groups are even greedier. When people discover that others in the group are leaning in the direction of maximizing gains by exploiting others, this social support spurs the group members on to greater levels of greed. When researchers changed

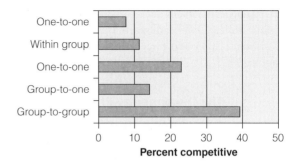

FIGURE 14.3 The level of competitiveness of five everyday situations ranging from one-to-one interactions to group-to-group interactions.

SOURCE: From tabled data in "Memory for and Experience of Differential Competitive Behavior of Individuals and Groups" by M. B. Pemberton, C. A. Insko, and J. Schopler, 1996, *Journal of Personality and Social Psychology, 71*, 953–966.

the PDG matrix payoff so that greed was no longer so lucrative, groups learned how to cooperate with each other to maximize joint gains (Wolf et al., 2008).

Second, people fear groups more than they fear individuals. They describe groups as more abrasive (competitive, aggressive, proud) and less agreeable (cooperative, trustworthy, helpful) than individuals. This pessimistic outlook also colors their expectations about specific group interactions, for people who were about to play the PDG against a group felt that the experience would be more abrasive than did individuals about to play the game as individuals (Hoyle, Pinkley, & Insko, 1989). People who are playing the PDG against a group also worry more about exploitation and fair play. They say such things as "We don't trust you" and "You better not cheat us" to their opponents, so communication between groups does little to quell tensions (Insko et al., 1990, 1993, 1994; Schopler & Insko, 1992; Schopler et al., 1995). This generalized distrust, in the extreme, has been termed *intergroup paranoia:* the belief held by the members of one group that they will be mistreated in some way by the members of a malevolent outgroup (Kramer, 2004).

Third, group members may feel that, as part of a group, they should do what they can to maximize the group's collective outcomes—that part of being good group members or leaders is to do what they can to increase the team's achievements, even if that comes at a cost to those outside of the group (Pinter et al., 2007). This sense of group duty may also trigger a stronger desire to outdo the other group as well as generate the best possible outcome for the ingroup. Groups playing a game where cooperation would have favored both groups equally seemed to transform, psychologically, the payoff matrix from a cooperation-favoring game into the more competitive PDG game (Wolf et al., 2008).

Fourth, diffusion of responsibility may also contribute to the discontinuity effect (Meier & Hinsz, 2004). In one experiment, investigators told individuals and groups they were studying people's reactions to different foods, but, for the purposes of experimental control, the subjects themselves would be selecting the amount of food given to others. All the subjects were led to believe that they had been assigned to the hot sauce condition, which involved giving helpings of painfully hot-spiced sauce to others to eat. They were also told that they were paired with either a group or an individual and that their partner had measured out a substantial portion of hot sauce for them to consume. They were then given the opportunity to select the amount of sauce to send back to their partner in the nearby room.

The study's results confirmed the discontinuity effect. Groups allocated, and received, more grams of hot sauce than individuals, with the result that group-to-group aggression was substantially higher than the individual-to-group and group-to-individual pairs. The greater aggressiveness did not appear to be due to the more aggressive group members convincing the others to dispense more punishment to their partners. Even though the researchers measured each group member's personal level of aggressiveness, groups with more aggressive individuals did not act more aggressively as a group. The researchers did find that those in groups reported feeling less responsible for their actions.

Deterring Discontinuity   What can be done to reduce the exaggerated competitiveness of groups relative to individuals? Insko and his associates find

that communication does little to reduce the effect, since in many cases the two factions communicate negative information or misinformation. Communication did lower the magnitude of the discontinuity, but not by lowering the level of conflict between groups. Instead, it tended to increase the level of conflict between individuals, to the point that they were as competitive as groups. This unexpected effect of communication was more likely to occur when communication was restricted in some way, as when interactants could only send written messages (Wildschut et al., 2003).

A tolerant appeasement approach to conflict also proved ineffective in reducing discontinuity. As with studies of individuals, when groups respond cooperatively even when the other party competes—hoping to signal their good intentions and inviting a reduction in conflict—the other group responds by exploiting the pacifistic group. A reciprocal strategy, such as *tit for tat* (TFT), was a more effective strategy to counter discontinuity. As noted in Chapter 13, TFT matches competition with competition and cooperation with cooperation. This strategy, Insko suggests, allays groups' fears that they will be exploited, for it reassures them that they can trust the other group. Other methods for reducing the discontinuity effect include decreasing the rewards of competition (by changing the values in the PDG matrix) and each member's anonymity (Wildschut et al., 2003).

Power and Domination

Intergroup conflicts, though initially rooted in competition for scarce resources, can escalate into *intergroup exploitation* as one group tries to dominate the other. Not only do groups wish to monopolize and control contested resources but they also wish to gain control over the other group's resources, which can include its wealth, land, peoples, and identity (Rouhana & Bar-Tal, 1998).

Social Dominance Theory   The Robbers Cave campground included three groups organized in a hierarchy of authority. The staff was more powerful than the campers, for they controlled all the camp's resources and mandated each day's activities. Neither the Rattlers nor the Eagles challenged the staff, but they did challenge each other as they struggled to rise above the other in the hierarchy (Sherif, White, & Harvey, 1955).

This hierarchical structure, and the tension that it produced, is explained by social psychologists Jim Sidanius, Felicia Pratto, and their colleagues' **social dominance theory**. This theory assumes that, just as some individuals within a group are more influential than others, groups within a community, organization, or society also vary in their capacity to influence other groups. Whereas some groups come to control more of the collective's resources (e.g., wealth, property, status, and protection), other groups occupy positions subordinate to these higher status groups and may even be oppressed by them. Sidanius and Pratto further suggest that members of the dominant groups tend to believe that this inequitable apportioning of resources is justified by precedent, by custom, or even by law. They may deny that the distribution of resources is actually unfair or claim that the dominance of one group over another is consistent with the natural order. The lower-status groups, however, often vie with other lower-ranked groups and with the dominant groups for power and resources (Sidanius et al., 2007; Sidanius & Pratto, 1999).

The Corruptive Effects of Dominance This cycle of domination and resistance occurs between nations, classes, ethnic groups, the sexes, and even small groups in controlled experimental situations. Chet Insko and his colleagues examined exploitation and conflict by creating a simulated social system in the laboratory. Insko's microsocieties included three interdependent groups, multiple generations of members, a communication network, products, and a trading system (Insko et al., 1980, 1983).

---

social dominance theory An approach to oppression and domination assuming that conflict between groups results from dynamic tensions between hierarchically ranked groups within society (developed by Sidanius, Pratto, and their colleagues).

Insko assigned the microsocieties to one of two experimental conditions. In the economic power condition, one group could produce more varied products, so it quickly became the center of all bargaining and trading. In the coercive power condition, the group whose members were supposedly better problem solvers was given the right to confiscate any products it desired from the other groups. (Insko referred to these conditions as the Service condition and the Carneiro condition, respectively.)

These differences in power had a dramatic effect on productivity and intergroup relations. In the economic power condition, all three groups reached very high levels of productivity, with the advantaged group slightly outperforming the others. In contrast, none of the groups in the coercive power condition were very productive. As the "idle rich" hypothesis suggests, the members of the powerful group spent less time working when they could confiscate others' work. But the other groups reacted very negatively to this exploitation, and as the powerful group continued to steal their work, the members of the other groups held strikes and work slowdowns and sabotaged their products. (Men, in particular, were more likely to strike back against the oppressive group.) Eventually, the groups worked so little that the dominant group could not confiscate enough products to make much profit. These results suggest that as with intragroup conflict, one sure way to create conflict is to give one party more coercive power than the other (Deutsch & Krauss, 1960). Apparently, when it comes to power, more is not always better.

Individual Differences in Social Dominance Social dominance theory recognizes that people differ from each other in their appraisal of the fairness of these disparities in power and status. Whereas some challenge this inequality, others recognize, and even support, the idea that some groups should be dominant and others oppressed. Do you, for example, agree with these statements?

- If certain groups of people stayed in their place, we would have fewer problems.

- Inferior groups should stay in their place.
- Sometimes other groups must be kept in their place.

Or, are these statements more consistent with your beliefs about groups?

- We should do what we can to equalize conditions for groups.
- Group equality should be our ideal.
- [We should] increase social equality.

These items are drawn from the *Social Dominance Orientation* (SDO) questionnaire. As noted in Chapter 8, individuals who are high in social dominance tend to be more interested in gaining and using power, whereas those who are low in social dominance are more likely to seek cooperative ways to handle conflicts. Men's SDO scores are generally higher than women's, and SDO levels are also higher in less economically prosperous countries and those with nondemocratic forms of government (Fisher, Hanke, & Sibley, 2012).

Individuals with high SDO scores are also strongly motivated to maximize their group's gains, particularly in relationship to other groups' outcomes. Sidanius, Pratto, and their colleagues examined this tendency by arranging for white college students who varied in SDO to play an experimental simulation they called Vladimir's Choice. The game is based on a Russian parable about a peasant named Vladimir. As the story goes, God visited Vladimir one day and told him he would grant him one wish. "However," God added: "There is one condition. Anything I give to you will be granted to your neighbor, Ivan, twice over." Vladimir's response, "Okay, take out one of my eyes" (Sidanius et al., 2007, p. 257). In the situation based on this fable, students made choices that would maximize their group's gains or those that would undermine other groups' outcomes. They were led to believe that they were being consulted by the school's administration regarding how student activity funds should be spent, with some options favoring White student interests over minority student interests. These options were contrived so that in order to receive the maximum allocation for their group—19 million dollars—it would mean that minority groups would receive 25 million dollars. In order to lower the amount given to the outgroup, the students had to choose an option that yielded less money for the ingroup.

The majority of the students, 56%, chose the option that split the funds equally between the two groups ($13 million to each). Many also favored allocations that would raise the amount given to both Whites and minorities, for they apparently were not concerned with getting more than the outgroup. Some, however, preferred receiving less money to ensure that their group received more than the minority group. And who was most likely to base their choice on the ingroup's gain over the outgroup's? Those who were high in social dominance orientation (Sidanius et al., 2007).

Eliminating Rivals How would the Rattlers have responded if the camp counselors had given them the option of removing their rivals from the Robbers Cave campground? Would a group, in its quest for social dominance, eliminate a rival altogether? And would the social dominance orientation of the members make a difference in how they reacted (Chirot & McCauley, 2006)?

Researchers studied these questions by arranging for individuals and groups to play a competitive game where winners would qualify for a raffle of $100. Players received feedback as they played each round, and this feedback was controlled so that some were told they were losing the competition, but others were led to believe they were winning. The players were also given the opportunity to punish their opponent by taking some or all of their points and by eliminating them from the competition altogether. Consistent with the discontinuity effect, groups exacted more severe punishments, and they also eliminated their rivals earlier in the contest than did individuals. Unexpectedly, this tendency was more pronounced for the teams that were winning rather than losing—apparently the successful groups felt as if their higher status earned them the privilege of eliminating the competition.

Not so unexpectedly, individuals who had higher SDO scores inflicted more punishment on their opponents, and they chose to eliminate their rivals sooner (McPherson & Parks, 2011).

Intergroup Aggression

Competition, alone, can trigger intergroup conflict, but it also sets in motion a number of other processes that can further aggravate the groups. The Rattlers, as the losers, experienced a high level of frustration, and that frustration triggered an increase in aggressive, hostile actions. They also felt deprived, relative to the Eagles, who had managed to secure the prizes that they sought. Rather than accept the blame for their failure, they denied having lost and tried to declare themselves the winners. Their loss, then, triggered a complicated emotional reaction that included frustration, anger, and a desire to find a scapegoat to blame for their loss (Meier, Hinsz, & Heimerdinger, 2008).

Anger and Retaliation The Rattlers were frustrated. They had set their sights on beating the Eagles, but on the final day of the competition their hopes were dashed; they had to watch as their enemies celebrated and accepted the trophy. When intergroup competitions end, one side is often branded the winner and one the loser. Like the victorious Eagles, winners experience a range of positive emotions, including pride, pleasure, happiness, and satisfaction. Losers, in contrast, experience the "agony of defeat"—humiliation, anger, embarrassment, and frustration (Brown & Dutton, 1995).

These emotions can contribute to the escalation of conflict between groups, for negative emotions have long been considered potent instigators of conflict and hostility. The **frustration-aggression hypothesis**, for example, argues that thwarting environmental conditions lead to feelings of frustration and that these feelings of frustration cause aggression. This view has been refined and extended through research, so that now the **general aggression model** recognizes that many aversive environmental factors—pain, threats, environmental stressors, and so on—can increase arousal, which, when paired with a negative appraisal of the situation, can generate aggression. And, as in the Robbers Cave experiment, once one group engages in aggression, the likelihood that the other group will respond aggressively increases, setting in motion a cycle of conflict escalation:

> Group A experiences Group B's retaliation, which causes Group A's members to have high levels of aggressive affect, to perceive Group B as hostile and aggressive, and to experience heightened arousal. These internal states cause members of Group A to act impulsively on their immediate appraisal of Group B as hostile and threatening. Group B then experiences the impulsively aggressive act from Group A, which sets in motion the same set of internal states and appraisal and decision processes that result in an even more aggressive retaliation (DeWall, Anderson, & Bushman, 2011, pp. 248–249).

Scapegoat Processes At Robbers Cave, the Rattlers attacked their enemy, the Eagles. In some cases, however, a group that experiences a privation will turn against a third party, rather than the group that originally caused the harm. The third group would be a *scapegoat*—a label derived from the biblical ritual of guilt transference—since anger originally aroused by one group becomes displaced on another, usually more defenseless

---

frustration–aggression hypothesis An early motivational model that argued that individuals become more aggressive whenever external conditions prevent them from reaching their goals.

general aggression model A framework for organizing biological, environmental, social, and psychological factors that influence the expression of hostile, negative behavior, including (a) person and situational inputs; (b) cognitive, affective, and arousal states, and (c) cognitive appraisals.

group. **Scapegoat theory** assumes that attacking a scapegoat provides an outlet for pent-up anger and frustration, and the aggressive group may then feel satisfied that justice has been done.

Scapegoating, as a possible cause of intergroup rather than interindividual conflict, requires a degree of consensus among group members. Individuals often blame others for their troubles and take out their frustrations on them, but group-level scapegoating occurs when the group, as a whole, has settled on a specific target group to blame for their problems (Glick, 2009). Scapegoating is more likely when a group has experienced difficult, prolonged negative experiences—not just petty annoyances or a brief economic downturn, but negative conditions that frustrate their success in meeting their most essential needs (Staub, 2004). In such cases, the group may develop a compelling, widely shared ideology, which, combined with political and social pressures, leads to the most extreme form of scapegoating: genocide. Scapegoating can also prompt oppressed groups to lash out at other oppressed groups. Even though the minority groups are is victimized by the majority group, minorities sometimes turn against other minority groups rather than confront the more powerful majority (Harding et al., 1969; Rothgerber & Worchel, 1997).

Norms of Engagement

Conflicts between groups—protests between rioters and police, war between nations, gang fights, or even the conflict between the Rattlers and the Eagles—are not out-of-control, atypical interpersonal actions that occur when the social order breaks down. Normatively, competition and hostility between groups are often completely consistent with the standards of conduct in that situation.

---

scapegoat theory An explanation of intergroup conflict arguing that hostility caused by frustrating environmental circumstances (such as abuse by others or failure) is released by taking hostile actions against members of other social groups.

Reciprocity   Groups, like individuals, tend to obey the *norm of reciprocity*. They answer threats with threats, insults with insults, and aggression with aggression. Consider, for example, the infamous Hatfield–McCoy feud that involved a dispute between two large families in a rural area of the United States in the late nineteenth century (Rice, 1978). The conflict originated with the theft of some hogs by Floyd Hatfield. The McCoys countered by stealing hogs from another member of the Hatfield clan, and soon members of the two families began taking potshots at one another. Between 1878 and 1890, more than 10 men and women lost their lives as a direct result of interfamily violence. Likewise, studies of gangs indicate that many street fights stem from some initial negative action that in reality may pose little threat to the offended group. The target of the negative action, however, responds to the threat with a counterthreat, and the conflict spirals. Battles resulting in the death of gang members have begun over an ethnic insult, the intrusion of one group into an area controlled by another group, or the theft of one gang's property by another gang (Gannon, 1966; Yablonsky, 1959). Large-scale intergroup conflicts, such as race riots and warfare between countries, have also been caused by gradually escalating hostile exchanges (Myers, 1997; Reicher, 2001).

An upward *spiral model of conflict intensification* accurately describes the unfolding of violence at Robbers Cave. The conflict began with minor irritations and annoyances but built in intensity. *Exclusion*, a mild form of rejection, occurred as soon as the boys realized that another group was sharing the camp. This antipathy escalated into *verbal abuse* when the groups met for the tournament. Insults were exchanged, members of the opposing team were given demeaning names, and verbal abuse ran high. Next, *intergroup discrimination* developed. The groups isolated themselves from each other at meals, and the boys expressed the belief that it was wrong for the other team to use the camp facilities or to be given an equal amount of food. Last came the acts of *physical violence*—the raids, thefts, and fistfights. Thus, the conflict at Robbers Cave built in a series of progressively more dangerous stages from exclusion to verbal abuse to discrimination and, finally, to physical assault (Streufert & Streufert, 1986).

Cultural Norms The extent to which groups respond in hostile ways to other groups varies from culture to culture. The Mbuti pygmies of Africa, !Kung, and many Native American tribes (e.g., the Blackfoot and Zuñi) traditionally avoided conflict by making concessions. In these societies, and those discussed in Focus 14.1, men were not regarded as brave or strong if they were aggressive, and lethal encounters between groups were rare (Bonta, 1997). In contrast, for the Yanomanö of South America and the Mundugumor of New Guinea, aggression is a cultural value (Chagnon, 1997; Mead, 1935). The anthropologist Napoleon Chagnon called the Yanomanö the "fierce people," for during the time he studied them they seemed to enjoy an armed conflict as much as a peaceful feast. Adjacent villages coexisted through times of uneasy cooperation, but any conflicts between tribes were often settled with a raid or ambush (Chirot & McCauley, 2006).

Regional differences in adherence to a *culture of honor* may also cause variations in intergroup conflict. As discussed in Focus 3.2, in some regions of the world, including the south of the United States, residents are more likely to respond negatively to challenges. Individuals in such cultures are not necessarily more positive about aggression, but they are more likely to recommend aggressive responses for self-defense and in response to insults (Nisbett & Cohen, 1996; Vandello & Cohen, 2003). These norms of the culture of honor are now anachronistic, but they are sustained by misperceptions about the commonness of aggressive behavior (Vandello, Cohen, & Ransom, 2008).

Group Norms Some groups within the larger society adopt unique norms and values pertaining to intergroup conflict. In the United States, the Mennonites and the Amish avoid interpersonal conflict and strive instead for cooperative, peaceful living. Other types of groups, such as urban youth gangs, sports fans, and cliques in schools, accept norms that emphasize dominance over other groups. Soccer fans show high levels of ingroup loyalty but equally intense forms of aggression against fans of rival clubs (Foer, 2004). Groups of young girls develop intricate patterns of ingroup favoritism and outgroup rejection (Wiseman, 2002). Even though they rarely engage in physical aggression, their relational aggression can be so pointed and unrelenting that it leads to long-term negative consequences for those they target. Studies of gangs living in urban areas suggest that these groups, although violent, use aggression in instrumental ways to maintain group structures and patterns of authority. Much of the most intense violence is intergroup conflict, when one gang must defend its area from another, or when the gang decides that it must inflict harm on someone who has acted in ways that undermine the local gang's authority (Venkatesh, 2008).

Evolutionary Perspectives

Evolutionary psychology offers a final set of causes, more distal than proximate, for conflict between groups. The tendency for conflict to emerge between groups is so pervasive that some experts believe that it may have a genetic basis. As noted in Chapter 3 and Focus 14.1, many theorists believe that contemporary humans' ancestors lived for much of their evolutionary past in small bands of between 50 and 150. These groups provided such an advantage to their members in terms of survival that, over time, humans became a social species— ready to cooperate with other humans in the pursuit of shared goals (Dunbar, 1998).

These same evolutionary pressures, however, also left humans ready to respond negatively to any human who was not a member of his or her group or tribe. Groups likely competed, forcefully, against other groups, claiming territories, plundering the resources of neighboring groups, and harming the members of those groups. In consequence, if a member strayed too far from the safety of his or her group, then the greatest danger was not from wild animals but from humans who were outsiders. Because outgroups were a substantial threat, the

F o c u s   **14.1**   **Cross-cultural Perspectives: Searching for a Peaceful People**

The encounter between the Rattlers and the Eagles resulted in conflict between these two groups, but is that not the way such encounters usually turn out? In centuries past, when one group encountered another, the result was often conflict with each group striving to take, by force if necessary, what it could from the other. The Yanomanö are not the world's only fierce people. But some cases groups have lived comfortably together, peacefully, in close proximity to each other, and have even helped one another in times of hardship and adversity. Are humans, by nature, peaceful or warlike?

This question has been debated for centuries. Thomas Hobbes, for example, argued that, were it not for the restraints of civilization, humans would live in "continual fear, and danger of violent death" and their lives would be "solitary, poor, nasty, brutish, and short" (1651/2008, p. 86). Jean-Jacques Rousseau disagreed and championed the basic goodness of humans who have lived free of the corruptive effects of complex societies: "So many authors have hastily concluded that man is naturally cruel, and requires a regular system of police to be reclaimed; whereas nothing can be more gentle than him in his primitive state, when placed by nature at an equal distance from the stupidity of brutes and the pernicious good sense of civilized man" (Rousseau, 1755/2008, p. 35).

The question Hobbes and Rousseau debated remains unsettled even today, with some arguing that intergroup conflict is a pervasive, and possibly instinctive, human tendency, but others arguing that conflict, when it does occur, is the result of situational circumstances rather than instinctual drives. Anthropological studies, for example, explore the question by examining instances of conflict and cooperation in ancient cultures as well as contemporary ones. Unfortunately, analysis of prehistoric human groups yields little in the way of definitive evidence of either habitual conflict or cooperation between groups. Most anthropologists believe that humans survived for much of the species' history in relatively small groups, but little is known about the relationships between these groups. When one clan would encounter another, did they welcome each other and share resources? Did they extend the same level of support for ingroup members to those in the outgroup? Or did these groups deal with each other in a more circumspect, and in some cases, hostile manner? Anthropologists have studied several locations where humans lived in ancient times, but they have yet to discover artifacts that suggest one group ever battled another group; if two groups entered into

lethal combat, they left behind few traces of the conflict (Festinger, 1983).

Cross-cultural studies of conflict between different societies also yield conflicting evidence on the question of humanity's intergroup tendencies. Two large databases of ethnographic records of the world's cultures—the Human Relations Areas Files (http://www.yale.edu/hraf/) and the Standard Cross-cultural Sample (http://escholarship.org/uc/wc_worldcultures)—include example after example of cultures that display combative reactions to other groups. Most cultures, for example, condone violence when perpetrated against the members of outgroups. Only 15.6% of the societies in the Standard Cross-cultural Sample value violence against subgroups within the community, but 61% value violence taken against members of other societies; another 25% consider it to be acceptable. Nearly half of the cultures surveyed considered warfare against other groups to be a socially valued activity and another 35% viewed it to be a necessary evil. Only 15% of the cultures in the survey avoided or openly denounced warfare. Nearly all known societies have engaged in an intergroup conflict that resulted in lethal outcomes in the last 50 years (Ember & Ember, 1994).

Intergroup conflict, however, is not a human universal, for some societies avoid entering into conflicts with other groups in any and all circumstances. Anthropologist Douglas Fry (2007), after scouring the ethnographic research literature, identified more than 70 societies—for example, the Martu and Arunta of Australia, the Saulteaux (a First Nation in Canada), and the Semai and Jahai of the Malay Peninsula—that avoid conflicts with other groups. The Semai, for example, value harmony in their interpersonal relations and rely on a group of tribal arbitrators to settle disputes that arise between group members. When other groups encroach upon their settlements, they usually respond by moving away from the intruding groups rather than defending their territories. Fry concludes that "not all societies make war. Humans have a solid capacity for getting along with each other peacefully, preventing physical aggression, limiting the scope and spread of violence, and restoring peace following aggression" (Fry, 2007, pp. 20–21).

Fry's findings indicate that intergroup conflict is not a necessary condition of human existence, but the societies he identified may be exceptions produced by unusual historical and environmental circumstances. Intergroup conflict, including warfare between

F o c u s   14.1   (Continued)

nations, has become increasingly commonplace in the last 10,000 years and shows little sign of decreasing. His findings do, however, offer some cause for optimism, for they suggest that while groups often resolve their conflicts with one another through violence, this choice is not one forced on them by genetic heritage. Nature may push groups into conflicts, but the push is not an irresistible one.

---

human mind developed the capacity to determine, with unerring accuracy, each person's tribal allegiance. Those who failed to distinguish between insiders and outsiders were less likely to survive.

According to evolutionary theory, these pressures also resulted in the gendering of intergroup biases. Men were, and continue to be, the warriors of human groups. In consequence, they are physically larger, stronger, and more biologically ready to aggress than are women. Humans are, in consequence, quicker to respond negatively to outgroup members who are male rather than female, and some evolutionary psychologists suggest that this reaction is produced by different psychological mechanisms for men as compared to women. Men respond negatively to outgroup males because they are viewed as possible enemies in violent confrontations of dominance. Women respond negatively to outgroup males because of a perceived vulnerability to sexual coercion (McDonald, Navarrete, & Van Vugt, 2012; Navarrete et al., 2010). In any case, men are more likely to encounter rejection by members of another group than are women.

Intergroup conflict was also instrumental in fostering the conditions needed to promote ingroup cooperation. Few experts believe that humans, as a species, could have survived had they not developed the means to cooperate with one another in the pursuit of joint outcomes. The development of this remarkable human capacity required a stable community of members, with care focused first on genetically related individuals and secondarily on group members who would be present on future occasions when helping could be reciprocated. These conditions, so essential to the survival of these fragile groups, could be maintained only if group members were well-known to one another and normatively bound to reciprocate exchanges without undue levels of selfishness. This capacity for intragroup cooperation may have been further enhanced by the presence of outgroups. Facing a threat from an outgroup, the ingroup became more unified, producing a level of solidarity that increased each member's likelihood of surviving by linking him or her to the survival of the group as a whole (Van Vugt, De Cremer, & Janssen, 2007).

These aspects of the evolutionary environment, over time, resulted in adaptations that increased the fitness of the individual, but at the price of creating a generalized hostility for members of other groups. The human species developed an extraordinary capacity for altruism, cooperation, and selflessness, but these prosocial behaviors are usually reserved for members of the ingroup and sustained by hostility toward the outgroup.

INTERGROUP BIAS: PERCEIVING US AND THEM

The boys in the Robbers Cave experiment displayed antipathy toward the other group even before the idea of a competitive tournament was mentioned. The Rattlers and Eagles had not even seen each other when they began to refer to "those guys" in a derogatory way:

> When the ingroup began to be clearly delineated, there was a tendency to consider all others as outgroup.... The Rattlers didn't know another group existed in the camp until they heard the Eagles on the ball diamond; but from that time on the outgroup figured prominently in their

lives. Hill (Rattler) said "They better not be in our swimming hole." The next day Simpson heard tourists on the trail just outside of camp and was convinced that "those guys" were down at "our diamond" again. (Sherif et al., 1961, p. 94)

The conflict at Robbers Cave was fueled by the competitive setting, situational norms, the struggle for power, and the frustrations that followed each loss, but these factors cannot fully account for the almost automatic rejection of members of the other group. Group members reject members of other groups not because they fear them or because they must compete with them, but simply because they belong to a different group.

Conflict and Categorization

When Mills, a Rattler, met Craig, an Eagle, on the path to the dining hall, he spontaneously classified him as an Eagle rather than a Rattler. This *social categorization* process, although adaptive in the long run, nonetheless provides a cognitive foundation for intergroup conflict. Once Mills realized the boy approaching him was an Eagle and not a Rattler, he considered him to be one of *them*—an outsider who was different from the Rattlers. As Sherif (1966, p. 12) explained, "Whenever individuals belonging to one group interact, collectively or individually, with another group or its members in terms of their group identification, we have an instance of intergroup behavior."

Does social categorization, in and of itself, cause conflict? Does the mere existence of identifiable groups within society, and the cognitive biases generated by this differentiation, inevitably push groups into conflict? Research by Henri Tajfel, John Turner, and their colleagues, as discussed in Chapter 3, demonstrated the pervasiveness of the intergroup bias in their studies of a minimal intergroup situation. Like the Sherifs, they examined groups that had no prior group history. But, unlike the Sherifs, they took this minimalism to its limit by creating groups that were hardly groups at all. Formed on the basis of some trivial similarity or

situational factor, the group members did not talk to each other, were anonymous throughout the study, and could not personally gain in any way from advantaging one person in the study over another. Even in these minimal groups, people favored their own; they gave more money to members of their own group and withheld money from the outgroup. Tajfel and Turner concluded that the "mere perception of belonging to two distinct groups—that is, social categorization per se—is sufficient to trigger intergroup discrimination favoring the ingroup" (Tajfel & Turner, 1986, p. 13).

Categorization sets in motion a number of affective, cognitive, emotional, and interpersonal processes that combine to sustain and encourage conflict between groups. People do not simply segment people into the categories "member of my group" and "member of another group" and then stop. Once people have categorized others according to group, they feel differently about those who are in the ingroup and those who are in the outgroup, and these evaluative biases are further sustained by cognitive and emotional biases that justify the evaluative ones—stereotypic thinking, misjudgment, and intensification of emotions. This section reviews these processes, beginning with the most basic: the tendency to favor one's own group.

The Ingroup–Outgroup Bias

The sociologist William Graham Sumner (1906) maintained that humans are, by nature, a species that joins together in groups. But he also noted a second, equally powerful, human tendency: favoring one's own group over all others. "Each group nourishes its own pride and vanity, boasts itself superior, exalts its own divinities, and looks with contempt on outsiders" (p. 13). At the group level, this tendency is called the *ingroup–outgroup bias*; at the tribal, ethnic, or national level, **ethnocentrism** (Sumner, 1906).

---

ethnocentrism The belief that one's own tribe, region, or country is superior to other tribes, regions, or countries.

The magnitude of the bias depends on a host of situational factors, including the group's outcomes, the way perceptions are measured, ambiguity about each group's characteristics, and members' identification with the group. Overall, however, the ingroup–outgroup bias is robust. A rock band knows its music is very good and that a rival band's music is inferior. A 70-year-old knows old people are wiser than the young, and an 18-year-old knows young people are smarter than the elderly. One ethnic group prides itself on its traditions and also views other groups' traditions with disdain. One team of researchers thinks that its theory explains intergroup conflict and criticizes other researchers' theories as inadequate. After a bean-collecting game, the Rattlers overestimated the number of beans collected by Rattlers and slightly underestimated the number of beans supposedly collected by Eagles. Across a range of group and organizational settings, members rate their own group as superior to other groups (Dasgupta, 2004).

Ingroup Positivity and Outgroup Negativity
The ingroup–outgroup bias is really two biases combined: (1) the selective favoring of the ingroup, its members, and its products, and (2) the derogation of the outgroup, its members, and its products. But at Robbers Cave, the pro-ingroup tendency went hand-in-hand with the anti-outgroup tendency. When they were asked to name their friends, 92.5% of the Eagles' choices were Eagles, and 93.6% of the Rattlers' choices were fellow Rattlers. When asked to pick the one person they disliked the most, 95% of the Eagles selected a Rattler, and 75% of the Rattlers identified an Eagle. In many intergroup conflicts, however, ingroup favoritism is stronger than outgroup rejection. For example, during a conflict between the United States and Iraq, U.S. citizens may feel very positive about the United States and its people, but they may not condemn Iraqis. Social psychologist Marilynn Brewer, after surveying a number of studies of intergroup conflict, concluded that the expression of hostility against the outgroup depends on the similarity of ingroup and outgroup members, anticipated future interactions, the type of evaluation being made, and the competitive or cooperative nature of the intergroup situation (see Brewer, 2010; Brewer & Brown, 1998; Hewstone, Rubin, & Willis, 2002).

Double-Standard Thinking   Craig, who was an Eagle, was proud of his group. He considered the Eagles to be superior, in every way, to the Rattlers. His ingroup favoritism, however, likely caused him to evaluate the actions taken by the Eagles more positively than the actions taken by the Rattlers, even when those actions were virtually identical. When people succumb to **double-standard thinking** they rationalize their own group's actions as generous and just, and condemn the actions of the outgroup as hostile and unjust. Our warnings are *requests*, but the other side calls them *threats*. We are *courageous*, though they consider us *stubborn*. Pride in our own group is *nationalism*, but the other group takes it as evidence of *ethnocentrism*. We offer them *concessions*, but they interpret them as *ploys* (De Dreu, Nauta, & Van de Vliert, 1995).

The **linguistic intergroup bias** also results in a subtle recasting of ingroup members' actions in a more positive light. When individuals display this bias, they describe actions differently depending on who performs it. If an ingroup member engages in a negative behavior, such as crying during a game, then members would describe that behavior very concretely—Elliott "shed some tears." If an outgroup member performed the same behavior, they would describe the action more abstractly—Elliott "acted like a baby." Positive behaviors, in contrast, are described in abstract terms when attributed to an ingroup member but in very concrete terms when performed by an outgroup member (Carnaghi et al., 2008; Maass, 1999).

---

double-standard thinking Judging the actions and attributes of one's own group positively, but viewing these very same behaviors or displays negatively when the outgroup performs them.

linguistic intergroup bias The tendency to describe positive ingroup and negative outgroup behaviors more abstractly, and negative ingroup and positive outgroup behaviors more concretely.

Implicit Intergroup Biases Group members often express their preferences openly. Sports fans cheer on their own team and boo their opponents. The Rattlers expressed pride in their own group's accomplishments and ridiculed the Eagles. Racists express support for members of their own group and speak harshly of people with racial backgrounds different from their own.

But in many cases, the ingroup–outgroup bias is an implicit one—subtle, unintentional, and even unconscious, operating below the level of awareness (Fiske, 2004). Even though people may, when asked, claim that they are not biased against outgroup members and do not favor their own group, their biases emerge when their implicit attitudes are measured. One such measure, the *Implicit Association Test* (IAT) developed by social psychologist Anthony Greenwald and his colleagues, assesses the extent to which people associate one concept—such as the ingroup—with another concept—such as goodness. When individuals are shown pairs of words or images that match their intuitive associations of these two concepts, such as ingroup/kind, outgroup/evil, they respond more quickly and without error. When, however, they respond to pairings of concepts that they do not associate with one another, such as ingroup/bad and outgroup/friendly, then they respond more slowly (Greenwald, McGhee, & Schwartz, 2008).

The IAT has revealed subtle ingroup–outgroup biases in dozens of studies using all types of social categories, including race, ethnicity, religion, nationality, age, and sex. Even when people deny any and all preferences based on race, color, or creed, the IAT tells a different story: whites favor whites over blacks; U.S. citizens favor Americans over Canadians; members of fraternities favor other fraternity members over independent students; Catholics favor Catholics over Protestants; the young favor the young over the old; and on and on. These biases occur even when people are striving to suppress their biases (Nosek, Greenwald, & Banaji, 2007).

The IAT also reveals biases in the most minimal of intergroup situations. In one study, participants were arbitrarily classified into one of two groups based on their art preferences (Ashburn-Nardo, Voils, & Monteith, 2001). When they then categorized other people on the basis of their art preferences, they were quicker when classifying (a) ingroup members (people who liked the same artist they did) when these people's names were paired with positive adjectives (e.g., joyous, loving, happy) and (b) outgroup members (people who liked the other artist) when these people's names were paired with negative adjectives (e.g., terrible, nasty, evil). Greenwald and his colleagues even find that just knowing the names of the individuals in a group is sufficient to create a favorable bias toward them and that people's explicit claims about their lack of bias do not always match their responses when tested with the IAT (Pinter & Greenwald, 2011).

Cognitive Biases

When Hill saw Craig, he did not merely judge him more negatively than he would one of his fellow Rattlers (the ingroup–outgroup bias). He probably made inferences about Craig—his physical strength, his athletic skill, even his morality—solely on the basis of one piece of information: Craig was an Eagle. When people categorize others, their perceptions of these individuals are influenced more by their category-based expectations than by the evidence of their senses.

Outgroup Homogeneity Bias Most group members are quick to point out the many characteristics that distinguish them from the other members of their own group ("Why, I'm not like them at all!"), but when they evaluate members of outgroups, they underestimate their variability ("They all look the same to me"). For example, Craig, an Eagle, would describe the Rattlers as poor sports who cheated whenever possible. When describing the Eagles, in contrast, he would admit that a few of the members were sissies and that maybe one Eagle liked to bend the rules, but Craig would probably argue that the Eagles were so heterogeneous that sweeping statements about their typical qualities could not be formulated. Studies of a variety of ingroups and outgroups—women versus men, physics majors versus dance majors, Sorority A versus Sorority B, Princeton students versus Rutgers students, Canadians versus Native Americans, and Blacks versus Whites—have documented this **outgroup homogeneity bias**. Group members' conceptualizations of other groups are simplistic and undifferentiated, but when they turn their eye to their own group, they note its diversity and complexity (see Boldry, Gaertner, & Quinn, 2007, and Linville & Fischer, 1998, for reviews).

The outgroup homogeneity bias does not emerge across all intergroup settings. The group that is disadvantaged in some way is usually viewed as more homogeneous, whereas the more powerful group is viewed as more variable (Guinote, Judd, & Brauer, 2002). The bias can also reverse entirely, resulting in *ingroup homogeneity bias* (Haslam & Oakes, 1995; Simon, Pantaleo, & Mummendey, 1995). Under conditions of extreme conflict, both tendencies may emerge, prompting group members to assume that "none of us deserves this treatment," and "they have harmed us; they must all be punished" (Rothgerber, 1997).

Group Attribution Error   Group members tend to make sweeping statements about the entire outgroup after observing one or two of the outgroup's members. If an African American employee is victimized by a European American boss, the victim may assume that all European Americans are racists. Similarly, a visitor to another country who is treated rudely by a passerby may leap to the conclusion that everyone who lives in that country is discourteous. Individuals in intergroup situations fall prey to the **law of small numbers** when they assume that the characteristics and qualities of all of the members of the outgroup can be accurately inferred

from information pertaining to just a few of its members (Quattrone & Jones, 1980).

The opposite process—assuming that the characteristics of a single individual in a group can be inferred from the general characteristics of the whole group—can also bias perceptions. Craig might know that the Eagles are opposed to swearing, but he would be reluctant to say each Eagle agrees on this rule. When he finds out the Rattlers, as a team, have chosen a snake as their emblem, he would be much more willing to assume that each and every member of the Rattlers likes the snake emblem. Social psychologist Scott Allison and his colleagues studied this **group attribution error** by telling students that an election had recently been held either at their college or at another college to determine how much funding should be given to the college's athletics programs. They then told the students the results of the vote and asked them to estimate the opinion of the "typical student" at the college where the vote was taken. When the students thought that the vote had been taken at their own college, they did not want to assume that the individual's opinion would match the group's opinion. But when they thought that the vote was taken at another college, they were much more confident that the individual's opinions would match the group's opinions (Allison & Messick, 1985b; Allison, Worth, & King, 1990).

Ultimate Attribution Error   When individuals form impressions of other individuals, the *fundamental attribution error* (FAE) prompts them to attribute the actions of others to their personal qualities rather than to the constraints of the situation. But when group members form impressions of outgroup members, the **ultimate attribution error** (UAE)

---

outgroup homogeneity bias The perceptual tendency to assume that the members of other groups are very similar to each other, whereas the membership of one's own group is more heterogeneous.
law of small numbers Basing generalizations about the outgroup on observations of a small number of individuals from that group.

group attribution error Mistakenly assuming that specific group members' personal characteristics and preferences, including their beliefs, attitudes, and decisions, are similar to the preferences of the group to which they belong.
ultimate attribution error Attributing negative actions performed by members of the outgroup to dispositional qualities and positive actions to situational, fluctuating circumstances.

prompts them to attribute only negative actions to outgroup members' dispositional qualities (Hewstone, 1990; Pettigrew, 2001). If outgroup members rob a bank or cheat on a test, then their actions are explained by reference to their personality, genetics, or fundamental lack of morality. But should an outgroup member perform a positive behavior, that action is attributed to a situational factor—perhaps good luck or a special advantage afforded the outgroup member. In any case, the perceiver will conclude that the good act, and the outgroup member who performed it, is just a special case. Because of the UAE, the perceiver concludes that there is no need to reappraise the group because the outgroup member is not responsible for the positive act (Doosje & Branscombe, 2003).

Stereotypes When an Eagle met another Eagle on the trail, he probably expected the boy to be friendly, helpful, and brave. But if he encountered a Rattler, he expected the boy to be unfriendly, aggressive, and deceitful. These expectations are based on **stereotypes**—cognitive generalizations about the qualities and characteristics of the members of a particular group or social category. In many ways, stereotypes function as cognitive labor-saving devices by helping perceivers make rapid judgments about people based on their category memberships (Schneider, 2004). Because they are widely adopted by most of the ingroup, stereotypes are group-level perceptions, shared social beliefs rather than individualistic expectations (Bar-Tal, 2000). But stereotypes tend to be exaggerated rather than accurate, negative rather than positive, and resistant to revision even when directly disconfirmed. People tend to cling to stereotypes so resolutely that they become unreasonable beliefs rather than honest misconceptions. As psychologist Gordon Allport (1954) wrote, "Prejudgments

become prejudices only if they are not reversible when exposed to new knowledge" (p. 8).

If stereotypes have all these perceptual and cognitive limitations, why do they persist? Walter Lippmann (1922), who first used the word *stereotype* to describe mental images of people, argued that the stereotype resists disconfirmation because "it stamps itself upon the evidence in the very act of securing the evidence." When group members see through eyes clouded by stereotypes, they misperceive and misremember people and events. Because individuals tend to interpret ambiguous information so that it confirms their expectations, stereotypes can act as self-fulfilling prophecies (Allport & Postman, 1947). Stereotypes also influence memory, so recall of information that is consistent with stereotypes is superior to recall of stereotype-inconsistent information (Howard & Rothbart, 1980; Rothbart, Sriram, & Davis-Stitt, 1996). Individuals who expect the worst from the outgroup can more easily remember the times that outgroup members acted negatively rather than positively (Hamilton & Sherman, 1989). Because stereotypes affect both the encoding of new information and the retrieval of old information, group membership is one of the most important cues that can influence judgment and memory (Bodenhausen, 1988; Heider et al., 2007).

Stereotype Content Model

Each one of the Rattlers stereotyped the Eagles, but they also applied stereotypes to all the other groups that populated their world: men, women, camp counselors, priests, parents, teachers, students, neighbors, baseball players, and on and on. Each one of these stereotypes likely included unique information pertaining to that group, but the **stereotype content model** suggests that these stereotypes also overlapped to a degree as well.

---

stereotype A socially shared set of cognitive generalizations (e.g., beliefs, expectations) about the qualities and characteristics of the members of a particular group or social category.

---

stereotype content model A theory of group perception positing that people's stereotyped views about social groups reflect their beliefs about the warmth and competence of the stereotyped group.

People do not assume that each group they encounter is utterly unique, but instead they intuitively estimate where the group falls along two basic dimensions: warmth and competence. Some groups (including the ingroup, in most cases) are viewed as warm, nice, friendly, and sincere, whereas other groups are considered to be filled with unpleasant, unfriendly, and even immoral people. The second dimension is competence: Some groups are thought to include competent, confident, skillful, able individuals, whereas other groups are viewed as incompetent or unintelligent. The Rattlers, for example, may have adopted a stereotypic view of the Eagles that rated them as neutral on the warm dimension but more negatively on the competence dimension (Cuddy, Fiske, & Glick, 2007, 2008; Fiske, 2010a; see Figure 14.4).

Conflict and Stereotypes The stereotype content model suggests that group members appraise the outgroup's standing on warmth and competency so as to answer two important questions: "Will this group attempt to harm me and my group?" and "Is this group capable of harming me and my group?" When two groups are competing for some scarce resource, it is essential for the members to have an accurate appraisal of the other group's willingness to inflict harm on their group (warmth), as well as the outgroups potential for effectively executing its plan to achieve that goal. In general, group members view competitors in a group conflict as lacking in warmth, but groups that are willing to collaborate with the ingroup are stereotyped as warm. Turning to the competency dimension, high-status, prestigious, or generally successful groups are viewed as competent, whereas groups that rarely find their way to victory are considered to be incompetent.

Stereotypes and Emotions The stereotype conflict model, in addition to identifying warmth and competence as the two basic dimensions that structure most people's stereotypes about other groups, suggests that these two dimensions also influence people's emotional reactions to other

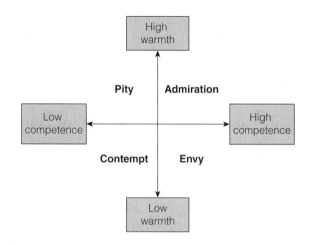

FIGURE 14.4   The stereotype content model.

SOURCE: "The BIAS Map: Behaviors from Intergroup Affect and Stereotypes," by Amy J. C. Cuddy, Susan T. Fiske, and Peter Glick, 2007, *Journal of Personality and Social Psychology, 92,* 631–648.

groups (Cuddy et al., 2009). Instead of assuming people's reactions to outgroups are generally negative, but their appraisal of the ingroup is generally positive, the stereotype conflict model breaks this general emotional reaction down into the following four more specific emotional states (see Figure 14.4):

- *Envy* is most likely when the outgroup, although judged negatively, is nonetheless higher in status than the ingroup and this status difference is thought to be due to the competence of the outgroup. The Eagles, when they lost a game to the Rattlers, were likely to be envious of the Rattlers' athleticism. They did not trust the Rattlers, however, and may have suspected that they gained their advantage unfairly. Groups who are envious of other groups covet what the outgroup has achieved and view the outgroup as a competitor.

- *Contempt* is one of the most common intergroup emotions, occurring when the outgroup is the most negatively stereotyped, that is, viewed as low in terms of both competence and warmth. The members of such an outgroup are viewed as responsible for their failings, and there is little consideration given to the idea that the division between the two groups can ever be lessened.

- *Pity*, as an intergroup emotion, is directed at outgroups that are viewed negatively in terms of competence, but are thought to also have positive, endearing qualities. Pity is usually directed downward, to outgroups that are low in the overall status ranking. Outgroups that evoke pity are not blamed for their plight, unlike outgroups that are held in contempt.

- *Admiration* is rare in intergroup contexts, for it is experienced when the outgroup is perceived as being both high in warmth and high in competence, an unusual occurrence. Intergroup admiration occurs when the outgroup is thought to be completely deserving of its accomplishments, when the outgroup's gains do not come at a cost to the ingroup, and when the outgroup members are generally judged positively. Such an emotion is most likely when individuals can take some pride in association with the outgroup, even though they are not an actual member of the group.

These emotional reactions also depend on the relative status of the ingroup and the outcome (Smith & Mackie, 2005). Fear and jealousy, for example, are more common emotions in members of the lower-status groups, whereas contempt or anger are characteristic of those who are members of higher-status groups.

Exclusion and Dehumanization

People do not just categorize and judge the outgroup. As the stereotype content model suggests, people respond emotionally to the outgroup, usually leaning in a negative direction. This negativity may be relatively mild, amounting to little more than unease when interacting with outgroup members or a general preference to be with someone from the ingroup rather than the outgroup. Such individuals may not even admit their negativity toward members of the other group, yet they display it through their nonverbal actions, social awkwardness, and nervousness when in the presence of

the outgroup (Dovidio et al., 2004). In other cases, however, individuals may display far more intense emotions in response to the outgroup, including hatred and disgust (Taylor, 2007).

Group Hate   Hatred, as Allport (1954) explained in *The Nature of Prejudice*, is usually a group-level emotion. Drawing on ideas discussed by Aristotle, Allport observed that "anger is customarily felt toward individuals only, whereas hatred may be felt toward whole classes of people" (1954, p. 363). And while individuals often regret giving way to anger directed at another person, they feel no such remorse about their group-level hatred. "Hatred is more deep-rooted, and constantly desires the extinction of the object of hate" (1954, p. 363).

   Hate causes a more violently negative reaction to the outgroup than such emotions as fear or anger. Often, group members fear the other group, for example, when outgroup members are viewed as competitors who may take harmful action toward the ingroup. Anger is also a dominant emotion in intergroup conflict settings, when previous negative exchanges between groups are a cause for irritation, annoyance, and hostility. Hate, however, is the feeling associated with many of the most negative consequences of intergroup conflict. Hate is expressed primarily when group members believe that previously harmful acts done by members of the outgroup were intentional ones that purposely harmed the ingroup and that the actions were caused by the intrinsically evil nature of the outgroup. In one study of people's reactions to terrorist attacks, fear was associated with avoiding the outgroup and anger with support for improved education to improve intergroup relations. Those who felt hatred for the other group, in contrast, advocated their destruction, expressed a desire to do evil against them, and called for physical violence against them (Halperin, 2008; Sternberg, 2003).

Moral Exclusion   Throughout history, the members of one group have done great harm to the members of other groups. When intergroup conflict reaches extreme levels, with members of one group attacking, harming, and killing members of other groups, the ingroup–outgroup bias becomes equally extreme. During extreme intergroup conflicts, group members view their own group as morally superior and members of the outgroup as less than human (Bandura, 1999; Reicher, Haslam, & Rath, 2008).

Such **moral exclusion** is more likely to occur in cases of extreme violence perpetrated by one group against another—European Americans enslaving Africans, Nazi Germany's attempted genocide of Jews, "ethnic cleansing" in Croatia and Serbia, and the continuing warfare between Israelis and Palestinians (Staub, 2004). Those who subjugate others tend to rationalize their violence by attributing it to the actions, intentions, or character of their victims. As their aggression intensifies, however, their rationalizations prompt them to increasingly devalue their victims. Eventually, the aggressors denigrate the outgroup so completely that the outsiders are excluded from moral concern, for it is difficult to savage whom one evaluates positively or strongly identifies with (Staub, 1990, p. 53). Groups that have a history of devaluing segments of their society are more likely to engage in moral exclusion, as are groups whose norms stress respect for authority and obedience. These groups, when they anticipate conflict with other groups, rapidly revise their opinions of their opponents so that they can take hostile actions against them (Opotow, 2000).

Dehumanization   Moral exclusion places the outgroup outside the *moral* realm. **Dehumanization** moves the outgroup outside the *human* realm.

---

moral exclusion A psychological process whereby opponents in a conflict come to view each other as undeserving of morally mandated rights and protections.
dehumanization Believing that other individuals or entire groups of individuals lack the qualities thought to distinguish human beings from other animals; such dehumanization serves to rationalize the extremely negative treatment often afforded to members of other groups.

Dehumanization occurs when the ingroup denies the outgroup those qualities thought to define the essence of human nature. Some of these qualities may be those thought to be uniquely human: culture, refinement, high moral standards, and the capacity to think rationally. Others are qualities that the ingroup associates with humanity's strengths, such as emotional responsiveness, warmth, openness, self-control, and depth (Haslam, 2006). The ingroup may also come to believe that the outgroup experiences raw, primary emotions such as anger or happiness, but not the more refined emotions that make humans truly human: affection, admiration, pride, conceit, remorse, guilt, and envy (Leyens et al., 2003). People describe dehumanized outgroup members as disgusting or revolting because they are thought to be sources of contamination and impurity (Chirot & McCauley, 2006; Maoz & McCauley, 2008).

This concept of dehumanization is no hyperbole. When researchers used an fMRI scanner to track perceivers' reactions to images of people from various groups, their results suggested that dehumanized outgroup members are no longer perceived to be humans. When individuals viewed general images of people, the areas of the brain that typically respond when people process social information (the medial prefrontal cortices) showed increased activity. However, when they were shown images of people from an extreme outgroup—homeless individuals and drug addicts—those same areas did not rise above their resting state of neuronal activity. The insula and amygdala were activated, however; these portions of the brain are most active when people are experiencing strong emotions, such as disgust and contempt (Harris & Fiske, 2006).

Dehumanization also increases the likelihood that the ingroup will aggress against the outgroup. Albert Bandura and his associates tested this possibility experimentally by giving groups the opportunity to deliver painful electric shocks to a second group each time it performed poorly. In reality, there was no other group, but participants nonetheless believed that they could control both the intensity and duration of the shocks they gave the group. In one condition, the experimenter mentioned that the outgroup members—who were similar to one another in background but different from the subjects—seemed like nice people. But in the other condition the experimenter mentioned, in an offhand remark, that they were an "animalistic, rotten bunch." As expected, when dehumanized by the experimenter, the groups increased their hostility and aggression, delivering more intense shocks (Bandura, Underwood, & Fromson, 1975).

Categorization and Identity

Social identity theory offers a compelling explanation for the robust relationship between categorization and conflict. This theory, as noted in Chapter 3, assumes that membership in groups can substantially influence members' sense of self. When the boys joined the Robbers Cave experiment and became firmly embedded in their groups, their identities changed. They came to think of themselves as Rattlers or Eagles, and they accepted the group's characteristics as their own. The theory also suggests that as the boys came to identify with their group, their own self-worth became more closely tied to the worth of the group. If a Rattler dedicated himself to the group and the Rattlers failed, the boy would likely experience a distressing reduction in his own self-esteem. Group members, therefore, stress the value of their own group relative to other groups as a means of indirectly enhancing their own personal worth (Tajfel & Turner, 1986).

Identity and Intergroup Conflict The basic premise of social identity theory is supported by evidence that people favor their group, even in minimal group conditions, and by the fact that the biasing effects of group membership are even more substantial when (a) individuals identify with their group rather than simply belonging to it and (b) the relative status of existing groups is salient (Kenworthy et al., 2008). Black Africans' attitudes toward an outgroup (Afrikaans Whites) were negatively associated with the strength of their ingroup identification (Duckitt & Mphuthing, 1998). British people's attitudes toward the French were negatively correlated with the strength of their British identities (Brown et al., 2001). When individuals feel that the value of their group is being questioned, they respond by underscoring the distinctiveness of their own group and by derogating others (Brown & Hewstone, 2005; Dietz-Uhler & Murrell, 1998).

Identity and Self-esteem Social identity theory's suggestion that ingroup favoritism is in the service of ingroup members' self-esteem is also consistent with findings that individuals who most need reassurance of their worth tend to be the most negative toward other groups. Individuals who experience a threat to their self-esteem tend to discriminate more against outgroups, and low-status, peripheral members of the group are often the most zealous in their defense of their group and in the rejection of the outgroup (Noel, Wann, & Branscombe, 1995). Individuals are also more likely to draw comparisons between their group and other groups in areas where the comparison favors the ingroup. The Rattlers, for example, lost the tournament, so they admitted that the Eagles were better than the Rattlers at sports. But the Rattlers could stress their superiority in other spheres unrelated to the games, such as toughness or endurance (Reichl, 1997). Group members also display group-level *schadenfreude*. They take pleasure when other groups fail, particularly when the failure is in a domain that is self-relevant and when the ingroup's superiority in this domain is uncertain (Leach et al., 2003).

But does condemning other groups raise one's self-esteem? The effectiveness of this technique for sustaining self-esteem has not been confirmed consistently by researchers. In some cases, derogating outgroup members raises certain forms of self-esteem, but praising the ingroup tends to bolster self-esteem more than condemning the outgroup (Brown & Zagefka, 2005). Also, though people are quick to praise their ingroup, they still think that they are superior to most people—including all the members of their own group (Lindeman, 1997).

INTERGROUP CONFLICT RESOLUTION: UNITING US AND THEM

What happens when one group encounters another? In many cases, conflict. Competition, differences in power, norms, and negative emotions combine to instigate intergroup hostilities. The tendency to distinguish between *us* from *them* creates divisions where none are warranted. Rejection and animosity flourish, and acceptance and support dwindle. But encounters between groups need not inevitably lead to conflict. First, contact between groups can, in the right circumstances, reduce tensions between groups rather than increase them. Second, the cognitive processes that often underscore the differences between people can also sustain collective, more inclusive, identities. Third, just as group members learn to respond to others who are outside of their groups in negative ways, so they can learn to respond positively when they encounter people from other groups. This section reviews these three approaches to promoting positive intergroup relations.

Intergroup Contact

The Robbers Cave researchers were left with a problem. The manipulations of the first two phases of the experiment had worked very well, for the Rattlers–Eagles war yielded a gold mine of data about intergroup conflict. Unfortunately, the situation had degenerated into a summer camp version of William Golding's (1954) *Lord of the Flies*. The two groups now despised each other. As conscientious social scientists, the Sherifs and their colleagues felt compelled to try to undo some of the negative effects of the study—to seek a method through which harmony and friendship could be restored at the Robbers Cave campsite.

The Contact Hypothesis The Robbers Cave researchers first tried to reduce the conflict by uniting the groups in shared activities. They based their

intervention on the **contact hypothesis**, which assumes that ingroup–outgroup biases will fade if people interact regularly with members of the outgroup. So the Sherifs arranged for the Rattlers and the Eagles to join in seven pleasant activities, such as eating, playing games, viewing films, and shooting off firecrackers. Unfortunately, this contact had little impact on the hostilities. During all these events, the lines between the two groups never broke, and antilocution, discrimination, and physical assault continued unabated. When contact occurred during meals, "food fights" were particularly prevalent:

> After eating for a while, someone threw something, and the fight was on. The fight consisted of throwing rolls, napkins rolled in a ball, mashed potatoes, etc. accompanied by yelling the standardized, unflattering words at each other. The throwing continued for about 8–10 minutes, then the cook announced that cake and ice cream were ready for them. Some members of each group went after their dessert, but most of them continued throwing things a while longer. As soon as each gobbled his dessert, he resumed throwing. (Sherif et al., 1961, p. 158)

The Sherifs discovered that bringing groups together, even in a relatively pleasant circumstance, was not sufficient to reduce conflict: The Eagles and Rattlers used the situation to continue their warfare.

Creating Positive Contact *Contact* lies at the heart of such social policies as school integration, foreign student exchange programs, and the Olympics, but simply throwing two groups together in an unregulated situation is a risky way to reduce intergroup tensions. Contact between racial groups at desegregated schools does not consistently lower levels of prejudice (Gerard, 1983; Schofield, 1986). When units of an organization

---

contact hypothesis The prediction that contact between the members of different groups will reduce intergroup conflict.

that clash on a regular basis are relocated in neighboring offices, the conflicts remain (Brown et al., 1986). In some cases students experience so much tumult during their semesters spent studying abroad that they become more negative toward their host countries rather than more positive (Stangor et al., 1996). Competing groups in laboratory studies remain adversaries if the only step taken to unite them is mere contact (Stephan, 1987). Even before they initiated the contact, the Sherifs predicted that a "contact phase in itself will not produce marked decreases in the existing state of tension between groups" (Sherif et al., 1961, p. 51).

Why does contact sometimes fail to cure conflict (Kenworthy et al., 2005)? Contact situations can create strong emotional reactions for group members: anger, fear, anxiety, and even shame and pity. If the contact situation is superficial or negative in tone, then these emotions will likely continue to disrupt the relationships between the groups (Tam et al., 2007). Moreover, if members of the two groups use the contact situation as one more opportunity to insult, argue with, physically attack, or discriminate against one another, then certainly such contact should not be expected to yield beneficial effects (Riordan & Riggiero, 1980).

The setting must, instead, create *positive contact* between groups. As psychologist Gordon Allport (1954) explained in his original statement of the contact hypothesis, the two groups should not be merely assembled in one place. They should, instead, be unified in a situation with the qualities listed in Table 14.1: equal status, common goals, intergroup cooperation, and support of authorities, law, or custom (Pettigrew, 1998). Several of these ingredients were also identified by a team of researchers led by Kenneth Clark and including Isidor Chein, Gerhart Saenger, and Stuart Cook. This group developed the social science statement filed in the U.S. Supreme Court case of *Brown vs. Board of Education*, which ruled that segregation of schools was unconstitutional (Benjamin & Crouse, 2002).

Contact and Superordinate Goals When the Sherifs ratcheted up the quality of the contact between the Eagles and the Rattlers, they achieved

TABLE 14.1   The Necessary Conditions for Creating Positive Contact Situation Identified by Allport (1954)

Condition	Description
Equal status	The members of the groups should be equal in terms of background, qualities, and characteristics that influence prestige and rank in the situation.
Common goals	The situation should involve a joint task with a common goal that is of equal interest to both groups.
Cooperation	The task should require cross-group interaction and high levels of interdependence.
Support of authorities, law, or custom	The norms of the situation should encourage positive interactions, and these norms must be endorsed explicitly by authorities and by the groups themselves.

the results they had hoped for: peace at Robbers Cave. Following the failure of simple contact, they arranged for the groups to work together in the pursuit of **superordinate goals**—goals that can be achieved only if two groups work together. The staff created these superordinate goals by staging a series of crises. They secretly sabotaged the water supply and then asked the boys to find the source of the problem by tracing the water pipe from the camp back to the main water tank, located about three-quarters of a mile away. The boys became quite thirsty during their search and worked together to try to correct the problem. Eventually, they discovered that the main water valve had been turned off by "vandals," and they cheered when the problem was repaired. Later in this stage, the boys pooled their monetary resources to rent a movie that they all wanted to see, worked together to

superordinate goal A goal that can only be attained if the members of two or more groups work together by pooling their efforts and resources.

pull a broken-down truck, prepared meals together, exchanged tent materials, and took a rather hot and dusty truck ride together. Like feuding neighbors who unite when a severe thunderstorm threatens to flood their homes or warring nations that pool their technological skills (in a recurring science fiction theme) to prevent the imagined collision of earth with an asteroid, the Rattlers and the Eagles were reunited when they sought goals that could not be achieved by a single group working alone.

Cooperation and Cohesion Superordinate goals create conditions favorable for the gradual reduction of tensions between groups, but in most cases several cooperative encounters will be needed before conflict is noticeably reduced. At Robbers Cave, the researchers used a series of superordinate goals to improve cross-group relationships. When students from two different colleges worked together on problems, the cooperative encounter led to increased liking for members of the outgroup only when it occurred twice (Wilder & Thompson, 1980). Students who worked with the outgroup just once or not at all rated the members of the outgroup more negatively than students who worked with the outgroup twice. Similarly, in public schools, a long period of cooperative intergroup contact is needed to reduce intergroup prejudice, and if cooperation is not constantly encouraged, then groups inevitably drift apart once again (Schofield, 1986; Schofield & Sagar, 1977).

Working together in the pursuit of superordinate goals is also more effective if the groups actually attain the goal; if the cooperative venture fails, then conflict will likely ensue. Cooperating groups who manage to succeed like one another, but when groups fail, the negative affect associated with a poor performance will spread to the outgroup with each group blaming the other for the outcome. Thus, cooperation is not enough: The cooperation must also lead to success rather than failure (Blanchard, Adelman, & Cook, 1975; Worchel, 1986).

A Common Enemy The Robbers Cave experiment was not the first time the Sherifs and their colleagues had used a summer camp to study intergroup

conflict processes. Their first field study, conducted in northern Connecticut, featured the two groups discussed in Chapter 5: the Red Devils and the Bull Dogs. These two groups experienced considerable levels of conflict, as did the Rattlers and the Eagles, but in this study, the Sherifs' reduced tension by introducing a common enemy (Sherif & Sherif, 1953). They arranged for the two warring groups to pick their best players for a camp-based all-star team who then played a game against the boys from another camp. This intervention was successful, for during the game the boys forgot about their previous group loyalties and cheered whenever their camp's team scored.

The Sherifs point out, however, that although combining groups in opposition to a common enemy worked for a short time (during the actual competition or crisis), once the enemy was removed, the groups returned to the status quo antebellum. In fact, the 1949 groups were never successfully reunited despite the experimenters' extended efforts. Also, the use of a common enemy to create cooperation actually enlarges a conflict; in the Sherifs' research, the tension that had divided a single camp came to divide two different camps. At the international level this method would amount to solving the disagreements between two nations by attacking a third (Kessler & Mummendey, 2001).

The Importance of Friendships Researchers have confirmed the importance of the four factors identified by Allport in his original statement of the contact hypothesis (see Table 14.1), but they have also identified other factors that, if not necessary conditions, are those that often turn an adequate contact situation into a highly successful one. Many researchers, for example, stress the extent to which the situation promotes informal, personal interactions with outgroup members rather than superficial, role-based contacts. If the members of the groups do not mingle with one another, they learn very little about the other group, and cross-group friendships do not develop (Cook, 1985; Schofield, 1986). Social psychologist Thomas Pettigrew (1997), for example, in a study of 3,806 people living in four countries in Europe, discovered that people who reported having friends who were members of an outgroup (another race, nationality, culture, religion, or social class) were less prejudiced than those who had no outgroup friends. Other investigations have confirmed this tendency, leading Pettigrew to conclude:

> The power of cross-group friendship to reduce prejudice and generalize to other outgroups demands a fifth condition for the contact hypothesis: The contact situation must provide the participants with the opportunity to become friends. Such opportunity implies close interaction that would make self-disclosure and other friendship-developing mechanisms possible. (Pettigrew, 1998, p. 76)

The Extended Contact Hypothesis   Cross-group friendships not only alleviate the negative intergroup biases of the two friends, but they can also lower the level of antipathy displayed by other group members—even those without friends in the outgroup. To test this **extended contact hypothesis**, social psychologist Stephen Wright and his colleagues (1997) conceptually replicated the Robbers Cave experiment with college students who spent an entire day working in one of two groups on a variety of tasks. Groups first developed a sense of cohesiveness by designing a logo for their team and sharing personal information. The groups then competed against each other, and during lunch, they watched as each group was given prizes and awards for defeating the other group. Later in the day, the groups worked on solitary tasks, except for two individuals who met together—supposedly to take part in an unrelated study. This meeting, however, was designed to

---

extended contact hypothesis: The prediction that cross-group friendships not only increase the two friends' acceptance of the respective outgroups, but also cause other members of their groups to become more positive toward the outgroups as well.

create a friendly relationship between these two individuals who then returned to their groups just before a final competition.

Wright discovered that the two group members who were turned into friends were more positive toward the outgroup. In addition, this positivity generalized throughout the rest of the groups. Even though the other group members had not themselves developed friendships with members of the outgroup, the knowledge that someone in their group considered an outgroup member to be likable moderated the ingroup–outgroup bias. Wright concluded that intergroup conflict sometimes prevents friendships from forming, but that friendships that cut across groups can undo some of the pernicious effects of the ingroup–outgroup bias. This effect is even more pronounced when a friend within one's group is a close friend, and their relationship with the outgroup member is a close one as well (Eller, Abrams, & Gomez, 2012).

The Effects of Contact   Does contact across various types of situations and between various kinds of groups stimulate conflict reduction? Thomas Pettigrew and Linda Tropp (2000, 2006, 2011) examined this question in a meta-analysis of 515 separate studies of contact and conflict. This massive pool of studies examined the responses of nearly a quarter of a million people from around the world. It included studies with tightly controlled methods as well as those with less stringent controls. Some studies measured contact directly, whereas others used participants' own self-reports. Some studies were experimental, with treatment and control conditions, but others were correlational or quasi-experimental. The studies examined a variety of intergroup conflicts, including those based on race, sexual orientation, age, and ethnicity.

Their careful meta-analysis (which took the researchers eight years to complete) confirmed the utility of the contact method in reducing conflict. They found that face-to-face contact between group members reduced prejudice in 94% of these studies and that the basic correlation between contact and conflict was $-.21$; the more contact, the less prejudice between groups. They also noted, however, that contact had a stronger impact on conflict when researchers studied high-quality contact situations that included equal status, cooperation between groups, and so on. In such studies, the correlation between contact and conflict climbed to −.29.

The effects of contact also varied across situations. Contact in recreational and work settings had the strongest impact on conflict, whereas contact that occurred when group members visited another group's country (i.e., as tourists) had the least impact (see Figure 14.5). The impact of contact on conflict also varied across countries. For example, it was greatest in Australia and New Zealand, followed by the United States and Europe. Contact worked to reduce conflict in all other countries, but its strength was less in some parts of the world (e.g., Africa, Asia, Israel). Some types of intergroup conflict were also more resistant to the curative power of contact than others. Heterosexuals' attitudes toward gay men and lesbians improved the most after contact, followed by attitudes related to race and ethnicity. Contact lost some of its strength in studies of contact between people of different ages. Also, contact had less effect on the attitudes of members of minority groups relative to members of majority groups (Pettigrew & Tropp, 2000).

Pettigrew and Tropp conclude that contact works best in situations that conform to Allport's original recommendations regarding positive contact situations, but they were also heartened by the positive effects obtained in less-than-ideal situations. Drawing on both their findings and social identity theory, they suggest that contact works most effectively when it helps reduce the anxiety associated with conflict between the groups and when membership in the two groups is salient to their members. They suspect that contact fails when members feel threatened by the outgroup and that the level of contact is not enough to assuage that anxiety (Brown & Hewstone, 2005). This suggestion is also consistent with research that finds that stress, as measured by levels of cortisol reactivity, decreases with each additional contact between people in a situation that encourages the formation of friendships (Page-Gould, Mendoza-Denton, & Tropp, 2008).

Cognitive Cures for Conflict

Intergroup contact does more than just promote positive interactions between people who were once antagonists. When individuals cooperate with the outgroup, their "us versus them" thinking fades, along with ingroup favoritism, outgroup rejection, and stereotyping (Brewer & Brown, 1998; Brewer & Miller, 1984; Crisp & Hewstone, 2007).

Decategorization During the waning days at Robbers Cave, the boys began to abandon their collective identities. Some boys became less likely to think of themselves as Rattlers, but instead viewed themselves as individuals with specific interests, skills, and abilities. This **decategorization**, or *personalization*, of group members reduces intergroup conflict by reminding group members to think of outgroup members as individuals rather

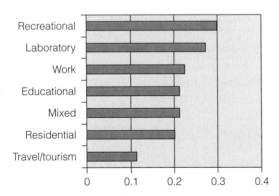

FIGURE 14.5 Degree of conflict reduction between groups across seven contact situations.

SOURCE: From tabled data in "A Meta-analytic Test of Intergroup Contact Theory" by T. F. Pettigrew and L. R. Tropp, 2006, *Journal of Personality and Social Psychology, 90,* 751–783.

decategorization Reducing social categorization tendencies by minimizing the salience of group memberships and stressing the individuality of each person in the group.

than as typical group members (Brewer, 2007). In one study, researchers personalized the outgroup by merging two distinct groups and giving them problems to solve. Some of the groups were urged to focus on the task, but others were encouraged to get to know one another. This latter manipulation decreased the magnitude of the ingroup–outgroup bias, although it did not eliminate it completely (Bettencourt et al., 1992). Individuation can also be increased by reducing the perceived homogeneity of the outgroup. When group members were told that one member of the outgroup strongly disagreed with his or her own group during an episode of intergroup conflict, ingroup–outgroup biases were muted (Wilder, 1986). The participants looked at the outgroup and saw a collection of individuals rather than a unified group (Wilder, Simon, & Faith, 1996).

Recategorization   The **common ingroup identity model**, developed by social psychologists Samuel Gaertner, John Dovidio, and their colleagues, recommends reducing bias by shifting group members' representations of themselves away from two separate groups into one common ingroup category. This **recategorization** will undo the conflict-exacerbating cognitive factors that are rooted in the ingroup–outgroup bias, but will also permit members to retain their original identities (so long as they do not conflict with the recategorized group). Because people belong to multiple groups, they may be able to conceive of themselves as members of different groups who are currently members of one, more superordinate group. Recategorization can also be achieved by systematically manipulating the perceptual cues that people use to

define "groupness." When the members of competing groups were urged to adopt a single name, space was minimized between the members, and their outcomes were linked; these cues increased the perceived unity (*entitativity*) of the group members, and ingroup–outgroup biases diminished (Gaertner & Dovidio, 2000; Gaertner, Dovidio, Nier et al., 1999; Gaertner, Dovidio, Rust et al., 1999; Gaertner et al., 2000).

Social psychologist Jason Nier and his colleagues (2001) confirmed this shifting of identities at a football game between the University of Delaware and Westchester State University. They arranged for European and African American interviewers to approach European American fans and ask them if they would answer a few questions about their food preferences. The interviewers manipulated shared social identity by wearing different hats. For example, when interviewers approached a Delaware fan, they wore a Delaware hat to signal their shared identity, or a Westchester hat to indicate they were members of the outgroup. Ingroup–outgroup identity did not influence European Americans' compliance with a European American interviewer's request. However, the participants were more likely to agree to be interviewed by an African American if the interviewer and interviewee apparently shared a common university affiliation. The Sherifs introducing a common enemy in their study of the Red Devils and the Bull Dogs would be an example of recategorization.

Cross-Categorization   Ingroup–outgroup biases are also minimized when group members' other classifications—in addition to their group identity that is the focus of the conflict—are made salient to them (Crisp & Hewstone, 2007). **Cross-categorization**, or multiple social categorization, instead of uniting all individuals in a single group or breaking down

---

common ingroup identity model An analysis of recategorization processes and conflict, predicting that intergroup conflict can be reduced by emphasizing membership in inclusive social categories and the interdependence of the individuals in the groups (developed by Samuel Gaertner, John Dovidio, and their colleagues).
recategorization A reduction of social categorization tendencies by collapsing groups in conflict into a single group or category.

---

cross-categorization A reduction of the impact of social categorization on individuals' perceptions by making salient their memberships in two or more social groups or categories that are not related to the categories that are generating ingroup–outgroup tensions.

groups altogether, decreases the power of the problematic group identity by shifting attention to alternative memberships that are less likely to provoke ingroup–outgroup tensions. The Sherifs, if they had implemented this strategy at Robbers Cave, would have introduced at least one other category and split the Rattlers and the Eagles into two new groups. The boys, for example, were drawn from both the north and the south side of Oklahoma City, so the Sherifs could have separated them into these two groups and introduced activities that would have made these identities salient.

When others are viewed as belonging to multiple categories rather than just one, intergroup differentiation decreases and with it goes intergroup bias. Cross-categorization also prompts individuals to develop a more complex conceptualization of the outgroup, which leads in some cases to decategorization. The effectiveness of cross-categorization depends, however, on individuals' willingness to do the cognitive work needed to rethink their conceptualization of the outgroup and their mood. If pressured by time constraints that placed demands on their ability to process information or a mood-souring situation, the boys at Robbers Cave may have fallen back on the older, better-known Eagles–Rattlers distinction (Brewer, 2000; Crisp & Hewstone, 2007; Urban & Miller, 1998).

Controlling Stereotyped Thinking   Rather than attacking the categorization process, social psychologist Patricia Devine (1989, 2005) recommended controlling the impact of stereotypes on perceptions. Although people may not be able to avoid the activation of stereotypes, they can control their subsequent thoughts to inhibit ingroup–outgroup biases. Devine found that the European Americans she studied could easily list the contents of their culture's stereotypes about African Americans. She also found that European Americans who were low in prejudice could describe the stereotype as accurately as those who were high in prejudice. The unprejudiced European Americans, however, could control their thoughts after the stereotypes were activated. When asked to list their thoughts about African Americans, the unprejudiced participants wrote such

things as "Blacks and Whites are equal" and "It's unfair to judge people by their color—they are individuals." Prejudiced people, in contrast, listed negative, stereotypical thoughts. Devine and her colleagues have also found that unprejudiced European Americans feel guilty when they respond to African Americans in stereotypical ways, whereas prejudiced European Americans do not (see Devine & Sharp, 2009, for a review).

Learning to Cooperate

Conflict between groups is one of the most complicated phenomena studied by social scientists, but the goal of greater understanding and the promise of reduced tension remain enticing. Schools, communities, businesses, and even nations, to deal with the problems that intergroup conflicts can create, have sought ways to help members recognize the sources of their disputes and learn to manage their differences successfully. Many of these approaches build on both the contact and cognitive approaches while adding elements designed to fit the given situation (for a comprehensive review, see Paluck & Green, 2009). These programs, when applied with diligence, often yield substantial reductions in conflict, although their success depends on their duration, their design, and their fidelity to the intervention strategy (Aberson, 2010; Stephan & Stephan, 2005).

Jigsaw Learning Groups   Studies of public schools in the United States suggest that desegregation often fails to eliminate racial and ethnic prejudices. Although integrated schools bring students from various groups into contact, they do not always promote cooperation between these groups. Instead of including the necessary ingredients for positive intergroup interactions, many school systems fail to encourage interaction among the members of various subgroups, and staff openly express hostile attitudes toward outgroup members. Some schools, too, group students on the basis of prior academic experiences; as a result, educationally deprived students are segregated from students with stronger academic backgrounds (Amir, 1969;

Brewer & Miller, 1984; Cook, 1985; Schofield, 1986).

Social psychologist Elliot Aronson and his colleagues developed the **jigsaw method** to increase collaborative learning and also reduce intergroup conflict (Aronson, 2000; Aronson & Patnoe, 1997; Aronson et al., 1978). Students from different racial or ethnic groups are assigned to a single learning group. These groups are then given an assignment that can be completed only if each individual member contributes his or her share. Study units are broken down into various subareas, and each member of a group must become an expert on one subject and teach that subject to other members of the group. In a class studying government, for example, the teacher might separate the pupils into three-person groups, with each member of the group being assigned one of the following topics: the judiciary system (the Supreme Court of the United States), the duties and powers of the executive branch (the office of the president), and the functions of the legislative branch (Congress). Students can, however, leave their three-person groups and meet with their counterparts from other groups. Thus, everyone assigned to study one particular topic, such as the Supreme Court, would meet to discuss it, answer questions, and decide how to teach the material to others. Once they have learned their material, these students rejoin their original groups and teach the other members of their group what they had learned. Thus, the jigsaw class uses both group learning and student teaching techniques. The technique can also be used in a variety of courses and grade levels and has even been adapted for use in online learning settings (Pozzi, 2010; see Focus 14.2).

Training in Conflict Resolution Intergroup conflicts resist resolution, despite the best intentions of those involved to settle the problem amicably. In

---

jigsaw method A team-learning technique that involves assigning topics to each student, allowing students with the same topics to study together, and then requiring these students to teach their topics to the other members of their groups (developed by Elliot Aronson and his colleagues).

one of the Sherifs' studies, for example, an informal attempt by one of the Bull Dogs' leaders to negotiate with the Red Devils ended in increased antagonism:

> Hall … was chosen to make a peace mission. He joined into the spirit, shouting to the Bull Dogs, "Keep your big mouths shut. I'm going to see if we can make peace. We want peace." Hall went to the Red Devil cabin. The door was shut in his face. He called up that the Bull Dogs had only taken their own [belongings] … and they wanted peace. His explanation was rejected, and his peaceful intentions were derided. He ran from the bunkhouse in a hail of green apples. (Sherif & Sherif, 1953, p. 283)

Conflict experts, such as Herbert Kelman (1992), recommend training people to be more effective managers of intergroup conflict. Kelman and his colleagues have met repeatedly with high-ranking representatives from countries in the Middle East to solve problems in that region of the world. Kelman has carefully structured the workshops so that participants can speak freely, and he intervenes only as necessary to facilitate the communication process. The workshops are completely confidential, discussion is open but focused on the conflict, and expectations are realistic. The workshops are not designed to resolve the conflict, but to give participants the behavioral skills needed to solve conflicts themselves (Rouhana & Kelman, 1994).

David and Roger Johnson (2009) have applied these principles in their school-based cooperative learning program. They designed their program to achieve three major goals: to decrease the amount of tension between groups in schools and colleges; to increase students' ability to solve problems without turning to authorities; and to give students skills they can use when they become adults. The program teaches students a five-step approach to resolving conflicts: (1) define the conflict; (2) exchange information about the nature of the conflict; (3) view the situation from multiple perspectives; (4) generate solutions to the conflict; and (5) select a solution that benefits all parties.

F o c u s   14.2   E-groups: Testing the Virtual Contact Hypothesis

---

When Zeina posted a link to a news report about Amsterdam's lax drug laws on Facebook, a friend who lives in Europe challenged the report's findings and a lively discussion ensued. Jim, growing up in Alabama, was set in his ways, and those ways were provincial ones. But Jim mellowed after playing an online game with people located in different parts of the world. Jackson is a diligent reader of his local newspaper, but he also stays informed by going online and reading posts and discussion threads at the Aljazeera news network and the BBC (British Broadcasting Corporation).

The contact hypothesis recommends reducing intergroup conflict by arranging for the members of different groups to interact with each other in cooperative, task-focused situations. In some cases, however, offline contact between group members is impossible. The counselors at Robbers Cave could require the Rattlers and the Eagles to watch a film together, but members of groups separated by great distances cannot convene easily in a single location. Nor is it ever easy for groups with a legacy of hostility to move easily from physical separation to positive contact (Amichai-Hamburger & McKenna, 2006).

In such cases, online collaboration provides an alternative way to bring groups together in cooperative contact. Social networking sites such as Facebook, gaming communities, discussion forums, and blogs all promote interaction among visitors to these sites and so provide the venue, if not the motivation, for contact. These sites also take much of the challenge out of contact, for the experience can be ended should it become uncomfortable. Online situations may, in fact, more easily meet the conditions required for successful contact. The playing field of the Internet is a relatively level one, for any indicators of status, wealth, or position, which would be obvious to group members if they met together in the same physical location, are hidden when people interact virtually. Moreover, the disinhibition that is so often problematic in Internet interactions may be of service during intergroup sessions, for individuals may be more willing to engage in intimate self-disclosures needed to create a more personal, rather than formal, connection. Interacting with others online may also take advantage of the positive effects of *imagined intergroup contact*. Even if

participants do not consider an online connection to another person to be a "real" relationship, if the interaction is a positively toned encounter, it should promote feelings of confidence about future offline interactions with the outgroup (e.g., Crisp & Turner, 2009; Husnu & Crisp, 2010).

Researchers have only begun to test the **virtual contact hypothesis**, but initial results are encouraging. Studies of multicultural virtual teams used in business and educational settings, for example, suggest that these groups become more cohesive if the factors identified by the contact hypothesis—task focus, collaborative orientation, and the support of the authority—are incorporated in the online contact situation. When groups are cautioned to interact with each other frequently, respectfully, and in supportive ways, virtual multicultural teams tend to be more productive, and members liking for one another increases (Walther, 2009).

The Internet has also been used as an online meeting place for groups with a history of intergroup hostility. Educators in Ireland, for example, developed an online program that linked students in the Republic of Ireland and North Ireland (Austin, 2006). Students from schools in the two countries worked collaboratively, at the group-level, on graded projects for at least one year in duration. By design, the class focused on academic content and the development of computer skills, but students also developed increased cultural awareness (Austin, 2006; Austin & Anderson, 2008). Another site, *Net Intergroup Contact* (located at http://www.intergroupcontact.com), facilitates intergroup contact by placing participants of varying ethnicity and cultural backgrounds into small groups of five to seven members. These groups work on collaborative tasks that require a high level of interaction for successful completion. Members share information about themselves through online profiles, and all sessions are supervised by a mediator (Amichai-Hamburger, 2012). A third example comes from the virtual community, *Second Life®*. In this avatar-based game environment, members of distributed, multicultural teams worked together to complete a virtual team-building exercise: building a bridge across a ravine on one of the Second Life® islands. Reactions to the experience were very positive: 95% of the participants agreed that the experience helped them

---

virtual contact hypothesis The prediction that online contact between the members of different groups will improve relations between these groups.

---

learn how to work with people from different cultures (Lewis, Ellis, & Kellogg, 2010).

These interventions are only at the experimental stage, but initial findings suggest that they may offer a possible alternative to traditional face-to-face inter-group contact procedures. They may, of course, prove to be untenable. Rather than an opportunity to act in

positive ways to resolve conflicts, the Internet may provide just another place where one group can enter into disputes with another. These projects may, how-ever, be the first in a long line of effective online methods for helping people move beyond bias to understanding and away from conflict toward reconciliation.

Johnson and Johnson, in evaluations of the program, reported substantial reductions in discipline problems after training, as well as increases in academic achievement (Roseth, Johnson, & Johnson, 2008). These programs can be made even more effective by structuring the task so that each group member makes a contribution, randomly assigning students to roles within the group, and making certain that all groups contain an equal number of representatives from the groups being merged. Too much of an emphasis on individual performance—created by assigning grades based on relative performance or degree of preparation—can undermine the effectiveness of the program, but research suggests that the intervention yields positive gains even in less-than-ideal settings (Miller & Davidson-Podgorny, 1987).

Resolving Conflict: Conclusions

In his classic treatise *The Nature of Prejudice*, Allport (1954) wrote that "conflict is like a note on an organ. It sets all prejudices that are attuned to it into simultaneous vibration. The listener can

scarcely distinguish the pure note from the sur-rounding jangle" (p. 996).

The Sherifs and their colleagues created just such a "jangle" at Robbers Cave. The Rattlers and the Eagles were only young boys camping, but their conflict followed patterns seen in disputes between races, between regions, and between countries. But just as the Robbers Cave experiment is a sobering commentary on the pervasiveness of conflict, the resolution of that conflict is cause for optimism. The Sherifs created conflict, but they also resolved it. When it came time to return to Oklahoma City, several of the group members asked if everyone could go in the same bus:

> When they asked if this might be done and received an affirmative answer from the staff, some of them actually cheered. When the bus pulled out, the seating arrangement did not follow group lines. Many boys looked back at the camp, and Wilson (E) cried because camp was over. (Sherif et al., 1961, p. 182)

If the Robbers Cave conflict can end peacefully, perhaps others can as well.

CHAPTER REVIEW

What interpersonal factors disrupt relations between groups?

1. Muzafer and Carolyn Sherif and their colleagues studied the causes of and remedies for inter-group conflict in their *Robbers Cave experiment.*

2. *Realistic group conflict theory* assumes that conflict occurs because groups must compete with one another for scarce resources. Blake and Mouton documented the effects of anticipated compe-tition on conflict.

3. Insko, Schopler, and their colleagues have documented the heightened competitiveness of groups, or the *discontinuity effect*.

   - When groups play the Prisoners Dilemma Game, they are more competitive than the individual members. People expect group-to-group interactions to be more competitive than individual-to-individual interactions.

   - The effect is due to individuals' desire to maximize profit (greed), distrust of groups (fear), group loyalty, and anonymity (diffusion of responsibility). Facilitating intergroup communication does not limit discontinuity, but a tit-for-tat strategy does.

4. Conflict increases when one group attempts to dominate and exploit another group, and the target group resists exploitation.

   - *Social dominance theory*, developed by Sidanius and Pratto, examines tensions between hierarchically ranked groups in society.

   - Groups exploit other groups both economically and coercively, but Insko's generational studies suggest that coercive influence is associated with greater increases in conflict.

   - Individuals who are high in social dominance orientation are more likely to prefer allocations that benefit their group relative to other groups, and they are more likely to eliminate rival groups.

5. Negative emotional reactions can trigger anti-outgroup reactions.

   - The emotional mechanisms described by the *frustration aggression hypothesis* and the *general aggression model* can trigger impulsive intergroup aggression.

   - *Scapegoat theory* explains why groups that experience setbacks sometimes fight other, more defenseless groups.

6. Normative processes instigate and sustain conflict.

   - Intergroup conflict, like intragroup conflict, tends to escalate over time.

The Hatfield-McCoy feud illustrates the influence of the norm of reciprocity and the use of contentious influence tactics on conflict spirals.

   - The extent to which groups respond in hostile ways to other groups varies from culture to culture, with some cultures eschewing intergroup conflict and others (such as the "fierce" Yanomanö studied by Chagnon) accepting it routinely.

   - Subgroups within the larger cultural context may adopt unique norms pertaining to violence. The "culture of honor," for example, may contribute to elevated intergroup conflict.

7. The instinctive roots of intergroup aggression have been debated by such sages as Hobbes and Rousseau.

   - Anthropological evidence suggests that human societies tend to be violent, but Fry's findings suggest that peaceful coexistence among cultures is a possibility.

   - Evolutionary psychology suggests intergroup conflict is the result of evolutionary pressures that favored individuals who preferred ingroup members over outgroup members.

   - In most cases, intergroup rejection is stronger for male members of the outgroup.

What are the psychological foundations of conflict between groups?

1. Social categorization leads perceivers to classify people into two mutually exclusive groups—the ingroup and the outgroup. Individuals in Tajfel and Turner's minimal intergroup situation displayed the *ingroup–outgroup bias*, leading them to conclude that social categorization may be sufficient to create conflict.

   - The ingroup–outgroup bias, when applied to larger groups such as tribes or nations, was labeled *ethnocentrism* by Sumner.

- Ingroup favoritism tends to be stronger than outgroup rejection, but both forms of ingroup–outgroup bias emerged at Robbers Cave.

- *Double-standard thinking*, as described by White, occurs when group members frame the behaviors and characteristics of the ingroup more positively than these same behaviors and characteristics displayed by the outgroup. Actions performed by the ingroup are described differently than actions performed by the outgroup (the *linguistic intergroup bias*).

- Implicit measures of bias, such as the Implicit Association Test (IAT) developed by Greenwald and his colleagues, can detect subtle, unconscious forms of bias.

2. During intergroup conflict, group members' judgments are often distorted by a number of cognitive biases:

- *Outgroup homogeneity bias:* The outgroup is assumed to be much more homogeneous than the ingroup. Members assume that their own group is diverse and heterogeneous, although when the group is threatened, members may exaggerate the similarity of everyone in their group.

- *Law of small numbers:* The behaviors and characteristics exhibited by a small number of outgroup members are generalized to all members of the outgroup.

- *Group attribution error:* Allison's work demonstrates that people assume group decisions reflect individual group members' attitudes, irrespective of the particular procedures used in making the decisions.

- *Ultimate attribution error:* Group members attribute the negative behaviors performed by outgroup members to internal dispositions, but their positive behaviors are explained away as situational aberrations.

- *Stereotypes:* Lippmann coined the word *stereotypes* to describe cognitive generalizations about the qualities and characteristics of the members of a particular group or social category.

- *Stereotype content model:* The contents of most stereotypes reflect judgments of the outgroup's competence and warmth, and they elicit four basic emotional reactions in intergroup situations: pity, admiration, envy, and contempt.

3. When conflicts become more intense, members may display more extreme emotional reactions to outgroups.

- As Allport observed, hatred tends to be directed at groups rather than individuals.

- Extreme conflict can result in both *moral exclusion* and *dehumanization* of members of the outgroup. Dehumanized individuals evoke a different reaction, at the neurological level, than those who are not dehumanized, and Bandura's research indicates that a group is likely to be treated more negatively when described as "animalistic."

4. Social identity theory suggests that individuals, by championing the ingroup, maintain and even raise their self-esteem.

How can intergroup relations be improved?

1. The *contact hypothesis* maintains that relations between groups are improved when the groups interact together in a positive contact situation. The Sherifs' first, relatively unsuccessful, attempt to reduce conflict was based on this hypothesis.

- The original hypothesis, proposed by Allport and referenced in the social science statement filed in *Brown vs. Board of Education*, indicated that contact is most effective in situations that maintain equal status, common goals, intergroup cooperation, and support of authorities, law, or custom.

- The Sherifs successfully reduced conflict in the Robbers Cave camp by prompting the boys to work toward *superordinate goals*.

- The effectiveness of contact increases if contact is lengthy in duration, results in success, and creates opportunities for the development of cross-group friendships. In Wright's studies of the *extended contact hypothesis*, friendships diffused throughout the group.

- Pettigrew and Tropp, using meta-analysis, concluded that contact is an effective means of reducing conflict, but its effects vary across contexts.

2. Cognitive approaches to conflict reduction seek to reverse the negative biases that follow from parsing individuals into ingroups and outgroups.

- *Decategorization* encourages members to recognize the individuality of the outgroup members.

- The *common ingroup identity model* developed by Gaertner and Dovidio suggests that *recategorization*—collapsing the boundaries between groups—reduces conflict yet can promote the retention of identities. The common-enemy approach is an example of recategorization.

- *Cross-categorization* involves making salient, multiple-group memberships.

- Devine's studies of stereotypic thinking indicate that even though individuals may be aware of the contents of stereotypes pertaining to outgroups, they can learn to control the impact of this biased cognitive response on their judgments.

3. Conflict experts such as Kelman recommend managing conflict by teaching group members the skills they need to resolve interpersonal disputes.

- Aronson's *jigsaw method* is an educational intervention that reduces prejudice by assigning students from different racial or ethnic groups to a single learning group.

- The *virtual contact hypothesis* suggests that online contact between members of groups experiencing intergroup tension will alleviate that tension.

- School-based conflict management programs, like those developed by Johnson and Johnson, are designed to reduce conflict between groups by teaching students to recognize conflict, communicate about the source of the conflict, and identify mutually acceptable solutions.

RESOURCES

Chapter Case: The Robbers Cave Experiment

- *Intergroup Conflict and Cooperation: The Robbers Cave Experiment* by Muzafer Sherif, O. J. Harvey, B. Jack White, William R. Hood, and Carolyn W. Sherif (1961) describes in detail the well-known study of conflict between two groups of boys at a summer camp.

Causes of Intergroup Conflict

- "Intergroup Relations," by Vincent Yzerbyt and Stephanie Demoulin (2010), is a theoretically sophisticated review of the latest theories and research pertaining to intergroup processes.

- "Beyond the Group Mind: A Quantitative Review of the Interindividual–Intergroup Discontinuity Effect" by Tim Wildschut,

Brad Pinter, Jack L. Vevea, Chester A. Insko, and John Schopler (2003) examines prior scholarly analyses of the transformation that occurs when conflict erupts between groups rather than individuals and provides a summary of work on the discontinuity effect.

Intergroup Relations

- *On the Nature of Prejudice: Fifty Years after Allport*, edited by John F. Dovidio, Peter Glick, and Laurie A. Rudman (2005), draws together papers on Allport's insights into the nature of intergroup conflict, with sections pertaining to preferential thinking, sociocultural factors, and prejudice reduction.

- *The Psychology of Stereotyping* by David J. Schneider (2004) examines issues of stereotype and bias, as well as a wide variety of cognitive processes that pertain to groups, including perceptions of entitativity, categorization, and ingroup–outgroup bias.

Resolving Intergroup Conflict

- "Prejudice Reduction: What Works? A Review and Assessment of Research and Practice," by Elizabeth Levy Paluck and Donald P. Green (2009) reviews a wide variety of methods used to reduce conflict between groups, with a focus on the rigor of the methods used to evaluate their efficacy.

- *The Psychology of Social and Cultural Diversity*, edited by Richard J. Crisp (2010), provides a balanced analysis of empirical studies of intergroup conflict, paired with practical applications for resolving such conflicts. This book is a publication of the Society for the Psychological Study of Social Issues (SPSSI), one of the oldest scientific societies devoted to the study of social problems and their solutions.

- *When Groups Meet: The Dynamics of Intergroup Contact* by Thomas F. Pettigrew and Linda R. Tropp (2011) examines the history and current empirical status of one of the most tried and tested methods for reducing conflict between groups: encouraging intergroup contact.

Groups in Context

CHAPTER OVERVIEW

Just as individuals are embedded in groups, so groups are embedded in physical and social environments. Groups alter their environments substantially, but in many cases, it's the place that shapes the group. As Lewin's law of interaction, $B = f(P, E)$, states, group behavior (B) is a function of the persons (P) who are in the group, but also the social and physical environment (E) where the group is located.

- How does the physical environment influence groups and their dynamics?

- What is the ecology of a group?

- What are the causes and consequences of a group's tendency to establish territories?

- How can group places, spaces, and locations be improved?

CHAPTER OUTLINE

Places: The Physical Context
   A Sense of Place
   Stressful Places
   Dangerous Places

Spaces: The Social Context
   Personal Space
   Reactions to Spatial Invasion
   Seating Arrangements

Locations: Group Territoriality
   Types of Territoriality
   Group Territories
   Territoriality in Groups

Designing Group Environments
   The Person-Place Fit
   Fitting Form to Function
  Chapter Review
  Resources

Apollo 13: The Group That Lost the Moon

In 1961, President John F. Kennedy set the goal: to send Americans to the surface of the moon by the end of the decade. His plan initiated the largest engineering project in modern history with as many as 400,000 individuals eventually working together to solve the endless technical, psychological, and medical problems posed by such an unprecedented undertaking. On July 20, 1969, Apollo 11 commander Neil Armstrong made history when he stepped on the moon's surface.

One year later, the crew of Apollo 13—James Lovell, John Swigert, and Fred Haise—also made history, but in their case by *not* stepping on the moon. On April 11, 1970, they piloted the National Aeronautics and Space Administration's (NASA) Apollo 13 into space without any sign of a problem. Lovell, Swigert, and Haise were to spend four days crowded together in their command module, named the *Odyssey*, before reaching the moon. The team members had trained for

years for the mission, and throughout the trip they would remain in constant communication with ground control teams in Houston, Texas. Once in orbit around the moon, Lovell and Haise would descend to the surface of the moon in the Lunar Excursion Module (LEM), the *Aquarius*.

But 56 hours into the mission, Swigert initiated a procedure designed to stir the cryogenic oxygen tanks. One of the tanks exploded. With oxygen escaping from their ship and battery power dwindling, Lovell coolly radioed NASA his famous understatement, "Houston, we have a problem." (Actually, he said, "Houston, we've had a problem.") During the next three days, the crew and the teams on the ground identified and responded to one life-threatening challenge after another, including near-freezing temperatures and a buildup of carbon dioxide in the cabin. The group managed to return to Earth and splashed down safely in the Pacific Ocean on April 17, 1970.

Groups exist in any number of distinct locations, ranging from classrooms, museums, factories, and boardrooms to copper mines, battlefields, and even space capsules. The impressionists thrived in Paris in the 1860s in the midst of its countless art schools, restaurants, bistros, and parks. The 1980 U.S. Olympic Hockey Team trained and played for hours and hours on hockey rinks across the world. The Bay of Pigs planners met in an elegantly appointed conference room, speaking to each other in subdued voices across an imposing mahogany table. The Rattlers and the Eagles met, fought, and befriended each other at the cabins and on the fields of the Robbers Cave State Park. The crew of Apollo 13 lived in a high-tech environment filled with multiple controls and few comforts. Each one of these groups slept, worked, played, interacted, argued, and fought in a specific environmental context, and these places substantially influenced their dynamics.

Many disciplines, including anthropology, architecture, demography, environmental psychology, ethology, human geography, interior design, and sociology, affirm the important impact of

environmental variables on human behavior. Just as a group-level orientation assumes that individuals' actions are shaped by the groups to which they belong, an environmental orientation assumes that groups are shaped by their environments. As Figure 15.1 suggests, a multilevel analysis of human behavior recognizes that individuals are nested in a hierarchy of increasingly inclusive social aggregates, such as groups, organizations, and communities. But individuals and their groups also exist in a physical setting located in a particular geographic locality in a specific region of the world, and that place will eventually influence the group's dynamics and outcomes. After all, did not Kurt Lewin (1951) remind us that $B = f(P, E)$: behavior (B) is a function of the persons (P) who are in the group, but also the social and physical environment (E) where the group is located?

This chapter, in reviewing theory and research dealing with the group–environment interface, focuses on group places, spaces, locations, and workspaces. It begins by examining the features of the physical place that influence the group (e.g., temperature, noise) before turning to the way group members

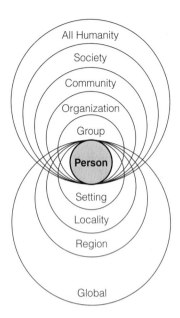

FIGURE 15.1 A multilevel model of both social aggregates (e.g., groups, organizations, communities) and geographic domains (e.g., settings, localities, regions).

SOURCE: © Cengage Learning

act within the space (personal distance, seating choices). The analysis then considers how individuals and groups come to develop a proprietary orientation to a given location—territoriality—before closing with a more practical question: Given what we know about group places, spaces, and locations, what features should be built into the group's habitat to ensure the members are contented and the group is productive? (For reviews, see Bell et al., 2006; Davis, Leach, & Clegg, 2011; Gieryn, 2000; Werner, Brown, & Altman, 2002.)

PLACES: THE PHYSICAL CONTEXT

Ecology is the science of organisms and their habitats. Ecologists examine how organisms—whether they are plant, animal, or microbe—interact with and adapt to other organisms in their environment and to the environment itself. Similarly, those who study the ecology of groups explore how individuals interact with and adapt to the group's habitat. In some cases, groups and the setting fit comfortably together. The place suits the group, leaving members free to focus on interpersonal and task dynamics. The materials they require are available, distractions are minimal, the temperature is comfortable, and the only sounds are those that the group members themselves create. But other environments are less hospitable. Humans have been remarkably successful in changing their environment to suit their preferences, but sometimes the place shapes the group rather than the group shaping the place.

A Sense of Place

Physical settings are often said to have **ambience**, or *atmosphere*, for they can create a distinctive cognitive and emotional reaction in people who occupy these spaces (Schroeder, 2007).

> We have strong feelings in and about places. Some places make us feel good: glad to be there, relaxed, excited, warm all over. We are drawn to these places and return to them as often as we can. Other places make us feel bad: uncomfortable, insignificant, unhappy, out of place. We avoid these places and suffer if we have to be in them. (Farbstein & Kantrowitz, 1978, p. 14)

The crew of the Apollo 13, for example, lived in a high-tech environment filled with various space-age gizmos: control panels, gauges, sensors, warning lights, and all sorts of buttons and switches. The space had been designed with meticulous care, but only an engineer or an astronaut would likely call it comfortable or beautiful.

Perceptions of Places A group's response to its environment is a subjective one, for the manifest physical features of the place are filtered through each member's personal preferences, expectations,

---

ambience The psychological reaction (mood, feelings, emotions) evoked by a setting.

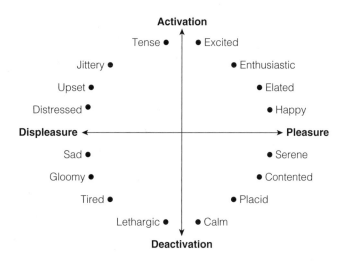

F I G U R E 15.2   Core affect experienced by people in various types of group environments.

SOURCE: Adapted from Russell, J. A. (2003). Core affect and the psychological construction of emotion. *Psychological Review, 110*, 145–172.

values, and attitudes. Their response is based more on their *image* of the place—their psychological representation of the physical location—as much as it is based on the place's physical features (Boulding, 1956). Furnishing, design, and landscaping practices all vary from one culture to the next, so a setting that is considered pleasant or comfortable in one country may be considered ugly and distressing in another. The very same aspects of a setting, such as the color of the walls or the way the table and chairs are arranged, will be considered ideal if the person chose these features, but not if they were imposed on the person by someone else (Rapoport, 1980). One's goals matter, as well. A person who wishes, for example, to study for an examination will respond very differently to a room with music, dancing, and party streamers than will a person whose goal is to have a good time (Herzog et al., 2011a). The beauty of a place is often in the eye of the beholder.

Psychologist James A. Russell and his colleagues, however, have found that people's perceptions of places are substantially influenced by their answers to two basic questions: How *pleasant* is the place (positive versus negative), and how *intense* is the place (arousing versus relaxing)? First, a group environment that is orderly, tastefully decorated, clean, and spacious usually prompts a more favorable reaction than one that is poorly designed, shabby, unkempt,

and odorous (see Figure 15.2). Second, whereas some places are restful, others are so stimulating that they arouse their occupants rather than relax them. The astronauts and engineers working in the control room at Houston all responded positively to their highly arousing habitat, and so they considered it an exhilarating place. Visitors to the control room, in contrast, often reacted negatively to its harsh lights, countless monitors, and a cacophony of voices issuing orders, relaying information, and asking questions. Few considered it boring or tranquil (Russell, 2003; Russell & Snodgrass, 1987; Widen & Russell, 2010; Yik, Russell, & Steiger, 2011).

Groups generally respond best, in terms of performance and satisfaction, in affectively pleasant situations. Studies of manufacturing teams in factories, students in classrooms, and workers in offices, for example, have found that they respond better when working in attractive spaces that are visually interesting rather than drab (Cabanac, 2005). Physical features that stimulate or provoke positive emotions—including music, furnishings, art, decor, decorations, color, and lighting—tend to be associated with a range of positive group dynamics, including increased cohesion, improved communication, productivity, and reduced absenteeism (Brief & Weiss, 2002). An attractive environment is not, however, a requirement for group effectiveness. Many successful groups work without problems in relatively shabby settings. A too-pleasant environment may distract the group from the task at hand, providing counterproductive levels of comfort. Highly effective groups may also be so focused on the task that they can work anywhere, since what matters is the quality of their tools and their personnel rather than the setting (Bennis & Biederman, 1997).

Groups also thrive in stimulating spaces. Studies of groups living in harsh circumstances, such as teams stationed in Antarctica and explorers living for months on end in a confined space, complain more about the monotony of the environment than about the danger, discomfort, or isolation (Stuster, 1996). During the *International Geophysical Year* (1957–1958), for example, several countries sent small groups of military and civilian personnel to outposts in Antarctica. These groups were responsible for collecting various data concerning that largely unknown continent, but the violent weather forced the staff to remain indoors most of the time. As months went by with little change in their situation, morale declined and group members found themselves arguing over trivial issues. The members summarized their group malaise with the term *antarcticitis*—lethargy, low morale, grouchiness, and boredom brought on by their unstimulating living conditions (Gunderson, 1973; see also Carrere & Evans, 1994; Stuster, 1996).

Cognitive Overload   Excessively stimulating settings can also be problematic. Groups experience cognitive **overload** if they are overwhelmed by the sheer volume of information in the environment (Greenberg & Firestone, 1977). Group members generally prefer to be located at the center of their group's communication network rather than on the periphery, but not if the flow of information is so great they cannot keep up with it (Shaw,

---

overload A psychological reaction to situations and experiences that are so cognitively, perceptually, or emotionally stimulating that they tax or even exceed the individual's capacity to process incoming information.

1964). College students who rated their environment as overly stimulating—they agreed with such items as "I was bothered by stimuli that were interesting but irrelevant" and "I couldn't think about something because there was too much going on around me"—also evidenced signs of mental fatigue, including an inability to concentrate and difficulty following directions (Herzog et al., 2011b). Novice automobile drivers (ages 16–18) traveling with young passengers (ages 16–18) create a group situation that is overly complex, resulting in increases in fatal accidents. In consequence, many states in the United States have banned these groups from the highway (Chen et al., 2000).

Even a highly effective team with a well-developed mental model (see Chapter 11) can experience a significant loss in functioning if the members are overloaded with information to process and decisions to enact. Researchers examined this process by bombarding expert teams of naval personnel with substantial amounts of information. The teams worked on a task that simulated a critically important naval decision—deciding on the basis of radar and database information whether an unidentified contact was a threat to the ship or nonhostile. The participants worked in teams of three, but in the coaction condition, members made their decisions independently of one another. In the interdependent condition, the members had to work together to gather information about the possible target. The researchers manipulated stress by exposing some of the groups to distracting sound and noise while they worked and by increasing the number of contacts presented on the radar screens. They also pressured these groups by telling members to "work harder" and to "hurry up."

The study's results confirmed the researchers' initial suspicions: Interdependent groups working in a stressful situation lost their group perspective. They were more likely to report feeling like three individuals rather than like a team, and they were not focused on the task. They were also less likely to use plural pronouns such as *we, us, our, ours,* and *ourselves* when describing their response to the simulation. Moreover, groups that lost their team perspective tended to perform more poorly—they were more likely to identify a harmless contact on their radar screens as hostile and less likely to correctly identify contacts that were dangerous. These findings suggest that a well-trained team may handle routine problems effectively, but that the advantages of extensive training may be lost when groups work in challenging environments (Driskell, Salas, & Johnston 1999).

Coping with Complexity   In everyday situations, people cope with overload by reducing their contact with others, limiting the amount of information they notice and process, or ignoring aspects of the situation. They can also cope by engaging in restorative practices. Psychologist Stephen Kaplan (1995, 2001), for example, maintains that one effective way of restoring cognitive resources is to spend time in an environment that does not demand high levels of directed attention. According to his **attention restoration theory**, or ART, directed attention is mentally draining, for it requires group members to monitor their attention, direct it to focus on a particular stimulus, and ignore other aspects of the environment. The crew monitoring their radar screens, students in their classrooms, and groups making complicated decisions may all be impressively productive, but they are also becoming cognitively depleted as these activities rely on finite and exhaustible psychological resources.

Other situations, in contrast, make far fewer cognitive demands on group members. People often report feeling rejuvenated and energized by the places that their groups occupy. They feel more at ease and content when they can spend time in places they feel attached to, including their homes, their rooms, or even cubicles in an office (Altman & Churchman, 1994; Carlopio, 1996). These settings require little in the way of directed attention, and so they serve a restorative function: They allow

cognitive resources to replenish themselves following depletion. Kaplan and his colleagues find that natural environments, in particular, are deeply restorative ones. Individuals who spend time walking in a park, sitting on a bench in a garden, or viewing photographs of nature scenes are better able to concentrate, control their thinking, tolerate frustration, and perform more successfully on a wide array of tests of mental acuity. Sleep and meditation may also serve to rejuvenate attention. Watching television, by the way, does not (Kaplan & Berman, 2010).

Stressful Places

Some settings sustain and restore, but others strain and stress. Groups do not exist in neutral, passive voids, but in fluctuating environments that are sometimes too hot, too cold, too impersonal, too intimate, too big, too little, too noisy, too quiet, too restrictive, or too open—but rarely just right. These settings are sources of **stress**—strain caused by environmental circumstances that threaten one's sense of well-being and safety (Evans & Stecker, 2004; Veitch et al., 2007).

Temperature   Temperature is a property of the environment, but this physical characteristic of a place influences its interpersonal properties (see Focus 15.1). People often describe other people, groups, and relationships as *warm* and *cold*. Warm people are thought to be intelligent, skillful, industrious, determined, practical, and cautious. Cold ones: ungenerous, unhappy, irritable, unsociable, unpopular, and humorless (Asch, 1946). Some groups, too, seem warm, friendly, and cozy, whereas others are cold, sterile, and chilly. People so closely associate ambient warmth with interpersonal warmth that they rate other people more positively when they themselves are feeling warm.

---

attention restoration theory A conceptual analysis of the cognitive processes that sustain high-level executive functioning, including attentional focus and self-regulation, which assumes that these cognitive resources can be replenished through an interaction with natural environments (developed by Stephen Kaplan).

---

stress Negative physiological, emotional, cognitive, and behavioral responses to circumstances that threaten—or are thought to threaten—one's sense of well-being and safety.

F o c u s 15.1 Cross-cultural Perspectives: Variations in Cultural Practices in Hot and Cold Climates

---

They say that there is no place like home, but where is home for the human species? People live in every part of the world, from the frozen Antarctic to its most arid deserts, and seem to manage wherever they go. But do these different climates change the groups within them? Do groups in Iceland or the Netherlands act differently than groups of Saudi Arabia and Chile? And are these variations the result of cultural differences or climatic factors that have influenced the people who live in hot places, warm places, and cold places?

Culture is the complex of relatively stable human values and practices of a given group that is passed from one generation to the next. Many forces influence a people's culture—political, economic, historical, sociological, and psychological—but social psychologist Evert Van de Vliert (2009) traces cultural variations back to an aspect of the physical world rather than the social world: temperature. His *climato-economic theory* argues that climate makes different demands on the people who live in a place, and the result is predictable differences in a variety of economic, political, and group-level processes.

Van de Vliert suggests that culture is the result of humans' response to dealing with the stress caused by having to live in difficult, challenging climates. Physically, humans are most comfortable in climates with temperatures of about 72°F, so groups who live in habitats where the temperature hovers near this mark experience less climate-related stress. Colder and hotter climates, in contrast, are more challenging, and so groups develop cultural practices to survive in such places. If the groups who live in a particular geographic area are economically prosperous, then the culture will likely develop production and trade systems to make or acquire the resources needed to deal with environmental challenges. Cultures that lack economic resources, including wealth or natural resources, cannot generate the food, clothing, shelter, and medical facilities they need by developing strong economies, so they instead shift toward self-sufficiency, localized trade, and a more communal orientation. In essence, less affluent cultures cope with living in a difficult environment by building social capital, whereas wealthier cultures rely on their economic capital.

Van de Vliert and his colleagues offer a number of compelling pieces of evidence in support of their theory. They discovered, for example, that they could predict a cultures' acceptance of an autocratic leader by taking into account the country's baseline level of wealth and the harshness of the climate where it is located. For example, Canada, Norway, Iran, and Russia all have challenging climates (too hot or too cold during some seasons), but only the residents of Russia and Iran express support for strong, autocratic, domineering leaders. These countries are also less economically prosperous, particularly in comparison to Canada and Norway (Van de Vliert, 2006). Van de Vliert also found that, when surveyed, the residents of relatively poorer countries tended to evidence higher levels of intergroup bias—but only if they were also located in a climate that was too hot or too cold. These countries' residents expressed more negative attitudes toward immigrant groups, were more supportive of nepotistic hiring practices, and also reported investing more time in their families (Van de Vliert, 2011). Countries where the climate was more temperate exhibited varying levels of support for authoritarian leaders and they also ranged from individualism to collectivism, but these variables were not related to the country's level of economic prosperity.

Some of Van de Vliert's other findings provide only partial support for his climato-economic theory. When, for example, he studied the sources of role stress in work groups in organizations, he discovered that conflict was associated with higher temperatures and so was not moderated either by wealth or harshness of the climate (Van de Vliert, 1996). And other investigators have suggested that factors that vary with temperature—such as susceptibility to infectious diseases—may be more causally influential factors (e.g., Fincher & Thornhill, 2012; Van de Vliert & Postmes, 2012). Researchers continue to test hypotheses derived from the theory, but it may be that global climate changes will provide the ultimate test. If the worldwide increase in temperatures continues for much longer, people living in colder climates may find that their climate is less of a challenge, whereas others may discover that their once temperate climate has become too hot to sustain their way of life. These countries, according to Van de Vliert, will undergo changes in their cultural traditions to deal with these climate changes, depending as well on their overall level of wealth. Time, then, and temperature, will tell (Fischer & Van de Vliert, 2011).

When researchers asked people to form an impression of a person they had just met, respondents evaluated the person more positively when they were holding a warm cup of coffee rather than a glass of iced coffee (Williams & Bargh, 2008). And, just as warm temperatures create increases in social warmth, social warmth causes people to misjudge ambient temperature. When individuals felt interpersonally closer to others in their group, they judged the room to be slightly warmer than did individuals who did not feel as close to others (IJzerman & Semin, 2010). Social neuroscience findings even suggest that areas of the brain that are responsible for processing information about ambient temperature also handle the processing of information about social warmth and trust (Kang et al., 2011).

One of the minor miseries of life, however, occurs when people must work in a room that is either too hot or too cold. Although people generally rate temperatures from the mid-60s to the mid-80s Fahrenheit as "comfortable," temperatures that fall outside this range cause discomfort, irritability, and reduced productivity (Bell, 1992). When groups were assigned to work either in a room at normal temperature (72.4°F) or in a hot room (93.5°F), the overheated group members reported feelings of fatigue, sadness, and discomfort, whereas participants in the normal-temperature room reported feeling more elated, vigorous, and comfortable (Griffitt & Veitch, 1971). Studies have also suggested that extremes in temperature can reduce interpersonal attraction (Griffitt, 1970) and interfere with successful task performance (Parsons, 1976). One of the concomitants of high temperatures in groups is exposure to others' body odors—a sensation that most people find objectionable (McBurney, Levine, & Cavanaugh, 1977). The odor of men's sweat and a stranger's sweat are perceived as particularly repugnant (Stevenson & Repacholi, 2003, 2005).

Groups tend to be more aggressive when they are hot; they get "hot under the collar," "steamed," and their "tempers flare." Heat and aggression are so closely linked, psychologically, that just thinking about hot temperatures can also trigger thoughts about aggression (DeWall & Bushman, 2009).

Collective violence tends to be seasonal, for people are more likely to riot in the warm days of the summer than they are in the colder winter months (Rotton & Cohn, 2002). Groups, too, tend to be more hostile when temperatures are high, but not extremely high. In one study, researchers created groups that worked on individual tasks in a comfortable room versus a hot room. The heat-stressed participants were angry, but they were so uncomfortable that their primary concern was to escape. They finished the experiment as quickly as possible and then left (Baron & Bell, 1975; Bell, 1992).

Extreme temperatures are also physically harmful (Folk, 1974). When temperatures are high, people are more likely to suffer from exhaustion, stroke, and heart attacks. Extreme cold can lead to hypothermia and death. The Apollo 13 astronauts, for example, struggled to maintain their body heat at healthy levels when the loss of power forced them to turn off the cabin heaters. It was, as Lovell characteristically understated, "very uncomfortable. Basically, the cold made it uncomfortable" (quoted in Godwin, 2000, p. 109). Accounts of groups struggling in extremely cold natural environments, such as teams wintering over in Antarctica or mountain climbers, document the lethal effects of exposure to extremely cold temperatures.

Noise The crew of Apollo 13 lived with constant noise during their five days in space. The Saturn V rockets were deafening, burning 3,400 gallons of fuel per second. Once in orbit, the cabin was filled with the humming of computers, the whirring of fans and pumps circulating air and liquids, and the crackling of transmissions between the crew and COMCON, the flight controller back in Houston. There was also the one sound that signaled to the crew that something was wrong; Lovell described the explosion as a "bang-whump-shudder" that was felt more than heard (Lovell & Kluger, 1994, p. 94).

Noise is any sound that is unwanted. Sounds in the range of 0–50 decibels (dB) are very soft and generally produce little irritation for the listener. Sounds of more than 80 dB, in contrast, may be bothersome enough to be called noise. In general, the louder the noise, the more likely it will produce distraction, irritation, and psychological stress (Cohen & Weinstein, 1981). Group communication becomes impossible in such environments, so members have problems coordinating their efforts. Coping with chronic noise also exacts a psychological toll. Groups in noisy places—people who work in noisy offices, families living in homes near airports, and children on playgrounds located near major highways—behave differently than groups in quieter contexts. People are less likely to interact with other people in noisy places, and they also tend to be less helpful (Edelstein, 2002; Mathews, Canon, & Alexander, 1974; Veitch, 1990). Over time, exposure to loud noise is associated with substantial threats to health, including physical illnesses (headaches, heart disease, allergies, and digestive disorders), infant and adult mortality rates, mental illness, interpersonal conflict, and even impotence (Bronzaft, 2002; Wallenius, 2004).

Not all noisy places are bad places, however. A moderate level of ambient noise, for example, may actually help people concentrate on their work. When attempting to perform a task that calls for creativity and divergent thinking, high levels and low levels of noise are deleterious, but a moderate level of background noise improves performance (Mehta, Zhu, & Cheema, 2012). If, however, the group is attempting a task that requires the accurate communication of information across members, then the less noise the better. Groups are particularly sensitive to noise because much of the unwanted sound in a group setting originates within the group itself. Depending on the qualities of the room, 15 people talking informally with one another will create so much noise that conversation between adjoining pairs is inhibited. When a conversing group passes by an individual who is attempting to perform a difficult task, the noise of the group can be distracting. People can often ignore ambient sounds, but overheard speech is another matter. Neurological evidence indicates that even when people strive to deliberately ignore speech by refocusing attention on the task at hand, some of their cognitive resources are being used to monitor the nearby conversations (Campbell, 2005).

People can cope with noise for short periods of time. When researchers bombarded people working on both simple and complex tasks with tape-recorded noise, the participants became so inured to the stimulus that it had no effect on their performance (Glass, Singer, & Pennebaker, 1977). Groups cannot, however, cope with noise for long periods of time. As "individuals expend 'psychic energy' in the course of the adaptive process," they become "less able to cope with subsequent environmental demands and frustrations" (Glass et al., 1977, p. 134). One investigation found that exposure to low levels of ambient noise in an office setting did not cause increases in stress, but people had trouble coping with other stressful events—an irritating boss or coworker, role ambiguities, or time pressures—when they worked in a noisy place (Leather, Beale, & Sullivan, 2003).

Dangerous Places

The astronauts sat atop millions of pounds of rocket fuel at launch, traveled through space in a thin-shelled spacecraft at speeds of nearly 25,000 miles an hour, and during reentry relied on a heat shield to deflect the heat away from the command module and parachutes that would slow the craft's descent. All the dangers were minimized through planning, design, and training, but one danger that all crews faced but could not protect themselves against was always present—a collision with a meteor.

EUEs: Extreme and Unusual Environments The Apollo 13 astronauts were not the first group to face difficult environmental circumstances. For centuries, explorers have hiked, sailed, flown, and ridden from their homes to distant lands and places, and many of these groups have endured long periods of isolation in **extreme and unusual environments**, or **EUE**s (Suedfeld & Steel,

---

extreme and unusual environments Environmental contexts that are unlike those where humans usually live, including confined and isolated environments.

2000). In some cases, a natural calamity, such as a flood, earthquake, or blizzard, may overtake a group, which must then struggle to survive. For example, Sir Ernest Shackleton and the crew of *Endurance* survived the destruction of their ship on an ice floe in the Antarctic. More recently, 33 miners in Chile survived the collapse of the mine where they worked, but all survived the cave-in and were reunited with their families after 69 days (Franklin, 2011). Some groups, too, work at jobs that are riskier than most: Ship crews, police officers, and military units often live and work in circumstances that can be life threatening. Teams of divers have lived for weeks on end in SEALAB, 200 feet beneath the ocean's surface. NASA's crews have endured months in space, and plans are being made for a three-year voyage to Mars (Bechtel, 2002; Stuster, 1996).

Surviving Environmental Challenges   Although technological innovations make survival in even the most hostile environments possible, groups living in these space-age settings must learn to cope with age-old problems of interpersonal adjustment. Whereas harsh environments and circumstances overwhelm lone individuals, groups are capable of overcoming the limiting conditions created by these environmental stressors. Groups generally cope with danger by taking precautions designed to make the situation safer. Astronauts, military combat squads, and explorers all minimize the danger by training, stressing cooperation among members, and monitoring each individual's connection to the group (Harrison & Connors, 1984; Suedfeld, 1987).

Groups that survive in EUEs respond by becoming better groups—more organized, more cohesive, and more efficient. Those that do not display breakdowns in team coordination, communication, and leadership. Journalist Jon Krakauer (1997), for example, describes the consequences of inattention to team functioning in his analysis of the events that led up to the loss of several members of two groups attempting to climb Mount Everest in 1996. Even though the climb is extremely dangerous and many who attempt it are killed, the groups

on Krakauer's summit did not practice together, establish routines for dealing with supplies, or set up contingency plans. A hierarchy of authority was not established, despite the possibility that one of the leaders could be injured. The leaders of both teams also made errors in judgment, possibly due to inexperience, the ill effects of too little oxygen (hypoxia), and the desire to outdo the other team. Both teams met with disaster (Burnette, Pollack, & Forsyth, 2011).

But many groups not only persevere in these adverse circumstances; they find the experience to be exhilarating. Groups like Apollo 13 and the Shackleton explorers have faced disaster, death, and ruin at each turn, yet their autobiographical accounts of their experiences speak eloquently about their adventures—which they do not regret—describing them as "a cherished and important part of their life, perceived as an impetus to growing, strengthening, and deepening, to be remembered with pride and enjoyment" (Suedfeld & Steel, 2000, p. 229).

SPACES: THE SOCIAL CONTEXT

Groups exist in any number of distinct locations, and the physical qualities of these places—temperature, noise, stress—substantially influence a group's dynamics. But the group's environment also includes the other people present in the physical space. Lovell was not alone in the Apollo 13 capsule but with Swigert and Haise; his fellow crewmen influenced his actions and outcomes as much as the physical features of the spacecraft did. This section examines two key aspects of **small group ecology**: the distances members maintain between

---

small group ecology The study of the interactions among the living (the group and its members) and the nonliving (the physical setting) components of a group's environment, with particular emphasis on the spatial arrangements of individuals in small groups.

T A B L E   15.1   **Types of Social Activities That Occur in Each Interpersonal Zone**

Zone	Distance	Characteristics	Typical Activities
Intimate	Touching to 18 inches	Sensory information concerning the other is detailed and diverse; stimulus person dominates the perceptual field	Sex, hugging, massage, comforting, jostling, handshakes, slow dancing
Personal	18 inches to 4 feet	Other person can be touched if desired; gaze can be directed away from the other person with ease	Conversations, discussion, car travel, viewing performances, watching television
Social	4 feet to 12 feet	Visual inputs begin to dominate other senses; voice levels are normal; appropriate distance for many informal social gatherings	Dining, meeting with business colleagues, interacting with a receptionist
Public	12 feet or more	All sensory inputs are beginning to become less effective; voices may require amplification; facial expressions unclear	Lectures, addresses, plays, dance recitals
Remote	Different locations	Primarily verbal inputs; facial and other behavioral and nonverbal cues unavailable	Electronic discussions, conference calls, telephone voice mail, e-mail, online gaming communities

SOURCE: Adapted from E. T. Hall, 1966.

each other—personal space—and the way they position themselves relative to one another—seating arrangements (Sommer, 1967).

Personal Space

Anthropologist Edward T. Hall (1966) argued that much of our behavior is shaped by a "hidden dimension." In Apollo 13, this dimension determined where each astronaut sat as he carried out his scheduled tasks; how crew members moved through the tunnel between the command module and the service module; where they positioned themselves when they looked out the windows of their ship as it passed over the surface of the moon. What is this hidden dimension? *Space.*

People prefer to keep some space between themselves and others. This **personal space** provides a boundary that limits the amount of physical contact between people. This boundary extends farther in front of a person than behind, but the

individual is always near the center of this invisible buffer zone. Personal space is portable, but it is actively maintained and defended. When someone violates our personal space, we tend to take steps to correct this problem (Aiello, 1987). The term *personal space* is something of a misnomer, as the process actually refers to distances that people maintain between one another. Hence, it is an *interpersonal space* (Patterson, 1975).

Interpersonal Zones   Different group activities require different amounts of personal space. Hall, in describing these variations, proposed four types of interpersonal zones (see Table 15.1). The *intimate zone* is appropriate only for the most involving and personal behaviors, such as arm wrestling and whispering. The *personal zone*, in contrast, is reserved for a wide range of small-group experiences, such as discussions with friends, interaction with acquaintances, and conversation. More routine transactions are conducted in the *social zone*. Meetings held over large desks, formal dining, and professional presentations to small groups generally take place in this zone. The *public zone* is reserved for even more formal meetings, such as stage presentations, lectures, or addresses.

---

personal   space   The   area   that   individuals   maintain around   themselves   into   which   others   cannot   intrude without   arousing   discomfort.

Table 15.1 adds a fifth zone to those described by Hall. In the years since Hall proposed his taxonomy of interpersonal zones, groups have begun to meet more frequently in the *remote zone*. Many groups now exist, in whole or in part, in a virtual environment. Instead of interacting face-to-face or even via voice communication, e-groups use computer-based tools such as e-mail, chat rooms, social networking sites, and other multiuser support interfaces. The members of these groups are not physically present with each other, making online groups considerably different—at least spatially— than face-to-face groups. The astronauts, for example, communicated with COMCON from a distance—a great distance, in fact. They used voice messages, in some cases, but they were also in touch using communication technologies that allowed them to send and receive information via computers.

Closer, smaller spaces are generally reserved for friendlier, more intimate interpersonal activities. As a result, cohesive groups tend to occupy smaller spaces than noncohesive gatherings (Evans & Howard, 1973); extraverted people maintain smaller distances from others than do introverted ones (Patterson & Sechrest, 1970); people who wish to create a friendly, positive impression usually choose smaller distances than do less friendly people (Evans & Howard, 1973); and groups of friends tend to stand closer to one another than do groups of strangers (Edney & Grundmann, 1979). Physical distance has less impact on remote groups, but even individuals who connect with one another via cell phones tend to be located close to one another geographically (Onnela et al., 2011). In general, individuals communicating via computer respond differently when their interface becomes informationally richer by including voice and video information (Thurlow, Lengel, & Tomic, 2004).

Men, Women, and Distance Would the amount of personal space maintained by the astronauts in Apollo 13 have differed if they had been women? Probably, for studies suggest that women's personal spaces tend to be smaller than men's (Hayduk,

1978; 1983). Relative to men, women allow others to get closer to them, and they approach other people more closely. Men also tend to approach women more closely than other men. Women tend to take up less space by sitting with their arms close to their sides and by crossing their legs, whereas men claim more space by assuming expansive, open positions (Henley, 1995). The interactions between the men of Apollo 13 occurred almost exclusively in the personal zone, except when Lovell hugged the shivering Haise, who had become increasingly ill during the mission.

Status People tend to "keep their distance" when interacting with higher status group members. Researchers documented this tendency by watching conversations between U.S. naval personnel that took place in nonwork settings, such as the cafeteria or a recreation center. The floors in these spaces were tiled, so observers measured distance by counting how many tiles separated the two individuals. As anticipated, rank determined distance: officers approached subordinates more closely than did individuals of a lower rank who were initiating a conversation with an officer (Dean, Willis, & Hewitt, 1975; see Hall, Coats, & LeBeau, 2005).

Culture Hall (1966) argued that cultures differ in their use of space. People socialized in the *contact cultures* of the Mediterranean, the Middle East, and Latin America prefer strong sensory involvement with others, and so they seek direct social contact whenever possible. In contrast, residents in such *noncontact cultures* as the United States, England, and Germany try to limit their spatial openness with others. Given that the crew of Apollo 13 included only Americans, they shared similar norms about how much distance should be maintained. Crews on space stations, such as Mir or Salyut, involve astronauts from different cultural backgrounds, so misunderstandings caused by spatial confusions may be more common (see Focus 12.1). Culture also influences how people interact in the remote zone, for people with different cultural backgrounds vary in how much emotion, personal information, and responsiveness to others they express when communicating via the Internet (Reeder et al., 2004).

Maintaining Equilibrium   Why does distance influence so many group processes? Most theories of nonverbal communication recognize that distance, like body orientation, eye contact, and physical touch, function to define the nature of the relationship between people. The **equilibrium model of communication**, for example, suggests that these nonverbal cues interact to influence perceptions of intimacy. If group members feel that a low level of intimacy is appropriate, they may sit far apart, make little eye contact, and assume a relatively formal posture. If, in contrast, the members are relaxing and discussing personal topics, they may move close together, make more eye contact, and adopt more relaxed postures (Argyle & Dean, 1965; Patterson, 1996). By continually adjusting their nonverbal and verbal behavior, group members can keep the intimacy of their interactions at the level they desire (Giles & Wadleigh, 1999).

Communication researcher Judee Burgoon's (1978, 1983) *expectancy violations theory* extends this analysis by identifying the types of messages that distance—taken in combination with other nonverbal cues—can signal. Sitting close to another person may indicate warmth and acceptance, but it may also be an indication of similarity, trust, composure (absence of nervousness), formality, dominance, equality, or task orientation. In one study, for example, she found that closer proximity signaled dominance, similarity, and composure, but that this meaning changed when one person in the group leaned forward, smiled, and briefly touched the other person. The interaction was transformed from one involving status and dominance to one suggesting informality and intimacy (Burgoon & Dillman, 1995; Burgoon & Hale, 1987).

---

equilibrium model of communication An explanation of distancing behavior in interpersonal settings arguing that the amount of eye contact and the intimacy of the topic influence the amount of personal space required by group members.

Reactions to Spatial Invasion

Individuals cannot always protect their personal space from intrusion by others. In some cases, group members may find themselves in places where the available space is so limited that people cannot maintain appropriate distances between one another. In other instances, the group may have sufficient space, but for some reason, a member approaches so closely that he or she seems "too close for comfort."

Density and Crowding   How do group members react to such intrusions? High density does not always lead to feelings of crowding and other negative interpersonal outcomes. **Density** refers to a characteristic of the environment—literally, the number of people per unit of space. **Crowding**, in contrast, refers to a psychological, experiential state that occurs when people *feel* that they do not have enough space (Stokols, 1972, 1978). Although the density of a given situation, such as a party, a rock concert, or Apollo 13, may be very high, the interactants may not feel crowded at all. Yet two people sitting in a large room may still report that they feel crowded if the other person is sitting too close to them, they expected to be alone, are engaged in some private activity, or dislike each other intensely. Passengers on a train where density was low—there were plenty of empty seats in the car—displayed the negative effects of crowding (e.g., more negative mood, evidence of stress, loss of motivation) if others were seated near them in their row (Evans & Wener, 2007).

Arousal and Stress   Unexpected and unwarranted violations of one's personal space needs are, in most cases, aversive experiences. When confederates approached too closely people studying in libraries, sitting outdoors, standing on escalators, or walking down the street, the targets displayed a number of

---

density The number of individuals per unit of space.
crowding A psychological reaction that occurs when individuals feel that the amount of space available to them is insufficient for their needs.

negative reactions, including reduced eye contact, shifts in body posture, verbal rebukes, and withdrawal from the situation (Sundstrom et al., 1996). People report the experience to be stressful, and measures of their physiological reactions confirm this description: Personal space violations cause increases in heart rate and blood pressure, more rapid breathing, and perspiration (Evans, 1979).

One of the more creative—if ethically controversial (see Koocher, 1977)—investigations of the arousal properties of personal space invasion was conducted in a men's restroom (Middlemist, Knowles, & Matter, 1976). Reasoning that arousal would lead to a general muscular contraction that would delay urination onset and reduce its duration, the researchers set up a situation in which men using wall-mounted urinals were joined by a confederate who used either the next receptacle (*near condition*) or one located farther down the wall (*far condition*). When onset times and duration for men in the near and far condition were compared with those same times for men in a no-confederate control condition, the researchers found that personal space invasion significantly increased general arousal.

One team of researchers identified the brain areas that govern how people respond to violations of their personal space by studying the neural functioning of a 42-year-old woman who showed no discomfort when others approached too closely. When asked to walk toward another person and stop when she reached a comfortable distance, she approached so closely she touched the other person and rated the experience as "completely comfortable." Upon analysis, the researchers found she had complete bilateral damage to her amygdala, which is the area of the brain that regulates strong emotions, including fear. The investigators also studied, using fMRI, healthy individuals' brain patterns when the experimenter stood close to the scanner and when he maintained a greater distance. These subjects evidenced increased activation of the amygdala, providing further corroboration of the source of the strong negative emotion most people experience when others approach too closely (Kennedy et al., 2009).

Causal Attributions   Every close encounter with another person is not necessarily a negative experience. If the intruder is a close friend, a relative, or an extremely attractive stranger, closeness can be a plus (Willis, 1966). Similarly, if we believe that the other person needs help or is attempting to initiate a friendly relationship, we tend to react positively rather than negatively (Murphy-Berman & Berman, 1978). These findings suggest that the label that individuals use to interpret their arousal determines the consequences of crowding. If people attribute the arousal to others' standing too close, they will conclude, "I feel crowded." If, in contrast, they explain the arousal in some other way—"I drank too much coffee," "I'm in love," "I'm afraid our ship will burn up in the atmosphere," and so on —they will not feel crowded.

Researchers tested this attributional model of crowding by seating five-person groups in chairs placed either 20 inches apart or touching at the legs. These researchers told the groups that an inaudible noise would be played in the room as they worked on several tasks. They told some groups that the noise was detectable at the unconscious level and would lead to stressful, discomforting effects. They told other groups that the noise would have relaxing and calming effects, or they gave no explanation for the noise at all. The groups were not actually exposed to any noise, but crowded groups who thought that the noise would arouse them felt less crowded. Why? Because they attributed the arousal caused by crowding to the supposed noise rather than to the proximity of other people (Worchel & Yohai, 1979; see also Worchel & Teddlie, 1976).

Intensity   Social psychologist Jonathan Freedman also argued that high-density situations are not always aversive situations. His **density–intensity hypothesis** suggested that high density merely

---

density–intensity hypothesis   An explanation of crowding that predicts that high density makes unpleasant situations more unpleasant but pleasant situations more pleasant (proposed by Jonathan Freedman).

intensifies whatever is already occurring in the group situation (Freedman, 1975, 1979). If something in the situation makes the group interaction unpleasant, high density will make the situation seem even more unpleasant. If the situation is a very pleasant one, however, high density will make the good situation even better. Freedman tested this notion by placing groups of people in large or small rooms and then manipulating some aspect of the group interaction to create either unpleasantness or pleasantness. In one investigation, groups of 6–10 high school students sat on the floor of either a large room or a small room. Each delivered a speech and then received feedback from the other group members. Freedman made certain that in some groups the feedback was always positive, whereas in other groups, the feedback was always negative. When the participants later rated the room and their group, Freedman discovered that crowding *intensified* the effects of the feedback: People liked their group the most when they received positive feedback under high-density conditions, and they liked their group the least when they got negative feedback when crowded. Furthermore, Freedman found that these effects were clearest for all-female groups as opposed to all-male or mixed-sex groups (see also Storms & Thomas, 1977).

Controllability Crowded situations are unsettling because they undermine group members' control over their experiences. Crowded situations bring people into contact with others they would prefer to avoid, and if working groups cannot cope with the constraints of their environment, they may fail at their tasks. Group members can therefore cope with crowding by increasing their sense of control over the situation. Just as a sense of high personal control helps people cope with a range of negative life events, including failure, divorce, illness, and accidents, people are less stressed by environmental threats when they feel they can control their circumstances (Evans & Lepore, 1992; Rodin & Baum, 1978; Schmidt & Keating, 1979; Sherrod & Cohen, 1979).

Researchers tested the benefits of controllability by asking groups of six men to work on tasks in either a small room or a large one. One task required participating in a 15-minute discussion of censorship, and the second involved blindfolding a member and letting him wander about within a circle formed by the rest of the group. To manipulate control, one of the participants was designated the *coordinator*; he was responsible for organizing the group, dealing with questions concerning procedures, and blindfolding members for the second task. A second participant, the *terminator*, was given control over ending the discussion and regulating each member's turn in the center of the circle. Significantly, the two group members who could control the group tasks through coordination or termination were not as bothered by the high-density situation as the four group members who were given no control (Rodin, Solomon, & Metcalf, 1978).

Interference Crowding is particularly troublesome when it interferes with the group's work. The Apollo 13 crew, for example, did not react negatively to their high-density living conditions so long as the crowding did not undermine their group's effectiveness. Difficulties only occurred when they needed to fix a problem—such as a hatch that would not secure properly when there was only enough room for one person to reach it. Similarly, studies that find no ill effects of crowding generally study groups working on coaction problems that require little interaction. Studies that require the participants to complete interactive tasks, in contrast, tend to find negative effects of crowding (e.g., Heller, Groff, & Solomon, 1977; Paulus et al., 1976).

Researchers demonstrated the importance of interference by deliberately manipulating both density and interaction. All-male groups worked in either a small laboratory room or in a large one collating eight-page booklets. The order of the pages was not constant, however, but was determined by first selecting a card that had the order of the pages listed in a random sequence. In the *low-interaction condition*, each person had all eight stacks of pages and a set of sequence cards. In the *high-interaction condition*, the stacks were located at points around the room, so participants had to walk around the room in unpredictable patterns. In fact, the participants often bumped into one another while trying to move from one stack to another. The interference created in the high-interaction condition led to decrements in task performance—provided that density was high (Heller et al., 1977).

Seating Arrangements

At launch and during most key maneuvers, the three Apollo 13 astronauts were seated side-by-side in front of the control panel, and the seat on the left was reserved for the mission commander or the officer who was piloting the ship. Each seat defined the role requirements of the person who occupied it, but the seat also defined his status in the group. Although often unrecognized, or simply taken for granted, seating patterns influence interaction, communication, and leadership in groups.

Seating Patterns and Social Interaction Social psychologist Robert Sommer (1967), after studying the ecology of small groups located in a variety of settings, drew a distinction between sociopetal spaces and sociofugal spaces. **Sociopetal spaces** promote interaction among group members by heightening eye contact, encouraging verbal communication, and facilitating the development of intimacy. **Sociofugal spaces**, in contrast, discourage interaction among group members and can even drive participants out of the situation altogether. A secluded booth in a quiet restaurant, a park bench, or five chairs placed in a tight circle are sociopetal environments, whereas classrooms organized in rows, movie theaters, waiting rooms, and airport waiting areas are sociofugal. Sommer concluded that airport seating was deliberately designed to disrupt interaction. He noted that even people seated side by side on airport chairs cannot converse comfortably:

> The chairs are either bolted together and arranged in rows theater-style facing the ticket counters, or arranged back-to-back, and even if they face one another they are at such distances that comfortable conversation is impossible. The motive for the sociofugal arrangement appears the same as that in hotels and other commercial places—to drive people out of the waiting areas into cafés, bars, and shops where they will spend money. (Sommer, 1969, pp. 121–122)

Group members generally prefer sociopetal arrangements (Batchelor & Goethals, 1972; Giesen & McClaren, 1976). This preference, however, depends in part on the type of task undertaken in the situation (Ryen & Kahn, 1975; Sommer, 1969). As Figure 15.3 shows, Sommer found that corner-to-corner and face-to-face arrangements were preferred for conversation, and side-by-side seating was selected for cooperation. Competing dyads either took a direct, face-to-face orientation (apparently to stimulate competition) or tried to increase interpersonal distance, whereas coacting dyads preferred arrangements that reduced eye contact. As one student stated, such an arrangement "allows staring into space and not into my neighbor's face" (Sommer, 1969, p. 63). Similar choices were found with round tables.

Groups in sociopetal environments act differently than groups in sociofugal spaces. In one study, dyads whose members sat facing each other seemed more relaxed, but dyads whose members sat at a 90-degree angle to each other were more affiliative (Mehrabian & Diamond, 1971). When researchers compared circle seating with L-shaped seating, the circle was associated with feelings of confinement but fostered greater interpersonal attraction (Patterson et al., 1979; Patterson, Roth, & Schenk, 1979). People seated in the L-shaped groups, on the other hand, engaged in more self-manipulative behaviors and fidgeting, and they

---

sociopetal spaces Environmental settings that promote interaction among group members, including seating arrangements that facilitate conversation.

sociofugal spaces Environmental settings that discourage or prevent interaction among group members.

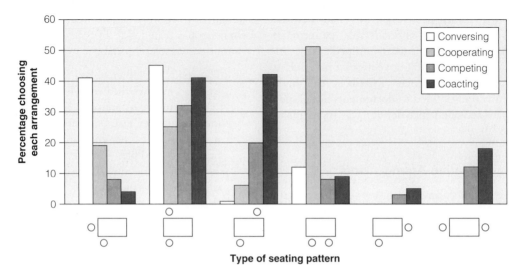

FIGURE 15.3 Preference for various types of seating arrangements when individuals expected to converse, cooperate, compete, or coact.

SOURCE: Personal Space by Robert Sommer, © 1969 by Prentice-Hall, Inc. Reprinted by permission of the author.

paused more during group discussions. Overall, the positive effects of the circle arrangement relative to the L-shaped arrangement were stronger in female groups than in male groups.

Men, Women, and Seating Preferences Women and men diverge, to a degree, in their preferences for seating arrangements. Men prefer to position themselves across from those they like, and women prefer adjacent seating positions (Sommer, 1959). Conversely, men prefer that strangers sit by their side, whereas women feel that strangers should sit across from them. Researchers studied the confusion that this difference can cause by sending confederates to sit at the same table as solitary women and men working in a library. After a brief and uneventful period, the confederate left. When a second researcher then asked the participant some questions about the confederate and the library, the researchers discovered that men were the least favorably disposed toward the stranger who sat across from them but that women reacted more negatively to the stranger who sat next to them (Fisher & Byrne, 1975). Clearly, group members should be sensitive

to the possibility that their spatial behaviors will be misinterpreted by others, and they should be willing to make certain that any possible misunderstandings will be short-lived.

Communication Patterns Psychotherapist Bernard Steinzor's early studies of face-to-face discussion groups indicated that spatial patterns also influence communication rates in groups. Although at first he could find few significant relationships between seat location and participation in the discussion, one day, while watching a group, he noticed a participant change his seat to sit opposite someone he had argued with during the previous meeting. Inspired by this chance observation, Steinzor (1950) reanalyzed his findings and discovered that individuals tended to speak after the person seated opposite them spoke. He reasoned that people have an easier time observing and listening to statements made by those who are seated in the center of the visual field, so that their remarks serve as stronger stimuli for listeners' ideas and statements. The tendency for members of a group to comment immediately after the person sitting opposite them is now termed the **Steinzor effect**. The phenomenon appears to occur primarily in leaderless discussion groups, for later research has suggested that when a leader is present group members direct more comments to their closest neighbor (Hearne, 1957).

Seating Locations   Where should the leader sit? At the head of the table or in one of the side chairs? With great consistency, leaders seek out the head of the table. Sommer (1969), for example, found that people appointed to lead small discussion groups tended to select seats at the head of the table. Those who move to this position of authority also tend to possess more dominant personalities (Hare & Bales, 1963), talk more frequently, and often exercise greater amounts of interpersonal influence (Strodtbeck & Hook, 1961). When people are shown pictures of groups with members seated around a rectangular table and are asked to identify the likely leader, they tend to settle on the person sitting at the head of the table (Jackson, Engstrom, & Emmers-Sommer, 2007).

Sommer suggested two basic explanations for this intriguing **head-of-the-table effect**—*perceptual prominence* and the *social meaning* associated with sitting at the head of the table. Looking first at prominence, Sommer suggested that in many groups, the chair at the end of the table is the most salient position in the group and that the occupant of this space can therefore easily maintain greater amounts of eye contact with more of the group members, can move to the center of the communication network, and (as the Steinzor effect suggests) can comment more frequently. Moreover, in Western cultures where most studies of leadership have been conducted, the chair at the head of the table is implicitly defined to be the most appropriate place for the leader to sit. Sommer was

---

Steinzor effect The tendency for members of a group to comment immediately after the person sitting opposite them (named for Bernard Steinzor).

head-of-the-table effect The tendency for group members to associate the leadership role and its responsibilities with the seat located at the head of the table; as a result, individuals who occupy such positions tend to emerge as leaders in groups without designated leaders.

careful to note that this norm may not hold in other societies, but in most Western cultures, leadership and the head of the table go together.

Both factors play a role in the head-of-the-table effect. Investigators manipulated salience by having two persons sit on one side of the table and three on the other side. Although no one sat in the end seat, those seated on the two-person side of the table could maintain eye contact with three of the group members, but those on the three-person side could focus their attention on only two members. Therefore, group members on the two-person side should be able to influence others more and hence be the more likely leaders. As predicted, 70% of the leaders came from the two-person side, and only 30% came from the three-person side (Howells & Becker, 1962).

In another study, the tendency for people to automatically associate the head of the table with leadership was examined by arranging for confederates to voluntarily choose or be assigned to the end position or to some other position around a table (Nemeth & Wachtler, 1974). These confederates then went about systematically disagreeing with the majority of the group members on the topic under discussion, and the extent to which the participants altered their opinions to agree with the deviant was assessed. Interestingly, the deviants succeeded in influencing the others only when they had freely chosen to sit in the head chair. Apparently, disagreeing group members sitting at the "side" locations around the table were viewed as "deviants," whereas those who had the confidence to select the end chair were viewed more as "leaders" (Riess, 1982; Riess & Rosenfeld, 1980).

LOCATIONS: GROUP TERRITORIALITY

Like so many animals—birds, wolves, lions, seals, geese, and even seahorses—human beings develop proprietary orientations toward certain geographical locations and defend these areas against intrusion by others. A person's home, a preferred seat in a

T A B L E 15.2   Three Types of Territories Established and Protected by Individuals and Groups

Type	Degree of Control	Duration of Claim	Examples
Primary	*High:* occupants control access and are very likely to actively defend this space.	*Long-term:* individuals maintain control over the space on a relatively permanent basis; ownership is often involved.	A family's house, a bedroom, a clubhouse, a dorm room, a study
Secondary	*Moderate:* individuals who habitually use a space come to consider it "theirs"; reaction to intrusions is milder.	*Temporary but recurrent:* others may use the space, but must vacate the area if the usual occupant requests.	A table in a bar, a seat in a classroom, a regularly used parking space, the sidewalk in front of your home
Public	*Low:* although the occupant may prevent intrusion while present, no expectation of future use exists.	*None:* the individual or group uses the space only on the most temporary basis and leaves behind no markers.	Elevator, beach, public telephone, playground, park, bathroom stall, restaurant counter

SOURCE: *The Environment and Social Behavior* by Irving Altman, Brooks/Cole Publishing Company, 1976.

classroom, a clubhouse, a football field, and a space capsule are all **territories**—specific areas that an individual or group claims, marks, and defends against intrusion by others. Since groups *and* group members develop attachment to places, this tendency influences both intragroup and intergroup functioning.

Types of Territoriality

When Lovell, Swigert, and Haise entered the Apollo 13 spaceship for their mission, they entered a cylinder filled with computers, controls, equipment, and supplies. But within days, this physical space was transformed into the group's territory. The men stowed personal gear in their lockers. The controls over which they had primary responsibility became "their controls," and they were wary when any of the other crew members would carry out procedures in their area. Haise, more so than either Lovell or Swigert, became attached to *Aquarius*, the lunar excursion module. When the time came to jettison the module prior to their descent, Haise collected small objects as

mementos, and mission control remarked, "Farewell, *Aquarius*, and we thank you" (Lovell & Kluger, 1994, p. 329).

When people establish a territory, they generally try to control who is permitted access. As environmental psychologist Irwin Altman noted, however, the degree of control depends on the type of territory (see Table 15.2). Control is highest for *primary territories*—areas that are maintained and "used exclusively by individuals or groups … on a relatively permanent basis" (Altman, 1975, p. 112). People develop *strong place attachments* to these areas, for they feel safe, secure, and comfortable when in them (Hernández et al., 2007). Individuals maintain only a moderate amount of control over their *secondary territories*. These areas are not owned by the group members, but because the members use such an area regularly, they come to consider it "theirs." College students, for example, often become very territorial about their seats in a class (Haber, 1980, 1982). **Third places**, identified by urban sociologist Ray Oldenburg (1999) and discussed in Focus 15.2, can

_____

territory A specific geographic area that individuals or groups of individuals claim, mark, and defend against intrusion by others.

_____

third places Semipublic places, such as bookstores, coffee shops, and taverns, where members of a community gather informally for conversation and camaraderie; often located close to individuals' homes (first places) and their work (second places).

F o c u s   **15.2   E-groups: Online Spaces as Third Places**

Have you ever frequented a third place? Third places are semipublic areas, usually in an urban location, where people go to meet their friends, socialize, and "hang out." They are usually located near people's homes (first places) and where they work (second places). As described by urban sociologist Ray Olden-burg (1999), they are typically businesses, but they welcome individuals who may not be customers. A third place might be a coffee shop, where people can spend time reading a book (about group dynamics) and talking to friends who stop by for a cup and a conver-sation. It might be the barbershop on the corner where people often stop to read the newspaper and talk sports and politics. But the prototypical third place is the neighborhood tavern, where people drink, social-ize, and entertain each other. The most famous third place is the bar depicted in the television program *Cheers.* At a third place, "everybody knows your name."

Not just any restaurant or bookstore qualifies as a third place (Mehta & Bosson, 2010). As Oldenburg (1999) explains, third places are uniquely hospitable, socially entertaining, and informal. They are places where people can come and go, unfettered by obliga-tions or the entanglements of roles and responsibilities. They are also egalitarian, in that people from all walks of life can walk in and feel at home—there are no dues, no membership requirements, nor much respect for wealth, professionalism, or breeding. But most of all, third places are a home away from home. Those who are regulars make newcomers feel welcome, and the norms of the setting stress connecting with others in a positive, playful way. Writes Oldenburg (1999, p. 29): "The atmosphere, both physical and social, is the trickiest and most essential part of creating a warm and welcoming third place. Both need constant attention and periodic tweaking. Both show signs of neglect and fatigue immediately" (Oldenburg, 1999, p. 29).

Not all third places, however, are located in phys-ical locations. In the not too distant past, people could only congregate in the confines of a friendly business place. Now, however, people can achieve this connec-tion to other people through online interactions in social networking sites, multiuser domains, and multi-player games. As these sites have increased in popular-ity, they have evolved from places where people post messages or acquire information into places that have many of the same characteristics Oldenburg attributes

to high-quality third places. As with real world third places, people can come and go as they please in online third places. In avatar-based games, in particular, peo-ple create identities that they use to interact with others, and others come to recognize them through their repeated use of these personas. The online world is also a leveler of status differences, for people are careful to not lay claim to privileges that are based on real-world wealth, status, or accomplishments. But most important of all, online third places generate conversation among the participants. People use e-mail, of course, to exchange messages, but on sites that qualify as third places, people are engaged in full conversations, often using any and all communication tools available to them: chat channels for voice, video-conferencing services such as Skype, instant text-based messaging, and back-and-forth postings on walls and forums (Soukup, 2006; Steinkuehler & Williams, 2006).

Online third places are also similar to real-world third places in that they both include regulars—people who are frequently present in the setting and who maintain its norms through good-natured teasing, conversation, and humor. Many online games, for example, offer players the opportunity to join smaller associations within the game, and the members of these groups are always quick to welcome familiar players when they log on to play. Most sites, too, have developed places within the game that have emerged as locations for socializing. Such online sites as World of Warcraft, BlueSky, Second Life®, Lineage, and Asheron's Call all have locations within them where players go to converse, tease, relax, dance, and joke with other players. In sites with graphics, these locations are often designed to resemble real-world third places; they are virtual pubs, bars, inns, coffee houses, and the like.

The relations that individuals establish in third places, whether online or offline, are not close ones. These are public places, and even though the people who join them support and entertain each other, they remain acquaintances rather than close friends. But in an evolving world where traditional forms of commu-nity, such as bridge clubs, civic associations, and sports leagues have dwindled, virtual third places "stand ready to serve people's needs for sociability and relaxation in the intervals before, between, and after their manda-tory appearances elsewhere" (Oldenburg, 1999, p. 32). At online third places, then, "everyone knows your (screen) name" (Steinkuehler & Williams, 2006, p. 885).

also function as secondary territories. Control *over public territories* is even more limited. Occupants can prevent intrusion while they are physically present, but they relinquish all claims when they leave. A bathroom stall or a spot on the beach can be claimed when occupied, but when the occupant leaves, another person can step in and claim the space. (Brown, 1987, thoroughly reviewed much of the work on human territoriality.)

Group Territories

Territoriality is, in many cases, a group-level process. Instead of an individual claiming an area and defending it against other individuals, a group will lay claim to its turf and prevent other groups from using it. South American howler monkeys, for example, live together in bands of up to 20 individuals, and these groups forage within a fairly well-defined region. The bands themselves are cohesive and free of internal strife, but when another group of howlers is encountered during the day's wandering, a fight begins. Among howlers, this territorial defense takes the form of a "shouting match," in which the members of the two bands simply howl at the opposing group until one band—usually the invading band—retreats. Boundaries are rarely violated, because each morning and night, the monkeys raise their voices in a communal and far-carrying howling session (Carpenter, 1958).

Human groups have also been known to territorialize areas. Classic sociological analyses of gangs, for example, often highlighted the tendency for young men to join forces in defense of a few city blocks that they considered to be their turf (Thrasher, 1927; Whyte, 1943; Yablonsky, 1962). Many gangs took their names from a street or park located at the very core of their claimed sphere of influence and sought to control areas around this base. Contemporary gangs, despite changes in size, violence, and involvement in crime, continue to be rooted to specific locations. Gangs in San Diego, California, for example, can be traced to specific geographical origins: the Red Steps and the Crips to Logan Heights and the Sidros to San Ysidro (Sanders, 1994).

Gangs mark their territories through the placement of graffiti, or "tags," and they also attack intruders. Philadelphia researchers found that the number of graffiti mentioning the local gang's name increased as one moved closer and closer to the gang's home base, suggesting that the graffiti served as *territorial markers*, warning intruders of the dangers of encroachment. This marking, however, was not entirely successful, for neighboring gangs would occasionally invade a rival's territory to spray-paint their own names over the territorial markers of the home gang or, at least, to append a choice obscenity. In fact, the frequency of graffiti attributable to outside groups provided an index of group power and prestige, for the more graffiti written by opposing gangs in one's territory, the weaker was the home gang (Ley & Cybriwsky, 1974).

Group Spaces   Human groups also maintain secondary and public territories. Groups at the beach, for example, generally stake out their claim by using beach towels, coolers, chairs, and other personal objects (Edney & Jordan-Edney, 1974). These temporary territories tend to be circular, and larger groups command bigger territories than smaller groups. Groups also create territories when they interact in public places, for, in most cases, nonmembers are reluctant to break through group boundaries. Just as individuals are protected from unwanted social contact by their invisible bubble of personal space, so groups seem to be surrounded by a sort of "shell" or "membrane" that forms an invisible boundary for group interaction. Various labels have been used to describe this public territory, including **group space** (Edney & Grundmann, 1979; Minami & Tanaka, 1995), *interactional territory* (Lyman & Scott, 1967), *temporary group territory* (Edney & Jordan-Edney, 1974), *jurisdiction* (Roos, 1968), and *group personal space* (Altman, 1975). No matter what this boundary is called, the evidence indicates that it often effectively serves to repel intruders.

---

group space A temporary spatial boundary that forms around interacting groups and serves as a barrier to unwanted intrusion by nonmembers.

Social psychologist Eric Knowles examined the impermeability of groups by placing two or four confederates in a hallway (Knowles, 1973). Participants who wished to move through this space were forced either to walk between the interactants or to squeeze through the approximately two-foot space between the group and the hallway wall. Knowles found that 75% of the passersby chose to avoid walking through the group, but this figure dropped to about 25% in a control condition in which the interacting individuals were replaced by waste barrels. Knowles and his colleagues (Knowles et al., 1976) also discovered that when passing by an alcove that was occupied by a group, people would shift their path to increase the distance between themselves and the group. People begin invading a group's public territory only if the distance between interactants becomes large (Cheyne & Efran, 1972) or if the group is perceived as a crowd rather than as a single entity (Knowles & Bassett, 1976). Furthermore, mixed-sex groups whose members are conversing with one another seem to have stronger boundaries (Cheyne & Efran, 1972), as do groups whose members are exhibiting strong emotions (Lindskold et al., 1976).

Benefits of Territories Studies of territoriality in prisons (Glaser, 1964), naval ships (Heffron, 1972; Roos, 1968), neighborhoods (Newman, 1972), and dormitories (Baum & Valins, 1977) have suggested that people feel far more comfortable when their groups can territorialize their living areas. For example, environmental psychologists Andrew Baum, Stuart Valins, and their associates confirmed the benefits of territories in their studies of college students who were randomly assigned to one of two types of dormitories. Some students lived in a traditionally designed, corridor-style dorm, which featured 17 double-occupancy rooms per floor. These residents could only claim the bedrooms they shared with their roommates as their territories. In contrast, students who lived in suite-style dorms controlled a fairly well-defined territory that included a private space shared with a roommate as well as a bathroom and lounge shared with several suitemates.

Even though nearly equal numbers of individuals lived on any floor in the two types of designs, students in the corridor-style dormitories reported feeling more crowded, complained of their inability to control their social interactions with others, and emphasized their unfulfilled needs for privacy. Suite-style dorm residents, on the other hand, developed deeper friendships with their suitemates, worked with one another more effectively, and even seemed more sociable when interacting with people outside the dormitory. Baum and Valins concluded that these differences stemmed from the corridor-style dorm residents' inability to territorialize areas that they had to use repeatedly (Baum & Davis, 1980; Baum, Davis, & Valins, 1979; Baum, Harpin, & Valins, 1975).

Territories and Intergroup Conflict Territories tend to reduce conflict between groups since they organize and regulate intergroup contact by isolating one group from another. Even in the absence of open conflict between groups, members tend to remain within their group's territories, and they avoid trespassing into other areas. Consider, for example, the distribution of people in a cafeteria of a public university in the United Kingdom. Over the course of two weeks when researchers studied where students sat for their meals, they discovered that White students tended to sit in one area of the cafeteria, but that Asian students tended to sit in a different area. Some members of one racial group moved across territorial lines, but for the most part students in this desegregated school tended to resegregate themselves by forming territories based on their race (Clack, Dixon, & Tredoux, 2005).

Group members often feel more comfortable when they can establish a territory for their group, but territoriality can cause conflict if the groups do not agree on their borders. All kinds of intergroup conflicts—from disputes between neighbors, to drive-by gang shootings, to civil wars, to wars between nations—are rooted in disputes over territories (Ardry, 1970). Such conflicts may be based on ancient group traditions. Because most human cultures harvest the animals and plants from the land around them, they establish control over certain geographical areas (Altman & Chemers, 1980). Territories also are defended for symbolic reasons. A group's power is often defined by the quality and size of the space it controls, so groups protect their turf as a means of protecting their reputations. An urban gang, for example, must be ready to attack intruding gangs because "a gang cannot lay any legitimate claim to public areas otherwise" (Sanders, 1994, p. 18). Most drive-by shootings are territorial disputes, occurring when the members of one gang deliberately enter an area controlled by a rival gang and shoot a member of that gang. Disputes over territories are often one-sided, however, for groups that are defending their territory usually triumph over groups that are invading territories.

The Home Advantage   When individuals and groups establish a proprietary claim to a place, they usually strive to control who is allowed to enter. Nations patrol their borders to make certain that people from neighboring countries cannot enter the country easily. Neighborhood associations erect fences and gates to keep others out. When families move into a new home or apartment, they often install locks and elaborate burglar alarms to prevent intrusions by nonmembers. Students who find someone sitting in their usual chair will ask the intruder to leave (Haber, 1980).

These territorial disputes, curiously enough, most often end with the defender of the territory vanquishing the intruder—the **home advantage**. Case studies of street gangs, for example, find that defending groups usually succeed in repelling invading groups, apparently because they are more familiar with the physical layout of the area and have access to necessary resources (Whyte, 1943). One member of the Nortons, a street gang discussed in Chapter 2, explained that his group

never lost a fight ("rally") so long as it took place on the group's turf:

> Once a couple of fellows in our gang tried to make a couple of girls on Main Street. The boyfriends of these girls chased our fellows back to Norton Street. Then we got together and chased the boyfriends back to where they came from. They turned around and got all Garden Street, Swift Street, and Main Street to go after us…. It usually started this way. Some kid would get beaten up by one of our boys. Then he would go back to his street and get his gang. They would come over to our street, and we would rally them…. I don't remember that we ever really lost a rally. Don't get the idea that we never ran away. We ran sometimes. We ran like hell. They would come over to our street and charge us. We might scatter, up roofs, down cellars, anywhere. We'd get ammunition there…. Then we would charge them—we had a good charge. They might break up, and then we would go back to our end of the street and wait for them to get together again…. It always ended up by us chasing them back to their street. We didn't rally them there. We never went looking for trouble. We only rallied on our own street, but we always won there. (Whyte, 1943, p. 51)

Individuals, too, are often more assertive when they are within their own territorial confines rather than encroaching on others' turf. College students working with another student on a cooperative task spent more time talking, felt more "resistant to control," and were more likely to express their own opinions when they were in their own room rather than in their partner's room (Conroy & Sundstrom, 1977; Edney, 1975; Taylor & Lanni, 1981). Individuals and groups seem to gain strength and resolve when the dispute takes place on their home territory, even if they are encountering an opponent who is physically stronger or more socially dominant.

---

home advantage   The tendency for individuals and groups to gain an advantage over others when interacting in their home territory; also known as the home field advantage.

This home advantage, becomes the *home field advantage* at sporting events, for the home team is more frequently the victor than the loser (Schlenker et al., 1995a). When a basketball team must travel to the rival team's home court to play, they often make more errors, score fewer points, and end up the losers rather than the winners of the contest (Schwartz & Barsky, 1977). This advantage becomes even greater when the visiting team must travel longer distances and when the fans watching the game support the home team and jeer the opponent (Courneya & Carron, 1991; Greer, 1983). Playing at home, however, can become something of a disadvantage in rare circumstances. When athletes play must-win games on their home field and they fear they will fail, the pressure to win may become too great. And when a team is playing a series of games and it loses an early game at home, it may lose its home advantage to the emboldened adversary. Overall, however, groups tend to win at home (for more details, see Baumeister, 1984, 1985, 1995; Baumeister & Showers, 1986; Schlenker et al., 1995a, 1995b).

Territoriality in Groups

Territoriality also operates at the level of each individual in the group. Although members develop attachment to the group's space, they also develop spatial attachments to specific areas within the group space (Moser & Uzzell, 2003). Such *individual territories*—a bedroom, a cubicle at work, a park bench no one else frequents, or one's car—can help group members maintain their privacy by providing them with a means of reducing contact with others (Fraine et al., 2007).

Territoriality and Privacy As Altman (1975) noted, depending on the situation, people prefer a certain amount of contact with others, and interaction in excess of this level produces feelings of crowding and privacy invasion. The student in the classroom who is distracted by a jabbering neighbor, employees who are unable to concentrate on their jobs because of their noisy officemates' antics, and the wife who cannot enjoy reading a novel because her husband is playing his music too loudly

are all receiving excessive inputs from another group member. If they moderated their accessibility by successfully establishing and regulating a territorial boundary, they could achieve a more satisfying balance between contact with others and solitude.

Territories also work as organizers of group members' relationships (Edney, 1976). Once we know the location of others' territories, we can find or avoid them with greater success. Furthermore, because we often grow to like people we interact with on a regular basis, people with contiguous territories tend to like one another (Moreland, 1987). Territories also work to regularize certain group activities. Students must return to a classroom regularly, but they do not spend time searching for an available seat each class session because they tend to return to the same seat over and over again. Finally, territories define what belongs to whom; without a sense of territory, the concept of stealing would be difficult to define, because one could not be certain that the objects carried off actually belonged to someone else.

Territories also help individual group members define and express a sense of personal identity. Office walls often display posters, diplomas, crude drawings produced by small children, pictures of loved ones, or little signs with trite slogans, even when company regulations specifically forbid such personalizing markings. Although such decorations may seem insignificant to the chance visitor, to the occupant of the space, they have personal meaning and help turn a drab, barren environment into home.

Researchers studied personal territories by photographing the walls over the beds of students living in campus dormitories. As an incidental finding, they discovered that most of the decorations on these walls fit into one of the categories listed in Table 15.3. They also found that students who eventually dropped out of school seemed to mark their walls more extensively—particularly in the categories of personal relations and music and theater—than students who stayed in school. Although "stay-ins" used fewer markers, their decorations revealed greater diversity, cutting across several categories. Whereas a dropout's wall would feature dozens of skiing posters or high school memorabilia, the

TABLE 15.3 **Displays and Decorations Used by Students to Mark Personal Territories in Dorm Rooms**

Category	Examples of Markers and Identifiers
Entertainment or equipment	Bicycles, skis, radios, stereos, climbing gear, tennis rackets, computers, phones
Personal relations	Pictures of friends and family, flowers, photographs of vacations, letters, drawings by siblings
Values	Religious or political posters, bumper stickers, ecology signs, flags, sorority signs
Abstract	Prints or posters of flowers, landscapes, art reproductions, cartoons
Reference items	Schedules, syllabi, calendars, maps
Music or theater	Posters of ballet, pictures of rock groups, theater posters
Sports	Ski posters, pictures of athletes, motorcycle races, magazine covers, hiking posters
Idiosyncratic	Handmade items (wall hangings, paintings), plants, unique items (e.g., stolen road signs), animal skins, stuffed animals

SOURCE: "Privacy Regulation, Territorial Displays, and Effectiveness of Individual Functioning" by A. Vinsel, B. B. Brown, I. Altman, and C. Foss, *Journal of Personality and Social Psychology*, 1980, 1104–1115. Copyright 1980 by the American Psychological Association.

stay-in's decorations might include syllabi, posters, wall hangings, plants, and family photos. The researchers concluded that the wall decorations of dropouts "reflected less imagination or diversity of interests and an absence of commitment to the new university environment" (Hansen & Altman, 1976; Vinsel et al., 1980, p. 1114).

Territory and Status The size and quality of individuals' territories within a group often indicates their social status within the group. In undifferentiated societies, people rarely divide up space into "yours," "mine," and "ours." The Basarwa of Africa, for example, do not make distinctions between people on the basis of age, sex, or prestige. Nor do they establish primary territories or build permanent structures (Kent, 1991). But stratified societies with leaders, status hierarchies, and classes are territorial. Moreover, the size and quality of the territories held by individuals tend to correspond to their status within society. The political and social elite in the community live in large, fine homes rather than small, run-down shacks (Cherulnik & Wilderman, 1986). Executives with large offices hold a higher, more prestigious position in the company than executives with small offices (Durand, 1977). Prison inmates who control the most desirable portions of the exercise yard enjoy higher status than individuals who cannot establish a territory (Esser, 1973). As one informal observer has noted, in many large corporations, the entire top floor of a company's headquarters is reserved for the offices of the upper-echelon executives and can only be reached by a private elevator (Korda, 1975). Furthermore, within this executive area, offices swell in size and become more lavishly decorated as the occupant's position in the company increases. Substantiating these informal observations, a study of a large chemical company headquarters, a university, and a government agency found a clear link between office size and status (Durand, 1977). The correlation between the size of the territory and the position in each group's organization chart was .81 for the company, .79 for the government agency, and .29 for the university.

The link between territory and dominance in small groups tends to be more variable. Several studies have suggested that territory size increases as status increases (Sundstrom & Altman, 1974). Other studies, however, indicated that territory size seems to decrease as status in the group increases (Esser, 1968; Esser et al., 1965). Psychologists Eric Sundstrom and Irwin Altman (1974) suggested that these contradictory results occur because territorial boundaries are more fluid in small groups. In one study conducted at a boys' rehabilitation center, they asked each participant to rank the other boys in terms of ability to influence others. Also, an observer regularly passed through the residence bedrooms, lounge, TV area, and bathrooms and recorded territorial behaviors. The boys evaluated each area to determine which territories were more desirable than others.

Sundstrom and Altman found evidence of the territory–dominance relation, but the strength of this relation varied over time. During the first phase of the project, the high-status boys maintained clear control over more desirable areas, but when two of the most dominant boys were removed from the group, the remaining boys competed with one another for both status and space. In time the group had quieted back down, although certain highly dominant members continued to be disruptive. When formal observations ended, the group's territorial structures were once more beginning to stabilize with higher-status members controlling the more desirable areas.

These findings suggest that dominance–territory relations, like most group processes, are dynamic. In many small groups, the higher-status members possess larger and more aesthetically pleasing territories, but chaotic intermember relations or abrupt changes in membership can create discontinuities in territorial behavior. Moreover, the hostility that surfaced in the group when spatial claims were disputed suggests that territories can work as tension reducers by clarifying the nature of the social situation and increasing opportunities for maintaining privacy.

Reactions to Territorial Intrusions Just as groups mark, protect, and defend their territories, so do individuals within groups mark, protect, and defend their individual spaces. This tendency serves to regulate relations within the group, but territoriality can also generate hostility and conflict when group members believe another group member has invaded an area that they consider to be their personal dominion.

Management researcher Graham Brown and his colleagues, for example, in their studies of territories in work settings, found that territorial intrusions are relatively common but that they are also quite irritating (Brown, 2009; Brown & Robinson, 2011). When they asked a sample of 180 adults who worked in business settings in the United States if they had ever experienced a territorial intrusion at work, 73.8% reported they had, and most of them were still angry about it. By far, the most frequent type of territorial intrusion was the use of one's tools, supplies, or equipment by others without the individual's explicit permission. A second category of territorial intrusions was spatial: people taking over another person's primary or secondary territory or intruding into that territory without permission. Other intrusions included people trying to take over duties or projects and plagiarism of their ideas and innovations. These infringements triggered all kinds of negative reactions, including complaints to supervisors, verbal rebukes, plots to seek revenge, and even physical confrontations. Most of these responses were mediated by one key psychological factor: anger. Some reported they felt "annoyed" or "irritated," but others were "upset" and "bitter." Still a third group reported feeling "irate" and "furious." Individuals in this third group rarely suffered the territorial intrusion in silence (Brown & Robinson, 2011).

Territory and Stress in Extreme and Unusual Environments The crew of the Apollo 13, like many other groups that must function in EUEs, were careful to monitor their territorial reactions, for attention to spatial concerns is critical for long-term success in such groups (Harrison, Clearwater, & McKay, 1991; Harrison & Connors, 1984; Leon, 1991; Palinkas, 1991).

Altman and his colleagues at the Naval Medical Research Institute in Bethesda, Maryland, studied territoriality in EUEs by confining pairs of volunteers to a 12-by-12-foot room equipped with beds, a toilet cabinet, and a table and chairs (see Altman, 1973, 1977). The groups worked for several hours each day at various tasks, but were left to amuse themselves with card games and reading the rest of the time. The men in the isolation condition never left their room during the 10 days of the experiment; matched pairs in a control condition were permitted to eat their meals at the base mess and sleep in their regular barracks.

The members of isolated groups quickly claimed particular bunks as theirs. Furthermore, this territorial behavior increased as the experiment progressed, with the isolated pairs extending their territories to include specific chairs and certain positions around the table. Not all of the groups, however, benefited by establishing territories. In some of the groups, territories structured the group dynamics and eased the stress of the situation, but in other dyads, these territories worked as barricades to social interaction and exacerbated the strain of isolation. Overall, withdrawal and time spent sleeping increased across the 10 days of the study, whereas time spent in social interaction decreased. Other measures revealed worsened task performance and heightened interpersonal conflicts, anxiety, and emotionality for isolates who drew a "psychological and spatial 'cocoon' around themselves, gradually doing more things alone and in their own part of the room" (Altman & Haythorn, 1967, p. 174).

Altman and his colleagues followed up these provocative findings in a second experiment by manipulating three aspects of the group environment: (1) availability of privacy (half of the groups lived and worked in a single room; the remaining groups had small adjoining rooms for sleeping, napping, reading, etc.); (2) expected duration of the isolation (pairs expected the study to last either 4 days or 20 days); and (3) amount of communication with the outside world. Although the study was to last for eight days for all the pairs, more than half terminated their participation early. Altman explained this high attrition rate by suggesting that the aborting groups tended to "misread the demands of the situation and did not undertake effective group formation processes necessary to cope with the situation" (1973, p. 249). On the first day of the study, these men tended to keep to themselves, never bothering to work out any plans for coping with what would become a stressful situation. Then, as the study wore on, they reacted to increased stress by significantly strengthening their territorial behavior, laying increased

claim to particular areas of the room. They also began spending more time in their beds, but they seemed simultaneously to be increasingly restless. Access to a private room and an expectation of prolonged isolation only added to the stress of the situation and created additional withdrawal, maladaptation, and eventual termination (Altman, Taylor, & Wheeler, 1971).

Groups that lasted the entire eight days seemed to use territoriality to their advantage in structuring their isolation. On the first day, they defined their territories, set up schedules of activities, and agreed on their plan of action for getting through the study. Furthermore, the successful groups tended to relax territorial restraints in the later stages of the project, thereby displaying a greater degree of positive interaction. As Altman (1977) described,

> The epitome of a successful group was one in which the members, on the first or second day, laid out an eating, exercise, and recreation schedule; constructed a deck of playing cards, a chess set, and a Monopoly game out of paper. (p. 310)

The men who adapted "decided how they would structure their lives over the expected lengthy period of isolation" (Altman, 1977, p. 310). Although territorial behavior worked to the benefit of some of the groups, the last-minute attempts of some of the faltering groups to organize their spatial relations failed to improve their inadequate adaptation to the isolation.

DESIGNING GROUP ENVIRONMENTS

Every square inch of the *Odyssey*, the Apollo 13 command module, and its landing craft, the *Aquarius*, was designed by considering how the group of astronauts would function within the confines of the spacecraft. Unfortunately, not all physical settings are designed so carefully as the Apollo 13: Many groups inhabit places that inhibit, rather than facilitate, their functioning. In the final section of this chapter, we consider ways to improve the fit between the group and its environment.

The Person-Place Fit

Ecological psychologist Roger Barker developed his concept of a behavior setting to describe the relationship between people and the places where they live and work. Barker, after studying offices, homes, schools, neighborhoods, communities, and entire towns, concluded that, across most situations, people adapt to fit the requirements of the place. For example, when people enter a fast-food restaurant, they join a line, place their order, pay for their food, and then find a table where they eat their meal. A group in a conference room sits in chairs, exchanges information, and eventually decides to adjourn. The astronauts, once they entered the Apollo 13, acted in ways that the situation required.

Behavior Settings   In Barker's theory, a **behavior setting** is a physical location where people's actions are prescribed by the features and functions of the situation. They tend to be specific spatial areas—actual places where group members interact with one another—with *boundaries* that identify the edge of one behavior setting and possibly the beginning of the next. Some boundaries can also be temporal, as when a group is present only during a certain time (e.g., a group may occupy a classroom only on Mondays and Wednesdays from 9 to 10:30). Most settings also include both people (group members) and things (equipment, chairs, etc.); Barker called them both *components* of the setting. Barker noted that individuals and settings are often inseparable, for the meaning of actions often depends on the physical features of the situation, just as a situation takes its meaning from the individuals in the setting. Barker believed that people routinely follow a *program* that

---

behavior setting In ecological psychology, a physically and temporally bounded social situation that determines the actions of the individuals in the setting (defined by Roger Barker).

sequences their actions and reactions in behavior settings. They may, for example, make use of the settings' objects in very predictable, routine ways, as when people who enter a room with chairs in it tend to sit on them (Barker, 1968, 1987, 1990; Barker et al., 1978).

Not every physical setting is a behavior setting. Some situations are novel ones that group members have never before encountered, so they have no expectations about how they should act. Some individuals, too, may enter a behavior setting but they are not aware of the norms of the situation, or they simply do not accept them as guides for their own actions. But in most cases, group members act in predictable, routine ways in such situations. Libraries, for example, are behavior settings because they create a readiness for certain types of action: One should be subdued, quiet, and calm when in a library. These normative expectations guide behavior directly, and, in many cases, group members are not even aware of how the situation automatically channels their actions. To demonstrate this automatic, unconscious impact of place on people, researchers first showed people a picture of either a library or a railroad station. Later, their reaction times to various words, including words relevant to libraries (e.g., *quiet, still, whisper*), were measured. As expected, people recognized library-related words more quickly after seeing the picture of a library, suggesting that the picture activated norms pertaining to the situation (Aarts & Dijksterhuis, 2003).

Synomorphy   Barker and his colleagues noted that in some behavior settings, people are seamlessly embedded in the place itself. The cockpit of the Apollo 13, for example, was designed so that the astronauts could monitor all their instruments and reach all their controls. A fast-food restaurant may use a system of guide chains and multiple cash registers to handle large numbers of customers efficiently. A classroom may contain areas where students can work on individual projects, a reading circle where the teacher can lead small groups, and an art area where students can easily access the supplies they need. In other behavior settings, however, the people do not fit the place. A classroom

T A B L E   15.4   **Group Members' Reactions to Understaffed and Overstaffed Work Settings**

Reaction	Understaffed Groups	Overstaffed Groups
Task performance	Members engage in diligent, consistent, goal-related actions	Members are perfunctory, inconsistent, and sloppy
Performance monitoring	Members provide one another with corrective, critical feedback as needed	Members exhibit little concern for the quality of the group's performance
Perceptions	Members are viewed in terms of the jobs they do rather than their individual qualities	Members focus on the personalities and uniqueness of members rather than on the group
Self-perceptions	Members feel important, responsible, and capable	Members feel lowered self-esteem with little sense of competence
Attitude toward the group	Members express concern over the continuation of the group	Members are cynical about the group and its functions
Supportiveness	Members are reluctant to reject those who are performing poorly	Members are less willing to help other members of the group

SOURCE: Adapted from Barker, 1968; Wicker, 1979.

may have chairs bolted to the floor in rows, so the teacher can never have students work in small groups. An office may have windows that provide workers with a view of the city, but the light from the windows prevents them from reading their computer screens. A concert hall may have so few doors that concertgoers clog the exits. Barker used the word **synomorphy** to describe the degree of fit between the setting and its human occupants. When settings are high in synomorphy, the people fit into the physical setting and use its objects appropriately. The people and the place are unified. Settings that are low in synomorphy lack this unity, for the people do not mesh well with the physical features and objects in the place.

Staffing Theory   Ecological psychologist Allan Wicker's **staffing theory** draws on the concept

---

synomorphy   In ecological psychology, the quality of the fit between the human occupants and the physical situation.

staffing theory   An ecological analysis of behavior settings arguing that both understaffing (not enough people) and overstaffing (too many people) can be detrimental (developed by Allan Wicker).

of synomorphy to explain group performance (Wicker, 1979, 1987, 2002). Consider office workers in a small business, university, or government agency who are responsible for typing papers and reports, answering the telephone, duplicating materials, and preparing paperwork on budgets, schedules, appointments, and so on. If the number of people working in the office is sufficient to handle all these activities, then the setting is *optimally staffed*. But if, for example, telephones are ringing unanswered, reports are days late, and the photocopier is broken and no one knows how to fix it, then the office lacks "enough people to carry out smoothly the essential program and maintenance tasks" and is *understaffed* (Wicker, 1979, p. 71). On the other hand, if the number of group members exceeds that needed in the situation, the group is *overstaffed* (Sundstrom, 1987).

Table 15.4 summarizes staffing theory's predictions about the relationship between staffing and performance. Overstaffed groups may perform adequately—after all, so many extra people are available to carry out the basic functions—but overstaffing can lead to dissatisfaction with task-related activities and heightened rejection among group members. Understaffed groups, in contrast, often respond positively to the challenging workload. Instead of complaining about the situation, under-staffed groups sometimes display increased involve-ment in their work and contribute more to the group's goals (Arnold & Greenberg, 1980; Wicker & August, 1995). Four-man groups, for example, when placed in an overstaffed situation (too few tasks to keep all members active), reported feeling less important, less involved in their work, less con-cerned with performance, and less needed. These effects were reversed in understaffed groups (Wicker et al., 1976). In another study, the increased workload brought on by understaffing increased professionals' and long-term employees' involvement in their work, but understaffing also led to decreased commitment among new employ-ees and blue-collar workers. Understaffing was also associated with more negative attitudes toward the group (Wicker & August, 1995). Staffing theory also explains why individuals who are part of smal-ler groups and organizations get more involved in their groups; for example, even though a large school offers more opportunities for involvement in small-group activities, the proportion of students who join school-based groups is higher in smaller schools (Gump, 1990).

How do groups cope with staffing problems? When researchers asked leaders of student groups this question, nearly 75% recommended recruiting more members or reorganizing the group as the best ways to deal with understaffing. Other solutions included working with other groups and adopting more modest group goals (see Figure 15.4). These leaders offered a wider range of solutions for over-staffing, including encouraging members to remain active in the group (often by assigning them specific duties), enforcing rules about participation, dividing the group, taking in fewer members, changing the group's structure to include more positions, and adopting more ambitious goals (Cini, Moreland, & Levine, 1993).

Fitting Form to Function

Groups that work in natural settings can exert little control over their workplace. Group members can dress more warmly when it is cold, carry lighting to illuminate the darkness, and adjust their work sche-dules to deal with inclement weather, but in many cases the group must work in whatever conditions it finds. Groups that work in indoor spaces, in contrast, expect their work spaces to be both comfortable and functional. Yet, studies of all types of behavior settings—classrooms, factories, offices, playgrounds, highways, theaters, and so on—frequently find that these areas need to be redesigned to maximize the fit between the people and the place (Davis, Leach, & Clegg, 2011; Vischer, 2008).

Hives, Cells, Dens, and Clubs What kind of spaces do groups need to be maximally productive? Architect Francis Duffy (1992), after examining a number of groups working in large corporations, concluded that the answer depends on the degree of interaction and level of individual autonomy the group's tasks require. Interaction is determined by the task's interdependency demands. If the group is working on a project that requires very little inter-action among members, the setting must provide for areas where the group members can work inde-pendently. But groups that work on more collabo-rate tasks require an office that facilitates productive interdependence. Autonomy refers to the group members', and the group's, control over the work itself: what tasks must be completed, as well as when and how. Autonomy is important because "the more autonomy office workers enjoy, the more they are likely to want to control their own working environments, singly and collectively, and the more discretion they are likely to want to exer-cise over the kind and quality of their surroundings in their places of work (Duffy, 1992, p. 60).

Duffy uses these two dimensions to identify four basic types of configurations of work and their ideal spatial arrangements: hives, cells, dens, and clubs.

- *Hives.* Members who function as "worker bees"—they perform individualized, routine tasks—require little interaction with other group members. Such groups function well in open, cubicle-type offices where each

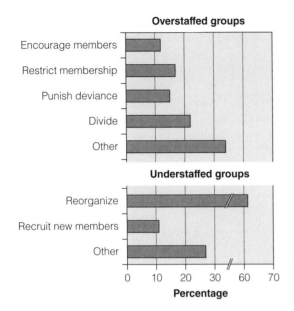

FIGURE 15.4 Leaders' recommendations for dealing with understaffed groups and overstaffed groups.

SOURCE: From Data in "Group Staffing Levels and Responses to Prospective and New Group Members" by M. A. Cini, R. L. Moreland, & J. M. Levine, *Journal of Personality and Social Psychology*, *65*. 1993 American Psychological Association. Reprinted by permission.

individual has a defined, relatively small work space (low interaction/low autonomy).

- *Cells.* Members working on complex, long-term, relatively individualized projects need private spaces to carry out their work. They may also be able to work by telecommuting from a home office (low interaction/high autonomy).

- *Dens.* When members who are similar in terms of skills and responsibilities work together on collective tasks and projects, they need an open space that all members share. Members may have individual areas within the collective space that they claim as their own, but boundaries do not separate these spaces from one another. These groups work on specific, relatively short-term projects where success depends on maintaining very high levels of information exchange (high interaction/low autonomy).

- *Clubs.* Members who are talented, well-trained, or possess very specialized skills often work on diverse tasks and projects that vary greatly in their collaborative demands. Their work space must be flexible, permitting them to collaborate as needed but also to secure privacy (high interaction/high autonomy).

Duffy found that club offices tend to be the most productive, but he added that nearly all group spaces must be changed to increase the fit between the group and its tasks. As the group and its tasks change, even the most carefully designed and implemented setting may fail to meet members' needs and would require revision.

Group Spaces in the Future More of the world's work is now being completed by teams, and as Duffy's work suggests, these groups require a different type of office than individuals required. Architects and designers, recognizing the need for innovative solutions, have begun to experiment with new types of spaces that promote group productivity rather than just individual productivity. The British Broadcasting Corporation (BBC), for example, redesigned its facility at Broadcast Center, being careful to make certain each work area corresponded to the interactional demands of the particular project group. The result was a highly effective and flexible space that includes spaces for meetings, seclusion, and for creative work (Harrison & Morgan, 2006). Another project, at NASA's Jet Propulsion Laboratory (JPL), relied on technological innovations to create close connections among collaborators: data visualization programs, shared spreadsheets, interactive graphic displays for modeling, and tools for building simulations. The team members, who were primarily engineers and computer scientists, had personal work stations within a larger room, as well as private offices elsewhere. They gathered at the main team room, however, for collaborative sessions that lasted for several hours. The room, and the group within in it, performed far more efficiently than similar types of teams, completing tasks in days that before took weeks or even months (Heerwagen et al., 2006).

These innovations are good news for one group that will need an improved habitat in the future: the crew that NASA will be sending to Mars. The team that takes on that mission will remain intact and functioning in a collocated setting longer than any other team or group ever has before. It will face extraordinary and unanticipated performance challenges that will likely require solutions and interventions unrelated to both training and experience. The group will be so small in size that it cannot fractionate into subgroups to deal with interpersonal conflict, and its habitat will be so restrictive that contact with other members is continual and unavoidable. The Mars mission team will live and work in conditions that no other group has ever experienced. That group is going to need a very nice habitat to survive the challenges of its extreme and unusual environment.

CHAPTER REVIEW

How does the physical environment influence groups and their dynamics?

1. An environmental approach recognizes that individuals and their groups are embedded in a physical and social setting and that the characteristics of that setting can substantially influence group dynamics.

2. Physical settings are often said to create a distinctive cognitive and emotional reaction in people (*ambience*).

    ■ Russell's studies indicate that people's affective reactions to environments range along two dimensions: pleasure–displeasure and activation–deactivation.

    ■ People generally prefer positive, stimulating environments, but excessive stimulation can lead to *overload*.

    ■ Kaplan's *attention restoration theory* assumes situations that require directed attention deplete cognitive resources, but that an effective way to replenish this resource is to spend time in the natural environment.

3. Features of the environment, such as extremes in temperature and noise and dangerousness, can engender *stress* in groups and undermine performance.

    ■ People associate warm temperatures with social warmth.

    ■ High temperatures are linked to loss of attention as well as a number of other unpleasant consequences, including discomfort and reduced productivity. Groups are more aggressive when they are hot, but not extremely hot. Extremes in heat and cold are also physically hazardous.

    ■ Van de Vliert's climato-economic theory assumes that cultures that exist in places with harsh climates cope by developing economically if wealthy and by becoming more collectivistic if not wealthy.

    ■ Group members can cope with exposure to noise for a short duration, but prolonged exposure is associated with psychological and physical difficulties.

    ■ Groups that must live or work in *extreme and unusual environments* (EUEs) adapt by improving communication and teamwork. Groups that do not emphasize a team approach in such environments, such as the 1996 expeditions to Mount Everest, are less likely to escape such situations unharmed.

What is the ecology of a group?

1. Researchers who study *small group ecology* explore how individuals interact with and adapt to the group habitat.

2. Studies of *personal space* suggest that group members prefer to keep a certain distance between themselves and others.

    ■ Closer distances are associated with greater intimacy, so space requirements tend to increase as the situation becomes less intimate. The four zones described by Hall are the intimate, personal, social, and public. Online groups meet in the remote zone.

- Spacing in groups is influenced by the sex, status, and cultural background of the group members.

- Both the *equilibrium model of communication* and Burgoon's expectancy violations model predict that individuals will moderate their distances to achieve the desired level of intimacy.

3. *Density* describes the number of people per unit of space, whereas *crowding* is a psychological reaction to high physical density.

4. Crowding is exacerbated by the following factors:

- cognitive processes that prompt individuals to make attributions about the causes of their arousal;

- group members' overall evaluation of the high-density setting (Freedman's *density–intensity hypothesis*);

- perceptions of control;

- the degree to which others interfere with task performance.

5. Sommer found that seating arrangements make up an important part of the ecology of small groups. *Sociopetal* spaces tend to encourage interaction, whereas *sociofugal* patterns discourage interaction. People generally prefer interaction-promoting, sociopetal patterns, but these preferences vary with the type of task being attempted and the sex of the group members.

6. Seating arrangements significantly influence patterns of attraction, communication, and leadership. For example, in many groups, individuals tend to speak immediately after the person seated opposite them (the *Steinzor effect*), and leadership is closely associated with sitting at the end of the table (the *head-of-the-table effect*).

What are the causes and consequences of a group's tendency to establish territories?

1. Like many other animals, humans establish *territories*—geographical locations that an individual or group defends against intrusion by others.

2. Altman distinguished between primary territories, secondary territories, and public territories.

- Oldenburg suggests that some secondary territories can serve as *third places* where individuals can gather to socialize and build community. Some third places are located in online communities.

- Various groups, including gangs, territorialize areas; they prevent nongroup members from entering them, and they mark them in various ways.

- Studies of *group space* suggest that, like individuals and their personal space, groups are surrounded by an interaction boundary that prevents nongroup members from approaching too closely.

- Individuals feel more comfortable when their groups can territorialize their living areas. Territories promote adjustment and reduce stress, but they also promote intergroup conflict, as in the case of gang-related territoriality.

- Groups with a *home advantage* tend to outperform groups that are outside their territories.

3. Individual members of the group establish their own personal territories within the group's territory.

- Personal territories fulfill privacy, organizing, and identity functions for individual members. Territorial markings, for example, are associated with membership stability.

- Higher-status individuals generally control larger and more desirable territories; Sundstrom and Altman's work suggests changes in status hierarchies can disrupt the allocation of territory.

- Brown's studies suggest that territorial intrusions are common in the workplace, and they generally generate strong, negative emotional reactions (anger).

4. A group's capacity to adapt and even thrive in extreme and unusual environments (EUEs) depends on its members' judicious management of the environment, including territories.

How can group places, spaces, and locations be improved?

1. Barker, after studying many groups in their natural locations, concluded that most behavior is determined by the *behavior setting* in which it occurs.

   - The boundaries, components, and programs of such settings define the functions of the situation and the type of behaviors performed in it.

- Behavior settings that lack *synomorphy* are inefficient and distressing.

- *Staffing theory*, developed by Wicker, describes the causes and consequences of understaffing and overstaffing.

2. Some groups work and interact in spaces that need to be redesigned to maximize the fit between the people and the place.

   - Duffy, differentiating between group tasks that call for more or less interaction and autonomy, identified four types of group workplaces; hives, cells, dens, and clubs.

   - Workplaces are currently being reconfigured to create spaces that will facilitate group productivity rather than individual productivity.

RESOURCES

Chapter Case: Apollo 13

- *Apollo 13: The NASA Mission Reports*, edited by Robert Godwin (2000), provides complete documentation of the mission, including press releases, transcripts of the crew debriefing, the text of the committee investigations of the cause of the accident, and recordings of the crew transmissions during the flight.

- *Lost Moon: The Perilous Journey of Apollo 13* by Jim Lovell and Jeffrey Kluger (1994) is a forthright summary of the Apollo 13 mission with details about the group's dynamics and relations with ground control teams and family members.

Groups in Context

- *Handbook of Environmental Psychology*, edited by Daniel Stokols and Irwin Altman (1987), contains chapters written by leading researchers and theorists in the field of person–environment relations. The 22 chapters in Volume One

focus on basic processes, and the 21 chapters in Volume Two consider applications and cross-cultural implications. The updated *Handbook of Environmental Psychology*, edited by Robert B. Bechtel and Arzah Churchman (2002), supplements the 1987 edition with expanded coverage of topics dealing with environmental preservation.

- *Environmental Psychology* by Paul A. Bell, Thomas C. Greene, Jeffery D. Fisher, and Andrew Baum (2006) is a comprehensive text dealing with environmental psychology in general, but with key chapters focusing on topics of interest to group researchers, including ecological perspectives, personal space, crowding, and territoriality.

Small-Group Ecology and Territoriality

- *The Environment and Social Behavior* by Irwin Altman (1975) remains the definitive analysis of privacy, personal space, territoriality, and crowding in groups.

- *The Great Good Place* by Ray Oldenburg (1999) is an inspiring analysis of third places where groups often congregate in comfortable, public establishments that provide the setting for socialization and support.

- *Personal Space* by Robert Sommer (1969) takes an entertaining look at interpersonal distancing processes.

Designing Group Spaces

- *Creating the Productive Workplace*, edited by Derek Clements-Croome (2006), is a compendium of chapters written by engineers, architects, and design experts who explore, in detail, the physical, psychological, and social demands of the 21st-century workplace.

- "Towards an Environmental Psychology of Workspace: How People are Affected by Environments for Work" by Jacqueline C.

Vischer (2008) provides a thorough and up-to-date review of the research literature examining how people's workplaces can be made both more comfortable and more efficient.

Groups in Extreme and Unusual Environments

- *Bold Endeavors: Lessons from Polar and Space Exploration* by Jack Stuster (1996) draws on interviews, historical documentation, and empirical research to develop a comprehensive, detailed analysis of the dynamics of groups that live and work in atypical environments, such as bases in Antarctica and space stations.

- "The Environmental Psychology of Capsule Habitats" by Peter Suedfeld and G. Daniel Steel (2000) examines the social and psychological consequences of prolonged stays in secluded and dangerous environments.

Groups and Change

CHAPTER OVERVIEW

The value of groups is nowhere more apparent than when they are used to help their members change for the better. Groups, by their very nature, provide their members with information, support, and guidance, and so many personal and interpersonal problems can be resolved when confronted in a group rather than alone. As Lewin's Law suggests, changing people one by one is difficult; changing them when they are part of a group is easier.

- What are some of the ways that groups are used to help members change?

- How do groups promote change?

- How effective are groups in bringing about change?

CHAPTER OUTLINE

Group Approaches to Change
   Therapeutic Groups
   Interpersonal Learning Groups
   Support Groups

Sources of Change in Groups
   Universality and Hope
   Social Learning
   Group Cohesion
   Disclosure and Catharsis
   Altruism
   Insight

The Effectiveness of Groups
   Empirical Support for Group Treatments
   Using Groups to Cure: Cautions
   The Value of Groups

Chapter Review

Resources

The Bus Group: Groups as Interpersonal Resources

The group had visited the Taj Mahal and was returning to the ship when the accident happened. They were teachers and students taking part in Semester-at-Sea: an educational program that combined classes on a floating university with tours to historic sites in countries throughout the world. Their bus fishtailed, flipped twice, and came to rest in a ravine by the roadside. Of the 25 students on the bus, 4 were killed. Three staff members also died in the crash.

The physicians in local clinics and on the Semester-at-Sea ship dealt with the survivors' physical injuries, and counselors and therapists sought to help them with their psychological problems. In the days immediately after the accident, the members of the "bus group," as they came to call themselves, met to deal with their emotions, pain, and uncertainties. The ship continued on its way, and the group met regularly in therapy sessions designed to help members cope with their grief and attempt to stave off the long-term

negative consequences of such a horrific experience. With great sensitivity, the therapists helped each survivor deal with the painful memories of that night, the recurrent nightmares most reported, and the inability to concentrate on normal activities. The group also examined ways to remain connected to the other students on the ship who were not involved in the accident, and explored existential issues related to their survival and the loss of the lives of their friends and classmates. Some had more difficulty than others in dealing with the tragedy; they worked with therapists individually as well as in the bus group. The group met for a dozen times on the ship, in sessions lasting approximately 90 minutes.

When the ship docked at Seattle, Washington, the members went their separate ways. They left behind the bus group, but it had served its purpose. A year after the tragedy, most "appeared to be coping well and getting on with their lives" (Turner, 2000, p. 147).

The idea that a group can be used for therapeutic purposes is not a new one. For centuries, people have sought help from groups in religious rites, community ceremonies, and tribal sessions for those suffering from both physical and psychological problems. These palliative and therapeutic effects of groups were rediscovered early in the twentieth century when health care providers began to use groups to help their patients better manage their illnesses (Pratt, 1922). At first, practitioners used groups to avoid meeting with each patient separately, but they soon realized that their patients were benefiting from the groups themselves. Members supported each other, shared nontechnical information about their illnesses and treatment and seemed to appreciate the opportunity to express themselves to attentive and sympathetic listeners. In time the veracity of Kurt **Lewin's law of change** became widely recognized: "It is usually

easier to change individuals formed into a group than to change any one of them separately" (Lewin, 1951, p. 228).

This chapter asks three questions about groups as agents of treatment and change. First, what are some of the ways that groups are used to achieve change in their members? Second, how do groups and group processes promote change? Third, are groups effective means of bringing about change? For example, did the bus group actually help the members, or did it do more harm than good?

GROUP APPROACHES
TO CHANGE

People join groups to solve many different kinds of problems. Some want to get rid of something— weight, sadness, irrational thoughts, or overwhelming feelings of worthlessness and despair. Others are seeking something—new skills and outlooks, insight into their own characteristics, or a new repertoire of behaviors they can use to improve their

---

Lewin's law of change A basic principle of attitude and behavioral change stating that individuals are more easily changed when they are part of a group (proposed by Kurt Lewin).

T A B L E 16.1   Varieties of Change-Promoting Groups

Type	Basic Goal	Leader	Examples
Therapeutic	Help members improve their psychological functioning and adjustment	Mental health professionals (e.g., psychologist, social worker, psychiatrist)	• group psychotherapy • cognitive-behavioral group therapy • trauma/disaster response groups
Interpersonal learning	Help members gain self-understanding and improve their interpersonal skills	Varies from trained and licensed professionals to untrained laypersons	• T-groups • encounter groups • experiential learning groups
Support	Help members cope with and identify solutions to specific problems or life crises	Usually a volunteer; some groups do not include a leadership position	• support groups • anti-addiction groups (e.g., AA) • advocacy groups

relationships with others. Still others seek the strength they need to cope with some challenge they face in their life—a serious illness, the loss of a loved one, or an addiction they have been unable to conquer on their own.

The variety of change-promoting groups reflects the variety of individuals' goals. The group formats devised by early psychologists and physicians have evolved into today's jogging and fitness clubs; consciousness-raising groups; support groups for parents, children, grandparents, and ex-spouses; workshops and leadership seminars; marriage and family counseling groups; religious retreats; mutual-support groups; psychotherapy groups; and so on. These groups, despite their many varieties, all help individuals to achieve goals that they cannot reach on their own. **Therapeutic groups** help their members overcome such psychological problems as depression, anxiety, personality disorders, and trauma-induced stress. **Interpersonal learning groups** help members gain self-understanding and improve their

relationships with others. **Support groups** help members cope with or overcome a problem all the members have in common. But not all change-promoting groups fall neatly into one and only one of the three categories shown in Table 16.1. Therapeutic groups, for example, provide members with the support they need when they encounter difficult, stressful circumstances, and, in many cases, interpersonal learning groups are quite therapeutic.

Therapeutic Groups

The therapists who worked with the bus group from Semester-at-Sea were trained to help people overcome psychological and personal problems. They worked with the students and the staff in one-to-one psychotherapy sessions, but they also treated the students "in groups, with the group itself constituting an important element in the therapeutic process" (Slavson, 1950, p. 42). When such groups were initially proposed, skeptics questioned the wisdom of putting people who were suffering from psychological problems together in one group. How, they asked, could troubled individuals

---

therapeutic group A group of individuals seeking treatment for a psychological problem who meet regularly with a trained mental health professional.
interpersonal learning group A group formed to help individuals extend their self-understanding and improve their relationships with others (e.g., experiential group, growth group).

---

support group A group of people who meet or communicate with one another regularly to help each other cope with or overcome a problem they hold in common.

be expected to cope in a group when they had failed individually? How could the therapist guide the therapeutic process in a group? History, however, has proved the skeptics wrong. Many mental health practitioners, including psychologists, psychiatrists, and clinical social workers, use group methods to treat a wide variety of psychological problems, including addictions, thought disorders, depression, eating disorders, posttraumatic stress disorder, and personality disorders (Barlow, Burlingame, & Fuhriman, 2000; Burlingame & Baldwin, 2011).

Group therapists vary widely in theoretical orientation. Some, for example, are primarily psychoanalytic, for their basic approach is based on Sigmund Freud's therapeutic principles. Others, in contrast, adopt a more interpersonal perspective that stresses the exploration of the social processes that unfold in the group. Other approaches are more behavioral; they teach group members specific behaviors they can use to cope with the problems they are facing. Most therapists, however, are eclectic: They base their work on a melding of many theoretical perspectives (Ettin, 1992). This section reviews these approaches, but the review must be selective given the many techniques that are currently in use (DeLucia-Waack & Kalodner, 2005). Also, just to be clear on one final point: Group therapy is a treatment for individuals rather than a way of treating dysfunctional groups. Group therapists are mindful of and make use of the group's interpersonal processes. As treatment progresses, the group as a whole generally becomes more adept in dealing with issues, providing support for its members, and acting sensibly (Bennis & Shepard, 1956). The goal of treatment, however, is not the creation of a well-functioning group, but the promotion of the adjustment of the individuals in the group.

Group Psychoanalysis   For many people, the psychoanalytic interview—complete with a note-taking therapist and a free-associating patient reclining on a comfortable couch—is the prototypical psychotherapy session. The client talks in detail about early life experiences, current problems and

difficulties, dreams, worries, and hopes, and the therapist provides interpretations and directions that help the client extract meaning from these materials. As the relationship between the therapist and client becomes stronger, the client unconsciously transfers feelings for and thoughts about others to the therapist. The therapist can use this **transference** to help the client understand his or her relations with others. With time, the client develops healthy insight into unresolved conflicts that have been repressed in the unconscious mind (Shedler, 2010).

But Freud's psychoanalysis can also be applied with individuals who take part in group sessions: **group psychoanalysis**. Psychoanalysis, by tradition, was used with the smallest of groups—one patient and one therapist. But Freud (1922) discussed the psychodynamic processes that occur in groups, and later psychoanalysts adapted his basic methods to groups with multiple clients. In such groups, the therapist is very much the leader, for he or she directs the group's discussion during the session, offers interpretations, and summarizes the group's efforts. Just as the goal of individual therapy is the gradual unfolding of repressed conflicts, in group therapy, as members talk about their memories, fantasies, dreams, and fears, they gain insight into their unconscious motivations. Some have suggested that Freud himself practiced group psychoanalysis when he and his students met to discuss his theories and cases (Roth, 1993).

As in one-to-one therapy, group psychoanalysis capitalizes on transference, for the group format provides the means for transferring external relationships onto the group itself. As Freud's (1922) replacement hypothesis suggests, the group

---

transference The displacement of emotions from one person to another during treatment, as when feelings for a parent are transferred to the analyst or feelings about siblings are transferred to fellow group members.
group psychoanalysis An approach to group therapy that is grounded in Sigmund Freud's method of treatment and so includes a directive therapist who makes use of free association, interpretation, and transference processes.

becomes a surrogate family with members serving as symbolic siblings and the group therapist acting as the primal authority figure. As transference develops, the group provides the therapist with the means of exploring the childhood roots of current adult anxieties. Members may find themselves reacting to one another inappropriately, but their actions, when examined more closely, may parallel the way they respond to people they know in their everyday lives. Hostilities, needs, and wants that are repressed in relationships with others outside of the group often surface within the group, and the therapist can use these experiences to help clients gain insight into their unconscious conflicts. Some therapists are more fully Freudian in their orientation than others, but rare is the therapist who does not deal with transference processes, the interpretation of fantasies or dreams, familial tensions, and other latent conflicts (Hopper, 2005).

Gestalt Groups   Psychiatrist Fritz Perls (1969), the founder of Gestalt therapy, frequently conducted his therapeutic sessions in groups rather than with single individuals. Perls drew his theoretical principles from Gestalt psychologists who argued that perception requires the active integration of perceptual information. The word *Gestalt*, which means both "whole" and "shape," suggests that people perceive the world as unified, continuous, and organized. Like Freud, Perls assumed that individuals often repress their emotions to the point that unresolved interpersonal conflicts turn into "unfinished business." Perls, however, believed that people are capable of self-regulation and great emotional awareness, and he used therapy to help patients reach their potential.

In some cases, **Gestalt group therapy** is individual-level therapy conducted in a group setting: Group members observe one another's

"work," but they do not interact with each other. More frequently, however, interaction takes place among group members with the therapist actively orchestrating the events. Many group therapists make use of unstructured interpersonal activities, such as the "hot seat" or the "empty chair," to stimulate members' emotional understanding. When using the *hot seat*, one person in the group sits in the center of the room and publicly works through his or her emotional experiences. The *empty chair* method involves imagining that another person or a part of oneself is sitting in an empty chair and then carrying on a dialogue with that person. These techniques, when properly applied, often elicit strong emotional reactions among members, but Gestalt therapists resist offering interpretations to their patients (Gaffney, 2012).

Psychodrama   Jacob Moreno (1934), one of the first therapists to treat his patients in groups, used special exercises to stimulate emotional experiences in group members. Moreno conducted therapeutic groups perhaps as early as 1910, and he used the term *group therapy* in print in 1932. Moreno believed that the interpersonal relations that developed in groups provided the therapist with unique insights into members' personalities and proclivities, and that by taking on roles, the members become more flexible in their behavioral orientations. He made his sessions more experientially powerful by developing **psychodrama** techniques. When *role playing*, for example, members take on the identity of someone else and then act as that person would in a simulated social situation. *Role reversal* involves playing a role for a period of time before changing roles with another group member. *Doubling* is the assignment of two group members to a single role, often with one member of the pair playing him- or herself. Moreno believed that the physical action of psychodrama helped members overcome

---

Gestalt group therapy An approach to group therapy in which clients are taught to understand the unity of their emotions and cognitions through a leader-guided exploration of their behavior in the group situation (developed by Fritz Perls and his associates).

---

psychodrama A therapeutic tool that stimulates active involvement in a group session through role playing (developed by Jacob Moreno).

their reluctance to discuss critical issues (Kipper & Ritchie, 2003; Sapp, 2009).

Interpersonal Group Psychotherapy Many therapeutic methods, including psychoanalysis and Gestalt therapy, trace difficulties in achieving well-being and adjustment back to psychological causes: inner conflicts, unmet needs, and functional but potentially unhealthy defense mechanisms. An interpersonal approach, in contrast, assumes that psychological problems are the result of *social* problems—difficulties relating to others, rejection by loved ones, abrasive interpersonal styles, and so on. Interpersonal therapists assume that maladaptive behavior results from "an individual's failure to attend to and correct the self-defeating, interpersonally unsuccessful aspects of his or her interpersonal acts" (Kiesler, 1991, pp. 442–443). Conversely, just as interpersonal processes are the source of individuals' problems, so submersion in a rich, interpersonally dynamic group provides the cure: by the group they have been broken, and by the group they will be healed (Marsh, 1931).

Psychiatrist Irvin Yalom's **interpersonal group psychotherapy** is perhaps the most influential of the interpersonal approaches (also called *interactive group psychotherapy* or *process groups*). Yalom uses the group as a "social microcosm" where members respond to one another in ways that are characteristic of their interpersonal tendencies outside of the group. Therapy groups, as groups, display a full array of group features and dynamics, including social influence, structure, conflict, and development. Yalom takes advantage of the group's dynamics to help members learn about how they influence others and how others influence them. Uniquely, members do not spend very much time discussing problems they are facing at home or at work—a *then and there* focus. Instead, the group members focus on each other and the

processes that sustain or detract from their relationships with one another: the *here and now* focus. Yalom's process approach assumes that, during the course of the group sessions, each member's interpersonal inclinations will express themselves, providing an opportunity to identify and possibly ameliorate those that are disadvantageous. As the group grapples with personal conflicts, problems of organization, goals, and communication failures, the members reveal their preferred interaction styles to others and to themselves. When, for example, two members begin criticizing each other, someone uses powerful or bizarre influence tactics, or another refuses to get involved in the group's process, the group members can discuss this shared experience and gain an understanding of both themselves and others (Yalom with Leszcz, 2005).

Cognitive-Behavioral Therapy Groups Some therapists, rather than searching for the cause of the problematic behavior in unseen, unconscious conflicts or interpersonal transactions, take a behavioral approach to mental health. This approach assumes that problematic thoughts and behaviors are acquired through experience, so behavior therapists encourage the development of healthy cognitions and behaviors and the avoidance of undesirable cognitions and behaviors. **Cognitive-behavioral therapy groups** use these principles with two or more individuals. A cognitive-behavioral approach to the Semester-at-Sea bus group, for example, may ask members to identify the thoughts that are triggered by their memory of their experiences and then provide them with the cognitive and behavioral skills they need to control those reactions. The therapist may ask the group members to focus their attention on the accident and then to share their reaction with the others in the group. When members report experiencing dysfunctional ideation—such as "I wonder why I survived and others didn't?" or "I wonder if

---

interpersonal group psychotherapy An approach to the treatment of psychological, behavioral, and emotional problems that emphasizes the therapeutic influence of interpersonal learning (developed by Irvin Yalom).

---

cognitive-behavioral therapy group The treatment of interpersonal and psychological problems through the application of behavioral principles in a group setting.

I deserve to live"—then the leader guides the group through the disputation of such thoughts. The leader might also model, with the group members assisting, methods of emotional and cognitive self-regulation such as mood monitoring, relaxation, and thought-stopping (Hollon & Beck, 2004).

A group format interfaces seamlessly with the process-structuring methods used in behavioral treatments. In many cases, therapists follow a series of standard procedures before, during, and after the group intervention. Prior to treatment, they can observe the reactions of each member to the group to index the degree of functioning prior to any intervention. Pretherapy reviews, in which the therapist reviews the theories and procedures that sustain the intervention, can be carried out in a psycho-educational group setting, and, through discussion, the members can clarify their expectations and goals. Therapists can also use public commitment to these goals to enhance the binding strengths of a *behavioral contract* that describes in objective terms the goals the group members are trying to achieve. During the therapeutic sessions themselves, the cognitive-behavioral group therapist can capitalize on the presence of multiple actors to magnify the effects of modeling, rehearsal, and feedback. Members of the group can practice interpersonal exchanges with other members, and other members can act as observers. These practice sessions can be recorded and played back to the group so that the participants can see precisely what they are doing correctly and what aspects of their behavior need improvement. During this feedback phase, the leader offers reassurance and praise, and members add their support and encouragement (Bieling, McGabe, & Antony, 2006; Whittal & McLean, 2002).

Process Debriefing Groups Groups are frequently used to lessen the likelihood of negative aftereffects following trauma. Although homo sapiens is a resilient species that can withstand great hardship, traumatic events—disasters, accidents, the loss of loved ones, physical assaults, victimization, and so on—can take a psychological toll. The students who survived the horrific night of the bus crash likely suffered from anxiety, sleeplessness, and fearfulness as they struggled to regain their psychological equilibrium. Given the severity of the trauma, had they not received treatment they would have likely exhibited symptoms of *posttraumatic stress disorder* (PTSD): a serious psychological reaction to stressful events characterized by high levels of anxiety, depression, fearfulness, and physical symptoms, such as migraines, sleep problems, and gastrointestinal distress (Bonanno et al., 2007).

These negative mental health consequences can be reduced through stress management crisis interventions. Variously termed **process debriefing groups**, critical incident stress debriefing groups, or trauma/disaster groups, these interventions were first used to help combat veterans deal with the psychological turmoil produced by the experience of combat. As the positive effects of these groups became evident, they came to be used to help individuals deal with traumatic community-level events, such as natural disasters, accidents, and school shootings (Foy, Drescher, & Watson, 2010).

These interventions—usually designed and implemented by community health professionals—generally make use of group-level therapeutic coping processes, including social comparison, social support, and social learning (Davies, Burlingame, & Layne, 2006; Layne et al., 2001). The members of the bus group, for example, met with therapists when they returned to the ship and collectively processed the experience, clarified the events leading up to the accident and after it, and began to prepare for the weeks of recover that lay before them. The ship's counselors also worked with the entire Semester-at-Sea community, providing information about the incident, initiating grief counseling, organizing the community response, and providing training for staff. This process debriefing phase was relatively brief, ending when the students transitioned to group therapy sessions (Turner, 2000).

---

process debriefing group Brief, highly structured interventions delivered by trained mental health professionals to members of a group or community who have experienced some type of traumatic experience, such as a natural disaster or fatal accident; these interventions are designed to help individuals deal with the emotional and cognitive consequences of the experience.

Interpersonal Learning Groups

Many psychologists are united in their belief that the human race too frequently fails to reach its full potential. Although human relationships should be rich and satisfying, they are more often than not superficial and limiting. People are capable of profound self-understanding and acceptance, yet most people are strangers to themselves. These limitations are not so severe that the help of a psychotherapist is needed, but people's lives would be richer if they could overcome these restraints.

Kurt Lewin was one of the first to suggest using small groups to teach people interpersonal skills and self-insight. Lewin believed that groups and organizations struggle because their members are not trained in human relations. He therefore recommended close examination of group experiences to give people a deeper understanding of themselves and their groups' dynamics. Other theorists expanded on this basic idea, which forms the basis of a number of approaches to maximize human potential. Although some of these methods, such as T-groups and growth groups, are primarily of historical interest, they nonetheless provide the basis for contemporary psycho-educational groups, including structured and experiential learning groups (Gazda & Brooks, 1985; Lakin, 1972).

Training Groups (T-Groups) How can people learn about group dynamics? Members could learn the facts about effective interpersonal relations by attending lectures or by reading books about group dynamics (as you are doing now), but Lewin argued that good group skills are most easily acquired by directly experiencing human relations. Hence, he developed specialized **training groups**, or **T-groups**. Lewin discovered the utility of such groups when running educational classes dealing with leadership and group dynamics. At the end of each day, he arranged for observers to discuss the dynamics of the

---

training group or **T-group** A skill development training intervention in which individuals interact in unstructured group settings and then analyze the dynamics of that interaction.

groups with the group leaders who conducted the training sessions. The group members themselves did not usually take part in the sessions, but that changed when several asked if they could listen to the observers' and leaders' interpretations. Lewin agreed to their request, but they took issue with the observers' and the leaders' interpretations of the events that transpired in the group. However, the animated discussion that followed proved to be highly educational, and Lewin realized that everyone in the group was benefiting enormously from the analysis of the group's processes and dynamics (Highhouse, 2002).

One of the most noteworthy aspects of T-groups was their lack of structure. Although, from time to time, the trainees would meet in large groups for lectures or presentations, most of the learning took place in small groups. Even though the group included a designated leader, often called a *facilitator* or *trainer*, this individual acted primarily as a catalyst for discussion rather than as a director of the group. Indeed, during the first few days of a T-group's existence, group members usually complain about the lack of structure and the ambiguity, blaming the trainer for their discomfort. This ambiguity was intentional, however, and was designed to shift responsibility for structuring, understanding, and controlling the group's activities to the members themselves. As the group grappled with problems of organization, agenda, goals, and structure, each member's preferred interaction style became apparent to others in the group. The members also learned to disclose their feelings honestly, gained conflict reduction skills, and found enjoyment from working in collaborative relationships.

Although T-groups and training groups are antiquated terms, the principles on which they were based continue to influence methods for training individuals to work more effectively in groups (Burke & Day, 1986; Kaplan, 1979). For example, T-groups provided the basic educational model for the National Training Laboratory (NTL). This facility, which was founded by Lewin's colleagues after his death, was jointly sponsored by the National Education Association, the Research Center for Group Dynamics, and the Office of Naval Research. Researchers and teachers at the center refined their training methods in special workshops, which they termed laboratories. Their approach stressed the importance of learning about groups by experiencing them and yielded Kenneth Benne and Paul Sheats (1948) well-known functional theory of roles discussed in Chapter 6. (Moreno [1953] provides a very different historical perspective on the development of interpersonal skill training.)

Growth Groups   The T-group was a precursor of group techniques designed to enhance spontaneity, increase personal growth, and maximize members' sensitivity to others. As the purpose of the group experience shifted from training in group dynamics to increasing sensitivity, the name changed from T-group to **sensitivity training group**, or **encounter group** (Johnson, 1988; Lieberman, 1994).

The humanistic therapist Carl Rogers (1970) was a leader in the development of encounter groups. Rogers believed that most people come to experience a loss of self-regard because their needs for approval and love are rarely satisfied. Encounter groups address this lack by helping people trust in their own feelings, accept themselves, and act more openly with others. Rogerian therapists focus on emotions and encourage members to "open up" to one another by displaying their inner feelings, thoughts, and worries. Recognizing that the group members probably feel insecure about their social competencies, therapists are sources of unconditional positive regard—meaning that they avoid criticizing group members if possible. Rogers believed that group members, in the security of the group, would drop their defenses and encounter each other "authentically" (Page, Weiss, & Lietaer, 2002). The encounter group movement reached the height of its popularity in the 1970s (Back, 1973).

Structured Learning Groups   Both T-groups and encounter groups are open-ended, unstructured

approaches to interpersonal learning. Members of such groups follow no agenda; they examine events that unfold spontaneously within the confines of the group itself, and give one another feedback about their interpersonal effectiveness when appropriate. **Structured learning groups**, in contrast, are planned interventions that focus on a specific interpersonal problem or skill. Integrating behavioral therapies with experiential learning, the group leaders identify specific learning outcomes before the sessions. They then develop exercises that will help members practice these targeted skills. In a session on nonverbal communication, for instance, group members may be assigned a partner and then be asked to communicate a series of feelings without using spoken language. During assertiveness training, members might practice saying no to one another's requests. In a leadership training seminar, group members may be asked to role-play various leadership styles in a small group. These exercises are similar in that they actively involve the group members in the learning process (Hill, 1969).

Thousands of local and national institutes use structured learning groups in their seminars and workshops. Although the formats of these structured experiences differ substantially, most include directly experiencing the targeted skill or process and then examining the experience through discussion, guided analysis, personal reflection, and so on. Figure 16.1 summarizes this process. The session generally begins with a brief *orientation* that reviews the critical issues and focuses members on the exercise's goals. Next, the group members *experience* the event or situation by carrying out a structured group exercise. When they have completed the exercise, the members engage in a general *discussion* of their experiences within the group. This phase can be open-ended, focusing on feelings and subjective interpretations, or it, too, can be structured through the use of questioning, information exchange procedures, or video recording. This

---

sensitivity training group An unstructured group designed to enhance spontaneity, increase personal awareness, and maximize members' sensitivity to others. **encounter group** A form of sensitivity training that provides individuals with the opportunity to gain deep interpersonal intimacy with other group members.

---

structured learning group A planned intervention, such as a workshop, seminar, or retreat, focusing on a specific interpersonal problem or skill.

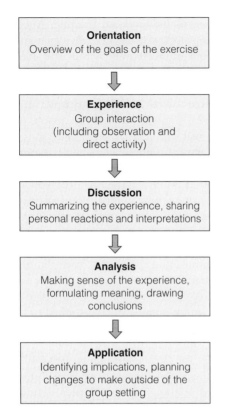

FIGURE 16.1   The experiential learning cycle.

SOURCE: © Cengage Learning 2014

discussion phase should blend into a period of *analysis*, during which the consultant helps group members to identify consistencies in their behavior and the behaviors of others. In many cases, the consultant guides the group's analysis of underlying group dynamics and offers a conceptual analysis that gives meaning to the event. The interpersonal learning cycle ends with *application*, as the group members use their new-found knowledge to enhance their relationships external to the group context. The model may also include a *reflection* component, in which participants examine the implications of their experience.

Kolb's Experiential Learning Model   Educator and social psychologist David Kolb (1984) has applied principles of experiential learning in organizational, educational, and governmental settings.

His **experiential learning theory** identifies two sets of polarities in the way people learn. The first polarity contrasts concrete, direct experiences with conceptual analysis. Through direct experiences people gain a firsthand understanding of the phenomenon they are examining, but by reflecting on the meaning of the experience, they transform these concrete data into abstract knowledge. The second polarity contrasts doing and observing. Like most analyses of experiential learning, Kolb stresses the importance of learning through action, engagement, and active experimentation, but he also suggests that considerable learning occurs through detached, objective observation—particularly because few individuals can act and accurately observe the effects of their action simultaneously. Kolb suggests that learning is deepest when individuals experience all four modes of learning: direct experience, observation, analysis, and action (Kayes, Kayes, & Kolb, 2005; see, too, Focus 10.1).

Support Groups

In times of trouble, such as illness, divorce, loss, or crisis, people tend to join with others rather than cope alone. Families, friends, and professional caregivers such as physicians and therapists are excellent sources of help and information in stressful, difficult circumstances, but some individuals' social networks may be too worn, too fragile, or too inexperienced to provide them with the solace they require. Sometimes, too, individuals may not wish to reveal their problems and their needs to their intimates and would prefer to unburden themselves with others who are knowledgeable but more objective and hence will be less likely to judge them harshly. In such circumstances, people join with others in support groups: voluntary groups whose members share a common

---

experiential learning theory A conceptual analysis of the experiential learning cycle that identifies four basic modes of acquiring information and transforming that information into knowledge: concrete experience, observation, active experimentation, and conceptual analysis (developed by David Kolb).

problem and meet for the purpose of exchanging social support (Borkman, 1999; Silverman, 2010).

Types of Support Groups   Support groups go by a variety of names, including *mutual aid groups* and *mutual help groups*. They are frequently called *self-help groups*, even though members of such groups are deliberately encouraged to rely on other group members for help and to provide those others with assistance in return. These groups meet at a wide variety of locations in the community, including churches, schools, universities, and private homes. They also meet, in some cases, using the Internet. As Focus 16.1 notes, Internet support groups provide individuals with advice, support, and information 24 hours a day, 7 days a week.

These groups generally began when individuals facing similar problems decided to share information with and support for one another. Because they are problem-focused, there are as many different support groups as there are specific problems that people encounter. However, most support groups fall into one of the four categories summarized in Table 16.2: mental and physical health, family and life transitions, advocacy, and addiction (Levy, 2000).

Defining Features of Support Groups   How do support groups help their members, given that they usually have no formally designated leaders, no professionally trained staff, and no facility or budget? No two support groups adopt identical procedures and structures, but most focus on a specific problem, encourage members to form personal relations with one another, and stress mutuality in helping. These often-seen features of support groups are as follows:

- **Problem-focused:** Support groups are communities of similar sufferers. Members may differ from one another in terms of age, sex, race, and wealth, but they share one important similarity: They are all coping with the same kind of problem. The members face a common predicament, so they are "psychologically bonded by the compelling similarity of member concerns" (Jacobs & Goodman, 1989, p. 537).

- **Relationship-oriented:** Support groups tend to be personally and interpersonally involving. Even though individuals' identities are often masked within such groups (e.g., Alcoholics Anonymous), members nonetheless establish personal relationships with one another that might continue outside of the confines of the group (unlike in psychotherapy groups). Members are expected to be honest and open, so that they learn to trust and rely on one another. Members are also expected to be respectful of one another and one another's needs and to treat people fairly.

- **Communal:** Most support groups develop a strong sense of community and sharing within the group. Members of the group draw support and encouragement from the group, but they are also expected to provide support and encouragement to others within the group. Each person, then, is both a provider and a recipient of help and support. The primary determinant of status in such groups is experience with the problem. Most support groups include veteran individuals who have more knowledge and experience with both the problem and with the means of dealing with the problem; these individuals serve as role models for others.

- **Autonomous:** Some support groups are created by health care practitioners, who use them to provide additional services to their patients. However, the traditional support group is a grassroots organization, initiated by members rather than an external coordinating professional. In fact, they often stand in contrast to more traditional forms of treatment, for they arise spontaneously because their members' needs are not being satisfied by existing educational, social, or health agencies. Local groups may be aligned to national organizations that mandate specific procedures for all their chapters, but even this standardization does not eliminate the emphasis on the local group's control of its methods.

Focus 16.1   E-groups: Seeking Support from Online Groups

It had been a long day, but her mother was asleep and the kids were in their rooms, maybe doing homework (but probably on Facebook with their friends). She opened her laptop, read her e-mail, and then signed into her account at Alzwell.com, which maintained resources and forums pertaining to Alzheimer's disease. She had gotten her free account a year ago, when her mother's Alzheimer's had progressed from mild to moderate. She logged in several times a week, sometimes asking questions, sometimes just reading other people's questions and the answers they received, and sometimes adding to the discussion, too. Tonight, someone had posted a question about medication. This topic always provoked considerable discussion, and sure enough: Eight people had offered their ideas, including Singlemom and BernardX, two regular contributors to the forum. But no one yet had talked about how important it is to make sure the medication fits the patient's needs—some drugs are better for depression, others for confusion—so she commented about that. She then switched over to Facebook, messaged her children to do their homework, and got ready for bed.

Just as the Internet offers new ways for groups to solve problems, collaborate on projects, and make decisions, so too has it opened up new possibilities for those seeking help and support for the problems they face. Members, instead of leaving their homes and traveling to a meeting, can now take part in a range of group activities using a computer and a connection to the Internet (Page, 2010). No matter what problem an individual faces—a serious physical illness, stress caused by providing care for an ill family member, a negative life event such as divorce or the death of a loved one, addiction and drug dependency, social rejection, prejudice, or problems of adjustment and mental health—an online group likely exists somewhere on the Internet that can provide self-care information, support, and referral services. Some of these sites are primarily repositories of information about the problem or issue and may be sponsored by professionals who treat these problems. Others, however, are unmoderated, self-sustaining mutual help groups, for they were created by individuals who all face the same difficulty and wish to connect to and support each other.

Most support groups create asynchronous communication among members who post their comments and questions on forums and discussion areas. Other sites set up meeting times when people can communicate synchronously, using video, audio, or text-only communication tools. Both synchronous and asynchronous groups can be moderated by a group leader who facilitates the discussion (and intervenes to remove content as necessary).

How helpful can these online support groups be, given that they meet in a relatively sterile online world? Studies of online groups for problems ranging from cancer to sexual abuse to psychological disorders suggest that these groups are surprisingly effective and may even rival face-to-face groups in terms of functionality. When researchers analyzed the content of two online support sites for cancer patients, they discovered that approximately 47% of the posts were informational (requesting and providing information about the disease), 15% discussed the effects of the disease, and 38% of the posts provided emotional support, including sharing the distress and expressions of concern (Gooden & Winefield, 2007). Participants report that they felt supported and valued by their group and, after taking part in an online session, felt more hopeful about their situation. Two issues that could cause problems—people posting inaccurate information or leaving comments that could be emotionally harmful—occur very rarely in such groups, and certainly no more frequently than in offline groups (Miller & Gergen, 1998; van Uden-Kraan et al., 2008).

Some aspects of the online format may even enhance aspects of a mutual help approach to coping with negative events (Tanis, 2008). Because members need not disclose their identity, they report being able to reveal more intimate information about their experiences and to respond more emotionally to others than they would if interacting face to face. Members of online sessions also tend to exchange more practical advice and factual information than they do in face-to-face sessions, and members value this aspect of online groups as well. They report that the information is useful to them in understanding their condition and in dealing more effectively with their health care providers (Houston, Cooper, & Ford, 2002). Internet support groups are also particularly valuable for individuals whose illness restricts their mobility and for those who are suffering from a stigmatized illness, such as prostate cancer or AIDS. Individuals may feel self-conscious about their condition, but the comfort they experience by joining with others who are "in the same boat" overwhelms this concern about embarrassment (Davison, Pennebaker, & Dickerson, 2000).

TABLE 16.2   Varieties of Support (Mutual Help) Groups

Type of Group	Examples
Mental and physical health: members dealing with psychological disorders, physical illness, and recovery from injury	• CARE (Cancer Aftercare and Rehabilitation Society) • Bell's Palsy Network • Recovery, Inc. (a mental health group)
Family and life transitions: individuals facing stressful life experiences, such as divorce, bereavement, ill family members	• In Touch (for parents of children with mental handicaps) • Parents without Partners • Alzheimer's Disease Support and Information Group
Advocacy: individuals advocating support for a personal and/or social issue	• Campaign for Homosexual Equality • Mothers Against Drunk Driving (MADD) • Gay Activists' Alliance
Addictions: members seeking to control intemperate behaviors and maladaptive dependencies	• AA (Alcoholics Anonymous) • NA (Narcotics Anonymous) • Weight Watchers

■ **Perspective-based:** Support groups' independence from more traditional approaches is also manifested in their adoption of a novel perspective with regard to their problem domain. A grief group may adopt fervently a particular model of the stages of grieving and base its interventions and recommendations on that perspective. A support group for alcoholics may maintain that recovery is never permanent, and so one must abstain from all forms of alcohol to overcome the addiction. These perspectives may not be complex nor are they always explicitly recognized by members, but, in many cases, the group's perspective on its affliction may become the centerpiece of the group's discussions with new members urged to adopt the group's worldview as a means of coping effectively with the problem.

Alcoholics Anonymous Alcoholics Anonymous (AA) is an example of a support group. AA was founded by Bill Wilson in 1935. Wilson had tried to quit drinking for years, but no matter what he tried, he always returned to his addiction. After a fourth hospital stay for acute alcoholism, Wilson became convinced that he could overcome his drinking problem and sought help from a small spiritual group, the Oxford Group Movement. With his physician and friend William D. Silkworth, he developed a support system that included self-examination, admitting past wrongs, rebuilding relationships and making amends, and reliance on and helping others.

Wilson's program formed the basis of Alcoholics Anonymous, which grew to be an international organization with millions of members. Despite AA's size, change is still achieved through local chapters of alcoholics who meet regularly to review their success in maintaining their sobriety. AA meetings emphasize testimonials, mutual help, and adherence to the 12-stage program (the "12 steps") described by the AA doctrine. These steps recommend admitting one's powerlessness over alcohol; surrendering one's fate to a greater power; taking an inventory of personal strengths, weaknesses, and moral failings; and helping others fight their addiction (Flores, 1997).

AA is a multipronged approach to addiction. It stresses the goal of total abstinence and the need to remain ever vigilant against the pressure to resume drinking. It asks members to take specific actions to prevent relapse and assigns veteran members to newcomers to help strengthen their resilience. Much of the success of the approach also rests on changing members' social networks. By participating actively in AA, members associate with people who are no longer drinking heavily, and the longer this positive association continues the more they can resist the "negative pull of 'wet' social circles that support drinking" (Bond, Kaskutas, & Weisner, 2003, p. 580). One team of researchers studied people one and three years after they first entered an AA-based treatment program. Those who remained abstinent after one year had attended far more AA meetings than those who were still drinking: an average of 93 meetings compared to only 25. They also reported having fewer heavy drinkers in their social network (7% vs. 17%) and more people who encouraged them to remain sober (see Figure 16.2; Bond et al., 2003; Kaskutas et al., 2005).

SOURCES OF CHANGE
IN GROUPS

Group approaches to change, despite their variations in goals and methods, have certain key elements in common. Some of these common **therapeutic factors** are equivalent to the change-promoting forces that operate in individual-level therapies, but others are unique to group-level approaches (Ingram, Hayes, & Scott, 2000). All therapies, for example, help clients gain self-insight, but only group approaches stimulate interpersonal comparisons and provide members with a forum for practicing their interpersonal skills. All therapies provide clients with support and help, but in groups, members don't just get help—they also give help to other group members.

Although no one list of therapeutic factors has been verified by researchers and accepted by practitioners, Table 16.3 lists the most frequently cited and empirically confirmed change-promoting factors. Some of these factors, such as giving hope to group members, are more influential during the early stages of the group's history, whereas others become more potent with time. Some focus on cognitive processes, whereas others promote changes in behavior directly. Some pertain more to task aspects of the group setting, such as guidance and gaining skills. Others originate from the positive social relations that unify the group. But all these processes combine to transform ordinary groups into therapeutic ones (Dierick & Lietaer,

---

therapeutic factor An aspect of group settings that aids and promotes personal growth and adjustment, including such factors as the installation of hope, universality, providing information, altruism, and interpersonal learning.

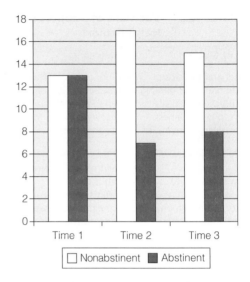

FIGURE 16.2 The percentage of abstinent and nonabstinent participants in AA who indicated they regularly interacted with a friend who was a heavy drinker when they began the program (Time 1), after one year (Time 2), and after three years (Time 3).

SOURCE: From tabled data in "The persistent influence of social networks and Alcoholics Anonymous on abstinence" by J. Bond, L. A. Kaskutas, & Weisner, C., 2003, in *Quarterly Journal of Studies on Alcohol, 64,* 579–588.

2008; Kivlighan, Miles, & Paquin, 2010; Yalom with Leszcz, 2005).

Universality and Hope

In the aftermath of the bus accident, the survivors coped with their physical injuries, their fears, and their grief. In unguarded moments, they may have flashed back to the accident and psychologically relived it. As they found that they could not concentrate on their work even months after the accident, they may have started to feel that they would never get over the anguish. They may also have found that their moods would take unexpected turns—they may have become angry for little reason or were disinterested in things that once fascinated them. If they never discussed these reactions with others, how would they know that these changes in mood, thinking, and memory are common occurrences for those who survive a traumatic experience?

T A B L E 16.3   Factors That Promote Change in Groups

Factor	Definition	Meaning to Member
Universality	Recognizing one is not the only one suffering; identification with others	I'm not alone; others in the group are dealing with the same problem I am.
Hope	Increasing optimism from seeing others improve	Others in the group are making progress; so can I.
Observational learning	Developing social skills through observation and imitation	By listening to others talk about their problems, I learn how to express myself.
Interpersonal learning	Developing social skills by interacting with others	Others let me know how my way of interacting with others causes problems and misunderstanding.
Guidance	Offering and accepting direction to and from the group	People in the group give me good suggestions.
Cohesion and support	Building strong, supportive relationships with others; acceptance	The group accepts, understands, and supports me.
Self-disclosure	Revealing personal information to others	I feel better for sharing things I've kept secret for too long.
Catharsis	Releasing pent-up emotions	It feels good to get things off my chest.
Altruism	Increasing sense of efficacy from helping others	Helping other people gives me more self-respect.
Insight	Gaining a deeper understanding of oneself	I am learning a lot about myself.

Universality and Identity   When suffering alone, individuals may not realize that their feelings and experiences are relatively common ones. But when surrounded by other people who are suffering similarly, members recognize the *universality* of the problems they face. Most people are careful to keep their negative emotions hidden from others, but they do not realize that others are doing this as well. In consequence, people tend to assume that their situation is a relatively bleak one, and this misperception can lead to self-blame, depressive rumination, and declines in overall well-being (Jordan et al., 2011). Research confirms that when people are with others who face similar problems or troubling events, they feel better, in terms of self-esteem and mood, than when they are with dissimilar people (Frable, Platt, & Hoey, 1998). People often enjoy feeling distinctive, unusual, and different from others,

but few people wish to feel uniquely singled out for misfortune (Snyder & Fromkin, 1980).

The AA "hello" ritual illustrates this collective sharing. Members, when addressing the group, state their first name, followed by the announcement "I am an alcoholic." This public declaration reassures all the other participants that their problem is shared by others, but also accentuates the members' identification with the group. Just as individuals who strongly identify with their racial and ethnic group show elevated levels of self-esteem, so do individuals who identify with their therapeutic group show greater well-being (Leach et al., 2010; Marmarosh, Holtz, & Schottenbauer, 2005). When researchers reinforced some members' identification with the group—by giving them a group identification card and telling them it symbolized their membership in the group—those members given an identity card reported greater collective self-esteem and displayed more positive treatment gains than members in a no-card control condition (Marmarosh & Corazzini, 1997).

Installation of Hope   Yalom believes that this collective process results in the *installation of hope* in members, and research confirms that group-derived hope contributes to well-being, life satisfaction, and inspiration. Members of a short-term therapeutic group that focused directly on members' sense of hope reported more optimism about reaching their goals, as well as reduced anxiety and depression, than did members of a control group (Cheavens et al., 2006). Groups that are designed so that they elevate members' sense of hope tend to be more powerful agents of change than groups that use other procedures (e.g., Worthington et al., 1997).

These therapeutic gains may be due, in part, to group members' tendencies to compare themselves to other members—the process of social comparison, as described in Chapter 4. Even when the group includes individuals who are experiencing particularly negative outcomes, these individuals can serve as targets for *downward social comparison*. Such comparisons reduce group members' own sense of victimization and can raise their overall sense of self-esteem (Wills & Filer, 2000). The group may also include individuals who are coping well with many difficulties, and these *upward social comparison* targets can encourage members by symbolizing the possibility of progress (Buunk & Gibbons, 2007). Although successful group members—the fellow cancer survivor who is in complete remission, the AA member who has stayed sober for three years, or the caregiver who is managing to care for her elderly mother and still attend college—may make some group members feel like failures, these successful outliers provide a standard for defining one's own goals (Tennen, McKee, & Affleck, 2000).

Social Learning

When people who are striving to change meet with one other person—whether a trained therapist, counselor, friend, or relative—they can discuss problems, identify solutions, and receive support and encouragement. But even in the most therapeutic of dyads, the individual shares perspectives, feedback, guidance, acceptance, and comfort with only one other person. A larger group, with its multiple members, is richer in terms of its interpersonal and therapeutic resources. Within the social microcosm of the group, individuals experience a fuller range of interpersonal processes, including feedback about their strengths and weaknesses, pressure to change originating from multiple sources, role models whose actions they can emulate, and opportunities to practice the very behaviors they are seeking to refine. Of the 10 therapeutic factors in Table 16.3, observational learning, interpersonal learning, and guidance all involve learning from other people: social learning.

Observational Learning   Albert Bandura (1986), like all learning theorists, assumes that people acquire new attitudes and behaviors through experience. His **social learning theory**, however, suggests that people also learn by observing and imitating other people. This theory explains how infants learn their native language, why adolescents adopt the unhealthy habits of their peers, and the acquisition of new, health-promoting skills in therapeutic groups. Social learning is more than imitation, however. If members are not motivated to learn from their peers or if they are distracted and so do not watch the modeled behavior closely, social learning is unlikely. Such learning also requires members be able to remember and reenact the behavior they observed. In general, people are more likely to learn through observation if they recognize that the actions they watch lead to positive consequences for the person who performs them (Shebilske et al., 1998).

Groups provide members with multiple models to emulate, including fellow group members and the group leaders. When, for example, members

---

social learning theory A conceptualization of learning developed by Albert Bandura that describes the processes by which new behaviors are acquired by observing and imitating the actions displayed by models, such as parents or peers.

who are skilled in expressing their feelings deftly describe their emotional reactions, the less verbally skilled members may learn how they, too, can put their feelings into words. When two members who regularly disagree with each other reach an accord, others, who watch this reconciliation unfold, learn how they can resolve interpersonal conflicts. Leaders can also model desirable behaviors by treating the group members in positive ways and avoiding behaviors that are undesirable (Dies, 1994). Researchers facilitated social learning in one study by arranging for the coleaders of therapy groups to model social interactions that the members considered difficult or anxiety-provoking. The leaders then helped the group members perform these same behaviors through role playing. Groups that used explicit modeling methods showed greater improvement than groups that only discussed the problematic behaviors (Falloon et al., 1977).

Interpersonal Learning   Most people believe that they can come to know themselves—their strengths, their weaknesses, their tendencies, and their satisfactions—through self-reflection. But much self-knowledge is gained socially; people implicitly monitor their impact on other people and draw conclusions about their own qualities from others' reactions to them. In therapeutic groups, the other members become, metaphorically, mirrors that members use to understand themselves (Cooley, 1902). A group member may begin to think that she has good social skills if the group always responds positively each time she contributes to the group discussion. Another member may decide that he is irritating if his comments are always met with anger and hostility. This interpersonal feedback helps members perceive themselves more accurately. Individuals who are socially withdrawn, for example, tend to evaluate their social skills negatively even though the other group members view them positively (Christensen & Kashy, 1998). Individuals also tend to rate themselves as more anxious than others perceive them to be (Marcus, 1998; Marcus & Wilson, 1996). Extended contact with others in a group setting helps repair these negative, inaccurate perceptions.

Groups are also very willing to give direct, unambiguous feedback to members when they engage in objectionable or praiseworthy actions (Kivlighan, 1985). Kurt Lewin was one of the first theorists to borrow the term *feedback* from engineering and use it to describe how others' responses to group members served as corrective guides for subsequent actions (Claiborn, Goodyear, & Horner, 2001). The individual who is lonely because he alienates everyone by acting rudely may be told, "You should try to be more sensitive" or "You are always so judgmental, it makes me sick." Some groups exchange so much evaluative information that members withdraw from the group rather than face the barrage of negative feedback (Scheuble et al., 1987). Skilled group leaders, however, are careful to monitor the exchange of information between members so that individuals receive the information they need in positive, supportive ways (Morran et al., 1998).

Guidance   When group members discuss issues, concerns, problems, and crises, other group members frequently help by providing advice, guidance, and direction. Members of support groups, for example, exchange considerable factual and personal information about their disorder or concern, as well as suggestions for problem management (e.g., LaBarge, Von Dras, & Wingbermuehle, 1998). Group leaders, in addition to guiding the flow of the session through questioning, summarizing, and rephrasing members' statements, also provide information, suggest solutions, confront the members' interpretations of problems, and offer their own interpretations (Hill et al., 1988). This guidance ranges from explicit suggestions and directions to more existentially challenging insights (Heppner et al., 1994).

Some therapists are more directive than others. Those who adopt a leader-centered approach—typical of psychoanalytic, Gestalt, and behavioral groups—guide the course of the interaction, assign various tasks to the group members, and occupy the hub of the centralized communication network. In some instances, the group members may not even communicate with one another, but only with the group leader. Other leaders, however, adopt a nondirected, democratic style of leadership. This more group-centered approach, which is more typical in interpersonal therapy groups, requires members to engage with one another rather than only with the leader. Such therapists function as facilitators and agenda setters; they help the members examine problems and generate alternatives, but their influence does not necessarily exceed that of any other member.

Both directive and nondirective approaches are effective, so long as the leaders are perceived to be caring, helpful in identifying the cause of members' problems, and skilled in keeping the group on task (Lieberman & Golant, 2002; Lieberman, Yalom, & Miles, 1973). Moreover, just as leaders in organizational settings sometimes vary their interventions to fit the situation, so effective leaders in therapeutic settings shift their methods over time. During the early stages of treatment, members may respond better to a more directive leader, whereas in the later stages, a less directive approach may yield more positive results (Kivlighan, 1997).

As in other groups, therapeutic ones often benefit from **coleadership**: having two rather than one leader (Miles & Kivlighan, 2010). The two leaders can lend support to each other, and they can also offer the group members their combined knowledge, insight, and experience. Male-female leadership teams are particularly beneficial, as they offer a fuller perspective on gender issues and serve as models of positive, nonromantic heterosexual relationships. In general, two cooks tend to improve, rather than spoil, the therapeutic broth, but the advantages of coleadership are lost if the leaders are unequal in status or engage in power struggles during group sessions (Arnardottir, 2002).

Group Cohesion

Just as cohesion is a key ingredient for effective military squads, production groups, and management

teams, so cohesion contributes to the effectiveness of change-promoting groups. Groups are more effective as change agents if they are unified and members feel tightly bonded to the group and its members (Cartwright, 1951). Without cohesion, feedback is not accepted, norms do not develop, and members to not attend with enough regularity to create a stable atmosphere for influence. Members are also more accepting of each other in cohesive groups. Cohesion creates the climate for acceptance that is so critical for therapeutic success.

Sources of Cohesion The concept of cohesion has generated considerable definitional and measurement debate among those who study therapeutic groups. To some, cohesion is the group-level equivalent of the working alliance that links therapist and client in one-to-one therapy. Others suggest that cohesiveness is what creates the psychological safety needed for members to feel comfortable revealing their weaknesses to other members. Still others suggest that the essence of cohesion is a sense of belonging to the group (see Marmarosh & Van Horn, 2010). However, as Chapter 5 noted, a group's cohesion is influenced by a number of factors, and no single factor can be named which is the critical ingredient that must be added to the group so that it can become a cohesive one. A therapeutic group, like any group, may exhibit both social and task cohesion: Social cohesion is defined by attraction to the group and its members whereas task cohesion is determined by a commitment to the group and its therapeutic processes. However, cohesion may also be based on identity and belonging (collective cohesion), shared feelings (emotional cohesion), and the integrity of the group's structural features—including the bond between the members and the leaders (structural cohesion).

Cohesion and Group Development Just as studies of all types of groups suggest that a group's cohesiveness depends on its longevity and stage of development, so studies of therapeutic groups suggest cohesion ebbs and flows across the life course of the group. Even when the group's task is a therapeutic one, time is needed to achieve cohesiveness.

coleadership Two or more individuals sharing the organizational, directive, and motivational duties of the leadership role.

Through continuous, guided, and increasingly skill-ful communication, group members come to iden-tify and better understand previously unrecognized motives and emotions, they become more rational in dealing with life's problems, and they acquire valuable interpersonal skills, but these gains will occur at a pace set by the group's gradual develop-ment. In one study, investigators observed and coded the behaviors displayed by adolescents in a program of behavioral change. These groups did not immedi-ately start to work on self-development issues nor did the members try to help one another. Rather, the groups first moved through orientation, conflict, and cohesion-building stages before they began to make therapeutic progress (Hill & Gruner, 1973).

These changes in cohesiveness that occur over time in therapeutic groups are largely consistent with Bruce Tuckman's five-stage theory of group development (see Chapters 1 and 5). During the forming stage, individual members are seeking to understand their relationship to the newly formed group and strive to establish clear inter-member relations. During the storming stage, group mem-bers often find themselves in conflict over status and group goals; consequently, hostility, disruption, and uncertainty dominate group discussions. During the norming phase, the group strives to develop a group structure that increases cohesiveness and harmony. The performing stage is typified by a focus on group productivity and decision making. Finally, when the group fulfills its goals, it reaches its last stage of development—adjourning. If a group does not move through these stages, its members will not be able to benefit from the experience (MacKenzie, 1994, 1997; Yalom with Leszcz, 2005).

Counseling psychologist Dennis Kivlighan and his colleagues (1984) illustrated the important impact of group development on therapeutic out-comes by matching interventions to the develop-mental stage of the group. Groups were given structured help in expressing either anger or inti-macy before either the fourth or the ninth group session of their therapy. The information dealing with anger clarified the value of anger as a natural part of group participation and provided suggestions for communicating it. The information dealing

with intimacy clarified the value of intimacy in groups and provided suggestions for its appropriate expression toward others. As anticipated, when the interventions matched the groups' developmental stage—for example, when group members received the information on anger during the storming phase (Session 4) and the information on intimacy during the norming phase (Session 9)—the participants dis-played more comfort in dealing with intimacy, more appropriate expressions of intimacy and anger, fewer inappropriate expressions of intimacy, and more congruence between self-ratings and other ratings of interpersonal style (Kivlighan, McGovern, & Corazzini, 1984).

Consequences of Cohesion   Cohesion, as noted in Chapter 5, can lead to negative consequences, particularly if social pressures become too powerful, if the group's norms are not productive ones, and if less-involved members feel as though they are out-siders in their own group. However, in groups with a therapeutic purpose, the positive consequences of cohesion far outnumber the negative. Cohesive groups tend to retain their members—attendance rates are higher and dropout rates lower. Members of cohesive therapy groups are more satisfied with their membership, and they describe the experience as more comfortable and less stressful. Communica-tion rates depend upon cohesiveness. The quantity of communication is greater in cohesive groups, participation is more equally distributed among all members, and members disclose more personal information. Cohesive groups are also superior sources of emotional and social support for their members. When a group is cohesive, the members are more engaged in the group and its change-promoting processes, they take part in the planning of the group's topics and activities, and they express a sense of closeness (rather than conflict) with the other members. Cohesive groups also exert a stron-ger influence on their members than noncohesive groups; members are more likely to internalize the group's norms and avoid dysfunctional behavior for fear of letting the group down. Of all the curative factors that work to promote change in groups, cohesion may be the only necessary condition for an effective change-promoting group: A therapeutic group that lacks cohesion may not be therapeutic (Higgenbotham, West, & Forsyth, 1988; Marmarosh & Van Horn, 2010).

Disclosure and Catharsis

Change-promoting groups provide members with the opportunity to disclose privately held information—about themselves and other people—with others in the group. As Yalom explains: "It is the affective sharing of one's inner world and then the acceptance by others that seem of paramount importance" in group therapy (Yalom with Leszcz, 2005, p. 56). This process of **self-disclosure** is one of the primary benefits of both support and therapeutic groups, for each new self-disclosure deepens the group's intimacy, and this increased closeness then makes further self-disclosures possible (Agazarian, 2001). In sharing information about themselves, members are expressing their trust in the group and signaling their commitment to the therapeutic process (Shechtman & Dvir, 2006). Disclosing troubling, worrisome thoughts also reduces the discloser's level of tension and stress. Individuals who keep their problems secret but continually ruminate about them display signs of physiological and psychological distress, whereas individuals who have the opportunity to disclose these troubling thoughts are healthier and happier (Pennebaker, 1997).

Disclosure over Time Group members generally need time to move from relatively superficial disclosures to more personal ones. When groups first convene, members usually focus on mundane topics and avoid saying anything too personal or provocative. In this *orientation stage*, members try to form a general impression of each other and also strive to make a good impression themselves. In the *exploratory affective stage*, members discuss their personal attitudes and opinions, but they avoid

intimate topics. This stage is often followed by the *affective stage* when a few topics still remain taboo. When the group reaches the final stage, *stable exchange*, all personal feelings are shared (Altman & Taylor, 1973).

Self-disclosure can be something of a challenge for some individuals. People experiencing personality or psychological disturbances, for example, often disclose the wrong sorts of information at the wrong time (McGuire & Leak, 1980). Men and boys, too, are generally more reserved in their self-disclosures (Brooks, 1996; Kilmartin, 1994; Shechtman, 1994). Thus, therapists must sometimes take special steps to induce males to share personal information about themselves and must model disclosure and incorporate disclosure rituals in the group (Horne, Jolliff, & Roth, 1996). Men's reluctance to disclose can even undermine the quality of the group experience for all participants: The more men in the therapeutic group, the fewer benefits are reported by participants (Hurley, 1997).

Expressing Strong Emotions Members do not only express insights, uncertainties, or worries that they usually keep to themselves. Sometimes, instead, they also disclose emotions that they usually keep hidden: anger, hostility, sadness, grief, and even sexual tensions. Some experts, accepting the psychoanalytic view that the buildup of such emotions is unhealthy, value this emotional release, which is called **catharsis**. Others, however, have suggested that "blowing off steam" is rarely helpful, for in the extreme, venting heightens members' psychological distress and upset (Ormont, 1984).

Altruism

The group's leader is not the only source of help available to group members. Other group members can draw on their own experiences to offer insights and advice to one another. This mutual assistance

---

self-disclosure The process of revealing personal, intimate information about oneself to others.

catharsis The release of emotional tensions.

benefits both parties. Even though the group's leader is the official expert in the group, people are often more willing to accept help from people who are similar to themselves (Wills & DePaulo, 1991). The helper, too, "feels a sense of being needed and helpful; can forget self in favor of another group member; and recognizes the desire to do something for another group member" (Crouch, Bloch, & Wanlass, 1994, p. 285). Mutual assistance teaches group members the social skills that are essential to psychological well-being (Ferencik, 1992).

Mutual assistance is particularly important in support groups. Mended Hearts—a support group that deals with the psychological consequences of open-heart surgery—tells its members that "you are not completely mended until you help mend others" (Lieberman, 1993, p. 297). AA groups formalize and structure helping in their 12-step procedures. Collective helping is also an essential component of group-level approaches to dealing with traumatic events.

Insight

Individuals' perceptions of their own personal qualities are generally accurate. People who think of themselves as assertive tend to be viewed that way by others, just as warm, outgoing individuals tend to be viewed as friendly and approachable (Kenny et al., 1996; Levesque, 1997). In some cases, however, individuals' self-perceptions are inaccurate (Andersen, 1984). An individual may believe himself to be attractive, socially skilled, and friendly, when in fact he is unattractive, interpersonally incompetent, and hostile.

Individuals are somewhat leery of joining therapeutic groups because they recognize that the group may see them for what they are—and that this appraisal may not match their own self-definition (Ringer, 2002). Although individuals tend to resist information that is discrepant from their self-views, when multiple individuals agree in their appraisals, the member is more likely to internalize this information (Jacobs, 1974; Kivlighan, 1985). Also, when the feedback is given in the context of a long-term, reciprocal relationship, it cannot be so easily dismissed as biased or subjective. Group leaders, too, often reward members for accepting rather than rejecting feedback, and the setting itself works to intensify self-awareness. In a supportive, accepting group, members can reveal hidden aspects of themselves, and, in so doing, further intensify the strength of their commitment to the group.

Even qualities that are unknown to others and to the individual can emerge and be recognized during group interactions (Luft, 1984). As self-perception theory suggests, people often "come to 'know' their own attitudes, emotions, and other internal states partially by inferring them from observations of their own overt behavior and/or the circumstances in which this behavior occurs" (Bem, 1972, p. 2). If individuals observe themselves acting in ways that suggest that they are socially skilled—for example, disclosing information about themselves appropriately and maintaining a conversation—then they may infer that they are socially skilled (Robak, 2001). Members may find that, as they act in ways that are inconsistent with their original self-conception, their self becomes increasingly complex and, in consequence, more stable (Vickery et al., 2006).

Studies of group members' evaluations of the therapeutic experience attest to the importance of insight. When participants in therapeutic groups were asked to identify the events that took place in their groups that helped them the most, they stressed incidents related to universality, interpersonal learning, cohesion (belonging), and insight (see Figure 16.3). But time and type of group also matter. For example, during later sessions, members value interpersonal learning more but universality less. Also, self-understanding is less important in support groups, but more important in affect-focused and interpersonal therapy groups (Kivlighan & Holmes, 2004). Also, some individuals are more concerned with gaining self-understanding than are others: Those who stress the value of self-understanding tend to benefit the most from participation in a therapeutic group (Butler & Fuhriman, 1983; MacNair-Semands & Lese, 2000).

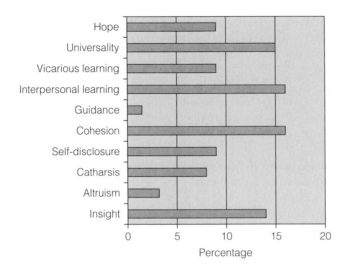

F I G U R E   16.3   Group members' ratings of the value of therapeutic factors in groups.

SOURCE: From "Participants perception of therapeutic factors in group counseling: The role of interpersonal style and stage of group development" by D. A. Kivlighan, Jr. & D. Mullison, 1988. *Small Group Behavior, 19*, 1988. Copyright 1988 by Sage Publications, Inc. Reprinted by permission of Sage Publications, Inc.

THE EFFECTIVENESS OF
GROUPS

What would you do if you were bothered by some personal problem? Perhaps you have trouble making friends. Maybe you are having difficulties adjusting to a new job or wish that you could be more productive when you are at work. Perhaps you have finally resolved to stop smoking or drinking, or you just cannot seem to get over the depression that has enveloped you since your mother passed away last year. Whatever the problem, you have not succeeded in changing on your own. So you decide to join a change-promoting group. Would this group really help you?

Empirical Support for
Group Treatments

Researchers and therapists have been debating the effectiveness of both individual and group treatment methods for years. As clinical studies of therapeutic outcomes have become increasingly sophisticated scientifically, treatment professionals have sought to

identify **evidence-based treatments** (EBTs): those that have been shown to be effective for specific problems and disorders using objective measures and evaluations (Kazdin, 2011). Do group methods deserve to be on the list of recognized EBTs?

Meta-analytic Reviews   Initial efforts to determine if group approaches qualify as EBTs were hampered by the methodological shortcomings of early studies of group effectiveness. Reviewers, after sifting through hundreds of studies evaluating the effectiveness of group interventions, rejected most as so methodologically flawed that they yielded no information whatsoever (Bednar & Kaul, 1978, 1979, 1994). But as researchers gathered more data using more precise scientific controls, including clinical trials, the results generally weighed in favor of group-level interventions. Although they rarely supported Lewin's law of change by finding group

_____
evidence-based treatment Clinical procedures whose effectiveness has been documented through objective, scientifically rigorous research procedures.

approaches were superior to individual-level methods, they indicated group-level and individual-level treatments were equal in effectiveness (Barlow, 2010).

Many of these reviews rely on meta-analysis to summarize the findings from multiple studies. Gary Burlingame and his colleagues, for example, statistically combined the results of hundreds of experimental, quasi-experimental, and correlational studies, before concluding that researchers had been more diligent in their studies of cognitive-behavioral therapies, and their review indicated such methods were superior to untreated control groups and equivalent in effectiveness to individual approaches (Fuhriman & Burlingame, 1994). These findings were generally sustained when Burlingame and his colleagues summarized findings from 107 studies and 14 meta-analyses of the use of group methods for treating a range of disorders, including anxiety, eating disorders, substance abuse, and personality disturbances. These analyses indicated that group methods are better for some problems than others—particularly social phobia and substance abuse (Burlingame, MacKenzie, & Strauss, 2004). The effectiveness of group treatment also depends on the nature of the group's structure and dynamics. Another Burlingame review indicates that groups that generate higher levels of member-to-member interpersonal feedback and stronger working relationships among members were more effective than other groups. The use of pregroup preparation and providing a higher level of structure during early group sessions also improved outcomes (Burlingame, Fuhriman, & Mosier, 2003; Burlingame & Krogel, 2005; Fuhriman & Burlingame, 1994; Kösters et al., 2006; McRoberts, Burlingame, & Hoag, 1998).

Types of Groups and Effectiveness Change-promoting groups conform to no single set of procedures: Some groups are leader centered, others group focused; a group's activities can range from the highly structured (interpersonal learning groups) to the wholly unstructured (encounter groups); in some groups, members themselves are responsible for running the meeting, whereas in other situations, the facilitator runs the session (structured groups). Group practitioners also vary greatly in their orientations and techniques: Some focus on emotions with Gestalt exercises, others concentrate on the here and now of the group's interpersonal processes, and still others train members to perform certain behaviors through videotaped feedback, behavioral rehearsal, and systematic reinforcement.

Given this diversity of purposes and procedures, one might expect some types of groups to emerge as more effective than others. Yet differences in treatment effectiveness are relatively rare. Group psychotherapists Morton Lieberman, Irvin Yalom, and Matthew Miles (1973), for example, investigated the overall impact of a 12-week experiential group on members' adjustment. They began by assigning 206 Stanford University students to 1 of 18 therapy groups representing 10 different theoretical orientations. Trained observers coded the groups' interactions, with particular attention given to leadership style. Before, during, immediately after, and six months following the participation, Lieberman and his colleagues gathered information about each group members' self-esteem, attitudes, self-satisfaction, and adjustment from the group leaders, the group members' acquaintances, and the group members themselves.

Somewhat unexpectedly, researchers discovered that no one theoretical approach had a monopoly on effectiveness. For example, two separate Gestalt groups with different leaders were included in the design, but the members of these two groups evidenced widely discrepant gains. One of the Gestalt groups ranked among the most successful in stimulating participant growth, but the other Gestalt group yielded fewer benefits than all of the other groups.

A number of factors could account for this apparent equivalence of therapies (Stiles, Shapiro, & Elliott, 1986). First, the various group therapies may be differentially effective, but researchers' measures may not be sensitive enough to detect these variations. Second, a group's effectiveness may depend as much on who is in the group and who leads the group as on the methods used. The question is not "Is Therapy X more effective than Therapy Y?" but,

"What type of group run by which therapist is effective for this individual with this type of problem?" (Paul, 1967). Third, although group interventions are based on widely divergent theoretical assumptions, these assumptions may not lead to differences in practice. The leader of a Gestalt group and the leader of a psychodynamic group, for example, may explain their goals and methods in very different theoretical terms, but they may nonetheless rely on identical methods in their groups. Fourth, as the concept of therapeutic factors suggests, despite their heterogeneity in purposes and procedures, therapeutic groups have certain characteristics in common, and these common aspects of groups and their dynamics may account for their therapeutic effects.

Participants' Appraisals   Most people, when asked if they would prefer to receive treatment in a private session with a therapist or in group sessions, express a strong preference for the one-to-one approach. This tendency depends, in part, on cultural factors—the idea of joining with other people who are initially strangers to discuss highly personal matters is viewed with more suspicion in some cultures than in others (see Focus 16.2). Even therapists themselves tend to favor individual methods over collective ones (Piper, 2008). However, those who have actually participated in group therapy—the consumers of group-based treatments—generally give group approaches high marks. One study, conducted by *Consumer Reports*, asked respondents to rate a variety of treatments. All psychological methods, including group interventions, were rated positively. AA received particularly positive evaluations in this study (Seligman, 1995, 1996; see also Christensen & Jacobson, 1994).

The effects of group approaches are also more evident when members themselves appraise the gains they have achieved through participation. One review, for instance, identified 26 controlled studies of personal growth groups that (1) used both pretest and posttest measures, (2) met for at least 10 hours, and (3) had a long-term follow-up (at least one month after termination). Summarizing these methodologically superior studies, the reviewers

concluded that group treatments did result in enduring positive changes, but primarily on self-report questionnaire data and not on behavioral measures (Berman & Zimpfer, 1980). These and other findings suggest that groups are most useful in promoting changes in "sensitivity, feeling management, directionality of motivation, attitudes towards the self, attitudes towards others, and interdependence," but that behavior is more resistant to change (Gibb, 1971, p. 855).

Using Groups to Cure: Cautions

Empirical evidence suggests that group approaches are generally effective—at least as effective as individual treatments and definitely better than no treatment at all. However, this positive appraisal is a qualified one. Although group approaches are often effective, they do not work for everyone or for all types of psychological difficulties.

Premature Terminations   Not everyone who joined the group following the bus accident remained in the group. Four individuals, after the first session, did not return to the group. Several members attended the sessions during the return trip only sporadically. One person, when later asked about the experience, said it did not help at all (Turner, 2000).

Any treatment will be ineffective if the treatment regimen is not followed—if people stop taking their medications, fail to comply with their physician's self-care instructions, or do not attend their group treatment sessions—and the results will likely be disappointing. However, because therapeutic groups are often volunteer associations—individuals can choose to attend or not attend meetings—those who lack commitment to treatment goals tend to attend meetings only sporadically or drop out altogether. Such **premature terminations** are problematic for any therapeutic intervention, but

---

premature termination The withdrawal of a participant from a change-promoting group that occurs before the individual has reached his or her therapeutic goals.

F o c u s 16.2   Cross-cultural Perspectives: Group Approaches Know No Cultural Boundaries

In 2004, a tsunami caused widespread devastation and loss of life in coastal areas of Asia. Given the likelihood of long-term negative psychological effects, school psychologists developed a group-level intervention program designed to help grade-school children in Sri Lanka better understand and express their feelings, identify sources of stress, and develop effective coping strategies (Nastasi et al., 2011). To assist in training in vocational choice in China, American researchers adapted the Hill (1969) Learning through Discussion system for use there by developing instructional materials that taught discussants to define terms, identify key themes and subthemes, and integrate concepts before evaluating or applying results (Conyne et al., 1999). In Israel, therapists worked with both Jewish and Arab students in experiential learning groups based on Yalom's interpersonal psychotherapy procedures. Some groups included both Jews and Arabs, but others were not culturally diverse (Shechtman, Goldberg, & Cariani, 2008). Women in remission from breast cancer were recruited to take part in psycho-educational groups that used cognitive behavior therapy methods to help participants deal with stress and anxiety, as well as improve communication with loved ones. The study was conducted in France, where "patients are not familiar with group approaches" to treatment (Dolbeault et al., 2009, p. 648).

Each of these examples illustrates the utility of group-level approaches for achieving positive social and psychological outcomes. Although psychodynamic methods originated in Western Europe, psycho-educational approaches to group effectiveness have their roots in England's Tavistock traditions, and support groups are primarily an American invention, these methods have been used with considerable success around the world. Their popularity and utility reflects, in part, their compatibility with most cultures' indigenous health-promoting practices. People relied on groups in difficult times long before there were group therapists, facilitators, or T-group trainers (McWhirter et al., 2010).

Each example is also a reminder of the importance of remaining sensitive to cultural differences in values, attitudes, and outlook. This sensitivity is perhaps best expressed in the distinction between emic and etic perspectives, first identified by anthropologist Kenneth Pike (1954). The **etic perspective** is the understanding gained by an outsider of the group, such as the scientist or observer who uses objective methods to study cultures around the world. The etic view examines the basic processes displayed by groups across cultures to test general principles about groups. The **emic perspective**, in contrast, is the equally valid perspective taken by those within the group and within the culture. The emic view examines the kinds of explanations, accounts, and practices that are considered meaningful by the members of the group, given their life experiences and their cultural backgrounds.

Researchers and group practitioners must consider both the etic and emic view when studying groups and using group methods for therapeutic purposes. Therapeutic methods are inevitably determined by the values of the culture where they were developed. Traditional therapeutic procedures—talking with a professional about one's psychological concerns, meeting with others in a group context to develop interpersonal and self-regulatory skills, and dealing with symptoms through medication—are all consistent with Western approaches to health and medicine, but these methods may seem foreign if applied in a different culture. The program used in Sri Lanka, for example, was based on methods used successfully in the United States, but it was modified after extensive analysis of the cultural practices and values of the people of Sri Lanka (Nastasi et al., 2011). Therapists used the Hill (1969) discussion technique in China only after they reviewed the procedure and developed materials that better suited the group-level tendencies of the Chinese. Given the current climate of hostility in Israel, combined with differences in the cultural tendencies of Arabs and Jews, these two groups were joined together into one for the purposes of therapy with considerable care. The groups were conducted by experts with experience working in multicultural groups, and techniques were adapted to minimize the negative impact of a set of cultural practices that warned against revealing vulnerabilities to nonfamily members.

In sum, good research and good practice require an understanding of both etics and emics (Cheung, van de Vijver, & Leong, 2011). The culturally competent researcher and group practitioner "must have a good understanding of the diversity of cultural worldviews and their potential impact on the relationships, behaviors, and willingness to participate in therapeutic group work" (DeLucia-Waack, 2010, p. 97). People the world over share a common desire to maximize their well-being, but how they achieve that goal will depend on where they are in the world.

---

etic perspective The nonmember's (outsider's) view of the group, organization, or culture developed through the application of objective, scientific methods for studying groups.

emic perspective The member's (insider's) view of the group, organization, or culture, grounded in the cultural beliefs, practices, and accounts accepted by the members of the group.

changes in membership are particularly disruptive for therapeutic groups because they create instability in the group's composition and dynamics (MacNair-Semands, 2002). Most premature terminations result from failed expectations about the purposes of the group or from an inadequate match between the group member's goals and the leader's methods. Dropout rates can be minimized by prescreening potential members, providing an initial briefing that describes the group's requirements, limiting conflict during sessions, and making certain that the group atmosphere is supportive, nonevaluative, and non-threatening (Burlingame et al., 2011; Mitchell & Mitchell, 1984).

Casualties   A participant who decides to leave the group before he or she has benefited in any way is a premature termination, or dropout, but a **casualty** is a member who is significantly harmed by the group experience. A casualty might, for example, attempt suicide as a result of the group experience, require individual therapy to correct harm caused by the group, or report continued deteriorations in adjustment over the course of the group experience. Casualties can most often be traced to a particularly negative event in the group. In one study, for example, an individual sought psychiatric treatment immediately after the group attacked her for being overweight:

> She stated that the group was an extremely destructive one for her. The group operated by everybody "ganging up on one another, thirteen to one, and bulldozing them until they were left on the ground panting." She was bitterly attacked by the group and finally dropped out after an attack on her in which she was labeled "a fat Italian mama with a big shiny nose." She was also told that she probably had "a hell of a time getting any man to look at her." (Lieberman et al., 1973, p. 189)

---

casualty An individual whose psychological well-being declines rather than improves as a result of his or her experiences in a change-promoting group.

The number of casualties reported in studies has ranged from a low of none among 94 participants in a human relations training lab followed up after five months (Smith, 1975, 1980) to a high of 8% of the participants in a study of 17 encounter groups (Lieberman et al., 1973). A relatively high casualty rate (18%) was obtained in one study of 50 married couples who participated in marathon encounter groups, but this rate was inflated by the problems the couples were experiencing before entering the group (Doherty, Lester, & Leigh, 1986). No evidence is available concerning the rate of casualties in support groups, but statistics maintained by the National Training Laboratory indicate that 25 individuals who participated in the program prior to 1974 experienced a severe psychological reaction (Back, 1974). This number represented less than 0.2% of the participants.

Overhelping   Joining in a therapeutic group generally yields positive outcomes for participants, but in some cases less is more. If individuals attribute their success in dealing with a problem to the group, and not to themselves, then they become dependent on the group—even if they themselves were the source of the successful coping outcomes. In such cases the group is engaged in *overhelping*—it appears to be rendering aid to the individual, but it is taking credit for success it did not earn (Gilbert & Silvera, 1996).

This criticism has been raised in evaluations of the effectiveness of process debriefings, which were discussed earlier in this chapter (Devilly, Gist, & Cotton, 2006). These interventions are usually enacted immediately following a traumatic event, but too often they use overly standardized methods that do not take into account the characteristics of the clients. Children and elderly people, for example, require a different set of group experiences than do adults, family members, and emergency personnel. Interventions must also be sensitive to each individual's reaction to the event. Some may appreciate the opportunity to interact with others who are coping with a disaster, but others may not respond well to the evocative demands of the group (Foy & Schrock, 2006). Not everyone can share their grief with others, and the continued discussion of the event may only exacerbate their anxieties and emotional reprocessing (Melamed & Wills, 2000). Given what is known about how people cope with trauma, superior benefits would likely be obtained if individuals seek support from their network of friends and family members rather than a too-brief, one-size-fits-all, intervention (McNally, Bryant, & Ehlers, 2003).

The Value of Groups

Groups are not all benefit with no cost. Groups can demand great investments of time and energy from their members. Although groups provide social support, they are also a source of considerable stress for their members. Groups, too, can socialize members in ways that are not healthy and set social identity processes in motion that increase conflict between groups (Forsyth & Elliott, 2000).

The checkered impact of groups, however, in no way detracts from their significance in shaping mental health. Groups help their members define and confirm their values, beliefs, and identities. When individuals are beset by problems and uncertainties, groups offer reassurance, security, support, and assistance. Groups are places where people can learn new social skills and discover things about themselves and others. Groups, too, can produce changes in members when other approaches have failed. Both researchers and mental health professionals who understand groups recognize their healing power, for groups help their members change for the better.

CHAPTER REVIEW

What are some of the ways that groups are used to help their members change?

1. Individuals often turn to groups for help in achieving personal and therapeutic change. As *Lewin's law of change* states, "It is usually easier to change individuals formed into a group than to change any one of them separately" (Lewin, 1951, p. 228).

2. Most change-oriented groups focus either on therapeutic adjustment (*therapy groups*), interpersonal and emotional growth (*interpersonal learning groups*), or overcoming addictions or other life stresses (*support groups*).

3. Therapeutic groups are usually conducted by a mental health professional and focus on psychological problems.

   - In *group psychoanalysis*, the therapist helps members to gain insight into their problems by offering interpretations and working through *transference* effects. Such therapies use a variety of analytic methods drawn from Freud's approach to treatment, including identifying unresolved conflicts.

   - *Gestalt group therapy*, developed by Perls, makes use of experiments, techniques, and extensive role-playing methods to stimulate emotional growth.

   - *Psychodrama*, developed by Moreno, also uses role play and physical activities.

   - In *interpersonal group psychotherapy*, the leader takes advantage of the group's dynamics to help members learn about how they influence others and how others influence them. This method was developed by Yalom.

   - In *cognitive-behavioral therapy groups*, the therapist uses principles derived from learning theory to encourage specific behaviors while extinguishing others. This approach makes use of behavioral methods, including behavioral contracts, modeling, behavior rehearsal, and feedback.

   - *Process debriefing groups* are used to help individuals who have experienced significant trauma cope with the event and are designed to reduce posttraumatic stress disorder (PTSD).

4. Interpersonal learning groups help relatively well-adjusted individuals improve their self-understanding and relationships with others.

- In *training groups*, or *T-groups*, developed by Lewin and his associates, members are encouraged to actively confront and resolve interpersonal issues through unstructured discussions.

- In growth groups, such as *sensitivity training groups* or *encounter groups*, individuals are urged to disclose personal aspects of themselves to others and to provide other members with positive feedback. Humanistic psychologist Rogers was a leader in the development of these groups.

- In *structured learning groups*, members take part in planned exercises that focus on a specific interpersonal problem or skill. Most of these interventions involve a learning cycle that begins with an orienting overview and then moves from experience to discussion to analysis to application. Kolb's *experiential learning theory* assumes individuals learn best through a combination of direct experience, observation, analysis, and action.

5. Support groups often form spontaneously when people combine their energies and efforts in an attempt to cope with or overcome a common problem. These groups tend to be problem-specific, highly interpersonal, communal, autonomous, and perspective-based.

- Many support groups, such as Alcoholics Anonymous (AA), emphasize inspirational testimonials, mutual help, shared similarities, collective encouragement, and changing the member's social networks.

- Studies of online support groups for problems ranging from cancer to sexual abuse to psychological disorders have suggested that these groups provide many of the same resources to members as do face-to-face support groups.

How do groups promote change?

1. A number of *therapeutic factors* operate in groups to promote change. They include hope, universality, observational learning, interpersonal learning, guidance, cohesion, self-disclosure, catharsis, altruism, and insight.

2. Hope and universality: Groups, by providing opportunities to engage in social comparison and mutual support, convince members of the universality of their problems, elevate their levels of hope, and instigate a shared, group-level identity.

3. Social learning: Because groups include multiple individuals, rather than just a single therapist/helper and a single client, they can make use of the sources of interpersonal learning described in Bandura's *social learning theory*.

- Groups facilitate observational learning (modeling of behaviors), interpersonal feedback, and guidance (direct instruction).

- *Coleadership* (two or more leaders are present at all sessions) provides more opportunities for social learning and feedback. Group facilitators, like all group leaders, vary considerably along the directive–nondirective dimension.

4. Group cohesion: Cohesion may be a necessary condition for an effective change-promoting group.

- As in all groups, cohesion can be based on attraction, task commitment, shared identity and emotion, and strong relational bonds.

- Therapeutic groups, like all groups, generally become more cohesive over time as they move through the basic forming-storming-norming-performing-adjourning stages of development identified by Tuckman.

- Kivlighan's work indicates that interventions are more effective when they match the developmental stage of the group.

- Cohesion yields a number of positive consequences for therapeutic groups, including membership retention, improved communication, and increased influence of the group on the individual.

5. Self-disclosure and catharsis: Groups become more intimate as members reveal private information about themselves (*self-disclosure*). When group members vent strong emotions, the resulting *catharsis* may reduce their stress.

6. Altruism and insight: Group members also benefit from the increased self-confidence produced by helping others and by gaining insight about their personal qualities from other group members.

   - People generally prefer individual-level treatment methods, in part because of uncertainty about what the group will reveal to them about themselves.

   - Individuals who have taken part in therapeutic groups rate insight as the most important of the curative factors.

How effective are groups in bringing about change?

1. Most group approaches are effective methods for helping individuals change their thoughts, emotions, and actions, and so qualify as *evidence-based treatments*.

   - Meta-analytic reviews, such as those conducted by Burlingame and his colleagues, indicate group approaches are more effective for certain problems (e.g., social anxiety, addictions) than for others (depression).

   - Although group approaches adopt a variety of methods, studies such as the one conducted by Lieberman, Yalom, and Miles, do not consistently identify one type of group method as superior to another.

   - Individuals who have participated in group-level interventions rate their effectiveness very positively, with one survey indicating that AA was rated as the most effective of all such groups.

2. Group approaches are generally effective, but they do not work for everyone or for all types of psychological problems.

   - The number of individuals who drop out of treatment, *premature terminations*, is higher in group treatments compared to individual treatment.

   - A small fraction of participants in groups experiences significant negative reactions to the experience and so are considered psychological *casualties*.

   - Interventions are more effective when they are consistent with both the *emic perspective* and *etic perspective* of a particular cultural context.

RESOURCES

Chapter Case: The Bus Group

- "Group Treatment of Trauma Survivors Following a Fatal Bus Accident: Integrating Theory and Practice" by Andrew L. Turner (2000) details the methods used to help college students recover from a tragic bus accident that occurred during a semester-abroad program.

Group Approaches to Changes

- *The Oxford Handbook of Group Counseling*, edited by Robert K. Conyne (2010), contains 31 chapters dealing with all types of change-focused groups with entire sections devoted to change processes, empirical analyses of group effectiveness, measurement issues, leadership, and applications in specific contexts.

- *Psychological Effects of Catastrophic Disasters: Group Approaches to Treatment*, edited by Leon A. Schein, Henry I. Spitz, Gary M. Burlingame, and Philip R. Muskin, with Shannon Vargo (2006), is a comprehensive compendium of group-based methods of dealing with traumatic events.

- *Understanding Self-help/mutual Aid: Experiential Learning in the Commons* by Thomasina Jo Borkman (1999) examines the sociological bases of support groups, and includes in-depth case analyses of two such groups (Caring Group on Stuttering and AA).

Therapeutic Factors in Groups

- "Group Process and Group Psychotherapy: Social Psychological Foundations of Change in Therapeutic Groups" by Donelson R. Forsyth (2010b) provides a general overview of the social psychological processes operating in group approaches to treatment.

- *The Theory and Practice of Group Psychotherapy* (5th ed.) by Irvin D. Yalom with Molyn Leszcz (2005) describes cases, theories, and syntheses of available research on Yalom's basic principles of interpersonal group therapy that stress the therapeutic factors common to all group approaches to change.

- *Group Development in Practice: Guidance for Clinicians and Researchers on Stages and Dynamics of Change* by Virginia Brabender and April Fallon (2009) reviews in detail previous theories pertaining to group development and identifies ways that therapists can both orchestrate, and adjust to, the inevitable changes that occur in groups over time.

Group Effectiveness

- "Evidence Bases for Group Practice" by Sally H. Barlow (2010) reviews the evidence-based movement in group approaches to health and well-being, providing both historical background factors as well as emerging scientific procedures and standards.

- "Small Group Treatment: Evidence for Effectiveness and Mechanisms of Change" by Gary Burlingame, K. Roy MacKenzie, and Berhard Strauss (2004) reviews 107 studies and 14 meta-analyses of the use of group approaches to treat six disorders and offers scientifically sound conclusions about the efficacy of group psychotherapy.

CHAPTER

Crowds and Collectives

CHAPTER OVERVIEW

A detailed study of groups would be incomplete if it did not consider the dynamics of larger social collectives. For centuries people have wondered at the seemingly inexplicable actions that people undertake when part of a large mass of humanity. Juries, teams, squads, clubs, and cults are all intriguing, but so are riots and rumors; crowds and crazes; and mobs and movements.

- What is collective behavior?
- What theories explain collective behavior?
- How different are collectives from other types of groups?

CHAPTER OUTLINE

Collectives: Forms and Features
- *What Are Collectives?*
- *Gatherings*
- *Crowds*
- *Mobs*
- *Panics*
- *Collective Movements*
- *Social Movements*

Collective Dynamics
- *Contagion*
- *Convergence*
- *Deindividuation*
- *Emergent Norms*
- *Social Identity*

Collectives Are Groups
- *The Myth of the Madding Crowd*
- *Studying Groups and Collectives*
- *Chapter Review*
- *Resources*

Arab Spring: Social Movement or Mob Rule?

The people of Egypt had suffered for too long. Inflation was driving up the cost of living, people were out of work, and those who did have jobs were paid too little. They could have sought a remedy through political action, but their basic civil rights were severely curtailed. Years before, the government had enacted a set of emergency procedures to stabilize the country—censorship, curfew, enhanced police power—but had never relaxed them. The police and other governmental agencies repressed dissent in any form. Anyone who sought to speak out against the ruling party, the National Democrats, and their leader, Hosni Mubarak, risked harassment, imprisonment, or death.

In January 2011, this smoldering state of discontent transformed into an active revolution in what has been called the Arab Spring or the Arab Revolution. Only a month before, the citizens of Tunisia had forced their country's president to resign through a series of demonstrations and protests. Possibly heartened by that success, millions of Egypt's citizens began to protest against Mubarak and his government through demonstrations, marches, labor strikes, and other forms of civil disobedience. These actions occurred across the country, but were centered in the nation's capital, Cairo, at Tahrir Square (Liberation Square). The citizens were, by law, not permitted to assemble, but on January 25, thousands converged on the square and refused to leave. Others soon joined them, with numbers reaching well above 100,000. The crowd called for the resignation of Mubarak and free elections with multiple candidates.

By January 28th, Tahrir Square had become "a sort of utopian mini-state" (Khalil, 2011, p. 245). Many different kinds of people mixed together in the square—men and women, young and old, well-to-do and poor—but all were united by their opposition to Mubarak. The mass of protestors spontaneously organized their political actions, including chants, demonstrations, and protests, as well as security, entertainment, and a supply system. They set up two wireless networks to facilitate communication and used Facebook to coordinate their activities.

Protest in a totalitarian regime, however, is dangerous. Most of the activists demonstrated peacefully, but they often encountered violent opposition; at least 800 people were killed during the 18 days of the uprising. The police brutality was indisputable: Video uploaded to Facebook and YouTube shared with a horrified world footage of police in riot gear severely beating and kicking unarmed protestors. Groups of violent men, labeled "thugs" by the local Egyptians, roamed the streets and sometimes the square, brutally beating protestors and broadcasters. On February 2nd, violence intensified when men armed with clubs, riding horses and camels, attacked the square, touching off a night of violence. The attack, however, may have worked to further solidify the protesters, hardening their resolve (Khalil, 2011).

On February 10th, the protest reached its climax. The relentless pressure of the protestors and the international community prompted Mubarak to announce his decision to not seek reelection. This concession, however, did not placate the April Spring protesters: They wanted him removed from office immediately. Faced with continuing bloodshed and instability, the Egyptian military forcibly removed Mubarak from office on February 11th and set up a provisional government.

The science of group dynamics is based on one core assumption: People act collectively. Much of this collective action occurs in relatively small groups, and the field of group dynamics (and this book as well) has concentrated on such groups—cliques, work squads, juries, sports teams, corporate boards, crews, bands of explorers, and so on. But individuals also—sometimes unwittingly and sometimes purposely—can become members of much larger groups. Some of these collectives, like the gathering of protesters at Tahrir Square, are concentrated in a specific location. Others, however, occur when widely dispersed individuals engage in markedly similar actions, as when vast numbers of Egyptian citizens throughout the country shifted from complacency to rebellion. Most collectives do not behave in odd, atypical ways. Each day, thousands upon thousands of collectives form and disband around the world and most help rather than hurt their members. But collectives are, at their core, groups, and, like any other group, they can do surprising things, including starting revolutions.

This chapter describes collectives, explains their dynamics, and tries to repair their reputation.

It begins by first describing the wide variety of collectives, for they can range from the accidental convergences of unrelated individuals to groups with faithful followers who remain members for many years. The chapter then considers both classic and contemporary theoretical analyses of collective behavior, beginning with the provocative arguments presented by Gustave Le Bon (1895/1960) in his book *The Crowd* and ending with new theories that strive to correct common misconceptions about these extraordinary forms of human association.

COLLECTIVES: FORMS AND FEATURES

Just as humans have lived in groups for all time, so have they also joined together with others in much larger gatherings. For as long as anyone can remember, religious devotees have joined together at the foot of Mount Kailash in Tibet, for the mountain is considered sacred by five religions. As many as 50,000 spectators gathered in the Roman Colosseum to watch exhibitions and gladiatorial competitions. In 1096, thousands upon thousands of Europeans, urged on by Pope Urban II, marched to Jerusalem to "free the Holy Land from the pagans." And even in ancient times, some of these collectives acted in unexpected ways. For example, the first entry in historian Hilary Evans and sociologist Robert Bartholomew's (2009) encyclopedia of extraordinary social behavior is the *Abdera Outbreak*, which occurred in the third century BC in Abdera, Greece. The populace developed an unusual fondness for the play *Andromeda* by Euripides and took to reciting lines from the play throughout the day and night, with people dressing to fit particular roles. Fast-forwarding to more modern times, Evans and Bartholomew end their listing with the *Zoot suit riots* of 1942 and 1943. Mobs of U.S. naval personnel stationed in Los Angeles, California, roamed through the city streets in search of Mexican Americans wearing zoot suits—a style of clothes featuring long suit coats and pleated trousers with tight cuffs, popular among men of the Mexican-American community. Once located, the "zooters" were surrounded, bullied, and in some cases beaten. The city ended the violence by banning zoot suits. Table 17.1 lists several other examples of recent collectives.

As these historical examples reveal, people not only join with others in small groups but also in very large ones, and the impact of these groups on their members can be large as well. This section considers the forms these collectives can take—the different types of collectives that researchers have identified—and their features—the qualities that are typical of these unique types of social aggregates.

What Are Collectives?

A **collective** is a relatively large group of people who display similarities in actions and outlook. Primary and social groups, such as families, best friends, clubs, juries, and work crews, are not collectives, for they are too small, too structured, and their membership too well-defined and stable. Neither are they categories, which include individuals who share some distinguishing quality in common such as nationality or eye color. The members of collectives, instead, are joined by some type of common interest or action. The men and women who gathered at Tahrir Square, for example, were unified by their desire to create social change, and that shared focus created commonalities in their thoughts, actions, and emotions (Martti, 2008).

The Characteristics of Collectives Collectives, like groups in general, vary considerably in size, duration, form, and function. They tend to be large, but some collectives are huge—as when millions of individuals respond similarly to some

---

collective A relatively large aggregation of people who are responding in a similar way to an event or situation, including people who all occupy the same location (a crowd), as well as mass phenomena in which individuals are dispersed across a wide area (collective movements).

TABLE 17.1 Examples of Collectives from the Last Century

Year	Event
1919	Reform movements, including the Women's Christian Temperance Union, the Prohibition Party, and the Anti-Saloon League, succeed in their efforts to ban alcoholic beverages in the United States. The ban's side effects include the rise of organized crime and willful violation of the law by citizens, and it is repealed in 1933.
1938	On Halloween night, Orson Welles broadcasts the radio program *The War of the Worlds*. Some listeners believe the dramatization is a real news broadcast, and react by warning relatives, taking defensive precautions, contemplating suicide, and fleeing from the invaded areas. The effect of the broadcast is exaggerated by the media, however.
1943	The citizens of Denmark, fearing that Germany would seize and kill its Jewish citizens, spontaneously organize the transportation of nearly all Jews to safety in Sweden (Abrahamsen, 1987).
1943	Mrs. Mullane, a contestant on a radio program, was told to collect pennies as a service to the nation's war effort. The announcer suggested that listeners should send Mrs. Mullane a penny and gave her address on the air. Within weeks, she received more than 200,000 letters and well over 300,000 pennies.
1954	Rumors that windshields were being damaged by nuclear fallout begin circulating in the Seattle, Washington, area. The rumors escalate into a mild mass hysteria as the media devote much attention to the issue, residents jam police telephone lines reporting damage, and civic groups demand government intervention. Subsequent investigation reveals that no damage at all has occurred (Medalia & Larsen, 1958).
1958	Wham-O Manufacturing Company begins selling a toy circular hoop made of plastic under the product name Hula-Hoop. Millions are sold within a four-month period, but the hoops' popularity ends abruptly. Some consider the hula-hoop to be the "greatest fad of the 20th century" (Evans & Bartholomew, 2009, p. 249).
1962	Sixty–two persons working in a manufacturing plant experience nausea, pain, disorientation, and muscular weakness; some collapse. Physicians can find no evidence of any physical illness. They conclude the episode to be completely due to psychological factors (Kerckhoff, Back, & Miller, 1965).
1970	The Brazilian soccer team defeats the Italian team in the World Cup Tournament, setting off a series of wild celebrations. Tragically, more than 100 people die and many more are injured by fireworks, brawls, automobile accidents, and shootings.
1979	A crowd in Cincinnati, waiting for a concert by the rock group The Who, panics when the ticket takers at the doors are unable to keep pace with the flow of the crowd into the arena. Eleven persons are killed and many others are injured.
2008	The prank known as "rickrolling" spreads across the Internet. When a viewer clicks a link that promises content on a particular topic, he or she is instead taken to a site that shows a video of British singer Rick Astley's 1987 song "Never Gonna Give You Up."
2011	An audience of 114,804, the largest number of spectators in the modern college football era, assembles on September 10 at Michigan Stadium in Ann Arbor to watch the University of Michigan team play rivals Notre Dame.
2012	On the ninth day of the month of hajj, at noon, more than two million people gather on the Plain of Arafat in Saudi Arabia, the site of the prophet Mohammad's final sermon—arguably the largest gathering of people to assemble in one place at any time in history.

fashion craze. In some cases, all the members of a collective are together in one place, and so they "can monitor each other by being visible to or within earshot of one another" (Snow & Oliver, 1995, p. 572). Some collectives, in contrast, involve individuals who are dispersed across great distances. All collectives, however, are distinguished by their members' "common or concerted" form of behavior or reaction (McPhail, 1991, p. 159). Members of a crowd, for example, may move in the same direction or perform the same general types of behaviors. Members of collective movements, although not interacting in face-to-face settings, act in similar ways to achieve a common purpose. They are moving in the same direction, psychologically and socially, even though they are dispersed.

Collectives also vary in their duration and cohesion. Some are planned groups created for a specific purpose, but most collectives result from the press of circumstances or through self-organizing dynamics (Arrow et al., 2000). They tend to be open groups, for they have no standards for defining membership and do not adopt operational strategies. In consequence, the relationships between members are more superficial and impersonal than those that link members of smaller groups. If a typical group is two or more individuals who are connected to one another by and within interpersonal relationships, a typical collective is a large number of individuals who are connected by similarity in action and outlook rather than by close, intimate relationships. Collectives, too, are by reputation more unconventional than other groups. They tend to exist outside of traditional forms of social structures and institutions, and, as a result, their members sometimes engage in atypical, unruly, unconventional, or even aberrant behaviors. Collectives often do surprising things (R. H. Turner, 2001a).

Types of Collectives   The diversity of collectives is so great that no single classification scheme is sufficient to categorize their many forms. But recognizing that any classification scheme will fail to do justice to their variety and complexity, Figure 17.1 distinguishes among gatherings, crowds, and collective movements. Gatherings include audiences and queues; they are relatively well-organized collectives, although they can transform from gatherings into crowds quickly. Crowds include various types of temporary assemblages, such as street crowds, mobs, riots, and panics. Sociologist Neil J. Smelser (1962), in his analyses of collective behavior, calls crowds "collective outbursts," for they can come into existence rapidly but often fade away just as quickly. Collective movements (or mass movements), he suggested, emerge over longer periods of time and can influence widely dispersed individuals. Collective movements include the diffusion of ideas and opinions throughout a populace—people passing rumors from one to another, for example, are engaged in collective behavior, as are those who change their preferences and practices to match some passing trend, fad, or craze. Social movements, in contrast, are more deliberate—and often more organized—attempts to achieve political, social, and economic reform. The following sections examine each of these types of collectives in more detail.

Gatherings

Gatherings combine aspects of smaller groups with qualities found in larger, more amorphous, crowds. Congregations listening to a sermon, wedding guests at the reception, audiences in a theater, and ticket-holders waiting patiently in line for admission to a baseball park have all deliberately assembled together for an express purpose; like small groups, they have boundaries, goals, and relatively clear structures that define how members should act. But, like crowds, the gathering's longevity is very limited, and individuals are linked by a common focus and not by their relations to one another.

Audiences   A gathering of individuals in a particular area to observe some event or activity is called an **audience** (or *conventional crowd*). Unlike a crowd

---

audience A gathering of onlookers who observe some performance, event, or activity; audiences tend to be conventional in behavior, and they disperse when the event they are watching concludes.

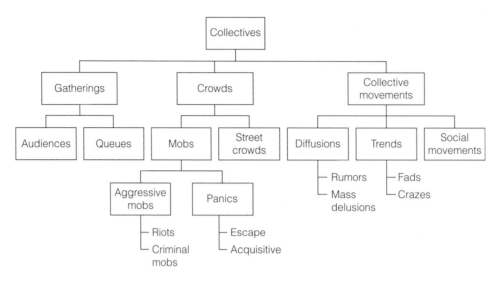

FIGURE 17.1 A classification of collectives.
SOURCE: © Cengage Learning 2014

that forms spontaneously when some event creates a shared focus, individuals join audiences deliberately, and they are bound more tightly by social conventions that dictate their location and movements (Blumer, 1946). They enter the focal area via aisles or pathways and occupy locations that are determined by seating arrangements or by custom. While observing, they may perform a variety of behaviors, including clapping, cheering, shouting, or questioning, but these actions are usually in accord with the norms of the particular setting. Moreover, when the event or performance has ended, the audience disperses in an orderly fashion (Hollingworth, 1935).

Audiences, although relatively staid collectives, nonetheless exert considerable social pressure on their members. Audience members expect each other to abide by the norms of the setting, and those who fail to do so—say, by speaking too loudly, using a cell phone, or otherwise flaunting the unspoken rules of the situation—put themselves at risk for a social rebuke (Goffman, 1971). Audience members also tend to act in relatively synchronized fashion—clapping, laughing, and exiting the situation in unison. Laughter, for example, is highly contagious within an audience: People are thirty times more likely to laugh when with others than when alone (Provine, 2004).

Queues An assemblage of people awaiting their turn—a **queue**—is a unique type of gathering. *Queue* comes from the French word for *a braid of hair* and so pays etymological homage to the queue's most common shape—a relatively straight line. But some settings, such as theme parks, lobbies, and registration offices, shape the queue into a zigzag pattern through the use of stanchions and ropes. Other establishments create dispersed queues by assigning queuers a number and then summoning them through a beeper or announcement when it is their turn. Queues can also be segmented into subgroups that are permitted to enter together, as when passengers board a plane in groups based on seat assignment. Some queues, too, are not at all linear, as when those waiting to board a bus or to enter a crowded concert venue move in a relatively unregulated way toward the entryway.

_____

queue A line, file, or set of people who are waiting for some service, commodity, or opportunity.

Members of a queue, like those in an audience, will probably never meet again. But also like an audience, those in a queue have joined deliberately to achieve a particular goal, and thus, as members of the collective, they are bound by certain norms of behavior (Mann, 1969, 1970). Queues are an interference, for they prevent people from immediately achieving their goal of acquiring tickets, services, or other commodities, but they also protect people from late-arriving competitors for these commodities. As social psychologist Stanley Milgram and his colleagues explain:

> As in the case of most social arrangements, people defer to the restraints of the form, but they are also its beneficiary. The queue thus constitutes a classic illustration of how individuals create social order, on the basis of a rudimentary principle of equity, in a situation that could otherwise degenerate into chaos. (Milgram et al., 1986, p. 683)

Social Order in Queues What prevents the queue from breaking down into a disorderly crowd? Milgram noted that in addition to environmental supports, such as ushers and ropes, queues are also protected by norms of civility and justice. People in many cultures implicitly recognize the basic fairness of the principle "first come, first served" (or "first in, first out") which the queue protects (Zhou & Soman, 2008). When members join the queue, they accept its rules, and even though the group will disband once it serves its purpose, members conform to its norms and enforce them as needed (Miller, 2001).

Milgram studied queues by having both male and female accomplices break into 129 lines waiting outside ticket offices and the like in New York City. Working either alone or in pairs, the accomplices would simply say, "Excuse me, I'd like to get in here," and then insert themselves in the line. In an attempt to determine who would be most likely to enforce the norm, Milgram also included either one or two passive confederates in some of the queues he studied. These individuals, who were planted in the line in advance, stood directly behind the point of intrusion (Milgram et al., 1986).

Objections occurred in nearly half of the lines studied. In a few cases (10.1%), queuers used physical action, such as a tap on the shoulder or a push. In 21.7% of the lines, the reaction was verbal, such as "No way! The line's back there. We've all been waiting and have trains to catch" or "Excuse me, it's a line." In another 14.7% of the lines, queuers used dirty looks, staring, and hostile gestures to object to the intrusion nonverbally. Objections were also more prevalent when two persons broke into the line rather than one, and they were least prevalent when two confederates separated the intruders from the other queuers. Overall, 73.3% of the complaints came from people standing behind the point of intrusion rather than from people standing in front of the intrusion.

Those who break into queues are not always socially condemned. If they appear to be joining someone who is holding a place for them in line or if they join a line near the rear where the tail's end is less well defined, then they are less likely to encounter resistance (Schmitt, Dubé, & Leclerc, 1992). Condemnation is swifter, however, if those in line believe that the line jumper, by inserting himself or herself into the line, may be increasing the chance that they will be disadvantaged in some way—say, by failing to gain admission or having to accept a lower-quality seating position (Helweg-Larsen & LoMonaco, 2008).

Crowds

Crowds tend to spring up, unexpectedly and spontaneously, when individuals who happen to be located in the same general vicinity share a common experience. Variously labeled *street crowds* or *public crowds*, these crowds form in public or semipublic places and are made up of people who are

---

crowd A gathering of individuals, usually in a public place, who are present in the same general vicinity and share a common focus.

strangers to one another—except for the clusters of intact groups that they enfold.

Crowd Formation   Individuals who are sitting on benches in a park, walking along a city sidewalk, or waiting for a bus may all occupy a common location, but they do not become a crowd unless something happens—a fire, a car collision, or street performance, for example—to create a common focus of attention (Milgram & Toch, 1969). Milgram and his colleagues examined this process by creating, experimentally, crowds on a street in New York City. On two winter afternoons in 1968, they had confederates stop in the middle of the sidewalk and stare, in rapt attention, at the sixth floor of a nearby building. They would remain in place as passersby flowed around them, and the researchers recorded—from that very same window of the nearby building—how many stopped. They selected a busy street for their study, for an average of 50 people passed by during any given observation period. And they varied the number of people who seeded the group. In some conditions just one person stood staring up, but other conditions included as many as 15 confederates.

How many would be drawn by the crowd, and how many would resist? When they counted the number of people who actually stopped walking and stood with the group, taking up the collective stare, they discovered that more and more people joined in as the stimulus crowd of confederates grew larger. Only 4% of the passersby joined a single starer, but 40% stopped in their tracks and joined the large crowd—swelling the group in size from 15 to about 35 people (see Figure 17.2). However, if a less stringent criterion for a crowd was used—people needed only to share the same focus of attention—then even a single individual was capable of influencing 42% of the passersby to look up. The crowd of 15 influenced even more—86% of the passersby also looked up (Milgram, Bickman, & Berkowitz, 1969). The crowds may have grown larger still, but for two factors. First, the confederates dispersed in different directions after one minute, and when they left the crowd usually dispersed quickly. Second, since there was nothing interesting to observe, these groups could not hold members' interest. When people realized there was nothing to see, they went on their way.

Milgram's study suggests that people, given their natural sociality, too easily fall under the influence of a crowd. Milgram and his colleagues, however, questioned this conclusion. Although there was nothing to be gained by joining the

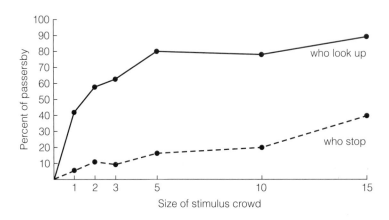

FIGURE 17.2   The mean percentage of people who looked up or stopped when they passed a single person or a group of 2, 3, 5, 10, or 15 people looking up at a building.

SOURCE: From "Note on the Drawing Power of Crowds of Different Size," by S. Milgram, L. Bickman, & L. Berkowitz, *Journal of Personality and Social Psychology, 13,* 1969. Copyright 1969 by the American Psychological Association.

crowds they created, the passersby did not know that; they naturally assumed that, "all other things being equal, the larger the crowd the more likely its members are attending to a matter of interest" (1969, pp. 81–82). Crowds, then, serve as signals to seek out information—in most cases what is of interest to those in the crowd will also be of interest to those who are outside of it.

Crowd Structure and Action Although such crowds are often short-lived, even these fleeting collectives possess a rudimentary social structure. Their boundaries are relatively permeable at the edges of the crowd where individuals are allowed to enter and exit freely, but permeability diminishes as one moves nearer the center of the crowd. Also, roles, status hierarchies, and other group structures may not be very evident in such crowds, but close probing usually reveals some underlying structure. For example, they usually take on one of two distinctive shapes—*arcs* (half-circles with all members facing some focal point) and *rings* (full circles). The focal point is known as a *crowd crystal*—one or more individuals who, by drawing attention to themselves or some event, prompt others to join them (Canetti, 1962). Evidence also indicates that those who occupy central positions in crowds are likely to be more actively involved in the experience than those who are content to remain on the fringes (Milgram & Toch, 1969).

Consistencies in action parallel these consistencies in structure. Sociologist Clark McPhail and his colleagues, after observing all kinds of public gatherings, identified a number of elementary behaviors common to such groups (McPhail, 1991, 2006, 2008; Tucker, Schweingruber & McPhail, 1999). Their listing includes:

- *Movement:* Actions taken in common by group members, such as clustering, queueing, surging, marching, jogging, and running.

- *Positioning:* The stance assumed by members in the space, including sitting, standing, jumping, bowing, and kneeling.

- *Manipulation:* Alteration of objects in the setting, such as throwing or moving objects.

- *Gesticulation:* Gesturing, such as saluting and signaling (e.g., the raised middle finger, power fist).

- *Verbalization:* Communicating through language forms, such as chanting, singing, praying, reciting, or pledging.

- *Vocalization:* Communicating with paralinguistic sounds, such as ooh-ing and ahh-ing, cheering, booing, whistling, laughing, or wailing.

- *Orientation:* Moving into a particular formation within the space, such as clustering, arcing, ringing, gazing, facing, or vigiling.

Mobs

When a gathering of people—a crowd, an audience, or even a queue—becomes emotionally charged, the collective can become a **mob**. Mobs tend to form when some event, such as a crime, a catastrophe, or a controversial action, evokes the same kind of affect and action in a substantial number of people. The hallmark of the mob is its emotion (Lofland, 1981). Early accounts of mobs argued that individuals in mobs were so overwhelmed by their emotions that they could no longer control their actions. Unless the situation is diffused, the mob becomes volatile, unpredictable, and capable of violent action. Mobs, as their name implies, are crowds that are in motion—they are *mobile*, with members moving together from one location to another, massing in a single location, or just milling about in unpatterned ways (Hughes, 2003).

Celebratory Mobs Mobs, even though they stimulate their members' emotions, are not necessarily irrational, nor are they necessarily violent. When teammates celebrate a victory, partiers parade in the streets of New Orleans during Mardi Gras, or

---

mob A disorderly, emotionally charged crowd; mobs tend to form when some event, such as a crime, a catastrophe, or a controversial action, evokes the same kind of affect and action in a substantial number of people.

patriots celebrate the end of a conflict, the members of a mob share positive emotions—joy, jubilation, and exhilaration—in a carnival-like atmosphere (Vider, 2004). Supporters of the winning team in a sports competition, for example, frequently gather in small mobs to express their happiness over the team's victory: cheering and shouting, hugging and gesturing to one another, waving the school banner or flag, and dancing. The displays of emotion are particularly robust in specific areas where fans congregate, suggesting they serve to bolster the celebrants' identification with the team. These after-victory rituals seem to be more theatrical than unguarded expressions of positive affect (Aveni, 1977; Snow, Zurcher, & Peters, 1981).

Flash mobs, too, tend to be emotionally positive crowds—although they are too contrived to be considered true mobs. Flash mobs are large groups of people who gather together, at a particular place and time, to perform some sort of pointless, obscure, or puzzling behavior before quickly dissembling. Most flash mobs are recreational, in that they are not intended to make any type of political statement or to significantly disrupt other social activities. Rather, they are usually harmless or playful group displays, such as dancing, chanting, or singing. In most cases these mobs are orchestrated through the use of communication technologies, including e-mail, instant messaging, and postings at Internet sites, and so participants are likely linked via social networks; they are not complete strangers to one another. Flash mobs are thought to have begun in New York City, but have been observed in public places throughout the world (Gore, 2010; Lemos, 2010).

Aggressive Mobs The night that Mubarak was forced from office, the crowds of people massed at Tahrir Square celebrated their victory with unreserved jubilation. But, mixed in with these celebratory mobs, were more malevolent ones. One of these mobs attacked and sexually assaulted a female reporter for a Western news agency. The mob of men beat her with sticks and poles, tore out her hair, ripped off her clothing, and assaulted her sexually until a group of Egyptian women formed a protective barrier around her (Lara Logan breaks silence, 2011).

Aggressive mobs engage in violent, criminal behaviors. Whereas the emotion of celebratory mobs is positive, the aggressive mob's dominant emotion is anger. These groups engage in a variety of unlawful actions, including destruction of property, looting, arson, assault, and rape. Their attacks on their victims are generally termed *mobbing*.

The *lynch mob* is an example of such a collective. White people in the southern areas of the United States joined together to form these mobs that attacked and killed African Americans, often by hanging. The first documented lynch mob occurred in 1882, but, by 1950, lynch mobs had killed thousands (Mullen, 1986; Tolnay & Beck, 1996). *Hooligans* are also examples of violent mobs. Hooligans are groups of violent sports fans and are usually associated with European football (soccer) teams. These mobs of fans, often intoxicated, mill about in the streets and pubs around the stadiums, attacking fans who support the opposing team (Braun & Vliegenthart, 2008).

Riots Riots can be construed as mobs on a much larger scale. They often begin when a relatively peaceful crowd is transformed by a negative experience into a violent mob. For example, on the final night of the 1999 Woodstock music festival, an antiviolence group named PAX asked the audience to light candles as an expression of unity. The concertgoers instead used the candles to burn down the outdoor venue. At sporting events, the violence of localized mobs sometimes diffuses through a much

---

flash mob A group, often recruited through social networks of peer-to-peer contacts or using computer-based technologies (e.g., cell phones, text messaging), that gathers at a particular place and time to perform some sort of innocuous behavior before quickly dissembling.

---

riot A large and often widely dispersed crowd whose wanton and unrestrained behavior violates rules of civil and legal authority (e.g., harassment, looting, destruction of property, assault, violence).

larger portion of the spectators, resulting in large-scale hostility, destruction, and harm. In Europe and South America, for example, riots during soccer matches frequently result in substantial injuries and death.

In other cases, riots are an expression of unrest and protest in the general population. In 1921, for example, Whites in Tulsa, Oklahoma, attacked the highly successful Black business community of Greenwood. Hundreds were killed, and 35 city blocks of Black-owned businesses were destroyed. In 1980 and 1992, residents of Liberty City, Florida, and Los Angeles, California, rioted when police officers charged with brutality were found not guilty. In 2011, riots occurred in a number of cities in England, including London. Analysis of these outbursts suggests that confrontations between police and local residents, who were already angered by police actions and substantial reductions in social services, resulted in open intergroup conflict (Reicher & Stott, 2011). Riots are also sometimes motivated by a collective desire to loot and steal. For example, in 1969, when the police force of Montreal went on strike for 17 hours, mayhem broke out all over the city. Professional crimes skyrocketed, but the noncriminal population also ran amok. A heterogeneous crowd, including impoverished, wealthy, and middle-class people, rampaged along the central business corridor, looting and vandalizing (Clark, 1969).

Panics

Some mobs are charged with a different set of emotions than anger; they are fearful, anxious, and frightened. These mobs have *panicked*, for they are either desperately seeking out a limited resource that they fear will run out (*acquisitive panics*) or, and more typically, fleeing from an aversive situation (*escape panics*).

Acquisitive Panics When large numbers of people face a situation of scarcity, their desire to acquire the resource sometimes triggers anxiety and a loss of self-regulation. Queues, for example, can break down, and individuals may be so intent on acquiring the scarce commodity that they act with callous disregard for others' well-being. Acquisitive panics are generally associated with consumer settings, when individuals are attempting to purchase scarce products or those that are priced below their value. For example, a number of retailers in the United States launch their winter holiday consumer season on the Friday following the national holiday Thanksgiving Day. This event, called "Black Friday," is sometimes marked by incidents of panic, as shoppers arrive at the retailers well before the scheduled opening and then crowd into the facility to make their purchase. When researchers stationed observers outside the doors of 21 large retailers in the early morning of Black Friday, in 80% of the locations, large crowds of 50 or more shoppers formed before the stores opened for business. At all the locations, the initial opening triggered a period of panic and crowd turbulence, and at 14% of the locations, the crowd was so large that it continued to push to gain entry for more than 30 minutes. Some of the shoppers in the group appeared to be excited by the situation, but many showed evidence of anxiety, irritability, frustration, and aggravation (Simpson et al., 2011).

Escape Panics When large numbers of people face danger, their desire to escape can result in a further decline of social coordination of the group's movement. Groups may react calmly during a catastrophe, such as a fire, flood, or earthquake, but if the situation is seen as very dangerous and the escape routes are limited, a crowd can become a panicked mob (Strauss, 1944). Members, fearing personal harm or injury, struggle to escape both from the situation and from the crowd itself:

> The individual breaks away and wants to escape from it because the crowd, as a whole, is endangered. But because he is still stuck in it, he must attack it…. The more fiercely each man "fights for his life," the clearer it becomes he is fighting against all the others who hem him in. They stand there like chairs, balustrades, closed doors, but different from these in that they are alive and hostile. (Canetti, 1962, pp. 26–27)

Panics often result in a staggering loss of life. In 1903, for example, a panic at Chicago's Iroquois Theater killed nearly 600 people. When a small fire broke out backstage, the management tried to calm the audience. But when the house lights when out and the fire was visible behind the stage, the crowd stampeded for the exits. Some were burned, and others died by jumping from the fire escapes to the pavement, but many more were killed as fleeing patrons trampled them. One observer described the panic this way:

> In places on the stairways, particularly where a turn caused a jam, bodies were piled seven or eight feet deep. Firemen and police confronted a sickening task in disentangling them. An occasional living person was found in the heaps, but most of these were terribly injured. The heel prints on the dead faces mutely testified to the cruel fact that human animals stricken in terror are as mad and ruthless as stampeding cattle. Many bodies had the clothes torn from them, and some had the flesh trodden from their bones. (Foy & Harlow, 1928/1956)

Panics as Queue Failures   As noted earlier in the chapter, queues serve to maintain social order and public safety, and their function becomes particularly clear when queues collapse into disorganized crowds. Such a queue failure occurred in 1979 in a gathering of concertgoers waiting to gain admission to a concert by the rock band The Who in Cincinnati. Many fans had general admission tickets rather than assigned seating. So, in order to get a spot near the stage, fans had come to the venue early so they could enter as soon as the doors opened. However, the queue was disorganized—no lines had formed, and when the doors opened, the group of 8,000 individuals pushed forward as a mass. The results were deadly. The back of the group moved faster than the front, and the flow jammed near the clogged doors. People were literally swept off their feet by the surge, and some slipped to the concrete floor. Those around them tried to pull them back to their feet, but the overcrowded

mass of people pushed on toward the open doors. As the rear of the crowd continued to push forward, the crowd swept past those who had fallen, and they were trampled underfoot. Eleven people were killed.

The group waiting for the Who concert was initially a queue—a disorganized queue, but a queue nonetheless. When the venue failed to open the doors on time, it is likely that a *queueing effect* occurred. Members of delayed queues tend to inch forward, creating the illusion of progress, but also compression of the crowd (Helbing & Mukerji, 2012). When the doors opened, the queue surged forward to release the pressure and jammed. Although the news media described the crowd as a drug-crazed stampede bent on storming into the concert, police interviews with survivors indicated that the crowd members in the center of the crush were trying to flee from the dangerous overcrowding rather than to get into the concert. Some individuals in the crowd were struggling to get out of danger, but others were Good Samaritans who helped the injured (Johnson, 1987).

Many municipalities and promoters, to prevent a repeat of this type of tragedy, have banned general admission seating: All tickets are for specific seats within the venue. However, in places where general admission seating is permitted, norms often develop to create queues to prevent crowding. Before shows by the band U2 in the United States, for example, fans holding general admission tickets arrive at the venue hours (or even days) before the doors open. They organize their wait, however, in a fairly elaborate, normative system, in which each person's order in the line is recorded by self-appointed "line Nazis." Line breaking is not tolerated, although friends are permitted to hold places for late-arriving friends, provided that others nearby in the line are fully informed about the later arrival of additional queue members. In general, more committed fans are more adamant about maintaining the queue's norms (Helweg-Larsen & LoManaco, 2008).

Crowd Management   Experimental simulations of panicked crowds suggest that individuals who must take turns exiting from a dangerous situation are most likely to panic when they believe that the time available to escape is limited and when they are fearful of the consequences of a failure to escape (Kelley et al., 1965; Mintz, 1951). Larger groups, even if given more time to effect their escape, are also more likely to panic than smaller ones (Chertkoff, Kushigian, & McCool, 1996). If a large group can be split up into smaller groups that are led separately to exits, the time taken to exit is reduced, but groups usually are unable to effect this level of control over their movements during a panic (Sugiman & Misumi, 1988). Other steps that can be taken to protect people when in crowds in public places are discussed in Focus 17.1.

Collective Movements

Not all collective phenomena transpire at close distances. In some cases, individuals who are dispersed may act and react in similar and often atypical ways. Such curious phenomena are variously termed **collective movements**, *mass movements*, or *dispersed collective behavior*, although this terminology is by no means formalized or universally recognized (Genevie, 1978; Smelser, 1962). But like crowds, collective phenomena come in many varieties, including (a) such social diffusions as rumors, mass delusions and trends, and (b) social movements.

Rumors The rumors had been circulating around the crowd of 100,000 gathered at Tahrir Square throughout the day. Mubarak was to address the nation that night, and the rumors all said the same thing: He was going to announce his resignation. These rumors built the throng's emotions up to a state of happy readiness that turned to anger when Mubarak promised, instead, to not seek another term in office.

Rumors provide people with a means of exchanging information about threatening situations and so have a calming effect on groups and communities. Sometimes, however, rumors can instigate more negative reactions to uncertainty and play a part in triggering riots and panics. Future rioters, for example, often mill about for hours swapping stories about injustices before taking any aggressive action. Panics and crazes, too, are often sustained by rumors, particularly when perpetuated by news reports and public announcements (Allport & Postman, 1947). A recent epidemic of *koro* (a rare delusion characterized by the fear that one's sex organs will disappear) that swept through the Han region of China, for example, was traced to exposure to rumors about the fictitious malady (Cheng, 1997). Similarly, the 1999 Woodstock music festival riots were preceded by a day of rumors circulating through the crowd about what the final night of the concert would bring (Vider, 2004).

Social psychologist Ralph Rosnow (1980) identified two conditions that influence the spread of rumors—the degree of *anxiety* that individuals are experiencing and their *uncertainty* about the true nature of the situation. He argued that just as individuals often affiliate with others in threatening situations, "ambiguous or chaotic" situations tend to generate rumors. By passing rumors, individuals convey information (albeit false) about the situation. Rumors also reduce anxiety by providing, in most cases, reassuring reinterpretations of the ambiguous event (Walker & Berkerle, 1987). After the Three Mile Island nuclear power plant accident, for example, authorities opened a rumor control center to supply more accurate information to the community. Rosnow, after studying this incident, maintained that even though many of the rumors were preposterous, they gave people a sense of security in a time of great anxiety (Rosnow & Kimmel, 1979; Rosnow, Yost, & Esposito, 1986).

Mass Delusions Rumors provide the basis for **mass delusion**—the spontaneous outbreak of atypical thoughts, feelings, or actions in a group

---

collective movement A large aggregation of individuals, widely dispersed across space and time, who display similarities in activities, reactions, interests, and so on.

mass delusion The spontaneous outbreak of atypical thoughts, feelings, or actions in a group or aggregation, including psychogenic illness, common hallucinations, and bizarre actions.

F o c u s 17.1 **Cross-cultural Perspectives: Universal Approaches to Crowd Safety**

It is said that there is safety in numbers, but there is danger as well. A dozen people were killed when a police raid triggered a panic in a crowded club in Mexico City, Mexico. When the thousands of pilgrims massed on a narrow road to the Chamunda Devi temple in India panicked 147 people were killed and scores injured. In Germany, at a street festival called the Love Parade, people crowding into the venue sought to escape up a narrow staircase, but when the flow jammed, 21 people were killed and 500 injured. In China, at least three shoppers died during a rush on sale items at a superstore located in Beijing. When a rumor raced through a huge gathering of Shiite Muslims in Baghdad that a suicide bomber was in their midst, the crowd panicked and pushed forward across a narrow bridge with concrete barriers for security. Nearly 1,000 people were killed.

Crowd disasters are a worldwide phenomenon because the primary ingredients for such tragedies—large numbers of people who gather in spaces that are too confining—are present in all cultures. Even when individuals planning such events are careful to engineer the site to fit the number of attendees, the dynamics of crowd movement, combined with unforeseen events, often result in uncontrolled, chaotic crowd occurrences. A relatively well-organized queue, for example, can become too compacted and so bottlenecks form along the group's path at points where its pathway is obstructed—even if the obstruction is a minor one. Organizers usually make certain that the entry points are smaller than the exit points, but arriving crowds may bypass the entry barricades, resulting in far greater pressure on the interior of the group. As the density of the group becomes greater, the crowd's capacity to move in a coordinated way becomes limited, and this instability causes density to rise even further. If the crowding is not relieved, crowd turbulence can cause people to lose their footing and fall. Once they fall, they may not be able to regain their footing, and so they are then trampled by the rest of the crowd as it passes over them. Most deaths, however, result from asphyxiation: People are jammed together so tightly that they cannot breathe (Helbing & Mukerji, 2012).

Researchers have studied this breakdown in how collectives move to identify ways to prevent tragedies due to overcrowding. Their work suggests that the principles that describe how fluids and gases flow through constrained spaces apply equally well to the movement of large groups. Most flow systems are stable and predictable, but when they are overloaded—too much fluid is pumped through too small a pipe—the system fails. Similarly, when too many people attempt to move through a constrained space, the system can be overwhelmed and the flow will jam. Once the clog occurs, those trapped in it are likely to be injured (Helbing et al., 2005; Hughes, 2003).

Sociologist and physicist Dirk Helbing and his colleagues (2007), for example, have examined the causes of fatal crowd disasters that occurred at the Jamarat Bridge in Saudi Arabia. This pedestrian bridge is used by Muslims visiting the three Jamrah Pillars during the ritual of the stoning of the devil. Helbing and his colleagues, to determine the source of the danger, conducted extensive analyses of video-recordings of a deadly crowd event in 2006. They discovered that, in most cases, the large group moved slowly, but inconsistently, through the crowded space. Some portions of the group moved more quickly than others, and density varied significantly across the entire crowd. As in vehicular traffic jams, when too crowded the group began to move in stop-and-go waves: Portions of the crowd would move forward more quickly than seemed prudent, given the congestion, and would then have to stop quickly when those in front of them were moving slower. Groups could tolerate these waves until density became extreme. But once density reached a very high level—as great as 10 people per square meter—the group transitioned into what Helbing calls the "turbulence phase." The crowd members collided with one another, people lost their footing, and, if they fell, the densely packed crowd unintentionally moved over them, killing or injuring them (Helbing, Johansson, & Al-Abideen, 2007; Johansson et al., 2008; Moussaïd et al., 2010).

These findings suggest one certain solution: Control the number of people entering the area by constricting the size of the entry points so that they are smaller than the size of the exits. Cross-flows within the crowd should also be minimized, if possible, by creating lanes within the space—similar to lanes on a highway. The researchers also recommend installing "pressure relief valves": structures that can be opened should the densities become too great. Helbing also recommends reviewing the space where events are to be held immediately before the event to identify any obstacles. Even minor changes to the space, such as a parked police car, a vendor's booth, or a misplaced trash barrel, can cause a crowd to slow, and a bottleneck can result (Helbing & Mukerji, 2012). These recommendations are being applied in the renovation of the Jamarat Bridge, which includes emergency exit ramps leading down from the sides of the bridge.

or aggregation, including psychogenic illness, common hallucinations, and bizarre actions (Pennebaker, 1982; Phoon, 1982). Such episodes are uncommon, but they have occurred regularly throughout the modern era. For example, the *Werther syndrome* is named for Johann Wolfgang von Goethe's (1749–1832) novel *The Sorrows of Young Werther*, which triggered a fashion fad (many young men of the time imitated the eccentric style of dress of the book's hero, Werther) but also led to cluster suicides—many readers also killed themselves in the same way as Werther did. *Choreomania* is the term used to describe the compulsive dancing crazes of the late Middle Ages. *Tulipmania* caused financial ruin for many who speculated in the tulip bulb market in Holland in the 1600s. Many traders lost their savings when the price of bulbs plummeted in 1637. *Biting mania* was a fifteenth-century epidemic of mass delusion that began when a German nun developed a compulsive urge to bite her associates, who in turn bit others, until the mania spread to convents throughout Germany, Holland, and Italy. Note, too, nearly all cases of mass delusions have been exaggerated in their retelling (see Evans & Bartholomew, 2009).

In some cases, unexplained epidemics of illnesses are thought to have been cases of **psychogenic illness** rather than organic illness. For example, in June 1962, workers at a garment factory began complaining of nausea, pain, disorientation, and muscular weakness; some actually collapsed at their jobs or lost consciousness. Rumors spread rapidly that the illness was caused by "some kind of insect" that had infested one of the shipments of cloth from overseas, and the owners began making efforts to eradicate the bug. No bug was ever discovered, however, and experts eventually concluded that the "June Bug incident" had been caused by mass delusion (Kerckhoff & Back, 1968; Kerckhoff, Back, & Miller, 1965).

---

psychogenic illness A set of symptoms of illness in a group of persons when there is no evidence of an organic basis for the illness and no identifiable environmental cause.

Researchers can never definitively determine which cases of widespread illness are socially produced rather than biologically produced, but one study of work groups identified 23 separate cases that involved large numbers of individuals afflicted with "physical symptoms ... in the absence of an identifiable pathogen" (Colligan & Murphy, 1982, p. 35). More than 1,200 people were affected by these outbreaks, with most reporting symptoms that included headaches, nausea, dizziness, and weakness. Many were women working in relatively repetitive, routinized jobs, and the illness often spread through friendship networks. Similarly, studies of pupils in school often conclude that many epidemics, such as outbreaks of fainting or nausea, are caused by hysterical contagion (Bartholomew, 1997; Bartholomew & Sirois, 1996; Lee et al., 1996). Some experts believe that many of the illnesses and medical complaints that are blamed on the presence of irritants in office buildings and schools—the so-called *sick building syndrome*—are actually psychogenic illnesses (Murphy, 2006).

How can group-level delusions be controlled? Organizational experts suggest that as soon as the possibility of a physical cause is eliminated, workers should be told that their problems are more psychological than physical. A second means of limiting the spread of such delusions involves altering the setting. The outbreaks often occur when employees have been told to increase their productivity or when they have been working overtime. Poor labor–management relations have also been implicated, as have negative environmental factors, such as noise, poor lighting, and exposure to dust, foul odors, or chemicals (Colligan, Pennebaker, & Murphy, 1982). Larger outbreaks of rumors and hysteria that sweep across whole regions and countries can be countered by providing citizens with clear, accurate information from trusted sources.

Trends In 1929, as the United States plunged into the Great Depression, people had little time or money to spend playing golf. But several entrepreneurs set up "miniature golf courses" in cities, and the idea took hold of the nation with a vengeance. Miniature golf spread over the entire country, and some people were predicting that the game would replace all other sports as the country's favorite form of recreation. The craze died out within six months (LaPiere, 1938).

Trends are changes in attitudes, actions, and behaviors that influence large segments of a population, such as whole communities or regions. Many of these changes are relatively ordinary ones; shifts in the use of the Internet and microwave ovens, for example, illustrate the diffusion of a technological innovation across the world. Others, in contrast, are more capricious and unpredictable. *A fad*, for example, is an unexpected, short-lived change in the opinions, behaviors, or lifestyles of a large number of widely dispersed individuals. Fads such as the hula hoop, Live Strong bracelets, and mood rings are remarkable both because they influence so many people so rapidly and because they disappear without leaving any lasting impact on society. *Crazes* are similar to fads in most respects, except that they are just a bit more irrational, expensive, or widespread. Swallowing live goldfish, streaking (running about naked in a public place), and the widespread use of cocaine in the 1980s all qualify as crazes. Finally, fads that pertain to styles of dress or manners are generally termed *fashion trends*. Ties and lapels expand and contract, women's hemlines move up and down, and last season's color takes a backseat to this season's shade (Bourdieu, 1984; see Table 17.2).

Social Movements

During the 2011 Occupy Wall Street movement in the United States, large numbers of citizens took up residence in the parks and plazas near the commercial centers of major cities to protest the exploitive practices of large corporations. In the spring of 2012, a strike by millions of workers in Spain closed most of the businesses in major cities and brought transportation to a standstill. In 2011, over one million individuals living in over 80 countries joined

TABLE 17.2   Various Types of Collectives

Type	Defining Characteristics
Audience	Spectators at an exhibition, performance, or event
Queue	A waiting line or file of individuals
Crowd	A temporary gathering of individuals who share a common focus or interest
Mob	An acting, moving crowd, often antagonistic or destructive
Riot	A large, less localized, and less organized mob
Panic	A threatened crowd, seeking to escape from danger or competing for a scarce commodity
Rumor	Unverified information passed from one person to another
Mass delusion	The spontaneous outbreak of atypical thoughts, feelings, or actions in a group or aggregate, including psychogenic illness and bizarre ideas and actions
Trend	An abrupt but short-lived change in the opinions, behaviors, lifestyle, or dress of a large number of dispersed individuals (includes fads, crazes, and fashions)
Social movement	A deliberate, organized attempt to achieve a change or resist a change in a social system

together to pressure their governments to intercede in the cases of 14 victims of civil rights abuse identified by the activist organization Amnesty International. The Arab Spring began when millions of citizens of Tunisia rose up and eventually overthrew their political leaders; uprisings, rebellions, and civil war in other Middle East countries, including Egypt, Bahrain, and Libya, soon followed.

A **social movement** is a deliberate, relatively organized attempt to achieve a change or resist a

---

trend The general direction in which the attitudes, interests, and actions of a large segment of a population change over time, including fashion trends, fads, and crazes.

social movement A collective movement making a deliberate, organized attempt to achieve a change or resist a change in a social system.

change in a social system. Social movements, like other forms of collective behavior, often arise spontaneously in response to some problem, such as unfair government policies, societal ills, or threats to personal values. Social movements are not short-lived, however. Over time, they tend to gain new members, set goals, and develop leadership structures, until eventually they change from spontaneous gatherings of people into *social movement organizations*, or *SMOs*. SMOs have all the structural characteristics of any organization, including goals and objectives, rational planning, and bureaucratic leadership structures (McAdam, McCarthy, & Zald, 1988).

Types of Social Movements   Social movements, like crowds, vary in their longevity and their goals (Appelbaum & Chambliss, 1995). *Reformist movements* seek to improve existing institutions, often through civil disobedience and demonstrations. The U.S. civil rights movement, for example, sought to change existing laws that gave unfair power to Whites, but the movement did not challenge the basic democratic principles of the country. *Revolutionary movements*, in contrast, seek more sweeping changes in existing social institutions. The revolts in France in the late 1700s and the Arab Spring of 2011 were revolutionary movements, for the protesters sought to change their existing system of government. *Reactionary movements*, instead of trying to achieve change, seek to resist it or even to reinstate extinct social systems. The Ku Klux Klan is one such movement, as are many militia groups and groups that argue against alternative lifestyles. *Communitarian movements* strive to create more ideal living conditions than currently exist in modern society, often by withdrawing from contact with nonmembers. The communes of the 1960s were communitarian movements, as are many alternative religious movements (cults).

The Politics of Social Movements   The Arab Spring was as much a political process as a social one. The protesters did not gather at Tahrir Square by happenstance; instead, the marches, demonstrations, and rallies were all part of a planned, organized, and orchestrated attempt to secure social change. According to *political opportunity theory*, to succeed the movement needed to take advantage of any and all political opportunities (Meyer, 2004). *Resource mobilization theory* stresses the importance of identifying and marshaling sources of support for the movement. Money must be raised; equipment, provisions, and, in some cases, weapons acquired; new recruits must be convinced to join; and allies need to be identified (McAdam, McCarthy, & Zald, 1988). Last, *framing theory* argues movements require a meaningful account of their nature, objectives, and goals. Before people join in a social movement, they must know what the movement stands for, and what it hopes to achieve (Walder, 2009).

The anti-Mubarak movement in Egypt's success was due, in part, to its navigating the political demands identified by these three overlapping theoretical perspectives. The initial revolution in the Arab Spring occurred in Tunisia and resulted in the overthrow of that country's government. These events upset the region's status quo, providing a temporary window of opportunity for the movement to engage in more forceful forms of protest. The movement also gained considerable strength when student protesters were joined by a number of different groups within that society, including labor groups, shopkeepers, professionals, Coptic Christians, and Islamists (Goldstone, 2011). The movement's leaders were also very successful in creating a coherent image for the group that stressed nonviolence, shared identity, and an end to the Mubarak regime. As Focus 17.2 suggests, technology also contributed to the movement's success by providing a means of disseminating its message widely (Diani, 2011).

COLLECTIVE DYNAMICS

Scholars have pondered and debated the vagaries of collectives for centuries, seeking to specify the factors that can transform individuals so thoroughly and so unexpectedly. Although many answers have been offered, this section narrows the analysis

---

Focus 17.2   E-groups: Social Movements as Smart Mobs

The Arab Spring—a cascade of demonstrations, protests, and riots in several countries in the Middle East—took many political analysts by surprise. The repressed citizens of these countries were discontented, but few thought the time was ripe for change. Countries such as Egypt were considered to be strong states and weak societies—two conditions that generally discourage social change. Strong states have powerful, centralized, autocratic forms of government. Such governments usually suppress rebellion through coercive means. These nations were also thought to be weak societies, in the sense that the citizens were divided among themselves. They lacked a sense of community and identity (Dupont & Passy, 2011). Yet, the events of the Arab Spring proved the experts wrong, for change not only happened—it happened quickly. It was as if some new social force, one that accelerated the process of change in those countries, was at work.

The surprising events of the Arab Spring are still being discussed and debated, but some political scientists have suggested that these were high-tech rebellions. The protesters became what technology expert Howard Rheingold (2002) calls a **smart mob**: a social movement organized through the use of information technology, including cell phones and the Internet. Although street demonstrations at the World Trade Organization summits, protestors camping out during Occupy Wall Street, and the roving mobs that formed during the recent English riots may have looked like traditional collectives, all were created—or, at least, organized—using communication technologies. Protesters in Manila, for example, used cell phone technology to organize a demonstration against the country's president, Joseph Estrada. Texting is a popular means of communication in the Philippines, so when organizers circulated the message "Go 2 EDSA, Wear blck" (Go to the Epifanio de los Santas Avenue and wear black clothing), a crowd estimated at nearly one million formed and forced the country's president from office.

Most people rely on the Internet to access news and entertainment resources, communicate with friends and family, and for shopping, but political activists use the Internet to mobilize, organize, and frame their social movement. During the Arab Spring, information about the growing levels of dissent in the nation was communicated widely using Facebook, Twitter, blog postings, and online satellite news services. When, for example, Egypt's state-run news service, Al-Ahram, published misleading information, reporters, citizens, and bloggers turned to technology to circumvent these controls and share information that would otherwise be suppressed. These tools also provided the leaders of the movement the means to articulate and discuss the basic premises of the movement and respond to challenges mounted by pro-Mubarak groups. It was through social media that the movement developed its identity—as a source of unification of Egypt that stood apart from political and religious practices or ideologies. Technology was also used for more practical, organizational purposes; participants for demonstrations, protests, and marches were in some cases recruited using tweets and Facebook event postings rather than through more traditional, word-of-mouth methods. Technology also appears to have played a role in overcoming barriers to cooperation among subgroups within the country (Rosiny, 2012).

The regimes of these countries, recognizing the threat posed by technology, intervened to limit access to the Internet and to cell phone networks. Mubarak, for example, cut all Internet access in late January, in an attempt to prevent communication and reduce protesters' ability to organize. Bloggers and online journalists, too, were frequently targeted by police, and those who worked for the Aljazeera news agency were assulted by pro-Mubarak gangs (Khalil, 2011). These interventions, however, failed when the protestors quickly identified technologically sophisticated ways to circumvent the state-imposed controls.

The Arab Spring social movement was not entirely a high-tech protest; activists made use of technology, but they also took to the streets, occupied Tahrir Square, confronted pro-Mubarak forces, and engaged in heroic acts of civil disobedience. Technology, however, significantly influenced the context and forms of the social movement, just as it is influencing nearly all types of groups. When the citizens of Paris stormed the Bastille in July of 1789, they managed it without cell phones, Twitter, and Facebook. Today's and tomorrow's rebellions, in contrast, will likely be wired (and wireless) ones.

---

smart mob Any group, including social movements, mobs, or crowds, that uses computer-based technologies (e.g., cell phones, text messaging, and the Internet) to organize and initiate its activities.

by focusing on five theoretical explanations that have stood the test of time and study. Each theory focuses on a different aspect of collective behavior, including motivational mechanisms, normative interpretations, and identity and its loss. Each one is selective in its focus, but taken together they provide considerable insight into a wide array of collective phenomena (Lang & Lang, 1961).

Contagion

People, when interacting with one another, do not only pass along germs, infections, and viruses; they also pass along ideas, actions, and outlooks. In Egypt during the Arab Spring uprising, for example, the people of Egypt interacted with one another constantly, and during the course of those daily interactions, they discussed the nation's problems, exchanged ideas, passed along rumors, and planned remedial actions. Through this process of **contagion**, interest in and support for the movement diffused throughout the nation, as one person influenced another.

Le Bon's Crowd Psychology The concept of contagion was popularized as an explanation of collective and crowd behavior by Gustave Le Bon in his book, *The Crowd*, in 1895. Le Bon was fascinated by large groups, but he also feared their tendency to erupt into violence. Perhaps because of these biases, he concluded that a crowd of people could, in certain instances, become a unified entity that acted as if guided by a single collective mind. Le Bon wrote,

> Whoever be the individuals that compose it, however like or unlike be their mode of life, their occupations, their character, or their intelligence, the fact that they have been transformed into a crowd puts them in possession of a sort of collective mind which makes them feel, think, and act in a

manner quite different from that in which each individual of them would feel, think, and act were he in a state of isolation. (1895/1960, p. 27)

Le Bon believed that no matter what the individual qualities of the people in the group, the crowd would transform them, changing them from rational, thoughtful individuals into impulsive, unreasonable, and extreme followers. Once people fall under the "law of the mental unity of crowds" (1895/1960, p. 24), they act as the collective mind dictates.

Le Bon was a physician, so he viewed the collective mind as a kind of disease that infected one part of the group and then spread throughout the rest of the crowd. After observing many crowds firsthand, Le Bon concluded that emotions and behaviors could be transmitted from one person to another just as germs can be passed along, and he believed that this process of contagion accounted for the tendency of group members to behave in very similar ways (Wheeler, 1966).

Contagion in Collectives Many of Le Bon's speculations have been discredited, but he was right about one thing: Contagion is common in groups (Chartrand & van Baaren, 2009; see Chapter 7). One person laughing in an audience will stimulate laughter in others. Question and answer sessions after a lecture usually begin very slowly, but they soon snowball as more and more questioners begin raising their hands. Individuals' emotions tend to converge over time when they interact frequently in groups. Mimicry of others is so basic a process that researchers believe that so-called *mirror neurons* are active when others' actions are observed and that these neurons play a role in producing the identical behavior in the observer (Semin, 2007). Mimicry explains why members of collectives act as if they are guided by a single mind: As one person imitates the next, the collective seems to act in a uniform manner.

Le Bon believed that such contagion processes reflected the heightened suggestibility of crowd members, but other processes may be at work as well. Because many crowd settings are ambiguous,

---

contagion The spread of behaviors, attitudes, and affect through crowds and other types of social aggregations from one member to another.

social comparison processes may prompt members to rely heavily on other members' reactions when they interpret the situation. Contagion may also arise in crowds through imitation, social facilitation, persuasion, or conformity (Freedman & Perlick, 1979; Tarde, 1903).

Sociologist Herbert Blumer combined these various processes when he argued that contagion involves circular reactions rather than interpretive reactions (Blumer, 1957). During interpretive interactions, group members carefully reflect on the meaning of others' behavior and try to formulate valid interpretations before making any kind of comment or embarking on a line of action. During circular reactions, however, the group's members fail to examine the meaning of others' actions cautiously and carefully and, therefore, tend to misunderstand the situation. When they act on the basis of such misunderstandings, the others in the group also begin to interpret the situation incorrectly, and a circular process is thus initiated that eventually culminates in full-blown behavioral contagion.

Contagion versus Diffusion Le Bon considered contagion to be a negative process; he likened the spread of ideas and information throughout a crowd to an infectious disease. Social network analysis, in contrast, discards the pejorative connotations of the concept of contagion by arguing that information diffuses throughout the network because its members are joined together in social relations. Diffusion, then, is not the result of the contamination of one person by another, but is instead due to the rational exchange of information within a network (Drury, 2002).

Diffusion starts when some bit of information, such as a rumor, information about an event, an interpretation, an emotion, or a description of an experience, is passed from individual (a node) to another. If that node does not pass along the information, diffusion ends—unless the initiator passes the information to other nodes in his or her network. If, however, the second individual passes the information onward to one or more contacts, then the information begins to propagate throughout the network. How quickly its spreads and how widely depends, in part, on the structure of the network. For example, information will diffuse more rapidly in networks that are dense and centralized and when the nodes are organized into clusters (Ugander et al., 2012).

All nodes within a network are not created equal, however, in terms of the capacity to influence the diffusion process. Journalist Malcolm Gladwell (2000), for example, distinguishes between people with large social networks (connectors), the individuals who are opinion authorities (mavens), and those who are able to persuade others to change their minds (salespeople). Relative to most people, these influential individuals can push an idea much more rapidly to many more people. Connectors, for example, have been identified as one source of the rapid shift in popularity of new musical groups. When investigators asked fans of a new musical group how many other people they told about the band, they discovered that most fans told only a few other people. But a small number of the fans—the connectors—told many more of their friends about the group, including one individual who claimed to have spread the message to more than 150 people (Reifman, Lee, & Apparala, 2004). Advertisers now target such influential persons, in the belief that if they win them over as customers, the rest of their network will follow (Watts & Dodds, 2007).

Convergence

Many explanations of collective behavior suggest that people are not changed by collectives, because they were similar to one another from the very start. **Convergence theory** assumes that individuals who join rallies, riots, movements, crusades, and the like all possess particular personal characteristics that influence their collective tendencies. Such aggregations are not haphazard gatherings of dissimilar strangers; rather, they represent the convergence of people with compatible needs, desires,

---

convergence theory An explanation of collective behavior assuming that individuals with similar needs, values, or goals tend to converge to form a single group.

motivations, and emotions. By joining in the group, the individual makes possible the satisfaction of these needs, and the crowd situation serves as a trigger for the spontaneous release of previously unexpressed desires. As social critic Eric Hoffer (1951) wrote, "All movements, however different in doctrine and aspiration, draw their early adherents from the same types of humanity; they all appeal to the same types of mind" (p. 9).

Who Joins Crowds and Collectives? Are people who take part in crowd activities different, in terms of their personalities and values, than people who do not join such groups? Early conceptions of crowds, which portrayed their members as less intelligent, more easily influenced, more impulsive, and more violent, have not received consistent empirical support (Martin, 1920; Meerloo, 1950). Nor have attempts to link participation in more unusual forms of collective behavior—such as cults or radical religious groups—to psychological problems. Those who join radical religious groups are usually teenagers or young adults, and although they tend to be more idealistic and open to new experiences and are higher in psychological dependency, they show no signs of psychological disturbance (Bromley, 2001, 2007; Walsh, Russell, & Wells, 1995). Those who take part in sports-related mobs and riots are usually younger men who have engaged in aggressive crowd activities in the past, but they are generally unremarkable in other respects (Russell & Arms, 1998).

Those who take part in social movements, in contrast, tend to be more politically engaged. In terms of basic personality, they are no more likely to be extraverted or introverted or stable or unstable, but they do tend to be open to new experiences. They also tend to have liberal rather than conservative political beliefs, and they are relatively engaged in political issues, in general. Even when political and social events do not directly influence them, they nonetheless consider them to be personally meaningful (Curtin, Stewart, & Duncan, 2010).

People who join social movements also tend to be higher in self-efficacy—they believe that through their personal involvement, they can make a difference (van Zomeren, Postmes, & Spears, 2008). Self-confidence, achievement orientation, a need for autonomy, dominance, self-acceptance, and maturity are all positively correlated with social activism (Werner, 1978). Individuals who have a history of taking part in collectives tend to jump at the chance to join new ones (Corning & Myers, 2002), but those who have a history of avoiding conflict are less likely to join (Ulbig & Funk, 1999).

Relative Deprivation People who feel that principles of fairness and justice are violated by the status quo are also more likely to take part in social movements. Collectives are often composed of those who are impoverished, persecuted, or endangered, but it is more the perceived unfairness of the deprivation that determines involvement in a collective rather than the deprivation itself. **Relative deprivation** is therefore more motivating than actual deprivation: Those who join social movements tend to be people who have higher expectations but who have not succeeded in realizing these expectations.

Individuals who take part in social movements are also more likely to be experiencing fraternal deprivation rather than egoistic deprivation. As sociologist Walter Runciman (1966) explains, **egoistic deprivation** (or personal deprivation) occurs when individuals are dissatisfied with their level of prosperity relative to other individuals. **Fraternal deprivation** (or group deprivation) occurs when the groups one belongs to do not enjoy the same level of prosperity as other groups. Both forms of deprivation can influence well-being,

---

relative deprivation The psychological state that occurs when individuals feel that, in comparison to others, their attainments, outcomes, status, recognition, and so on are inadequate.

egoistic deprivation The psychological state that occurs when one feels one's outcomes are inferior relative to other individuals' outcomes.

fraternal deprivation The psychological state that occurs when a group member feels his or her group's outcomes are inferior relative to other groups' outcomes.

satisfaction, and happiness, but fraternal deprivation is associated with a collective response. Individuals experiencing egoistic deprivation may be angry and disappointed, but those experiencing fraternal deprivation (a) join with other group members to take action against other groups or organizations and (b) express more negative attitudes and opinions about those groups (Smith et al., 2012). Individuals who are active in revolutionary social movements, such as the national separatist movements in Quebec and Ireland, are more likely to be dissatisfied with their group's outcomes than with their own personal outcomes (Abrams, 1990; Guimond & Dubé–Simard, 1983).

Deindividuation

Like Le Bon, social psychologist Philip Zimbardo believes that in some cases the group can become more powerful than the individual. But Zimbardo did not believe that the group's power comes from contagion. Instead, Zimbardo hypothesized that people, when they become too deeply submerged in a group, experience **deindividuation**: They lose their sense of personal identity and become one with the group. Once deindividuated, they no longer feel compelled to act in accord with social norms. They also lack self-control and self-regulation, so their actions become highly emotional, impulsive, and atypical. While deindividuation may lead to increasingly positive behaviors, it usually leads to "aggression, vandalism, stealing, cheating, rudeness, as well as a general loss of concern for others" (Zimbardo, 1969, 1975, p. 53).

Zimbardo's theory is an input–process–output model, for it identifies factors that cause deindividuation (inputs), the process of deindividuation itself, and the consequences of deindividuation (outputs). The inputs include situational factors, such as the degree of anonymity and the size of the group, as well as more psychological factors: sense of responsibility, degree of arousal, and altered states of consciousness due to the use of drugs or alcohol. These factors, in turn, lead to deindividuation and irrational, emotional, and impulsive actions (Zimbardo, 1969).

Anonymity   When individuals join a large collective, they feel less identifiable, and this sense of anonymity may cause them to engage in behavior that they would never consider undertaking if alone. Zimbardo confirmed anonymity's impact experimentally by comparing the aggressiveness of anonymous groups to those whose members were identifiable. Under an elaborate pretense, he asked all-female groups to give 20 electric shocks to two women. *Anonymous* groups wore large lab coats (size 44) and hoods over their heads, and they were not permitted to use their names. Those in groups that were *identifiable* were greeted by name and wore large name tags; the experimenter emphasized their uniqueness and individuality. Although identifiability was unrelated to the number of shocks given (the average was 17 of 20), the unidentifiable participants held their switches down nearly twice as long as the identifiable participants (0.90 seconds versus 0.47 seconds).

Any situational factor that increases members' sense of anonymity may also increase levels of deindividuation. For example, crowds and mobs that form at night tend to be more unruly and aggressive than daylight crowds (e.g., Mann, 1981). Disguises, too, can increase anonymity. According to anthropological evidence, warriors in 92.3% (12 out of 13) of the most highly aggressive cultures—those known to practice headhunting and to torture captives—disguise themselves prior to battle, whereas only 30% (3 out of 10) of the low-aggression cultures feature similar rituals (Watson, 1973).

Responsibility   As Le Bon argued many years ago, the crowd is "anonymous, and in consequence irresponsible" (1895/1960, p. 30). This *diffusion of responsibility* has been verified in dozens of studies of people who faced various emergencies alone or in a

----

deindividuation An experiential state caused by a number of input factors, such as group membership and anonymity, that is characterized by the loss of self-awareness, altered experiencing, and atypical behavior.

group (see Chapter 7). Members of groups may also experience a reduction in responsibility if an authority demands compliance (Milgram, 1974) or if they do not recognize the connections between their personal actions and their final consequences. Some groups actually take steps to ensure the diffusion of responsibility, as when murderers pass around their weapons from hand to hand so that responsibility for the crime is distributed through the entire group rather than concentrated in the one person who pulls the trigger or wields the knife (Zimbardo, 1969, 2007).

Group Membership Deindividuation is a group-level process. Single individuals may feel unrecognizable or uncertain as to their identity, but Zimbardo considers membership in a collective to be a necessary condition for deindividuation. Social psychologist Edward Diener and his associates (1976) tested this assumption in an ingenious study of Halloween trick-or-treating. Their participants were 1,352 children from the Seattle area who visited one of the 27 experimental homes scattered throughout the city. Observers hidden behind decorative panels recorded the number of extra candy bars and money (pennies and nickels) taken by the trick-or-treaters who were told to take one candy bar each. The children came to the house alone or in small groups (exceedingly large groups were not included in the study nor were groups that included an adult). An experimenter manipulated anonymity by asking some children to give their names and addresses. As expected, the children who were members of groups took more money and candy than children who were alone. So did the anonymous children compared to those children who gave their names. But when these two factors were combined—children were part of a group and they were anonymous—transgressions more than doubled (see Figure 17.3). These findings, which have been supported by other investigations, suggest that the term *deindividuation* is used most appropriately in reference to people who perform atypical behavior while they are members of a group (Cannavale, Scarr, & Pepitone, 1970; Mathes & Kahn, 1975).

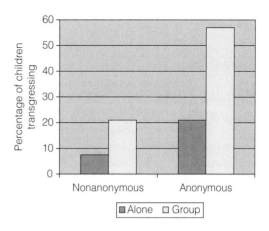

FIGURE 17.3 The combined effects of anonymity and group membership on counternormative behavior.

SOURCE: From data from "Effects of deindividuating variables on stealing by Halloween trick-or-treaters," by E. Diener, S. C. Fraser, A. L. Beaman, & R. T. Kelem, *Journal of Personality and Social Psychology, 33*, 1976. Copyright 1976 by the American Psychological Association. Reprinted by permission.

Group Size Are larger groups more likely to act in unusual ways? Social psychologist Leon Mann discovered that people are more likely to respond to religious messages when they are part of a larger rather than a smaller group (Newton & Mann, 1980). At the end of many religious meetings, audience members are invited to become "inquirers" by coming forward and declaring their dedication to Christ. In 57 religious meetings, the correlation between crowd size and the proportion of people who moved down to the stage to become inquirers was .43. On Sundays, the correlation rose to .78. Larger lynch mobs are also more violent than smaller ones. A review of historical records of 60 such groups reveals that they ranged in size from 4 to 15,000, but that larger mobs were more likely to attack more victims (Mullen, 1986).

Arousal Zimbardo listed a number of other variables that can contribute to deindividuation, including altered temporal perspectives, sensory overload, a lack of situational structure, and the use of drugs. Many of these factors, he suggested, function by both arousing and distracting group members. Zimbardo even suggested that certain rituals, such as war dances and group singing, are actually designed to arouse participants and enable them to be deindividuated when the fighting starts: "Among cannibals, like the Cenis or certain Maori and Nigerian tribes, the activity of ritual bonfire dance which precedes eating the flesh of another human being is always more prolonged and intense when the victim is to be eaten alive or uncooked" (1969, p. 257). Aroused individuals, as deindividuation theory suggests, tend to respond more aggressively, particularly when in a group (Goldstein, 2002).

Self-Awareness Zimbardo's deindividuation theory posits that situational variables, such as anonymity and membership in a group, can in some cases combine to induce psychological changes in group members. Deindividuated people, Zimbardo predicted, should feel very little self-awareness, and this minimization of self-scrutiny is the most immediate cause of the atypical behaviors seen in collectives.

Diener (1979, 1980) tested this hypothesis by making use of an Asch-type experimental situation. He created eight-person groups, but he included in each group six accomplices trained to facilitate or inhibit the development of deindividuation. In the *self-aware condition*, the confederates seemed restless and fidgety. Everyone wore name tags as they worked on tasks designed to heighten self-awareness, such as providing personal responses to questions, sharing their opinions on topics, and disclosing personal information about themselves. In the *non-self-aware condition*, Diener shifted the participants' focus of attention outward by having them perform a series of mildly distracting tasks. The problems were not difficult, but they required a good deal of concentration and creativity. In the *deindividuation condition*, Diener tried to foster feelings of group cohesiveness, unanimity, and anonymity by treating the members as interchangeable and by putting the groups through a variety of arousing activities.

When Diener asked the participants to describe how they felt during the study, he identified the two clusters, or factors, shown in Table 17.3. The first factor, *loss of self-awareness*, encompasses a lack

T A B L E 17.3 Characteristics of Factors That Combine to Create a State of Deindividuation

Factor	Typical Characteristics
Loss of self-awareness	• Minimal self-consciousness • Lack of conscious planning as behavior becomes spontaneous • Lack of concern for what others think of one • Subjective feeling that time is passing quickly • Liking for the group and feelings of group unity • Uninhibited speech • Performing uninhibited tasks
Altered experiencing	• Unusual experiences, such as hallucinations • Altered states of consciousness • Subjective loss of individual identity • Feelings of anonymity • Liking for the group and feelings of group unity

SOURCE: "Deindividuation, Self-Awareness, and Disinhibition," by E. Diener, *Journal of Personality and Social Psychology, 37*, 1160–1171. Copyright 1979 by the American Psychological Association. Adapted by permission.

of self-consciousness, little planning of action, high group unity, and uninhibited action. The second factor, *altered experiencing*, is also consistent with deindividuation theory in that it ties together a number of related processes, such as "unusual" experiences, altered perceptions, and a loss of individual identity. When Diener compared the responses of participants in the three conditions of his experiment, he discovered that (1) deindividuated participants displayed a greater loss of self-awareness than both the non-self-aware and the self-aware participants and (2) deindividuated participants reported more extreme altered experiencing than the self-aware participants.

Other investigators have replicated these findings. For example, in one study, members of four-man groups were led to believe that they were going to deliver electric shocks to another person. Half of the participants were prompted to focus their attention on the situation, whereas the others were frequently reminded to pay attention

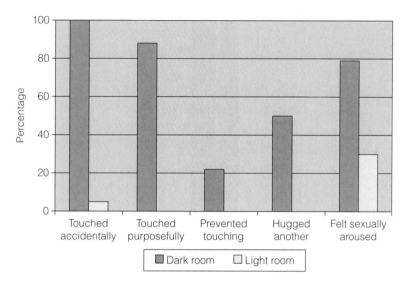

FIGURE 17.4   The reactions reported by participants in the dark room or the light room.

SOURCE: From data presented in "Deviance in the Dark" by K. J. Gergen, M. M. Gergen, & W. H. Barton. Reprinted with permission from *Psychology Today magazine.* Copyright © 1973 (Sussex Publishers, Inc.).

to their personal feelings. Moreover, some participants were told that their actions would be carefully monitored, whereas others were led to believe that their actions were not going to be linked to them personally. The results of the study supported Diener's two-factor model of deindividuation and suggested that both low self-awareness and altered experiencing caused increased aggressiveness (Prentice-Dunn & Rogers, 1980, 1982, 1983; Prentice-Dunn & Spivey, 1986).

Positive Deindividuation   Deindividuation usually leads to negative, antisocial behavior, but not if cues that serve to prime aggressive responses are removed from the situation. In such circumstances, people who feel anonymous may act in positive, even prosocial, ways (Johnson & Downing, 1979). Researchers, to examine this possibility, simply placed some groups in totally darkened rooms and other groups in well-lit rooms and recorded how the groups responded. All who participated in the study were anonymous: they were escorted individually to and from the room and were assured that the other participants would not be told their identities. The individuals in the dark room reported

feeling aroused, but in no case did they exhibit hostility, aggressiveness, or violence. Rather, nearly everyone felt relaxed and at ease in the darkness, surrounded by strangers. In the words of one participant, a "group of us sat closely together, touching, feeling a sense of friendship and loss as a group member left. I left with a feeling that it had been fun and nice" (Gergen, Gergen, & Barton, 1973, p. 129). Apparently, the situation helped people express feelings that they would have otherwise kept hidden, but these feelings were positive rather than negative (see Figure 17.4).

Emergent Norms

Ralph Turner and Lewis Killian's **emergent norm theory** questions the idea that unusual psychological and social processes operate in crowds and collectives (Turner, 1964; Turner & Killian, 1972).

---

emergent norm theory An explanation of collective behavior suggesting that the uniformity in behavior often observed in collectives is caused by members' conformity to unique normative standards that develop spontaneously in those groups.

They reject one of the fundamental assumptions of both Le Bon's contagion theory and Zimbardo's deindividuation theory—that people in crowds have lost self-control. Instead, they conclude that members of collectives act in ways that are consistent with the norms that are salient in the situation. They are not acting in random, unpredictable ways, but rather are following the example set by others in the group. Granted, these *emergent norms* may be unique and sharply contrary to more general societal standards, but they nonetheless exert a powerful influence on behavior.

Consider, for example, the unusual behavior of some crowds that form near buildings where a person is threatening to commit suicide by leaping from a window or ledge. In some cases these crowds transform from relatively passive audiences into **baiting crowds** whose members urge the jumpers to take their life. When Mann studied members of such crowds, he was unable to identify any similarities in personality or demographic characteristics (as convergence theory would suggest). He did note, however, that baiting became more likely as crowd size increased. Mann suggested that larger crowds are more likely to include at least one person who introduces the baiting norm into the group. "In a large crowd at least one stupid or sadistic person will be found who is prepared to cry 'Jump!' and thereby provide a model for suggestible others to follow" (Mann, 1981, p. 707). Mann reported evidence of conformity to the baiting norm in crowds that not only encouraged the victim to "end it all" but also jeered and booed as rescuers attempted to intervene.

Emergent norm theory, in contrast to other analyses of crowds and collectives, argues that collectives are not out of control or normless. Rather, they are socially structured groups, but by an unusual, temporary, or group-specific norm rather than by more traditional social standards. For example, some cults condone mass suicide. Hooligans at British soccer matches consider violence a normal

part of the event. When riots occur, it becomes commonplace to loot stores. After a week, the protesters in Egypt did not think it was unusual to be living in the open air at Tahrir Square. Although these events—when viewed from a more objective perspective—may seem out of control and very strange, for the group members they are literally "normal."

Social Identity

Social identity theory, like emergent norm theory, takes issue with one of deindividuation theory's core assumptions. Deindividuation theory suggests that people in collectives experience a loss of identity, but the *Social Identity Model of Deindividuation Effects* (SIDE) argues that people's social identities are actually amplified when they are members of a collective (Postmes & Spears, 1998; Reicher, Spears, & Postmes, 1995). For example, each individual who took part in the protests at Tahrir Square likely had many unique qualities—some were lawyers, others were students, some were religious, others were suspicious by nature, others were kindly—but when they gathered together they all became anti-Mubarak protesters, and they acted in ways that were consistent with that identity (Polletta & Jasper, 2001). Thus, social identity theory argues that joining a collective does not lead to deindividuation but to a depersonalized sense of self that reflects group-level qualities rather than individual ones.

Social Identity and Intergroup Conflict Studies of both social movements as well as such fast-forming collectives as riots and mobs suggest that social identity processes significantly influence who joins collectives and how people act once they become members. Like the protesters in Egypt, members usually recognize the characteristics expected of the prototypical member, and they define themselves in terms of those qualities. They identify with the group, and experience positive effects—including an increased sense of efficacy—by joining together with other like-minded individuals. When, for example, social psychologist

---

baiting crowd A gathering of people in a public location whose members torment, tease, or goad others.

Stephen Reicher asks individuals who have taken part in riots to describe the experience, few report feeling emotionally overwrought, impulsive, or out of control. Instead, they describe themselves and their comembers as taking collective action in an attempt to reach a goal that all members recognized as appropriate in the given context (e.g., Reicher, 1984, 1987, 1996, 2001; Reicher & Stott, 2011).

Social identity theory stresses one aspect of collective settings frequently overlooked by other theoretical perspectives: collective behavior is usually intergroup behavior (Reicher et al., 1995; Waddington, 2008). Riots in inner cities, for example, usually occur when inner-city residents contend against another group: the police (Goldberg, 1968). Violence during athletic competitions often occurs when the fans of one team attack, en masse, the fans or players of another team (Leonard, 1980). Protests on college campuses pit students against the university administration (Lipset & Wolin, 1965). Gangs vie for turf against other gangs (Sanders, 1994). Militia groups rise up to confront civil and judicial authorities (Flynn & Gerhardt, 1989). Lynch mobs were crowds of Whites with high solidarity who attacked Blacks (de la Roche, 2002). The presence of an outgroup increases the salience of the collective identity and members begin to perceive themselves and the situation in ways that reflect the ingroup–outgroup bias: Other members of the ingroup are viewed positively, as are their actions, whereas outgroup members and their actions are denigrated (see Chapter 14).

Reicher's analyses of riots underscore collectives' intergroup character. For example, one riot occurred when members of the National Union of Students organized a demonstration in London. The leaders of the group planned to march to the Houses of Parliament, but the police blocked their path. As the tension between the groups escalated, the students became more unified. When one member of the group was arrested by the police, students attacked the police unit as a group. They also felt that the police were behaving violently and that they themselves only responded in self-defense. As one student put it, "To some extent there was a feeling of there was the students and there was the police and you knew which side you were on so you had to be up in the front with students, you know. And there was a lot of crowd empathy" (quoted in Reicher, 1996, p. 126).

Individuation A paradox permeates the analysis of individuality and collectives. On the one hand, many theorists assume that submersion in a group results in the attainment of power and an escape from societal inhibitions; hence, group members seek and try to maintain the experience of deindividuation. On the other hand, many psychologists believe that people can enjoy psychological well-being only when they are able to establish and maintain their own unique identities: "A firm sense of one's own autonomous identity is required in order that one may be related as one human being to another. Otherwise, any and every relationship threatens the individual with loss of identity" (Laing, 1960, p. 44; see, too, Dipboye, 1977).

An *identity affirmation* approach to collective behavior suggests that group members who feel "lost" in a group will try to reestablish their individual identities. People in large crowds, for example, may act oddly to regain a sense of individuality, not because they feel anonymous. Individuals who take part in riots may do so not to protest their group's unfair treatment, but to reaffirm their individual identities. As one resident of the riot-torn community of Watts (in Los Angeles) explained, "I don't believe in burning, stealing, or killing, but I can see why the boys did what they did. They just wanted to be noticed, to let the world know the seriousness of their state of life" (Milgram & Toch, 1969, p. 576). Similarly, members of large groups, such as industrial workers, students in large classrooms, people working in bureaucratic organizations, and employees in companies with high turnover rates, may perform atypical actions just to stand apart from the crowd.

Psychologist Christina Maslach (1972) examined this *individuation* process by making two people in a four-person group feel individuated; she referred to them by name, made more personal comments to them, and maintained a significant amount of eye contact. She made the other two feel deindividuated by avoiding close contact with them and addressing them impersonally. When these individuals were later given the opportunity to engage in a free-response group discussion and to complete some questionnaires, the deindividuated participants evidenced various identity-seeking reactions. Some attempted to make themselves seem as different as possible from the other group members by giving more unusual answers to the questions, making longer comments, joining in the discussion more frequently, and attempting to capture the attention of the experimenter. Other participants seemed to redefine their identities by revealing more intimate details of their personalities and beliefs through longer and more unusual self-descriptions.

COLLECTIVES ARE GROUPS

All groups are intriguing, but groups that undertake extreme or unexpected actions—cults, mobs, crowds, and the like—fascinate both layperson and researcher. Although groups are so commonplace that they often go unnoticed and unscrutinized, atypical groups invite speculation and inquiry. But are such groups mad? Do human beings lose their rationality when they are immersed in gatherings, crowds, mobs, and movements?

The Myth of the Madding Crowd

For well over a century, most theorists and researchers have assumed that crowds are unique social aggregations; a "perversion of human potential" (Zimbardo, 1969, p. 237) where impulse and chaos replace reason and order. Le Bon argued that crowds develop a collective mind that leaves individual members unable to think for themselves. Convergence theories assume atypical groups are staffed by atypical people. Groups often develop odd, unusual norms, and members may forget who they are when they sink too deeply into their groups. This belief in the "madness of crowds"

is so deeply ingrained in common conceptions of collectives that some individuals who commit violent crimes in groups are given more lenient punishments. Deindividuated and driven to conform to their group's norms, they are not held personally responsible for their actions (Colman, 1991).

Yet collectives are, at their core, groups, and so the processes that shape group behaviors also shape collective behaviors. Many contemporary theorists, rather than assuming collectives are atypical groups that require special theories that include novel or even mysterious processes, argue the "madding crowd" is more myth than reality. Collective behavior is not bizarre, but instead a rational attempt by a number of individuals to seek change through united action. These groups form, change, and disband following the same patterns that govern other groups, and the internal structures and processes of collectives and more mundane groups are more similar than they are different.

Sociologist Clark McPhail (1991) elaborated this viewpoint in his book *The Myth of the Madding Crowd*. McPhail maintained that early theorists were too biased by their preconceived belief that crowds are crazed. McPhail himself carried out extensive field studies of actual collective movements over a 10-year period so he could determine firsthand what such groups do. His conclusions were threefold:

> First, individuals are not driven mad by crowds; they do not lose cognitive control! Second, individuals are not compelled to participate by some madness-in-common, or any other sovereign psychological attribute, cognitive style, or predisposition that distinguishes them from nonparticipants. Third, the majority of behaviors in which members of these crowds engaged are neither mutually inclusive nor extraordinary, let alone mad. (McPhail, 1991, p. xxii)

Social psychologist John Drury (2002) reiterates this message in his critique of the continuing use of the word "contagion" to describe the flow of information through a crowd. As he explains, the term is hopelessly derogatory and will forever be associated with disease, corruption, illness, and pathology. He recommends using more positive terms such as identification and empowerment:

> Lone individuals endorsing a reactionary and mystifying ideology have little power to act upon it. The most that they can do, perhaps, is to act under cover of night.... However, collective support enables people to put their beliefs into practice in broad daylight, even in the face of opposition from the police (Drury and Reicher, 1999). In short, the crowd empowers. (Drury, 2002, p. 69)

A hundred years of theory and research that have pushed the "crowd-as-mad" position is a stalwart legacy that cannot be easily dismissed. Yet the available evidence favors the view that the crowd is a group. When scholars have reviewed some of the famous examples of crowd delusions, such as dancing mania and the supposed panic during the *War of the Worlds* broadcast, they have discovered that these events were sensationalized (Bartholomew & Goode, 2000). The dancers who were viewed as a pathological mob were, in all likelihood, members of a religious sect who were passing through the area on a pilgrimage (Evans & Bartholomew, 2009). Many of the Dutch merchants who invested in the tulip bulb market prospered, and while some may have lost money, they probably fared better than many investors in the stock market during the 2000–2002 bubble market (Menschel, 2002). And the story of the mass panic following the broadcast of the War of the Worlds is nearly entirely fictional: Farmers did not stand in their yards with shotguns, people did not flee from their homes in terror, and no one was injured in panicky mobs fleeing the invaders (Socolow, 2008).

A closer look at the work of Le Bon's (1895/1960) crowd psychology also reveals weaknesses, both in terms of scholarship and scientific objectivity. Although his writings did much to popularize such concepts as group mind and contagion, he borrowed heavily—some say, too heavily—from the work of earlier scholars (van Ginneken, 2007).

Moreover, his dire predictions about crowds and mobs were driven more by his racial and class-based prejudices than the facts (Bendersky, 2007).

Yet, people are quick to call crowds irrational and mad, even though the data do not support this conjecture. Violence occurs in crowds and mobs, but it is relatively rare (McPhail, 1991). In most cases, individuals in collectives seek specific goals and, by joining with others, they improve their chances of reaching those goals. Even when people are trapped in dangerous situations, such as the crowd at The Who concert in the United States or the Love Parade in Germany, the crowd does not behave badly. Many condemn such crowds, saying that they stampeded, but when researchers consider the evidence, they usually conclude that the crowd panicked, but did not engage in selfish, destructive behavior. Indeed, the amount of helping shown by the people in such crowds exceeds levels of helping documented in studies of bystander interventions in emergencies (see Chapter 7).

Moreover, when crowds do engage in violence, it takes the form of intergroup conflict rather than mindless savagery. Studies of riots, social movements, and even criminal mobs, suggest that violence occurs when these groups confront other groups—and the conflict between the two escalates. In many cases one of the group is a recognized authority within the society—such as a police force or a militia. These socially sanctioned groups are generally judged more positively than the activists, protestors, and rebels, even though in many cases they are more violent than the "mindless mob."

The crowd-as-mad and the crowd-as-group views must be reconciled in a more complete understanding of collective behavior. Individuals, when immersed in a collective, do sometimes perpetrate great wrongs, yet most gatherings, crowds, and social movements act in ways that are unremarkable. Crowds are groups, and collective dynamics are for the most part the same as small group dynamics. Hence, the next time you hear of a crowd behaving oddly, do not dismiss its actions as one more illustration of a group gone wrong.

Studying Groups and Collectives

In this book, we have examined many different groups—a search and rescue squad; a band of outcasts from the art community that generated a cohesive movement that redefined the world of art; a sports team that survived against all odds when their plane crashed in the Andes; a cohesive hockey team that outperformed a superior opponent; a jury reaching a verdict by carefully reviewing its mission and the evidence it was given; a group led by a powerful authority figure who manipulated the members through deceit and subterfuge; teams that worked to make products and decisions, including military and political experts who planned an ill-fated invasion; groups that had to deal with conflict within their ranks and conflict with other groups; a heroic group trying to return to Earth after circling the Moon; and a group of people who made use of the restorative, curative impact of a group to gain self-understanding and improve their well-being. In this final chapter, we have turned to examine crowds, mobs, and social movements.

These analyses have illuminated many of a group's most basic processes—how groups take in and reject members; evolve over time; organize their members in hierarchies of authority; perform tasks, both effectively and ineffectively; make plans and decisions; and succor their members and regulate their behavior in context. But these analyses have also revealed that groups, like large collectives, are often misunderstood and mismanaged. It is ironic that whereas scientists have studied aspects of the physical world for centuries, only in the last hundred years have they turned their attention to human experiences and human groups in particular. Yet the theories and studies of group dynamics we have examined here repeatedly confirm the important role that groups play in all aspects of social life. Human beings are in many ways individuals who are seeking their personal, private objectives, yet they are also members of larger social units that may be seeking collective outcomes. As social creatures, embedded in a rich network of mutual, collective, and reciprocal relationships, individuals cannot be understood fully without considering the social groups to which they belong.

Fortunately, the field of group dynamics offers the means of reducing our ignorance of this fundamental aspect of the human condition. Stanley Milgram and Hans Toch, writing nearly 50 years ago, asked this question: If we "do not take up the job of understanding riots, panics, and social movements, who will?" (1969, p. 590). Their question applies, with equal force, to the study of groups in general. If we do not take up the job of understanding groups, who will?

CHAPTER REVIEW

What is collective behavior?

1. The term *collective behavior* has many interpretations, but in general, it describes instances in which a relatively large group of people respond in a similar way to an event or situation. *Collectives* differ from other types of groups in terms of:

   - Size: Collectives tend to be large rather than small.

   - Proximity: In some cases, members of a collective are together in one place (e.g., crowds), but other collectives involve individuals who are dispersed across great distances (e.g., social movements).

   - Duration: Collectives sometimes, but not always, form and disband rapidly. Smelser distinguished between collective outbursts and collective movements.

   - Conventionality: Members sometimes engage in atypical, unconventional, or even aberrant behaviors.

   - Relationships between members: Collectives are often weak associations of individuals rather than cohesive groups.

2. Gatherings combine aspects of smaller groups with qualities found in larger, more amorphous, crowds.

   - *Audiences* and *queues* are more normatively regulated than crowds. Violations of norms in either type of collective generally lead to negative sanctioning.

   - Milgram's studies of line breaking suggest that queue members are both group- and self-motivated.

3. *Crowds* include common crowds, such as street crowds or public gatherings, audiences, queues, and mobs (aggressive mobs and panics).

   - Milgram and his associates created crowds on a New York City street by having people stare up at a building. The larger the initial seed group, the more people who joined the crowd.

   - Crowds, although unstable and short-lived, display consistent structures and behavioral tendencies. McPhail has documented the types of behaviors common in such groups (e.g., movement, position, manipulation, gesticulation, etc.).

4. *Mobs* include both positive and negative types of crowds.

   - The emotional state of celebratory mobs, including *flash mobs*, is generally very positive—one of elation and joy rather than anger and hostility.

   - Aggressive mobs, such as lynch mobs and hooligans, engage in aggressive, violent actions, including mobbing.

   - *Riots* are large, disbursed, and typically hostile mobs.

5. *Panics* occur when crowds seek to escape a situation (escape panics) or when fearful a valued resource will run out (acquisitive panics).

   - Group panics are dangerous situations. Eleven people were killed when a group waiting to gain admission to The Who concert panicked due to overcrowding.

   - Crowd disasters are common across the world. The queueing effect, turbulence, and overcrowding all combine to create dangerous crowd situations.

   - Studies of very large crowds, such as those conducted by Helbing at the Jamarat Bridge, have identified the factors that contribute to injury in such crowds and ways to reduce the danger.

6. Individuals need not be concentrated in a single location to display convergence in action, for such *collective movements* as rumors, *trends* (fads, crazes, fashion trends), *mass delusions, psychogenic illness*, and *social movements* can influence widely dispersed individuals.

   - Rosnow suggests that anxiety and uncertainty are key triggers for rumor transmission.

   - The Arab Spring and Occupy Wall Street are examples of social movements. Researchers have identified four types of social movements: reformist, revolutionary, reactionary, and communitarian.

   - Political opportunity theory, resource mobilization theory, and framing theory examine the political factors that influence the success of social movements.

   - Recent movements have made use of information technologies, as described in Rheingold's concept of a *smart mob*.

What theories explain collective behavior?

1. Le Bon maintained that crowds are governed by a collective mind and that *contagion* causes crowd members to experience similar thoughts and emotions.

   - People tend to imitate each other, thereby increasing the likelihood that their actions will become unified and coordinated.

   - Social network theory considers contagion to result from relatively common network processes. As Gladwell points out, some individuals in social networks (e.g., connectors) are more influential than are others.

2. *Convergence theories* propose that the individuals who join groups often possess similar needs and personal characteristics.

   - Involvement in social movements is related to individuals' personalities, sense of injustice, self-efficacy, and identity.

   - Studies of *relative deprivation*, for example, suggest that people whose attainments fall below their expectations are more likely to join social movements. As Runciman notes, individuals are more likely to take action when they are experiencing *fraternal deprivation* rather than *egoistic deprivation*.

3. Zimbardo's deindividuation theory traces collective phenomena back to *deindividuation*, which can be broken down into three components—inputs, internal changes, and behavioral outcomes. Inputs, or causes, of deindividuation include feelings of anonymity, reduced responsibility (diffusion of responsibility), membership in large groups, and a heightened state of physiological arousal.

   - Zimbardo's study of aggression in hooded college students, Diener's study of Halloween trick-or-treaters, and Mann's studies of religious groups, all support the basic model.

   - Diener's work indicates that the deindividuated state has two basic components—reduced self-awareness (minimal self-consciousness, etc.) and altered experiencing (disturbances in concentration and judgment, etc.).

   - Deindividuation is most likely to generate negative outcomes when individuals are part of a group and anonymous. However, in some cases deindividuation can lead to positive, rather than negative, reactions.

4. Turner and Killian's *emergent norm theory* argues that crowds often develop unique standards for behavior and that these atypical norms exert a powerful influence on behavior. The *baiting crowd*, for example, forms when a group of onlookers collectively urges someone to injure him- or herself.

5. Social identity theory suggests that much of the behavior of individuals in collectives can be explained by basic identity mechanisms.

   - As Reicher notes, collective behavior is often intergroup behavior, and so individuals maximize their individual sense of worth by identifying with the ingroup.

   - Work by Maslach and others indicates that collective behavior in some cases represents an attempt to reestablish a sense of individuality.

How different are collectives from other types of groups?

1. Recent analyses of crowds and collectives have questioned the "crowd-as-mad" assumption. Collectives differ from more routine groups in degree rather than in kind.

2. Collectives, like groups in general, are often misunderstood and mismanaged, but the field of group dynamics offers a means of dispelling this ignorance.

RESOURCES

Chapter Case: The Arab Spring

- *Liberation Square: Inside the Egyptian Revolution and the Rebirth of a Nation* by Ashraf Khalil

(2011) provides a detailed, street-level view into the dynamics of Egypt's 2011 revolutionary social movement.

Collective Behavior

- *Markets, Mobs, & Mayhem: A Modern Look at the Madness of Crowds* by Robert Menschel (2002) draws on literature, case studies, and even cartoons to provide a general overview and analysis of collective action.

- *Outbreak! The Encyclopedia of Extraordinary Social Behavior* by Hilary Evans and Robert Bartholomew (2009) is a comprehensive and well-researched analysis of all manner of collective behavior that corrects many misconceptions and myths about famous cases.

Theoretical Perspectives

- "Collective Behavior: Crowds and Social Movements" by Stanley Milgram and Hans Toch (1969), although written over 40 years ago, still offers fundamental insights into collective behavior.

- *Collective Behavior* by Ralph H. Turner (2001a) is a succinct yet comprehensive overview of the key theories of "those forms of social behavior in which the usual conventions cease to guide social action and people collectively transcend, bypass, or subvert established institutional patterns and structures" (p. 348).

- "The Human Choice: Individuation, Reason, and Order Versus Deindividuation, Impulse,

and Chaos" by Philip G. Zimbardo (1969) is a wide-ranging analysis of the causes and consequences of the loss of identity that sometimes occurs in groups.

- "Toward an Integrative Social Identity Model of Collective Action: A Quantitative Research Synthesis of Three Socio-Psychological Perspectives" by Martijn van Zomeren, Tom Postmes, and Russell Spears (2008) provides a scholarly review of the vast literature on social movements, as well as results from their meta-analysis of the impact of injustice, efficacy, and identity on social participation.

Collectives as Groups

- *The Myth of the Madding Crowd* by Clark McPhail (1991) expertly synthesizes prior theoretical work on crowds with McPhail's field studies of actual crowds to dispel many absurd myths about crowds and replace them with data-based propositions.

- *Mad Mobs and Englishmen? Myths and Realities of the 2011 Riots* by Steve Reicher and Cliff Stott (2011) provides a theoretically insightful description of the events leading up to the 2011 protests and riots in England, casting those events into a modern, crowd-as-group perspective.

References

Aarts, H., & Dijksterhuis, A. (2003). The silence of the library: Environment, situational norm, and social behavior. *Journal of Personality and Social Psychology, 84*, 18–28.

Aarts, H., Dijksterhuis, A., & Custers, R. (2003). Automatic normative behavior in environments: The moderating role of conformity in activating situational norms. *Social Cognition, 21*, 447–464.

Abele, A. E. (2003). The dynamics of masculine-agentic and feminine-communal traits: Findings from a prospective study. *Journal of Personality and Social Psychology, 85*, 768–776.

Aberson, C. L. (2010). Diversity experiences and intergroup attitudes. In R. J. Crisp (Ed.), *The psychology of social and cultural diversity* (pp. 171–189). New York: Wiley-Blackwell.

Abrahamsen, S. (1987). The rescue of Denmark's Jews. In L. Goldberger (Ed.), *The rescue of the Danish Jews: Moral courage under stress* (pp. 3–12). New York: New York University.

Abrams, D. (1990). *Political identity: Relative deprivation, social identity, and the case of Scottish nationalism.* London: Economic and Social Research Council.

Abrams, D., & Hogg, M. A. (2001). Collective identity: Group membership and self–conception. In M. A. Hogg & R. S. Tindale (Eds.), *Blackwell handbook of social psychology: Group processes* (pp. 425–460). Malden, MA: Blackwell.

Abrams, D., Hogg, M. A., Hinkle, S., & Often, S. (2005). The social identity perspective on small groups. In M. S. Poole & A. B. Hollingshead (Eds.), *Theories of small groups: Interdisciplinary perspectives* (pp. 99–137). Thousand Oaks, CA: Sage.

Abrams, D., Randsley de Moura, G., Marques, J. M., & Hutchison, P. (2008). Innovation credit: When can leaders oppose their group's norms? *Journal of Personality and Social Psychology, 95*(3), 662–678.

Adams, R. B. (1998). Inciting sociological thought by studying the Deadhead community: Engaging publics in dialogue. *Social Forces, 77*, 1–25.

Adler, P. A., & Adler, P. (1995). Dynamics of inclusion and exclusion in preadolescent cliques. *Social Psychology Quarterly, 58*, 145–162.

Agazarian, Y. M. (2001). *A systems-centered approach to inpatient group psychotherapy.* Philadelphia: Jessica Kingsley.

Aiello, J. R. (1987). Human spatial behavior. In D. Stokols & I. Altman (Eds.), *Handbook of environmental psychology* (Vol. 1, pp. 389–504). New York: Wiley.

Aiello, J. R., & Douthitt, E. A. (2001). Social facilitation: From Triplett to electronic performance monitoring. *Group Dynamics: Theory, Research, and Practice, 5*, 163–180.

Aiello, J. R., & Kolb, K. J. (1995). Electronic performance monitoring and social context: Impact on productivity and stress. *Journal of Applied Psychology, 80*, 339–353.

Albright, L., Kenny, D. A., & Malloy, T. E. (1988). Consensus in personality judgments at zero acquaintance. *Journal of Personality and Social Psychology, 55*, 387–395.

Alge, B. J. (2001). Effects of computer surveillance on perceptions of privacy and procedural justice. *Journal of Applied Psychology, 86*, 797–804.

Alicke, M. D., Braun, J. C., Glor, J. E., Klotz, M. L., Magee, J., Sederholm, H., & Siegel, R. (1992). Complaining behavior in social interaction. *Personality and Social Psychology Bulletin, 18*, 286–295.

Allen, K., Blascovich, J., & Mendes, W. B. (2002). Cardiovascular reactivity in the presence of pets, friends, and spouses: The truth about cats and dogs. *Psychosomatic Medicine, 64*, 727–739.

Allen, K., Blascovich, J., Tomaka, J., & Kelsey, R. M. (1991). Presence of human friends and pet dogs as moderators of autonomic responses to stress in women. *Journal of Personality and Social Psychology, 61*, 582–589.

Allen, N. J., & Hecht, T. D. (2004). The 'romance of teams': Toward an understanding of its psychological underpinnings and implications. *Journal of Occupational and Organizational Psychology, 77*, 439–461.

Allen, V. L. (1975). Social support for nonconformity. *Advances in Experimental Social Psychology, 8,* 2–43.

Allison, G., & Zelikow, P. (1999). *Essence of decision: Explaining the Cuban missile crisis* (2nd ed.). New York: Longman.

Allison, S. T., McQueen, L. R., & Schaerfl, L. M. (1992). Social decision making processes and the equal partitionion of shared resources. *Journal of Experimental Social Psychology, 28,* 23–42.

Allison, S. T., & Messick, D. M. (1985a). Effects of experience on performance in a replenishable resource trap. *Journal of Personality and Social Psychology, 49,* 943–948.

Allison, S. T., & Messick, D. M. (1985b). The group attribution error. *Journal of Experimental Social Psychology, 21,* 563–579.

Allison, S. T., & Messick, D. M. (1990). Social decision heuristics in the use of shared resources. *Journal of Behavioral Decision Making, 3,* 195–204.

Allison, S. T., Worth, L. T., & King, M. C. (1990). Group decisions as social inference heuristics. *Journal of Personality and Social Psychology, 58,* 801–811.

Allmendinger, J., Hackman, J. R., & Lehman, E.V. (1996). Life and work in symphony orchestras. *Musical Quarterly, 80,* 194–219.

Allport, F. H. (1920). The influence of the group upon association and thought. *Journal of Experimental Psychology, 3,* 159–182.

Allport, F. H. (1924). *Social psychology.* Boston: Houghton Mifflin.

Allport, F. H. (1934). The J-curve hypothesis of conforming behavior. *Journal of Social Psychology, 5,* 141–183.

Allport, F. H. (1961). The contemporary appraisal of an old problem. *Contemporary Psychology, 6,* 195–197.

Allport, F. H. (1962). A structuronomic conception of behavior: Individual and collective. I. Structural theory and the master problem of social psychology. *Journal of Abnormal and Social Psychology, 64,* 3–30.

Allport, F. H., & Lepkin, M. (1943). Building war morale with news-headlines. *Public Opinion Quarterly, 7,* 211–221.

Allport, G. W. (1954). *The nature of prejudice.* New York: Addison-Wesley.

Allport, G. W. (1968). The historical background of modern social psychology. In G. Lindzey & E. Aronson (Eds.), *The handbook of social psychology* (Vol. 1, 2nd ed., pp. 1–80). New York: Addison-Wesley.

Allport, G. W., & Postman, L. J. (1947). *The psychology of rumor.* New York: Holt.

Alonso, O., & Mizzaro, S. (2009). Can we get rid of TREC assessors? Using Mechanical Turk for relevance assessment. *SIGIR 2009 Proceedings: The Future of IR Evaluation,* Boson. Retrieved from staff.science.uva.nl/~kamps/publications/2009/

Altemeyer, B. (1988). *Enemies of freedom: Understanding right-wing authoritarianism.* San Francisco: Jossey-Bass.

Alter, A. L., & Darley, J. M. (2009). When the association between appearance and outcome contaminates social judgment: A bidirectional model linking group homogeneity and collective treatment. *Journal of Personality and Social Psychology, 97*(5), 776–795.

Alterman, E. (2004). *When presidents lie: A history of official deception and its consequences.* New York: Viking.

Altman, I. (1973). An ecological approach to the functioning of socially isolated groups. In J. E. Rasmussen (Ed.), *Man in isolation and confinement* (pp. 241–269). Chicago: Aldine.

Altman, I. (1975). *The environment and social behavior.* Pacific Grove, CA: Brooks/Cole.

Altman, I. (1977). Research on environment and behavior: A personal statement of strategy. In D. Stokols (Ed.), *Perspectives on environment and behavior* (pp. 303–324). New York: Plenum Press.

Altman, I., & Chemers, M. M. (1980). *Culture and environment.* Pacific Grove, CA: Brooks/Cole.

Altman, I., & Churchman, A. S. (Eds.). (1994). *Human behavior and the environment: Place attachment* (Vol. 12). New York: Plenum Press.

Altman, I., & Haythorn, W. W. (1967). The ecology of isolated groups. *Behavioral Science, 12,* 169–182.

Altman, I., & Taylor, D. A. (1973). *Social penetration: The development of interpersonal relationships.* New York: Holt, Rinehart & Winston.

Altman, I., Taylor, D. A., & Wheeler, L. (1971). Ecological aspects of group behavior in social isolation. *Journal of Applied Social Psychology, 1,* 76–100.

Alvares, G. A., Hickie, I. B., & Guastella, A. J. (2010). Acute effects of intranasal oxytocin on subjective and behavioral responses to social rejection. *Experimental and Clinical Psychopharmacology, 18*(4), 316–321.

Amegashie, J. A., & Runkel, M. (2007). Sabotaging potential rivals. *Social Choice and Welfare, 28,* 143–162.

Ames, C. (1987). The enhancement of student motivation. In M. L. Maehr & D. A. Kleiber (Eds.), *Advances in motivation and achievement* (Vol. 5, pp. 123–148). Greenwich, CT: JAI Press.

Ames, D. R., & Flynn, F. J. (2007). What breaks a leader: The curvilinear relation between assertiveness and leadership. *Journal of Personality and Social Psychology, 92,* 307–324.

Amichai-Hamburger, Y. (2012). Reducing intergroup conflict in the digital age. In H. Giles (Ed.), *The handbook of intergroup communication* (pp. 181–193). New York: Routledge.

Amichai-Hamburger, Y., & McKenna, K. Y. A. (2006). The contact hypothesis reconsidered: Interacting via the Internet. *Journal of Computer-Mediated Communication, 11*(3), 825–843.

Amir, Y. (1969). Contact hypothesis in ethnic relations. *Psychological Bulletin, 71,* 319–342.

Andersen, S. M. (1984). Self-knowledge and social inference: II. The diagnosticity of cognitive/affective and behavioral data. *Journal of Personality and Social Psychology, 46,* 294–307.

Anderson, C., & Galinsky, A. D. (2006). Power, optimism, and risk-taking. *European Journal of Social Psychology, 36,* 511–536.

Anderson, C., John, O. P., Keltner, D., & Kring, A. M. (2001). Who attains social status? Effects of personality and physical attractiveness in social groups. *Journal of Personality and Social Psychology, 81,* 116–132.

Anderson, C., & Kilduff, G. J. (2009). The pursuit of status in social groups. *Current Directions in Psychological Science, 18*(5), 295–298.

Anderson, C., Srivastava, S., Beer, J. S., Spataro, S. E., & Chatman, J. A. (2006). Knowing your place: Self-perceptions of status in face-to-face groups. *Journal of Personality and Social Psychology, 91*(6), 1094–1110.

Anderson, C. J. (2003). The psychology of doing nothing: Forms of decision avoidance result from reason and emotion. *Psychological Bulletin, 129*(1), 139–166.

Anderson, L. R. (1978). Groups would do better without humans. *Personality and Social Psychology Bulletin, 4,* 557–558.

Andersson, J., Hitch, G., & Meudell, P. (2006). Effects of the timing and identity of retrieval cues in individual recall: An attempt to mimic cross-cueing in collaborative recall. *Memory, 14,* 94–103.

Annett, J., & Stanton, N. (2001). Team work—a problem for ergonomics? *Ergonomic, 43,* 1045–1051.

APA (2007). *APA dictionary of psychology.* Washington, DC: American Psychological Association.

Apodoca v. Oregon, 406 U.S. 404(1972).

Appelbaum, R. P., & Chambliss, W. J. (1995). *Sociology.* New York: HarperCollins.

Applebaum, E., & Blatt, R. (1994). *The new American workplace.* Ithaca, NY: ILR.

Ardry, R. (1970). *The territorial imperative: A personal inquiry into the animal origins of property and nations.* New York: Atheneum.

Argyle, M., & Dean, J. (1965). Eye-contact, distance, and affiliation. *Sociometry, 28,* 289–304.

Argyle, M., Henderson, M., Bond, M., Iizuka, Y., Contarello, A. (1986). Cross-cultural variations in relationship rules. *International Journal of Psychology, 21*(3), 287–315.

Arkes, H. R., & Blumer, C. (1985). The psychology of sunk cost. *Organizational Behavior and Human Decision Processes, 35,* 124–140.

Arkin, R. M., & Burger, J. M. (1980). Effects of unit relation tendencies on interpersonal attraction. *Social Psychology Quarterly, 43,* 380–391.

Arnardottir, A. A. (2002). *Leadership style in colead psychotherapy groups, assessed from leaders', co-leaders', and group members' perspective.* Unpublished doctoral dissertation. Richmond: Virginia Commonwealth University.

Arnold, D. W., & Greenberg, C. I. (1980). Deviate rejection within differentially manned groups. *Social Psychology Quarterly, 43,* 419–424.

Aronson, E. (2000). *Nobody left to hate: Teaching compassion after Columbine.* New York: Henry Holt.

Aronson, E., & Mills, J. (1959). The effects of severity of initiation on liking for a group. *Journal of Abnormal and Social Psychology, 59,* 177–181.

Aronson, E., & Patnoe, S. (1997). *Cooperation in the classroom: The jigsaw method.* New York: Longman.

Aronson, E., Stephan, C., Sikes, J., Blaney, N., & Snapp, M. (1978). *The jigsaw classroom.* Thousand Oaks, CA: Sage.

Arriaga, X. B., & Agnew, C. R. (2001). Being committed: Affective, cognitive, and conative components of relationship commitment. *Personality and Social Psychology Bulletin, 27,* 1190–1203.

Arrow, H. (1997). Stability, bistability, and instability in small group influence patterns. *Journal of Personality and Social Psychology, 72,* 75–85.

Arrow, H., Henry, K. B., Poole, M. S., Wheelan, S., & Moreland, R. (2005). Traces, trajectories, and timing: The temporal perspective on groups. In M. S. Poole & A. B. Hollingshead (Eds.), *Theories of small groups: Interdisciplinary perspectives* (pp. 313–367). Thousand Oaks, CA: Sage.

Arrow, H., & McGrath, J. E. (1995). Membership dynamics in groups at work: A theoretical framework. *Research in Organizational Behavior, 17,* 373–411.

Arrow, H., McGrath, J. E., & Berdahl, J. L. (2000). *Small groups as complex systems: Formation, coordination, development, and adaptation.* Thousand Oaks, CA: Sage.

Arterberry, M. E., Cain, K. M., & Chopko, S. A. (2007). Collaborative problem solving in five-year-old children: Evidence of social facilitation and social loafing. *Educational Psychology, 27,* 577–596.

Arvey, R., & Chaturvedi, S. (2011). Examining the genetic basis of leadership. In S. E. Murphy & R. J. Reichard (Eds.), *Series in applied psychology. Early development and leadership: Building the next generation of leaders* (pp. 59–69). New York: Routledge/ Taylor & Francis Group.

Arvey, R. D., Rotundo, M., Johnson, W., Zhang, Z., & McGue, M. (2006). The determinants of leadership role occupancy: Genetic and personality factors. *Leadership Quarterly, 17,* 1–20.

Arvey, R. D., Zhang, Z., Krueger, R. E., & Avolio, B. (2007). Developmental and genetic determinants of leadership role occupancy among women. *Journal of Applied Psychology, 92,* 693–706.

Asch, S. E. (1946). Forming impressions of personality. *Journal of Abnormal and Social Psychology, 41*(3), 258–290.

Asch, S. E. (1952). *Social psychology.* Upper Saddle River, NJ: Prentice-Hall.

Asch, S. E. (1955). Opinions and social pressures. *Scientific American, 193,* 31–35.

Asch, S. E. (1956). Studies of independence and conformity: I. A minority of one against a unanimous majority. *Psychological Monographs: General and Applied, 70*(9), 1–70. Whole No. 416.

Asendorpf, J. B., & Meier, G. H. (1993). Personality effects on children's speech in everyday life: Sociability-mediated exposure and shyness-mediated reactivity in social situations. *Journal of Personality and Social Psychology, 64,* 1072–1083.

Asendorpf, J. B., & Wilpers, S. (1998). Personality effects on social relationships. *Journal of Personality and Social Psychology, 74,* 1531–1544.

Ashburn-Nardo, L., Voils, C. I., & Monteith, M. J. (2001). Implicit associations as the seeds of intergroup bias: How easily do they take root? *Journal of Personality and Social Psychology, 81,* 789–799.

Asher, S. R., & Paquette, J. A. (2003). Loneliness and peer relations in childhood. *Current Directions in Psychological Science, 12,* 75–78.

Ashmore, R. D., Deaux, K., & McLaughlin-Volpe, T. (2004). An organizing framework for collective identity: Articulation and significance of multidimensionality. *Psychological Bulletin, 130,* 80–114.

Aubé, C., & Rousseau, V. (2005). Team goal commitment and team effectiveness: The role of task interdependence and supportive behaviors. *Group Dynamics: Theory, Research, and Practice, 9*(3), 189–204.

Aubé, C., Rousseau, V., & Tremblay, S. (2011). Team size and quality of group experience: The more the merrier? *Group Dynamics: Theory, Research, and Practice, 15*(4), 357–375.

Aubert, B. A., & Kelsey, B. L. (2003). Further understanding of trust and performance in virtual teams. *Small Group Research, 34*(5), 575–618.

Augustine, A. A., & Hemenover, S. H. (2008). Extraversion and the consequences of social interaction on affect repair. *Personality and Individual Differences, 44,* 1151–1161.

Austin, R. (2006). The role of ICT in bridge-building and social inclusion: Theory, policy and practice issues. *European Journal of Teacher Education, 29*(2), 145–161.

Austin, R., & Anderson, J. (2008). Building bridges online: Issues of pedagogy and learning outcomes in intercultural education through citizenship. *International Journal of Information and Communication Technology Education, 4*(1), 86–94.

Aveni, A. (1977). The not-so-lonely crowd: Friendship groups in collective behavior. *Sociometry, 40,* 96–99.

Averill, J. R. (1983). Studies on anger and aggression: Implications for theories of emotion. *American Psychologist, 38,* 1145–1160.

Avolio, B. J. (2004). Transformational and transactional leadership. In G. R. Goethals, G. J. Sorenson, & J. M. Burns (Eds.), *The encyclopedia of leadership* (pp. 1558–1566). Thousand Oaks, CA: Sage.

Avolio, B. J., & Bass, B. M. (1995). Individual consideration viewed at multiple levels of analysis: A multi-level framework for examining the diffusion of transformational leadership. *Leadership Quarterly, 6,* 199–218.

Avolio, B. J., & Locke, E. E. (2002). Contrasting different philosophies of leader motivation: Altruism versus egoism. *Leadership Quarterly, 13,* 169–191.

Avolio, B. J., Walumbwa, F. O., & Weber, T. J. (2009). Leadership: Current theories, research, and future directions. *Annual Review of Psychology, 60,* 421–449.

Axelrod, R. (1984). *The evolution of cooperation.* New York: Basic Books.

Axelrod, R., & Hamilton, W. D. (1981). The evolution of cooperation. *Science, 211,* 1390–1396.

Ayduk, Ö., Gyurak, A., & Luerssen, A. (2008). Individual differences in the rejection-aggression link in the hot sauce paradigm: The case of rejection sensitivity. *Journal of Experimental Social Psychology, 44*(3), 775–782.

Ayman, R., Chemers, M. M., & Fiedler, F. (2007). The contingency model of leadership effectiveness: Its levels of analysis. In R. P. Vecchio (Ed.), *Leadership: Understanding the dynamics of power and influence in organizations* (2nd ed., pp. 335–360). Notre Dame, IN: University of Notre Dame Press.

Ayoko, O. B., Konrad, A. M., & Boyle, M. V. (2012). Online work: Managing conflict and emotions for performance in virtual teams. *European Management Journal, 30*(2), 156–174.

Back, K. W. (1951). Influence through social communication. *Journal of Abnormal and Social Psychology, 46,* 9–23.

Back, K. W. (1973). *Beyond words: The story of sensitivity training and the encounter movement.* Baltimore: Penguin.

Back, K. W. (1974). Intervention techniques: Small groups. *Annual Review of Psychology, 25,* 367–387.

Back, M. D., Schmukle, S. C., & Egloff, B. (2008). How extraverted is honey.bunny77@hotmail.de? Inferring personality from e-mail addresses. *Journal of Research in Personality, 42*(4), 1116–1122.

Backstrom, L., Kumar, R., Marlow, C., Novak, J., & Tomkins, A. (2008). Preferential behavior in online groups. Proceedings of the 1st ACM WSDM International Conference on Web Search and Data Mining. Retrieved from www.cs.cornell.edu/~lars/wsdm08.pdf

Bahns, A. J., Pickett, K. M., & Crandall, C. S. (2012). Social ecology of similarity: Big schools, small schools and social relationships. *Group Processes & Intergroup Relations, 15*(1), 119–131.

Bahrami, B., Olsen, K., Latham, P. E., Roepstorff, A., Rees, G., & Frith, C. D. (2010). Optimally interacting minds. *Science, 329,* 1081–1085.

Bainbridge, W. S. (2007). The scientific research potential of virtual worlds. *Science, 317*(5837), 472–476.

Bainbridge, W. S. (2010). *The warcraft civilization: Social science in a virtual world.* Boston: MIT Press.

Bakeman, R. (2000). Behavioral observation and coding. In H. T. Reis & C. M. Judd (Eds.), *Handbook of research methods in social and personality psychology* (pp. 138–159). New York: Cambridge University Press.

Baldwin, M. W. (1992). Relational schemas and the processing of social information. *Psychological Bulletin, 112*(3), 461–484.

Bales, R. F. (1950). *Interaction process analysis: A method for the study of small groups.* Reading, MA: Addison-Wesley.

Bales, R. F. (1955). How people interact in conferences. *Scientific American, 192,* 31–35.

Bales, R. F. (1958). Task roles and social roles in problem-solving groups. In E. E. Maccoby, T. M. Newcomb, & E. L. Hartley (Eds.), *Readings in social psychology* (pp. 437–447). New York: Holt, Rinehart & Winston.

Bales, R. F. (1965). The equilibrium problem in small groups. In A. P. Hare, E. F. Borgatta, & R. F. Bales (Eds.), *Small groups: Studies in social interaction* (Revised ed., pp. 444–483). New York: Knopf.

Bales, R. F. (1970). *Personality and interpersonal behavior.* New York: Holt, Rinehart & Winston.

Bales, R. F. (1980). *SYMLOG case study kit*. New York: Free Press.

Bales, R. F. (1999). *Social interaction systems: Theory and measurement*. New Brunswick, NJ: Transaction.

Bales, R. F., & Cohen, S. P. with Williamson, S. A. (1979). *SYMLOG: A system for the multiple level observation of groups*. New York: Free Press.

Bales, R. F., & Hare, A. P. (1965). Diagnostic use of the interaction profile. *Journal of Social Psychology, 67*, 239–258.

Bales, R. F., & Slater, P. E. (1955). Role differentiation in small decision-making groups. In T. Parsons & R. F. Bales (Eds.), *Family, socialization, and interaction process* (pp. 259–306). New York: Free Press.

Bales, R. F., & Strodtbeck, F. L. (1951). Phases in group problem solving. *Journal of Abnormal and Social Psychology, 46*, 485–495.

Balkundi, P., & Harrison, D. A. (2006). Ties, leaders, and time in teams: Strong inference about network structure's effects on team viability and performance. *Academy of Management Journal, 49*(1), 49–68.

Balliet, D., Li, N. P., Macfarlan, S. J., & Van Vugt, M. (2011). Sex differences in cooperation: A meta-analytic review of social dilemmas. *Psychological Bulletin, 137*(6), 881–909.

Balliet, D., Mulder, L. B., & Van Lange, P. A. M. (2011). Reward, punishment, and cooperation: A meta-analysis. *Psychological Bulletin, 137*(4), 594–615.

Balliet, D., Parks, C., & Joireman, J. (2009). Social value orientation and cooperation in social dilemmas: A meta-analysis. *Group Processes & Intergroup Relations, 12*(4), 533–547.

Baltes, B. B., Dickson, M. W., Sherman, M. P., Bauer, C. C., & LaGanke, J. (2002). Computer-mediated communication and group decision making: A meta-analysis. *Organizational Behavior and Human Decision Processes, 87*, 156–179.

Bandura, A. (1986). *Social foundations of thought and action: A social cognitive theory*. Upper Saddle River, NJ: Prentice Hall.

Bandura, A. (1997). *Self-efficacy: The exercise of control*. New York: Freeman.

Bandura, A. (1999). Moral disengagement in the perpetration of inhumanities. *Personality and Social Psychology Review, 3*, 193–209.

Bandura, A., Underwood, B., & Fromson, M. E. (1975). Disinhibition of aggression through diffusion of responsibility and dehumanization of victims. *Journal of Research in Personality, 9*, 253–269.

Barabási, A. (2003). *Linked: How everything is connected to everything else and what it means for business, science, and everyday life*. New York: Plume.

Bargal, D. (2008). Action research: A paradigm for achieving social change. *Small Group Research, 39*, 17–27.

Bargh, J. A., & McKenna, K. Y. A. (2004). The Internet and social life. *Annual Review of Psychology, 55*, 573–590.

Barker, R. G. (1968). *Ecological psychology*. Stanford, CA: Stanford University Press.

Barker, R. G. (1987). Prospecting in ecological psychology: Oskaloosa revisited. In D. Stokols & I. Altman (Eds.), *Handbook of environmental psychology* (Vol. 2, pp. 1413–1432). New York: Wiley.

Barker, R. G. (1990). Recollections of the Midwest Psychological Field Station. *Environment and Behavior, 22*, 503–513.

Barker, R. G., & Associates. (1978). Habitats, environments, and human behavior: Studies in ecological psychology and eco-behavioral sciences from the Midwest Psychological Field Station, 1947–1972. San Francisco: Jossey-Bass.

Barlow, S. H. (2010). Evidence bases for group practice. In R. K. Conyne (Ed.), *The Oxford handbook of group counseling* (pp. 207–230). New York: Oxford University Press.

Barlow, S. H., Burlingame, G. M., & Fuhriman, A. (2000). Therapeutic applications of groups: From Pratt's "thought control classes" to modern group psychotherapy. *Group Dynamics: Theory, Research, and Practice, 4*, 115–134.

Barnett, L. A. (2006). Flying high or crashing down: Girls' accounts of trying out for cheerleading and dance. *Journal of Adolescent Research, 21*, 514–541.

Baron, R. A., & Bell, P. A. (1975). Aggression and heat: Mediating effects of prior provocation and exposure to an aggressive model. *Journal of Personality and Social Psychology, 31*, 825–832.

Baron, R. S. (1986). Distraction-conflict theory: Progress and problems. *Advances in Experimental Social Psychology, 19*, 1–40.

Baron, R. S. (2000). Arousal, capacity, and intense indoctrination. *Personality and Social Psychology Review, 4*, 238–254.

Baron, R. S. (2005). So right it's wrong: Groupthink and the ubiquitous nature of polarized group decision making. *Advances in Experimental Social Psychology, 37*, 219–253.

Baron, R. S., Kerr, N. L., & Miller, N. (1992). *Group process, group decision, group action*. Pacific Grove, CA: Brooks/Cole.

Baron, R. S., Vandello, J. A., & Brunsman, B. (1996). The forgotten variable in conformity research: Impact of task importance on social influence. *Journal of Personality and Social Psychology, 71*, 915–927.

Barsade, S. G., & Gibson, D. E. (2012). Group affect: Its influence on individual and group outcomes. *Current Directions in Psychological Science, 21*(2), 119–123.

Barsade, S. G., Ward, A. J., Turner, J. D. F., & Sonnenfeld, J. A. (2000). To your heart's content: A model of affective diversity in top management teams. *Administrative Science Quarterly, 45*, 802–836.

Bar-Tal, D. (2000). *Shared beliefs in a society: Social psychological analysis*. Thousand Oaks, CA: Sage.

Bar-Tal, D. (2007). Sociopsychological foundations of intractable conflicts. *American Behavioral Scientist, 50*, 1430–1453.

Bartels, L. (May, 2001). No looking back. *Rocky Mountain News*. Retrieved from www.rockymountainnews.com/

Bartholomew, R. E. (1997). Mass hysteria. *British Journal of Psychiatry, 170*, 387–388.

Bartholomew, R. E., & Goode, E. (2000). Mass delusions and hysterias: Highlights from the past millennium. *Skeptical Inquirer, 24*, 20–28.

Bartholomew, R. E., & Sirois, F. (1996). Epidemic hysteria in schools: An international and historical overview. *Educational Studies, 22,* 285–311.

Bartis, S., Szymanski, K., & Harkins, S. G. (1988). Evaluation and performance: A two-edged knife. *Personality and Social Psychology Bulletin, 14,* 242–251.

Bartlem, C. S., & Locke, E. A. (1981). The Coch and French study: A critique and reinterpretation. *Human Relations, 34,* 555–566.

Basden, B. H., Basden, D. R., Bryner, S. & Thomas, R. L. (1997). A comparison of group and individual remembering: Does collaboration disrupt retrieval strategies? *Journal of Experimental Psychology: Learning, Memory and Cognition, 23,* 1176–1189.

Basow, S. A., Foran, K. A., & Bookwala, J. (2007). Body objectification, social pressure, and disordered eating behavior in college women: The role of sorority membership. *Psychology of Women Quarterly, 31,* 394–400.

Bass, B. M. (1997). Does the transactional-transformational leadership paradigm transcend organizational and national boundaries? *American Psychologist, 52,* 130–139.

Bass, B. M., & Ryterband, E. C. (1979). *Organizational psychology* (2nd ed.). Boston: Allyn & Bacon.

Bass, B. M., with R. Bass. (2008). *The Bass handbook of leadership: Theory, research, and managerial applications* (4th ed.). New York: Free Press.

Batchelor, J. P., & Goethals, G. R. (1972). Spatial arrangements in freely formed groups. *Sociometry, 35,* 270–279.

Bateman, P. J., Gray, P. H., & Butler, B. S. (2011). The impact of community commitment on participation in online communities. *Information Systems Research, 22,* 841–854.

Batson, C. D. (1975). Rational processing or rationalization? The effect of disconfirming information on a stated religious belief. *Journal of Personality and Social Psychology, 32*(1), 176–184.

Baum, A., & Davis, G. E. (1980). Reducing the stress of high-density living: An architectural intervention. *Journal of Personality and Social Psychology, 38,* 471–481.

Baum, A., Davis, G. E., & Valins, S. (1979). Generating behavioral data for the design process. In J. R. Aiello & A. Baum (Eds.), *Residential crowding and design* (pp. 175–196). New York: Plenum.

Baum, A., Harpin, R. E., & Valins, S. (1975). The role of group phenomena in the experience of crowding. *Environment and Behavior, 7*(2), 185–198.

Baum, A., & Valins, S. (1977). *Architecture and social behavior: Psychological studies of social density.* Mahwah, NJ: Erlbaum.

Baumeister, R. F. (1984). Choking under pressure: Self-consciousness and paradoxical effects of incentives on skillful performance. *Journal of Personality and Social Psychology, 46,* 610–620.

Baumeister, R. F. (1985). The championship choke. *Psychology Today, 19,* 48–52.

Baumeister, R. F. (1995). Disputing the effects of championship pressures and home audiences. *Journal of Personality and Social Psychology, 68,* 644–648.

Baumeister, R. F. (2010). *Is There Anything Good About Men?: How Cultures Flourish by Exploiting Men.* New York: Oxford University Press.

Baumeister, R. F., Chesner, S. P., Senders, P. S., & Tice, D. M. (1988). Who's in charge here? Group leaders do lend help in emergencies. *Personality and Social Psychology Bulletin, 14,* 17–22.

Baumeister, R. F., & Leary, M. R. (1995). The need to belong: Desire for interpersonal attachments as a fundamental human motivation. *Psychological Bulletin, 117,* 497–529.

Baumeister, R. F., & Showers, C. J. (1986). A review of paradoxical performance effects: Choking under pressure in sports and mental tests. *European Journal of Social Psychology, 16,* 361–383.

Baumeister, R. F., & Sommer, K. L. (1997). What do men want? Gender differences and two spheres of belongingness. *Psychological Bulletin, 122,* 38–44.

Bavelas, A. (1948). A mathematical model for group structures. *Applied Anthropology, 7,* 16–30.

Bavelas, A. (1950). Communication patterns in task-oriented groups. *Journal of the Acoustical Society of America, 22,* 725–730.

Bavelas, A., & Barrett, D. (1951). An experimental approach to organization communication. *Personnel, 27,* 367–371.

Bayazit, M., & Mannix, E. A. (2003). Should I stay or should I go? Predicting team members' intent to remain in the team. *Small Group Research, 34,* 290–321.

Beach, S. R. H., & Tesser, A. (2000). Self-evaluation maintenance and evolution: Some speculative notes. In J. Suls & L. Wheeler (Eds.), *Handbook of social comparison: Theory and research* (pp. 123–140). New York: Kluwer Academic.

Beach, S. R. H., Tesser, A., Fincham, F. D., Jones, D. J., Johnson, D., & Whitaker, D. J. (1998). Pleasure and pain in doing well, together: An investigation of performance-related affect in close relationships. *Journal of Personality and Social Psychology, 74,* 923–938.

Beal, D. J., Cohen, R. R., Burke, M. J., & McLendon, C. L. (2003). Cohesion and performance in groups: A meta-analytic clarification of construct relations. *Journal of Applied Psychology, 88,* 989–1004.

Beaman, A. L., Cole, C. M., Preston, M., Klentz, B., & Steblay, N. M. (1983). Fifteen years of foot-in-the door research: A meta-analysis. *Personality and Social Psychology Bulletin, 9,* 181–196.

Beaton, E. A., Schmidt, L. A., Schulkin, J., Antony, M. M., Swinson, R. P., & Hall, G. B. (2008). Different neural responses to stranger and personally familiar faces in shy and bold adults. *Behavioral Neuroscience, 122,* 704–709.

Bechky, B. A. (2006). Gaffers, gofers, and grips: Role-based coordination in temporary organizations. *Organization Science, 17*(1), 3–21.

Bechtel, R. B. (2002). On to Mars! In R. B. Bechtel & A. Churchman (Eds.), *Handbook of environmental psychology* (pp. 676–685). New York: Wiley.

Bechtel, R. B., & Churchman, A. (Eds.). (2002). *Handbook of environmental psychology.* New York: Wiley.

Bedeian, A. G., & Day, D. V. (2004). Can chameleons lead? *Leadership Quarterly*, *15*, 687–718.

Bedeian, A. G., & Hunt, J. G. (2006). Academic amnesia and vestigial assumptions of our forefathers. *Leadership Quarterly*, *17*, 190–205.

Bednar, R. L., & Kaul, T. (1978). Experiential group research: Current perspectives. In S. L. Garfield & A. E. Bergin (Eds.), *Handbook of psychotherapy and behavior change* (2nd ed., pp. 769–815). New York: Wiley.

Bednar, R. L., & Kaul, T. (1979). Experiential group research: What never happened. *Journal of Applied Behavioral Science*, *15*, 311–319.

Bednar, R. L., & Kaul, T. (1994). Experiential group research: Can the canon fire? In S. L. Garfield and A. E. Bergin (Eds.), *Handbook of psychotherapy and behavior change* (4th ed., pp. 631–663). New York: Wiley.

Behfar, K. J., Mannix, E. A., Peterson, R. S., & Trochim, W. M. (2011). Conflict in small groups: The meaning and consequences of process conflict. *Small Group Research*, *42*(2), 127–176.

Behfar, K. J., Peterson, R. S., Mannix, E. A., & Trochim, W. M. K. (2008). The critical role of conflict resolution in teams: A close look at the links between conflict type, conflict management strategies, and team outcomes. *Journal of Applied Psychology*, *93*, 170–188.

Bell, P. A. (1992). In defense of the negative affect escape model of heat and aggression. *Psychological Bulletin*, *111*, 342–346.

Bell, P. A., Green, T. C., Fisher, J. D., & Baum, A. (2006). *Environmental psychology* (6th ed.). New York: Psychology Press.

Bell, S. T.. (2007). Deep-level composition variables as predictors of team performance: A meta-analysis. *Journal of Applied Psychology*, *92*, 595–615.

Bellah, R. N., Madsen, R., Sullivan, W. M., Swidler, A., & Tipton, S. M. (1985). *Habits of the heart: Individualism and commitment in American life*. New York: Harper & Row.

Bem, D. J. (1972). Self-perception theory. *Advances in Experimental Social Psychology*, *6*, 2–62.

Bem, S. L. (1982). Gender schema theory and self-schema theory compared: A comment on Markus, Crane, Bernstein, and Siladi's "Self-schemas and gender." *Journal of Personality and Social Psychology*, *43*, 1192–1194.

Bem, S. L. (1985). Androgyny and gender schema theory: A conceptual and empirical integration. *Nebraska Symposium on Motivation*, *32*, 179–226.

Bendersky, J. W. (2007). "Panic": The impact of Le Bon's crowd psychology on U.S. military thought. *Journal of the History of the Behavioral Sciences*, *43*, 257–283.

Benjamin, L. T., Jr., & Crouse, E. M. (2002). The American Psychological Association's response to *Brown v. Board of Education*: The case of Kenneth B. Clark. *American Psychologist*, *57*, 38–50.

Benne, K. D., & Sheats, P. (1948). Functional roles of group members. *Journal of Social Issues*, *4*, 41–49.

Bennett, H. S. (1980). *On becoming a rock musician*. Amherst: University of Massachusetts Press.

Bennett, M., & Sani, F. (2008). Children's subjective identification with social groups: A self-stereotyping approach. *Developmental Science*, *11*, 69–75.

Bennis, W., & Biederman, P. W. (1997). *Organizing genius: The secrets of creative collaboration*. Reading, MA: Addison-Wesley.

Bennis, W. G. (1975). *Where have all the leaders gone?* Washington, DC: Federal Executive Institute.

Bennis, W. G., & Shepard, H. A. (1956). A theory of group development. *Human Relations*, *9*, 415–437.

Berdahl, J. L., & Anderson, C. (2005). Men, women, and leadership centralization in groups over time. *Group Dynamics: Theory, Research, and Practice*, *9*, 45–57.

Berdahl, J. L., & Henry, K. (2005). Contemporary issues in group research. In S. A. Wheelan (Ed.), *Handbook of group research and practice* (pp. 19–37). Thousand Oaks, CA: Sage.

Berdahl, J. L., & Martorana, P. (2006). Effects of power on emotion and expression during a controversial group discussion. *European Journal of Social Psychology*, *36*, 497–509.

Berger, J., Ridgeway, C. L., & Zelditch, M. (2002). Construction of status and referential structure. *Sociological Theory*, *20*, 157–179.

Berger, R. E. (1981). *Heart rate, arousal, and the "mere presence" hypothesis of social facilitation*. Unpublished doctoral dissertation, Virginia Commonwealth University, Richmond, VA.

Berger, S. M., Carli, L. L., Garcia, R., & Brady, J. J., Jr. (1982). Audience effects in anticipatory learning: A comparison of drive and practice-inhibition analyses. *Journal of Personality and Social Psychology*, *42*, 478–486.

Berger, S. M., Hampton, K. L., Carli, L. L., Grandmaison, P. S., Sadow, J. S., Donath, C. H., & Herschlag, L. R. (1981). Audience-induced inhibition of overt practice during learning. *Journal of Personality and Social Psychology*, *40*, 479–491.

Berkowitz, L. (1953). Sharing leadership in small, decision-making groups. *Journal of Abnormal and Social Psychology*, *48*, 231–238.

Berkowitz, L. (1954). Group standards, cohesiveness, and productivity. *Human Relations*, *7*, 509–519.

Berman, J. J., & Zimpfer, D. G. (1980). Growth groups: Do the outcomes really last? *Review of Educational Research*, *50*, 505–524.

Berns, G. S., Chappelow, J., Zink, C. F., Pagnoni, G., Martin-Skurski, M. E., & Richards, J. (2005). Neurobiological correlates of social conformity and independence during mental rotation. *Biological Psychiatry*, *58*, 245–253.

Bernstein, M. J., & Claypool, H. M. (2012). Social exclusion and pain sensitivity: Why exclusion sometimes hurts and sometimes numbs. *Personality and Social Psychology Bulletin*, *38*(2), 185–196.

Bernstein, M. J., Young, S. G., Brown, C. M., Sacco, D. F., & Claypool, H. M. (2008). Adaptive responses to social exclusion: Social rejection improves detection of real and fake smiles. *Psychological Science*, *19*(10), 981–983.

Bernthal, P. R., & Insko, C. A. (1993). Cohesiveness without groupthink: The interactive effects of social and task cohesion. *Group and Organizational Management, 18*, 66–87.

Berry, C. M., Ones, D. S., & Sackett, P. R. (2007). Interpersonal deviance, organizational deviance, and their common correlates: A review and meta-analysis. *Journal of Applied Psychology, 92*(2), 410–424.

Betancourt, H., & Blair, I. (1992). A cognition (attribution)-emotion model of violence in conflict situations. *Personality and Social Psychology Bulletin, 18*, 343–350.

Bettencourt, B. A., Brewer, M. B., Croak, M. R., & Miller, N. (1992). Cooperation and the reduction of intergroup bias: The role of reward structure and social orientation. *Journal of Experimental Social Psychology, 28*, 301–309.

Bettencourt, B. A., & Sheldon, K. (2001). Social roles as mechanisms for psychological need satisfaction within social groups. *Journal of Personality and Social Psychology, 81*, 1131–1143.

Bezrukova, K., Jehn, K. A., Zanutto, E. L., & Thatcher, S. M. B. (2009). Do workgroup faultlines help or hurt? A moderated model of faultlines, team identification, and group performance. *Organization Science, 20*(1), 35–50.

Bhatt, M. A., Lohrenz, T., Camerer, C. F., & Montague, P. R. (2010). Neural signatures of strategic types in a two-person bargaining game. *PNAS: Proceedings of the National Academy of Sciences, 107*(46), 19720–19725.

Bianchi, A. J., Kang, S. M., & Stewart, D. (2012). The organizational selection of status characteristics: Status evaluations in an open source community. *Organization Science, 23*(2), 341–354.

Bicchieri, C. (2006). *The grammar of society: The nature and dynamics of social norms.* New York: Cambridge University Press.

Biddle, B. J. (1986). Recent developments in role theory. *Annual Review of Sociology, 12*, 67–92.

Biddle, B. J. (2001). Role theory. In E. F. Borgatta & R. J. V. Montgomery (Eds.), *Encyclopedia of sociology* (Vol. 4, 2nd ed., pp. 2415–2420). New York: Macmillan Reference.

Bieling, P., McGabe, R., & Antony, M. (2006). *Cognitive-behavioral therapy in groups.* New York: Guilford.

Biernat, M., Crandall, C. S., Young, L. V., Kobrynowicz, D., & Halpin, S. M. (1998). All that you can be: Stereotyping of self and others in a military context. *Journal of Personality and Social Psychology, 75*, 301–317.

Biernat, M., & Kobrynowicz, D. (1997). Gender- and race-based standards of competence: Lower minimum standards but higher ability standards for devalued groups. *Journal of Personality and Social Psychology, 72*, 544–557.

Biernat, M., Vescio, T. K., & Green, M. L. (1996). Selective self-stereotyping. *Journal of Personality and Social Psychology, 71*, 1194–1209.

Birnbaum, M. L., & Cicchetti, A. (2005). A model for working with the group life cycle in each group session across the life span of the group. *Groupwork, 15*, 23–43.

Black, L. W., Welser, H. T., Cosley, D., & DeGroot, J. M. (2011). Self-governance through group discussion in Wikipedia: Measuring deliberation in online groups. *Small Group Research, 42*(5), 595–634.

Blader, S. L., & Tyler, T. R. (2003). What constitutes fairness in work settings? A four-component model of procedural justice. *Human Resource Management Review, 13*, 107–126.

Blader, S. L., & Tyler, T. R. (2009). Testing and extending the group engagement model: Linkages between social identity, procedural justice, economic outcomes, and extrarole behavior. *Journal of Applied Psychology, 94*(2), 445–464.

Blake, R. R., & McCanse, A. A. (1991). *Leadership dilemmas—Grid solutions.* Houston, TX: Gulf.

Blake, R. R., & Mouton, J. S. (1964). *The managerial grid.* Houston, TX: Gulf.

Blake, R. R., & Mouton, J. S. (1982). How to choose a leadership style. *Training and Development Journal, 36*, 39–46.

Blake, R. R., & Mouton, J. S. (1984). *Solving costly organizational conflicts: Achieving intergroup trust, cooperation, and teamwork.* San Francisco: Jossey-Bass.

Blake, R. R., & Mouton, J. S. (1986). From theory to practice in interface problem solving. In S. Worchel & W. G. Austin (Eds.), *Psychology of intergroup relations* (2nd ed., pp. 67–87). Chicago: Nelson-Hall.

Blanchard, A. L. (2007). Developing a sense of virtual community measure. *Cyberpsychology & Behavior, 10*(7), 827–830.

Blanchard, F. A., Adelman, L., & Cook, S. W. (1975). Effect of group success and failure upon interpersonal attraction in cooperating interracial groups. *Journal of Personality and Social Psychology, 31*, 1020–1030.

Blanchard, K., & Johnson, S. (1981). *The one minute manager.* New York: Berkley.

Blascovich, J., Ginsburg, G. P., & Howe, R. C. (1975). Blackjack and the risky shift, II: Monetary stakes. *Journal of Experimental Social Psychology, 11*, 224–232.

Blascovich, J., Ginsburg, G. P., & Howe, R. C. (1976). Blackjack, choice shifts in the field. *Sociometry, 39*, 274–276.

Blascovich, J., Loomis, J., Beall, A. C., Swinth, K. R., Hoyt, C. L., & Bailenson, J. N. (2002). Immersive virtual environment technology as a methodological tool for social psychology. *Psychological Inquiry, 13*, 103–124.

Blascovich, J., Mendes, W. B., Hunter, S. B., & Salomon, K. (1999). Social "facilitation" as challenge and threat. *Journal of Personality and Social Psychology, 77*, 68–77.

Blascovich, J., Nash, R. F., & Ginsburg, G. P. (1978). Heart rate and competitive decision making. *Personality and Social Psychology Bulletin, 4*, 115–118.

Blass, T. (1991). Understanding behavior in the Milgram obedience experiment: The role of personality, situations, and their interactions. *Journal of Personality and Social Psychology, 60*, 398–413.

Blass, T. (2000a). The Milgram paradigm after 35 years: Some things we now know about obedience to authority. In T. Blass (Ed.). *Obedience to authority: Current perspectives on the Milgram paradigm* (pp. 35–59). Mahwah, NJ: Erlbaum.

Blass, T. (Ed.). (2000b). *Obedience to authority: Current perspectives on the Milgram paradigm*. Mahwah, NJ: Erlbaum.

Blass, T. (2004). *The man who shocked the world: The life and legacy of Stanley Milgram*. New York: Basic Books.

Blass, T. (2009). From New Haven to Santa Clara: A historical perspective on the Milgram obedience experiments. *American Psychologist, 64*, 37–45.

Blass, T. (2012). A cross-cultural comparison of studies of obedience using the Milgram paradigm: A review. *Social and Personality Psychology Compass, 6*(2), 196–205.

Blau, P. (1964). *Exchange and power in social life*. New York: Wiley.

Bligh, M. C., Kohles, J. C., & Pillai, R. (2011). Romancing leadership: Past, present, and future. *The Leadership Quarterly, 22*(6), 1058–1077.

Blumberg, H., Kent, M. V., Hare, A. P., & Davies, M. F. (2012). *Small group research: Implication for peace psychology and conflict resolution*. New York: Springer.

Blumer, H. (1946). Collective behavior. In A. M. Lee (Ed.), *New outline of the principles of sociology*. New York: Barnes & Noble.

Blumer, H. (1951). Collective behavior. In A. M. Lee (Ed.), *Principles of sociology* (pp. 167–224). New York: Barnes & Noble.

Blumer, H. (1957). Collective behavior. In J. B. Gittler (Ed.), *Review of sociology: Analysis of a decade* (pp. 127–158). New York: Wiley.

Bó, P. D. (2005). Cooperation under the shadow of the future: Experimental evidence from infinitely repeated games. *American Economic Review, 95*, 1591–1604.

Bodenhausen, G. V. (1988). Stereotypic biases in social decision making and memory: Testing process models of stereotype use. *Journal of Personality and Social Psychology, 55*(5), 726–737.

Bogardus, E. S. (1928). World leadership types. *Sociology and Social Research, 12*, 573–579.

Bogardus, E. S. (1954). Group behavior and groupality. *Sociology and Social Research, 38*, 401–403.

Boldry, J. G., Gaertner, L., & Quinn, J. (2007). Measuring the measures: A meta-analytic investigation of the measures of outgroup homogeneity. *Group Processes & Intergroup Relations, 10*, 157–178.

Bollen, K. A., & Hoyle, R. H. (1990). Perceived cohesion: A conceptual and empirical examination. *Social Forces, 69*, 479–504.

Bonacich, P. (1987). Communication networks and collective action. *Social Networks, 9*, 389–396.

Bonanno, G. A., Brewin, C. R., Kaniasty, K., & La Greca, A. M. (2010). Weighing the costs of disaster: Consequences, risks, and resilience in individuals, families, and communities. *Psychological Science in the Public Interest, 11*(1), 1–49.

Bonanno, G. A., Galea, S., Bucciarelli, A., & Vlahov, D. (2007). What predicts psychological resilience after disaster? The role of demographics, resources, and life stress. *Journal of Consulting and Clinical Psychology, 75*, 671–682.

Bond, C. F., Atoum, A. O., & VanLeeuwen, M. D. (1996). Social impairment of complex learning in the wake of public embarrassment. *Basic and Applied Social Psychology, 18*, 31–44.

Bond, C. F., & Titus, L. J. (1983). Social facilitation: A meta-analysis of 241 studies. *Psychological Bulletin, 94*, 265–292.

Bond, J., Kaskutas, L. A., & Weisner, C. (2003). The persistent influence of social networks and Alcoholics Anonymous on abstinence. *Quarterly Journal of Studies on Alcohol, 64*, 579–588.

Bond, M. H. (2002). Reclaiming the individual from Hofstede's ecological analysis—A 20-year odyssey: Comment on Oyserman et al. (2002). *Psychological Bulletin, 128*, 73–77.

Bond, R. (2005). Group size and conformity. *Group Processes & Intergroup Relations, 8*, 331–354.

Bond, R., & Smith, P. B. (1996). Culture and conformity: A meta-analysis of studies using Asch's (1952b, 1956) line judgment task. *Psychological Bulletin, 119*, 111–137.

Bonebright, D. A. (2010). 40 years of storming: A historical review of Tuckman's model of small group development. *Human Resource Development International, 13*(1), 111–120.

Bonikowski, B., & McPherson, M. (2007). The sociology of voluntary associations. In C. D. Bryant & D. L. Peck (Eds.), *21st Century Sociology: A reference handbook* (Vol. 1, pp. 197–207). Thousand Oaks, CA: Sage.

Bonito, J. A., & Hollingshead, A. B. (1997). Participation in small groups. *Communication Yearbook, 20*, 227–261.

Bonner, B. L., & Baumann, M. R. (2008). Informational intragroup influence: The effects of time pressure and group size. *European Journal of Social Psychology, 38*, 46–66.

Bonner, B. L., & Baumann, M. R. (2012). Leveraging member expertise to improve knowledge transfer and demonstrability in groups. *Journal of Personality and Social Psychology, 102*(2), 337–350.

Bonta, B. D. (1997). Cooperation and competition in peaceful societies. *Psychological Bulletin, 121*, 299–320.

Boone, C., Van Olffen, W., & Van Witteloostuijn, A. (2005). Team locus-of-control composition, leadership structure, information acquisition, and financial performance: A business simulation study. *Academy of Management Journal, 48*(5), 889–909.

Booth, A. (1972). Sex and social participation. *American Sociological Review, 37*, 183–193.

Borah, L. A., Jr. (1963). The effects of threat in bargaining: Critical and experimental analysis. *Journal of Abnormal and Social Psychology, 66*, 37–44.

Borgatta, E. F., & Bales, R. F. (1953). Task and accumulation of experience as factors in the interaction of small groups. *Sociometry, 16*, 239–252.

Borgatta, E. F., Couch, A. S., & Bales, R. F. (1954). Some findings relevant to the great man theory of leadership. *American Sociological Review, 19*, 755–759.

Borgatti, S. P. (2002). A statistical method for comparing aggregate data across a priori groups. *Field Methods, 14*, 88–107.

Borgatti, S. P. (2005). Centrality and network flow. *Social Networks, 27*, 55–71.

Borgatti, S. P., Mehra, A., Brass, D. J., & Labianca, G. 2009. Network analysis in the social sciences. *Science, 323*, 892–895.

Borkman, T. J. (1999). *Understanding self-help/mutual aid: Experiential learning in the common.* Piscataway, NJ: Rutgers University Press.

Bornstein, G. (2003). Intergroup conflict: Individual, group, and collective interests. *Personality and Social Psychology Review, 7,* 129–145.

Bornstein, R. F. (1989). Exposure and affect: Overview and meta-analysis of research, 1968–1987. *Psychological Bulletin, 106,* 265–289.

Bornstein, R. F. (1992). The dependent personality: Developmental, social, and clinical perspectives. *Psychological Bulletin, 112,* 3–23.

Bouchard, T. J. (1972). A comparison of two group brainstorming procedures. *Journal of Applied Psychology, 56,* 418–421.

Boulding, K. E. (1956). *The image: Knowledge in life and society.* Ann Arbor: University of Michigan Press.

Bourdieu, P. (1984). *Distinction: A social critique of the judgment of taste* (Trans. R. Nice). Boston: Harvard University Press.

Bourgeois, P., & Hess, U. (2008). The impact of social context on mimicry. *Biological Psychology, 77,* 343–352.

Bowers, C. A., Pharmer, J. A., & Salas, E. (2000). When member homogeneity is needed in work teams: A meta-analysis. *Small Group Research, 31,* 305–327.

Bowers, D. G., & Seashore, S. E. (1966). Predicting organizational effectiveness with a four-factor theory of leadership. *Administrative Science Quarterly, 11,* 238–263.

Bowlby, J. (1980). *Attachment and loss* (Vol. 1). London: Hogarth.

Bowling, N. A., Beehr, T. A., Johnson, A. L., Semmer, N. K., Hendricks, E. A., & Webster, H. A. (2004). Explaining potential antecedents of workplace social support: Reciprocity or attractiveness? *Journal of Occupational Health Psychology, 9,* 339–350.

Bowman, J. M., & Wittenbaum, G. M. (2012). Time pressure affects process and performance in hidden-profile groups. *Small Group Research, 43*(3), 295–314.

Boyd, J. E., Kanas, N. A., Salnitskiy, V. P., Gushin, V. I., Saylor, S. A., Weiss, D. S., Marmar, C. R. (2009). Cultural differences in crewmembers and mission control personnel during two space station programs. *Aviation, Space, and Environmental Medicine, 80*(6), 532–40.

Brabender, V. M., & Fallon, A. (2009). *Group development in practice: Guidance for clinicians and researchers on stages and dynamics of change.* Washington, DC: American Psychological Association.

Bradshaw, S. D. (1998). I'll go if you will: Do shy persons utilize social surrogates? *Journal of Social and Personal Relationships, 15,* 651–669.

Bramel, D., & Friend, R. (1981). Hawthorne, the myth of the docile worker, and class bias in psychology. *American Psychologist, 36,* 867–878.

Brandon, D. P. & Hollingshead, A. B. (2007). Categorizing on-line groups. In A. Joinson, K. McKenna, T. Postmes, & U. Reips (Eds.), *The Oxford Handbook of Internet Psychology* (pp. 105–120). Oxford, England: Oxford University Press.

Branscombe, N. R. (1998). Thinking about one's gender group's privileges or disadvantages: Consequences for well-being in women and men. *British Journal of Social Psychology, 37,* 167–184.

Brauer, M., Judd, C. M., & Gliner, M. D. (1995). The effects of repeated expressions on attitude polarization during group discussions. *Journal of Personality and Social Psychology, 68,* 1014–1029.

Braun, D. E., Prusaczyk, W. K., & Pratt, N. C. (1992). *Personality profiles of U.S. Navy Sea-Air-Land (SEAL) personnel.* San Diego: Naval Health Research Center.

Braun, R., and Vliegenthart, R. (2008) The contentious fans: The impact of repression, media coverage, grievances and aggressive play on supporters' violence. *International Sociology 23*(6), 796–818.

Bray, R. M., Johnson, D., & Chilstrom, J. T., Jr. (1982). Social influence by group members with minority opinions: A comparison of Hollander & Moscovici. *Journal of Personality and Social Psychology, 43,* 78–88.

Brazy, D. P. (2009). *Group chairman's factual report of investigation: Cockpit voice recorder* (DCA09MA026). Washington, DC: National Transportation Safety Board.

Brechner, K. C. (1977). An experimental analysis of social traps. *Journal of Experimental Social Psychology, 13,* 552–564.

Brehm, J. W., & Sensenig, J. (1966). Social influence as a function of attempted and implied usurpation of choice. *Journal of Personality and Social Psychology, 4,* 703–707.

Brehm, S. S., & Brehm, J. W. (1981). *Psychological reactance: A theory of freedom and control.* New York: Academic Press.

Brenner, O. C., & Vinacke, W. E. (1979). Accommodative and exploitative behavior of males versus females and managers versus nonmanagers as measured by the Test of Strategy. *Social Psychology Quarterly, 42,* 289–293.

Brew, F. P., Tan, J., Booth, H., & Malik, I. (2011). The effects of cognitive appraisals of communication competence in conflict interactions: A study involving western and chinese cultures. *Journal of Cross-Cultural Psychology, 42*(5), 856–874.

Brewer, M. B. (2000). Reducing prejudice through cross-categorization: Effects of multiple social identities. In S. Oskamp (Ed.), *Reducing prejudice and discrimination* (pp. 165–183). Mahwah, NJ: Erlbaum.

Brewer, M. B. (2007). The social psychology of intergroup relations: Social categorization, ingroup bias, and outgroup prejudice. In A. W. Kruglanski & E. T. Higgins (Eds.), *Social psychology: Handbook of basic principles* (2nd ed., pp. 695–715). New York: Guilford.

Brewer, M. B. (2010). Intergroup relations. In R. F. Baumeister & E. J. Finkel (Eds.), *Advanced social psychology: The state of the science* (pp. 535–571). New York: Oxford University Press.

Brewer, M. B. (2012). Optimal distinctiveness theory: Its history and development. In P. A. M. Van Lange, A. W. Kruglanski, & E. T. Higgins (Eds.), *Handbook of theories of social psychology* (Vol. 2, pp. 81–98). Thousand Oaks, CA: Sage.

Brewer, M. B., & Brown, R. J. (1998). Intergroup relations. In D. T. Gilbert, S. T. Fiske, & G. Lindzey (Eds.), *The handbook of* social psychology (Vol. 2, 4th ed., pp. 554–594). New York: McGraw-Hill.

Brewer, M. B., & Campbell, D. T. (1976). *Ethnocentrism and intergroup attitudes: East African evidence.* New York: Halsted Press.

Brewer, M. B., & Chen, Y.-R. (2007). Where (who) are collectives in collectivism? Toward conceptual clarification of individualism and collectivism. *Psychological Review, 114,* 133–151.

Brewer, M. B., Hong, Y.-Y., & Li, Q. (2004). Dynamic entitativity: Perceiving groups as actors. In V. Yzerbyt, C. M. Judd, & O. Corneille (Eds.), *The psychology of group perception: Perceived variability, entitativity, and essentialism* (pp. 25–38). New York: Psychology Press.

Brewer, M. B., & Kramer, R. M. (1986). Choice behavior in social dilemmas: Effects of social identity, group size, and decision framing. *Journal of Personality and Social Psychology, 50,* 543–549.

Brewer, M. B., & Miller, N. (1984). Beyond the contact hypothesis: Theoretical perspectives on desegregation. In N. Miller & M. Brewer (Eds.), *Groups in contact: The psychology of desegregation* (pp. 281–302). New York: Academic Press.

Brewer, S., & Klein, J. D. (2006). Type of positive interdependence and affiliation motive in an asynchronous, collaborative learning environment. *Educational Technology Research and Development, 54*(4), 331–354.

Brickner, M. A., Harkins, S. G., & Ostrom, T. M. (1986). Effects of personal involvement: Thought-provoking implications for social loafing. *Journal of Personality and Social Psychology, 51,* 763–770.

Brief, A. P., Schuler, R. S., & Van Sell, M. (1981). *Managing job stress.* Boston: Little, Brown.

Brief, A. P., & Weiss, H. M. (2002). Organizational behavior: Affect in the workplace. *Annual Review of Psychology, 53,* 279–307.

Brinthaupt, T. M., Moreland, R. L., & Levine, J. M. (1991). Sources of optimism among prospective group members. *Personality and Social Psychology Bulletin, 17,* 36–43.

Brockner, J. (1995). How to stop throwing good money after bad: Using theory to guide practice. In D. A. Schroeder (Ed.), *Social dilemmas: Perspectives on individuals and groups* (pp. 163–182). Westport, CT: Praeger.

Brockner, J., & Rubin, J. Z. (1985). *The social psychology of conflict escalation and entrapment.* New York: Springer Verlag.

Brockner, J., & Wiesenfeld, B. M. (1996). An integrative framework for explaining reactions to decisions: Interactive effects of outcomes and procedures. *Psychological Bulletin, 120,* 189–208.

Bromley, D. G. (2001). A tale of two theories: Brainwashing and conversion as competing political narratives. In B. Zablocki & T. Robbins (Eds.), *Misunderstanding cults* (pp. 318–348). Toronto: University of Toronto Press.

Bromley, D. G. (2007). Methodological issues in the study of new religious movements. In D. G. Bromley (Ed.), *Teaching new religious movements* (pp. 65–89). New York: Oxford University Press.

Bronzaft, A. L. (2002). Noise pollution: A hazard to physical and mental well-being. In R. B. Bechtel & A. Churchman (Eds.),

Handbook of environmental psychology (pp. 499–510). New York: Wiley.

Brooks, G. R. (1996). Treatment for therapy-resistant men. In M. P. Andronico (Ed.), *Men in groups: Insights, interventions, and psychoeducational work* (pp. 7–19). Washington, DC: American Psychological Association.

Brosnan, S. F., & de Waal, F. B. M. (2003). Monkeys reject unequal pay. *Nature, 425,* 297–299.

Brown, B. B. (1987). Territoriality. In D. Stokols & I. Altman (Eds.), *Handbook of environmental psychology* (Vol. 1, pp. 505–531). New York: Wiley.

Brown, B. B., & Lohr, N. (1987). Peer group affiliation and adolescent self-esteem: An integration of ego-identity and symbolic-interaction theories. *Journal of Personality and Social Psychology, 52,* 47–55.

Brown, D. E. (1991). *Human universals.* New York: McGraw-Hill.

Brown, G. (2009). Claiming a corner at work: Measuring employee territoriality in their workspaces. *Journal of Environmental Psychology, 29*(1), 44–52.

Brown, G., & Robinson, S. L. (2011). Reactions to territorial infringement. *Organization Science, 22*(1), 210–224.

Brown, J. D., & Dutton, K. A. (1995). The thrill of victory, the complexity of defeat: Self-esteem and people's emotional reactions to success and failure. *Journal of Personality and Social Psychology, 68,* 712–722.

Brown, L. H., Silvia, P. J., Myin-Germeys, I., & Kwapil, T. R. (2007). When the need to belong goes wrong: The expression of social anhedonia and social anxiety in daily life. *Psychological Science, 18,* 778–782.

Brown, R. (1974). Further comment on the risky shift. *American Psychologist, 29,* 468–470.

Brown, R. (2000). *Group processes* (2nd ed.). Malden, MA: Blackwell.

Brown, R., Condor, S., Matthews, A., Wade, G., & Williams, J. A. (1986). Explaining intergroup differentiation in an industrial organization. *Journal of Occupational Psychology, 59,* 273–286.

Brown, R., & Hewstone, M. (2005). An integrative theory of intergroup contact. *Advances In Experimental Social Psychology, 37,* 255–343.

Brown, R., Maras, P., Masser, B., Vivian, J., & Hewstone, M. (2001). Life on the ocean wave: Testing some intergroup hypotheses in a naturalistic setting. *Group Processes & Intergroup Relations, 4,* 81–97.

Brown, R., & Zagefka, H. (2005). Ingroup affiliations and prejudice. In J. F. Dovidio, P. Glick & L. A. Rudman (Eds.), *On the nature of prejudice: Fifty years after Allport* (pp. 54–70). Malden, MA: Blackwell.

Brown, T. M., & Miller, C. E. (2000). Communication networks in task-performing groups: Effects of task complexity, time pressure, and interpersonal dominance. *Small Group Research, 31*(2), 131–157.

Brown, V., & Paulus, P. B. (1996). A simple dynamic model of social factors in group brainstorming. *Small Group Research, 27,* 91–114.

Brucks, W. M., Reips, U., & Ryf, B. (2007). Group norms, physical distance, and ecological efficiency in common pool resource management. *Social Influence, 2*(2), 112–135.

Bryant, E. M., & Marmo, J. (2012). The rules of Facebook friendship: A two-stage examination of interaction rules in close, casual, and acquaintance friendships. *Journal of Social and Personal Relationships.* In press.

Buchan, N. R., Croson, R. T. A., & Dawes, R. M. (2002). Swift neighbors and persistent strangers: A cross-cultural investigation of trust and reciprocity in social exchange. *American Journal of Sociology, 108*(1), 168–206.

Buckley, W. (1967). *Sociology and modern systems theory.* Upper Saddle River, NJ: Prentice Hall.

Buehler, R., Messervey, D., & Griffin, D. (2005). Collaborative planning and prediction: Does group discussion affect optimistic biases in time estimation? *Organizational Behavior and Human Decision Processes, 97*(1), 47–63.

Bugental, D. B. (2010). Paradoxical power manifestations: Power assertion by the subjectively powerless. In A. Guinote & T. K. Vescio (Eds.), *The social psychology of power* (pp. 209–230). New York: Guilford Press.

Bunderson, J. S. (2003). Recognizing and utilizing expertise in work groups: A status characteristics perspective. *Administrative Science Quarterly, 48*, 557–591.

Bunderson, J. S., & Boumgarden, P. (2010). Structure and learning in self-managed teams: Why "bureaucratic" teams can be better learners. *Organization Science, 21*(3), 609–624.

Buote, V. M., Pancer, S. M., Pratt, M. W., Adams, G., Birnie-Lefcovitch, S., Polivy, J., & Wintre, M. G. (2007). The importance of friends: Friendship and adjustment among 1st-year university students. *Journal of Adolescent Research, 22*, 665–689.

Burger, J. M. (2009). Replicating Milgram: Would people still obey today? *American Psychologist, 64*(1), 1–11.

Burger, J. M., LaSalvia, C. T., Hendricks, L. A., Mehdipour, T., & Neudeck, E. M. (2011). Partying before the party gets started: The effects of descriptive norms on pregaming behavior. *Basic and Applied Social Psychology, 33*(3), 220–227.

Burgoon, J. K. (1978). A communication model of personal space violation: Explication and an initial test. *Human Communication Research, 4*, 129–142.

Burgoon, J. K. (1983). Nonverbal violations of expectations. In J. M. Wiemann & R. R. Harrison (Eds.), *Nonverbal interaction* (pp. 11–77). Thousand Oaks, CA: Sage.

Burgoon, J. K., & Dillman, L. (1995). Gender, immediacy, and nonverbal communication. In P. J. Kalbfleisch & M. J. Cody (Eds.), *Gender, power, and communication in human relationships* (pp. 63–81). Hillsdale, NJ: Erlbaum.

Burgoon, J. K., & Hale, J. L. (1987). Validation and measurement of the fundamental themes of relational communication. *Communication Monographs, 54*(1), 19–41.

Burke, M. J., & Day, R. R. (1986). A cumulative study of the effectiveness of managerial training. *Journal of Applied Psychology, 71*, 232–245.

Burke, P. J. (1967). The development of task and social-emotional role differentiation. *Sociometry, 30*, 379–392.

Burkley, M., & Blanton, H. (2008). Endorsing a negative in-group stereotype as a self-protective strategy: Sacrificing the group to save the self. *Journal of Experimental Social Psychology, 44*, 37–49.

Burlingame, G. M., & Baldwin, S. (2011). Group therapy. In J. C. Norcross, G. R. VandenBos, & D. K. Freedheim (Eds.), *History of psychotherapy: Continuity and change* (2nd ed., pp. 505–515). Washington, DC: American Psychological Association.

Burlingame, G. M., Cox, J. C., Davies, D. R., Layne, C. M., & Gleave, R. (2011). The Group Selection Questionnaire: Further refinements in group member selection. *Group Dynamics: Theory, Research, and Practice, 15*(1), 60–74.

Burlingame, G. M., Fuhriman, A., & Mosier, J. (2003). The differential effectiveness of group psychotherapy: A meta-analytic perspective. *Group Dynamics: Theory, Research, and Practice, 7*, 3–12.

Burlingame, G. M., & Krogel, J. (2005). Relative efficacy of individual versus group psychotherapy. *International Journal of Group Psychotherapy, 55*, 607–611.

Burlingame, G. M., MacKenzie, K. R., & Strauss, B. (2004). Small group treatment: Evidence for effectiveness and mechanisms of change. In M. J. Lambert (Ed.), *Bergin & Garfield's handbook of psychotherapy and behavior change* (5th ed., pp. 647–696). New York: Wiley & Sons.

Burnette, J. L., & Forsyth, D. R. (2008). "I didn't do it": Responsibility biases in open and closed groups. *Group Dynamics: Theory, Research, and Practice, 12*, 210–222.

Burnette, J. L., McCullough, M. E., Van Tongeren, D. R., & Davis, D. E. (2012). Forgiveness results from integrating information about relationship value and exploitation risk. *Personality and Social Psychology Bulletin, 38*(3), 345–356.

Burnette, J. L., Pollack, J. M., & Forsyth, D. R. (2011). Leadership in extreme contexts: A groupthink analysis of the May 1996 Mount Everest disaster. *Journal of Leadership Studies, 4*(4), 29–40.

Burney, C. (1961). *Solitary confinement* (2nd ed.). New York: St. Martin's Press.

Burnham, T., McCabe, K., & Smith, V. L. (2000). Friend-or-foe intentionality priming in an extensive form trust game. *Journal of Economic Behavior & Organization, 43*, 57–73.

Burns, J. M. (1978). *Leadership.* New York: Harper.

Burns, J. M. (2003). *Transforming leadership: The pursuit of happiness.* New York: Atlantic Monthly Press.

Burnstein, E., & Vinokur, A. (1973). Testing two classes of theories about group-induced shifts in individual choice. *Journal of Experimental Social Psychology, 9*, 123–137.

Burnstein, E., & Vinokur, A. (1977). Persuasive arguments and social comparison as determinants of attitude polarization. *Journal of Experimental Social Psychology, 13*, 315–332.

Burnstein, E., & Worchel, P. (1962). Arbitrariness of frustration and its consequences for aggression in a social situation. *Journal of Personality, 30*, 528–540.

Burt, R. S. (1997). The contingent value of social capital. *Administrative Science Quarterly, 42*(2), 339–365.

Bushe, G. R., & Coetzer, G. H. (2007). Group development and team effectiveness: Using cognitive representations to measure group development and predict task performance and group viability. *Journal of Applied Behavioral Science, 43,* 184–212.

Buss, D. M., & Duntley, J. D. (2008). Adaptations for exploitation. *Group Dynamics: Theory, Research, and Practice, 12*(1), 53–62.

Butkovic, A., & Bratko, D. (2007). Family study of manipulation tactics. *Personality and Individual Differences, 43,* 791–801.

Butler, D., & Geis, F. L. (1990). Nonverbal affect responses to male and female leaders: Implications for leadership evaluations. *Journal of Personality and Social Psychology, 58,* 48–59.

Butler, T., & Fuhriman, A. (1983). Level of functioning and length of time in treatment variables influencing patients' therapeutic experience in group psychotherapy. *International Journal of Group Psychotherapy, 33,* 489–505.

Buton, F., Fontayne, P., Heuzé, J., Bosselut, G., & Raimbault, N. (2007). The QAG-a: An analog version of the Questionnaire sur l'Ambiance du Groupe for measuring the dynamic nature of group cohesion. *Small Group Research, 38,* 235–264.

Buunk, A. P., & Gibbons, F. X. (2007). Social comparison: The end of a theory and the emergence of a field. *Organizational Behavior and Human Decision Processes, 102,* 3–21.

Buxant, C., Saroglou, V., & Tesser, M. (2010). Free-lance spiritual seekers: self-growth or compensatory motives? *Mental Health, Religion & Culture 13*(2), 209–222.

Buys, C. J. (1978a). Humans would do better without groups. *Personality and Social Psychology Bulletin, 4,* 123–125.

Buys, C. J. (1978b). On humans would do better without groups: A final note. *Personality and Social Psychology Bulletin, 4,* 568.

Byrne, D. (1961). Anxiety and the experimental arousal of affiliation need. *Journal of Abnormal and Social Psychology, 63,* 660–662.

Byrne, D. (1971). *The attraction paradigm.* New York: Academic Press.

Byrne, Z. S., & LeMay, E. (2006). Different media for organizational communication: Perceptions of quality and satisfaction. *Journal of Business and Psychology, 21,* 149–173.

Cabanac, M. (2006). Pleasure and joy, and their role in human life. In D. Clements-Croome (Ed.), *Creating the productive workplace* (2nd. ed., pp. 3–13). New York: Taylor & Francis.

Cacioppo, J. T., Fowler, J. H., & Christakis, N. A. (2009). Alone in the crowd: The structure and spread of loneliness in a large social network. *Journal of Personality and Social Psychology, 97*(6), 977–991.

Cadinu, M. R., & Cerchioni, M. (2001). Compensatory biases after ingroup threat: 'Yeah, but we have a good personality'. *European Journal of Social Psychology, 31,* 353–367.

Cai, D. A., & Fink, E. L. (2002). Conflict style differences between individualists and collectivists. *Communication Monographs, 69*(1), 67–87.

Cain, S. (2012). *Quiet: The power of introverts in a world that can't stop talking.* New York: Crown Publishers.

Caldwell, D. F., & Burger, J. M. (1997). Personality and social influence strategies in the workplace. *Personality and Social Psychology Bulletin, 23,* 1003–1012.

Callaway, M. R., Marriott, R. G., & Esser, J. K. (1985). Effects of dominance on group decision making: Toward a stress-reduction explanation of groupthink. *Journal of Personality and Social Psychology, 49,* 949–952.

Camacho, L. M., & Paulus, P. B. (1995). The role of social anxiousness in group brainstorming. *Journal of Personality and Social Psychology, 68,* 1071–1080.

Campbell, D. T. (1958a). Common fate, similarity, and other indices of the status of aggregates of persons as social entities. *Behavioral Science, 3,* 14–25.

Campbell, D. T. (1958b). Systematic error on the part of human links in communication systems. *Information and Control, 1,* 334–369.

Campbell, D. T. (1965). Ethnocentric and other altruistic motives. *Nebraska Symposium on Motivation, 13,* 283–311.

Campbell, L., Simpson, J. A., Stewart, M., & Manning, J. G. (2002). The formation of status hierarchies in leaderless groups: The role of male waist-to-hip ratio. *Human Nature, 13,* 345–362.

Campbell, T. (2005). The cognitive neuroscience of auditory distraction. *Trends in Cognitive Sciences, 9,* 3–5.

Canetti, E. (1962). *Crowds and power.* London: Gollancz.

Cannavale, F. J., Scarr, H. A., & Pepitone, A. (1970). Deindividuation in the small group: Further evidence. *Journal of Personality and Social Psychology, 16,* 141–147.

Cannon, M. D., & Edmondson, A. C. (2005). Failing to learn and learning to fail (intelligently): How great organizations put failure to work to innovate and improve. *Long Range Planning: International Journal of Strategic Management, 38,* 299–319.

Cannon-Bowers, J. A., & Salas, E. (2001). Reflections on team cognition. *Journal of Organizational Behavior, 22,* 195–202.

Cannon-Bowers, J. A., Tannenbaum, S. I., Salas, E., & Volpe, C. E. (1995). Defining team competencies and establishing team training requirements. In R. Guzzo, E. Salas, & Associates, *Team effectiveness and decision making in organizations* (pp. 333–380). San Francisco: Jossey-Bass.

Caporael, L. R. (2007). Evolutionary theory for social and cultural psychology. In A. W. Kruglanski & E. T. Higgins (Eds.), *Social psychology: Handbook of basic principles* (2nd ed., pp. 3–18). New York: Guilford Press.

Carey, H. R., & Laughlin, P. R. (2012). Groups perform better than the best individuals on letters-to-numbers problems: Effects of induced strategies. *Group Processes & Intergroup Relations, 15*(2), 231–242.

Carless, S. A., & De Paola, C. (2000). The measurement of cohesion in work teams. *Small Group Research, 31*(1), 71–88.

Carli, L. L. (2001). Gender and social influence. *Journal of Social Issues, 57,* 725–741.

Carli, L. L., & Eagly, A. H. (2011). Gender and leadership. In A. Bryman, D. Collinson, K. Grint, B. Jackson, & M. Uhl-Bien

(Eds.), *The Sage handbook of leadership* (pp. 269–285). London: Sage.

Carlopio, J. R. (1996). Construct validity of a physical work environment satisfaction questionnaire. *Journal of Occupational Health Psychology, 1,* 330–344.

Carlyle, T. (1841). *On heroes, hero-worship, and the heroic.* London: Fraser.

Carnaghi, A., Maass, A., Gresta, S., Bianchi, M., Cadinu, M., & Arcuri, L. (2008). Nomina sunt omina: On the inductive potential of nouns and adjectives in person perception. *Journal of Personality and Social Psychology, 94,* 839–859.

Carneiro, R. L. (1970). A theory of the origin of the state. *Science, 169,* 239–249.

Carnevale, P. J. (2008). Theory of conflict in the workplace: Whence and whither. In C. K. W. De Dreu & M. J. Gelfand (Ed.), *The psychology of conflict and conflict management in organizations* (pp. 435–444). New York: Taylor & Francis Group/ Lawrence Erlbaum Associates.

Carnevale, P. J., & Pruitt, D. G. (1992). Negotiation and mediation. *Annual Review of Psychology, 43,* 531–582.

Carpenter, C. R. (1958). Territoriality: A review of concepts and problems. In A. Roe & G. G. Simpson (Eds.), *Behavior and evolution* (pp. 224–250). New Haven, CT: Yale University Press.

Carrere, S., & Evans, G. W. (1994). Life in an isolated and confined environment: A qualitative study of the role of the designed environment. *Environment and Behavior, 26,* 707–741.

Carron, A. V., & Brawley, L. R. (2000). Cohesion: Conceptual and measurement issues. *Small Group Research, 31*(1), 89–106.

Carron, A. V., Colman, M. M., Wheeler, J., & Stevens, D. (2002). Cohesion and performance in sport: A meta-analysis. *Journal of Sport and Exercise Psychology, 24,* 168–188.

Carson, J., Barling, J., & Turner, N. (2007). Group alcohol climate, alcohol consumption, and student performance. *Group Dynamics: Theory, Research, and Practice, 11*(1), 31–41.

Carson, P. P., Carson, K. D., & Roe, C. W. (1993). Social power bases: A meta-analytic examination of interrelationships and outcomes. *Journal of Applied Social Psychology, 23,* 1150–1169.

Carson, R. C. (1969). *Interaction concepts of personality.* Chicago: Aldine.

Carton, A. M., & Rosette, A. S. (2011). Explaining bias against Black leaders: Integrating theory on information processing and goal-based stereotyping. *Academy of Management Journal, 54,* 1141–1158.

Cartwright, D. (1951). Achieving change in people: Some applications of group dynamics theory. *Human Relations, 4,* 381–392.

Cartwright, D. (1959). A field theoretical conception of power. In D. Cartwright (Ed.), *Studies in social power.* Ann Arbor, MI: Institute for Social Research.

Cartwright, D., & Harary, F. (1956). Structural balance: A generalization of Heider's theory. *Psychological Review, 63,* 277–293.

Cartwright, D., & Harary, F. (1970). Ambivalence and indifference in generalizations of structural balance. *Behavioral Science, 14,* 497–513.

Cartwright, D., & Zander, A. (Eds.). (1953). *Group dynamics: Research and theory.* New York: Row, Peterson.

Cartwright, D., & Zander, A. (Eds.). (1968). *Group dynamics: Research and theory* (3rd ed.). New York: Harper & Row.

Caruso, E., Epley, N., & Bazerman, M. H. (2006). The costs and benefits of undoing egocentric responsibility assessments in groups. *Journal of Personality and Social Psychology, 91,* 857–871.

Carvalho, E. R., & Brito, V. C. A. (1995). Sociometric intervention in family therapy: A case study. *Journal of Group Psychotherapy, Psychodrama & Sociometry, 47,* 147–164.

Cascio, W. F. (1995). Whither industrial and organizational psychology in a changing world of work? *American Psychologist, 50,* 928–939.

Casey-Campbell, M., & Martens, M. L. (2009). Sticking it all together: A critical assessment of the group cohesion-performance literature. *International Journal of Management Reviews, 11,* 223–246.

Castano, E., Yzerbyt, V., & Bourguignon, D. (2003). We are one and I like it: The impact of ingroup entitativity on ingroup identification. *European Journal of Social Psychology, 33,* 735–754.

Castore, C. H., & Murnighan, J. K. (1978). Determinants of support for group decisions. *Organizational Behavior and Human Performance, 22,* 75–92.

Cattell, R. B. (1948). Concepts and methods in the measurement of group syntality. *Psychological Review, 55,* 48–63.

Cattell, R. B. (1951). New concepts for measuring leadership in terms of group syntality. *Human Relations, 4,* 161–184.

Cecil, J. S., Hans, V. P., & Wiggins, E. C. (1991). Citizen comprehension of difficult issues: Lessons from civil jury trials. *American University Law Review, 40,* 727–774.

Chagnon, N. A. (1997). *Yanomamö* (5th ed.). Fort Worth, TX: Harcourt Brace.

Chamley, C. P. (2004). *Rational herds: Economic models of social learning.* Cambridge, UK: Cambridge University Press.

Chansler, P. A., Swamidass, P. M., & Cammann, C. (2003). Self-managing work teams: An empirical study of group cohesiveness in "natural work groups" at a Harley-Davidson motor company plant. *Small Group Research, 34,* 101–120.

Chaplin, W. F., Phillips, J. B., Brown, J. D., Clanton, N. R., & Stein, J. L. (2000). Handshaking, gender, personality, and first impressions. *Journal of Personality and Social Psychology, 79,* 110–117.

Chartrand, T. L., & Bargh, J. A. (1999). The chameleon effect: The perception–behavior link and social interaction. *Journal of Personality and Social Psychology, 76*(6), 893–910.

Chartrand, T. L., & van Baaren, R. (2009). Human mimicry. *Advances in Experimental Social Psychology, 41,* 219–274.

Charuvastra, A., & Cloitre, M. (2008). Social bonds and posttraumatic stress disorder. *Annual Review of Psychology, 59,* 301–328.

Chatman, J. A., & Spataro, S. E. (2005). Using self-categorization theory to understand relational demography-based variations in people's responsiveness to organizational culture. *Academy of Management Journal, 48,* 321–331.

Cheavens, J. S., Feldman, D. B., Gum, A., Michael, S. T., & Snyder, C. R. (2006). Hope therapy in a community sample: A pilot investigation. *Social Indicators Research, 77*, 61–78.

Chemers, M. M. (1997). *An integrative theory of leadership*. Mahwah, NJ: Erlbaum.

Chemers, M. M. (2000). Leadership research and theory: A functional integration. *Group Dynamics: Theory, Research, and Practice, 4*, 27–43.

Chen, F. F., & West, S. G. (2008). Measuring individualism and collectivism: The importance of considering differential components, reference groups, and measurement invariance. *Journal of Research in Personality, 42*, 259–294.

Chen, H., & Duh, H.B.L. (2007). Understanding social interaction in World of Warcraft. In *Proceedings of the 4th International Conference on Advances in Computer Entertainment Technology* (pp. 21–24). New York: Association for Computing Machinery.

Chen, L-H., Baker, S. P., Braver, E. R., & Li, G. (2000). Carrying passengers as a risk factor for crashes fatal to 16- and 17-year-old drivers. *Journal of the American Medical Association, 283*, 1578–1582.

Chen, S., Chen, K. Y., & Shaw, L. (2004). Self-verification motives at the collective level of self-definition. *Journal of Personality and Social Psychology, 86*(1), 77–94.

Chen, S., Lee-Chai, A. Y., & Bargh, J. A. (2001). Relationship orientation as a moderator of the effects of social power. *Journal of Personality and Social Psychology, 80*, 173–187.

Chen, S., Shechter, D., & Chaiken, S. (1996). Getting at the truth or getting along: Accuracy-versus impression-motivated heuristic and systematic processing. *Journal of Personality and Social Psychology, 71*, 262–275.

Chen, X. (2011). Culture, peer relationships, and human development. In L. A. Jensen (Ed.) *Bridging cultural and developmental approaches to psychology: New syntheses in theory, research, and policy* (pp. 92–112). New York: Oxford University Press.

Chen, Y., Tjosvold, D., & Su, S. F. (2005). Goal interdependence for working across cultural boundaries: Chinese employees with foreign managers. *International Journal of Intercultural Relations, 29*(4), 429–447.

Chen, Z., Lawson, R. B., Gordon, L. R., & McIntosh, B. (1996). Groupthink: Deciding with the leader and the devil. *Psychological Record, 46*, 581–590.

Cheng, S. (1997). Epidemic genital retraction syndrome: Environmental and personal risk factors in southern China. *Journal of Psychology and Human Sexuality, 9*, 57–70.

Chernyak, N., & Zayas, V. (2010). Being excluded by one means being excluded by all: Perceiving exclusion from inclusive others during one-person social exclusion. *Journal of Experimental Social Psychology, 46*(3), 582–585.

Chertkoff, J. M., Kushigian, R. H., & McCool, M. A., Jr. (1996). Interdependent exiting: The effects of group size, time limit, and gender on the coordination of exiting. *Journal of Environmental Psychology, 16*, 109–121.

Cherulnik, P., & Wilderman, S. (1986). Symbols of status in urban neighborhoods. *Environment and Behavior, 18*, 604–622.

Cheung, F. M., van de Vijver, F. J. R., & Leong, F. T. L. (2011). Toward a new approach to the study of personality in culture. *American Psychologist, 66*(7), 593–603.

Cheyne, J. A., & Efran, M. G. (1972). The effect of spatial and interpersonal variables on the invasion of group controlled territories. *Sociometry, 35*, 477–487.

Chiaburu, D. S., & Harrison, D. A. (2008). Do peers make the place? Conceptual synthesis and meta-analysis of coworker effects on perceptions, attitudes, OCBs, and performance. *Journal of Applied Psychology, 93*(5), 1082–1103.

Chiao, J. Y. (2006). Building blocks to human social hierarchy: Psychological and neural investigations of social dominance perception. *Dissertation Abstracts International: Section B: The Sciences and Engineering, 67*(5-B), 2851. (UMI No. AAI3217697)

Chiocchio, F., & Essiembre, H. (2009). Cohesion and performance: A meta-analytic review of disparities between project teams, production teams, and service teams. *Small Group Research, 40*(4), 382–420.

Chirot, D., & McCauley, C. (2006). *Why not kill them all*. Princeton, NJ: Princeton University Press.

Chiu, C., Hong, Y., & Dweck, C. S. (1997). Lay dispositionism and implicit theories of personality. *Journal of Personality and Social Psychology, 73*, 19–30.

Chow, R. M., Tiedens, L. Z., & Govan, C. L. (2008). Excluded emotions: The role of anger in antisocial responses to ostracism. *Journal of Experimental Social Psychology, 44*(3), 896–903.

Christakis, N. A., & Fowler, J. H. (2007). The spread of obesity in a large social network over 32 years. *New England Journal of Medicine, 357*, 370–379.

Christensen, A., & Jacobson, N. S. (1994). Who (or what) can do psychotherapy: The status and challenge of nonprofessional therapies. *Psychological Science, 5*, 8–12.

Christensen, P. N., & Kashy, D. A. (1998). Perceptions of and by lonely people in initial social interaction. *Personality and Social Psychology Bulletin, 24*, 322–329.

Christensen, P. N., Rothgerber, H., Wood, W., & Matz, D. C. (2004). Social norms and identity relevance: A motivational approach to normative behavior. *Personality and Social Psychology Bulletin, 30*(10), 1295–1309.

Cialdini, R. B. (2009). *Influence: Science and practice* (6th ed.). Boston: Allyn and Bacon.

Cialdini, R. B., Borden, R., Thorne, A., Walker, M., Freeman, S., & Sloane, L. R. (1976). Basking in reflected glory: Three (football) field studies. *Journal of Personality and Social Psychology, 34*, 366–375.

Cialdini, R. B., & Goldstein, N. J. (2004). Social influence: Compliance and conformity. *Annual Review of Psychology, 55*, 591–621.

Cialdini, R. B., & Griskevicius, V. (2010). Social influence. In R. F. Baumeister & E. J. Finkel (Eds.), *Advanced social psychology: The state of the science* (pp. 385–417). New York: Oxford University Press.

Cialdini, R. B., Kallgren, C. A., & Reno, R. R. (1991). A focus theory of normative conduct: A theoretical refinement and reevaluation of the role of norms in human behavior. *Advances in Experimental Social Psychology, 24,* 201–234.

Cialdini, R. B., Reno, R. R., & Kallgren, C. A. (1990). A focus theory of normative conduct: Recycling the concept of norms to reduce littering in public places. *Journal of Personality and Social Psychology, 58,* 1015–1026.

Cialdini, R. B., & Trost, M. R. (1998). Social influence: Social norms, conformity and compliance. In D. T. Gilbert, S. T. Fiske, & G. Lindzey (Eds.), *The handbook of social psychology* (Vol. 2, 4th ed., pp. 151–192). New York: McGraw-Hill.

Cianni, M., & Romberger, B. (1995). Interactions with senior managers: Perceived differences by race/ethnicity and by gender. *Sex Roles, 32,* 353–373.

Cigler, A., & Joslyn, M. R. (2002). The extensiveness of group membership and social capital: The impact on political tolerance attitudes. *Political Research Quarterly, 55,* 7–25.

Cimino, A. (2011). The evolution of hazing: Motivational mechanisms and the abuse of newcomers. *Journal of Cognition and Culture, 11*(3-4), 241–267.

Cini, M. A., Moreland, R. L., & Levine, J. M. (1993). Group staffing levels and responses to prospective and new group members. *Journal of Personality and Social Psychology, 65,* 723–734.

Ciulla, J. B., & Forsyth, D. R. (2011). Leadership ethics. In A. Bryman, D. Collinson, K. Grint, B. Jackson, & M. Uhl-Bien (Eds.), *The Sage handbook of leadership* (pp. 229–241). London: Sage.

Clack, B., Dixon, J., & Tredoux, C. (2005). Eating together apart: Patterns of segregation in a multi-ethnic cafeteria. *Journal of Community & Applied Social Psychology, 15,* 1–16.

Claiborn, C. D., Goodyear, R. K., & Horner, P. A. (2001). Feedback. *Psychotherapy: Theory, Research, Practice, Training, 38,* 401–405.

Clapp, J. D., Holmes, M. R., Reed, M. B., Shillington, A. M., Freisthler, B., & Lange, J. E. (2007). Measuring college students' alcohol consumption in natural drinking environments: Field methodologies for bars and parties. *Evaluation Review, 31,* 469–489.

Clapp, J. D., Min, J. W., Shillington, A. M., Reed, M. B., & Croff, J. K. (2008). Person and environment predictors of blood alcohol concentrations: A multi-level study of college parties. *Alcoholism: Clinical and Experimental Research, 32,* 100–107.

Clark, G. (1969, November). What happens when the police strike? *New York Times Magazine,* p. 45.

Clark, K. B. (1971). The pathos of power. *American Psychologist, 26,* 1047–1057.

Clark, M. S., & Lemay Jr., E. P. (2010). Close relationships. In S. T. Fiske, D. T. Gilbert, & G. Lindzey (Eds.), *Handbook of social psychology* (Vol. 2, 5th ed., pp. 898–940). Hoboken, NJ: John Wiley & Sons Inc.

Clark, M. S., & Mills, J. R. (2012). A theory of communal (and exchange) relationships. In P. A. M. Van Lange, A. W. Kruglanski, & E. T. Higgins (Eds.), *Handbook of theories of social psychology* (Vol. 2, pp. 232–250). Thousand Oaks, CA: Sage.

Clark, N. K., Stephenson, G. M., & Kniveton, B. (1990). Social remembering: Quantitative aspects of individual and collaborative remembering by police officers and students. *British Journal of Psychology, 81,* 73–94.

Clark, R. D. (1971). Group induced shift toward risk: A critical appraisal. *Psychological Bulletin, 76*(4), 251–270.

Clark, R. D. (1990). Minority influence: The role of argument refutation of the majority position and social support for the minority position. *European Journal of Social Psychology, 20,* 489–497.

Clark, R. D. (1999). Effect of number of majority defectors on minority influence. *Group Dynamics: Theory, Research, and Practice, 3,* 303–312.

Clark, R. D. (2001). Effects of majority defection and multiple minority sources on minority influence. *Group Dynamics: Theory, Research, and Practice, 5,* 57–62.

Clark, R. D., & Sechrest, L. B. (1976). The mandate phenomenon. *Journal of Personality and Social Psychology, 34,* 1057–1061.

Clark, R. D., & Word, L. E. (1972). Why don't bystanders help? Because of ambiguity? *Journal of Personality and Social Psychology, 24,* 392–400.

Clark, R. D., & Word, L. E. (1974). Where is the apathetic bystander? Situational characteristics of the emergency. *Journal of Personality and Social Psychology, 29,* 279–287.

Clark, S. (1998). International competition and the treatment of minorities: Seventeenth-century cases and general propositions. *American Journal of Sociology, 103,* 1267–1308.

Clayton, D. A. (1978). Socially facilitated behavior. *The Quarterly Review of Biology, 53,* 373–392.

Clements-Croome, D. (Ed.). (2006). *Creating the productive workplace* (2nd ed.). New York: Taylor & Francis.

Clendenen, V. I., Herman, C. P., & Polivy, J. (1994). Social facilitation of eating among friends and strangers. *Appetite, 23,* 1–13.

Cleveland, C., Blascovich, J., Gangi, C., & Finez, L. (2011). When good teammates are bad: Physiological threat on recently formed teams. *Small Group Research, 42*(1), 3–31.

Coch, L., & French, J. R. P., Jr. (1948). Overcoming resistance to change. *Human Relations, 1,* 512–532.

Cohen, D., Nisbett, R. E., Bowdle, B. F., & Schwarz, N. (1996). Insult, aggression, and the southern culture of honor: An "experimental ethnography." *Journal of Personality and Social Psychology, 70,* 945–960.

Cohen, F., Ogilvie, D. M., Solomon, S., Greenberg, J., & Pyszczynski, T. (2005). American roulette: The effect of reminders of death on support for George W. Bush in the 2004 presidential election. *Analyses of Social Issues and Public Policy, 5,* 177–187.

Cohen, F., Solomon, S., Maxfield, M., Pyszczynski, T., & Greenberg, J. (2004). Fatal attraction: The effects of mortality salience on evaluations of charismatic, task-oriented, and relationship-oriented leaders. *Psychological Science, 15,* 846–851.

Cohen, S., & Weinstein, N. (1981). Nonauditory effects of noise on behavior and health. *Journal of Social Issues, 37,* 36–70.

Cohen, S. G., & Bailey, D. E. (1997). What makes teams work: Group effectiveness research from the shop floor to the executive suite. *Journal of Management, 23,* 239–290.

Cohen, T. R., Wildschut, T., & Insko, C. A. (2010). How communication increases interpersonal cooperation in mixed-motive situations. *Journal of Experimental Social Psychology, 46*(1), 39–50.

Coleman, P. T. (2000). Intractable conflict. In M. Deutsch & P. T. Coleman (Eds.), *The handbook of conflict resolution: Theory and practice* (pp. 428–450). San Francisco: Jossey-Bass.

Colligan, M. J., & Murphy, L. R. (1982). A review of mass psychogenic illness in work settings. In M. J. Colligan, J. W. Pennebaker, & L. R. Murphy (Eds.), *Mass psychogenic illness: A social psychological analysis* (pp. 33–52). Mahwah, NJ: Erlbaum.

Colligan, M. J., Pennebaker, J. W., & Murphy, L. R. (Eds.). (1982). *Mass psychogenic illness: A social psychological analysis.* Mahwah, NJ: Erlbaum.

Collins, B. E., & Guetzkow, H. (1964). *A social psychology of group processes for decision-making.* New York: Wiley.

Collins, R. (2004). *Interaction ritual chains.* Princeton, NJ: Princeton University Press.

Collins, R. L. (2000). Among the better ones: Upward assimilation in social comparison. In J. Suls & L. Wheeler (Eds.), *Handbook of social comparison: Theory and research* (pp. 159–171). New York: Kluwer Academic.

Colman, A. M. (1991). Crowd psychology in South African murder trials. *American Psychologist, 46,* 1071–1079.

Colquitt, J. A., & Greenberg, J. (2003). Organizational justice: A fair assessment of the state of the literature. In J. Greenberg (Ed.), *Organizational behavior: The state of the science* (2nd. ed., pp. 165–209). Mahwah, NJ: Erlbaum.

Conger, J. A. (2011). Charismatic leadership. In A. Bryman, D. Collinson, K. Grint, B. Jackson, & M. Uhl-Bien (Eds.), *The Sage handbook of leadership.* London: Sage.

Conroy, J., & Sundstrom, E. (1977). Territorial dominance in a dyadic conversation as a function of similarity of opinion. *Journal of Personality and Social Psychology, 35,* 570–576.

Conyne, R. K. (Ed.). (2010). *The Oxford handbook of group counseling.* New York: Oxford University Press.

Conyne, R. K., Wilson, F. R., Tang, M., & Shi, K. (1999). Cultural similarities and differences in group work: Pilot study of a U.S.–Chinese group comparison. *Group Dynamics: Theory, Research, and Practice, 3*(1), 40–50.

Cook, K. S., Cheshire, C., & Gerbasi, A. (2006). Power, dependence, and social exchange. In P. J. Burke (Ed.), *Contemporary social psychological theories* (pp. 194–216). Stanford, CA: Stanford University Press.

Cook, K. S., & Rice, E. (2006). Social exchange theory. In J. Delamater (Ed.), *Handbook of social psychology* (pp. 53–76). New York: Kluwer Academic/Plenum.

Cook, S. W. (1985). Experimenting on social issues: The case of school desegregation. *American Psychologist, 40,* 452–460.

Cooley, C. H. (1902). *Human nature and the social order.* New York: Scribner.

Cooley, C. H. (1909). *Social organization.* New York: Scribner.

Cooper, H. M. (1979). Statistically combining independent studies: A meta-analysis of sex differences in conformity research. *Journal of Personality and Social Psychology, 37,* 131–146.

Coovert, M., & Burke, J. (2005). Leadership and decision making. In Y. Amichai-Hamburger (Ed.), *The social net: Understanding human behavior in cyberspace* (pp. 219–246). Oxford: Oxford University Press.

Cope, C. J., Eys, M. A., Beauchamp, M. R., Schinke, R. J., & Bosselut, G. (2011). Informal roles on sport teams. *International Journal of Sport and Exercise Psychology, 9*(1), 19–30.

Cordery, J. (2004). Another case of the emperor's new clothes? *Journal of Occupational and Organizational Psychology, 77,* 481–484.

Corning, A. F., & Myers, D. J. (2002). Individual orientation toward engagement in social action. *Political Psychology, 23,* 703–729.

Coser, L. A. (1956). *The functions of social conflict.* New York: Free Press.

Costanzo, P. R. (1970). Conformity development as a function of self-blame. *Journal of Personality and Social Psychology, 14,* 366–374.

Costanzo, P. R., & Shaw, M. E. (1966). Conformity as a function of age level. *Child Development, 37,* 967–975.

Côté, S., Kraus, M. W., Cheng, B. H., Oveis, C., van der Löwe, I., Lian, H., & Keltner, D. (2011). Social power facilitates the effect of prosocial orientation on empathic accuracy. *Journal of Personality and Social Psychology, 101*(2), 217–232.

Cottrell, N. B. (1972). Social facilitation. In C. G. McClintock (Ed.), *Experimental social psychology* (pp. 185–236). New York: Holt, Rinehart & Winston.

Coughlin, B. C., & Venkatesh, S. A. (2003). The urban street gang after 1970. *Annual Review of Sociology, 29,* 41–64.

Courneya, K. S., & Carron, A. V. (1991). Effects of travel and length of home stand/road trip on the home advantage. *Journal of Sport and Exercise Psychology, 13,* 42–49.

Cousins, S. D. (1989). Culture and self-perception in Japan and the United States. *Journal of Personality and Social Psychology, 56,* 124–131.

Covey, S. R. (2004). *The 8th habit: From effectiveness to greatness.* New York: Free Press.

Crandall, C. S. (1988). Social contagion of binge eating. *Journal of Personality and Social Psychology, 55,* 588–598.

Crano, W. D., & Seyranian, V. (2007). Majority and minority influence. *Social and Personality Psychology Compass, 1,* 572–589.

Crano, W. D., & Seyranian, V. (2009). How minorities prevail: The context/comparison-leniency contract model. *Journal of Social Issues, 65,* 335–363.

Crawford, M. T., Sherman, S. J., & Hamilton, D. L. (2002). Perceived entitativity, stereotype formation, and the interchangeability of group members. *Journal of Personality and Social Psychology, 83,* 1076–1094.

Cress, D. M., McPherson, J. M., & Rotolo, T. (1997). Competition and commitment in voluntary memberships: The paradox of persistence and participation. *Sociological Perspectives, 40,* 61–79.

Cress, U. (2005). Ambivalent effect of member portraits in virtual groups. *Journal of Computer Assisted Learning, 21,* 281–291.

Crisp, R. J. (Ed.). (2010). *Social issues and interventions. The psychology of social and cultural diversity.* New York: Wiley-Blackwell.

Crisp, R. J., Heuston, S., Farr, M. J., & Turner, R. N. (2007). Seeing red or feeling blue: Differentiated intergroup emotions and ingroup identification in soccer fans. *Group Processes & Intergroup Relations, 10*(1), 9–26.

Crisp, R. J., & Hewstone, M. (2007). Multiple social categorization. *Advances in Experimental Social Psychology, 39,* 163–254.

Crisp, R. J., & Turner, R. N. (2009). Can imagined interactions produce positive perceptions?: Reducing prejudice through simulated social contact. *American Psychologist, 64*(4), 231–240.

Crocker, J., & Luhtanen, R. (1990). Collective self-esteem and ingroup bias. *Journal of Personality and Social Psychology, 58,* 60–67.

Crocker, J., Luhtanen, R., Blaine, B., & Broadnax, S. (1994). Collective self-esteem and psychological well-being among White, Black, and Asian college students. *Personality and Social Psychology Bulletin, 20,* 503–513.

Crocker, J., & Major, B. (1989). Social stigma and self-esteem: The self-protective properties of stigma. *Psychological Review, 96,* 608–630.

Crocker, J., & McGraw, K. M. (1984). What's good for the goose is not good for the gander: Solo status as an obstacle to occupational achievement for males and females. *American Behavioral Scientist, 27,* 357–369.

Cross, S. E., & Madson, L. (1997). Models of the self: Self-construals and gender. *Psychological Bulletin, 122,* 5–37.

Crouch, E. C., Bloch, S., & Wanlass, J. (1994). Therapeutic factors: Interpersonal and intrapersonal mechanisms. In A. Fuhriman & G. M. Burlingame (Eds.), *Handbook of group psychotherapy* (pp. 269–315). New York: Wiley.

Crutchfield, R. S. (1955). Conformity and character. *American Psychologist, 10,* 191–198.

Cuddy, A. J. C., Fiske, S. T., & Glick, P. (2007). The BIAS map: Behaviors from intergroup affect and stereotypes. *Journal of Personality and Social Psychology, 92,* 631–648.

Cuddy, A. J. C., Fiske, S. T., & Glick, P. (2008). Warmth and competence as universal dimensions of social perception: The stereotype content model and the BIAS map. *Advances in Experimental Social Psychology, 40,* 61–149.

Cuddy, A. J. C., Fiske, S. T., Kwan, V. S. Y., Glick, P., Demoulin, S., Leyens, J-P., Bond, M. H., Croizet, J-C., Ellemers, N., Sleebos, E., Htun, T. T. Kim, H-J., Maio, G., Perry, J., Petkova, K., Todorov, V., Rodríguez-Bailón, R., Morales, E., Moya, M., Palacios, M., Smith, V., Perez, R., Vala, J., & Ziegler, R. (2009). Stereotype content model across cultures: Universal similarities and some differences. *British Journal of Social Psychology, 48,* 1–33.

Cullum, J., & Harton, H. C. (2007). Cultural evolution: Interpersonal influence, issue importance, and the development of shared attitudes in college residence halls. *Personality and Social Psychology Bulletin, 33,* 1327–1339.

Cunningham, G. B. (2005). The importance of a common ingroup identity in ethnically diverse groups. *Group Dynamics: Theory, Research, and Practice, 9*(4), 251–260.

Curhan, J. R., Neale, M. A., & Ross, L. (2004). Dynamic valuation: Preference changes in the context of face-to-face negotiation. *Journal of Experimental Social Psychology, 40,* 142–151.

Curtin, N., Stewart, A. J., & Duncan, L. E. (2010). What makes the political personal? Openness, personal political salience, and activism. *Journal of Personality, 78*(3), 943–968.

Curtis, J. E., Baer, D. E., & Grabb, E. G. (2001). Nations of joiners: Explaining voluntary association membership in democratic societies. *American Sociological Review, 66,* 783–805.

Dabbs, J. M., & Dabbs, M. G. (2000). *Heroes, rogues, and lovers: Testosterone and behavior.* New York: McGraw-Hill.

Dabbs, J. M., Jr., & Ruback, R. B. (1987). Dimensions of group process: Amount and structure of vocal interaction. *Advances in Experimental Social Psychology, 20,* 123–169.

Dahl, R. A. (1957). The concept of power. *Behavioral Science, 2,* 201–215.

Dale, R. (1952). *Planning and developing the company organization structure.* New York: American Management Association.

Dane, F. C., & Wrightsman, L. S. (1982). Effects of defendants' and victims' characteristics on jurors' verdicts. In N. L. Kerr & R. M. Bray (Eds.), *Psychology of the courtroom* (pp. 83–115). New York: Academic Press.

Daniels, E. (2011). A brief history of individualism in American thought. In D. R. Forsyth & C. L. Hoyt (Eds.), *For the greater good of all: Perspectives on individualism, society, and leadership* (pp. 69–84). New York: Palgrave-MacMillan.

Dansereau, F., Graen, G. C., & Haga, W. (1975). A vertical dyad linkage approach to leadership in formal organizations. *Organizational Behavior and Human Performance, 13,* 46–78.

Darley, J. M. (1992). Social organization for the production of evil. *Psychological Inquiries, 3,* 199–218.

Darley, J. M. (1995). Constructive and destructive obedience: A taxonomy of principal-agent relationships. *Journal of Social Issues, 51,* 125–154.

Darley, J. M., & Latané, B. (1968). Bystander intervention in emergencies: Diffusion of responsibility. *Journal of Personality and Social Psychology, 8,* 377–383.

Dasgupta, N. (2004). Implicit ingroup favoritism, outgroup favoritism, and their behavioral manifestations. *Social Justice Research, 17*(2), 143–169.

Dasgupta, N., Banaji, M. R., & Abelson, R. P. (1999). Group entitativity and group perception: Associations between physical features and psychological judgment. *Journal of Personality and Social Psychology, 77,* 991–1003.

David, E. M., Rubino, C., Keeton, K. E., Miller, C. A., & Patterson, H. N. (2010). An examination of cross-cultural interactions aboard the International Space Station (ISS). Houston, TX: National Aeronautics and Space Administration. Retrieved from lsda.jsc.nasa.gov/

Davidson-Shivers, G. V., Morris, S. B., & Sriwongkol, T. (2003). Gender differences: Are they diminished in online discussions? *International Journal on E-Learning, 2,* 29–36.

Davies, D. R., Burlingame, G. M., & Layne, C. M. (2006). Integrating small-group process principles into trauma-focused group psychotherapy: What should a group trauma therapist know? In L. A. Schein, H. I. Spitz, G. M. Burlingame, & P. R. Muskin (Eds.), with S. Vargo, *Psychological effects of catastrophic disasters: Group approaches to treatment* (pp. 385–423). New York: Haworth Press.

Davis, J. A., & Smith, T. W. (2007). *General social surveys (1972–2006).* [machine-readable data file]. Chicago: National Opinion Research Center & Storrs, CT: The Roper Center for Public Opinion Research. Available at www.norc.uchicago.edu.

Davis, J. H. (1973). Group decision and social interaction: A theory of social decision schemes. *Psychological Review, 80,* 97–125.

Davis, J. H., Bray, R. M., & Holt, R. W. (1977). The empirical study of decision processes in juries: A critical review. In J. L. Tapp & F. J. Levine (Eds.), *Law, justice, and the individual in society* (pp. 326–361). New York: Holt, Rinehart & Winston.

Davis, J. H., Kameda, T., & Stasson, M. (1992). Group risk taking: Selected topics. In J. F. Yates (Ed.), *Risk-taking behavior* (pp. 163–199). Chichester, England: Wiley.

Davis, J. H., Kerr, N. L., Atkin, R. S., Holt, R., & Meek, D. (1975). The decision processes of 6- and 12-person mock juries assigned unanimous and two-thirds majority rules. *Journal of Personality and Social Psychology, 32,* 1–14.

Davis, J. H., Stasson, M., Ono, K., & Zimmerman, S. (1988). Effects of straw polls on group decision making: Sequential voting pattern, timing, and local majorities. *Journal of Personality and Social Psychology, 55,* 918–926.

Davis, J. R. (1982). *Street gangs: Youth, biker, and prison groups.* Dubuque, IO: Kendall/Hunt.

Davis, M. C., Leach, D. J., & Clegg, C. W. (2011). The physical environment of the office: Contemporary and emerging issues. *International Review of Industrial and Organizational Psychology, 26,* 193–237.

Davis, M. S., & Schmidt, C. J. (1977). The obnoxious and the nice: Some sociological consequences of two psychological types. *Social Psychology Quarterly, 40*(3), 201–213.

Davison, K. P., Pennebaker, J. W., & Dickerson, S. S. (2000). Who talks? The social psychology of illness support groups. *American Psychologist, 55,* 205–217.

Dawes, R. M. (1988). *Rational choice in an uncertain world.* San Diego: Harcourt Brace Jovanovich.

Dawkins, R. (1989) Darwinism and human purpose. In J. R. Durant (Ed.), *Human origins* (pp. 137–143). Oxford: Oxford University Press.

de Castro, J. M., Bellisle, F., Feunekes, G. L. J., Dalix, A. M., & de Graaf, C. (1997). Culture and meal patterns: A comparison of the food intake of free-living Americans, Dutch, and French students. *Nutrition Research, 17,* 807–829.

De Dreu, C. K. W. (1997). Productive conflict: The importance of conflict management and conflict issue. In C. K. W. De Dreu & E. Van de Vliert (Eds.), *Using conflict in organizations* (pp. 9–22). Thousand Oaks, CA: Sage.

De Dreu, C. K. W. (2003). Time pressure and closing of the mind in negotiation. *Organizational Behavior and Human Decision Processes, 91,* 280–295.

De Dreu, C. K. W. (2010). Social conflict: The emergence and consequences of struggle and negotiation. In S. T. Fiske, D. T. Gilbert, & G. Lindzey (Eds.), *Handbook of social psychology* (Vol. 2, 5th ed., pp. 983–1023). Hoboken, NJ: John Wiley.

De Dreu, C. K. W., Beersma, B., Steinel, W., & Van Kleef, G. A. (2007). The psychology of negotiation: Principles and basic processes. In A. W. Kruglanski & E. T. Higgins (Eds.), *Social psychology: Handbook of basic principles* (2nd ed., pp. 608–629). New York: Guilford.

De Dreu, C. K. W., & Gelfand, M. J. (Eds.). (2008). *The psychology of conflict and conflict management in organizations.* New York, NY: Taylor & Francis Group/Erlbaum.

De Dreu, C. K. W., Greer, L. L., Handgra, M. J. J., Shalvi, S., Van Kleef, G. A., Baas, M., Ten Velden, F. S., Van Dijk, E., & Feith, S. W. W. (2010). The neuropeptide oxytocin regulates parochial altruism intergroup conflict among humans. *Science, 328*(5984), 1408–1411.

De Dreu, C. K. W., Nauta, A., & Van de Vliert, E. (1995). Self-serving evaluations of conflict behavior and escalation of the dispute. *Journal of Applied Social Psychology, 25,* 2049–2066.

De Dreu, C. K. W., & Van Vianen, A. E. M. (2001). Responses to relationship conflict and team effectiveness. *Journal of Organizational Behavior, 22,* 309–328.

De Dreu, C. K. W., & Weingart, L. R. (2003). Task versus relationship conflict, team performance, and team member satisfaction: A meta-analysis. *Journal of Applied Psychology, 88,* 741–749.

De Dreu, C. K. W., Weingart, L. R., & Kwon, S. (2000). Influence of social motives on integrative negotiation: A meta-analytic review and test of two theories. *Journal of Personality and Social Psychology, 78,* 889–905.

De Grada, E., Kruglanski, A. W., Mannetti, L., & Pierro, A. (1999). Motivated cognition and group interaction: Need for closure affects the contents and processes of collective negotiations. *Journal of Experimental Social Psychology, 35,* 346–365.

de Kwaadsteniet, E. W., & van Dijk, E. (2010). Social status as a cue for tacit coordination. *Journal of Experimental Social Psychology, 46*(3), 515–524.

de la Roche, R. S. (2002). Why is collective violence collective? *Sociological Theory, 19,* 126–144.

de Tocqueville, A. (1969). *Democracy in America* (G. Lawrence, Trans.). New York: Doubleday. (original work published in 1831)

de Waal, F. B. M. (2006). *Primates and philosophers: How morality evolved*. Princeton, NJ: Princeton University Press.

Dean, L. M., Willis, F. N., & Hewitt, J. (1975). Initial interaction distance among individuals equal and unequal in military rank. *Journal of Personality and Social Psychology, 32*, 294–299.

Decety, J., Jackson, P. L., Sommeerville, J. A., Chaminade, T., & Meltzoff, A. N. (2004). The neural bases of cooperation and competition: An fMRI investigation. *NeuroImage, 23*, 744–751.

DeChurch, L. A., & Haas, C. D. (2008). Examining team planning through an episodic lens: Effects of deliberate, contingency, and reactive planning on team effectiveness. *Small Group Research, 39*(5), 542–568.

DeChurch, L. A., Hamilton, K. L., & Haas, C. (2007). Effects of conflict management strategies on perceptions of intragroup conflict. *Group Dynamics: Theory, Research, and Practice, 11*(1), 66–78.

DeChurch, L. A., & Mathieu, J. E. (2009). Thinking in terms of multiteam systems. In E. Salas, G. F. Goodwin, & C. S. Burke (Eds.), *Team effectiveness in complex organizations: Cross-disciplinary perspectives and approaches* (pp. 267–292). New York: Routledge/Taylor & Francis Group.

DeChurch, L. A., & Mesmer-Magnus, J. R. (2010). Measuring shared team mental models: A meta-analysis. *Group Dynamics: Theory, Research, and Practice, 14*(1), 1–14.

Delbecq, A. L., & Van de Ven, A. H. (1971). A group process model for problem identification and program planning. *Journal of Applied Behavioral Science, 7*, 466–492.

Delton, A. W., Cosmides, L., Guemo, M., Robertson, T. E., & Tooby, J. (2012). The psychosemantics of free riding: Dissecting the architecture of a moral concept. *Journal of Personality and Social Psychology, 102*(6), 1252–1270.

DeLucia-Waack, J. (2010). Diversity in groups. In R. K. Conyne (Ed.), *The Oxford handbook of group counseling* (pp. 83–101). New York: Oxford University Press.

DeLucia-Waack, J. L., & Kalodner, C. R. (2005). Contemporary issues in group practice. In S. A. Wheelan (Ed.), *The handbook of group research and practice* (pp. 65–84). Thousand Oaks, CA: Sage.

DeMatteo, J. S., Eby, L. T., & Sundstrom, E. (1998). Team-based rewards: Current empirical evidence and directions for future research. *Research in Organizational Behavior, 20*, 141–183.

Denissen, J. J. A., Penke, L., Schmitt, D. P., & van Aken, M. A. G. (2008). Self-esteem reactions to social interactions: Evidence for sociometer mechanisms across days, people, and nations. *Journal of Personality and Social Psychology, 95*(1), 181–196.

Denrell, J., & Le Mens, G. (2007). Interdependent sampling and social influence. *Psychological Review, 114*, 398–422.

Denson, T. F., Lickel, B., Curtis, M., Stenstrom, D. M., & Ames, D. R. (2006). The roles of entitativity and essentiality in judgments of collective responsibility. *Group Processes & Intergroup Relations, 9*, 43–61.

Denvir, B. (1993). *The chronicle of impressionism*. New York: Little, Brown.

Derks, B., Scheepers, D., Van Laar, C., & Ellemers, N. (2011). The threat vs. challenge of car parking for women: How self- and group affirmation affect cardiovascular responses. *Journal of Experimental Social Psychology, 47*(1), 178–183.

Derlega, V. J., Cukur, C., Kuang, J. C. Y., & Forsyth, D. R. (2002). Interdependent construal of self and the endorsement of conflict resolution strategies in interpersonal, intergroup, and international disputes. *Journal of Cross-cultural Psychology, 33*, 610–625.

DeRosa, D. M., Smith, C. L., & Hantula, D. A. (2007). The medium matters: Mining the long-promised merit of group interaction in creative idea generation tasks in a meta-analysis of the electronic group brainstorming literature. *Computers in Human Behavior, 23*, 1549–1581.

DeRue, D. S., Nahrgang, J. D., Wellman, N., & Humphrey, S. E. (2011). Trait and behavioral theories of leadership: An integration and meta-analytic test of their relative validity. *Personnel Psychology, 64*(1), 7–52.

Deutsch, M. (1949a). An experimental study of the effects of cooperation and competition upon group process. *Human Relations, 2*, 199–231.

Deutsch, M. (1949b). A theory of cooperation and competition. *Human Relations, 2*, 129–152.

Deutsch, M. (1973). *The resolution of conflict: Constructive and destructive processes*. New Haven, CT: Yale University Press.

Deutsch, M. (1980). Fifty years of conflict. In L. Festinger (Ed.), *Retrospections on social psychology* (pp. 46–77). New York: Oxford University Press.

Deutsch, M., & Coleman, P. T. (Eds.). (2000). *The handbook of conflict resolution: Theory and practice*. San Francisco: Jossey-Bass.

Deutsch, M., & Gerard, H. B. (1955). A study of normative and informational social influences upon individual judgment. *Journal of Abnormal and Social Psychology, 51*(3), 629–636.

Deutsch, M., & Krauss, R. M. (1960). The effect of threat upon interpersonal bargaining. *Journal of Abnormal and Social Psychology, 61*, 181–189.

Deutsch, M., & Lewicki, R. J. (1970). "Locking in" effects during a game of Chicken. *Journal of Conflict Resolution, 14*, 367–378.

Devilly, G., Gist, R., & Cotton, P. (2006). Ready! Aim! Fire! The status of psychological debriefing and therapeutic interventions: In the work place and after disasters. *Review of General Psychology, 10*, 318–345.

Devine, D. J. (2002). A review and integration of classification systems relevant to teams in organizations. *Group Dynamics: Theory, Research, and Practice, 6*, 291–310.

Devine, D. J., Clayton, L. D., Dunford, B. B., Seying, R., & Pryce, J. (2001). Jury decision making: 45 years of empirical research on deliberating groups. *Psychology, Public Policy, & Law, 7*, 622–727.

Devine, D. J., Clayton, L. D., Philips, J. L., Dunford, B. B., & Melner, S. B. (1999). Teams in organizations: Prevalence, characteristics, and effectiveness. *Small Group Research, 30*, 678–711.

Devine, D. J., & Philips, J. L. (2001). Do smarter teams do better: A meta-analysis of cognitive ability and team performance. *Small Group Research, 32,* 507–532.

Devine, P. G. (1989). Stereotypes and prejudice: Their automatic and controlled components. *Journal of Personality and Social Psychology, 56,* 5–18.

Devine, P. G. (2005). Breaking the prejudice habit: Allport's "inner conflict" revisited. In J. F. Dovidio, P. Glick & L. A. Rudman (Eds.), *On the nature of prejudice: Fifty years after Allport* (pp. 327–342). Malden, MA: Blackwell.

Devine, P. G., & Sharp, L. B. (2009). Automaticity and control in stereotyping and prejudice. In T. D. Nelson (Ed.), *Handbook of prejudice, stereotyping, and discrimination* (pp. 61–88). New York: Psychology Press.

DeWall, C. N., Anderson, C. A., & Bushman, B. J. (2011). The general aggression model: Theoretical extensions to violence. *Psychology of Violence, 1*(3), 245–258.

DeWall, C. N., & Baumeister, R. F. (2006). Alone but feeling no pain: Effects of social exclusion on physical pain tolerance and pain threshold, affective forecasting, and interpersonal empathy. *Journal of Personality and Social Psychology, 91,* 1–15.

DeWall, C. N., Baumeister, R. F., Mead, N. L., & Vohs, K. D. (2011). How leaders self-regulate their task performance: Evidence that power promotes diligence, depletion, and disdain. *Journal of Personality and Social Psychology, 100*(1), 47–65.

DeWall, C. N., & Bushman, B. J. (2009). Hot under the collar in a lukewarm environment: Words associated with hot temperature increase aggressive thoughts and hostile perceptions. *Journal of Experimental Social Psychology, 45*(4), 1045–1047.

DeWall, C. N., MacDonald, G., Webster, G. D., Masten, C. L., Baumeister, R. F., Powell, C., Combs, D., Schurtz, D. R., Stillman, T. F., Tice, D. M., Eisenberger, N. I. (2010). Acetaminophen reduces social pain: Behavioral and neural evidence. *Psychological Science, 21*(7), 931–937.

DeWall, C. N., Maner, J. K., & Rouby, D. A. (2009). Social exclusion and early-stage interpersonal perception: Selective attention to signs of acceptance. *Journal of Personality and Social Psychology, 96*(4), 729–741.

DeYoung, C. G., Peterson, J. B., & Higgins, D. M. (2002). Higher-order factors of the Big Five predict conformity: Are there neuroses of health? *Personality and Individual Differences, 33,* 533–552.

Di Salvo, V. S., Nikkel, E., & Monroe, C. (1989). Theory and practice: A field investigation and identification of group members' perceptions of problems facing natural work groups. *Small Group Behavior, 20,* 551–567.

Diamond, S. S., Vidmar, N., Rose, M., Ellis, L., & Murphy, B. (2003). Inside the jury room: Evaluating juror discussions during trial. *Judicature, 87,* 54–58.

Diani, M. (2011). Networks and Internet into perspective. *Swiss Political Science Review, 17,* 469–474.

Diehl, M., & Stroebe, W. (1987). Productivity loss in brainstorming groups: Toward the solution of a riddle. *Journal of Personality and Social Psychology, 53,* 497–509.

Diehl, M., & Stroebe, W. (1991). Productivity loss in idea-generating groups: Tracking down the blocking effect. *Journal of Personality and Social Psychology, 61,* 392–403.

Diener, E. (1979). Deindividuation, self-awareness, and disinhibition. *Journal of Personality and Social Psychology, 37,* 1160–1171.

Diener, E. (1980). Deindividuation: The absence of self-awareness and self-regulation in group members. In P. B. Paulus (Ed.), *Psychology of group influence* (pp. 209–242). Mahwah, NJ: Erlbaum.

Diener, E., Fraser, S. C., Beaman, A. L., & Kelem, R. T. (1976). Effects of deindividuating variables on stealing by Halloween trick-or-treaters. *Journal of Personality and Social Psychology, 33,* 178–183.

Dienesch, R. M., & Liden, R. C. (1986). Leader/member exchange model of leadership: A critique and further development. *Academy of Management Review, 11,* 618–634.

Dierdorff, E. C., Bell, S. T., & Belohlav, J. A. (2011). The power of "we": Effects of psychological collectivism on team performance over time. *Journal of Applied Psychology, 96*(2), 247–262.

Dierick, P., & Lietaer, G. (2008). Client perception of therapeutic factors in group psychotherapy and growth groups: An empirically-based hierarchical model. *International Journal of Group Psychotherapy, 58,* 203–230.

Dies, R. R. (1994). Therapist variables in group psychotherapy research. In A. Fuhriman & G. M. Burlingame (Eds.), *Handbook of group psychotherapy* (pp. 114–154). New York: Wiley.

Dietz-Uhler, B., & Murrell, A. (1998). Effects of social identity and threat on self-esteem and group attributions. *Group Dynamics: Theory, Research, and Practice, 2,* 24–35.

DiFonzo, N. (2008). *The watercooler effect: A psychologist explores the extraordinary power of rumors.* New York: Penguin.

Dillard, J. P. (1991). The current status of research on sequential-request compliance techniques. *Personality and Social Psychology Bulletin, 17,* 283–288.

Dion, K. L. (2000). Group cohesion: From "field of forces" to multidimensional construct. *Group Dynamics: Theory, Research, and Practice, 4,* 7–26.

Dionne, S. D., Yammarino, F. J., Howell, J. P., & Villa, J. (2005). Theoretical letters: Substitutes for leadership, or not. *Leadership Quarterly, 16,* 169–193.

Dipboye, R. L. (1977). Alternative approaches to deindividuation. *Psychological Bulletin, 84,* 1057–1075.

Dishion, T. J., & Dodge, K. A. (2005). Peer contagion in interventions for children and adolescents: Moving towards an understanding of the ecology and dynamics of change. *Journal of Abnormal Child Psychology, 33,* 395–400.

Dobbins, G. H., & Platz, S. J. (1986). Sex differences in leadership: How real are they? *Academy of Management Review, 11,* 118–127.

Doherty, W. J., Lester, M. E., & Leigh, G. K. (1986). Marriage encounter weekends: Couples who win and couples who lose. *Journal of Marital and Family Therapy, 12,* 49–61.

Doise, W. (1969). Intergroup relations and polarization of individual and collective judgments. *Journal of Personality and Social Psychology, 12,* 136–143.

Dolbeault, S., Cayrou, C., Brédart, A., Viala, A-L., Desclaux, B., Saltel, P., Gauvain-Piquard, A., Hardy, P., Dickes, P. (2009). The effectiveness of a psycho-educational group after early breast cancer treatment: Results of a randomized French study. *Psycho-Oncology, 18,* 647–656.

Doll, B., Murphy, P., & Song, S. Y. (2003). The relationship between children's self-reported recess problems, and peer acceptance and friendships. *Journal of School Psychology, 41,* 113–130.

Dollar, N. J., & Merrigan, G. M. (2002). Ethnographic practices in group communication research. In L. R. Frey (Ed.), *New directions in group communication* (pp. 59–78). Thousand Oaks, CA: Sage.

Doosje, B. J., & Branscombe, N. R. (2003). Attributions for the negative historical actions of a group. *European Journal of Social Psychology, 33,* 235–248.

Dorfman, P. W., Hanges, P. J., & Brodbeck, F. C. (2004). Leadership and cultural variation: The identification of culturally endorsed leadership profiles. In R. J. House, P. J. Hanges, M. Javidan, P. W. Dorfman, & V. Gupta (Eds.), *Culture, leadership, and organizations: The GLOBE study of 62 societies* (pp. 669–719). Thousand Oaks, CA: Sage.

Douthitt, E. A., & Aiello, J. R. (2001). The role of participation and control in the effects of computer monitoring on fairness perceptions, task satisfaction, and performance. *Journal of Applied Psychology, 86,* 867–874.

Dovidio, J. F., Gaertner, S. L., Nier, J. A., Kawakami, K., & Hodson, G. (2004). Contemporary racial bias: When good people do bad things. In A. G. Miller (Ed.), *The social psychology of good and evil* (pp. 141–167). New York: Guilford.

Dovidio, J. F., Glick, P., & Rudman, L. A. (Eds.). (2005). *On the nature of prejudice: Fifty years after Allport.* Malden, MA: Blackwell.

Drigotas, S. M. (1993). Similarity revisited: A comparison of similarity-attraction versus dissimilarity-repulsion. *British Journal of Social Psychology, 32*(4), 365–377.

Driskell, J. E., Goodwin, G. F., Salas, E., & O'Shea, P. G. (2006). What makes a good team player? Personality and team effectiveness. *Group Dynamics: Theory, Research, and Practice, 10,* 249–271.

Driskell, J. E., & Mullen, B. (1990). Status, expectations, and behavior: A meta-analytic review and test of theory. *Personality and Social Psychology Bulletin, 16,* 541–553.

Driskell, J. E., & Salas, E. (1992). Can you study real teams in contrived settings? The value of small group research to understanding teams. In R. W. Swezey & E. Salas (Eds.), *Teams: Their training and performance* (pp. 101–124). Norwood, NJ: Ablex.

Driskell, J. E., Salas, E., & Hughes, S. (2010). Collective orientation and team performance: Development of an individual differences measure. *Human Factors, 52*(2), 316–328.

Driskell, J. E., Salas, E., & Johnston, J. (1999). Does stress lead to a loss of team perspective? *Group Dynamics: Theory, Research, and Practice, 3*(4), 291–302.

Drury, J. (2002). "When the mobs are looking for witches to burn, nobody's safe:" Talking about the reactionary crowd. *Discourse & Society, 13,* 41–73.

Drury, J. & Reicher, S. (1999). The intergroup dynamics of collective empowerment: Substantiating the social identity model of crowd behavior. *Group Processes and Intergroup Relations, 2,* 1–22.

Dryer, D. C., & Horowitz, L. M. (1997). When do opposites attract? Interpersonal complementarity versus similarity. *Journal of Personality and Social Psychology, 72,* 592–603.

Dubrovsky, V. J., Kiesler, S., & Sethna, B. N. (1991). The equalization phenomenon: Status effects in computer-mediated and face-to-face decision-making groups. *Human-Computer Interaction, 6,* 119–146.

Ducheneaut, N., Yee, N., Nickell, E., & Moore, R. J. (2006). Alone together? Exploring the social dynamics of massively multiplayer games. In *Proceedings of CHI2006* (pp. 407–416). New York: ACM.

Duckitt, J., & Mphuthing, T. (1998). Group identification and intergroup attitudes: A longitudinal analysis in South Africa. *Journal of Personality and Social Psychology, 74,* 80–85.

Duffy, F. (1992). *The new office.* London: Conran Octopus.

Dugosh, K. L., Paulus, P. B., Roland, E. J., & Yang, H. (2000). Cognitive stimulation in brainstorming. *Journal of Personality and Social Psychology, 79,* 722–735.

Dulebohn, J. H., Bommer, W. H., Liden, R. C., Brouer, R. L., & Ferris, G. R. (2011). A meta-analysis of antecedents and consequences of leader-member exchange: Integrating the past with an eye toward the future. *Journal of Management,* in press.

Dunbar, R. I. M. (1998). The social brain hypothesis. *Evolutionary Anthropology, 6,* 178–190.

Dunbar, R. I. M. (2008). Cognitive constraints on the structure and dynamics of social networks. *Group Dynamics: Theory, Research, and Practice, 12*(1), 7–16.

Dunning, D. (2007). Prediction: The inside view. In A. W. Kruglanski & E. T. Higgins (Eds.), *Social psychology: Handbook of basic principles* (2nd ed., pp. 69–90). New York: Guilford.

Dupont, C., & Passy, F. (2011). The Arab Spring or how to explain those revolutionary episodes. *Swiss Political Science Review, 17,* 447–451.

Dupue, R. L. (2007). A theoretical profile of Seung Hui Cho: From the perspective of a forensic behavioral scientist. In *Mass shootings at Virginia Tech: Report of the review panel.* Retrieved from www.governor.virginia.gov

Durand, D. E. (1977). Power as a function of office space and physiognomy: Two studies of influence. *Psychological Reports, 40,* 755–760.

Durkheim, É. (1965). *The elementary forms of religious life.* New York: Free Press. (original work published in 1912)

Durkheim, É. (1966). *Suicide*. New York: Free Press. (original work published in 1897)

Durkheim, É. (1973). *Emile Durkheim on morality and society*. Chicago: University of Chicago Press. (original work published in 1900)

Durkheim, É. (2005). The rules of sociological method. In K. Thompson (Ed.), *Readings from Emile Durkheim* (rev. ed., pp. 53–80). New York: Routledge. (original work published 1892)

Dvir, T., Eden, D., Avolio, B. J., & Shamir, B. (2002). Impact of transformational leadership on follower development and performance: A field experiment. *Academy of Management Journal*, *45*, 735–744.

Eagly, A. H., Johannesen-Schmidt, M. C., & van Engen, M. L. (2003). Transformational, transactional, and laissez-faire leadership styles: A meta-analysis comparing women and men. *Psychological Bulletin*, *129*, 569–591.

Eagly, A. H. (1987). *Sex differences in social behavior: A social-role interpretation*. Mahwah, NJ: Erlbaum.

Eagly, A. H., & Carli, L. L. (1981). Sex of researchers and sex-typed communications as determinants of sex differences in influenceability: A meta-analysis of social influence studies. *Psychological Bulletin*, *90*, 1–20.

Eagly, A. H., & Carli, L. L. (2007). *Through the labyrinth: The truth about how women become leaders*. Boston: Harvard Business School Press.

Eagly, A. H., & Johnson, B. T. (1990). Gender and leadership style: A meta-analysis. *Psychological Bulletin*, *108*, 233–256.

Eagly, A. H., & Karau, S. J. (2002). Role congruity theory of prejudice toward female leaders. *Psychological Review*, *109*, 573–598.

Eagly, A. H., Karau, S. J., & Makhijani, M. (1995). Gender and the effectiveness of leaders: A meta-analysis. *Journal of Personality and Social Psychology*, *117*, 125–145.

Eagly, A. H., Makhijani, M. G., & Klonsky, B. G. (1992). Gender and the evaluation of leaders: A meta-analysis. *Psychological Bulletin*, *111*, 3–22.

Eagly, A. H., Wood, W., & Fishbaugh, L. (1981). Sex differences in conformity: Surveillance by the group as a determinant of male nonconformity. *Journal of Personality and Social Psychology*, *40*, 384–394.

Earley, P. C., & Gibson, C. B. (1998). Taking stock in our progress on individualism-collectivism: 100 years of solidarity and community. *Journal of Management*, *24*(3), 265–304.

Eaton, J. W. (1947). Experiments in testing for leadership. *American Journal of Sociology*, *52*, 523–535.

Ebbesen, E. B., Kjos, G. L., & Konečni, V. J. (1976). Spatial ecology: Its effects on the choice of friends and enemies. *Journal of Experimental Social Psychology*, *12*, 505–518.

Echterhoff, G., Higgins, E. T., & Levine, J. M. (2009). Shared reality: Experiencing commonality with others' inner states about the world. *Perspectives on Psychological Science*, *4*(5), 496–521.

Edelstein, M. R. (2002). Contamination: The invisible built environment. In R. B. Bechtel & A. Churchman (Eds.), *Handbook of environmental psychology* (pp. 559–588). New York: Wiley.

Edmondson, A., Bohmer, R., & Pisano, G. (2001). Speeding up team learning. *Harvard Business Review*, *79*(9), 125–132.

Edmondson, A. C. (2011). Crossing boundaries to investigate problems in the field: An approach to useful research. In S. A. Mohrman & E. E. Lawler III (Eds.), *Useful research: Advancing theory and practice* (pp. 37–55). San Francisco: Berrett-Koehler.

Edney, J. J. (1975). Territoriality and control: A field experiment. *Journal of Personality and Social Psychology*, *31*, 1108–1115.

Edney, J. J. (1976). Human territories: Comment on functional properties. *Environment and Behavior*, *8*, 31–48.

Edney, J. J., & Grundmann, M. J. (1979). Friendship, group size, and boundary size: Small group spaces. *Small Group Behavior*, *10*, 124–135.

Edney, J. J., & Jordan-Edney, N. L. (1974). Territorial spacing on a beach. *Sociometry*, *37*, 92–104.

Egan, V., & Beadman, M. (2011). Personality and gang embeddedness. *Personality and Individual Differences*, *51*(6), 748–753.

Ehrhart, M. G., & Naumann, S. E. (2004). Organizational citizenship behavior in work groups: A group norms approach. *Journal of Applied Psychology*, *89*, 960–974.

Eisenberger, N. I. (2011). Why rejection hurts: What social neuroscience has revealed about the brain's response to social rejection. In J. Decety & J. Cacioppo (Eds.), *The Handbook of Social Neuroscience* (pp. 586–598). New York: Oxford University Press.

Eisenberger, N. I. & Lieberman, M. D. (2004). Why rejection hurts: A common neural alarm system for physical and social pain. *Trends in Cognitive Sciences*, *8*, 294–300.

Eisenberger, N. I., Lieberman, M. D., & Williams, K. D. (2003). Does rejection hurt? An fMRI study of social exclusion. *Science*, *302*, 290–292.

Eisenberger, R., Lynch, P., Aselage, J., & Rohdieck, S. (2004). Who takes the most revenge? Individual differences in negative reciprocity norm endorsement. *Personality and Social Psychology Bulletin*, *30*, 789–799.

Eldredge, N., & Gould, S. J. (1972). Punctuated equilibria: An alternative to phyletic gradualism. In T. M. Schopf (Ed.), *Models in palaeobiology* (pp. 82–115). New York: Freeman.

Ellemers, N., & Haslam, S. A. (2012). Social identity theory. In P. A. M. Van Lange, A. W. Kruglanski & E. T. Higgins (Eds.), *Handbook of theories of social psychology* (Vol. 2, pp. 379–398). Thousand Oaks, CA: Sage.

Ellemers, N., Spears, R., & Doosje, B. (1997). Sticking together or falling apart: In-group identification as a psychological determinant of group commitment versus individual mobility. *Journal of Personality and Social Psychology*, *72*, 617–626.

Ellemers, N., Spears, R., & Doosje, B. (2002). Self and social identity. *Annual Review of Psychology*, *53*, 161–186.

Eller, A., Abrams, D., & Gomez, A. (2012). When the direct route is blocked: The extended contact pathway to improving intergroup relations. *International Journal of Intercultural Relations*. In press.

Ellis, A. P. J., Hollenbeck, J. R., Ilgen, D. R., Porter, C. O. L. H., West, B. J., & Moon, H. (2003). Team learning: Collectively connecting the dots. *Journal of Applied Psychology, 88*, 821–835.

Ellison, N. B., Steinfield, C., & Lampe, C. (2007). The benefits of Facebook "friends": Social capital and college students' use of online social network sites. *Journal of Computer-Mediated Communication, 12*(4), 1143–1168.

Ellsworth, P. C. (1989). Are twelve heads better than one? *Law and Contemporary Problems, 52*, 205–224.

Ellsworth, P.C. (2003). One inspiring jury. *Michigan Law Review, 101*(6), 1387–1407.

Ellsworth, P. C., & Reifman, A. (2000). Juror comprehension and public policy: Perceived problems and proposed solutions. *Psychology, Public Policy, & Law, 6*, 788–821.

Elms, A. C. (1972). *Social psychology and social relevance.* Boston: Little, Brown.

Elms, A. C. (1995). Obedience in retrospect. *Journal of Social Issues, 51*, 21–31.

Elms, A. C. (2009). Obedience lite. *American Psychologist, 64*(1), 32–36.

Elster, J. 1989. *The cement of society: A study of social order.* New York: Cambridge University Press.

Ember, M., & Ember, C. R. (1994). Prescriptions for peace: Policy implications of cross-cultural research on war and interpersonal violence. *Cross-Cultural Research: The Journal of Comparative Social Science, 28*(4), 343–350.

Emerson, R. M. (1962). Power-dependence relations. *American Sociological Review, 27*, 31–40.

Emerson, R. M., Fretz, R. I., & Shaw, L. L. (2011). *Writing ethnographic fieldnotes* (2nd ed.). Chicago: University of Chicago Press.

Emler, N., & Cook, T. (2001). Moral integrity in leadership: Why it matters and why it may be difficult to achieve. In B. W. Roberts & R. Hogan (Eds.), *Personality psychology in the workplace* (pp. 277–298). Washington, DC: American Psychological Association.

Emrich, C. G. (1999). Context effects in leadership perception. *Personality and Social Psychology Bulletin, 25*, 991–1006.

Engeström, Y. (2008). *From teams to knots.* Cambridge, UK: Cambridge University Press.

Epitropaki, O., & Martin, R. (2004). Implicit leadership theories in applied settings: Factor structure, generalizability, and stability over time. *Journal of Applied Psychology, 89*, 293–310.

Epley, N., & Gilovich, T. (1999). Just going along: Nonconscious priming and conformity to social pressure. *Journal of Experimental Social Psychology, 35*, 578–589.

Ericksen, J., & Dyer, L. (2004). Right from the Start: Exploring the Effects of Early Team Events on Subsequent Project Team Development and Performance. *Administrative Science Quarterly, 49*(3), 438–471.

Esser, A. H. (1968). Dominance hierarchy and clinical course of psychiatrically hospitalized boys. *Child Development, 39*, 147–157.

Esser, A. H. (1973). Cottage Fourteen: Dominance and territoriality in a group of institutionalized boys. *Small Group Behavior, 4*, 131–146.

Esser, A. H., Chamberlain, A. S., Chapple, E. D., & Kline, N. S. (1965). Territoriality of patients on a research ward. In J. Wortis (Ed.), *Recent advances in biological psychiatr* (Vol. 7, pp. 36–44). New York: Plenum.

Esser, J. K. (1998). Alive and well after 25 years: A review of groupthink research. *Organizational Behavior and Human Decision Processes, 73*, 116–141.

Esses, V. M., Jackson, L. M., Dovidio, J. F., & Hodson, G. (2005). Instrumental relations among groups: Group competition, conflict, and prejudice. In J. F. Dovidio, P. Glick & L. A. Rudman (Eds.), *On the nature of prejudice: Fifty years after Allport* (pp. 227–243). Malden, MA: Blackwell.

Estellés-Arolas, E., & González-Ladrón-de-Guevara, F. (2012). *Journal of Information Science, 38*(2), 189–200.

Ettin, M. F. (1992). *Foundations and applications of group psychotherapy: A sphere of influence.* Boston: Allyn & Bacon.

Etzioni, A. (1968). A model of significant research. *International Journal of Psychiatry, 6*, 278–280.

Euwema, M. C., & Van Emmerik, I. H. (2007). Intercultural competencies and conglomerated conflict behaviors in intercultural conflicts. *International Journal of Intercultural Relations, 31*(4), 427–441.

Evans, G. W. (1979). Behavioral and physiological consequences of crowding in humans. *Journal of Applied Social Psychology, 9*, 27–46.

Evans, G. W., & Cohen, S. (1987). Environmental stress. In D. Stokols & I. Altman (Eds.), *Handbook of environmental psychology* (Vol. 1, pp. 571–610). New York: Wiley.

Evans, G. W., & Howard, R. B. (1973). Personal space. *Psychological Bulletin, 80*, 334–344.

Evans, G. W., & Lepore, S. J. (1992). Conceptual and analytic issues in crowding research. *Journal of Environmental Psychology, 12*, 163–173.

Evans, G. W., & Stecker, R. (2004). Motivational consequences of environmental stress. *Journal of Environmental Psychology, 24*, 143–165.

Evans, G. W., & Wener, R. E. (2007). Crowding and personal space invasion on the train: Please don't make me sit in the middle. *Journal of Environmental Psychology, 27*, 90–94.

Evans, H., & Bartholomew, R. (2009). *Outbreak! The encyclopedia of extraordinary social behavior.* New York: Anomalist Books.

Evans, N. J., & Jarvis, P. A. (1986). The Group Attitude Scale: A measure of attraction to group. *Small Group Behavior, 17*, 203–216.

Eys, M. A., & Carron, A. V. (2001). Role ambiguity, task cohesion, and task self-efficacy. *Small Group Research, 32*(3), 356–373.

Eysenck, H. (1990). Biological dimensions of personality. In L. A. Pervin (Ed.), *Handbook of personality: Theory and research* (pp. 244–276). New York: Guilford.

Falbo, T. (1977). The multidimensional scaling of power strategies. *Journal of Personality and Social Psychology, 35,* 537–548.

Falbo, T., & Peplau, L. A. (1980). Power strategies in intimate relationships. *Journal of Personality and Social Psychology, 38,* 618–628.

Falk, A., & Fischbacher, U. (2006). A theory of reciprocity. *Games and Economic Behavior, 54,* 293–315.

Falloon, I. R. H., Lindley, P., McDonald, R., & Marks, I. M. (1977). Social skills training of outpatient groups: A controlled study of rehearsal and homework. *British Journal of Psychiatry, 131,* 599–609.

Fanon, F. (1963). *The wretched of the earth.* New York: Grove.

Faraj, S., & Johnson, S. L. (2011). Network exchange patterns in online communities. *Organization Science, 22*(6), 1464–1480.

Farbstein, J., & Kantrowitz, M. (1978). *People in places: Experiencing, using, and changing the built environment.* Upper Saddle River, NJ: Prentice Hall.

Farrell, M. P. (1982). Artists' circles and the development of artists. *Small Group Behavior, 13,* 451–474.

Farrell, M. P. (2001). *Collaborative circles: Friendship dynamics & creative work.* Chicago: University of Chicago Press.

Farrell, M. P., Schmitt, M. H., & Heinemann, G. D. (2001). Informal roles and the stages of interdisciplinary team development. *Journal of Interprofessional Care, 15*(3), 281–295.

Feather, N. T. (1994). Human values and their relation to justice. *Journal of Social Issues, 50*(4), 129–151.

Feeley, T. H. (2000). Testing a communication network model of employee turnover based on centrality. *Journal of Applied Communication Research, 28,* 262–277.

Feigenson, N. (2000). *Legal blame: How jurors think and talk about accidents.* Washington, DC: American Psychological Association.

Feld, S. L. (1982). Social structural determinants of similarity among associates. *American Sociological Review, 47,* 797–801.

Feldman, R. E. (1968). Response to compatriot and foreigner who seek assistance. *Journal of Personality and Social Psychology, 10*(3), 202–214.

Feldman, S. (2003). Enforcing social conformity: A theory of authoritarianism. *Political Psychology, 24,* 41–74.

Ferencik, B. M. (1992). The helping process in group therapy: A review and discussion. *Group, 16,* 113–124.

Ferreira, M. C., Fischer, R., Porto, J. B., Pilati, R., & Milfont, T. L. (2012). Unraveling the mystery of Brazilian Jeitinho: A cultural exploration of social norms. *Personality and Social Psychology Bulletin, 38*(3), 331–344.

Ferris, D. L., Brown, D. J., Berry, J. W., & Lian, H. (2008). The development and validation of the Workplace Ostracism Scale. *Journal of Applied Psychology, 93*(6), 1348–1366.

Ferris, G. R., & Rowland, K. M. (1983). Social facilitation effects on behavioral and perceptual task performance measures: Implications for work behavior. *Group and Organization Studies, 8,* 421–438.

Ferris, G. R., Treadway, D. C., Kolodinsky, R. W., Hochwarter, W. A., Kacmar, C. J., Douglas, C., & Frink, D. D. (2005). Development and validation of the Political Skill Inventory. *Journal of Management, 31*(1), 126–152.

Ferris, G. R., Treadway, D. C., Perrewé, P. L., Brouer, R. L., Douglas, C., & Lux, S. (2007). Political skill in organizations. *Journal of Management, 33*(3), 290–320.

Festinger, L. (1950). Informal social communication. *Psychological Review, 57,* 271–282.

Festinger, L. (1954). A theory of social comparison processes. *Human Relations, 7,* 117–140.

Festinger, L. (1957). *A theory of cognitive dissonance.* Stanford, CA: Stanford University Press.

Festinger, L. (1983). *The human legacy.* New York: Columbia University Press.

Festinger, L., Pepitone, A., & Newcomb, T. (1952). Some consequences of deindividuation in a group. *Journal of Abnormal and Social Psychology, 47,* 382–389.

Festinger, L., Riecken, H. W., & Schachter, S. (1956). *When prophecy fails.* Minneapolis: University of Minnesota Press.

Festinger, L., Schachter, S., & Back, K. (1950). *Social pressures in informal groups.* New York: Harper.

Festinger, L., & Thibaut, J. (1951). Interpersonal communication in small groups. *Journal of Abnormal and Social Psychology, 46,* 92–99.

Fiedler, F. E. (1955). The influence of leader-keyman relations on combat crew effectiveness. *Journal of Abnormal and Social Psychology, 51,* 227–235.

Fiedler, F. E. (1964). A contingency model of leadership effectiveness. *Advances in Experimental Social Psychology, 1,* 150–190.

Fiedler, F. E. (1967). *A theory of leadership effectiveness.* New York: McGraw-Hill.

Fiedler, F. E. (1978). The contingency model and the dynamics of the leadership process. *Advances in Experimental Social Psychology, 12,* 59–112.

Fiedler, F. E. (1986). The contribution of cognitive resources to leadership performance. *Journal of Applied Social Psychology, 16,* 532–548.

Fiedler, F. E. (1996). Research on leadership selection and training: One view of the future. *Administrative Science Quarterly, 41,* 241–250.

Fiedler, F. E., Chemers, M. M., & Mahar, L. (1976). *Improving leadership effectiveness: The Leader Match concept.* New York: Wiley.

Filkins, J. W., Smith, C. M., & Tindale, R. S. (1998). An evaluation of the biasing effects of death qualification: A meta-analytic/computer simulation approach. In R. S. Tindale, L. Heath, J. Edwards, E. J. Posavac, F. B. Bryant, Y. Suarez-Balcazar, E. Henderson-King, & J. Myers (Eds.), *Social psychological applications to social issues: Theory and research on small groups* (Vol. 4, pp. 153–175). New York: Plenum Press.

Fincham, F. D., & Bradbury, T. N. (1992). Assessing attributions in marriage: The Relationship Attribution Measure. *Journal of Personality and Social Psychology, 62,* 457–468.

Fincham, F. D., & Bradbury, T. N. (1993). Marital satisfaction, depression, and attributions: A longitudinal analysis. *Journal of Personality and Social Psychology, 64,* 442–452.

Fincher, C. L., & Thornhill, R. (2012). Parasite-stress promotes in-group assortative sociality: The cases of strong family ties and heightened religiosity. *Behavioral and Brain Sciences, 35*(2), 61–79.

Fine, G. A. (1987). *With the boys: Little League baseball and preadolescent culture.* Chicago: University of Chicago Press.

Fine, G. A. (2003). Morel tales: The culture of mushrooming. Champaign: University of Illinois Press. (original work published 1998)

Fine, G. A., & Holyfield, L. (1996). Secrecy, trust, and dangerous leisure: Generating group cohesion in voluntary organizations. *Social Psychology Quarterly, 59,* 22–38.

Finkel, M. A. (2002). Traumatic injuries caused by hazing practices. *American Journal of Emergency Medicine, 20,* 228–233.

Finlay, F., Hitch, G., & Meudell, P. R. (2000). Mutual inhibition in collaborative recall: Evidence for a retrieval-based account. *Journal of Experimental Psychology: Learning, Memory, and Cognition, 26,* 1556–1567.

Fiore, S. M. (2008). Interdisciplinarity as teamwork: How the science of teams can inform team science. *Small Group Research, 39*(3), 251–277.

Fischer, A. H., & Roseman, I. J. (2007). Beat them or ban them: The characteristics and social functions of anger and contempt. *Journal of Personality and Social Psychology, 93*(1), 103–115.

Fischer, R., Hanke, K. and Sibley, C. G. (2012), Cultural and institutional determinants of social dominance orientation: A cross-cultural meta-analysis of 27 societies. *Political Psychology, 33,* 437–467.

Fischer, R., Smith, P. B., Richey, B., Ferreira, M. C., Assmar, E. M. L., Maes, J., & Stumpf, S. (2007). How do organizations allocate rewards? The predictive validity of national values, economic and organizational factors across six nations. *Journal of Cross-Cultural Psychology, 38,* 3–18.

Fischer, R., & Van de Vliert, E. (2011). Does climate undermine subjective well-being? A 58-nation study. *Personality and Social Psychology Bulletin, 37*(8), 1031–1041.

Fisher, B. A. (1980). *Small group decision making* (2nd ed.). New York: McGraw-Hill.

Fisher, J. D., & Byrne, D. (1975). Too close for comfort: Sex differences in response to invasions of personal space. *Journal of Personality and Social Psychology, 32,* 15–21.

Fisher, R. (1983). Negotiating power. *American Behavioral Science, 27,* 149–166.

Fisher, R., & Ury, W., with B. Patton (Ed.). (1981). *Getting to YES: Negotiating agreement without giving in.* Boston: Houghton-Mifflin.

Fiske, A. P. (1992). The four elementary forms of sociality: Framework for a unified theory of social relations. *Psychological Review, 99,* 689–723.

Fiske, A. P. (2002). Using individualism and collectivism to compare cultures—A critique of the validity and measurement of the constructs: Comment on Oyserman et al. (2002). *Psychological Bulletin, 128,* 78–88.

Fiske, S. T. (2004). What's in a category? Responsibility, intent, and the avoidability of bias against outgroups. In A. G. Miller (Ed.), *The social psychology of good and evil* (pp. 127–140). New York: Guilford.

Fiske, S. T. (2010a). Envy up, scorn down: How comparison divides us. *American Psychologist, 65*(8), 698–706.

Fiske, S. T. (2010b). Interpersonal stratification: Status, power, and subordination. In S. T. Fiske, D. T. Gilbert, & G. Lindzey (Eds.), *Handbook of social psychology* (Vol. 2, 5th ed., pp. 941–982). Hoboken, NJ: John Wiley.

Fiske, S. T., & Berdahl, J. (2007). Social power. In A. W. Kruglanski & E. T. Higgins (Eds.), *Social psychology: Handbook of basic principles* (2nd ed., pp. 678–692). New York: Guilford.

Fiske, S. T., Harris, L. T., & Cuddy, A. J. C. (2004). Why ordinary people torture enemy prisoners. *Science, 306,* 1482–1483.

Fleeson, W., Malanos, A. B., & Achille, N. M. (2002). An intraindividual process approach to the relationship between extraversion and positive affect: Is acting extraverted as "good" as being extraverted? *Journal of Personality and Social Psychology, 83,* 1409–1422.

Fleishman, E. A. (1953). The description of supervisory behavior. *Journal of Applied Psychology, 37,* 1–6.

Flores, P. J. (1997). *Group psychotherapy with addicted populations: An integration of twelve step and psychodynamic theory.* Binghamton, NY: Haworth Press.

Flowers, M. L. (1977). A laboratory test of some implications of Janis' groupthink hypothesis. *Journal of Personality and Social Psychology, 35,* 888–896.

Flynn, F. J. (2010). Power as charismatic leadership: A significant opportunity (and a modest proposal) for social psychology research. In A. Guinote & T. K. Vescio (Eds.), *The social psychology of power* (pp. 284–309). New York: Guilford Press.

Flynn, K., & Gerhardt, G. (1989). The silent brotherhood: Inside America's racist underground. New York: Penguin.

Foddy, M., & Smithson, M. (1996). Relative ability, paths of relevance, and influence in task-oriented groups. *Social Psychology Quarterly, 59,* 140–153.

Fodor, E. M. (2009). Power motivation. In M. R. Leary & R. H. Hoyle (Eds.), *Handbook of individual differences in social behavior* (pp. 426–440). New York: Guilford Press.

Fodor, E. M., & Riordan, J. M. (1995). Leader power motive and group conflict as influences on leader behavior and group member self-affect. *Journal of Research in Personality, 29,* 418–431.

Fodor, E. M., & Smith, T. (1982). The power motive as an influence on group decision making. *Journal of Personality and Social Psychology, 42,* 178–185.

Fodor, E. M., & Wick, D. P. (2009). Need for power and affective response to negative audience reaction to an extemporaneous speech. *Journal of Research in Personality, 43*(5), 721–726.

Fodor, E. M., Wick, D. P., & Hartsen, K. M. (2006). The power motive and affective response to assertiveness. *Journal of Research in Personality, 40*(5), 598–610.

Foer, F. (2004). *How soccer explains the world.* New York: HarperCollins.

Folk, G. E., Jr. (1974). *Textbook of environmental physiology.* Philadelphia: Lea & Febiger.

Fontana, D. (1990). *Social skills at work.* Exeter: British Printing and Publishing Communication Corporation.

Forbes, D. L. (2011). Toward a unified model of human motivation. *Review of General Psychology, 15*(2), 85–98.

Ford, M. T., Heinen, B. A., & Langkamer, K. L. (2007). Work and family satisfaction and conflict: A meta-analysis of cross-domain relations. *Journal of Applied Psychology, 92*(1), 57–80.

Forgas, J. P. (1998). On feeling good and getting your way: Mood effects on negotiator cognition and bargaining strategies. *Journal of Personality and Social Psychology, 74*, 565–577.

Forsyth, D. R. (2010a). Delphi technique. In J. M. Levine & M. A. Hogg (Eds.), *Encyclopedia of group process and intergroup relations* (pp. 195–197). Thousand Oaks, CA: Sage.

Forsyth, D. R. (2010b). Group process and group psychotherapy: Social psychological foundations of change in therapeutic groups. In J. E. Maddux & J. P. Tangney (Eds.), *Social psychological foundations of clinical psychology* (pp. 497–513). New York: Guilford.

Forsyth, D. R., Berger, R. E., & Mitchell, T. (1981). The effects of self-serving vs. other-serving claims of responsibility on attraction and attribution in groups. *Social Psychology Quarterly, 44*, 59–64.

Forsyth, D. R., & Burnette, J. L. (2005). The history of group research. In S. A. Wheelan (Ed.), *The handbook of group research and practice* (pp. 3–18). Thousand Oaks, CA: Sage.

Forsyth, D. R., & Elliott, T. R. (1999). Group dynamics and psychological well-being: The impact of groups on adjustment and dysfunction. In R. Kowalski & M. R. Leary (Eds.), *The social psychology of emotional and behavioral problems: Interfaces of social and clinical psychology* (pp. 339–361). Washington, DC: American Psychological Association.

Forsyth, D. R., Heiney, M. M., & Wright, S. S. (1997). Biases in appraisals of women leaders. *Group Dynamics: Theory, Research, and Practice, 1*, 98–103.

Forsyth, D. R., & Hoyt, C. L. (Eds.). (2011). *For the greater good of all.* New York: Palgrave MacMillan.

Forsyth, D. R., & Nye, J. L. (2008). Seeing and being a leader: The perceptual, cognitive, and interpersonal roots of conferred influence. In C. L. Hoyt, G. R. Goethals, & D. R. Forsyth (Eds.), *Leadership at the crossroads: Leadership and psychology* (Vol. 1, pp. 116–131). Westport, CT: Praeger.

Forsyth, D. R., Schlenker, B. R., Leary, M. R., & McCown, N. E. (1985). Self-presentational determinants of sex differences in leadership behavior. *Small Group Behavior, 16*, 197–210.

Forsyth, D. R., Zyzniewski, L. E., & Giammanco, C. A. (2002). Responsibility diffusion in cooperative collectives. *Personality and Social Psychology Bulletin, 28*, 54–65.

Fortin, M., & Fellenz, M. R. (2008). Hypocrisies of fairness: Towards a more reflexive ethical base in organizational justice research and practice. *Journal of Business Ethics, 78*, 415–433.

Foschi, M. (1996). Double standards in the evaluation of men and women. *Social Psychology Quarterly, 59*, 237–254.

Foschi, M., Warriner, G. K., & Hart, S. D. (1985). Standards, expectations, and interpersonal influence. *Social Psychology Quarterly, 48*, 108–117.

Foss, R. D. (1981). Structural effects in simulated jury decision making. *Journal of Personality and Social Psychology, 40*, 1055–1062.

Foti, R. J., & Hauenstein, N. M. A. (2007). Pattern and variable approaches in leadership emergence and effectiveness. *Journal of Applied Psychology, 92*, 347–355.

Foti, R. J., & Lord, R. G. (1987). Prototypes and scripts: The effects of alternative methods of processing information on rating accuracy. *Organizational Behavior and Human Decision Processes, 39*, 318–340.

Foushee, H. C. (1984). Dyads and triads at 35,000 feet: Factors affecting group process and aircrew performance. *American Psychologist, 39*, 886–893.

Foy, D. W., Drescher, K. D., & Watson, P. J. (2010). Groups for trauma/disaster. In R. K. Conyne (Ed.), *The Oxford handbook of group counseling* (pp. 534–550). New York: Oxford University Press.

Foy, D. W., & Schrock, D. A. (2006). Future directions. In L. A. Schein, H. I. Spitz, G. M. Burlingame, & P. R. Muskin (Eds.), with S. Vargo, *Psychological effects of catastrophic disasters: Group approaches to treatment* (pp. 879–903). New York: Haworth Press.

Foy, E., & Harlow, A. F. (1956). *Clowning through life.* New York: Dutton. (original work published in 1928)

Frable, D. E. S., Platt, L., & Hoey, S. (1998). Concealable stigmas and positive self-perceptions: Feeling better around similar others. *Journal of Personality and Social Psychology, 74*, 909–922.

Frager, R. (1970). Conformity and anticonformity in Japan. *Journal of Personality and Social Psychology, 15*, 203–210.

Fraine, G., Smith, S. G., Zinkiewicz, L., Chapman, R., & Sheehan, M. (2007). At home on the road? Can drivers' relationships with their cars be associated with territoriality? *Journal of Environmental Psychology, 27*, 204–214.

Francis, L. J. (1998). Self-esteem as a function of personality and gender among 8-11 year olds: Is Coopersmith's index fair? *Personality and Individual Differences, 25*, 159–165.

Francis, R. C. (2004). *Why men won't ask for directions: The seduction of sociobiology.* Princeton, NJ: Princeton University Press.

Franke, R. H., & Kaul, J. D. (1978). The Hawthorne experiments: First statistical interpretation. *American Sociological Review, 43*, 623–643.

Franklin, J. (2011). *33 men: Inside the miraculous survival and dramatic rescue of the Chilean miners.* New York: Putnam.

Freedman, J. L. (1975). *Crowding and behavior.* San Francisco: Freeman.

Freedman, J. L. (1979). Reconciling apparent differences between responses of humans and other animals to crowding. *Psychological Review, 86*, 80–85.

Freedman, J. L., & Fraser, S. C. (1966). Compliance without pressure: The foot-in-the-door technique. *Journal of Personality and Social Psychology, 4*, 195–202.

Freedman, J. L., & Perlick, D. (1979). Crowding, contagion, and laughter. *Journal of Experimental Social Psychology, 15*, 295–303.

Freeman, L. C. (1979). Centrality in social networks: I. Conceptual clarification. *Social Networks, 1*, 215–239.

Freeman, L. C. (2004). *The development of social network analysis: A study in the sociology of science*. Vancouver, British Columbia: Empirical Press.

French, J. R. P., Jr. (1941). The disruption and cohesion of groups. *Journal of Abnormal and Social Psychology, 36*, 361–377.

French, J. R. P., Jr., & Raven, B. (1959). The bases of social power. In D. Cartwright (Ed.), *Studies in social power*. Ann Arbor, MI: Institute for Social Research.

Freud, S. (1922). *Group psychology and the analysis of the ego* (J. Strachey, Trans.). London: Hogarth Press and the Institute of Psycho-analysis.

Frey, L. R. (Ed.). (2003). *Group communication in context: Studies of bona fide groups* (2nd ed.). Mahwah, NJ: Erlbaum.

Frey, L. R., & Konieczka, S. P. (2010). Group identity. In R. L. Jackson (Ed.), *Encyclopedia of identity* (Vol. 1, pp. 316–319). Thousand Oaks, CA: Sage.

Friedkin, N. E. (1999). Choice shift and group polarization. *American Sociological Review, 64*, 856–875.

Friedkin, N. E. (2004). Social cohesion. *Annual Review of Sociology, 30*, 409–425.

Friedland, N. (1976). Social influence via threats. *Journal of Experimental Social Psychology, 12*, 552–563.

Friedman, S. D., & Saul, K. (1991). A leader's wake: Organization member reactions to CEO succession. *Journal of Management, 17*, 619–642.

Friedman, T. L. (2005). *The world is flat: A brief history of the twenty-first century*. New York: Farrar, Straus and Giroux.

Froman, L. A., Jr., & Cohen, M. D. (1969). Threats and bargaining efficiency. *Behavioral Science, 14*, 147–153.

Fry, D. P. (2007). *Beyond war*. New York: Oxford.

Fuegen, K., & Biernat, M. (2002). Reexamining the effects of solo status for women and men. *Personality and Social Psychology Bulletin, 28*, 913–925.

Fuhriman, A., & Burlingame, G. M. (1994). Group psychotherapy: Research and practice. In A. Fuhriman & G. M. Burlingame (Eds.), *Handbook of group psychotherapy: An empirical and clinical synthesis* (pp. 3–40). New York: Wiley.

Furman, W., & Buhrmester, D. (2009). The Network of Relationships Inventory: Behavioral Systems Version. *International Journal of Behavioral Development, 33*(5), 470–478.

Furnham, A. (2008). Psychometric correlates of FIRO-B scores: Locating the FIRO-B scores in personality factor space. *International Journal of Selection and Assessment, 16*(1), 30–45.

Gabarro, J. J. (1987). The development of working relationships. In J. W. Lorsch (Ed.), *Handbook of organizational behavior* (pp. 172–189). Upper Saddle River, NJ: Prentice Hall.

Gabriel, S., & Gardner, W. L. (1999). Are there "his" and "her" types of interdependence? The implications of gender differences in collective versus relational interdependence for affect, behavior, and cognition. *Journal of Personality and Social Psychology, 77*, 642–655.

Gaertner, L., Iuzzini, J., & O'Mara, E. M. (2008). When rejection by one fosters aggression against many: Multiple-victim aggression as a consequence of social rejection and perceived groupness. *Journal of Experimental Social Psychology, 44*(4), 958–970.

Gaertner, L., Iuzzini, J., Witt, M. G., & Oriña, M. M. (2006). Us without them: Evidence for an intragroup origin of positive in-group regard. *Journal of Personality and Social Psychology, 90*(3), 426–439.

Gaertner, L., & Sedikides, C. (2005). A hierarchy within: On the motivational and emotional primacy of the individual self. In M. D. Alicke, D. A. Dunning, & J. I. Krueger (Eds.), *The self in social judgment* (pp. 213–239). New York: Psychology Press.

Gaertner, L., Sedikides, C., Vevea, J. L., & Iuzzini, J. (2002). The "I," the "we," and the "when": A meta-analysis of motivational primacy in self-definition. *Journal of Personality and Social Psychology, 83*, 574–591.

Gaertner, S. L., & Dovidio, J. F. (2000). *Reducing intergroup bias: The common ingroup identity model*. Philadelphia: Psychology Press.

Gaertner, S. L., Dovidio, J. F., Banker, B. S., Houlette, M., Johnson, K. M., & McGlynn, E. A. (2000). Reducing intergroup conflict: From superordinate goals to decategorization, recategorization, and mutual differentiation. *Group Dynamics: Theory, Research, and Practice, 4*, 98–114.

Gaertner, S. L., Dovidio, J. F., Nier, J. A., Ward, C. M., & Banker, B. S. (1999). Across cultural divides: The value of a superordinate identity. In D. A. Prentice & D. T. Miller (Eds.), *Cultural divides: Understanding and overcoming group conflict* (pp. 173–212). New York: Russell Sage Foundation.

Gaertner, S. L., Dovidio, J. F., Rust, M. C., Nier, J. A., Banker, B. S., Ward, C. M., Mottola, G. R., & Houlette, M. (1999). Reducing intergroup bias: Elements of intergroup cooperation. *Journal of Personality and Social Psychology, 76*, 388–402.

Gaffney, S. (2012). A neo-Lewinian perspective on gestalt group facilitation. In T. B. Y. Levine (Ed.), *Gestalt therapy: Advances in theory and practice* (pp. 149–159). New York: Routledge/ Taylor & Francis Group.

Gaines, S. O., Jr., & Reed, E. S. (1995). Prejudice: From Allport to DuBois. *American Psychologist, 50*, 96–103.

Galinsky, A. D., Gruenfeld, D. H., & Magee, J. C. (2003). From power to action. *Journal of Personality and Social Psychology, 85*, 453–466.

Galinsky, A. D., Jordan, J., & Sivanathan, N. (2008). Harnessing power to capture leadership. In C. L. Hoyt, G. R. Goethals, & D. R. Forsyth (Eds.), *Leadership at the crossroads: Leadership and psychology* (Vol. 1, pp. 283–299). Westport, CT: Praeger.

Galinsky, A. D., Ku, G., & Wang, C. S. (2005). Perspective-taking and self-other overlap: Fostering social bonds and facilitating social coordination. *Group Processes & Intergroup Relations, 8,* 109–124.

Galinsky, A. D., Magee, J. C., Inesi, M. E., & Gruenfeld, D. H. (2006). Power and perspectives not taken. *Psychological Science, 17,* 1068–1074.

Gallo, P. S., Jr. (1966). Effects of increased incentives upon the use of threat in bargaining. *Journal of Personality and Social Psychology, 4,* 14–20.

Gammage, K. L., Carron, A. V., & Estabrooks, P. A. (2001). Team cohesion and individual productivity: The influence of the norm for productivity and the identifiability of individual effort. *Small Group Research, 32,* 3–18.

Gannon, T. M. (1966). Emergence of the "defensive" group norm. *Federal Probation, 30,* 44–47.

Garcia, S. M., Song, H., & Tesser, A. (2010). Tainted recommendations: The social comparison bias. *Organizational Behavior and Human Decision Processes, 113*(2), 97–101.

Garcia, S. M., Weaver, K., Moskowitz, G. B., & Darley, J. M. (2002). Crowded minds: The implicit bystander effect. *Journal of Personality and Social Psychology, 83,* 843–853.

Gardikiotis, A. (2011). Minority influence. *Social and Personality Psychology Compass, 5*(9), 679–693.

Gardner, B., & Korth, S. (1998). A framework for learning to work in teams. *Journal of Education for Business, 74*(1), 28–33.

Gardner, J. W. (1965). The antileadership vaccine. *Annual Report of the Carnegie Corporation.* New York: Carnegie Corporation.

Gardner, W. L., & Knowles, M. L. (2008). Love makes you real: Favorite television characters are perceived as "real" in a social facilitation paradigm. *Social Cognition, 26,* 156–168.

Gastil, J., Black, L. W., Deess, E. P., & Leighter, J. (2008). From group member to democratic citizen: How deliberating with fellow jurors reshapes civic attitudes. *Human Communication Research, 34*(1), 137–169.

Gastil, J., Burkhalter, S., & Black, L. W. (2007). Do juries deliberate? A study of deliberation, individual difference, and group member satisfaction at a municipal courthouse. *Small Group Research, 38*(3), 337–359.

Gawronski, B., Walther, E., & Blank, H. (2005). Cognitive consistency and the formation of interpersonal attitudes: Cognitive balance affects the encoding of social information. *Journal of Experimental Social Psychology, 41,* 618–626.

Gazda, G. M., & Brooks, D. K. (1985). The development of the social/life skills training movement. *Journal of Group Psychotherapy, Psychodrama, and Sociometry, 38,* 1–10.

Geffner, R. Braverman, M. Galasso, J., & Marsh, J. (Eds.). (2004). *Aggression in organizations: Violence, abuse, and harassment at work and in schools.* Binghamton, NY: Haworth.

Gelfand, M. J., Bhawak, D. P. S., Nishii L. H., & Bechtold, D. (2004). Individualism and collectivism. In R. M. House, P. J. Hanges, M. Javidan, P. W. Dorfman, & V. Gupta (Eds.), *Cultures, leadership, and organizations: A 62 nation study* (pp. 437–512). Thousand Oaks, CA: Sage.

Gelfand, M. J., Leslie, L. M., & Keller, K. (2008). On the etiology of organizational conflict cultures. *Research in Organizational Behavior, 28,* 137–166.

Gemmill, G. (1986). The mythology of the leader role in small groups. *Small Group Behavior, 17,* 41–50.

Genevie, L. E. (Ed.). (1978). *Collective behavior and social movements.* Itasca, IL: Peacock.

George, J. M. (1995). Leader positive mood and group performance: The case of customer service. *Journal of Applied Social Psychology, 25,* 778–794.

George, J. M., & Brief, A. P. (1992). Feeling good/doing good: A conceptual analysis of the mood at work/organizational spontaneity relationship. *Psychological Bulletin, 112,* 310–329.

Gerard, H. B. (1953). The effect of different dimensions of disagreement on the communication process in small groups. *Human Relations, 6,* 249–271.

Gerard, H. B. (1964). Conformity and commitment to the group. *Journal of Abnormal and Social Psychology, 68,* 209–211.

Gerard, H. B. (1983). School desegregation: The social science role. *American Psychologist, 38,* 869–877.

Gerard, H. B., & Mathewson, G. C. (1966). The effects of severity of initiation on liking for a group: A replication. *Journal of Experimental Social Psychology, 2,* 278–287.

Gerard, H. B., & Orive, R. (1987). The dynamics of opinion formation. *Advances in Experimental Social Psychology, 20,* 171–202.

Gerber, G. L. (1996). Status in same-gender and mixed-gender police dyads: Effects on personality attributions. *Social Psychology Quarterly, 59*(4), 350–363.

Gerber, J., & Wheeler, L. (2009). On being rejected: A meta-analysis of experimental research on rejection. *Perspectives on Psychological Science, 4*(5), 468–488.

Gergen, K. J., Gergen, M. M., & Barton, W. H. (1973). Deviance in the dark. *Psychology Today, 7,* 129–130.

Gersick, C. J. G. (1989). Marking time: Predictable transitions in task groups. *Academy of Management Journal, 32,* 274–309.

Gerstner, C. R., & Day, D. V. (1997). Meta-analytic review of leader-member exchange theory: Correlates and construct issues. *Journal of Applied Psychology, 82,* 827–844.

Gevers, J. M. P., van Eerde, W., & Rutte, C. G. (2009). Team self-regulation and meeting deadlines in project teams: Antecedents and effects of temporal consensus. *European Journal of Work and Organizational Psychology, 18,* 295–321.

Giacalone, R. A., & Promislo, M. D. (2010). Unethical and unwell: Decrements in well-being and unethical activity at work. *Journal of Business Ethics, 91*(2), 275–297.

Giannetti, C. C., & Sagarese, M. (2001). *Cliques.* New York: Broadway Books.

Gibb, C. A. (1969). Leadership. In G. Lindzey & E. Aronson (Eds.), *The handbook of social psychology* (Vol. 4, 2nd ed., pp. 205–282). Reading, MA: Addison-Wesley.

Gibb, J. R. (1971). Effects of human relations training. In A. E. Bergin & S. L. Garfield (Eds.), *Handbook of psychotherapy and behavior change* (pp. 839–862). New York: Wiley.

Gibbons, D., & Olk, P. M. (2003). Individual and structural origins of friendship and social position among professionals. *Journal of Personality and Social Psychology, 84*, 340–351.

Gibson, C. B., & McDaniel, D. M. (2010). Moving beyond conventional wisdom: Advancements in cross-cultural theories of leadership, conflict, and teams. *Perspectives on Psychological Science, 5*(4), 450–462.

Gibson, D. R. (2003). Participation shifts: Order and differentiation in group conversation. *Social Forces, 81*, 1335–1380.

Gibson, L. L., Mathieu, J. E., Shalley, C. E., & Ruddy, T. M. (2005). Creativity and standardization: Complementary or conflicting drivers of team effectiveness. *Academy of Management Journal, 48*, 521–531.

Gieryn, T. F. (2000). A space for place in sociology. *Annual Review of Sociology, 26*, 463–496.

Giesen, M., & McClaren, H. A. (1976). Discussion, distance, and sex: Changes in impressions and attraction during small group interaction. *Sociometry, 39*, 60–70.

Gigone, D. (2010). Common knowledge effect. In J. M. Levine & M. A. Hogg (Eds.), *Encyclopedia of group process and intergroup relations* (Vol. 1, pp. 123–125). Thousand Oaks, CA: Sage.

Gigone, D., & Hastie, R. (1997). Proper analysis of the accuracy of group judgments. *Psychological Bulletin, 121*, 149–167.

Gilbert, D. T., & Silvera, D. H. (1996). Overhelping. *Journal of Personality and Social Psychology, 70*, 678–690.

Gilbert, S. J. (1981). Another look at the Milgram obedience studies: The role of the graduated series of shocks. *Personality and Social Psychology Bulletin, 7*, 690–695.

Gilboa, S., Shirom, A., Fried, Y., & Cooper, C. (2008). A meta-analysis of work demand stressors and job performance: Examining main and moderating effects. *Personnel Psychology, 61*, 227–271.

Giles, H., & Wadleigh, P.M. (1999). Accommodating nonverbally. In L. K. Guerrero, J. A. DeVito, & M. L. Hecht (Eds.), *The nonverbal communication reader: Classic and contemporary readings* (2nd. ed., pp. 425–436). Prospect Heights, IL: Waveland Press.

Gill, D. L. (1984). Individual and group performance in sport. In J. M. Silva & R. S. Weinberg (Eds.), *Psychological foundations of sport* (pp. 315–328). Champaign, IL: Human Kinetics.

Gillies, R. M. (2007). *Cooperative learning: Integrating theory and practice.* Thousand Oaks, CA: Sage.

Ginnett, R. C. (2010). Crews as groups: Their formation and their leadership. In B. G. Kanki, R. L. Helmreich, & J. Anca (Eds.), *Crew resource management* (2nd ed., pp. 79–110). New York: Academic Press.

Giordano, P. C. (2003). Relationships in adolescence. *Annual Review of Sociology, 29*, 257–281.

Gire, J. T. (1997). The varying effect of individualism-collectivism on preference for methods of conflict resolution. *Canadian Journal of behavioral Science/Revue Canadienne Des Sciences Du Comportement, 29*(1), 38–43.

Gladwell, M. (2000). *The tipping point: How little things can make a big difference.* Boston: Little, Brown.

Gladwell, M. (2005). *Blink: The power of thinking without thinking.* Boston: Little, Brown.

Glaser, D. (1964). *The effectiveness of a prison and parole system.* Indianapolis, IN: Bobbs-Merrill.

Glass, D. C., Singer, J. E., & Pennebaker, J. W. (1977). Behavioral and physiological effects of uncontrollable environmental events. In D. Stokols (Ed.), *Perspectives on environment and behavior* (pp. 131–151). New York: Plenum Press.

Gleijeses, P. (1995). Ships in the night: The CIA, the White House and the Bay of Pigs. *Journal of Latin American Studies, 27*(1), 1–42.

Glick, J. C., & Staley, K. (2007). Inflicted traumatic brain injury: Advances in evaluation and collaborative diagnosis. *Pediatric Neurosurgery, 43*, 436–441.

Glick, P. (2009). When neighbors blame neighbors: Scapegoating and the breakdown of ethnic relations. In V. M. Esses & R. A. Vernon (Eds.), *Explaining the breakdown of ethnic relations: Why neighbors kill* (pp. 121–146). Oxford, UK: Blackwell.

Gockel, C., Kerr, N. L., Seok, D., & Harris, D. W. (2008). Indispensability and group identification as sources of task motivation. *Journal of Experimental Social Psychology, 44*, 1316–1321.

Godfrey, D. K., Jones, E. E., & Lord, C. G. (1986). Self-promotion is not ingratiating. *Journal of Personality and Social Psychology, 50*, 106–115.

Godwin, R. (Ed.). (2000). *Apollo 13: The NASA mission reports.* Burlington, Ontario: Apogee.

Goethals, G. R., & Hoyt, C. L. (2011). What makes leadership necessary, possible and effective: The psychological dimensions. In M. Harvey & R. E. Riggio (Eds.), *Leadership studies: The dialogue of disciplines* (pp. 101–118). Northampton, MA: Edward Elgar.

Goethals, G. R., Sorenson, G. J., & Burns, J. M. (Eds.). (2004). *Encyclopedia of leadership.* Thousand Oaks, CA: Sage.

Goethals, G. R., & Zanna, M. P. (1979). The role of social comparison in choice shifts. *Journal of Personality and Social Psychology, 37*, 1469–1476.

Goetsch, G. G., & McFarland, D. D. (1980). Models of the distribution of acts in small discussion groups. *Social Psychology Quarterly, 43*, 173–183.

Goffman, E. (1959). *The presentation of self in everyday life.* Garden City, NY: Doubleday.

Goffman, E. (1971). *Relations in public: Microstudies of the public order.* New York: Basic Books.

Goldberg, L. C. (1968). Ghetto riots and others: The faces of civil disorder in 1967. *Journal of Peace Research, 2*, 116–132.

Goldberg, L. R. (1993). The structure of phenotypic personality traits. *American Psychologist, 48*(1), 26–34.

Golden, T. D., & Veiga, J. F. (2008). The impact of superior–subordinate relationships on the commitment, job satisfaction, and performance of virtual workers. *The Leadership Quarterly, 19*(1), 77–88.

Goldhammer, J. (1996). *Under the influence: The destructive effects of group dynamics.* Amherst, NY: Prometheus Books.

Golding, W. (1954). *Lord of the flies*. New York: Putnam.

Goldman, M., & Fraas, L. A. (1965). The effects of leader selection on group performance. *Sociometry, 28*, 82–88.

Goldstein, A. P. (2002). *The psychology of group aggression*. New York: Wiley.

Goldstein, N. J., & Cialdini, R. B. (2011). Managing normative influences in organizations. In D. De Cremer, R. van Dick, & J. K. Murnighan (Eds.), *Social psychology and organizations* (pp. 67–86). New York: Routledge/Taylor & Francis Group.

Goldstone, J. A. (2011). Cross-class coalitions and the making of the Arab revolts of 2011. *Swiss Political Science Review, 17*, 457–462.

Goleman, D., Boyatzis, R., & McKee, A. (2002). *Primal leadership: Learning to lead with emotional intelligence*. Boston: Harvard Business School Press.

Gómez, Á., Brooks, M. L., Buhrmester, M. D., Vázquez, A., Jetten, J., & Swann, W. B., Jr. (2011). On the nature of identity fusion: Insights into the construct and a new measure. *Journal of Personality and Social Psychology, 100*(5), 918–933.

Gómez, Á., Seyle, D. C., Huici, C., & Swann Jr., W. B. (2009). Can self-verification strivings fully transcend the self–other barrier? Seeking verification of ingroup identities. *Journal of Personality and Social Psychology, 97*(6), 1021–1044.

Goncalo, J. A., & Staw, B. M. (2006). Individualism–collectivism and group creativity. *Organizational Behavior and Human Decision Processes, 100*(1), 96–109.

Gonsalkorale, K., & Williams, K. D. (2007). The KKK won't let me play: Ostracism even by a despised outgroup hurts. *European Journal of Social Psychology, 37*(6), 1176–1186.

Goodacre, D. M. (1953). Group characteristics of good and poor performing combat units. *Sociometry, 16*, 168–178.

Goodall, J. (1986). Social rejection, exclusion, and shunning among the Gombe chimpanzees. *Ethology & Sociobiology, 7*(3-4), 227–236.

Gooden, R. J., & Winefield, H. R. (2007). Breast and prostate cancer online discussion boards: A thematic analysis of gender differences and similarities. *Journal of Health Psychology, 12*(1), 103–114.

Goodwin, D. K. (2005). *Team of rivals: The political genius of Abraham Lincoln*. New York: Simon & Schuster.

Gordijn, E. H., De Vries, N. K., & De Dreu, C. K. W. (2002). Minority influence on focal and related attitudes: Change in size, attributions and information processing. *Personality and Social Psychology Bulletin, 28*, 1315–1326.

Gore, G. (2010). Flash mob dance and the territorialization of urban movement. *Anthropological Notebooks, 16*, 125–131.

Gore, J. S., & Cross, S. E. (2006). Pursuing goals for us: Relationally autonomous reasons in long-term goal pursuit. *Journal of Personality and Social Psychology, 90*, 848–861.

Gorse, C. A., & Emmitt, S. (2009). Informal interaction in construction progress meetings. *Construction Management and Economics, 27*, 983–993.

Gosling, S. D., Rentfrow, P. J., & Swann, W. B., Jr. (2003). A very brief measure of the Big Five personality domains. *Journal of Research in Personality, 37*, 504–528.

Gould, C. C. (2004). *Globalizing democracy and human rights*. New York: Cambridge University Press.

Gouldner, A. W. (1960). The norm of reciprocity: A preliminary statement. *American Sociological Review, 25*, 161–178.

Gouran, D. S., & Hirokawa, R. Y. (1996). Functional theory and communication in decision-making and problem-solving groups: An expanded view. In R. Y. Hirokawa & M. S. Poole (Eds.), *Communication and group decision making* (2nd ed., pp. 55–80). Thousand Oaks, CA: Sage.

Graen, G. B., & Uhl-Bien, M. (1991). The transformation of professionals into self-managing and partially self-designing contributors: Toward a theory of leadership making. *Journal of Management Systems, 3*, 33–48.

Graen, G. B., & Uhl-Bien, M. (1995). Relationship-based approach to leadership: Development of leader-member exchange (LMX) theory of leadership over 25 years: Applying a multi-level multi-domain perspective. *Leadership Quarterly, 6*, 219–247.

Granovetter, M. S. (1973). The strength of weak ties. *American Journal of Sociology, 78*, 1360–1380.

Graziano, W. G., Jensen-Campbell, L. A., & Hair, E. C. (1996). Perceiving interpersonal conflict and reacting to it: The case for agreeableness. *Journal of Personality and Social Psychology, 70*, 820–835.

Graziano, W. G., & Tobin, R. M. (2009). Agreeableness. In M. R. Leary & R. H. Hoyle (Eds.), *Handbook of individual differences in social behavior* (pp. 46–61). New York: Guilford.

Green, L. R., Richardson, D. S., Lago, T., & Schatten-Jones, E. C. (2001). Network correlates of social and emotional loneliness in young and older adults. *Personality and Social Psychology Bulletin, 27*, 281–288.

Green, R. B., & Mack, J. (1978). Would groups do better without social psychologists? *Personality and Social Psychology Bulletin, 4*, 561–563.

Greenberg, C. I., & Firestone, I. J. (1977). Compensatory responses to crowding: Effects of personal space intrusion and privacy reduction. *Journal of Personality and Social Psychology, 35*, 637–644.

Greenberg, J. (1996). "Forgive me, I'm new": Three experimental demonstrations of the effects of attempts to excuse poor performance. *Organizational Behavior and Human Decision Processes, 66*, 165–178.

Greenberg, J., Solomon, S., & Pyszczynski, T. (1997). Terror management theory of self-esteem and cultural worldviews: Empirical assessments and conceptual refinements. *Advances in Experimental Social Psychology, 29*, 61–139.

Greenwald, A. G., McGhee, D. E., & Schwartz, J. L. K. (2008). Measuring individual differences in implicit cognition: The implicit association test. In R. H. Fazio, & R. E. Petty (Eds.), *Attitudes: Their structure, function, and consequences* (pp. 109–131). New York: Psychology Press.

Greenwood, J. D. (2004). *The disappearance of the social in American social psychology*. New York: Cambridge University Press.

Greer, D. L. (1983). Spectator booing and the home advantage: A study of social influence in the basketball arena. *Social Psychology Quarterly, 46*, 252–261.

Greer, L. L., Jehn, K. A., & Mannix, E. A. (2008). Conflict transformation: A longitudinal investigation of the relationships between different types of intragroup conflict and the moderating role of conflict resolution. *Small Group Research, 39*(3), 278–302.

Greitemeyer, T., Schulz-Hardt, S., Brodbeck, F. C., & Frey, D. (2006). Information sampling and group decision making: The effects of an advocacy decision procedure and task experience. *Journal of Experimental Psychology: Applied, 12*, 31–42.

Griffin, C., & Bengry-Howell, A. (2008). Ethnography. In C. Willig & W. Stainton-Rogers (Eds.), *The Sage handbook of qualitative research in psychology* (pp. 15–31). Los Angeles: Sage.

Griffitt, W. (1970). Environmental effects on interpersonal affective behavior: Ambient effective temperature and attraction. *Journal of Personality and Social Psychology, 15*, 240–244.

Griffitt, W., & Veitch, R. (1971). Hot and crowded: Influence of population density and temperature on interpersonal affective behavior. *Journal of Personality and Social Psychology, 17*, 92–98.

Griskevicius, V., Goldstein, N. J., Mortensen, C. R., Cialdini, R. B., & Kenrick, D. T. (2006). Going along versus going alone: When fundamental motives facilitate strategic (non) conformity. *Journal of Personality and Social Psychology, 91*, 281–294.

Grose, M. (2003). *Why first-borns rule the world and last-borns want to change it*. New York: Random House.

Guastello, S. J. (2007). Non-linear dynamics and leadership emergence. *Leadership Quarterly, 18*, 357–369.

Guerin, B., & Innes, J. M. (1982). Social facilitation and social monitoring: A new look at Zajonc's mere presence hypothesis. *British Journal of Social Psychology, 21*, 7–18.

Guetzkow, H., & Gyr, J. (1954). An analysis of conflict in decision-making groups. *Human Relations, 7*, 367–382.

Guimond, A., & Dubé-Simard, L. (1983). Relative deprivation theory and the Quebec nationalist movement: The cognitive-emotion distinction and the personal-group deprivation issue. *Journal of Personality and Social Psychology, 44*, 526–535.

Guinote, A. (2007). Power affects basic cognition: Increased attentional inhibition and flexibility. *Journal of Experimental Social Psychology, 43*, 685–697.

Guinote, A. (2008). Power and affordances: When the situation has more power over powerful than powerless individuals. *Journal of Personality and Social Psychology, 95*, 237–252.

Guinote, A., Brown, M., & Fiske, S. T. (2006). Minority status decreases sense of control and increases interpretive processing. *Social Cognition, 24*, 169–186.

Guinote, A., Judd, C. M., & Brauer, M. (2002). Effects of power on perceived and objective group variability: Evidence that more powerful groups are more variable. *Journal of Personality and Social Psychology, 82*, 708–721.

Guinote, A., & Vescio, T. K. (Eds.). (2010). *The social psychology of power*. New York: Guilford Press.

Gulati, R., Sytch, M., & Tatarynowicz, A. (2012). The dynamics of social structure: The emergence and decline of small worlds. *Organization Science, 23*, 449–471.

Gullahorn, J. T. (1952). Distance and friendship as factors in the gross interaction matrix. *Sociometry, 15*, 123–134.

Gully, S. M., Devine, D. J., & Whitney, D. J. (1995). A meta-analysis of cohesion and performance: Effects of level of analysis and task interdependence. *Small Group Research, 26*, 497–520.

Gump, P. V. (1990). A short history of the Midwest Psychological Field Station. *Environment and Behavior, 22*, 436–457.

Gunderson, E. K. E. (1973). Individual behavior in confined or isolated groups. In J. E. Rasmussen (Ed.), *Man in isolation and confinement* (pp. 145–164). Chicago: Aldine.

Gurr, T. R. (1970). *Why men rebel*. Princeton, NJ: Princeton University Press.

Gustafson, D. H., Shukla, R. M., Delbecq, A. L., & Walster, G. W. (1973). A comparative study of differences in subjective likelihood estimates made by individuals, interacting groups, Delphi groups, and nominal groups. *Organizational Behavior and Human Performance, 9*, 280–291.

Guthman, E. (1971). *We band of brothers*. New York: Harper & Row.

Guzzo, R. A., Yost, P. R., Campbell, R. J., & Shea, G. P. (1993). Potency in groups: Articulating a construct. *British Journal of Social Psychology, 32*, 87–106.

Haas, D. F., & Deseran, F. A. (1981). Trust and symbolic exchange. *Social Psychology Quarterly, 44*, 3–13.

Haber, G. M. (1980). Territorial invasion in the classroom: Invadee response. *Environment and Behavior, 12*, 17–31.

Haber, G. M. (1982). Spatial relations between dominants and marginals. *Social Psychology Quarterly, 45*, 219–228.

Hackman, J. R. (1986). The psychology of self-management in organizations. In M. S. Pallak & R. O. Perloff (Eds.), *Psychology and work: Productivity, change, and employment* (pp. 89–136). Washington, DC: American Psychological Association.

Hackman, J. R. (Ed.). (1990). *Groups that work (and those that don't)*. San Francisco: Jossey-Bass.

Hackman, J. R. (2002). *Leading teams: Setting the stage for greater performances*. Boston: Harvard Business School Press.

Hackman, J. R. (2003). Learning more by crossing levels: Evidence from airplanes, hospitals, and orchestras. *Journal of Organizational Behavior, 24*, 905–922.

Hackman, J. R. (2011). *Collaborative intelligence: Using teams to solve hard problems*. San Francisco: Berrett-Koehler.

Hackman, J. R., Brousseau, K. R., & Weiss, J. A. (1976). The interaction of task design and group performance strategies in determining group effectiveness. *Organizational Behavior and Human Performance, 16*, 350–365.

Hackman, J. R., & Katz, N. (2010). Group behavior and performance. In S. T. Fiske, D. T. Gilbert, & G. Lindzey (Eds.), *Handbook of social psychology* (Vol. 2, 5th ed., pp. 1208–1251). Hoboken, NJ: John Wiley.

Hackman, J. R., & Morris, C. G. (1975). Group tasks, group interaction process, and group performance effectiveness: A review and proposed integration. *Advances in Experimental Social Psychology, 8*, 47–99.

Haines, V. Y., & Taggar, S. (2006). Antecedents of team reward attitude. *Group Dynamics: Theory, Research, and Practice, 10*, 194–205.

Hains, S. C., Hogg, M. A., & Duck, J. M. (1997). Self-categorization and leadership: Effects of group prototypicality and leader stereotypicality. *Personality and Social Psychology Bulletin, 23*, 1087–1099.

Halevy, N., Berson, Y., & Galinsky, A. (2011). The mainstream is not electable: When vision triumphs over representativeness in leader emergence and effectiveness. *Personality and Social Psychology Bulletin, 37*, 893–904.

Hall, E. T. (1966). *The hidden dimension*. New York: Doubleday.

Hall, E. T. (1976). *Beyond culture*. New York: Anchor.

Hall, E. T. (1996). *The hidden dimension*. New York: Doubleday.

Hall, J. A. (2006). Nonverbal behavior, status, and gender: How do we understand their relations? *Psychology of Women Quarterly, 30*, 384–391.

Hall, J. A. (2011). Sex differences in friendship expectations: A meta-analysis. *Journal of Social and Personal Relationships, 28*(6), 723–747.

Hall, J. A., Coats, E. J., & LeBeau, L. S. (2005). Nonverbal behavior and the vertical dimension of social relations: A meta-analysis. *Psychological Bulletin, 131*(6), 898–924.

Hallinan, M. T. (1981). Recent advances in sociometry. In S. R. Asher & J. M. Gottman (Eds.), *The development of children's friendships* (pp. 91–115). New York: Cambridge University Press.

Halperin, E. (2008). Group-based hatred in intractable conflict in Israel. *Journal of Conflict Resolution, 52*, 713–736.

Halpin, A. W., & Winer, B. J. (1952). *The leadership behavior of the airplane commander*. Columbus: Ohio State University Research Foundation.

Halverson, C. B. (2008). Team development. In C. B. Halverson & S. A. Tirmizi (Eds.), *Effective multicultural teams: Theory and practice* (pp. 81–110). New York: Springer.

Ham v. S. Carolina, 409 U.S. 524 (1973).

Hamaguchi, E. (1985). A contextual model of the Japanese: Toward a methodological innovation in Japanese studies. *Journal of Japanese Studies, 11*, 289–321.

Hamilton, D. L., & Sherman, S. J. (1989). Illusory correlations: Implications for stereotype theory and research. In D. Bar-Tal, C. F. Graumann, A. W. Kruglanski, & W. Stroebe (Eds.), *Stereotyping and prejudice: Changing conceptions* (pp. 59–82). New York: Springer-Verlag.

Hamilton, V. L., & Sanders, J. (1995). Crimes of obedience and conformity in the workplace: Surveys of Americans, Russians, and Japanese. *Journal of Social Issues, 51*, 67–88.

Hamilton, V. L., & Sanders, J. (1999). The second face of evil: Wrongdoing in and by the corporation. *Personality and Social Psychology Review, 3*, 222–233.

Hammer, M. R. (2005). The intercultural conflict style inventory: A conceptual framework and measure of intercultural conflict resolution approaches. *International Journal of Intercultural Relations, 29*(6), 675–695.

Haney, C., Banks, C., & Zimbardo, P. (1973). Interpersonal dynamics in a simulated prison. *International Journal of Criminology and Psychology, 1*, 69–97.

Hans, V. P., Hannaford-Agor, P. L., Mott, N. L., & Munsterman, G. T. (2003). The hung jury: The American Jury's insights and contemporary understanding. *Criminal Law Bulletin, 39*, 33–50.

Hans, V. P., & Vidmar, N. (1982). Jury selection. In N. L. Kerr & R. M. Bray (Eds.), *Psychology of the courtroom* (pp. 39–82). New York: Academic Press.

Hans, V. P., & Vidmar, N. (1991). The *American Jury* at twenty-five years. *Law & Social Inquiry, 16*, 323–353.

Hansen, W. B., & Altman, I. (1976). Decorating personal places: A descriptive analysis. *Environment and Behavior, 8*, 491–504.

Hardin, G. (1968). The tragedy of the commons. *Science, 162*, 1243–1248.

Harding, J., Proshansky, H., Kutner, B., & Chein, I. (1969). Prejudice and ethnic relations. In G. Lindzey & E. Aronson (Eds.), *The handbook of social psychology* (Vol. 5, 2nd ed., pp. 1–76). Reading, MA: Addison-Wesley.

Hardy, C., & Latané, B. (1986). Social loafing on a cheering task. *Social Science, 71*(2-3), 165–172.

Hardyck, J. A., & Braden, M. (1962). Prophecy fails again: A report of a failure to replicate. *Journal of Abnormal and Social Psychology, 65*(2), 136–141.

Hare, A. P. (1967). Small group development in the relay assembly testroom. *Sociological Inquiry, 37*, 169–182.

Hare, A. P. (1976). *Handbook of small group research* (2nd ed.). New York: Free Press.

Hare, A. P. (1982). *Creativity in small groups*. Thousand Oaks, CA: Sage.

Hare, A. P. (1999). Understanding Paul Moxnes (1999). *Group Dynamics: Theory, Research, and Practice, 3*(2), 116–117.

Hare, A. P. (2005). Analysis of social interaction systems. In A. P. Hare, E. Sjøvold, H. G. Baker, & J. Powers (Eds.), *Analysis of social interaction systems: SYMLOG research and applications* (pp. 1–14). Lanham, MD: University Press of America.

Hare, A. P., & Bales, R. F. (1963). Seating position and small group interaction. *Sociometry, 26*, 480–486.

Hare, A. P., Borgatta, E. F., & Bales, R. F. (1955). Preface to the revised edition. In A. P. Hare, E. F. Borgatta, & R. F. Bales (Eds.), *Small groups: Studies in social interaction* (Revised ed., pp. v–ix). New York: Knopf.

Hare, A. P., & Hare, J. R. (1996). *J. L. Moreno*. Thousand Oaks, CA: Sage.

Hare, A. P., & Naveh, D. (1986). Conformity and creativity: Camp David, 1978. *Small Group Behavior, 17,* 243–268.

Hare, A. P., Sjovold, E., Baker, H. G., & Powers, J. (Eds.). (2005). *Analysis of social interaction systems: SYMLOG research and applications.* Lanham, MD: University Press of America.

Hare, S. E., & Hare, A. P. (2005). Role repertoires of members in an effective small group: A simulation. In A. P. Hare, E. Sjovold, H. G. Baker, & J. Powers (Eds.), *Analysis of social interaction systems: SYMLOG research and applications* (pp. 273–298). Lanham, MD: University Press of America.

Hareli, S., & Parkinson, B. (2008). What's social about social emotions? *Journal for the Theory of Social Behavior, 38,* 131–156.

Harinck, F. (2004). Persuasive arguments and beating around the bush in negotiations. *Group Processes & Intergroup Relations, 7,* 5–18.

Harkins, S. G. (2006). Mere effort as the mediator of the evaluation-performance relationship. *Journal of Personality and Social Psychology, 91*(3), 436–455.

Harkins, S. G., & Jackson, J. M. (1985). The role of evaluation in eliminating social loafing. *Personality and Social Psychology Bulletin, 11,* 457–465.

Harkins, S. G., Latané, B., & Williams, K. (1980). Social loafing: Allocating effort or taking it easy. *Journal of Experimental Social Psychology, 16,* 457–465.

Harkins, S. G., & Szymanski, K. (1987). Social loafing and social facilitation: New wine in old bottles. In C. Hendrick (Ed.), *Review of Personality and Social Psychology: Group Process and Intergroup Relations* (Vol. 9, pp. 167–188). Thousand Oaks, CA: Sage.

Harkins, S. G., & Szymanski, K. (1988). Social loafing and self-evaluation with an objective standard. *Journal of Experimental Social Psychology, 24,* 354–365.

Harkins, S. G., & Szymanski, K. (1989). Social loafing and group evaluation. *Journal of Personality and Social Psychology, 56,* 934–941.

Harlow, R. E., & Cantor, N. (1995). To whom do people turn when things go poorly? Task orientation and functional social contacts. *Journal of Personality and Social Psychology, 69,* 329–340.

Harlow, R. E., & Cantor, N. (1996). Still participating after all these years: A study of life task participation in later life. *Journal of Personality and Social Psychology, 71,* 1235–1249.

Harms, P. D., Roberts, B. W., & Wood, D. (2007). Who shall lead? An integrative personality approach to the study of the antecedents of status in informal social organizations. *Journal of Research in Personality, 41,* 689–699.

Harrington, B., & Fine, G. A. (2000). Opening the "black box": Small groups and twenty-first-century sociology. *Social Psychology Quarterly, 63*(4), 312–323.

Harris, C. B., Paterson, H. M., & Kemp, R. I. (2008). Collaborative recall and collective memory: What happens when we remember together? *Memory, 16,* 213–230.

Harris, J. R. (1995). Where is the child's environment? A group socialization theory of development. *Psychological Review, 102,* 458–489.

Harris, L. T., & Fiske, S. T. (2006). Dehumanizing the lowest of the low: Neuroimaging responses to extreme out-groups. *Psychological Science, 17,* 847–853.

Harrison, A. A., Clearwater, Y. A., & McKay, C. P. (Eds.). (1991). *From Antarctica to outer space: Life in isolation and confinement.* New York: Springer-Verlag.

Harrison, A. A., & Connors, M. M. (1984). Groups in exotic environments. *Advances in Experimental Social Psychology, 18,* 50–87.

Harrison, A., & Morgan, N. (2006). The narrative office: BBC case study. In D. Clements-Croome (Ed.), *Creating the productive workplace* (2nd. ed., pp. 257–276). New York: Taylor & Francis.

Harrison, D. A., & Klein, K. J. (2007). What's the difference? Diversity constructs as separation, variety, or disparity in organizations. *Academy of Management Review, 32,* 1199–1228.

Harrison, D. A., Price, K. H., Gavin, J. H., & Florey, A. T. (2002). Time, teams, and task performance: Changing effects of surface- and deep-level diversity on group functioning. *Academy of Management Journal, 45,* 1029–1045.

Harrod, W. J., Welch, B. K., & Kushkowski, J. (2009). Thirty-one years of group research in Social Psychology Quarterly (1975–2005). *Current Research in Social Psychology, 14,* Article ID 6.

Hart, J. W., Bridgett, D. J., & Karau, S. J. (2001). Coworker ability and effort as determinants of individual effort on a collective task. *Group Dynamics: Theory, Research, and Practice, 5,* 181–190.

Harton, H. C., & Bullock, M. (2007). Dynamic social impact: A theory of the origins and evolution of culture. *Social and Personality Psychology Compass, 1,* 521–540.

Harton, H. C., Green, L. R., Jackson, C., & Latané, B. (1998). Demonstrating dynamic social impact: Consolidation, clustering, correlation, and (sometimes) the correct answer. *Teaching of Psychology, 25,* 31–35.

Harvey, J. B. (1988). *The Abilene paradox and other meditations on management.* New York: Wiley.

Haslam, N. (2006). Dehumanization: An integrative review. *Personality and Social Psychology Review, 10,* 252–264.

Haslam, N., Rothschild, L., & Ernst, D. (2002). Are essentialist beliefs associated with prejudice? *British Journal of Social Psychology, 41,* 87–100.

Haslam, S. A. (2004). *Psychology in organizations: The social identity approach* (2nd ed.). Thousand Oaks, CA: Sage.

Haslam, S. A., & Oakes, P. J. (1995). How context-independent is the outgroup homogeneity effect? A response to Bartsch and Judd. *European Journal of Social Psychology, 12,* 469–475.

Haslam, S. A., & Reicher, S. D. (2006). Stressing the group: Social identity and the unfolding dynamics of responses to stress. *Journal of Applied Psychology, 91,* 1037–1052.

Haslam, S. A., & Reicher, S. D. (2012). When prisoners take over the prison: A social psychology of resistance. *Personality and Social Psychology Review, 16*(2), 154–179.

Haslam, S. A., Reicher, S. D., & Platow, M. J. (2011). *The new psychology of leadership: Identity, influence and power.* New York: Psychology Press.

Haslam, S. A., Ryan, M. K., Postmes, T., Spears, R., Jetten, J., & Webley, P. (2006). Sticking to our guns: Social identity as a basis for the maintenance of commitment to faltering organizational projects. *Journal of Organizational Behavior, 27,* 607–628.

Hastie, R., & Kameda, T. (2005). The robust beauty of majority rules in group decisions. *Psychological Review, 112,* 494–508.

Hastie, R., Penrod, S. D., & Pennington, N. (1983). *Inside the jury.* Boston: Harvard University Press.

Hastorf, A. H., & Cantril, H. (1954). They saw a game. *Journal of Abnormal and Social Psychology, 49,* 129–134.

Hawkley, L. C., & Cacioppo, J. T. (2010). Loneliness matters: A theoretical and empirical review of consequences and mechanisms. *Annals of Behavioral Medicine, 40*(2), 218–227.

Hayduk, L. A. (1978). Personal space: An evaluative and orienting overview. *Psychological Bulletin, 85,* 117–134.

Hayduk, L. A. (1983). Personal space: Where we now stand. *Psychological Bulletin, 94*(2), 293–335.

Hazan, C., & Shaver, P. (1987). Romantic love conceptualized as an attachment process. *Journal of Personality and Social Psychology, 52,* 511–524.

Healey, A. N., Undre, S., & Vincent, C. A. (2006). Defining the technical skills of teamwork in surgery. *Quality & Safety in Health Care, 15,* 231–234.

Hearne, G. (1957). Leadership and the spatial factor in small groups. *Journal of Abnormal and Social Psychology, 54,* 269–272.

Hechter, M., & Op, K. (Eds.). (2001). *Social norms.* New York: Russell Sage Foundation.

Heerwagen, J. H., Kelly, K. V., Kampschroer, K., & Powell, K. M. (2006). The cognitive workplace. In D. Clements-Croome (Ed.), *Creating the productive workplace* (2nd. ed., pp. 136–149). New York: Taylor & Francis.

Heffron, M. H. (1972). The naval ship as an urban design problem. *Naval Engineers Journal, 12,* 49–64.

Heider, F. (1958). *The psychology of interpersonal relations.* New York: Wiley.

Heider, J. D., Scherer, C. R., Skowronski, J. J., Wood, S. E., Edlund, J. E., & Hartnett, J. L. (2007). Trait expectancies and stereotype expectancies have the same effect on person memory. *Journal of Experimental Social Psychology, 43*(2), 265–272.

Heilman, M. E., Block, C. J., & Martell, R. F. (1995). Sex stereotypes: Do they influence perceptions of managers? *Journal of Social Behavior and Personality, 10,* 237–252.

Heinicke, C. M., & Bales, R. F. (1953). Developmental trends in the structure of small groups. *Sociometry, 16,* 7–38.

Helbing, D., Buzna, L., Johansson, A., Werner, T. (2005). Self-organized pedestrian crowd dynamics: Experiments, simulations, and design solutions. *Transportation Science, 39*(1), 1–24.

Helbing, D., Johansson, A., & Al-Abideen, H. Z. (2007). *Crowd turbulence: The physics of crowd disasters.* Paper presented at the Fifth International Conference on Nonlinear Mechanics (ICNM-V), Shanghai.

Helbing, D., & Mukerji, P. (2012). Crowd disasters as systemic failures: Analysis of the Love Parade disaster. *Arxiv,* 1206.5856.

Heller, J. F., Groff, B. D., & Solomon, S. H. (1977). Toward an understanding of crowding: The role of physical interaction. *Journal of Personality and Social Psychology, 35,* 183–190.

Helliwell, J. F., & Putnam, R. D. (2004). The social context of well-being. *Philosophical Transactions of the Royal Society B: Biological Sciences, 359,* 1435–1446.

Helman, C. (2011). The world's happiest (and saddest) countries. *Forbes* (December 7, 2011). Retrieved from www.forbes.com/sites/christopherhelman/2011/12/07/the-worlds-happiest-and-saddest-countries/

Helmreich, R. L., & Foushee, H. C. (2010). Why CRM? Empirical and theoretical bases of human factors training. In B. G. Kanki, R. L. Helmreich, & J. Anca (Eds.), *Crew resource management* (2nd ed., pp. 3–58). New York: Academic Press.

Helweg-Larsen, M., LoMonaco, B. L. (2008). Queuing among U2 fans: Reactions to social norm violations. *Journal of Applied Social Psychology, 38,* 2378–2393.

Hembroff, L. A. (1982). Resolving status inconsistency: An expectation states theory and test. *Social Forces, 61,* 183–205.

Hemphill, J. K. (1950). Relations between the size of the group and the behavior of "superior" leaders. *Journal of Social Psychology, 32,* 11–22.

Henchy, T., & Glass, D. C. (1968). Evaluation apprehension and the social facilitation of dominant and subordinate responses. *Journal of Personality and Social Psychology, 10,* 446–454.

Henley, N. M. (1995). Body politics revisited: What do we know today? In P. J. Kalbfleisch & M. J. Cody (Eds.), *Gender, power, and communication in human relationships* (pp. 27–61). Mahwah, NJ: Erlbaum.

Henningsen, D. D., & Henningsen, M. L. M. (2007). Do groups know what they don't know? Dealing with missing information in decision-making groups. *Communication Research, 34,* 507–525.

Henrich, J., Boyd, R., Bowles, S., Camerer, C., Fehr, E., Gintis, H., & McElreath, R. (2004). Overview and synthesis. In J. Henrich, R. Boyd, S. Bowles, C. Camerer, E. Fehr, & H. Gintis (Eds.), *Foundations of human sociality: Economic experiments and ethnographic evidence from fifteen small-scale societies* (pp. 8–54). New York: Oxford University Press.

Henry, K. B., Arrow, H., & Carini, B. (1999). A tripartite model of group identification: Theory and measurement. *Small Group Research, 30,* 558–581.

Heppner, P. P., Kivlighan, D. M., Burnett, J. W., Berry, T. R., Goedinghaus, M., Doxsee, D. J., Hendricks, F. M., Krull, L. A., Wright, G. E., Bellatin, A. M., Durham, R. J., Tharp, A., Kim, H., Brossart, D. F., Wang, L., Witty, T. E., Kinder, M. H., Hertel, J. B., & Wallace, D. L. (1994). Dimensions that characterize supervisor interventions delivered in the context of live supervision of practicum counselors. *Journal of Counseling Psychology, 41,* 227–235.

Herek, G., Janis, I. L., & Huth, P. (1987). Decision-making during international crises: Is quality of process related to outcome? *Journal of Conflict Resolution, 31,* 203–226.

Herek, G. M., Janis, I. L., & Huth, P. (1989). Quality of U.S. decision making during the Cuban missile crisis: Major errors in Welch's reassessment. *Journal of Conflict Resolution, 33,* 446–459.

Herman, C. P., Roth, D. A., & Polivy, J. (2003). Effects of the presence of others on food intake: A normative interpretation. *Psychological Bulletin, 129,* 873–886.

Hernández, B., Carmen Hidalgo, M., Salazar-Laplace, M. E., & Hess, S. (2007). Place attachment and place identity in natives and non-natives. *Journal of Environmental Psychology, 27,* 310–319.

Hersey, P., & Blanchard, K. H. (1976). Leader effectiveness and adaptability description (LEAD). In J. W. Pfeiffer & J. E. Jones (Eds.), *The 1976 annual handbook for group facilitators* (Vol. 5, pp. 133–142). La Jolla, CA: University Associates.

Hersey, P., Blanchard, K. H., & Johnson, D. E. (2001). *Management of organizational behavior: Leading human resources* (8th ed.). Upper Saddle River, NJ: Prentice Hall.

Herzog, T. R., Hayes, L. J., Applin, R. C., & Weatherly, A. M. (2011a). Compatibility: An experimental demonstration. *Environment and Behavior, 43*(1), 90–105.

Herzog, T. R., Hayes, L. J., Applin, R. C., & Weatherly, A. M. (2011b). Incompatibility and mental fatigue. *Environment and Behavior, 43*(6), 827–847.

Hess, J. A., Fannin, A. D., & Pollom, L. H. (2007). Creating closeness: Discerning and measuring strategies for fostering closer relationships. *Personal Relationships, 14*(1), 25–44.

Hess, Y. D., & Pickett, C. L. (2010). Social rejection and self- versus other-awareness. *Journal of Experimental Social Psychology, 46*(2), 453–456.

Hewstone, M. (1990). The "ultimate attribution error"? A review of the literature on intergroup causal attribution. *European Journal of Social Psychology, 20,* 311–335.

Hewstone, M., Rubin, M., & Willis, H. (2002). Intergroup bias. *Annual Review of Psychology, 53,* 575–604.

Heyel, C. (1949). *The foreman's handbook.* New York: McGraw-Hill.

Higginbotham, H. N., West, S. G., & Forsyth, D. R. (1988). *Psychotherapy and behavior change: Social, cultural, and methodological perspectives.* New York: Pergamon.

Highhouse, S. (2002). A history of the T-group and its early applications in management development. *Group Dynamics: Theory, Research, and Practice, 6,* 277–290.

Hill, C. A. (1991). Seeking emotional support: The influence of affiliative need and partner warmth. *Journal of Personality and Social Psychology, 60,* 112–121.

Hill, C. A. (2009). Affiliation motivation. In M. R. Leary & R. H. Hoyle (Eds.), *Handbook of individual differences in social behavior* (pp. 410–425). New York: Guilford Press.

Hill, C. E., Helms, J. E., Tichenor, V., Spiegel, S. B., O'Grady, K. E., & Perry, E. S. (1988). Effects of therapist response modes in brief psychotherapy. *Journal of Counseling Psychology, 35,* 222–233.

Hill, W. F. (1969). *Learning thru discussion: Guide for leaders and members of discussion groups* (2nd ed.). Thousand Oaks, CA: Sage.

Hill, W. F., & Gruner, L. (1973). A study of development in open and closed groups. *Small Group Behavior, 4,* 355–381.

Hillyard, C., Gillespie, D., & Littig, P. (2010). University students' attitudes about learning in small groups after frequent participation. *Active Learning in Higher Education, 11*(1), 9–20.

Hinds, P. J., & Mortensen, M. (2005). Understanding conflict in geographically distributed teams: The moderating effects of shared identity, shared context, and spontaneous communication. *Organization Science, 16*(3), 290–307.

Hingson, R. W., Edwards, E. M., Heeren, T., & Rosenbloom, D. (2009). Age of drinking onset and injuries, motor vehicle crashes, and physical fights after drinking and when not drinking. *Alcoholism: Clinical and Experimental Research, 33*(5), 783–790.

Hinrichs, K. T. (2007). Follower propensity to commit crimes of obedience: The role of leadership beliefs. *Journal of Leadership & Organizational Studies, 14,* 69–76.

Hinrichs, K. T., Wang, L., Hinrichs, A., & Romero, E. J. Moral disengagement through displacement of responsibility: The role of leadership beliefs. *Journal of Applied Social Psychology, 42*(1), 62–80.

Hinsz, V. B. (1995). Goal setting by groups performing an additive task: A comparison with individual goal setting. *Journal of Applied Social Psychology, 25,* 965–990.

Hinsz, V. B. (2005). The influences of social aspects of competition in goal-setting situations. *Current Psychology: Developmental, Learning, Personality, Social, 24,* 258–273.

Hinsz, V. B., Tindale, R. S., & Vollrath, D. A. (1997). The emerging conceptualization of groups as information processors. *Psychological Bulletin, 121,* 43–64.

Hirokawa, R. Y. (1980). A comparative analysis of communication patterns within effective and ineffective decision-making groups. *Communication Monographs, 47,* 312–321.

Hirst, W., & Manier, D. (2008). Towards a psychology of collective memory. *Memory, 16,* 183–200.

Hirt, E. R., Zillmann, D., Erickson, G. A., & Kennedy, C. (1992). Costs and benefits of allegiance: Changes in fans' self-ascribed competencies after team victory versus defeat. *Journal of Personality and Social Psychology, 63,* 724–738.

Hobbes, T. (2008). *Leviathan.* Hong Kong: Forgotten Books. (original work published 1651)

Hodges, B. H., & Geyer, A. L. (2006). A nonconformist account of the Asch experiments: Values, pragmatics, and moral dilemmas. *Personality and Social Psychology Review, 10*, 2–19.

Hodgkinson, G. P., & Healey, M. P. (2008). Cognition in organizations. *Annual Review of Psychology, 59*, 387–417.

Hodson, G., & Sorrentino, R. M. (1997). Groupthink and uncertainty orientation: Personality differences in reactivity to the group situation. *Group Dynamics: Theory, Research, and Practice, 1*, 144–155.

Hoel, H., Glasø, L., Hetland, J., Cooper, C. L., & Einarsen, S. (2010). Leadership styles as predictors of self-reported and observed workplace bullying. *British Journal of Management, 21*(2), 453–468.

Hoffer, E. (1951). *The true believer.* New York: Harper & Row.

Hoffman, J. R., & Rogelberg, S. G. (2001). All together now? College students' preferred project group grading procedures. *Group Dynamics: Theory, Research, and Practice, 5*, 33–40.

Hofstede, G. (1980). *Culture's consequences: International differences in work-related values.* Thousand Oaks, CA: Sage.

Hofstede, G., Hofstede, G. J., & Minkov, M. (2010). *Cultures and organizations: Software of the mind* (3rd ed.). New York: McGraw-Hill.

Hogan, R. (2005). In defense of personality measurement: New wine for old whiners. *Human Performance, 18*, 331–341.

Hogan, R., & Kaiser, R. B. (2005). What we know about leadership. *Review of General Psychology, 9*, 169–180.

Hogg, M. A. (1992). *The social psychology of group cohesiveness: From attraction to social identity.* New York: New York University Press.

Hogg, M. A. (2001). Social categorization, depersonalization, and group behavior. In M. A. Hogg & R. S. Tindale (Eds.), *Blackwell handbook of social psychology: Group processes* (pp. 56–85). Malden, MA: Blackwell.

Hogg, M. A. (2005). *The social identity perspective.* In S. Wheelan (Ed.), The handbook of group research and practice (pp. 133–157). Thousand Oaks, CA: Sage.

Hogg, M. A. (2010). Influence and leadership. In S. T. Fiske, D. T. Gilbert, & G. Lindzey (Eds.), *Handbook of social psychology* (Vol. 2, 5th ed., pp. 1166–1207). Hoboken, NJ: John Wiley.

Hogg, M. A., Sherman, D. K., Dierselhuis, J., Maitner, A. T., & Moffitt, G. (2007). Uncertainty, entitativity, and group identification. *Journal of Experimental Social Psychology, 43*, 135–142.

Hogg, M. A., & Tindale, S. (Eds.). (2001). *Blackwell handbook of social psychology: Group processes.* Malden, MA: Blackwell.

Hogg, M. A., & Turner, J. C. (1987). Intergroup behavior, self-stereotyping and the salience of social categories. *British Journal of Social Psychology, 26*, 325–340.

Hogg, M. A., Turner, J. C., & David, B. (1990). Polarized norms and social frames of references: A test of the self-categorization theory of group polarization. *Basic and Applied Social Psychology, 11*, 77–100.

Hollander, E. P. (1965). Validity of peer nominations in predicting a distance performance criterion. *Journal of Applied Psychology, 49*, 434–438.

Hollander, E. P. (1971). *Principles and methods of social psychology* (2nd ed.). New York: Oxford University Press.

Hollander, E. P. (1985). Leadership and power. In G. Lindzey & E. Aronson (Eds.), *Handbook of social psychology* (Vol. 2, 3rd ed., pp. 485–537). New York: Random House.

Hollander, E. P. (2006). Influence processes in leadership–followership: Inclusion and the idiosyncrasy credit model. In D. A. Hantula (Ed.), *Advances in social & organizational psychology: A tribute to Ralph Rosnow* (pp. 293–312). Mahwah, NJ: Erlbaum.

Hollenbeck, J. R., Beersma, B., & Schouten, M. E. (2012). Beyond team types and taxonomies: A dimensional scaling conceptualization. *Academy of Management Review, 37*(1), 82–106.

Hollingshead, A. B. (2001a). Cognitive interdependence and convergent expectations in transactive memory. *Journal of Personality and Social Psychology, 81*, 1080–1089.

Hollingshead, A. B. (2001b). Communication technologies, the Internet, and group research. In M. A. Hogg & R. S. Tindale (Eds.), *Blackwell handbook of social psychology: Group processes* (pp. 557–573). Malden, MA: Blackwell.

Hollingshead, A. B., Wittenbaum, G. M., Paulus, P. B., Hirokawa, R. Y., Ancona, D. G., Peterson, R. S., Jehn, K. A., & Yoon, K. (2005). A look at groups from the functional perspective. In M. S. Poole & A. B. Hollingshead (Eds.), *Theories of small groups: Interdisciplinary perspectives* (pp. 21–62). Thousand Oaks, CA: Sage.

Hollingworth, H. L. (1935). *The psychology of the audience.* New York: American Books.

Hollon, S. D., & Beck, A. T. (2004). Cognitive and cognitive behavioral therapies. In M. J. Lambert (Ed.), *Bergin & Garfield's handbook of psychotherapy and behavior change* (5th ed., pp. 447–492). New York: Wiley & Sons.

Holmes, J. G., Miller, D. T. (1976). *Interpersonal conflict.* Morristown, NJ: General Learning Press.

Homan, A. C., Greer, L. L., Jehn, K. A., & Koning, L. (2010). Believing shapes seeing: The impact of diversity beliefs on the construal of group composition. *Group Processes & Intergroup Relations, 13*(4), 477–493.

Homans, G. C. (1950). *The human group.* New York: Harcourt, Brace & World.

Homans, G. C. (1961). *Social behavior: Its elementary forms.* New York: Harcourt, Brace.

Homans, G. C. (1967). *The nature of social science.* New York: Harcourt, Brace & World.

Honeywell-Johnson, J. A., & Dickinson, A. M. (1999). Small group incentives: A review of the literature. *Journal of Organizational Behavior Management, 19*, 89–120.

Hong, L. K. (1978). Risky shift and cautious shift: Some direct evidence on the culture-value theory. *Social Psychology, 41*(4), 342–346.

Hooijberg, R., & DiTomaso, N. (1996). Leadership in and of demographically diverse organizations. *Leadership Quarterly, 7*, 1–19.

Hooper, D. T., & Martin, R. (2008). Beyond personal Leader–Member Exchange (LMX) quality: The effects of perceived LMX variability on employee reactions. *The Leadership Quarterly, 19*, 20–30.

Hopper, E. (2005). Countertransference in the context of the fourth basic assumption in the unconscious life of groups. *International Journal of Group Psychotherapy, 55*, 87–113.

Horne, A. M., Jolliff, D. L., & Roth, E. W. (1996). Men mentoring men in groups. In M. P. Andronico (Ed.), *Men in groups: Insights, interventions, and psychoeducational work* (pp. 97–112). Washington, DC: American Psychological Association.

Horne, A. M., Stoddard, J. L., & Bell, C. D. (2007). Group approaches to reducing aggression and bullying in school. *Group Dynamics: Theory, Research, and Practice, 11*, 262–271.

Hornsey, M. J., & Jetten, J. (2004). The individual within the group: Balancing the need to belong with the need to be different. *Personality and Social Psychology Review, 8*(3), 248–264.

Horowitz, I. A., & Kirkpatrick, L. C. (1996). A concept in search of a definition: The effects of reasonable doubt instructions on certainty of guilt standards and jury verdicts. *Law and Human Behavior, 20*(6), 655–670.

Horwitz, S. K., & Horwitz, I. B. (2007). The effects of team diversity on team outcomes: A meta-analytic review of team demography. *Journal of Management, 33*, 987–1015.

Houle, C. O. (1989). *Governing boards: Their nature and nurture.* San Francisco: Jossey-Bass.

House, R. J. (2004). Preface. In R. J. House, P. J. Hanges, M. Javidan, P. W. Dorfman, & V. Gupta (Eds.), *Culture, leadership, and organizations: The GLOBE study of 62 societies* (pp. xxi–xxvii). Thousand Oaks, CA: Sage.

House, R. J., Hanges, P. J., Javidan, M., Dorfman, P. W., & Gupta, V. (Eds.). (2004). *Culture, leadership, and organizations: The GLOBE study of 62 societies.* Thousand Oaks, CA: Sage.

Houston, T. K., Cooper, L. A., & Ford, D. E. (2002). Internet support groups for depression: A 1-year prospective cohort study. *American Journal of Psychiatry, 159*, 2062–2068.

Howard, J. W., & Rothbart, M. (1980). Social categorization and memory for in-group and out-group behavior. *Journal of Personality and Social Psychology, 38*, 301–310.

Howe, J. (2008). *Crowdsourcing: Why the power of the crowd is driving the future of business.* New York: Three Rivers Press.

Howell, J. P., Bowen, D. E., Dorfman, P. W., Kerr, S., & Podsakoff, P. M. (1990). Substitutes for leadership: Effective alternatives to ineffective leadership. *Organizational Dynamics, 19*(1), 21–38.

Howells, L. T., & Becker, S. W. (1962). Seating arrangement and leadership emergence. *Journal of Abnormal and Social Psychology, 64*(2), 148–150.

Hoyle, R. H. (2005). Design and analysis of experimental research on groups. In S. A. Wheelan (Ed.), *The handbook of group research and practice* (pp. 223–239). Thousand Oaks, CA: Sage.

Hoyle, R. H., & Crawford, A. M. (1994). Use of individual-level data to investigate group phenomena: Issues and strategies. *Small Group Research, 25*, 464–485.

Hoyle, R. H., Pinkley, R. L., & Insko C. A. (1989). Perceptions of behavior: Evidence of differing expectations for interpersonal and intergroup interactions. *Personality and Social Psychology Bulletin, 15*, 365–376.

Hoyt, C. L. (2010). Women, men, and leadership: Exploring the gender gap at the top. *Social and Personality Psychology Compass, 4*, 484–498.

Hoyt, C. L. (in press). Leadership within virtual contexts. In Y. Amichai-Hamburger (Ed.), *The social net: Human behavior in cyberspace* (2nd edition). New York: Oxford University Press.

Hoyt, C. L., & Blascovich, J. (2007). Leadership efficacy and women leaders' responses to stereotype activation. *Group Processes & Intergroup Relations, 10*, 595–616.

Hoyt, C. L., & Chemers, M. M. (2008). Social stigma and leadership: A long climb up a slippery ladder. In C. L. Hoyt, G. R. Goethals, & D. R. Forsyth (Eds.), *Leadership at the crossroads: Leadership and psychology* (Vol. 1, pp. 165–180). Westport, CT: Praeger.

Hoyt, C. L., Goethals, G. R., & Forsyth, D. R. (Eds.). (2008). *Leadership at the crossroads: Leadership and psychology* (Vol. 1). Westport, CT: Praeger.

Hoyt, C. L., Simon, S., & Innella, A. N. (2011). Taking a turn toward the masculine: The impact of mortality salience on implicit leadership theories. *Basic and Applied Social Psychology, 33*(4), 374–381.

Hughes, R. L. (2003). The flow of human crowds. *Annual Review of Fluid Mechanics, 35*, 169–182.

Huguet, P., Galvaing, M. P., Monteil, J. M., & Dumas, F. (1999). Social presence effects in the Stroop task: Further evidence for an attentional view of social facilitation. *Journal of Personality and Social Psychology, 77*, 1011–1025.

Human Area Relations Files. (2012). Database available at www.yale.edu/hraf/

Humphreys, L. (1975). *Tearoom trade* (enlarged ed.). Hawthorne, NY: Aldine.

Hurley, J. R. (1997). Interpersonal theory and measures of outcome and emotional climate in 111 personal development groups. *Group Dynamics: Theory, Research, and Practice, 1*, 86–97.

Husnu, S., & Crisp, R. J. (2010). Elaboration enhances the imagined contact effect. *Journal of Experimental Social Psychology, 46*(6), 943–950.

Hyman, H. (1942). The psychology of status. *Archives of Psychology, 38*(269).

Hyman, H. M., & Tarrant, C. M. (1975). Aspects of American trial jury history. In R. J. Simon (Ed.), *The jury system in America: A critical overview* (pp. 21–44). Thousand Oaks, CA: Sage.

Iacoboni, M., Liberman, M. D., Knowlton, B. J., Molnar-Szakas, I., Moritz, M., Throop, C. J., Fiske, A. P. (2004). Watching social interactions produces dorsomedial prefrontal and medial parietal BOLD fMRI signal increases compared to a resting baseline. *NeuroImage, 21,* 1167–1173.

Iannaccone, L. R. (1994). Why strict churches are strong. *American Journal of Sociology, 99,* 1180–1211.

IJzerman, H., & Semin, G. R. (2010). Temperature perceptions as a ground for social proximity. *Journal of Experimental Social Psychology, 46*(6), 867–873.

Ilgen, D. R., Hollenbeck, J. R., Johnson, M., & Jundt, D. (2005). Teams in organizations: From input-process-output models to IMOI models. *Annual Review of Psychology, 56,* 517–543.

Ilgen, D. R., Mitchell, T. R., & Fredrickson, J. W. (1981). Poor performances: Supervisors' and subordinates' responses. *Organizational Behavior and Human Performance, 27,* 386–410.

Ilies, R., Morgeson, F. P., & Nahrgang, J. D. (2005). Authentic leadership and eudaemonic well-being: Understanding leader-follower outcomes. *Leadership Quarterly, 16,* 373–394.

Ilies, R., Nahrgang, J. D., & Morgeson, F. P. (2007). Leader-member exchange and citizenship behaviors: A meta-analysis. *Journal of Applied Psychology, 92,* 269–277.

Imhoff, R., & Erb, H-P. (2009). What motivates nonconformity? Uniqueness seeking blocks majority influence. *Personality and Social Psychology Bulletin, 35*(3), 309–320.

Indik, B. P. (1965). Organization size and member participation: Some empirical tests of alternate explanations. *Human Relations, 15,* 339–350.

Ingham, A. G., Levinger, G., Graves, J., & Peckham, V. (1974). The Ringelmann effect: Studies of group size and group performance. *Journal of Experimental Social Psychology, 10*(4), 371–384.

Ingram, R. E., Hayes, A., & Scott, W. (2000). Empirically supported treatments: A critical analysis. In C. R. Snyder & R. E. Ingram (Eds.). *Handbook of psychological change: Psychotherapy processes & practices for the 21st century* (pp. 40–60). New York: Wiley.

Insko, C. A., Gilmore, R., Drenan, S., Lipsitz, A., Moehle, D., & Thibaut, J. (1983). Trade versus expropriation in open groups: A comparison of two types of social power. *Journal of Personality and Social Psychology, 44,* 977–999.

Insko, C. A., Pinkley, R. L., Hoyle, R. H., Dalton, B., Hong, G., Slim, R., Landry, P., Holton, B., Ruffin, P. F., & Thibaut, J. (1987). Individual-group discontinuity: The role of intergroup contact. *Journal of Experimental Social Psychology, 23,* 250–267.

Insko, C. A., & Schopler, J. (1972). *Experimental social psychology.* New York: Academic Press.

Insko, C. A., Schopler, J., Drigotas, S. M., Graetz, K., Kennedy, J., Cox, C., & Bornstein, G., (1993). The role of communication in interindividual–intergroup discontinuity. *Journal of Conflict Resolution, 37,* 108–138.

Insko, C. A., Schopler, J., Graetz, K. A., Drigotas, S. M., Currey, K. P., Smith, S. L., Brazil, D., & Bornstein, G. (1994).

Interindividual–intergroup discontinuity in the Prisoner's Dilemma Game. *Journal of Conflict Resolution, 38,* 87–116.

Insko, C. A., Schopler, J., Hoyle, R. H., Dardis, G. J., & Graetz, K. A., (1990). Individual–group discontinuity as a function of fear and greed. *Journal of Personality and Social Psychology, 58,* 68–79.

Inkso, C. A., Thibaut, J. W., Moehle, D., Wilson, M., Diamond, W. D., Gilmore, R., Solomon, M. R., & Lipsitz, A. (1980). Social evolution and the emergence of leadership. *Journal of Personality and Social Psychology, 39,* 431–448.

Instone, D., Major, B., & Bunker, B. B. (1983). Gender, self-confidence, and social influence strategies: An organizational simulation. *Journal of Personality and Social Psychology, 44,* 322–333.

Ioakimidis, M., & Myloni, B. (2010). Good fences make good classes: Greek tertiary students' preferences for instructor teaching method. *International Online Journal of Educational Sciences, 2*(2), 290–308.

Ip, G. W., Chiu, C., & Wan, C. (2006). Birds of a feather and birds flocking together: Physical versus behavioral cues may lead to trait- versus goal-based group perception. *Journal of Personality and Social Psychology, 90,* 368–381.

Isenberg, D. J., & Ennis, J. G. (1981). Perceiving group members: A comparison of derived and imposed dimensions. *Journal of Personality and Social Psychology, 41,* 293–305.

Isidore, C. (2012, March 22). African-American CEOs still rare. *CNNMoney.* Retrieved from money.cnn.com

Islam, G., & Zyphur, M. J. (2005). Power, voice, and hierarchy: Exploring the antecedents of speaking up in groups. *Group Dynamics: Theory, Research, and Practice, 9,* 93–103.

Ito, H., Yamauchi, H., Kaneko, H., Yoshikawa, T., Nomura, K., & Honjo, S. (2011). Prefrontal overactivation, autonomic arousal, and task performance under evaluative pressure: A near-infrared spectroscopy (NIRS) study. *Psychophysiology, 48*(11), 1563–1571.

Jablin, F. M. (1979). Superior-subordinate communication: The state of the art. *Psychological Bulletin, 86,* 1201–1222.

Jackson, D., Engstrom, E., & Emmers-Sommer, T. (2007). Think leader, think male and female: Sex vs. seating arrangement as leadership cues. *Sex Roles, 57,* 713–723.

Jackson, J. M. (1987). Social impact theory: A social forces model of influence. In B. Mullen & G. R. Goethals (Eds.), *Theories of group behavior* (pp. 112–124). New York: Springer-Verlag.

Jackson, J. M., & Latané, B. (1981). All alone in front of all those people: Stage fright as a function of number and type of co-performances and audience. *Journal of Personality and Social Psychology, 40,* 73–85.

Jackson, S. E. (1992). Team composition in organizational settings: Issues in managing an increasingly diverse workforce. In S. Worchel, S. Wood, & J. A. Simpson (Eds.), *Group process and productivity* (pp. 138–172). Thousand Oaks, CA: Sage.

Jackson, T. (1996). European management learning: A cross-cultural interpretation of Kolb's learning cycle. *Journal of Management Development, 14*(6), 42–50.

Jacobs, A. (1974). The use of feedback in groups. In A. Jacobs & W. W. Spradlin (Eds.), *Group as an agent of change* (pp. 408–448). New York: Behavioral Publications.

Jacobs, D., & O'Brien, R. M. (1998). The determinants of deadly force: A structural analysis of police violence. *American Journal of Sociology, 103,* 837–862.

Jacobs, M. K., & Goodman, G. (1989). Psychology and self-help groups: Predictions on a partnership. *American Psychologist, 44,* 536–545.

Jacobs, R. C., & Campbell, D. T. (1961). The perpetuation of an arbitrary tradition through several generations of a laboratory microculture. *Journal of Abnormal and Social Psychology, 62,* 649–658.

Jahoda, G. (2007). *A history of social psychology: From the eighteenth-century enlightenment to the Second World War.* Cambridge, UK: Cambridge University Press.

James, J. (1951). A preliminary study of the size determinant in small group interaction. *American Sociological Review, 16,* 474–477.

James, R. (1959). Status and competency of jurors. *American Journal of Sociology, 64,* 563–570.

James, W. (1961). *Psychology.* New York: Harper & Row. (original work published 1892)

Janicik, G. A., & Bartel, C. A. (2003). Talking about time: Effects of temporal planning and time awareness norms on group coordination and performance. *Group Dynamics: Theory, Research, and Practice, 7,* 122–134.

Janis, I. L. (1972). *Victims of groupthink.* Boston: Houghton-Mifflin.

Janis, I. L. (1982). *Groupthink: Psychological studies of policy decisions and fiascos* (2nd ed.). Boston: Houghton Mifflin.

Janis, I. L. (1983). Groupthink. In H. H. Blumberg, A. P. Hare, V. Kent, & M. F. Davis (Eds.), *Small groups and social interaction* (Vol. 2, pp. 39–46). New York: Wiley.

Janis, I. L. (1989). *Crucial decisions: Leadership in policy making and crisis management.* New York: Free Press.

Janis, I. L., & Mann, L. (1977). *Decision making: A psychological analysis of conflict, choice, and commitment.* New York: Free Press.

Jans, L., Postmes, T., & Van der Zee, K. I. (2011). The induction of shared identity: The positive role of individual distinctiveness for groups. *Personality and Social Psychology Bulletin, 37*(8), 1130–1141.

Janssen, L., Fennis, B. M., & Pruyn, A. T. H. (2010). Forewarned is forearmed: Conserving self-control strength to resist social influence. *Journal of Experimental Social Psychology, 46*(6), 911–921.

Jarboe, S. C., & Witteman, H. R. (1996). Intragroup conflict management in task-oriented groups: The influence of problem sources and problem analyses. *Small Group Research, 27,* 316–338.

Jarman, R. (2005). When success isn't everything: Case studies of two virtual teams. *Group Decision and Negotiation, 14*(4), 333–354.

Jarvenpaa, S. L., Knoll, K., & Leidner, D. E. (1998). Is anybody out there? Antecedents of trust in global virtual teams. *Journal of Management Information Systems, 14*(4), 29–64.

Jarvenpaa, S. L., Shaw, T. R., & Staples, D. S. (2004). Toward contextualized theories of trust: The role of trust in global virtual teams. *Information Systems Research, 15*(3), 250–267.

Jehn, K. A. (1995). A multimethod examination of the benefits and detriments of intragroup conflict. *Administrative Science Quarterly, 40,* 256–282.

Jehn, K. A. (1997). Affective and cognitive conflict in work groups: Increasing performance through value-based intragroup conflict. In C. K. W. De Dreu & E. Van de Vliert (Eds.), *Using conflict in organizations* (pp. 87–100). Thousand Oaks, CA: Sage.

Jehn, K. A., & Bendersky, C. (2003). Intragroup conflict in organizations: A contingency perspective on the conflict-outcome relationship. In R. M. Kramer & B. M. Staw (Eds.), *Research in organizational behavior* (Vol. 25, pp. 187–242). Oxford: Elsevier Science.

Jehn, K. A., & Mannix, E. A. (2001). The dynamic nature of conflict: A longitudinal study of intragroup conflict and group performance. *Academy of Management Journal, 44,* 238–251.

Jehn, K. A., & Shah, P. P. (1997). Interpersonal relationships and task performance: An examination of mediating processes in friendship and acquaintance groups. *Journal of Personality and Social Psychology, 72,* 775–790.

Jetten, J., & Hornsey, M. J. (Eds.). (2011). *Rebels in groups: Dissent, deviance, difference and defiance.* Malden, MA: Wiley-Blackwell.

Jetten, J., Hornsey, M. J., & Adarves-Yorno, I. (2006). When group members admit to being conformist: The role of relative intragroup status in conformity self-reports. *Personality and Social Psychology Bulletin, 32,* 162–173.

Johansson, A., Helbing, D., Al-Abideen, H. Z., & Al-Bosta, S. (2008). From crowd dynamics to crowd safety: A video-based analysis. *Advances in Complex Systems, 11,* 497–527.

John, P. F. U., Mandal, M. K., Ramachandran, K., & Panwar, M. R. (2010). Interpersonal behavior in an isolated and confined environment. *Environment and Behavior, 42,* 707–717.

Johnson, C., Gadon, O., Carlson, D., Southwick, S., Faith, M., & Chalfin, J. (2002). Self-reference and group membership: Evidence for a group-reference effect. *European Journal of Social Psychology, 32*(2), 261–274.

Johnson, D. W., & Johnson, R. T. (2009). An educational psychology success story: Social interdependence theory and cooperative learning. *Educational Researcher, 38*(5), 365–379.

Johnson, F. (1988). Encounter group therapy. In S. Long (Ed.), *Six group therapies* (pp. 115–158). New York: Plenum Press.

Johnson, N. R. (1987). Panic at "The Who concert stampede": An empirical assessment. *Social Problems, 34,* 362–373.

Johnson, R. D., & Downing, L. L. (1979). Deindividuation and valence of cues: Effects on prosocial and antisocial behavior. *Journal of Personality and Social Psychology, 37,* 1532–1538.

Johnson, S. E., & Richeson, J. A. (2009). Solo status revisited: Examining racial group differences in the self-regulatory consequences of self-presenting as a racial solo. *Journal of Experimental Social Psychology, 45*(4), 1032–1035.

Johnstone, R. A., & Manica, A. (2011). Evolution of personality differences in leadership. *PNAS: Proceedings of the National Academy of Sciences, 108*(20), 8373–8378.

Joinson, A. N. (2007). Disinhibition and the Internet. In J. Gackenbach (Ed.), *Psychology and the Internet: Intrapersonal, interpersonal, and transpersonal implications* (2nd ed., pp. 75–92). San Diego: Academic Press.

Jones, E. E., Carter-Sowell, A. R., & Kelly, J. R. (2011). Participation matters: Psychological and behavioral consequences of information exclusion in groups. *Group Dynamics: Theory, Research, and Practice, 15*(4), 311–325.

Jones, E. E., Carter-Sowell, A. R., Kelly, J. R., & Williams, K. D. (2009). 'I'm out of the loop': Ostracism through information exclusion. *Group Processes & Intergroup Relations, 12*(2), 157–174.

Jones, E. E., & Kelly, J. R. (2007). Contributions to a group discussion and perceptions of leadership: Does quantity always count more than quality? *Group Dynamics: Theory, Research, and Practice, 11*, 15–30.

Jones, E. S., Gallois, C., Callan, V. J., & Barker, M. (1995). Language and power in an academic context: The effects of status, ethnicity, and sex. *Journal of Language & Social Psychology, 14*, 434–461.

Jones, J. T., Pelham, B. W., Carvallo, M., & Mirenberg, M. C. (2004). How do I love thee? Let me count the js: Implicit egotism and interpersonal attraction. *Journal of Personality and Social Psychology, 87*(5), 665–683.

Jones, M. B. (1974). Regressing group on individual effectiveness. *Organizational Behavior and Human Decision Processes, 11*, 426–451.

Jordan, A. H., Monin, B., Dweck, C. S., Lovett, B. J., John, O. P., & Gross, J. J. (2011). Misery has more company than people think: Underestimating the prevalence of others' negative emotions. *Personality and Social Psychology Bulletin, 37*(1), 120–135.

Jorgenson, D. O., & Dukes, F. O. (1976). Deindividuation as a function of density and group membership. *Journal of Personality and Social Psychology, 34*, 24–29.

Joseph, D. L., & Newman, D. A. (2010). Emotional intelligence: An integrative meta-analysis and cascading model. *Journal of Applied Psychology, 95*(1), 54–78.

Jourard, S. (1971). *Self-disclosure: An experimental analysis of the transparent self.* New York: Wiley.

Joyce, E., & Kraut, R. E. (2006). Predicting continued participation in newsgroups. *Journal of Computer-Mediated Communication, 11*(3), 723–747.

Judge, T. A., Bono, J. E., Ilies, R., & Gerhardt, M. W. (2002). Personality and leadership: A qualitative and quantitative review. *Journal of Applied Psychology, 87*, 765–780.

Judge, T. A., & Cable, D. M. (1997). Applicant personality, organizational culture, and organization attraction. *Personnel Psychology, 50*, 359–394.

Judge, T. A., & Piccolo, R. F. (2004). Transformational and transactional leadership: A meta-analytic test of their relative validity. *Journal of Applied Psychology, 89*, 755–768.

Judge, T. A., Piccolo, R. F., & Ilies, R. (2004). The forgotten ones? The validity of consideration and initiating structure in leadership research. *Journal of Applied Psychology, 89*(1), 36–51.

Jung, D., Wu, A., & Chow, C. W. (2008). Towards understanding the direct and indirect effects of CEOs' transformational leadership on firm innovation. *The Leadership Quarterly, 19*, 582–594.

Kagan, J., Snidman, N., & Arcus, D. M. (1992). Initial reactions to unfamiliarity. *Current Directions in Psychological Science, 1*, 171–174.

Kagitçibasi, C. (1997). Individualism and collectivism. In J. W. Berry, M. H. Segall, & C. Kagitçibasi (Eds.), *Handbook of cross-cultural psychology: Social behavior and applications* (Vol. 3, pp. 1–49). Boston: Allyn & Bacon.

Kahn, A., Hottes, J., & Davis, W. L. (1971). Cooperation and optimal responding in the Prisoner's Dilemma Game: Effects of sex and physical attractiveness. *Journal of Personality and Social Psychology, 17*, 267–279.

Kahn, R. L., Wolfe, D. M., Quinn, R. P., Snoek, J. D., & Rosenthal, R. A. (1964). *Organizational stress: Studies in role conflict and ambiguity.* New York: Wiley.

Kahneman, D., & Tversky, A. (1973). On the psychology of prediction. *Psychological Review, 80*(4), 237–251.

Kaiser, R. B., Hogan, R., & Craig, S. B. (2008). Leadership and the fate of organizations. *American Psychologist, 63*, 96–110.

Kalven, H., Jr., & Zeisel, H. (1966). *The American jury.* Boston: Little, Brown.

Kamarck, T. W., Manuck, S. B., & Jennings, J. R. (1990). Social support reduces cardiovascular reactivity to psychological challenge: A laboratory model. *Psychosomatic Medicine, 52*, 42–58.

Kameda, T. (1994). Group decision making and social sharedness. *Japanese Psychological Review, 37*, 367–385.

Kameda, T., Stasson, M. F., Davis, J. H., Parks, C. D., & Zimmerman, S. K. (1992). Social dilemmas, subgroups, and motivation loss in task-oriented groups: In search of an "optimal" team size in division of work. *Social Psychology Quarterly, 55*, 47–56.

Kameda, T., Takezawa, M., & Hastie, R. (2005). Where do social norms come from? The example of communal sharing. *Current Directions in Psychological Science, 14*, 331–334.

Kameda, T., Takezawa, M., Tindale, R. S., & Smith, C. M. (2002). Social sharing and risk reduction: Exploring a computational algorithm for the psychology of windfall gains. *Evolution and Human Behavior, 23*, 11–33.

Kameda, T., & Tamura, R. (2007). "To eat or not to be eaten?" collective risk-monitoring in groups. *Journal of Experimental Social Psychology, 43*, 168–179.

Kameda, T., & Tindale, R. S. (2006). Groups as adaptive devices: Human docility and group aggregation mechanisms in evolutionary context. In M. Schaller, J. A. Simpson & D. T. Kenrick (Eds.), *Evolution and social psychology* (pp. 317–341). Madison, WI: Psychosocial Press.

Kameda, T., Tsukasaki, T., Hastie, R., & Berg, N. (2011). Democracy under uncertainty: The wisdom of crowds and the free-rider problem in group decision making. *Psychological Review, 118*(1), 76–96.

Kampmeier, C., & Simon, B. (2001). Individuality and group formation: The role of independence and differentiation. *Journal of Personality and Social Psychology, 81*(3), 448–462.

Kandel, D. B. (1978). Similarity in real-life adolescent friendship pairs. *Journal of Personality and Social Psychology, 36*, 306–312.

Kang, Y., Williams, L. E., Clark, M. S., Gray, J. R., & Bargh, J. A. (2011). Physical temperature effects on trust behavior: The role of insula. *Social Cognitive and Affective Neuroscience, 6*(4), 507–515.

Kanki, B. G., Helmreich, R. L., & Anca, J. (Eds.). (2010). *Crew resource maintenance* (2nd ed.). New York: Academic Press.

Kaplan, M. F., & Miller, C. E. (1987). Group decision making and normative versus informational influence: Effects of type of issue and assigned decision rule. *Journal of Personality and Social Psychology, 53*, 306–313.

Kaplan, R. E. (1979). The conspicuous absence of evidence that process consultation enhances task performance. *Journal of Applied Behavioral Science, 15*, 346–360.

Kaplan, S. (1995). The restorative benefits of nature: Toward an integrative framework. *Journal of Environmental Psychology, 15*(3), 169–182.

Kaplan, S. (2001). Meditation, restoration, and the management of mental fatigue. *Environment and Behavior, 33*(4), 480–506.

Kaplan, S., & Berman, M. G. (2010). Directed attention as a common resource for executive functioning and self-regulation. *Perspectives on Psychological Science, 5*(1), 43–57.

Kaplowitz, S. A. (1978). Towards a systematic theory of power attribution. *Social Psychology, 41*, 131–148.

Karau, S. J., & Elsaid, A. M. M. K. (2009). Individual differences in beliefs about groups. *Group Dynamics: Theory, Research, and Practice, 13*(1), 1–13.

Karau, S. J., & Williams, K. D. (1993). Social loafing: A meta-analytic review and theoretical integration. *Journal of Personality and Social Psychology, 65*, 681–706.

Karau, S. J., & Williams, K. D. (2001). Understanding individual motivation in groups: The collective effort model. In M. E. Turner (Ed.), *Groups at work: Theory and research* (pp. 113–141). Mahwah, NJ: Erlbaum.

Karremans, J. C., Verwijmeren, T., Pronk, T. M., & Reitsma, M. (2009). Interacting with women can impair men's cognitive functioning. *Journal of Experimental Social Psychology, 45*(4), 1041–1044.

Kashima, Y., Kashima, E., Chiu, C.-Y., Farsides, T., Gelfand, M., Hong, Y-Y., Kim, U., Strack, F., Werth, L., Yuki, M., Yzerbyt, V. (2005). Culture, essentialism, and agency: Are individuals universally believed to be more real entities than groups? *European Journal of Social Psychology, 35*, 147–169.

Kashima, Y., Yamaguchi, S., Kim, U., Choi, S., Gelfand, M. J., & Yuki, M. (1995). Culture, gender, and self: A perspective from individualism-collectivism research. *Journal of Personality and Social Psychology, 69*, 925–937.

Kaskutas, L. A., Ammon, L., Delucchi, K., Room, R., Bond, J., & Weisner, C. (2005). Alcoholics Anonymous careers: Patterns of AA involvement five years after treatment entry. *Alcoholism: Clinical and Experimental Research, 29*, 1983–1990.

Katz, D., & Kahn, R. L. (1978). *The social psychology of organizations* (2nd ed.). New York: Wiley.

Katz, R. (1977). The influence of group conflict on leadership effectiveness. *Organizational Behavior and Human Performance, 20*, 265–286.

Katz, R., & Tushman, M. (1979). Communication patterns, project performance, and task characteristics: An empirical evaluation and integration in an R & D setting. *Organization Behavior and Group Performance, 23*, 139–162.

Katzenbach, J. R., & Smith, D. K. (2001). *The discipline of teams.* New York: Wiley.

Kauffeld, S., & Lehmann-Willenbrock, N. (2012). Meetings matter: Effects of team meetings on team and organizational success. *Small Group Research, 43*(2), 130–158.

Kayes, A. B., Kayes, D. C., & Kolb, D. A. (2005). Experiential learning in teams. *Simulation and Gaming, 36*, 330–354.

Kayes, D.C. (2006). *Destructive goal pursuit: The Mount Everest disaster.* New York: Palgrave-Macmillan.

Kazdin, A. E. (2011). Evidence-based treatment research: Advances, limitations, and next steps. *American Psychologist, 66*(8), 685–698.

Keating, C. F., Pomerantz, J., Pommer, S. D., Ritt, S. J. H., Miller, L. M., & McCormick, J. (2005). Going to college and unpacking hazing: A functional approach to decrypting initiation practices among undergraduates. *Group Dynamics: Theory, Research, and Practice, 9*(2), 104–126.

Keinan, G., & Koren, M. (2002). Teaming up Type As and Bs: The effects of group composition on performance and satisfaction. *Applied Psychology: An International Review, 51*, 425–445.

Kellermanns, F. W., Walter, J., Floyd, S. W., Lechner, C., & Shaw, J. C. (2011). To agree or not to agree? A meta-analytical review of strategic consensus and organizational performance. *Journal of Business Research, 64*(2), 126–133.

Kelley, H. H. (1952). Two functions of reference groups. In G. E. Swanson, T. M. Newcomb, & E. L. Hartley (Eds.), *Readings in social psychology* (2nd ed., pp. 410–414). New York: Holt.

Kelley, H. H. (1979). *Personal relationships: Their structures and processes.* Mahwah, NJ: Erlbaum.

Kelley, H. H., Contry, J. C., Dahlke, A. E., & Hill, A. H. (1965). Collective behavior in a simulated panic situation. *Journal of Experimental Social Psychology, 1*, 20–54.

Kelley, H. H., Holmes, J. G., Kerr, N. L., Reis, H. T., Rusbult, C. E. & Van Lange, P. A. M. (2003). *An atlas of interpersonal situations.* New York: Cambridge University Press.

Kelley, H. H., & Stahelski, A. J. (1970a). Errors in perceptions of intentions in a mixed-motive game. *Journal of Experimental Social Psychology, 6*, 379–400.

Kelley, H. H., & Stahelski, A. J. (1970b). Social interaction basis of cooperators' and competitors' beliefs about others. *Journal of Personality and Social Psychology, 16*, 66–91.

Kelley, H. H., & Stahelski, A. J. (1970c). The inference of intentions from moves in the Prisoner's Dilemma Game. *Journal of Experimental Social Psychology*, *6*, 401–419.

Kelley, R. E. (1988). In praise of followers. *Harvard Business Review*. *66*(6), 142–148.

Kelley, R. E. (2004). Followership. In G. R. Goethals, G. J. Sorenson, & J. M. Burns (Eds.), *The encyclopedia of leadership* (pp. 504–513). Thousand Oaks CA: Sage.

Kelly, J. R. (2001). Mood and emotion in groups. In M. A. Hogg & R. S. Tindale (Eds.), *Blackwell handbook of social psychology: Group processes* (pp. 164–181). Malden, MA: Blackwell.

Kelly, J. R., Futoran, G. C., & McGrath, J. E. (1990). Capacity and capability: Seven studies of entrainment of task performance rates. *Small Group Research*, *21*, 283–314.

Kelly, J. R., & Karau, S. J. (1993). Entrainment of creativity in small groups. *Small Group Research*, *24*, 179–198.

Kelly, J. R., & Karau, S. J. (1999). Group decision making: The effects of initial preferences and time pressure. *Personality and Social Psychology Bulletin*, *25*, 1342–1354.

Kelly, J. R., & Loving, T. J. (2004). Time pressure and group performance: Exploring underlying processes in the attentional focus model. *Journal of Experimental Social Psychology*, *40*, 185–198.

Kelly, T. (2002, April 21). Reginald Rose, 81, TV writer noted for 'Twelve Angry Men'. *The New York Times*. Retrieved from www.nytimes.com

Kelman, H. C. (1958). Compliance, identification, and internalization: Three processes of attitude change. *Journal of Conflict Resolution*, *2*, 51–60.

Kelman, H. C. (1961). Processes of opinion change. *Public Opinion Quarterly*, *25*, 57–78.

Kelman, H. C. (1992). Informal mediation by the scholar/practitioner. In J. Bercovitch & J. Rubin (Eds.), *Mediation in international relations: Multiple approaches to conflict management* (pp. 64–96). New York: St. Martin's Press.

Kelman, H. C., & Hamilton, V. L. (1989). *Crimes of obedience: Toward a social psychology of authority and responsibility*. New Haven, CT: Yale University Press.

Kelman, H.C. (2006). Interests, relationships, identities: Three central issues for individuals and groups in negotiating their social environment. *Annual Review of Psychology*, *57*, 1–26.

Keltner, D., Gruenfeld, D. H., & Anderson, C. (2003). Power, approach, and inhibition. *Psychological Review*, *110*, 265–284.

Keltner, D., Gruenfeld, D., Galinsky, A., & Kraus, M. W. (2010). Paradoxes of power: Dynamics of the acquisition, experience, and social regulation of social power. In A. Guinote & T. K. Vescio (Eds.), *The social psychology of power* (pp. 177–208). New York: Guilford Press.

Keltner, D., Van Kleef, G. A., Chen, S., & Kraus, M. W. (2008). A reciprocal influence model of social power: Emerging principles and lines of inquiry. *Advances in Experimental Social Psychology*, *40*, 151–192.

Kennedy, D. P., Gläscher, J., Tyszka, J. M., & Adolphs, R. (2009). Personal space regulation by the human amygdala. *Nature Neuroscience*, *12*(10), 1226–1227.

Kennedy, F. A., Loughry, M. L., Klammer, T. P., & Beyerlein, M. M. (2009). Effects of organizational support on potency in work teams: The mediating role of team processes. *Small Group Research*, *40*(1), 72–93.

Kennedy, R. F. (1969). *Thirteen days*. New York: Norton.

Kenny, D. A., Kieffer, S. C., Smith, J. A., Ceplenski, P., & Kulo, J. (1996). Circumscribed accuracy among well-acquainted individuals. *Journal of Experimental Social Psychology*, *32*, 1–12.

Kenrick, D. T., Griskevicius, V., Neuberg, S. L., & Schaller, M. (2010). Renovating the pyramid of needs: Contemporary extensions built upon ancient foundations. *Perspectives on Psychological Science*, *5*(3), 292–314.

Kent, S. (1991). Partitioning space: Cross-cultural factors influencing domestic spatial segmentation. *Environment and Behavior*, *23*, 438–473.

Kenworthy, J. B., Popan, J. R., Moerhl, T. G., Holovics, M. A., Jones, J. R., & Diamon, S. (2008). *Antecedents, correlates, and consequences of social identity strength: A meta-analytic review.* Presented at the Annual Meeting of the Society of Personality and Social Psychology, Albuquerque, NM.

Kenworthy, J. B., Turner, R. N., Hewstone, M., & Voci, A. (2005). Intergroup contact: When does it work, and why? In J. F. Dovidio, P. Glick & L. A. Rudman (Eds.), *On the nature of prejudice: Fifty years after Allport* (pp. 278–292). Malden, MA: Blackwell.

Kerckhoff, A. C., & Back, K. W. (1968). *The June Bug: A study of hysterical contagion*. New York: Appleton-Century-Crofts.

Kerckhoff, A. C., Back, K. W., & Miller, N. (1965). Sociometric patterns in hysterical contagion. *Sociometry*, *28*, 2–15.

Kerr, N. L., Aronoff, J., & Messe, L. A. (2000). Methods of small group research. In H. T. Reis & C. M. Judd (Eds.), *Handbook of research methods in social and personality psychology* (pp. 160–189). New York: Cambridge University Press.

Kerr, N. L., Atkin, R. S., Stasser, G., Meek, D., Holt, R. W., & Davis, J. H. (1976). Guilt beyond a reasonable doubt: Effect of concept definition and assigned decision rule on the judgments of mock jurors. *Journal of Personality and Social Psychology*, *34*, 282–294.

Kerr, N. L., & Bruun, S. E. (1981). Ringelmann revisited: Alternative explanations for the social loafing effect. *Personality and Social Psychology Bulletin*, *7*, 224–231.

Kerr, N. L., & Bruun, S. E. (1983). Dispensability of member effort and group motivation losses: Free-rider effects. *Journal of Personality and Social Psychology*, *44*, 78–94.

Kerr, N. L., & Huang, J. Y. (1986). Jury verdicts: How much difference does one juror make? *Personality and Social Psychology Bulletin*, *12*, 325–343.

Kerr, N. L., & Levine, J. M. (2008). The detection of social exclusion: Evolution and beyond. *Group Dynamics: Theory, Research, and Practice*, *12*(1), 39–52.

Kerr, N. L., & MacCoun, R. J. (1985). The effects of jury size and polling method on the process and product of jury deliberation. *Journal of Personality and Social Psychology, 48,* 349–363.

Kerr, N. L., MacCoun, R. J., & Kramer, G. P. (1996a). Bias in judgment: Comparing individuals and groups. *Psychological Review, 103,* 687–719.

Kerr, N. L., MacCoun, R. J., & Kramer, G. P. (1996b). "When are *N* heads better (or worse) than one?" Biased judgment in individuals and groups. In E. H. Witte & J. H. Davis (Eds.), *Understanding group behavior: Consensual action by small groups* (Vol. 1, pp. 105–136). Mahwah, NJ: Erlbaum.

Kerr, N. L., Messé, L. A., Seok, D., Sambolec, E. J., Lount Jr., Robert B., & Park, E. S. (2007). Psychological mechanisms underlying the Köhler motivation gain. *Personality and Social Psychology Bulletin, 33,* 828–841.

Kerr, N. L., & Tindale, R. S. (2004). Group performance and decision making. *Annual Review of Psychology, 55,* 623–655.

Kerr, S., & Jermier, J. M. (1978). Substitutes for leadership: Their meaning and measurement. *Organizational Behavior and Human Performance, 22,* 375–403.

Kerr, S., Schriesheim, C. A., Murphy, C. J., & Stogdill, R. M. (1974). Toward a contingency theory of leadership based upon the consideration and initiating structure literature. *Organizational Behavior and Human Performance, 12,* 62–82.

Keshet, S., Kark, R., Pomerantz-Zorin, L., Koslowsky, M., & Schwarzwald, J. (2006). Gender, status and the use of power strategies. *European Journal of Social Psychology, 36,* 105–117.

Kessler, T., & Cohrs, J. C. (2008). The evolution of authoritarian processes: Fostering cooperation in large-scale groups. *Group Dynamics: Theory, Research, and Practice, 12*(1), 73–84.

Kessler, T., & Mummendey, A. (2001). Is there any scapegoat around? Determinants of intergroup conflicts at different categorization levels. *Journal of Personality and Social Psychology, 81,* 1090–1102.

Keyton, J. (2002). *Communicating in groups: Building relationships for effective decision making.* New York: McGraw-Hill.

Keyton, J., & Beck, S. J. (2008). Team components, processes, and values: A pedagogical matrix. *Business Communication Quarterly, 71,* 488–504.

Keyton, J., & Beck, S. J. (2010). Examining laughter functionality in jury deliberations. *Small Group Research, 41*(4), 386–407.

Khalil, A. (2011). *Liberation square: Inside the Egyptian revolution and the rebirth of a nation.* New York: St. Martin's Press.

Kiesler, C. A., Corbin, L. H. (1965). Commitment, attraction, and conformity. *Journal of Personality and Social Psychology, 2,* 890–895.

Kiesler, C. A., Zanna, M., & Desalvo, J. (1966). Deviation and conformity: Opinion change as a function of commitment, attraction, and presence of a deviate. *Journal of Personality and Social Psychology, 3,* 458–467.

Kiesler, D. J. (1991). Interpersonal methods of assessment and diagnosis. In C. R. Snyder & D. R. Forsyth (Eds.), *Handbook of social and clinical psychology: The health perspective* (pp. 438–468). Elmsford, NY: Pergamon Press.

Kilham, W., & Mann, L. (1974). Level of destructive obedience as a function of transmitter and executant roles in the Milgram obedience paradigm. *Journal of Personality and Social Psychology, 29,* 696–702.

Kilmartin, C. T. (1994). *The masculine self.* New York: Macmillan.

Kim, H., & Markus, H. R. (1999). Deviance or uniqueness, harmony or conformity? A cultural analysis. *Journal of Personality and Social Psychology, 77,* 785–800.

Kim, K., & Bonk, C. J. (2002). Cross-cultural comparisons of online collaboration. *Journal of Computer-Mediated Communication, 8*(1). Retrieved from jcmc.indiana.edu/vol8/issue1/kimandbonk.html

Kim, Y., Cohen, D., & Au, W. (2010). The jury and abjury of my peers: The self in face and dignity cultures. *Journal of Personality and Social Psychology, 98*(6), 904–916.

Kim, Y., Jung, J., Cohen, E. L., & Ball-Rokeach, S. J. (2004). Internet connectedness before and after September 11, 2001. *New Media & Society, 6,* 611–631.

King, A. J., & Cowlishaw, G. (2009). All together now: Behavioral synchrony in baboons. *Animal Behavior, 78*(6), 1381–1387.

King, G. A., & Sorrentino, R. M. (1983). Psychological dimensions of goal-oriented interpersonal situations. *Journal of Personality and Social Psychology, 44,* 140–162.

King, L. A. (2004). Measures and meaning: The use of qualitative data in social and personality psychology. In C. Sansone, C. C. Morf, & A. T. Panter (Eds.), *The Sage handbook of methods in social psychology* (pp. 173–194). Thousand Oaks, CA: Sage.

Kipnis, D. (1974). *The powerholders.* Chicago: University of Chicago Press.

Kipnis, D. (1984). The use of power in organizations and in interpersonal settings. *Applied Social Psychology Annual, 5,* 179–210.

Kipnis, D., Castell, P. J., Gergen, M., & Mauch, D. (1976). Metamorphic effects of power. *Journal of Applied Psychology, 61,* 127–135.

Kipnis, D., Schmidt, S. M., Swaffin-Smith, C., & Wilkinson, I. (1984). Patterns of managerial influence: Shotgun managers, tacticians, and bystanders. *Organizational Dynamics, 12,* 58–67.

Kipper, D. A., & Ritchie, T. D. (2003). The effectiveness of psychodramatic techniques: A meta-analysis. *Group Dynamics: Theory, Research, and Practice, 7,* 13–25.

Kirkpatrick, L. A., & Shaver, P. (1988). Fear and affiliation reconsidered from a stress and coping perspective: The importance of cognitive clarity and fear reduction. *Journal of Social & Clinical Psychology, 7,* 214–233.

Kishida, K. T., Yang, D., Quartz, K. H., Quartz, S. R., & Montague, P. R. (2012). Implicit signals in small group settings and their impact on the expression of cognitive capacity and associated brain responses. *Philosophical Transactions of the Royal Society B: Biological Sciences, 367*(1589), 704–716.

Kitayama, S. (2002). Culture and basic psychological theory—Toward a system view of culture: Comment on Oyserman et al. (2002). *Psychological Bulletin, 128,* 89–96.

Kitayama, S., Markus, H. R., & Kurokawa, M. (2000). Culture, emotion, and well-being: Good feelings in Japan and the United States. *Cognition and Emotion, 14*(1), 93–124.

Kivlighan, D. M., Jr. (1985). Feedback in group psychotherapy: Review and implications. *Small Group Behavior, 16*, 373–386.

Kivlighan, D. M., Jr. (1997). Leader behavior and therapeutic gain: An application of situational leadership theory. *Group Dynamics: Theory, Research, and Practice, 1*, 32–38.

Kivlighan, D. M., Jr., & Holmes, S. E. (2004). The importance of therapeutic factors: A typology of therapeutic factors studies. In J. L. Delucia-Waak, D. A. Gerrity, C. R. Kalodner, & M. T. Riva (Eds.), *Handbook of group counseling and psychotherapy* (pp. 23–48). Thousand Oaks, CA: Sage.

Kivlighan, D. M., Jr., McGovern, T. V., & Corazzini, J. G. (1984). Effects of content and timing of structuring interventions on group therapy process and outcome. *Journal of Counseling Psychology, 31*, 363–370.

Kivlighan, D. M., Jr., Miles, J. R., & Paquin, J. D. (2010). Therapeutic factors in group-counseling: Asking new questions. In R. K. Conyne (Ed.), *The Oxford handbook of group counseling* (pp. 121–136). New York: Oxford University Press.

Kivlighan, D. M., Jr., & Mullison, D. (1988). Participants' perception of therapeutic factors in group counseling: The role of interpersonal style and stage of group development. *Small Group Behavior, 19*, 452–468.

Klauer, K. C., Herfordt, J., & Voss, A. (2008). Social presence effects on the Stroop task: Boundary conditions and an alternative account. *Journal of Experimental Social Psychology, 44*, 469–476.

Klein, C., DiazGranados, D., Salas, E., Le, H., Burke, C. S., Lyons, R., & Goodwin, G. F. (2009). Does team building work? *Small Group Research, 40*(2), 181–222.

Klein, K. J., Knight, A. P., Ziegert, J. C., Lim, B. C., & Saltz, J. L. (2011). When team members' values differ: The moderating role of team leadership. *Organizational Behavior and Human Decision Processes, 114*, 25–36.

Klein, M. (1948). *Contributions to psychoanalysis, 1921–1945.* London: Hogarth Press.

Kleingeld, A., van Mierlo, H., & Arends, L. (2011). The effect of goal setting on group performance: A meta-analysis. *Journal of Applied Psychology, 96*, 1289–1304.

Klinenberg, E. (2002). *Heatwave: A social autopsy of disaster in Chicago.* Chicago: University of Chicago Press.

Klinenberg, E. (2012). *Going solo: The extraordinary rise and surprising appeal of living alone.* New York: Penguin.

Klocke, U. (2007). How to improve decision making in small groups: Effects of dissent and training interventions. *Small Group Research, 38*, 437–468.

Klocke, U. (2009). 'I am the best': Effects of influence tactics and power bases on powerholders' self-evaluation and target evaluation. *Group Processes & Intergroup Relations, 12*(5), 619–637.

Knight, G. P., & Dubro, A. F. (1984). Cooperative, competitive, and individualistic social values: An individualized regression and clustering approach. *Journal of Personality and Social Psychology, 46*, 98–105.

Knowles, E. S. (1973). Boundaries around group interaction: The effect of group size and member status on boundary permeability. *Journal of Personality and Social Psychology, 26*, 327–331.

Knowles, E. S., & Bassett, R. L. (1976). Groups and crowds as social entities: Effects of activity, size, and member similarity on nonmembers. *Journal of Personality and Social Psychology, 34*(5), 837–845.

Knowles, E. S., Condon, C. A. (1999). Why people say "yes": A dual-process theory of acquiescence. *Journal of Personality and Social Psychology, 77*, 379–386.

Knowles, E. S., Kreuser, B., Haas, S., Hyde, M., & Schuchart, G. E. (1976). Group size and the extension of social space boundaries. *Journal of Personality and Social Psychology, 33*, 647–654.

Koenig, A. M., Eagly, A. H., Mitchell, A. A., & Ristikari, T. (2011). Are leader stereotypes masculine? A meta-analysis of three research paradigms. *Psychological Bulletin, 137*(4), 616–642.

Köhler, O. (1926). Kraftleistungen bei Einzel- und Gruppenarbeit. *Industrielle Psychotechnik, 3*, 274–282.

Köhler, W. (1959). Gestalt psychology today. *American Psychologist, 14*, 727–734.

Kohut, H. (1984). *How does analysis cure?* A. Goldberg (Ed.), with Paul E. Stepansky. Chicago: University of Chicago Press.

Kojima, H. (1984). A significant stride toward the comparative study of control. *American Psychologist, 39*, 972–973.

Kolb, D. A. (1984). *Experiential learning: Experience as the source of learning and development.* Englewood Cliffs, NJ: Prentice Hall.

Kolb, D. M., & Williams, J. (2003). *Everyday negotiation: Navigating the hidden agendas in bargaining.* San Francisco: Jossey-Bass.

Komorita, S. S., Hilty, J. A., & Parks, C. D. (1991). Reciprocity and cooperation in social dilemmas. *Journal of Conflict Resolution, 35*, 494–518.

Komorita, S. S., & Parks, C. D. (1994). *Social dilemmas.* Dubuque, IA: Brown & Benchmark.

Komorita, S. S., Parks, C. D., & Hulbert, L. G. (1992). Reciprocity and the induction of cooperation in social dilemmas. *Journal of Personality and Social Psychology, 62*, 607–617.

Koocher, G. P. (1977). Bathroom behavior and human dignity. *Journal of Personality and Social Psychology, 35*(2), 120–121.

Kopp, W. (2003). *One day, all children … The unlikely triumph of Teach for America and what I learned along the way.* New York: Public Affairs.

Korda, M. (1975). *Power! How to get it, how to use it.* New York: Ballantine.

Koriat, A. (2012). The self-consistency model of subjective confidence. *Psychological Review, 119*(1), 80–113.

Kösters, M., Burlingame, G. M., Nachtigall, C., & Strauss, B. (2006). A meta-analytic review of the effectiveness of inpatient group psychotherapy. *Group Dynamics: Theory, Research, and Practice, 10*, 146–163.

Kotter, J. P. (1990). *A force for change: How leadership differs from management.* New York: Free Press.

Kounin, J. S. (1970). *Discipline and group management in classrooms*. New York: Holt, Rinehart & Winston.

Kounin, J. S., & Gump, P. V. (1958). The ripple effect in discipline. *Elementary School Journal, 59*, 158–160.

Kowalski, R. M. (1996). Complaints and complaining: Functions, antecedents, and consequences. *Psychological Bulletin, 119*, 179–196.

Kowert, P. A. (2002). *Groupthink or deadlock: When do leaders learn from their advisors?* Albany: State University of New York Press.

Kozlowski, S. W. J., Gully, S. M., Nason, E. R., & Smith, E. M. (1999). Developing adaptive teams: A theory of compilation and performance across levels and time. In D. R. Ilgen & E. D. Pulakos (Eds.), *The changing nature of work performance: Implications for staffing, personnel actions, and development* (pp. 240–292). San Francisco: Jossey-Bass.

Kozlowski, S. W. J., & Ilgen, D. R. (2006). Enhancing the effectiveness of work groups and teams. *Psychological Science in the Public Interest, 7*, 77–124.

Krackhardt, D. (1996). Social networks and the liability of newness for managers. In C. L. Cooper & D. M. Rousseau (Eds.), *Trends in organizational behavior* (Vol. 3, pp. 159–173). Hoboken, NJ: John Wiley.

Krackhardt, D., & Hanson, J. R. (1993). Informal networks: The company behind the chart. *Harvard Business Review, 71*(4), 104–111.

Krackhardt, D., & Porter, L. W. (1986). The snowball effect: Turnover embedded in communication networks. *Journal of Applied Psychology, 71*, 50–55.

Kraft, R. (2012, February 6). Robert Kraft press conference [video]. Retrieved from www.patriots.com/media-center/videos/

Krakauer, J. (1997). *Into thin air*. New York: Random House.

Kramer, R. M. (1998). Paranoid cognition in social systems: Thinking and acting in the shadow of doubt. *Personality and Social Psychology Review, 2*, 251–275.

Kramer, R. M. (1999). Trust and distrust in organizations: Emerging perspectives, enduring questions. *Annual Review of Psychology, 50*, 569–598.

Kramer, R. M. (2004). The "dark side" of social context: The role of intergroup paranoia in intergroup negotiations. In M. J. Gelfand, & J. M. Brett (Eds.), *The handbook of negotiation and culture* (pp. 219–237). Stanford, CA: Stanford University Press.

Kramer, R. M. (2006). The great intimidators. *Harvard Business Review, 84*, 88–96.

Kramer, R. M. (2008). Presidential leadership and group folly: Reappraising the role of groupthink in the Bay of Pigs decisions. In C. L. Hoyt, G. R. Goethals, & D. R. Forsyth (Eds.), *Leadership at the crossroads: Leadership and psychology* (Vol. 1, pp. 230–249). Westport, CT: Praeger.

Kramer, R. M. (2011). Cooperation and the commons: Laboratory and field investigations of a persistent dilemma. In R. M. Kramer, G. J. Leonardelli, & R. W. Livingston

(Eds.), *Social cognition, social identity, and intergroup relations: A Festschrift in honor of Marilynn B. Brewer* (pp. 297–317). New York: Psychology Press.

Kraus, L. A., Davis, M. H., Bazzini, D. G., Church, M., & Kirchman, C. M. (1993). Personal and social influences on loneliness: The mediating effect of social provisions. *Social Psychology Quarterly, 56*, 37–53.

Kraus, M. W., Chen, S., & Keltner, D. (2011). The power to be me: Power elevates self-concept consistency and authenticity. *Journal of Experimental Social Psychology, 47*(5), 974–980.

Krause, D. E., & Kearney, E. (2006). The use of power bases in different contexts: Arguments for a context-specific perspective. In C. A. Schriesheim & L. L. Neider (Eds.), *Power and influence in organizations: New empirical and theoretical perspectives* (pp. 59–86). Greenwich, CT: Information Age Publishing.

Krause, N., & Wulff, K. M. (2005). Church-based social ties, A sense of belonging in a congregation, and physical health status. *International Journal for the Psychology of Religion, 15*, 73–93.

Krause, S., James, R., Faria, J. J., Ruxton, G. D., & Krause, J. (2011). Swarm intelligence in humans: Diversity can trump ability. *Animal Behavior, 81*, 941–948.

Krauss, R. M., & Morsella, E. (2000). Communication and conflict. In M. Deutsch & P. T. Coleman (Eds.), *The handbook of conflict resolution: Theory and practice* (pp. 131–143). San Francisco: Jossey-Bass.

Kravitz, D. A., Cohen, J. L., Martin, B., Sweeney, J., McCarty, J., Elliott, E., & Goldstein, P. (1978). Humans would do better without other humans. *Personality and Social Psychology Bulletin, 4*, 559–560.

Kravitz, D. A., & Martin, B. (1986). Ringelmann rediscovered: The original article. *Journal of Personality and Social Psychology, 50*, 936–941.

Kreager, D. (2004). Strangers in the halls: Isolation and delinquency in school networks. *Social Forces, 83*, 351–390.

Kressel, K. (2000). Mediation. In M. Deutsch & P. T. Coleman (Eds.), *The handbook of conflict resolution: Theory and practice* (pp. 522–545). San Francisco: Jossey-Bass.

Kristof-Brown, A., Barrick, M. R., & Stevens, C. K. (2005). When opposites attract: A multi-sample demonstration of complementary person-team fit on extraversion. *Journal of Personality, 73*, 935–958.

Krueger, J., & Clement, R. W. (1997). Estimates of social consensus by majorities and minorities: The case for social projection. *Personality and Social Psychology Review, 1*, 299–312.

Kruglanski, A. W., Pierro, A., Mannetti, L., & De Grada, E. (2006). Groups as epistemic providers: Need for closure and the unfolding of group-centrism. *Psychological Review, 113*, 84–100.

Kruglanski, A. W., Shah, J. Y., Pierro, A., & Mannetti, L. (2002). When similarity breeds content: Need for closure and the allure of homogeneous and self-resembling groups. *Journal of Personality and Social Psychology, 83*, 648–662.

Kruglanski, A. W., & Webster, D. M. (1991). Group members' reactions to opinion deviates and conformists at varying degrees of proximity to decision deadline and of environmental noise. *Journal of Personality and Social Psychology, 61,* 212–225.

Kuchinke, K. P., Cornachione, E. B., Oh, S. Y., & Kang, H.-S. (2010). All work and no play? The meaning of work and work stress of mid-level managers in the United States, Brazil, and Korea. *Human Resource Development International, 13*(4), 393–408.

Kuhn, M. H., & McPartland, T. S. (1954). An empirical investigation of self-attitudes. *American Sociological Review, 19,* 68–76.

Kuhn, T. S. (1970). *The structure of scientific revolutions* (2nd ed., enlarged). Chicago: University of Chicago Press.

Kulik, J. A., & Mahler, H. I. M. (1989). Stress and affiliation in a hospital setting: Preoperative roommate preference. *Personality and Social Psychology Bulletin, 15,* 183–193.

Kulik, J. A., & Mahler, H. I. M. (2000). Social comparison, affiliation, and emotional contagion under threat. In J. Suls & L. Wheeler (Eds.), *Handbook of social comparison: Theory and research* (pp. 295–320). New York: Kluwer Academic.

Kulik, J. A., Mahler, H. I. M., & Moore, P. J. (1996). Social comparison and affiliation under threat: Effects on recovery from major surgery. *Journal of Personality and Social Psychology, 71,* 967–979.

Kurebayashi, K., Hoffman, L., Ryan, C. S., & Murayama, A. (2012). Japanese and American perceptions of group entitativity and autonomy: A multilevel analysis. *Journal of Cross-Cultural Psychology, 43,* 349–364.

Kurland, N. B., & Pelled, L. H. (2000). Passing the word: Toward a model of gossip and power in the workplace. *Academy of Management Review, 25,* 428–438.

Kurzban, R., & Leary, M. R. (2001). Evolutionary origins of stigmatization: The functions of social exclusion. *Psychological Bulletin, 127*(2), 187–208.

Kushnir, T. (1984). Social psychological factors associated with the dissolution of dyadic business partnerships. *Journal of Social Psychology, 122,* 181–188.

Kuypers, B. C., Davies, D., & Glaser, K. H. (1986). Developmental arrestations in self-analytic groups. *Small Group Behavior, 17,* 269–302.

LaBarge, E., Von Dras, D., & Wingbermuehle, C. (1998). An analysis of themes and feelings from a support group for people with Alzheimer's disease. *Psychotherapy: Theory, Research, Practice, Training, 35,* 537–544.

LaBrie, J. W., Hummer, J. F., Neighbors, C., & Larimer, M. E. (2010). Whose opinion matters? The relationship between injunctive norms and alcohol consequences in college students. *Addictive Behaviors, 35*(4), 343–349.

Lacoursiere, R. B. (1980). *The life cycle of groups.* New York: Human Sciences Press.

Ladbury, J. L., & Hinsz, V. B. (2009). Individual expectations for group decision processes: Evidence for overestimation of majority influence. *Group Dynamics: Theory, Research, and Practice, 13*(4), 235–254.

Laing, R. D. (1960). *The divided self.* London: Tavistock.

Lakens, D. (2010). Movement synchrony and perceived entitativity. *Journal of Experimental Social Psychology, 46,* 701–708.

Lakin, J. L., Chartrand, T. L., & Arkin, R. M. (2008). I am too just like you: Nonconscious mimicry as an automatic behavioral response to social exclusion. *Psychological Science, 19*(8), 816–822.

Lakin, M. (1972). *Experiential groups: The uses of interpersonal encounter, psychotherapy groups, and sensitivity training.* Morristown, NJ: General Learning Press.

Lal Goel, M. (1980). Conventional political participation. In D. H. Smith, J. Macaulay, & Associates (Eds.), *Participation in social and political activities: A comprehensive analysis of political involvement, expressive leisure time, and helping behavior* (pp. 108–132). San Francisco: Jossey-Bass.

Lalonde, R. N. (1992). The dynamics of group differentiation in the face of defeat. *Personality and Social Psychology Bulletin, 18,* 336–342.

Lam, S. K., & Schaubroeck, J. (2000). Improving group decisions by better pooling information: A comparative advantage of group decision support systems. *Journal of Applied Psychology, 85,* 565–573.

Lambert, A. J., Cronen, S., Chasteen, A. L., & Lickel, B. (1996). Private vs. public expressions of racial prejudice. *Journal of Experimental Social Psychology, 32,* 437–459.

Lambert, A. J., Payne, B. K., Jacoby, L. L., Shaffer, L. M., Chasteen, A. L., & Khan, S. R. (2003). Stereotypes as dominant responses: On the "social facilitation" of prejudice in anticipated public contexts. *Journal of Personality and Social Psychology, 84,* 277–295.

Lamm, H., & Myers, D. G. (1978). Group-induced polarization of attitudes and behavior. *Advances in Experimental Social Psychology, 11,* 145–195.

Lammers, J., Galinsky, A. D., Gordijn, E. H., & Otten, S. (2008). Illegitimacy moderates the effects of power on approach. *Psychological Science, 19,* 558–564.

Landau, J. (1995). The relationship of race and gender to managers' ratings of promotion potential. *Journal of Organizational Behavior, 16,* 391–401.

Landau, M. J., Johns, M., Greenberg, J., Pyszczynski, T., Martens, A., Goldenberg, J. L., & Solomon, S. (2004). A function of form: Terror management and structuring the social world. *Journal of Personality and Social Psychology, 87,* 190–210.

Lang, K., & Lang, G. E. (1961). *Collective dynamics.* New York: Crowell.

Langer, E. J. (1989). Minding matters: The consequences of mindlessness-mindfulness. *Advances in Experimental Social Psychology, 22,* 137–173.

Langer, E. J., Blank, A., & Chanowitz, B. (1978). The mindlessness of ostensibly thoughtful action: The role of "placebic" information in interpersonal interaction. *Journal of Personality and Social Psychology, 36*(6), 635–642.

Langfred, C. W. (1998). Is group cohesiveness a double-edged sword? An investigation of the effects of cohesiveness on performance. *Small Group Research, 29,* 124–143.

Langner, C. A., & Keltner, D. (2008). Social power and emotional experience: Actor and partner effects within dyadic interactions. *Journal of Experimental Social Psychology, 44*, 848–856.

Lanzetta, J. T., & Roby, T. B. (1960). The relationship between certain group process variables and group problem-solving efficiency. *Journal of Social Psychology, 52*, 135–148.

LaPiere, R. (1938). *Collective behavior.* New York: McGraw-Hill.

Lara Logan breaks silence (2011, April 28). *CBS Interactive.* Retrieved from www.cbsnews.com/2100-18560_162-20058368.html

Larsen, K. S. (1982). Cultural conditions and conformity: The Asch effect. *Bulletin of the British Psychological Society, 35*, 347.

Larson, J. R., Jr. (2010). *In search of synergy in small group performance.* New York: Psychology Press.

Larson, J. R., Jr., Christensen, C., & Abbott, A. S., & Franz, T. M. (1996). Diagnosing groups: Charting the flow of information in medical decision-making teams. *Journal of Personality and Social Psychology, 71*, 315–330.

Latané, B. (1981). The psychology of social impact. *American Psychologist, 36*, 343–356.

Latané, B. (1996). Strength from weakness: The fate of opinion minorities in spatially distributed groups. In E. Witte & J. Davis (Eds.), *Understanding group behavior: Consensual action by small groups* (Vol. 1, pp. 193–219). Mahwah, NJ: Erlbaum.

Latané, B. (1997). Dynamic social impact: The societal consequences of human interaction. In C. McGarty & S. A. Haslam (Eds.), *The message of social psychology: Perspectives on mind and society* (pp. 200–220). Malden, MA: Blackwell.

Latané, B., & Bourgeois, M. J. (1996). Experimental evidence for dynamic social impact: The emergence of subcultures in electronic groups. *Journal of Communication, 46*, 35–47.

Latané, B., & Bourgeois, M. J. (2001). Dynamic social impact and the consolidation, clustering, correlation, and continuing diversity of culture. In M. A. Hogg & R. S. Tindale (Eds.), *Blackwell handbook of social psychology: Group processes* (pp. 235–258). Malden, MA: Blackwell.

Latané, B., & Darley, J. M. (1970). *The unresponsive bystander: Why doesn't he help?* New York: Appleton-Century-Crofts.

Latané, B., & Nida, S. A. (1981). Ten years of research on group size and helping. *Psychological Bulletin, 89*, 308–324.

Latané, B., Williams, K., & Harkins, S. (1979). Many hands make light the work: The causes and consequences of social loafing. *Journal of Personality and Social Psychology, 37*, 822–832.

Latané, B., & Wolf, S. (1981). The social impact of majorities and minorities. *Psychological Review, 88*, 438–453.

Latham, G. P., & Baldes, J. J. (1975). The "practical significance" of Locke's theory of goal settings. *Journal of Applied Psychology, 60*, 122–124.

Latham, G. P., & Locke, E. A. (2007). New developments in and directions for goal-setting research. *European Psychologist, 12*, 290–300.

LaTour, S. (1978). Determinants of participant and observer satisfaction with adversary and inquisitorial modes of adjudication. *Journal of Personality and Social Psychology, 36*, 1531–1545.

LaTour, S., Houlden, P., Walker, L., & Thibaut, J. (1976). Some determinants of preference for modes of conflict resolution. *Journal of Conflict Resolution, 20*, 319–356.

Lau, D. C., & Murnighan, J. K. (1998). Demographic diversity and faultlines: The compositional dynamics of organizational groups. *Academy of Management Review, 23*, 325–340.

Laughlin, P. R. (1980). Social combination processes of cooperative problem solving groups on verbal intellective tasks. In M. Fishbein (Ed.), *Progress in social psychology* (pp. 127–155). Mahwah, NJ: Erlbaum.

Laughlin, P. R., Bonner, B. L., & Miner, A. G. (2002). Groups perform better than the best individuals on letters-to-numbers problems. *Organizational Behavior and Human Decision Processes, 88*, 605–620.

Laughlin, P. R., & Hollingshead, A. B. (1995). A theory of collective induction. *Organizational Behavior and Human Decision Processes, 61*, 94–107.

Laughlin, P. R., Zander, M. L., Knievel, E. M., & Tan, T. K. (2003). Groups perform better than the best individuals on letters-to-numbers problems: Informative equations and effective strategies. *Journal of Personality and Social Psychology, 85*, 684–694.

Lawler, E. E. and Mohrman, S. A. (1985). Quality circles after the fad. *Harvard Business Review, 85*, 64–71.

Lawler, E. J., Ford, R. S., & Blegen, M. A. (1988). Coercive capability in conflict: A test of bilateral deterrence versus conflict spiral theory. *Social Psychology Quarterly, 51*, 93–107.

Lawler, E. J., & Thompson, M. E. (1978). Impact of a leader's responsibility for inequity on subordinate revolts. *Social Psychology Quarterly, 41*, 264–268.

Lawler, E. J., & Thompson, M. E. (1979). Subordinate response to a leader's cooptation strategy as a function of type of coalition power. *Representative Research in Social Psychology, 9*, 69–80.

Lawler, E. J., Thye, S. R., & Yoon, J. (2000). Emotion and group cohesion in productive exchange. *American Journal of Sociology, 106*(3), 616–657.

Lawler, E. J., Thye, S. R., & Yoon, J. (2008). Social exchange and micro social order. *American Sociological Review, 73*(4), 519–542.

Lawler, E. J., & Yoon, J. (1996). Commitment in exchange relations: Test of a theory of relational cohesion. *American Sociological Review, 61*, 89–108.

Layne, C. M., Pynoos, R. S., Saltzman, W. R., Arslanagić, B., Black, M., Savjak, N., Popović, T., Duraković, E., Mušić, M., Ćampara, N., Djapo, N., & Houston, R. (2001). Trauma/grief-focused group psychotherapy: School-based postwar intervention with traumatized Bosnian adolescents. *Group Dynamics: Theory, Research, and Practice, 5*, 277–290.

Lazarsfeld, P. F., & Merton, R. K. (1954). Friendship as a social process: A substantive and methodological analysis. In M. Berger, T. Abel & C. H. Page (Eds.), *Freedom and control in modern society* (pp. 18–66). New York: Van Nostrand.

Lazonder, A. W. (2005). Do two heads search better than one? Effects of student collaboration on web search behavior and search outcomes. *British Journal of Educational Technology*, *36*, 465–475.

Le Bon, G. (1960). *The crowd: A study of the popular mind [La psychologie des foules]*. New York: Viking Press. (original work published in 1895)

Leach, C. W., Mosquera, P. M. R., Vliek, M. L. W., & Hirt, E. (2010). Group devaluation and group identification. *Journal of Social Issues*, *66*, 535–552.

Leach, C. W., Spears, R., Branscombe, N. R., & Doosje, B. (2003). Malicious pleasure: Schadenfreude at the suffering of another group. *Journal of Personality and Social Psychology*, *84*, 932–943.

Leach, C. W., van Zomeren, M., Zebel, S., Vliek, M. L. W., Pennekamp, S. F., Doosje, B., Ouwerkerk, J. W., & Spears, R. (2008). Group-level self-definition and self-investment: A hierarchical (multicomponent) model of in-group identification. *Journal of Personality and Social Psychology*, *95*, 144–165.

Leach, L. S., Myrtle, R. C., Weaver, F. A., & Dasu, S. (2009). Assessing the performance of surgical teams. *Health Care Management Review*, *34*(1), 29–41.

Leaper, C., & Ayres, M. M. (2007). A meta-analytic review of gender variations in adults' language use: Talkativeness, affiliative speech, and assertive speech. *Personality and Social Psychology Review*, *11*, 328–363.

Leary, M. R. (1983). *Understanding social anxiety*. Thousand Oaks, CA: Sage.

Leary, M. R. (1990). Responses to social exclusion: Social anxiety, jealousy, loneliness, depression, and low self-esteem. *Journal of Social & Clinical Psychology*, *9*, 221–229.

Leary, M. R. (2007). Motivational and emotional aspects of the self. *Annual Review of Psychology*, *58*, 317–344.

Leary, M. R. (2012). Sociometer theory. In P. A. M. Van Lange, A. W. Kruglanski, & E. T. Higgins (Eds.), *Handbook of theories of social psychology* (Vol. 2, pp. 151–159). Thousand Oaks, CA: Sage.

Leary, M. R. & Baumeister, R. F. (2000). The nature and function of self-esteem: Sociometer theory. *Advances in Experimental Social Psychology*, *32*, 1–62.

Leary, M. R., & Forsyth, D. R. (1987). Attributions of responsibility for collective endeavors. *Review of Personality and Social Psychology*, *8*, 167–188.

Leary, M. R., & Kowalski, R. M. (1995). *Social anxiety*. New York: Guilford.

Leary, M. R., Kowalski, R. M., Smith, L., & Phillips, S. (2003). Teasing, rejection, and violence: Case studies of the school shootings. *Aggressive Behavior*, *29*, 202–214.

Leary, M. R., Rogers, P. A., Canfield, R. W., & Coe, C. (1986). Boredom in interpersonal encounters: Antecedents and social implications. *Journal of Personality and Social Psychology*, *51*, 968–975.

Leary, M. R., Tambor, E. S., Terdal, S. K., & Downs, D. L. (1995). Self-esteem as an interpersonal monitor: The sociometer hypothesis. *Journal of Personality and Social Psychology*, *68*, 518–530.

Leather, P., Beale, D., & Sullivan, L. (2003). Noise, psychosocial stress and their interaction in the workplace. *Journal of Environmental Psychology*, *23*, 213–222.

Leavitt, H. J. (1951). Some effects of certain communication patterns on group performance. *Journal of Abnormal and Social Psychology*, *46*, 38–50.

Lee, I.-C., Pratto, F., & Johnson, B. T. (2011). Intergroup consensus/disagreement in support of group-based hierarchy: An examination of socio-structural and psycho-cultural factors. *Psychological Bulletin*, *137*(6), 1029–1064.

Lee, P. W. H., Leung, P. W. L., Fung, A. S. M., & Low, L. C. K. (1996). An episode of syncope attacks in adolescent schoolgirls: Investigations, intervention and outcome. *British Journal of Medical Psychology*, *69*, 247–257.

Lee, R. M., Dean, B. L., & Jung, K. (2008). Social connectedness, extraversion, and subjective well-being: Testing a mediation model. *Personality and Individual Differences*, *45*, 414–419.

Lee-Kelley, L., & Sankey, T. (2008). Global virtual teams for value creation and project success: A case study. *International Journal of Project Management*, *26*(1), 51–62.

Lemos, A. (2010). Post–mass media functions, locative media, and informational territories: New ways of thinking about territory, place, and mobility in contemporary society. *Space and Culture*, *12*, 403–420.

Leon, G. R. (1991). Individual and group process characteristics of polar expedition teams. *Environment and Behavior*, *23*, 723–748.

Leonard, W. M., II. (1980). *A sociological perspective on sport*. Minneapolis: Burgess.

LePine, J. A. (2003). Team adaptation and postchange performance: Effects of team composition in terms of members' cognitive ability and personality. *Journal of Applied Psychology*, *88*, 27–39.

LePine, J. A., Piccolo, R. F., Jackson, C. L., Mathieu, J. E., & Saul, J. R. (2008). A meta-analysis of teamwork processes: Tests of a multidimensional model and relationships with team effectiveness criteria. *Personnel Psychology*, *61*, 273–307.

Leung, A. K., & Cohen, D. (2011). Within- and between-culture variation: Individual differences and the cultural logics of honor, face, and dignity cultures. *Journal of Personality and Social Psychology*, *100*(3), 507–526.

Leung, A. S. M. (2008). Matching ethical work climate to in-role and extra-role behaviors in a collectivist work setting. *Journal of Business Ethics*, *79*, 43–55.

Leung, K. (1988). Some determinants of conflict avoidance. *Journal of Cross-Cultural Psychology*, *19*(1), 125–136.

Leung, K. (1997). Negotiation and reward allocations across cultures. In P. C. Earley & M. Erez (Eds.), *New perspectives on international industrial/organizational psychology* (pp. 640–675). San Francisco: The New Lexington Press/Jossey-Bass.

Levesque, M. J. (1997). Meta-accuracy among acquainted individuals: A social relations analysis of interpersonal perception and metaperception. *Journal of Personality and Social Psychology*, *72*, 66–74.

Levett, L. M., Danielsen, E. M., Kovera, M. B., & Cutler, B. L. (2005). The psychology of jury and juror decision making. In N. Brewer & K. D. Williams (Eds.), *Psychology and law: An empirical perspective* (pp. 365–406). New York: Guilford Press.

Levin, H. M. (2006). Worker democracy and worker productivity. *Social Justice Research, 19*, 109–121.

Levine, J. M. (1980). Reaction to opinion deviance in small groups. In P. B. Paulus (Ed.), *Psychology of group influence* (pp. 375–429). Mahwah, NJ: Erlbaum.

Levine, J. M., & Hogg, M. A. (Eds.). (2010). *Encyclopedia of group processes and intergroup relations.* Thousand Oaks, CA: Sage.

Levine, J. M., & Kerr, N. L. (2007). Inclusion and exclusion: Implications for group processes. In A. W. Kruglanski & E. T. Higgins (Eds.), *Social psychology: Handbook of basic principles* (2nd ed., pp. 759–784). New York: Guildford.

Levine, J. M., & Moreland, R. L. (2012). A history of small group research. In A. W. Kruglanski & W. Stroebe (Eds.), *Handbook of the history of social psychology* (pp. 383–405). New York: Psychology Press.

Levine, J. M., Moreland, R. L., & Choi, H. (2001). Group socialization and newcomer innovation. In M. A. Hogg & R. S. Tindale (Eds.), *Blackwell handbook of social psychology: Group processes* (pp. 86–106). Malden, MA: Blackwell.

Levine, J. M., & Russo, E. M. (1987). Majority and minority influence. *Review of Personality and Social Psychology, 8*, 13–54.

Levine, M., Cassidy, C., & Jentzsch, I. (2010). The implicit identity effect: Identity primes, group size, and helping. *British Journal of Social Psychology, 49*(4), 785–802.

Levine, M., & Crowther, S. (2008). The responsive bystander: How social group membership and group size can encourage as well as inhibit bystander intervention. *Journal of Personality and Social Psychology, 95*(6), 1429–1439.

Levine, M., Prosser, A., Evans, D., & Reicher, S. (2005). Identity and emergency intervention: How social group membership and inclusiveness of group boundaries shapes helping behavior. *Personality and Social Psychology Bulletin, 31*, 443–453.

Levine, R. V., Norenzayan, A., & Philbrick, K. (2001). Cross-cultural differences in helping strangers. *Journal of Cross-Cultural Psychology, 32*(5), 543–560.

Levy, L. H. (2000). Self-help groups. In J. Rappaport & E. Seidman (Eds.), *Handbook of community psychology* (pp. 591–613). Dordrecht, Netherlands: Kluwer Academic.

Lewicki, R. J., Saunders, D. M., & Barry, B. (2010). *Negotiation* (6th ed.). New York: McGraw-Hill/Irwin.

Lewin, K. (1943). Psychology and the process of group living. *Journal of Social Psychology* (*S.P.S.S.I Bulletin*), *17*, 113–131.

Lewin, K. (1948). *Resolving social conflicts: Selected papers on group dynamics.* New York: Harper.

Lewin, K. (1951). *Field theory in social science.* New York: Harper.

Lewin, K., Lippitt, R., & White, R. (1939). Patterns of aggressive behavior in experimentally created "social climates." *Journal of Social Psychology, 10*, 271–299.

Lewis, S., Ellis, J. B., & Kellogg, W. A. (2010). Using virtual interactions to explore leadership and collaboration in globally distributed teams. *Proceedings of the 3rd International Conference on Intercultural Collaboration, ICIC 2010* (pp. 9–18). New York: ACM.

Ley, D., & Cybriwsky, R. (1974). Urban graffiti as territorial markers. *Annals of the Association of American Geographers, 64*, 491–505.

Leyens, J.-P., Cortes, B., Demoulin, S., Dovidio, J. F., Fiske, S. T., Gaunt, R., Paladino, M., Rodriguez-Perez, A., Rodriguez-Torres, R., & Vaes, J. (2003). Emotional prejudice, essentialism, and nationalism: The 2002 Tajfel Lecture. *European Journal of Social Psychology, 33*, 703–717.

Li, N. P., Halterman, R. A., Cason, M. J., Knight, G. P., & Maner, J. K. (2008). The stress-affiliation paradigm revisited: Do people prefer the kindness of strangers or their attractiveness? *Personality and Individual Differences, 44*(2), 382–391.

Lickel, B., Hamilton, D. L., & Sherman, S. J. (2001). Elements of a lay theory of groups: Types of groups, relationship styles, and the perception of group entitativity. *Personality and Social Psychology Review, 5*, 129–140.

Lickel, B., Hamilton, D. L., Wieczorkowska, G., Lewis, A., Sherman, S. J., & Uhles, A. N. (2000). Varieties of groups and the perception of group entitativity. *Journal of Personality and Social Psychology, 78*, 223–246.

Liden, R. C., Erdogan, B., Wayne, S. J., & Sparrowe, R. T. (2006). Leader–member exchange, differentiation, and task interdependence: Implications for individual and group performance. *Journal of Organizational Behavior, 21*, 723–746.

Liden, R. C., Wayne, S. J., Jaworski, R. A., & Bennett, N. (2004). Social loafing: A field investigation. *Journal of Management, 30*, 285–304.

Lieberman, M. A. (1993). Self-help groups. In H. I. Kaplan & M. J. Sadock (Eds.), *Comprehensive group psychotherapy* (3rd ed., pp. 292–304). Baltimore: Williams & Wilkins.

Lieberman, M. A. (1994). Growth groups in the 1980s: Mental health implications. In A. Fuhriman & G. M. Burlingame (Eds.), *Handbook of group psychotherapy* (pp. 527–558). New York: Wiley.

Lieberman, M. A., & Golant, M. (2002). Leader behaviors as perceived by cancer patients in professionally directed support groups and outcomes. *Group Dynamics: Theory, Research, and Practice, 6*, 267–276.

Lieberman, M. A., Yalom, I., & Miles, M. (1973). *Encounter groups: First facts.* New York: Basic Books.

Likert, R. (1967). *The human organization.* New York: McGraw-Hill.

Lindblom, C. E. (1965). *The intelligence of democracy.* New York: Free Press.

Lindeman, M. (1997). Ingroup bias, self-enhancement and group identification. *European Journal of Social Psychology, 27*, 337–355.

Lindskold, S. (1978). Trust development, the GRIT proposal, and the effects of conciliatory acts on conflict and cooperation. *Psychological Bulletin, 85*, 772–793.

Lindskold, S., Albert, K. P., Baer, R., & Moore, W. C. (1976). Territorial boundaries of interacting groups and passive audiences. *Sociometry, 39,* 71–76.

Linville, P. W., & Fischer, G. W. (1998). Group variability and covariation: Effects on intergroup judgment and behavior. In C. Sedikides, J. Schopler, & C. A. Insko (Eds.), *Intergroup cognition and intergroup behavior* (pp. 123–150). Mahwah, NJ: Erlbaum.

Linzmayer, O. W. (2004). *Apple confidential 2.0: The definitive history of the world's most colorful company.* New York: No Starch Press.

Lippitt, R., & White, R. K. (1943). The "social climate" of children's groups. In R. G. Barker, J. S. Kounin, & M. F. Wright (Eds.), *Child behavior and development: A course of representative studies* (pp. 485–508). New York: McGraw-Hill.

Lippmann, W. (1922). *Public opinion.* New York: Harcourt & Brace.

Lipset, S. M., & Wolin, S. S. (1965). *The Berkeley student revolt.* Garden City, NY: Anchor.

Lipton, J. (1991). *An exaltation of larks.* New York: Penguin.

Lischetzke, T., & Eid, M. (2006). Why extraverts are happier than introverts: The role of mood regulation. *Journal of Personality, 74,* 1127–1162.

List, J. A. (2006). Friend or foe? A natural experiment of the prisoner's dilemma. *Review of Economics and Statistics, 88,* 463–471.

Littlepage, G. E. (1991). Effects of group size and task characteristics on group performance: A test of Steiner's model. *Personality and Social Psychology Bulletin, 17,* 449–456.

Littlepage, G. E., Hollingshead, A. B., Drake, L. R., & Littlepage, A. M. (2008). Transactive memory and performance in work groups: Specificity, communication, ability differences, and work allocation. *Group Dynamics: Theory, Research, and Practice, 12,* 223–241.

Littlepage, G. E., & Mueller, A. L. (1997). Recognition and utilization of expertise in problem-solving groups: Expert characteristics and behavior. *Group Dynamics: Theory, Research, and Practice, 1,* 324–328.

Littlepage, G. E., Robison, W., & Reddington, K. (1997). Effects of task experience and group experience on group performance, member ability, and recognition of expertise. *Organizational Behavior and Human Decision Processes, 69,* 133–147.

Littlepage, G. E., Schmidt, G. W., Whisler, E. W., & Frost, A. G. (1995). An input-process-output analysis of influence and performance in problem-solving groups. *Journal of Personality and Social Psychology, 69,* 877–889.

Littlepage, G. E., & Silbiger, H. (1992). Recognition of expertise in decision-making groups: Effects of group size and participation patterns. *Small Group Research, 23,* 344–355.

Littlewood, W. (2001). Students' attitudes to classroom English learning: A cross-cultural study. *Language Teaching Research, 5*(1), 3–28.

Liu, J. H., & Latané, B. (1998). Extremitization of attitudes: Does thought- and discussion-induced polarization cumulate? *Basic and Applied Social Psychology, 20,* 103–110.

Locke, E. A., Tirnauer, D., Roberson, Q., Goldman, B., Latham, M. E., & Weldon, E. (2001). The importance of the individual in an age of groupism. In M. E. Turner (Ed.), *Groups at work: Theory and research* (pp. 501–528). Mahwah, NJ: Erlbaum.

Lodewijkx, H. F. M., & Syroit, J. E. M. M. (1997). Severity of initiation revisited: Does severity of initiation increase attractiveness in real groups? *European Journal of Social Psychology, 27,* 275–300.

Lodewijkx, H. F. M., van Zomeren, M., & Syroit, J. E. M. M. (2005). The anticipation of a severe initiation: Gender differences in effects on affiliation tendency and group attraction. *Small Group Research, 36*(2), 237–262.

Lofland, J. (1981). Collective behavior: The elementary forms. In M. Rosenberg & R. H. Turner (Eds.), *Social psychology* (pp. 411–446). New York: Basic Books.

Lois, J. (1999). Socialization to heroism: Individualism and collectivism in a voluntary search and rescue group. *Social Psychology Quarterly, 62,* 117–135.

Lois, J. (2003). *Heroic efforts: The emotional culture of search and rescue volunteers.* New York: New York University Press.

Long, C. R., Seburn, M., Averill, J. R., & More, T. A. (2003). Solitude experiences: Varieties, settings, and individual differences. *Personality and Social Psychology Bulletin, 29,* 578–583.

Longley, J., & Pruitt, D. G. (1980). Groupthink: A critique of Janis's theory. In L. Wheeler (Ed.), *Review of personality and social psychology* (Vol. 1). Thousand Oaks, CA: Sage.

Lopes, P. N., & Salovey, P. (2008). Emotional intelligence and leadership: Implications for leader development. In C. L. Hoyt, G. R. Goethals, & D. R. Forsyth (Eds.), *Leadership at the crossroads: Leadership and psychology* (Vol. 1, pp. 78–98). Westport, CT: Praeger.

Lord, R. G. (1977). Functional leadership behavior: Measurement and relation to social power and leadership perceptions. *Administrative Science Quarterly, 22,* 114–133.

Lord, R. G. (2005). Preface: Implicit leadership theory. In B. Schyns & J. R. Meindl (Eds.), *Implicit leadership theories: Essays and explorations* (pp. ix–xiv). Charlotte, NC: Information Age.

Lord, R. G., De Vader, C. L., & Alliger, G. M. (1986). A meta-analysis of the relation between personality traits and leadership perceptions: An application of validity generalization procedures. *Journal of Applied Psychology, 71,* 402–410.

Lord, R. G., Foti, R. J., & De Vader, C. L. (1984). A test of leadership categorization theory: Internal structure, information processing, and leadership perceptions. *Organization Behavior and Human Performance, 34,* 343–378.

Lord, R. G., & Maher, K. J. (1991). *Leadership and information processing: Linking perceptions and performance.* Boston: Unwin Hyman.

Lott, A. J., & Lott, B. E. (1961). Group cohesiveness, communication level, and conformity. *Journal of Abnormal and Social Psychology, 62*(2), 408–412.

Lott, A. J., & Lott, B. E. (1965). Group cohesiveness as interpersonal attraction: A review of relationships with antecedent and consequent variables. *Psychological Bulletin, 64*, 259–309.

Lovaglia, M. J., & Houser, J. A. (1996). Emotional reactions and status in groups. *American Sociological Review, 61*, 867–883.

Lovell, J., & Kluger, J. (1994). *Lost moon: The perilous journey of Apollo 13.* New York: Houghton Mifflin.

Lu, L., Yuan, Y. C., & McLeod, P. L. (2012). Twenty-five years of hidden profiles in group decision making: A meta-analysis. *Personality and Social Psychology Review, 16*(1), 54–75.

Lucas, R. E. (2008). Personality and subjective well-being. In M. Eid & R. J. Larsen (Eds.), *The science of subjective well-being* (pp. 171–194). New York: Guilford.

Lucas, R. E., & Diener, E. (2001). Understanding extraverts' enjoyment of social situations: The importance of pleasantness. *Journal of Personality and Social Psychology, 81*, 343–356.

Lucas, R. E., Diener, E., Grob, A., Suh, E. M., & Shao, L. (2000). Cross-cultural evidence for the fundamental features of extraversion. *Journal of Personality and Social Psychology, 79*, 452–468.

Luce, R. D., & Raiffa, H. (1957). *Games and decisions.* New York: Wiley.

Ludwig, D. C., & Longenecker, C. O. (1993). The Bathsheba Syndrome: The ethical failure of successful leaders. *Journal of Business Ethics, 12*, 265–273.

Luft, J. (1984). *Groups process: An introduction to group dynamics* (3rd ed.). Palo Alto, CA: Mayfield.

Luhtanen, R., & Crocker, J. (1992). A collective self-esteem scale: Self-evaluation of one's social identity. *Personality and Social Psychology Bulletin, 18*, 302–318.

Lun, J., Sinclair, S., Whitchurch, E. R., & Glenn, C. (2007). (Why) do I think what you think? Epistemic social tuning and implicit prejudice. *Journal of Personality and Social Psychology, 93*(6), 957–972.

Luong, A., & Rogelberg, S. G. (2005). Meetings and more meetings: The relationship between meeting load and the daily well-being of employees. *Group Dynamics: Theory, Research, and Practice, 9*, 58–67.

Lutsky, N. (1995). When is "obedience" obedience? Conceptual and historical commentary. *Journal of Social Issues, 51*, 55–65.

Lyman, S. M., & Scott, M. B. (1967). Territoriality: A neglected sociological dimension. *Social Problems, 15*, 236–249.

Maass, A. (1999). Linguistic intergroup bias: Stereotype perpetuation through language. *Advances In Experimental Social Psychology, 31*, 79–121.

Maass, A., West, S. G., & Cialdini, R. B. (1987). Minority influence and conversion. *Review of Personality and Social Psychology, 8*, 55–79.

Maassen, G. H., Akkermans, W., & van der Linden, J. L. (1996). Two-dimensional sociometric status determination with rating scales. *Small Group Research, 27*, 56–78.

Maccoby, E. E. (2002). Gender and group process: A developmental perspective. *Current Directions in Psychological Science, 11*, 54–58.

MacCoun, R. J. (2012). The burden of social proof: Shared thresholds and social influence. *Psychological Review, 119*(2), 345–372.

MacCoun, R. J., Kier, E., & Belkin, A. (2005). Does social cohesion determine motivation in combat? *Armed Forces & Society, 32*, 1–9.

MacCracken, M. J., & Stadulis, R. E. (1985). Social facilitation of young children's dynamic balance performance. *Journal of Sport Psychology, 7*, 150–165.

MacDonald, G., & Leary, M. R. (2005). Why does social exclusion hurt? The relationship between social and physical pain. *Psychological Bulletin, 131*, 202–223.

MacIver, R. M., & Page, C. H. (1937). *Society: An introductory analysis.* New York: Rinehart.

MacKenzie, K. R. (1994). Group development. In A. Fuhriman & G. M. Burlingame (Eds.), *Handbook of group psychotherapy* (pp. 223–268). New York: Wiley.

MacKenzie, K. R. (1997). Clinical application of group development ideas. *Group Dynamics: Theory, Research, and Practice, 1*, 275–287.

Mackie, D. (1987). Systematic and nonsystematic processing of majority and minority persuasive communications. *Journal of Personality and Social Psychology, 53*, 41–52.

Mackie, D. M., & Queller, S. (2000). The impact of group membership on persuasion: Revisiting "who says what to whom with what effect?" In D. J. Terry & M. A. Hogg (Eds.), *Attitudes, behavior, and social context: The role of norms and group membership* (pp. 135–155). Mahwah, NJ: Erlbaum.

Mackie, M. (1980). The impact of sex stereotypes upon adult self imagery. *Social Psychology Quarterly, 43*, 121–125.

MacKinnon, C. A. (2003). The social origin of sexual harassment. In M. Silberman (Ed.), *Violence and society: A reader* (pp. 251–258). Upper Saddle River, NJ: Prentice Hall.

MacNair-Semands, R. R. (2002). Predicting attendance and expectations for group therapy. *Group Dynamics: Theory, Research, and Practice, 6*, 219–228.

MacNair-Semands, R. R., & Lese, K. P. (2000). Interpersonal problems and the perception of therapeutic factors in group therapy. *Small Group Research, 31*, 158–174.

MacNeil, M. K., & Sherif, M. (1976). Norm change over subject generations as a function of arbitrariness of prescribed norm. *Journal of Personality and Social Psychology, 34*, 762–773.

Macy, B. A., & Izumi, H. (1993). Organizational change, design, and work innovation: A meta-analysis of 131 North American field studies—1961–1991. *Research in Organizational Change and Development, 7*, 235–313.

Magee, J. C., Galinsky, A. D., & Gruenfeld, D. H. (2007). Power, propensity to negotiate, and moving first in competitive interactions. *Personality and Social Psychology Bulletin, 33*, 200–212.

Magee, J. C., & Tiedens, L. Z. (2006). Emotional ties that bind: The roles of valence and consistency of group emotion in inferences of cohesiveness and common fate. *Personality and Social Psychology Bulletin, 32*(12), 1703–1715.

Maier, N. R. F., & Solem, A. R. (1952). The contribution of a discussion leader to the quality of group thinking: The effective use of minority opinions. *Human Relations, 5,* 277–288.

Majchrzak, A. Ba, S., Rice, R. E., Malhotra, A., & King, N. (2000). Technology adaptation: The case of a computer-supported inter-organizational virtual team. *MIS Quarterly, 24*(4), 569–600.

Major, D. A., Kozlowski, S. W. J., Chao, G. T., & Gardner, P. D. (1995). A longitudinal investigation of newcomer expectations, early socialization outcomes, and the moderating effects of role development factors. *Journal of Applied Psychology, 80,* 418–431.

Maki, J. E., Thorngate, W. B., & McClintock, C. G. (1979). Prediction and perception of social motives. *Journal of Personality and Social Psychology, 37,* 203–220.

Malhotra, A., Majchrzak, A., & Rosen, B. (2007). Leading virtual teams. *Academy of Management Perspectives, 21*(1), 60–70.

Mallett, K. A., Varvil-Weld, L., Turrisi, R., & Read, A. (2011). An examination of college students' willingness to experience consequences as a unique predictor of alcohol problems. *Psychology of Addictive Behaviors, 25*(1), 41–47.

Malloy, T. E., & Janowski, C. L. (1992). Perceptions and meta-perceptions of leadership: Components, accuracy, and dispositional correlates. *Personality and Social Psychology Bulletin, 18,* 700–708.

Malone, K.-L. (2009). Dragon kill points: The economics of power gamers. *Games and Culture: A Journal of Interactive Media, 4*(3), 296–316.

Maner, J. K., DeWall, C. N., Baumeister, R. F., & Schaller, M. (2007). Does social exclusion motivate interpersonal reconnection? Resolving the "porcupine problem." *Journal of Personality and Social Psychology, 92,* 42–55.

Mann, F. C. (1965). Toward an understanding of the leadership role in formal organizations. In R. Dubin, G. C. Homans, F. C. Mann, & D. C. Miller (Eds.), *Leadership and productivity.* San Francisco: Chandler.

Mann, J. H. (1959). A review of the relationships between personality and performance in small groups. *Psychological Bulletin, 56,* 241–270.

Mann, L. (1969). Queue culture. The waiting line as a social system. *American Journal of Sociology, 75,* 340–354.

Mann, L. (1970). The psychology of waiting lines. *American Scientist, 58,* 390–398.

Mann, L. (1981). The baiting crowd in episodes of threatened suicide. *Journal of Personality and Social Psychology, 41,* 703–709.

Mann, L. (1986). Cross-cultural studies of rules for determining majority and minority decision rights. *Australian Journal of Psychology, 38,* 319.

Mann, L. (1988). Cultural influence on group processes. In M. H. Bond (Ed.), *The cross-cultural challenge to social psychology* (pp. 182–195). Thousand Oaks, CA: Sage.

Manning, R., Levine, M., & Collins, A. (2007). The Kitty Genovese murder and the social psychology of helping: The parable of the 38 witnesses. *American Psychologist, 62*(6), 555–562.

Mannix, E. A. (1993). Organizations as resource dilemmas: The effects of power balance on coalition formation in small groups. *Organizational Behavior and Human Decision Processes, 55,* 1–22.

Mannix, E., & Neale, M. A. (2005). What differences make a difference? The promise and reality of diverse teams in organizations. *Psychological Science in the Public Interest, 6,* 31–55.

Mantell, D. M. (1971). The potential for violence in Germany. *Journal of Social Issues, 27*(4), 101–112.

Maoz, I., & McCauley, C. (2008). Threat, dehumanization, and support for retaliatory aggressive policies in asymmetric conflict. *Journal of Conflict Resolution, 52,* 93–116.

Marcus, D. K. (1998). Studying group dynamics with the social relations model. *Group Dynamics: Theory, Research, and Practice, 2,* 230–240.

Marcus, D. K., & Wilson, J. R. (1996). Interpersonal perception of social anxiety: A social relations analysis. *Journal of Social & Clinical Psychology, 15,* 471–487.

Marks, M. A., Mathieu, J. E., & Zaccaro, S. J. (2001). A temporally based framework and taxonomy of team processes. *Academy of Management Review, 26,* 356–376.

Markus, H. (1978). The effect of mere presence on social facilitation: An unobtrusive test. *Journal of Experimental Social Psychology, 14,* 389–397.

Marmarosh, C. L., & Corazzini, J. G. (1997). Putting the group in your pocket: Using collective identity to enhance personal and collective self-esteem. *Group Dynamics: Theory, Research, and Practice, 1,* 65–74.

Marmarosh, C. L., Holtz, A., & Schottenbauer, M. (2005). Group cohesiveness, group-derived collective self-esteem, group-derived hope, and the well-being of group therapy members. *Group Dynamics: Theory, Research, and Practice, 9,* 32–44.

Marmarosh, C. L., & Markin, R. D. (2007). Group and personal attachments: Two is better than one when predicting college adjustment. *Group Dynamics: Theory, Research, and Practice, 11*(3), 153–164.

Marmarosh, C. L., & Van Horn, S. M. (2010). Cohesion in counseling and psychotherapy groups. In R. K. Conyne (Ed.), *The Oxford handbook of group counseling* (pp. 137–163). New York: Oxford University Press.

Marques, J. M. (2010). Black sheep effect. In J. M. Levine & M. A. Hogg (Eds.), *Encyclopedia of group process and intergroup relations* (pp. 55–57). Thousand Oaks, CA: Sage.

Marsh, H. W., Trautwein, U., Lüdtke, O., Baumert, J., & Köller, O. (2007). The big-fish-little-pond effect: Persistent negative effects of selective high schools on self-concept after graduation. *American Educational Research Journal, 44*(3), 631–669.

Marsh, L. C. (1931). Group treatment for the psychoses by the psychological equivalent of revival. *Mental Hygiene, 15,* 328–349.

Marsh, P., & Morris, D. (1988). *Tribes.* Layton, UT: Gibbs Smith.

Martens, R., Landers, D. M., & Loy, J. (1972). *Sports cohesiveness questionnaire.* Reston, VA: American Association of Health, Physical Education, and Recreation.

Martin, E. D. (1920). *The behavior of crowds*. New York: Harper.

Martin, J., Lobb, B., Chapman, G. C., & Spillane, R. (1976). Obedience under conditions demanding self-immolation. *Human Relations, 29*(4), 345–356.

Martin, L. J., Carron, A. V., Eys, M. A., & Loughead, T. M. (2012). Development of a cohesion inventory for children's sport teams. *Group Dynamics: Theory, Research, and Practice, 16*(1), 68–79.

Martin, R., & Hewstone, M. (2008). Majority versus minority influence, message processing and attitude change: The Source-Context-Elaboration Model. *Advances in Experimental Social Psychology, 40,* 237–326.

Martti, M. (2008). Continuing validity of the collective behavior approach. *Sociology Compass, 5,* 1553–1564.

Marx, K., & Engels, F. (1947). *The German ideology*. New York: International Publishers.

Maslach, C. (1972). Social and personal bases of individuation. *Proceedings of the 80th Annual Convention of the American Psychological Association, 7,* 213–214.

Maslach, C., Stapp, J., & Santee, R. T. (1985). Individuation: Conceptual analysis and assessment. *Journal of Personality and Social Psychology, 49,* 729–738.

Maslow, A. H. (1943). A theory of human motivation. *Psychological Review, 50*(4), 370–396.

Mason, C. M., & Griffin, M. A. (2002). Group task satisfaction: Applying the construct of job satisfaction to groups. *Small Group Research, 33,* 271–312.

Mathes, E. W., & Kahn, A. (1975). Diffusion of responsibility and extreme behavior. *Journal of Personality and Social Psychology, 5,* 881–886.

Mathews, E., Canon, L. K., & Alexander, K. R. (1974). The influence of level of empathy and ambient noise on body buffer zone. *Personality and Social Psychology Bulletin, 1,* 367–369.

Mathieu, J., Maynard, M. T., Rapp, T., & Gilson, L. (2008). Team effectiveness 1997–2007: A review of recent advancements and a glimpse into the future. *Journal of Management, 34,* 410–476.

Matthews, M. D., Eid, J., Kelly, D., Bailey, J. K. S., & Peterson, C. (2006). Character strengths and virtues of developing military leaders: An international comparison. *Military Psychology, 18*(Suppl.), S57–S68.

Matz, D. C., Hofstedt, P. M., & Wood, W. (2008). Extraversion as a moderator of the cognitive dissonance associated with disagreement. *Personality and Individual Differences, 45,* 401–405.

Matz, D. C., & Wood, W. (2005). Cognitive dissonance in groups: The consequences of disagreement. *Journal of Personality and Social Psychology, 88,* 22–37.

Mausner, B. (1954). The effect of one partner's success in a relevant task on the interaction of observer pairs. *Journal of Abnormal and Social Psychology, 49,* 557–560.

May, G. L., Carter, T. J., & Dewey, J. D. (2002). Collaboration in a virtual team environment: A case study in planning the ASTD/AHRD 2001 Future Search Conference. Retrieved from www.itapintl.com

Mayer, R. C., Davis, J. H., & Schoorman, F. D. (1995). An integrative model of organizational trust. *The Academy of Management Review, 20*(3), 709–734.

Maynard, M. T., Mathieu, J. E., Rapp, T. L., & Gilson, L. L. (2012). Something(s) old and something(s) new: Modeling drivers of global virtual team effectiveness. *Journal of Organizational Behavior, 33*(3), 342–365.

Mayo, E. (1945). *The social problems of an industrial civilization*. Boston: Harvard University Press.

Mazar, N., & Aggarwal, P. (2011). Greasing the palm: Can collectivism promote bribery? *Psychological Science, 22*(7), 843–848.

McAdam, D., McCarthy, J. D., & Zald, M. N. (1988). Social movements. In N. J. Smelser (Ed.), *Handbook of sociology* (pp. 695–737). Thousand Oaks, CA: Sage Publications.

McAdams, D. P. (1982). Experiences of intimacy and power: Relationships between social motives and autobiographical memory. *Journal of Personality and Social Psychology, 42,* 292–301.

McAdams, D. P. (1995). What do we know when we know a person? *Journal of Personality, 63,* 365–396.

McAdams, D. P., & Constantian, C. A. (1983). Intimacy and affiliation motives in daily living: An experience sampling analysis. *Journal of Personality and Social Psychology, 45,* 851–861.

McAdams, D. P., Healy, S., & Krause, S. (1984). Social motives and patterns of friendship. *Journal of Personality and Social Psychology, 47,* 828–838.

McBurney, D. H., Levine, J. M., & Cavanaugh, P. H. (1977). Psychophysical and social ratings of human body odor. *Personality and Social Psychology Bulletin, 3*(1), 135–138.

McCallin, A., & Bamford, A. (2007). Interdisciplinary teamwork: Is the influence of emotional intelligence fully appreciated? *Journal of Nursing Management, 15*(4), 386–391.

McClelland, D. C. (1975). *Power: The inner experience*. New York: Irvington.

McClelland, D. C. (1985). How motives, skills, and values determine what people do. *American Psychologist, 40,* 812–825.

McClelland, D. C., & Boyatzis, R. E. (1982). Leadership motive pattern and long-term success in management. *Journal of Applied Psychology, 67,* 737–743.

McClintock, C. G., Stech, F. J., & Keil, L. J. (1983). The influence of communication on bargaining. In P. B. Paulus (Ed.), *Basic group processes* (pp. 205–233). New York: Springer-Verlag.

McCrae, R. R. (1996). Social consequences of experiential openness. *Psychological Bulletin, 120,* 323–337.

McCrae, R. R., & Costa, P. T. Jr. (1997). Personality trait structure as a human universal. *American Psychologist, 52*(5), 509–516.

McCullough, M. E., Kurzban, R., & Tabak, B. A. (2011). Evolved mechanisms for revenge and forgiveness. In M. Mikulincer & P. R. Shaver (Eds.), *Human aggression and violence: Causes, manifestations, and consequences* (pp. 221–239). Washington, DC: American Psychological Association.

McDonald, M. M., Navarrete, C. D., & Vugt, M. V. (2012). Evolution and the psychology of intergroup conflict: the male warrior hypothesis. *Philosophical Transactions of the Royal Society B: Biological Sciences, 367*(1589), 670–679.

McDougall, W. (1908). *An introduction to social psychology.* London: Methuen.

McFall, S. R., Jamieson, J. P., & Harkins, S. G. (2009). Testing the mere effort account of the evaluation-performance relationship. *Journal of Personality and Social Psychology, 96*(1), 135–154.

McGillicuddy, N. B., Pruitt, D. G., & Syna, H. (1984). Perceptions of firmness and strength in negotiation. *Personality and Social Psychology Bulletin, 10,* 402–409.

McGrath, J. E. (1984). *Groups: Interaction and performance.* Upper Saddle River, NJ: Prentice Hall.

McGrath, J. E., & Altermatt, T. W. (2001). Observation and analysis of group interaction over time: Some methodological and strategic choices. In M. A. Hogg & R. S. Tindale (Eds.), *Blackwell handbook of social psychology: Group processes* (pp. 525–556). Malden, MA: Blackwell.

McGraw, K. M., & Bloomfield, J. (1987). Social influence on group moral decisions: The interactive effects of moral reasoning and sex role orientation. *Journal of Personality and Social Psychology, 53,* 1080–1087.

McGregor, D. (1960). *The human side of enterprise.* New York: McGraw-Hill.

McGrew, J. F., Bilotta, J. G., & Deeney, J. M. (1999). Software team formation and decay: Extending the standard model for small groups. *Small Group Research, 30,* 209–234.

McGuire, G. M. (2007). Intimate work: A typology of the social support that workers provide to their network members. *Work and Occupations, 34*(2), 125–147.

McGuire, J. P., & Leak, G. K. (1980). Prediction of self-disclosure from objective personality assessment techniques. *Journal of Clinical Psychology, 36,* 201–204.

McGuire, W. J., & McGuire, C. V. (1988). Content and process in the experience of self. *Advances in Experimental Social Psychology, 21,* 97–144.

McIntyre, M. H., Li, A. Y., Chapman, J. F., Lipson, S. F., & Ellison, P. T. (2011). Social status, masculinity, and testosterone in young men. *Personality and Individual Differences, 51*(4), 392–396.

McKenna, K. Y. A., & Seidman, G. (2005). You, me and we: Self, identity and interpersonal processes in electronic groups. In Y. A. Hamburger (Ed.), *The social net: The social psychology of the Internet* (pp. 191–217). Oxford: Oxford Press.

McLeod, P. L. (2011). Effects of anonymity and social comparison of rewards on computer-mediated group brainstorming. *Small Group Research, 42*(4), 475–503.

McLeod, P. L., Lobel, S. A., & Cox, T. H. (1996). Ethnic diversity and creativity in small groups. *Small Group Research, 27,* 248–264.

McNally, R. J., Bryant, R. A., & Ehlers, A. (2003). Does early psychological intervention promote recovery from posttraumatic stress? *Psychological Science in the Public Interest, 4,* 45–79.

McNeill, W. H. (1995). *Keeping together in time: Dance and drill in human history.* Boston: Harvard University Press.

McNiel, J. M., & Fleeson, W. (2006). The causal effects of extraversion on positive affect and neuroticism on negative affect: Manipulating state extraversion and state neuroticism in an experimental approach. *Journal of Research in Personality, 40,* 529–550.

McPhail, C. (1991). *The myth of the madding crowd.* Hawthorne, NY: Aldine de Gruyter.

McPhail, C. (2006). The crowd and collective behavior: Bringing symbolic interaction back in. *Symbolic Interaction, 29,* 433–464.

McPhail, C. (2008). Gatherings as patchworks. *Social Psychology Quarterly, 71*(1), 1–5.

McPherson, M., & Smith-Lovin, L. (2002). Cohesion and membership duration: Linking groups, relations and individuals in an ecology of affiliation. In S. R. Thye & E. J. Lawler (Eds.), *Group cohesion, trust and solidarity* (pp. 1–36). New York: Elsevier Science/JAI Press.

McPherson, M., Smith-Lovin, L., & Cook, J. M. (2001). Birds of a feather: Homophily in social networks. *Annual Review of Sociology, 27,* 415–444.

McPherson, S., & Joireman, J. (2009). Death in groups: Mortality salience and in the interindividual– intergroup discontinuity effect. *Group Processes & Intergroup Relations, 12*(4), 419–429.

McPherson, S., & Parks, C. D. (2011). Intergroup and interindividual resource competition escalating into conflict: The elimination option. *Group Dynamics: Theory, Research, and Practice, 15*(4), 285–296.

McRoberts, C., Burlingame, G. M., & Hoag, M. J. (1998). Comparative efficacy of individual and group psychotherapy: A meta-analytic perspective. *Group Dynamics: Theory, Research, and Practice, 2,* 101–117.

McWhirter, J. J., McWhirter, P. T., McWhirter, B. T., & McWhirter, E. H. (2010). International group counseling. In R. K. Conyne (Ed.), *The Oxford handbook of group counseling* (pp. 469–486). New York: Oxford University Press.

Mead, G. H. (1934). *Mind, self, and society: From the standpoint of a social behaviorist.* Chicago: University of Chicago Press.

Mead, M. (1935). *Sex and temperament.* Oxford: Morrow.

Medalia, N. Z., & Larsen, O. N. (1958). Diffusion and belief in a collective delusion: The Seattle windshield pitting epidemic. *American Sociological Review, 23,* 180–186.

Meece, J. L., Anderman, E. M., & Anderman, L. H. (2006). Classroom goal structure, student motivation, and academic achievement. *Annual Review of Psychology, 57,* 487–503.

Meerloo, J. A. (1950). *Patterns of panic.* New York: International Universities Press.

Megargee, E. I. (1969). Influence of sex roles on the manifestation of leadership. *Journal of Applied Psychology, 53,* 377–382.

Mehrabian, A., & Diamond, S. G. (1971). Effects of furniture arrangement, props, and personality on social interaction. *Journal of Personality and Social Psychology, 20,* 18–30.

Mehta, R., Zhu, R., & Cheema, A. (2012). Is noise always bad? Exploring the effects of ambient noise on creative cognition. *Journal of Consumer Research*, in press.

Mehta, V., & Bosson, J. K. (2010). Third places and the social life of streets. *Environment and Behavior, 42*(6), 779–805.

Meier, B. P., & Hinsz, V. B. (2004). A comparison of human aggression committed by groups and individuals: An interindividual–intergroup discontinuity. *Journal of Experimental Social Psychology, 40*, 551–559.

Meier, B. P., Hinsz, V. B., & Heimerdinger, S. R. (2008). A framework for explaining aggression involving groups. *Social and Personality Psychology Compass, 2*, 298–312.

Meindl, J. R., Ehrlich, S. B., & Dukerich, J. M. (1985). The romance of leadership and the evaluation of organizational performance. *Academy of Management Journal, 30*, 90–109.

Melamed, B. G., & Wills, T. A. (2000). Comment on Turner (2000). *Group Dynamics: Theory, Research, and Practice, 4*, 150–156.

Mendes, W. B., Major, B., McCoy, S., & Blascovich, J. (2008). How attributional ambiguity shapes physiological and emotional responses to social rejection and acceptance. *Journal of Personality and Social Psychology, 94*(2), 278–291.

Menon, T., Morris, M. W., Chiu, C.-Y., & Hong, Y.-Y (1999). Culture and the construal of agency: Attribution to individual versus group dispositions. *Journal of Personality and Social Psychology, 76*, 701–717.

Menschel, R. (2002). *Markets, mobs, & mayhem: A modern look at the madness of crowds.* New York: Wiley.

Merton, H. W. (1917). *How to choose the right vocation: Vocational self-measurement based upon natural abilities* (5th ed.). New York: Funk and Wagnalls.

Merton, R. K. (1976). *Sociological ambivalence and other essays.* New York: Free Press.

Messick, D. M. (1999). Dirty secrets: Strategic uses of ignorance and uncertainty. In L. L. Thompson, J. M. Levine, & D. M. Messick (Eds.), *Shared cognition in organizations: The management of knowledge* (pp. 71–87). Mahwah, NJ: Erlbaum.

Messick, D. M. (2005). On the psychological exchange between leaders and followers. In D. M. Messick & R. M. Kramer (Eds.), *The psychology of leadership: New perspectives and research* (pp. 81–96). Mahwah, NJ: Erlbaum.

Messick, D. M., & Brewer, M. B. (1983). Solving social dilemmas: A review. In L. Wheeler & P. Shaver (Eds.), *Review of Personality and Social Psychology* (Vol. 4, pp. 11–44). Thousand Oaks, CA: Sage.

Meudell, P. R., Hitch, G. J., & Kirby, P. (1992). Are two heads better than one? Experimental investigations of the social facilitation of memory. *Applied Cognitive Psychology, 6*, 525–543.

Meumann, E. (1904). Haus- und Schularbeit: Experimente an Kindern der Volkschule. *Die Deutsche Schule, 8*, 278–303, 337–359, 416–431.

Meyer, D. S. (2004). Protest and political opportunities. *Annual Review of Sociology, 30*, 125–145.

Meyer, P. (1970, February). If Hitler asked you to electrocute a stranger, would you? Probably. *Esquire*, pp. 73–80, 128, 130, 132.

Meyers, R. A., Seibold, D. R., & Kang, P. (2010). Examining argument in a naturally occurring jury deliberation. *Small Group Research, 41*(4), 452–473.

Michaels, J. W., Blommel, J. M., Brocato, R. M., Linkous, R. A., & Rowe, J. S. (1982). Social facilitation and inhibition in a natural setting. *Replications in Social Psychology, 2*, 21–24.

Michaelsen, L. K., Watson, W. E., & Black, R. H. (1989). A realistic test of individual versus group consensus decision making. *Journal of Applied Psychology, 74*, 834–839.

Michels, R. (1959). *Political parties: A sociological study of the oligarchical tendencies of modern democracy.* New York: Dover. (original work published in 1915)

Michener, H. A., & Burt, M. R. (1975). Use of social influence under varying conditions of legitimacy. *Journal of Personality and Social Psychology, 32*, 398–407.

Michener, H. A., & Lawler, E. J. (1975). The endorsement of formal leaders: An integrative model. *Journal of Personality and Social Psychology, 31*, 216–223.

Michinov, N. (2012). The use of electronic brainstorming for collecting ideas in scientific research teams: A challenge for future online research. In C. Silva (Ed.), *Online research methods in urban and planning studies: Design and outcomes* (pp. 157–172). Hershey, PA: Information Science Reference.

Middlemist, R. D., Knowles, E. S., & Matter, C. F. (1976). Personal space invasions in the lavatory: Suggestive evidence for arousal. *Journal of Personality and Social Psychology, 33*, 541–546.

Mikolic, J. M., Parker, J. C., & Pruitt, D. G. (1997). Escalation in response to persistent annoyance: Groups versus individuals and gender effects. *Journal of Personality and Social Psychology, 72*, 151–163.

Milanovich, D. M., Driskell, J. E., Stout, R. J., & Salas, E. (1998). Status and cockpit dynamics: A review and empirical study. *Group Dynamics: Theory, Research, and Practice, 2*, 155–167.

Miles, J. R., & Kivlighan, D. M., Jr. (2010). Co-leader similarity and group climate in group interventions: Testing the co-leadership, team cognition-team diversity model. *Group Dynamics: Theory, Research, and Practice, 14*(2), 114–122.

Milgram, S. (1963). Behavioral study of obedience. *Journal of Abnormal and Social Psychology, 67*, 371–378.

Milgram, S. (1965). Some conditions of obedience and disobedience to authority. *Human Relations, 18*(1), 57–76.

Milgram, S. (1974). *Obedience to authority.* New York: Harper & Row.

Milgram, S. (1992). *The individual in a social world: Essays and experiments* (2nd ed.). New York: McGraw-Hill.

Milgram, S., Bickman, L., & Berkowitz, L. (1969). Note on the drawing power of crowds of different size. *Journal of Personality and Social Psychology, 13*, 79–82.

Milgram, S., Liberty, H. J., Toledo, R., & Wackenhut, J. (1986). Response to intrusion into waiting lines. *Journal of Personality and Social Psychology, 51*, 683–689.

Milgram, S., & Toch, H. (1969). Collective behavior: Crowds and social movements. In G. Lindzey & E. Aronson (Eds.), *The handbook of social psychology* (Vol. 4, 2nd ed., pp. 507–610). Reading, MA: Addison Wesley.

Miller, A. G. (2004). What can the Milgram obedience experiments tell us about the Holocaust? Generalizing from the social psychology laboratory. In A. G. Miller (Ed.), *The social psychology of good and evil* (pp. 193–239). New York: Guilford.

Miller, D. T. (2001). Disrespect and the experience of injustice. *Annual Review of Psychology, 52,* 527–553.

Miller, G. A., Galanter, E., & Pribram, K. H. (1960). *Plans and the structure of behavior.* New York: Holt.

Miller, J. G. (2002). Bringing culture to basic psychological theory —Beyond individualism and collectivism: Comment on Oyserman et al. (2002). *Psychological Bulletin, 128,* 97–109.

Miller, J. K., & Gergen, K. J. (1998). Life on the line: The therapeutic potentials of computer-mediated conversation. *Journal of Marital and Family Therapy, 24,* 189–202.

Miller, K. I., & Monge, P. R. (1986). Participation, satisfaction, and productivity: A meta-analytic review. *Academy of Management Journal, 29,* 727–753.

Miller, M. D., & Brunner, C. C. (2008). Social impact in technologically-mediated communication: An examination of online influence. *Computers in Human Behavior, 24*(6), 2972–2991.

Miller, N., & Davidson-Podgorny, G. (1987). Theoretical models of intergroup relations and the use of cooperative teams as an intervention for desegregated settings. In C. Hendrick (Ed.), *Review of Personality and Social Psychology: Group Process* (Vol. 9, pp. 41–67). Thousand Oaks, CA: Sage.

Miller, R. S. (2012). *Intimate relationships* (5th ed.). Boston: McGraw-Hill.

Minami, H., & Tanaka, K. (1995). Social and environmental psychology: Transaction between physical space and group-dynamic processes. *Environment and Behavior, 27,* 43–55.

Mintz, A. (1951). Non-adaptive group behavior. *Journal of Abnormal and Social Psychology, 46,* 150–159.

Mintzberg, H. (1973). *The nature of managerial work.* New York: Harper & Row.

Mintzberg, H. (2009). *Managing.* San Francisco: Berrett-Koehler.

Miracle on the Hudson Survivors with Prochnau, W. W., & Parker, L. (2009). *Miracle on the Hudson: The extraordinary real-life story behind Flight 1549, by the survivors.* New York: Ballantine.

Mischel, W. (1977). On the future of personality measurement. *American Psychologist, 32,* 246–254.

Mischel, W., & DeSmet, A. L. (2000). Self-regulation in the service of conflict resolution. In M. Deutsch & P. T. Coleman (Eds.), *The handbook of conflict resolution: Theory and practice* (pp. 256–275). San Francisco: Jossey-Bass.

Misumi, J. (1995). The development in Japan of the performance-maintenance (PM) theory of leadership. *Journal of Social Issues, 51,* 213–228.

Mitchell, R. C., & Mitchell, R. R. (1984). Constructive management of conflict in groups. *Journal for Specialists in Group Work, 9,* 137–144.

Mobley, W. H., Griffeth, R. W., Hand, H. H., & Meglino, B. M. (1979). Review and conceptual analysis of employee turnover process. *Psychological Bulletin, 86,* 493–522.

Modigliani, A., & Rochat, F. (1995). The role of interaction sequences and the timing of resistance in shaping obedience and defiance to authority. *Journal of Social Issues, 51,* 107–123.

Moehrle, M. G. (2005). What is TRIZ? From conceptual basics to a framework for research. *Creativity and Innovation Management, 14,* 3–13.

Mohammed, S., Hamilton, K., & Lim, A. (2009). The incorporation of time in team research: Past, current, and future. In E. Salas, G. F. Goodwin, & C. S. Burke (Eds.), *Team effectiveness in complex organizations: Cross-disciplinary perspectives and approaches* (pp. 321–348). New York: Routledge/Taylor & Francis Group.

Molden, D. C., Lucas, G. M., Gardner, W. L., Dean, K., & Knowles, M. L. (2009). Motivations for prevention or promotion following social exclusion: Being rejected versus being ignored. *Journal of Personality and Social Psychology, 96*(2), 415–431.

Molm, L. D. (1986). Gender, power, and legitimation: A test of three theories. *American Journal of Sociology, 91,* 1156–1186.

Molm, L. D. (1997). Risk and power use: Constraints on the use of coercion in exchange. *American Sociological Review, 62,* 113–133.

Montoya, R. M., & Insko, C. A. (2008). Toward a more complete understanding of the reciprocity of liking effect. *European Journal of Social Psychology, 38,* 477–498.

Moody, J., & White, D. R. (2003). Structural cohesion and embeddedness: A hierarchical concept of social groups. *American Sociological Review, 68*(1), 103–127.

Moos, R. H., Insel, P. M., & Humphrey, B. (1974). *Preliminary manual for family environment scale, work environment scale, and group environment scale.* Palo Alto, CA: Consulting Psychologists Press.

Moreland, R. L. (1985). Social categorization and the assimilation of "new" group members. *Journal of Personality and Social Psychology, 48,* 1173–1190.

Moreland, R. L. (1987). The formation of small groups. *Review of Personality and Social Psychology, 8,* 80–110.

Moreland, R. L. (2010). Are dyads really groups? *Small Group Research, 41,* 251–267.

Moreland, R. L., Argote, L., & Krishnan, R. (1996). Socially shared cognition at work: Transactive memory and group performance. In J. L. Nye & A. M. Brower (Eds.), *What's social about social cognition? Research on socially shared cognitions in small groups* (pp. 57–84). Thousand Oaks, CA: Sage.

Moreland, R. L., & Levine, J. M. (1982). Socialization in small groups: Temporal changes in individual-group relations. *Advances in Experimental Social Psychology, 15,* 137–192.

Moreland, R. L., & Levine, J. M. (2002). Socialization and trust in work groups. *Group Processes & Intergroup Relations, 5,* 185–201.

Moreland, R. L., Levine, J. M., & Cini, M. A. (1993). Group socialization: The role of commitment. In M. Hogg & D. Abrams (Eds.), *Group motivation: Social psychological perspectives* (pp. 105–129). London: Harvester Wheatsheaf.

Moreland, R. L., Levine, J. M., & Wingert, M. L. (1996). Creating the ideal group: Composition effects at work. In E. H. Witte & J. H. Davis (Eds.), *Understanding group behavior: Small group processes and interpersonal relations* (Vol. 2, pp. 11–35). Mahwah, NJ: Erlbaum.

Moreno, J. L. (1934). *Who shall survive? A new approach to the problem of human interrelations.* Washington, DC: Nervous and Mental Disease Publishing Co.

Moreno, J. L. (1953). How Kurt Lewin's "Research Center for Group Dynamics" started. *Sociometry, 16,* 101–104.

Morgeson, F. P., Reider, M. H., & Campion, M. A. (2005). Selecting individuals in team settings: The importance of social skills, personality characteristics, and teamwork knowledge. *Personnel Psychology, 58,* 583–611.

Morran, K. D., Stockton, R., Cline, R. J., & Teed, C. (1998). Facilitating feedback exchange in groups: Leader interventions. *Journal for Specialists in Group Work, 23,* 257–268.

Morrill, C. (1995). *The executive way.* Chicago: University of Chicago Press.

Morris, C. G. (1966). Task effects on group interaction. *Journal of Personality and Social Psychology, 4*(5), 545–554.

Morris, R. T. (1956). A typology of norms. *American Sociological Review, 21,* 610–613.

Morris, W. N., Worchel, S., Bois, J. L., Pearson, J. A., Rountree, C. A., Samaha, G. M., Wachtler, J., & Wright, S. L. (1976). Collective coping with stress: Group reactions to fear, anxiety, and ambiguity. *Journal of Personality and Social Psychology, 33,* 674–679.

Morrison, K. R., & Miller, D. T. (2011). Innovation credit: When and why do group members give their leaders license to deviate from group norms? In J. Jetten & M. J. Hornsey (Eds.), *Rebels in groups: Dissent, deviance, difference, and defiance* (pp. 238–257). Malden, MA: Wiley-Blackwell.

Moscovici, S. (1976). *Social influence and social change.* New York: Academic Press.

Moscovici, S. (1980). Toward a theory of conversion behavior. *Advances in Experimental Social Psychology, 13,* 209–239.

Moscovici, S. (1985). Social influence and conformity. In G. Lindzey & E. Aronson (Eds.), *Handbook of social psychology* (Vol. 2, pp. 397–412). New York: Random House.

Moscovici, S. (1994). Three concepts: Minority, conflict, and behavioral styles. In S. Moscovici, A. Mucchi-Faina, & A. Maass (Eds.), *Minority influence* (pp. 233–251). Chicago: Nelson-Hall.

Moscovici, S., Lage, E., & Naffrechoux, M. (1969). Influence of a consistent minority on the responses of a majority in a color perception task. *Sociometry, 12,* 365–380.

Moscovici, S., & Personnaz, B. (1980). Studies in social influence. V. Minority influence and conversion behavior in a perceptual task. *Journal of Experimental Social Psychology, 16,* 270–282.

Moscovici, S., & Zavalloni, M. (1969). The group as a polarizer of attitudes. *Journal of Personality and Social Psychology, 12,* 125–135.

Moser, G., & Uzzell, D. L. (2003). Environmental psychology. In T. Millon, M. J. Lerner, & I. B. Weiner (Eds.), *Handbook of psychology: Personality and social psychology* (Vol. 5, pp. 419–445). New York: Wiley.

Moskowitz, G. B., & Chaiken, S. (2001). Mediators of minority social influence: Cognitive processing mechanisms revealed through a persuasion paradigm. In C. K. W. De Dreu & N. K. De Vries (Eds.). *Group consensus and minority influence: Implications for innovation* (pp. 60–90). Malden, MA: Blackwell.

Moussaïd, M., Perozo, N., Garnier, S., Helbing, D., & Theraulaz, G. (2010). The walking behavior of pedestrian social groups and its impact on crowd dynamics, *PLoS One, 5*(4), e10047.

Moxnes, P. (1999). Understanding roles: A psychodynamic model for role differentiation in groups. *Group Dynamics: Theory, Research, and Practice, 3,* 99–113.

Moxnes, P. (2011). Deep roles: Are they real? A model of positive and negative interpersonal fantasies. *Poster presented at the 12th European Congress of Psychology,* Istanbul, Turkey.

Mudrack, P. E. (1989). Defining group cohesiveness: A legacy of confusion? *Small Group Behavior, 20,* 37–49.

Mudrack, P. E., & Farrell, G. M. (1995). An examination of functional role behavior and its consequences for individuals in group settings. *Small Group Behavior, 26,* 542–571.

Mullen, B. (1986). Atrocity as a function of lynch mob composition: A self-attention perspective. *Personality and Social Psychology Bulletin, 12,* 187–197.

Mullen, B. (1991). Group composition, salience, and cognitive representations: The phenomenology of being in a group. *Journal of Experimental Social Psychology, 27,* 297–323.

Mullen, B., Anthony, T., Salas, E., & Driskell, J. E. (1994). Group cohesiveness and quality of decision making: An integration of tests of the groupthink hypothesis. *Small Group Research, 25,* 189–204.

Mullen, B., & Baumeister, R. F. (1987). Group effects on self-attention and performance: Social loafing, social facilitation, and social impairment. *Review of Personality and Social Psychology, 9,* 189–206.

Mullen, B., & Copper, C. (1994). The relation between group cohesiveness and performance: An integration. *Psychological Bulletin, 115,* 210–227.

Mullen, B., Johnson, C., & Salas, E. (1991). Productivity loss in brainstorming groups: A meta-analytic review. *Basic and Applied Social Psychology, 12,* 3–23.

Muller, D., & Butera, F. (2007). The focusing effect of self-evaluation threat in coaction and social comparison. *Journal of Personality and Social Psychology, 93,* 194–211.

Mumford, E. (1906). The origins of leadership. *American Journal of Sociology, 12*(2), 216–240.

Munro, M., & Aouni, B. (2012). Group decision makers' preferences modeling within the goal programming model: An overview and a typology. *Journal of Multi-Criteria Decision Analysis*, in press.

Murnighan, J. K. (1986). Organizational coalitions: Structural contingencies and the formation process. *Research on Negotiation in Organizations*, 1, 155–174.

Murnighan, J. K., & Conlon, D. E. (1991). The dynamics of intense work groups: A study of British string quartets. *Administrative Science Quarterly*, 36, 165–186.

Murphy, M. (2006). *Sick building syndrome and the problem of uncertainty*. Durham, NC: Duke University Press.

Murphy, S. A., & Keating, J. P. (1995). Psychological assessment of postdisaster class action and personal injury litigants: A case study. *Journal of Traumatic Stress*, 8, 473–482.

Murphy-Berman, V., & Berman, J. (1978). Importance of choice and sex invasions of personal space. *Personality and Social Psychology Bulletin*, 4, 424–428.

Myers, A. E. (1962). Team competition, success, and the adjustment of group members. *Journal of Abnormal and Social Psychology*, 65, 325–332.

Myers, D. G. (1978). The polarizing effects of social comparison. *Journal of Experimental Social Psychology*, 14, 554–563.

Myers, D. G. (1982). Polarizing effects of social interaction. In H. Brandstätter, J. H. Davis, & G. Stocker-Kreichgauer (Eds.), *Group decision making* (pp. 125–161). New York: Academic Press.

Myers, D. G., & Bishop, G. D. (1970). Discussion effects on racial attitudes. *Science*, 169, 778–789.

Myers, D. G., & Lamm, H. (1976). The group polarization phenomenon. *Psychological Bulletin*, 83, 602–627.

Myers, D. J. (1997). Racial rioting in the 1960s: An event history analysis of local conditions. *American Sociological Review*, 62, 94–112.

Nagasundaram, M., & Dennis, A. R. (1993). When a group is not a group: The cognitive foundation of group idea generation. *Small Group Research*, 24, 463–489.

Nagler, J., Levina, A., & Timme, M. (2011). Impact of single links in competitive percolation. *Nature Physics*, 7, 265–270.

Nail, P. R., & MacDonald, G. (2007). On the development of the social response context model. In A. R. Pratkanis (Ed.), *The science of social influence: Advances and future progress* (pp. 193–221). New York: Psychology Press.

Nardi, B. (2010). *My life as a night elf priest: An anthropological account of World of Warcraft*. Ann Arbor: University of Michigan Press.

Nardi, B., & Harris, J. (2006). Strangers and friends: Collaborative play in World of Warcraft. In *Proceedings of CSCW2006* (pp. 149–158). New York: Association for Computing Machinery.

Nario-Redmond, M. R., Biernat, M., Eidelman, S., & Palenske, D. J. (2004). The social and personal identities scale: A measure of the differential importance ascribed to social and personal self-categorizations. *Self and Identity*, 3(2), 143–175.

Nastasi, B. K., Jayasena, A., Summerville, M., & Borja, A. P. (2011). Facilitating long-term recovery from natural disasters: Psychosocial programming for tsunami-affected schools of Sri Lanka. *School Psychology International*, 32(5), 512–532.

National Transportation Safety Board. (1994). A review of flight crew-involved, major accidents of U.S. air carriers, 1978 through 1990 (Safety Study NTSB/SS-94/01). Washington, DC: NTSB.

Navarrete, C. D., McDonald, M. M., Molina, L. E., & Sidanius, J. (2010). Prejudice at the nexus of race and gender: An outgroup male target hypothesis. *Journal of Personality and Social Psychology*, 98(6), 933–945.

Neighbors, C., Lee, C. M., Lewis, M. A., Fossos, N., & Larimer, M. E. (2007). Are social norms the best predictor of outcomes among heavy-drinking college students? *Journal of Studies on Alcohol and Drugs*, 68(4), 556–565.

Neighbors, C., O'Connor, R. M., Lewis, M. A., Chawla, N., Lee, C. M., & Fossos, N. (2008). The relative impact of injunctive norms on college student drinking: The role of reference group. *Psychology of Addictive Behaviors*, 22(4), 576–581.

Nemeth, C., & Goncalo, J. A. (2011). Rogues and heroes: Finding value in dissent. In J. Jetten & M. J. Hornsey (Eds.), *Rebels in groups: Dissent, deviance, difference, and defiance* (pp. 17–35). Malden, MA: Wiley-Blackwell.

Nemeth, C. J., Endicott, J., & Wachtler, J. (1976). From the '50s to the '70s: Women in jury deliberations. *Sociometry*, 39, 293–304.

Nemeth, C. J., & Wachtler, J. (1974). Creating the perceptions of consistency and confidence: A necessary condition for minority influence. *Sociometry*, 37, 529–540.

Neuberg, S. L., & Cottrell, C. A. (2008). Managing the threats and opportunities afforded by human sociality. *Group Dynamics: Theory, Research, and Practice*, 12(1), 63–72.

Newcomb, T. M. (1943). *Personality and social change*. New York: Dryden.

Newcomb, T. M. (1960). Varieties of interpersonal attraction. In D. Cartwright & A. Zander (Eds.), *Group dynamics: Research and theory* (2nd ed., pp. 104–119). Evanston, IL: Row, Peterson.

Newcomb, T. M. (1961). *The acquaintance process*. New York: Holt, Rinehart & Winston.

Newcomb, T. M. (1963). Stabilities underlying changes in interpersonal attraction. *Journal of Abnormal and Social Psychology*, 66, 376–386.

Newcomb, T. M. (1979). Reciprocity of interpersonal attraction: A nonconfirmation of a plausible hypothesis. *Social Psychology Quarterly*, 42, 299–306.

Newcomb, T. M. (1981). Heiderian balance as a group phenomenon. *Journal of Personality and Social Psychology*, 40, 862–867.

Newcomb, T. M., Koenig, K., Flacks, R., & Warwick, D. (1967). *Persistence and change: Bennington College and its students after 25 years*. New York: Wiley.

Newman, K. S., Fox, C., Harding, D. J., Mehta, J., & Roth, W. (2004). *Rampage: The social roots of school shootings*. New York: Basic Books.

Newman, O. (1972). *Defensible space*. New York: Macmillan.

Newsom, J. T., Mahan, T. L., Rook, K. S., & Krause, N. (2008). Stable negative social exchanges and health. *Health Psychology*, 27(1), 78–86.

Newton, J. W., & Mann, L. (1980). Crowd size as a factor in the persuasion process: A study of religious crusade meetings. *Journal of Personality and Social Psychology*, 39, 874–883.

Nezlek, J. B., Kowalski, R. M., Leary, M. R., Blevins, T., & Holgate, S. (1997). Personality moderators of reactions to interpersonal rejection: Depression and trait self-esteem. *Personality and Social Psychology Bulletin*, 23(12), 1235–1244.

Nielsen, M. E., & Miller, C. E. (1997). The transmission of norms regarding group decision rules. *Personality and Social Psychology Bulletin*, 23, 516–525.

Nier, J. A., Gaertner, S. L., Dovidio, J. F., Banker, B. S., Ward, C. M., & Rust, M. C. (2001). Changing interracial evaluations and behavior: The effects of a common group identity. *Group Processes & Intergroup Relations*, 4, 299–316.

Nieva, V. F., Fleishman, E. A., & Rieck, A. M. (1978). *Team dimensions: Their identity, their measurement, and their relationships*. Technical report. Washington, DC: ARRO.

Niiya, Y., Ellsworth, P. C., & Yamaguchi, S. (2006). Amae in Japan and the United States: An exploration of a "culturally unique" emotion. *Emotion*, 6, 279–295.

Nijstad, B. A. (2009). *Group performance*. New York: Psychology Press.

Nijstad, B. A., & Stroebe, W. (2006). How the group affects the mind: A cognitive model of idea generation in groups. *Personality and Social Psychology Review*, 10, 186–213.

Nijstad, B. A., Stroebe, W., & Lodewijkx, H. F. M. (2006). The illusion of group productivity: A reduction of failures explanation. *European Journal of Social Psychology*, 36, 31–48.

Nisbett, R. E., & Cohen, D. (1996). *Culture of honor: The psychology of violence in the south*. Boulder, CO: Westview.

Nisbett, R. E., Peng, K., Choi, I., & Norenzayan, A. (2001). Culture and systems of thought: Holistic versus analytic cognition. *Psychological Review*, 108(2), 291–310.

Nisbett, R. E., & Storms, M. D. (1974). Cognitive and social determinants of food intake. In H. London & R. E. Nisbett (Eds.), *Thought and feeling: Cognitive alteration of feeling states* (pp. 190–208). Chicago: Aldine.

Nixon, A. E., Mazzola, J. J., Bauer, J., Krueger, J. R., & Spector, P. E. (2011). Can work make you sick? A meta-analysis of the relationships between job stressors and physical symptoms. *Work & Stress*, 25(1), 1–22.

Noel, J. G., Wann, D. L., & Branscombe, N. R. (1995). Peripheral ingroup membership status and public negativity toward outgroups. *Journal of Personality and Social Psychology*, 68, 127–137.

Norris, F. H., & Murrell, S. A. (1990). Social support, life events, and stress as modifiers of adjustment to bereavement by older adults. *Psychology and Aging*, 5, 429–436.

Norton, M. I., Frost, J. H., & Ariely, D. (2007). Less is more: The lure of ambiguity, or why familiarity breeds contempt. *Journal of Personality and Social Psychology*, 92, 97–105.

Nosek, B. A., Greenwald, A. G., & Banaji, M. R. (2007). The implicit association test at age 7: A methodological and conceptual review. In J. A. Bargh (Ed.), *Social psychology and the unconscious: The automaticity of higher mental processes* (pp. 265–292). New York: Psychology Press.

Nowak, A., Vallacher, R. R., & Miller, M. E. (2003). Social influence and group dynamics. In T. Millon, M. J. Lerner, & I. B. Weiner (Eds.), *Handbook of psychology: Social psychology* (Vol. 5, pp. 383–418). New York: Wiley.

Nunamaker, J. F., Jr., Briggs, R. O., Mittleman, D. D., Vogel, D. R., & Balthazard, P. A. (1997). Lessons from a dozen years of group systems research: A discussion of lab and field findings. *Journal of Management Information Systems*, 13, 163–207.

Nutt, P. C. (2002). *Why decisions fail: Avoiding the blunders and traps that lead to debacles*. San Francisco: Berrett-Koehler.

Nuwer, H. (1999). *Wrongs of passage: Fraternities, sororities, hazing, and binge drinking*. Indianapolis: Indiana University Press.

Nyquist, L. V., & Spence, J. T. (1986). Effects of dispositional dominance and sex role expectations on leadership behaviors. *Journal of Personality and Social Psychology*, 50, 87–93.

Oberholzer-Gee, F., Waldfogel, J., & White, M. W. (2010). Friend or foe? Cooperation and learning in high-stakes games. *Review of Economics and Statistics*, 92(1), 179–187.

O'Boyle, E. H., Jr., Forsyth, D. R., Banks, G. C., & McDaniel, M. A. (2012). A meta-analysis of the Dark Triad and work behavior: A social exchange perspective. *Journal of Applied Psychology*, 97(3), 557–579.

OED Online (1989). Teams. *Oxford English Dictionary*, retrieved from dictionary.oed.com

Offerman, T. (2002). Hurting hurts more than helping helps. *European Economic Review*, 46(8), 1423–1437.

O'Gorman, R., Sheldon, K. M., & Wilson, D. S. (2008). For the good of the group? Exploring group-level evolutionary adaptations using multilevel selection theory. *Group Dynamics: Theory, Research, and Practice*, 12(1), 17–26.

Ohbuchi, K., Chiba, S., & Fukushima, O. (1996). Mitigation of interpersonal conflicts: Politeness and time pressure. *Personality and Social Psychology Bulletin*, 22, 1035–1042.

Oishi, S., Lun, J., & Sherman, G. D. (2007). Residential mobility, self-concept, and positive affect in social interactions. *Journal of Personality and Social Psychology*, 93, 131–141.

Oldenburg, R. (1999). *The great good place: Cafes, coffee shops, bookstores, bars, hair salons, and other handouts at the heart of a community*. New York: Marlowe & Co.

Oldmeadow, J. (2007). Status generalization in context: The moderating role of groups. *Journal of Experimental Social Psychology*, 43, 273–279.

Oliver, L. W., Harman, J., Hoover, E., Hayes, S. M., & Pandhi, N. A. (1999). A quantitative integration of the military cohesion literature. *Military Psychology*, 11, 57–83.

Olson, R., Verley, J., Santos, L., & Salas, C. (2004). What we teach students about the Hawthorne studies: A review of content within a sample of introductory I-O and OB textbooks. *The Industrial-Organizational Psychologist*, 41, 23–39.

Olweus, D. (1997). Tackling peer victimization with a school-based intervention program. In D. P. Fry & K. Björkqvist (Eds.), *Cultural variation in conflict resolution: Alternatives to violence* (pp. 215–231). Mahwah, NJ: Erlbaum.

Ong, J. (2012). Former Apple CEO John Sculley says he never fired co-founder Steve Jobs. *Apple Insider*. Retrieved from www.appleinsider.com

Onnela, J.-P., Arbesman, S., González, M. C., Barabási, A.-L., & Christakis, N. A. (2011) Geographic constraints on social network groups. *PLoS ONE 6*(4): e16939, 1–7.

Opotow, S. (2000). Aggression and violence. In M. Deutsch & P. T. Coleman (Eds.), *The handbook of conflict resolution: Theory and practice* (pp. 403–427). San Francisco: Jossey-Bass.

Ormont, L. R. (1984). The leader's role in dealing with aggression in groups. *International Journal of Group Psychotherapy, 34*, 553–572.

Orne, M. T., & Holland, C. H. (1968). On the ecological validity of laboratory deceptions. *International Journal of Psychiatry, 6*, 282–293.

Örtqvist, D., & Wincent, J. (2006). Prominent consequences of role stress: A meta-analytic review. *International Journal of Stress Management, 13*, 399–422.

Osborn, A. F. (1957). *Applied imagination.* New York: Scribner.

Osgood, D. W., Wilson, J. K., O'Malley, P. M., Bachman, J. G., & Johnson, L. D. (1996). Routine activities and individual deviant behavior. *American Sociological Review, 61*, 635–655.

O'Sullivan, P. B., & Flanagin, A. J. (2003). Reconceptualizing 'flaming' and other problematic messages. *New Media & Society, 5*(1), 69–94.

Overbeck, J. R., & Park, B. (2001). When power does not corrupt: Superior individuation processes among powerful perceivers. *Journal of Personality and Social Psychology, 81*, 549–565.

Oyserman, D., Coon, H. M., & Kemmelmeier, M. (2002). Rethinking individualism and collectivism: Evaluation of theoretical assumptions and meta-analyses. *Psychological Bulletin, 128*(1), 3–72.

Oyserman, D., & Lee, S. W. S. (2008). Does culture influence what and how we think? Effects of priming individualism and collectivism. *Psychological Bulletin, 134*, 311–342.

Ozer, D. J., & Benet-Martínez, V. (2006). Personality and the prediction of consequential outcomes. *Annual Review of Psychology, 57*, 401–421.

Pace, J. L., & Hemmings, A. (2007). Understanding authority in classrooms: A review of theory, ideology, and research. *Review of Educational Research, 77*, 3–27.

Packer, D. J. (2008a). Identifying systematic disobedience in Milgram's obedience experiments: A meta-analytic review. *Perspectives on Psychological Science, 3*, 301–304.

Packer, D. J. (2008b). On being both with us and against us: A normative conflict model of dissent in social groups. *Personality and Social Psychology Review, 12*(1), 50–72.

Packer, D. J. (2009). Avoiding groupthink: Whereas weakly identified members remain silent, strongly identified members dissent about collective problems. *Psychological Science, 20*(5), 546–548.

Packer, D. J., & Chasteen, A. L. (2010). Loyal deviance: Testing the normative conflict model of dissent in social groups. *Personality and Social Psychology Bulletin, 36*(1), 5–18.

Page, B. J. (2010). Online groups. In R. K. Conyne (Ed.), *The Oxford handbook of group counseling* (pp. 520–533). New York: Oxford University Press.

Page, R. C., Weiss, J. F., & Lietaer, G. (2002). Humanistic group psychotherapy. In D. J. Cain & J. Seeman (Eds.), *Humanistic psychotherapies: Handbook of research and practice* (pp. 339–368). Washington, DC: American Psychological Association.

Page-Gould, E., Mendoza-Denton, R., & Tropp, L. R. (2008). With a little help from my cross-group friend: Reducing anxiety in intergroup contexts through cross-group friendship. *Journal of Personality and Social Psychology, 95*, 1080–1094.

Palinkas, L. A. (1991). Effects of physical and social environments on the health and well-being of Antarctic winter-over personnel. *Environment and Behavior, 23*, 782–799.

Palmer, G. J. (1962). Task ability and effective leadership. *Psychological Reports, 10*, 863–866.

Paluck, E. L., & Green, D. P. (2009). Prejudice reduction: What works? A review and assessment of research and practice. *Annual Review of Psychology, 60*, 339–367.

Pandey, C., & Kapitanoff, S. (2011). The influence of anxiety and quality of interaction on collaborative test performance. *Active Learning in Higher Education, 12*(3), 163–174.

Panksepp, J., Nelson, E., & Bekkedal, M. (1997). Brain systems for the mediation of social separation-distress and social-reward: Evolutionary antecedents and neuropeptide intermediaries. In C. S. Carter, I. I. Lederhendler, & B. Kirkpatrick (Eds.), *The integrative neurobiology of affiliation* (pp. 78–100). New York: New York Academy of Sciences.

Paris, C. R., Salas, E., & Cannon-Bowers, J. A. (1999). Human performance in multi-operator systems. In P. A. Hancock (Ed.), *Human performance and ergonomics* (2nd ed., pp. 329–386). San Diego: Academic Press.

Park, E. S., & Hinsz, V. B. (2006). "Strength and safety in numbers": A theoretical perspective on group influences on approach and avoidance motivation. *Motivation and Emotion, 30*(2), 135–142.

Park, L. E., & Pinkus, R. T. (2009). Interpersonal effects of appearance-based rejection sensitivity. *Journal of Research in Personality, 43*, 602–612.

Parker, K. C. (1988). Speaking turns in small group interaction: A context-sensitive event sequence model. *Journal of Personality and Social Psychology, 54*, 965–971.

Parkinson, C. N. (1957). *Parkinson's law and other studies in administration.* Boston: Houghton Mifflin.

Parks, C. D., & Komorita, S. S. (1997). Reciprocal strategies for large groups. *Personality and Social Psychology Review, 1*, 314–322.

Parks, C. D., & Stone, A. B. (2010). The desire to expel unselfish members from the group. *Journal of Personality and Social Psychology, 99*(2), 303–310.

Parks, M. R. (2007). *Personal relationships and personal networks.* Mahwah, NJ: Erlbaum.

Parks, S. D. (2005). *Leadership can be taught: A bold approach for a complex world.* Boston: Harvard Business School Press.

Parkum, K. H., & Parkum, V. C. (1980). Citizen participation in community planning and decision making. In D. H. Smith, J. Macaulay, & Associates (Eds.), *Participation in social and political activities: A comprehensive analysis of political involvement, expressive leisure time, and helping behavior* (pp. 153–167). San Francisco: Jossey-Bass.

Parrado, N., with Rause, V. (2006). *Miracle in the Andes.* New York: Crown.

Parsons, H. M. (1976). Work environments. In I. Altman & J. Wohlwill (Eds.), *Human behavior and environment* (Vol. 1, pp. 163–209). New York: Plenum Press.

Parsons, T., Bales, R. F., & Shils, E. (Eds.). (1953). *Working papers in the theory of action.* New York: Free Press.

Paskevich, D. M., Brawley, L. R., Dorsch, K. D., & Widmeyer, W. N. (1999). Relationship between collective efficacy and team cohesion: Conceptual and measurement issues. *Group Dynamics: Theory, Research, and Practice, 3,* 210–222.

Patel, K. A., & Schlundt, D. G. (2001). Impact of moods and social context on eating behavior. *Appetite, 36,* 111–118.

Patterson, M. L. (1975). Personal space—Time to burst the bubble? *Man-Environment Systems, 5,* 67.

Patterson, M. L. (1996). Social behavior and social cognition: A parallel process approach. In J. L. Nye & A. M. Brower (Eds.), *What's social about social cognition? Research on socially shared cognitions in small groups* (pp. 87–105). Thousand Oaks, CA: Sage.

Patterson, M. L., Kelley, C. E., Kondracki, B. A., & Wulf, L. J. (1979). Effects of seating arrangement on small group behavior. *Social Psychology Quarterly, 42,* 180–185.

Patterson, M. L., Roth, C. P., & Schenk, C. (1979). Seating arrangement, activity, and sex differences in small group crowding. *Personality and Social Psychology Bulletin, 5,* 100–103.

Patterson, M. L., & Sechrest, L. B. (1970). Interpersonal distance and impression formation. *Journal of Personality, 38,* 161–166.

Paul, G. L. (1967). Strategy of outcome research in psychotherapy. *Journal of Consulting Psychology, 31,* 109–118.

Paulus, P. B., Annis, A. B., Seta, J. J., Schkade, J. K., & Matthews, R. W. (1976). Density does affect task performance. *Journal of Personality and Social Psychology, 34,* 248–353.

Paulus, P. B., & Brown, V. R. (2007). Toward more creative and innovative group idea generation: A cognitive-social-motivational perspective of brainstorming. *Social and Personality Psychology Compass, 1,* 248–265.

Paulus, P. B., Dzindolet, M. T., Poletes, G., & Camacho, L. M. (1993). Perception of performance in group brainstorming: The illusion of group productivity. *Personality and Social Psychology Bulletin, 19,* 78–89.

Paulus, P. B., Nakui, T., Putman, V. L., & Brown, V. R. (2006). Effects of task instructions and brief breaks on brainstorming. *Group Dynamics: Theory, Research, and Practice, 10,* 206–219.

Pavelchak, M. A., Moreland, R. L., & Levine, J. M. (1986). Effects of prior group memberships on subsequent reconnaissance activities. *Journal of Personality and Social Psychology, 50,* 56–66.

Paxton, P., & Moody, J. (2003). Structure and sentiment: Explaining emotional attachment to group. *Social Psychology Quarterly, 66,* 34–47.

Pazos, P., & Beruvides, M. G. (2011). Performance patterns in face-to-face and computer-supported teams. *Team Performance Management, 17,* 83–101.

Pearce, C. L., & Conger, J. A. (Eds.). (2003). *Shared leadership: Reframing the hows and whys of leadership.* Thousand Oaks, CA: Sage.

Pearce, C. L., Conger, J. A., & Locke, E. A. (2008). Shared leadership theory. *The Leadership Quarterly, 19,* 622–628.

Pearsall, M. J., & Ellis, A. P. J. (2006). The effects of critical team member assertiveness on team performance and satisfaction. *Journal of Management, 32,* 575–594.

Pedersen, D. M. (1999). Model for types of privacy by privacy functions. *Journal of Environmental Psychology, 19,* 397–405.

Peeters, M. A. G., Van Tuijl, H. F. J. M., Rutte, C. G., & Reymen, I. M. M. J. (2006). Personality and team performance: A meta-Analysis. *European Journal of Personality, 20,* 377–396.

Pelled, L. H., Eisenhardt, K. M., & Xin, K. R. (1999). Exploring the black box: An analysis of work group diversity, conflict, and performance. *Administrative Science Quarterly, 44,* 1–28.

Pelz, D. C. (1956). Some social factors related to performance in a research organization. *Administrative Science Quarterly, 1,* 310–325.

Pelz, D. C. (1967). Creative tensions in the research and development climate. *Science, 157,* 160–165.

Pemberton, M., Insko, C. A., & Schopler, J. (1996). Memory for and experience of differential competitive behavior of individuals and groups. *Journal of Personality and Social Psychology, 71,* 953–966.

Pemberton, M., & Sedikides, C. (2001). When do individuals help close others improve? The role of information diagnosticity. *Journal of Personality and Social Psychology, 81,* 234–246.

Pennebaker, J. W. (1982). Social and perceptual factors affecting symptom reporting and mass psychogenic illness. In M. J. Colligan, J. W. Pennebaker, & L. R. Murphy (Eds.), *Mass psychogenic illness: A social psychological analysis* (pp. 139–153). Mahwah, NJ: Erlbaum.

Pennebaker, J. W. (1997). *Opening up: The healing power of expressing emotions* (rev. ed.). New York: Guilford.

Pennington, D. C. (2002). *The social psychology of behavior in small groups.* New York: Psychology Press.

Pennington, N., & Hastie, R. (1986). Evidence evaluation in complex decision-making. *Journal of Personality and Social Psychology, 51,* 242–258.

Pennington, N., & Hastie, R. (1992). Explaining the evidence: Tests of the Story Model for juror decision making. *Journal of Personality and Social Psychology, 62,* 189–206.

Pepitone, A., & Reichling, G. (1955). Group cohesiveness and the expression of hostility. *Human Relations, 8,* 327–337.

Pepitone, A., & Wilpinski, C. (1960). Some consequences of experimental rejection. *Journal of Abnormal and Social Psychology, 60,* 359–364.

Perls, F. (1969). *Gestalt therapy verbatim.* Lafayette, CA: Real People Press.

Perrin, S., & Spencer, C. P. (1980). The Asch effect—A child of its time? *Bulletin of the British Psychological Society, 32,* 405–406.

Perrin, S., & Spencer, C. P. (1981). Independence or conformity in the Asch experiment as a reflection of cultural and situational factors. *British Journal of Social Psychology, 20,* 205–210.

Pescosolido, A. T. (2003). Group efficacy and group effectiveness: The effects of group efficacy over time on group performance and development. *Small Group Research, 34*(1), 20–42.

Peterson, M. F., Smith, P. B., Akande, A., Ayestaran, S., Bochner, S., Callan, V., Cho, N. G., Iscte, J. C. J., D'Amorim, M., Francois, P-H., Hofmann, K., Koopman, P. L., Leung, K., Lim, T. K.,Mortazavi, S., Munene, J., Ranford, M., Ropo, A., Savage, G., Setiadi, B., Sinha, T. N., Sorenson, R., & Viedge, C. (1995). Role conflict, ambiguity, and overload: A 21-nation study. *Academy of Management Journal, 38,* 429–452.

Peterson, R. S. (1997). A directive leadership style in group decision making can be both virtue and vice: Evidence from elite and experimental groups. *Journal of Personality and Social Psychology, 72,* 1107–1121.

Peterson, R. S., & Behfar, K. J. (2003). The dynamic relationship between performance feedback, trust, and conflict in groups: A longitudinal study. *Organizational Behavior and Human Decision Processes, 92,* 102–112.

Peterson, R. S., & Nemeth, C. J. (1996). Focus versus flexibility: Majority and minority influence can both improve performance. *Personality and Social Psychology Bulletin, 22,* 14–23.

Peterson, R. S., Owens, P. D., Tetlock, P. E., Fan, E. T., & Martorana, P. (1998). Group dynamics in top management teams: Groupthink, vigilance, and alternative models of organizational failure and success. *Organizational Behavior and Human Decision Processes, 73,* 272–305.

Petrie, T. A., & Greenleaf, C. A. (2007). Eating disorders in sport: From theory to research to intervention. In G. Tenenbaum & R. C. Eklund (Eds.), *Handbook of sport psychology* (3rd ed., pp. 352–378). Hoboken, NJ: John Wiley.

Pettigrew, T. F. (1997). Generalized intergroup contact effects on prejudice. *Personality and Social Psychology Bulletin, 23,* 173–185.

Pettigrew, T. F. (1998). Intergroup contact theory. *Annual Review of Psychology, 49,* 65–85.

Pettigrew, T. F. (2001). The ultimate attribution error: Extending Allport's cognitive analysis of prejudice. In M. A. Hogg & D. Abrams (Eds.), *Intergroup relations: Essential readings* (pp. 162–173). Philadelphia: Psychology Press.

Pettigrew, T. F., & Tropp, L. R. (2000). Does intergroup contact reduce prejudice: Recent meta-analytic findings. In S. Oskamp (Ed.), *Reducing prejudice and discrimination* (pp. 93–114). Mahwah, NJ: Erlbaum.

Pettigrew, T. F., & Tropp, L. R. (2006). A meta-analytic test of intergroup contact theory. *Journal of Personality and Social Psychology, 90,* 751–783.

Pettigrew, T. F., & Tropp, L. R. (2011). *When groups meet: The dynamics of intergroup contact.* New York: Psychology Press.

Pettit, G. S., Erath, S. A., Lansford, J. E., Dodge, K. A., & Bates, J. E. (2011). Dimensions of social capital and life adjustment in the transition to early adulthood. *International Journal of Behavioral Development, 35,* 482–489.

Phillips, K. W. (2003). The effects of categorically based expectations on minority influence: The importance of congruence. *Personality and Social Psychology Bulletin, 29,* 3–13.

Phinney, J. S., & Ong, A. D. (2007). Conceptualization and measurement of ethnic identity: Current status and future directions. *Journal of Counseling Psychology, 54,* 271–281.

Phoon, W. H. (1982). Outbreaks of mass hysteria at workplaces in Singapore: Some patterns and modes of presentation. In M. J. Colligan, J. W. Pennebaker, & L. R. Murphy (Eds.), *Mass psychogenic illness: A social psychological analysis* (pp. 21–31). Mahwah, NJ: Erlbaum.

Pierro, A., Cicero, L., & Raven, B. H. (2008). Motivated compliance with bases of social power. *Journal of Applied Social Psychology, 38,* 1921–1944.

Pierro, A., Kruglanski, A. W., & Raven, B. H. (2012). Motivational underpinnings of social influence in work settings: Bases of social power and the need for cognitive closure. *European Journal of Social Psychology, 42*(1), 41–52.

Pike, K. L. (1954). *Language in relation to a unified theory of the structure of human behavior.* Dallas, TX: Summer Institute of Linguistics.

Piliavin, J. A., & Siegl, E. (2007). Health benefits of volunteering in the Wisconsin Longitudinal Study. *Journal of Health and Social Behavior, 48*(4), 450–464.

Pillutla, M. M., & Murnighan, J. K. (1996). Unfairness, anger, and spite: Emotional rejections of ultimatum offers. *Organizational Behavior and Human Decision Processes, 68,* 208–224.

Pinter, B., & Greenwald, A. G. (2011). A comparison of minimal group induction procedures. *Group Processes & Intergroup Relations, 14*(1), 81–98.

Pinter, B., Insko, C. A., Wildschut, T., Kirchner, J. L., Montoya, R. M., & Wolf, S. T. (2007). Reduction of interindividual-intergroup discontinuity: The role of leader accountability and proneness to guilt. *Journal of Personality and Social Psychology, 93,* 250–265.

Piper, W. E. (2008). Underutilization of short-term group therapy: Enigmatic or understandable? *Psychotherapy Research, 18,* 127–138.

Pisano, G. P., Bohmer, R. M. J., & Edmondson, A. C. (2001). Organizational differences in rates of learning: Evidence from the adoption of minimally invasive cardiac surgery. *Management Science, 47,* 752–768.

Pittard-Payne, B. (1980). Nonassociational religious participation. In D. H. Smith, J. Macaulay, & Associates (Eds.), *Participation in social and political activities: A comprehensive analysis of political involvement, expressive leisure time, and helping behavior* (pp. 214–243). San Francisco: Jossey-Bass.

Pittinsky, T. L. (2010). A two-dimensional model of intergroup leadership: The case of national diversity. *American Psychologist, 65,* 194–200.

Pittman, T. S., & Zeigler, K. R. (2007). Basic human needs. In A. W. Kruglanski & E. T. Higgins (Eds.), *Social psychology: Handbook of basic principles* (2nd ed., pp. 473–489). New York: Guilford Press.

Platania, J., & Moran, G. P. (2001). Social facilitation as a function of mere presence of others. *Journal of Social Psychology, 141,* 190–197.

Polletta, F., & Jasper, J. M. (2001). Collective identity and social movements. *Annual Review of Sociology, 27,* 283–305.

Polley, R. B. (1989). On the dimensionality of interpersonal behavior: A reply to Lustig. *Small Group Behavior, 20,* 270–278.

Polzer, J. T. (1996). Intergroup negotiations: The effects of negotiating teams. *Journal of Conflict Resolution, 40,* 678–698.

Polzer, J. T., Kramer, R. M., & Neale, M. A. (1997). Positive illusions about oneself and one's group. *Small Group Research, 28,* 243–266.

Poole, M. S., & Dobosh, M. (2010). Exploring conflict management processes in jury deliberations through interaction analysis. *Small Group Research, 41*(4), 408–426.

Poole, M. S., & Hollingshead, A. B. (Eds.). (2005). *Theories of small groups: Interdisciplinary perspectives.* Thousand Oaks, CA: Sage.

Porter, N., Geis, F. L., Cooper, E., & Newman, E. (1985). Androgyny and leadership in mixed-sex groups. *Journal of Personality and Social Psychology, 49,* 808–823.

Postmes, T., & Spears, R. (1998). Deindividuation and antinormative behavior: A meta-analysis. *Psychological Bulletin, 123,* 238–259.

Postmes, T., Spears, R., & Cihangir, S. (2001). Quality of decision making and group norms. *Journal of Personality and Social Psychology, 80,* 918–930.

Postmes, T., Spears, R., & Lea, M. (2000). The formation of group norms in computer-mediated communication. *Human Communication Research, 26,* 341–371.

Poulin, M. J., Holman, E. A., & Buffone, A. (2012). The neurogenetics of nice receptor genes for oxytocin and vasopressin interact with threat to predict prosocial behavior. *Psychological Science, 23*(5), 446–452.

Poundstone, W. (1992). *Prisoner's dilemma.* New York: Doubleday.

Pozzi, F. (2010). Using Jigsaw and case study for supporting online collaborative learning. *Computers & Education, 55*(1), 67–75.

Prapavessis, H., & Carron, A. V. (1997). Sacrifice, cohesion, and conformity to norms in sport teams. *Group Dynamics: Theory, Research, and Practice, 1,* 231–240.

Pratkanis, A. R. (Ed.). (2007). *The science of social influence: Advances and future progress.* New York: Psychology Press.

Pratt, J. H. (1922). The principle of class treatment and their application to various chronic diseases. *Hospital Social Services, 6,* 401–417.

Prentice, D. A. (2007). Pluralistic ignorance. In R. F. Baumeister & K. D. Vohs (Eds.), *Encyclopedia of social psychology* (pp. 673–674). Thousand Oaks, CA: Sage.

Prentice, D. A., & Miller, D. T. (1993). Pluralistic ignorance and alcohol use on campus: Some consequences of misperceiving the social norm. *Journal of Personality and Social Psychology, 64,* 243–254.

Prentice-Dunn, S., & Rogers, R. W. (1980). Effects of deindividuating situation cues and aggressive models on subjective deindividuation and aggression. *Journal of Personality and Social Psychology, 39,* 104–113.

Prentice-Dunn, S., & Rogers, R. W. (1982). Effects of public and private self-awareness on deindividuation and aggression. *Journal of Personality and Social Psychology, 43,* 503–513.

Prentice-Dunn, S., & Rogers, R. W. (1983). Deindividuation and aggression. In R. G. Geen & E. I. Donnerstein (Eds.), *Aggression: Theoretical and empirical reviews* (Vol. 1). New York: Academic Press.

Prentice-Dunn, S., & Spivey, R. W. (1986). Extreme deindividuation in the laboratory: Its magnitude and subjective components. *Personality and Social Psychology Bulletin, 12,* 206–215.

Prislin, R., Brewer, M., & Wilson, D. J. (2002). Changing majority and minority positions within a group versus an aggregate. *Personality and Social Psychology Bulletin, 28,* 640–647.

Prislin, R., & Crano, W. D. (2012). A history of social influence research. In A. W. Kruglanski & W. Stroebe (Eds.), *Handbook of the history of social psychology* (pp. 321–339). New York: Psychology Press.

Prislin, R., Limbert, W. M., & Bauer, E. (2000). From majority to minority and vice versa: The asymmetrical effects of losing and gaining majority position within a group. *Journal of Personality and Social Psychology, 79,* 385–397.

Pritchard, R. D., Harrell, M. M., DiazGranados, D., & Guzman, M. J. (2008). The productivity measurement and enhancement system: A meta-analysis. *Journal of Applied Psychology, 93,* 540–567.

Probst, T., Carnevale, P. J., & Triandis, H. C. (1999). Cultural values in intergroup and single-group social dilemmas. *Organizational Behavior and Human Decision Processes, 77*(3), 171–191.

Pronin, E. (2008). How we see ourselves and how we see others. *Science, 320*(5880), 1177–1180.

Provine, R. R. (2004). Laughing, tickling, and the evolution of speech and self. *Current Directions in Psychological Science, 13,* 215–218.

Pruitt, D. G. (1971). Choice shifts in group discussion: An introductory review. *Journal of Personality and Social Psychology, 20,* 339–360.

Pruitt, D. G. (1983). Strategic choice in negotiation. *American Behavioral Science, 27,* 167–194.

Pruitt, D. G. (1998). Social conflict. In D. T. Gilbert, S. T. Fiske, & G. Lindzey (Eds.), *The handbook of social psychology* (4th ed., Vol. 2, 470–503). New York: McGraw-Hill.

Pruitt, D. G. (2012). A history of social conflict and negotiation research. In A. W. Kruglanski & W. Stroebe (Eds.), *Handbook of the history of social psychology* (pp. 431–452). New York: Psychology Press.

Pruitt, D. G., & Kim, S. H. (2004). *Social conflict: Escalation, stalemate, and settlement* (3rd ed.). New York: McGraw-Hill.

Pruitt, D. G., Parker, J. C., & Mikolic, J. M. (1997). Escalation as a reaction to persistent annoyance. *International Journal of Conflict Management, 8*(3), 252–270.

Putnam, R. D. (2000). *Bowling alone: The collapse and revival of American community*. New York: Simon & Schuster.

Quattrone, G. A., & Jones, E. E. (1980). The perception of variability within in-groups and out-groups: Implications for the law of small numbers. *Journal of Personality and Social Psychology, 38*, 141–152.

Quinn, A., Schlenker, B. R. (2002). Can accountability produce independence? Goals as determinants of the impact of accountability on conformity. *Personality and Social Psychology Bulletin, 28*, 472–483.

Raafat, R. M., Chater, N., & Frith, C. (2009). Herding in humans. *Trends in Cognitive Sciences, 13*(10), 420–428.

Rabbie, J. (1963). Differential preference for companionship under stress. *Journal of Abnormal and Social Psychology, 67*, 643–648.

Radloff, R., & Helmreich, R. (1968). *Groups under stress: Psychological research in SEALAB II*. New York: Irvington.

Raghubir, P., & Valenzuela, A. (2010). Male–female dynamics in groups: A field study of The Weakest Link. *Small Group Research, 41*(1), 41–70.

Ragone, G. (1981). Fashion, "crazes," and collective behavior. *Communications, 7*, 249–268.

Rakoczy, H., Brosche, N., Warneken, F., & Tomasello, M. (2009). Young children's understanding of the context-relativity of normative rules in conventional games. *British Journal of Developmental Psychology, 27*(2), 445–456.

Randsley de Moura, G., Leader, T., Pelletier, J., & Abrams, D. (2008). Prospects for group processes and intergroup relations research: A review of 70 years' progress. *Group Processes & Intergroup Relations, 11*, 575–596.

Rantilla, A. K. (2000). Collective task responsibility allocation: Revisiting the group-serving bias. *Small Group Research, 31*, 739–766.

Rapee, R. M., Kim, J., Wang, J., Liu, X., Hofmann, S. G., Chen, J., Oh, K. Y., Bögels, S., Arman, S., Heinrichs, N., & Alden, L. E. (2011). Perceived impact of socially anxious behaviors on individuals' lives in Western and East Asian countries. *Behavior Therapy, 42*(3), 485–492.

Rapoport, A. (1980). Environmental preference, habitat selection and urban housing. *Journal of Social Issues, 36*(3), 118–134.

Ratner, R. K., & Miller, D. T. (2001). The norm of self-interest and its effects on social action. *Journal of Personality and Social Psychology, 81*, 5–16.

Raven, B. H. (1965). Social influence and power. In I. D. Steiner & M. Fishbein (Eds.), *Current studies in social psychology* (pp. 371–382). New York: Holt, Rinehart & Winston.

Raven, B. H. (1992). A power/interaction model of interpersonal influence: French and Raven thirty years later. *Journal of Social Behavior and Personality, 7*, 217–244.

Raven, B. H., Schwarzwald, J., & Koslowsky, M. (1998). Conceptualizing and measuring a power/interaction model of interpersonal influence. *Journal of Applied Social Psychology, 28*, 307–332.

Rawls, J. (1971). *A theory of justice*. Cambridge, MA: Belknap Press of Harvard University Press.

Read, K. E. (1986). *Return to the high valley: Coming full circle*. Berkeley: University of California Press.

Read, P. P. (1974). *Alive*. New York: Avon.

Redl, F. (1942). Group emotion and leaders. *Psychiatry, 5*, 573–596.

Reeder, G. D., Monroe, A. E., & Pryor, J. B. (2008). Impressions of Milgram's obedient teachers: Situational cues inform inferences about motives and traits. *Journal of Personality and Social Psychology, 95*(1), 1–17.

Reeder, K., Macfadyen, L., Roche, J., & Chase, M. (2004). Negotiating cultures in cyberspace: Participation patterns and problematics. *Language Learning & Technology, 8*, 88–105.

Rees, C. R., & Segal, M. W. (1984). Role differentiation in groups: The relationship between instrumental and expressive leadership. *Small Group Behavior, 15*, 109–123.

Reichard, R. J., Riggio, R. E., Guerin, D. W., Oliver, P. H., Gottfried, A. W., & Gottfried, A. E. (2011). A longitudinal analysis of relationships between adolescent personality and intelligence with adult leader emergence and transformational leadership. *The Leadership Quarterly, 22*(3), 471–481.

Reicher, S. D. (1984). The St. Paul's riot: An explanation of the limits of crowd action in terms of a social identity model. *European Journal of Social Psychology, 14*, 1–21.

Reicher, S. D. (1987). Crowd behavior as social action. In J. C. Turner, M. A. Hogg, P. J. Oakes, S. D. Reicher, & M. S. Wetherell (Eds.), *Rediscovering the social group: A self-categorization theory* (pp. 171–202). Oxford, UK: Blackwell.

Reicher, S. D. (1996). "The Battle of Westminster": Developing the social identity model of crowd behavior in order to explain the initiation and development of collective conflict. *European Journal of Social Psychology, 26*, 115–134.

Reicher, S. D. (2001). The psychology of crowd dynamics. In M. A. Hogg & R. S. Tindale (Eds.), *Blackwell handbook of social psychology: Group processes* (pp. 182–208). Malden, MA: Blackwell.

Reicher, S. D., Haslam, S. A., & Rath, R. (2008). Making a virtue of evil: A five-step social identity model of the development of collective hate. *Social and Personality Psychology Compass, 2*, 1313–1344.

Reicher, S. D., Spears, R., & Postmes, T. (1995). A social identity model of deindividuated phenomena. In W. Stroebe & M. Hewstone (Eds.), *European review of social psychology* (Vol. 6, pp. 161–198). Chichester, UK: Wiley.

Reicher, S. D., & Stott, C. (2011). *Mad mobs and Englishmen? Myths and realities of the 2011 riots*. London: Constable & Robinson.

Reichl, A. J. (1997). Ingroup favoritism and outgroup favoritism in low status minimal groups: Differential responses to status-related and status-unrelated measures. *European Journal of Social Psychology, 27*, 617–633.

Reifman, A., Lee, L., & Apparala, M. (2004). *Spreading popularity of two musical artists: A "tipping point" study*. Poster presented at the Annual Meeting of the Society for Personality and Social Psychology, Austin, TX.

Reimer, T., Reimer, A., & Czienskowski, U. (2010). Decision-making groups attenuate the discussion bias in favor of shared information: A meta-analysis. *Communication Monographs, 77*(1), 121–142.

Reimer, T., Reimer, A., & Hinsz, V. B. (2010). Naïve groups can solve the hidden-profile problem. *Human Communication Research, 36*(3), 443–467.

Reinig, B. A., Horowitz, I., & Whittenburg, G. E. (2011). A longitudinal analysis of satisfaction with group work. *Group Decision and Negotiation, 20*(2), 215–237.

Reis, H. T., & Gosling, S. D. (2010). Social psychological methods outside the laboratory. In S. T. Fiske, D. T. Gilbert, & G. Lindzey (Eds.), *Handbook of social psychology* (Vol. 1, 5th ed., pp. 82–114). Hoboken, NJ: John Wiley.

Reis, H. T., Maniaci, M. R., Caprariello, P. A., Eastwick, P. W., & Finkel, E. J. (2011). Familiarity does indeed promote attraction in live interaction. *Journal of Personality and Social Psychology, 101*(3), 557–570.

Reno, R. R., Cialdini, R. B., & Kallgren, C. A. (1993). The transsituational influence of social norms. *Journal of Personality and Social Psychology, 64*, 104–112.

Rentsch, J. R., & Steel, R. P. (1998). Testing the durability of job characteristics as predictors of absenteeism over a six-year period. *Personnel Psychology, 51*, 165–190.

Reston, J., Jr. (2000). *Our father who art in hell*. Lincoln, NE: iUniverse.com

Rhee, E., Uleman, J. S., Lee, H. K., & Roman, R. J. (1995). Spontaneous self-descriptions and ethnic identities in individualistic and collectivistic cultures. *Journal of Personality and Social Psychology, 69*, 142–152.

Rheingold, H. (2002). *Smart mobs: The next social revolution*. New York: Basic Books.

Riaño, J., & Hodess, R. (2008). *Bribe payers index 2008*. Berlin, Germany: Transparency International.

Rice, O. K. (1978). *The Hatfields and the McCoys*. Lexington: University Press of Kentucky.

Rice, R. W. (1979). Reliability and validity of the LPC Scale: A reply. *Academy of Management Review, 4*, 291–294.

Rice, R. W., Instone, D., & Adams, J. (1984). Leader sex, leader success, and leadership process: Two field studies. *Journal of Applied Psychology, 69*, 12–31.

Richard, F. D., Bond, C. F., Jr., & Stokes-Zoota, J. J. (2003). One hundred years of social psychology quantitatively described. *Review of General Psychology, 7*, 331–363.

Ridgeway, C. L. (1989). Understanding legitimation in informal status orders. In J. Berger & M. Zelditch (Eds.), *Sociological theories in progress* (Vol. 3, pp. 131–159). Thousand Oaks, CA: Sage.

Ridgeway, C. L. (2001). Social status and group structure. In M. A. Hogg & R. S. Tindale (Eds.), *Blackwell handbook of social psychology: Group processes* (pp. 352–375). Malden, MA: Blackwell.

Ridgeway, C. L., Backor, K., Li, Y. E., Tinkler, J. E., & Erickson, K. G. (2009). How easily does a social difference become a status distinction: Gender matters. *American Sociological Review, 74*(1), 44–62.

Ridgeway, C. L., & Balkwell, J. W. (1997). Group processes and the diffusion of status beliefs. *Social Psychology Quarterly, 60*, 14–31.

Riess, M. (1982). Seating preferences as impression management: A literature review and theoretical integration. *Communication, 11*, 85–113.

Riess, M., & Rosenfeld, P. (1980). Seating preferences as nonverbal communication: A self-presentational analysis. *Journal of Applied Communications Research, 8*, 22–30.

Riggio, H. R., & Kwong, W. Y. (2009). Social skills, paranoid thinking, and social outcomes among young adults. *Personality and Individual Differences, 47*(5), 492–497.

Rimal, R. N., & Real, K. (2005). How behaviors are influenced by perceived norms: A test of the theory of normative social behavior. *Communication Research, 32*, 389–414.

Ringelmann, M. (1913). Research on animate sources of power: The work of man. *Annales de l'Institut National Agronomique, 2e serié—tome XII*, 1–40.

Ringer, T. M. (2002). *Group action: The dynamics of groups in therapeutic, educational, and corporate settings*. Philadelphia: Jessica Kingsley Publishers.

Rink, F., & Ellemers, N. (2011). From current state to desired state: How compositional changes affect dissent and innovation in work groups. In J. Jetten & M. J. Hornsey (Eds.), *Rebels in groups: Dissent, deviance, difference, and defiance* (pp. 54–72). Malden, MA: Wiley-Blackwell.

Riordan, C., & Riggiero, J. (1980). Producing equal-status interracial interaction: A replication. *Social Psychology Quarterly, 43*, 131–136.

Rivera, A. N., & Tedeschi, J. T. (1976). Public versus private reactions to positive inequity. *Journal of Personality and Social Psychology, 34*, 895–900.

Rivers, J. J., & Josephs, R. A. (2010). Dominance and health: The role of social rank in physiology and illness. In A. Guinote & T. K. Vescio (Eds.), *The social psychology of power* (pp. 87–112). New York: Guilford Press.

Robak, R. W. (2001). Self-definition in psychotherapy: Is it time to revisit self-perception theory? *North American Journal of Psychology, 3*, 529–534.

Robbins, A. (2004). *Pledged: The secret life of sororities*. New York: Hyperion.

Robert, C., & Wasti, S. A. (2002). Organizational individualism and collectivism: Theoretical development and an empirical test of a measure. *Journal of Management, 28*(4), 544–566.

Robert, H. M. (1971). *Robert's rules of order* (Rev. ed.). New York: Morrow. (original work published in 1915)

Robinson, T. T., & Carron, A. V. (1982). Personal and situational factors associated with dropping out versus maintaining participation in competitive sport. *Journal of Sport Psychology, 4*(4), 364–378.

Robison, F. F. (1999). Commentary on "Understanding roles: A psychodynamic model for role differentiation in groups," by Moxnes (1999). *Group Dynamics: Theory, Research, and Practice, 3*(2), 114–115.

Roccas, S., Sagiv, L., Schwartz, S., Halevy, N., & Eidelson, R. (2008). Toward a unifying model of identification with groups: Integrating theoretical perspectives. *Personality and Social Psychology Review, 12*, 280–306.

Rodin, J., & Baum, A. (1978). Crowding and helplessness: Potential consequences of density and loss of control. In A. Baum & Y. Epstein (Eds.), *Human responses to crowding* (pp. 389–401). Mahwah, NJ: Erlbaum.

Rodin, J., Solomon, S. K., & Metcalf, J. (1978). Role of control in mediating perceptions of density. *Journal of Personality and Social Psychology, 36*, 988–999.

Roethlisberger, F. J., & Dickson, W. J. (1939). *Management and the worker*. Boston: Harvard University Press.

Rofé, Y. (1984). Stress and affiliation: A utility theory. *Psychological Review, 91*, 235–250.

Rogelberg, S. G., Leach, D. J., Warr, P. B., & Burnfield, J. L. (2006). "Not another meeting!" Are meeting time demands related to employee well-being? *Journal of Applied Psychology, 91*, 83–96.

Rogelberg, S. G., & O'Connor, M. S. (1998). Extending the step-ladder technique: An examination of self-paced stepladder groups. *Group Dynamics: Theory, Research, and Practice, 2*, 82–91.

Rogelberg, S. G., & Rumery, S. M. (1996). Gender diversity, team decision quality, time on task, and interpersonal cohesion. *Small Group Research, 27*, 79–90.

Rogers, C. (1970). *Encounter groups*. New York: Harper & Row.

Rohrmann, B. (2000). Cross-cultural studies of the perception and evaluation of hazards. In O. Renn & B. Rohrmann (Eds.), *Cross-cultural risk perception: A survey of empirical studies* (pp. 103–144). Dordrecht, The Netherlands: Kluwer.

Roll, S., McClelland, G., & Abel, T. (1996). Differences in susceptibility to influence in Mexican American and Anglo females. *Hispanic Journal of Behavioral Sciences, 18*, 13–20.

Rom, E., & Mikulincer, M. (2003). Attachment theory and group processes: The association between attachment style and group-related representations, goals, memories, and functioning. *Journal of Personality and Social Psychology, 84*, 1220–1235.

Ronay, R., Greenaway, K., Anicich, E. M., & Galinsky, A. D. (2012). The path to glory is paved with hierarchy: When hierarchical differentiation increases group effectiveness. *Psychological Science, 23*(6), 669–677.

Roos, P. D. (1968). Jurisdiction: An ecological concept. *Human Relations, 21*, 75–84.

Rose, R., & Sergel, S. L. (1958). *Twelve angry men: A play in three acts*. New York: The Dramatic Publishing Co.

Rose-Krasnor, L. (2009). Future directions in youth involvement research. *Social Development, 18*(2), 497–509.

Rosenbloom, T., Shahar, A., Perlman, A., Estreich, D., & Kirzner, E. (2007). Success on a practical driver's license test with and without the presence of another testee. *Accident Analysis & Prevention, 39*, 1296–1301.

Rosenthal, S. A., & Pittinsky, T. L. (2006). Narcissistic leadership. *Leadership Quarterly, 17*, 617–633.

Roseth, C. J., Johnson, D. W., & Johnson, R. T. (2008). Promoting early adolescents' achievement and peer relationships: The effects of cooperative, competitive, and individualistic goal structures. *Psychological Bulletin, 134*, 223–246.

Rosiny, S. (2012). The Arab Spring: Triggers, dynamics, and prospects. *GIGA Focus International Edition, 5*(1), 1–7. Retrieved from www.giga-hamburg.de/giga-focus

Rosnow, R. L. (1980). Psychology of rumor reconsidered. *Psychological Bulletin, 87*, 578–591.

Rosnow, R. L., & Kimmel, A. J. (1979). Lives of a rumor. *Psychology Today, 13*, 88–92.

Rosnow, R. L., Yost, J. H., & Esposito, J. L. (1986). Belief in rumor and likelihood of rumor transmission. *Language and Communication, 6*, 189–194.

Ross, L. (1977). The intuitive psychologist and his shortcomings: Distortions in the attribution process. *Advances in Experimental Social Psychology, 10*, 173–220.

Ross, L., Bierbrauer, G., & Hoffman, S. (1976). The role of attribution processes in conformity and dissent: Revisiting the Asch situation. *American Psychologist, 31*, 148–157.

Ross, L., Greene, D., & House, P. (1977). The false consensus effect: An egocentric bias in social perception and attribution processes. *Journal of Experimental Social Psychology, 13*(3), 279–301.

Ross, L., & Ward, A. (1995). Psychological barriers to dispute resolution. *Advances in Experimental Social Psychology, 27*, 255–304.

Ross, M., & Sicoly, E. (1979). Egocentric biases in availability and attribution. *Journal of Personality and Social Psychology, 37*, 322–336.

Ross, T. M., Jones, E. C., & Adams, S. (2008). Can team effectiveness be predicted? *Team Performance Management, 14*, 248–268.

Ross, W. H., Brantmeier, C., & Ciriacks, T. (2002). The impact of hybrid dispute-resolution procedures on constituent fairness judgments. *Journal of Applied Social Psychology, 32*, 1151–1188.

Ross, W. H., & Conlon, D. E. (2000). Hybrid forms of dispute resolution: Theoretical implications of combining mediation and arbitration. *Academy of Management Review, 25*, 416–427.

Rossano, M. J. (2012). The essential role of ritual in the transmission and reinforcement of social norms. *Psychological Bulletin, 138*(3), 529–549.

Rost, J. C. (1993). *Leadership for the twenty-first century*. Westport, CT: Praeger.

Rost, J. C. (2008). Followership: An outmoded concept. In R. E. Riggio, I. Chaleff, & J. Lipman-Blumen (Eds.), *The art of followership: How great followers create great leaders and organizations* (pp. 53–64). San Francisco: Jossey-Bass.

Roth, B. E. (1993). Freud: The group psychologist and group leader. In H. I. Kaplan & M. J. Sadock (Eds.), *Comprehensive group psychotherapy* (3rd. ed., pp. 10–21). Baltimore: Williams & Wilkins.

Rothbart, M., Sriram, N., & Davis-Stitt, C. (1996). The retrieval of typical and atypical category members. *Journal of Experimental Social Psychology, 32*, 309–336.

Rothgerber, H. (1997). External intergroup threat as an antecedent to perceptions in in-group and out-group homogeneity. *Journal of Personality and Social Psychology, 73*, 1206–1212.

Rothgerber, H., & Worchel, S. (1997). The view from below: Intergroup relations from the perspective of the disadvantaged group. *Journal of Personality and Social Psychology, 73*, 1191–1205.

Rotton, J., & Cohn, E. G. (2002). Climate, weather, and crime. In R. B. Bechtel & A. Churchman (Eds.), *Handbook of environmental psychology* (pp. 481–498). New York: Wiley.

Rouhana, N. N., & Bar-Tal, D. (1998). Psychological dynamics of intractable ethnonational conflicts: The Israeli-Palestinian case. *American Psychologist, 53*, 761–770.

Rouhana, N. N., & Kelman, H. C. (1994). Promoting joint thinking in international conflicts: An Israeli-Palestinian continuing workshop. *Journal of Social Issues, 50*, 157–178.

Rousseau, V., Aubé, C., & Savoie, A. (2006). Teamwork behaviors: A review and an integration of frameworks. *Small Group Research, 37*(5), 540–570.

Rousseau, J.-J. (2008). *A discourse upon the origin and foundation of the inequality among mankind.* New York: Cosimo. (original work published 1755)

Roy, D. F. (1959). "Banana time": Job satisfaction and informal interaction. *Human Organization, 18*, 158–168.

Roy, M. C., Gauvin, S., & Limayem, M. (1996). Electronic group brainstorming: The role of feedback and productivity. *Small Group Research, 27*, 214–247.

Rozin, P., Lowery, L., Imada, S., & Haidt, J. (1999). The CAD triad hypothesis: A mapping between three moral emotions (contempt, anger, disgust) and three moral codes (community, autonomy, divinity). *Journal of Personality and Social Psychology, 76*, 574–586.

Ruback, R. B., Dabbs, J. M., Jr., & Hopper, C. H. (1984). The process of brainstorming: An analysis with individual and group vocal parameters. *Journal of Personality and Social Psychology, 47*, 558–567.

Rubin, K. H., Wojslawowicz, J. C., Rose-Krasnor, L., Booth-LaForce, C., & Burgess, K. B. (2006). The best friendships of shy/withdrawn children: Prevalence, stability, and relationship quality. *Journal of Abnormal Child Psychology, 34*(2), 143–157.

Rubin, R. B. (1985). The validity of the Communication Competency Assessment Instrument. *Communication Monographs, 52*, 173–185.

Rudman, L. A., & Glick, P. (2001). Prescriptive gender stereotypes and backlash toward agentic women. *Journal of Social Issues, 57*, 743–762.

Ruef, M., Aldrich, H. E., & Carter, N. M. (2003). The structure of founding teams: Homophily, strong ties, and isolation among U.S. entrepreneurs. *American Sociological Review, 68*, 195–222.

Rufus, A. S. (2003). *Party of one: The loners' manifesto.* New York: Marlowe and Co.

Runciman, W. G. (1966). *Relative deprivation and social justice.* London: Routledge & Kegan Paul.

Rusbult, C. E., Agnew, C. R., & Arriaga, X. B. (2012). The investment model of commitment processes. In P. A. M. Van Lange, A. W. Kruglanski, & E. T. Higgins (Eds.), *Handbook of theories of social psychology* (Vol. 2, pp. 218–231). Thousand Oaks, CA: Sage.

Ruscher, J. B., & Hammer, E. D. (2006). The development of shared stereotypic impressions in conversation: An emerging model, methods, and extensions to cross-group settings. *Journal of Language and Social Psychology, 25*, 221–243.

Russell, B. (2004). *Power.* London: Allen & Unwyn. (original work published in 1938)

Russell, G. W., & Arms, R. L. (1998). Toward a social psychological profile of would-be rioters. *Aggressive Behavior, 24*, 219–226.

Russell, J. A. (2003). Core affect and the psychological construction of emotion. *Psychological Review, 110*, 145–172.

Russell, J. A., & Snodgrass, J. (1987). Emotion and the environment. In D. Stokols & I. Altman (Eds.), *Handbook of environmental psychology* (pp. 245–280). New York: Wiley.

Russell, N. J. C., & Gregory, R. J. (2011). Spinning an organizational "web of obligation"? Moral choice in Stanley Milgram's "obedience" experiments. *The American Review of Public Administration, 41*(5), 495–518.

Ryan, M. K., Haslam, S. A., Hersby, M. D., & Bongiorno, R. (2011). Think crisis–think female: The glass cliff and contextual variation in the think manager–think male stereotype. *Journal of Applied Psychology, 96*(3), 470–484.

Rydell, R. J., Hugenberg, K., Ray, D., & Mackie, D. M. (2007). Implicit theories about groups and stereotyping: The role of group entitativity. *Personality and Social Psychology Bulletin, 33*, 549–558.

Ryen, A. H., & Kahn, A. (1975). The effects of intergroup orientation on group attitudes and proxemic behavior: A test of two models. *Journal of Personality and Social Psychology, 31*, 302–310.

Saavedra, R., Earley, P. C., & Van Dyne, L. (1993). Complex interdependence in task-performing groups. *Journal of Applied Psychology, 78*(1), 61–72.

Saavedra, R., & Van Dyne, L. (1999). Social exchange and emotional investment in work groups. *Motivation and Emotion, 23*(2), 105–123.

Sabini, J., Garvey, B., & Hall, A. L. (2001). Shame and embarrassment revisited. *Personality and Social Psychology Review, 27*, 104–117.

Sadler, M. S., & Judd, C. M. (2001). Overcoming dependent data: A guide to the analysis of group data. In M. A. Hogg & R. S. Tindale (Eds.), *Blackwell handbook of social psychology: Group processes* (pp. 497–524). Malden, MA: Blackwell.

Sadler, P., & Woody, E. (2003). Is who you are who you're talking to? Interpersonal style and complementarily in mixed-sex interactions. *Journal of Personality and Social Psychology*, *84*, 80–95.

Saks, M. J. (1977). *Jury verdicts*. Lexington, MA: Heath.

Saks, M. J., & Hastie, R. (1978). *Social psychology in court*. New York: Van Nostrand Reinhold.

Saks, M. J., & Marti, M. W. (1997). A meta-analysis of the effects of jury size. *Law and Human Behavior*, *21*, 451–467.

Salas, E., Goodwin, G. F., & Burke, C. S. (Eds.). (2009). *Team effectiveness in complex organizations: Cross-disciplinary perspectives and approaches*. New York: Routledge/Taylor & Francis Group.

Salas, E., Nichols, D. R., & Driskell, J. E. (2007). Testing three team training strategies in intact teams: A meta-analysis. *Small Group Research*, *38*, 471–488.

Salas, E., Priest, H. A., & DeRouin, R. E. (2005). Team building. In N. Stanton, A. Hedge, K. Brookhuis, E. Salas, & H. Hendrick (Eds.), *Handbook of human factors and ergonomics methods* (pp. 465–470). Boca Raton, FL: CRC Press.

Salas, E., Rosen, M. A., Burke, C. S., & Goodwin, G. F. (2009). The wisdom of collectives in organizations: An update of the teamwork competencies. In E. Salas, G. F. Goodwin, & C. S. Burke (Eds.), *Team effectiveness in complex organizations: Cross-disciplinary perspectives and approaches* (pp. 39–79). New York: Routledge/Taylor & Francis Group.

Salas, E., Rozell, D., Mullen, B., & Driskell, J. E. (1999). The effect of team building on performance: An integration. *Small Group Research*, *30*, 309–329.

Salas, E., Tannenbaum, S. I., Kraiger, K., & Smith-Jentsch, K. A. (2012). The science of training and development in organizations: What matters in practice. *Psychological Science in the Public Interest*, *13*(2), 74–101.

Salas, E., Wilson, K. A., Burke, C. S., & Wightman, D. C. (2006). Does crew resource management training work? An update, an extension, and some critical needs. *Human Factors*, *48*, 392–412.

Samaranayake, V., & Gamage, C. (2012). Employee perception towards electronic monitoring at work place and its impact on job satisfaction of software professionals in Sri Lanka. *Telematics and Informatics*, *29*(2), 233–244.

Sampson, E. E., & Brandon, A. C. (1964). The effects of role and opinion deviation on small group behavior. *Sociometry*, *27*, 261–281.

Samuelson, C. D., & Allison, S. T. (1994). Cognitive factors affecting the use of social decision heuristics in resource-sharing tasks. *Organizational Behavior and Human Decision Processes*, *58*, 1–27.

Sandelands, L., & St. Clair, L. (1993). Toward an empirical concept of group. *Journal for the Theory of Social Behavior*, *23*(4), 423–458.

Sanders, G. S., Baron, R. S., & Moore, D. L. (1978). Distraction and social comparison as mediators of social facilitation effects. *Journal of Experimental Social Psychology*, *14*, 291–303.

Sanders, W. B. (1994). *Gangbangs and drive-bys: Grounded culture and juvenile gang violence*. New York: Aldine de Gruyter.

Sanna, L. J. (1992). Self-efficacy theory: Implications for social facilitation and social loafing. *Journal of Personality and Social Psychology*, *62*, 774–786.

Sanna, L. J., Parks, C. D., Chang, E. C., & Carter, S. E. (2005). The hourglass is half full or half empty: Temporal framing and the group planning fallacy. *Group Dynamics: Theory, Research, and Practice*, *9*, 173–188.

Sapp, M. (2009). *Psychodynamic, affective, and behavioral theories of psychotherapy*. Springfield, IL: Charles C. Thomas.

Sapp, S. G., Harrod, W. J., & Zhao, L. (1996). Leadership emergence in task groups with egalitarian gender-role expectations. *Sex Roles*, *34*, 65–83.

Sarbin, T. R., & Allen, V. L. (1968). Increasing participation in a natural group setting: A preliminary report. *Psychological Record*, *18*, 1–7.

Sattler, D. N., & Kerr, N. L. (1991). Might versus morality explored: Motivational and cognitive bases for social motives. *Journal of Personality and Social Psychology*, *60*, 756–765.

Saucier, G. (1994). Mini-Markers: A brief version of Goldberg's unipolar Big-Five markers. *Journal of Personality Assessment*, *63*, 506–516.

Saunders, C., Van Slyke, C., & Vogel, D. (2004). My time or yours? Managing time visions in global virtual teams. *Academy of Management Executive 18*(1), 19–31.

Savitsky, K. (2007). Egocentrism. In R. F. Baumeister & K. D. Vohs (Eds.), *Encyclopedia of social psychology* (p. 278). Thousand Oaks, CA: Sage.

Savitsky, K., Van Boven, L., Epley, N., & Wight, W. (2005). The unpacking effect in responsibility allocations for group tasks. *Journal of Experimental Social Psychology*, *41*, 447–457.

Scandura, T. A., & Lankau, M. J. (1996). Developing diverse leaders: A leader-member exchange approach. *Leadership Quarterly*, *7*, 243–263.

Schachter, S. (1951). Deviation, rejection, and communication. *Journal of Abnormal and Social Psychology*, *46*, 190–207.

Schachter, S. (1959). *The psychology of affiliation*. Stanford, CA: Stanford University Press.

Schachter, S., Ellertson, N., McBride, D., & Gregory, D. (1951). An experimental study of cohesiveness and productivity. *Human Relations*, *4*, 229–238.

Schafer, M., & Crichlow, S. (2010). *Groupthink vs. high quality decision making in international relations*. New York: Columbia University Press.

Schauer, A. H., Seymour, W. R., & Geen, R. G. (1985). Effects of observation and evaluation on anxiety in beginning counselors: A social facilitation analysis. *Journal of Counseling and Development*, *63*, 279–285.

Scheepers, D., de Wit, F., Ellemers, N., & Sassenberg, K. (2012). Social power makes the heart work more efficiently: Evidence from cardiovascular markers of challenge and threat. *Journal of Experimental Social Psychology*, *48*(1), 371–374.

Scheeres, J. (2011). *A thousand lives: The untold story of hope, deception, and survival at Jonestown.* New York: Free Press.

Schei, V., Rognes, J., & Shapiro, D. L. (2011). Can individualists and cooperators play together? The effect of mixed social motives in negotiations. *Journal of Experimental Social Psychology, 47*(2), 371–377.

Schein, E. H. (1961). *Coercive persuasion.* New York: Norton.

Schein, E. H. (1990). Organizational culture. *American Psychologist, 45*(2), 109–119.

Schein, L. A., Spitz, H. I., Burlingame, G. M., & Muskin, P. R. (Eds.), with S. Vargo (2006). *Psychological effects of catastrophic disasters: Group approaches to treatment.* New York: Haworth Press.

Schein, V. (2007). Women in management: Reflections and projections. *Women in Management Review, 22,* 6–8.

Schelling, T. C. (1960). *The strategy of conflict.* Cambridge, MA: Harvard University Press.

Scheuble, K. J., Dixon, K. N., Levy, A. B., & Kagan-Moore, L. (1987). Premature termination: A risk in eating disorder groups. *Group, 11,* 85–93.

Schlenker, B. R. (1975). Liking for a group following an initiation: Impression management or dissonance reduction? *Sociometry, 38,* 99–118.

Schlenker, B. R., Phillips, S. T., Boniecki, K. A., & Schlenker, D. R. (1995a). Championship pressures: Choking or triumphing in one's own territory. *Journal of Personality and Social Psychology, 68,* 632–643.

Schlenker, B. R., Phillips, S. T., Boniecki, K. A., & Schlenker, D. R. (1995b). Where is the home choke? *Journal of Personality and Social Psychology, 68,* 649–652.

Schlenker, B. R., Pontari, B. A., & Christopher, A. N. (2001). Excuses and character: Personal and social implications of excuses. *Personality and Social Psychology Review, 5,* 15–32.

Schlesinger, A. M., Jr. (1965). *A thousand days.* Boston: Houghton Mifflin.

Schmid Mast, M., Jonas, K., & Hall, J. A. (2009). Give a person power and he or she will show interpersonal sensitivity: The phenomenon and its why and when. *Journal of Personality and Social Psychology, 97*(5), 835–850.

Schmid Mast, M. S. (2002). Female dominance hierarchies: Are they any different from males? *Personality and Social Psychology Bulletin, 28,* 29–39.

Schmidt, D. E., & Keating, J. P. (1979). Human crowding and personal control: An integration of the research. *Psychological Bulletin, 86,* 680–700.

Schmidt, N., & Sermat, V. (1983). Measuring loneliness in different relationships. *Journal of Personality and Social Psychology, 44,* 1038–1047.

Schmitt, B. H., Dubé, L., & Leclerc, F. (1992). Intrusions into waiting lines: Does the queue constitute a social system? *Journal of Personality and Social Psychology, 63,* 806–815.

Schmitt, B. H., Gilovich, T., Goore, N., & Joseph, L. (1986). Mere presence and social facilitation: One more time. *Journal of Experimental Social Psychology, 22,* 242–248.

Schmitt, D. P., Realo, A., Voracek, M., & Allik, J. (2008). Why can't a man be more like a woman? Sex differences in big five personality traits across 55 cultures. *Journal of Personality and Social Psychology, 94*(1), 168–182.

Schneebaum, T. (1969). *Keep the river on your right.* New York: Grove Press.

Schneider, D. J. (2004). *The psychology of stereotyping.* New York: Guilford.

Schneider, J., & Cook, K. (1995). Status inconsistency and gender: Combining revisited. Special Issue: Extending interaction theory. *Small Group Research, 26,* 372–399.

Schofield, J. W. (1986). Black-White contact in desegregated schools. In M. Hewstone & R. Brown (Eds.), *Social psychology and society. Contact and conflict in intergroup encounters* (pp. 79–92). Cambridge, MA: Basil Blackwell.

Schofield, J. W., & Sagar, H. A. (1977). Peer interaction patterns in an integrated middle school. *Sociometry, 40,* 130–138.

Schofield, J. W., & Whitley, B. E., Jr. (1983). Peer nomination vs. rating scale measurement of children's peer preferences. *Social Psychology Quarterly, 46,* 242–251.

Scholten, L., van Knippenberg, D., Nijstad, B. A., & De Dreu, C. K. W. (2007). Motivated information processing and group decision-making: Effects of process accountability on information processing and decision quality. *Journal of Experimental Social Psychology, 43,* 539–552.

Schoorman, F. D., Mayer, R. C., & Davis, J. H. (2007). An integrative model of organizational trust: Past, present, and future. *The Academy of Management Review, 32*(2), 344–354.

Schopler, J., & Insko, C. A. (1992). The discontinuity effect in interpersonal and intergroup relations: Generality and mediation. In W. Stroebe & M. Hewstone (Eds.), *European Review of Social Psychology* (Vol. 3, pp. 121–151). Chichester, England: Wiley.

Schopler, J., Insko, C. A., Drigotas, S. M., Wieselquist, J., Pemberton, M., & Cox, C. (1995). The role of identifiability in the reduction of interindividual-intergroup discontinuity. *Journal of Experimental Social Psychology, 31,* 553–574.

Schriesheim, C. A., Castro, S. L., & Cogliser, C. C. (1999). Leader-member exchange (LMX) research: A comprehensive review of theory, measurement, and data-analytic practices. *The Leadership Quarterly, 10,* 63–113.

Schriesheim, C. A., & Eisenbach, R. J. (1995). An exploratory and confirmatory factor-analytic investigation of item wording effects on the obtained factor structures of survey questionnaire measures. *Journal of Management, 21,* 1177–1193.

Schroeder, H. W. (2007). Place experience, gestalt, and the human–nature relationship. *Journal of Environmental Psychology, 27,* 293–309.

Schulz-Hardt, S., Frey, D., Luethgens, C., & Moscovici, S. (2000). Biased information search in group decision making. *Journal of Personality and Social Psychology, 78,* 655–669.

Schulz-Hardt, S., Jochims, M., & Frey, D. (2002). Productive conflict in group decision making: Genuine and contrived dissent as strategies to counteract biased information seeking.

Organizational Behavior and Human Decision Processes, 88, 563–586.

Schumann, K., & Ross, M. (2010). The benefits, costs, and paradox of revenge. *Social and Personality Psychology Compass, 4*(12), 1193–1205.

Schuster, M. A., Stein, B. D., Jaycox, L. H., Collins, R. L., Marshall, G. N., Elliott, M. N., Zhou, A. J., Kanouse, D. E., Morrison, J. L., & Berry, S. H. (2001). A national survey of stress reactions after the September 11, 2001, terrorist attacks. *New England Journal of Medicine, 345,* 1507–1512.

Schutz, W. C. (1958). *FIRO: A three-dimensional theory of interpersonal behavior.* New York: Rinehart.

Schutz, W. C. (1992). Beyond FIRO-B. Three new theory-driven measures—Element B: behavior, Element F: feelings, Element S: self. *Psychological Reports, 70,* 915–937.

Schwartz, B., & Barsky, S. F. (1977). The home advantage. *Social Forces, 55,* 641–661.

Schwartz, S. H. (1994). Are there universal aspects in the structure and contents of human values? *Journal of Social Issues, 50,* 19–45.

Schwartz, S. H., & Gottlieb, A. (1976). Bystander reactions to a violent theft: Crime in Jerusalem. *Journal of Personality and Social Psychology, 34,* 1188–1199.

Schweiger, D. M., Sandberg, W. R., & Ragan, J. W. (1986). Group approaches for improving strategic decision making: A comparative analysis of dialectical inquiry, devil's advocacy, and consensus. *Academy of Management Journal, 29*(1), 51–71.

Schyns, B., & Hansbrough, T. (Eds.). (2010). *When leadership goes wrong: Destructive leadership, mistakes, and ethical failures.* Charlotte, NC: Information Age.

Sculley, J. (2011). John Sculley on Steve Jobs. *Bloomberg Businessweek,* October 6, 2011. Retrieved from www.businessweek.com

Sculley, J. (with J. A. Byrne). (1987). *Odyssey: Pepsi to Apple … A journey of adventure, ideas, and the future.* New York: Harper & Row.

Seal, D. W., Bogart, L. M., & Ehrhardt, A. A. (1998). Small group dynamics: The utility of focus group discussion as a research method. *Group Dynamics: Theory, Research, and Practice, 2,* 253–267.

Seashore, S. E. (1954). *Group cohesiveness in the industrial work group.* Ann Arbor, MI: Institute for Social Research.

Seashore, S. E., & Bowers, D. G. (1970). Durability of organizational change. *American Psychologist, 25,* 227–233.

Sedgwick, J. (1982). *Night vision.* New York: Simon & Schuster.

Sedikides, C., Gaertner, L., & Toguchi, Y. (2003). Pancultural self-enhancement. *Journal of Personality and Social Psychology, 84,* 60–79.

Seers, A., Keller, T., & Wilkerson, J. M. (2003). Can team members share leadership? Foundations in research and theory. In C. L. Pearce & J. A. Conger (Eds.), *Shared leadership: Reframing the hows and whys of leadership* (pp. 77–102). Thousand Oaks, CA: Sage.

Seers, A., & Woodruff, S. (1997). Temporal pacing in task forces: Group development or deadline pressure? *Journal of Management, 23,* 169–187.

Segal, H. A. (1954). Initial psychiatric findings of recently repatriated prisoners of war. *American Journal of Psychiatry, 111,* 358–363.

Segal, M. W. (1974). Alphabet and attraction: An unobtrusive measure of the effect of propinquity in a field setting. *Journal of Personality and Social Psychology, 30,* 654–657.

Sekaquaptewa, D., & Thompson, M. (2003). Solo status, stereotype threat, and performance expectancies: Their effects on women's performance. *Journal of Experimental Social Psychology, 39,* 68–74.

Seligman, M. E. P. (1995). The effectiveness of psychotherapy: The *Consumer Reports* study. *American Psychologist, 50,* 965–974.

Seligman, M. E. P. (1996). Science as an ally of practice. *American Psychologist, 51,* 1072–1079.

Sell, J., Lovaglia, M. J., Mannix, E. A., Samuelson, C. D., & Wilson, R. K. (2004). Investigating conflict, power, and status within and among groups. *Small Group Research, 35,* 44–72.

Semin, G. R. (2007). Grounding communication: Synchrony. In A. W. Kruglanski & E. T. Higgins (Eds.), *Social psychology: Handbook of basic principles* (2nd ed., pp. 630–649). New York: Guilford.

Semin, G. R., & Rubini, M. (1990). Unfolding the concept of person by verbal abuse. *European Journal of Social Psychology, 20,* 463–474.

Sessa, V. I., & London, M. (2008). Group learning: An introduction. In V. I. Sessa & M. London (Eds.), *Work group learning: Understanding, improving and assessing how groups learn in organizations* (pp. 3–13). New York: Taylor & Francis Group.

Seta, C. E., & Seta, J. J. (1995). When audience presence is enjoyable: The influences of audience awareness of prior success on performance and task interest. *Basic and Applied Social Psychology, 16,* 95–108.

Seta, J. J., Crisson, J. E., Seta, C. E., & Wang, M. A. (1989). Task performance and perceptions of anxiety: Averaging and summation in an evaluative setting. *Journal of Personality and Social Psychology, 56,* 387–396.

Seta, J. J., Seta, C. E., & Donaldson, S. (1991). The impact of comparison processes on coactors' frustration and willingness to expend effort. *Personality and Social Psychology Bulletin, 17,* 560–568.

Seta, J. J., Seta, C. E., & McElroy, T. (2006). Better than better-than-average (or not): Elevated and depressed self-evaluations following unfavorable social comparisons. *Self and Identity, 5,* 51–72.

Shachaf, P. (2008). Cultural diversity and information and communication technology impacts on global virtual teams: An exploratory study. *Information & Management, 45*(2), 131–142.

Shaver, P., & Buhrmester, D. (1983). Loneliness, sex-role orientation, and group life: A social needs perspective. In P. B. Paulus (Ed.), *Basic group processes* (pp. 259–288). New York: Springer-Verlag.

Shaver, P., Schwartz, J., Kirson, D., & O'Connor, C. (1987). Emotion knowledge: Further exploration of a prototype approach. *Journal of Personality and Social Psychology, 52,* 1061–1086.

Shaw, J. D., Duffy, M. K., & Stark, E. M. (2001). Team reward attitude: Construct development and initial validation. *Journal of Organizational Behavior, 22*(8), 903–917.

Shaw, M. E. (1932). A comparison of individuals and small groups in the rational solution of complex problems. *American Journal of Psychology, 44,* 491–504.

Shaw, M. E. (1964). Communication networks. *Advances in Experimental Social Psychology, 1,* 111–147.

Shaw, M. E. (1978). Communication networks fourteen years later. In L. Berkowitz (Ed.), *Group processes* (pp. 351–361). New York: Academic Press.

Shaw, M. E. (1981). *Group dynamics: The psychology of small group behavior* (3rd ed.). New York: McGraw-Hill.

Shaw, M. E., & Shaw, L. M. (1962). Some effects of sociometric grouping upon learning in a second grade classroom. *Journal of Social Psychology, 57,* 453–458.

Sheatsley, P. B., & Feldman, J. J. (1964). The assassination of President Kennedy: A preliminary report on public attitudes and behavior. *Public Opinion Quarterly, 28,* 189–215.

Shebilske, W. L., Jordon, J. A., Goettl, B. P., & Paulus, L. E. (1998). Observation versus hands-on practice of complex skills in dyadic, triadic, and tetradic training-teams. *Human Factors, 40,* 525–540.

Shechtman, Z. (1994). The effect of group psychotherapy on close same-gender friendships among boys and girls. *Sex Roles, 30,* 829–834.

Shechtman, Z., & Dvir, V. (2006). Attachment style as a predictor of behavior in group counseling with preadolescents. *Group Dynamics: Theory, Research, and Practice, 10*(1), 29–42.

Shechtman, Z., Goldberg, A., & Cariani, R. (2008). Arab and Israeli counseling trainees: A comparison of ethnically homogeneous and heterogeneous groups. *Group Dynamics: Theory, Research, and Practice, 12*(2), 85–95.

Shedler, J. (2010). The efficacy of psychodynamic psychotherapy. *American Psychologist, 65*(2), 98–109.

Shelly, R. K., Troyer, L., Munroe, P. T., & Burger, T. (1999). Social structure and the duration of social acts. *Social Psychology Quarterly, 62,* 83–95.

Shelton, G. A. (1982). *The generalization of understanding to behavior: The role of perspective in enlightenment.* Unpublished Doctoral Thesis, University of British Columbia.

Sheppard, B. H. (1983). Managers as inquisitors: Some lessons from the law. In H. Bazerman & R. J. Lewicki (Eds.), *Negotiating in organizations* (pp. 193–213). Thousand Oaks, CA: Sage.

Shepperd, J. A. (1993). Productive loss in performance groups: A motivational analysis. *Psychological Bulletin, 113,* 67–81.

Shepperd, J. A. (1995). Remedying motivation and productivity loss in collective settings. *Current Directions in Psychological Science, 5,* 131–133.

Shepperd, J. A., & Wright, R. A. (1989). Individual contributions to a collective effort: An incentive analysis. *Personality and Social Psychology Bulletin, 15,* 141–149.

Sherif, M. (1936). *The psychology of social norms.* New York: Harper & Row.

Sherif, M. (1966). *In common predicament: Social psychology of intergroup conflict and cooperation.* Boston: Houghton Mifflin.

Sherif, M., Harvey, O. J., White, B. J., Hood, W. R., & Sherif, C. W. (1961). *Intergroup conflict and cooperation. The Robbers Cave Experiment.* Norman, OK: Institute of Group Relations.

Sherif, M., & Sherif, C. W. (1953). *Groups in harmony and tension.* New York: Harper & Row.

Sherif, M., & Sherif, C. W. (1956). *An outline of social psychology* (rev. ed.). New York: Harper & Row.

Sherif, M., White, B. J., & Harvey, O. J. (1955). Status in experimentally produced groups. *American Journal of Sociology, 60,* 370–379.

Sherrod, D. R., & Cohen, S. (1979). Density, personal control, and design. In J. R. Aiello & A. Baum (Eds.), *Residential crowding and design* (pp. 217–227). New York: Plenum.

Shipper, F., & Davy, J. (2002). A model and investigation of managerial skills, employees' attitudes, and managerial performance. *Leadership Quarterly, 13,* 95–120.

Shuffler, M. L., DiazGranados, D., & Salas, E. (2011). There's a science for that: Team development interventions in organizations. *Current Directions in Psychological Science, 20*(6), 365–372.

Shure, G. H., & Meeker, J. R. (1967). A personality/attitude scale for use in experimental bargaining studies. *Journal of Psychology, 65,* 233–252.

Shure, G. H., Rogers, M. S., Larsen, I. M., & Tassone, J. (1962). Group planning and task effectiveness. *Sociometry, 25,* 263–282.

Sias, P. M. (2009). Social ostracism, cliques, and outcasts. In P. Lutgen-Sandvik & B. D. Sypher (Eds.), *Destructive organizational communication: Processes, consequences, and constructive ways of organizing* (pp. 145–163). New York: Routledge/Taylor & Francis Group.

Sias, P. M., Krone, K. J., & Jablin, F. M. (2002). An ecological systems perspective on workplace relationships. In M. L. Knapp & J. A. Daly (Eds.), *Handbook of interpersonal communication* (3rd ed., pp. 615–642). Thousand Oaks, CA: Sage.

Sibona, C., & Walczak, S. (2011). Unfriending on Facebook: Friend request and online/offline behavior analysis. *Hawaii International Conference on Systems Science (HICSS-44 2011) Proceedings,* January 2011. Retrieved from IEEE.org

Sidanius, J., Haley, H., Molina, L., & Pratto, F. (2007). Vladimir's choice and the distribution of social resources: A group dominance perspective. *Group Processes & Intergroup Relations, 10,* 257–265.

Sidanius, J., & Pratto, F. (1999). *Social dominance: An intergroup theory of social hierarchy and oppression.* New York: Cambridge University Press.

Siebold, G. L. (2007). The essence of military group cohesion. *Armed Forces & Society, 33,* 286–295.

Sigall, H., Mucchi-Faina, A., & Mosso, C. (2006). Minority influence is facilitated when the communication employs linguistic abstractness. *Group Processes & Intergroup Relations, 9*(3), 443–451.

Silver, W. S., & Bufanio, K. A. (1996). The impact of group efficacy and group goals on group task performance. *Small Group Research, 27,* 347–349.

Silverman, P. R. (2010). Mutual help groups: What are they and what makes them work? In R. K. Conyne (Ed.), *The Oxford handbook of group counseling* (pp. 511–519). New York: Oxford University Press.

Silvia, P. J., & Kwapil, T. R. (2011). Aberrant asociality: How individual differences in social anhedonia illuminate the need to belong. *Journal of Personality, 79,* 1013–1030.

Simmel, G. (1902). The number of members as determining the sociological form of the group. *American Journal of Sociology, 8,* 1–46, 158–196.

Simon, B., Glässner-Bayerl, B., & Stratenwerth, I. (1991). Stereotyping and self-stereotyping in a natural intergroup context: The case of heterosexual and homosexual men. *Social Psychology Quarterly, 54,* 252–266.

Simon, B., & Hamilton, D. L. (1994). Self-stereotyping and social context: The effects of relative in-group size and in-group status. *Journal of Personality and Social Psychology, 66*(4), 699–711.

Simon, B., Pantaleo, G., & Mummendey, A. (1995). Unique individual or interchangeable group member? The accentuation of intragroup differences versus similarities as an indicator of the individual self versus the collective self. *Journal of Personality and Social Psychology, 69,* 106–119.

Simon, R. J. (1980). *The jury: Its role in American society.* Lexington, MA: Heath.

Simonton, D. K. (1985). Intelligence and personal influence in groups: Four nonlinear models. *Psychological Review, 92,* 532–547.

Simpson, B. (2003). Sex, fear, and greed: A social dilemma analysis of gender and cooperation. *Social Forces, 82,* 35–52.

Simpson, J. A. (2007). Psychological foundations of trust. *Current Directions in Psychological Science, 16,* 264–268.

Simpson, L., Taylor, L., O'Rourke, K., & Shaw, K. (2011). An analysis of consumer behavior on Black Friday. *American International Journal of Contemporary Research, 1,* 1–5.

Singer, E. (1990). Reference groups and social evaluations. In M. Rosenberg & R. H. Turner (Eds.), *Social psychology: Sociological perspectives* (pp. 66–93). New Brunswick, NJ: Transaction Publishers.

Sivuneun, A., & Hakonen, M. (2011). Review of virtual environment studies on social and group phenomena. *Small Group Research, 42,* 405–457.

Skinner, B. F. (1953). *Science and human behavior.* New York: Macmillan.

Skinner, B. F. (1971). *Beyond freedom and dignity.* New York: Knopf.

Skitka, L. J., Winquist, J., & Hutchinson, S. (2003). Are outcome fairness and outcome favorability distinguishable psychological constructs? A meta-analytic review. *Social Justice Research 16*(4), 309–341.

Slavson, S. R. (1950). Group psychotherapy. *Scientific American, 183,* 42–45.

Smeesters, D., Warlop, L., Van Avermaet, E., Corneille, O., & Yzerbyt, V. (2003). Do not prime hawks with doves: The interplay of construct activation and consistency of social value orientation on cooperative behavior. *Journal of Personality and Social Psychology, 84,* 972–987.

Smelser, N. J. (1962). *Theory of collective behavior.* New York: Free Press.

Smith, C. B., McLaughlin, M. L., & Osborne, K. K. (1997). Conduct control on Usenet. *Journal of Computer-Mediated Communication, 2*(4). Retrieved from jcmc.indiana.edu/vol2/issue4/smith.html

Smith, C. M. (2008). Adding minority status to a source of conflict: An examination of influence processes and product quality in dyads. *European Journal of Social Psychology, 38,* 75–83.

Smith, D. H. (1980). Participation in outdoor recreation and sports. In D. H. Smith, J. Macaulay, & Associates (Eds.), *Participation in social and political activities: A comprehensive analysis of political involvement, expressive leisure time, and helping behavior* (pp. 177–201). San Francisco: Jossey-Bass.

Smith, E. R., & Mackie, D. M. (2005). Aggression, hatred, and other emotions. In J. F. Dovidio, P. Glick & L. A. Rudman (Eds.), *On the nature of prejudice: Fifty years after Allport* (pp. 361–376). Malden, MA: Blackwell.

Smith, E. R., Murphy, J., & Coats, S. (1999). Attachment to groups: Theory and management. *Journal of Personality and Social Psychology, 77,* 94–110.

Smith, E. R., Seger, C. R., & Mackie, D. M. (2007). Can emotions be truly group level? Evidence regarding four conceptual criteria. *Journal of Personality and Social Psychology, 93,* 431–446.

Smith, H. J., Pettigrew, T. F., Pippin, G. M., & Bialosiewicz, S. (2012). Relative deprivation: A theoretical and meta-analytic review. *Personality and Social Psychology Review,* in press.

Smith, J. A., & Foti, R. J. (1998). A pattern approach to the study of leader emergence. *The Leadership Quarterly, 9*(2), 147–160.

Smith, K. B., Larimer, C. W., Littvay, L., & Hibbing, J. R. (2007). Evolutionary theory and political leadership: Why certain people do not trust decision makers. *Journal of Politics, 69,* 285–299.

Smith, M. (1935). Leadership: The management of social differentials. *Journal of Abnormal and Social Psychology, 30*(3), 348–358.

Smith, M. (1945). Social situation, social behavior, social group. *Psychological Review, 52,* 224–229.

Smith, M. B. (1972). Is experimental social psychology advancing? *Journal of Experimental Social Psychology, 8,* 86–96.

Smith, P. B. (1975). Controlled studies of the outcome of sensitivity training. *Psychological Bulletin, 82,* 597–622.

Smith, P. B. (1980). The outcome of sensitivity training and encounter. In P. B. Smith (Ed.), *Small groups and personal change* (pp. 25–55). New York: Methuen.

Smith, P. B., & Bond, M. H. (1993). *Social psychology across cultures: Analysis and perspectives.* Boston: Allyn & Bacon.

Smith, P. B., Peterson, M. F., & Schwartz, S. H., with Ahmad, A. H., Akande, D., Andersen, J. A., Ayestaran, S. Bochner, S., Callan, V., Davila, C., Ekelund, B., François, P-H., Graversen, G., Harb, C., Jesuino, J., Kantas, A., Karamushka, L., Koopman, P., Leung, K., Kruzela, P., Malvezzi, S., Mogaji, A., Mortazavi, S., Munene, J., Parry, K., Punnett, B. J., Radford, M., Ropo, A., Saiz, J., Savage, G., Setiadi, B., Sorenson, R., Szabo, E., Teparakul, P., Tirmizi, A., Tsvetanova, S., Viedge, C., Wall, W., & Yanchuk, V. (2002). Cultural values, sources of guidance, and their relevance to managerial behavior: A 47-nation study. *Journal of Cross-Cultural Psychology, 33*(2), 188–208.

Smith, P. K., Jostmann, N. B., Galinsky, A. D., & van Dijk, W. W. (2008). Lacking power impairs executive functions. *Psychological Science, 19*, 441–447.

Smith, R. H. (2000). Assimilative and contrastive emotional reactions to upward and downward social comparisons. In J. Suls & L. Wheeler (Eds.), *Handbook of social comparison: Theory and research* (pp. 173–200). New York: Kluwer Academic.

Smoke, W. H., & Zajonc, R. B. (1962). On the reliability of group judgments and decisions. In J. H. Criswell, H. Solomon, & P. Suppes (Eds.), *Mathematical methods in small group processes.* Stanford, CA: Stanford University Press.

Smokowski, P. R., Rose, S. D., & Bacallao, M. L. (2001). Damaging experiences in therapeutic groups: How vulnerable consumers become group casualties. *Small Group Research, 32*(2), 223–251.

Smrt, D. L., & Karau, S. J. (2011). Protestant work ethic moderates social loafing. *Group Dynamics: Theory, Research, and Practice, 15*(3), 267–274.

Sniezek, J. A. (1992). Groups under uncertainty: An examination of confidence in group decision making. *Organizational Behavior and Human Decision Processes, 52*, 124–155.

Snow, D. A., & Oliver, P. E. (1995). Social movements and collective behavior: Social psychological dimensions and considerations. In K. S. Cook, G. A. Fine, & J. S. House (Eds.), *Sociological perspectives on social psychology* (pp. 571–599). Needham Heights, MA: Allyn and Bacon.

Snow, D. A., Zurcher, L. A., & Peters, R. (1981) Victory celebrations as theater: A dramaturgical approach to crowd behavior. *Symbolic Interaction, 4*, 21–42.

Snyder, C. R., & Fromkin, H. L. (1980). *Uniqueness: The human pursuit of difference.* New York: Plenum.

Sobel, R. (1947). The "Old Sergeant" syndrome. *Psychiatry: Journal for the Study of Interpersonal Processes, 10*, 315–321.

Socolow, M. J. (2008, October 24). The hyped panic over "War of the Worlds." *The Chronicle of Higher Education, 55*(9), B16.

Sommer, R. (1959). Studies in personal space. *Sociometry, 22*, 247–260.

Sommer, R. (1967). Small group ecology. *Psychological Bulletin, 67*, 145–152.

Sommer, R. (1969). *Personal space.* Englewood Cliffs, NJ: Prentice Hall.

Son Hing, L. S., Bobocel, D. R., Zanna, M. P., Garcia, D. M., Gee, S. S., & Orazietti, K. (2011). The merit of meritocracy. *Journal of Personality and Social Psychology, 101*(3), 433–450.

Son Hing, L. S., Bobocel, D. R., Zanna, M. P., & McBride, M. V. (2007). Authoritarian dynamics and unethical decision making: High social dominance orientation leaders and high right-wing authoritarianism followers. *Journal of Personality and Social Psychology, 92*(1), 67–81.

Sorrels, J. P., & Kelley, J. (1984). Conformity by omission. *Personality and Social Psychology Bulletin, 10*, 302–305.

Sorrentino, R. M., & Boutillier, R. G. (1975). The effect of quantity and quality of verbal interaction on ratings of leadership ability. *Journal of Experimental Social Psychology, 11*, 403–411.

Sorrentino, R. M., & Field, N. (1986). Emergent leadership over time: The functional value of positive motivation. *Journal of Personality and Social Psychology, 50*, 1091–1099.

Soukup, C. (2006). Computer-mediated communication as a virtual third place: Building Oldenburg's great good places on the World Wide Web. *New Media & Society, 8*(3), 421–440.

Spears, R., Lea, M., & Postmes, T. (2007). CMC and social identity. In A. N. Joinson, K. Y. A. McKenna, T. Postmes, & U.-D. Reips (Eds.), *The Oxford handbook of Internet psychology* (pp. 253–269). Oxford: Oxford University Press.

Spears, R., Lea, M., Postmes, T., & Wolbert, A. (2011). A SIDE look at computer-mediated interaction: Power and the gender divide. In Z. Birchmeier, B. Dietz-Uhler, & G. Stasser (Eds.), *Strategic uses of social technology: An interactive perspective of social psychology* (pp. 16–39). New York: Cambridge University Press.

Spears, R., Postmes, T., Lea, M., & Wolbert, A. (2002). When are net effects gross products? The power of influence and the influence of power in computer-mediated communication. *Journal of Social Issues, 58*, 91–107.

Spell, C. S., Bezrukova, K., Haar, J., & Spell, C. (2011). Faultlines, fairness, and fighting: A justice perspective on conflict in diverse groups. *Small Group Research, 42*(3), 309–340.

Spencer Stuart. (2004). The 2004 Spencer Stuart route to the top: Our survey of Fortune 700 CEOs provides a snapshot of today's CEOs and the major trends emerging. Retrieved from www.spencerstuart.com/

Spencer, R. W., & Huston, J. H. (1993). Rational forecasts: On confirming ambiguity as the mother of conformity. *Journal of Economic Psychology, 14*, 697–709.

Spencer-Rodgers, J., Hamilton, D. L., & Sherman, S. J. (2007). The central role of entitativity in stereotypes of social categories and task groups. *Journal of Personality and Social Psychology, 92*(3), 369–388.

Spisak, B. R., Dekker, P. H., Krüger, M., & Van Vugt, M. (2012). Warriors and peacekeepers: Testing a biosocial implicit leadership hypothesis of intergroup relations using masculine and feminine faces. *PLoS ONE, 7*(1), e30399.

Spoor, J. R., & Kelly, J. R. (2004). The evolutionary significance of affect in groups: Communication and group bonding. *Group Processes & Intergroup Relations, 7*, 398–412.

Sprinthall, N. A. (2009). Milgram, Kohlberg, and Dostoevsky. *American Psychologist, 64*(7), 620–621.

Srivastava, S., & Beer, J. S. (2005). How self-evaluations relate to being liked by others: Integrating sociometer and attachment perspectives. *Journal of Personality and Social Psychology, 89*, 966–977.

St. John, W. (2004). *Rammer jammer yellow hammer: A journey into the heart of fan mania.* New York: Crown.

Stager, S. F., Chassin, L., & Young, R. D. (1983). Determinants of self-esteem among labeled adolescents. *Social Psychology Quarterly, 46*, 3–10.

Stahl, G. K., Maznevski, M. L., Voigt, A., & Jonsen, K. (2010). Unraveling the effects of cultural diversity in teams: A meta-analysis of research on multicultural work groups. *Journal of International Business Studies, 41*, 690–709.

Stajkovic, A. D., Lee, D., & Nyberg, A. J. (2009). Collective efficacy, group potency, and group performance: Meta-analyses of their relationships, and test of a mediation model. *Journal of Applied Psychology, 94*(3), 814–828.

Stangor, C., Jonas, K., Stroebe, W., & Hewstone, M. (1996). Influence of student exchange on national stereotypes, attitudes, and perceived group variability. *European Journal of Social Psychology, 26*, 663–675.

Stanton, S. J., & Schultheiss, O. C. (2009). The hormonal correlates of implicit power motivation. *Journal of Research in Personality, 43*(5), 942–949.

Stark, E. M., Shaw, J. D., & Duffy, M. K. (2007). Preference for group work, winning orientation, and social loafing behavior in groups. *Group & Organization Management, 32*, 699–723.

Starks, T. J., Golub, S. A., Kelly, B. C., & Parsons, J. T. (2010). The problem of "just for fun": Patterns of use situations among active club drug users. *Addictive Behaviors, 35*(12), 1067–1073.

Stasser, G. (1992). Pooling of unshared information during group discussions. In S. Worchel, W. Wood, & J. A. Simpson (Eds.), *Group process and productivity* (pp. 48–67). Thousand Oaks, CA: Sage.

Stasser, G., & Dietz-Uhler, B. (2001). Collective choice, judgment, and problem solving. In M. A. Hogg & R. S. Tindale (Eds.), *Blackwell handbook of social psychology: Group processes* (pp. 31–55). Malden, MA: Blackwell.

Stasser, G., Kerr, N. L., & Bray, R. M. (1982). The social psychology of jury deliberations: Structure, process, and product. In N. L. Kerr & R. M. Bray (Eds.), *Psychology of the courtroom* (pp. 221–256). New York: Academic Press.

Stasser, G., & Titus, W. (1985). Pooling of unshared information in group decision making: Biased information sampling during discussion. *Journal of Personality and Social Psychology, 48*, 1467–1478.

Stasser, G., & Titus, W. (1987). Effects of information load and percentage of shared information on the dissemination of unshared information during group discussion. *Journal of Personality and Social Psychology, 53*, 81–93.

Stasson, M. F., & Bradshaw, S. D. (1995). Explanations of individual-group performance differences: What sort of "bonus" can be gained through group interaction? *Small Group Research, 26*(2), 296–308.

Stasson, M. F., Kameda, T., & Davis, J. H. (1997). A model of agenda influences on group decisions. *Group Dynamics: Theory, Research, and Practice, 1*, 316–323.

Staub, E. (1989). *The roots of evil: The origins of genocide and other group violence.* New York: Cambridge University Press.

Staub, E. (1990). Moral exclusion, personal goal theory, and extreme destructiveness. *Journal of Social Issues, 46*, 47–64.

Staub, E. (2004). Basic human needs, altruism, and aggression. In A. G. Miller (Ed.), *The social psychology of good and evil* (pp. 51–84). New York: Guilford.

Staw, B. M., & Ross, J. (1987). Behavior in escalation situations: Antecedents, prototypes, and solutions. *Research in Organizational Behavior, 9*, 39–78.

Steele, C. M., & Aronson, J. (1995). Stereotype threat and the intellectual test performance of African Americans. *Journal of Personality and Social Psychology, 69*, 797–811.

Steele, G. L. (1983). *The Hacker's dictionary.* New York: Harper & Row.

Stein, R. T., & Heller, T. (1979). An empirical analysis of the correlations between leadership status and participation rates reported in the literature. *Journal of Personality and Social Psychology, 37*, 1993–2002.

Steinel, W., & De Dreu, C. K. (2004). Social motives and strategic misrepresentation in social decision making. *Journal of Personality and Social Psychology, 86*, 419–434.

Steiner, I. D. (1972). *Group process and productivity.* New York: Academic Press.

Steiner, I. D. (1974). Whatever happened to the group in social psychology? *Journal of Experimental Social Psychology, 10*, 94–108.

Steiner, I. D. (1976). Task-performing groups. In J. W. Thibaut, J. T. Spence, & R. C. Carson (Eds.), *Contemporary topics in social psychology* (pp. 393–422). Morristown, NJ: General Learning Press.

Steiner, I. D. (1983). What ever happened to the touted revival of the group? In H. Blumberg, A. Hare, V. Kent, & M. Davies (Eds.), *Small groups and social interaction* (Vol. 2, pp. 539–547). New York: Wiley.

Steiner, I. D. (1986). Paradigms and groups. *Advances in Experimental Social Psychology, 19*, 251–289.

Steinkuehler, C. A., & Williams, D. (2006). Where everybody knows your (screen) name: Online games as "Third Places." *Journal of Computer-Mediated Communication, 11*(4), 885–909.

Steinzor, B. (1950). The spatial factor in face to face discussion groups. *Journal of Abnormal and Social Psychology, 45*, 552–555.

Stempfle, J., Hübner, O., & Badke-Schaub, P. (2001). A functional theory of task role distribution in work groups. *Group Processes & Intergroup Relations, 4,* 138–159.

Stephan, F. F., & Mischler, E. G. (1952). The distribution of participation in small groups: An exponential approximation. *American Sociological Review, 17,* 598–608.

Stephan, W. G. (1987). The contact hypothesis in intergroup relations. In C. Hendrick (Ed.), *Review of personality and social psychology: Group process* (Vol. 9, pp. 13–40). Thousand Oaks, CA: Sage.

Stephan, W. G., & Stephan, C. W. (2005). Intergroup relations program evaluation. In J. F. Dovidio, P. Glick, & L. A. Rudman (Eds.), *On the nature of prejudice: Fifty years after Allport* (pp. 431–446). Malden, MA: Blackwell.

Stern, E. K. (1997). Probing the plausibility of newgroup syndrome: Kennedy and the Bay of Pigs. In P. 't Hart, E. K. Stern, & B. Sundelius (Eds.), *Beyond groupthink: Political group dynamics and foreign policy-making* (pp. 153–189). Ann Arbor: University of Michigan Press.

Sternberg, R. J. (2003). A duplex theory of hate: Development and application to terrorism, massacres, and genocide. *Review of General Psychology, 7,* 299–328.

Sternberg, R. J. (2007). A systems model of leadership: WICS. *American Psychologist, 62*(1), 34–42.

Sternberg, R. J. (2011). The purpose of college education: Producing a new generation of positive leaders. In S. E. Murphy & R. J. Reichard (Eds.), *Early development and leadership: Building the next generation of leaders* (pp. 293–308). New York: Routledge/Taylor & Francis Group.

Sternberg, R. J., & Dobson, D. M. (1987). Resolving interpersonal conflicts: An analysis of stylistic consistency. *Journal of Personality and Social Psychology, 52,* 794–812.

Stets, J. E., & Thai, Y. (2010). Roles. In J. Levine & M. Hogg (Eds.), *Encyclopedia of group processes and intergroup relations* (pp. 709–713). Thousand Oaks, CA: Sage.

Stevens, M. J., & Campion, M. A. (1994). The knowledge, skill, and ability requirements for teamwork: Implications for human resource management. *Journal of Management, 20,* 503–530.

Stevens, M. J., & Campion, M. A. (1999). Staffing work teams: Development and validation of a selection test for teamwork settings. *Journal of Management, 25,* 207–228.

Stevenson, R. J., & Repacholi, B. M. (2003). Age-related changes in children's hedonic response to male body odor. *Developmental Psychology, 39,* 670–679.

Stevenson, R. J., & Repacholi, B. M. (2005). Does the source of an interpersonal odor affect disgust? A disease risk model and its alternatives. *European Journal of Social Psychology, 35*(3), 375–401.

Stevenson, W. B., Pearce, J. L., & Porter, L. W. (1985). The concept of "coalition" in organization theory and research. *Academy of Management Journal, 10,* 256–268.

Stewart, D. D., & Stasser, G. (1998). The sampling of critical, unshared information in decision-making groups: The role of an informed minority. *European Journal of Social Psychology, 28,* 95–113.

Stewart, G. L. (2006). A meta-analytic review of relationships between team design features and team performance. *Journal of Management, 32,* 29–55.

Stewart, G. L., & Manz, C. C. (1995). Leadership for self-managing work teams: A typology and integrative model. *Human Relations, 48,* 747–770.

Stewart, P. A., & Moore, J. C. (1992). Wage disparities and performance expectations. *Social Psychology Quarterly, 55,* 78–85.

Stice, E., Marti, C. N., Spoor, S., Presnell, K., & Shaw, H. (2008). Dissonance and healthy weight eating disorder prevention programs: Long-term effects from a randomized efficacy trial. *Journal of Consulting and Clinical Psychology, 76,* 329–340.

Stiles, W. B., Lyall, L. M., Knight, D. P., Ickes, W., Waung, M., Hall, C. L., & Primeau, B. E. (1997). Gender differences in verbal presumptuousness and attentiveness. *Personality and Social Psychology Bulletin, 23,* 759–772.

Stiles, W. B., Shapiro, D. A., & Elliott, R. (1986). Are all psychotherapies equivalent? *American Psychologist, 41,* 165–180.

Stillwell, A. M., Baumeister, R. F., & Del Priore, R. E. (2008). We're all victims here: Toward a psychology of revenge. *Basic and Applied Social Psychology, 30*(3), 253–263.

Stinson, D. A., Logel, C., Zanna, M. P., Holmes, J. G., Cameron, J. J., Wood, J. V., et al. (2008). The cost of lower self-esteem: Testing a self- and social-bonds model of health. *Journal of Personality and Social Psychology, 94,* 412–428.

Stogdill, R. M. (1948). Personal factors associated with leadership. *Journal of Psychology, 23,* 35–71.

Stogdill, R. M. (1974). *Handbook of leadership.* New York: Free Press.

Stokes, J. P. (1983). Components of group cohesion: Intermember attraction, instrumental value, and risk taking. *Small Group Behavior, 14,* 163–173.

Stokes, J. P. (1985). The relation of social network and individual difference variables to loneliness. *Journal of Personality and Social Psychology, 48,* 981–990.

Stokols, D. (1972). On the distinction between density and crowding: Some implications for future research. *Psychological Review, 79,* 275–278.

Stokols, D. (1978). In defense of the crowding construct. In A. Baum, J. E. Singer, & S. Valins (Eds.), *Advances in environmental psychology* (Vol. 1, pp. 111–130). Mahwah, NJ: Erlbaum.

Stokols, D., & Altman, I. (Eds.). (1987). *Handbook of environmental psychology* (Vols. 1 & 2). New York: Wiley.

Stokols, D., Misra, S., Moser, R. P., Hall, K. L., & Taylor, B. K. (2008). The ecology of team science. *American Journal of Preventive Medicine, 35*(2), S96–S115.

Stoner, J. A. (1961). *A comparison of individual and group decisions involving risk.* Unpublished master's thesis, Massachusetts Institute of Technology.

Stoner, J. A. (1968). Risky and cautious shifts in group decisions: The influence of widely held values. *Journal of Experimental Social Psychology, 4*, 442–459.

Stones, C. R. (1982). A community of Jesus people in South Africa. *Small Group Behavior, 13*, 264–272.

Stoop, J. R. (1932). Is the judgment of the group better than that of the average member of the group? *Journal of Experimental Psychology, 15*, 550–562.

Storms, M. D., & Thomas, G. C. (1977). Reactions to physical closeness. *Journal of Personality and Social Psychology, 35*, 319–328.

Storr, A. (1988). *Solitude: A return to the self.* New York: Free Press.

Stratham, A. (1987). The gender model revisited: Differences in the management styles of men and women. *Sex Roles, 16*, 409–429.

Straus, S. G. (1997). Technology, group process, and group outcomes: Testing the connections in computer-mediated and face-to-face groups. *Human-Computer Interaction, 12*, 227–266.

Strauss, A. L. (1944). The literature on panic. *Journal of Abnormal and Social Psychology, 39*, 317–328.

Strauss, B. (2002). Social facilitation in motor tasks: A review of research and theory. *Psychology of Sport & Exercise, 3*, 237–256.

Streufert, S., & Streufert, S. C. (1986). The development of international conflict. In S. Worchel & W. G. Austin (Eds.), *Psychology of intergroup relations* (2nd ed., pp. 134–152). Chicago: Nelson-Hall.

Strickland, L. H., Barefoot, J. C., & Hockenstein, P. (1976). Monitoring behavior in the surveillance and trust paradigm. *Representative Research in Social Psychology, 7*, 51–57.

Strodtbeck, F. L., & Hook, L. H. (1961). The social dimensions of a twelve-man jury table. *Sociometry, 24*, 397–415.

Strodtbeck, F. L., James, R. M., & Hawkins, C. (1957). Social status in jury deliberations. *American Sociological Review, 22*, 713–719.

Strodtbeck, F. L., & Lipinski, R. M. (1985). Becoming first among equals: Moral considerations in jury foreman selection. *Journal of Personality and Social Psychology, 49*, 927–936.

Strodtbeck, F. L., & Mann, R. D. (1956). Sex role differentiation in jury deliberations. *Sociometry, 19*, 3–11.

Stroebe, M. S. (1994). The broken heart phenomenon: An examination of the mortality of bereavement. *Journal of Community and Applied Social Psychology, 4*, 47–61.

Stroebe, W. (2012). The truth about Triplett (1898), but nobody seems to care. *Perspectives on Psychological Science, 7*, 54–57.

Stroebe, W., Diehl, M., & Abakoumkin, G. (1992). The illusion of group effectivity. *Personality and Social Psychology Bulletin, 18*, 643–650.

Stroebe, W., Stroebe, M. S., Abakoumkin, G., & Schut, H. (1996). The role of loneliness and social support in adjustment to loss: A test of attachment versus stress theory. *Journal of Personality and Social Psychology, 70*, 1241–1249.

Strong, S. R., Hills, H. I., Kilmartin, C. T., DeVries, H., Lanier, K., Nelson, B. N., Strickland, D., & Meyer, C. W. (1988). The dynamic relations among interpersonal behaviors: A test

of complementarity and anticomplementarity. *Journal of Personality and Social Psychology, 54*, 798–810.

Stroud, L. R., Tanofsky-Kraff, M., Wilfley, D. E., & Salovey, P. (2000). The Yale Interpersonal Stressor (YIPS): Affective, physiological, and behavioral responses to a novel interpersonal rejection paradigm. *Annals of Behavioral Medicine, 22*(3), 204–213.

Strube, M. J. (2005). What did Triplett really find? A contemporary analysis of the first experiment in social psychology. *The American Journal of Psychology, 118*, 271–286.

Stryker, S., & Burke, P. J. (2000). The past, present, and future of an identity theory. *Social Psychology Quarterly, 63*(4), 284–297.

Stryker, S., & Vryan, K. D. (2006). The symbolic interactionist framework. In J. Delamater (Ed.), *Handbook of social psychology* (pp. 3–28). New York: Plenum.

Stuster, J. (1996). *Bold endeavors: Lessons from polar and space exploration.* Annapolis, MD: Naval Institute Press.

Suedfeld, P. (1987). Extreme and unusual environments. In D. Stokols & I. Altman (Eds.), *Handbook of environmental psychology* (Vol. 1, pp. 863–887). New York: Wiley.

Suedfeld, P. (1997). The social psychology of "invictus": Conceptual and methodological approaches to indomitability. In C. McGarty & S. A. Haslam (Eds.), *The message of social psychology: Perspectives on mind in society* (pp. 329–341). Malden, MA: Blackwell.

Suedfeld, P., & Steel, G. D. (2000). The environmental psychology of capsule habitats. *Annual Review of Psychology, 51*, 227–253.

Sugiman, T., & Misumi, J. (1988). Development of a new evacuation method for emergencies: Control of collective behavior by emergent small groups. *Journal of Applied Psychology, 73*, 3–10.

Suleiman, R., Aharonov-Majar, E., & Luzon, P. (2011). The sharing dilemma: Joining groups and sharing resources as a means of coping with environmental risk. *Social Science Research Network.* Retrieved from ssrn.com/abstract=1955813

Sullenberger, C. B., with Zaslow, J. (2009). *Highest duty: My search for what really matters.* New York: Harper Collins.

Sulloway, F. J. (1996). *Born to rebel: Birth order, family dynamics, and creative lives.* New York: Pantheon Books.

Suls, J., Martin, R., & David, J. P. (1998). Person-environment fit and its limits: Agreeableness, neuroticism, and emotional reactivity to interpersonal conflict. *Personality and Social Psychology Bulletin, 24*, 88–98.

Suls, J., & Wheeler, L. (Eds.). (2000). *Handbook of social comparison: Theory and research.* New York: Kluwer Academic.

Suls, J., & Wheeler, L. (2012). Social comparison theory. In P. A. M. Van Lange, A. W. Kruglanski, & E. T. Higgins (Eds.), *Handbook of theories of social psychology* (Vol. 1., pp. 460–482). Thousand Oaks, CA: Sage.

Sumner, W. G. (1906). *Folkways.* New York: Ginn.

Sundstrom, E. (1987). Work environments: Offices and factories. In D. Stokols & I. Altman (Eds.), *Handbook of environmental psychology* (Vol. 1, pp. 733–782). New York: Wiley.

Sundstrom, E. & Altman, I. (1974). Field study of dominance and territorial behavior. *Journal of Personality and Social Psychology, 30*, 115–125.

Sundstrom, E., Bell, P. A., Busby, P. L., & Asmus, C. (1996). Environmental psychology: 1989-1994. *Annual Review of Psychology, 47*, 485–512.

Sundstrom, E., McIntyre, M., Halfhill, T., & Richards, H. (2000). Work groups: From the Hawthorne studies to work teams of the 1990s and beyond. *Group Dynamics: Theory, Research, and Practice, 4*, 44–67.

Sunstein, C. R. (2002). The law of group polarization. *The Journal of Political Philosophy, 10*, 175–195.

Sunwolf, T. (2002). Getting to "Group Aha!": Provoking creative processes in task groups. In L. R. Frey (Ed.), *New directions in group communication* (pp. 203–217). Thousand Oaks, CA: Sage.

Sunwolf (2010). Investigating jury deliberation in a capital murder case. *Small Group Research, 41*(4), 380–385.

Surowiecki, J. (2004). *The wisdom of crowds: Why the many are smarter than the few and how collective wisdom shapes business, economies, societies, and nations.* New York: Random House.

Susarla, A., Oh, J.-H., & Tan, Y. (2012). Social networks and the diffusion of user-generated content: Evidence from YouTube. *Information Systems Research, 23*, 23–41.

Sussman, S., Pokhrel, P., Ashmore, R. D., & Brown, B. B. (2007). Adolescent peer group identification and characteristics: A review of the literature. *Addictive Behaviors, 32*, 1602–1627.

Swann, W. B., Jr., Gómez, Á., Huici, C., Morales, J. F., & Hixon, J. G. (2010). Identity fusion and self-sacrifice: Arousal as a catalyst of pro-group fighting, dying, and helping behavior. *Journal of Personality and Social Psychology, 99*(5), 824–841.

Swann, W. B., Jr., Gómez, Á., Seyle, D. C., Morales, J. F., & Huici, C. (2009). Identity fusion: The interplay of personal and social identities in extreme group behavior. *Journal of Personality and Social Psychology, 96*(5), 995–1011.

Swann, W. B., Jr., Jetten, J., Gómez, Á., Whitehouse, H., & Bastian, B. (2012). When group membership gets personal: A theory of identity fusion. *Psychological Review, 119*(3), 441–456.

Swift, E. M. (1980, December). A reminder of what we can be. *Sports Illustrated*, December 22, 1980. Retrieved from sportsillustrated.cnn.com/vault/article/magazine/MAG1124069/index.htm

't Hart, P. (1998). Preventing groupthink revisited: Evaluating and reforming groups in government. *Organizational Behavior and Human Decision Processes, 73*, 306–326.

Tajfel, H. (1974). Social identity and intergroup behavior. *Social Science Information, 13*, 65–93.

Tajfel, H. (1981). *Human groups and social categories.* Cambridge, England: Cambridge University Press.

Tajfel, H., & Turner, J. C. (1979). An integrative theory of intergroup conflict. In W. G. Austin & S. Worchel (Eds.), *Psychology of intergroup relations* (pp. 33–47). Monterey, CA: Brooks/Cole.

Tajfel, H., & Turner, J. C. (1986). The social identity theory of intergroup behavior. In S. Worchel & W. G. Austin (Eds.), *Psychology of intergroup relations* (2nd ed., pp. 7–24). Chicago: Nelson-Hall.

Takeda, M. B., Helms, M. M., & Romanova, N. (2006). Hair color stereotyping and CEO selection in the United Kingdom. *Journal of Human Behavior in the Social Environment, 13*, 85–99.

Talley, A. E., Kocum, L., Schlegel, R. J., Molix, L., & Bettencourt, B. A. (2012). Social roles, basic need satisfaction, and psychological health: The central role of competence. *Personality and Social Psychology Bulletin, 38*(2), 155–173.

Tal-Or, N. (2008). Communicative behaviors of outperformers and their perception by the outperformed people. *Human Communication Research, 34*, 234–262.

Tam, T., Hewstone, M., Cairns, E., Tausch, N., Maio, G., & Kenworthy, J. (2007). The impact of intergroup emotions on forgiveness in Northern Ireland. *Group Processes & Intergroup Relations, 10*(1), 119–136.

Tang, J. (1997). The Model Minority thesis revisited: (Counter) evidence from the science and engineering fields. *Journal of Applied Behavioral Science, 33*, 291–314.

Tang, T. L., & Butler, E. A. (1997). Attributions of quality circles' problem-solving failure: Differences among management, supporting staff, and quality circle members. *Public Personnel Management, 26*, 203–225.

Tanis, M. (2008). Health-related on-line forums: What's the big attraction? *Journal of Health Communication, 13*(7), 698–714.

Tanis, M., & Postmes, T. (2005). Short communication: A social identity approach to trust: Interpersonal perception, group membership and trusting behavior. *European Journal of Social Psychology, 35*, 413–424.

Taras, V., Kirkman, B. L., & Steel, P. (2010). Examining the impact of culture's consequences: A three-decade, multilevel, meta-analytic review of Hofstede's cultural value dimensions. *Journal of Applied Psychology, 95*, 405–439.

Tarde, G. (1903). *The laws of imitation.* New York: Holt.

Tarnow, E. (2000). Self-destructive obedience in the airplane cockpit and the concept of obedience optimization. In T. Blass (Ed.), *Obedience to authority: Current perspectives on the Milgram paradigm* (pp. 111–123). Mahwah, NJ: Erlbaum.

Tata, J., Anthony, T., Hung-yu, L., Newman, B., Tang, S., Millson, M., & Sivakumar, K. (1996). Proportionate group size and rejection of the deviate: A meta-analytic integration. *Journal of Social Behavior and Personality, 11*, 739–752.

Tausch, N., Becker, J. C., Spears, R., Christ, O., Saab, R., Singh, P., & Siddiqui, R. N. (2011). Explaining radical group behavior: Developing emotion and efficacy routes to normative and nonnormative collective action. *Journal of Personality and Social Psychology, 101*(1), 129–148.

Taylor, F. W. (1923). *The principles of scientific management.* New York: Harpers.

Taylor, H. F. (1970). *Balance in small groups.* New York: Van Nostrand Reinhold.

Taylor, K. (2007). Disgust is a factor in extreme prejudice. *British Journal of Social Psychology, 46*(3), 597–617.

Taylor, P. J., Russ-Eft, D. F., & Taylor, H. (2009). Transfer of management training from alternative perspectives. *Journal of Applied Psychology, 94*(1), 104–121.

Taylor, R. B., & Lanni, J. C. (1981). Territorial dominance: The influence of the resident advantage in triadic decision making. *Journal of Personality and Social Psychology, 41*, 909–915.

Taylor, S. E. (2002). *The tending instinct: How nurturing is essential for who we are and how we live.* New York: Henry Holt.

Taylor, S. E. (2006). Tend and befriend: Biobehavioral bases of affiliation under stress. *Current Directions in Psychological Science, 15*(6), 273–277.

Taylor, S. E., Klein, L. C., Lewis, B. P., Gruenewald, T. L., Gurung, R. A. R., & Updegraff, J. A. (2000). Biobehavioral responses to stress in females: Tend-and-befriend, not fight-or-flight. *Psychological Review, 107*, 411–429.

Teger, A. (1980). *Too much invested to quit.* New York: Pergamon.

Tekleab, A. G., Quigley, N. R., & Tesluk, P. E. (2009). A longitudinal study of team conflict, conflict management, cohesion, and team effectiveness. *Group & Organization Management, 34*(2), 170–205.

Ten Velden, F. S., Beersma, B., & De Dreu, C. K. W. (2007). Majority and minority influence in group negotiation: The moderating effects of social motivation and decision rules. *Journal of Applied Psychology, 92*, 259–268.

Tennen, H., McKee, T. E., & Affleck, G. (2000). Social comparison processes in health and illness. In J. Suls & L. Wheeler (Eds.), *Handbook of social comparison: Theory and research* (pp. 443–483). New York: Kluwer Academic/Plenum.

Teppner, B. J. (2006). What do managers do when subordinates just say, "No?" An analysis of incidents involving refusal to perform downward requests. In C. A. Schriesheim & L. L. Neider (Eds.), *Power and influence in organizations: New empirical and theoretical perspectives* (pp. 1–20). Greenwich, CT: Information Age Publishing.

Terry, D. J., & Callan, V. J. (1998). In-group bias in response to an organizational merger. *Group Dynamics: Theory, Research, and Practice, 2*, 67–81.

Tesser, A. (1988). Toward a self-evaluation maintenance model of social behavior. *Advances in Experimental Social Psychology, 21*, 181–227.

Tesser, A. (1991). Emotion in social comparison and reflection processes. In J. Suls & T. A. Wills (Eds.), *Social comparison: Contemporary theory and research* (pp. 117–148). Mahwah, NJ: Erlbaum.

Tesser, A., Campbell, J., & Smith, M. (1984). Friendship choice and performance: Self-evaluation maintenance in children. *Journal of Personality and Social Psychology, 46*, 561–574.

Tetlock, P. E. (1979). Identifying victims of groupthink from public statements of decision makers. *Journal of Personality and Social Psychology, 37*, 1314–1324.

Tetlock, P. E., Peterson, R. S., McGuire, C., Chang, S., & Feld, P. (1992). Assessing political group dynamics: A test of the groupthink model. *Journal of Personality and Social Psychology, 63*, 403–425.

Thayer, B. A., & Hudson, V. M. (2010). Sex and the Shaheed: Insights from the life sciences on Islamic suicide terrorism. *International Security, 34*(4), 37–62.

Thibaut, J. W., & Kelley, H. H. (1959). *The social psychology of groups.* New York: Wiley.

Thomas, K. W. (1992). Conflict and negotiation processes in organizations. In M. D. Dunnette & L. M. Hough (Eds.), *Handbook of industrial and organizational psychology* (2nd ed., Vol. 3, pp. 651–717). Palo Alto, CA: Consulting Psychologists Press.

Thomas, W. I., & Thomas, D. S. (1928). *The child in America: Behavior problems and programs.* New York: Knopf.

Thomas-Hunt, M. C., & Phillips, K. W. (2004). When what you know is not enough: Expertise and gender dynamics in task groups. *Personality and Social Psychology Bulletin, 30*, 1585–1598.

Thompson, L. (1991). Information exchange in negotiation. *Journal of Experimental Social Psychology, 27*, 161–179.

Thompson, L., & Nadler, J. (2000). Judgmental biases in conflict resolution and how to overcome them. In M. Deutsch & P. T. Coleman (Eds.), *The handbook of conflict resolution: Theory and practice* (pp. 213–235). San Francisco: Jossey-Bass.

Thompson, L. L., Mannix, E. A., & Bazerman, M. H. (1988). Group negotiation: Effects of decision rule, agenda, and aspiration. *Journal of Personality and Social Psychology, 54*, 86–95.

Thoreau, H. D. (1962). *Walden and other writings.* New York: Bantam.

Thorne, B. (1993). *Gender play.* New Brunswick, NJ: Rutgers University Press.

Thrasher, F. M. (1927). *The gang.* Chicago: University of Chicago Press.

Thurlow, C., Lengel, L., & Tomic, A. (2004). *Computer mediated communication: Social interaction and the Internet.* Thousand Oaks, CA: Sage.

Thye, S. R. (2000). A status value theory of power in exchange relations. *American Sociological Review, 65*, 407–432.

Tiedens, L. Z. (2001). Anger and advancement versus sadness and subjugation: The effect of negative emotion expressions on social status conferral. *Journal of Personality and Social Psychology, 80*, 86–94.

Tiedens, L. Z., Ellsworth, P. C., & Mesquita, B. (2000). Stereotypes about sentiments and status: Emotional expectations for high- and low-status group members. *Personality and Social Psychology Bulletin, 26*, 560–574.

Tiedens, L. Z., & Fragale, A. R. (2003). Power moves: Complementarity in dominant and submissive nonverbal behavior. *Journal of Personality and Social Psychology, 84*, 558–568.

Tiedens, L. Z., Unzueta, M. M., & Young, M. J. (2007). An unconscious desire for hierarchy? The motivated perception of dominance complementarity in task partners. *Journal of Personality and Social Psychology, 93*(3), 402–414.

Tiger, L., & Fox, R. (1998). *The imperial animal.* New Brunswick, NJ: Transaction.

Tindale, R. S., Meisenhelder, H. M., Dykema-Engblade, A. A., & Hogg, M. A. (2001). Shared cognitions in small groups. In M. A. Hogg & R. S. Tindale (Eds.), *Blackwell handbook in social psychology: Group processes* (pp. 1–30). Malden, MA: Blackwell.

Tindale, R. S., Stawiski, S., & Jacobs, E. (2008). Shared cognition and group learning. In V. I. Sessa & M. London (Eds.), *Work group learning: Understanding, improving and assessing how groups learn in organizations* (pp. 73–90). New York: Taylor & Francis Group.

Tjosvold, D. (1995). Cooperation theory, constructive controversy, and effectiveness: Learning from crisis. In R. A. Guzzo, E. Salas, & Associates, *Team effectiveness and decision making in organizations* (pp. 79–112). San Francisco: Jossey-Bass.

Tjosvold, D., Johnson, D. W., Johnson, R. T., & Sun, H. (2006). Competitive motives and strategies: Understanding constructive competition. *Group Dynamics: Theory, Research, and Practice, 10,* 87–99.

Tobin, K. (2008). *Gangs: An individual group perspective.* Upper Saddle River, NJ: Prentice-Hall.

Toennies, F. (1963). *Community and society [Gemeinscheaft and Gesellschaft].* New York: Harper & Row. (original work published in 1887)

Tolnay, S. E., & Beck, E. M. (1996). Vicarious violence: Spatial effects on southern lynchings, 1890–1919. *American Journal of Sociology, 102,* 788–815.

Tolstoy, L. (1952). *War and peace.* Chicago: Encyclopedia Britannica. (original work published in 1887)

Tong, E. M. W., Tan, C. R. M., Latheef, N. A., Selamat, M. F. B., & Tan, D. K. B. (2008). Conformity: Moods matter. *European Journal of Social Psychology, 38,* 601–611.

Toobin, J. (2007). *The nine: Inside the secret world of the Supreme Court.* New York: Doubleday.

Torrance, E. P. (1954). The behavior of small groups under the stress conditions of "survival." *American Sociological Review, 19,* 751–755.

Tracey, T. J., Ryan, J. M., & Jaschik-Herman, B. (2001). Complementarity of interpersonal circumplex traits. *Personality and Social Psychology Bulletin, 27,* 786–797.

Travis, L. E. (1928). The influence of the group upon the stutterer's speed in free association. *Journal of Abnormal and Social Psychology, 23,* 45–51.

Treadwell, T., Lavertue, N., Kumar, V. K., & Veeraraghavan, V. (2001). The group cohesion scale-revised: Reliability and validity. *International Journal of Action Methods: Psychodrama, Skill Training, and Role Playing, 54,* 3–12.

Triandis, H. C. (1995). *Individualism and collectivism.* Boulder, CO: Westview Press.

Triandis, H. C. (1996). The psychological measurement of cultural syndromes. *American Psychologist, 51,* 407–415.

Triandis, H. C., & Gelfand, M. J. (2012). A theory of individualism and collectivism. In P. A. M. Van Lange, A. W. Kruglanski, & E. T. Higgins (Eds.), *Handbook of theories of social psychology* (Vol. 2, pp. 498–520). Thousand Oaks, CA: Sage.

Triandis, H. C., Leung, K., Villareal, M. J., & Clack, F. L. (1985). Allocentric versus idiocentric tendencies: Convergent and discriminant validation. *Journal of Research in Personality, 19*(4), 395–415.

Triandis, H. C., McCusker, C., & Hui, C. H. (1990). Multimethod probes of individualism and collectivism. *Journal of Personality and Social Psychology, 59,* 1006–1013.

Triandis, H. C., & Suh, E. M. (2002). Cultural influences on personality. *Annual Review of Psychology, 53,* 133–160.

Triplett, N. (1898). The dynamogenic factors in pacemaking and competition. *American Journal of Psychology, 9,* 507–533.

Tschan, F., Semmer, N. K., Gurtner, A., Bizzari, L., Spychiger, M., Breuer, M., & Marsch, S. U. (2009). Explicit reasoning, confirmation bias, and illusory transactive memory: A simulation study of group medical decision making. *Small Group Research, 40*(3), 271–300.

Tsui, A. S. (1984). A role-set analysis of managerial reputation. *Organizational Behavior and Human Performance, 34,* 64–96.

Tsui, A. S., Egan, T. D., & O'Reilly, C. A. (1992). Being different: Relational demography and organizational attachment. *Administrative Science Quarterly, 37,* 549–579.

Tucker, C. W., Schweingruber, D., & McPhail, C. (1999). Simulating arcs and rings in gatherings. *International Journal of Human-Computer Studies, 50,* 581–588.

Tuckman, B. W. (1965). Developmental sequences in small groups. *Psychological Bulletin, 63,* 384–399.

Tuckman, B. W., & Jensen, M. A. C. (1977). Stages of small group development revisited. *Group and Organizational Studies, 2,* 419–427.

Turnage, A. K. (2007). Email flaming behaviors and organizational conflict. *Journal of Computer-Mediated Communication, 13*(1), 43–59.

Turner, A. L. (2000). Group treatment of trauma survivors following a fatal bus accident: Integrating theory and practice. *Group Dynamics: Theory, Research, and Practice, 4,* 139–149.

Turner, J. C. (1982). Toward a cognitive redefinition of the social group. In H. Tajfel (Ed.), *Social identity and intergroup behavior* (pp. 15–40). New York: Cambridge University Press.

Turner, J. C. (1991). *Social influence.* Belmont, CA: Wadsworth/ Cengage.

Turner, J. C. (1999). Some current issues in research on social identity and self-categorization theories. In N. Ellemers, R. Spears, & B. Doosje (Eds.), *Social identity* (pp. 6–34). Malden, MA: Blackwell.

Turner, M. E. (Ed.). (2001). *Groups at work: Theory and research.* Mahwah, NJ: Erlbaum.

Turner, M. E., & Pratkanis, A. R. (1998a). A social identity maintenance model of groupthink. *Organizational Behavior and Human Decision Processes, 73*(2-3), 210–235.

Turner, M. E., & Pratkanis, A. R. (1998b). Twenty-five years of groupthink theory and research: Lessons from the evaluation of a theory. *Organizational Behavior and Human Decision Processes, 73*(2-3), 105–115.

Turner, R. H. (1964). Collective behavior. In R. E. L. Faris (Ed.), *Handbook of modern sociology*. Chicago: Rand McNally.

Turner, R. H. (2001a). Collective behavior. In E. F. Borgatta & R. J. V. Montgomery (Eds.), *Encyclopedia of sociology* (Vol. 1, 2nd ed., pp. 348–354). New York: Macmillan Reference.

Turner, R. H. (2001b). Role theory. In J. H. Turner (Ed.), *Handbook of sociological theory* (pp. 233–254). New York: Springer Science+Business Media.

Turner, R. H., & Colomy, P. (1988). Role differentiation: Orienting principles. *Advances in Group Processes, 5*, 1–27.

Turner, R. H., & Killian, L. M. (1972). *Collective behavior* (2nd ed.). Englewood Cliffs, NJ: Prentice Hall.

Twenge, J. M. (1997). Changes in masculine and feminine traits over time: A meta-analysis. *Sex Roles, 36*, 305–325.

Twenge, J. M. (2001). Changes in women's assertiveness in response to status and roles: A cross-temporal meta-analysis, 1931–1993. *Journal of Personality and Social Psychology, 81*, 133–145.

Twenge, J. M. (2006). *Generation me: Why today's young Americans are more confident, assertive, entitled—and more miserable than ever before*. New York: Free Press.

Twenge, J. M. (2009). Change over time in obedience: The jury's still out, but it might be decreasing. *American Psychologist, 64*(1), 28–31.

Twenge, J. M., Baumeister, R. F., DeWall, C. N., Ciarocco, N. J., & Bartels, J. M. (2007). Social exclusion decreases prosocial behavior. *Journal of Personality and Social Psychology, 92*, 56–66.

Twenge, J. M., Baumeister, R. F., Tice, D. M., & Stucke, T. S. (2001). If you can't join them, beat them: Effects of social exclusion on aggressive behavior. *Journal of Personality and Social Psychology, 81*, 1058–1069.

Twenge, J. M., Campbell, W. K., & Freeman, E. C. (2012). Generational differences in young adults' life goals, concern for others, and civic orientation, 1966–2009. *Journal of Personality and Social Psychology, 102*(5), 1045–1062.

Twenge, J. M., & Crocker, J. (2002). Race and self-esteem: Meta-analyses comparing Whites, Blacks, Hispanics, Asians, and American Indians and comment on Gray-Little and Hafdahl (2000). *Psychological Bulletin, 128*, 371–408.

Tyler, T. R. (2005). Introduction: Legitimating ideologies. *Social Justice Research, 18*, 211–215.

Tyler, T. R. (2011). Justice theory. In P. A. M. V. Lange, A. W. Kruglanski, & E. T. Higgins (Eds.), *Handbook of theories of social psychology* (Vol. 2, pp. 344–362). Thousand Oaks, CA: Sage.

Tyler, T. R., & Blader, S. L. (2003). The group engagement model: Procedural justice, social identity, and cooperative behavior. *Personality and Social Psychology Review, 7*, 349–361.

Uchino, B. N. (2004). *Social support and physical health: Understanding the health consequences of relationships*. New Haven, CT: Yale University Press.

Ugander, J., Backstrom, L., Marlow, C., & Kleinberg, J. (2012). Structural diversity in social contagion. *PNAS: Proceedings of the National Academy of Sciences, 109*(16), 5962–5966.

Uglow, J. S. (2002). *Lunar men: Five friends whose curiosity changed the world*. New York: Farrar, Straus, Giroux.

Ulbig, S. G., & Funk, C. L. (1999). Conflict avoidance and political participation. *Political Behavior, 21*, 265–282.

Umble, E. J., Haft, R. R., & Umble, M. M. (2003). Enterprise resource planning: Implementation procedures and critical success factors. *European Journal of Operational Research, 146*, 241–257.

Urban, L. M., & Miller, N. (1998). A theoretical analysis of crossed categorization effects: A meta-analysis. *Journal of Personality and Social Psychology, 74*, 894–908.

Uris, A. (1978). *Executive dissent: How to say no and win*. New York: AMACOM.

U.S. Senate Select Committee on Intelligence (2004). *Report of the Select Committee on Intelligence on the U.S. intelligence community's prewar intelligence assessments on Iraq together with additional views*. Retrieved from intelligence.senate.gov/108301.pdf

Utman, C. H. (1997). Performance effects of motivational state: A meta-analysis. *Personality and Social Psychology Review, 1*, 170–182.

Utz, S., & Sassenberg, K. (2002). Distributive justice in common-bond and common-identity groups. *Group Processes & Intergroup Relations, 5*, 151–162.

Uziel, L. (2007). Individual differences in the social facilitation effect: A review and meta-analysis. *Journal of Research in Personality, 41*, 579–601.

Uziel, L. (2010). Look at me, I'm happy and creative: The effect of impression management on behavior in social presence. *Personality and Social Psychology Bulletin, 36*(12), 1591–1602.

Vaillancourt, T., Hymel, S., & McDougall, P. (2003). Bullying is power: Implications for school-based intervention strategies. *Journal of Applied School Psychology, 19*, 157–176.

Valdesolo, P., & DeSteno, D. (2011). Synchrony and the social tuning of compassion. *Emotion, 11*(2), 262–266.

Vallacher, R. R., & Nowak, A. (2007). Dynamical social psychology: Finding order in the flow of human experience. In A. W. Kruglanski & E. T. Higgins (Eds.), *Social psychology: Handbook of basic principles* (2nd ed., pp. 734–758). New York: Guilford.

van de Ven, N., Zeelenberg, M., & Pieters, R. (2011). Why envy outperforms admiration. *Personality and Social Psychology Bulletin, 37*(6), 784–795.

Van de Vliert, E. (2006). Autocratic leadership around the globe: Do climate and wealth drive leadership culture? *Journal of Cross-Cultural Psychology, 37*(1), 42–59.

Van de Vliert, E. (2009). *Climate, affluence, and culture*. New York: Cambridge University Press.

Van de Vliert, E. (2011). Climato-economic origins of variation in ingroup favoritism. *Journal of Cross-Cultural Psychology, 42*(3), 494–515.

Van de Vliert, E., & Euwema, M. C. (1994). Agreeableness and activeness as components of conflict behaviors. *Journal of Personality and Social Psychology, 66*, 674–687.

Van de Vliert, E., & Janssen, O. (2001). Description, explanation, and prescription of intragroup conflict behaviors. In M. E. Turner (Ed.), *Groups at work: Theory and research* (pp. 267–297). Mahwah, NJ: Erlbaum.

Van de Vliert, E., & Postmes, T. (2012). Climato-economic livability predicts societal collectivism and political autocracy better than parasitic stress does. *Behavioral and Brain Sciences, 35*(2), 94–95.

Van de Vliert, E., & Van Yperen, N. (1996). Why cross-national differences in role overload? Don't overlook ambient temperature! *Academy of Management Journal, 39*(4), 986–1004.

Van der Toorn, J., Tyler, T. R., & Jost, J. T. (2011). More than fair: Outcome dependence, system justification, and the perceived legitimacy of authority figures. *Journal of Experimental Social Psychology, 47*(1), 127–138.

van Dijke, M., & Poppe, M. (2004). Social comparison of power: Interpersonal versus intergroup effects. *Group Dynamics: Theory, Research, and Practice, 8*, 13–26.

van Dijke, M., & Poppe, M. (2006). Striving for personal power as a basis for social power dynamics. *European Journal of Social Psychology, 36*, 537–556.

van Dijke, M., & Poppe, M. (2007). Motivation underlying power dynamics in hierarchically structured groups. *Small Group Research, 38*, 643–669.

Van Doorn, E. A., Heerdink, M. W., & Van Kleef, G. A. (2012). Emotion and the construal of social situations: Inferences of cooperation versus competition from expressions of anger, happiness, and disappointment. *Cognition and Emotion, 26*(3), 442–461.

van Ginneken, J. (2007). *Mass movements in Darwinist, Freudian, and Marxist perspective: Trotter, Freud, and Reich on war, revolution and reaction, 1900–1933*. Apeldoorn, NL: Het Spinhuis.

Van Hiel, A., & Franssen, V. (2003). Information acquisition bias during the preparation of group discussion: A comparison of prospective minority and majority members. *Small Group Research, 34*, 557–574.

Van Kleef, G. A. (2010). The emerging view of emotion as social information. *Social and Personality Psychology Compass, 4/5*, 331–343.

Van Kleef, G. A., & Côté, S. (2007). Expressing anger in conflict: When it helps and when it hurts. *Journal of Applied Psychology, 92*(6), 1557–1569.

Van Kleef, G. A., & De Dreu, C. K. (2002). Social value orientation and impression formation: A test of two competing hypotheses about information search in negotiation. *International Journal of Conflict Management, 13*, 59–77.

Van Kleef, G. A., De Dreu, C. K., & Manstead, A. S. (2004). The interpersonal effects of anger and happiness in negotiations. *Journal of Personality and Social Psychology, 86*, 57–76.

Van Kleef, G. A., Oveis, C., van der Löwe, I., LuoKogan, A., Goetz, J., & Keltner, D. (2008). Power, distress, and compassion: Turning a blind eye to the suffering of others. *Psychological Science, 19*(12), 1315–1322.

van Knippenberg, D., De Dreu, C. K. W., & Homan, A. C. (2004). Work group diversity and group performance: An integrative model and research agenda. *Journal of Applied Psychology, 89*, 1008–1022.

van Knippenberg, D., & Schippers, M. C. (2007). Work group diversity. *Annual Review of Psychology, 58*, 515–541.

Van Lange, P. A. M., De Cremer, D., Van Dijk, E., & Van Vugt, M. (2007). Self-interest and beyond: Basic principles of social interaction. In A. W. Kruglanski & E. T. Higgins (Eds.), *Social psychology: Handbook of basic principles* (2nd ed., pp. 540–561). New York: Guildford.

Van Lange, P. A. M., Klapwijk, A., & Van Munster, L. M. (2011). How the shadow of the future might promote cooperation. *Group Processes and Intergroup Relations, 14*, 857–870.

Van Lange, P. A. M., Ouwerkerk, J. W., & Tazelaar, M. J. (2002). How to overcome the detrimental effects of noise in social interaction: The benefits of generosity. *Journal of Personality and Social Psychology, 82*, 768–780.

van Oostrum, J., & Rabbie, J. M. (1995). Intergroup competition and cooperation within autocratic and democratic management regimes. *Small Group Research, 26*, 269–295.

Van Overwalle, F., & Heylighen, F. (2006). Talking nets: A multiagent connectionist approach to communication and trust between individuals. *Psychological Review, 113*, 606–627.

Van Pelt, S. (2009). *The complexities of leading virtual teams: A phenomenological study*. Unpublished dissertation, University of Phoenix.

van Prooijen, J., De Cremer, D., van Beest, I., Ståhl, T., van Dijke, M., & Van Lange, P. A. M. (2008). The egocentric nature of procedural justice: Social value orientation as moderator of reactions to decision-making procedures. *Journal of Experimental Social Psychology, 44*(5), 1303–1315.

Van Raalte, J. L., Cornelius, A. E., Linder, D. E., & Brewer, B. W. (2007). The relationship between hazing and team cohesion. *Journal of Sport Behavior, 30*, 491–507.

Van Swol, L. M. (2008). Performance and process in collective and individual memory: The role of social decision schemes and memory bias in collective memory. *Memory, 16*, 274–287.

van Uden-Kraan, C. F., Drossaert, C. H. C., Taal, E., Lebrun, C. E. I., Drossaers-Bakker, K. W., Smit, W. M., & van de Laar, M. A. F. J. (2008). Coping with somatic illnesses in online support groups: Do the feared disadvantages actually occur? *Computers in Human Behavior, 24*(2), 309–324.

Van Vugt, M., & Ahuja, A. (2011). *Naturally selected: The evolutionary science of leadership*. New York: HarperCollins.

Van Vugt, M., De Cremer, D., & Janssen, D. P. (2007). Gender differences in cooperation and competition: The male-warrior hypothesis. *Psychological Science, 18*, 19–23.

Van Vugt, M., & Hart, C. M. (2004). Social identity as social glue: The origins of group loyalty. *Journal of Personality and Social Psychology, 86*, 585–598.

Van Vugt, M., Hogan, R., & Kaiser, R. B. (2008). Leadership, followership, and evolution: Some lessons from the past. *American Psychologist, 63*(3), 182–196.

Van Vugt, M., & Schaller, M. (2008). Evolutionary approaches to group dynamics: An introduction. *Group Dynamics: Theory, Research, and Practice, 12*(1), 1–6.

Van Vugt, M., & Spisak, B. R. (2008). Sex differences in the emergence of leadership during competitions within and between groups. *Psychological Science, 19*(9), 854–858.

Van Zelst, R. H. (1952). Sociometrically selected work teams increase production. *Personnel Psychology, 5,* 175–185.

van Zomeren, M., Postmes, T., & Spears, R. (2008). Toward an integrative social identity model of collective action: A quantitative research synthesis of three socio-psychological perspectives. *Psychological Bulletin, 134,* 504–535.

Vandello, J. A., & Cohen, D. (1999). Patterns of individualism and collectivism across the United States. *Journal of Personality and Social Psychology, 77,* 279–292.

Vandello, J. A., & Cohen, D. (2003). Male honor and female fidelity: Implicit cultural scripts that perpetuate domestic violence. *Journal of Personality and Social Psychology, 84,* 997–1010.

Vandello, J. A., & Cohen, D. (2004). When believing is seeing: Sustaining norms of violence in cultures of honor. In M. Schaller & C. S. Crandall (Eds.), *The psychological foundations of culture* (pp. 281–304). Mahwah, NJ: Erlbaum.

Vandello, J. A., Cohen, D., & Ransom, S. (2008). U.S. southern and northern differences in perceptions of norms about aggression: Mechanisms for the perpetuation of a culture of honor. *Journal of Cross-Cultural Psychology, 39,* 162–177.

Vandenberghe, C., & Bentein, K. (2009). A closer look at the relationship between affective commitment to supervisors and organizations and turnover. *Journal of Occupational and Organizational Psychology, 82*(2), 331–348.

Varela, J. A. (1971). *Psychological solutions to social problems.* New York: Academic Press.

Varvel, S. J., He, Y., Shannon, J. K., Tager, D., Bledman, R. A., Chaichanasakul, A., Mendoza, M. M., & Mallinckrodt, B. (2007). Multidimensional, threshold effects of social support in firefighters: Is more support invariably better? *Journal of Counseling Psychology, 54,* 458–465.

Vecchio, R. P. (1987). Situational leadership theory: An examination of a prescriptive theory. *Journal of Applied Psychology, 72,* 444–451.

Vecchio, R. P., & Boatwright, K. J. (2002). Preferences for idealized styles of supervision. *Leadership Quarterly, 13,* 327–342.

Vecchio, R. P., Bullis, R. C., & Brazil, D. M. (2006). The utility of situational leadership theory: A replication in a military setting. *Small Group Research, 37*(5), 407–424.

Veitch, J. A. (1990). Office noise and illumination effects on reading comprehension. *Journal of Environmental Psychology, 10,* 209–217.

Veitch, J. A., Charles, K. E., Farley, K. M. J., & Newsham, G. R. (2007). A model of satisfaction with open-plan office conditions: COPE field findings. *Journal of Environmental Psychology, 27*(3), 177–189.

Venkatesh, S. (2008). *Gang leader for a day: A rogue sociologist takes to the streets.* New York: Penguin.

Verhofstadt, L. L., Buysse, A., & Ickes, W. (2007). Social support in couples: An examination of gender differences using self-report and observational methods. *Sex Roles, 57*(3-4), 267–282.

Vertue, F. M. (2003). From adaptive emotion to dysfunction: An attachment perspective on social anxiety disorder. *Personality and Social Psychology Review, 7,* 170–191.

Vickery, C. D., Gontkovsky, S. T., Wallace, J. J., & Caroselli, J. S. (2006). Group psychotherapy focusing on self-concept change following acquired brain injury: A pilot investigation. *Rehabilitation Psychology, 51,* 30–35.

Vider, S. (2004). Rethinking crowd violence: Self-categorization theory and the Woodstock 1999 riot. *Journal for the Theory of Social Behavior, 34,* 141–166.

Vidmar, N., & Hans, V. P. (2007). *American juries: The verdict.* Amherst, NY: Prometheus Books.

Vinokur, A., & Burnstein, E. (1974). The effects of partially shared persuasive arguments on group-induced shifts: A group-problem-solving approach. *Journal of Personality and Social Psychology, 29,* 305–315.

Vinokur, A., & Burnstein, E. (1978). Depolarization of attitudes in groups. *Journal of Personality and Social Psychology, 36,* 872–885.

Vinokur, A., Burnstein, E., Sechrest, L., & Wortman, P. M. (1985). Group decision making by experts: Field study of panels evaluating medical technologies. *Journal of Personality and Social Psychology, 49,* 70–84.

Vinsel, A., Brown, B. B., Altman, I., & Foss, C. (1980). Privacy regulation, territorial displays, and effectiveness of individual functioning. *Journal of Personality and Social Psychology, 39,* 1104–1115.

Vischer, J. C. (2008). Towards an environmental psychology of workspace: How people are affected by environments at work. *Architectural Science Review, 51*(2), 97–108.

Vroom, V. H. (2003). Educating managers in decision making and leadership. *Management Decision, 10,* 968–978.

Vroom, V. H., & Jago, A. G. (2007). The role of the situation in leadership. *American Psychologist, 62,* 17–24.

Vroom, V. H., & Mann, F. C. (1960). Leader authoritarianism and employee attitudes. *Personnel Psychology, 13,* 125–140.

Waber, B. N., Olguin, D. O., Kim, T., & Pentland, A. (2010). Productivity through coffee breaks: Changing social networks by changing break structure. *SSRN eLibrary.* Retrieved from papers.ssrn.com/sol3/papers.cfm?abstract_id=1586375

Waddington, D. (2008). The madness of the mob? Explaining the "irrationality" and destructiveness of crowd violence. *Sociology Compass, 2,* 675–687.

Wagner, D. G. (1995). Gender differences in reward preference: A status-based account. *Small Group Research, 26,* 353–371.

Walder, A. G. (2009). Political sociology and social movements. *Annual Review of Sociology, 35,* 393–412.

Walker, C. J., & Berkerle, C. A. (1987). The effect of state anxiety on rumor transmission. *Journal of Social Behavior and Personality, 2,* 353–360.

Walker, H. A., Ilardi, B. C., McMahon, A. M., & Fennell, M. L. (1996). Gender, interaction, and leadership. *Social Psychology Quarterly, 59,* 255–272.

Wall, V. D., Jr., & Nolan, L. L. (1987). Small group conflict: A look at equity, satisfaction, and styles of conflict management. *Small Group Behavior, 18,* 188–211.

Wallach, M. A., Kogan, N., & Bem, D. J. (1962). Group influence on individual risk taking. *Journal of Abnormal and Social Psychology, 65,* 75–86.

Wallenius, M. A. (2004). The interaction of noise stress and personal project stress on subjective health. *Journal of Environmental Psychology, 24,* 167–177.

Walsh, Y., Russell, R. J. H., & Wells, P. A. (1995). The personality of ex-cult members. *Personality and Individual Differences, 19,* 339–344.

Walters, S., Barr-Anderson, D., Wall, M., & Neumark-Sztainer, D. (2009). Does participation in organized sports predict future physical activity for adolescents from diverse economic backgrounds? *Journal of Adolescent Health, 44*(3), 268–274.

Walther, E., Bless, H., Strack, F., Rackstraw, P., Wagner, D., & Werth, L. (2002). Conformity effects in memory as a function of group size, dissenters and uncertainty. *Applied Cognitive Psychology, 16,* 793–810.

Walther, J. B. (2009). In point of practice: Computer-mediated communication and virtual groups: Applications to inter-ethnic conflict. *Journal of Applied Communication Research, 37*(3), 225–238.

Wang, A. Y., Newlin, M. H., & Tucker, T. L. (2001). A discourse analysis of online classroom chats: Predictors of cyber-student performance. *Teaching of Psychology, 28,* 222–226.

Warburton, W. A., Williams, K. D., & Cairns, D. R. (2006). When ostracism leads to aggression: The moderating effects of control deprivation. *Journal of Experimental Social Psychology, 42*(2), 213–220.

Warner HBO (Production Company). (2001). *Do you believe in miracles? The story of the 1980 U.S. Hockey Team* [Videotape]. New York: HBO Studios.

Warr, M. (2002). *Companions in crime: The social aspects of criminal conduct.* New York: Cambridge University Press.

Wasserman, S., & Faust, K. (1994). *Social network analysis: Methods and applications.* New York: Cambridge University Press.

Watson, C., & Hoffman, L. R. (1996). Managers as negotiators: A test of power versus gender as predictors of feelings, behavior, and outcomes. *Leadership Quarterly, 7,* 63–85.

Watson, D., & Clark, L. A. (1997). Extraversion and its positive emotional core. In R. Hogan & J. A. Johnson (Eds.), *Handbook of personality psychology* (pp. 767–793). San Diego: Academic Press.

Watson, R. I., Jr. (1973). Investigation into deindividuation using a cross-cultural survey technique. *Journal of Personality and Social Psychology, 25,* 342–345.

Watson, W. E., & Kumar, K. (1992). Differences in decision making regarding risk taking: A comparison of culturally diverse and culturally homogeneous task groups. *International Journal of Intercultural Relations, 16*(1), 53–65.

Watts, D. J., & Dodds, P. S. (2007). Influentials, networks, and public opinion formation. *Journal of Consumer Research, 34*(4), 441–458.

Waytz, A., & Young, L. (2012). The group-member mind trade-off: Attributing mind to groups versus group members. *Psychological Science, 23*(1), 77–85.

Webb, N. M., Troper, J. D., & Fall, R. (1995). Constructive activity and learning in collaborative small groups. *Journal of Educational Psychology, 87,* 406–423.

Weber, B., & Hertel, G. (2007). Motivation gains of inferior group members: A meta-analytical review. *Journal of Personality and Social Psychology, 93,* 973–993.

Weber, J. M., & Messick, D. M. (2004). Conflicting interests in social life: Understanding social dilemma dynamics. In M. J. Gelfand & J. M. Brett (Eds.), *The handbook of negotiation and culture* (pp. 374–394). Stanford, CA: Stanford University Press.

Weber, J. M., & Murnighan, J. K. (2008). Suckers or saviors? Consistent contributors in social dilemmas. *Journal of Personality and Social Psychology, 95*(6), 1340–1353.

Weber, M. (1946). The sociology of charismatic authority. In H. H. Gert & C. W. Mills (Trans. & Eds.), *From Max Weber: Essay in Sociology* (pp. 245–252). New York: Oxford University Press. (original work published in 1921)

Weber, M. (1978). *Economy and society* (G. Roth & C. Wittich, Trans.). Los Angeles: University of California Press. (original work published 1956)

Webster, G. D. (2008). The kinship, acceptance, and rejection model of altruism and aggression (KARMAA): Implications for interpersonal and intergroup aggression. *Group Dynamics: Theory, Research, and Practice, 12*(1), 27–38.

Webster, M., Jr., & Driskell, J. E., Jr. (1983). Processes of status generalization. In H. H. Blumberg, A. P. Hare, V. Kent, & M. F. Davies (Eds.), *Small groups and social interaction* (Vol. 1, pp. 57–67). New York: Wiley.

Wech, B. A., Mossholder, K. W., Steel, R. P., & Bennett, N. (1998). Does work group cohesiveness affect individuals' performance and organizational commitment? A cross-level examination. *Small Group Research, 29,* 472–494.

Wechsler, H., & Nelson, T. F. (2008). What we have learned from the Harvard School of Public Health College Alcohol Study: Focusing attention on college student alcohol consumption and the environmental conditions that promote it. *Journal of Studies on Alcohol and Drugs, 69*(4), 481–490.

Wegge, J., & Haslam, S. A. (2005). Improving work motivation and performance in brainstorming groups: The effects of three group goal-setting strategies. *European Journal of Work and Organizational Psychology, 14,* 400–430.

Wegner, D. M. (1987). Transactive memory: A contemporary analysis of the group mind. In B. Mullen & G. R. Goethals (Eds.), *Theories of group behavior* (pp. 185–208). New York: Springer Verlag.

Wegner, D. M., Giuliano, T., & Hertel, P. T. (1985). Cognitive interdependence in close relationships. In W. Ickes (Ed.), *Compatible and incompatible relationships* (pp. 253–276). New York: Springer-Verlag.

Weick, M., & Guinote, A. (2010). How long will it take? Power biases time predictions. *Journal of Experimental Social Psychology, 46*(4), 595–604.

Weigold, M. F., & Schlenker, B. R. (1991). Accountability and risk taking. *Personality and Social Psychology Bulletin, 17,* 25–29.

Weingart, L. R. (1992). Impact of group goals, task component complexity, effort, and planning on group performance. *Journal of Applied Psychology, 77,* 682–693.

Weingart, L. R. (1997). How did they do that? The ways and means of studying group process. *Research in Organizational Behavior, 19,* 189–239.

Weingart, L. R., Brett, J. M., Olekalns, M., & Smith, P. L. (2007). Conflicting social motives in negotiating groups. *Journal of Personality and Social Psychology, 93*(6), 994–1010.

Weingart, L. R., & Olekalns, M. (2004). Communication processes in negotiation: Frequencies, sequences, and phases. In M. J. Gelfand & J. M. Brett (Eds.), *The handbook of negotiation and culture* (pp. 143–157). Stanford, CA: Stanford University Press.

Weingart, L. R., & Weldon, E. (1991). Processes that mediate the relationship between a group goal and group member performance. *Human Performance, 4,* 33–54.

Weiss, T. (2011). The blurring border between the police and the military: A debate without foundations. *Cooperation and Conflict, 46*(3), 396–405.

Welch, D. A. (1989). Crisis decision making reconsidered. *Journal of Conflict Resolution, 33,* 430–445.

Weldon, E., Jehn, K. A., & Pradhan, P. (1991). Processes that mediate the relationship between a group goal and improved group performance. *Journal of Personality and Social Psychology, 61,* 555–569.

Weldon, E., & Weingart, L. R. (1993). Group goals and group performance. *British Journal of Social Psychology, 32,* 307–334.

Weldon, M. S., & Bellinger, K. D. (1997). Collective memory: Collaborative and individual processes in remembering. *Journal of Experimental Psychology: Learning, Memory, and Cognition, 23,* 1160–1175.

Weldon, M. S., Blair, C., & Huebsch, D. (2000). Group remembering: Does social loafing underlie collaborative inhibition? *Journal of Experimental Psychology: Learning, Memory, & Cognition, 26,* 1568–1577.

Werner, C. M., Brown, B. B., & Altman, I. (2002). Transactionally oriented research: Examples and strategies. In R. Bechtel & A. Churchman (Eds.), *Handbook of environmental psychology* (pp. 203–221). New York: Wiley.

Werner, P. (1978). Personality and attitude-activism correspondence. *Journal of Personality and Social Psychology, 36,* 1375–1390.

Wesselmann, E. D., & Williams, K. D. (2011). Ostracism in Cyberspace: Being ignored and excluded on the Internet. In Z. Birchmeier, B. Dietz-Uhler, and G. Stasser, (Eds.), *Strategic uses of social technology: An interactive perspective of social psychology* (pp. 127–144). New York: Cambridge University Press.

West, M. A., & Lyubovnikova, J. (2012). Real teams or pseudo teams? The changing landscape needs a better map. *Industrial and Organizational Psychology: Perspectives on Science and Practice, 5*(1), 25–55.

Wheelan, S. A. (2005). *Group processes: A developmental perspective* (2nd ed.). Boston: Allyn & Bacon.

Wheelan, S. A. (Ed.). (2005). *The handbook of group research and practice.* Thousand Oaks, CA: Sage.

Wheelan, S. A., Davidson, B., & Tilin, F. (2003). Group development across time: Reality or illusion? *Small Group Research, 34,* 223–245.

Wheelan, S. A., & Hochberger, J. M. (1996). Validation studies of the group development questionnaire. *Small Group Research, 27,* 143–170.

Wheelan, S. A., & McKeage, R. L. (1993). Developmental patterns in small and large groups. *Small Group Research, 24,* 60–83.

Wheeler, D. D., & Janis, I. L. (1980). *A practical guide for making decisions.* New York: Free Press.

Wheeler, L. (1966). Toward a theory of behavioral contagion. *Psychological Review, 73,* 179–192.

Wheeler, L., & Miyake, K. (1992). Social comparison in everyday life. *Journal of Personality and Social Psychology, 62,* 760–773.

White, R. K. (1990). Democracy in the research team. In S. A. Wheelan, E. Pepitone, & V. Abt (Eds.), *Advances in field theory* (pp. 19–26). Thousand Oaks, CA: Sage.

White, R. K., & Lippitt, R. (1960). *Autocracy and democracy.* New York: Harper & Row.

White, R. K., & Lippitt, R. (1968). Leader behavior and member reaction in three "social climates." In D. Cartwright & A. Zander (Eds.), *Group dynamics: Research and theory* (3rd ed., pp. 318–335). New York: Harper & Row.

Whitley, B. E., Jr. (1999). Right-wing authoritarianism, social dominance orientation, and prejudice. *Journal of Personality and Social Psychology, 77,* 126–134.

Whitney, K., & Sagrestano, L. M., & Maslach, C. (1994). Establishing the social impact of individuation. *Journal of Personality and Social Psychology, 66,* 1140–1153.

Whittal, M. L., & McLean, P. D. (2002). Group cognitive behavioral therapy for obsessive compulsive disorder. In R. O. Frost & G. Steketee (Eds.), *Cognitive approaches to obsessions and compulsions: Theory, assessment, and treatment* (pp. 417–433). Amsterdam: Pergamon/Elsevier Science.

Whyte, W. F. (1943). *Street corner society.* Chicago: University of Chicago Press.

Whyte, W. F. (1955). *Street corner society* (2nd ed.). Chicago: University of Chicago Press.

Whyte, W. F., Greenwood, D. J., & Lazes, P. (1991). Participatory action research: Through practice to science in social research. In W. F. Whyte (Ed.), *Participatory action research* (pp. 19–55). Thousand Oaks, CA: Sage.

Wicker, A. W. (1979). *An introduction to ecological psychology.* Pacific Grove, CA: Brooks/Cole.

Wicker, A. W. (1987). Behavior settings reconsidered: Temporal stages, resources, internal dynamics, context. In D. Stokols & I. Altman (Eds.), *Handbook of environmental psychology* (Vol. 1, pp. 613–653). New York: Wiley.

Wicker, A. W. (2002). Ecological psychology: Historical contexts, current conception, prospective directions. In R. Bechtel & A. Churchman (Eds.), *Handbook of environmental psychology* (pp. 114–126). New York: Wiley.

Wicker, A. W., & August, R. A. (1995). How far should we generalize? The case of a workload model. *Psychological Science, 6,* 39–44.

Wicker, A. W., Kirmeyer, S. L., Hanson, L., & Alexander, D. (1976). Effects of manning levels on subjective experiences, performance, and verbal interaction in groups. *Organizational Behavior and Human Performance, 17,* 251–274.

Widen, S. C., & Russell, J. A. (2010). Descriptive and prescriptive definitions of emotion. *Emotion Review, 2*(4), 377–378.

Widmeyer, W. N. (1990). Group composition in sport. *International Journal of Sport Psychology, 21,* 264–285.

Widmeyer, W. N., Brawley, L. R., & Carron, A. V. (1992). Group dynamics in sports. In T. S. Horn (Ed.), *Advances in sport psychology* (pp. 163–180). Champaign, IL: Human Kinetics Publishers.

Wilder, D. A. (1977). Perception of groups, size of opposition, and social influence. *Journal of Experimental Social Psychology, 13,* 253–268.

Wilder, D. A. (1986). Social categorization: Implications for creation and reduction of intergroup bias. *Advances in Experimental Social Psychology, 19,* 293–355.

Wilder, D. A., Simon, A. F., & Faith, M. (1996). Enhancing the impact of counterstereotypic information: Dispositional attributions for deviance. *Journal of Personality and Social Psychology, 71,* 276–287.

Wilder, D. A., & Thompson, J. E. (1980). Intergroup contact with independent manipulations of in-group and out-group interaction. *Journal of Personality and Social Psychology, 38,* 589–603.

Wildman, J. L., Thayer, A. L., Rosen, M. A., Salas, E., Mathieu, J. E., & Rayne, S. R. (2012). Task types and team-level attributes: Synthesis of team classification literature. *Human Resource Development Review, 11*(1), 97–129.

Wildschut, T., Pinter, B., Vevea, J. L., Insko, C. A., & Schopler, J. (2003). Beyond the group mind: A quantitative review of the interindividual-intergroup discontinuity effect. *Psychological Bulletin, 129,* 698–722.

Wilgus, A. J. (2003). Lone wolves and rogue elephants: Emotional cutoff among animals. In P. Titelman (Ed.), *Emotional cutoff* (pp. 67–81). Binghamton, NY: Haworth.

Wilke, H. A. M. (1996). Status congruence in small groups. In E. Witte & J. H. Davis (Eds.), *Understanding group behavior: Small group processes and interpersonal relations* (Vol. 2, pp. 67–91). Mahwah, NJ: Erlbaum.

Wilkinson-Weber, C. M. (2010). From commodity to costume: Productive consumption in the production of Bollywood film "looks". *Journal of Material Culture, 15,* 1–28.

Williams v. Florida, 399 U.S. 78(1970).

Williams, D., Ducheneaut, N., Xiong, L., Zhang, Y., Yee, N., & Nickell, E. (2006). From tree house to barracks: The social life of guilds in World of Warcraft. *Games & Culture, 1*(4), 338–361.

Williams, J. E., & Best, D. L. (1990). *Measuring sex stereotypes: A multination study.* Thousand Oaks, CA: Sage.

Williams, K. D. (2007). Ostracism. *Annual Review of Psychology, 58,* 425–452.

Williams, K. D. (2009). Ostracism: A temporal need-threat model. *Advances in Experimental Social Psychology, 41,* 275–314.

Williams, K. D. (2010). Dyads can be groups (and often are). *Small Group Research, 41,* 268–274.

Williams, K. D., Cheung, C. K. T., & Choi, W. (2000). Cyberostracism: Effects of being ignored over the Internet. *Journal of Personality and Social Psychology, 79,* 748–762.

Williams, K. D., Govan, C. L., Croker, V., Tynan, D., Cruickshank, M., & Lam, A. (2002). Investigations into differences between social- and cyber-ostracism. *Group Dynamics: Theory, Research, and Practice, 6,* 65–77.

Williams, K. D., Harkins, S., & Latané, B. (1981). Identifiability as a deterrent to social loafing: Two cheering experiments. *Journal of Personality and Social Psychology, 40,* 303–311.

Williams, K. D., & Karau, S. J. (1991). Social loafing and social compensation: The effects of expectations of co-worker performance. *Journal of Personality and Social Psychology, 61,* 570–581.

Williams, K. D., & Sommer, K. L. (1997). Social ostracism by coworkers: Does rejection lead to loafing or compensation? *Personality and Social Psychology Bulletin, 23,* 693–706.

Williams, K. Y., & O'Reilly, C. A. (1998). Demography and diversity in organizations: A review of 40 years of research. *Research in Organizational Behavior, 20,* 77–140.

Williams, L. E., & Bargh, J. A. (2008). Experiencing physical warmth promotes interpersonal warmth. *Science, 322*(5901), 606–607.

Willig, C., & Stainton-Rogers, W. (Eds.). (2008). *The Sage handbook of qualitative research in psychology.* Thousand Oaks, CA: Sage.

Willis, F. N. (1966). Initial speaking distance as a function of the speakers' relationship. *Psychonomic Science, 5,* 221–222.

Wills, T. A. (1991). Social comparison processes in coping and health. In C. R. Snyder, & D. R. Forsyth (Eds.), *Handbook of social and clinical psychology: The health perspective* (pp. 376–394). Elmsford, NY: Pergamon.

Wills, T. A., & DePaulo, B. M. (1991). Interpersonal analysis of the help-seeking process. In C. R. Snyder & D. R. Forsyth (Eds.), *Handbook of social and clinical psychology: The health perspective* (pp. 350–375). New York: Pergamon Press.

Wills, T. A., & Filer, M. (2000). Social networks and social support. In A. Baum & T. Revenson (Eds.), *Handbook of health psychology* (pp. 209–232). Mahwah, NJ: Erlbaum.

Wilson, S. R. (1992). Face and facework in negotiation. In L. L. Putnam & M. E. Roloff (Eds.), *Communication and negotiation* (pp. 176–205). Thousand Oaks, CA: Sage.

Wiltermuth, S. S., & Heath, C. (2009). Synchrony and cooperation. *Psychological Science, 20*(1), 1–5.

Winquist, J. R., & Larson, J. R., Jr. (1998). Information pooling: When it impacts group decision making. *Journal of Personality and Social Psychology, 74,* 371–377.

Winter, D. G. (1973). *The power motive.* New York: Free Press.

Winter, D. G. (2010). Power in the person: Exploring the motivational underground of power. In A. Guinote & T. K. Vescio (Eds.), *The social psychology of power* (pp. 113–140). New York: Guilford Press.

Wiseman, R. (2002). *Queen bees and wannabes: Helping your daughter survive cliques, gossip, boyfriends, and other realities of adolescence.* New York: Crown.

Wisman, A., & Koole, S. L. (2003). Hiding in the crowd: Can mortality salience promote affiliation with others who oppose one's worldviews? *Journal of Personality and Social Psychology, 84,* 511–526.

Witte, E. H. (1989). Köhler rediscovered: The anti-Ringelmann effect. *European Journal of Social Psychology, 19,* 147–154.

Witteman, H. (1991). Group member satisfaction: A conflict-related account. *Small Group Research, 22,* 24–58.

Wittenbaum, G. M. (1998). Information sampling in decision-making groups: The impact of members' task-relevant status. *Small Group Research, 29,* 57–84.

Wittenbaum, G. M., Hollingshead, A. B., & Botero, I. C. (2004). From cooperative to motivated information sharing in groups: Moving beyond the hidden profile paradigm. *Communication Monographs, 71,* 286–310.

Wittenbaum, G. M., Hollingshead, A. B., Paulus, P. B., Hirokawa, R. Y., Ancona, D. G., Peterson, R. S., Jehn, K. A., & Yoon, K. (2004). The functional perspective as a lens for understanding groups. *Small Group Research, 35,* 17–43.

Wittenbaum, G. M., Hubbell, A. P., & Zuckerman, C. (1999). Mutual enhancement: Toward an understanding of the collective preference for shared information. *Journal of Personality and Social Psychology, 77,* 967–978.

Wittenbaum, G. M., Stasser, G., & Merry, C. J. (1996). Tacit coordination in anticipation of small group task completion. *Journal of Experimental Social Psychology, 32,* 129–152.

Wolf, S. (1987). Majority and minority influence: A social impact analysis. In M. P. Zanna, J. M. Olson, & C. P. Herman (Eds.), *Social influence: The Ontario Symposium* (Vol. 5, pp. 207–235). Mahwah, NJ: Erlbaum.

Wolf, S. T., Insko, C. A., Kirchner, J. L., & Wildschut, T. (2008). Interindividual-intergroup discontinuity in the domain of correspondent outcomes: The roles of relativistic concern, perceived categorization, and the doctrine of mutual assured destruction. *Journal of Personality and Social Psychology, 94,* 479–494.

Wood, A. M., Linley, P. A., Maltby, J., Baliousis, M., & Joseph, S. (2008). The authentic personality: A theoretical and empirical conceptualization and the development of the authenticity scale. *Journal of Counseling Psychology, 55,* 385–399.

Wood, W. (1987). A meta-analytic review of sex differences in group performance. *Psychological Bulletin, 102,* 53–71.

Wood, W., Polek, D., & Aiken, C. (1985). Sex differences in group task performance. *Journal of Personality and Social Psychology, 48,* 63–71.

Wooldridge, B., Schmid, T., & Floyd, S. W. (2008). The middle management perspective on strategy process: Contributions, synthesis, and future research. *Journal of Management, 34*(6), 1190–1221.

Woolley, A. W., Chabris, C. F., Pentland, A., Hashmi, N., & Malone, T. W. (2010). Evidence for a collective intelligence factor in the performance of human groups. *Science, 333*(6004), 686–688.

Woolley, A. W., Gerbasi, M. E., Chabris, C. F., Kosslyn, S. M., & Hackman, J. R. (2008). Bringing in the experts: How team composition and collaborative planning jointly shape analytic effectiveness. *Small Group Research, 39*(3), 352–371.

Worchel, S. (1986). The role of cooperation in reducing intergroup conflict. In S. Worchel & W. G. Austin (Eds.), *Psychology of intergroup relations* (2nd ed., pp. 288–304). Chicago: Nelson-Hall.

Worchel, S., & Brehm, J. W. (1971). Direct and implied social restoration of freedom. *Journal of Personality and Social Psychology, 18,* 294–304.

Worchel, S., & Teddlie, C. (1976). The experience of crowding: A two-factor theory. *Journal of Personality and Social Psychology, 34,* 30–40.

Worchel, S., & Yohai, S. (1979). The role of attribution in the experience of crowding. *Journal of Experimental Social Psychology, 15,* 91–104.

Worringham, C. J., & Messick, D. M. (1983). Social facilitation of running: An unobtrusive study. *Journal of Social Psychology, 121,* 23–29.

Worthington, E. L., Jr., Hight, T. L., Ripley, J. S., Perrone, K. M., Kurusu, T. A., & Jones, D. R. (1997). Strategic hope-focused relationship-enrichment counseling with individual couples. *Journal of Counseling Psychology, 44,* 381–389.

Wosniak, S., & Smith, G. (2006). *iWoz.* New York: Norton.

Wright, S. C., Aron, A., McLaughlin-Volpe, T., & Ropp, S. A. (1997). The extended contact effect: Knowledge of cross-group friendships and prejudice. *Journal of Personality and Social Psychology, 73,* 73–90.

Wright, S. C., Aron, A., & Tropp, L. R. (2002). Including others (and groups) in the self: Self-expansion and intergroup relations. In J. P. Forgas & K. D. Williams (Eds.), *The social self: Cognitive, interpersonal and intergroup perspectives* (pp. 343–363). Philadelphia: Psychology Press.

Wright, S. S., & Forsyth, D. R. (1997). Group membership and collective identity: Consequences for self-esteem. *Journal of Social & Clinical Psychology, 16,* 43–56.

Wrightsman, L. S., Nietzel, M. T., & Fortune, W. H. (1998). *Psychology and the legal system* (4th ed.). Pacific Grove, CA: Brooks/Cole.

Wu, J. Z., & Axelrod, R. (1995). How to cope with noise in the iterated prisoner's dilemma. *Journal of Conflict Resolution, 39,* 183–189.

Wundt, W. (1916). *Elements of folk psychology.* New York: MacMillan.

Wyden, P. H. (1979). *Bay of Pigs: The untold story.* New York: Simon & Schuster.

Xu, Y., Schneier, F., Heimberg, R. G., Princisvalle, K., Liebowitz, M. R., Wang, S., & Blanco, C. (2012). Gender differences in social anxiety disorder: Results from the national epidemiologic sample on alcohol and related conditions. *Journal of Anxiety Disorders, 26*(1), 12–19.

Yablonsky, L. (1959). The delinquent gang as a near group. *Social Problems, 7,* 108–117.

Yablonsky, L. (1962). *The violent gang.* New York: Macmillan.

Yakovleva, M., Reilly, R. R., & Werko, R. (2010). Why do we trust? Moving beyond individual to dyadic perceptions. *Journal of Applied Psychology, 95*(1), 79–91.

Yalom, I. D., with Leszcz, M. (2005). *The theory and practice of group psychotherapy* (5th ed.). New York: Basic Books.

Yamagishi, K. (1994). Social dilemmas. In K. S. Cook, G. A. Fine, & J. S. House (Eds.), *Sociological perspectives on social psychology* (pp. 311–334). Boston: Allyn & Bacon.

Yamazaki, Y. (2005). Learning styles and typologies of cultural differences: A theoretical and empirical comparison. *International Journal of Intercultural Relations, 29*(5), 521–548.

Yammarino, F. J., & Bass, B. M. (1990). Long-term forecasting of transformational leadership and its effects among naval officers: Some preliminary findings. In K. E. Clark & M. B. Clark (Eds.), *Measure of leadership* (pp. 151–169). West Orange, NJ: Leadership Library of America.

Yammarino, F. J., & Dansereau, F. (2008). Multi-level nature of and multi-level approaches to leadership. *Leadership Quarterly, 19,* 135–141.

Yammarino, F. J., Dionne, S. D., Chun, J. U., & Dansereau, F. (2005). Leadership and levels of analysis: A state-of-the-science review. *Leadership Quarterly, 16,* 879–919.

Yang, J., & Mossholder, K. W. (2004). Decoupling task and relationship conflict: The role of intragroup emotional processing. *Journal of Organizational Behavior, 25,* 589–605.

Yang, K., & Bond, M. H. (1990). Exploring implicit personality theories with indigenous or imported constructs: The Chinese case. *Journal of Personality and Social Psychology, 58*(6), 1087–1095.

Yik, M., Russell, J. A., & Steiger, J. H. (2011). A 12-point circumplex structure of core affect. *Emotion, 11*(4), 705–731.

Yin, R. K. (2009). *Case study research: Design and methods* (4th ed.). Thousand Oaks, CA: Sage.

York, E. and Cornwell, B. (2006). Status on trial: Social characteristics and influence in the jury room. *Social Forces, 85,* 455–477.

Youngs, G. A., Jr. (1986). Patterns of threat and punishment reciprocity in a conflict setting. *Journal of Personality and Social Psychology, 51,* 541–546.

Yuki, M. (2003). Intergroup comparison versus intragroup relationships: A cross-cultural examination of social identity theory in North American and East Asian cultural contexts. *Social Psychology Quarterly, 66,* 166–183.

Yukl, G., Kim, H., & Falbe, C. (1996). Antecedents of influence outcomes. *Journal of Applied Psychology, 81,* 309–317.

Yukl, G., & Michel, J. W. (2006). Proactive influence tactics and leader member exchange. In C. A. Schriesheim & L. L. Neider (Eds.), *Power and influence in organizations: New empirical and theoretical perspectives* (pp. 87–104). Greenwich, CT: Information Age Publishing.

Yukl, G. A. (2013). *Leadership in organizations* (8th ed.). Boston: Pearson.

Yzerbyt, V., & Demoulin, S. (2010). Intergroup relations. In S. T. Fiske, D. T. Gilbert, & G. Lindzey (Eds.), *Handbook of social psychology* (Vol. 2, 5th ed., pp. 1024–1083). Hoboken, NJ: John Wiley.

Yzerbyt, V., Judd, C. M., & Corneille, O. (Eds.). (2004). *The psychology of group perception: Perceived variability, entitativity, and essentialism.* New York: Psychology Press.

Zaccaro, S. J. (2007). Trait-based perspectives of leadership. *American Psychologist, 62,* 6–16.

Zaccaro, S. J., Foti, R. J., & Kenny, D. A. (1991). Self-monitoring and trait-based variance in leadership: An investigation of leader flexibility across multiple group situations. *Journal of Applied Psychology, 76,* 308–315.

Zaccaro, S. J., Gulick, L. M., & Khare, V. P. (2008). Personality and leadership. In C. L. Hoyt, G. R. Goethals, & D. R. Forsyth (Eds.), *Leadership at the crossroads: Leadership and psychology* (Vol. 1, pp. 14–29). Westport, CT: Praeger.

Zaccaro, S. J., Kemp, C., & Bader, P. (2004). Leader traits and attributes. In J. Antonakis, A. T. Cianciolo, & R. J. Sternberg (Eds.), *The nature of leadership* (pp. 101–124). Thousand Oaks, CA: Sage.

Zajonc, R. B. (1965). Social facilitation. *Science, 149,* 269–274.

Zajonc, R. B. (1980). Compresence. In P. B. Paulus (Ed.), *Psychology of group influence* (pp. 35–60). Mahwah, NJ: Erlbaum.

Zajonc, R. B., Heingartner, A., & Herman, E. M. (1969). Social enhancement and impairment of performance in the cockroach. *Journal of Personality and Social Psychology, 13,* 83–92.

Zander, A. F. (1971). *Motives and goals in groups.* New York: Academic Press.

Zander, A. F. (1985). *The purposes of groups and organizations.* San Francisco: Jossey-Bass.

Zander, A. F., Stotland, E., & Wolfe, D. (1960). Unity of group, identification with group, and self-esteem of members. *Journal of Personality, 28,* 463–478.

Zhou, R., & Soman, D. (2008). Consumers' waiting in queues: The role of first-order and second-order justice. *Psychology and Marketing, 25,* 262–279.

Zhou, W., & Shi, X. (2011). Special review article: Culture in groups and teams: A review of three decades of research. *International Journal of Cross Cultural Management, 11*(1), 5–34.

Ziller, R. C. (1965). Toward a theory of open and closed groups. *Psychological Bulletin, 64,* 164–182.

Zimbardo, P. G. (1969). The human choice: Individuation, reason, and order versus deindividuation, impulse, and chaos. *Nebraska Symposium on Motivation, 11,* 237–307.

Zimbardo, P. G. (1975). Transforming experimental research into advocacy for social change. In M. Deutsch & H. A. Hornstein (Eds.), *Applying social psychology* (pp. 33–66). Mahwah, NJ: Erlbaum.

Zimbardo, P. G. (1977). *Shyness: What it is and what to do about it.* Cambridge, MA: Perseus.

Zimbardo, P. G. (2004). A situationist perspective on the psychology of evil: Understanding how good people are transformed into perpetrators. In A. G. Miller (Ed.), *The social psychology of good and evil* (pp. 21–50). New York: Guilford.

Zimbardo, P. G. (2007). *The Lucifer effect.* New York: Random House.

Zimbardo, P. G., Butler, L. D., & Wolfe, V. A. (2003). Cooperative college examinations: More gain, less pain when students share information and grades. *Journal of Experimental Education, 71,* 101–125.

Zimbardo, P. G., Maslach, C., & Haney, C. (2000). Reflections on the Stanford Prison Experiment: Genesis, transformations, consequences. In T. Blass (Ed.). *Obedience to authority: Current perspectives on the Milgram paradigm.* Mahwah, NJ: Erlbaum.

Zimmermann, P., Wit, A., & Gill, R. (2008). The relative importance of leadership behaviors in virtual and face-to-face communication settings. *Leadership, 4*(3), 321–337.

Zitek, E. M., & Tiedens, L. Z. (2012). The fluency of social hierarchy: The ease with which hierarchical relationships are seen, remembered, learned, and liked. *Journal of Personality and Social Psychology, 102*(1), 98–115.

Zubek, J. P. (1973). Behavioral and physiological effects of prolonged sensory and perceptual deprivation: A review. In J. E. Rasmussen (Ed.), *Man in isolation and confinement* (pp. 9–83). Chicago: Aldine.

Zuber, J. A., Crott, H. W., & Werner, J. (1992). Choice shift and group polarization: An analysis of the status of arguments and social decision schemes. *Journal of Personality and Social Psychology, 62,* 50–61.

Zurcher, L. A., Jr. (1969). Stages of development in poverty program neighborhood action committees. *Journal of Applied Behavioral Science, 15,* 223–258.

Zyphur, M. J., Kaplan, S. A., & Christian, M. S. (2008). Assumptions of cross-level measurement and structural invariance in the analysis of multilevel data: Problems and solutions. *Group Dynamics: Theory, Research, and Practice, 12,* 127–140.

Author Index

Aarts, H., 169, 533
Abakoumkin, G., 68, 350
Abbott, A. S., 280, 376
Abel, T., 293
Abele, A. E., 89, 285
Abelson, R. P., 16
Aberson, C. L., 498
Abrahamsen, S., 574
Abrams, D., 13, 29, 32, 89, 218, 495, 592
Achille, N. M., 103
Adams, G., 67
Adams, J., 291
Adams, R. B., 45
Adams, S., 420
Adarves-Yorno, I., 209
Adelman, L., 494
Adler, P., 45, 69, 189
Adler, P. A., 45, 69, 189
Adolphs, R., 519
Affleck, G., 556
Agazarian, Y. M., 560
Aggarwal, P., 230
Agnew, C. R., 129, 153
Aharonov-Majar, E., 115
Ahmad, A. H., 185
Ahuja, A., 276, 301
Aiello, J. R., 325, 327, 332, 333, 356, 516
Aiken, C., 416–417
Akande, A., 185
Akande, D., 185
Akkermans, W., 191
Al-Abideen, H. Z., 584
Albert, K. P., 527
Al-Bosta, S., 584
Albright, L., 102

Alden, L. E., 108
Aldrich, H. E., 4
Alexander, D., 535
Alexander, K. R., 514
Alge, B. J., 333
Alicke, M. D., 448
Allen, K., 329
Allen, N. J., 427, 432
Allen, V. L., 186, 208
Alliger, G. M., 288
Allik, J., 104
Allison, G., 45
Allison, S. T., 442, 444, 486
Allmendinger, J., 23, 24, 417
Allport, F. H., 19, 20, 63, 324, 326
Allport, G. W., 5, 32, 487, 489, 501, 583
Alonso, O., 366, 367
Altemeyer, B., 214
Alter, A. L., 16
Alterman, E., 393
Altermatt, T. W., 35, 61
Altman, I., 508, 511, 524, 526, 528–532, 539, 560
Alvares, G. A., 76
Amegashie, J. A., 441
Ames, C., 441
Ames, D. R., 16, 288
Amichai-Hamburger, Y., 500
Amir, Y., 498
Ammon, L., 554
Anca, J., 345
Ancona, D. G., 360, 397
Anderman, E. M., 441
Anderman, L. H., 441
Andersen, J. A., 185
Andersen, S. M., 561

Anderson, C., 258, 262, 266, 267, 270, 279
Anderson, C. A., 478
Anderson, C. J., 374
Anderson, J., 500
Anderson, L. R., 27
Andersson, J., 363
Anicich, E. M., 265, 410
Annett, J., 401
Annis, A. B., 520
Anthony, T., 145, 227, 390
Antony, M. M., 107, 547
Aouni, B., 361
APA, 153
Apodaca v. Oregon, 406 U.S. 404, 236
Apparala, M., 590
Appelbaum, R. P., 587
Applebaum, E., 426
Applin, R. C., 509, 510
Arbesman, S., 517
Arcuri, L., 484
Arcus, D. M., 107
Ardry, R., 527
Arends, L., 337
Argote, L., 421
Argyle, M., 152, 518
Ariely, D., 122
Arkes, H. R., 380
Arkin, R. M., 71, 122, 125
Arman, S., 108
Arms, R. L., 591
Arnardottir, A. A., 558
Arnold, D. W., 535
Aron, A., 90, 495
Aronoff, J., 49, 61
Aronson, E., 159, 499

Aronson, J., 94
Arriaga, X. B., 129, 153
Arrow, H., 5, 56, 61, 123, 139, 145, 146, 150, 320, 405–407, 575
Arslanagić, B., 547
Arterberry, M. E., 337
Arvey, R. D., 279
Asch, S. E., 204–208, 211, 212, 389, 511
Aselage, J., 454
Asendorpf, J. B., 102, 107
Ashburn-Nardo, L., 485
Asher, S. R., 67
Ashmore, R. D., 88, 91
Asmus, C., 519
Assmar, E. M. L., 444
Atkin, R. S., 236
Atoum, A. O., 328, 329
Au, W., 87
Aubé, C., 402, 404, 428
Aubert, B. A., 424
August, R. A., 535
Augustine, A. A., 103
Austin, R., 500
Aveni, A., 580
Averill, J. R., 64, 454
Avolio, B. J., 279, 281, 307, 312, 313
Axelrod, R., 58, 462, 463
Ayduk, Ö., 71
Ayestaran, S., 185
Ayman, R., 302
Ayoko, O. B., 455
Ayres, M. M., 213, 285

Ba, S., 307
Baas, M., 58
Bacallao, M. L., 111
Bachman, J. G., 104
Back, K. W., 121, 136, 154, 549, 556, 574, 585
Back, M. D., 121
Backor, K., 262
Backstrom, L., 142, 590
Bader, P., 287
Badke-Schaub, P., 175
Baer, D. E., 65
Baer, R., 527
Bahns, A. J., 125
Bahrami, B., 348
Bailenson, J. N., 50
Bailey, D. E., 418
Bailey, J. K. S., 288
Bainbridge, W. S., 37–39
Bakeman, R., 41
Baker, H. G., 198, 201
Baker, S. P., 510
Baldes, J. J., 337
Baldwin, M. W., 80
Baldwin, S., 544

Bales, R. F., 3, 7, 22, 24, 39, 40, 41, 149, 151, 175–177, 195, 287, 363, 402, 435, 523
Baliousis, M., 214
Balkundi, P., 424
Balkwell, J. W., 262
Balliet, D., 439, 440, 443
Ball-Rokeach, S. J., 116
Baltes, B. B., 364
Balthazard, P. A., 373
Bamford, A., 410
Banaji, M. R., 16, 485
Bandura, A., 138, 490, 491, 556
Banker, B. S., 497
Banks, C., 272
Banks, G. C., 289
Barabási, A-L., 25, 517
Barefoot, J. C., 268
Bargal, D., 26
Bargh, J. A., 212, 221, 266, 269, 513
Barker, M., 293
Barker, R. G., 533–534
Barling, J., 173
Barlow, S. H., 544, 563, 570
Barnett, L. A., 91
Baron, R. A., 513
Baron, R. S., 210, 272, 329, 331, 391, 392, 398
Barr-Anderson, D., 111
Barrett, D., 194
Barrick, M. R., 126
Barry, B., 457, 468
Barsade, S. G., 140, 414
Barsky, S. F., 529
Bar-Tal, D., 451, 475, 487
Bartel, C. A., 361
Bartels, J. M., 69–70
Bartels, L., 232
Bartholomew, R. E., 573, 574, 585, 599, 603
Bartis, S., 328
Bartlem, C. S., 369
Barton, W. H., 595
Basden, B. H., 379
Basden, D. R., 379
Basow, S. A., 174
Bass, B. M., 278, 304, 312, 313, 317, 426
Bass, R., 278, 317, 304
Bassett, R. L., 14, 527
Bastian, B., 139
Batchelor, J. P., 521
Bateman, P. J., 142
Bates, J. E., 66
Batson, C. D., 159
Bauer, C. C., 364
Bauer, E., 227
Bauer, J., 186
Baum, A., 508, 520, 527, 539

Baumann, M. R., 344, 362, 363
Baumeister, R. F., 64, 69–71, 75, 77, 104, 131, 267, 280, 329, 454, 529
Baumert, J., 119
Bavelas, A., 186, 194
Bayazit, M., 460
Bazerman, M. H., 219, 445
Bazzini, D. G., 67
Beach, S. R. H., 119, 120
Beadman, M., 103
Beal, D. J., 155, 156, 164
Beale, D., 514
Beall, A. C., 50
Beaman, A. L., 257, 593
Beaton, E. A., 107
Beauchamp, M. R., 183
Bechky, B. A., 179–180
Bechtel, R. B., 515, 539
Bechtold, D., 81
Beck, A. T., 547
Beck, E. M., 580
Beck, S. J., 221, 406
Becker, J. C., 112
Becker, S. W., 523
Bedeian, A. G., 281, 288
Bednar, R. L., 562
Beehr, T. A., 115
Beer, J. S., 76, 258
Beersma, B., 219, 403, 454
Behfar, K. J., 446, 447, 464–465
Bekkedal, M., 118
Belkin, A., 137
Bell, C. D., 260
Bell, P. A., 508, 513, 519, 539
Bell, S. T., 149, 410, 409
Bellah, R. N., 78
Bellatin, A. M., 557
Bellinger, K. D., 378
Bellisle, F., 332
Belohlav, J. A., 149, 410
Bem, D. J., 381, 561
Bem, S. L., 213, 214
Bendersky, C., 464
Bendersky, J. W., 599
Benet-Martínez, V., 101
Bengry-Howell, A., 45
Benjamin, L. T., Jr., 493
Benne, K. D., 10, 177–178, 549
Bennett, H. S., 45
Bennett, M., 90
Bennett, N., 153, 338
Bennett, W., 412, 510
Bennis, W. G., 148, 279
Bentein, K., 150
Berdahl, J. L., 27, 56, 61, 123, 255, 267, 269, 270, 279, 406, 407, 575
Berg, N., 365
Berger, J., 261

Berger, R. E., 329, 379, 446
Berger, S. M., 333
Berkerle, C. A., 583
Berkowitz, L., 157, 280, 578–579
Berman, J., 519
Berman, J. J., 564
Berman, M. G., 511
Berns, G. S., 225
Bernstein, M. J., 71
Bernthal, P. R., 391
Berry, C. M., 410
Berry, J. W., 69
Berry, S. H., 116
Berry, T. R., 557
Berson, Y., 298
Beruvides, M. G., 142
Best, D. L., 299
Betancourt, H., 463
Bettencourt, B. A., 184, 497
Beyerlein, M. M., 428
Bezrukova, K., 144, 447
Bhatt, M. A., 436
Bhawak, D. P. S., 81
Bialosiewicz, S., 592
Bianchi, A. J., 264
Bianchi, M., 484
Bicchieri, C., 171
Bickman, L., 578–579
Biddle, B. J., 166, 177, 200
Biederman, P. W., 412, 510
Bieling, P., 547
Bierbrauer, G., 208
Biernat, M., 79, 90, 262, 263
Bilotta, J. G., 151
Birnbaum, M. L., 150
Birnie-Lefcovitch, S., 67
Bishop, G. D., 382
Bizzari, L., 364
Black, L. W., 234, 361, 456
Black, M., 547
Black, R. H., 348
Blader, S. L., 252, 444
Blaine, B., 92, 93
Blair, C., 378
Blair, I., 463
Blake, R. R., 304–306, 472
Blanchard, A. L., 7
Blanchard, F. A., 494
Blanchard, K. H., 305
Blanco, C., 109
Blaney, N., 499
Blank, A., 221–222
Blank, H., 192
Blanton, H., 93
Blascovich, J., 50, 57, 76, 120, 288, 327, 329, 383
Blass, T., 247–249, 254, 276
Blatt, R., 426

Blau, P., 53, 127
Bledman, R. A., 118
Blegen, M. A., 453
Bless, H., 223
Blevins, T., 69
Bligh, M. C., 281
Bloch, S., 561
Block, C. J., 293
Blommel, J. M., 326
Bloomfield, J., 387
Blumberg, H., 177
Blumer, C., 380
Blumer, H., 13, 576, 590
Bó, P. D., 438
Boatwright, K. J., 305
Bobocel, D. R., 260, 264
Bochner, S., 185, 185
Bodenhausen, G. V., 487
Bogardus, E. S., 27, 282
Bogart, L. M., 45
Bögels, S., 108
Bohmer, R., 422–423, 432
Bohmer, R. M. J., 400, 408–409, 418, 422
Bois, J. L., 114–115
Boldry, J. G., 486
Bollen, K. A., 139, 145
Bommer, W. H., 307
Bonacich, P., 192
Bonanno, G. A., 115, 118, 547
Bond, C. F., 26, 326, 328, 329
Bond, J., 174, 553–554
Bond, M., 152
Bond, M. H., 98, 101, 293, 488
Bond, R., 208, 210, 213, 215
Bonebright, D. A., 150
Bongiorno, R., 298
Boniecki, K. A., 529
Bonikowski, B., 65, 111
Bonito, J. A., 259, 264
Bonk, C. J., 264
Bonner, B. L., 344, 362, 363
Bono, J. E., 288, 289
Bonta, B. D., 480
Bookwala, J., 174
Boone, C., 410
Booth, A., 104
Booth, H., 461
Booth-LaForce, C., 107
Borah, L. A., Jr., 453
Borden, R., 138
Borgatta, E. F., 24, 149, 176, 287
Borgatti, S. P., 43, 186, 188, 201
Borja, A. P., 565
Borkman, T. J., 551, 570
Bornstein, G., 473–475
Bornstein, R. F., 122, 214
Bosselut, G., 145, 183
Bosson, J. K., 525

Botero, I. C., 374, 375
Bouchard, T. J., 353
Boulding, K. E., 509
Boumgarden, P., 403
Bourdieu, P., 586
Bourgeois, M. J., 210, 219
Bourgeois, P., 221
Bourguignon, D., 16
Boutillier, R. G., 291
Bowdle, B. F., 87–88
Bowen, D. E., 285
Bowers, C. A., 414
Bowers, D. G., 283, 426
Bowlby, J., 58, 109
Bowles, S., 84
Bowling, N. A., 115
Bowman, J. M., 376
Boyatzis, R., 290
Boyatzis, R. E., 259
Boyd, J. E., 415
Boyd, R., 84
Boyle, M. V., 455
Brabender, V. M., 146, 570
Bradbury, T. N., 451
Braden, M., 159
Bradshaw, S. D., 107, 348
Brady, J. J., Jr., 333
Bramel, D., 36
Brandon, A. C., 227
Brandon, D. P., 7
Branscombe, N. R., 91, 487, 491
Brantmeier, C., 464
Brass, D. J., 186, 201
Bratko, D., 256
Brauer, M., 383, 486
Braun, D. E., 103
Braun, J. C., 448
Braun, R., 580
Braver, E. R., 510
Braverman, M., 260
Brawley, L. R., 144, 145
Bray, R. M., 218, 236
Brazil, D., 474–475
Brazil, D. M., 305
Brazy, D. P., 319
Brechner, K. C., 442
Brédart, A., 565
Brehm, J. W., 450
Brehm, S. S., 450
Brenner, O. C., 439
Brett, J. M., 440
Breuer, M., 364
Brew, F. P., 461
Brewer, B. W., 161
Brewer, M., 217
Brewer, M. B., 14, 79, 82, 442, 459, 471, 472, 484, 496–499
Brewer, S., 105

Brewin, C. R., 115
Brickner, M. A., 338
Bridgett, D. J., 337
Brief, A. P., 183, 423, 509
Briggs, R. O., 373
Brinthaupt, T. M., 111–112, 127
Brito, V. C. A., 45
Broadnax, S., 92, 93
Brocato, R. M., 326
Brockner, J., 369, 380
Brodbeck, F. C., 296–297, 376
Bromley, D. G., 591
Bronzaft, A. L., 514
Brooks, D. K., 548
Brooks, G. R., 560
Brooks, M. L., 139
Brosche, N., 171
Brosnan, S. F., 444–445
Brossart, D. F., 557
Brouer, R. L., 259, 307
Brousseau, K. R., 361
Brown, B. B., 91, 508, 526, 529–530
Brown, C. M., 71
Brown, D. E., 278
Brown, D. J., 69
Brown, G., 531
Brown, J. D., 258, 478
Brown, L. H., 109
Brown, M., 218
Brown, R., 3, 383, 491, 493
Brown, R. J., 484, 496
Brown, T. M., 194
Brown, V. R., 338, 349, 350, 356
Brucks, W. M., 442
Brunner, C. C., 220
Brunsman, B., 211
Bruun, S. E., 337
Bryant, E. M., 172
Bryant, R. A., 557
Bryner, S., 379
Bucciarelli, A., 118, 547
Buchan, N. R., 230
Buckley, W., 250
Buehler, R., 372
Bufanio, K. A., 386
Buffone, A., 118
Bugental, D. B., 252
Buhrmester, D., 66, 67
Buhrmester, M. D., 139
Bullis, R. C., 305
Bullock, M., 210, 219, 240
Bunderson, J. S., 291, 403
Bunker, B. B., 256
Buote, V. M., 67
Burger, J. M., 122, 125, 173, 248–250, 256
Burger, T., 193
Burgess, K. B., 107
Burgoon, J. K., 518

Burke, C. S., 345, 402, 421, 428, 432
Burke, J., 313
Burke, M. J., 155, 156, 164, 303, 548
Burke, P. J., 175, 177
Burkhalter, S., 234
Burkley, M., 93
Burlingame, G. M., 544, 547, 556, 563, 570
Burnett, J. W., 557
Burnette, J. L., 18, 142, 391, 463, 515
Burney, C., 64
Burnfield, J. L., 373
Burnham, T., 438
Burns, J. M., 278, 281, 282, 311–312, 317
Burnstein, E., 361, 383, 448
Burt, M. R., 270
Burt, R. S., 189
Busby, P. L., 519
Bushe, G. R., 149
Bushman, B. J., 478, 513
Buss, D. M., 97
Butera, F., 330
Butkovic, A., 256
Butler, B. S., 142
Butler, D., 293
Butler, E. A., 428
Butler, L. D., 359
Butler, T., 561
Buton, F., 145
Buunk, A. P., 119, 131, 556
Buxant, C., 103
Buys, C. J., 27
Buysse, A., 117
Buzna, L., 584
Byrne, D., 105, 125, 522
Byrne, Z. S., 195

Cabanac, M., 509
Cable, D. M., 102
Cacioppo, J. T., 67
Cadinu, M., 484
Cadinu, M. R., 93
Cai, D. A., 461
Cain, K. M., 337
Cain, S., 108
Cairns, D. R., 70
Cairns, E., 493
Caldwell, D. F., 256
Callan, V., 185
Callan, V. J., 93, 293
Callaway, M. R., 390
Camacho, L. M., 350
Camerer, C., 84
Camerer, C. F., 436
Cameron, J. J., 118
Cammann, C., 426
Ćampara, N., 547
Campbell, D. T., 14, 171, 372, 472

Campbell, J., 119–120
Campbell, L., 292, 294
Campbell, R. J., 423
Campbell, T., 514
Campbell, W. K., 81
Campion, M. A., 409, 412–413
Canetti, E., 579, 581
Canfield, R. W., 127
Cannavale, F. J., 593
Cannon, M. D., 419
Cannon-Bowers, J. A., 361, 364, 418
Canon, L. K., 514
Cantor, N., 67, 115
Cantril, H., 39
Caporael, L. R., 58
Caprariello, P. A., 123
Carey, H. R., 347
Cariani, R., 565
Carini, B., 139, 145
Carless, S. A., 137
Carli, L. L., 213, 262, 293, 317, 333
Carlopio, J. R., 511
Carlson, D., 56–57
Carmen Hidalgo, M., 524
Carnaghi, A., 484
Carneiro, R. L., 472
Carnevale, P. J., 451, 461, 464
Caroselli, J. S., 561
Carpenter, C. R., 526
Carrere, S., 510
Carron, A. V., 141, 144, 145, 153, 154, 155, 157, 529
Carson, J., 173
Carson, K. D., 256
Carson, P. P., 256
Carson, R. C., 263
Carter, N. M., 4
Carter, S. E., 361
Carter, T. J., 307–308
Carter-Sowell, A. R., 69
Carton, A. M., 293
Cartwright, D., 18, 32, 192, 242, 282, 558
Caruso, E., 445
Carvalho, E. R., 45
Carvallo, M., 125
Cascio, W. F., 369
Casey-Campbell, M., 144
Cason, M. J., 115
Cassidy, C., 230
Castano, E., 16
Castell, P. J., 268
Castore, C. H., 367
Castro, S. L., 307
Cattell, R. B., 3, 27
Cavanaugh, P. H., 513
Cayrou, C., 565
Cecil, J. S., 234

Ceplenski, P., 561
Cerchioni, M., 93
Chabris, C. F., 321–322, 412
Chagnon, N. A., 300, 480
Chaichanasakul, A., 118
Chaiken, S., 214, 223
Chalfin, J., 56–57
Chamberlain, A. S., 530
Chambliss, W. J., 587
Chaminade, T., 436
Chamley, C. P., 223
Chang, E. C., 361
Chang, S., 390
Chanowitz, B., 221–222
Chansler, P. A., 426
Chao, G. T., 182
Chaplin, W. F., 258
Chapman, G. C., 249
Chapman, J. F., 259
Chapman, R., 529
Chappelow, J., 225
Chapple, E. D., 530
Charles, K. E., 511
Chartrand, T. L., 71, 221, 589
Charuvastra, A., 67
Chase, M., 518
Chassin, L., 92
Chasteen, A. L., 228, 332
Chater, N., 223
Chatman, J. A., 258, 416
Chaturvedi, S., 279
Chawla, N., 171, 174
Cheavens, J. S., 556
Cheema, A., 514
Chein, I., 479
Chemers, M. M., 299, 302–304, 528
Chen, F. F., 79
Chen, H., 38
Chen, J., 108
Chen, K. Y., 93
Chen, L-H., 510
Chen, S., 93, 214, 266, 267, 269, 276
Chen, X., 108
Chen, Y., 461
Chen, Y-R., 79
Chen, Z., 391
Cheng, B. H., 267
Cheng, S., 583
Chernyak, N., 72
Chertkoff, J. M., 583
Cherulnik, P., 530
Cheshire, C., 251
Chesner, S. P., 280
Cheung, C. K. T., 73
Cheung, F. M., 565
Cheyne, J. A., 527
Chiaburu, D. S., 185, 186
Chiao, J. Y., 258

Chiba, S., 448
Chilstrom, J. T., Jr., 218
Chiocchio, F., 155, 423
Chirot, D., 477, 480, 490
Chiu, C., 14, 86
Chiu, C-Y., 17
Cho, N. G., 185
Choi, H., 182
Choi, I., 17
Choi, S., 81
Choi, W., 73
Chopko, S. A., 337
Chow, C. W., 280
Chow, R. M., 71
Christ, O., 112
Christakis, N. A., 67, 174, 517
Christensen, A., 564
Christensen, C., 280, 376
Christensen, P. N., 168, 557
Christian, M. S., 51
Christopher, A. N., 446
Chun, J. U., 307
Church, M., 67
Churchman, A. S., 511, 539
Churchman, C. W., 508, 535
Cialdini, R. B., 138, 168, 200, 211, 213, 217, 222, 225, 240, 257, 277
Cianni, M., 293
Ciarocco, N. J., 69–70
Cicchetti, A., 150
Cicero, L., 270
Cigler, A., 66
Cihangir, S., 375
Cimino, A., 161
Cini, M. A., 127, 535–536
Ciriacks, T., 464
Ciulla, J. B., 270
Clack, B., 527
Clack, F. L., 80
Claiborn, C. D., 557
Clanton, N. R., 258
Clapp, J. D., 173
Clark, G., 581
Clark, K. B., 273
Clark, L. A., 267
Clark, M. S., 83, 121, 127, 513
Clark, N. K., 362
Clark, R. D., 208, 223–224, 228, 268, 382
Clark, S., 472
Claypool, H. M., 71
Clayton, D. A., 325
Clayton, L. D., 236, 401, 428
Clearwater, Y. A., 531
Clegg, C. W., 508, 535
Clement, R. W., 211, 222
Clements-Croome, D., 540
Clendenen, V. I., 332
Cleveland, C., 120
Cline, R. J., 557

Cloitre, M., 67
Coats, E. J., 258, 517
Coats, S., 109–110
Coch, L., 369
Coe, C., 127
Coetzer, G. H., 149
Cogliser, C. C., 307
Cohen, D., 87–88, 480
Cohen, E. L., 116
Cohen, F., 300
Cohen, J. L., 27
Cohen, M. D., 453
Cohen, R. R., 155, 156, 164
Cohen, S., 57, 514, 520
Cohen, S. G., 418
Cohen, S. P., 151, 195
Cohen, T. R., 459
Cohn, E. G., 513
Cohrs, J. C., 97
Cole, C. M., 257
Coleman, P. T., 446, 468
Colligan, M. J., 585
Collins, A., 228
Collins, B. E., 347, 372
Collins, R., 148, 171
Collins, R. L., 116, 119
Colman, A. M., 598
Colman, M. M., 155
Colomy, P., 176
Colquitt, J. A., 369
Combs, D., 77
Condon, C. A., 214
Condor, S., 493
Conger, J. A., 310
Conger, J. A., 311
Conlon, D. E., 462, 464
Connors, M. M., 515, 531
Conroy, J., 528
Constantian, C. A., 105
Contarello, A., 152
Contractor, N., 5
Contry, J. C., 583
Conyne, R. K., 565, 569
Cook, J. M., 125
Cook, K., 262
Cook, K. S., 55, 251
Cook, S. W., 494, 499
Cook, T., 268
Cooley, C. H., 11–12, 25, 557
Coon, H. M., 79, 80, 83, 85, 86, 88, 98
Cooper, C., 201
Cooper, C. L., 260
Cooper, E., 293
Cooper, H. M., 213
Cooper, L. A., 552
Coovert, M., 313
Cope, C. J., 183
Copper, C., 155–156, 424

Corazzini, J. G., 556, 559
Corbin, L. H., 211
Cordery, J., 427
Cornachione, E. B., 185
Corneille, O., 16, 439
Cornelius, A. E., 161
Corning, A. F., 591
Cornwell, B., 234, 262
Cortes, B., 490
Coser, L. A., 148
Cosley, D., 456
Cosmides, L., 443
Costa, P. T., Jr., 101
Costanzo, P. R., 214
Côté, S., 267, 454
Cotton, P., 556
Cottrell, C. A., 97
Cottrell, N. B., 328, 331
Couch, A. S., 176, 287
Coughlin, B. C., 154
Courneya, K. S., 529
Cousins, S. D., 86
Covey, S. R., 426, 428
Cowlishaw, G., 300
Cox, C., 474–475
Cox, J. C., 556
Cox, T. H., 414
Craig, S. B., 280
Crandall, C. S., 125, 174, 262
Crano, W. D., 204, 217, 240
Crawford, A. M., 153
Crawford, M. T., 16
Cress, D. M., 55
Cress, U., 212
Crichlow, S., 390
Crisp, R. J., 91, 471, 496–498, 500, 505
Crisson, J. E., 328
Croak, M. R., 497
Crocker, J., 91–93, 293
Croff, J. K., 173
Croizet, J-C., 488
Croker, V., 73
Cronen, S., 332
Croson, R. T. A., 230
Cross, S. E., 81, 104
Crott, H. W., 383
Crouch, E. C., 561
Crouse, E. M., 493
Crowther, S., 230
Cruickshank, M., 73
Crutchfield, R. S., 210, 214
Cuddy, A. J. C., 248, 488–489
Cukur, C., 461
Cullum, J., 220
Cunningham, G. B., 416
Curhan, J. R., 450
Currey, K. P., 474–475
Curtin, N., 591

Curtis, J. E., 65
Curtis, M., 16
Custers, R., 169
Cutler, B. L., 231, 235
Cybriwsky, R., 526
Czienskowski, U., 375

Dabbs, J. M., 58
Dabbs, J. M., Jr., 264, 351
Dabbs, M. G., 58
Dahl, R. A., 242
Dahlke, A. E., 583
Dale, R., 190
Dalix, A. M., 332
Dalton, B., 474–475
D'Amorim, M., 185
Dane, F. C., 234
Daniels, E., 85
Danielsen, E. M., 231, 234
Dansereau, F., 306, 307
Dardis, G. J., 474–475
Darley, J. M., 16, 228–229, 231, 271, 273
Dasgupta, N., 16, 484
Dasu, S., 405
David, B., 385
David, E. M., 415
David, J. P., 449
Davidson, B., 149
Davidson-Podgorny, G., 501
Davidson-Shivers, G. V., 264
Davies, D., 149
Davies, D. R., 547, 556
Davies, M. F., 177
Davila, C., 185
Davis, D. E., 463
Davis, G. E., 527
Davis, J. A., 65
Davis, J. H., 236, 337, 344, 367, 383, 389, 424
Davis, J. R., 160
Davis, M. C., 508, 535
Davis, M. H., 67
Davis, M. S., 101–102
Davis, W. L., 440
Davison, K. P., 115, 552
Davis-Stitt, C., 487
Davy, J., 283
Dawes, R. M., 230, 378
Dawkins, R., 8
Day, D. V., 288, 307
Day, R. R., 303, 548
de Castro, J. M., 332
De Cremer, D., 439, 443, 482
De Dreu, C. K. W., 58, 148, 219, 224, 375, 392, 406, 414, 434, 439, 448, 451, 454, 460, 462, 464, 468, 484
de Graaf, C., 332
De Grada, E., 214, 392

de Kwaadsteniet, E. W., 263
de la Roche, R. S., 597
De Paola, C., 137
de Tocqueville, A., 85
De Vader, C. L., 288, 295
De Vries, N. K., 224
de Waal, F. B. M., 58, 444–445
de Wit, F., 267
Dean, B. L., 103
Dean, J., 518
Dean, K., 69
Dean, L. M., 517
Deaux, K., 88
Decety, J., 436
DeChurch, L. A., 361, 372, 401, 464
Deeney, J. M., 151
Deess, E. P., 361
DeGroot, J. M., 456
Dekker, P. H., 301
Del Priore, R. E., 454
Delbecq, A. L., 351, 353
Delton, A. W., 443
Delucchi, K., 554
DeLucia-Waack, J. L., 544, 565
DeMatteo, J. S., 338
Demoulin, S., 471, 488, 490, 504
Denissen, J. J. A., 76
Dennis, A. R., 352
Denrell, J., 222
Denson, T. F., 16
Denvir, B., 128, 131
DePaulo, B. M., 561
Derks, B., 94
Derlega, V. J., 461
DeRosa, D. M., 352
DeRouin, R. E., 428
DeRue, D. S., 283–284
Desalvo, J., 211
Desclaux, B., 565
Deseran, F. A., 462
DeSmet, A. L., 463
DeSteno, D., 141
Deutsch, M., 221, 436, 441, 452–453, 459, 468, 476
Devilly, G., 556
Devine, D. J., 155–156, 236, 401, 404, 411, 428
Devine, P. G., 498
DeVries, H., 265
DeWall, C. N., 69–72, 77, 267, 478, 513
Dewey, J. D., 307–308
DeYoung, C. G., 214
Di Salvo, V. S., 372–373
Diamon, S., 219, 491
Diamond, S. G., 521
Diamond, S. S., 231
Diamond, W. D., 476
Diani, M., 587

DiazGranados, D., 186, 428
Dickerson, S. S., 115, 552
Dickes, P., 565
Dickinson, A. M., 338
Dickson, M. W., 364
Dickson, W. J., 36
Diehl, M., 349–350
Diener, E., 101, 103, 593–595
Dienesch, R. M., 307
Dierdorff, E. C., 149, 410
Dierick, P., 554
Dierselhuis, J., 16
Dies, R. R., 557
Dietz-Uhler, B., 93, 359, 491
DiFonzo, N., 254
Dijksterhuis, A., 169, 533
Dillard, J. P., 257
Dillman, L., 518
Dion, K. L., 10, 164
Dionne, S. D., 285, 307
Dipboye, R. L., 597
Dishion, T. J., 174
DiTomaso, N., 293
Dixon, J., 527
Dixon, K. N., 557
Djapo, N., 547
Dobbins, G. H., 285
Dobosh, M., 235
Dobson, D. M., 459, 460
Dodds, P. S., 590
Dodge, K. A., 66, 174
Doherty, W. J., 556
Doise, W., 382
Dolbeault, S., 565
Doll, B., 71, 448
Dollar, N. J., 37
Donaldson, S., 350
Donath, C. H., 333
Doosje, B., 91, 94, 491
Doosje, B. J., 487
Dorfman, P. W., 285, 295–297, 317
Dorsch, K. D., 145
Douglas, C., 259
Douthitt, E. A., 325, 327, 333, 356
Dovidio, J. F., 472, 489, 490, 497, 505
Downing, L. L., 595
Downs, D. L., 76
Doxsee, D. J., 557
Drake, L. R., 421
Drenan, S., 476
Drescher, K. D., 547
Drigotas, S. M., 125, 474–475
Driskell, J. E., 47, 145, 261, 293, 345, 390, 410, 411, 428, 511
Drossaers-Bakker, K. W., 552
Drossaert, C. H. C., 552
Drury, J., 590, 598–599
Dryer, D. C., 126

Dubé, L., 577
Dubé-Simard, L., 592
Dubro, A. F., 440
Dubrovsky, V. J., 264
Ducheneaut, N., 38, 142, 143
Duck, J. M., 298
Duckitt, J., 491
Duffy, F., 535–536
Duffy, M. K., 322, 338
Dugosh, K. L., 351, 352
Duh, H. B. L., 38
Dukerich, J. M., 280
Dukes, F. O., 4
Dulebohn, J. H., 307
Dumas, F., 329
Dunbar, R. I. M., 97, 480
Duncan, L. E., 591
Dunford, B. B., 236, 401, 428
Dunning, D., 371
Duntley, J. D., 97
Dupont, C., 588
Dupue, R. L., 72
Duraković, E., 547
Durand, D. E., 530
Durham, R. J., 557
Durkheim, É., 19, 20, 139
Dutton, K. A., 478
Dvir, T., 313
Dvir, V., 560
Dweck, C. S., 86, 119, 555
Dyer, L., 361
Dykema-Engblade, A. A., 371
Dzindolet, M. T., 350

Eagly, A. H., 213, 262, 285, 293, 294, 299, 312, 314, 317
Earley, P. C., 82, 403
Eastwick, P. W., 123
Eaton, J. W., 290
Ebbesen, E. B., 122
Eby, L. T., 338
Echterhoff, G., 169
Edelstein, M. R., 514
Eden, D., 313
Edlund, J. E., 487
Edmondson, A. C., 400, 408–409, 414, 418–419, 422–423, 432
Edney, J. J., 517, 526, 528, 529
Edwards, E. M., 171
Efran, M. G., 527
Egan, T. D., 414
Egan, V., 103
Egloff, B., 121
Ehlers, A., 557
Ehrhardt, A. A., 45
Ehrhart, M. G., 137
Ehrlich, S. B., 280
Eid, J., 288

Eid, M., 103
Eidelman, S., 79
Eidelson, R., 88
Einarsen, S., 260
Eisenbach, R. J., 283
Eisenberger, N. I., 76, 77
Eisenberger, R., 454
Eisenhardt, K. M., 414
Ekelund, B., 185
Eldredge, N., 151
Ellemers, N., 88, 94, 98, 227, 267, 488
Eller, A., 495
Ellertson, N., 157
Elliott, E., 27
Elliott, M. N., 116
Elliott, R., 563
Elliott, T. R., 153, 557
Ellis, A. P. J., 410, 411
Ellis, J. B., 501
Ellis, L., 231
Ellison, N. B., 123
Ellison, P. T., 259
Ellsworth, P. C., 17, 217, 231, 234, 236, 258
Elms, A. C., 244, 248, 249
Elsaid, A. M. M. K., 111, 411
Elster, J., 167
Ember, C. R., 481
Ember, M., 481
Emerson, R. M., 36, 250
Emler, N., 268
Emmers-Sommer, T., 523
Emmitt, S., 151, 402
Emrich, C. G., 280
Endicott, J., 234
Engels, F., 472
Engeström, Y., 405
Engstrom, E., 523
Ennis, J. G., 197
Epitropaki, O., 295
Epley, N., 211, 445
Erath, S. A., 66
Erb, H-P., 214
Erdogan, B., 306–307
Ericksen, J., 361
Erickson, G. A., 91
Erickson, K. G., 262
Ernst, D., 16
Esposito, J. L., 583
Esser, A. H., 530
Esser, J. K., 390
Esses, V. M., 472
Essiembre, H., 155, 423
Estabrooks, P. A., 157
Estellés-Arolas, E., 366
Estreich, D., 326
Ettin, M. F., 544
Etzioni, A., 276

Euwema, M. C., 460
Evans, D., 230
Evans, G. W., 57, 510, 511, 517–520
Evans, H., 573, 574
Evans, H., 585
Evans, H., 599, 603
Evans, N. J., 145
Eys, M. A., 141, 145, 183
Eysenck, H., 102

Faith, M., 56–57, 497
Falbe, C., 270
Falbo, T., 255, 256
Falk, A., 438
Fall, R., 334
Fallon, A., 146, 570
Falloon, I. R. H., 557
Fan, E. T., 390
Fannin, A. D., 117
Fanon, F., 273
Faraj, S., 142
Farbstein, J., 508
Faria, J. J., 342–343
Farley, K. M. J., 511
Farr, M. J., 91
Farrell, G. M., 176, 177
Farrell, M. P., 11, 45, 100, 124, 131, 183
Farsides, T., 17
Faust, K., 188
Feather, N. T., 120
Feeley, T. H., 194
Fehr, E., 84
Feigenson, N., 229
Feith, S. W. W., 58
Feld, P., 390
Feld, S. L., 125
Feldman, D. B., 556
Feldman, J. J., 116
Feldman, R. E., 230
Feldman, S., 214
Fellenz, M. R., 444
Fennell, M. L., 293
Fennis, B. M., 211
Ferencik, B. M., 561
Ferreira, M. C., 230, 444
Ferris, D. L., 69
Ferris, G. R., 259, 307, 333
Festinger, L., 37, 45, 113, 121, 127, 136, 158–159, 224, 225, 481
Feunekes, G. L. J., 332
Fiedler, F. E., 282, 301–304, 306
Field, N., 288
Filer, M., 556
Filkins, J. W., 237
Fincham, F. D., 120, 451
Fincher, C. L., 512
Fine, G. A., 26, 37, 45, 145, 254, 424
Finez, L., 120

Fink, E. L., 461
Finkel, E. J., 123
Finkel, M. A., 161
Finlay, F., 378
Fiore, S. M., 427
Firestone, I. J., 510
Fischbacher, U., 438
Fischer, A. H., 454
Fischer, G. W., 486
Fischer, R., 230, 444, 477, 512
Fishbaugh, L., 213
Fisher, B. A., 148
Fisher, J. D., 508, 522, 539
Fisher, R., 457–458, 468
Fiske, A. P., 84, 86, 98, 327
Fiske, S. T., 9, 218, 248, 255, 258, 269, 270, 276, 485, 488–490
Flacks, R., 48
Flanagin, A. J., 455
Fleeson, W., 103
Fleishman, E. A., 283, 420
Flores, P. J., 553
Florey, A. T., 416
Flowers, M. L., 391
Floyd, S. W., 185, 368
Flynn, F. J., 253, 288
Flynn, K., 597
Foddy, M., 261
Fodor, E. M., 106, 259, 268, 391
Foer, F., 480
Folk, G. E., Jr., 513
Fontana, D., 412
Fontayne, P., 145
Foran, K. A., 174
Forbes, D. L., 105
Ford, D. E., 552
Ford, M. T., 185
Ford, R. S., 453
Forgas, J. P., 463
Forsyth, D. R., 18, 79, 91, 142, 153, 155, 270, 285, 289, 298, 299, 317, 353, 379, 391, 446, 461, 515, 557, 560, 570
Fortin, M., 444
Fortune, W. H., 234, 237
Foschi, M., 253, 262
Foss, C., 529–530
Foss, R. D., 236
Fossos, N., 171, 174
Foti, R. J., 287, 288, 295, 298, 305
Foushee, H. C., 345
Fowler, J. H., 67, 174
Fox, C., 72
Fox, R., 416
Foy, D. W., 547, 556
Foy, E., 582
Fraas, L. A., 290
Frable, D. E. S., 555

Fragale, A. R., 190, 265
Frager, R., 215
Fraine, G., 529
Francis, L. J., 214
Francis, R. C., 58
Francois, P-H., 185
Franke, R. H., 36
Franklin, J., 515
Franssen, V., 218
Franz, T. M., 280, 376
Fraser, S. C., 257, 593
Fredrickson, J. W., 448
Freedman, J. L., 257, 519–520, 590
Freeman, E. C., 81
Freeman, L. C., 187, 188
Freeman, S., 138
Freisthler, B., 173
French, J. R. P., Jr., 155, 250, 254, 369, 435
Fretz, R. I., 36
Freud, S., 180, 544
Frey, D., 376, 378
Frey, L. R., 3, 45
Fried, Y., 201
Friedkin, N. E., 135, 382
Friedland, N., 270
Friedman, S. D., 280
Friedman, T. L., 415
Friend, R., 36
Frink, D. D., 259
Frith, C., 223
Frith, C. D., 348
Froman, L. A., Jr., 453
Fromkin, H. L., 82, 555
Fromson, M. E., 491
Frost, A. G., 56
Frost, J. H., 122
Fry, D. P., 481
Fuegen, K., 263
Fuhriman, A., 544, 561, 563
Fukushima, O., 448
Fung, A. S. M., 585
Funk, C. L., 591
Furman, W., 67
Furnham, A., 106
Futoran, G. C., 351

Gabarro, J. J., 149
Gabriel, S., 81
Gadon, O., 56–57
Gaertner, L., 72, 90, 93, 94, 486
Gaertner, S. L., 489, 497
Gaffney, S., 545
Gaines, S. O., Jr., 472
Galanter, E., 360
Galasso, J., 260
Galea, S., 118, 547
Galinsky, A. D., 13, 252, 263, 265–268, 298, 410

Gallo, P. S., Jr., 453
Gallois, C., 293
Galvaing, M. P., 329
Gamage, C., 333
Gammage, K. L., 157
Gangi, C., 120
Gannon, T. M., 479
Garcia, D. M., 264
Garcia, R., 333
Garcia, S. M., 120, 231
Gardikiotis, A., 217, 240
Gardner, B., 334
Gardner, J. W., 279
Gardner, P. D., 182
Gardner, W. L., 69, 81, 326
Garnier, S., 584
Garvey, B., 208
Gastil, J., 234, 361
Gaunt, R., 490
Gauvain-Piquard, A., 565
Gauvin, S., 352
Gavin, J. H., 416
Gawronski, B., 192
Gazda, G. M., 548
Gee, S. S., 264
Geen, R. G., 333
Geffner, R., 260
Geis, F. L., 293
Gelfand, M. J., 17, 81, 98, 461, 468
Gerbasi, A., 251
Gerbasi, M. E., 412
Gerber, G. L., 261
Gerber, J., 71
Gergen, K. J., 552, 595
Gergen, M., 268
Gergen, M. M., 595
Gerhardt, G., 597
Gerhardt, M. W., 288, 289
Gersick, C. J. G., 151
Gerstner, C. R., 307
Gevers, J. M. P., 140–141
Geyer, A. L., 207
Giacalone, R. A., 260
Giammanco, C. A., 155, 446
Giannetti, C. C., 260
Gibb, C. A., 290
Gibb, J. R., 564
Gibbons, D., 124
Gibbons, F. X., 119, 131, 556
Gibson, C. B., 82, 461
Gibson, D. E., 140
Gibson, D. R., 264
Gibson, L. L., 420
Gieryn, T. F., 121, 508

Giesen, M., 521
Gigone, D., 374
Gilbert, D. T., 556
Gilbert, S. J., 257
Gilboa, S., 201
Giles, H., 518
Gill, D. L., 411
Gill, R., 308
Gillespie, D., 334
Gillies, R. M., 334
Gilmore, R., 476
Gilovich, T., 211, 327
Gilson, L., 428
Gilson, L. L., 401, 425
Ginnett, R. C., 345
Ginsburg, G. P., 57, 383
Gintis, H., 84
Giordano, P. C., 154
Gire, J. T., 461
Gist, R., 556
Giuliano, T., 363
Gladwell, M., 297, 590
Gläscher, J., 519
Glaser, D., 527
Glaser, K. H., 149
Glasø, L., 260
Glass, D. C., 329, 514
Glässner-Bayerl, B., 93
Gleave, R., 556
Gleijeses, P., 397
Glenn, C., 169
Glick, J. C., 359
Glick, P., 299, 479, 488–489, 505
Gliner, M. D., 383
Glor, J. E., 448
Gockel, C., 339
Godfrey, D. K., 259
Godwin, R., 513, 539
Goedinghaus, M., 557
Goethals, G. R., 280, 317, 383, 521
Goetsch, G. G., 194
Goettl, B. P., 556
Goetz, J., 268–269
Goffman, E., 179, 186, 328, 576
Golant, M., 558
Goldberg, A., 565
Goldberg, L., 597
Goldberg, L. R., 101
Golden, T. D., 307–308
Goldenberg, J. L., 300
Goldhammer, J., 154
Golding, W., 492
Goldman, B., 427
Goldman, M., 290
Goldstein, A. P., 161, 594
Goldstein, N. J., 200, 210, 211, 213, 227
Goldstein, P., 27
Goldstone, J. A., 587

Goleman, D., 290
Golub, S. A., 174
Gómez, Á., 93, 139, 495
Goncalo, J. A., 216, 223, 351
Gonsalkorale, K., 70
González, M. C., 517
González-Ladrón-de-Guevara, F., 366
Goodacre, D. M., 149
Goodall, J., 69
Goode, E., 599
Gooden, R. J., 552
Goodman, G., 551
Goodwin, D. K., 45
Goodwin, G. F., 402, 410, 421, 428, 432
Goodyear, R. K., 557
Goore, N., 327
Gordijn, E. H., 224, 252
Gordon, L. R., 391
Gore, G., 580
Gore, J. S., 104
Gorse, C. A., 151, 402
Gosling, S. D., 47, 102
Gottfried, A. E., 287
Gottfried, A. W., 287
Gottlieb, A., 229
Gould, C. C., 3
Gould, S. J., 151
Gouldner, A. W., 84
Gouran, D. S., 359, 360
Govan, C. L., 71, 73
Grabb, E. G., 65
Graen, G. B., 307
Graen, G. C., 306
Graetz, K. A., 474–475
Grandmaison, P. S., 333
Granovetter, M. S., 5, 186, 192
Graversen, G., 185
Graves, J., 335
Gray, J. R., 513
Gray, P. H., 142
Graziano, W. G., 101, 449
Green, D. P., 498, 505
Green, L. R., 66, 220
Green, M. L., 90
Green, R. B., 27
Green, T. C., 508, 539
Greenaway, K., 265, 410
Greenberg, C. I., 510, 535
Greenberg, J., 299, 300, 369, 446
Greene, D., 222
Greenleaf, C. A., 174
Greenwald, A. G., 485
Greenwood, D. J., 35
Greenwood, J. D., 6
Greer, D. L., 529
Greer, L. L., 58, 416, 448
Gregory, D., 157

Gregory, R. J., 247
Greitemeyer, T., 376
Gresta, S., 484
Griffeth, R. W., 137
Griffin, C., 45
Griffin, D., 372
Griffin, M. A., 145
Griffitt, W., 513
Griskevicius, V., 53, 211, 213, 257
Grob, A., 103
Groff, B. D., 520–521
Grose, M., 288
Gross, J. J., 119, 555
Gruenewald, T. L., 71, 116
Gruenfeld, D. H., 263, 266, 267, 268, 270
Grundmann, M. J., 517, 526
Gruner, L., 146, 559
Guastella, A. J., 76
Guastello, S. J., 279
Guemo, M., 443
Guerin, B., 329
Guerin, D. W., 287
Guetzkow, H., 347, 372, 448
Guimond, A., 592
Guinote, A., 218, 267, 268, 276, 486
Gulati, R., 154
Gulick, L. M., 288
Gullahorn, J. T., 122
Gully, S. M., 155, 156, 407
Gum, A., 556
Gump, P. V., 270, 535
Gunderson, E. K. E., 510
Gupta, V., 295–297, 317
Gurr, T. R., 472
Gurtner, A., 364
Gurung, R. A. R., 71, 116
Gushin, V. I., 415
Gustafson, D. H., 353
Guthman, E., 389
Guzman, M. J., 186
Guzzo, R. A., 423
Gyr, J., 448
Gyurak, A., 71

Haar, J., 447
Haas, C., 464
Haas, C. D., 372
Haas, D. F., 462
Haas, S., 527
Haber, G. M., 524, 528
Hackman, J. R., 3, 8, 23–24, 32, 356, 361,
    371, 402–408, 412, 417, 422, 424,
    426–427, 432
Haft, R. R., 379
Haga, W., 306
Haidt, J., 83
Haines, V. Y., 322
Hains, S. C., 298

Hair, E. C., 449
Hakonen, M., 50
Hale, J. L., 518
Halevy, N., 88, 298
Haley, H., 476, 477
Halfhill, T., 401, 405, 426
Hall, A. L., 208
Hall, C. L., 259
Hall, E. T., 152, 415, 516–517
Hall, G. B., 107
Hall, J. A., 104, 258, 267, 285, 517
Hall, K. L., 359
Hallinan, M. T., 189
Halperin, E., 489
Halpin, A. W., 283
Halpin, S. M., 262
Halterman, R. A., 115
Halverson, C. B., 164
Ham v. S. Carolina, 409 U.S. 524, 236,
Hamaguchi, E., 86
Hamilton, D. L., 12, 14–16, 17, 91, 487
Hamilton, K., 151–152
Hamilton, K. L., 464
Hamilton, V. L., 272
Hamilton, W. D., 58
Hammer, E. D., 359
Hammer, M. R., 461
Hampton, K. L., 333
Hand, H. H., 137
Haney, C., 272
Hanges, P. J., 317, 295–297
Hanke, K., 477
Hannaford-Agor, P. L., 232
Hans, V. P., 51, 231–236, 240
Hansbrough, T., 280
Hansen, W. B., 530
Hanson, J. R., 190
Hanson, L., 535
Hantula, D. A., 352
Harary, F., 192
Harb, C., 185
Hardin, G., 442
Harding, D. J., 72
Harding, J., 479
Hardy, C., 337
Hardy, P., 565
Hardyck, J. A., 159
Hare, A. P., 4, 24, 41, 42, 45, 146, 149,
    177, 180, 197, 198, 201, 435, 523
Hare, J. R., 42
Hare, S. E., 197
Hareli, S., 53
Harinck, F., 459
Harkins, S., 337
Harkins, S. G., 328, 330, 331, 335–338
Harlow, A. F., 582
Harlow, R. E., 67, 115

Harman, J., 156
Harms, P. D., 259
Harpin, R. E., 527
Harrell, M. M., 186
Harrington, B., 26
Harris, C. B., 362
Harris, D. W., 339
Harris, J., 38
Harris, J. R., 25
Harris, L. T., 248, 490
Harrison, A., 536
Harrison, A. A., 515, 531
Harrison, D. A., 185, 186, 414, 416, 424
Harrod, W. J., 29, 294
Hart, C. M., 92
Hart, J. W., 337
Hart, S. D., 253
Hartnett, J. L., 487
Harton, H. C., 210, 219, 220, 240
Hartsen, K. M., 106
Harvey, J. B., 379–380
Harvey, O. J., 470–472, 483, 492–494,
    497, 499, 501, 504
Hashmi, N., 321–322
Haslam, N., 16, 490
Haslam, S. A., 88, 98, 118, 271, 298, 338–
    339, 349, 384, 392, 423, 486, 490
Hastie, R., 84, 231–232, 234–236, 240,
    365, 367, 374
Hastorf, A. H., 39
Hauenstein, N. M. A., 287
Hawkins, C., 233–234, 261
Hawkley, L. C., 67
Hayduk, L. A., 517
Hayes, A., 554
Hayes, L. J., 509, 510
Hayes, S. M., 156
Haythorn, W. W., 532
Hazan, C., 109
He, Y., 118
Healey, A. N., 400
Healey, M. P., 56
Healy, S., 106
Hearne, G., 523
Heath, C., 141
Hecht, T. D., 427, 432
Hechter, M., 166, 200
Heerdink, M. W., 454
Heeren, T., 171
Heerwagen, J. H., 536
Heffron, M. H., 527
Heider, F., 17, 192, 449
Heider, J. D., 487
Heilman, M. E., 293
Heimberg, R. G., 109
Heimerdinger, S. R., 478
Heinemann, G. D., 183
Heinen, B. A., 185

Heiney, M. M., 299
Heingartner, A., 326
Heinicke, C. M., 149
Heinrichs, N., 108
Helbing, D., 582, 584
Heller, J. F., 520–521
Heller, T., 291
Helliwell, J. F., 53
Helman, C., 230
Helmreich, R. L., 45, 345, 509
Helms, J. E., 557
Helms, M. M., 292
Helweg-Larsen, M., 577, 582
Hembroff, L. A., 262
Hemenover, S. H., 103
Hemmings, A., 248
Hemphill, J. K., 279
Henchy, T., 329
Henderson, M., 152
Hendricks, E. A., 115
Hendricks, F. M., 557
Hendricks, L. A., 173
Henley, N. M., 517
Henningsen, D. D., 362
Henningsen, M. L. M., 362
Henrich, J., 84
Henry, K., 27
Henry, K. B., 139, 145, 146
Heppner, P. P., 557
Herek, G. M., 390
Herfordt, J., 329
Herman, C. P., 332
Herman, E. M., 326
Hernández, B., 524
Hersby, M. D., 298
Herschlag, L. R., 333
Hersey, P., 305
Hertel, G., 346
Hertel, J. B., 557
Hertel, P. T., 363
Herzog, T. R., 509, 510
Hess, J. A., 117
Hess, S., 524
Hess, U., 221
Hess, Y. D., 71
Hetland, J., 260
Heuston, S., 91
Heuzé, J., 145
Hewitt, J., 517
Hewstone, M., 217, 223, 484, 487, 491,
    493, 496–498
Heyel, C., 307
Heylighen, F., 363
Hibbing, J. R., 265, 301
Hickie, I. B., 76
Higginbotham, H. N., 560
Higgins, D. M., 214
Higgins, E. T., 169

Highhouse, S., 548
Hight, T. L., 556
Hill, A. H., 583
Hill, C. A., 105
Hill, C. E., 557
Hill, W. F., 146, 549, 559, 565
Hills, H. I., 265
Hillyard, C., 334
Hilty, J. A., 463
Hinds, P. J., 423
Hingson, R. W., 171
Hinkle, S., 13
Hinrichs, A., 272
Hinrichs, K. T., 248, 272
Hinsz, V. B., 56, 70, 338, 362, 367, 376,
    475, 478
Hirokawa, R. Y., 359–361, 397
Hirst, W., 362
Hirt, E., 555
Hirt, E. R., 91
Hitch, G. J., 363, 378
Hixon, J. G., 139
Hoag, M. J., 563
Hobbes, T., 481
Hochberger, J. M., 149–150
Hochwarter, W. A., 259
Hockenstein, P., 268
Hodess, R., 230
Hodges, B. H., 207
Hodgkinson, G. P., 56
Hodson, G., 391, 472, 489
Hoel, H., 260
Hoey, S., 555
Hoffer, E., 591
Hoffman, J. R., 337
Hoffman, L., 17
Hoffman, L. R., 293
Hoffman, S., 208
Hofmann, K., 185
Hofmann, S. G., 108
Hofstede, G., 54–55, 85, 185
Hofstede, G.J., 54–55, 185
Hofstedt, P. M., 214
Hogan, R., 58, 263, 280, 289, 301
Hogg, M. A., 13, 16, 21, 32, 88, 89, 91, 98,
    137, 164, 298, 371, 385
Holgate, S., 69
Holland, C. H., 248
Hollander, E. P., 218, 281, 282, 290
Hollenbeck, J. R., 56, 403, 408, 411
Hollingshead, A. B., 7, 61, 259, 264, 360,
    363, 364, 374–376, 397, 421
Hollingworth, H. L., 576
Hollon, S. D., 547
Holman, E. A., 118
Holmes, J. G., 118, 434, 436
Holmes, M. R., 173
Holmes, S. E., 561

Holovics, M. A., 219, 491
Holt, R., 236
Holt, R. W., 236
Holton, B., 474–475
Holtz, A., 555
Holyfield, L., 145, 254
Homan, A. C., 414, 416
Homans, G. C., 34, 53, 58, 127
Honeywell-Johnson, J. A., 338
Hong, G., 474–475
Hong, L. K., 384
Hong, Y., 86
Hong, Y-Y., 14, 17
Honjo, S., 328
Hood, W. R., 470–472, 483, 492–494,
    497, 499, 501, 504
Hooijberg, R., 293
Hook, L. H., 233, 523
Hooper, D. T., 307
Hoover, E., 156
Hopper, C. H., 351
Hopper, E., 545
Horne, A. M., 260, 560
Horner, P. A., 557
Hornsey, M. J., 82, 209, 240
Horowitz, I., 111
Horowitz, I. A., 236
Horowitz, L. M., 126
Horwitz, I. B., 414
Horwitz, S. K., 414
Hottes, J., 440
Houlden, P., 464
Houle, C. O., 447
Houlette, M., 497
House, P., 222
House, R. J., 282, 295–297, 317
Houser, J. A., 194
Houston, R., 547
Houston, T. K., 552
Howard, J. W., 487
Howard, R. B., 517
Howe, J., 366
Howe, R. C., 383
Howell, J. P., 285
Howells, L. T., 523
Hoyle, R. H., 47, 139, 145, 153, 474–475
Hoyt, C. L., 50, 79, 280, 288, 299, 300,
    307, 317
Htun, T. T. Kim, H-J., 488
Huang, J. Y., 235
Hubbell, A. P., 375
Hübner, O., 175
Hudson, V. M., 440
Huebsch, D., 378
Hugenberg, K., 16
Hughes, R. L., 579, 584
Hughes, S., 411
Huguet, P., 329

Hui, C. H., 86
Huici, C., 93, 139
Hulbert, L. G., 463
Hummer, J. F., 171
Humphrey, B., 145
Humphrey, S. E., 283–284
Humphreys, L., 51
Hung-yu, L., 227
Hunt, J. G., 281
Hunter, S. B., 327
Hurley, J. R., 560
Husnu, S., 500
Huston, J. H., 211
Hutchinson, S., 369
Hutchison, P., 218
Huth, P., 390
Hyde, M., 527
Hyman, H., 48
Hyman, H. M., 231
Hymel, S., 260

Iacoboni, M., 327
Iannaccone, L. R., 158
Ickes, W., 117, 259
Iizuka, Y., 152
IJzerman, H., 513
Ilardi, B. C., 293
Ilgen, D. R., 56
Ilgen, D. R., 408, 411, 420, 422, 427, 428, 432, 448
Ilies, R., 284, 288, 289, 307
Imada, S., 83
Imhoff, R., 214
Indik, B. P., 145
Inesi, M. E., 268
Ingham, A. G., 335
Ingram, R. E., 554
Innella, A. N., 300
Innes, J. M., 329
Insel, P. M., 145
Insko, C. A., 125, 127, 391, 459, 473–476, 505
Instone, D., 256, 291
Ioakimidis, M., 334
Ip, G. W., 14
Iscte, J. C. J., 185
Isenberg, D. J., 197
Isidore, C., 293
Islam, G., 259
Ito, H., 328
Iuzzini, J., 72, 90, 93, 94
Izumi, H., 426

Jablin, F. M., 195
Jackson, C., 220
Jackson, C. L., 420
Jackson, D., 523
Jackson, J. M., 208, 210, 337

Jackson, L. M., 472
Jackson, P. L., 436
Jackson, S. E., 414
Jackson, T., 334
Jacobs, A., 561
Jacobs, D., 472
Jacobs, E., 421
Jacobs, M. K., 551
Jacobs, R. C., 171
Jacobson, N. S., 564
Jacoby, L. L., 332
Jago, A. G., 370
Jahoda, G., 20, 32
James, J., 4
James, R., 234, 342–343
James, R. M., 233–234, 261
James, W., 79
Jamieson, J. P., 330
Janicik, G. A., 361
Janis, I. L., 12, 44–46, 50, 154, 358, 374, 385–393
Janowski, C. L., 291
Jans, L., 16
Janssen, D. P., 482
Janssen, L., 211
Janssen, O., 459
Jarboe, S. C., 460
Jarman, R., 307
Jarvenpaa, S. L., 425
Jarvis, P. A., 145
Jaschik-Herman, B., 126
Jasper, J. M., 596
Javidan, M., 295–297, 317
Jaworski, R. A., 338
Jayasena, A., 565
Jaycox, L. H., 116
Jehn, K. A., 144, 337, 360, 361, 364, 397, 416, 448, 464, 472
Jennings, J. R., 327, 329
Jensen, M. A. C., 22, 146
Jensen-Campbell, L. A., 449
Jentzsch, I., 230
Jermier, J. M., 285
Jesuino, J., 185
Jetten, J., 82, 139, 209, 240, 392
Jochims, M., 378
Johannesen-Schmidt, M. C., 294, 312
Johansson, A., 584
John, O. P., 119, 258, 555
John, P. F. U., 127
Johns, M., 300
Johnson, A. L., 115
Johnson, B. T., 260, 285, 312
Johnson, C., 56–57, 349–350
Johnson, D., 120, 218
Johnson, D. E., 305
Johnson, D. W., 436, 441, 499, 501
Johnson, F., 549

Johnson, K. M., 497
Johnson, L. D., 104
Johnson, M., 56, 408
Johnson, N. R., 582
Johnson, R. D., 595
Johnson, R. T., 436, 441, 499, 501
Johnson, S. E., 262, 417
Johnson, S., 305
Johnson, S. L., 142
Johnson, W., 279
Johnston, J., 511
Johnstone, R. A., 300
Joinson, A. N., 212
Joireman, J., 439, 474
Jolliff, D. L., 560
Jonas, K., 267, 493
Jones, D. J., 120
Jones, D. R., 556
Jones, E. C., 420
Jones, E. E., 69, 291–292,
Jones, Ed. E., 259, 486
Jones, E. S., 293
Jones, J. R., 219, 491
Jones, J. T., 125
Jones, M. B., 411
Jonsen, K., 416, 432
Jordan, A. H., 119, 555
Jordan, J., 268
Jordan-Edney, N. L., 526
Jordon, J. A., 556
Jorgenson, D. O., 4
Joseph, D. L., 290
Joseph, L., 327
Joseph, S., 214
Josephs, R. A., 259
Joslyn, M. R., 66
Jost, J. T., 251
Jostmann, N. B., 267
Jourard, S., 147
Joyce, E., 123
Judd, C. M., 16, 51, 61, 383, 486
Judge, T. A., 102, 284, 288, 289, 312
Jundt, D., 56, 408
Jung, D., 280
Jung, J., 116
Jung, K., 103

Kacmar, C. J., 259
Kagan, J., 107
Kagan-Moore, L., 557
Kagitçibasi, C., 79
Kahn, A., 440, 521, 593
Kahn, R. L., 135, 183, 184
Kahneman, D., 371
Kaiser, R. B., 58, 263, 280, 301
Kallgren, C. A., 225
Kalodner, C. R., 544

Kalven, H., 231, 234
Kamarck, T. W., 327, 329
Kameda, T., 74, 84, 232, 337, 365, 367, 383, 385, 389
Kampmeier, C., 78
Kampschroer, K., 536
Kanas, N. A., 415
Kandel, D. B., 127
Kaneko, H., 328
Kang, H-S., 185
Kang, P., 236
Kang, S. M., 264
Kang, Y., 513
Kaniasty, K., 115
Kanki, R. L., 345
Kanouse, D. E., 116
Kantas, A., 185
Kantrowitz, M., 508
Kapitanoff, S., 343
Kaplan, M. F., 368
Kaplan, R. E., 548
Kaplan, S., 511
Kaplan, S. A., 51
Kaplowitz, S. A., 253
Karamushka, L., 185
Karau, S. J., 111, 299, 314, 336–339, 351, 356, 391, 411
Kark, R., 256
Karremans, J. C., 417
Kashima, E., 17
Kashima, Y., 17, 81
Kashy, D. A., 557
Kaskutas, L. A., 174, 553–554
Katz, D., 135, 184
Katz, N., 3, 5, 356, 432
Katz, R., 287, 364
Katzenbach, J. R., 8, 402
Kauffeld, S., 428
Kaul, J. D., 36
Kaul, T., 562
Kawakami, K., 489
Kayes, A. B., 550
Kayes, D. C., 45, 550
Kazdin, A. E., 562
Kearney, E., 256
Keating, C. F., 160
Keating, J. P., 45, 520
Keeton, K. E., 415
Keil, L. J., 459
Keinan, G., 410–411
Kelem, R. T., 593
Keller, K., 461
Keller, T., 310
Kellermanns, F. W., 368
Kelley, C. E., 521
Kelley, H. H., 53, 55, 127, 128, 221, 436, 438, 448, 451, 583
Kelley, J., 167

Kelley, R. E., 310–311
Kellogg, W. A., 501
Kelly, B. C., 174
Kelly, D., 288
Kelly, J. R., 69, 140, 291–293, 351, 391, 454
Kelly, K. V., 536
Kelly, T., 203
Kelman, H. C., 271–272, 499
Kelsey, B. L., 424
Kelsey, R. M., 329
Keltner, D., 258, 263, 266–270, 276
Kemmelmeier, M., 79, 80, 83, 85, 86, 88, 98
Kemp, C., 287
Kemp, R. I., 362
Kennedy, C., 91
Kennedy, D. P., 519
Kennedy, F. A., 428
Kennedy, J., 474–475
Kennedy, R. F., 394
Kenny, D. A., 102, 305, 561
Kenworthy, J. B., 219, 491, 493
Kerckhoff, A. C., 574, 585
Kerr, N. L., 49, 61, 97, 227, 235, 236, 272, 337, 339, 346, 377, 397, 436, 451
Kerr, S., 283, 285
Keshet, S., 256
Kessler, T., 97, 494
Keyton, J., 3, 221, 406
Khalil, A., 572, 588, 602
Khan, S. R., 332
Khare, V. P., 288
Kieffer, S. C., 561
Kier, E., 137
Kiesler, C. A., 211
Kiesler, D. J., 287, 546
Kiesler, S., 264
Kilduff, G. J., 262
Kilham, W., 249
Killian, L. M., 595–596
Kilmartin, C. T., 265, 560
Kim, H., 214, 270, 557
Kim, J., 108
Kim, K., 264
Kim, S. H., 380, 434, 468
Kim, T., 341
Kim, U., 17, 81
Kim, Y., 87, 116
Kimmel, A. J., 583
Kinder, M. H., 557
King, A. J., 300
King, G. A., 436
King, L. A., 41
King, M. C., 486

King, N., 307
Kipnis, D., 256, 266, 268, 269
Kipper, D. A., 546
Kirby, P., 363
Kirchman, C. M., 67
Kirchner, J. L., 474–475
Kirkman, B. L., 55
Kirkpatrick, L. A., 114
Kirkpatrick, L. C., 236
Kirmeyer, S. L., 535
Kirson, D., 454
Kirzner, E., 326
Kishida, K. T., 265, 267
Kitayama, S., 53–54, 98–98
Kivlighan, D. M., Jr., 554, 557–562
Kjos, G. L., 122
Klammer, T. P., 428
Klapwijk, A., 438
Klauer, K. C., 329
Klein, C., 428
Klein, J. D., 105
Klein, K. J., 313, 414
Klein, L. C., 71, 116
Klein, M., 180
Kleinberg, J., 590
Kleingeld, A., 337
Klentz, B., 257
Kline, N. S., 530
Klinenberg, E., 64, 67, 108
Klocke, U., 269, 376
Klonsky, B. G., 299
Klotz, M. L., 448
Kluger, J., 513, 524, 539
Knievel, E. M., 344
Knight, A. P., 313
Knight, D. P., 259
Knight, G. P., 115, 440
Kniveton, B., 362
Knoll, K., 425
Knowles, E. S., 14, 214, 519, 527
Knowles, M. L., 69, 326
Knowlton, B. J., 327
Kobrynowicz, D., 262
Kocum, L., 184
Koenig, A. M., 299
Koenig, K., 48
Kogan, N., 381
Köhler, O., 346
Köhler, W., 14
Kohles, J. C., 281
Kohut, H., 138
Kojima, H., 86
Kolb, D. A., 334, 550
Kolb, D. M., 458
Kolb, K. J., 332
Köller, O., 119
Kolodinsky, R. W., 259
Komorita, S. S., 443, 456, 463

Kondracki, B. A., 521
Konečni, V. J., 122
Konieczka, S. P., 3
Koning, L., 416
Konrad, A. M., 455
Koocher, G. P., 519
Koole, S. L., 115
Koopman, P., 185
Koopman, P. L., 185
Kopp, W., 278, 285, 311
Korda, M., 530
Koren, M., 410–411
Koriat, A., 348
Korth, S., 334
Koslowsky, M., 255, 256
Kosslyn, S. M., 412
Kösters, M., 563
Kotter, J. P., 281
Kounin, J. S., 270
Kovera, M. B., 231, 234
Kowalski, R. M., 69, 72, 109, 127
Kowert, P. A., 361, 389
Kozlowski, S. W. J., 182, 407, 420, 422,
　　427, 428, 432
Krackhardt, D., 190, 191, 194
Kraft, R., 34
Kraiger, K., 428
Krakauer, J., 515
Kramer, G. P., 377
Kramer, R. M., 46, 181, 252, 350, 374,
　　388, 389, 398, 424, 442, 474
Kraus, L. A., 67
Kraus, M. W., 263, 266, 267, 276
Krause, D. E., 256
Krause, J., 342–343
Krause, N., 116–117
Krause, S., 106, 342–343
Krauss, R. M., 452–453, 459, 476
Kraut, R. E., 123
Kravitz, D. A., 27, 335
Kreager, D., 73
Kressel, K., 463
Kreuser, B., 527
Kring, A. M., 258
Krishnan, R., 421
Kristof-Brown, A., 126
Krogel, J., 563
Krone, K. J., 195
Krueger, J., 211, 222
Krueger, J. R., 186
Krueger, R. E., 279
Krüger, M., 301
Kruglanski, A. W., 214, 252, 255, 392, 448
Krull, L. A., 557
Kruzela, P., 185
Ku, G., 13
Kuang, J. C. Y., 461
Kuchinke, K. P., 185

Kuhn, M. H., 79
Kuhn, T. S., 18
Kulik, J. A., 114
Kulo, J., 561
Kumar, K., 384
Kumar, R., 142
Kumar, V. K., 145
Kurebayashi, K., 17
Kurland, N. B., 254
Kurokawa, M., 53–54
Kurusu, T. A., 556
Kurzban, R., 74, 463
Kushigian, R. H., 583
Kushkowski, J., 29
Kushnir, T., 150
Kutner, B., 479
Kuypers, B. C., 149
Kwan, V. S. Y., 488
Kwapil, T. R., 2, 109
Kwon, S., 439
Kwong, W. Y., 412

La Greca, A. M., 115
LaBarge, E., 557
Labianca, G., 186, 201
LaBrie, J. W., 171
Lacoursiere, R. B., 146
Ladbury, J. L., 367
LaGanke, J., 364
Lage, E., 216–217
Lago, T., 66
Laing, R. D., 597
Lakens, D., 14–15
Lakin, J. L., 71
Lakin, M., 548
Lal Goel, M., 104
Lalonde, R. N., 93
Lam, A., 73
Lam, S. K., 376
Lambert, A. J., 332
Lamm, H., 380–382
Lammers, J., 252
Lampe, C., 123
Landau, J., 293
Landau, M. J., 300
Landers, D. M., 145
Landry, P., 474–475
Lang, G. E., 589
Lang, K., 589
Lange, J. E., 173
Langer, E. J., 221–222
Langfred, C. W., 157
Langkamer, K. L., 185
Langner, C. A., 268
Lanier, K., 265
Lankau, M. J., 293
Lanni, J. C., 528
Lansford, J. E., 66

Lanzetta, J. T., 364
LaPiere, R., 586
Larimer, C. W., 265, 301
Larimer, M. E., 171, 174
Larsen, I. M., 371
Larsen, K. S., 215
Larsen, O. N., 574
Larson, J. R., 21, 280, 347, 356, 376
LaSalvia, C. T., 173
Latané, B., 208–210, 219–220, 228–32,
　　335–336, 337, 382
Latham, G. P., 337, 338
Latham, M. E., 427
Latham, P. E., 348
Latheef, N. A., 223
LaTour, S., 464
Lau, D. C., 414
Laughlin, P. R., 8, 344, 347, 364
Lavertue, N., 145
Lawler, E. E., 428
Lawler, E. J., 140, 252, 270, 271, 453
Lawson, R. B., 391
Layne, C. M., 547
Layne, C. M., 556
Lazarsfeld, P. F., 125
Lazer, D., 5
Lazes, P., 35
Lazonder, A. W., 359
Le, H., 428
Le Bon, G., 19, 573, 598, 599
Le Mens, G., 222
Lea, M., 212, 264
Leach, C. W., 91, 491, 555
Leach, D. J., 373, 508, 535
Leach, L. S., 405
Leader, T., 29, 32
Leak, G. K., 560
Leaper, C., 213, 285
Leary, M. R., 64, 68, 69, 72, 74–76, 97–
　　98, 109, 127, 285, 379, 446
Leather, P., 514
Leavitt, H. J., 186, 194
LeBeau, L. S., 258, 517
Lebrun, C. E. I., 552
Lechner, C., 368
Leclerc, F., 577
Lee, C. M., 171
Lee, D., 138
Lee, H. K., 80
Lee, I-C., 260
Lee, L., 590
Lee, P. W. H., 585
Lee, R. M., 103
Lee, S. W. S., 81
Lee-Chai, A. Y., 266, 269
Lee-Kelley, L., 308
Lehman, E.V., 23–24, 417
Lehmann-Willenbrock, N., 428

Leidner, D. E., 425
Leigh, G. K., 556
Leighter, J., 361
LeMay, E., 195
Lemay, E. P., Jr., 121, 127
Lemos, A., 580
Lengel, L., 517
Leon, G. R., 531
Leonard, W. M., 597
Leong, F. T. L., 565
LePine, J. A., 410, 420
Lepkin, M., 20
Lepore, S. J., 520
Lese, K. P., 561
Leslie, L. M., 461
Lester, M. E., 556
Leszcz, M., 546, 554, 559, 560, 570
Leung, A. K., 87
Leung, A. S. M., 81
Leung, K., 80, 84, 185, 461
Leung, P. W. L., 585
Levesque, M. J., 561
Levett, L. M., 231, 234
Levin, H. M., 310
Levina, A., 123
Levine, J. M., 4, 32, 97, 111–112, 127, 169, 181–183, 217, 227, 409, 513, 535–536
Levine, M., 228, 230
Levine, R. V., 86, 230
Levinger, G., 335
Levy, A. B., 557
Levy, L. H., 551
Lewicki, R. J., 453, 457, 468
Lewin, K., 3, 16, 18, 21, 24, 26, 27, 46–47, 308–310, 313, 507, 542
Lewis, A., 15–16
Lewis, B. P., 71, 116
Lewis, M. A., 171, 174
Lewis, S., 501
Ley, D., 526
Leyens, J-P., 488, 490
Li, A. Y., 259
Li, G., 510
Li, N. P., 115, 440
Li, Q., 14
Li, Y. E., 262
Lian, H., 69, 267
Liberman, M. D., 327
Liberty, H. J., 577
Lickel, B., 12, 15–16, 332
Liden, R. C., 306–307, 338
Lieberman, M. A., 549, 556, 558, 561, 563
Lieberman, M. D., 77
Liebowitz, M. R., 109
Lietaer, G., 549, 554
Likert, R., 283, 401
Lim, A., 151–152

Lim, B. C., 313
Lim, T. K., 185
Limayem, M., 352
Limbert, W. M., 227
Lindblom, C. E., 374
Lindeman, M., 491
Linder, D. E., 161
Lindley, P., 557
Lindskold, S., 462, 527
Linkous, R. A., 326
Linley, P. A., 214
Linville, P. W., 486
Linzmayer, O. W., 434, 468
Lipinski, R. M., 233, 261
Lippitt, R., 46–47, 308–310
Lippmann, W., 487
Lipset, S. M., 597
Lipsitz, A., 476
Lipson, S. F., 259
Lipton, J., 2
Lischetzke, T., 103
List, J. A., 440–441
Littig, P., 334
Littlepage, A. M., 421
Littlepage, G. E., 56, 253, 291, 344, 421
Littlewood, W., 334
Littvay, L., 265, 301
Liu, J. H., 382
Liu, X., 108
Lobb, B., 249
Lobel, S. A., 414
Locke, E. A., 310, 338, 369, 427
Locke, E. E., 281
Lodewijkx, H. F. M., 160–161, 350
Lofland, J., 579
Logel, C., 118
Lohr, N., 91
Lohrenz, T., 436
Lois, J., 37, 45, 63, 68, 97
LoMonaco, B. L., 577, 582
London, M., 422
Long, C. R., 64
Longenecker, C. O., 269
Longley, J., 386
Loomis, J., 50
Lopes, P. N., 290
Lord, C. G., 259
Lord, R. G., 282–283, 288, 295, 298
Lott, A. J., 136, 211
Lott, B. E., 136, 211
Loughead, T. M., 145
Loughry, M. L., 428
Lount, R. B., Jr., 346
Lovaglia, M. J., 194, 446
Lovell, J., 513, 524, 539
Lovett, B. J., 119, 555
Loving, T. J., 391
Low, L. C. K., 585

Lowery, L., 83
Loy, J., 145
Lu, L., 375, 376
Lucas, G. M., 69
Lucas, R. E., 101, 103
Luce, R. D., 427
Lüdtke, O., 119
Ludwig, D. C., 269
Luerssen, A., 71
Luethgens, C., 378
Luft, J., 561
Luhtanen, R., 91–93
Lun, J., 81, 169
LuoKogan, A., 268–269
Luong, A., 373
Lutsky, N., 271
Lux, S., 259
Luzon, P., 115
Lyall, L. M., 259
Lyman, S. M., 526
Lynch, P., 454
Lyons, R., 428
Lyubovnikova, J., 403–404

Maass, A., 217, 484
Maassen, G. H., 191
Maccoby, E. E., 285
MacCoun, R. J., 137, 210, 235, 377
MacCracken, M. J., 333
MacDonald, G., 76, 77, 205
Macfadyen, L., 518
Macfarlan, S. J., 440
MacIver, R. M., 12
Mack, J., 27
MacKenzie, K. R., 559, 563, 570
Mackie, D., 223
Mackie, D. M., 16, 139, 385, 489
Mackie, M., 89
MacKinnon, C. A., 269
MacNair-Semands, R. R., 556, 561
MacNeil, M. K., 21, 171
Macy, B. A., 426
Madsen, R., 78
Madson, L., 81
Maes, J., 444
Magee, J., 448
Magee, J. C., 14, 267, 268
Mahan, T. L., 117
Mahar, L., 303
Maher, K. J., 295
Mahler, H. I. M., 114
Mai-Dalton, R. R., 293
Maier, N. R. F., 344
Maio, G., 488, 493
Maitner, A. T., 16
Majchrzak, A., 307
Major, B., 76, 92, 256
Major, D. A., 182

Makhijani, M. G., 299, 314
Maki, J. E., 451
Malanos, A. B., 103
Malhotra, A., 307
Malik, I., 461
Mallett, K. A., 171
Mallinckrodt, B., 118
Malloy, T. E., 102, 291
Malone, K-L., 143
Malone, T. W., 321–322
Maltby, J., 214
Malvezzi, S., 185
Mandal, M. K., 127
Maner, J. K., 71, 72, 115
Maniaci, M. R., 123
Manica, A., 300
Manier, D., 362
Mann, F. C., 283, 310
Mann, J. H., 287
Mann, L., 58, 249, 365, 374, 577, 592, 593, 596
Mann, R. D., 233–234
Mannetti, L., 214, 392
Manning, J. G., 292, 294
Manning, R., 228
Mannix, E. A., 219, 413–414, 446, 447, 448, 456, 460, 464–465, 472
Manstead, A. S., 454
Mantell, D. M., 249
Manuck, S. B., 327, 329
Manz, C. C., 280
Maoz, I., 490
Maras, P., 491
Marcus, D. K., 557
Markin, R. D., 110
Marks, I. M., 557
Marks, M. A., 407, 418–420, 432
Markus, H., 326
Markus, H. R., 53–54, 214
Marlow, C., 142, 590
Marmar, C. R., 415
Marmarosh, C. L., 110, 555–556, 558, 560
Marmo, J., 172
Marques, J. M., 218, 228
Marriott, R. G., 390
Marsch, S. U., 364
Marsh, H. W., 119
Marsh, J., 260
Marsh, L. C., 546
Marsh, P., 74
Marshall, G. N., 116
Martell, R. F., 293
Martens, A., 300
Martens, M. L., 144
Martens, R., 145
Marti, C. N., 174
Marti, M. W., 235
Martin, B., 27, 335

Martin, E. D., 591
Martin, J., 249
Martin, L. J., 145
Martin, R., 217, 223, 295, 307, 449
Martin-Skurski, M. E., 225
Martorana, P., 267, 390
Martti, M., 573
Marx, K., 472
Maslach, C., 82, 214, 272, 597–598
Maslow, A. H., 52–53
Mason, C. M., 145
Masser, B., 491
Masten, C. L., 77
Mathes, E. W., 593
Mathews, E., 514
Mathewson, G. C., 160
Mathieu, J., 428
Mathieu, J. E., 320, 401, 405, 407, 418–420, 425, 432
Matter, C. F., 519
Matthews, A., 493
Matthews, M. D., 288
Matthews, R. W., 520
Matz, D. C., 168, 214, 224
Mauch, D., 268
Mausner, B., 211
Maxfield, M., 300
May, G. L., 307–308
Mayer, R. C., 424
Maynard, M. T., 401, 425, 428
Mayo, E., 36
Mazar, N., 230
Maznevski, M. L., 416, 432
Mazzola, J. J., 186
McAdam, D., 587
McAdams, D. P., 105–106
McBride, D., 157
McBride, M. V., 260
McBurney, D. H., 513
McCabe, K., 438
McCallin, A., 410
McCanse, A. A., 304–305
McCarthy, J. D., 587
McCarty, J., 27
McCauley, C., 477, 480, 490
McClaren, H. A., 521
McClelland, D. C., 106, 259, 270
McClelland, G., 293
McClintock, C. G., 451, 459
McCool, M. A., Jr., 583
McCormick, J., 160
McCown, N. E., 285
McCoy, S., 76
McCrae, R. R., 101, 214
McCullough, M. E., 463
McCusker, C., 86
McDaniel, D. M., 461
McDaniel, M. A., 289

McDonald, M. M., 482
McDonald, R., 557
McDougall, P., 260
McDougall, W., 74
McElreath, R., 84
McElroy, T., 119
McFall, S. R., 330
McFarland, D. D., 194
McGabe, R., 547
McGhee, D. E., 485
McGillicuddy, N. B., 462
McGlynn, E. A., 497
McGovern, T.V., 559
McGrath, J. E., 3, 8, 35, 50, 56, 61, 123, 320–321, 351, 405, 406, 407, 575
McGraw, K. M., 293, 387
McGregor, D., 401
McGrew, J. F., 151
McGue, M., 279
McGuire, C., 390
McGuire, C. V., 90
McGuire, G. M., 115, 117
McGuire, J. P., 560
McGuire, W. J., 90
McIntosh, B., 391
McIntyre, M., 401, 404, 426
McIntyre, M. H., 259
McKay, C. P., 531
McKeage, R. L., 148
McKee, A., 290
McKee, T. E., 556
McKenna, K. Y. A., 7, 212, 500
McLaughlin, M. L., 455
McLaughlin-Volpe, T., 88, 495
McLean, P. D., 547
McLendon, C. L., 155, 156, 164
McLeod, P. L., 352, 375, 376, 414
McMahon, A. M., 293
McNally, R. J., 557
McNeill, W. H., 141
McNiel, J. M., 103
McPartland, T. S., 79
McPhail, C., 575, 579, 599, 603
McPherson, J. M., 55
McPherson, M., 65, 111, 125, 136, 144
McPherson, S., 474, 478
McQueen, L. R., 444
McRoberts, C., 563
McWhirter, B. T., 565
McWhirter, E. H., 565
McWhirter, J. J., 565
McWhirter, P. T., 565
Mead, G. H., 179
Mead, M., 480
Mead, N. L., 267
Medalia, N. Z., 574
Meece, J. L., 441
Meek, D., 236

Meeker, J. R., 439
Meerloo, J. A., 591
Megargee, E. I., 294
Meglino, B. M., 137
Mehdipour, T., 173
Mehra, A., 186, 201
Mehrabian, A., 521
Mehta, J., 72
Mehta, R., 514
Mehta, V., 525
Meier, B. P., 475, 478
Meier, G. H., 107
Meindl, J. R., 280
Meisenhelder, H. M., 371
Melamed, B. G., 557
Melner, S. B., 401, 428
Meltzoff, A. N., 436
Mendes, W. B., 76, 327, 329
Mendoza, M. M., 118
Mendoza-Denton, R., 496
Menon, T., 17
Menschel, R., 599, 603
Merrigan, G. M., 37
Merry, C. J., 376
Merton, H. W., 282
Merton, R. K., 16, 125
Mesmer-Magnus, J. R., 361
Mesquita, B., 258
Messé, L. A., 61, 49, 346
Messervey, D., 372
Messick, D. M., 254, 281, 326, 438, 442, 444, 459, 486
Metcalf, J., 520
Meudell, P., 363
Meudell, P. R., 363, 378
Meumann, E., 324
Meyer, C. W., 265
Meyer, D. S., 587
Meyer, P., 249
Meyers, R. A., 236
Michael, S. T., 556
Michaels, J. W., 326
Michaelsen, L. K., 348
Michel, J. W., 256
Michels, R., 263
Michener, H. A., 270
Michinov, N., 352
Middlemist, R. D., 519
Mikolic, J. M., 452
Mikulincer, M., 110
Milanovich, D. M., 345
Miles, J. R., 554, 558
Miles, M., 556, 558, 563
Milfont, T. L., 230
Milgram, S., 25, 51, 168–169, 243–250, 263, 272, 276, 577–579, 593, 597, 600, 603
Miller, A. G., 247

Miller, C. A., 415
Miller, C. E., 171, 194, 368
Miller, D. T., 83, 173–174, 218, 434, 577
Miller, G. A., 360
Miller, J. G., 86
Miller, J. K., 552
Miller, K. I., 310
Miller, L. M., 160
Miller, M. D., 220
Miller, M. E., 220
Miller, N., 272, 496–499, 501, 574, 585
Miller, R. S., 126, 132
Mills, J., 159
Mills, J. R., 83
Millson, M., 227
Min, J. W., 173
Minami, H., 526
Miner, A. G., 344
Minkov, M., 54–55, 185
Mintz, A., 583
Mintzberg, H., 281, 282
Miracle on the Hudson Survivors, 341, 356
Mirenberg, M. C., 125
Mischel, W., 210, 463
Mischler, E. G., 264
Misra, S., 359
Misumi, J., 283, 583
Mitchell, A. A., 299
Mitchell, R. C., 556
Mitchell, R. R., 556
Mitchell, T., 379, 446
Mitchell, T. R., 448
Mittleman, D. D., 373
Miyake, K., 119
Mizzaro, S., 366–367
Mobley, W. H., 137
Modigliani, A., 257
Moehle, D., 476
Moehrle, M. G., 353
Moerhl, T. G., 219, 491
Moffitt, G., 16
Mogaji, A., 185
Mohammed, S., 151
Mohrman, S. A., 428
Molden, D. C., 69
Molina, L., 476, 477
Molina, L. E., 482
Molix, L., 184
Molm, L. D., 252, 262, 293
Molnar-Szakas, I., 327
Monge, P. R., 310
Monin, B., 119, 555
Monroe, A. E., 273
Monroe, C., 372–373
Montague, P. R., 265, 267, 436
Monteil, J. M., 329
Monteith, M. J., 485
Montoya, R. M., 127, 474–475

Moody, J., 141, 191
Moon, H., 411
Moore, D. L., 329, 329
Moore, J. C., 261
Moore, P. J., 114
Moore, R., 142
Moore, R.J., 38
Moore, W. C., 527
Moos, R. H., 145
Morales, E., 488
Morales, J. F., 139
Moran, G. P., 329
More, T. A., 64
Moreland, R. L., 4, 32, 111–112, 127, 132, 146, 181–183, 409, 421, 529, 535–536
Moreno, J. L., 42, 186, 189, 192, 545, 549
Morgan, N., 536
Morgeson, F. P., 288, 307, 409, 413
Moritz, M., 327
Morran, K. D., 557
Morrill, C., 446
Morris, C. G., 8, 320, 371, 408
Morris, D., 74
Morris, M. W., 17
Morris, R. T., 168
Morris, S. B., 264
Morris, W. N., 114–115
Morrison, J. L., 116
Morrison, K. R., 218
Morsella, E., 453
Mortazavi, S., 185
Mortensen, C. R., 211, 213
Mortensen, M., 423
Moscovici, S., 215–217, 378, 382
Moser, G., 529
Moser, R. P., 359
Mosier, J., 563
Moskowitz, G. B., 223, 231
Mosquera, P. M. R., 555
Mossholder, K. W., 153, 463
Mosso, C., 223
Mott, N. L., 232
Mottola, G. R., 497
Moussaïd, M., 584
Mouton, J. S., 304, 306, 472
Moxnes, P., 180, 181
Moya, M., 488
Mphuthing, T., 491
Mucchi-Faina, A., 223
Mudrack, P. E., 144, 176, 177
Mueller, A. L., 253, 291
Mukerji, P., 582, 584
Mulder, L. B., 443
Mullen, B., 16, 145, 155–156, 261, 329, 349–350, 390, 424, 428, 580, 593
Muller, D., 330
Mullison, D., 561, 562
Mumford, E., 282

Mummendey, A., 486, 494
Munene, J., 185
Munro, M., 361
Munroe, P. T., 193
Munsterman, G. T., 232
Murayama, A., 17
Murnighan, J. K., 367, 414, 443, 454, 456, 462
Murphy, B., 231
Murphy, C. J., 283
Murphy, J., 109–110
Murphy, L. R., 585
Murphy, M., 585
Murphy, P., 71, 448
Murphy, S. A., 45
Murphy-Berman, V., 519
Murrell, A., 93, 491
Murrell, S. A., 118
Mušić, M., 547
Muskin, P. R., 570
Myers, A. E., 153
Myers, D. G., 380–383
Myers, D. J., 479, 591
Myin-Germeys, I., 109
Myloni, B., 334
Myrtle, R. C., 405

Nachtigall, C., 563
Nadler, J., 451
Naffrechoux, M., 216–217
Nagasundaram, M., 352
Nagler, J., 123
Nahrgang, J. D., 283–284, 288, 307
Nail, P. R., 205
Nakui, T., 350
Nardi, B., 38, 45
Nario-Redmond, M. R., 79
Nash, R. F., 57
Nason, E. R., 407
Nastasi, B. K., 565
National Transportation Safety Board, 345
Naumann, S. E., 137
Nauta, A., 484
Navarrete, C. D., 482
Naveh, D., 45, 149
Neale, M. A., 350, 413, 414, 450
Neighbors, C., 171, 174
Nelson, B. N., 265
Nelson, E., 118
Nelson, T. F., 171
Nemeth, C., 216
Nemeth, C. J., 223, 234, 523
Neuberg, S. L., 53, 97
Neudeck, E. M., 173
Neumark-Sztainer, D., 111
Newcomb, T. M., 25, 47–49, 121, 124, 126–127, 192, 204, 227
Newlin, M. H., 264

Newman, B., 227
Newman, D. A., 290
Newman, E., 293
Newman, K. S., 72
Newman, O., 527
Newsham, G. R., 511
Newsom, J. T., 117
Newton, J. W., 593
Nezlek, J. B., 69
Nichols, D. R., 428
Nickell, E., 38, 142
Nida, S. A., 229
Nielsen, M. E., 171
Nier, J. A., 489, 497
Nietzel, M. T., 234, 237
Nieva, V. F., 420
Niiya, Y., 17
Nijstad, B. A., 349, 350, 375, 397
Nikkel, E., 372–373
Nisbett, R. E., 17, 87–88, 332, 480
Nishii, L. H., 81
Nixon, A. E., 186
Noel, J. G., 491
Nolan, L. L., 435, 443, 448
Nomura, K., 328
Norenzayan, A., 17, 86, 230
Norris, F. H., 118
Norton, M. I., 122
Nosek, B. A., 485
Novak, J., 142
Nowak, A., 219, 220
Nunamaker, J. F. Jr., 373
Nutt, P. C., 380, 397
Nuwer, H., 160, 161, 164
Nyberg, A. J., 138
Nye, J. L., 298
Nyquist, L. V., 294

Oakes, P. J., 486
Oberholzer-Gee, F., 440–441
O'Boyle, E. H., Jr., 289
O'Brien, R. M., 472
O'Connor, C., 454
O'Connor, M. S., 353
O'Connor, R. M., 171, 174
OED Online, 401
Offerman, T., 438
Often, S., 13
Ogilvie, D. M., 300
O'Gorman, R., 97
O'Grady, K. E., 557
Oh, J-H., 212
Oh, K. Y., 108
Oh, S. Y., 185
Ohbuchi, K., 448
Oishi, S., 81
Oldenburg, R., 524, 525, 540
Oldmeadow, J., 261

Olekalns, M., 440, 459
Olguin, D. O., 341
Oliver, L. W., 156
Oliver, P. E., 575
Oliver, P. H., 287
Olk, P. M., 124
Olsen , K., 348
Olson, R., 36
Olweus, D., 260
O'Malley, P. M., 104
O'Mara, E. M., 72
Ones, D. S., 410
Ong, A. D., 90
Ong, J., 443
Onnela, J-P., 517
Ono, K., 367
Op, K., 166, 200
Opotow, S., 490
Orazietti, K., 264
O'Reilly, C. A., 414
Oriña, M. M., 90, 93
Orive, R., 222
Ormont, L. R., 560
Orne, M. T., 248
O'Rourke, K., 581
Örtqvist, D., 185
Osborn, A. F., 348
Osborne, K. K., 455
Osgood, D. W., 104
O'Shea, P. G., 410
Ostrom, T. M., 338
O'Sullivan, P. B., 455
Otten, S., 252
Ouwerkerk, J. W., 91, 463
Oveis, C., 267–269
Overbeck, J. R., 268
Owens, P. D., 390
Oyserman, D., 79, 80, 81, 83, 85, 86, 88, 98
Ozer, D. J., 101

Pace, J. L., 248
Packer, D. J., 207, 228, 245
Page, B. J., 552
Page, C. H., 12
Page, R. C., 549
Page-Gould, E., 496
Pagnoni, G., 225
Palacios, M., 488, 490
Palenske, D. J., 79
Palinkas, L. A., 531
Palmer, G. J., 291
Paluck, E.L., 498, 505
Pancer, S. M., 67
Pandey, C., 343
Pandhi, N. A., 156
Panksepp, J., 118
Pantaleo, G., 486

Panwar, M. R., 127
Paquette, J. A., 67
Paquin, J. D., 554
Paris, C. R., 364
Park, B., 268
Park, E. S., 70, 346
Park, L. E., 71
Parker, J. C., 452
Parker, K. C., 264
Parker, L., 341, 356
Parkinson, B., 53
Parkinson, C. N., 373
Parks, C., 439
Parks, C. D., 337, 361, 443, 456, 463, 478
Parks, M. R., 123
Parks, S. D., 281
Parkum, K. H., 104
Parkum, V. C., 104
Parrado, N., 169, 200
Parry, K., 185
Parsons, H. M., 513
Parsons, J. T., 174
Parsons, T., 177
Paskevich, D. M., 145
Passy, F., 588
Patel, K. A., 332
Paterson, H. M., 362
Patnoe, S., 499
Patterson, H. N., 415
Patterson, M. L., 516–518, 521
Patton, B., 457–458, 468
Paul, G. L., 564
Paulus, L. E., 556
Paulus, P. B., 338, 349–352, 356, 360, 397, 520
Pavelchak, M. A., 111–112
Paxton, P., 191
Payne, B. K., 332
Pazos, P., 142
Pearce, C. L., 310
Pearce, J. L., 456
Pearsall, M. J., 410
Pearson, J. A., 114–115
Peckham, V., 335
Pedersen, D. M., 64
Peeters, M. A. G., 410
Pelham, B. W., 125
Pelled, L. H., 254, 414
Pelletier, J., 29, 32
Pelz, D. C., 414
Pemberton, M., 120, 474–475
Peng, K., 17
Penke, L., 76
Pennebaker, J. W., 115, 514, 552, 560, 585
Pennekamp, S. F., 91
Pennington, D. C., 3
Pennington, N., 231–232, 234, 240
Penrod, S. D., 231–232, 234, 240

Pentland, A., 321–322, 341
Pepitone, A., 127, 155, 227, 593
Peplau, L. A., 255, 256
Perez, R., 488
Perlick, D., 590
Perlman, A., 326
Perls, F., 545
Perozo, N., 584
Perrewé, P. L., 259
Perrin, S., 215
Perrone, K. M., 556
Perry, E. S., 557
Perry, J., 488
Personnaz, B., 217
Pescosolido, A. T., 138
Peters, R., 580
Peterson, C., 288
Peterson, J. B., 214
Peterson, M. F., 185
Peterson, R. S., 223, 360, 390, 391, 397, 446, 447, 464–465
Petkova, K., 488
Petrie, T. A., 174
Pettigrew, T. F., 487, 493–496, 505, 592
Pettit, G. S., 66
Pharmer, J. A., 414
Philbrick, K., 86, 230
Philips, J. L., 401, 411, 428
Phillips, J. B., 258
Phillips, K. W., 217
Phillips, K. W., 262
Phillips, S., 72
Phillips, S. T., 529
Phinney, J. S., 90
Phoon, W. H., 585
Piccolo, R. F., 284, 312, 420
Pickett, C. L., 71
Pickett, K. M., 125
Pierro, A., 214, 252, 255, 270, 392
Pieters, R., 119
Pike, K. L., 565
Pilati, R., 230
Piliavin, J. A., 67
Pillai, R., 281
Pillutla, M. M., 454
Pinkley, R. L., 474–475
Pinkus, R. T., 71
Pinter, B., 473–475, 485, 505
Piper, W. E., 564
Pippin, G. M., 592
Pisano, G. P., 400, 408–409, 418, 422–423, 432
Pittard-Payne, B., 104
Pittinsky, T. L., 288, 313
Pittman, T. S., 52
Platania, J., 329
Platow, M. J., 298
Platt, L., 555

Platz, S. J., 285
Podsakoff, P. M., 285
Pokhrel, P., 91
Polek, D., 416–417
Poletes, G., 350
Polivy, J., 67, 332
Pollack, J. M., 391, 515
Polletta, F., 596
Polley, R. B., 197
Pollom, L. H., 117
Polzer, J. T., 350, 473
Pomerantz, J., 160
Pomerantz-Zorin, L., 256
Pommer, S. D., 160
Pontari, B. A., 446
Poole, M. S., 61, 146, 234
Popan, J. R., 219, 491
Popović, T., 547
Poppe, M., 259, 270, 271
Porter, C. O. L. H., 411
Porter, L. W., 194, 456
Porter, N., 293
Porto, J. B., 230
Postman, L. J., 487, 583
Postmes, T., 16, 212, 264, 375, 392, 512, 591, 596–597, 603
Poulin, M. J., 118
Poundstone, W., 427
Powell, C., 77
Powell, K. M., 536
Powers, J., 198, 201
Pozzi, F., 499
Pradhan, P., 337, 361
Prapavessis, H., 153, 154
Pratkanis, A. R., 240, 390, 391, 392
Pratt, J. H., 542
Pratt, M. W., 67
Pratt, N. C., 103
Pratto, F., 259–260, 475–477
Prentice, D. A., 173–174
Prentice-Dunn, S., 594–595
Presnell, K., 174
Preston, M., 257
Pribram, K. H., 360
Price, K. H., 416
Priest, H. A., 428
Primeau, B. E., 259
Princisvalle, K., 109
Prislin, R., 204, 217, 227
Pritchard, R. D., 186
Probst, T., 461
Prochnau, W. W., 341, 356
Promislo, M. D., 260
Pronin, E., 221
Pronk, T. M., 417
Proshansky, H., 479
Prosser, A., 230
Provine, R. R., 576

Pruitt, D. G., 380, 381, 386, 434, 442, 451, 452, 457, 459, 462, 468
Prusaczyk, W. K., 103
Pruyn, A. T.H., 211
Pryce, J., 236
Pryor, J. B., 273
Punnett, B. J., 185
Putman, V. L., 350
Putnam, R. D., 53, 66, 81
Pynoos, R. S., 547
Pyszczynski, T., 299, 300

Quartz, K. H., 265, 267
Quartz, S. R., 265, 267
Quattrone, G. A., 486
Queller, S., 385
Quigley, N. R., 148
Quinn, A., 211
Quinn, J., 486
Quinn, R. P., 183

Raafat, R. M., 223
Rabbie, J., 115
Rabbie, J. M., 473
Rackstraw, P., 223
Radford, M., 185
Radloff, R., 45, 509
Ragan, J. W., 367
Raghubir, P., 417
Raiffa, H., 427
Raimbault, N., 145
Rakoczy, H., 171
Ramachandran, K., 127
Randsley de Moura, G., 29, 32, 218
Ranford, M., 185
Ransom, S., 480
Rantilla, A. K., 446
Rapee, R. M., 108
Rapoport, A., 509
Rapp, T., 428
Rapp, T. L., 401, 425
Rath, R., 490
Ratner, R. K., 83
Rause, V., 169, 200
Raven, B. H., 250, 252–255, 270
Rawls, J., 384
Ray, D., 16
Rayne, S. R., 320, 405
Read, A., 171
Read, K. E., 86
Read, P. P., 166, 169, 176, 200
Real, K., 168
Realo, A., 104
Reddington, K., 291, 421
Redl, F., 124, 282
Reed, E. S., 472
Reed, M. B., 173
Reeder, G. D., 273

Reeder, K., 518
Rees, C. R., 176
Rees, G., 348
Reichard, R. J., 287
Reicher, S., 230
Reicher, S. D., 118, 271, 298, 479, 490, 581, 596–597, 599, 603
Reichl, A. J., 491
Reichling, G., 155
Reider, M. H., 409, 413
Reifman, A., 235, 236, 590
Reilly, R. R., 424
Reimer, A., 375, 376
Reimer, T., 375, 376
Reinig, B. A., 111
Reips, U., 442
Reis, H. T., 47, 123, 436
Reitsma, M., 417
Reno, R. R., 225
Rentfrow, P. J., 102
Rentsch, J. R., 183
Repacholi, B. M., 513
Reston, J. R., Jr., 253, 276
Reymen, I. M. M. J., 410
Rhee, E., 80
Rheingold, H., 12, 588
Riaño, J., 230
Rice, E., 55
Rice, O. K., 479
Rice, R. E., 307
Rice, R. W., 291, 304
Richard, F. D., 26
Richards, H., 401, 405, 426
Richards, J., 224–225
Richardson, D. S., 66
Richeson, J. A., 262, 417
Richey, B., 444
Ridgeway, C. L., 261, 262, 263
Rieck, A. M., 420
Riecken, H. W., 37, 45, 158–159
Riess, M., 523
Riggiero, J., 493
Riggio, H. R., 412
Riggio, R. E., 287
Rimal, R. N., 168
Ringelmann, M., 333
Ringer, T. M., 561
Rink, F., 227
Riordan, C., 493
Riordan, J. M., 268
Ripley, J. S., 556
Ristikari, T., 299
Ritchie, T. D., 546
Ritt, S. J. H., 160
Rivera, A. N., 444
Rivers, J. J., 259
Robak, R. W., 561
Robbins, A., 45

Roberson, Q., 427
Robert, C., 83
Robert, H. M., 447
Roberts, B. W., 259
Robertson, T. E., 443
Robinson, S. L., 531
Robinson, T. T., 154
Robison, F. F., 180
Robison, W., 291, 421
Roby, T. B., 364
Roccas, S., 88
Rochat, F., 257
Roche, J., 518
Rodin, J., 520
Rodríguez-Bailón, R., 488
Rodriguez-Perez, A., 490
Rodriguez-Torres, R., 490
Roe, C. W., 256
Roepstorff, A., 348
Roethlisberger, F. J., 36
Rofé, Y., 115
Rogelberg, S. G., 337, 353, 373, 417
Rogers, C., 549
Rogers, M. S., 371
Rogers, P. A., 127
Rogers, R. W., 594–595
Rognes, J., 436
Rohdieck, S., 454
Rohrmann, B., 384
Roland, E. J., 351, 352
Roll, S., 293
Rom, E., 110
Roman, R. J., 80
Romanova, N., 292
Romberger, B., 293
Romero, E. J., 272
Ronay, R., 265, 410
Rook, K. S., 117
Room, R., 554
Roos, P. D., 526, 527
Ropo, A., 185
Ropp, S. A., 495
Rose, M., 231
Rose, R., 203, 240
Rose, S. D., 111
Rose-Krasnor, L., 107
Roseman, I. J., 454
Rosen, B., 307
Rosen, M. A., 320, 402, 405, 421
Rosenbloom, D., 171
Rosenbloom, T., 326
Rosenfeld, P., 523
Rosenthal, R. A., 183
Rosenthal, S. A., 288
Roseth, C. J., 501
Rosette, A. S., 293
Rosiny, S., 588
Rosnow, R. L., 583

Ross, J., 450
Ross, L., 208, 222, 438, 450, 450, 451
Ross, M., 445, 454
Ross, T. M., 420
Ross, W. H., 464
Rossano, M. J., 171
Rost, J. C., 281, 282
Roth, B. E., 544
Roth, C. P., 521
Roth, D. A., 332
Roth, E. W., 560
Roth, W., 72
Rothbart, M., 487
Rothgerber, H., 168, 479, 486
Rothschild, L., 16
Rotolo, T., 55
Rotton, J., 513
Rotundo, M., 279
Rouby, D. A., 71, 72
Rouhana, N. N., 475, 499
Rountree, C. A., 114–115
Rousseau, J-J., 481
Rousseau, V., 402, 404, 428
Rowe, J. S., 326
Rowland, K. M., 333
Roy, D. F., 37, 153
Roy, M. C., 352
Rozell, D., 428
Rozin, P., 83
Ruback, R. B., 264, 351
Rubin, J. Z., 380
Rubin, K. H., 107
Rubin, M., 484
Rubin, R. B., 372
Rubini, M., 86
Rubino, C., 415
Ruddy, T. M., 420
Rudman, L. A., 299, 505
Ruef, M., 4
Ruffin, P. F., 474–475
Rufus, A. S., 108
Rumery, S. M., 417
Runciman, W. G., 591
Runkel, M., 441
Rusbult, C. E., 129, 436
Ruscher, J. B., 359
Russ-Eft, D. F., 303
Russell, B., 250
Russell, G. W., 591
Russell, J. A., 509
Russell, N. J. C., 247
Russell, R. J. H., 591
Russo, E. M., 217
Rust, M. C., 497
Rutte, C. G., 140–141, 410
Ruxton, G. D., 342–343
Ryan, C. S., 17
Ryan, J. M., 126

Ryan, M. K., 298, 392
Rydell, R. J., 16
Ryen, A. H., 521
Ryf, B., 442
Ryterband, E. C., 426

Saab, R., 112
Saavedra, R., 128, 403
Sabini, J., 208
Sacco, D. F., 71
Sackett, P. R., 410
Sadler, M. S., 51, 61
Sadler, P., 265
Sadow, J. S., 333
Sagar, H. A., 494
Sagarese, M., 260
Sagiv, L., 88
Sagrestano, L. M., 214
Saiz, J., 185
Saks, M. J., 235, 236
Salas, C., 36
Salas, E., 47, 145, 320, 345, 349–350, 361,
    364, 390, 402, 405, 410, 411, 414,
    418, 421, 428, 432, 511
Salazar-Laplace, M. E., 524
Salnitskiy, V. P., 415
Salomon, K., 327
Salovey, P., 76, 290
Saltel, P., 565
Saltz, J. L., 313
Saltzman, W. R., 547
Samaha, G. M., 114–115
Samaranayake, V., 333
Sambolec, E. J., 346
Sampson, E. E., 227
Samuelson, C. D., 444, 446
Sandberg, W. R., 367
Sandelands, L., 21
Sanders, G. S., 329
Sanders, J., 272
Sanders, W. B., 526, 528, 597
Sani, F., 90
Sankey, T., 308
Sanna, L. J., 329, 337, 361
Santee, R. T., 82
Santos, L., 36
Sapp, M., 546
Sapp, S. G., 294
Sarbin, T. R., 186
Saroglou, V., 103
Sassenberg, K., 85, 267
Sattler, D. N., 451
Saucier, G., 102
Saul, J. R., 420
Saul, K., 280
Saunders, C., 151, 152
Saunders, D. M., 457, 468
Savage, G., 185

Savitsky, K., 445
Savjak, N., 547
Savoie, A., 402
Saylor, S. A., 415
Scandura, T. A., 293
Scarr, H. A., 593
Schachter, S., 37, 45, 113–115, 121, 136,
    145, 157–159, 168, 226–227
Schaerfl, L. M., 444
Schafer, M., 390
Schaller, M., 53, 71, 97
Schatten-Jones, E. C., 66
Schaubroeck, J., 376
Schauer, A. H., 333
Scheepers, D., 94, 267
Scheeres, J., 242, 276
Schei, V., 436
Schein, E. H., 82, 258
Schein, L. A., 570
Schein, V., 293, 299
Schelling, T. C., 435
Schenk, C., 521
Scherer, C. R., 487
Scheuble, K. J., 557
Schinke, R. J., 183
Schippers, M. C., 414
Schkade, J. K., 520
Schlegel, R. J., 184
Schlenker, B. R., 160, 211, 285, 383,
    446, 529
Schlenker, D. R., 529
Schlesinger, A. M., Jr., 387
Schlundt, D. G., 332
Schmid, T., 185
Schmid Mast, M. S., 259, 267, 279
Schmidt, C. J., 101–102
Schmidt, D. E., 520
Schmidt, G. W., 56
Schmidt, L. A., 107
Schmidt, N., 67
Schmidt, S. M., 256
Schmitt, B. H., 327, 577
Schmitt, D. P., 76, 104
Schmitt, M. H., 183
Schmukle, S. C., 121
Schneebaum, T., 86
Schneider, D. J., 487, 505
Schneider, J., 262
Schneier, F., 109
Schofield, J. W., 189, 492, 494, 499
Scholten, L., 375
Schoorman, F. D., 424
Schopler, J., 125, 473–475, 505
Schottenbauer, M., 555
Schouten, M. E., 403
Schriesheim, C. A., 283, 307
Schrock, D. A., 556
Schroeder, H. W., 508

Schuchart, G. E., 527
Schuler, R. S., 183
Schulkin, J., 107
Schultheiss, O. C., 106
Schulz-Hardt, S., 376, 378
Schumann, K., 454
Schurtz, D. R., 77
Schuster, M. A., 116
Schut, H., 68
Schutz, W. C., 106–107, 126, 410
Schwartz, B., 529
Schwartz, J., 454
Schwartz, J. L. K., 485
Schwartz, S., 88
Schwartz, S. H., 83, 185, 229
Schwarz, N., 87–88
Schwarzwald, J., 255, 256
Schweiger, D. M., 367
Schweingruber, D., 579
Schyns, B., 280
Scott, M. B., 526
Scott, W., 554
Sculley, J., 434, 443
Seal, D. W., 45
Seashore, S. E., 153, 157, 283, 426
Seburn, M., 64
Sechrest, L., 361
Sechrest, L. B., 268, 517
Sederholm, H., 448
Sedgwick, J., 13
Sedikides, C., 94, 120
Seers, A., 151, 310
Segal, H. A., 258
Segal, M. W., 121, 176
Seger, C. R., 139
Seibold, D. R., 236
Seidman, G., 7
Sekaquaptewa, D., 262
Selamat, M. F. B., 223
Seligman, M. E. P., 564
Sell, J., 446
Semin, G. R., 86, 140, 221, 513, 589
Semmer, N. K., 115, 364
Senders, P. S., 280
Sensenig, J., 450
Seok, D., 339, 346
Sergel, S. L., 203, 240
Sermat, V., 67
Sessa, V. I., 422
Seta, C. E., 119, 328, 350
Seta, J. J., 119, 328, 350, 520
Sethna, B. N., 264
Setiadi, B., 185
Seying, R., 236
Seyle, D. C., 93, 139
Seymour, W. R., 333
Seyranian, V., 217, 240
Shachaf, P., 152–153

Shaffer, L. M., 332
Shah, J. Y., 392
Shah, P. P., 364
Shahar, A., 326
Shalley, C. E., 420
Shalvi, S., 58
Shamir, B., 313
Shannon, J. K., 118
Shao, L., 103
Shapiro, D. A., 563
Shapiro, D. L., 436
Sharp, L. B., 498
Shaver, P., 66–67, 109, 114, 454
Shaw, H., 174
Shaw, J. C., 368
Shaw, J. D., 322, 338
Shaw, K., 581
Shaw, L., 93
Shaw, L. L., 36
Shaw, L. M., 153
Shaw, M. E., 153, 193–194, 214, 322, 510
Shaw, Ma. E., 364
Shaw, T. R., 425
Shea, G. P., 423
Sheats, P., 10, 177–178, 549
Sheatsley, P. B., 116
Shebilske, W. L., 556
Shechter, D., 214
Shechtman, Z., 560, 565
Shedler, J., 544
Sheehan, M., 529
Sheldon, K., 184
Sheldon, K. M., 97
Shelly, R. K., 193
Shelton, G. A., 249
Shepard, H. A., 148
Sheppard, B. H., 459
Shepperd, J. A., 338
Sherif, C. W., 3, 136, 143–144, 470–472,
    483, 492, 493, 494, 497, 499, 501, 504
Sherif, M., 3, 21, 136, 143–144, 169–171,
    204, 470–472, 476, 483, 492, 493,
    494, 497, 499, 501, 504
Sherman, D. K., 16
Sherman, G. D., 81
Sherman, M. P., 364
Sherman, S. J., 12, 15–17, 487
Sherrod, D. R., 520
Shi, K., 565
Shi, X., 82
Shillington, A. M., 173
Shils, E., 177
Shipper, F., 283
Shirom, A., 201
Showers, C. J., 529
Shuffler, M. L., 428
Shukla, R. M., 353
Shure, G. H., 371, 439

Sias, P. M., 195
Sibley, C. G., 477
Sibona, C., 142
Sicoly, E., 445
Sidanius, J., 259–260, 475–477, 482
Siddiqui, R. N., 112
Siebold, G. L., 144–145, 164
Siegel, R., 448
Siegl, E., 67
Sigall, H., 223
Sikes, J., 499
Silbiger, H., 291, 421
Silver, W. S., 386
Silvera, D. H., 556
Silverman, P. R., 551
Silvia, P. J., 2, 109
Simmel, G., 4, 78
Simon, A. F., 497
Simon, B., 78, 91, 93, 486
Simon, R. J., 234
Simon, S., 300
Simonton, D. K., 289
Simpson, B., 440
Simpson, J. A., 292, 458
Simpson, L., 581
Sinclair, S., 169
Singer, E., 48
Singer, J. E., 514
Singh, P., 112
Sinha, T. N., 185
Sirois, F., 585
Sivakumar, K., 227
Sivanathan, N., 268
Sivuneun, A., 50
Sjovold, E., 198, 201
Skinner, B. F., 53
Skitka, L.J., 369
Skowronski, J. J., 487
Slater, P. E., 176
Slavson, S. R., 543
Sleebos, E., 488
Slim, R., 474–475
Sloane, L. R., 138
Smeesters, D., 439
Smelser, N. J., 575, 583
Smit, W. M., 552
Smith, C. B., 455
Smith, C. L., 352
Smith, C. M., 237, 367, 376
Smith, D. H., 104
Smith, D. K., 8, 402
Smith, E. M., 407
Smith, E. R., 109–110, 139, 489
Smith, G., 108
Smith, H. J., 592
Smith, J. A., 288, 561
Smith, K. B., 265, 301
Smith, L., 72

Smith, M., 3, 119–120, 282
Smith, M. B., 381
Smith, P. B., 185, 210, 213, 215, 293, 444, 556
Smith, P. K., 267
Smith, P. L., 440
Smith, R. H., 119
Smith, S. G., 529
Smith, S. L., 474–475
Smith, T., 391
Smith, T. W., 65
Smith, V., 488
Smith, V. L., 438
Smith-Jentsch, K. A., 428
Smith-Lovin, L., 125, 136, 144
Smithson, M., 261
Smoke, W. H., 447
Smokowski, P. R., 111
Smrt, D. L., 338
Snapp, M., 499
Snidman, N., 107
Sniezek, J. A., 392
Snodgrass, J., 509
Snoek, J. D., 183
Snow, D. A., 575, 580
Snyder, C. R., 82, 555, 556
Sobel, R., 154
Socolow, M. J., 599
Solem, A. R., 344
Solomon, M. R., 476
Solomon, S., 299, 300
Solomon, S. H., 520–521
Solomon, S. K., 520
Soman, D., 577
Sommeerville, J. A., 436
Sommer, K. L., 71, 104
Sommer, R., 516, 521–522, 540
Son Hing, L. S., 260, 264
Song, H., 120
Song, S. Y., 71, 448
Sonnenfeld, J. A., 414
Sorenson, G. J., 317
Sorenson, R., 185
Sorrels, J. P., 167
Sorrentino, R. M., 288, 291, 391, 436
Soukup, C., 525
Southwick, S., 56–57
Sparrowe, R. T., 306–307
Spataro, S. E., 258, 416
Spears, R., 91, 94, 112, 212, 264, 375, 392, 491, 591, 596–597, 603
Spector, P. E., 186
Spell, C., 447
Spell, C. S., 447
Spence, J. T., 294
Spencer, C. P., 215
Spencer, R. W., 211
Spencer-Rodgers, J., 15, 17

Spencer Stuart., 292
Spiegel, S. B., 557
Spillane, R., 249
Spisak, B. R., 301
Spitz, H. I., 570
Spivey, R. W., 595
Spoor, J. R., 140
Spoor, S., 174
Sprinthall, N. A., 250
Spychiger, M., 364
Sriram, N., 487
Srivastava, S., 76, 258
Sriwongkol, T., 264
St. Clair, L., 21
St. John, W., 45
Stadulis, R. E., 333
Stager, S. F., 92
Stahelski, A. J., 438, 451
Stahl, G. K., 416, 432
Ståhl, T., 443
Stainton-Rogers, W., 61
Stajkovic, A. D., 138
Staley, K., 359
Stangor, C., 493
Stanton, N., 401
Stanton, S. J., 106
Staples, D. S., 425
Stapp, J., 82
Stark, E. M., 322, 338
Starks, T. J., 174
Stasser, G., 236, 359, 374–376
Stasson, M. F., 337, 348, 367, 383, 389
Staub, E., 271, 479, 490
Staw, B. M., 351, 450
Stawiski, S., 421
Steblay, N. M., 257
Stech, F. J., 459
Stecker, R., 511
Steel, G. D., 514, 515, 540
Steel, P., 55
Steel, R. P., 153, 183
Steele, C. M., 94
Steele, G. L., 455
Steiger, J. H., 509
Stein, B. D., 116
Stein, J. L., 258
Stein, R. T., 291
Steinel, W., 451, 454
Steiner, I. D., 19, 323, 333, 339–341, 344–348, 356
Steinfield, C., 123
Steinkuehler, C. A., 525
Steinzor, B., 522
Stempfle, J., 175
Stenstrom, D. M., 16
Stephan, C., 499
Stephan, C. W., 498
Stephan, F. F., 264

Stephan, W. G., 493, 498
Stephenson, G. M., 362
Stern, E. K., 371
Sternberg, R. J., 290, 459, 460, 489
Stets, J. E., 175
Stevens, C. K., 126
Stevens, D., 155
Stevens, M. J., 412–413
Stevenson, R. J., 513
Stevenson, W. B., 456
Stewart, A. J., 591
Stewart, D., 264
Stewart, D. D., 375
Stewart, G. L., 280, 406, 414
Stewart, M., 292, 294
Stewart, P. A., 261
Stice, E., 174
Stiles, W. B., 259, 563
Stillman, T. F., 77
Stillwell, A. M., 454
Stinson, D. A., 118
Stockton, R., 557
Stoddard, J. L., 260
Stogdill, R. M., 283, 287, 289, 292
Stokes, J. P., 67, 145
Stokes-Zoota, J. J., 26
Stokols, D., 359, 518, 539
Stone, A. B., 443, 463
Stoner, J. A., 380
Stones, C. R., 45
Stoop, J. R., 342
Storms, M. D., 332, 520
Storr, A., 64
Stotland, E., 16
Stott, C., 581, 597, 603
Stout, R. J., 345
Strack, F., 17, 223
Stratenwerth, I., 93
Stratham, A., 285
Straus, S. G., 212
Strauss, A. L., 581
Strauss, B., 327, 563, 570
Streufert, S., 472, 480
Streufert, S. C., 472, 480
Strickland, D., 265
Strickland, L. H., 268
Strodtbeck, F. L., 149, 233–234, 261, 523
Stroebe, M. S., 67, 68
Stroebe, W., 24, 68, 349–350, 493
Strong, S. R., 265
Stroud, L. R., 76
Strube, M. J., 324
Stryker, S., 175, 179
Stucke, T. S., 70
Stumpf, S., 444
Stuster, J., 510, 540
Su, S. F., 461
Suedfeld, P., 64, 514, 515, 540

Sugiman, T., 583
Suh, E. M., 17, 79, 86, 103
Suleiman, R., 115
Sullenberger, C. B., 319, 333, 338, 356
Sullivan, L., 514
Sullivan, W. M., 78
Sulloway, F. J., 214
Suls, J., 113–115, 131, 449
Summerville, M., 565
Sumner, W. G., 167, 483
Sun, H., 436
Sundstrom, E., 338, 401, 405, 426, 519, 528, 530–531, 534
Sunstein, C. R., 385
Sunwolf, 235, 351
Surowiecki, J., 342
Susarla, A., 212
Sussman, S., 91
Swaffin-Smith, C., 256
Swamidass, P. M., 426
Swann, W. B., Jr., 93, 102, 139
Sweeney, J., 27
Swidler, A., 78
Swift, E. M., 134, 138, 164
Swinson, R. P., 107
Swinth, K. R., 50
Syna, H., 462
Syroit, J. E. M. M., 160, 161
Sytch, M., 154
Szabo, E., 185
Szymanski, K., 328, 337

't Hart, P., 393
Taal, E., 552
Tabak, B. A., 463
Tager, D., 118
Taggar, S., 322
Tajfel, H., 13, 88, 90, 483, 491
Takeda, M. B., 292
Takezawa, M., 84, 367
Talley, A. E., 184
Tal-Or, N., 120
Tam, T., 493
Tambor, E. S., 76
Tamura, R., 385
Tan, C. R. M., 223
Tan, D. K. B., 223
Tan, J., 461
Tan, T. K., 344
Tan, Y., 212
Tanaka, K., 526
Tang, J., 293
Tang, M., 565
Tang, S., 227
Tang, T. L., 428
Tanis, M., 212, 552
Tannenbaum, S. I., 418, 428
Tanofsky-Kraff, M., 76

Taras, V., 55
Tarde, G., 590
Tarnow, E., 345
Tarrant, C. M., 231
Tassone, J., 371
Tata, J., 227
Tatarynowicz, A., 154
Tausch, N., 112, 493
Taylor, B. K., 359
Taylor, D. A., 532, 560
Taylor, F. W., 401
Taylor, H., 303
Taylor, H. F., 192, 449–450
Taylor, K., 489
Taylor, L., 581
Taylor, P. J., 303
Taylor, R. B., 528
Taylor, S. E., 71, 76, 104, 116, 131–132
Tazelaar, M. J., 463
Teddlie, C., 519
Tedeschi, J. T., 444
Teed, C., 557
Teger, A., 450
Tekleab, A. G., 148
Ten Velden, F. S., 58, 219
Tennen, H., 556
Teparakul, P., 185
Teppner, B. J., 256
Terdal, S. K., 76
Terry, D. J., 93
Tesluk, P. E., 148
Tesser, A., 119–120
Tesser, M., 103
Tetlock, P. E., 386, 390
Thai, Y., 175
Tharp, A., 557
Thatcher, S. M. B., 144
Thayer, A. L., 320, 405
Thayer, B. A., 440
Theraulaz, G., 584
Thibaut, J. W., 53, 55, 127, 128, 227, 464, 474–476
Thomas, D. S., 16
Thomas, G. C., 520
Thomas, K. W., 459
Thomas, R. L., 379
Thomas, W.I., 16
Thomas-Hunt, M. C., 262
Thompson, J. E., 494
Thompson, L., 451, 459
Thompson, L. L., 219
Thompson, M., 262
Thompson, M. E., 271
Thoreau, H. D., 64
Thorne, A., 138
Thorne, B., 189
Thorngate, W. B., 451
Thornhill, R., 512

Thrasher, F. M., 526
Throop, C. J., 327
Thurlow, C., 517
Thye, S. R., 140, 251
Tichenor, V., 557
Tice, D. M., 70, 77, 280
Tiedens, L. Z., 14, 71, 126, 190, 258, 263, 265
Tiger, L., 416
Tilin, F., 149
Timme, M., 123
Tindale, R. S., 32, 56, 74, 237, 362, 367, 371, 397, 421
Tinkler, J. E., 262
Tipton, S. M., 78
Tirmizi, A., 185
Tirnauer, D., 427
Titus, L. J., 326
Titus, W., 374–375
Tjosvold, D., 436, 461
Tobin, K., 124
Tobin, R. M., 101
Toch, H., 578, 597, 600, 603
Todorov, V., 488
Toennies, F., 12
Toguchi, Y., 94
Toledo, R., 577
Tolnay, S. E., 580
Tolstoy, L., 286
Tomaka, J., 329
Tomasello, M., 171
Tomic, A., 517
Tomkins, A., 142
Tong, E. M. W., 223
Toobin, J., 45
Tooby, J., 443
Torrance, E. P., 261
Tracey, T. J., 126
Trautwein, U., 119
Travis, L. E., 326
Treadway, D. C., 259
Treadwell, T., 145
Tredoux, C., 527
Tremblay, S., 404
Triandis, H. C., 17, 79, 80, 81, 83, 86, 98, 461
Triplett, N., 24, 324
Trochim, W. M. K., 447, 464–465
Troper, J. D., 334
Tropp, L. R., 90, 495–496, 505
Trost, M. R., 210
Troyer, L., 193
Tschan, F., 364
Tsui, A. S., 291, 414
Tsukasaki, T., 365
Tsvetanova, S., 185
Tucker, C. W., 579
Tucker, T. L., 264

Tuckman, B. W., 22, 146–148
Turnage, A. K., 455
Turner, A. L., 45, 542, 547, 564, 569
Turner, J. C., 3, 88–91, 385, 483, 491
Turner, J. D. F., 414
Turner, M. E., 356, 390–392
Turner, N., 173
Turner, R. H., 176, 177, 179, 575, 595–596, 603
Turner, R. N., 91, 493, 500
Turrisi, R., 171
Tushman, M., 364
Tversky, A., 371
Twenge, J. M., 69–70, 81, 93, 104, 213, 248
Tyler, T. R., 251, 252, 368, 444
Tynan, D., 73
Tyszka, J. M., 519

U.S. Senate Select Committee on Intelligence, 391
Uchino, B. N., 117
Ugander, J., 590
Uglow, J. S., 45
Uhl-Bien, M., 307
Uhles, A. N., 15–16
Ulbig, S. G., 591
Uleman, J. S., 80
Umble, E. J., 379
Umble, M. M., 379
Underwood, B., 491
Undre, S., 400
Unzueta, M. M., 126, 263
Updegraff, J. A., 71, 116
Urban, L. M., 498
Uris, A., 388
Ury, W., 457–458, 468
Utman, C. H., 333
Utz, S., 85
Uziel, L., 330–331
Uzzell, D. L., 529

Vaes, J., 490
Vaillancourt, T., 260
Vala, J., 488
Valdesolo, P., 141
Valenzuela, A., 417
Valins, S., 527
Vallacher, R. R., 219, 220
van Aken, M. A. G., 76
Van Avermaet, E., 439
van Baaren, R., 221, 589
van Beest, I., 443
Van Boven, L., 445
van de Laar, M. A. F. J., 552
Van de Ven, A. H., 351, 353
van de Ven, N., 119
van de Vijver, F. J. R., 565

Van de Vliert, E., 459, 460, 484, 512
van der Linden, J. L., 191
van der LÖwe, I., 267–269
van der Toorn, J., 251
Van der Zee, K. I., 16
Van Dijk, E., 58, 263, 439
van Dijk, W. W., 267
van Dijke, M., 259, 270, 271, 443
Van Doorn, E. A., 454
Van Dyne, L., 128, 403
van Eerde, W., 140–141
Van Emmerik, I. H., 460
van Engen, M. L., 294, 312
van Ginneken, J., 599
Van Hiel, A., 218
Van Horn, S. M., 558, 560
Van Kleef, G. A., 58, 266, 268–269, 276, 451, 454
van Knippenberg, D., 375, 414
Van Laar, C., 94
Van Lange, P. A. M., 436, 438, 439, 443, 463
van Mierlo, H., 337
Van Munster, L. M., 438
Van Olffen, W., 410
van Oostrum, J., 473
Van Overwalle, F., 363
Van Pelt, S., 308
van Prooijen, J., 443
Van Raalte, J. L., 161
Van Sell, M., 183
Van Slyke, C., 152
Van Swol, L. M., 378
Van Tongeren, D. R., 463
Van Tuijl, H. F. J. M., 410
van Uden-Kraan, C. F., 552
Van Vianen, A. E. M., 460, 462
Van Vugt, M., 58, 92, 97, 263, 276, 301, 439, 440, 482
Van Witteloostuijn, A., 410
van Yperen, N., 512
Van Zelst, R. H., 153
van Zomeren, M., 91, 161, 591, 603
Vandello, J. A., 87, 210, 480
Vandenberghe, C., 150
VanLeeuwen, M. D., 328, 329
Varela, J. A., 361
Varvel, S. J., 118
Varvil-Weld, L., 171
Vázquez, A., 139
Vecchio, R. P., 305
Veeraraghavan, V., 145
Veiga, J. F., 307–308
Veitch, J. A., 511, 514
Veitch, R., 513
Venkatesh, S., 37, 45, 480
Venkatesh, S. A., 154
Verhofstadt, L. L., 117

Verley, J., 36
Vertue, F. M., 108
Verwijmeren, T., 417
Vescio, T. K., 90, 276
Vevea, J. L., 94, 473–475, 505
Viala, A-L., 565
Vickery, C. D., 561
Vider, S., 580
Vidmar, N., 51, 231, 234, 236, 240
Viedge, C., 185
Villa, J., 285
Villareal, M. J., 80
Vinacke, W. E., 439
Vincent, C. A., 400
Vinokur, A., 361, 383
Vinsel, A., 529–530
Vischer, J. C., 535, 540
Vivian, J., 491
Vlahov, D., 118, 547
Vliegenthart, R., 580
Vliek, M. L. W., 91, 555
Voci, A., 493
Vogel, D., 152
Vogel, D. R., 373
Vohs, K. D., 267
Voigt, A., 416, 432
Voils, C. I., 485
Vollrath, D. A., 56, 362
Volpe, C. E., 418
Von Dras, D., 557
Voracek, M., 104
Voss, A., 329
Vroom, V. H., 310, 370–371
Vryan, K. D., 179

Waber, B. N., 341
Wachtler, J., 114–115, 234, 523
Wackenhut, J., 577
Waddington, D., 597
Wade, G., 493
Wadleigh, P. M., 518
Wagner, D., 223
Wagner, D. G., 444
Walczak, S., 142
Walder, A. G., 587
Waldfogel, J., 440–441
Walker, C. J., 583
Walker, H. A., 293
Walker, L., 464
Walker, M., 138
Wall, M., 111
Wall, V. D., Jr., 435, 443, 448
Wall, W., 185
Wallace, D. L., 557
Wallace, J. J., 561
Wallach, M. A., 381
Wallenius, M. A., 514
Walsh, Y., 591

Walster, G. W., 353
Walter, J., 368
Walters, S., 111
Walther, E., 192, 223
Walther, J. B., 500
Walumbwa, F. O., 307, 313
Wan, C., 14
Wang, A. Y., 264
Wang, C. S., 13
Wang, J., 108
Wang, L., 272, 557
Wang, M. A., 328
Wang, S., 109
Wanlass, J., 561
Wann, D. L., 491
Warburton, W. A., 70
Ward, A., 438, 450
Ward, A. J., 414
Ward, C. M., 497
Warlop, L., 439
Warneken, F., 171
Warner HBO, 138, 149
Warr, M., 359
Warr, P. B., 373
Warriner, G. K., 253
Warwick, D., 48
Wasserman, S., 187
Wasti, S. A., 83
Watson, C., 293
Watson, D., 267
Watson, P. J., 547
Watson, R. I., Jr., 592
Watson, W. E., 348, 384
Watts, D. J., 590
Waung, M., 259
Wayne, S. J., 306–307
Wayne, S. J., 338
Waytz, A., 16, 20–21
Weatherly, A. M., 509
Weatherly, A. M., 510
Weaver, F. A., 405
Weaver, K., 231
Webb, N. M., 334
Weber, B., 346
Weber, J. M., 438, 443
Weber, M., 253, 311
Weber, T. J., 307, 313
Webley, P., 392
Webster, D. M., 448
Webster, G. D., 77, 97
Webster, H. A., 115
Webster, M., Jr., 293
Wech, B. A., 153
Wechsler, H., 171
Wegge, J., 349
Wegner, D. M., 363, 421
Weick, M., 268
Weigold, M. F., 383

Weingart, L. R., 39, 338, 361, 364, 439,
    440, 448, 459, 460, 464
Weinstein, N., 514
Weisner, C., 174, 553–554
Weiss, D. S., 415
Weiss, H. M., 509
Weiss, J. A., 361
Weiss, J. F., 549
Weiss, T., 321
Welch, B. K., 29
Welch, D. A., 390
Weldon, E., 337, 338, 361, 364, 427
Weldon, M. S., 378
Wellman, N., 283–284
Wells, P. A., 591
Welser, H. T., 456
Wener, R. E., 518
Werko, R., 424
Werner, C. M., 508
Werner, J., 383
Werner, P., 591
Werner, T., 584
Werth, L., 17, 223
Wesselmann, E. D., 73
West, B. J., 411
West, M. A., 403–404
West, S. G., 79, 217, 560
Wheelan, S. A., 61, 146, 148–150, 164
Wheeler, D. D., 386, 393
Wheeler, J., 155
Wheeler, L., 71, 113–115, 119, 131,
    532, 589
Whisler, E. W., 56
Whitaker, D. J., 120
Whitchurch, E. R., 169
White, B. J., 470–472, 476, 483, 492, 493,
    494, 497, 499, 501, 504
White, D. R., 141
White, M. W., 440–441
White, R., 308–310
Whitehouse, H., 139
Whitley, B. E., Jr., 189, 260
Whitney, D. J., 155–156
Whitney, K., 214
Whittal, M. L., 547
Whittenburg, G. E., 111
Whyte, W. F., 35–37, 42, 61, 526, 528
Wick, D. P., 106, 259
Wicker, A. W., 534–535
Widen, S. C., 509
Widmeyer, W. N., 145, 411
Wieczorkowska, G., 15–16
Wieselquist, J., 474–475
Wiesenfeld, B. M., 369
Wiggins, E. C., 235
Wight, W., 445
Wightman, D. C., 345
Wilder, D. A., 208, 494, 497

Wilderman, S., 530
Wildman, J. L., 320, 405
Wildschut, T., 459, 473–475, 504
Wilfley, D. E., 76
Wilgus, A. J., 69
Wilke, H. A. M., 261
Wilkerson, J. M., 310
Wilkinson, I., 256
Wilkinson-Weber, C. M., 45
Williams v. Florida, 399 U.S. 78, 235
Williams, D., 142, 525
Williams, J. A., 493
Williams, J. E., 299
Williams, J., 458
Williams, K. D., 3, 4, 69, 70, 71, 73, 77,
    97, 335–339, 356
Williams, K. Y., 414
Williams, L. E., 513
Williamson, S. A., 151, 195
Willig, C., 61
Willis, F. N., 517, 519
Willis, H., 484
Wills, T. A., 119, 556, 557, 561
Wilpers, S., 102
Wilpinski, C., 127
Wilson, D. J., 217
Wilson, D. S., 97
Wilson, F. R., 565
Wilson, J. K., 104
Wilson, J. R., 557
Wilson, K. A., 345
Wilson, M., 476
Wilson, R. K., 446
Wilson, S. R., 450
Wiltermuth, S. S., 141
Wincent, J., 185
Winefield, H. R., 552
Winer, B. J., 283
Wingbermuehle, C., 557
Wingert, M. L., 409
Winquist, J., 369
Winquist, J. R., 376
Winter, D. G., 259, 270
Wintre, M. G., 67
Wiseman, R., 480
Wisman, A., 115
Wit, A., 308
Witt, M. G., 90, 93
Witte, E. H., 346
Witteman, H., 435
Witteman, H. R., 460
Wittenbaum, G. M., 360, 37
Witty, T. E., 557
Wojslawowicz, J. C., 107
Wolbert, A., 212
Wolf, S., 208, 210
Wolf, S. T., 474–475
Wolfe, D., 16

Wolfe, D. M., 183
Wolfe, V. A., 359
Wolin, S. S., 597
Wood, A. M., 214
Wood, D., 259
Wood, J. V., 118
Wood, S. E., 487
Wood, W., 168, 213, 214, 224, 416–417
Woodruff, S., 151
Woody, E., 265
Wooldridge, B., 185
Woolley, A. W., 321–322, 412
Worchel, P., 448
Worchel, S., 114–115, 450, 479, 494, 519
Word, L. E., 229
Worringham, C. J., 326
Worth, L. T., 486
Worthington, E. L., Jr., 556
Wortman, P. M., 361
Wosniak, S., 108
Wright, G. E., 557
Wright, R. A., 338
Wright, S. C., 90, 495
Wright, S. L., 114–115
Wright, S. S., 91, 299
Wrightsman, L. S., 234, 237
Wu, A., 280
Wu, J. Z., 463
Wulf, L. J., 521
Wulff, K. M., 116–117
Wundt, W., 19
Wyden, P. H., 358, 369, 392, 397

Xin, K. R., 414
Xiong, L., 142
Xu, Y., 109

Yablonsky, L., 479, 526
Yakovleva, M., 424

Yalom, I. D., 546, 554, 556, 558, 559, 560, 563, 570, 558
Yamagishi, K., 442
Yamaguchi, S., 17, 81
Yamauchi, H., 328
Yamazaki, Y., 334
Yammarino, F. J., 285, 307, 312
Yanchuk, V., 185
Yang, D., 265, 267
Yang, H., 351, 352
Yang, J., 463
Yang, K., 101
Yee, N., 38, 142
Yik, M., 509
Yin, R. K., 45, 61
Yohai, S., 519
Yoon, J., 140, 252
Yoon, K., 360, 397
York, E., 234, 262
Yoshikawa, T., 328
Yost, J. H., 583
Yost, P. R., 423
Young, L., 16, 20–21
Young, L. V., 262
Young, M. J., 126, 263
Young, R. D., 92
Young, S. G., 71
Youngs, G. A., Jr., 270, 454
Yuan, Y. C., 375, 376
Yuki, M., 17, 81
Yukl, G. A., 256, 270, 282–283, 317
Yzerbyt, V., 16, 17, 439, 471, 504

Zaccaro, S. J., 287, 288, 305, 407, 418–420, 432
Zagefka, H., 491
Zajonc, R. B., 325–327, 331, 333, 447
Zald, M. N., 587
Zander, A. F., 16, 18, 32, 137, 282, 322

Zander, M. L., 344
Zanna, M. P., 118, 211, 260, 264, 383
Zanutto, E. L., 144
Zaslow, J., 320, 333, 338, 356
Zavalloni, M., 382
Zayas, V., 72
Zebel, S., 91
Zeelenberg, M., 119
Zeigler, K. R., 52
Zeisel, H., 231, 234
Zelditch, M., 261
Zelikow, P., 45
Zhang, Y., 142
Zhang , Z., 279
Zhao, L., 294
Zhou, A. J., 116
Zhou, R., 577
Zhou, W., 82
Zhu, R., 514
Ziegert, J. C., 313
Ziegler, R., 488
Ziller, R. C., 142
Zillmann, D., 91
Zimbardo, P. G., 107, 272, 276, 359, 592–594, 603
Zimmerman, S., 367
Zimmerman, S. K., 337
Zimmermann, P., 308
Zimpfer, D. G., 564
Zink, C. F., 225
Zinkiewicz, L., 529
Zitek, E. M., 190
Zubek, J. P., 64
Zuber, J. A., 383
Zuckerman, C., 375
Zurcher, L. A., 149
Zurcher, L. A., 580
Zyphur, M. J., 51, 259
Zyzniewski, L. E., 155, 446

Subject Index

Page numbers for definitions are in boldface.

Abdera outbreak, 573
Abilene paradox, **379**
Acquaintance process, 121
Acquisitive panics, 581
Action research, **26**
Ad hoc teams, **405**
Additive task, **341**
Adjustment and well-being, 53, 64, 66,
    153–154
  affiliation, 117–118
  alternative groups and, 591
  anxiety disorders, 108–109
  attachment styles, 109–110
  bullying, 260
  extraversion and happiness, 103
  loneliness and, 66–67
  roles and, 184–186
  shyness, 107–108
  social anxiety, 105, 107–108
Affiliation, **112**, 112–120
  attraction and, 121–129
  disaffiliation, 109
  during group development, 147
  joining groups, 101–110
  need for, 105
  social exchange theory of, 127–129
Agentic state, **272**
Aggression
  culture of honor, 87
  deindividuation, 592–595
  general aggression model, 478
  group-level, 72
  intergroup, 478–479
  scapegoat theory of, 479

  temperature and, 513
Agreeableness (trait of), **101**
Alcohol use in groups, 171, 173–174, 199
Alcoholics Anonymous, 174, 553–556,
    561, 564
Ambience, **508**
Amygdala, 107, 225, 267, 335, 436,
    490, 519
Anonymity, 173, 211, 474–475, 592
Anterior insula, 77, 490
Anticonformity, **207**
Apodaca v. Oregon, 236
Approach/inhibition theory, **266**
Arab Spring, 572, 580, 588, 602
Arbitration, 464
Aristotle, 34, 64, 279, 489
Artists circle, 11, **100**
Asch situation, **205**, 204–206
Assembly bonus effect, 347
Attachment, 109–110
Attention restoration theory, **511**
Attitude(s)
  polarization of, 382
  popularity and, 43–44, 48–49
  prejudice, 331–332, 487–495
  reference groups and, 48
  toward groups, 111
  toward women leaders, 315
Attraction
  acquaintance process, 121–122
  conflict and, 448–449
  familiarity principle of, 122
  group cohesion and, 136–137, 153
  homophily, 124–125

  in e-groups, 122–123
  nonconformists and, 227
  power and, 253
  principles of, 121–129
  seating arrangements and, 122
  social exchange theory of, 53–54
  social structure, 191–192
  sociometric measures of, 42–44
  temperature and, 512
Attribution
  during conflict, 451
  fundamental attribution error, 273, 377,
    451, 486
  group attribution error, 486
  of rejection to prejudice, 76
  of responsibility, 379, 396, 445–446
  overhelping, 556–557
  ultimate attribution error, 486
Audience(s), 324, **575**
Authoritarianism, and conformity, 214
Authority relations, *see* Status
Autokinetic effect, 169–170

$B = f (P, E)$, **21**, 287, 507
Babble effect, **291**
Baiting crowd(s), **596**
Balance theory, **192**
Bases of power, 250–254
Bathsheba syndrome, **269**
Bay of Pigs, 12, 358–363, 387
Bazille, Frederic, 100, 101, 120–121
Behavior setting, **533**
Behavioral assimilation, **438**
Behavioral study of obedience, 342–350

Behavioral synchrony, **140**
Behaviorism, **53**
Bennington College, 47–48
Beowulf, 278
Betweenness, **188**
Big five personality theory, 101–102
Biting mania, 585
Black-sheep effect, **228**
Bona fide groups, **45**, 155
Borda count method, 367
Brainstorming, **348**–353
    methods for, 350–351
    production blocking, 349
    rules of, 348–349
Brainwashing, 257–258
Brainwriting, **351**
Brooks, Herb, 134, 137, 138, 140, 146,
    148, 149, 151, 161
Brown v. Board of Education, 493
Bullying, **260**, 566
Bush, George W., 299–300
Bystander effect, **229**, 280

Caillebotte, Gustave, 100
Canessa, Roberto, 166
Cannibalism, 169, 594
Carlyle, Thomas, 286
Case study methods, 44–46
Cases
    1980 U.S. Olympic Hockey Team, 134
    Andes rugby team, 166
    Apollo 13, 507
    Arab Spring, 572
    Bay of Pigs planners, 358
    Bus group, 542
    Impressionists, 100
    Jobs vs. Sculley, 434
    Miracle on the Hudson, 319
    Mountain Medical, 400
    Peak Search and Rescue, 63
    People's Temple, 242
    Robbers Cave Experiment, 470
    Teach for America (Wendy Kopp), 278
    Twelve angry men jury, 203
Cassatt, Mary, 103–104
Castro, Fidel, 358, 362, 365, 387, 393
Casualty, **566**
Catharsis, **560**
Central Intelligence Agency (CIA), 358,
    362–363
Cézanne, Paul, 100, 102, 107
Challenger, 359
Challenge-threat responses, 327
Charisma, **253**, 300, 311
Children's groups
    acceptance of norms, 171
    conformity, 214
    extraversion and popularity, 108

inclusion/exclusion in, 69
    leadership in hobby groups, 46
    shy children and, 107–108
    social identity and, 90
Cho, Seung Hui, 72
Choice-Dilemmas Questionnaire, **380**–381
Choreomania, 585
Climato-economic theory, 512
Cliques, 39–42, **189**, 191, 320–321
Closed groups, **142**
Closeness, **188**
Coaction, **324**
Coalitions, 189, 271, 456
Coercive power, **252**
Cognitive closure, **392**
Cognitive dissonance, **158**, 224
Cognitive-behavioral therapy group(s),
    546–547
Cohesion, 10, 136–144
    commitment and, 137–138, 143, 153,
        157–160
    faultlines and, 414
    group development and, 145–151,
        155–158
    groupthink and, 154, 388–391
    intergroup conflict and, 482
    measures of, 145
    military squads and, 141, 144–145, 154
    performance and, 137–138, 155–158
    severe initiations and, 158–161
    social structure, 191–192
    team performance and, 422–424
    therapeutic groups and, 558–559
    trust and, 424–425
Coleadership, **558**
Collaboration, in online groups, 455–456
Collective cohesion, **138**
Collective conscious, 20
Collective effervescence, 139
Collective efficacy, **138**
Collective effort model (CEM), **339**
Collective induction, 364
Collective information processing model,
    362–369
Collective intelligence (c-factor), 321–322
Collective movements, **583**, 585
Collective self-esteem, **91**–92
Collective(s), **13**, 573–604
    characteristics, 573–575
    composition of, 590–592
    crowds, 577–579
    deindividuation theory of, 592–595
    early crowd studies, 19–20
    emergent norms, 595–596
    examples of, 574, 576, 586
    mobs, 579–583
    social identity and, 596–597
    theories of, 589–598

violence and temperature, 512
Collectivism and individualism, **78**–87
    altruism, 230
    cohesion and, 138–139
    conflict, 436, 461–462
    conformity, 214
    cultural differences, 54, 512
    leadership expectations, 296–297
    multicultural teams, 415
    multi-level model of, 78–79
    role conflict, 185
    shyness, 108
    vertical and horizontal, 86
Collectivists, **80**
Columbia, 359
Comcon, 193
Common ingroup identity model, **497**
Common knowledge effect, 374–376
Communal relationship, **83**
Communication
    argumentation, 218
    coding systems of, 39–41
    conflict and, 59, 435, 452–453
    disagreement, 213, 215–217
    discussion, 361–365
    in e-groups, 73, 455–456
    in juries, 221
    in noisy environments, 514
    in social networking sites, 122–123,
        172, 212,
    in teams, 418–420
    leaders and followers, 282–284, 300
    negotiation, 457–458
    networks, 5, 192–194
    nonverbal, 142, 143, 258, 264–265, 293,
        415–416
    of anger, 454–456
    of normative information, 157
    out-of-the-loop, 69
    power and, 253–254, 259
    problems, 345, 364, 372–374, 415–416
    public speaking, 326
    reactions to deviants, 226–227
    relationship and task, 6
    rules of order, 447
    rumors, 583
    self-disclosure, 147, 560
    sex differences, 213
    shared information bias, 374–376
    social comparison, 113–115
    speaking orders, 264
    Steinzor effect, 522–523
    supportive, 117
    SYMLOG measures of, 195–198
    vocalizations of crowds, 579
Communication network, **192**
Comparison level for alternatives, **128**
Comparison level, **128**

Compatibility, 126
Compensatory task, **341**
Competition, **436**, 472–475
Complementarity principle, **125**
Compliance (acquiescence), **205**
Compliance tactics, **257–258**
Compresence, 327
Confirmation bias, **377**
Conflict (in groups), **434**–468; *see also*
    Intergroup conflict
  causes of, 435–450
  competition and, 435–436
  cultural differences, 461–462
  culture of honor and, 87
  diversity and, 414, 416
  escalation, 450–456
  group development and, 148–149, 559
  influence tactics and, 270–271
  negotiation and, 451, 457–458
  regulatory norms and, 455
  resolution, 456–464
  sex differences, 444
  social justice and, 368–369, 457
  social value orientation and, 438–440
  soft and hard power tactics, 457–458
  task vs. process, 447–448, 464–465
  territoriality and, 527
  value of, 447–448, 464–465
Conflict resolution, 456–464
  emotions and, 454–455, 463
  negotiation, 457–458
  styles of, 459–460
  third parties and, 463–464
Conformity, **204**, 203–209; *see also* Social
    influence
  Asch's studies of, 204–208
  automaticity and, 221–223
  cohesive groups and, 154–155
  collectivism and, 82–83
  groupthink and, 386
  herding, 223
  majority influence, 203–215
  mindlessness and mimicry, 221
  minority influence, 215–220
  personality differences in, 211–214
  power and resistance, 267
  sex differences in, 213
  situational influences, 210–211
  size of group and, 208–210
Congregations, 26
Congruence (uniformity), **207**
Conjunctive task, **345**
Contact cultures, 517
Contact hypothesis, **492**
Contagion, 576, **589**–590
Contingency theory, **302**
Convergence theory, **590**
Conversion (private acceptance), **207**

Conversion theory, **215**
Conversion, 216–217
Cooperation, **436**
  egocentrism vs. sociocentrism, 84–85
  collectivism and, 83–84
  leadership and, 280
Correlation coefficient, **48**
Correlational study, **48**
Counterconformity, 207
Court cases
  Apodaca vs. Oregon, 236, 404
  Brown v. Board of Education, 493
  Ham v. S. Carolina, 236, 524
  Terry Nichols and the Oklahoma City
    bombing, 232
  Williams v. Florida, 78, 235
Covert observation, **35**
Crazes, 586
Crew resource management (CRM), **345**,
  428
Crews, **405**
Cross-categorization, **497**
Cross-cueing, **363**
Cross-functional teams, **406**
Crowd stampedes, 581–584
Crowd turbulence, 584
Crowd(s), **577**–579
  collectives, 12–13
  density, 518
  early theories of, 19–20
  neuropsychology of, 519
  personal space and, 516–518
  sex differences and, 517
  stampedes, 582–584
Crowding, 188, **519**
Crowdsourcing, 338, 345–346, **366**, 365–367
Crutchfield situation, **210**
Cults, 25, 154, 158–159
Culture, 512
  collectivism and individualism, 85–86
  conformity, 213–215
  contact and noncontact, 517
  cooperation, 84
  crowd disasters and, 584
  culture-sensitive group treatments, 565
  differences in self-esteem, 76
  emphasis on groups, 65
  etic-emic distinction, 565
  extraversion and popularity, 108
  group polarization, 384
  group-level learning methods, 334
  helping, 86, 230
  Hofstede's dimensions, 54, 85, 185
  honor, dignity, and face, 87, 480
  implicit leadership theories, 296–297
  intergroup conflict, 480–482
  multicultural teams, 415–416
  online teams, 424–425

  orchestras and, 23–24
  perceptions of groups, 17
  perceptions of time, 152–153
  polychronic and monochronic, 142–143
  reactions to role conflict, 185
  social loafing, 339
  syndromes, 87
  temperature and, 512
Cyberball, 73, 77
Cyberostracism, **73**

Darwin, Charles, 74
Decategorization, **496**
Decision rules, 219, 343–344, 365–366
Decision-making
  biases and pitfalls, 371–380
  brainstorming methods for, 348–353
  collective induction, 364
  dealing with dissent during, 225–228
  Delphi technique, 353
  effective methods for, 393–394
  functional model of, 359
  groupthink, 385–394
  in centralized groups, 192–194
  juries, 234–236
  memory in groups, 56–57
  nominal group technique (NGT), 351
  polarization and risky-shift, 380–385
  post-decisional regret, 379–380
  rules of, 219, 343–344
  stress, 322
  task type and, 339–347
  voting, 365–366
Degas, Edgar, 100, 128–129
Degree centrality, **187**
Degrees of separation, 68
Dehumanization, **490**
Deindividuation, **592**–595
Delphi technique, **353**
Density, social network, **188**
Density, **518**
Density-intensity hypothesis, **519**
Dependent variable, **46**
Depersonalization, 90
Descriptive norm(s), **167**, 225
Deviancy, 168, 208, 215–218, 224–228
Diffuse status characteristic(s), **261**
Diffusion of responsibility, **231**, 475, 592
Discontinuity effect, **473**
Discretionary task, **347**
Discussion, **361**–365; *see also*
    Communication
Disjunctive task, **343**
Dissent and rejection, 448
Dissent, 215–217, 219
Distraction-conflict theory, **329**
Distributed teams, 424–425
Distributive justice, 443–444

Distributive negotiation, **457**
Diversity
  cultural, 415–416
  deep and surface, 414, 416
  in orchestras, 23–24
  in teams, 413–417
  leadership and, 292–294
Divisible task, **340**
Dominance
  hierarchies, 259
  leadership and, 300–301
  and submission, 293–294
  team composition, 411
  territorial disputes and, 530–531
Dorsal cingulate cortex (dACC), 77
Double-standard thinking, **484**
Downward social comparison, 119–120
Drive theory, **327**
Dual concern model, **459**
Dual process theories of influence, **223**
Dynamic social impact theory, 219–220

Eating disorders, 174
Educational settings
  bullying in, 260
  collaborative testing, 359
  cooperative classrooms, 441, 499
  dynamic social impact in, 220
  experiential learning, 549–550
  group-level learning methods, 334
  jigsaw learning groups, 498–499
  online project teams, 424–425
  ripple effect, 270
  role differentiation in, 176–177
  social facilitation, 333–334
Egocentric, **84**
Egocentrism, **445**
Egoistic deprivation, **591**
e-groups, *see* Online groups
Elaboration principle, **124**
e-leadership, **307**–308, 313
Electronic brainstorming, **352**
Electronic performance monitoring
  (EPM), **332**
Emergent norm theory, **595**–596
Emerson, Ralph Waldo, 34
Emic perspective, **565**
Emotion(s), **52**
  anger, 70–71, 83, 112, 258, 260, 446,
    454, 478, 580, 581
  arousal and, 593–594
  catharsis, 560
  celebratory crowds, 579–580
  cohesion and, 139–141
  contagion of, 580
  conflict and, 454–455, 463
  cultural differences in the expression of,
    54–55, 152

discomfort of disagreement, 224
  emotional intelligence, 290
  emotional loneliness, 66
  environments and, 508–510
  fear, 105, 109, 115–117, 436, 474
  greed, 436, 474
  norm violations and, 168
  group affective tone, 423
  group hate, 489
  in online groups, 455–456
  intergroup contact, 487–489, 493
  marching and, 141
  moods and conflict, 449
  neural mechanisms, 519
  positive, 140–141
  power and, 266–270
  ostracism and, 69–71
  social comparison and, 119
Emotional cohesion, **139**
Encounter group(s), **549**
Endurance, 155, 515
Entitativity, **14**–16
  blame, punishment, and, 72
  Campbell's theory of, 14–16
  cross-cultural differences, 17
  group cohesion and, 135
  group mind and, 20–21
  types of groups and, 14–16
Entrapment, **380**
Environment(s)
  ambient, 508–515
  behavior settings, 533–535
  crowded, 516–521
  designed, 532–537
  extreme and unusual, 64–65, 514–515,
    531–532
  personal space, 516–518
  proximity and attraction, 121–122
  restorative effects of, 511
  seating, 122, 521–523
  sick building syndrome, 585
  small group ecology, 515
  territoriality, 168, 523–532
Environment of evolutionary adaptation
  (EEA), 300
Equality norm, **85**
Equifinality, **135**
Equilibrium model, **151**
Equilibrium model of communication, **518**
Equity and equality, sex differences, 444
Equity norm, **85**
Escape panics, 581
Essentialism, 16
e-teams, 142–143, 424–425, *see also* Online
  groups
Ethnocentrism, **483**
Etic perspective, **565**
Evaluation apprehension, **328**

Evidence-based treatment, **562**
Evolution
  cheater (free-rider) detection, 443
  dominance hierarchies, 263
  Dunbar number, 480
  evolutionary psychology, 73–75
  gregariousness and, 58, 73–76
  intergroup conflict and, 480–481
  leadership and, 300–301
  mistmatch hypothesis, 301
Exchange relationship, **83**
Exclusion, *see* Ostracism
Expectation-states theory, **261**–262
Experience sampling, **105**
Experiential learning theory, **550**
Experiments and experimentation, **46**–47
Expert power, **253**
Extended contact hypothesis, **495**
Extraversion, **101**–103
  group membership and, 101–102
  happiness and, 103
  leadership and, 289
  popularity and, 108
Extreme and unusual environments,
  64–65, **514**–515, 531–532

Facebook, 2, 20, 38, 123–124, 142, 172,
  212, 500, 552, 616, 628, 676, 572, 588
Fads, 586
False consensus effect, **222**
Faultlines, **414**
Field research, 36–38, 45
Fight-or-flight response, **70**–71, 116, 148
Five factor model (FFM) of personality,
  101–102, 288–289
Five-stage model of group development, **147**
Flaming, **455**
Flash mob(s), 12, **580**
fMRI research, 77, 95, 224, 327, 436, 490,
  519, 624, 627, 643
Focus theory of normative conduct, **225**
Folkways, **167**
Followership, **281**, 300, 310–311
Foot-in-the-door technique, **257**
Forbidden triad, 192
Forgiveness, 462–463
Formation, 99–131; *see also* Affiliation
  attraction and, 121–129
  cult recruitment and conversion, 272
  dissolution of the group, 149
  experiences in groups, 111–112
  group development, 147
  group-level attachment, 109–110
  joining groups, 101–110
  psychological needs and, 105–106
  social movements, 586–587, 591
Framing theory, 587
Fraternal deprivation, **591**

Free riding, **337**, 443
Friend or foe, 440–441
Frustration-aggression hypothesis, **478**
Functional theory of group decision
    making, **359**–369
Fundamental attribution error, **273**, 451
Fundamental Interpersonal Relations
    Orientation (FIRO), **106**, 126

Group(s), **4**
Galton, Francis, 341–342
Gangs, 35–37, 480, 526, 528
Gatekeepers, 43–44
General aggression model, **478**
Generation Me, 81
Generational effects, 81, 214–215
Gephi (computer program), 43
Gestalt group therapy, **545**
Glass ceiling, 293, 299
GLOBE (Global Leadership and
    Organization Behavior
    Effectiveness), 296–297
Goals, 8
    group, 320–325
    in teams, 402, 418–419
    planning fallacy, 371–372
    power and goal-striving, 267
    setting and decision making, 360–361
    superordinate, 493
Great leader theory, **286**
Gregariousness, 106
Group affective tone, **423**
Group attribution error, **486**
Group composition, 439–440, 449–450
Group culture, **82**, 167–169
Group decision support systems, 352, **376**
Group development, 145–151
    course of conflict in groups, 434–435
    cyclical theories of, 150–151
    leadership across time, 305
    role socialization, 180–183
    stages of self-disclosure, 560
    therapeutic groups and, 558–559
    Tuckman's theory of, 22
Group dynamics, **2**, 18–24
    action research, 26
    cultural variations in, 54–55, 152–153
    group development and, 152
    interdisciplinary nature of, 24–25
    power of, 24–25
    research topics in, 27–29
    subjective, 227–228
    theories of, 146–151
Group fallacy, **19**
Group mind, **20**
Group Networks Laboratory, 186
Group polarization, **382**–384
    Choice-Dilemmas Questionnaire, 380–381

cultural influences on group, 384
discontinuity and, 473–475
risky/cautious shifts, 380–385
theories of, 382–383
Group potency, **138**
Group Process and Productivity, 323
Group psychoanalysis, **544**
Group serving biases, 379
Group socialization, **181**
Group space, **526**
Groupality, 27
Group-centrism, **392**
Groupness, *see* Entitativity
Group-reference effect, **56**–57
GroupSystems, 352
Groupthink, **44**
    causes of, 388–390
    cohesion and, 154
    Janis' model of, 386
    preventing, 392–394
    symptoms of, 386–387
Groupware, 352

Haise, F., 507, 515, 517, 524
Ham v. S. Carolina, 236
Happiness, *see* Adjustment and well-being
Hatfield and McCoy feud, 479
Hawthorne effects, **36**
Hazing, **160**
Head-of-the-table effect, **523**
Health
    alcohol use and groups, 171–172, 553–554
    challenge-threat response, 327
    cohesion and members', 153–155
    crowd safety, 584
    hazing and, 160–161
    heat and, 513
    interpersonal approaches to, 546
    noise and, 514
    norms and, 174
    psychogenic illnesses, 585
    psychotherapy and, 562–567
    role-stress, 185
    social comparison and, 114
    overeating, 332
    territoriality and, 527, 531–532
    traumatic life events and, 547
Helping
    bystander effect, 228–229
    in crowds, 599
    in therapeutic groups, 560–561
    overhelping, 556–567
Herd instinct, 74
Herding, 223
Heuristic, **223**
Hidden profiles, 374–375
Hierarchy of needs, **53**
Hofstede's dimensions, 54, 85, 185

Holes (in social networks), **189**
Home advantage, **528**
Home field advantage, 529
Homophily, **125**
Horse-trading problem, 344
Hudson School for Girls, 189
Human Relations Area Files, 54, 481
Hung juries, 232

Identify fusion theory, **139**
Identify; *see also* Social identity
    fusion, 139
    online groups and, 212
    power and, 271
    territorial displays and, 529–530
    therapeutic groups and, 555–556
Idiosyncrasy credit, **218**
Illusion of group productivity, **350**
Implicit Association Test, 485
Implicit leadership theories (ILTs), **295**
Implicit leadership theory, **295**
Impressionists, 11, 100, 101, 113, 118
Inclusion and exclusion, 63–77; *see also*
    Ostracism
    continuum, 68
    loneliness and, 66–68
    physiological response to, 76–77
    response to, 70–72
    self-esteem and, 75–76
Indegree, **188**
Independence, **436**
Independence (dissent), **207**
Independent variable, **46**
Individual mobility, **94**
Individualism, **78**, 85, *see also* Collectivism
    and individualism
Individualists, **80**
Information saturation, 194
Informational influence, **222**
Informational power, **253**
Ingroup-outgroup bias, **92**, 85, 484–485
Initiations, 158–161
Injunctive norm, **168**, 225
Innocuous sociability, 109
Input-process-output models, **56**,
    407–408, 592
Institutional Review Board (IRB), **51**
Integrative negotiation, **457**
Intellective task, **344**
Intelligence
    collective, 321
    emotional, 290
    leadership and, 289–90
    swarm, 341–343
Interaction Process Analysis (IPA), 8,
    39–41, 176, 363, 402
Interaction, 6–8, 140, 402
Interactionism, 21

Interchange compatibility, **125**
Interdependence, 2, **8**–9, 50, 156, 322, 402–403
Intergroup biases, 482–491; *see also* Prejudice
  dehumanization, 490
  double-standard thinking, 448
  ethnocentrism, 443
  exclusion and, 489
  group attribution error, 486
  implicit, 485
  ingroup-outgroup, 484
  linguistic, 484
  outgroup homogeneity, 485
  stereotypes, 487–488
  ultimate attribution error, 486
Intergroup conflict, **435**, 470–501; *see also* Conflict
  categorization and, 483, 491, 496–498
  causes of, 471–482
  collectivism and, 85, 461
  culture of honor and, 87
  discontinuity effect and, 473–475
  intergroup biases, 482–491
  moral exclusion and, 489–490
  relative deprivation and, 591–592
  resolution of, 492–501
  Robbers Cave study of, 470–501
  social identity, 88–94, 596–597
International Space Station, 415–416
Internet groups; *see* Online groups
Interpersonal complementarity hypothesis, **263**–264
Interpersonal group psychotherapy, **546**
Interpersonal influence, **225**
Interpersonal learning group(s), **543**
Interpersonal trust, **424**
Interpersonal zones, 516–517
Interrole conflict, **183**
Intra-class correlations, 51
Intragroup conflict, **435**
Intrarole conflict, **184**
Iron law of oligarchy, **263**
Isolation, effects of, 64–65, 510

James, William, 79
Jigsaw method, **499**
Jobs, Steve, 434, 435, 437–438, 441, 443–456, 465
Joining, *see* Affiliation; Formation
Judgmental task, **344**
Juries, 231–237
  death qualified, 237
  effectiveness of, 234–236
  hung, 232
  minority influence in, 232
  sex differences in, 234
  status effects, 233

story model, 231–232
studying (ethics of), 51
systematic jury selection, 236–237
Twelve angry men, 203

Keech, Marion, 158–159
Kennedy, J. F., 44, 115–116, 358, 363, 368, 369, 371–374, 379, 380, 385, 388, 389, 392, 393
Kennedy, R., 388, 389, 394
Kitty Genovese, 228–229
Knots, 405
Köhler effect, **346**
Kopp, W., 278, 280–282, 284–286, 289, 290, 292, 293, 301, 302, 308, 311, 314, 317
Krakauer, J., 515
KSAs, **411**
Ku Klux Klan, 69, 587

Law of small numbers, **486**
Law of triviality, **373**
Leader Behavior Description Questionnaire (LBDQ), 283–284
LeaderMatch program, 303
Leader–member exchange theory (LMX), **306**
Leadership, **278**–317
  autocratic/democratic, 46, 308–309
  charismatic, 253
  defined, 278, 281–282
  effectiveness, 301–313
  emergence, 286–301
  great-leader theory, 286
  groupthink and, 391
  heat-of-the-table effect, 523
  idiosyncrasy credits and, 218
  in brainstorming groups, 351
  in therapeutic groups, 557–558
  informal status structures and, 190–191
  misconceptions about, 278–281
  normative model, 369–370
  overconfidence, 344–345
  personality and, 279, 287–290
  physical characteristics of, 292–294
  presidential, 299–300, 358–391
  role differentiation, 176
  self-managing teams and, 406–407
  sex differences in, 285, 293–294, 298–301
  shared (or distributed), 46, 308–311, 368–369, 558
  social dominance orientation and, 260
  substitutes for, 284–285
  task and relationship, 282–284, 300
  theories of, 294–313
  transformational, 311–314
  twin-studies of, 279

Leadership emergence, **286**–301, 233, 548
Leadership Grid, **304**
Leadership substitutes theory, **284**–285
Learning styles, 334
Least Preferred Coworker Scale (LPC), **302**
Legitimate power, **252**
Level of analysis, **19**, 23, 50–51, 78
Lewin's law of change, **542**
Linguistic intergroup bias, **484**
Loneliness, **66**–67
Lord of the Flies, 492
Lovell, J., 507, 513, 515, 517, 524, 539
Lucifer effect, **273**
Lynch mob(s), 580, 593, 597

Machiavelli, Niccolo, 34
Majority influence, **203**–215
Majority decision rule, 219
Male bonding, 416–417, 440
Manet, Edouard, 100
Mass delusion, **583**, 585
Master problem of social life, 63
Maximizing task, **341**
Measurement
  cultural differences, 54–55
  experience sampling methods, 105
  multilevel, 50–51
  of group structure, 191–198
  reliability and validity, 41
  structuring coding systems, 39–41
  SYMLOG, 195–198
Mechanical Turk, 266–267
Mediator, **463**
Meetings, 218, 387–388
Membership, 5–**6**, 142–143
Mental models, 361–362, 431, 510
Mere-effort model, 330
Metacontrast principle, 89
Mimicry, **140**, 221
Mindguard, **388**
Mindlessness, **221**
Minimal intergroup situation, **88**
Minimax principle, **127**
Minority influence, **204**, 215–220, 232, 377–378
Mismatch hypothesis, 301
Missionary-cannibal dilemma, 364
Mixed-motive situation, **437**
Mob(s), **579**–580, 597
Monet, Claude, 11, 100, 101, 113, 118
Monochronic cultures (M-time cultures), **152**
Moral exclusion, **490**
Mores, **167**
Morisot, Berthe, 103–104

Motivation, **52**–53
  collective, 137–138, 335–336
  fight or flight, 116
  joining groups, 105–106
  misperceiving, 451
  mixed motive situations, 437–439
  social facilitation and, 328–329
  tend and befriend, 116
Multifactor Leadership Questionnaire, 312
Multilevel perspective, **22**–23, 144–145,
  508
Myth of the madding crowd, 598–599

Narcissism, 288, 289
National Training Laboratory (NTL), 177,
  548, 556
Natural selection, 73–75
Need for affiliation, **105**
Need for intimacy, **105**
Need for power, **106**, 259
Need to belong, **64**
Negotiation, **457**
  hard and soft tactics, 255
  impact of anger on, 454–455
  integrative, 457–458
  tasks, 320
Neuroscience
  conflict, 436
  crowding, 42
  exclusion, 57–58
  fMRI methods, 77, 95, 224, 327, 436,
    490, 519, 624, 627, 643
  inclusion and exclusion, 76–77
  interpersonal distance, 519
  ostracism, 62
  outgroup exclusion, 490
  oxytocin, 58
  perception of status, 258
  power, 267
  reactions to dissent, 224–225
  response to affiliation, 118
  shyness, 107
  social facilitation, 327–328
Nominal group(s), **349**
Nominal group technique (NGT), **351**
Nonhuman groups, 63–64, 263, 444–445
  howler monkeys, 526
  productivity, 336
  social facilitation in, 325–326
Nonverbal communication
  complementarity, 264–265
  cross-cultural differences in pace,
    142–143
  cultural misunderstandings and, 415–416
  distance, 518
  facial reactions to leaders, 293
  mimicry as, 140, 221
  status cues, 258

Norm(s), **10**, 167–174
  changes over time, 215
  characteristics of, 173
  development and transmission of, 21,
    169–171
  distributive, 443–444
  emergent, 595
  equality and equity, 85
  group development, 148–149
  and helping in emergency situations, 229
  in online groups, 172, 212, 455–456
  intergroup conflict, 479–480, 493
  internalization of, 168–169, 173
  performance, 139–140, 157
  social dilemmas and, 442–443
  types of, 167–168
Norm of reciprocity, **84**, 438
Normative influence, **224**, 168–169, 375
Normative model of decision making, **370**
Nucleus accumbens, 107

Obedience to authority, 242–250
Obedience, 242–273
  conversion theory of extreme, 271–272
  destructive, 272
  hazing and, 161
Observation, **34**–41
Observational learning, 556–557
Occupy Wall Street, 586, 588
Odyssey, 278
Offline groups, **7**
Old Christians (rugby team), 166
Old sergeant syndrome, **154**
Oligarchy, 365
Online groups, **7**
  attraction in, 122–123
  cohesiveness of, 142–143
  conformity in, 212
  cyberostracism, 73
  disinhibition, 455
  e-brainstorming, 352
  e-leadership, 307–308
  e-nominal groups, 352
  flaming in, 455–456
  gaming groups, 38–39
  group decision support systems (GDSS),
    352, 376
  normative influence in, 172, 212
  performance monitoring, 332–333
  smart mobs, 588
  status organizing processes in, 264
  support, 552
  teams, 424–425
  third places, 525
  virtual intergroup contact, 500–501
  virtual reality groups, 50
Open groups, **142**
Optimal distinctiveness theory, 81–82

Optimizing task, **341**
Organizational contexts
  citizenship behaviors, 306
  Hawthorne studies, 36
  leadership in, 286–313
  noise in the workplace, 514
  office design, 535–536
  organizational structures, 23, 190–191
  participation in decisions, 368–369
  performance monitoring in, 332–333
  political skill in, 259
  role stress, 185
  scientific management, 401
  sex differences in leadership, 285, 293
  territoriality in, 530–531
  use of teams in, 401, 425–428
Organizational trust model, **424**
Originator compatibility, **125**
Ostracism, **69**, 68–77
  communication and exclusion, 226–227
  dissent and, 224–227
  fight-or-flight response to, 70–72
  neurological reactions to, 76–77
  temporal need-threat model of, 70
  tend-and-befriend response to, 71
Outdegree, **188**
Outgroup homogeneity bias, **486**
Overhelping, 566–567
Overload, **510**, 194
Overt observation, **35**
Oxytocin, 58, 76, 118

Palo Alto Research Center (PARC), 155, 412
Panic(s), **581**–583
Paradigm, **18**
Parkinson's Law, **373**
Parrado, Fernando, 166, 187, 190
Participant observation, **35**–37, 179
Participation equalization effect, 264
Patton, General George S., 301
Pecking order, **258**, 189–191
Performance; *see also* Teams,
    Decision-making
  beliefs about groups and, 111
  circumplex model of group tasks, 9
  clarity of role responsibilities and, 184, 186
  cognitive overload and, 510
  cohesion and, 137–138, 155–158
  collective effort model of, 339
  compensatory processes, 338,
    345–346, 365
  composition and, 23–24, 409–413
  creativity and, 348–353
  crowdsourcing, 366–367
  diversity and, 413–417
  free riding, 337, 443
  goal setting and, 9, 337, 360–361
  group development and, 149

Performance (*continued*)
  Hawthorne studies of, 36
  home advantage, 528–529
  illusion of, 350
  in centralized and decentralized
      groups, 194
  in online groups, 307–308
  in open groups, 142
  in overcrowded situations, 520–521
  in P-time and M-time groups, 152
  I-P-O models of, 56, 407–408
  norms of, 157
  of juries, 234–235
  personality and, 103, 409–413
  process loss and planning, 372–373, 412
  productivity losses, 333–339
  Ringelmann effect, 323, 325–336
  social facilitation and, 327–336
  social loafing, 335–339
  stable status structures and, 265
  staffing and, 534–535
  Steiner's theory of productivity,
      322–323, 339–348
  synergistic effectives, 347–348
  type of task and, 320–322
  when to work in groups, 322
Personal conflict, **448**
Personal identity, **80**–81
Personal space, **516**
Personality, **101**
  attachment styles, 109–110
  extraversion, 101–102
  five factor model (FFM), 101–102,
      288–289, 409–410
  individualism/collectivism, 80
  and joining groups, 74–75, 591
  motivational style and leadership, 302
  need for cognitive closure, 392
  self-esteem, 74–76, 91–94, 214,
      268–269, 441, 491
  sense of uniqueness, 82
  shyness, 107–108
  social anxiety, 108–109
  social dominance orientation, 259–260,
      476–477
  social value orientation, 438–440
  team orientation, 411
  traits associated with leadership,
      287–288, 296–297
  Type A, 410–411
Persuasive-arguments theory, **383**
Pissarro, Camille, 11, 100, 102, 107
Planning fallacy, **371**
Pluralistic ignorance, **173**, 229
Political opportunity theory, 587
Polychronic cultures (P-time cultures), **152**
Posttraumatic Stress Disorder (PTSD), 547
Power, 243–278

authority, 242–250
bases, 250–254
conflict and control, 446, 451–453
dynamics in flight crews, 345
in group hierarchies, 189–191
intergroup dominance, 475–477
leadership and, 279
metamorphic effects of, 265–273
Milgram's studies of obedience, 242–250
need for, 106, 259
power distance, 334
power of the situation, 210–211, 272
priming, 266
seeking, 269–270
social dominance orientation and,
    475–477
social justice and, 443–444
tactics, 254–257, 268, 270 451–452
unilateral and bilateral, 453
Power bases, **250**
Power tactics, **254**–257
Prejudice, 13; *see also* Intergroup bias
  intergroup contact and, 495–496
  scapegoat theory of, 479
  social dominance orientation and, 475–477
  social facilitation and, 331–332
Premature termination, **564**
Prescriptive norm, **167**
Primary groups, **11**–12
Principles of Psychology, 79
Prisoner's dilemma game (PDG), **437**–440,
    473–474
Privacy, 64, 529
Procedural justice, **368**, 443–444
Process conflict (procedural), **447**
Process debriefing group(s), **547**, 566–567
Process loss, **323**
Production blocking, **349**
Productivity in groups, *see* Performance
Proscriptive norm, **167**
Prototype-matching hypothesis, 295
Psychoanalytic approaches, 138, 180–181,
    544–545
Psychodrama, 545–546
Psychogenic illness, **585**
Psychologie des Foules, 10
Public goods dilemma, **442**
Punctuated equilibrium model, **151**

Qualitative study, **37**
Quality circles, **429**
Quantitative study, **39**
Queue(s), **576**–577, 12
Queueing effect, 582

Race riots, 580–581
Reactance, **450**
Real teams model, **402**

Realistic group conflict theory, **472**
Recategorization, **497**
Reciprocity principle, **125**
Reciprocity, 8
  attraction and, 126–127
  intergroup conflict and, 479
  negative and positive, 438, 444
  overmatching and undermatching, 454
  retaliation as, 454
  rough and exact, 454
  social justice, 443–444
Reference group(s), **48**
Referent power, **253**
Relational cohesion theory, **140**
Relationality, **104**
Relationship interaction, **8**
Relationship role, **176**
Relationship(s)
  amae, 17
  balance theory of, 191–192
  directed and undirected, 186–187
  exchange and communal, 83–84
  leadership style, 282–284, 300
  loneliness, 66–67
  relational conflict, 448–449
  relationship interaction, 7–8, 39–41
  social exchange, 53–54
  social network analysis of, 186–189
  social networking and, 122–123, 172
  ties, 5
  well-being and, 64–66
Relative deprivation, **591**
Reliability, **41**, 43–44
Remote Associates Test, 333
Renoir, Auguste, 100, 101, 113, 118, 120–121
Research Center for Group Dynamics, 548
Research methods, 33–60
  case study method, 44–46
  cluster analysis, 15
  correlational, 47–49
  ethics of research, 51
  evidence-based treatments, 562
  experience sampling methods, 105
  experimental games, 83
  experimentation, 46–47
  field research methods, 36–38, 45–46, 230
  fMRI methods, 77, 95, 224, 327, 436,
      490, 519, 624, 627, 643
  generational paradigms, 170–171
  measurement, 34–44, 54–55, 145
  meta-analytic methods, 155
  multilevel analysis, 19–20
  observational methods, 34–41
  rotational designs, 287
  social network analysis, 186–188
  statistical approaches to interdependence, 50
  SYMLOG, 195–198
Resource mobilization theory, 587

Responsibility
conflict and, 445–446
cultural differences in perceptions of, 17
deindividuation and, 592–593
self-serving attributions, 84, 379, 396,
445–446
unpacking effect, 445
Revolutionary coalition, **271**
Reward power, **250**–251
Ringelmann effect, **335**
Riot(s), 512, **580**–581
Ripple effect, 270
Risky-shift effect, **380**
Robbers Cave experiment, **470**
Robert's Rules of Order, 447
Role(s), **10**, 174–186
characteristics of, 174–175
deep, 180–181
in online groups, 308
incongruity, 299
role theory of leadership, 299
social identity, and, 79
SYMLOG measures of, 195–198
theories of, 177–181
transition during socialization, 181–183
types of role stress, 183–186
types of, 175–176, 178–179
Role ambiguity, **183**
Role conflict, **183**
Role differentiation, **175**
Role fit, **184**
Role stress, 183–186, 512
Role-taking, **179**
Romance of leadership, **280**–281
Romance of teams, **427**
Romeo and Juliet, 175, 181
Rules of order, **447**
Rumors, 254, 583

Safety in numbers, 115–116
Scapegoat, **46**, 155
Scapegoat theory, **479**
Schadenfreude, 491
Schlesinger, A., 387
School shootings, 72
Scientific management, **401**
Sculley, John, 434, 435, 437–438, 441,
443–451, 456, 465
SEALAB, 515
Seating, 205, 266, 521–523
Second Life, 38, 500, 525
Self, **79**
awareness and deindividuation, 594
collective, 79–80, 88–92
cultural differences in the, 86–87
disclosure, 147, 560
egocentrism vs. sociocentrism, 84–85
identity, 138–139, 597–598

identity fusion theory, 139
inclusion of the group in the, 90
insight, 561
self-stereotyping, 89
social identity theory, 88–94
Self-censorship, 387
Self-disclosure, **560**
Self-esteem
collective, 91–92
conformity and, 214
cooperative classrooms, 441
individual vs. collective, 94
intergroup rejection and, 491
minority members', 92–93
power and, 268–269
social comparison and, 119–120
sociometer theory of, 74–76
stereotype threat, 93–94
Self-evaluation maintenance model,
119–120
Self-managing teams, 406–407
Self-organizing systems, 56–57
Self-presentation, 160, **179**, 298, 328
Self-presentation theory, **328**
Self-reference effect, **56**
Self-report measure(s), **42**
Self-serving biases, 379, 445–446
Self-stereotyping, **89**
Semester-at-Sea, 542, 543, 546
Sensitivity training group, **549**
Sex differences
acceptance of leadership, 279
collective intelligence, 322
conformity, 213
culture and, 54
individualism and collectivism, 81
intergroup hostily, 482
joining groups, 103–104
leadership, 285. 293–204, 298–301
male bonding, 416
need for power, 106
participation in jury deliberations, 234
personal space, 517
reactions to ostracism, 71
relationality, 104
seating preferences, 522
social dominance orientation, 260
teamwork, 416–417
testerone, 58, 87, 106, 259, 265
use of power tactics, 256
Sexism, 24, 104, 213, 292–294, 299, 417
Shackleton, E., 155, 515
Shared information bias, **374**
Shared mental model, 156, **361**, 421
Shyness, **107**
Sick building syndrome, 585
Simpatia (or simpatico), 230
Sisley, Alfred, 100, 101, 118

Situational leadership theory, **305**
Size
coalitions and subgrouping, 456
and conformity, 208–210
crowd formation and, 578
deindividuation and, 593
dyads and triads, 4
groups and collectives, 6, 573
leadership emergence, 279
need for power, 106
performance on additive tasks, 341
productivity losses, 338
restrictions in automobiles, 510
staffing and performance, 534–535
Skiles, J. B., 319, 320–324, 328, 338,
342, 344
Small group ecology, **515**–523
Smart mob(s), **588**
Social anxiety, 101, **108**–109, 113–117,
210
Social anxiety disorder (SAD), **109**
Social capital, **66**
Social categorization, **89**
Social category, **13**
Social cognition
attentional processes and performance,
329
collective memory, 362
depth of processing, 56–57
entitativity, 14–16
essentialism, 16
implicit leadership theories, 294–295
individual differences in, 80
intergroup perceptions, 483–490
leadership and, 280, 295
memory errors, 378–379
mere-effort model, 330
nonconscious reactions to settings, 533
overload, 510
shared mental models, 361–362, 431,
510
social comparison, 112–120
stereotyped thinking, 498
stereotypes, 16, 487
transactive memory, 362–363
uncertainty , 54, 450–451
Social cohesion, **136**
Social comparison, **113**
affiliation and, 112–120
bystander effect and, 229
downward and upward, 119–120
false consensus and, 222
Festinger's theory of, 113
informational influence and, 222–223
minority influence, 215–217
polarization in groups, 382–383
therapeutic groups, 556
Social compensation, **338**

Social creativity, **93**
Social decision scheme, **365**
Social diffusion, 590
Social dilemma, **442**
Social dominance orientation (SDO), **259**–260
Social dominance theory, **476**
Social exchange theory, **53**, 55
Social exchange, 127–129, 150, 250–251, 306
Social facilitation, **324**
  coaction and audiences, 324
  personality and, 330–331
  prejudice and, 331–332
  theories of, 327–331
  Triplett's early study of, 24, 324
  Zajonc's resolution, 325
Social identification, 89–90
Social Identity Model of Deindividuation Effects, 596
Social identity, **13, 80**–81
  categorization, 13, 89–90
  cohesion and, 137
  collective movements and, 596–597
  identification, 89–90
  intergroup conflict, 483, 491
  leader prototypicality and, 298
  relative deprivation, 591–592
  self-esteem and, 92–93
  social loafing and, 341–342
  team identity, 423
Social identity theory, **88**–94, 491
Social impact theory, **209**
Social influence, **203**–231
  alcohol use and, 171, 173–174
  Asch's studies of, 204–208
  black-sheep effect and, 227–228
  communication and dissent, 226–227
  dynamic social impact theory of, 219–220
  helping and, 228–231
  idiosyncrasy credits, 217–218
  in cohesive groups, 154–155
  in collectivistic groups, 83–84
  informational, 222–224
  interpersonal, 225–227
  majority influence, 203–215
  minority influence, 215–220
  normative, 224–225
  obedience, 242–250
  peer groups and, 21
  principle of social proof, 222
  proximity and, 121–122
  reference groups, 48
  social impact theory of, 209–210
  sources of, 220–226
  via social comparison, 112–120
  viral, 212

Social justice
  conflict and, 443–444, 457
  distributive and procedural, 368–369
  in nonhuman species, 444–445
  intergroup conflict and, 472–474, 476
  moral exclusion, 489–491
  social movements and, 112, 572, 586–587
  voice and fairness judgments, 369
Social laboring, 338
Social learning theory, **556**
Social learning, 556–558
Social loafing, **335**–339
  collective effort model of, 339
  free riding and, 337
  helping, 231
  social identity and, 338–339
  ways to reduce, 336–339
Social loneliness, 66
Social matching effect, **350**
Social movement(s), **112, 586**–587
  Arab Spring, 572
  joining, 586–587, 591
  smart mobs and, 588
  theories of, 587
Social network(s), **6**
  analysis, 186–189
  attraction in, 123–124
  communication networks, 193–196
  loneliness, 68
  mass delusions and, 583, 585
  open, 142
Social network analysis (SNA), 5, **42**, 68, 186–188
Social networking, 122–123, 172, 590
Social orientation theory, **330**
Social perception
  during social conflict, 439–440
  entitativity, 14–16
  fundamental attribution error, 273
  implicit leadership theories, 295–296
  misperception during conflict, 458–459
  observers' inaccuracies, 39
  of free-riders, 443
  of leadership qualities, 280
  of leaders, 299
  of members' abilities, 291, 421
  perceiving groups, 13–16
  power and, 253, 268–269
  social warmth, 512
  status signals, 258–259
Social power, **242**, *see also* Power
Social proof, 168
Social psychophysiology, *see* Neuroscience
Social role theory, **299**
Social support, **116**, 332
  affiliation and, 116–117
  forms of, 117–118

support groups, 543–554, 559
  team backup behavior as, 420
Social surrogates, 107
Social trap (or commons dilemma), **442**
Social tuning, **169**, 220
Social values orientation (SVO), **439**
Socialization, group, 181–183
Sociocentric, **84**
Socioemotional communication, 39–41
Sociofugal spaces, **521**
Sociogram, **42**
Sociometer theory, **75**, 74–76
Sociometric differentiation, **191**
Sociometry, **42**, 43–44, 186–188
Sociopetal spaces, **521**
Solitude, 64, 104, 108
Solo status, **262**
Song of Roland, 278
Specific status characteristics, **261**
Spiral model of conflict intensification, 479
Sports fans, 34, 45, 91, 228, 480, 497, 580, 582
Sports teams, 324, 326, 411–412, 529
Staffing theory, **534**
Stanford Prison study, 272
Statisticized group decisions, 342
Status differentiation, **189**
Status generalization, **262**
Status, 189–193
  biases in allocation, 261–262, 292–294, 299, 417
  claiming, 258
  conformity, 217–218
  cultural differences in, 54–55, 86
  differentiation, 189–190
  dominance-submission, 195, 293–294
  hierarchies, 189–191
  in online groups, 264
  influence and juror, 232–233
  information flow in hierarchical networks, 194
  obedience to authority, 242–250
  organizing processes, 258–265
  personal space and, 517
  personality differences in seeking, 259
  power tactic use and, 256
  seating choices and, 523
  sociometric measures of, 42–43
  territoriality and, 530–531
Steinzor effect, **523**
Stepladder technique, 353
Stereotype content model, **487**
Stereotype threat, 93–**94**
Stereotype(s), 13, **16**, 387, **487**, 498
Story model of jury deliberation, **231**–232
Street Corner Society, 35–36
Strength of weak ties, 154, 186

Stress, **511**; *see also* Health
   affiliation and, 115–117
   challenge-threat responses, 327
   cognitive overload, 510–511
   environmental stressors, 511–515
   fight, flight, tend and befriend responses
      to, 116–117
   groupthink and decisional, 390
   need for leadership, 279–281
   overcrowding, 515–520
   physiological reactions to, 518–519
   PTSD, 547
   role, 512
   therapeutic treatments for, 543–570
   time-pressure and groupthink, 391
Structural cohesion, **141**
Structure, **10**, 167–198
   balance theory analysis of,
      191–192
   cohesion and, 141–142
   communication networks, 193
   development of, 147–149
   formal and informal, 190–191
   groupthink and 389, 391
   indexes of, 186–188
   intermember relations, 186–198
   norms, 10, 167–174
   of queues and crowds, 577, 579
   performance and, 403
   performance, 186
   roles, 10, 174–186
   rules of order, 447
Structured learning group(s), **549**
Structured observational methods, 37
Study group, **334**
Subjective group dynamics, **228**
Sucker effect, **337**, 443
Sullenberger, C. B., 319, 320–324, 328,
      330, 333, 338, 342–344, 356
Sunk cost, **380**
Superordinate goal, **493**
Support features, 551, 553
Support group(s), **543**–554, 559
Support online, 552
Swigert, J., 507, 515, 524
Synergy, 139–141, **347**–348
Synomorphy, **534**
Syntality, 27
Systematic Multiple Level Observation of
      Groups (SYMLOG), **41**, 195
Systems theory, **55**–56, 135, 150–151

Tahrir Square, 572, 573, 580, 583, 587,
      588, 596
Task(s), 339–347
   circumplex model, 9, 320–321
   competence and leadership, 290–291,
      302

complexity and performance, 329
conformity across, 211
efficacy and performance, 138
intellectual and judgmental, 244
interaction, 7, 35–36, 402
interaction process, 39–41
interdependency, 322, 535–536
leadership, 282–284, 300
relationship and task roles, 176–177
task and process conflict, 447
types of, 320–321
Task cohesion, **137**
Task conflict, **447**
Task demands, **339**
Task-relationship model of leadership,
      282–283
Task role, **176**
Teach for America (TFA), 278, 281, 282,
      284–286, 289, 290, 292, 301, 308,
      311, 317
Team building, **428**
Team science, 359, 427
Team training, **428**
Team(s), **400**, 401–429
   autonomous work groups, 369
   building, 428–429
   cohesion and performance, 137–138,
      153, 156–157, 422–424
   collective efficacy, 138
   communication in, 39–41, 192–194
   conflict in, 460–461, 464–465
   crew resource management
      (CRM), 345
   designing team settings, 536–537
   diversity in, 292–293, 413–416
   evaluating, 426–427
   flight crews, 322–344
   in extreme environments, 514–515
   leading, 296–297, 301–304,
      307–308
   learning, 421–423, 427
   mental models, 510
   multicultural, 415–416
   norms and productivity, 156–157
   online, 142–143, 424–425
   open and closed, 142–143
   performance monitoring, 332–333
   performance, 510
   player personality, 409–410
   potency and performance, 138
   process model of, 418–421
   role stress in, 184–186
   romance of, 427
   self-managed teams, 406–407
   sex differences, 416–417
   shared mental models, 361–362, 431,
      510
   social comparison and, 120

social loafing in, 336–339
sports, 324, 326, 411–412, 529
systems model (I-P-O), 407–408
training in teamwork skills, 428
types, 403–406
Teamwork, **418**
Teamwork-KSA Test of team knowledge,
      412–413
Tend and befriend response, **71**, 116
Territoriality, **524**, 523–532
   functions of, 527,
   group, 526–529
   home advantage, 528–529
   member, 529–531
   third places, 525
   types, 524
Terror management theory (TMT),
      299–300
Testosterone, 58, 106
   need for power and, 259
   status and, 265
   culture of honor and, 87
Therapeutic group(s), **543**–570
   Alcoholics Anonymous, 553–556,
      561, 564
   cognitive-behavioral, 546–547
   effectiveness of, 562–567
   interpersonal learning groups,
      548–550
   leadership in, 557–558, 563
   psychoanalytic, 544–546
   social learning in, 556–558
   support, 550–554
   therapeutic factors, 554–562
   types of, 543–554
T-groups, 177–178, **548**
The World is Flat, 415
Therapeutic factor(s), **554**–562
Third places, **524**
Thomas Theorem, 16
Thoreau, Henry David, 64
Time
   cultural differences in the perception of,
      152–153
   group development over, 145–151
   in groups, 146–152
   planning use of, 361, 371–372
   pressure and decision-making, 391
   wasting, 373
Tit for tat (TFT), **462**
Tocqueville, Alex de, 85
Tokens, 417
Tolstoy, Leo, 286
Tragedy of the commons, 442
Training group or T-group, 177–178, **548**
Transactional leadership, **311**
Transactive memory processes, **362**, 421
Transference, **544**

Transformational leadership, **312**, 311–313
Trend, **586**
Trolley-car dilemma, 139
Trucking game experiment, **452**
Truth-wins rule, 343–344
Tulipmania, 585
Twelve Angry Men, 203, 205, 208, 209, 215, 217, 222–225, 232, 234, 240
Twelve-step programs, 553

Ultimate attribution error, **486**
Ultimatum game, **83**
Unanimity rule, 219, 236
Unit of analysis, 19, 50–51
Unitary task, **340**

Upward social comparison, **119**–120

Validity, **41**, 43–44
Van Gogh, Vincent, 100–101, 107
Viral social media processes, 212
Virginia Tech shooting, 72
Virtual contact hypothesis, **500**
Virtual reality groups, 50
Virtual teams, 424–425
Vladimir's choice, 477
voir dire, **236**
Volkerpsychologie, 19
Voluntary associations, 65, 111

Warren Harding effect, 297

Well-being, *see* Adjustment and Well-being
Werther syndrome, 585
Wikipedia, 212, 455–456
Williams v. Florida, 235
Wisdom of crowds effect, 341
Within-and-between analysis (WABA), 51
Workshops, 549–550
World of Warcraft, 37–38, 142–143, 525

Yanomamö, 300–301, 480
YouTube, 212

Zeitgeist theory, **286**
Zoot suit riots, 573